THE OXFORD INTERNATIONAL ENCYCLOPEDIA OF LEGAL HISTORY

EDITORIAL BOARD

EDITOR IN CHIEF
Stanley N. Katz
Princeton University

AREA EDITORS
Barbara Aronstein Black
Columbia Law School

Lawrence M. Friedman
Stanford Law School

Michael Gagarin
University of Texas, Austin

David Ibbetson
University of Cambridge, England

Baber Johansen
Harvard Divinity School

Laura Kalman
University of California, Santa Barbara

Andrew Lewis
University College London, England

Klaus Luig
Universität zu Köln, Germany

Geoffrey D. MacCormack
University of Aberdeen, Scotland

Werner Menski
*School of Oriental and African Studies,
University of London, England*

ADVISORY EDITOR
M. C. Mirow
Florida International University

THE OXFORD INTERNATIONAL ENCYCLOPEDIA OF LEGAL HISTORY

STANLEY N. KATZ

EDITOR IN CHIEF

VOLUME 6

Training–Zivilgesetzbuch
Topical Outline of Contents
Directory of Contributors
Index of Legal Cases
Index

OXFORD
UNIVERSITY PRESS

2009

OXFORD
UNIVERSITY PRESS

Oxford University Press, Inc., publishes works that further
Oxford University's objective of excellence
in research, scholarship, and education.

Oxford   New York
Auckland   Cape Town   Dar es Salaam   Hong Kong   Karachi
Kuala Lumpur   Madrid   Melbourne   Mexico City   Nairobi
New Delhi   Shanghai   Taipei   Toronto

With offices in
Argentina   Austria   Brazil   Chile   Czech Republic   France   Greece
Guatemala   Hungary   Italy   Japan   Poland   Portugal   Singapore
South Korea   Switzerland   Thailand   Turkey   Ukraine   Vietnam

Copyright © 2009 by Oxford University Press

Published by Oxford University Press, Inc.
198 Madison Avenue, New York, NY 10016
www.oup.com

Oxford is a registered trademark of Oxford University Press

All rights reserved. No part of this publication may be reproduced,
stored in a retrieval system, or transmitted, in any form or by any means,
electronic, mechanical, photocopying, recording, or otherwise,
without the prior permission of Oxford University Press.

The Library of Congress Cataloging-in-Publication Data
The Oxford international encyclopedia of legal history /
Stanley N. Katz, editor in chief.
p. cm. Includes bibliographical references and index.
ISBN 978-0-19-513405-6 (set : alk. paper)
1. Law—History—Terminology. 2. Historical jurisprudence. I. Katz, Stanley Nider.
K50.O94 2009
340'.03—dc22
2008036797

1 2 3 4 5 6 7 8 9

Printed in the United States of America
on acid-free paper

COMMON ABBREVIATIONS USED IN THIS WORK

ABGB	Allgemeines Bürgerliches Gesetzbuch Österreich, Austrian General Civil Code	EU	European Union
A.D.	*anno Domini*, in the year of the Lord	f.	and following (pl., ff.)
ADHGB	Allgemeines Deutsches Handelsgesetzbuch, General German Commercial Code	fl.	*floruit*, flourished
		GG	Grundgesetz, Basic Law for the Federal Republic of Germany
A.H.	*anno Hegirae*, in the year of the Hajj	HRE	Holy Roman Empire
ALR	Allgemeines Landrecht für die Preussischen Staaten, Prussian Civil Code or General Territorial Law for the Prussian States	I	*Institutes* (of Justinian)
		IPL	International Private Law
A.M.	*Artium magister*, Master of Arts	l	line (pl., ll.)
b.	born; ibn (in Arab names)	LL.D.	*Legum doctor*, Doctor of Laws
B.C.	before Christ	n.	note
B.C.E.	before the common era (= BC)	NBW	Nieuw Burgerlijk Wetboek, Dutch New Civil Code
BGB	Bürgerliches Gesetzbuch, German Civil Code		
c.	*circa*, about, approximately	n.d.	no date
C	Codex (of Justinian)	no.	number
C.E.	common era (= AD)	n.p.	no place
cf	*confer*, compare	n.s.	new series
CIC	Codex Iuris Canonici, Code of Canon Law	p.	page (pl., pp.)
CMBC	Codex Maximilianeus Bavaricus Civilis, Civil Code of Bavaria	pt.	part
		rev.	revised
d.	died	ser.	series
D	Digest (of Justinian)	supp.	supplement
diss.	dissertation	UCC	Uniform Commercial Code
EC	European Community	USSR	Union of Soviet Socialist Republics
ed.	editor (pl., eds), edition	vol.	volume (pl., vols.)
EEC	European Economic Community	ZGB	Zivilgesetzbuch, Swiss Civil Code

THE OXFORD INTERNATIONAL ENCYCLOPEDIA OF LEGAL HISTORY

TRAINING. *See* Education and Training.

TREASON. This article deals with "high" treason—treason against the sovereign—as distinct from "petty" treason—the killing of a husband by his wife (though not the reverse), of a master by his servant, or of a prelate by a person in holy orders—which no longer forms part of English law, having become subsumed in the offense of murder.

High treason was historically regarded as a crime of peculiar gravity. It remained a capital offense until the Crime and Disorder Act of 1998 substituted life imprisonment for death by hanging, and for many years was tried under procedures separate from those of the ordinary criminal courts and which greatly restricted the accused's ability to mount an effective defense. Treason involves the principle that one person may automatically owe loyalty to another by virtue of the relationship between them; certain acts become criminal offenses, or assume much greater gravity, where such a relationship exists. In high treason, that relationship arises when a person owes *allegiance* to the sovereign.

Beginnings. The English law of treason emerged during the late-twelfth and early-thirteenth centuries and was first given statutory definition—a definition that remains in force today—by the parliament of 1351–1352. Its roots, however, are much older. In his seminal work in this area, J. G. Bellamy sees the concept as an amalgam of ancient Germanic ideals of loyalty from a man to his lord, seen, inter alia, in the *Germania* of Tacitus, and the Roman legal principle of *maiestas*, which first emerged in the third century B.C.E. In the Roman Republic, offenses that fell within the concept of *maiestas* involved disloyalty to the state but were mainly military in nature: desertion, giving up fortresses or standards to the enemy, and communicating with the enemy. Gradually thereafter, *maiestas* came to encompass a number of offenses against the emperor and the emperor's government. Again, many of these were military, including the raising of armies or making war without the command of the emperor, and the failure of a provincial governor to leave his province at the end of his term or to deliver his army to his successor. Others involved political challenge to the regime: questioning the emperor's choice of successor, occupation of public places, and incitement to sedition. From the reign of Tiberius (14–37 C.E.), convicted traitors were punished not only by death, but by forfeiture of all property and the imposition of complete civil disability, so that before his execution the traitor was unable to make a will or to manumit his slaves—both matters of vital importance in that day.

Although the English law of treason in medieval times has many similarities to the law of *maiestas*, and though the Roman concept seems to have been transmitted into medieval thought via Justinian's sixth-century *Institutes*, the one is not simply an evolved version of the other. From the time of Alfred the Great (r. 871–899), apparently independently of *maiestas*, Anglo-Saxon law codes began to distinguish explicitly between plotting against the life of the king and the more general offense of plotting against the life of one's lord. The laws of Aethelred "the Unready" (978–1016) imposed special penalties for desertion from an army when the king was present and the same penalties for false coining as for plotting against the king's life—coinage was of great political and symbolic significance, since it was produced by official moneyers and bore an image of the king.

Much the most frequent form of treason found in medieval times was armed rebellion against the king. However, the feudal system that took effect in England after the Norman Conquest did not initially make any distinction between the king as sovereign and the king as feudal lord. A point often neglected is that the feudal relationship was reciprocal; lord and vassal each owed the other a duty of faith. If the lord failed to keep faith, his vassal had recourse to *diffidatio*—formal defiance—and could then make war against him without penalty, although he thus deprived himself of lands he held from that lord. In twelfth-century feudal law the position of the king was no different from that of any other lord; indeed, it was argued by some writers that a vassal wronged by his king was not merely entitled but duty bound to seek justice through rebellion: God would judge the rightness of his cause on the battlefield. As late as 1266, the surviving adherents of Simon de Montfort—who had not only been in armed rebellion against Henry III (r. 1216–1272), but after the Battle of Lewes (1264) had held the king; his heir apparent the future Edward I; and Henry's brother, Richard, Earl of Cornwall and King of the Romans, prisoner for some months—were not tried for any offense. Instead, under the Dictum of Kenilworth (October 31, 1266) they were allowed to regain their lands on payment of a fee calculated according to the degree of their personal involvement in the rebellion.

Before the end of the twelfth century, however, it was recognized that the position of the king was unique; faith between subjects was always qualified by the faith each subject owed to the king, and by the mid-thirteenth century a concept of treason had emerged that encompassed the procuring of the king's death, the betrayal of armies, and the giving of aid to the king's enemies. When Dafydd ap Gruffydd, the last native Prince of Wales, was convicted of treason by a specially summoned parliament in the autumn of 1283, the ambit of treason was extended to armed rebellion against the king. In English eyes Edward was feudal overlord of Wales. There was also a personal relationship between the king and Dafydd: Edward had earlier knighted Dafydd and had given him refuge during his disputes with his elder brother, Llywelyn (killed 1282). Dafydd ap Gruffydd also became the first man known to have suffered the gruesome penalty specifically ordained for treason until 1814—hanging, drawing, and quartering. In a similar fashion, the Scottish patriot William Wallace was executed in 1305 as a traitor to Edward I, who had declared himself the feudal overlord of Scotland.

The Statute of Treasons. The law of treason was invoked on a number of occasions in the later years of the reign (1307–1327) of Edward II and the minority of his son Edward III (r. 1327–1377) to deal not only with armed rebellion but with matters falling well short. In the course of events leading to Edward II's deposition and murder the Despensers, who had made themselves virtual rulers of the country by dominating the king, were condemned by their enemies on charges of accroaching (usurping) royal power; in 1330, Edward III's mother, Queen Isabella, and her lover, Roger de Mortimer, secured the execution of the king's uncle Edmund, Earl of Kent, younger son of Edward I by his second marriage, on charges that he was plotting to restore Edward II to the throne.

The Statute of Treasons, passed by the parliament of 1351–1352 and still in force, was theoretically declaratory of the existing common law, as were all medieval statutes, but seems in fact to have narrowed the scope of treason. It has been linked to the political events of the 1340s and to a petition of 1348 requesting the king to provide a definition of the offense of accroaching royal power; it seems ultimately to have represented a concession made by Edward III in return for a grant of extraordinary revenues to enable continued prosecution of war against France. It provides (in translation from the Norman French):

> When a man doth compass or imagine the death of our lord the King, or of our lady his Queen, or of their eldest son and heir; or if a man do violate the King's companion, or the King's eldest daughter unmarried, or the wife of the King's eldest son and heir; or if a man do levy war against our lord the King in his realm, giving to them aid and comfort in the realm, or elsewhere, and . . . if a man slay the chancellor or the treasurer, or the King's justices of the one bench or the other, justices in eyre, or justices of assize, and all other justices assigned to hear or determine, being in their places, doing their offices..., that ought to be judged treason which extends to our lord the King, and his royal majesty. . . .

High treason therefore takes four forms: (a) conspiring to kill the sovereign, his queen, or the heir apparent; (b) compromising the royal succession by sexual intercourse with the queen, the wife of the heir apparent, or the sovereign's eldest daughter while unmarried; (c) levying war against the sovereign within the sovereign's realms, or adhering to or giving aid and comfort to the sovereign's enemies; and (d) the killing of the Lord Chancellor, Lord High Treasurer, or certain judges, when they are carrying out the functions of their office.

Although it is accepted that under the normal principles of statutory interpretation the use of the word "king" in historic statutes encompasses a queen regnant, there has been doubt as to whether there is any liability under the Statute of Treasons for compassing the death of the husband of a queen regnant. In his *Pleas of the Crown*, Sir Matthew Hale stated explicitly that liability did not arise, but he seemed to have based this view entirely on the Treason Act of 1555, which declared that compassing the death of Philip II of Spain, husband of Mary I (r. 1553–1558), was treasonable. However, when this provision is placed in the context of the 1555 act as a whole, it becomes clear that it cannot be relied on as evidence of any general principle. The act's purpose was to make provision for a regency should Mary, then in the later stages of what proved to be a phantom pregnancy, die in childbirth leaving an infant heir. Philip was the obvious regent, but he was a foreign king with a claim by blood to the English throne in his own right (through Catherine of Lancaster, daughter of John of Gaunt and wife of Henry III of Castile), and the English strongly suspected him of seeking to use the resources of England for his own purposes elsewhere in his domains. It was thus essential that Parliament set strict limitations on Philip's powers as regent, but also proper to give him the same legal protection against insurrection as if he had been sovereign in his own right.

Violating royal chastity. No prosecutions have ever taken place under the second category.

Levying war. Levying war against the sovereign encompasses not only armed rebellion against the sovereign or his forces or government but also, according to seventeenth-century authorities, a rising "for some general public purpose," such as to effect an alteration of the law, to open all prisons, or to alter the religion established by law. Convictions under this head include those of the Cato

Street Conspirators, who plotted to murder the cabinet at dinner on February 23, 1820—the plan was betrayed and the conspirators arrested in flagrante delicto as had been the 1605 Gunpowder Plotters—and the leaders of an 1839 insurrection at Newport, Monmouthshire, North Wales, when extreme Chartists attempted to take over the town. In 1781 Lord George Gordon was tried but acquitted on charges of levying war after members of his Protestant Association had rioted in London for several days against a bill for Catholic relief.

Adhering to the enemy and giving aid and comfort to the enemy. This head brought all the treason charges of the twentieth century, including the two most famous, those against Sir Roger Casement in 1916 and William Joyce in 1945. "Adhering" and "giving aid and comfort" are broad concepts, though it seems from *R v Casement* (1917) 1 K.B. 98 that the latter is simply a gloss on the former. According to Chief Justice the Marquess of Reading, whose definition was upheld by Justice Darling on appeal, a person is adherent to the sovereign's enemies when he commits an act that strengthens or tends to strengthen them in the conduct of a war against the sovereign or that weakens or tends to weaken the power of the sovereign to resist or attack his enemies or those of the country, although there must be an overt act with intent to assist the enemy. "Enemy" means a foreign state in actual hostility against the sovereign, with or without a formal declaration of war. Early cases (*R v Preston*, 1691; *R v Crosby*, 1695) involved communicating military information to the French when they were at war with William III (r. 1688–1714). It is not necessary that the communication actually reach the enemy; a communication that is intercepted is sufficient (*R v Hensey* [1758] 19 State Tr 1341). Serving in the armed forces of an enemy clearly constitutes adherence (*R v DeJager* [1907] A.C.), as does becoming naturalized in an enemy country in time of war (*R v Lynch* [1903] 1 K.B. 444). When the German consul in Sunderland, who had been naturalized as a British subject in 1905, acted on instructions from Berlin and provided money and train and ferry tickets to Germans of military age to enable them to return to Germany on the outbreak of World War I, he was held to have been giving aid and comfort to the enemy, provided he intended to assist the enemy rather than to simply do part of what he believed was his duty as consul (*R v Ahlers* [1915] 1 K.B. 616). The central issue in *Casement* was whether a person could be liable under this head where the actions forming the basis of the indictment were committed outside the sovereign's realms. Sir Roger Casement had enjoyed a distinguished career in the British Consular Service and as an opponent of slavery, but after retirement became an extreme Irish nationalist. After World War I broke out, he went to Germany, and with the active support of the Kaiser's government sought to persuade Irish prisoners of war to join an Irish brigade equipped and maintained by the Germans. The purpose of this brigade was "to fight solely for the cause of Ireland," and evidence given at the trial of Irish POWs repatriated to the United Kingdom was that there was no intention it should fight under German command or for German objectives; the original plan was presumably that it would at some stage make an armed landing in Ireland—though clearly this would be of considerable indirect benefit to the German war effort.

Casement's efforts garnered few recruits, and the Germans turned to supporting the Irish nationalists themselves. They agreed to provide a shipment of arms for what became the Easter Rising, timed to begin on April 24, 1916. British Naval Intelligence became aware of the plan, and Casement was arrested as he came ashore from a U-boat near Tralee on the morning of April 21. One of the two men who landed with him was arrested a few hours later. The same day HMS *Bluebell* intercepted the

The Trial of Roger Casement. Roger Casement (*left*) with a police officer, c. 1916. Photograph from *Trial of Roger Casement* by H. Montgomery Hyde, 1960. PRINTS AND PHOTOGRAPHS DIVISION, LIBRARY OF CONGRESS

ship carrying German rifles and ammunition some ninety miles off the Irish coast.

Perhaps surprisingly, the Law Officers of the Crown chose not to proceed on the basis that landing from an enemy vessel with equipment provided by the enemy—a map, codes, and ammunition—constituted an overt act of adhering to the enemy, and charged Casement only in respect of acts carried out in Germany. One charge was based on his "setting out from Germany as a member of a warlike and hostile expedition undertaken and equipped by the enemy with a view to landing arms and ammunition on the coast of Ireland for use in the prosecution of the war by the enemy"; the remainder addressed his attempts to subvert prisoners of war from their allegiance to the British Crown.

The Crown's case was that the relevant wording of the Statute of Treasons defining liability should be read as, "If a man be adherent to the King's enemies in his realm (giving to them aid and comfort in the realm) or elsewhere"; the words in parentheses were simply a glossing of the main provision, and it was irrelevant whether the acts constituting adherence to the enemy took place within the realm or elsewhere. In any case, acts constituting adherence to a foreign enemy were far more likely than not to be committed outside the realm, and it was inconceivable that Parliament could have intended to exclude a person committing such acts from liability. For their part the defense contended that the words "or elsewhere" also formed part of the gloss, so that treason in this form was possible only when the overt acts constituting adherence were committed within the realm. They also argued that the ordinary criminal courts—the trial had taken place at the Royal Courts of Justice—had no jurisdiction, since trials for treason, other than those taking place via bill of attainder or impeachment, were the sole province of the constable and marshal under the law of arms.

The prosecution produced precedents demonstrating that numerous convictions had been based on overt acts outside the realm, and that trial before the constable and marshal had been the practice only in dealing with those taken in armed rebellion against the Crown—the best example that following the Battle of Tewksbury in May 1471. These were accepted by the jury, who found Casement guilty after only fifty-five minutes.

Casement's legal team, headed by Serjeant Sullivan of the Irish bar, appealed to the Court of Criminal Appeal on the grounds that the offense of adhering to the enemy could not be committed abroad, and that Chief Justice Lord Reading had misdirected the jury in defining acts that constituted adherence. But Casement's junior counsel, Artemus Jones, was unable to cite a single case in support of a definition of "giving aid and comfort to the enemy" that was limited to espionage and serving in the armed forces of an enemy, rather than Reading's broad definition. It is fair to say, however, that the issue had not previously been considered, as all cases of adherence since 1688 had involved espionage or service in enemy forces. Justice Darling, giving the judgment of the court, upheld Reading's definition and dismissed the appeal. After a request for a further appeal to the House of Lords had been rejected (and the government had used Casement's "black" diaries, which detailed homosexual encounters, to bolster public opinion against him), he was hanged at Pentonville Prison on August 3.

Murder of specific officeholders. This category is obsolete, as any such killing would be dealt with as murder or manslaughter under the ordinary criminal law.

The Requirement of Allegiance. No person may be liable for high treason who does not owe allegiance to the sovereign. This requirement, not stated in the Statute of Treasons, had emerged by the time Hale (1609–1676) was writing, and he saw it as the quid pro quo of the protection a subject was entitled to from the sovereign. At common law, indeed, a subject could never divest himself of the duty of allegiance, even by becoming the naturalized subject of another state—a difficulty not resolved until the Aliens Act of 1870. The circumstances in which this concept emerged are not entirely clear, since the defendant's allegiance was not raised expressly as an issue in treason trials until much later. However, the idea of allegiance as a subject's duty seems to have emerged as a consequence of the development of a concept of nationality and thus of a legal distinction between the English subject and the alien, which dates from the fourteenth and fifteenth centuries. Under English law an alien, whether or not resident in England, was at a considerable disadvantage as compared with a subject; but as no man could owe allegiance to a king not his own, prima facie an alien could not be a traitor, as case law arising from the Perkin Warbeck insurrection in the 1490s makes clear. Though Warbeck had claimed to be Richard, Duke of York, the younger of the "Princes in the Tower," he admitted following his capture to being an impostor born at Tournai, in Flanders. Though his actions were clearly overt acts of treason, as an alien he owed no allegiance to Henry VII (r. 1485–1509), and thus could not be liable; as a foreign enemy taken in arms, though, he might be put to death.

Though an alien did not owe allegiance automatically—as did an English subject—if resident in England in time of peace he enjoyed a degree of protection from the sovereign, since he then came within the king's peace; on this basis he owed a duty of allegiance. This form of allegiance, first enunciated by Hale, was the central issue in the trial of William Joyce, known as "Lord Haw-Haw."

Joyce (1906–1946) spent World War II broadcasting propaganda from Berlin, being employed as an announcer on German radio from September 20, 1939. At times he encouraged British prisoners of war to join a "British Free

Corps" under German command. Though reviled as a British renegade, he had in fact been born in New York of an Irish father and an English mother. As an alien he owed no automatic duty of allegiance to George VI (r. 1936–1952) and, his defense argued at trial, any duty he owed as a resident alien had lapsed on his departure from the United Kingdom for Germany in August 1939. But the formulation that allegiance was the quid pro quo of protection accorded by the British Crown was applied here. In 1933, Joyce had obtained a British passport, stating that he had been born in Galway, Ireland, which, if true, would have made him a natural-born British subject. This passport was renewed twice, and only expired finally on July 2, 1940, by which time he had been working to promote the German war effort for over nine months. Though Joyce was not in fact entitled to the protection of the Crown, the jury accepted the prosecution case that by producing his improperly obtained passport he could have obtained the protection of the British Crown in a foreign country—even after the outbreak of war—until its expiry, although no evidence was produced that he had actually made use of it after August 1939. On this basis, the jury convicted Joyce on two charges predicated on his not being a British subject but one who nevertheless owed a duty of allegiance at the time of overt acts of adhering to the enemy between September 20, 1939 and July 2, 1940. He was hanged in January 1946.

Attainder. The penalties imposed under the Statute of Treasons included not only death by hanging, drawing, and quartering (sentences on peers and other men of rank were customarily commuted to beheading) but forfeiture to the Crown of all property and any titles of honor. The law of attainder that developed from the late fourteenth century added the "corrupting" of blood, so that the traitor's heirs could not inherit property or titles from or through him. Since this provided the king with a valuable source of lands and honors with which to reward those whose loyalty he wished to secure, those killed while in armed rebellion were customarily attainted posthumously; there are many examples dating from the Wars of the Roses (1455–1485). An act of attainder might be reversed by a second act, following a petition by the traitor's heirs, restoring lands and honors to those heirs, but this was by no means inevitable (the attainder against James, Duke of Monmouth, passed in 1685, is still in force), and the delay might be lengthy—that against the 11th Lord Lovat was reversed in 1857 after 110 years—32 years after his heir's petition.

Attainder, a procedure in which Parliament passed an act of attainder against a named person or persons at the request of the king, also enabled the Crown to secure the condemnation of enemies for actions falling outside the normal scope of treason, as a particular act or omission could be designated high treason in respect only of the persons named. During the fifteenth and sixteenth century acts of attainder were used extensively against peers who had committed a variety of acts that aroused the king's wrath. The attainder passed in February 1478 against George, Duke of Clarence, younger brother of Edward IV, refers, inter alia, to Clarence's intending to send his heir abroad, issuing indentures to his retainers that did not reserve allegiance to the king, and claiming that the king was a bastard. Henry Howard, Earl of Surrey, was attainted in January 1547 on charges that included his adopting the attributed arms of Edward the Confessor, thus in the eyes of the increasingly paranoid Henry VIII proclaiming his own right to the crown; he was beheaded. His father, the third Duke of Norfolk, was also attainted, on January 27, but escaped execution when the king died the next day. Surrey's son, Thomas Howard, 4th Duke of Norfolk, was attainted in January 1572 after being drawn into the Ridolfi Plot, which was designed to replace Elizabeth I with the captive Mary Queen of Scots, with Norfolk as her husband. The charges against Norfolk were that he had:

> conspired and imagined to deprive the queen of her crown and dignity, and compassed to excite sedition, to cause great slaughter amongst the queen's lieges, to levy war and rebellion against the queen, to subvert the government, to change and alter the pure religion established in the kingdom, and to bring in strangers and aliens to invade the realm, and to carry on a bitter war against the queen (Cooper, *Athenae Cantabrigienses*).

Most of these charges fell within the scope of the Statute of Treasons, but by no means all.

Acts of attainder were also passed at the behest of Henry VIII against two of his queens, Anne Boleyn (1536, on charges of adultery) and Catherine Howard (1542, not only of adultery during, but sexual relations before, the marriage).

The last acts of attainder were passed in 1746, following the failure of the Jacobite rising known as "the Forty Five." The last peer beheaded for treason, on Tower Hill on April 9, 1747, was Simon Fraser, 11th Lord Lovat, who had been impeached by the House of Commons after a long career of walking a tightrope between Hanoverians and Jacobites, which had brought a previous attainder as far back as 1697.

Other Treason Legislation. Not only was attainder used extensively by the Tudor monarchs, but the scope of treason under the Statute of Treasons was considerably extended by a series of acts, although a concession was made by Henry VII in 1495, specifically declaring service in war under a "king for the time being" not to be treason. This is somewhat ironic given that Henry had earlier dated the commencement of his reign to the day before the Battle of Bosworth Field (August 22, 1485) so that those who had fought in that battle for Richard III could be attainted. There was a further flurry of legislation in the 1790s as a result of fears of violent insurrection inspired by the French Revolution, but all this has since been repealed, so that the scope of treason is once more defined by the original statute. Two other acts, however, remain in force imposing liability for actions outside the statute. After a series of incidents in 1842 when Queen Victoria was shot at with pistols that may or may not have been loaded with "ball" as distinct from powder alone, the Treason Act of 1842 made it an offense to discharge a firearm in the vicinity of the sovereign. This act has been applied once in recent years, after Marcus Simon Serjeant fired a starting pistol as Elizabeth II rode down the Mall in London after the 1981 Trooping of the Colour ceremony. The Treason Felony Act of 1848, passed during a wave of revolutionary risings on the Continent and the abdications of two kings (Louis Philippe of France and Ludwig I of Bavaria), made it an offense, punishable by imprisonment for life, to publicly advocate the establishment of a republican government in the United Kingdom. Though there have been no prosecutions under this act since the 1880s, an attempt was made in 2002 to secure a "declaration of incompatibility"—under the Human Rights Act of 1998—between the 1848 act and Article 10 of the European Convention on Human Rights. The Divisional Court declined the application, and its decision was upheld by the House of Lords.

[*See also* Nationality in English Common Law.]

BIBLIOGRAPHY

Bellamy, John G. *The Law of Treason in England in the Later Middle Ages*. Cambridge, U.K.: Cambridge University Press, 1970. The leading work on medieval treason, but written by a general historian rather than a legal historian.

Bellamy, John G. *The Tudor Law of Treason: An Introduction*. London: Routledge & Keegan Paul, 1979.

Gunn, M. J. and Ann E. Lyon. "'Compassing the Death of the Queen's Consort'; Would It Be High Treason." *Nottingham Law Journal* 34 (1998).

Halsbury's Laws of England, vol. 11(1). 5th ed. Edited by Lord Mackay of Clashfern. London: LexisNexis, 2008.

Kim, Keechang. *Aliens in Medieval Law: The Origins of Modern Citizenship*. New York: Cambridge University Press, 2000. A fascinating study of a highly complex area.

Lyon, Ann E. "From Daffydd ap Gruffydd to Law Haw-Haw: The Concept of Allegiance in the Law of Treason." *Cambrian Law Review* 33 (2002): 35–52.

Ann E. Lyon

TRIAL. *See* Judges; Jury; *and* Procedure.

TRIAL BY BATTLE. Introduced into England by William the Conqueror, trial by battle was used in two types of lawsuit at common law: actions on the writs of right and appeals of felony. It was also used in England in the courts of the Constable and Marshal.

Battle and the Writs of Right. The writs of right were original writs issued by the king's chancery to initiate actions asserting claims to land. They were of two main forms: patent and praecipe. The patent writ was addressed from the king to the lord from whom the plaintiff—sometimes known as the "demandant"—claimed to hold the land, ordering the lord to "do right" or else let the local sheriff do it. The matter could be handled in the lord's court or, if not resolved there, transferred to the sheriff's court by a procedure called tolt and then to the king's court by a writ of *pone*. The three-step process of patent writ, tolt, and *pone* became a regular method by which demandants obtained access to the king's court to litigate claims to land. The second type of writ of right, the praecipe writ, was addressed from the king to the local sheriff, ordering him to command the defendant either to render the land the demandant claimed or to come before the king's justices and explain why he had not done so. The praecipe writ was used in place of the patent writ when the lord had waived jurisdiction or when the demandant claimed to hold from the king.

Trial on the writs of right was by battle between the two parties' champions. Details of the proceedings from the eleventh and twelfth centuries do not survive. Over time there developed an elaborate procedure of pledges, gloves, oaths, and batons, with battle lasting until surrender, death, or sunset, whichever came first. The party whose champion was victorious—the victor being the defendant if the battle remained unresolved at sunset—won the litigation.

Trial by Battle. Hamo Stare (*right*) claiming the right to prove his innocence by trial by combat, 1249. THE NATIONAL ARCHIVES

Almost from the outset there were concerns about the use of trial by battle to determine claims to land. From 1179, Henry II provided an alternative: the "grand assize" in which four knights from the neighborhood of the land in question would elect from the same neighborhood twelve knights, who would then declare on oath which party had the better right to the land. Henry II also created procedures other than the writs of right for litigating claims to land: the petty assizes of mort d'ancestor and novel disseisin, neither of which permitted trial by battle.

The use of battle on the writs of right soon fell into decline. The last fight on a writ of right seems to have occurred around the year 1300. The last attempt to use battle in civil litigation came in *Claxton v. Lilburn* (1638), a case that dragged on for years to avoid any fighting. By statute, Parliament abolished trial by battle in 1819.

Battle and the Appeal of Felony. The appeal of felony was a procedure for the private prosecution of a serious criminal offense. The appeal began with an oral accusation against the suspected felon, the "appellee." The accusation was made by the "appellor": normally the victim but in the event of homicide the victim's surviving spouse or heir. The appeal could also be brought by an "approver"—an accomplice of the accused felon—in exchange for leniency.

In an appeal brought by the victim or the victim's spouse or heir, the appellee was permitted to elect trial by battle, though not against a woman or a man elderly or infirm. In an appeal brought by an approver, the approver was required to prove the accusation by battle. Battle on an appeal was fought in person, not by champion. If the appellee lost, he was drawn and hanged, and his estate was forfeited. If the appellor lost, he could be fined or imprisoned.

As with battle on a writ of right, battle on an appeal raised concerns nearly from the outset. Judges and appellors distrusted it, and by the early thirteenth century most appeals were tried by jury. But the theoretical possibility of trial by battle was one factor leading to the replacement of the appeal by the writ of trespass.

Battle on an appeal fell into total disuse, but it remained technically available until the nineteenth century. An inventive litigant sought to resurrect trial by battle in the Court of King's Bench in *Ashford v. Thornton* (1818). Parliament responded by abolishing it the following year.

Battle in the Courts of the Constable and Marshal. Trial by battle was also available in England in the Court of the Lord High Constable and Earl Marshal, later the Court of the Earl Marshal also known as the Court of Chivalry. The constable and marshal were senior officers of state; their courts were conciliar courts outside the common law. Among other matters, these courts handled disputes over honors and coats of arms; they also heard complaints of treason. The last attempt at battle, averted by a letter from the king, was in *Lord Rea v. Ramsey* (1631).

[*See also* Anglo-Saxon Law; Evidence, *subentry on* English Common Law; Ordeal in English Common Law; *and* Petty Assizes.]

BIBLIOGRAPHY

Baker, John H. *An Introduction to English Legal History*. 4th ed. London: Butterworths, 2002.

Hudson, John. *The Formation of the English Common Law: Law and Society in England from the Norman Conquest to Magna Carta*. London: Longman, 1996.

Russell, M. J. "Trial by Battle and the Writ of Right." *Journal of Legal History* 1, no. 2 (1980): 111–134.

Russell, M. J. "Trial by Battle Procedure in Writs of Right and Criminal Appeals." *Legal History Review* 51 (1983): 123–134.

Thomas P. Gallanis

TRIBONIAN (c. 470–541/543? C.E.) The jurist and statesman Tribonian was the most substantial collaborator with the emperor Justinian in the editing of the Codex, the *Institutes*, and the Digest. Born in Pamphylia (now in southwestern Turkey), perhaps educated at the law school of Beirut, he began practice as an attorney before the praetorian prefect of the East, whose court was the most important after that of the emperor. He entered into the circle of the court in 528 as one of seven functionaries and three legal experts commissioned to reorganize the imperial constitutions under John of Cappadocia. Having completed the Codex Iustinianus quickly and successfully (in April 529), Tribonian was nominated *quaestor sacri palatii* (quaestor of the sacred palace), no later than November 17, 529. This office had been created in the fourth century by Constantine, perhaps to parallel the *quaestor Augusti*, who spoke for the emperor in the Senate; its principal duty was drafting and compiling "beneficial laws" for his subjects. The quaestor was therefore defined as the "voice of the emperor," "privy to his thoughts," and "treasure of the good reputation of the state." In translating the will of the emperor into persuasive legal form, the quaestor needed skill in technical rhetoric as well as knowledge of laws and jurisprudence; this ideal—sketched by Cassiodorus, who was active in the same period in Rome—was met in Tribonian, who had a reputation for culture and peerless knowledge of juristic writing.

In his new position (possibly as late as August 1, 530, until perhaps April 30, 531), he issued fifty constitutions to repeal obsolete institutions and to settle controversial issues—the *Quinquaginta decisiones* (perhaps circulated in a compilation). This paved the way for consolidating the writings of jurists. Charged with forming a commission for the Digest, he enlisted four professors, eleven attorneys, and a lone bureaucrat, Constantinus, master of petitions. He also took on many assistants, five of whom are mentioned in *Novel* 35.

While work was in full swing, accompanied by the introduction of numerous constitutions intended to handle emerging issues, a revolt began in January 532 in Constantinople. This continued even after the resignation of the praetorian prefect, John; of the prefect of Constantinople, Eudaimon; and of Tribonian himself. In the end, the generals Belisarius and Narses quelled the revolt.

Despite his resignation as quaestor, Tribonian remained chairman of the commission for the Digest, and was quickly promoted to *magister officiorum*. With this post he received the duty of preparing a didactic guide, the *Institutes*, which he completed in November 533 with the collaboration of two professors, Theophilus, from the school in Constantinople, and Dorotheus, from Beirut. The Digest (or Pandects) an anthology of the writings of jurists, was published that December. Perhaps in the interval between the two projects, he was named an honorary consul.

He was still *magister officiorum* when he presided over a modest commission (comprising Dorotheus and three attorneys) for the second edition of the Codex. Completed in November 534, this added constitutions subsequent to the first edition that rectified dated law (making up the *Quinquaginta decisiones* and *Extravagantes*) and several others of contemporary significance, such as two laws of 534 that established civil and military order in Roman Africa, recently reconquered from the Vandals. The Digest now superseded the Law of Citations (*lex citationum*), which had from 426 regulated judicial use of legal works. Having completed this enterprise, Tribonian was in 535 renamed quaestor of the sacred palace (a post he perhaps briefly combined with that of *magister officiorum*). As quaestor, he drew up numerous laws (called *Novels* because they were new compared with those compiled in the Codex), reforming public administration and several institutions of private law. The constitutions of this period were mostly in Greek, or bilingual; this interruption of the Latinate tradition has been ascribed to John of Cappadocia, but Tribonian himself was aware that, in reality, Greek promoted the promulgation of imperial norms. His intense legislative activity brought him a reputation for corruption—for repealing laws and creating others for personal benefit; this seems confirmed by the hostility of the insurgents of January 532 and by the confiscation of part of Tribonian's patrimony, ordered by Justinian upon his death, which came between the end of 541 and 543 and perhaps owing to a wave of plague that killed a third of the population in Constantinople.

Methods of Compilation. It is probable (if disputed) that Justinian planned his reorganization of constitutions and jurisprudence from the beginning, and that Tribonian was a determining factor in its formulation. It is certain that Justinian credited him most for its actualization (probably also for the first Codex, created under the direction of John of Cappadocia). The Justinianic stamp appears in several forms: elimination of the superfluous, and of outdated, redundant, and contradictory regulations; modification of texts; and distribution of texts within pertinent titles. It is most evident, however, in the compilation's divergences from the original order of its models; one clue is the transfer of religious and ecclesiastical laws from the final book of Theodosius's compilation to the first book of Justinian's.

The loss of the first edition of the Codex (with the exception of the index to Titles 11–16 of the first book and another fragment) hinders evaluation of the modifications introduced in its revision. But beside the inclusion of constitutions introduced between 529 and 534 and several retouches, it is probable that Tribonian left the structure virtually unaltered.

The *Institutes* (or *Elements*), issued in 530 and quickly compiled while the Digest was being finalized, were mainly used as a first-year manual for a reformed legal-studies curriculum (as prescribed in the constitution Omnem). The principal sources of the *Institutes* were two brilliant second-century manuals by Gaius, compiled from the *Institutes* of Florentinus, Ulpian, Paul, and Marcianus, which had consulted different models than those used in compiling the Digest. For the most part, only excerpts not of an introductory nature were used in the Digest, patched together and modified so that the narrating voice was that of the emperor. The editor Philip E. Huschke (1868) held that Dorotheus had drawn up books I and II and Theophilus the remainder, Tribonian limiting himself to supervision. Tony Honoré and others argued that Tribonian personally added the "emperor's" amendments in an early draft prepared by Dorotheus and Theophilus.

The Digest reduces a library that would have included 1,528 volumes, by thirty-eight or thirty-nine jurists writing from the first century B.C.E. to the fourth century C.E., to about one-twentieth its size; it was compiled with the utmost generosity by Tribonian, as the restoration of even annotations by Ulpian, Paul, and Marcianus to the writings of Papinian—which had been eliminated by Constantine—demonstrates. The hypothesis that the compilers utilized preceding compilations is not substantiated by sources. What allowed Tribonian to carry out, in just three years, an undertaking that had been deemed impossible was discovered in 1820 by Friedrich Bluhme (1797–1874), who noted that the order of the fragments within the titles is constant. Bluhme understood this to be the order in which the commission members read the works. More precisely, Tribonian had divided the works into three groups ("Bluhmian masses"), the Sabinian (which begins with comments *ad Sabinum*), the edictal (opening with comments on the edict), and the Papinian (opening with works on Papinian). Each mass was assigned a subcommittee that worked simultaneously with the others. In the end, the fragments selected by each subcommittee under specific rubrics were united with those compiled by the others, giving way to the titles of the Digest (the internal order of which, therefore, is owed to the order in which they were read).

Later Evaluation of Tribonian's Work. In the sixteenth century Tribonian became the lightning rod for critics of the defects of common law, the legal system based on Justinianic texts. The influential pamphlet *Anti-Tribonian* by François Hotman (published in 1603), an anthem to the liberation of France from the "domination" of the law of Rome, especially attacks the Digest (the "Tribonian reliquary"), chiding its defective arrangement, the selection of jurists of Eastern origin who did not command the Latin language, and inept modifications (*emblemata Triboniani*) to the original texts. As to the first accusation, the order of titles follows the perpetual edict and other traditional models (there is however, some basis regarding the order of fragments within the titles). The accusation of impure Latin should be contrasted with the high praise the great humanist Lorenzo Valla had bestowed on the elegance of the same jurists Hotman criticized. The hypothesis of widespread interpolation appeared to have been confirmed by studies at the end of the nineteenth century, but these also were based on preconceptions. Anti-Tribonianism wrongly presupposed that classical jurists were isolated from contemporary culture (above all philosophical and rhetorical) and that their Latin followed an abstract, puristic model. The "hunt for interpolation" also indulged in conjecture and in oversimplification of the historical and cultural background of the various phases of Roman law. After having dominated the first half of the twentieth century (and having progressively shifted the responsibility for interpolations from Tribonian to presumed reissues of the legal texts in the fourth and fifth centuries), Anti-Tribonianism died out. Comparisons with texts surviving from outside the Digest demonstrate that the compilers rarely modified contents (especially eliminating obsolete matter like the *formulae*); more often, they trimmed tedious disagreements between jurists, faithful to the goal of reducing ambiguity and conflict. It is clear that the Digest and the *Institutes* transformed a legally uncertain set of regulations into a normative system. Historical evaluation must nonetheless refer to the conditions of late antiquity. Judicial use of the writings of jurists had continued even after the dying away of original legal literature in the third century; legal training is striking, as well, for the importance it assigned to classical jurists. Thus, the attempt to guarantee the authenticity of texts, to render them accessible at reasonable cost and to reduce their bulk, to simplify the variety of opinions, and especially to coordinate ancient law with the innovations introduced by specific imperial initiatives (an aspect not yet adequately analyzed) was a reform that was not only rational but sensational, given the conditions of its time.

[*See also* Humanism; Jurists; Justinian; Praetorian Edict; *and* Roman Law, *subentry on* The Age of Justinian.]

BIBLIOGRAPHY

Bluhme, Friedrich. "Die Ordnung der Fragmente in den Pandectentiteln. Ein Beitrag zur Entsehungsgeschichte der Pandecten." *Zeitschrift für geschichtliche Rechtswissenschaft* 4 (1820): 257–472.

Giomaro, Anna Maria. *Codex Repetitae Praelectionis*. Rome: Pontificia Università Lateranense, 2001.

Honoré, Tony. "How Tribonian Organised the Compilation of Justinian's Digest." *Zeitschrift der Savigny-Stiftung für Rechtsgeschichte. Romanistische Abteilung* 121 (2004): 1–43.

Honoré, Tony. *Tribonian*. London: Duckworth; Ithaca, N.Y.: Cornell University Press, 1978.

Mantovani, Dario. *Digesto e masse bluhmiane*. Milan: Giuffrè, 1987.

Osler, Douglas. "The Compilation of Justinian's Digest." *Zeitschrift der Savigny-Stiftung für Rechtsgeschichte. Romanistische Abteilung* 102 (1985): 129–184.

Russo Ruggeri, Carmela. *Studi sulle* Quinquaginta decisiones. Milan, Italy: Giuffrè, 1999.

Varvaro, Mario. "Contributo allo studio delle *Quinquaginta decisiones*." *Annali del Seminario Giuridico dell'Università di Palermo* 46 (2000): 361–539.

Wallinga, Tammo. *Tanta/Dedōken: Two Introductory Constitutions to Justinian's Digest*. Groningen, Netherlands: E. Forsten, 1989.

Wieacker, Franz. "Zur Herstellung der Digesten." In *Ars boni et aequi. Festschrift für Wolfgang Waldstein zum 65. Geburtstag*, edited by Martin Josef Schermaier and Zoltan Végh, pp. 417–442. Stuttgart, Germany: Steiner, 1993.

DARIO MANTOVANI
Translated from the Italian by Joe Jackson

TRINIDAD AND TOBAGO. The Republic of Trinidad and Tobago consists of two main and twenty-one smaller islands. Trinidad was first claimed by Christopher Columbus for Spain on July 31, 1498. Early Spanish colonizers wiped out most original inhabitants, Arawaks and Carib Indians. While Trinidad remained under Spanish rule until the British captured it on February 18, 1797, Tobago changed hands twenty-two times between the British, French, and Dutch, until Britain consolidated the two islands into one colony in 1889.

Population. The ethnic composition reflects a history of conquest and immigration. Between 1783 and 1797, 10,000 slaves were imported from Africa; there were twice as many by 1806. The Abolition Act of 1834, proclaimed in Trinidad in 1838 while Africans were a majority population, led to a system of apprenticeship until August 1, 1838. Between 1845 and 1917, approximately 145,000 Indians were introduced into Trinidad to save the British sugar industry. These technically free Indian laborers could return to India when their contract ended, but were offered land grants as inducements and about 110,000 Indians remained. Today, the dense population of Trinbagonians (2006 estimate 1,297,944) comprises about 40.3 percent descendents of Indians, about 39.5 percent people of African origin, 18.4 percent of mixed race, 0.6 percent Europeans, with the remaining 1.2 percent mainly Chinese and Syrians. Major religious groups are Roman Catholics (26 percent), Hindus (22 percent), Anglicans (8 percent), Muslims (6 percent) and Seventh-day Adventists (4 percent).

Plural Legal Structure. Over time, the people developed a marked legal pluralism to validate religio-cultural practices, reflected in today's hybrid legal system. Faced with social diversity and racial and religious tensions, Britain devised a form of colonial constitution under a Crown Colony government in which control was exercised by an appointed governor without the assistance of an elected Assembly, subject to directions from the Colonial Office in London. Local legislatures were presided over by the governor and consisted at first entirely of officials who took their instructions from him.

Indian settlers evolved a "creolized" lifestyle, mixing elements of the local culture with uniquely Indian characteristics, including important sociocultural differences between North and South Indians. Since the post-indenture period, there has been an increasingly well-organized reconstruction of Indian identity within the islands' multicultural setting.

In 1890 a consolidated Indian Marriage Law was passed by the Trinidad Legislative Council, providing for the recovery by immigrants of any presents given in connection with marriage, but this law proved ineffective. Most Indian marriages remained outside the law and the Colony did not consider them legal. The Immigrants' Marriage and Divorce Ordinances 6/1881 and 23/1891 attempted to place Indian marriages on a legal basis, provided certain registration requirements were fulfilled, but both ordinances proved ineffective. To the Indians it seemed unfair that customary Hindu marriages were recognised in India but not in Trinidad, though both countries were ruled by the British. Conflicts over minimum marriage ages and age of consent brought many Indians before the courts. Not registering marriages had a huge impact on property law, as illegitimate children could not inherit property and much land reverted to state ownership. This unsatisfactory state of affairs continued until May 13, 1946, when Hindu marriages received legal recognition under the Hindu Marriage Act of 1945. The Muslim Marriage and Divorce Act of December 1, 1964 recognized Muslim practices, while Orisa marriages of traditional Africans have only been accepted since August 16, 1999.

Hindus had protested since 1938 that they were unable to dispose legally of their dead in accordance with

First Prime Minister of Trinidad. Eric Williams, 1962. NEW YORK WORLD-TELEGRAM AND THE SUN NEWSPAPER PHOTOGRAPH COLLECTION/PRINTS AND PHOTOGRAPHS DIVISION, LIBRARY OF CONGRESS

religious customs. By 1948 the debate had escalated, the government was prepared to approve cremation by modern methods, but Hindus wanted approval for burning dead bodies on pyres and disposing the ashes in flowing water. A Cremation Committee, created in 1950, reached an agreement with the government, and after much debate Ordinance 16/1953 for the Regulation of Burning of Human Remains in Crematoria or Otherwise legalized both systems. To cremate a person, one must first obtain a licence under these Regulations.

Independence. Trinidad and Tobago became independent in 1962, but retained allegiance to the British monarch. On August 1, 1976, the country became a Republic under the Constitution of September 24, 1976, with a president and a prime minister. Section 4 of the 1976 Constitution contains nondiscrimination guarantees, but politics in Trinidad remain deeply divided by racial distinctions. The People's National Movement (PNM) draws support mostly from Africans, while the United National Congress (UNC) has mostly Indian supporters. Various moves to bridge the divide resulted in the formation of the Organisation of National Reconstruction party (September 1981) and more recently the creation of a new Congress of the People (September 2006) to include citizens of all colors, ethnic groups, and creeds. Both parties sought to include a greater mix of the ethnic groups but their attempts ended in failure at the polls.

Dr. Eric Williams was prime minister from 1962 until his death in 1981. In 1986, A. N. R. Robinson of the National Alliance for Reconstruction became prime minister. Patrick Manning then served as prime minister from 1991 to 1995, was again appointed after inconclusive elections in December 2001, and returned to power after elections in October 2002, the third poll in three years. The first Indo-Trinbagonian prime minister, Basdeo Panday, served from November 10, 1995 until December 23, 2001. Sir Ellis Clarke the first president of the Republic was appointed on August 1, 1976 and served in that capacity until 1987. The first Indo-Trinbagonian president, Justice Noor Hassanali, was elected on March 19, 1987 and served until March 19, 1997.

The bicameral Parliament has thirty-six members in the House of Representatives (to be increased in 2007 to forty-one), elected for five years. The Senate's thirty-one members are appointed by the president for up to five years, sixteen on the advice of the prime minister, six on advice of the opposition leader, with nine independent members of the community selected by the president. The country's judicial system consists of a Supreme Court, composed of the High Court of Justice and the Court of Appeal, whose Chief Justice is appointed by the president. The Judicial Committee of the Privy Council in London still decides final appeals on some matters. Member states of the Caribbean Community (CARICOM) selected Trinidad as the headquarters for the new Caribbean Court of Justice, which heard its first case in August 2005 and is intended to replace the Privy Council for all CARICOM states.

[*See also* British Commonwealth.]

BIBLIOGRAPHY

Tikasingh, Gerad I. M. *The Establishment of Indians in Trinidad 1870–1900*. St Augustine, Trinidad: The University of the West Indies, 1973. Unpublished PhD thesis. A detailed account of the racial and cultural integration of East Indians in Trinidad.

Williams, Eric. *From Columbus to Castro: The History of the Caribbean 1492–1969*. New York: Harper & Row, 1970. An authoritative history of the Caribbean from the first European contact to the turbulent 1960s.

Wood, Donald. *Trinidad in Transition: The Years After Slavery*. Oxford: Oxford University Press, 1968. A meticulously documented account of life in Trinidad from slavery to the turn of the century with an emphasis on racial and cultural elements of modern Trinidad.

ARSHA GOSINE

TRUSTS AND ESTATES. *See* Inheritance *and* Succession.

TRUSTS IN ENGLISH COMMON LAW. The law of trusts is perhaps English law's most distinctive contribution to jurisprudence. Its origins lie in conscience, and, later, in equity: common-law attribution of ownership would not suffice where property had been acquired on the understanding that it would be held for the benefit of another (the beneficiary), and a court of conscience, or equity, would intervene to prevent unconscientious exploitation of the legal position by the trustee who would be required to exercise his common-law ownership of the trust property for the beneficiary's benefit.

Origins in conscience suggest obligation, but regular enforcement against both trustees and strangers, the beneficiary's capacity to assign his interest and pass it by will, and its protection from external claims on the trust property, led to a strong proprietary aspect to the beneficial interest, the nature and limits of which continue to be debated. This has been accompanied by a movement from emphasis upon personal trust and confidence, from vernacular "trust," toward an institutional understanding of trusts, in which, despite judicial reassertion of its relevance, emphasis upon conscience, of the court or of the trustee, has been seen as tending to an undue width of discretion. The movement from personal trust and confidence has seen also the rise of trusts constructed by the courts, or supplied by statute.

While the core of trusts lies in conscience, or in equity, their boundaries have never been simple. The action of account, for example, may be regarded as a common-law action for breach of trust, while distinctions between trusts and such transactions as contracts, conditional transfers, or bailments, when drawn, are not straightforward.

While their flexibility and versatility are well known, trusts have tended to be concentrated in particular contexts, the balance between them shifting over time: the handling of family wealth, finance and commerce, and charity. The historical development of trusts may be divided into three: the period before the Statute of Uses (1536), in which uses originated and developed; the period after 1536, in which the statute's effects were worked out and the groundwork of the modern law was laid; and the period from the earlier nineteenth century in which trusts law was adapted to a new economic and social climate.

Uses before 1536. Modern trusts have their roots in medieval "uses," land being transferred by feoffment with livery of seisin from a settlor ("feoffor to uses") to a trustee ("feoffee to uses"), to the use of (that is, *ad opus*, for the benefit of) a beneficiary (*cestui que use*)—either the feoffor or a third party.

Origins. Uses' remoter origins have been variously sought, in Roman *fideicommissa*, in canonical conceptions of stewardship, in the Germanic *Salman* (or *Treuhand*), or in the Islamic waqf. In thirteenth-century England temporary uses were encountered in transfer of land by substitution. Enduring uses appeared from the 1220s in the case of Franciscan friars, living in hostels held to their use. Use-like arrangements were also made in the thirteenth century by landowners going abroad, or for management of land for an infant, though frequently the "settlor" retained ownership: these were custody arrangements.

Development and enforcement. Following the statute *Quia Emptores* (1290) freehold land (not held immediately of the king) was freely transferable between the living, and the concept of various times or estates in the land was emerging. These developments encouraged landowners to change their estates: a tenant in fee simple might become a tenant for life jointly with his wife, with remainder in fee tail to a younger son (in consequence of primogeniture otherwise unprovided for). This necessitated a grant in fee simple to another, and regrant as required. This was a transaction, not a lasting relationship, but during the fourteenth century testamentary executors were becoming common. If a grant might be made for regrant, it might be made for longer, even until after the grantor's death, the feoffees to uses behaving as executors. The devolution of land might thus be directed across generations, and provision made for the payment of debts from landed wealth, despite the common-law prohibition upon wills of freehold land.

As uses became more common in the later fourteenth century, court interpretation and enforcement became available. The consistory courts of Rochester and Canterbury (and perhaps elsewhere) enforced uses of land, after the feoffor's death, from the 1370s until the mid-fifteenth century. The court of Chancery also began to enforce uses at this time, perhaps as early as the 1370s, with a settled jurisdiction in the first decades of the fifteenth century.

Rules began to develop. If the feoffees died the use was enforceable against the last surviving feoffee's heir, and the feoffees' grantee was bound by the use unless he acquired the land for value, without notice. Uses could arise by implication: a bargain and sale for pecuniary consideration raised an implied use for the purchaser, while a conveyance for no consideration with no use expressed raised a resulting use for the grantor. The beneficiary acquired a kind of ownership, but tension remained between property and the role of the feoffee's conscience: a corporation, having no conscience, could not be a feoffee to uses, and notice of the use would not bind those, such as feudal lords taking by escheat, who did not come to the land through the feoffees.

The sub-plot: Uses and the feudal revenue. The evasion of the feudal revenue was not the primary aim of creating feoffments to uses, but uses' capacity to deprive feudal lords, and particularly the king, of feudal revenue played a significant role in the development of the law.

Of particular importance here were wardship and *primer seisin*. Wardship applied to land, held by a military tenure (i.e., in return for the provision of feudal military service) that descended to an infant heir upon the ancestor's death, giving the lord custody of the heir's lands or body, or both, until majority, with no obligation to account for the income. *Primer seisin* was a royal prerogative, giving the king the profits of the land of an adult heir for a defined period upon inheritance. Where a tenant died having made a feoffment to the uses of his last will of land held in fee simple or fee tail, no wardship or *primer seisin* would arise since nothing descended to the heir. Some protection against the consequent loss of revenue was provided by the Statute of Marlborough (1267), but legislative activity concerning uses began again in the later fifteenth century. A statute of 1484, concerned to protect purchasers, gave beneficiaries of uses power to convey a legal title, thus bringing uses before the common-law judges; and a statute of 1490 plugged a gap in the Statute of Marlborough, where a feoffor to uses of land held by military tenure died leaving an infant heir and no will.

In the context of renewed emphasis on the royal feudal revenue in the early decades of the sixteenth century two lines of thinking developed concerning uses. One, supported by the statute of 1484, saw uses as "at common law"; the other saw them as fraudulent and uncertain. The latter was more obviously a Crown line of argument, but if uses were "at common law" should they not obey the common-law prohibition on wills of freehold land? Limited revenue-protection legislation having failed in parliament in 1532, royal attention turned to changing the common law. In 1535 in a test case over the will of Thomas Fiennes, Lord Dacre of the South, the judges were persuaded to hold that a use of freehold land, following the nature of the land, could not be devised (i.e., passed by will). This startling decision cast into doubt most titles in England, giving the Crown the leverage to push through the Statute of Uses (1536), which included a clause removing any retrospective effect of *Lord Dacre's Case*, (1535) 105 B. & M. 109.

The Statute of Uses (1536) and Its Aftermath. The Statute of Uses' mechanism completed the assimilation of the position of the beneficiary of a use to that of a legal owner begun by the statute of 1484. Now the beneficiary was not merely empowered to convey a legal title, but was the legal owner, the statute "executing" the use and passing legal title from the feoffees to the beneficiary. Wills of freehold land now seemed impossible, as the uses which had enabled them in effect to be made would be executed by the statute. But the position proved unsustainable, and in 1540 the Statute of Wills gave power to make a will of one-third of lands held by military tenure (and of the whole of land not so held). From 1540 until military tenure's abolition in the mid-seventeenth century, the Statute of Wills (not the Statute of Uses) defined the scope of the feudal revenue.

The Statute of Uses did not apply to all uses. In the exceptions (which came commonly to be known as trusts) lie the origins of modern trusts. It was clear that uses were unexecuted where the feoffees had active management duties (for example, where they were required to raise money from the land and pay it over to the beneficiary). Also, the statute did not apply to uses of personal property or of copyhold land (land held according to the custom of the manor). The position of uses of leases for terms of years was initially doubtful, but by the 1590s it was clear that they were unexecuted. Also unexecuted were uses upon uses, arising expressly, for example by transfer from *X* to *A*, to the use of *A*, to the use of (or upon trust for) *B*; or impliedly, as in a bargain and sale enrolled from *X* to *A*, to the use of (or upon trust for) *B* (the bargain and sale raising an implied use for *A*). The form "to *A*, to the use of *A*, to the use of *B*" became standard, though too much should not be claimed for uses upon uses: active uses alone would have secured the survival of trusts after 1536.

The purposes for which trusts were created after 1536 were in some respects unchanged: charitable provision, for example, continued uninterrupted (though the Reformation altered the definition of charity, which was set on a long-term course by the Statute of Charitable Uses (1601). The Statute of Wills had removed the role of uses in making wills of freehold land, but trusts, some temporary, some longer-term, found diverse employment after 1536, including secrecy under persecution (by hiding assets); payment of debts; evasion of creditors (a recurring theme, legislated against from the 1370s); provision for the incapable; restraint of spendthrifts (a purpose resonating with nineteenth-century development of protective trusts); avoidance of dower (again by placing assets out of reach); and the enabling of married women to manage property independently of their husbands. In the seventeenth century trusts began to play a significant role in landed estates as a key element in strict settlements.

Enforcement of trusts of both personalty and realty in the court of Chancery continued after 1536, the feudal revenue being governed by the Statute of Wills, which was relatively difficult to evade using trusts. The concept of notice was applied by the 1570s, and though it was said at common law in the later sixteenth century and early seventeenth century that the trust beneficiary's interest was no more than the benefit of an obligation (a constant theme in discussion of trusts), it seems that even at this time the interest was both assignable and devisable in Chancery.

After the Restoration, Lord Chancellor Nottingham (1673–1682) played a significant role in giving substance to interests under trusts and in setting out the framework of the law, though not all that he did was new and the doctrines of the pre-1536 use cast a long shadow. In some aspects Nottingham dispelled that shadow, for example, in promoting the availability of the trust estate for the payment of the beneficiary's debts (the corollary of which was protection of the trust property from claims against the trustee personally). In other aspects he drew upon the learning of uses, drawing, for example, upon the old law of resulting uses in analyzing resulting trusts. Another category of implied trusts, now called constructive, was also recognized by Nottingham, though it predated him. Its primary function was in regulating existing trusts, as in the case of trustees seeking to profit from the trust (now usually associated with the decision in *Keech v. Sandford*, [1726] Sel Cas Ch. 61; 25 ER 223). Secret trusts of property left by will also appeared in Nottingham's time. Beyond implied trusts, express trusts gave rise to difficulties over "precatory" words, expressing hope or desire, which Nottingham did not readily permit to give rise to trusts.

In Nottingham's time also, the Statute of Frauds (1677) (for which he was responsible) introduced formality requirements for the creation of trusts, requiring evidence in writing, with an exception for trusts arising or resulting by implication or construction of law, a provision which survives. In Nottingham's time emphasis was upon the duties, rather than the rights, of the trustees, but an honest mistake would not be penalized, and no more than reasonable skill and care seems to have been required. Generally trustees would be charged only for actual receipts, though Nottingham laid down the enduring principle that they would be allowed reimbursement for costs, but not for work in managing the trust.

During the eighteenth century, in particular under Lord Chancellor Hardwicke (1737–1756), Nottingham's work was developed and refined. Trusts played a (debated) role in eighteenth-century unincorporated deed-of-settlement companies, but a model centered upon land settlement continued to exert a powerful influence. Trusteeship's voluntary nature was reemphasized, and rules governing the conduct of trustees stiffened, in part in consequence of the financial collapse after the South Sea Bubble of 1720. To ensure safety, only an extremely narrow range of investments was permitted to trustees in the absence of express provision.

The Nineteenth Century and Later. In the first half of the nineteenth century the work of assimilating the trust beneficiary's interest to common-law rules, and of defining trusts as a legal category, was largely completed: apart from the separate property of married women, the legal rules preventing restraints on alienation were applied to trusts; beneficiaries of full age and absolutely entitled were enabled to terminate the trust by demanding conveyance of the trust property; an abstract conception of trusts, independent of any actual relationship of trusting, appeared in the development of the possibility of declaring oneself a trustee; and the requirements of certainty of objects (i.e., that the beneficiaries be ascertainable), and that noncharitable trusts must have human beneficiaries, were established (though discretionary trusts developed, initially linked to protective trusts intended to place income and capital beyond the reach of creditors).

During the nineteenth century investment opportunities widened dramatically, stimulated by the development of railways, and by legislation allowing the free formation of limited-liability joint-stock companies. As trusts expanded beyond the landed gentry and aristocracy and became increasingly centered upon interchangeable investments, the old tie with uses and conveyancing was cut, and from the 1830s appeared the first texts on trusts, rather than uses, or uses and trusts. Changing social and economic conditions demanded reevaluation of the rights and duties of trustees, who were increasingly professionals required to actively manage a fund. In turn the scope of permitted investments was slowly widened, in part by legislation (though lists of permitted investments endured until the Trustee Act [2000]). With wider powers of investment, questions arose as to how far agents might be employed and functions delegated, and as to the degree of skill and care which should be required of trustees both generally, and in investment decisions, the last being set in the 1880s at the standard of an ordinary prudent man of business acting on behalf of those for whom he felt morally bound to provide.

Development in the first half of the nineteenth century was largely judicial. The first general trusts statute was the Trustee Act (1850), largely concerned with the transfer of trust property. A series of statutes from 1859 concerned trustee investment. Provision was made in the Conveyancing and Law of Property Act (1881) for the appointment and removal of trustees, and the Trustee Act (1888) was motivated by concern to increase protection against liability for honest trustees. Trusts legislation was consolidated in 1893 and again in the Trustee Act (1925), now modified and to some extent replaced by the Trustee Act (2000), which together with wider powers of investment, makes provision in relation to remuneration of trustees, the appointment of nominees and custodians, delegation, and insurance. Provision is also made for a new standard duty of such care and skill as is reasonable in the circumstances.

The abolition of the separate courts of common law and equity in the Judicature Acts of the 1870s left trusts unscathed, though in modern debate over "fusion" of law and equity even trusts are not universally regarded as incapable of practical integration. But the flexibility of trusts, reemphasized in the twentieth century as they have adapted to modern taxation regimes, unit trusts, family breakdown, and occupational pension provision, may owe much to their conceptual complexity and ambiguity, rendering any disassembly and reintegration a challenging undertaking.

[*See also* Chancery; Charities; Conveyancing; Equity, *subentry on* English Common Law; Feudal Law, *subentry on* English Common Law; Land, *subentry on* Leases of Land in English Common Law; Property, *subentry on* Real Property in English Common Law; Tenure, Doctrine of; *and* Wills, *subentry on* English Common Law.]

BIBLIOGRAPHY

Alexander, G. S. "The Transformation of Trusts as a Legal Category, 1800–1914." *Law and History Review* 5 (1987): 303–350.

Baker, J. H. *An Introduction to English Legal History*. 4th ed. London: Butterworths, 2002. An introductory survey of the history of uses and trusts to the eighteenth century. See chap. 14 and pp. 290–297. Includes bibliographies at pp. 258 and 296.

Bean, John M. W. *The Decline of English Feudalism, 1215–1540*. Manchester, U.K.: Manchester University Press, 1968. See chaps. 3 and 4. Concerns the origins and development of uses and their effect upon the feudal revenue. To be read in the light of Biancalana (in *Itinera Fiduciae*), but still useful.

Helmholz, Richard, and Reinhard Zimmermann, eds. *Itinera Fiduciae: Trust and Treuhand in Historical Perspective*. Berlin: Duncker & Humblot, 1998. See in particular: Joseph Biancalana, "Medieval Uses," pp. 111–152; Richard Helmholz, "Trusts in the English Ecclesiastical Courts, 1300–1600," pp. 153–172; Neil Jones, "Trusts in England after the Statute of Uses: A View from the 16th Century," pp. 173–205; and Michael Macnair, "The Conceptual Basis of Trusts in the Later 17th and Early 18th Centuries," pp. 207–236.

Jones, N. G. "The Use Upon a Use in Equity Revisited." *Cambrian Law Review* 33 (2002): 67–80.

Lord Nottingham's Chancery Cases. Edited by D. E. C. Yale. Vol. 2, pp. 87–194. London: B. Quaritch, 1961. This section of Mr. Yale's introduction to the second volume of his edition of Lord Nottingham's reports amounts to a small monograph on the law concerning trusts in England in the later seventeenth century.

Milsom, S. F. C. *Historical Foundations of the Common Law*. 2d ed. London: Butterworths, 1981. See chapter 9, which includes (at pp. 222–233) material on the effects of the Statute of Uses at law (as opposed to in equity).

Stebbings, Chantal. *The Private Trustee in Victorian England*. Cambridge, U.K.: Cambridge University Press, 2002. A history of the state of trusts law, and of its reform, in nineteenth-century England, from the point of view of trustees.

N. G. Jones

TURKEY. [*This entry contains two subentries, on Islamic law and Turkish law in Turkey.*]

Islamic Law

The legal system of the Ottoman Empire (1299–1918) was based on Islamic law, which applied to all Muslims in every field and to non-Muslims in the field of public law. The non-Muslims (*dhimmī*s) were subject to the rules of religious law applied by their own community courts in such private areas of law as personal status, family, and inheritance. In the Ottoman Empire, the *ḳānūnnāme*s (basic laws) that included rules other than Islamic Law were established in the areas of criminal and fiscal law. For example, in the Islamic criminal law, Muslims and *dhimmī*s were punished under the same rules, but the Ottoman *ḳānūnnāme*s gave less (about half) punishments to the *dhimmī*s when compared to Muslims. In the area of fiscal law, some of the taxes were kept the same as in the Islamic law. However, some new taxes, such as the traditional taxes, were established in the *ḳānūnnāme*s. The new rules instituted in the *ḳānūnnāme*s are called *örfī* law. Foreigners were tried at the consular courts operating in accordance with the judicial and financial capitulations granted to some European countries. The Ottoman legal and judiciary structure was thus fragmented, with the community and consular courts dealing with non-Muslims and the qadi courts applying Islamic law to Muslims.

In an attempt to save the state, which was in decline by the early nineteenth century, reforms were made in the field of law, as they were in every field. The aim was to realize equality and to ensure that the non-Muslims influenced by the principles of nationalism of the French Revolution remained loyal to the state.

Equality was emphasized in the 1839 Tanzimat reform (Hatt-ı Şerif [order of the sultan] of Gülhane) and 1856 Islahat (reform) decrees (Hatt-ı Hümayun [order of the sultan]). With the Hatt-ı Şerif of Gülhane, equality was declared among all citizens. With the 1856 Islahat Decree, equality was guaranteed and existing privileges were confirmed. Secular laws, mostly adopted from France, were intended to ensure equality before the law; examples are the 1850 Commercial Code and the 1858 Criminal Code. The incorporation of these new laws, and the new civil courts (*nizamiye*) that were to apply them, into the existing legal and judicial system created conflicts of jurisdiction and power among the *şeriat* (Islamic law), non-Muslim, consular, and *nizamiye* courts that persisted until the fall of the empire.

The War of Independence brought about in 1920 a new state on the ruins of the Ottoman state. Mustafa Kemal Atatürk (1881–1938), the founder of the new state, decided to bring about a revolution in law: in 1926, the Swiss Civil Code was adopted in Turkey as a model. Article 1 of the Swiss Civil Code states that the judge, when exercising his discretionary power, shall take as his basis the settled court decisions and established doctrine. In contrast, article 1 of the Turkish Civil Code avoided the terms "legal tradition" and "established court opinions," stating instead that "the judge will make use of jurisprudence and case law." The only rule transferred from Islamic law into the new Turkish system was the procedure of the separation of property in the administration of the property of husband and wife. This article was later repealed as well, when the Turkish Civil Code entered into force on January 1, 2002.

Other basic laws came into the Turkish legal system by way of the translation of relevant laws of the Western European countries. Such laws as the Italian Criminal Law, the German Criminal Procedure Code, and the Swiss Execution-Bankruptcy Law were adopted, with some amendments, and were not at all affected by Islamic law.

Although in most respects Turkish citizens adapted themselves rapidly to the new system of law, there were a few rules in the field of family law whose application was blocked by social reality. For example, people in rural areas continued to rely on the religious marriage ceremony instead of the civil ceremony. Uneducated people continued to consider the religious ceremonies legally valid. Special laws of remission, enacted on several dates, allowed these marriages to be registered by the birth registration offices just like civil marriages. These laws are temporary, however, and the number of such religious marriage ceremonies has decreased over time. The new Turkish Civil Law provides for the imprisonment of parties who perform a religious marriage ceremony without a civil marriage ceremony, but the punishment is remitted when a civil marriage ceremony is then performed.

One other area where Islamic law persists is inheritance law. The estates of those who died before 1926 (the year when the Civil Code entered into force) are distributed according to the rules of Islamic inheritance law.

[*See also* Ottoman Empire, Islamic Law in Asia Minor (Turkey); *and* Personal Status Law: Personal Status Law in Islamic Countries.]

BIBLIOGRAPHY

Bozkurt, Gülnihal. *Alman-Ingiliz Belgelerinin ve Siyasi Gelismelerin Isigi Altinda Gayrimüslim Osmanli Vatandaslarinin Hukuki Durumu (1839–1914)*. Ankara: Türk Tarih Kurumu Publications, 1989.

Bozkurt, Gülnihal. *Bati Hukukunun Türkiye'de Benimsenmesi (1839–1939)*. Ankara: Türk Tarih Kurumu Publications, 1996. This book analyses reasons for the adoption of European law, from the Ottoman Empire to the Turkish Republic.

Özkorkut, Ünal Nevin, and Korkut Özkorkut. "Die Entwicklung des türkischen Handelsrechts in der Türkei seit osmanischer Zeit bis heute im Hinblick auf den Prozess einer Mitgliedschaf in der EU." In *Rechstpfleger-Studienheft*, Vol. 2, pp. 48–54. Bielefeld, Germany: Gieseking Verlag, 2005.

Öztan, Bilge. "Türkisches Familienrecht nach 70 Jahren ZGB." In *Westliches Recht in der Republik Türkei 70 Jahre nach der Gründung*, edited by Heinrich Scholler and Silvia Tellenbach, pp. 85–124. Baden-Baden, Germany: Nomos, 1996.

GÜLNIHAL BOZKURT

Turkish Law

Following the earlier Ottoman period of Islamic law, based upon principles of Koran and Sunna (the body of traditional sayings and customs attributed to Muhammad) and administered by religious courts throughout the Ottoman Empire, the first reformist and tentatively secular period of Turkish law began in 1839 under the Tanzimat (reorganization) government and extended until the establishment of the new Turkish Republic in 1923 and the enactment of a Civil Code adopted from Switzerland. The Ottoman Empire was abolished in 1924, and the Turkish Republic then sought to implement a nationalistic vision of complete westernization in a secular state in which the vast majority of citizens are Muslims, and the pace of legal reforms quickened. Turkey is today eager to join the European Union (EU) and is engaged in a complex process to change its laws to that end.

Early Steps. Attempts at modernization in Turkey had begun in the seventeenth century. Beneath the Ottoman Empire's ostensibly religious superstructure, a national secular system of law was developing, based on *firmān*s (edicts), *qānūn*s (state-made laws), judicial decisions, custom, and the doctrines of Turkish jurists. A product of the realism of the Turkish people, it was dictated largely by the administrative, military, and economic needs of the declining Ottoman Empire, which was then still a superpower. Throughout the late nineteenth century, Ottoman civil servants enforced a top-down revolution by constructing national secular legal institutions parallel to the existing Islamic ones. While most reformers wanted to copy the West to achieve progress, wholesale abandonment of Islamic foundations and culture was considered excessive.

The Tanzimat reforms of 1839 commenced with the Gülhane Hatt-i Hümayunu (Gülhane Imperial Edict), a charter protecting the basic rights of all Ottoman subjects, including religious minorities who lived under the *millet* system (which divided the population according to religious or ethnic affiliation) of personal status laws administered by their own leaders under Ottoman rule. The 1856 Ferman of Islahat reconfirmed equality between Muslims and non-Muslims. Such measures reflect European pressures over extraterritoriality and trade concessions imposed on the Ottoman Empire, which was losing strength and now sought to reform from within in order to avoid collapse. New secular courts were established, compilations of secular laws were made, and transplantation of European laws and regulations began. Secular schools were opened, and Turks went abroad to study, bringing back new ideas for reforms.

The gradual process of the disestablishment of Islamic law and the creation of a nonreligious state began in earnest after 1839, supported by the army and a new elite of Young Ottomans with a utopian vision of Ottoman nationalism. The Ottoman Penal Code of 1840, influenced by French criminal law, introduced for the first time an Ottoman *qānūn* in the form of a secular European code. A Commercial Code, adopted under pressure from France (1850), was followed by a Maritime Code (1863), also based on French law. The Ottoman Land Code of 1858 was inspired by the French freehold farming system. The Penal Code of 1858, based on the Napoleonic Code of 1810, put aside Islamic punishments and established a French-type system of secular courts, with a separate hierarchy operating until 1923. Reforms of criminal-procedure law in 1879 paved the way for the transplantation of the French Code of Criminal Procedure. The Majalla, the famous Ottoman Civil Code, designed to be compatible with Islamic law, codified the official Hanafi Muslim law but included many divergent opinions through the process of selection (*takhayyur*). Developed between 1867 and 1876, it codified the Muslim law of obligations and some elements of civil procedure, but not family law.

Major Reforms. Though secular commercial and criminal courts had been established earlier, the true beginning of a secular legal system was in the governance reforms starting in 1868 which divided the Supreme Council of Judicial Ordinances (Meclis-i Vala) into two organs: the Council of State (Şuray-i Devlet, now the Danıştay) as a legislative body, and a Court of Appeal (the Divan-i Ahkam-i Adliyye), divided into civil and criminal sections and later renamed Adliyye Nezareti (Ministry of Justice). Reformers, especially the nationalistic Young Turks, pressed for more democratic reforms and a constitutional government.

First and Second Constitutional Periods. The first Ottoman Constitution (Kanun-i Esasi) was promulgated in 1876, starting the period known as the First Meshrutiyet (First Constitutional Period), during which pressure was exerted for a liberal constitutional monarchy that was not to the liking of the Sultan. The 1876 Constitution, the first constitution of any Islamic state, was modeled on the Prussian Constitution (1851) and Belgian elements. All subjects were declared to be Ottomans regardless of religion, all subjects were equal and free, and a person's home was declared inviolable. The 1876 Constitution also protected the independence of courts and the safety of judges, and it recognized a legislative assembly. This new Parliament was divided into two chambers, an elected Meclis-i Mebusan (Chamber of Deputies) and the Meclis-i Ayan (Chamber of Notables), appointed by the Sultan, and a grand vizier would perform the duties of a prime minister. The Şuray-i Devlet (Council of State) was retained as the supreme court of appeal for administrative law cases and was to continue its legislative function. A new High Court (Divan-i Ali) was also established to hear cases against members of the government. The Meclis-i Mebusan was granted powers to enact certain laws and to exercise control over the executive. The entire secular court system which had evolved during the Tanzimat period was incorporated into the Constitution. Judges were to be appointed for life and courts to be organized by law.

The first secular law-school had been established in 1875 to train judges, advocates, and public prosecutors for the non-Islamic courts. The Ministries of Justice and Religious Affairs were united in one ministry. While Sultan Abdülhamit II dissolved the Parliament in 1878 and ended this period, the influence of liberalism continued, and the Sultan was eventually forced to restore the Constitution in 1908, marking the beginning of the Second Meshrutiyet period. The 1876 Constitution was substantially amended in 1909 to increase the power of the legislature and restrict that of the Sultan, and a truly constitutional system was established. In 1879, the French Criminal Procedure Code, introducing public prosecutors, had become the basis for modern criminal courts. In the same year, the Civil Procedure Code was enacted, also modeled on French law. In 1911, nearly seventy articles were transplanted from the Italian Zanardelli Criminal Code into the Ottoman Criminal Code.

Religious courts had been retained in matters of religion and family law. Despite secularization in several areas of law under the Tanzimat, the laws of marriage, divorce, inheritance, and custody of children for Muslims continued as before. Following much debate, however, the Ottoman Family Laws Ordinance was enacted in 1917, the first codification of Muslim family law in history, eclectically amalgamating the views of various juristic schools. This law placed religious qadi (a Muslim judge) courts under the authority of the Ministry of Justice, but also made non-Muslims subject to its rules, for which reason this law was repealed under foreign pressure in 1919.

The Kemalist Agenda. Legal reforms and borrowings in the nineteenth century had aimed to increase the efficiency of the state machinery, not to change society and culture. When the new Republic was established by Kemal Atatürk in 1923, however, the nationalist Kemalist elite decided that to reach the level of contemporary European civilization, Turkey would have to adopt a western way of life. The Kemalists imported all kinds of institutions including laws to achieve such transformations. In the mid-1920s, new commercial, penal, and civil codes were transplanted from Europe at which time the Turkish courts ceased to operate under a dual legal system. The adoption of the Swiss Civil Code (1923) and Swiss Code of Obligations (1926) represented a serious attempt by the Kemalist elite to change Turkish society. In 1926, for the first time, Islam was clearly separated from the secular law and confined to its religious sphere, and an entirely secular legal system was established. Turkey's legal culture became an amalgam of mostly Swiss, German, Italian, and French elements, a legal system based totally on the extensive eclectic adoption of components from Western models. To promote secularization of the legal system, a law school was opened in Ankara in 1925 to train judges and lawyers in the new secular laws.

Twentieth-Century Constitutions. The Constitution of 1921 (Teskilat-i Esasiye), consisting of twenty-four articles, established a legal system radically different from that of Ottoman times. While the power to legislate belongs to Parliament, executive power can be exercised only by an Executive Council to be elected by majority vote from among members of Parliament. Under the 1961 Constitution, Parliament was divided into two chambers: the National Assembly of 450 deputies elected by universal suffrage, and the Republican Senate of 150 senators elected by universal suffrage plus fifteen presidential appointees. The 1961 Constitution also fully separated the judiciary from the other branches of government and established a Constitutional Court. The third Constitution, promulgated in 1982, abolished the Republican Senate. Widely considered a military constitution, it restricted many fundamental rights and emphasized the interests and protection of the state, giving precedence to the responsibilities and duties of citizens rather than to their rights.

Part One of the Constitution details the general principles alluded to in the Preamble: Turkey is a Republic (Article 1), and a "democratic, secular, and social state governed by the rule of law; bearing in mind the concepts of public peace, national solidarity, and justice; respecting human rights; loyal to the nationalism of Atatürk, and based on the fundamental tenets set forth in the preamble" (Article 2). Article 4 protects these characteristics of the Republic (Articles 1–3) from amendment. Articles 7–9 establish the three separate branches of government. Article 10 ensures equality before the law, and Article 11 makes the Constitution the supreme rule of law.

The legal state foreseen in the Constitution is based on the principle of the protection of fundamental rights and freedoms and the separation of powers. Legislative procedures are subject to the control of the Constitutional Court, and executive procedures and activities to that of the Administrative Court. Under the principle of secularism, no one can make the basic social, economic, political, and legal system of the State dependent on religious rules nor abuse religious beliefs with the objective of obtaining political or personal advantages or influence. The original major elements underpinning modern Turkish legal developments can be summarized as nationalism, laicism, republicanism, populism, statism, and reformism.

Turkish Secularism. Turkey cultivates a unique version of secularism officially based on French *laicisme*. Soon after the establishment of the Republic, the Directorate of Religious Affairs was established; all Islamic activities and mosques were placed under the auspices of this state organ, including imams and muftis (as salaried employees). With secularism and with tight controls on education, the modern Turkish state has assumed the role of a secular *mujtahid* (originally a jurist recognized by Shiites as an authority on the interpretation of Islamic law), providing authoritative interpretations consonant with Turkish nationalist principles. Ongoing tensions between different visions of Turkish secularism emerge, for example, in conflicts over headscarves. It is also apparent that the reforms in family laws intended for all Turks are not being followed rigorously in rural areas and in the many large migrant communities of Turkey's major cities.

Many changes have been made recently in Turkish law, for example, the totally new Civil Code introduced in 2001. Today, Turkish nationalism remains strong, as does Westernization, but the rule of law, the welfare state, democracy, and human rights have moved up on the agenda, partly under EU pressure. During the current preparations for anticipated EU entry, many changes to Turkish laws are being considered, showing that Turkey is attempting to move away from authoritarian rule toward the recognition of human rights.

[*See also* Ottoman Empire, Islamic Law in Asia Minor (Turkey) and the.]

BIBLIOGRAPHY

Adal, E. *Fundamentals of Turkish Private Law*. 3d ed. Istanbul: Legal Yayıncılık, 1991. Useful collection of legal materials. The eighth edition was published in 2005.

Ansay, T., and D. Wallace, Jr., eds. *Introduction to Turkish Law*. The Hague: Kluwer Law International, 1996. A good overview.

Bozkurt, G. "The Reception of Western European Law in Turkey (From the Tanzimat to the Turkish Republic, 1839–1939)." *Der Islam* 75 (1998): 283–95. Well-focused, concise analysis.

McCarthy, Justin. *The Ottoman Turks: An Introductory History to 1923*. London and New York: Longman, 1997. Historically focused analysis of developments in Turkish law.

Starr, J. *Law as Metaphor: From Islamic Courts to the Palace of Justice*. Albany: State University of New York Press, 1992. The leading study of Turkish legal developments.

Yilmaz, I. *Muslim Laws, Politics, and Society in Modern Nation States: Dynamic Legal Pluralisms in England, Turkey, and Pakistan*. Aldershot, U.K.: Ashgate, 2005. Contains a chapter on Turkish legal developments to the present.

IHSAN YILMAZ

TUSI, MUHAMMAD IBN AL-HASAN AL-, SHAYKH AL-TA'IFA (d. A.H. 460 / 1067 C.E.).

Muhammad ibn al-Hasan al-Tusi was a prolific Imami Shi'i jurist and theologian based for most of his academic life in Baghdad. His legal writings fall into three groups.

First, *Al-tahdhib* and *Al-istibsar* are compilations of reports of the actions and sayings of the Prophet and Shi'i Imams (hadiths or *akhbār*). Although often referred to as hadith collections, these works do, in fact, contain extensive legal argumentation. *Al-tahdhib* is a commentary on al-Shaykh al-Mufid's *Al-muqni'a*, a breviary of Shi'i *fiqh*, in which the relevant *akhbār* are listed for each legal issue. In *Al-istibsar* al-Tusi studies the many legal problems caused by conflicting reports (in which the Shi'i Imams give contradictory rulings). In both works, al-Tusi not only lists reports but uses them as the starting point for a process of intricate legal reasoning resulting in clear legal rulings despite the ambiguity of the sources.

Second, al-Tusi wrote legal theory (*uṣūl al-fiqh*). These works are scattered across a number of sources (including his various "answers to questions" from fellow scholars), though his main work in this area is *Al-'udda fi usul al-fiqh*. Al-Tusi consistently argues for a report-based jurisprudence. The law should, he argues, be based on the explicit rulings of the Imams as found in the *akhbār*, and other techniques of legal reasoning (analogy, linguistic exegesis, and the like) should be employed only with extreme caution. This position leads him to restrict the direct interpretation of the Qur'an, for the true meaning of the Qur'an can only be understood in the light of the Imams' statements (i.e., the *akhbār*). He criticizes those who reject reports as inauthentic. In al-Tusi's view, the *akhbār* should be treated as authentic and their message as clear. He is consequently forced to explain in some detail the procedures for solving contradictions within the *akhbār*.

Finally, there are his works of law proper (*fiqh*). The most important are *Al-mabsut* ("The Expanded," which, as its name suggests, is an impressive compendium of all areas of Muslim law) and *Al-nihaya* ("The Utmost," a reference to its extreme brevity). In these works, and in contrast to his legal theory and *akhbār* collections, al-Tusi's legal reasoning consists of testing general legal maxims against hard cases, and direct reference to the *akhbār* is rare. Both works were the subject of commentary by subsequent scholars, and both became standard elements of the advanced Imami legal curriculum.

Al-Tusi's principal legal achievement was to give Shi'i law a sound revelatory base in the *akhbār*. This enabled later Imami jurists to participate in broader Muslim legal discussions without losing their distinctive Shi'i character. His efforts enabled Imami law to establish itself as a legal tradition alongside the four Sunni schools of thought. His *akhbār*-based style of jurisprudence, although not universally popular among his Imami successors, experienced a revival in the sixteenth-century Akhbariyya. This new school aimed to revive the "way of the early scholars," the most important of whom was al-Tusi.

[*See also* Islamic Schools of Sacred Law, *subentry on* Shi'i Schools: The Imami School of Law.]

BIBLIOGRAPHY

Gleave, Robert. "Between Hadith and *Fiqh*: Early Imami Collections of *Akhbār*." *Islamic Law and Society* 8 (2001): 350–382. An analysis of al-Tusi's legal and hadith works.

Stewart, Devin J. *Islamic Legal Orthodoxy: Twelver Shiite Responses to the Sunni Legal System*. Salt Lake City: University of Utah Press, 1998. The most comprehensive English-language work on Shi'i jurisprudence in recent times.

ROBERT GLEAVE

TWELVE TABLES. The Twelve Tables were a codification of various rules of Roman law created in the middle of the fifth century B.C.E. The traditional date is 451–450 B.C.E. Little is known of Roman law in the period before the Twelve Tables. As H. Maine wrote, in a well-known quotation in *Lectures on the Early History of Institutions*, "Roman law begins, as it ends, with a Code." Our detailed knowledge of the Twelve Tables derives from three types of sources:

1. The annalistic accounts of the late Roman Republic, chiefly Livy (c. 59 B.C.E.–17 C.E.), contain description of the process and Cicero (106–43 B.C.E.) provides interpretation based upon these understandings. These accounts date from a period long after the events in question and need to be read carefully for the influence of contemporary political and social issues.
2. The legal sources, chiefly Gaius (fl. c. 180 C.E.), *Institutes* and *Commentary on the Twelve Tables*, preserved in Justinian's Digest, contain references to the content and occasionally the form of individual provisions.
3. Roman philologists, chiefly Festus (fl. c. 180 C.E.), and antiquarians like Aulus Gellius (fl. c. 150 C.E.), preserve a lot of information about the supposed original form of the Tables. As law their formulation was typically preserved as unaltered as possible and attracted attention for their archaic vocabulary and grammar.

The Twelve Tables constitute a collection of *leges*, or legal provisions, the whole collection being known in Latin as *leges duodecim tabularum*, the laws of the Twelve Tables.

The Making of the Twelve Tables. According to the Roman annalists, the period following the expulsion of the kings in 510 B.C.E. was characterized by uncertainty and conflict between the patrician, or ruling, class and the plebeians, which resulted in the concession by the former of a publication of the law in the form of the Twelve Tables. It should perhaps be noted that nothing in the content of the surviving provisions of the Twelve Tables would justify this interpretation: it is as likely that they are the product of a process of "self regulation by a patrician elite," as Crawford writes in *Roman Statutes*.

Pomponius, in his account of Roman legal history in his *Enchiridion*, reports that a commission of ten was appointed to make the laws. They were expected to study the laws of the Greek city-states (probably the cities of Magna Graecia in southern Italy are intended). They first promulgated ten tablets of laws to which they in the

The Twelve Tables. Nineteenth-century illustration of Rome's first legal code being drawn up by a commission. MARY EVANS PICTURE LIBRARY

subsequent year added two more, making twelve in all. Although few fragments of the last two tables can be identified, it is possible to say that they are concerned with matters already dealt with earlier in the sequence, which makes Pomponius's statement possible.

Pomponius, writing in the second century C.E., was probably indebted to the earlier annalistic accounts himself. In Livy the creation of the Twelve Tables is linked to a temporary change of government. On the expulsion of the kings the state was headed by two consuls, elected annually. Now the consuls were to be replaced by a Council of Ten (*decemviri*): it is not clear whether this was done for its own sake—the people are said to have been unhappy with the system of consuls—or solely for the purpose of creating the Twelve (or Ten) Tables. Livy reports that three of the decemvirs were ambassadors who had visited Athens to study the laws of Solon. All went well for a year but then it was decided that the system should be continued for a further year, possibly in order to supplement the first Ten Tables with two more. Violence was associated with the election of the second Council of Ten. The second council abused its powers and one man, Appius Claudius, who was a member of both councils and a leading figure, prompted a revolt when as magistrate he condemned to slavery the daughter of a leading Roman, Verginius. In consequence the regime of two consuls was reestablished but not before the additional two tables had been approved to create twelve in all. Livy is careful to stress that the Twelve Tables, both the original ten and the two supplements, were passed through the regular legislative assembly of the people, the *comitia centuriata*. To this extent the creation of the decemvirs was a mere device to bring about change rather than the means for achieving it.

The Transmission of the Twelve Tables. We do not possess any fragments of the Twelve Tables. Gaius in the second century C.E. was confident enough in his knowledge to produce six books on the Twelve Tables, and we know of the existence of a commentary by the Augustan jurist Labeo at the turn of the eras on which it is likely that Gaius relied. Both were probably indebted to an even older commentary, the *Tripartita* (three parts) of Sextus Aelius Paetus (consul 198 B.C.E. and censor 194 B.C.E). According to Pomponius (*Enchiridion* preserved in Dig.1.2.2.38) this text was still in existence in his own day, the second century C.E., and consisted of a lemmatic commentary on the individual provisions of the Tables accompanied by procedural details. Cicero (*de legibus* 2.23.59) refers to this text indicating that where Sextus Aelius was uncertain of an obsolete phrase he was not above guessing its meaning, sometimes wrongly. Apart from anything else, this indicates that by Aelius's day at the close of the second century B.C.E. some provisions of the Twelve Tables were already incomprehensible and presumably ineffective. Others had been replaced by subsequent legislation, such as, according to Crawford, the provisions on damage to property at VIII.3–6 by the Lex Aquilia of after 287 B.C.E.

The Content of the Twelve Tables. None of our sources clearly locates the fragments they cite or appear to quote in any part of the document. (A partial exception in Festus 336L, which may identify II.2, the second law of the second table, is marred by a corruption that makes it appear to refer to legislation of King Numa and a careless transmission of the text itself.) Any attempt at reconstruction is therefore wholly speculative. However, the sheer bulk of the surviving evidence requires some ordering of the information, and editors since Jacques Godefroy (1616) have not shirked the challenge of placing the fragments in a plausible order.

Clues are provided as follows. The jurist Gaius's *Commentary on the Twelve Tables*, extracts from which, possibly interpolated, are preserved in the Digest together with references to their place in Gaius's original, may be presumed to have followed the order of the original (though it should be noted that it is only a supposition that Gaius had access to a complete text of the Tables). Similar considerations apply to the less extensive references in Gellius. Cicero famously alludes to his having learned the "*si in ius vocat*" ("If anyone summons to court") as a child, implying that he knew the whole by heart and that these were the opening words of the text; in other places (*Topica* 26–7, *De oratore* I.173) Cicero gives lists of legal terms seemingly in the order in which they appeared in the Tables.

The Structure of the Twelve Tables. The first three tables were concerned with procedure, starting with the summons to court and trial in the first table and proceeding to matters involving witnesses and postponements of the suit in the second. The third table deals with execution of judgment. The first table also probably contained a series of rules relating to penalties: these have traditionally been placed in table eight on the basis that they can be understood in later terms as substantive provisions on delictual wrongs of *iniuria* and theft, but in Crawford's reconstruction they are restored to the beginning of the Tables.

The fourth table contained provisions on status within the family, and the fifth dealt with succession to property. The sixth and seventh tables treated issues of the law of property. The eighth table contained provisions relating to delictual or criminal liability. The ninth table, of which there is little trace, may have dealt with constitutional matters. The tenth table dealt with rules on burial. The eleventh and twelfth tables were, on the traditional account, added the following year to amend and supplement several of the provisions of the first ten tables, an understanding that the surviving evidence does nothing to disprove.

It should be noted that the use of modern terminology for identifying parts of the law, such as "delict," "property," and so on, though inevitable, is anachronistic and potentially misleading. These divisions, now universally adopted, were the product of scientific reflection by subsequent generations of Roman jurists.

The Function of the Twelve Tables. Assuming that we are dissatisfied with the fables of the Roman annalists, what understandings of the function of the Twelve Tables are open to us? We cannot suppose that they were the first law in Rome: apart from any other consideration, they presuppose an existing sophisticated legal terminology containing such concepts as *conubium* (capacity to intermarry) in XI.1 (see extracts below); *auctoritas* (guarantee of ownership) in VI.3 & 4; and *intestatus* (intestate) in V.4. The Roman historians naturally stress those features of the law that relate to personal status and constitutional strife; but as Watson points out in *Rome of the Twelve Tables*, a significant part of the provisions of the Twelve Tables refers to highly technical matters of property and obligations, which presupposes an existing framework of interpretation, albeit not by specialist lawyers. It is possible that some of the provisions relate to actual decisions in past cases now generalized: this form of legislative provision is well attested in the ancient Near Eastern codes. The possibility of influence from this quarter, though widely canvassed and indeed suggested by the Romans' own account of the visit to Athens for instruction, does not seem likely in point of detail.

The Language of the Twelve Tables. It will be noticed that nearly all our evidence is very late; most is at best some six hundred years after the compilation was made. We know that Roman culture and the Latin language developed considerably over this period. The somewhat elliptical and abrupt style of the clauses in the Tables is probably original: there could be no good reason to make more obscure what was formerly plainer. But the language has inevitably been modernized by the time it reaches our sources.

The Legacy of the Twelve Tables. The Twelve Tables functioned in the Romans' legal imagination rather as Magna Carta does in English law. Although none of the provisions remained in force in the classical period there was an observable continuity in ideas and, to an extent, in terminology, which reinforced the Romans' sense that their law extended in an unbroken chain since the earliest days of their existence as a people.

Some Extracts. The best modern text and English translation of the Twelve Tables is to be found in M. H. Crawford, *Roman Statutes*, vol. 2, pp. 555–721. The English translation there is designed to be read alongside the Latin original. Some extracts of better-known passages are here quoted in a simplified version (together with Crawford's numbering of the Tables). Terms in parentheses are added for explanation, words in square brackets are presumed to have existed.

I.1 If anyone summons to court, he (the defendant) is to go; if he does not go, he (the plaintiff) is to call to witness; then he is to take him.

I.2 If he (the defendant) delays or drags his feet, he (the plaintiff) is to lay a hand on (him).

I.3 If there is illness or age, he (the plaintiff) is to provide a beast of burden; if he be unwilling, he is not to prepare a carriage. [. . .]

I.17 If he commit theft by night and he killed him, he is to be lawfully killed.

I.18 If he commit theft by day and he defend himself with a weapon, . . . he is to call out. [. . .]

IV.2 If a father thrice sell a son, from the father the son is to be free. [. . .]

V.4 If one dies intestate to whom there is no *suus heres*, the nearest agnate is to have the family property.

V.5 If there be no agnate, the *gentiles* are to have the family property.

VI.1 When he shall perform *nexum* and *mancipium* as his tongue has pronounced so is there to be a source of rights. [. . .]

VI.3 For an estate *auctoritas* is to be two years. [For other things it is to be one year.]

VI.4 Against a foreigner, *auctoritas* is to be everlasting. [. . .]

X.4 Women are not to mutilate their cheeks or hold a wake for the purpose of holding a funeral.

XI.1 [There is not to be *conubium*] with the plebs.

[*See also* Cicero; Digest; Lex; *and* Roman Law 753–27 B.C.E.]

BIBLIOGRAPHY

Crawford, M. H., ed. *Roman Statutes*. Vol. 2. London: Institute of Classical Studies, School of Advanced Study, University of London, 1996.

Kaser, Max. *Das altrömische Ius: Studien zur Rechtsvorstellung und Rechtsgeschichte der Römer*. Göttingen, Germany: Vandenhoeck & Ruprecht, 1949.

Watson, Alan. *Rome of the XII Tables: Persons and Property*. Princeton, N.J.: Princeton University Press, 1975.

Wieacker, F. "Die XII Tafeln in ihrem Jahrhundert." In *Fondation Hardt: Entretiens sur l'Antiquité classique* 13. Geneva, Switzerland: Vandoeuvres, 1967.

Andrew Lewis

UGANDA. *See* African Law, Sub-Saharan, *subentries on* The Precolonial Period; The Colonial Period; *and* After Independence.

ULPIAN (c. 170 C.E.–223–224 C.E.). Ulpian (Domitius Ulpianus) was a prolific legal author and prominent officeholder under the Severan dynasty (193–235 C.E.). His massive exposition of Roman law in over two hundred books (*libri* of ten thousand to twelve thousand words) was mainly composed in the sole reign of Antoninus Caracalla (211–217 C.E.). In this, he reflected the cosmopolitan outlook of which the political expression was extension of citizenship by Caracalla to all free people in the Roman Empire in 212 C.E. His work, composed in a clear, relaxed style, was chosen by Justinian's compilers as a main source of the Digest (530–533 C.E.), the collection of private writings of an earlier age to which Justinian gave legislative authority. Just over two-fifths of it is drawn from Ulpian's works and three-quarters of the 432 chapters ("titles") in the Digest begin with a text of Ulpian.

Ulpian, whose full name was perhaps Gnaeus Domitius Annius Ulpianus, was born ca. 170 C.E. and was by origin a citizen of Tyre in Syria. He was proud of his connection with Tyre and its long-standing alliance with Rome. A marble column with an inscription in his honor was found there in 1988. He followed an equestrian career in Rome in the reign of Septimius Severus (193–211 C.E.) and was never raised to the higher rank of senator. His rise to prominence was probably connected with Septimius' marriage in 187 to the Syrian Julia Domna, mother of the later emperors Antoninus (Caracalla) and Geta and aunt of Julia Mammaea, who promoted Ulpian's career in the early part of the reign of her son, Alexander Severus.

The unusually forthright and incisive style of imperial rescripts of the period 202–209, some ninety of which have survived, points to the conclusion that Ulpian was drafting replies to petitions on behalf of Septimius Severus from 202 to 209. He did so, at least from 205 onward, as secretary for petitions (*a libellis*). He was a member of Aemilius Papinianus' council of advisers (*consilium*) when Papinian was praetorian prefect (205–211). He accompanied Septimius on his expedition to Britain in 209–211. In the conflict after the death of Severus at York in February 211 between his two sons, Ulpian, in contrast with Papinian, who favored joint rule, sided with the elder, Antoninus Carcacalla (emperor 212–217), to whom he refers in flattering terms, even giving him precedence over his father, Severus. By the *Constitutio Antoniniana* of 212, Caracalla extended Roman citizenship to all free inhabitants of the Empire. At a modest reckoning, this doubled or tripled the number of Roman citizens and consequently of persons subject to Roman law. Presumably in response to this extension, which suited his cosmopolitan outlook, Ulpian was spurred into literary activity in the ensuing years. The bulk of his work was composed in Caracalla's reign between 213 and 217. It was a comprehensive exposition of Roman law and was specially aimed at expounding to the new citizens the principles of the system to which they were now subject. Particularly in his commentary on the praetor's edict, he seeks to persuade readers of the rational character of the law, rooted in Stoic ideas of natural law.

Although reports conflict, under the emperor Elagabal (also called Antoninus [218–222]), Ulpian may have been promoted to a prefecture, probably as prefect of supply (*praefectus annonae*), when in 221 Elagabal was obliged to accept his cousin Alexander as coruler. Ulpian is recorded as holding that office three weeks into Alexander Severus's reign in March 222. In December of that year, he is described as praetorian prefect (the emperor's chief minister) and the young emperor's protector (*parens*). The initiative for this promotion perhaps came from Julia Mammaea, Alexander's mother. Ulpian was placed over the two existing praetorian prefects as a sort of superprefect, a constitutional innovation. Both these prefects were then tried and sentenced to death. This led to unrest among the praetorian troops. As a civilian, Ulpian was unable to stop disorders breaking out between the praetorian guards and the populace. He was murdered by mutinous guards in a revolt instigated by a powerful freedman, Epagathus, in 223 or early 224. Neither the emperor nor his mother was able to protect him from them.

In his short period of high office, Ulpian was able to correct some of the abuses of Elagabal's reign and to ensure that the young emperor attended to his civil duties, such as answering petitions, in a conscientious way.

Ulpian's writing was on a grand scale. It comprises two major commentaries, on the praetor's edict (*ad edictum praetoris*) in eighty-one books and on Sabinus's Civil Law (*ius civile*) in fifty-one books. The first of these was particularly important because a version of the praetor's edict was in force in all the provinces of the Empire, so that his commentary on its provisions constituted an up-to-date handbook that could guide provincial governors in their administration. Ulpian also wrote a series of shorter works, which cover public as well as private law, including criminal law and taxation. There are manuals on the duties of consuls, prefects, and other officeholders, of which one, of particular importance, is on the duties of provincial governors. The manuals take account of political as well as legal factors, for instance, the need for a provincial governor to respect public opinion and custom in his province. Ulpian also wrote on important statutes. Finally he wrote works for teaching, including an introductory book for students (*Institutiones*) and, for the more advanced, ten books of discussions on difficult points of law (*Disputationes*). By contrast, hardly any of the opinions (*responsa*) that Ulpian gave to private clients and officials have survived. Indeed, the two books of *Responsa* from which there are excerpts in the Digest are of doubtful authenticity. As with other prominent authors, some spurious works were attributed to him, whereas others may have been written by an author of the same last name, Ulpianus, which was a common name. The compilers of Justinian's Digest were not, however, in a position to distinguish the genuine majority from the spurious minority.

In parallel with what his elder contemporary Galen says of medicine, Ulpian treats law as both an art and a true philosophy. It is the art or technique of doing justice, and is a true philosophy based on reason, not sophistry, and as such capable of being put into practice. His philosophical outlook rests in part on the Stoic idea that human beings are born free and equal; indeed, he holds that natural law extends to animals. To him, Roman law is based on reason and equity, and should be acceptable to the enlarged body of citizens created by the Constitutio Antoniniana, whatever their cultural or linguistic background or gender. Roman law possessed a remedy in the form of the action for wrongs (*actio iniuriarum*) that was available to vindicate the dignity of free people and, in principle, slaves.

Ulpian's works were mostly composed in no more than five or six years and were of necessity largely dictated. One sign of this is the number of sentences that begin with a conjunction such as "*et*" (and). His prose has almost a conversational feel, as if the author is engaged in a dialogue with the reader, although as a careful scholar he freely cites the opinions of earlier writers. His works are, as with most Roman legal writings, written in Latin but, more than other writers, he introduces Greek words or phrases in a way that suggests that he had in mind a partly bilingual readership. His texts are notable for the many illustrations the author gives, and for his habit of asking whether, if the facts were slightly different from the previous example, the law would be the same. Of all the Roman jurists whose work has survived, his lies closest in style and method to contemporary legal writing. Ulpian is ingenious in finding ways to avoid an apparently unfair conclusion, while at the same time respecting the procedural requirements of the Roman system of formulary actions. He combines a philosophical framework with an acute feeling for the just solution to a specific problem.

He was not regarded by Tribonian and Justinian as the subtlest of Roman legal authors. That accolade was reserved for Julian (Salvius Julianus), the second-century author from Africa of ninety books of *Digesta*, and, second, Papinian, whose practice yielded a wealth of difficult cases subjected to expert analysis, but Ulpian was as lucid, fair-minded, and influential an expositor of the law as any.

Politically, Ulpian's career was a failure. The historian Syme pilloried him as "the scholar who deserts his books for favour of princes and governmental employment, to a calamitous end." But, given the importance of his writings both in the ancient world and, through Justinian's Digest, in medieval and renaissance law, he has proved to be among the most influential of legal writers. He also may be accounted a supporter, in embryo, of the egalitarian ideal of human rights.

BIBLIOGRAPHY

PRIMARY WORKS

Early: Notes on Marcellus' *Digesta*, Papinian's *Responsa*. Monograph *De excusationibus* 1. Rescripts composed on behalf of Septimius Severus 202–209 C.E. Later (mainly under Caracalla): *Ad edictum praetoris* 81; *Ad Masurium Sabinum* 51; *Ad legem Iuliam et Papiam* 20; *De officio proconsulis* 10; *De omnibus tribunalibus* 10; *Publicae disputationes* 10; *De censibus* 6; *Fideicommissa* 6; *Ad legem Iuliam de adulteriis* 5; *De appellationibus* 4; *Ad legem Aeliam Sentiam* 4; *De officio consulis* 3; *Institutiones* 2; *Ad edictum aedilium curulium* 2; and several one-book monographs. Works spuriously attributed to him: *Opiniones* 6; *Regulae* 7; *Liber singularis regularum* 1; *Pandectae* 1; *Responsa* 2.

SECONDARY WORKS

O. Lenel, *Palingenesia Iuris Civilis* 2 (1889): 379–1200; A. Pernice, *Ulpian als Schriftsteller* (1885): 443–484 = 8 *Labeo* (1962): 351–389; P. Jörs, *Domitius 88*, RE 5 (1903): 1435–1509; R. Syme, "Lawyers in Government: The Case of Ulpian," *Proceedings of the American Philosophical Society* 116 (1972): 406–409 = *Roman Papers* (1984): III.863–8; G. Crifò, "Ulpiano: Esperienze e responsibilità del giurista," *Aufstieg und Niedergang der römischen Welt* 2.15 (1976): 708–789; R. Syme, "Fiction about Roman Jurists," *Zeitschrift der Savigny-Stiftung für Rechtsgeschichte* (Rom. Abt.) 97 (1980): 78–104 = *Roman Papers* (1984): III: 1393–1414; D. Liebs, "Zur Laufbahn Ulpians," *Bonner Historia-Augusta-Colloquium* 1984/5 (1987): 175–181; idem., "Domitius Ulpianus," *Handbuch der Lateinischen Literatur der Antike* 4 (Munich, Germany: C. H. Beck, 1997), section 424; V. Marotta, *Ulpiano e l'Impero* (Naples: Loffredo Editore, 2000); T. Honoré, *Ulpian: Pioneer of Human Rights* (New York: Oxford University Press, 1982; 2d ed., 2002); D. Liebs, "Mein Ulpian," in *Altera Ratio: Klassische Philologie zwischen Subjectivität und Wissenschaft*, edited by M. Schauer and G. Thome (Stuttgart, Germany: Franz Steiner Verlag, 2003), pp. 74–81.

TONY HONORÉ

UNDUE INFLUENCE IN MEDIEVAL AND POST-MEDIEVAL ROMAN LAW.

Unlike the common law, the civil law has not developed a specific legal instrument aimed at providing relief if a person in a relationship of dependence towards another is unduly influenced into concluding a detrimental contract. The remedial response to these situations, which cannot easily be accommodated under the law of *dolus* (fraud) or *metus* (duress), has been sporadic and fragmented.

Roman law generally did not release a person from contractual liability merely because it was concluded due to reverence or awe of another. However, the thirteenth-century Accursian gloss reflects a more accommodating approach: it states that a married woman who sells or encumbers an object belonging to her under the influence of fear or reverence (*metu vel reverentia*) may revoke the transaction. Although it further states that this could even be done if there was no threat of physical harm, the fourteenth-century commentator Bartolus de Saxoferrato emphasized that a position of authority, or reverence as such, does not provide the other party to the contract with a ground for rescission. Some additional factors, such as previous abuse or a reputation for violence, had to be present. Nonetheless, Bartolus cautioned that it would still be best to have witnesses present when a wife or minor concluded a transaction.

Civil lawyers now proceeded to work out in detail when presumptions of duress and fraud would arise in situations involving reverence. While a gross disparity between the performances (*laesio enormis*) was obviously relevant, it is particularly significant that the fifteenth-century author Marianus Socinus regarded excessive flattery and persuasion as circumstances which indicated the existence of *metus*. Given the absence of actual threats of physical harm in these cases, it can be said that the civil law had by now developed to provide relief in cases of "undue influence."

However, somewhat curiously, these developments were not reflected in seventeenth-century Roman-Dutch law. The notion that reverence could be a source of fear was either ignored, or rejected, and the inchoate civilian notion of undue influence withered away. It is only in the latter half of the nineteenth century that it came to be appreciated again that some relief needs to be provided to persons who are unduly influenced by others to conclude disadvantageous contracts. In German law, victims can nowadays either rely on paragraph 138 II of the civil code, which is aimed at protecting weak parties who conclude such contracts, or on the general requirement encapsulated in paragraph 138 I that contracts should not be contrary to public policy. In mixed legal systems, such as those of South Africa and Scotland, the civil law of fraud and duress was in turn supplemented by the adoption of the common law doctrine of undue influence, while Dutch law has drawn on both the civil law and common law in formulating "abuse of circumstances" as a ground for avoiding contractual liability.

The phenomenon of undue influence by third parties, such as husbands, to induce their wives to provide security for their debts, is of great importance in modern contract law. Some modern systems, as in medieval times, protect the victim by way of presumptions of impropriety, and, like Bartolus, stress the importance of taking safeguards to ensure that persons who may have been unduly influenced acted freely.

BIBLIOGRAPHY

Bell, A. P. "Abuse of Relationship: Undue Influence in English Law and French Law." *European Review of Private Law* 3 (2007): 555–599.

Du Plessis, Jacques, and Reinhard Zimmermann. "The Relevance of Reverence: Undue Influence Civilian Style." *Maastricht Journal of European and Comparative Law* 10: 4 (2003): 345–380.

Scholtens, J. E. "Undue Influence." *Acta Juridica* (1960): 276–288.

JACQUES E. DU PLESSIS

UNGER, JOSEF (1828–1913).

Josef Unger was born July 2, 1828, in Vienna as the son of a merchant. He first studied philosophy, then law, and received a PhD on March 4, 1850, in Königsberg for his "historical-philosophical treatise on 'Marriage as it developed in its world-historical context'"; on April 11, 1852, he received the Juris Doctor degree in Vienna. Unger converted from Judaism to Catholicism. He undertook studies on the history of law as seen in works by Eduard Gans and Friedrich Carl von Savigny. He was appointed *Privatdozent* (instructor) in 1853 in recognition of his programmatic critical work *Der Entwurf eines bürgerlichen Gesetzbuches für das Königreich Sachsen mit bes. Rücksicht auf das Österreichische Allgemeine Bürgerliche Gesetzbuch* (1853; English trans., Draft for a Civil Law Code for the Kingdom of Saxony with Special Consideration of the Austrian Civil Law Code). In the same year he was appointed adjunct professor at the university in Prague as part of curriculum reform by Minister Leo Graf Thun-Hohenstein to help promote the "historical treatment of Austrian civil law." He was appointed extraordinary professor in 1856 and granted full professorship in Vienna in 1857.

Involved in the events of 1848, but as a moderate, he later adopted a conservative-liberal position; after 1870, with growing influence, he became increasingly active in politics: in 1867 as a member of the state parliament and Reichstag, and after 1869 as a lifelong member of the *Herrenhaus* (upper chamber). He was appointed *Sprechminister* (minister without portfolio) in 1871. He was one of the first members of the Reichsgericht (supreme court constituted in 1869 with constitutional functions) and became its president in 1881; additionally, he was involved with constituting the court of administration, 1875–1876. After 1859 he edited the collection of civil law rulings of the supreme court and the court of cassation, together with Julius Glaser (known as "Glaser-Unger").

His name is connected with the "pandectization" or "historization" of Austrian civil law following the example of Savigny's conceptual-systematic method. In his work *Über den Entwicklungsgang der österreichischen Civiljurisprudenz* (1855; English trans., On the Development of Austrian Civil Jurisprudence), he demanded a unified German civil-law code for the states of the German Confederation; under this aspect he pleaded for a convergence of Austrian and German civil-law studies. After rejecting the demand for a total revision of the ABGB (Allgemeines Bürgerliches Gesetzbuch, the civil code of Austria) according to the historic school of law, and after the idea of a national German civil code including Austria became obsolete in 1866, he initiated a revision and modernization of the ABGB at the beginning of the twentieth century (publishing a call for revision of the ABGB in 1904), which resulted in the partial revision of 1914–1916. On account of his comprehensive work in legislative and judiciary studies, Unger was one of the most influential Austrian jurists in the second half of the nineteenth century. He died on February 5, 1913, in Vienna.

[*See also* Austria.]

BIBLIOGRAPHY

PRIMARY WORKS

Unger, Josef. *Die Ehe in ihrer welthistorischen Entwicklung: Ein Beitrag zur Philosophie der Geschichte*. Vienna: Jasper, Hügel, and Mainz, Germany, 1850.

Unger, Josef. *System des österreichischen allgemeinen Privatrechts 1–2*. Leipzig, Germany: Breitkopf & Härtel, 1856–1859.

Unger, Josef. *Über die wissenschaftliche Behandlung des österreichischen gemeinen Privatrechts*. Inaugural Lecture. Vienna: F. Manz, 1853.

Unger, Josef. "Zur Revision des allgemeinen bürgerlichen Gesetzbuches." *GrünhutsZS* (1904): 389–406.

SECONDARY WORKS

Brauneder, Wilhelm, ed. *Juristen in Österreich 1200–1980*. Vienna: Orax, 1987. See especially pp. 177–183. Contains further literature.

Lentze, Hans. "Josef Unger—Leben und Werk." In *Festschrift for H. Arnold*, pp. 219–232. 1963.

Losano, Mario G. *Der Briefwechsel Jherings mit Unger und Glaser*. Ebelsbach, Germany: Aktiv Druck & Verlag, 1996.

Sinzheimer, Hugo. *Jüdische Klassiker der deutschen Rechtswissenschaft*. 2d ed. Frankfurt am Main, Germany: V. Klostermann, 1953. See pp. 83ff.

BARBARA DOLEMEYER
Translated from the German by Alexa Nieschlag

UNIFORM CIVIL CODE IN INDIAN LAW.
See Personal Law and General Law.

UNITED STATES LAW. [*This entry contains six subentries, an introduction and historical overview of United States law during the colonial period and discussions of the sources of colonial law, the colonies in the empire, the American Revolution, the nineteenth century, and the twentieth century.*]

The Colonial Period: General Introduction and Historical Overview

The Colonial period of American history covers almost two centuries, stretching from the first European settlements in the early seventeenth century to the American Revolution at the end of the eighteenth. Although we think, appropriately enough, of the American Colonies as having been English—it was, after all, the king of England from whom the colonists declared their independence in 1776—it must at least be noted that among the earliest European settlers were the Spanish, the French, the Swedish, and the Dutch, as well as the English, and that here and there we can identify concrete ways in which some of these cultures influenced what was to become the legal heritage of the United States (most dramatically the French influence in Louisiana). And of course the first Europeans to arrive were not the first people to arrive: the Indians preceded them. Native American culture did not, however, leave an imprint on American law, and the fact is that overwhelmingly, American legal heritage is indeed English, and an overview of Colonial legal history must begin with a capsule account of English legal history.

English Common Law. At the core of English legal history is the common law, one of the two great systems of jurisprudence of the Western world (the civil law being the other). The origins of the common law lie in custom that is said to be common to all in the land and is adopted, adapted, and applied by courts. The common law is the law of the king's courts, and it is the law that both binds and protects all the king's subjects. It is judge made (often imprecisely called "unwritten") law: common-law method is judicial method, and it involves the case-by-case development of rules and principles. The common law is said to rest on the bedrock of precedent: in theory—a theory that finds expression in the phrase *stare decisis*—the judge is bound, in deciding the case before the court, to follow those rules and principles earlier enunciated in, or legitimately to be drawn from, like cases. The extent to which stare decisis actually operates (or ever has operated) to determine decision is a much-vexed issue; that it has and always has had *some*, at times considerable, force is hard to dispute.

Manifestly, such a system is resistant to change, but no law is static; all law changes. In a common-law system, change will come gradually, incrementally, but change there will be, whether resulting from the abandonment, or loose application, of the doctrine of stare decisis; from the time-honored technique of distinguishing cases on the basis of facts said to be different from those in the instant case; or, *ex necessitate*, from the formulation of new rules to resolve novel issues presented by novel circumstances, such as those appearing in the wake of technological invention or, more to the point for us at the moment, in the struggle to settle a wilderness.

The common law, destined to achieve dominance in the administration of justice in England, may be thought of as the central strand of English legal history, but it is not the only one. This royal justice was by no means the only form of justice in the realm of England; nor indeed was it the one reaching most of the people who sought, or found themselves in the toils of, justice. For the most part it was the landed gentry who availed themselves of the king's justice; the general run of Englishmen encountered justice at the local level, in manorial, borough, and other courts. Then, too, there was a network of courts with special competence: mercantile tribunals, for example, administered the law merchant, that is, rules that flowed from the customs of the merchants; ecclesiastical courts, administering church law (canon law), had jurisdiction over marriage and probate; and maritime law was centered in admiralty courts. And then there is the story of equity.

The early common law operated through what is known as a formulary system, and in its beginnings is best understood as a set of procedures, rather than as the body of rules and principles that it became as the centuries wore on. To initiate an action at common law, a party purchased a writ that set out the predicates for the action; only those whose complaint fit within the description of one of the available writs were entitled to be heard at common law. Since the number of available writs was, at first, severely limited, so were the available actions, or—as they were called—forms of action.

Equity. Even this most formalistic system permitted, and underwent, change, but its high technicality and relative rigidity did produce dissatisfaction in some litigants who felt that they had been unable to obtain justice at common law. These disaffected parties often petitioned the king for (in the well-worn phrase) "relief from the rigours of the common law"; they sought equitable dispensation or intervention. Such petitions were heard by the chancellor (a high royal functionary), who exercised what is often called a conscience jurisdiction, in which individual hardship, fairness, and the like were prominent decisional considerations. From this ad hoc process there evolved chancery, or equity, courts. And over time, by a process once dubbed "hardening of the categories," the original case-by-case, individualized, fact-specific, equitable justice dispensed by the chancellor gave way to an equity jurisprudence; realistically, there then existed two systems of law, side by side, administered in separate court systems. This state of affairs survived, not only in England but in America as well, until the so-called merger of law and equity in the nineteenth century. That "merger,"

however, was more administrative than conceptual, and anything but complete; thus in the twenty-first century, although most states no longer have separate courts of equity, the dichotomy retains considerable power, with certain actions, procedures, and remedies indelibly stamped "equitable," and afforded distinctive treatment: there was, for example, no jury in equity cases, and consequently cases that historically would have been "equitable" are still largely tried without a jury.

Legislation. As judge-made law, the common law is to be distinguished from legislation, either a single statute or a code. And in this respect the common law as a system differs from that other great Western legal system, the civil law, which roots in Roman law and remains to this day the law of Western European nations—and of Louisiana. The civil law is to be found in codes; the judge seeking applicable law must look to the code, locate, and apply the appropriate provision. "The civil law system . . . trusted in legislative action and the scholarly endeavors of academic lawyers rather than judges to systematize, criticize and develop it" (Hall, p. 10).

Legislation had not achieved major significance in England in the era of colonization, but it was not negligible even then. Enactment of statutes required both the concurrence of the two houses of Parliament and the royal assent. At the time of the settlement of the first American Colonies, the royal assent to parliamentary action was a real, rather than merely formal, requirement: the royal prerogative was alive and well, and the royal assent to legislation might be, and often was, withheld. The progressive whittling away of the royal prerogative and the shift of sovereignty from the king to the king-in-Parliament (realistically, to Parliament) that culminated in the modern British constitutional monarchy were yet to come. When Virginia and Massachusetts were founded, sovereignty resided in the king, and nowhere did this fact have more force than in the Colonies, or (as they were known to the law) the dominions. The dominions were understood to belong to the king, not to the people of England or their representatives. The colonists were subjects of the king, not citizens of England; their relationship was with the king and their allegiance was personal to the king. Thus the usual legal foundation of a colony was a royal charter, or patent; many Colonial officials, including governors, were appointed by the king, and instructions to royal governors were foundational documents as well.

Development of Colonial Legal Systems. Tasks in bewildering multitude, of crushing magnitude, confronted those who would settle a wilderness: one such task was the creation of a legal system. Each colony faced this task, and each independently developed its legal system. Thus, we do not have one body of law, or one legal system, during the Colonial period: we speak of "Colonial law" or "the Colonial legal system" at our (or our readers') peril, loosely and perhaps misleadingly. A moment's reflection will reveal that this must be the case: the Colonies were settled at different times, by people with different capacities, backgrounds, objectives, and by people of different faiths—Puritans in New England, Quakers in Pennsylvania, Anglicans in Virginia, Roman Catholics in Maryland. And the settlers of the different Colonies were confronted with the challenges of different physical environments, in the land, in the climate.

There are, to be sure, certain features of Colonial life and law that span the Colonies, though not affecting all equally: for example, there was less inflexible social stratification, more social fluidity, than was the case in England; with land in abundance we find broad property ownership, a sturdy middle class, and a relatively extensive franchise. Still, class distinctions held, and each Colonial society recognized a "better sort" and a "lesser sort." As in England, the Colonies adopted an adversary system, and many of the fundamentals of the English legal system, including petit and grand juries, and writs, were in use throughout the Colonies. But we also find much informal process, both within courts and in the use of alternative modes of dispute resolution. Colonial courts were from the start hierarchical: in most of the Colonies, at the lowest tier a magistrate or justice of the peace exercised jurisdiction over small civil causes and petty crime, and then came the county, or quarter, courts with general jurisdiction; appeal then lay to a single appellate court. With few lawyers available, lay judges perforce were the rule, but the gentlemen who administered justice were knowledgeable about law to a degree not to be found among lay persons in the twenty-first century. Since governmental powers were distributed without much regard to the principle of separation of powers, the highest ruling body, the "chiefe civill power," of a colony tended to be a body that served not merely as legislature and executive but also as the colony's "Supreme Court." Similarly, lower courts typically had an administrative as well as a judicial function. Legislation was important in the Colonies, many of which adopted codes of law as a measure both to ensure an informed populace and to constrain magisterial discretion. Colonial governments did not hesitate to regulate the economy, legislating to safeguard the public health and safety and to protect the colonists from "oppression"; they experimented with price and quality control, setting up public markets for the sale of food and other critical commodities, licensing inns, enacting inspection and branding laws, and more. Elements of crime and punishment spanned the Colonies: criminal law was less harsh than in England, and control of morality, eradication of sin, was as much its aim as was prevention of economic crime; punishment was public, involving the pillory, stocks, public whipping, and the like.

Frequently, when we do discover commonalities, they are regional: New England, the Middle Atlantic Colonies, the South. Geophysical determinism set the North in one direction, the South in another: "The rough soils, heavy forests, and few navigable waterways of New England encouraged the exploitation of natural resources—fish, timber and furbearing animals—and an agricultural system that produced foodstuffs and grazing animals for export" (Hall, p. 13); in New England we find "small independent towns based on the common field system of agriculture and pasturage" (Hall, p. 13), while in the South "rich soil and a mild climate . . . favor[ed] certain crops—tobacco, cotton, rice. Climate and soil make a plantation economy possible. This kind of economy deeply affects social conditions. Slavery, for example, made sense in the South, less sense in communities of small patchwork farms" (Friedman, p. 7).

Complicating the picture yet further is the fact that this "Colonial period" to which we so glibly refer covers some 170 years, over a century and a half; another moment's reflection tells us that a lot must have happened over this time, and that it is hardly to be expected that the story—of law or any other feature of society—will be at the end the same as it was at the beginning. Thus even if we confine ourselves to the law of an individual colony, we must be clear on whether we are addressing ourselves to, for example, 1620 or 1776. In that century and a half we find, of course, the basic demographic and geographic facts of major population growth and territorial expansion. We also find two other significant factors. First, the growing complexity of the Colonial economy, or more precisely economies, as struggling settlements evolved into sophisticated commercial entities. And then, the shifting attitude of imperial authorities, from the "benign neglect" of early decades, through attempts at effective imperial supervision from about 1660 on, to a serious crackdown in the pre-Revolutionary era.

Grappling with this problem of change over time, historians tend to treat "the Colonial period" as two distinct periods, that is, the seventeenth century and the eighteenth century; this approximation is very rough indeed, but useful nonetheless. Thus, for example, modes of dispute resolution and legal process in general became more formal in the eighteenth century; a legal profession did develop, and separation of powers in the form of institutional differentiation took hold to a marked degree. More comprehensively, we see in the eighteenth century a process aptly dubbed "Anglicization," when Colonies grew more English in their law and legal systems and thus in a sense more like each other. Ironically, this growing sameness by way of Anglicization was a critical factor in enabling the Colonies, finally, to break their ties with the mother country.

As subordinate units of government, colonies were in theory not free simply to set up the governmental institutions, or adopt the laws, that suited them. Governing structure, for a start, was largely predetermined. A colony might be either "royal" or "private," and if private, then either "corporate" or "proprietary": in the first instance, the foundational document—the royal charter, the letters patent, that authorized the venture—dictated which of these the colony was to be. By those documents the king invested lawmaking authority in some person or body: in some cases, as in the corporate colony of Massachusetts Bay, the authority was bestowed upon a group of "adventurers"—that is, businessmen investing in a corporate enterprise that envisaged settlement of some area of North America and the reaping of profits by exploitation of the natural resources of the region and by trade. In the proprietary colonies, lawmaking authority was granted to a private individual, a wealthy, perhaps titled, proprietor, such as Lord Baltimore in Maryland, while in royal colonies, such as Virginia, the authority was vested in a royal governor and council. Along with the lawmaking power, in whomever vested, went the power to appoint others to essential government positions, to create governmental offices and fill them, to provide for the administration of justice, to establish court structures, and to establish the forms and powers of local government, the focus of which in the North tended to be the town, and in the South, the county.

The Colonies all either began life with a legislative body or shortly developed one, most of them bicameral. As the decades wore on, these bodies became self-consciously imitative of the prototype, that is, Parliament; the lower houses, the representative assemblies, were the locus of popular opposition to imposition of imperial control.

Just as the forms of government were to a degree predetermined, so, to a degree, was the law of the Colonies—but to *what* degree? First, and crucially, the question is to what extent the colonists were tied to English law itself: Were English statutes in force in the Colonies? Were Colonial judges bound to apply the common law? Or were the colonists truly free to make law as it suited them? In the era of settlement, given the virtually unfettered royal prerogative in the dominions, it was undoubtedly open to the monarch to direct that English law *be* the law of the Colonies; for complex reasons, kings did not do that, but instead stipulated in the founding documents only that Colonial laws be "not contrary or repugnant to the lawes and statutes of this our realme of England" or "as neer as may be" to the laws of England. Thus English law was simply set up as a standard to keep Colonial laws from straying too far from its guiding rules and principles.

Just how much of a constraint these clauses were intended to impose on Colonial lawmaking authority one cannot, certainly, tell from the wording itself, which is

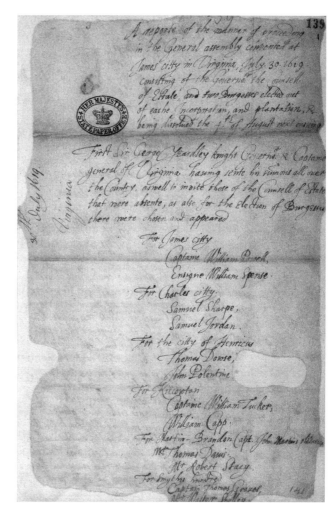

Jamestown. List of burgesses elected to the first assembly at Jamestown, 1619. HIP/ART RESOURCE, NY

nothing if not ambiguous: "contrary or repugnant to," for example, is hardly self-explanatory—is "different from" contrary or repugnant to? And exactly how "neer" is "as neer as may be"? And "the lawes and statutes of this our realme of England" is not exactly a model of clarity: "Lawes" meaning common law? Local law? "Statutes" meaning those enacted before settlement? After settlement? Both? It is not surprising that by the early eighteenth century we hear that "no one can tell what is law and what is not in the plantations. Some hold that the law of England is chiefly to be respected . . . others are of the opinion that the laws of the Colonies are to take first place" (Wright, p. 23).

The critical point, however, is that for some decades the precise meaning of these clauses did not terribly matter: they could not operate *at all* as a constraint upon Colonial lawmaking unless they were enforced, and at first they were not. The seventeenth century was a time of turmoil in England—of rebellion, civil war, the beheading of a king, and more—and that fact of life within the realm had a profound effect on the facts of life within the dominions. No one in England really had time to worry about whether, over in those small scattered struggling settlements, they were passing laws contrary or repugnant, or not near enough, to English law. There was no effective enforcement of the clauses, no effective imperial supervision of lawmaking in the Colonies, nothing, indeed, that can be called imperial policy for some decades after the founding of Virginia, Massachusetts Bay, and other such places. In the meanwhile, the Colonies by and large went their merry way.

Where then, did the colonists get their law and legal institutions? At one time, tracing the source of Colonial law was a major industry. Justice Joseph Story started the inquiry off by opining that Colonial law was from the beginning "common law"; this was problematic in its oversimplification, but perhaps more so in its suggestion that Colonial law was in nature and origin unitary, that the historian ought to look for *the* source of law, for a "single monopolistic factor." And Justice Story set the mood: historians might not agree on what the single monopolistic factor was, but they assumed that a successful search would reveal *the*, one and only, source of Colonial law. So, the so-called indigenous school, rejecting Justice Story's common-law thesis, said that early Colonial law was a home-grown, crude, unsophisticated American law. Columbia Law School professor Julius Goebel then took on both the common-law and the indigenous schools, insisting that "resort was to the law with which the colonists had grown up," that is, to English law, but to English *local* law rather than the law of the king's courts.

Finally, Harvard Law School professor Zechariah Chafee successfully issued a plea for a "synthetic-rubber hypothesis," that is, for accepting that Colonial law contained a number of elements, displayed a number of influences, and historians have for some time recognized that the settlers were as unlikely to cast off all that they knew as they were to not respond to new conditions (including the freedom to cast off some of what they knew); scholars are no more eager to detect English than religious (or other cultural) influence, and they accord respectful consideration to common law, local law, ancient custom, and frontier conditions.

One can, indeed, occasionally see the convergence of multiple influences in a single law, for example, the New England law of intestacy. By the English common law of primogeniture, a decedent's land went to the eldest son, and primogeniture was the rule in the southern and middle Colonies. The New England colonists, however, adopted partible inheritance, by which the real property of a decedent parent is divided among the sons, sometimes with a double portion to the eldest son. Now, partible inheritance did have English—local-law rather than common-law—roots: the practice of gavelkind, in Kent, was a form of partible inheritance. And scripture prescribes division of the estate with a double portion to the eldest son. And finally, we can see the pressure exerted by the living conditions confronting the colonists: at first glance it may seem that primogeniture made more sense in New England, with its abundance of land, than it did in land-sparse England, but the realities of farming dictated partible inheritance; many hands were needed to ensure success in the tough New England soil, and a way had to be found to keep sons down on the farm. In the eighteenth century, when English authorities tried to impose primogeniture on New England, the colonists pleaded that if there were to be no reward in prospect, their sons would leave. (Note that we see here a picture of a social system in which tight control is kept by the father, who does not, for example, parcel out land to his sons while he is alive; New England Puritans constructed a society of small tight units, built around the church, with the family as primary locus of authority.)

The Role of Religion. It is worth noting the extent to which religion drove law in such a colony as early Massachusetts Bay, long labeled a "Bible Commonwealth." There were those in the colony who urged adoption of scripture as law, and the introductory epistle to the code of 1648 read: "This hath been no small privilege, and advantage to us in New-England . . . to frame our lawes according to the rules of His most holy word." But exhortations to biblical literalism did not prevail, and it is only in the peculiarly sensitive area of capital crime that we find something approaching true fidelity to scripture. Where God's law demanded the taking of a life, the colony would in most instances so prescribe; capital laws were cited to scripture, and capital crimes included idolatry, witchcraft, sodomy, adultery, and rebellion against parental authority. Massachusetts did, however, mitigate the severity of God's law in this area in a couple of ways. First, the colony did not *prescribe* the death penalty in all cases where it was called for by scripture—incest, for example, was not a capital crime in Massachusetts. Second, *prescription* did not necessarily bring *enforcement*: rebellion against parents was never punished as a capital crime. Moreover, conversely, Puritans were reluctant to take life *without* scriptural warrant: in England, theft was a capital crime, but in Massachusetts, it was not, "because we read otherwise in Scripture."

Indentured Servitude and Slavery. Colonial labor systems included both free and bound labor, the latter in the forms of indentured servitude and slavery. The indentured servant, a "slave for the time being" (Friedman, p. 45), was the property of his master for a term of years—typically four to seven—at the end of which he was free. Although usually voluntary, indentured servitude might also be prescribed as punishment for crime and was employed as a means of dealing with orphaned or abandoned children.

Indentured servants could be bought, sold, and traded, and often suffered cruelly, though they did have rights of redress for ill treatment at law; they could not marry without the master's consent or vote or engage in trade.

Slavery as a legal status did not exist in England, but in the Colonies it was found both in the North and the South; in the South, black slavery replaced white servitude. Slaves were property and as such could be bought, sold, traded, mortgaged, given away, and bequeathed. Slaves could not vote, own property, testify against whites in court, or marry. Slave codes in the Southern Colonies were far more repressive than those in the North, and increasingly so with the decades, imposing a wide variety of restrictions on slaves and on free whites, who were forbidden, for example, to trade with slaves or to teach them to read or write. Slaves were subject to corporal punishment by masters, and if death resulted, the master was not punished. Slave courts sentenced slaves to whippings, and for serious crimes, to death. There were free blacks in the Colonies, but racism, which drove the system of slavery, also found expression in discrimination against free blacks: "By 1776, the free black was a kind of half slave in many parts of the country" (Friedman, p. 49).

Land Ownership. In theory, all land in England was owned by the king; others held of the king, or held of intermediate tenants. This was a tenurial system, and the key concept was tenure rather than ownership. Land in the Colonies also belonged to the king, whose grants, whether to the Governor and Company of Massachusetts Bay in New England or to Lord Baltimore, were not absolute. In some of the Colonies annual rents, called quitrents, were due the king; in others quitrents were owed the proprietor.

Early on, land systems varied widely throughout the Colonies, reflecting impulses as divergent as communitarianism on the one hand and on the other hand a desire to follow English ways by importing the complex organization and structures of English land law. After a certain amount of trial and error, the Colonies found their way to satisfactory positions. In the end, with the abundance of land as the major factor, most of the Colonies adopted relatively simple land policies and procedures. The consequence was, in most Colonies, a level of widespread ownership of land unknown in England. Larger estates did obtain in the South and in New York, where the Dutch had instituted a "patroon" system, putting enormous amounts of land in individuals' hands. This system of concentration of land ownership continued even after the colony became English, with huge grants of land made to a few favored personages, producing a manorial system of vast estates with tenant farmers who paid rent to the "lord of the manor."

Land was conveyed for the most part in simplified ways, fostering free alienation and facilitating informal transfer. An innovative system of land recordation began in New England and spread to other Colonies. The English system of totally separate rules for land on the one hand and personalty on the other began to break down in the Colonies.

Development of the Legal Profession. Among the most critical developments in the maturity of the Colonies was the growth of a legal profession. Antilawyer sentiment is a phenomenon whose roots are deep and branches widespread; it was perhaps particularly acute among the early colonists, and some of them ventured upon a society without lawyers. But such experimentation was short-lived, and as the decades wore on, as Colonial economies grew increasingly complex, and as the outside world more and more intruded, it became ever more evident that a vigorous legal profession was, if a necessary evil as the saying went, necessary nonetheless. From the latter decades of the seventeenth century through the eighteenth century, a profession evolved. There were no law schools, and legal training was largely through apprenticeship in the office of a practitioner or judge; in addition, some number of young aspiring lawyers went off to study at the Inns of Court in London. "There were upper and lower lawyers, rich and poor, exclusive lawyers and lawyers hungry for clients, just as there are today" (Friedman, p. 59). And lawyers played a central, indispensable role in the movements toward independence and toward the creation of a new nation.

Courts. The court structure continued basically hierarchic in the eighteenth century, but the "cheife civill power," once functionally undifferentiated, evolved into what we would recognize as a legislature, *simpliciter*, as its judicial function virtually disappeared. Governor and council often did sit as a court, with jurisdiction in such matters as probate and divorce, but this was quite different from the possession of the judicial power, and the supreme judicial power at that, by the representatives of the people in the lower house of the legislature. Specialized courts of vice admiralty administered maritime law, and chancery courts dispensed equity; both of these sat without a jury.

Imperial Attempts to Limit Colonial Autonomy. As we have seen, there was at first little attempt by authorities in the mother country to impose either authority or uniformity on the Colonies; after the Glorious Revolution of 1688, however, the mind-set of empire took hold. And to the mercantilist mentality that dominated that mind-set it was indisputable that colonies existed for the benefit of the mother country. At the least, imperial authorities insisted, colonists who enjoyed the benefits of empire ought to pay their fair share of the costs; and in British eyes, the American Colonies were doing no such thing. Thus we see ever-increasing, more and more frenetic, attempts by the metropolitan authorities to control their dominions. The colonists were unable to accept the version of mercantilist theory that resulted in what they perceived as their virtual submergence, and they denied that they were failing to contribute their fair share of imperial costs. Thus, imperial initiatives provoked resentment, encountered resistance, produced disparate and conflicting understandings of the imperial constitution, and culminated in the shattering loss of empire.

An early step was the "Dominion of New England," a restructuring of the governments of several Colonies that included, most dramatically, the elimination of representative government in the affected Colonies. This particular experiment failed, but imperial authorities had other strings to their bow. From the imperial perspective, the royal colony was the ideal, the structure most amenable to effective supervision, since the charters of private colonies, whether corporate or proprietary, tended to grant privileges of one kind or another to the inhabitants or to the proprietors—privileges that made it difficult to crack down on them. Thus, in the late seventeenth and the early eighteenth centuries, imperial government by one method or another transformed all but five Colonies into royal colonies. Connecticut and Rhode Island remained corporate colonies, Pennsylvania and Maryland proprietary. Massachusetts was a hybrid, its 1692 charter providing for a governor appointed by the king, but with popular participation in the selection of the council.

In the imperial effort to limit the autonomous lawmaking power of the colonists, the primary resort was the royal governor, who had veto power over Colonial legislation; repeatedly outmaneuvered by the ingenuity of Colonial assemblies, this official proved a weak reed. Then there were two types of review of Colonial legislation by the Privy Council. Legislative review required that Colonial laws be sent to the Privy Council for approval; disallowance of a law acted as a repeal of the statute, which was deemed in effect until the date of the disallowance. Pursuant to judicial review, certain cases might go on appeal from a colony's highest court to the Privy Council. When, in such a case, a Colonial statute was declared invalid, that law was deemed to be null and void ab initio, that is, never to have been in effect at all. In the end, the Colonial assemblies were able to render these supervisory mechanisms ineffectual as well.

It did not escape the attention of the British authorities that the way to put teeth into imperial government was for the king to depart from traditional royal government and turn to Parliament—or perhaps one should say turn Parliament loose on the Colonies. Perhaps royal governors, and even the Privy Council, could be dealt with handily, but up against the British Parliament the colonists might find that something more than ingenuity was required to retain the lawmaking autonomy they had come to think of as theirs by inalienable right. And the story of the pre-Revolutionary decades, and of the American Revolution, is the story of the relationship between Parliament and the Colonies. In the end, the colonists took the position that under the constitution of empire, Parliament had no authority over the Colonies. George III and his Parliaments and his Privy Council and his judges and his English subjects thought otherwise. In 1776 the Colonial period ended with a declaration of independence; colonists no longer, Americans would wage and win their war and go on to create a nation.

[*See also* Civil Law, *subentry on* Colonial United States; Common Law, *subentry on* English Common Law; Criminal Law, *subentry on* Colonial United States; Land, *subentry on* Land Registration in English Common Law; *and* Slavery, *subentry on* Slavery and Other Labor Systems in the Colonial United States.]

BIBLIOGRAPHY

Black, Barbara A. "The Constitution of Empire: The Case for the Colonists." *Pennsylvania Law Review* 124 (1976): 1157–1211.
Friedman, Lawrence M. *A History of American Law*. 3d ed. New York: Simon & Schuster, 2005.
Hall, Kermit L. *The Magic Mirror: Law in American History*. New York: Oxford University Press, 1989.
Haskins, George Lee. *Law and Authority in Early Massachusetts: A Study in Tradition and Design*. Hamden, Conn.: Archon Books, 1968.
Wright, Louis B., ed. *An Essay upon the Government of the English Plantations on the Continent of American (1701): Au Anonymous Virginian's Proposals for Liberty under the British Crown*. San Marino, Calif.: Huntington Library, 1945.

BARBARA ARONSTEIN BLACK

The Colonial Period: The Sources of Colonial Law

Between the sixteenth and late eighteenth centuries, Spain, France, the Netherlands, and England expanded into the area that would form the United States. Before European contact, between two and ten million people lived in this area. The many tribes and extended family groups had legal and governing practices that differed from each other and from the European models. The legal culture of these societies was not incorporated by European colonizers and settlers. Although these legal practices continued to govern many matters relating to tribal members, what became known as "Colonial law" arose from the relationship between European law and the local legal practices of European settlers.

Spanish and French Sources of Law. Although Spanish and French sources of law did not directly affect the thirteen American Colonies, they influenced the development of diverse state law in the United States. During the Colonial period, Spain controlled Florida and parts of the Southeast and Southwest (in particular, New Mexico and Texas). At the imperial level, Spain established a centralized colonial bureaucracy of Spanish officials. At the local level, however, governance often was placed with

Catholic missionaries or Spanish colonists who governed the native population in a system of labor known as the *encomienda*. The French colonial presence remained most dominant in trading settlements along the Mississippi valley. Unlike the English, Spanish and French officials and settlers drew on Roman law (in particular, the idea of a code-based legal system and the structure of law established in Justinian's *Institutes*) as well as the canon law and practices of the imperial Catholic church. These influences led to, among other things, Louisiana's civil code (1808) and the retention of community-property (marital) law in certain states.

Dutch Sources of Law. The legal practices of the Netherlands played a significant, albeit narrow, role in New York's legal development. Dutch settlements in Manhattan and Long Island arose from trade, and governance drew on the practices of mercantile trading corporations and Dutch localities. Dutch colonial policy permitted the establishment of large landholders (patroons) who held extensive local governance authority. Dutch law was based on Roman civil law, but Protestant Dutch legal reformers drew more heavily on Germanic practices and rejected canon law. Dutch legal practices differed from those of the English: women were treated more favorably under Dutch law; juries were not essential parts of the Dutch legal system; and slaves possessed some legal rights under Dutch law. When New York became an English colony, Dutch legal practices faded. Nevertheless, the continued existence of the patroon landholding eventually gave rise to mid-nineteenth-century property controversies referred to as the anti-rent wars.

English Law as a Source of Colonial Law. Although new immigrants from non-English legal traditions affected particular areas of Colonial law and legal practice, English law established the constitutional structure of American Colonial law. This constitutional structure was written into Colonial patents, charters, and Crown instructions. Historians refer to this structure as the transatlantic constitution, the constitution of empire, or the imperial constitution. The complexities in applying the laws of England to diverse Colonial circumstances lay at the center of this Colonial constitutional law. The precedent of English corporate law; the idea of the common law; English imperial practices in Ireland, Wales, Scotland, and the Channel Islands; and early experience in the colonies themselves soon established two principles. First, Colonial law could not be repugnant to the laws of England but should be as near as possible to, or agreeable to, English law. Second, Colonial law could diverge from English law to reflect local circumstances. These principles attempted to create uniformity in the laws and practices that defined the English people while simultaneously recognizing that the law should respond to local concerns. The temporal and physical distance created by the Atlantic Ocean permitted significant divergences from English law but also produced deep tensions among the English colonists and the English in England over the need to retain English identity through legal structures.

Of course, many aspects of Colonial law responded to local circumstances and appear on their face to have had little relationship to the laws of England. Examples of such local legislation include acts relating to internal improvements such as the laying out of highways; statutes encouraging various industries such as water mills; certain types of environmental laws such as those regulating the killing of wild animals; and many laws addressing relationships with indigenous peoples. In this area, however, the breadth and diversity of English law suggests caution. It is difficult to neatly divide laws that originated wholly from local Colonial ideologies and circumstances from those that related to English laws or English legal reform. For example, Colonial laws often required that deeds to land be recorded. Although this requirement responded to the complexities of new Colonial land titles, it also drew on mid-seventeenth-century English law-reform efforts.

In the colonies, English statutes were important sources of law. English colonists and officials claimed that very old English statutes understood to constitute the unwritten ancient constitution—for example, the Magna Carta (1215)—had been brought with the settlers. Various proprietary charters, however, explicitly rejected one particular property reform statute, *Quia Emptores* (1290), in order to resurrect ancient feudal landholding practices barred in England by the statute. Statutes passed after early Colonial settlement had more controversial status. For example, colonists in New England and Virginia argued over whether the Statute of Frauds (1677) applied to Colonial wills. After 1681 English officials concluded that the colonies had to be specifically named in an English statute for it to apply to the colonies. In the 1720s, English officials concluded that English statutes would also apply if explicitly adopted by the Colonial legislature or if it could be established that the statute had been implicitly adopted through long usage and practice.

The colonists and English officials also debated the relevance of English common law. Colonial settlement coincided with the expansion of the concept of the common law in an outpouring of English law books aimed at legal practitioners by Sir Edward Coke, Sir Matthew Hale, and others. In these texts, English common law was imagined as a body of law centered on property law that defined Englishness and was the right of English people. Although the common law was the theoretical product of judicial decisions, Colonial law relied on the description of common law in treatises and abridgments. From a Colonial perspective, English common law thus appeared to consist of largely stable legal terms, concepts, and rules.

By the eighteenth century, Colonial lawyers often referred to English common-law cases in arguments before appellate courts. English common-law court decisions also may have prompted Colonial divergences from English law. For example, Colonial statutes legalizing and regulating slavery implicitly responded to English common-law court decisions, suggesting that baptism might free a slave (*Butts v. Penny* [1677]) or that slaves became free upon setting foot on English soil (*Smith v. Brown and Cooper* [1701] and *Smith v. Gould* [1705]).

English statutory and common law also become part of Colonial law through Colonial reception statutes, which gave legal effect to, or received, existing English law. Rhode Island, for example, passed a statute in 1700 authorizing the "laws of England" to be introduced where Colonial law or custom did not apply. In 1712, South Carolina passed a statute that gave legal effect to certain English statutes and the English common law. North Carolina passed a similar statute in 1715. After 1750, however, some of these types of reception statutes were disallowed by the English Privy Council.

Colonial arguments for divergence from the laws of England often intertwined arguments based on local Colonial circumstances with arguments drawn from the richness and diversity of the laws of England themselves. The term "laws of England" included statutes and the common law, but it also encompassed the customary law of particular areas of England, canon law, the law merchant, and other bodies of law. Martial law, for example, briefly served as a source for the first collection of Virginia laws written by the colony's English governors, although these laws were later supplanted by the local assembly. Colonists appropriated the language of ancient customary practices to justify other divergences. In New England, colonists claimed that a presumption in favor of tenancy in common had been the ancient practice and usage, rather than the English preference for joint tenancy. New England colonists likewise successfully justified their rejection of primogeniture (the practice of the eldest son alone inheriting) in favor of partible inheritance, the division of property equally among children. Their arguments included the right to follow gavelkind (a custom of partible inheritance followed in the English region of Kent), customary local Colonial practices and usages, and an emphasis on the ways in which local Colonial circumstances favored equal division.

Eventually, local Colonial practices arising from the varied circumstances of the colonies became the most important source for Colonial law. The repugnancy and divergence principles permitted Colonial law to differ across the colonies in order to accommodate local differences but still maintain crucial uniformities that allowed Colonial law to remain English. For example, some colonies concluded that two witnesses were required for a will; others insisted on three. Primogeniture remained dominant in the southern colonies, whereas partible inheritance came to dominate the New England colonies. Although some colonies retained the Church of England as the legally established religion, others rejected it and, in Rhode Island, even legally proclaimed no establishment. Despite court decisions that questioned the legality of slavery on English soil, many colonies legalized slavery through increasingly complex slave codes. After the Revolution, this pattern continued to influence American state law and resulted in the clash between so-called American and English doctrinal rules.

[*See also* Common Law, *subentry on* English Common Law.]

BIBLIOGRAPHY

Benton, Lauren. *Law and Colonial Cultures: Legal Regimes in World History: 1400–1900*. Cambridge, U.K., and New York: Cambridge University Press, 2001.

Biemer, Linda Briggs. *Women and Property in Colonial New York: The Transition from Dutch to English Law, 1643–1727*. Ann Arbor, Mich.: UMI Research Press, 1983.

Bilder, Mary Sarah. *The Transatlantic Constitution: Colonial Legal Culture and the Empire*. Cambridge, Mass.: Harvard University Press, 2004.

Haskins, George Lee. *Law and Authority in Early Massachusetts: A Study in Tradition and Design*. New York: Macmillan, 1960.

Hulsebosch, Daniel J. *Constituting Empire: New York and the Transformation of Constitutionalism in the Atlantic World, 1664–1830*. Chapel Hill: University of North Carolina Press, 2005.

Konig, David T. "The Virgin and the Virgin's Sister: Virginia, Massachusetts, and the Contested Legacy of Colonial Law." In *The History of the Law in Massachusetts: The Supreme Judicial Court, 1692–1992*, edited by Russell K. Osgood, pp. 81–115. Boston: Supreme Judicial Court Historical Society, 1992.

Muldoon, James. *The Americas in the Spanish World Order: The Justification for Conquest in the Seventeenth Century*. Philadelphia: University of Pennsylvania Press, 1994.

Sullivan, Dennis. *The Punishment of Crime in Colonial New York: The Dutch Experience in Albany during the Seventeenth Century*. New York: Peter Lang, 1997.

Tomlins, Christopher L., and Bruce H. Mann, eds. *The Many Legalities of Early America*. Chapel Hill: University of North Carolina Press, 2001.

Williams, Robert A. *The American Indian in Western Legal Thought: The Discourses of Conquest*. New York: Oxford University Press, 1990.

Mary Sarah Bilder

The Colonial Period: The Colonies in the Empire

Colonial lawmaking in the British Empire is a story of how traditional notions of English constitutionalism intersected with opportunity and accident to create not one but a number of forms of governance exercised through several competing institutions within the colonies and across the empire that had overlapping jurisdiction and that competed for authority. The government of each North American colony originated in a formal royal document, either a proprietary grant to individuals, like that used for any grant of royal property; a charter incorporating a company for overseas exploration, trade, and settlement; or a royal charter like that of a municipality. Some of these grants contained broader delegations of internal authority than others. But generally they shared a similar structure: the proprietor, company, or royal governor received direct authority from the king to govern the territory and control the allotment of land and commercial privileges within it. The royal grant always made some provision for colonial government. Typically, though not always, the company or governor was instructed to govern with the aid or a local council, assembly, or both. The rules so made could not be inconsistent with or repugnant to the laws of England. Among the powers delegated to the company or governor was judicial power.

Despite this formal pyramid, power did not flow down smoothly. Each institution was answerable to one above it, but to what degree and in what ways was unclear; this hampered central authority while allowing fairly free rein to local government. Government in North America was a continuous negotiation not just between the center of empire and its periphery but also within each territory, between imperial officials and colonists. There were conflicts between those who believed that colonies existed primarily to serve imperial interests and those who believed that the colonists were carrying English civilization—its commerce, law, and culture—into new worlds and deserved great freedom as they struggled to do so. In short, almost everyone who participated in colonial government—administrators, representatives, petitioners, and litigants—thought they were doing the good work of the empire.

An example of the compromises necessary to keep the empire working was the creation of the New York colonial assembly in 1683. When Charles II granted New York to his brother, James, Duke of York, in 1664, he did not provide for the establishment of a local assembly. And the duke had no desire to create one. "[A]n assembly," James told his governor in 1676, "would be of dangerous consequences, nothing being more known than the aptness of such bodies to assume privileges destructive to the peace of the government." But years of colonial protest and tax evasion forced the duke to capitulate in 1683, when he instructed the then governor to call elections for a colonial assembly. The assembly divided the colony into counties on the English model, and with them came a system in imitation of the English common law. In addition, the assembly declared that its own existence, the new courts it created, and several "liberties of Englishmen" were constitutionally required in the province and unalterable—something the metropolitan officials were reluctant to concede. Meanwhile, Parliament claimed ever greater power to legislate for the colonies, often in derogation of colonial autonomy. For the next century, colonial disputes throughout America often turned on this claim that the colonists deserved all the rights of Englishmen, especially legal rights like the jury trial and political representation as a prerequisite for taxation.

These conflicts bred widespread debate about imperial government within the colonies and between them and the metropolitan government in Britain. A few formal venues existed for transatlantic dialogue. First, the king and his Privy Council appointed imperial agents who served in the colonies. They received commissions that described their role, and regular instructions for carrying them out. In return, these officials reported regularly to the Privy Council on the state of the colonies and the problems of imperial administration. Sometimes these were official reports. More often they were included in letters to members of the council or others of influence in the metropolis. These reports constituted the primary lens through which the Crown viewed the colonies.

The Privy Council's dual review process, over colonial statutes and judicial decisions, created a second forum for transatlantic discussion of imperial government. The council regularly reviewed most of the colonies' statutes and heard appeals from the highest court in each. Most (though not all) colonial legislatures were required to send their statutes to the council for review, and it would consider whether they were "repugnant" to the laws of England, a vague standard that could be used to disallow statutes that deviated too far from some domestic norm or that, paradoxically, presumed too much of domestic law. The practice and the standard of review had originated in the medieval kingdom to supervise the lawmaking of largely self-governing corporate bodies within and just outside the realm, such as the Channel Islands. The American colonies were not part of the realm of England, and could not presume to enjoy its law unless it was granted to them. Yet neither could they innovate in ways that contradicted some underarticulated baseline of English legality. In practice, claims of presumption and deviation were used by local adversaries to vindicate their interests, and it does not appear that the council generated much consistent jurisprudence defining the meaning of "repugnance to the laws of England."

Similarly, the Privy Council retained appellate jurisdiction over judicial decisions. Litigants were permitted to appeal beyond a colony's highest court (in the royal colonies, the governor and his council) to the council in London in cases that involved a minimum amount in controversy. This limitation varied but was usually the considerable sum of 300 pounds sterling, thus excluding the majority of civil and criminal cases. The transatlantic appeal was an expensive option that few litigants pursued, but it reminded everyone of the existence of a superior royal tribunal in England.

Third, although the colonies did not send representatives to the English (and, after 1707, British) Parliament, most colonial legislatures had official agents in London. Typically these were members of the Commons who, in exchange for a salary, represented colonial interests in Parliament. Edmund Burke, for example, served as the New York assembly's colonial agent on the eve of the Revolution. Along with these official agents, interest groups within the colonies, from merchants to churches and colleges, had lobbyists in London too, some them also members of Parliament.

During the eighteenth century it became increasingly important for colonial interests to have some influence in Parliament as that body took a larger role in governing the empire. The Parliament, and especially the House of Commons, had since the Glorious Revolution of 1688–1689 become the dominant force in domestic politics; by 1765, William Blackstone could refer to Parliament's lawmaking power as "sovereign and uncontrollable." Although the Commons began regulating colonial trade after the English Civil War of the 1640s, it only gradually increased its jurisdiction over the internal governance of the colonies. It began to enlarge that control in the 1760s, inspiring the colonists to draw new and problematic distinctions between internal and external legislation or, alternatively, between taxation and regulation. It also provoked increased evasion of statutes.

There was, in sum, no fully authoritative institution for defining the place of the colonies within the empire and the liberties that colonists enjoyed. Royal documents and parliamentary legislation set loose boundaries on what actually transpired on the ground. In this large gap between the theory of royal authority and the practice of colonial administration emerged competing visions of the imperial constitution that metropolitan officials, overseas imperial agents, provincial elites, and local settlers used to their advantage in conflicts that pitted one claim of authority against another. Typical disputes included those over the validity of private transactions with Native Americans for land and goods; the nature of land tenure; the autonomy of colonial churches; provincial control over the salaries of the imperial agents; the problem of jury nullification; and the personnel of the colonial legal system. While many factors were at work in these disputes, a common theme was the conflict between different visions of the empire. Whose interests was the empire supposed to serve? And how?

Disagreements embraced not only the content of the imperial constitution but also its nature and sources. Both the provincial elite and ordinary colonists conceived of their constitution as fluid in source and rigid in substance. They drew on a wide range of English constitutional resources but held firm to the particular liberties they claimed. Imperial agents, on the other hand, relied on fixed sources but wished to keep its substance fluid, to permit administrative flexibility. In other words, provincial versions of the imperial constitution were essentially lists of political and legal liberties selected from English tradition that defined local government and individual freedom, while the agents' versions identified hierarchical procedures that would ensure that the right personnel controlled government. One group upheld definitions of substantive liberties of localism; the other, the authority of imperial personnel and procedure.

These differing visions of the imperial constitution coexisted for many years, until the events of the 1760s forced their contradictions into stark relief. Indeed, the modus vivendi of imperial governance—discussions and practices that emerged in the gaps between static theories of royal power—operated to prevent clear definitions. The fact that contestants drew on similar, overlapping constitutional traditions helped mask the fundamental differences between rival interpretations of the imperial constitution. When in the 1760s and 1770s Parliament asserted absolute sovereignty over the colonies, the colonists responded by demanding precise definition of their liberties, and a civil war—the American Revolution—ensued.

Only from the perspective of the thirteen rebellious colonies did the story end in the Revolution. For people in the rest of the British Empire—from London and Dublin to Jamaica and India—that revolution was one passage in a long, not yet completed journey toward more rationalized government in which the imperial territories were aligned in a hierarchy of liberty, with settler colonies obtaining greater internal autonomy while control over indigenous populations became tighter. Both strategies—greater liberty for the white settlers, less for other people—were attempts to preempt future declarations of independence. Both were conceived by Britons who tried to govern and live within the North American colonies in the eighteenth century.

[*See also* United States Law, *subentry on* American Revolution; Constitution; *and* Constitutional Law, *subentry on* English Common Law.]

BIBLIOGRAPHY

Gould, Eliga H. *The Persistence of Empire: British Political Culture in the Age of the American Revolution*. Chapel Hill: University of North Carolina Press, 2000.

Greene, Jack P. *Peripheries and Center: Constitutional Development in the Extended Polities of the British Empire and the United States, 1607–1788*. Athens: University of Georgia Press, 1986.

Hulsebosch, Daniel J. *Constituting Empire: New York and the Transformation of Constitutionalism in the Atlantic World, 1664–1830*. Chapel Hill: University of North Carolina Press, 2005.

Reid, John Phillip. *Constitutional History of the American Revolution*. 4 vols. Madison: University of Wisconsin Press, 1986–1993.

Smith, Joseph H. *Appeals to the Privy Council from the American Plantations*. New York: Columbia University Press, 1950.

DINIEL J. HULSEBOCH

The American Revolution

The American Revolution affected all levels of American law. At the national level, a new nation emerged in 1776, and within a little more than a decade it had adopted a national constitution that embodied much of the philosophy of the Revolution. The Revolution also affected the states, as the individual colonies asserted their independence by writing constitutions and to differing degrees changing the common and statutory law they had inherited from England. Legal change that is tied to the Revolution began to emerge even before the war and continued until the eve of the War of 1812.

Most obviously, the Revolution altered the very nature of the political and philosophical basis for law itself. The creation of an independent nation led to the development of governmental powers and new laws to support and implement those powers. Law at the national level affected both foreign and domestic policy as well as the relationships between the newly independent states. During and after the Revolution, the legislators in the new American states reconsidered much of their English legal heritage, rejecting many common-law and statutory rules that had existed in the colonies. In the aftermath of the Revolution, Americans rewrote or at least altered significant aspects of English property law and criminal law. At both the national and the state levels, changes in law also reflected Americans' desire for liberty. This was the most problematic part of the revolutionary change in law. For free people—especially free white men—the Revolution created a regime of unprecedented legally protected liberty. Free women shared some of this growth in liberty but not all of it. The experience for slaves was more complicated and in the end more bleak. For some slaves the Revolution led to freedom and, especially in the North, limited legal protections and equality. For most slaves, however, the new legal regimes created during the Revolution left their chains even more secure than they might have been under royal authority.

Law and the Philosophy of the Revolution. In the period leading up to the Revolution, Americans argued that they should be represented in the English Parliament. They objected to laws passed by a parliament in which they could not participate. They asserted that taxation without representation is tyranny. Americans also objected to a distant king overturning the laws passed by the popularly elected colonial legislatures. The English Parliament, for example, had overturned Virginia's Two Penny Act, which set the value of a pound of tobacco at two pennies for all contracts. Virginians were furious, because the law was a legitimate response by the popularly elected colonial legislature to the economic turmoil caused by a tobacco-crop failure in a colony where most contracts used tobacco, rather than money, as a form of payment.

American Revolution. Five men forcing a tarred and feathered customs officer to drink from a teapot. "The Bostonian's paying the excise-man, or tarring & feathering," mezzotint by Philip Dawe, 1774. DEFENSE VISUAL INFORMATION DIRECTORATE

The Parliament did not understand the economic issues or the local needs of Virginia. Similarly, in the 1770s, for purely economic reasons, Virginia banned the importation of slaves, but the king overturned the law to protect the English slave trade. These examples illustrate why the Americans wanted self-government.

This desire for self-government provided the theoretical basis for the Revolution. The Declaration of Independence set out two separate but interrelated theories for law and a well-ordered society. First, the Declaration asserted that "governments are instituted among Men, deriving their just powers from the consent of the governed." This theory of government rejected the idea of a monarchy or a nobility ruling over the people. It also rejected the idea that laws could come from God or some religious leader or church. Rather, the Declaration presumed that the people would govern themselves. The theory rejected not only the British monarchy and a House of Lords whose seats were gained through inheritance, but also such British institutions as virtual representation and rotten boroughs. (Many parts of England, including some large cities like Manchester, had no members in Parliament, but according to English theory were "virtually represented" because Parliament governed for the entire nation. Similarly, because there had been no redistricting for centuries, some places in England sent members to Parliament even though almost no one lived in these places; these were known as "rotton boroughs." The U.S. Constitution would prevent both of these problems by requiring the reallocation of seats in Congress every ten years after a national census.)

The notion that governments were just only if they were based on the "consent of the governed" set the stage for representative democracy—what the U.S. Constitution would call a "republican form of government"—in every one of the new states and, after 1787, in the new nation itself. All but two of the newly independent states adopted constitutions that provided for representation based on population.

The second theory of law in the Declaration was based on the assertion of self-evident truths—that "all men are created equal and are endowed. . . with certain unalienable rights," including "life, liberty, and the pursuit of happiness." The principle of equality would be contested in the period after the war, and debate over its meaning and implementation would continue long after the Revolutionary period ended.

Changing the Law in the New Nation. All but two states (Connecticut and Rhode Island) adopted new constitutions. Initially they were written and promulgated by the state legislatures. In 1778 the Massachusetts legislature sent its constitution to the state's town meetings for ratification. The town meetings, however, rejected the document for a number of reasons, including its failure to end slavery and grant universal adult male suffrage. In 1780 the people of the state approved a new constitution, written mostly by John Adams, which both ended slavery and granted universal adult male suffrage.

All the new governments had elected legislatures, and except for a brief time in Pennsylvania, all were bicameral. Most had governors, but with fewer powers than royal governors had had. Most of the new state constitutions had restrictions on suffrage, usually based on property and sometimes on race. New Jersey allowed women to vote, but no other new state did. About half the states, mostly in the North, allowed free black males to vote. All the states allowed the free exercise of religion, but most maintained their existing religious establishments. Every state but Virginia and New York had a religious test for office holding, limiting such jobs to Protestants, Christians (which would have included Catholics), or in Delaware, to Trinitarians. A number of the state constitutions exempted Quakers and other pacifists from military service. Almost all had some form of a declaration of rights or a bill of rights. Collectively, these contained almost all the rights that would later be found in the federal Bill of Rights, but no state had them all. The most common civil liberty, protected by almost every state, was freedom of the press. However, the meaning of that freedom was uncertain, since all the states also continued to allow the prosecution of publications that offended the government. These prosecutions were for the old common law crime of "seditious libel," which is essentially the crime of libeling the government or undermining support for the government through publications that embarrassed those in power. Ironically, in a traditional seditious libel case, it did not matter whether the publication was true or not, but only whether it diminished respect for the government or those in high office.

On the eve of the Revolution, the First Continental Congress had claimed that all Americans were entitled to the protections and rights in the common law of England. Nine states adopted the common law of England, either through a statute or a constitutional provision. But these "reception statutes" (called this because they "received" the common law) always contained a provision limiting the date of the reception (often to the common law as of July 4, 1776) and also asserting that the common law was received except where superseded by state law or where the common law conflicted with the new state constitution. Other states implied some recognition of the common law without using the phrase. Massachusetts, for example, retained those "laws which have heretofore been adopted, and approved" in the colony and states. Revolutionaries were also aware of the problematic nature of the common law because of its origin and imprecision. The common law had developed under a monarchy with an established church, an elite body of titled nobles, and a minuscule electorate. Thus, many aspects of the common law were seen as protective of elites and those with vested interests and unsuitable for a growing, dynamic nation where there were no formal class distinctions or established churches. In addition, much of the common law was developed by judges on a case-by-case basis, making it impossible for those not trained in the law to fully know what the law meant. Unlike a statute, common law precedents were imprecise and not created by democratically elected legislatures. When the framers drafted the national Constitution in 1787, they gave the courts jurisdiction over cases in "law and equity" but did not use the term "common law." Thus, in his American edition of *Blackstone's Commentaries*, St. George Tucker noted that "the common law is a collection of *general* customs" and thus that "it might not be amiss to inquire whether *particular* customs have any, or what force, among us." Tucker's goal in writing his own *Commentaries* was to provide an American guide to law that would not be tainted by the royal regime of England. Similarly, in his 1798 introduction to the reports of the Connecticut Supreme Court, Jesse Root said that his state court was "forming a system of jurisprudence congenial to the spirit of our own government."

States began to rewrite their laws and thus change the common law. In 1778 Virginia appointed a committee—chaired by Thomas Jefferson—to rewrite all of the state's laws. Famously, Virginia altered the law of land ownership and inheritance by banning primogeniture and entail. Most of the states reduced the severity of the criminal law. In England one might still be hanged for stealing a lamb or a sheep, but not in America. Most of the southern states even reduced the severity of their slave codes. North Carolina, for example, made it a crime to murder a slave, thus giving slaves some legal protections (although not legal rights). Some of the new states instituted divorce laws that shifted divorces from the legislatures to the courts; some state courts recognized common-law marriages. On the other hand, although legal commentators expressed doubts that a husband could still legally chastise his wife, the formal law did not change and few wife beaters faced punishment in the Revolutionary era.

Slavery and Race. The Revolution led to dramatic changes in the law of race and slavery. During the Revolution, Pennsylvania passed the nation's first gradual abolition act, which provided that the children of all slave women born after March 1, 1780, would be free, subject to an indenture. Massachusetts and New Hampshire ended slavery in 1780 and 1783, respectively. Rhode Island and Connecticut followed Pennsylvania's model, passing gradual emancipation acts in 1784, as did New York in 1799 and New Jersey in 1804. Although some blacks lingered in slavery for another half century, the institution of slavery itself was destroyed in the North in this period. In 1787 Congress, under the Northwest Ordinance, prohibited slavery north and west of the Ohio River. This provision had no immediate impact on the slaves in the area, but it did set the stage for that region to eventually become free soil. Vermont (1791) and Ohio (1803) came into the union as free states.

Free blacks could vote in most of the North as well as in North Carolina and Tennessee (which became a state in 1798). They would lose the vote in a number of states after 1830, as Revolutionary sentiments faded and Jacksonian democracy undermined black rights, by expanding the right of white men to vote while simultaneously taking the vote away from black men in a number of states. But in the Revolutionary period the law in the North reflected some of the principles of the Declaration of Independence.

In the South the Revolution had less of an impact on slavery, but even that region saw some changes. In 1782 Virginia allowed masters to emancipate slaves within the states. The state repealed this law in 1806 and for the next four decades passed various laws trying to regulate private manumission. But in the Revolutionary period the law had a significant impact for some slaves, as the free black population grew from two thousand in 1780 to over thirty thousand by 1810. Delaware (1787) and Maryland (1790) adopted similar laws, and the free black population grew even more rapidly in those states. In addition to manumission, many southern states in this period reduced the harshness of their slave codes, banning such practices as branding and mutilation. The slave states also extended some legal protections to slaves accused of crimes, giving them fairer trials.

During the Revolution all the states banned the African slave trade. This was not antislavery per se, but rather part of the general nonimportation agreements among the colonies and independent states. Since most new slaves came to America in British ships, a ban on the trade was part of the economic war on Britain. After the war all the states except Georgia and North Carolina continued the ban, and by the mid-1790s both states had reinstated the ban. At the Constitutional Convention the delegates from the Carolinas and Georgia insisted on prohibiting Congress from ending the African trade before 1808, even though no state was at the time importing slaves. Starting in 1794 Congress passed a series of laws preventing American ships and sailors from participating in the trade. In 1803 South Carolina reopened the trade, and the state imported about sixty thousand slaves before Congress finally banned the trade altogether, starting on January 1, 1808.

In another area, most of the northern states cooperated with the return of fugitive slaves in the Revolutionary period. The Northwest Ordinance provided for the return of fugitive slaves escaping into the region, and the Constitution written that summer also provided for the return of fugitive slaves. In 1793 Congress enforced that provision with the Fugitive Slave Act of 1793. Few slaves were actually returned in the Revolutionary period, but the federal constitutional provision and the law enacted in this period would have a major impact on American society in the mid-nineteenth century.

Federal Law. The Continental Congress, which operated from the beginning of the Revolution until the summer of 1787, was relatively weak and enacted few laws of any consequence. Most importantly, after the war the Continental Congress enacted legislation for the sale of western lands and the settlement of those lands as a prelude toward statehood. The Continental Congress wrote the Articles of Confederation during the Revolution, and the states adopted them in 1781. Creating a weak national government, the Articles nevertheless provided the institutional mechanisms that allowed the nation to win the Revolution, successfully conclude a peace treaty with England, and begin the business of creating a more stable nation Thus, the Articles allowed for the creation of a national army, a rudimentary foreign service, a treasury department that could issue bonds to fund the Revolution, and most of all a national Congress that could pass laws, own property in the name of the whole nation, and help guide the former colonies in the development of new state constitutions. After the war the Congress under the Articles passed a series of laws culminating in the Northwest Ordinance (1787), which set the stage for the settlement of the Ohio valley and the eventual addition of new states to the Union. The Constitutional Convention (1787) was called to remedy defects in the Articles, but the delegates ended up writing an entirely new constitution and system of government.

The new government under the Constitution created new laws with breathtaking speed. Congress established government departments and agencies, passed new laws to collect taxes, and established a national system of courts with the Judiciary Act of 1789, a post office, an army and a navy, and some limited law-enforcement mechanisms. In 1789 Congress proposed twelve amendments to the Constitution, ten of which were ratified as the Bill of Rights. In 1791 Congress passed legislation creating a national bank. In its early years, Congress passed laws to acquire lands from Indians, build a military college (West Point), institute a system of copyright and patent, provide for the interstate extradition of criminals and the return of fugitive slaves, and punish treason, forgery and counterfeiting, piracy, and participation in the African slave trade. Congressional taxation led to the Whiskey Rebellion, when western farmers armed themselves to prevent the collection of taxes on the whiskey they produced from surplus corn. The rebellion was short lived and easily suppressed by the national army led by Washington's former aide-de-camp, Alexander Hamilton. The end result of the Whiskey Rebellion further strengthened national power as the rebels were suppressed but in the end pardoned rather than hanged.

In 1798 Congress passed a series of acts, known as the Alien and Sedition Acts, to regulate aliens and one law to prohibit speech hostile to the administration. The Alien Acts were designed to slow down naturalization of aliens and allow their expulsion during wartime. The Federalists who passed these laws believed that most new citizens were joining the opposition party led by Thomas Jefferson. The Sedition Act prohibited criticism of the president and the government in the period before the election of 1800; it was designed to help reelect John Adams. All the laws were also passed in response to tense international relations, a "quasi-war" with France and the likelihood of a real war with either France or Britain, or both. In the end the arrest under the Alien and Sedition Acts of a handful of publishers and politicians who opposed Adams, discredited the Adams administration, and helped establish the notion among Americans that they were free to criticize their government. The Jeffersonians denounced these laws not as a violation of the First Amendment in the newly adopted Bill of Rights but rather as a violation of states' rights. Once in power, Jefferson urged state authorities to prosecute his critics, but this Jeffersonian war on free speech also failed, and by 1810, Americans had accepted that the English common law of seditious libel had no place in a democracy. This was accomplished without any intervention by the Supreme Court and illustrates the way politics and accepted practice helped shape the law at this time.

The weakest branch of the national government in this period was in fact the judiciary. The Supreme Court heard relatively few cases in the 1790s. In *Chisholm v. Georgia*, 2 U.S. (2 Dall.) 419 (1793), the Court ordered Georgia to pay a debt owed to a man from South Carolina. Rather than establishing the authority of the Supreme Court to "establish justice"—as the preamble to the Constitution phrased it—this case led to a political reaction against the Court that undermined its credibility as Congress quickly passed, and the states quickly ratified, a constitutional amendment (the Eleventh Amendment) that effectively overturned the decision by prohibiting citizens of one state from suing another state.

In *Marbury v. Madison*, 5 U.S. (1 Cranch) 137 (1803), the Supreme Court established its right to overturn federal law ("judicial review"), but the Court would not actually exercise that power again until *Dred Scott v. Sandford*, 60 U.S. (19 How.) 393 (1857). However, in a series of very important cases, the Court under Chief Justice John Marshall established its power to overrule state laws and state courts. In *Martin v. Hunter's Lessee*, 14 U.S. (1 Wheat.) 304 (1816), the Court established that under the supremacy clause of Article VI of the Constitution the states could not overrule a treaty ratified by Congress. In *Sturges v. Crowninshield*, 17 U.S. (4 Wheat.) 122 (1819), the Court struck down a state bankruptcy law as violating the Contracts Clause of Article I, Section 10. Using the same clause, in *Dartmouth College v. Woodward*, 17 U.S. (4 Wheat.) 518 (1819), the Court prevented the state of New Hampshire from taking over Dartmouth College against the will of the trustees. In *McCulloch v. Maryland*, 17 U.S. (4 Wheat.) 316 (1819), arguably Chief Justice Marshall's most important decision, the Court upheld the constitutionality of the Second Bank of the United States and at the same time made clear that the state could not pass laws interfering with the legitimate power of the national government. Marshall found that the Constitution's implied powers gave Congress enormous power to pass laws "necessary and proper" for a national state. His reading of the Constitution set the stage for an expansive national government and emphatically confirmed that the Supreme Court was the ultimate arbiter of the Constitution (short of an amendment) and that the states were subordinate to the national government. As the Revolutionary period faded from memory, Marshall held, in *Cohens v. Virginia*, 19 U.S. (6 Wheat.) 264 (1821), that the federal courts were superior to the state courts and that the federal courts (or Congress), not the state courts, would decide where the jurisdiction of the federal courts began and ended.

Assessment. By 1820 American law had evolved and changed in dramatic ways. Written constitutions could be found in every state but Rhode Island. Freedom had been expanded to most white men and some blacks. Women had more rights than under British rule, although far fewer than they would have in the future. Slavery was strong and powerful in the South; in the North it was dead or dying. The Supreme Court was an integral part of the legal and political culture, and law was emerging as a dynamic force that would enable economic growth and social change. Many of the elements of the common law that had protected vested interests were gone. But the liberties of the common law were increasingly spreading to more people. Religious tests for office holding—banned in the Constitution—had all but died out, as had most state support for established churches. Tucker's *Blackstone* and Kent's *Commentaries* provided the basis for an *American* law that still retained some of its British heritage but was dramatically different in many ways.

[*See also* Articles of Confederation *and* Constitution of the United States.]

BIBLIOGRAPHY

Bailyn, Bernard. *The Ideological Origins of the American Revolution*. Cambridge, Mass.: Belknap Press of Harvard University Press, 1967.

Finkelman, Paul. *An Imperfect Union: Slavery, Federalism, and Comity*. Chapel Hill: University of North Carolina Press, 1981.

Finkelman, Paul. *Slavery and the Founders: Race and Liberty in the Age of Jefferson*. 2d ed. Armonk, N.Y.: M. E. Sharpe, 2001.

Friedman, Lawrence M. *A History of American Law*. 2d ed. New York: Simon & Schuster, 1985.

Fritz, Christian G. *American Sovereigns: The People and America's Constitutional Tradition before the Civil War*. Cambridge, U.K., and New York: Cambridge University Press, 2008.

Hall, Kermit L. *The Magic Mirror: Law in American History*. New York: Oxford University Press, 1989.

Hartog, Hendrik, ed. *Law in the American Revolution and the Revolution in the Law*. New York: New York University Press, 1981.

Horwitz, Morton J. *The Transformation of American Law, 1780–1860*. Cambridge, Mass.: Harvard University Press, 1977.

Kerber, Linda K. *Women of the Republic: Intellect and Ideology in Revolutionary America*. Chapel Hill: University of North Carolina Press, 1997.

Nelson, William E. *Americanization of the Common Law: The Impact of Legal Change on Massachusetts Society, 1760–1830*. Cambridge, Mass.: Harvard University Press, 1975.

Reid, John Phillip. *Constitutional History of the American Revolution: The Authority of Law*. Madison: University of Wisconsin Press, 1993.

Tomlins, Christopher L., and Bruce H. Mann, eds. *The Many Legalities of Early America*. Chapel Hill: University of North Carolina Press, 2001.

Urofsky, Melvin I., and Paul Finkelman. *A March of Liberty: A Constitutional History of the United States*. 2d ed. New York: Oxford University Press, 2002.

Watkins, William J., Jr. *Reclaiming the American Revolution: The Kentucky and Virginia Resolutions and Their Legacy*. New York: Palgrave Macmillan, 2004.

Wood, Gordon S. *The Creation of the American Republic*. Chapel Hill: University of North Carolina Press, 1969.

Wood, Gordon S. *The Radicalism of the American Revolution*. New York: Vintage Books, 1993.

PAUL FINKELMAN

The Nineteenth Century

The United States changed more in the nineteenth century than in any other century. With these changes came dramatic developments in law. In 1799, the handful of states that made up the new United States looked much like the Colonies of a century before. With the exception of Kentucky and Tennessee, all the American states were huddled along the Atlantic coast, and the nation's territory only extended west to the Mississippi River and south to what is now the border of Georgia and Florida. In this respect, the political geography of the nation in 1800 looked much like that of the British Colonies a century earlier. Similarly, the nation's population in 1700 and 1799 was mostly of British and African origin, with a small minority of people who were of Irish, German, or other western European ancestry. Almost all Americans—white and black—were Protestants. There were a few Catholics and only a smattering of Jews. There were almost no people of southern or eastern European background and none from Asia or the Middle East. With the exception of a few slaves who were Muslim, there were no Hindus, Buddhists, Sikhs, or Muslims in the nation. Slavery was legal everywhere in 1700, and in 1799 it was still legal in most places, although three states had abolished the institution and four more were gradually ending it. The free black population was higher in 1799 than in 1700, but in both years, the overwhelming majority of blacks were slaves with no legal or political rights. Although not quite as ubiquitous in 1799, established churches could be found in most states, and religious tests for office holding were prevalent in most places. Women had almost no political rights in 1700 or 1799 and when married were almost universally limited in their legal rights.

Travel in 1799 was much like it had been in 1700. People and goods moved by animal power, wind, or oars. Roads were undeveloped. Almost all Americans were rural. The few cities—Philadelphia, New York, Boston, Charleston—were small. Goods were made by hand; large-scale manufacturing was unknown. Mills were few and depended on water for their operation. Wood was the most common fuel, supplemented by whale oil. The workday and life itself were regulated by the rising and setting sun.

The Revolution of 1775–1783 had been fought with weapons that would have been familiar to people in 1700. Even the military tactics of the Revolution were almost identical to those of a century before. Armies were small, professional soldiers were almost unknown, and citizen militias were the first—and often only—line of defense against Indians or European enemies.

The Revolution had changed the political structure and had also created a new ideology of liberty and self-government. But the franchise was limited by wealth, gender, and race, and office holding was often restricted by faith. In these ways, the America of 1799 looked a lot like the America of 1700. The national and state constitutions adopted after the Revolution held the promise of more profound political changes, but these for the most part had not yet matured. Similarly, the Declaration of Independence held out the promise of more fundamental changes in society while underscoring the importance of liberty in the new nation. But this promise remained unfulfilled in 1799. Also unfulfilled was the potential for a strong national government under the Constitution of 1787.

Not surprisingly, with the exception of a national constitution and republican self-government, the legal system and laws of 1799 looked very much like those of 1700. Lawyers were trained in 1799 almost exactly as they had been in 1700. There were few colleges at the time, and only William and Mary, in Virginia, offered any formal legal training. A few proprietary law schools, like Litchfield in Connecticut, also offered the opportunity for formal legal training. All lawyers in 1700 or 1799 were white men, and almost all were of at least middle-class backgrounds. The Revolution had led to some important changes in law, such as the abolition of entail and primogeniture, the abolition of religious restrictions on voting, and the abolition of slavery either immediately or gradually in New England and some of the middle states. The late-eighteenth-century legal changes—although incredibly important for the development of the nation—seem minor compared with the huge revolution in law that would take place in the nineteenth century.

Changes in a New Century. America in 1899 looked almost nothing like the America of 1800. The nation spanned the continent. The strong opponent of colonialism in 1799 had an overseas empire a century later. A weak, powerless nation, protected from its enemies mostly by a large ocean, was now a world power with vast military potential, well-trained officers, and a navy sailing on two oceans. A nation once dependent on imported weapons was now a manufacturer of cutting-edge military hardware. In 1799, American Indians had posed a great threat to the new nation and to its citizens ambitious to move to lands they then occupied. By 1899, the frontier had ceased to exist; Indians had been shunted off to isolated and harsh reservations and been reduced to almost anthropological curiosities. Slavery on the other hand had been abolished, and although most blacks lived in poverty and political isolation, they had enjoyed substantial participation in the political system from the 1870s to the early 1890s, despite increasing efforts at intimidation and ultimately disfranchisement in the South. Other races and ethnic groups—from East Asia, the Caribbean, southern and eastern Europe, and the Middle East—had profoundly altered the social and demographic landscape. So too had the emergence of huge cities. In 1800, only one city, New York, had a population greater than 50,000. By 1899, the populations of Chicago and Philadelphia exceeded a million, and the population of New York City was over 3 million. Seven other cities had populations of more than 300,000.

Animal transportation was still important in 1899, but steam had replaced sails on the nation's waters and, more importantly, on the land, as railroads crisscrossed the nation. Automobiles were just being manufactured. Agriculture had been transformed by giant machines and national and international markets. Commerce itself had been altered in ways that would have bewildered all but the most astute and prescient businessman of 1800. With the exception of a few larger trading companies and a small number of ship captains who sailed overseas, few Americans in 1800 had commercial connections beyond their own neighborhoods. By 1899, Americans bought and sold goods to people they had never met, using catalogs, trains, telegraphs, and telephones to communicate. Commerce in 1899 looked far more like the Internet commerce of the twenty-first century than the commerce of 1800. For example, the emergence of the bill of lading in the nineteenth century as a significant legal tool allowed transactions to take place over vast distances between parties who had never met. The rule of caveat emptor—buyer beware—doubtless led to fraudulent and unscrupulous behavior by some economic actors, but it also led to a vigorous development of contract law as economic actors tried to protect their interests. The American economy of 1899 looked very modern, with stock markets, complicated banking, huge companies, general incorporation laws, holding companies, and threats of monopolies. The major industries of the next century—steel, oil, rubber, telecommunications, banking, and publishing—had all emerged in the nineteenth century. Labor unions were essentially illegal conspiracies in 1800; by 1899 they were legal and sometimes successful in changing the work environment. New forms of communication—the telephone, the telegraph, penny newspapers, postage stamps and then inexpensive mail, photographs—had all emerged in the nineteenth century. So too did a vibrant field of personal-injury law—tort law. The simple action of a tort suit did not even exist in 1800. Satisfaction for an injury was gained, if at all, through a cumbersome form of action known as "trespass on the case." But by the end of the nineteenth century, the field of torts was established as a significant field of law.

The economic, demographic, and social transformation of the century led to profound changes in American law. A lawyer in 1800 would most likely have been trained in a law office and have "read" the law as an apprentice. Among universities and colleges only the College of William and Mary in Virginia formally taught law—and its law department consisted of just one professor. Before the Civil War there were about twenty law schools in the nation, but by 1900 there were over one hundred, with some ten thousand students. By 1899 many lawyers had attended law school. In addition to the college and university training, in the late eighteenth and early nineteenth century there were a number of private proprietary law schools, usually founded by judges or lawyers and usually operated for a profit. The first, and most important, proprietary school was the Litchfield Law School in Connecticut, founded by Tapping Reeve in 1784. The school closed in 1833, a decade after Reeve's death, having trained nearly a thousand men in the law. Other proprietary schools lasted much longer by merging with existing universities. For example, the Lumpkin Law School in Georgia, founded by the chief justice of the state in the 1850s, eventually became the law school at the University of Georgia. A few independent law schools, like Albany Law School, founded in 1851, remained private and continue to operate independently in the twenty-first century. Before the Civil War a number of legal periodicals, edited by practitioners, were published. One, the *American Law Register*, began publication in 1852 and in the 1890s became the *University of Pennsylvania Law Review*, making it the oldest continuously published law review in the nation. By the end of the century, a number of law schools published such journals, which were part scholarly and part designed to aid practitioners. Harvard Law School began with a chair in law in 1817, which for many years was held by Supreme Court justice Joseph Story. By mid-century Harvard Law School had emerged as a separate college within the university, attracting students from throughout the United States. In the 1870s, the school adopted the case method of teaching law, setting the basic curriculum for most law schools into the twenty-first century.

At about this time Harvard also began to require new law students either to have a bachelor's degree or to pass a difficult entrance exam. Other law schools followed suit. The American Bar Association, founded in 1878, pressured schools to raise their admissions standards and require undergraduate degrees for all students. This movement for new standards reflected a desire for greater professionalization. But this professionalization of law practice was also designed to prevent immigrants and economically disadvantaged men from entering the profession. This movement dovetailed with other attempts to discourage immigrants from mixing with more elite Americans, as well as with rising anti-Semitism and anti-Catholic sentiment among upper-class Americans. By the end of the century, the poor boys who read law—embodied by men like Abraham Lincoln—were being increasingly shut out of the legal profession. This ABA-sponsored movement to raise "standards" was also focused on eliminating a number of night schools, YMCA-sponsored law schools, and other programs designed to open legal education to immigrants, African Americans, and the working class. Many of these law schools would continue to produce lawyers through the end of the century, but in the early years of the twentieth century the ABA and most of the elite bar would successfully force most of them out of existence or force them to affiliate with colleges and universities.

Political Rights and the Law. A lawyer from 1800 would have recognized the courts and political apparatus of American law in 1899, but not the legal regulation of political life. Property requirements for voting and office holding disappeared in the first part of the nineteenth century, as did established churches and religious tests for office holding. Three constitutional amendments passed after the Civil War (the Thirteenth, Fourteenth, and Fifteenth amendments) had ended slavery, made blacks citizens of the nation, and provided black men with the right to vote. By 1899, women could vote in a few states.

Legal developments in the nineteenth century were directly connected to political change and were influenced by the relationship between law and political structures. This was true at the most basic level, for example, changes in the laws regarding who could vote, and at the highest level of the legal system, for example, the power and importance of the U.S. Supreme Court.

The Revolutionary era saw some dramatic changes in the nature of the franchise and office holding. Massachusetts, for example, provided for universal adult male suffrage in its Constitution of 1780, and in the same period Virginia, New York, and the U.S. government under the Constitution of 1787 prohibited religious tests for office holding. But these Revolutionary-era changes were incomplete. The law of voting began to change in the nineteenth century, both expanding and contracting the franchise.

Two of the first new states—Vermont (1791) and Tennessee (1796)—provided for adult male suffrage without regard to property or race, following the standard set by Massachusetts and New Hampshire during the Revolution. This policy changed in the new century when Ohio, in 1803, allowed universal adult suffrage only for whites. With the exception of Maine, which would break off from Massachusetts in

The Fifteenth Amendment. President Ulysses S. Grant signing the Fifteenth Amendment, 1870. Vignettes show African Americans in military service, at school, on the farm, and voting. Print published by C. Rogan, c. 1871. PRINTS AND PHOTOGRAPHS DIVISION, LIBRARY OF CONGRESS

1820, no new state would allow black suffrage until after the Civil War. From the War of 1812 until the end of the 1830s, most states followed Ohio's lead. New Jersey, which had allowed women and blacks to vote, took the franchise from both. In 1821, New York removed property qualifications for whites but left them in place for blacks. In the 1830s, Jacksonian democracy brought the franchise to all white men, while blacks lost the vote in Pennsylvania, North Carolina, and Tennessee. In the 1840s, Rhode Island broke this trend by enfranchising all adult men. Black men would not gain the right to vote in any other state until the Civil War era, although in Michigan they were granted some limited suffrage rights in the 1850s.

With the end of slavery, black men gained full legal citizenship and the right to vote through federal acts during Reconstruction and with the ratification of the Fourteenth and Fifteenth amendments. Blacks would vigorously engage in politics until the last decade of the century, despite intimidation and violence. In *Ex parte Yarbrough* (1884), the Supreme Court upheld the federal conviction of members of the Ku Klux Klan for beating a black man to prevent him from voting—a rare instance of the federal courts supporting black voting rights. Within a few years, the Court had virtually abandoned blacks to the tender mercies of Southern whites. When whites regained political control in the Southern states, starting in the late 1870s, they used voting laws, literacy tests, poll taxes, and various discriminatory provisions in newly written state constitutions, and where necessary violence, to disfranchise most blacks. The Court never ruled directly on the disfranchisement of blacks, but in *Williams v. Mississippi* (1898), it refused to interfere with Mississippi's use of a poll tax and literacy requirements to prevent blacks from voting and serving as jurors. In the 1890s, Republicans in Congress tried to protect black voting rights with the Lodge Bill, which passed the House but not the Senate.

The new constitutional amendments applied to all people in the United States, and thus laws in California, Oregon, and other western states prohibiting Americans of Asian ancestry from voting were also no longer constitutional. However, Congress refused to allow Asian immigrants to become naturalized citizens, and thus the Fifteenth Amendment enfranchised very few Asians until the twentieth century, when significant American-born children of Asian immigrants reached age twenty-one.

In this period Congress passed laws making it a felony for polygamists—or even those who believed in polygamy but did not practice it—to vote in territorial elections. In *Davis v. Beason* (1890), the Court upheld the conviction of a Mormon who had voted in the Idaho Territory simply because he believed in plural marriage even though he did not practice it.

Starting with the Seneca Falls Convention of 1848, some women began to demand the right to vote, but except for a few western territories and states—Wyoming was the first to allow women to vote, in 1869—most states refused to allow women to vote until the second decade of the twentieth century. Federal and state courts rejected feminist claims to the vote, most notably when a federal court convicted Susan B. Anthony of illegally voting in 1873 and when the Supreme Court, in *Minor v. Happersett* (1875), held that the Fourteenth Amendment did not prevent states from prohibiting women from voting. The Court later held that although women were citizens of the United States under the Fourteenth Amendment, the states were free to deny them numerous rights, including the right to vote and the right to practice law. By midcentury, a number of states had passed married-women's property acts, giving women who married greater control over property they owned before their marriages. Some states removed various restrictions on divorce by midcentury. In *Prince v. Prince* (1845), for example, South Carolina allowed women to receive alimony from the deserting husband's income, rather than just his estate as had been the English rule. This allowed for greater opportunities for divorce. During this period, Indiana permitted divorce for almost any reason, after a short residency requirement, thus giving some American women and men a way of ending marriages in an age when most states made divorce very difficult. In the twentieth century Nevada would have similarly lax divorce laws. After the Civil War and by the end of the century, a few states had begun to move away from the traditional English notion that fathers would always gain custody of their children in a divorce. In 1879 the Rhode Island Supreme Court held in *McKim v. McKim* that child custody should be based on the best interests of the child. This became the universal standard in the twentieth century, although its implementation has always been difficult and sometimes quite problematic.

In the last years of the century, while women remained disfranchised in all but a few western territories and states, most African Americans lost the right to vote, and Mormons faced jail terms for voting, millions of new immigrants gained the right to vote. Equally important, the states had removed religious tests for office holding in the first thirty years of the century. Thus, the right to vote, and to serve on juries, expanded for new Americans even as it remained nonexistent or contracted for many whose families had been in the country for generations.

National Law and the Supreme Court under John Marshall. At the beginning of the century, the U.S. Supreme Court was a virtually powerless institution, with little prestige or influence. In 1801, John Marshall became chief justice, bringing to the Court political savvy, a shrewd legal mind, great energy, and a determination to strengthen the national government. In *Marbury v. Madison* (1803), Marshall established the power of the Court—known as judicial review—to overturn an act of Congress. Marshall would never exert this power again—and indeed the Court would not declare another act of Congress unconstitutional until 1857—but the successful assertion of power, in a politically charged case, enhanced the prestige of the Court. More significant in the short run was Marshall's opinion in *Ex parte Bollman* (1807), which successfully undermined President Jefferson's attempt to use treason prosecutions to punish his political enemies and rivals, including former vice president Aaron Burr.

Marshall's most important contribution in the long run was to establish the supremacy of the U.S. government and the Supreme Court over the states. Many of these decisions were unpopular at the time, but in the long run they helped create a rule of law that was based on the U.S. Constitution. In *Fletcher v. Peck* (1810), the Court ruled that the states could not undo private sales of land as long as the sale was legal at the time. The land in question had been purchased from the State of Georgia at an absurdly low price after almost every member of the Georgia legislature was bribed in what became known as the Yazoo Land Fraud. A subsequent legislature rescinded these sales, but by that time the land had been resold to purchasers not involved in the original corrupt sale. The Court ruled that the contracts clause of the Constitution prevented the state from undoing the sales, which were legal at the time they were made. The Court continued to support vested property rights in *Terrett v. Taylor* (1813), *Sturges v. Crowninshield* (1819), and *Dartmouth College v. Woodward* (1819). These cases ensured that Americans could make business decisions—buying and selling land or investing in other property—without fear that changing political circumstances would undermine their investments. At the same time, the Court asserted that when states granted corporate charters they had the power to reserve the right to alter corporate charters or to change the rules of contract for future business arrangements. In *Martin v. Hunter's Lessee* (1816), the Court upheld the supremacy of the national government over the states in those areas, like treaty making, that belonged wholly to the national government. In his most important opinion, in *McCulloch v. Maryland* (1819), Marshall further expanded on the power of Congress to pass any legislation that was "necessary and proper" to carry out the tasks assigned to Congress by the Constitution. He acknowledged that under the Constitution the national government was "limited in its powers," but where it had powers it was "supreme" in "its sphere of action." Marshall asserted that the "great principle" of the American government was "that the Constitution and the laws made in pursuance thereof are supreme; that they control the Constitution and laws of the respective States, and cannot be controlled by them." He also read the Constitution to be a flexible document "intended to endure for ages to come." In *Cohens v. Virginia* (1821), Marshall asserted the power of the Court to review any action by a state court that affected the Constitution. He heard this case over the protests of Virginia's highest court, which denied that the U.S. Supreme Court could review its decision in a minor criminal case. In the end, Marshall upheld the Virginia court's ruling, but in doing so he reaffirmed the power of his court to hear any case under the U.S. Constitution. In his most popular opinion, *Gibbons v. Ogden* (1824), Marshall ruled that the states could not regulate interstate commerce, even if they did so in the guise of just regulating commerce within their own state. The Court struck down New York laws giving certain companies a monopoly to operate a steamboat in the state, because the monopoly prevented out-of-state operators from bringing goods and passengers into New York.

As a whole, the jurisprudence of the Marshall Court strengthened the power of Congress to regulate the economy and negotiate treaties and limited the powers of the states. Marshall left a legacy of a Supreme Court that would interpret the Constitution to ensure economic development while protecting investors and vested interests.

Economic Development and Law. Under Chief Justice Roger Taney, the Court remained supportive of economic development while ensuring that the states had sufficient power to regulate their economies as they wished. In *Charles River Bridge v. Warren Bridge* (1837), the Taney Court refused to construe a corporate charter to limit competition because specific language to that effect was not found in the original charter. This decision left it up to the states to develop economic rules and laws that would best serve their needs. In *Mayor of the City of New York v. Miln* (1837), the Court created the concept of state police powers to counter the Marshall Court's strong view of the commerce clause. Under the doctrine of state police power, the states were free to regulate significant amounts of commerce within their own boundaries, even if those regulations affected interstate or international commerce. Thus, in *Cooley v. Board of Wardens* (1851), the Court allowed Pennsylvania to require that all ships entering the port of Philadelphia hire a local pilot to guide the ship to the dock, even if its captain was perfectly able to do so. A minority on the Court believed that this law interfered with the right of Congress to regulate all interstate commerce. However, there were limits to how much power the states had. In *Bank of Augusta v. Earle* (1839), the Court ruled that corporations chartered in one state could conduct business in any state unless that state specifically prohibited out-of-state corporations from doing so. This helped pave the way toward the development of a national market. After the Civil War, and the adoption of the Fourteenth Amendment, states were no longer able to prohibit out-of-state corporations from doing business in their jurisdictions—except in the case of banks and insurance companies, where Congress specifically granted the states the power to restrict out-of-state corporations. Indeed, late in the century, the Court would hold in such cases as *Santa Clara County v. Southern Pacific Railroad* (1886) that corporations were "persons" under the Fourteenth Amendment and as such had due process protections.

Although the Supreme Court often interpreted the Constitution to set general rules and guidelines for law and economic development, it was in the states that new law developed in the nineteenth century in contract law, tort law, property law, corporation law, and labor law. Treatise writers, such as St. George Tucker, James Kent, Joseph Story, William Wetmore Story, Simon Greenleaf, and Joseph K. Angell, set out theories of law that were later adopted by state jurists and state legislatures. At the end of the century, these treatises were still around, having been updated and reedited by leading scholars. Oliver Wendell Holmes Jr., for example, brought out the twelfth edition of Kent's *Commentaries on American Law* in 1873, and John Henry Wigmore worked on the sixteenth edition of Greenleaf's treatise on evidence in 1899. The treatises were particularly important before the West Publishing Company began its National Reporter System in 1876, because lawyers and judges had little access to most law from other states. Thus the treatise writers were able to both report the law and shape it. Equally important in the development of law were leading state supreme court justices, such as Lemuel Shaw and Oliver Wendell Holmes Jr. of Massachusetts, James Kent of New York, and Thomas Ruffin of North Carolina.

The state supreme courts and state legislatures shaped the nature of the new industrial economy from the end of the War of 1812 until the end of the century. As new industries emerged, especially railroads and manufacturing companies, the states adopted rules and statutes to facilitate economic growth. Typical charters for railroads gave the companies a monopoly on routes and granted them important powers, such as the right to seize land through eminent domain. However, in return for these rights, the states retained the power to regulate rates, require equality of access for shippers and passengers, and even take over the company after a fixed number of years. State-court judges, like Chief Justice Shaw of Massachusetts, upheld these charters in numerous cases, such as *Boston Water Power v. Boston & Worcester Railroad* (1839) and *Boston & Lowell Railroad v. Salem & Lowell Railroad* (1854). In *McCulloch v. Maryland* (1819), Chief Justice John Marshall had prohibited a state from taxing the Bank of the United States, which had been created by a federal charter. Marshall argued that state taxation could destroy the bank and thus frustrate the will of Congress. In *Inhabitants of Worcester v. Western Railroad* (1842), Chief Justice Shaw reached a similar conclusion, prohibiting a city from

McCulloch v. Maryland. The Court's decision in the handwritten minutes of the Supreme Court, February 1819. NATIONAL ARCHIVES AND RECORDS ADMINISTRATION

taxing land of the Western Railroad because such taxation could undermine the state's ability to ensure that railroads could operate in the state. Most other states adopted similar laws as railroads and other industries boomed. By the end of the century, railroad regulation posed different problems. No longer part of an infant industry in need of the protection of courts and legislatures, railroads were now huge, powerful, and wealthy. Through political clout and sometimes political corruption, they had vast influence over politics and the economy. States passed laws requiring that railroads charge the same rates to all customers, which the Supreme Court upheld in *Munn v. Illinois* (1877). However, in *Wabash, St. Louis & Pacific Railway v. Illinois* (1886), the Court held that the commerce clause of the Constitution prohibited states from setting freight rates. This led, in 1887, to the creation of the Interstate Commerce Commission to regulate railroad rates.

Business corporations were almost unknown in 1799—just a few banks and insurance companies existed as corporations—but by midcentury there were thousands of them. Until late in the century, in most states corporations were chartered one by one, through special statutes (often called private laws) passed by the legislature. In the 1870s and 1880s, some states passed hundreds of these private acts annually. But by the end of the century, almost all states had passed general incorporation laws, allowing for the rapid development of companies. Late in the century some states, especially New Jersey and later Delaware, specialized in serving as the host states where businesses could be incorporated even though those businesses might have actually had little presence in those states. Corporations often did business in more than one state; by the end of the century national corporations were common. These developments—especially some of the lax rules for incorporation in New Jersey and Delaware—also led to national monopolies. Congress attempted to regulate the emerging giants of business with the Sherman Antitrust Act in 1890, but the act had little impact on law and the economy until the next century. In *United States v. E. C. Knight Co.* (1895) the Supreme Court held that manufacturing was not "commerce" and could not be regulated by the Sherman Act. Thus, the court rejected an attempt to break up the American Sugar Refining Company—incorporated in New Jersey—which controlled 90 percent of all sugar refining in the United States and thus was able to force the price of sugar higher because it had a monopoly on the supply of the refined product.

At the beginning of the century, labor unions were considered to be unlawful conspiracies, as illustrated by the conviction of shoemakers in the *Philadelphia Cordwainers' Case* (*Commonwealth v. Pullis*) in 1806. Courts in New York and other states followed the logic that in striking, a union engaged in a criminal activity. However, in *Commonwealth v. Hunt* (1842), Chief Justice Shaw of Massachusetts rejected this long-held notion, asserting that if workers could individually leave their employer, they could collectively leave him, and that if they could individually ask for a change in working conditions or for more wages, they could collectively do this as well. This was not the "emancipation proclamation" for the American worker—labor unions would struggle until the 1930s to gain full legal recognition. But the case did mean that in the future most courts, following Shaw's lead, would accept the idea that labor unions were not in fact illegal conspiracies. Toward the end of the nineteenth century, federal courts used injunctions to stop strikes that affected interstate commerce. In *In re Debs* (1895), the Supreme Court upheld the conviction of the labor leader Eugene V. Debs for organizing a railroad strike. Ironically, the federal government used the recently enacted Sherman Antitrust Act, which was aimed at the monopoly power of large corporations, to break the strike on the grounds that the railway workers' union constituted an unlawful conspiracy in restraint of trade. The same year that the Court upheld a contempt citation and a six-month prison sentence for Debs, the Court refused to allow the prosecution of the sugar trust in *United States v. E.C. Knight Co.* (1895). By the end of the century, labor unions had more rights than they had had in 1800, and were more successful, but they would have to wait until the 1930s to win the real freedom to strike and negotiate contracts without government interference.

Chief Justice Shaw also altered traditional workplace law to the great detriment of workers in *Farwell v. Boston & Worcester Railroad* (1842), a case involving a railroad engineer who was permanently injured because of the negligence of a switchman working for the railroad. Farwell sued, arguing that his employer was responsible for maintaining a safe workplace. In a decision that defied the realities of emerging industries, Chief Justice Shaw held that the employer could not be responsible for the acts of every employee if those acts harmed a fellow employee, or, as Shaw called them, "a fellow servant." Shaw was not the first judge to apply the fellow-servant rule—it had been applied in England and South Carolina. But his use of the rule set the standard for most of the United States because of his prestige. The "fellow-servant rule" meant that employees who were injured on the job could only sue their coworkers and thus that men like Farwell would have no chance of recovering for their workplace injuries because their coworkers (fellow servants) would have no money to recover—the would be, in modern parlance, judgment proof. After this decision Farwell could have sued the railroad switchman who failed to do his job, which resulted in the accident in which Farwell lost his hand. But that switchman would not have had sufficient assets to compensate Farwell. Initially, almost all American courts followed this rule—although Southern courts did not apply it to injuries caused to

In re Debs. Eugene V. Debs leaving the federal penitentiary in Atlanta, 25 December 1921. PHOTOGRAPH BY UNDERWOOD & UNDERWOOD. PRINTS AND PHOTOGRAPHS DIVISION, LIBRARY OF CONGRESS

workers by the negligence of slaves. However, by the end of the nineteenth century, a number of courts had refined and altered the rule through exceptions that favored some injured workers. More importantly, state legislatures stepped in by passing workers' compensation acts early in the next century. Legislatures also began to regulate working conditions, starting with a Massachusetts act of 1877 requiring factory inspections. In *Holden v. Hardy* (1898), the U.S. Supreme Court upheld a Utah law that regulated mine safety, including the number of hours a miner could work. This law was similar to the law limiting the number of hours bakers could work that the Court would strike down in *Lochner v. New York* (1905). The Court saw a difference in the two laws: mines, unlike bakeries, were inherently unsafe, and therefore a limit on the number of hours a miner could work was reasonable. By the end of the century, many states had put into place all sorts of regulations on workplaces, including some prohibiting child labor.

Western Settlement. Much of the history of the nineteenth century was the history of western migration and settlement. New states entered the union throughout the century, usually borrowing laws and constitutions from older states but often adding their own particular nuances to them. Physical geography led to dramatic changes in the common law, especially in water law. A "western water law" emerged that allowed settlers to use existing supplies without regard to how this might affect others. This allowed for growth in mining and agriculture that might have been impossible under older common-law rules on water use.

American Indians stood in the way of settlement. Warfare and treaties eventually pushed most Indians out of the South and Midwest. Some Indians remained in the upper Midwest and a few in the Deep South, and a considerable number remained in upstate New York, but otherwise, Indians were pushed west, to what became Iowa, Kansas, and most of all Oklahoma. Beginning in the Jefferson administration, Congress enacted various Indian removal acts and ratified numerous treaties. In *Johnson v. M'Intosh* (1823), the Court held that Indian tribes had only a "right of occupancy" and could never actually own the land they were on. Rather, the U.S. government, through the "doctrine of discovery," had "an exclusive right to extinguish the Indian title of occupancy, either by purchase or by conquest"; discovery "gave also a right to such a degree of sovereignty as the circumstances of the people would allow them to exercise." Chief Justice Marshall further asserted that "the tribes of Indians inhabiting this country were fierce savages, whose occupation was war, and whose subsistence was drawn chiefly from the forest." This case helped set a tone that allowed the government to take Indian land through force, treaty, or purchase, as it wished. In the 1820s, the Southeastern states encroached on Indian land and even defied the U.S. Supreme Court in refusing to stay proceedings or executions in order for the Court to review their activities. In *Cherokee Nation v. Georgia* (1831), the Court held that Indian tribes had no standing to sue in federal court as foreign nations. A year later, in *Worcester v. Georgia* (1832), the Court attempted to prevent the states from trampling on the rights of Indian tribes as set out in treaties, but this decision did not protect the Indians from any actions Congress or the president might choose to take. Congress, meanwhile, continued to pass legislation enabling removal. After 1832 Congress and the executive branch continued to force eastern Indians to the Indian Territory (present-day Oklahoma) and later did the same to western Indians.

After the Civil War, Congress experimented with various rules to "civilize" Indians and, in 1871, abandoned the charade of treaties and simply took land from Indian tribes through depredation claims. Under this process the U.S. government essentially condemned the land and then went to court to determine the value to pay the Indian tribe. The tribe had no right or power to resist this process but could dispute the amount paid for the land. After 1885 the United States used the Court of Claims to take Indian lands. Under this process the government would simply take the land without a hearing and the tribe could then make a claim for the value of the land. "Civilizing" the Indians, however, did not mean making them citizens. In *Elk v. Wilkins* (1884), the Supreme Court held that Indians were not citizens of the United States under the Fourteenth Amendment and therefore could not vote. In 1885, Congress enacted the Indian Major Crimes Act, giving the federal courts jurisdiction over a number of crimes committed on Indian lands. The General Allotment Act of 1887 (also known as the Dawes Act) required that Indians cease to own lands as tribes; instead, tribal lands, mostly in Indian country (present-day Oklahoma) was to be parceled out to individual tribe members. By the end of the century, Native Americans had mostly been reduced to isolation on reservations where they were legally marginalized and subject to the acts of Congress, in which they had no representation.

Crime and Punishment. At the beginning of the century, most criminals were punished in local jails or by fines, corporal punishment, or hanging. There were relatively few theories of crime and few defenses for those charged with a crime. By the end of the century, most courts had accepted the insanity defense—that a defendant could not be convicted of a capital offense if he was insane and did not know right from wrong. Some states went further. For example, in *State v. Felter* (1868), the chief justice of Iowa said that a defendant had the right to have a jury decide "whether *passion* or *insanity* was the ruling force and controlling agency," that led to a homicide. In the antebellum period most states adopted a rule that people had a "duty to retreat" to avoid a violent or lethal confrontation unless they were in their own home. However, most of the slave states accepted the "Texas rule" that every man had a legal right to "stand one's ground," and if confronted in public had a right to use lethal force to stop an aggressor, even if the aggressor was unarmed.

Meanwhile, states built larger, fortresslike prisons, such as New York's Auburn (1817) and Sing Sing (1825) prisons and Pennsylvania's giant Eastern State Penitentiary, which opened in 1829. In 1876, New York opened its Elmira prison as a "reformatory," designed to reform as much as punish. The new prisons, like Elmira, provided vocational training and granted prisoners early release for "good time." Meanwhile, the number of crimes, which had decreased after the Revolution, increased throughout the century. For example, in 1822 Rhode Island had only 50 criminal acts on its books, but by 1872 there were 128. At the beginning of the century, executions were public events, outdoors, sometimes with sermons and even gallows confessions by the person being executed. In 1846 Michigan became the first political entity in the Western world to ban the death penalty. A few other states followed this lead, but most then retreated from it. Late in the century, states moved executions inside prisons, away from public view. The electric chair replaced the gallows. In *In re Kemmler* (1890), the Supreme Court rejected a claim that the electric chair constituted cruel and unusual punishment. By the end of the century, the use of the electric chair was common, although it often produced grisly results as executioners miscalculated the amount of electricity needed to accomplish their task. Sometimes prisoners writhed in agony but did not die; others literally caught on fire from the bursts of electricity.

Throughout the century, criminal justice was tainted by racism; blacks and members of other minorities were always more likely to be arrested, jailed, and executed. In the last quarter of the century, the Southern states used the criminal-justice system to jail tens of thousands of black men on minor offenses and then either sell their labor to business under the convict-lease system or use them as laborers for the state itself on prison farms, or in prison factories, and in the early part of the next century on roads, as part of chain gangs.

Liberty and Law. The nineteenth-century United States witnessed sweeping changes in how law affected liberty in the nation. In 1800, the Sedition Act of 1798 was still in force and the Adams administration used it to prosecute a few supporters of Thomas Jefferson. The law expired in 1801. Jefferson opposed the use of national power to regulate civil liberties, but he did urge that the states prosecute his critics. Such prosecutions occurred early in his administration in New York and Pennsylvania, but they soon ceased. In Connecticut, where the Federalists still held power, the Jeffersonians initiated common-law seditious libel prosecutions in the federal courts to suppress their critics. In *United States v. Hudson and Goodwin* (1812), the Supreme Court held that there was no common law of crimes in the nation, and the cases were dropped. There were no more attempts by the national government to regulate expression until the Civil War. In the North there were few criminal prosecutions for speech, although as late as 1838 the Supreme Judicial Court of Massachusetts upheld a blasphemy conviction in *Commonwealth v. Kneeland*.

From 1820 until the end of the Civil War, the Southern states passed laws restricting speech that questioned slavery. There were numerous prosecutions of ministers, abolitionists, and others for antislavery speech and the possession of antislavery or abolitionist materials. By the eve of the Civil War, freedom of speech and the press was severely limited in the South. A number of Southern states banned *Uncle Tom's Cabin* (1852), which at the time was the most popular book in the nation's history, despite almost no sales in the South. Even in Washington, D.C., freedom of expression was proscribed by local law. In 1836, authorities there charged Dr. Reuben Crandall of Connecticut with sedition after he was found in possession of antislavery literature. The prosecutor was that city's district attorney, Francis Scott Key, the author of "The Star-Spangled Banner," a poem honoring the national flag and liberty, which would become the national anthem. The irony of Key's prosecuting a man for possession of literature advocating liberty for *all* Americans boldly illustrates the way in which slavery shaped American law and liberty in this period. In the late 1850s, a North Carolina man, Hinton Rowan Helper, was forced to leave his home state after he published *The Impending Crisis of the South*, in which he argued that slavery was detrimental to the interest of non slaveholding whites like himself.

During the Civil War, there was some suppression of newspapers in the North that criticized the Lincoln administration, but Lincoln usually opposed such actions by his generals and often countermanded orders to close newspapers. In the Confederacy, the administration of Jefferson Davis was far more aggressive in suppressing dissent. The Civil War also saw the institution of the draft in both the Confederacy and the United States. This innovation, along with the vast growth of the federal government in this period, affected law and liberty in many ways.

After the Civil War, the U.S. government actively suppressed information about birth control, abortion, and human anatomy under the Comstock Act (1873), which was purportedly aimed at "obscene" materials. The Supreme Court rejected a First Amendment challenge to this law in *Ex parte Jackson* (1878). Both the states and the federal government moved to suppress anarchists and socialists late in the century as well. The Haymarket Square bombing in Chicago (1886), which killed seven policemen and injured seventy more, led to the prosecution and conviction of eight anarchists and socialists. Prosecutions for the underlying offense—the bombing—were perfectly reasonable and would not have raised issues of freedom of expression. However, none of the defendants were actually tied to the bombing. Thus, they were prosecuted and convicted—and four were executed—for their ideas and their advocacy of socialism. In *Spies v. Illinois* (1887), the Supreme Court refused to interfere with these convictions and hangings.

By the 1830s, most states had abolished their religious tests for office holding, and most states no longer gave financial or other support to religious groups. The emergence of the Church of Jesus Christ of Latter-Day Saints—the Mormons—led to open religious persecution. Eventually the Mormons moved to the Utah Territory, which was subject to federal law. Starting with the Morrill Act of 1862, Congress enacted a series of laws designed to marginalize, persecute, and destroy the Mormon Church. In *Reynolds v. United States* (1879), the Supreme Court upheld the federal ban on polygamy in the Morrill Act. Under the Edmunds Act (1882) and the Edmunds-Tucker Act (1887), federal authorities prosecuted numerous Mormons for cohabitation. In *Davis v. Beason* (1890), the Supreme Court upheld the conviction of a Mormon man who had voted in the Idaho Territory, for merely believing in polygamy even though he did not practice it. At the same time, in *The Late Corporation of the Church of Jesus Christ of Latter-Day Saints v. United States* (1890), the Court allowed the U.S. government to revoke the corporate charter of the Mormon Church and seize all its assets. Shortly after that, the Mormons renounced polygamy, and by 1896 Congress had restored all the church's property.

Mormons were not the only people to face religious discrimination. In the early part of the century, Jews in Pennsylvania were fined for refusing to serve on juries, and in Maryland a Jew was not permitted to hold public office. In North Carolina, a Jew who was elected to the state legislature faced a challenge on the grounds that the state constitution limited office holding to Christians. Fortunately, his party was in the majority, and the legislature ruled that this provision applied only to the executive branch. By the eve of the Civil War, most formal discrimination against Jews had ceased, although during the war General Grant issued an order expelling all Jews from his military district, which Lincoln countermanded as soon as it was brought to his attention. The origin of this order is unclear, since Grant himself never displayed any anti-Semitic prejudices. The influx of Chinese in the 1840s and 1850s raised other issues of religious persecution. In *People v. Hall* (1854), the California Supreme Court ruled that Chinese immigrants could not testify in court, on the grounds that because they were not Christians their oath to tell the truth was meaningless. While statutory discrimination on the basis of religion had disappeared by the end of the century, private discrimination on the basis of religion and ethnicity (as well as race) was rampant, as Jews and other ethnic groups and racial minorities were kept out of housing markets through private agreements known as restrictive covenants.

The influx of Chinese also led to the first federal restriction on immigration in 1882, the Chinese Exclusion Act. Congress had not previously banned immigration of any kind. This law was the beginning of immigration restrictions that, by the 1920s, had closed America's "Golden Door" to most foreigners. The Supreme Court upheld the Chinese Exclusion Act, and subsequent amendments to it, in a number of cases in the 1880s and 1890s. The Court was generally unsympathetic to claims of Chinese aliens and allowed Congress plenary and arbitrary power to exclude people. In 1870 Congress extended the right of naturalization to foreign-born blacks and in 1875 specifically limited naturalization to "free white persons" and "aliens of African nativity and to persons African descent." Thus, Chinese immigrants were not permitted to become citizens, no matter how long they lived in the United States. However, in *United States v. Wong Kim Ark* (1898), the Court refused to accept the proposition that native-born children of Chinese parents were not citizens. The Court held that under both the common law and the Fourteenth Amendment, *all* persons born in the nation (except perhaps the children of diplomats) were citizens of the United States and the states in which they lived.

The central liberty issue of the century was of course slavery. In 1807 Congress banned the importation of new slaves from Africa, effective January 1, 1808. However, in the first six decades of the century, slavery expanded rapidly within the South and the slave population grew through natural increase. After the War of 1812, slavery also spread into the West. The Missouri Compromise (1820) restricted the growth of slavery, but that was the last substantive limitation on slavery until the Civil War. In 1845 Congress annexed Texas and in 1850 it opened up the newly acquired Mexican territories to slavery. In the Kansas-Nebraska Act (1854) Congress repealed the Missouri Compromise, and in 1857 the Supreme Court ruled in *Dred Scott v. Sandford* that Congress had no power to prohibit slavery in the federal territories. Meanwhile, in 1850, Congress had enacted a draconian fugitive-slave law to help masters recover runaway slaves.

The proslavery stance of the federal government ended with the election of Lincoln in 1860. His election led to civil war, which in turn led to dramatic changes in law, especially for African Americans. The Confiscation Acts of 1861 and 1862 set the stage for the Emancipation Proclamation, which was perhaps the most important executive order ever issued in the United States. By the end of the war, millions of slaves had been freed, and the remaining slaves gained their freedom through the Thirteenth Amendment, ratified in 1865. Two more amendments made blacks citizens of the United States (the Fourteenth Amendment) and prohibited discrimination in voting based on race or "previous condition of servitude" (the Fifteenth Amendment). Between 1864 and 1875 Congress enacted numerous laws to guarantee the civil rights of former slaves and to counteract black codes passed by former Confederate states that were designed to permanently make blacks second-class citizens.

For a brief moment, between 1868 and 1875, the United States flirted with the idea of making legal equality permanent and moving toward social equality. This was followed by a slow decline as former Confederates and their sons gained power in the South and instituted thorough segregation and political and legal discrimination. The Supreme Court generally turned a blind eye to the evisceration of black rights. In the *Slaughterhouse Cases* (1873), the Court offered a cramped and narrow interpretation of the privileges or immunities clause of the Fourteenth Amendment that prevented the national government from protecting black civil liberties in the South. In the *Civil Rights Cases* (1883), the Court struck down the 1875 Civil Rights Act, which had prohibited private discrimination in restaurants, theaters, hotels, railroads, and other public accommodations. The Court held that Congress lacked the power to regulate private behavior, and thus gave the states the right to allow private discrimination as long as there was no direct state action. The Southern states immediately took advantage of this decision to increasingly marginalize and segregate blacks. Almost every Northern state, however, passed laws prohibiting racial discrimination in public accommodations and transportation and requiring integrated schools. Enforcement of these laws proved to be difficult and unsatisfactory, but Northern state courts upheld them. For example, in upholding Michigan's 1885 civil-rights law in *Ferguson v. Gies* (1890), Justice Allen B. Morse, who had lost an arm in the Civil War, wrote that "the humane and enlightened judgment of our people has decided—although it cost blood and treasure so to determine—that the negro is a man; a freeman; a citizen; and entitled to equal rights before the law with the white man. This decision was a just one." Unfortunately, only about 5 percent of the nation's black population lived in the North, where such protections were available. Emboldened by the Supreme Court's refusal to protect black rights and the failure of Congress to enact new legislation, the South moved aggressively to disfranchise and segregate blacks in the last decade of the nineteenth century. The Court approved this trend in *Plessy v. Ferguson* (1896).

That decision suggested how much had changed in America—a free black could sue in a federal court, with his case financed by other free blacks and aided by sympathetic whites. But it also illustrated how little had changed, since in the end the Court emphatically supported segregation. Justice John Marshall Harlan's dissent—arguing that the Constitution was "color-blind"—was a harbinger of a more egalitarian legal system that would live up to the assertions of equality in the Declaration of Independence. But that world would not emerge for more than half a century.

[*See also* Constitution of the United States, *subentry on* The Constitution; Discrimination, Race and Sex; Education and Training, *subentry on* United States; Native American Law; Slavery, *subentries on* Slavery and Other Labor Systems in the Colonial United States *and* United States Law; *and* Women, *subentry on* United States Law.]

BIBLIOGRAPHY

Bloomfield, Maxwell. *American Lawyers in a Changing Society, 1776–1876*. Cambridge, Mass.: Harvard University Press, 1976.

Finkelman, Paul. *An Imperfect Union: Slavery, Federalism, and Comity*. Chapel Hill: University of North Carolina Press, 1981.

Friedman, Lawrence M. *A History of American Law*. 3d ed. New York: Simon & Schuster, 2005.

Garrison, Tim Alan. *The Legal Ideology of Removal: The Southern Judiciary and the Sovereignty of Native American Nations*. Athens: University of Georgia Press, 2002.

Hall, Kermit L. *The Magic Mirror: Law in American History*. New York: Oxford University Press, 1989.

Horwitz, Morton J. *The Transformation of American Law, 1780–1860*. Cambridge, Mass.: Harvard University Press, 1977.

Horwitz, Morton J. *The Transformation of American Law, 1870–1960: The Crisis of Legal Orthodoxy*. New York: Oxford University Press, 1992.

Huebner, Timothy. *The Southern Judicial Tradition: State Judges and Sectional Distinctiveness, 1790–1890*. Athens: University of Georgia Press, 1999.

Hurst, James Willard. *Law and the Conditions of Freedom in the Nineteenth-Century United States*. Madison: University of Wisconsin Press, 1964.

Karsten, Peter. *Heart versus Head: Judge-Made Law in Nineteenth-Century America*. Chapel Hill: University of North Carolina Press, 1997.

Scheiber, Harry N. *The State and Freedom of Contract*. Stanford, Calif.: Stanford University Press, 1998.

Stevens, Robert. *Law School: Legal Education in the United States from the 1850s to the 1980s*. Chapel Hill: University of North Carolina Press, 1983.

Urofsky, Melvin I., and Paul Finkelman. *A March of Liberty: A Constitutional History of the United States*. 2d ed. 2 vols. New York: Oxford University Press, 2002.

Paul Finkelman

The Twentieth Century

In geologic time, a century is nothing. In legal history, especially modern legal history, it can be an eternity. The American legal system in the twentieth century was built, of course, on nineteenth-century foundations. The nineteenth century was itself a century of massive change; the twentieth was even more so. In its course, field after field of law was transformed, sometimes root and branch. The old house still stood where it had always stood: its basic plan was unaltered; the walls and roof and facade were still what they were; but the kitchens and bathrooms were totally remodeled, the furniture changed, the wiring brought up to date, and air conditioning installed. The story of the law in the twentieth century is a story of change; it is also a story of mind-numbing complexity. This essay seeks to pick out a few of the highlights of the century.

The Law Explosion. There is a good deal of talk about a litigation explosion in the late twentieth century. The idea is that the rate of litigation (cases filed per 1,000 population, say) rose during the century. The actual evidence for such an "explosion" is thin. On the other hand, we can speak, quite confidently, of a *law* explosion. The number of reported cases, statutes, ordinances, rules, and regulations grew tremendously between 1900 and 2000. To be sure, so did the population—from about 100 million to almost 300 million; but the sheer amount of "law," even as crudely measured by cases, statutes, ordinances, and rules and regulations, outstripped population growth. This reflects a dramatic increase in the scope and scale of government, at all levels. It continues, of course, a trend well under way in the previous century. If there ever was a pure laissez-faire state, it had eroded greatly by 1900, and eroded even further by 2000. There was a great deal of talk about privatization in the late twentieth century, and even some action; but the public sector was still amazingly large in 2000, and showed no sign of disappearing.

One aspect of the growth of law and government deserves special mention. This is the vast expansion of the national government, one of the most obvious trends of the twentieth century. We can chart this growth with a few crude figures. In 1900, something on the order of 13,600 cases were filed in federal courts; in 1999, over 260,000. Federal statute making also increased dramatically. Dozens and dozens of federal administrative agencies came into being and produced tons of rules and regulations. All proposed rules, final rules, and executive orders, under a law of 1946, must be published in the *Federal Register*, and this has run to as much as a gargantuan 75,000 pages a year.

The shift to the center, to the national government, has been a relative shift. The legal systems of the states have by no means shrunk. Most litigation was and is state litigation: If you want a divorce, if you need a zoning change, if you want to incorporate a small business, if you want to sue a driver who backed into your car, if you want a marriage license or a hunting license or a license to practice medicine, your business is with the state. The states, like the federal government, have dozens and dozens of administrative agencies. But the biggest action, as far as regulation of business and the economy is concerned, centers on Washington. The New Deal of the 1930s was a watershed; among other things, it gave us insurance on bank deposits, a Labor Relations Act to strengthen the unions, and a Social Security law, for old-age pensions and pensions for people with disabilities. Social Security and other government programs replaced the old, local poor laws, and centralized the process. But even before the New Deal, the federal government had become increasingly active—with laws like the Pure Food and Drug Act (1906) and the Federal Trade Commission Act (1914). Nor was the New Deal the end of the process: later presidents and Congresses added substantially to the national structure of welfare and regulatory law. Medicare and Medicaid, for example, were added to the list of key programs in the 1960s.

This shift to the center was, perhaps, inevitable. External events played a part. In the twentieth century the United States became a world power; and world powers go to war. There were two gigantic world wars, and lesser but bloody wars—including Korea in the 1950s and Vietnam in the 1960s and 1970s. War is a centralizer. It sucks power into the capital, into the nerve center of a country; it breeds regulation and taxation to feed and maintain the war effort. Some wartime programs had lasting effects. The so-called GI Bill of Rights, passed during World War II, promised free education, home loans, and other benefits to millions of veterans. Its impact on the economy, and on higher education, was enormous.

Wars perhaps accelerated a trend, but one that would have taken place even without the military stimulus. In 1800, travel and communication among the states was slow and difficult. The railroad, telegraph, and telephone helped turn the country into a single trade and culture area. In the twentieth century came the automobile and the airplane, radio, television, and the Internet. Time and space became less important as barriers to trade, and were no cultural barriers at all. Thanks to the media, the United States became more and more a single culture area. Americans saw the same movies, sang the same songs, cheered the same sports events, all over the country. They shopped in malls that looked much the same, and contained much the same stores; only the climate varied.

New modes of communication also made the president more and more the central figure in the government, the overwhelming leader. Before the twentieth century, only a small number of people ever actually saw the president, or heard his voice. Photographs and newsreels, though, made Franklin D. Roosevelt, a master politician, familiar to the public, to whom he also spoke directly in his "fireside chats" on the radio. Television made the presidency even more vividly familiar. Local politics and local lawmaking have receded to the background; most people could not name their representative in the state capital, or in city hall, to save their lives; but they see the president every day on television. They know the way he walks and talks; they know about his habits, his family, and his dogs. The United States' position as a superpower accentuates this fact: It is the president who controls the armed forces, whose finger is on the nuclear button. He commands atom bombs and aircraft carriers; the governors do not.

Modern communications and transportation explain why the center of gravity of the welfare-regulatory state has shifted from the states to the federal government. They do not, however, explain why the welfare-regulatory state has grown so greatly. Changes in both technology and culture account for this, at least partly. To begin with, there are much higher expectations from government. Generally speaking, people in the nineteenth century, when personal calamities struck, did not expect help from the state—or from anyone else except family, friends, and churches. There was no welfare state, medicine was crude and ineffective, and ordinary people carried no insurance. By the late twentieth century, all this had changed, and with change had come a general expectation that somebody, somehow, would make good, if personal or social disaster occurred. This new ethos lay behind the welfare state itself, and behind the development of many national programs—disaster relief, for example.

Another factor in the growth of the welfare-regulatory state was the enormous amount of social interdependence. Human beings have always depended on each other; but in modern society they depend more and more on total strangers. The lives of riders on a passenger jet are in the hands of the pilot—and of the mechanics who service the craft. If the passengers feel safe, it is because of law. They assume, for the most part correctly, that there are rules and regulations that make sure pilots know what they are doing, and that they are in good physical shape (and stay away from drugs and liquor); they can also assume that the planes are regularly serviced, and that air traffic controllers are doing their job.

This last example shows, too, how modern technology generates a felt need for regulatory law. And the technology itself needs legal protection. Much of the wealth of developed countries rests on new discoveries, new ideas, new devices. This became particularly true in the age of the computer and the Internet. Patents and copyrights had always been important to industry; but by the end of the twentieth century these fields of law had become pillars of the new economy, along with the trademarks and brand names on which so many companies had long depended.

In 1900, only a few rich people owned the newfangled horseless carriage. By the 1920s, millions of people drove cars, and their numbers snowballed as the century went on. The automobile liberates and can enrich one's life; but it also brings into being a huge new body of law. "Traffic law" in the age of the horse and buggy consisted of a few simple, rudimentary rules. But automobiles are fast and potentially deadly; they need better roads than horses do; and they can create chaos on the streets. Drivers' licenses, auto insurance, car safety rules, traffic lights—all these were unknown in 1900 but today are part of a field that law schools never discuss, but that touches on the lives of almost everybody in the country, every day of the year.

Safety is a consideration; but traffic law also helps keep order on the streets, and regulates the flow of traffic. The invention of the radio, and later of television, created a similar problem—possible gridlock on the airwaves. Here too the law stepped in, with the Federal Radio Commission (FRC), created by Congress in 1927, and then its successor, the Federal Communications Commission (FCC) of 1934—which, among other things, allocated wavelengths and controlled the radio spectrum. Later, the FCC extended its mandate to television channels.

American society in the last half of the twentieth century was enormously affluent. There were, to be sure, millions of poor people; but they were outnumbered by a vast middle class. A rich society can afford to think about things beyond one's daily bread. Nobody before the twentieth century had imagined the field of "environmental law." A society that once tore down beautiful buildings, and that slaughtered the bison almost into extinction, now began to worry about historic preservation. A society that once offered bounties for the killing of wolves now made it a crime to kill one.

The environmental movement was more than aesthetics and nostalgia. There was a hard core of human self-interest too. A giant industrial economy produces, along with all its goods, toxic wastes, pollution, environmental degradation. In 1948, the "Donora death fog" engulfed the town of Donora, Pennsylvania: poisonous fog from zinc and steel factories and a freakish weather condition resulted in kind of darkness at noon; twenty people died and half the town ended up in the hospital. The continual smog in Los Angeles was notorious for decades. Eventually, Congress passed clear-air and clean-water laws. President Richard Nixon created the Environmental Protection Agency. The worst sins of the profligate past could no longer be committed.

Taxation. Regulation costs money, the welfare state costs even more, and aircraft carriers and atom bombs are obscenely expensive. The budgets of nineteenth-century governments, state and federal, today seem almost laughably small; the federal government then got by on tariffs and excise taxes. But the twentieth century needed an enormous increase in taxes to fuel Leviathan's huge maw. Congress had passed an income tax law in 1895, but the Supreme Court had promptly declared it unconstitutional. The Sixteenth Amendment, which went into effect in 1913, undid this decision. The rates under the first income tax law were modest—the top was 6 percent, and only very wealthy people had to pay it. In 1916, Congress also enacted a modest estate tax. Income tax rates rose, at first quite modestly. During the Second World War, the government, for good reason, was particularly hungry for revenue. Rates zoomed upward, and for the first time millions of ordinary people felt the sting of the income tax. At this time, the government adopted the pay-as-you-go or withholding system. The text of the Internal Revenue Code grew even faster than revenues. As people squirmed and plotted to evade the sharp bite of the taxman, the Internal Revenue Service fought back with more rules, regulations, and statutory amendments. Each discovery by some bright tax lawyer of a new loophole led to a scramble to close the loophole. Every administration talks about simplifying the code, but it does not happen. The code is a monster—huge, unwieldy, arcane—but we seem unable to chop it down to size.

The Legal Profession. Along with the legal system itself, the legal profession grew enormously in the twentieth century. This continued a trend that was already clear in the previous century. In 1900, there were about 100,000 lawyers in the United States; by the early 1980s, this had grown to about 600,000, and by the end of the century, to more than a million.

The character of the profession changed dramatically, too. In 1900, it was basically a club of white men. Black lawyers were scarce, and law schools in the South were strictly segregated. In the last third of the century, law schools were desegregated, and many had programs to encourage and recruit students from racial minorities; their numbers began to grow.

Women had been entering the bar since the 1870s, but in the merest trickle: in Philadelphia, in 1905, there were exactly three women lawyers. In the 1960s and 1970s, the tide turned dramatically. By 2000, about a quarter of the profession was made up of women, who had been 4 percent of law students in 1965 but had become 42 percent by 1995. As old men retired or died off, more and more were replaced by women. Women also became much more common as law school professors and deans, and as judges. In 1981, Sandra Day O'Connor became the first woman to sit on the United States Supreme Court. A woman chief justice of a state high court is no longer a rarity. Still, at the end of the century, women seemed to face what came to be called the "glass ceiling" in law firms. Less likely than men to become partners of big law firms, they were more likely to drop out of this particular rat race. Why this was true was much discussed and much disputed.

The large law firms themselves represent another dramatic change in the profession in the twentieth century. In 1900, most lawyers were solo practitioners. A handful of

First Woman Supreme Court Justice. Sandra Day O'Connor being sworn in as a Supreme Court Justice by Chief Justice Warren Burger, September 1981. John O'Connor, her husband, looks on. COURTESY RONALD REAGAN LIBRARY

firms, mostly in New York, had more than a dozen lawyers. In 1935, the largest Chicago law firm had forty-three lawyers. Giant firms (one hundred or more) were still mostly confined to New York. But by 2000, the largest, Baker & McKenzie, had over three thousand lawyers. Big firms were everywhere in the country—the largest in Richmond, Virginia, for example, had more than five hundred lawyers in the year 2000—and they tended now to have branch offices, in other cities in the United States or abroad, in Europe, or Asia, or Latin America. Not all lawyers worked for big firms: substantial numbers were house counsel—lawyers employed by companies—or worked for government at various levels. A sizeable number worked either for small general or small, specialized ("boutique") firms, or practiced entirely on their own.

In 1900, law schools were a dominant factor in legal education, but still hardly a monopoly. A century later, the apprenticeship system was virtually dead. There were about one hundred law schools in 1910, some of them night schools. In 1980, there were more than two hundred. In 1900, quite a few states had no law schools at all; by 2000, Alaska was the only state in this benighted condition. California could boast of at least thirty-five law schools. (Not all of these were accredited.) In the second half of the century, schools became more and more selective. The Law School Admission Test (LSAT) was launched in 1948. Eventually, all schools signed on. Before the LSAT, many schools routinely admitted great numbers of students, and flunked out a third of them, or more. In 2000, it was harder to get in—but also very much harder, in fact almost impossible, to flunk out.

Why are there so many lawyers in the United States? Many countries—Japan, very notably—are rich and developed but seem to get along with a much smaller cadre. There are indeed scholars who argue that American lawyers are a drag on the economy; or that they are parasitic, or troublemakers. American society, however, is complex: the law is complex, government is complex, and complexity breeds work for lawyers—or rather, work that has to be done, whether by lawyers (as in the United States), or by somebody else (as in Japan). American lawyers have been innovative and nimble at finding new ways to make a dollar, new ways to make themselves useful. The profession is supple. Its boundaries are porous and indistinct, and the best lawyers act as legal engineers, rather than as learned experts; they are problem solvers and advisers, indispensable to economy and polity. It is worth pointing out that the profession is growing rapidly in other developed countries, too—and even, modestly, in Japan.

The Liability Explosion. In some fields of law, the twentieth century continued nineteenth-century trends; in others, it turned them upside down. Tort law was essentially a nineteenth-century invention. Much of its complex fabric of rules tilted the law toward protecting defendants—corporations and other business enterprises, for the most part. This fabric was already in decay in the late-nineteenth century; and it was ripped to shreds in the twentieth. Workers injured on the job in the earlier century for the most part got no compensation at all; they were barred by the so-called fellow-servant rule. In 1908, the Federal Employers' Liability Act abolished that rule for interstate railroad workers. In the states, from about the time of World War I, workers' compensation systems replaced the old tort rules entirely in dealing with injuries on the job. Compensation was reckoned by a statutory formula, and paid for through an insurance scheme. Negligence or fault no longer mattered. By 1948 every state had a compensation statute.

MacPherson v. Buick Motor Co., 217 N.Y. 382 (111 N.E. 1050) (1916), decided by the New York Court of Appeals in 1916, was the leading case on products liability. Under an old rule (the "privity" doctrine), a person injured by a defective product could sue only whoever had sold it to him. In the *MacPherson* case, plaintiff bought a car from a dealer; he was injured because of a defective wheel, and he sued the manufacturer, Buick. Benjamin N. Cardozo, who wrote the opinion, swept the privity doctrine aside: MacPherson could sue Buick directly. In an age of advertising, brand names, and mass production, this made perfect sense.

Malpractice cases also exemplify the liability explosion. In the nineteenth century, cases against doctors were rare, and usually unsuccessful. By the end of the twentieth century, they were common enough to alarm the medical profession, and doctors complained about staggering insurance bills. Indeed, the liability explosion set off a serious backlash in the last quarter of the century; many states passed laws that, in one way or another, tried to rein in what business and the medical profession saw as an epidemic of dangerous lawsuits. Many ordinary people, too, seemed to feel that the system had gone amok. But the same cultural and social factors that undergird the welfare state itself—the rising expectation of compensation, in the event of disaster—have influenced the law of torts as well.

Race Relations and Civil Rights. It would be hard to find a field of law that changed more dramatically in the twentieth century than race relations. Four years before the start of the new century, the Supreme Court, in *Plessy v. Ferguson*, 163 U.S. 537 (1896), had launched the "separate but equal" doctrine, recognizing the legitimacy of segregating by race. In 1900, blacks in the South did not vote or hold office. Most were little better than peons on white-owned farms. There was little or no justice for blacks in Southern courts, and the curse of the lynch mob was at its height. The situation outside the South was only somewhat better. Northern blacks voted, but most good jobs were closed to them. The armed forces were segregated. Most institutions, from major league baseball to the Metropolitan Opera, were for whites only.

This situation changed only slowly. White Southerners held key positions in Congress, and resisted any move toward racial equality—or even measures against lynching. For want of anything better, the National Association for the Advancement of Colored People (NAACP), formed in 1909, made good use of a litigation strategy. They won a fair number of victories in court—though these victories had, on the whole, little impact on the life of Southern blacks.

There was a dramatic turnaround in the second half of the century. Blacks in substantial numbers had moved north; there they had at least a small degree of political leverage. The Second World War was a war against a racist enemy. Civil rights became an issue in the Cold War, especially after the African colonies became independent states. In any event, opinion outside the South slowly turned against segregation and race discrimination. President Harry Truman, with a stroke of the pen in 1948, ordered an end to segregation in the armed forces though full implementation took time. Meanwhile, some northern states enacted "fair employment" laws.

Brown v. Board of Education, 347 U.S. 483 (1954; Brown I), thus did not come out of nowhere; it rested, in part, on a line of Supreme Court cases. Nonetheless, it was a bombshell. Segregation by race, in public schools, was declared unconstitutional. In quick succession, the Supreme Court barred all forms of segregation, and, in *Loving v. Virginia*, 388 U.S. 1 (1967), even struck down laws against racial intermarriage—the last, and strongest, of racial taboos. The Southern states resisted change, sometimes with brute force. But they faced a strong and determined civil-rights movement. Moreover, President Lyndon Johnson rammed through Congress a powerful civil-rights law in 1964, followed, in 1965, by a tough new law on voting rights. The old order in the South was doomed. By the end of the century, affirmative action, not segregation or discrimination, was the major disputed legal issue—whether government and institutions could tilt the scales toward racial minorities, not against them.

The civil-rights movement was only one of a linked set of revolts against subordinate status. The Civil Rights Act of 1964 barred sex discrimination in the job market. The Supreme Court, in *Reed v. Reed*, 404 U.S. 71 (1971), in one of its magical fits of discovery, read a ban on sex discrimination into the Fourteenth Amendment. Here too a strong social movement lay behind the legal developments. Congress also outlawed age discrimination (for people over forty) in the 1960s, and eventually ended mandatory retirement. In 1990, the Americans with Disabilities Act gave job rights—within, of course, certain limits—to people with physical and mental handicaps.

For Native Americans, the nineteenth century had been an unbroken string of calamities and outrages. Shrunken in numbers, herded into reservations, they stared extinction in the face. Government policy was sometimes well meaning, but almost always disastrous in practice. Many of the tribes were destitute, and assimilation was the

Thurgood Marshall. Marshall (*left*) with client Donald Gaines Murray (*center*), who was denied entry into the University of Maryland Law School, and attorney Charles Houston during court proceedings, Maryland, c. 1935. VISUAL MATERIALS FROM THE NATIONAL ASSOCIATION FOR THE ADVANCEMENT OF COLORED PEOPLE RECORDS/PRINTS AND PHOTOGRAPHS DIVISION, LIBRARY OF CONGRESS

government's dominant policy—which meant a war on native languages, customs, and religions. During the New Deal, the commissioner of Indian Affairs, John Collier, tried to reverse this policy. In the 1950s, though, policy reverted to assimilation, and Congress voted to "terminate" a long list of tribes. Yet in the 1960s, here too a social movement, more or less on the civil-rights model, struggled to reverse the policy of assimilation once and for all. Congress granted more autonomy. Some tribes began to grow in size. Languages and religions were now safe from government interference—their main enemy now, and a powerful one, was American mass culture, TV, and the lure of urban life.

For Asian-Americans, too, the century saw a classic reversal. Chinese exclusion was the norm in the early 1900s. Asians were barred from owning land in California, and from marrying Caucasians. Japanese-Americans on the West Coast were callously driven from their homes during World War II, and interned in remote camps. But China was an American ally in this war, and Japan became an American fief in 1945. Immigration restrictions ended in 1965. The climate of opinion in the late twentieth century also benefited Hispanics, the fastest growing, and indeed the largest, of American minorities by 2000; at the end of the century, their influence was beginning to be felt in the political process.

An Activist Court. An expanded role for judicial review was a striking trait of twentieth-century courts. High courts had always been strong institutions, but in this century they used their ultimate weapon more frequently, voiding, as unconstitutional, acts of the executive and other branches of government. The legal realist school of the 1920s and 1930s confirmed what the keenest judges and jurists had always known: that judges were political actors, and that their views and ideologies mattered. Perhaps the public knew this too. American judges, in the states, were mostly elected; this made their power, in theory at least, responsive to the public will.

The United States Supreme Court was, of course, the court of courts. In the early part of the century, many of its boldest decisions were conservative. A notorious instance was *Lochner v. New York*, 198 U.S. 45 (1905). Here the Supreme Court struck down a New York statute that regulated health and safety conditions in bakeries and fixed maximum hours of work for employees. Later, in *Hammer v. Dagenhart*, 247 U.S. 251 (1918), the Court confronted an act of Congress, which barred from interstate commerce goods made with child labor, and voided it. These cases aroused intense opposition from the progressive left.

During the 1930s, the "nine old men" of the Court struck down a number of key New Deal statutes. President Roosevelt hatched a plan to pack the Court with new, and more pliant, justices—one of this master politician's few serious errors—that was vilified and buried in Congress. Roosevelt, however, lost the battle but won the war. He was in office more than twelve years, and by the end had all the justices he needed. The Supreme Court essentially stopped intruding into the legality of the regulatory state.

In the second half of the twentieth century, the Court shifted focus. Now it became the champion of the underdog, the shield and sword of the oppressed. This was particularly the case in the years (1953–1969) when Earl Warren was chief justice. The *Brown* case was an outstanding example. But the Court also laid down new rules for the protection of criminal defendants. It extended the Bill of Rights, in essence, to the states; and interpreted rights language very broadly. Everybody who watches television knows about the Miranda warning—"you have the right to remain silent"—and other curbs on police behavior. How effective these are in practice is another question.

The Supreme Court also boldly entered what it had once called a "political thicket": the boundary lines of electoral districts, once a taboo subject for the courts. But starting with *Baker v. Carr*, 369 U.S. 186 (1962), the Court insisted that courts could and should intervene in these questions, and that citizens of the states had a right to electoral districts that were roughly equal in population—that in general the principle of "one person, one vote" should prevail.

The Court also invented, and developed, a constitutional right of "privacy." What this came to mean was the right to make decisions about sex, lifestyle, and reproduction, free from the heavy hand of the state. The first major case was *Griswold v. Connecticut*, 381 U.S. 479 (1965); this struck down a Connecticut law that, in essence, outlawed contraception and family planning. And in *Roe v. Wade*, 410 U.S. 113 (1973), the Court stepped into a genuine minefield—the issue of abortion. The case gave women a constitutional right to an abortion, at least during the early months of pregnancy. No case since *Brown* was so controversial, and aroused such opposition. *Brown*, though, within a generation, had entered the pantheon of Great Decisions; nobody criticizes the result any more. But the passage of more than thirty years has done nothing to still the uproar over *Roe v. Wade*. Religious people still dream of overturning it. Compared with *Roe*, the reaction to *Lawrence v. Texas*, 539 U.S. 558 (2003)—a decision that voided every remaining sodomy law, and forbade the states from punishing same-sex behavior—was mild and restrained.

Criminal Justice. The privacy cases remind us of the Court's role in regulating, or at least trying to regulate, criminal justice. Crime and punishment remained, as before, primarily a state issue. The basic crimes—murder, rape, arson, burglary, robbery, assault, and the like—were state crimes, punished by the state. There were, in fact, no federal prisons before 1895, when Leavenworth opened; the few federal prisoners before that date were boarded in state prisons. A second federal prison opened in Atlanta in 1902; by 1930, there were five.

The state role in criminal justice remained dominant throughout the century; but the federal role grew relatively stronger. Prohibition, in the 1920s, and drug laws, through to the present, swelled the ranks of federal prisoners. The regulatory state also created a certain number of new crimes: insider trading, for example, under the Securities Act of 1933 and the Securities and Exchange Act of 1934. Income tax frauds were federal crimes. The federal government also became in time a more sophisticated crime fighter. Crime, like commerce, had gone interstate—another contribution of the automotive society. Bank robbers, for example, could easily cross state borders. In 1908, a Bureau of Investigation was formed within the Department of Justice; in 1935 this became the Federal Bureau of Investigation (the famous FBI).

On a number of issues involving criminal justice, the century breaks almost neatly into two rather discordant pieces. This is the case, for example, with so-called victimless crimes. During the first part of the century, laws against these tightened: there was a massive campaign to wipe out prostitution, red-light districts, and vice and debauchery in general. This grew out of a sense of national crisis, a feeling that, in times of rapid social change, massive immigration, and urbanization, the old American values were threatened with extinction. These values had to be enforced, and vigorously, by the state. Prohibition itself was perhaps the crown jewel of this movement.

A political disaster, Prohibition died fairly quickly, lasting little more than a decade. And the last years of the twentieth century undid the work of the early years—and then some. In a permissive age, the age of the "sexual revolution," of rampant consumerism and expressive individualism, the old rules reflecting traditional morality could not survive. This was true not only for criminal law. In this period, too, strict divorce laws collapsed. So-called no-fault divorce began in California, in 1970; but it soon swept most of the nation. No-fault put an end to a rotting system of collusion and perjury, and allowed men and women to unmarry as the spirit moved them, which it seemed to do quite often.

The impact of the new social ethos was dramatic. State after state reformed its penal code to get rid of laws against adultery, fornication, and sodomy: the sex life of consenting adults was, essentially, no longer the business of the state. Early in the twentieth century there had been widespread censorship of movies; obscene literature was taboo, and even mild allusions to sex on the stage were out of the question. All this was gone by 2000. In theory, pornography remains subject to legal regulation, or outright ban; in practice, though, almost anything goes, and nobody would dream of applying the rules to D. H. Lawrence or Rabelais. In an age when entertainment was perhaps the biggest industry in the country, old strictures against gambling collapsed as well. Before the 1950s only Nevada, a barren desert state, made a living out of casino gambling. Now other states—and many Indian tribes—have gotten into the act; and state after state have rushed into the business themselves by peddling lottery tickets.

Drug laws were the great exception. They not only survived, but flourished; they became, in fact, harsher and harsher over the years. Today, prisons and jails house hundreds of thousands of men and women convicted of nonviolent drug crimes. The government spends billions every year trying to cut off the supply of drugs at their sources in distant countries, or to stop them at the borders.

Crime was a political issue throughout the century; Prohibition made it a federal issue as well. After the Second World War, the violent crime rate seemed to spin out of control. This put tremendous pressure on government, at all levels; no politician wanted to seem soft on crime. Because the federal government was so salient and visible, candidates for national office began to promise to confront street crime, even though this remained largely a state matter. The federal government began to shovel a certain amount of cash into local law enforcement—for example, through the 1965 Law Enforcement Assistance Act. Ironically, at the same time that the Warren Court was trying to expand defendants' rights, states and the federal government were trying to tighten the screws.

Early in the century, reforms in the criminal-justice system were aimed at individualizing punishment and correction. This was the era of parole, probation, and the indeterminate sentence. Young offenders went to the new juvenile courts, where, in theory, they were not treated as criminals at all. Emphasis shifted, in other words, from what had been done, to who had done it—at least relatively. The second half of the century reversed this trend. Some states abolished parole, and got rid of the indeterminate sentence. In many states, violent juveniles could be tried as if they were adults. In the panic over crime, emphasis shifted back to the offense, rather than the offender. At the end of the century, prisons and jails were bursting at the seams. Prisoners, and ex-prisoners under parole supervision, formed a kind of nation within a nation, more than two million strong.

The death penalty was in decline through much of the century, and in *Furman v. Georgia*, 408 U.S. 238 (1972), the Supreme Court struck down all existing laws on capital punishment, on various constitutional grounds. Four years later, it reinstated the death penalty—but only for states that provided certain safeguards. About a dozen states never had the death penalty, and still do not. Most executions take place in Southern and Border states, and one state, Texas, accounts for about a third of all executions. Capital punishment remains controversial, and the process is amazingly slow: If a prisoner dies, it is only after years and years of appeals, delays, writs, and maneuvers. More than ten years on death row is normal; twenty years is far from rare.

Business Law. Big constitutional issues and sensational trials make the headlines; but the main business of American law and American lawyers is business. There are perhaps millions of businesses in the United States, ranging from mom-and-pop stores to giant multinationals. Almost all of them need help from lawyers—to incorporate or not, to work out their tax problems, and to navigate the straits and shoals of regulation. The most prominent lawyers, and the big law firms, represent the large, publicly traded corporations. The nineteenth century developed a massive body of law on corporations—on their structure and their internal operations. Corporations were business associations that were allowed to last forever; they had stockholders and managers, and limited liability. This last feature is particularly important. If a company goes bankrupt, stockholders lose their investment, but nothing more—they are not liable for the company's debts.

Corporations were and are created state by state. But the United States is a federal union, and a giant free-trade area. A company can incorporate in one state and do business in all the others. This gave an opening to one small but enterprising state, Delaware; in 1899, it adopted easy corporation laws, threw in a package of low fees and taxes, and declared itself open for business. It beat out all its rivals: Throughout the twentieth century, the Delaware Corporation Law was the corporation law for the United States; the decisions of the Delaware Chancery Court, an archaic remnant in one of the tiniest states of the union, meant more for American corporations than all the decisions of courts in New York or California.

Corporation law is essentially permissive. Corporations can be formed for any purpose, and on the whole, no one can question what the officers decide, in their general business judgment. The law, of course, regulates with some vigor particular kinds of corporations—banks, for example, or railroads. And after passage of the Securities and Exchange act in the 1930s, the federal government insisted that companies selling stock, and reporting to stockholders on their finances, income, and debts, must tell the truth, the whole truth, and nothing but the truth. The Sherman Act (1890) had been aimed at curbing "trusts" and monopolies. Enforcement was fitful; the early Supreme Court cases were crabbed and narrow. In 1911, however, the Court upheld the breakup of the Standard Oil monopoly. In 1914, Congress created a Federal Trade Commission;

and the Clayton Act of the same year prohibited unfair business practices, and strengthened and added detail to national antitrust law. Much later, the government would successfully attack the telephone monopoly; but a lawsuit against the computer giant IBM ended in failure.

In the twentieth century, business and trade paid less and less attention to state borders. Yet each state had its own dialect of commercial law. To many legal scholars, this mélange of laws was a problem, for businesses sold goods in all parts of the country. One solution, early in the century, was to draft "uniform" laws and try to induce the states to pass them. A few of these laws—on sales and on negotiable instruments, for example—were quite successful. Even more successful was the Uniform Commercial Code (UCC), drafted for the American Law Institute in the 1940s, which aimed to supersede the specific uniform laws, and to cover all of commercial law, presumably in a rational and efficient way. Pennsylvania adopted the UCC in 1953. Other states were more hesitant, but by the late 1960s, it had become the basic law in every state but Louisiana, and even Louisiana law has been heavily influenced by the UCC.

The Constitution gave Congress power to pass a national bankruptcy law. In the nineteenth century, there were three such laws—all of them short-lived and quickly repealed. The law of 1898, however, proved to have greater staying power. Since that year there has never been a period without federal bankruptcy laws and procedures. Under the 1898 law, bankruptcy could be voluntary or involuntary. In 1904, there were over 13,000 petitions in bankruptcy. The numbers rose and fell—quite high during the Depression, but very low in 1945, a year of wartime prosperity. The end of the century saw an astonishing increase. Society floated on a sea of credit; individuals freely went into debt; and bankruptcy seemed to have lost whatever stigma it once had. There were more than 1,400,000 filings in 1990. Over 90 percent of these were by individuals, not businesses.

The American Empire. In the nineteenth century, the United States spread from the Atlantic to the Pacific; and at the very end of the century, even beyond. In 1898 Hawaii was annexed, and the United States seized Puerto Rico and the Philippines from the decaying Spanish empire. In the twentieth century there were no new acquisitions of territory—indeed, the Philippines gained their independence after the Second World War. But the sheer size, wealth, and power of the United States, by 2000, made much of the world, in a sense, part of an American empire. American movies and music could be heard all over the world. After the collapse of the Soviet Union, America was the only superpower, militarily speaking. American law firms had branches all over the globe, and law firms on the American model were springing up in all developed countries. The world has become a single giant stage, on which America plays a starring role.

But in some ways, the rest of the world is catching up. America invented or perfected judicial review; now most European countries have it too, and for the same complex reasons—the spread of a global culture of human rights, beyond the power of governments to alter, which only courts can enforce. America was the first automotive society; and made more cars than anybody else. But Tokyo's traffic jams are now as good as New York's—and Japanese cars are "stealing" the market from Detroit. No empire lasts forever. What will happen to America's empire—and America's law—in the twenty-first century is anybody's guess.

BIBLIOGRAPHY

Auerbach, Jerold. *Unequal Justice: Lawyers and Social Change in Modern America*. New York: Oxford University Press, 1976.
Friedman, Lawrence M. *American Law in the Twentieth Century*. New Haven, Conn.: Yale University Press, 2002.
Friedman, Lawrence M. *The Horizontal Society*. New Haven, Conn.: Yale University Press, 1999.
Friedman, Lawrence M. *Private Lives: Families, Individuals, and the Law*. Cambridge, Mass.: Harvard University Press, 2004.
Garrow, David J. *Liberty and Sexuality: The Right to Privacy and the Making of Roe v. Wade*. Berkeley: University of California Press, 1998.
Harrison, Robert. *State and Society in Twentieth-Century America*. London: Longman, 1997.
Hovenkamp, Herbert. *Enterprise and American Law, 1836–1937*. Cambridge, Mass.: Harvard University Press, 1991.
Jacob, Herbert. *Silent Revolution: The Transformation of Divorce Law in the United States*. Chicago and London: University of Chicago Press, 1988.
Klarman, Michael. *From Jim Crow to Civil Rights: The Supreme Court and the Struggle for Racial Equality*. Oxford and New York: Oxford University Press, 2004.
Powe, Lucas A. (Scot), Jr. *The Warren Court and American Politics*, Cambridge, Mass.: Harvard University Press, 2000.
Stevens, Robert B. *Law School: Legal Education in America from the 1850s to the 1980s*. Chapel Hill: University of North Carolina Press, 1983.
Urofsky, Melvin I. and Paul Finkelman. *A March of Liberty: A Constitutional History of the United States*, 2nd ed., 2 vols. New York: Oxford University Press, 2002.

LAWRENCE FRIEDMAN

UNIVERSITIES.

The university in western Europe arose in the twelfth century, as an institution that grew organically and was not established by decree. In no other culture was the transmission of knowledge organized in this manner, not even in antiquity. The university is an institution of the medieval papal world. Its members were first legally acknowledged in 1158 by the Authentica "Habita," a decree of Emperor Friedrich I. They were guaranteed imperial protection, their own court of jurisdiction, and the *privilegium fori* (privilege of the forum) of clerics was extended to instructors and students. The *universitas magistrorum et scholarium* (corporation of masters and scholars) or the *studium generale* (general studies) designated a privileged community or confraternity of teachers and students at one location. They possessed the *libertas scholastica*, a corporate autonomy which later developed into the freedom of instruction.

The oldest universities are Bologna (earliest statutes in 1252), a union of famous private law schools, as well as Paris (1215), which arose from theological schools. Oxford and Cambridge had similarly early foundations. Paris and Bologna stand for different types of university organizations. In the Parisian model (*modus Parisiensis*) the master led the corporation (also true of Oxford), while in Bologna the students were in charge (*universitas scholarium*). Here the teachers were not part of the university, they were employed by it and were organized into a *collegium doctorum* (college of teachers). Bologna was the leading university for law, attracting students from all over Europe. Faculties of law following this example were established in Padua, Pavia, Perugia, and Siena, as well as in Montpellier, Orléans, and Toulouse in France. Not until 1368 did Bologna acquire a theological faculty; in Paris the theological faculty was the germ cell of the university and long served as the authority of Western Christianity. A law faculty, especially for canon law, was not established until later.

By the middle of the thirteenth century most of the new institutes of education were organized as legal persons. As signs of autonomy, they had their own seals; a scepter stood for independent jurisdiction. From the fourteenth century, their own statutes and constitutions governed their internal affairs. They possessed papal or imperial privileges and thus the right to grant academic degrees. Their degrees commanded respect—after the fifteenth century they increasingly opened doors to careers in church and state and were acknowledged throughout Christianity. This corresponded to the universalism of their teachings, which itself was considered one of their sciences. From this they derived the right of cooptation and to appoint additional members of the faculty.

Along with those earliest universities, which arose *ex consuetudine* (by custom), there were soon those that were formally established by a ruler or a city and given privileges, such as Salamanca (1243), Sevilla (1254), Coimbra (1290), or—from the fourteenth century—those in eastern or northern Europe. The establishment of universities was promoted by scientific schisms and disputes (*via antiqua* / *via moderna*) as well as by the prestige generated for the founders/cities of the empire, such as Prague (1348), Vienna (1365–1383), Heidelberg (1386), Cologne (1388), or Louvain (1425). Such foundings increased throughout Europe—with the exception of England and Italy—in the fifteenth century, generally following the Parisian model of the magisterial university. Around 1500 there were approximately sixty universities in Europe. This corresponded to the progressive scientification and tendency toward the recording of knowledge in written form in the communities of the late Middle Ages and early modern times, and thus established the aspiration to a knowledge-based, rational organization of the human community that persists to this day.

A (full) university consisted of four faculties. Up to early modern times the first was generally theology, the second law—considered the finest and with the highest social standing—the third was the smallest, that of medicine. These formed the higher faculties that were served by the fourth and lowest, the arts (so named because of the *septem artes liberales* [seven liberal arts]) faculty. For a long time it was also called *ancilla theologiae* (servant of theology). This division reflected the rating of the sciences, comprising the entire cosmos of possible knowledge as the classical authorities had described it, in previously unattained completeness. There were also exceptions. Thus in England jurists were educated at the Inns of Court. Although Oxford had a chair of canon law and one of civil law, it had no law faculty. Some French and Italian universities initially had only two or three faculties.

Academic activity did not—as in the nineteenth century—consist of researching, discovering the unknown. The Bible, the Corpus Juris, the writings of Galen and Aristotle remained the basic authorities until the eighteenth century. The authoritative texts were taught in lectures and disputations; rote learning played a decisive role. The use of Latin and the generally accepted authority of the texts guaranteed the ubiquity of the sciences and also, initially, the degrees. Until late in the eighteenth century, outstanding students considered a degree from a recognized foreign university an advantage. For jurists, the Italian universities along with Orléans and Bourges were preferred goals of the *peregrinatio academia* (academic pilgrimage), for physicians they were Padua, Montpellier, and later Leiden, which was also attractive for the arts and jurisprudence following the *usus modernus* (modern use of Roman law) and natural and international law.

The university was governed by a president or vice chancellor elected for a year or half a year. The faculties were led by a dean, and a senate implemented the self-administration of the autonomous institution, along with various officials. Matriculation—free of charge only for the so-called *pauperes* (poor students)—was the act by which students became members of the corporation and eligible for its many privileges. At the early universities the students were initially organized into *nationes* (countries) according to their national origins and they lived in hostels, colleges, or halls. In Paris and Oxford and Cambridge these developed increasingly into the actual universities and the faculty dealt only with the awarding of degrees. Often these were sanctioned by a chancellor, the local bishop, or high officials of the church. Of course only a minority actually got a degree, not least because of the costs, but also because documentation of course participation was sufficient proof of having attended university. Bachelor, master, licentiate (for theologians), and doctorate became differentiated degrees. Masters had the right and the obligation to teach for two years at their university, which they customarily took advantage of to study at the one of the upper faculties. The doctorate/licentiate was required only for an academic career or was useful for one at court, from which some—especially jurists—derived the notion that they were equal to the aristocracy.

The humanists opposed the increasingly esoteric-scholastic education mills of the late Middle Ages. Without presenting an alternative scientific system or even one of their own, they postulated that merely the correct use of language would make comprehension and knowledge and even civilization possible. Moreover, the academic disciplines were to be made more practical. Their model was antiquity, which they believed had been lost, but should be revived. They took up a kind of historicizing method known as *ad fontes* (back to the sources). Improved texts and more precise insights into the circumstances of its origins resulted from humanistic jurisprudence, a method known in France as the *mos gallicus* (French method).

This outlook, ethical and esoteric and with cosmopolitan tendencies, was repressed by the Reformation, depending on the country. In England the break was less drastic than in the Empire. In all countries, the end of the unity, ideally speaking, of Christianity led to increased efforts to stabilize the respective confessions by scientific means, that is, with the help of the universities. The new believers forged ahead; the Catholic countries caught up after the Council of Trent. The newly founded Society of Jesus with its *ratio studiorum* (plan of studies, 1599) controlled the artistic and theological faculties throughout Europe and abroad. These were important for the faith; they were forbidden to interfere with the faculties of law and medicine, which remained in secular hands. In some places there existed purely Jesuit universities with only artistic and theological faculties. The goal—and often the method—was the same in all confessions: the creation of a *sapiens et eloquens pietas* (a wise and eloquent piety). This led to a unification of humanistic and theologic interests, and the universities were considered ecclesiastical and state seminaries (*seminaria ecclesiae et reipublicae*). Thereafter, control by the state increased everywhere. Matriculation as well as graduation was tied to oaths of religious allegiance, which in practice could often be flouted.

Formerly the period between the sixteenth and eighteenth centuries was considered a time of decline or stagnation of the universities. This may be true of some universities. However, recent work shows that important and outstanding contributions were made during this time, that certain directions were determined at German and Dutch universities that were to be important for the rise of the universities in the nineteenth and twentieth centuries. The Iberian peninsula remained a stronghold of canon law and of late Scholasticism. Italy and France were important for jurisprudence and medicine. In Bourges and Orléans, humanistic jurisprudence of the *mos gallicus* influenced many other universities; followers of the *mos italicus* (Italian method) left their mark on other universities of the Continent and Scotland, while the medical schools of Montpellier, Padua, Bologna, and Pavia retained their leading positions. The number of universities promoted the professionalization of jurists, physicians, and theologians throughout Europe.

With the spread of the Enlightenment the prominent role played by the theological faculties and the confessional usurpation of the universities had to appear dated. The universities were to become more practice oriented and more useful. In many places the sciences became more secular and as a result the state took precedence in questions of education. At reform-oriented universities the faculty of law frequently assumed the leading position and methodologically determined the understanding of science. This was of course not true of all countries. In France and England, the leading states in Europe, the Enlightenment remained a phenomenon taking place outside the universities. In France they diminished to vocational schools, and the new ideas gave rise to special schools, the predecessors of the *grandes écoles*. In England, Oxford and Cambridge remained training grounds for the gentry, while the Scottish system, previously unsuccessful, experienced an upturn thanks to a new moral philosophy and sciences following Dutch models.

In the Protestant realm *jus publicum* (public law), *usus modernus*, natural and international law (as in the Netherlands), administration, and classical studies led to an enlightened understanding of science. Increasingly, aristocrats returned to the universities, abandoning the academies for the noble. The Catholic universities adopted this new educational system in the eighteenth century, which included the faculties of theology. Universities with four faculties remained the model, unlike in England and France, and proved reformable. Even in Mediterranean countries, reforms could be instituted after the Jesuit order was dissolved, even if only with temporary success. In Halle, Göttingen, Jena, Mainz, Ingolstadt, Vienna, and Salzburg, the universities were rejuvenated and served as preliminary models for a new kind of university that culminated in the foundation of the university in Berlin in 1810. While in France the decree of September 15, 1793, established specialized education at the Écoles Centrales and abolished the universities, Wilhelm von Humboldt and Friedrich Schleiermacher upheld the traditional four-faculty university. The faculty of philosophy, now on equal footing with the other faculties, indeed now intellectually superior to the other so-called Brotwissenschaften (bread-and-butter courses) legitimized the new concept behind the university. Along with academic freedom, freedom of research and teaching, and scientific self-determination, research and scientific content were established as the backbone of the universities. The state should be responsible for organization and finances, as it would profit most when it did not interfere with the contents of education, as neo-humanist reformers thought. As previously, the universities in Germany remained the stronghold of intellectual self-assurance.

Initially the French model had more rapid success, especially in medicine and natural sciences. Paris became the leader in these and other disciplines. Over the course of the century, however, especially in its second half, the German model turned out to be the more successful in all sciences. In an analogy to the federalist organization of government, German universities were quietly supported by the states and had no centralized organization, which stimulated competition. This remained true even after the unification of 1870–1871—and the extensive development of old and many new fields, largely left to the universities themselves, caused the Empire to temporarily become the leading center of science. Many foreign teachers and students visited Germany, and in many disciplines the German language was considered indispensable. There was talk of a "major educational production site," both in qualitative as well as in quantitative terms, and even France adopted this model in 1896, as did Swiss and Italian universities. In England new universities broke the monopoly of Oxbridge and altered academic and vocational education, in part following the Continental model. In many countries universities became places of national self-assurance and prestige. In Russia universities were founded in the attempt to connect with the European model. In the United States, English and German models were important, even if the organization of leading institutions as privately founded institutions remained an important characteristic.

World War I destroyed the supposedly purely objectively oriented, tolerant, international scientific community. Only gradually did mutual opposition subside during the 1920s as connections with the former *respublica litteraria* (republic of letters) were reestablished. The emergence of the Soviet Union and of the National Socialists of course split the scientific community anew and ultimately World War II led to drastic upheavals. In the meantime, the United States assumed the leading position among scientific nations; Germany had lost its former status. The fact that after 1945 a new beginning and broader international and more humane university education of as many as possible was sought after everywhere, though not necessarily in the Eastern bloc, led to comparable educational policies and to the establishment of further universities with a multitude of new disciplines.

[*See also* International Law: Roman Law; *and* Natural Law: Medieval and Post-Medieval Roman Law.]

BIBLIOGRAPHY

Rüegg, Walter, general editor. *A History of the University in Europe*, 4. vols. Cambridge, U.K.: Cambridge University Press, 1992–2006. Also available in German, Spanish, and Portuguese translations.

NOTKER HAMMERSTEIN
Translated from the German by Alexa Nieschlag

UNJUST ENRICHMENT IN ROMAN LAW. *See* Contract, *subentry on* Ancient Roman Law.

UNJUST ENRICHMENT IN MEDIEVAL AND POST-MEDIEVAL ROMAN LAW.

Article 6: 212 § 1 of the new Dutch Civil code states explicitly that "a person who has been unjustifiably enriched at the expense of another is obliged, so far as reasonable, to make good the other's loss, up to the amount of his enrichment." At first glance, there is nothing peculiar about this provision. It could have been taken directly from Roman law, since the *Digest*, that inexhaustible source of juridical wisdom, contains two similar texts, transmitted under the name of Sextus Pomponius (D. 50.17.206; Pomponius in the ninth book of his various lessons): According to natural law it is equitable that nobody enriches himself at the expense of another.

Pomponius was a very influential Roman lawyer. He drew in his *Liber singularis enchiridii* a picture of legal history in terms of the progress of the offices of lawyers and jurists which via D. 1.2.2 through the ages dominated the image of the development of substantive law and its sources in Rome. By way of the text just cited Pomponius seems to have been influential already in classical Roman law: in the context of unjustified enrichment Paul discusses natural law (D. 12.6.15*pr.*). Natural equity is the guiding principle for Celsus and Ulpian (D. 12.4.3.7), whereas Celsus invokes the good and the equitable (D.12.1.32), just like Paul (D. 12.6.65.4) and Papinianus (D. 12.6.66). Good faith plays a similar role with Africanus (D. 23.3.50), whereas Celsus (D. 12.6.47) and Marcianus (D. 25.5.25) found this rule in *ius gentium*. It is tempting to identify the statements dating back to antiquity and the provisions found in the most modern codification of the European continent.

Upon closer view, however, important differences are to be noticed. The Dutch provision leaves no doubt that the impoverished can bring an action against the unjustly enriched party, who, in his turn, is obliged to convey the amount of his enrichment. Pomponius' text is a legal principle, *regula iuris*. The compilers of the *Digest* placed the quotation in D. 50.17, *De diversis regulis iuris*, a collection of phrases that offer little support in decision making. In Roman law the structure of civil procedure, more in particular the wording of specific remedies, dominate over the substantive law. Access to justice was reserved to claimants who brought an action that the *praetor* had mentioned in his *Edict*. Remarkably the *Edict* of the *praetor* does not contain a general remedy for cases of unjust enrichment. The Latin language does not even have an equivalent expression. In the *Institutes* of Gaius or Justinian, the chapters on the sources of obligations other than contract or tort do not mention unjustified enrichment. Nevertheless, the Romans were aware of the type of problems that we are currently subsume under this label. Mistaken payments belong to all times and the Romans knew remedies to undo them (*condictio indebiti*). Management of another person's affairs gave rise to an action (*actio negotiorum contraria*). The *pater familias* is liable for the debts incurred by his son or his slave in as far he is enriched (*action de in rem verso*). The scope of these various actions, however, was rather limited. One of the most intriguing questions in legal history is concerned with the development of these (and other) specific remedies into one general action for unjust enrichment, as it is nowadays found in several civil law jurisdictions.

This development started in the Middle Ages. An important text to the glossators was Inst. 2.1.30. According to the Justinian original one who built on another person's property lost ownership in the building materials and was unable to bring an action for compensation, not only during the time of his possession, but all not after having lost possession. Only in case he had acted bona fide, for example, if he had a mistaken belief that he himself had full title in the building site, he was given a defense to raise when the genuine owner reclaimed his assets. The difference between the two situations is obvious. Once the owner had regained possession of his property the builder had lost every possibility to claim compensation for his expenses. Glossators such as Johannes Bassianus, Azo, and Accursius followed this line of reasoning and accepted fully every harsh consequence. Martinus Gosia, however, was of the opinion that the builder should even be allowed to bring an action for the expenses he had incurred.

Of all glossators Gosia is the scholar who made the most use of the general concept of equity (*aequitas Gosiana*) and with the help thereof he often reaches surprising conclusions given Justinian's text. He was one of the rare supporters of the buyer's right to specific performance, of the binding nature of contracts in favor of third parties, and a few other examples of equitable doctrines for which support in Justinian's text was very hard to find. The great canon lawyer Hostiensis (d. 1271) stated that Gosia took his inspiration for an important part from the Bible and canon law. Indeed, discussing the problem of the building on another person's property Gosia invokes the eighth commandment: *furtum non facies*. By giving the notion of *furtum* an extensive interpretation he reached the conclusion that the owner should in any case compensate the impoverished builder and that the latter could bring an action for this compensation.

Although Gosia did not convince his contemporaries, the point he made remained continuously under scrutiny. Angelus de Gambilionibus (Aretinus, d. 1451) remarks that Accursius followed Johannes Bassianus, but Cynus de Pistoia (d. 1336) preferred Gosia's doctrinal point of view.

Three centuries later, Hugo Grotius (1583–1645) felt the need to write for his son a systematic introduction to the jurisprudence of his day encompassing elements derived from Roman law, canon law, and contemporary indigenous law. Consequently he devoted much attention to the problem of building on another person's property and, combining the three realms of the law of the day, he chose unequivocally to allow the builder not only to raise a defense, but even to bring an action for compensation, which is a general remedy covering an area that in medieval Roman law was still divided among the specific remedies. Symon à Groenewegen van der Made (1642–1695) agreed completely and consequently he considered the text of Inst. 1.2.30 abolished for Holland and the other united provinces.

Hugo Grotius has certainly been influential on the European level, maybe less by his Introduction than by his main work *De iure belli ac pacis*. In that book he also pleaded the general remedy for unjust enrichment. Nevertheless, the main current of European jurisprudence adhered to the earlier doctrine of separate remedies of a specific nature in particular cases. Several writers felt that a well-balanced system of remedies like that found in Roman law could have been blown up only once the floodgates of a general action for unjust enrichment were opened. The French considered the general remedy as a sort of Trojan horse that would, after having been introduced within the walls, destroy the legal system from within. Consequently the French civil code followed the footsteps of Robert Joseph Pothier and laid down only a small number of specific remedies, for example, for mistaken payment and management of another person's affairs, the remedies that had survived from the Roman times onward. Several other codifications followed this example. Nevertheless many jurisdictions kept asking the question as to whether one general principle unites these specific remedies. The German BGB (1900) was the first to codify one general remedy in § 812; other codifications followed soon, notably the Greek and the Italian codification and the 1992 Dutch codification. A legal discourse that found its source in Roman times and took its modern shape in the Middle Ages, seems to have been decided in the twentieth century.

[*See also* Accursius, Franciscus; Azo; Celsus the Younger; Grotius, Hugo; Natural Law, *subentry on* Medieval and

Post-Medieval Roman Law; Pothier, Robert Joseph; *and* Ulpian.]

BIBLIOGRAPHY

Beatson, Jack, and Eltjo J. H. Schrage, eds. *Unjustified Enrichment. Cases Materials and Texts*. Ius Commune Casebooks for the Common law of Europe. Oxford, U.K., and Portland, Ore.: Hart Publications, 2003.

Flume, Werner. *Studien zur Lehre von der ungerechtfertigten Bereicherung*, edited by Wolgang Ernst. Tübingen, Germany: Mohr Siebeck, 2003.

Mitchell, Charles, and Paul Mitchell. *Landmark Cases in the Law of Restitution*. Oxford, U.K., and Portland, Ore.: Hart Publications, 2006.

Schlechtriem, P. *Restitution und Bereicherungsausgleich in Europa*. 2 vols. Tübingen, Germany: Mohr Siebeck, 2000.

Schrage, Eltjo J. H.. ed. *Unjust Enrichment and the Law of Contract*. Proceedings of a Conference in Memory of Marcel Henri Bregstein. The Hague and New York: Kluwer Law International, 2001.

Schrage, Eltjo J. H., ed. *Unjust Enrichmen:. The Comparative Legal History of the Law of Restitution*. Comparative Studies in Continental and Anglo-American Legal History/Vergleichende Untersuchungen zur kontinentaleuropäischen und anglo-amerikanischen Rechtsgeschichte, vol. 15. Berlin: Duncker und Humblot, 1995.

Schrage, Eltjo J. H. "Unjustified Enrichment. Recent Dutch Developments from a Comparative and Historical Perspective." *Netherlands International Law Review* 46 (1999): 57–86.

Eltjo J. H. Schrage

UPPER VOLTA. *See* African Law, Sub-Saharan, *subentries on* The Colonial Period *and* After Independence.

URUGUAY. Officially known as the Oriental Republic of Uruguay, this small country in southeastern Latin America possesses a predominantly civil law system, although elements from common law countries like the United States have also influenced the evolution of the country's legal institutions.

The Uruguayan legal system first developed as part of the Spanish empire. For much of the colonial period, the provincial territory was primarily a military outpost on the periphery of the Spanish realm, with sparse settlements. The principal civil institutions during this period were municipal town councils (*cabildos*), which exercized both administrative and legal authority over their respective jurisdictions. By the end of the eighteenth century, Uruguay possessed five such *cabildos*, most important the provincial (and later, national) capital of Montevideo.

The collapse of Spanish authority in 1808 inaugurated a prolonged series of domestic and international conflicts over the territory. For the first twenty years, control over Uruguay shifted between various governments in Buenos Aires and the Brazilian Empire, punctuated by a brief period of political independence under José Gervasio Artigas between 1815 and 1816. In 1828 Uruguay finally obtained formal independence as part of the Preliminary Peace Convention between Brazil and Argentina.

In preparation for independence, Uruguayan leaders engaged in a series of important legal reforms to establish basic institutional elements, many of which remain in place today. A series of enactments replaced the colonial *cabildos* with a dual system of Justices of the Peace and Local Magistrates (*Alcaldes Ordinarios*), along with a three-judge Court of Appeals.

These piecemeal reforms were formalized in the new Republic's first Constitution of July 18, 1830. In addition to confirming the established delineations of lower judicial personnel, this Constitution also created Uruguay's first Supreme Court (*Alte Corte de Justicia*). Reflecting the Constitution's emphasis on consolidating political authority in the hands of the country's conservative elites, Court members had to be persons possessing at least six years of legal experience and substantial property.

Although the 1830 Constitution had established an institutional judicial framework, the widespread militarization of the countryside forced these nascent formal legal institutions to compete with the informal, personalist justice of military leaders (*caudillos*). A chronic shortage of trained lawyers to serve in judicial posts only exacerbated this problem. Combined with widespread opposition to the formal judiciary, this meant that even the Supreme Court's inauguration had to be delayed until 1907.

By the second half of the nineteenth century, decades of endemic violence prompted a series of reformers to refashion the legal system and implant the rule of law. As part of this effort, jurists such as Eduardo Acevedo and Tristán Narvaja sought to break with antiquated legal norms by enacting new codes. The reformist drive culminated in adoption of the first Commercial Code in 1865, quickly followed by a Civil Code in 1868. These reform-minded jurists also sought to streamline the administration of justice, promulgating a Code of Civil Procedure in 1878. By 1900, the reformers had succeeded in forging at least a partially functional legal system throughout the country.

With the ascension of José Battle y Ordóñez in 1903 to the Presidency, reform accelerated. Breaking with the orthodox economic liberalism that had characterized the country's jurisprudence throughout the nineteenth century, Battle and his followers enacted a variety of broad-based social and legal reforms over the next two decades, culminating in the 1918 Constitution. The new Constitution's most important innovations, adoption of universal male suffrage and creation of a plural executive, established also a division of powers between the

President and a National Administrative Council of nine members. Under Battle, the formal structure of the judiciary remained largely unchanged, but commitment to the rule of law and establishment of the long-delayed Supreme Court gradually increased the importance of the courts.

Following the global depression of the early 1930s, a coup d'etat removed Battle's followers from power on March 30, 1933, resulting in a new Constitution that eliminated the plural executive. Though substantially more authoritarian in nature, the new Constitution, which came into effect on May 18, 1934, retained many of the social and political rights enacted under Battle. It also left the judicial branch mostly unchanged, though the document established specific procedures, for the first time, for declaring laws unconstitutional in either form or content. The steady growth in judicial authority and independence over the course of the twentieth century abruptly ended with the military coup of June 27, 1973, and the subsequent dictatorship. The new regime stripped the judiciary of its status as an independent branch of government and even shortened the Supreme Court's title to "Court." The return to democracy in 1985 brought a return to the rule of law and an independent judiciary. Since the democratic restoration, reformers have again sought to modernize the country's court system, introducing procedural reforms, as well as a system of dispute mediation.

BIBLIOGRAPHY

Barrán, José Pedro, and Benjamín Nahum. *Historia Rural Del Uruguay Moderno*. Montevideo: Ediciones de la Banda Oriental, 1967–1978. Excellent, exhaustive study of rural conditions in Uruguay throughout the latter half of the nineteenth century, stressing economic themes.

Benton, Lauren A. *Law and Colonial Cultures: Legal Regimes in World History, 1400–1900*. Cambridge, U.K., and New York: Cambridge University Press, 2002. Though only chapter 6 focuses directly on Uruguay, this is the best single source in English describing the condition of the Uruguayan legal system in the nineteenth century.

Caetano, Gerardo, and José Pedro Rilla. *História Contemporánea Del Uruguay: De La Colonia Al Siglo XXI*. Montevideo: Editorial Fin de Siglo, 2005. Excellent overview of Uruguay's history from the colonial period to the present.

Gros Espiell, Hector. *Las Constituciones Del Uruguay (Exposición, Crítica y Textos)* (Constitutions of Uruguay (Exposition, Criticism and Texts). Madrid: Ediciones Cultura Hispánica, 1956. Definitive source for Uruguay's constitutional history, especially the 1830, 1918, and 1934 constitutions.

Servicio Paz y Justicia (Uruguay). *Uruguay Nunca Más: Human Rights Violations, 1972–1985*. Philadelphia: Temple University Press, 1992. English transition of the Uruguayan government's official report on human rights violations under the 1974 to 1985 dictatorship, with interesting discussions on the suppression of the judiciary and military justice during the period.

JOSEPH P. YOUNGER

USUCAPIO. See Property, *subentry on* Roman Law.

UṢŪL AL-FIQH. See Islamic Law, *subentry on* Genres of Legal Literature.

USURPATION (GHAṢB). Usurpation (*ghaṣb*) is defined as "the illegitimate establishing of possession over the property of another person." Some authors add "by force but without causing a fear of death" or similar wordings to distinguish it from robbery and theft, for the robber and the thief are punished with a *ḥadd* punishment, whereas the usurper incurs a discretionary punishment (*taʿzīr*), which is less severe than a *ḥadd* punishment.

Jurists are concerned primarily with the rights and obligations arising from usurpation, which are common to robbery and theft. They unanimously obligate the usurper to restore the usurped thing to the owner or, according to the majority view, the legitimate possessor such as a depositary or a lessee if it remains physically and legally in the same status as it was in before the usurpation, and hold the usurper liable for the total loss or destruction that occurs to it: the usurper should pay its value if it is a nonfungible thing or provide an object of the same kind if it is a fungible thing. Although the term *ghaṣb* itself appears in the Qur'an (18:79) and possession of a usurper is regarded as representative of *yad ḍamān*—that is, usurpers are held liable for any fortuitous loss or destruction that occurs to the usurped thing—very few opinions are attributed to jurists prior to Abu Hanifa on the subject of usurpation.

It appears that the eighth-century Iraqi jurists, including Abu Hanifa, were the first to develop the cluster of rules regulating usurpation in a short period of time by applying the existing rules governing pledge, rent, the sale of a specified object, and unauthorized agency to usurpation. The eighth-century Medinese jurists, in particular Malik ibn Anas, accepted their system, to which they brought some modifications, whereas al-Shafi'i created an entirely new system based on the idea that the usurper because of the illegality of his act can by no means benefit from the usurped thing. His system was accepted by the Shafi'is and the Hanbalis. It follows that the Hanafi and Maliki rules on the one hand, and the Shafi'i and Hanbali rules on the other, are different in some important points. In the following, let us consider how the Hanafi and the Shafi'i ideas led to different positives rule, on the supposition that the usurped object is a nonfungible thing (except for item 6).

1. In case of total loss of the usurped thing, the Hanafis enable the owner to demand that the usurper pay the value as evaluated at the moment of usurpation, with the result that the usurper "proves to have been its

owner retroactively from the moment of usurpation," as a Hanafi jurist puts it. Certain Hanafi solutions indicate, however, that the retroactive attribution of ownership is fictitious. For example, if the usurper of a slave declared the slave to be free before the slave died, and subsequently the usurper paid the slave's value to his owner, the manumission proves to be null and void, so that the usurper is not the *mawlā* (patron) of the slave's offspring. The Shafi'is permit the owner to demand that the usurper pay the highest value reached by the usurped thing between the date of usurpation and that of the demand. In contrast with the Hanafis, the Shafi'is never attribute ownership to the usurper.

2. If the usurper uses the usurped thing, the Hanafis hold that the owner cannot demand that the usurper pay a rent for it, because the use of a thing, which does not represent a commodity value, cannot be the subject of indemnification without a contract that transforms the use into a commodity, as Hanafi authors put it. This rule derived, however, originally from the principle first applied to a rent that a person who profits from a thing assumes the risk of loss, and vice versa. That is to say, the eighth-century Iraqi jurists permitted usurpers to enjoy the use of the usurped thing in order to compensate for the loss that it incurs in their possession. Later Hanafis introduced a change to this classical rule by obligating the usurper of waqf land or an orphan's land to pay a fair rent. The Shafi'is enable the owner to demand that the usurper pay a fair rent in any situation.

3. If the usurper materializes the use of the usurped thing by renting it to a third party to receive a rent, the Hanafis attribute the rent to the usurper for the reason referred to in (b). However, they require it to be given as *ṣadaqa* (charity) as an unlawful gain. According to the Shafi'is, the owner can demand that the usurper pay whichever is the higher of a fair rent and the rent that the usurper received.

4. If *fructus* are produced from the usurped thing in the usurper's possession, the Hanafis and the Shafi'is unanimously hold that they belong to the owner. But according to the Hanafis, they perish at the risk of the owner; that is, the usurper's possession of the *fructus* is *yad amāna*. This rule derived originally from a rule regarding *fructus* produced from a pledge. According to the Shafi'is, they perish at the risk of the usurper, that is, possession is *yad ḍamān*.

5. If the usurper sells the usurped thing to a third party, the Hanafi rule is that the owner can choose between canceling the sale, to demand that the buyer return the object, and ratifying it. In other words, the sale is regarded as suspended (*mawqūf*). In case of ratification, the sale becomes valid as from the moment when it was concluded by the usurper. This may be an application of the rule governing unauthorized agency. The Shafi'is hold that the sale concluded by the usurper, who did not have the right to dispose of it, is null and void, so that it cannot be ratified.

6. If the usurped thing is transformed into a thing of a different kind or species—for example, the usurper uses a usurped beam to build a ship—the Hanafi rule is that the new product belongs to the usurper, who is required to compensate for the loss to the (original) owner. The Shafi'is obligate the usurper to dismantle the ship to return the beam unless it has rotted or the demand has been made at a moment when it would cause danger to persons or goods on the ship. Finally, *ghaṣb* as a legal term is used also in the meaning of rape.

[*See also* Abu Hanifa, al-Nuʿman ibn Thabit; Islamic Schools of Sacred Law, *subentries on* Sunni Schools: The Hanafi School of Law *and* Sunni Schools: The Maliki School of Law, Part 1; Malik ibn Anas ibn Malik al-Asbahi; Obligations, *subentry on* Islamic Law; *and* Shafi'i, Muhammad ibn Idris al-.]

BIBLIOGRAPHY

Hakim, Jacques el-. *Le dommage de source délictuelle en droit musulman: Survivance en droit syrien et libanais*. Paris: Librairie Générale de Droit et de Jurisprudence, 1964.

Ibn Rushd. *The Distinguished Jurist's Primer: A Translation of Bidayat al-Mujtahid*. Translated by Imran Ahsan Khan Nyazee. 2 vols. Reading, U.K.: Garnet Publishing, 1996.

Johansen, Baber. *The Islamic Law on Land Tax and Rent: The Peasants' Loss of Property Rights as Interpreted in the Hanafite Legal Literature of the Mamluk and Ottoman Periods*. London and New York: Croom Helm, 1988.

Schacht, Joseph. *An Introduction to Islamic Law*. Oxford, U.K.: Clarendon Press, 1964.

Yanagihashi, Hiroyuki. *A History of the Early Islamic Law of Property: Reconstructing the Legal Development, 7th–9th Centuries*. Leiden, Netherlands, and Boston: E. J. Brill, 2004.

Hiroyuki Yanagihashi

USURY. [*This entry contains two subentries, on usury in Islamic law and in medieval and post-medieval Roman law.*]

Illicit Commercial Gain (*Ribā*) in Islamic Law

"God hath permitted sale and forbidden usury" (Qurʾan 2:275). According to Muslim scholars, this verse was revealed after some of the Prophet's contemporaries questioned the relevance of *ribā* and affected to see in the condemnation of *ribā* the disapproval of profit generated by sale transactions. As a matter of fact, verse 275 is interpreted to say that gain from commercial dealing, such as sale, is approved, whereas gain derived from a loan agreement is prohibited because it is not the product of entrepreneurial skill in a legitimate business endeavor.

Early History. The Qur'anic prohibition of *ribā* is limited to loan agreements and is found in four suras (30:39, 4:161, 3:130, 2:275–279). The first sura was revealed in Mecca and the remaining three in Medina.

Sunna (the deeds, utterances, and unspoken approvals of the Prophet as reported by his Companions in hadith) extended the Qur'anic prohibition to the exchange of currencies (gold and silver) and denominated articles (wheat, barley, dates, and salt).

Nearly all Islamic schools of law widened the prohibition of *ribā* beyond the six articles mentioned by the Sunna, on the ground of analogy. Nonetheless, they often dissented when it came to the interpretation of the underlying principle or objective of a shari'a injunction, that is, its efficient cause (*'illat al-ḥukm*), which should connect the object of the analogy with its subject.

Definition. In view of the Qur'anic prohibition, which is limited to loan agreements, and in view of the widening of the *ribā* prohibition by the Sunna and its further widening by jurisprudence, *ribā* can be defined as follows:

Ribā by way of excess (*ribā al-faḍl*) is the unlawful gain derived from the inequality of the countervalues in any transaction purporting to effect the exchange of two or more species that belong to the same genus and are governed by the same efficient cause (*'illat*). *Ribā* by way of deferment (*ribā al-nasī'a*) results from the deferral of the completion of the exchange of species that belong to the same genus, or even of species that belong to different genera but are governed by the same efficient cause, whether or not the deferment is accompanied by an increase in any of the exchanged countervalues.

For the Hanafi school of law, *ribā* by way of excess takes place when, in a hand-to-hand transaction involving an excess in one of the countervalues, the two elements of the Hanafi efficient cause exist, namely that the exchanged countervalues belong to the same genus and have the property of both being weighable or measurable when they change hands. It is not required that the quality be identical; otherwise, the exchange would be meaningless. A deferred transaction gives rise to *ribā al-nasī'a* for the Hanafis if and when articles of the same genus, or with the property of being both weighable or both measurable, are exchanged with deferment, whether or not there is an excess in one of the countervalues.

Shafi'is see *ribā* by way of excess (*ribā al-faḍl*) as occurring when, in a hand-to-hand transaction which involves an excess in one of the countervalues, their *'illat*—that is, their being currency or their being foodstuffs—and their requisite for the purpose of *ribā*—that is, their being species subordinate to the same genus—are both present. There is *ribā* by way of deferment (*ribā al nasī'a*) for the Shafi'is when the exchange of countervalues which are all foodstuffs or all currencies, whether or not they belong to the same genus, is delayed.

Legal Stratagems. From the outset the prohibition of *ribā* was a great burden to Muslims in their daily dealings. Scholars, as we will see immediately below, endeavored to interpret that prohibition in a restricted sense. In addition, a carefully contrived range of legal stratagems (*ḥiyal*) through which various transactions could take place, developed in countries where the Hanafi and Shafi'i schools were prevalent. One of these stratagems is *mukhāṭara* or *'īna*, in which the borrower buys a trivial object from the lender on credit for, say, 110 dinars, then on the spot the lender buys back the same object for 100 dinars payable immediately; as a result the lender has effectively lent 110 dinars to the borrower at 10% interest. Another way of securing a markup on the price, which often includes a surcharge for deferred payment, is nonetheless acceptable to most scholars: person A entrusts person B to buy an object from person C for, say, 100 dinars in cash on the understanding that person A will buy the same object from person B for 110 dinars, which is often paid at a later date or by installments. That is the *murābaha* transaction favored by modern Islamic banks.

Restricted Interpretations. A few Companions of the Prophet, most prominent among them Ibn 'Abbas, considered that the only unlawful *ribā* is the pre-Islamic one manifested by the lender when he or she asks the borrower at maturity date: will you settle the debt or increase it? For them, *ribā al-nasī'a* as well as *ribā al-faḍl*, object of the famous hadith, are lawful. Ibn 'Abbas's view was taken up by a contemporary Muslim scholar, Zaydan Abu al-Karim Hassan, in 1980, in the magazine *Al-Azhar*.

Ibn Qayyin al-Jawziyya, a famous Hanbali scholar, taught that *ribā al-nasi'a* cannot become lawful except in the case of pressing necessity (*ḍarūra muljī'a*), like that which allows the eating of carrion. On the other hand, *ribā al-faḍl* can be lawful in case of need (*ḥāja*) only.

Sheikh Mohammed 'Abduh (1849–1905), who ended his life as Grand Mufti of Egypt, considered that the only disallowed *ribā* is the pre-Islamic one which is the manifest (*jali*) *ribā* and consequently is prohibited not as a way of performing a usurious transaction but as a usurious transaction in itself. As for the two other sorts of *ribā*, namely *ribā al-faḍl* and *ribā al-nasī'a* (both provided for in hadith and not in the Qur'an), their prohibition tends to close the loopholes which otherwise might allow manifest *ribā* (*ribā jali*). Thus the sale of any of the six articles mentioned in the hadith, with an increase and whether in a hand-to-hand transaction or in a deferred one, is disallowed only if it is intended to lead to manifest *ribā* (*ribā jali*), which takes place when interest occurs on interest already accounted by the time the transaction was concluded. Faithful to his view, Sheikh 'Abduh declared that "moderate" interest on deposited capital was legal.

Recent Developments. Following the demise of the Ottoman Empire (1918), countries of the Levant (Lebanon,

Syria, Palestine), as well as Iraq, legalized, or at least tolerated, the collection of interest on commercial loans.

Decades later, the Gulf States achieved independence (Kuwait was the first, in 1961) and turned toward Egypt—which already had a developed legal system in the Arabic language—to organize their own legal system. Egyptian law had been inspired for hundreds of years by French law. This in turn was transmitted to the sets of laws of the newly independent states.

Following the French model, the Gulf States—with the exception of Saudi Arabia, where shariʻa has remained paramount—distinguish two branches of the law: commercial law, which applies to merchants and governs acts of trade; and civil law, which governs ordinary consumer transactions. Taking advantage of this distinction, the authorities of the Gulf States legalized the collection of interest on commercial loans (Article 102 of the 1980 Kuwaiti Commercial Code; Article 81, amended in 1992, of the 1987 Bahraini Commercial Code; Articles 80 and 81 of the 1990 Omani Commercial Code). Collecting interest on noncommercial transactions remained prohibited.

Most controversial was the fatwa on *riba* issued in 1989 by the Mufti of Egypt, Sheikh Muhammad Sayyid Tantawi, in which he declared that interest, or certain interest-based government investments, were not disallowed *ribā*. Tantawi based his opinion on Qurʼan and hadith, the search for the truth, personal reasoning, rejection of fanaticism, and the need to resort to experts in their field to unravel arcane issues.

[*See also* Banking and Finance in Islamic Law; Commercial Law, *subentries on* Islamic Law; *and* Loan, *subentry on* Islamic Law.]

BIBLIOGRAPHY

Ray, Nicholas Dylan. *Arab Islamic Banking and the Renewal of Islamic Law*. London: Graham & Trotman, 1995.

Saleh, Nabil A. *Unlawful Gain and Legitimate Profit in Islamic Law: Riba, Gharar, and Islamic Banking*. 2d ed. London: Graham & Trotman, 1992.

Sanhuri, ʻAbd al-Razzaq al-. *Masadir al-haqq fi al-fiqh al-Islami: Dirasah muqaranah fi-al-fiqh al-gharbi*. 6 vols. Beirut: Manshurat Muhammad al-Dayah, n.d.

Vogel, Frank E., and Samuel L. Hayes III. *Islamic Law and Finance: Religion, Risk, and Return*. The Hague: Kluwer Law International, 1998.

Warde, Ibrahim. *Islamic Finance in the Global Economy*. Edinburgh: Edinburgh University Press, 2000.

NABIL SALEH

Medieval and Post-Medieval Roman Law

The Latin term *usura* denotes, generally, the use of an object. In relation to money, *usurae* are the interests accruing—as though measuring use into the money itself—during a specified period of time, such as a month or a year; similarly, *faenus* (or *foenus*) refers generally to earnings and specifically to interest. Rules about these are to be found, above all, in Justinian's *Digests* (D.22.1) and *Codex* (C.4.32).

The payment of interest could be legally compulsory. Regional practices were incorporated into the *Digest*'s judgments on this. An especially important instance of legally compulsory interest was when a debtor went into arrears (*mora*, delay). The rate of default interest was, already in antiquity and still in the Middle Ages and into modernity, in a constant state of flux: these interest rates were generally between 4 and 12 percent per year. Default interest was seen as a flat adjustment to make up for the losses incurred by the creditor through the delay.

The question of to what extent one could contractually set interest rates was of extraordinary economic and social importance. *Usurae* (*faenus*) and the respective words in the national languages—for example, in German *Wucher*, in English "usury"—denote, alongside interest, also the transaction of rate setting, and there, most particularly, credit with interest. Because transactions with interest were seen as offensive and were allowed within only narrow bounds, the word *usurae* and its national-language counterparts also gained the general meaning of an unbalanced, exploitative contract.

Roman law allowed a pledge of interest to be included in a contract. If the payment in question was through a consensual contract (*obligatio consensu, contractus bonae fidei*), such as sale, then the pledge of interest was informal, though the boundaries of good morality (*boni mores*) were to be maintained. For other contracts a person pledged interest through a stipulation. All these contracts required an *obligatio verbis*: that is, a formal oral transaction—if possible, accomplished before a witness—or a written transaction set down in a legal document (*instrumentum*) or in another sort of writ (*alia scriptura*).

A transaction was, above all, required for contracts of credit (*mutuum*). In principle such contracts engendered no obligations of interest, but the receiver of credit could pledge interest to the creditor in a stipulation to the actual contract of *mutuum*. For this, however, it was not sufficient for the receiver of credit simply to make a promise upon receipt of the sum of credit—that is, where the pledge of interest was solely an aspect of the contract of credit; rather, a separate pledge was necessary. That said, if the receiver of credit did pay interest that had been informally pledged (i.e., without a stipulation), then that receiver could not demand the interest back as a payment that was not legally required. Throughout history, up to the twenty-first century, there has remained a conceptual separation between credit itself and an agreement upon interest for credit. Since the end of the twentieth century, consumer-protection laws have required that credit with interest be agreed upon in writing, in a way reminiscent of the stipulation.

Free or informal agreements of interest have been mistrusted since Roman law in antiquity. Both under Christian rulership and before that, there were caps on interest rates, which were differentiated according to person and circumstances. Further, interest was not allowed to rise above the principal sum (*sors*). This latter condition was interpreted as meaning that creditors could insist on interest from an unlimited stipulation only until the sum of all paid and remaining interest reached the original capital sum. Thus not only was back interest limited, but the creditor was also forced after a certain time—in the course of normal repayment—either to insist on a return of the money or to let it stand with the receiver of credit, without interest. In addition, any pledge to pay interest upon interest (*usurarum usurae*, or compound interest) was legally void. One could, however, retroactively combine the interest (when it was paid, at any rate) to form a new credit, and then could agree upon interest for that credit.

The provisos against collecting interest were strengthened in the Middle Ages and modernity, influenced by the bans on interest in the Bible and in canon law. Clerics were stripped of their positions if they offered credit with interest or did so through intermediaries. In the confrontation between Roman law, which was fundamentally tolerant of interest, and canon law, canon law was considered stronger because it was divine law (*ius divinum*); the ban on interest was enforced not only in the church court but also in the secular court. No one, whether Christian or not, was to require interest of a Christian. Interest was forbidden in order to prevent people from becoming covetous instead of diligent. To take interest on credit was seen as selling time itself; time, however, could not be sold, because it was at the disposition of everyone. A further argument was that money was, by nature, barren (*sterilis*). This particular basis for a ban on interest was later withdrawn because it was realized that many things become fruitful through human diligence.

In early modern times, interest on credit at moderate rates came to be seen as not necessarily forbidden by canon law, divine law, or natural law (*ius naturale*). This depended on the credit's use (*lucrum*, or gain) by the recipient and the outlay (*impensa*), waiver (*lucrum cessans*), or loss (*damnum*) to the creditor, as well as on the risk that the creditor would lose his or her capital outright (*periculum amittendae sortis*); this was also restricted by the injunction that one not demand credit of a poor person, to whom one should rather be giving alms. The inherent risk had already brought forth in antiquity special regulations for nautical credit (*faenus nauticum*). During the Middle Ages and early modernity countless regulations developed that allowed interest up to certain limits, as well as special terms for Jewish moneylenders. In addition to interest for nautical credit, traders in antiquity could often demand up to 12 percent per year, while others might demand up to 8 percent; this was antiquity's provision for traders. Grotius saw the interpretation of interest as a risk premium, to be described alongside the insurance contract (*assecuratio*).

Creditors sought through numerous contractual configurations to bypass the strict limits on interest. They stipulated reimbursement of capital through the delivery of goods of a higher value, or insisted that goods be pledged in addition to the return of the capital. Or credit was disguised as a sale to the creditor with the understanding that repurchase would take place at a higher price. In cases where the recipient of credit truly had an object of some value, this served the creditor as security; for fictitious sales, an object of no great value sufficed, which the creditor would nonetheless dispose of in extreme circumstances. Another popular strategy was the masking of credit as the sale of a pension. Such practices were forbidden, to the extent that they gutted the regulation of interest.

One may see how enduring was the animus against transactions of interest in that the laws of the nineteenth century still found it necessary expressly to allow the taking of interest. The question of interest-taking was shunted, though, to the field of ideological conflict—with Karl Marx in his description of finance capitalists as those with whom industrial capitalists share the excess value extracted from the production of the workers, and under German Nazism with the anti-Semitic position seen in the "breaking of the thralldom to interest" that was described as a "steel axis" and in the "abolition of work-free and effortless income" (point 11 of the party program of the German National Socialist Workers' Party, 1920).

Pledges of compound interest are today still fundamentally legally void in Germany. Banks, however, may pledge interest on the interest that accrues on and is added into accounts. The open account, too, makes it possible to add interest to the capital and pay interest on both; this option is, however, closed in cases of consumer credit as soon as the consumer's account falls in arrears. The clause that did not allow interest to grow to be greater than the capital sum has now been abandoned.

[*See also* Baldus de Ubaldis, Petrus; Bartolus of Saxoferrato; Credit in Medieval and Post-Medieval Roman Law; Grotius, Hugo; Natural Law, *subentry on* Medieval and Post-Medieval Roman Law; Pufendorf, Samuel von; and Wolff, Christian von.]

BIBLIOGRAPHY

PRIMARY WORKS

Accursius, Franciscus (1182–1260). [Corpus Iuris Civilis.] Lyon, France, 1589. See columns 2038–2065 (on D.22.1).

Azo, Portius (d. c. 1230). *Summa aurea*. Lyon, France, 1557. See folios 97–99 (on C.4.32).

Baldus de Ubaldis, Petrus (1320/1327–1400). *In quartum et quintum codicis libros commentaria*. Venice, Italy, 1586. See folios 87–95 (on C.4.32).

Bartolus de Saxoferrato (1313–1357). *Commentaria in primam codicis partem*. Lyon, France, 1547. See folios 180–183 (on C.4.32).

Denari, Odofredo (d. 1265). *In primam codicis partem*. Lyon, France, 1552. See folios 234–237 (on C.4.32).

Grotius, Hugo (1583–1645). *The Rights of War and Peace*. Edited by Richard Tuck. Indianapolis: Liberty Fund 2005. See sections 2.12.20–2.12.23.

Molinaeus, Carolus (1500–1566). *Tractatus commerciorum, contractuum et usurarum, redituumque pecunia constitutorum et monetarum*. Cologne, Germany, 1606.

Pufendorf, Samuel (1632–1694). *On the Duty of Man and Citizen according to Natural Law*. Edited by James Tully and translated by Michael Silverthorne. Cambridge: Cambridge University Press, 1991. See p. 101 (section 1.15.11).

Wolff, Christian (1679–1754). *Institutiones juris naturae et gentium*. Halle, Germany, 1750. See pp. 367–369 (sections 649–651).

SECONDARY LITERATURE

Coing, Helmut. *Europäisches Privatrecht*. 2 vols. Munich, Germany: Beck, 1985–1989. See vol. 1, pp. 437, 478–480, 535, and 553, and vol. 2, pp. 492–493 and 553.

Noonan, John. *The Scholastic Analysis of Usury*. Cambridge, Mass.: Harvard University Press, 1957.

Tafaro, Sebastiano, ed. *L'usura ieri and oggi* (Usury Yesterday and Today). Bari, Italy: Cacucci, 1997.

Zimmermann, Reinhard. *The Law of Obligations: Roman Foundations of the Civilian Tradition*. Cape Town, South Africa: Juta, 1990. See pp. 166–177.

CHRISTOPH BECKER
Translated from the German by Ira Allen

USUS MODERNUS PANDECTARUM. *See* Civil Law, *subentry on* Medieval and Post-Medieval Roman Law.

VANUATU. *See* Melanesia.

VATTEL, EMER DE (1714–1767). Swiss specialist in international law. Emer de Vattel was born on April 25, 1714, at Couvet in Neuchâtel, at the time a principality of Prussia that was also associated with the Swiss cantons. This is important to note because it explains his liberalism and lack of prejudice: "I am born," he wrote later, "in a country in which freedom is the soul, the treasure, and the fundamental law; due to my origin I could be the friend of all nations." Vattel's father was a priest at Couvet and later on at Saint Aubin, also in Neuchâtel. For this reason, Vattel was destined to become a priest, too. He started his studies of theology at the University of Basel and went to Geneva in 1733 with the intention of consolidating his knowledge in theology and metaphysics. In Geneva he turned toward philosophy and became a supporter of the German scholars Gottfried Wilhelm Leibniz and Christian von Wolff, whom he defended against criticism, especially by theologians.

In 1742, Vattel traveled to Berlin, hoping in vain to be assigned diplomatic functions by the Prussian king Frederick II. In Berlin he stayed with his friend Jean-Henri-Samuel Formey, the secretary of the Prussian Academy of Sciences and a supporter of Christian Wolff as well. At the invitation of Heinrich, Count von Brühl, the prime minister of the elector of Saxony, Vattel went to Dresden in 1743 and 1746. In 1747 he was appointed minister resident of Frederick Augustus II, the king of Poland and the elector of Saxony, for the canton of Bern for the period from 1749 to 1758. Being irregularly or not remunerated in this function, Vattel was forced to live in Neuchâtel. It was during this period and because of his not being kept very busy by his diplomatic charge that he wrote his masterpiece *Le droit des gens, ou Principes de la loi naturelle, appliqués à la conduite et aux affaires des nations et des souverains* (The Law of Nations, or Principles of Natural Law Applied to the Conduct and Affairs of Nations and Sovereigns), which he published in 1758 in London.

In 1763, Frederick Augustus called Vattel back to Dresden and appointed him his secret counsel. In l764, Vattel married Marie-Anne, Baronne du Chêne de Ramelot, and in 1766 his son Charles Adolphe Maurice was born. In the same year Vattel traveled to Neuchâtel for recreation as his health weakened; he returned to Dresden only to come back to Neuchâtel in 1767, where he died December 28.

Vattel also wrote a great number of essays on literary and aesthetic subjects, but *Le droit des gens*, influenced by the ideas of Christian von Wolff, remains the most renowned of his works. It was published in three volumes and went through twenty-one editions in the original French version, twenty-one editions in English, and six in Spanish, as well as one in German and one in Italian. *Le droit des gens* had a great influence on the development of international law, especially in the United States, where it was quoted not only by secretaries of state but also by federal judges in cases involving international and intrastate law.

[*See also* International Law; Leibniz, Gottfried Wilhelm; Natural Law, *subentry on* Medieval and Post-Medieval Roman Law; *and* Wolff, Christian von.]

BIBLIOGRAPHY

Béguelin, Édouard. "En souvenir de Vattel." In *Recueil des travaux offert par la Faculté de droit de l'Université de Neuchâtel à la Société Suisse des Juristes à l'occasion de sa réunion à Neuchâtel, 15–17 septembre 1929*, pp. 33–176. Neuchâtel, Switzerland: Imprimerie P. Attinger, 1929.

Guggenheim, Paul. *Emer de Vattel et l'étude des relations internationales en Suisse*. Geneva, Switzerland: Georg et Cie, 1956.

Manz, Johannes J. *Emer de Vattel: Versuch einer Würdigung*. Zurich, Switzerland: Schulthess, 1971.

Theodor Bühler

VENEZUELA. The territory of the present Bolivarian Republic of Venezuela was conquered by Spain in the sixteenth century, but colonization proceeded slowly; not until the eighteenth century did Venezuela become a prosperous colony. A university with a legal faculty was founded in Caracas in 1724, and the Audiencia (High Court) was established there in 1786.

After Independence. Venezuela declared independence on July 5, 1811, and approved the first constitution in December 1811. A bloody civil war ensued. Between 1821 and 1830, Venezuela was part of Colombia, under the leadership of Simón Bolívar. The Venezuelan Congress approved a new constitution in 1830 and in the following three decades passed a number of statutes, including a procedural code (1836). Spanish law remained in force until the 1860s when modern codes were adopted

(Commercial Code, 1862; Civil Code, 1867; Penal Code, 1873). After an extended period of war, Venezuela adopted a federal constitution in 1864. Even though there were nominally organs of national power, this Constitution embodied the acceptance of the disintegration of the country and domination by regional war lords (*caudillos*). Civil wars continued until the early twentieth century.

Twentieth Century. This situation changed during the rule of General Juan Vicente Gómez from 1909 to 1935. Building a national army and police force, he centralized the country and disposed of the *caudillos* and any other opposition with brutal methods. He became the quintessential dictator, though elected president several times by constitutional procedures. At the same time Gómez called upon the most important jurists of his time to modernize legislation and the legal system. Under his successors a liberalization of the regime ensued. After a short and disorderly revolution in 1945, Venezuela experienced another period of military dictatorship between 1948 and 1958. Democracy was reestablished in 1958, but corruption and human rights abuses by the police and the army alienated the population from the political parties and other representative institutions. In 1998 the population elected Hugo Chávez, who promoted a change of constitution in 1999. A radical change proposed in 2007 was not accepted in referendum.

Venezuela clearly is part of the civil-law tradition. It adopted modern constitutions and codes, as well as the style of teaching and legal literature of continental Europe. In comparison with other civil-law countries, substantive legal rules were progressive. Torture and punishments attaching infamy to family members were prohibited from the early constitutions onward, slavery was suppressed in 1854 and the death penalty in 1864, elementary education became mandatory and free of charge in the 1870s, and civil marriage and civil registries were established in the 1880s and divorce in 1904. But as the country was engulfed in civil wars and had an antiquated economic structure, its modern legal paraphernalia and courts had little social significance in the nineteenth century. The number of lawyers was small, at about the ratio of late colonial society (ten for every 100,000 inhabitants).

The Law Revived. In the twentieth century, civil peace and the subsequent discovery of oil allowed rapid economic growth. The state apparatus grew, and services like health and education were provided by the state. During the second half of the century the state became highly regulatory and interventionist, which made law very complicated. Many universities and law schools were created and lawyers' numbers increased rapidly, reaching 290 per 100,000 inhabitants in the year 2000. Legal scholarship developed, especially during the democratic regime. In this period (1958–1998) Venezuela signed all human rights treaties and promoted legislation for protection against abuses. In practice, however, many human rights abuses occurred, particularly affecting the poor. Regulatory policies, though initially very successful, became a source of corruption and an obstacle to economic development, particularly during the 1980s.

The 1990s were particularly rich from the perspective of a movement for law and judicial reform. The country became decentralized and free-market policies opened the economy. Innovative law schools opened their doors. The Supreme Court became an important arbiter of political and economic conflicts, and the judiciary gained in importance, exposing the inadequacies of the law and the judicial system. A comprehensive judicial reform was attempted along the lines of World Bank policies. A new criminal procedure, oral and accusatorial, was established. But all these reforms failed to overcome the intense political crisis.

As a consequence of the political turmoil, a complete outsider was elected president in 1998. Lieutenant Colonel Chávez was an unknown quantity when he became a candidate but emerged a strong leader with enormous appeal to much of the population. A new constituent assembly was convened in 1999 and produced a new constitution which increased the power of the executive, and converted the legislative to a unicameral body and decreased its power.

Venezuela has had universal suffrage since 1947. All citizens over eighteen years of age vote directly for the president, deputies of the National Assembly, state governors, state legislative councils, and mayors. According to the 1999 Constitution, the president is the head of state and the head of the government. He appoints the vice-president and determines the size and composition of his cabinet. The National Assembly has 167 deputies with three seats reserved for indigenous people (one percent of the population). Deputies are elected for five-year terms, the president for six-year terms, renewable once, and the Supreme Court justices are elected by the National Assembly for twelve-year terms, which are not renewable. A constitutional amendment is under consideration to increase the president's term in office to seven years, eliminate any limit on his reelection, and increase his power.

Socialist Venezuela. President Chávez has proclaimed a socialist revolution. Rule of law and judicial independence are no longer valued. The Supreme Court has been purged three times and staffed with more compliant justices and has consequently diminished in importance. Most of the problems of the 1990s, particularly high rates of violent crime and corruption scandals, have worsened. Corruption scandals have affected even the justices of the Supreme Court. Human rights violations, especially crimes by the police, are on the rise, and property rights have been curtailed. Foreign investments in oil have been restricted, and businesses in important areas like telecommunications, agriculture, electricity, and television have come under direct state control.

[*See also* Colombia *and* South and Central America, *subentry* Overview.]

Venezuelan Election. Venezuelan President Hugo Chávez (*left*) speaks with Christopher Thomas, under-secretary of the Organization of American States and head of the OAS election observers, following Venezuela's constitutional assembly election, Caracas, July 1999. AP PHOTO

BIBLIOGRAPHY

Bello Lozano, Humberto. *Historia de las fuentes e instituciones jurídicas venezolanas* (History of the Juridical Sources and Institutions of Venezuela). Caracas: Editorial Estrados, 1966. Although dated, it is the only book that attempts to cover the entire history of law in Venezuela. A fifth edition was published in 1983.

Carrera Damas, Germán. *Una nación llamada Venezuela* (A Nation Called Venezuela). Caracas: Universidad Central de Venezuela, 1980. A general history of Venezuela by the most noted Venezuelan contemporary historian.

Clagett, Helen L. *A Guide to the Law and Legal Literature of Venezuela*. Washington, D.C.: Library of Congress, 1947. Very useful for the legal literature until the mid-1940s.

Lombardi, John V. *Venezuela: The Search for Order, the Dream of Progress*. New York: Oxford University Press, 1982. A useful general history in English.

Pérez Perdomo, Rogelio. *Los abogados en Venezuela: Estudio de una elite intelectual y política 1780–1980* (Attorneys in Venezuela: A Study of an Intellectual and Political Elite 1780–1980). Caracas: Monte Ávila Editores, 1981. A history of legal education and lawyers' occupational and political roles.

Pérez Perdomo, Rogelio. "Judicialization and Regime Change: The Venezuelan Supreme Court." In *The Judicialization of Politics in Latin America*, edited by Rachel Sieder, L. Schjolden and A. Angell. Basingstoke, U.K.: Palgrave Macmillan, 2005. A history of the ups and downs of the Supreme Court in the last fifteen years.

ROGELIO PÉREZ PERDOMO

VICARIOUS LIABILITY. [*This entry contains two subentries, on vicarious liability in English common law and in medieval and post-medieval Roman law.*]

English Common Law

"Vicarious liability" is a concept deployed in the modern law of torts, comprehending the imposition of liability as a result of a tortious act or omission of another with whom the defendant had some preexisting legal relationship, such as that of master and servant, where that relationship had some connection with the circumstances leading up to the commission of the tort sufficient that it is not necessary to demonstrate the defendant's personal blameworthiness. As such, vicarious liability (generally in addition to, rather than in the place of, the servant's own liability) is perceived to be an exception to a supposed general principle of "no liability without fault" that—despite the fragmentation of remedies by the different forms of action, concealment arising from the inarticulate role of the jury, and distortion consequent upon allegations in pleadings not required to be proved in evidence—is discernible in England by around the early eighteenth century, if not earlier.

Origins. The history of the liability of masters for the wrongful acts and omissions of servants is closely linked with the wider history of what became the action for damages for negligence. So what has often, despite the pointed absence of any allegation of negligence, been regarded as the first case in which the common law recognized liability for negligence in carrying on one's own affairs (that is, in the absence of a positive assumption of responsibility to the plaintiff or a custom of the realm), *Mitchell v. Allestry* (1676), has also been regarded as the beginning of the line of cases settling the scope of a master's liability for a servant's wrongs. Previously, such a claim might have taken the form of trespass, making no mention of the involvement of any servant, with any issue about a master's liability for the wrong of his servant concealed by the usual general plea of "not guilty" and left to the jury's assessment of the evidence at trial. The use of actions on the case, necessarily accompanied by greater elaboration of the facts in the pleadings, made it easier for the true basis of the claim to be stated. From the late eighteenth century, a line of cases articulated rules concerning a master's tortious liability for servants' wrongs. This was in part due to the trend toward more explicit pleading, the increasing use of the device of reserving points of law arising on the evidence at trial, and the expansion of nisi prius reporting.

The scope of liability, when not presented as the result of natural reasoning or derived from general reference to considerations of public policy and convenience, was justified by reference to the maxims *respondeat superior* (let the superior answer) and *qui facit per alium facit per se* (who acts through another acts for himself), whereby a master was regarded as acting through the instrumentality of a servant or agent. These maxims, derived from early medieval canon law and long part of the common learning of English judges, found new applications in the context of the shifts in the forms of pleadings and practice, bringing to the surface issues about the responsibility of one person for the acts of another that had formerly been latent in the pleadings or left to the jury.

Disquiet about the apparent expansion of liability was being articulated from early in the nineteenth century, as in the complaint by the editor of the report of *Weyland v. Elkins* (1816), where the proprietor of a wagon was held liable for the negligence and misconduct of the driver, despite having had no actual control over the driver at the time of the accident, and despite the driver's having being hired and paid by the defendant's partner, the horse's owner, who was not sued. According to the reporter, the responsibility of the master for the acts of his servant had been extended by recent cases "to a length beyond the ordinary course of practice," including even cases where a contractor had been engaged and the wrong was not committed by an agent or servant in the master's direct employment. Lest this responsibility be carried further, contrary to both reason and the principles of general equity, the editor emphasized that the principle must be duly understood to be that liability depended upon express command, a reasonable presumption of a general command, or some absence of due care and control by the master, either in choice of servant or in the immediate act itself; thus, liability should not be imposed where the injury could not be foreseen or prevented by the master, in the sense of "growing out of the particular service" and occurring during its performance, contrasting this with a willful and independent act committed by a servant from his or her own malice, without reference to the master's business. Furthermore, it is generally supposed that the midcentury articulation of the doctrine of common employment (in America, the fellow-servant rule), whereby a master would not be liable, in the absence of personal fault, for injuries sustained by one employee through the fault of another employee (based upon a supposed consensual submission to risk), was a device to limit the scope of the emergent modern rules about masters' liability. Yet the pattern of imposing tortious liability on masters for physical and economic injuries suffered in consequence of the acts of servants and agents continued, especially, from midcentury, in litigation against railway and other companies created following the enactment of modern companies legislation; and despite a vociferous defense by employer interests before an 1877 Select Committee of the House of Commons on Employers' Liability for Injuries to Their Servants, the doctrine of common employment was ameliorated by workmen's compensation legislation and eventually abolished.

The Modern Analysis. By the 1870s there was a developing recognition that the routine citation of the maxims (one a bald statement of conclusion, the other being based on a fiction) was an inadequate basis upon which to explain the trends in the case law, whereby, for example, liability might be imposed even though the servant had acted directly contrary to instructions or where the court chose to discern a nondelegable duty incumbent upon the employer, and where a less than strict view was often taken of when a servant had "deviated onto a frolic." Perhaps influenced by terminological usage in Scottish judicial reasoning and legal writing concerning delictual liability, the 1870s marked the beginning of the displacement of the maxims through a process of infiltration of the concept of "vicarious liability" into the position of being, by the early to mid-twentieth century, the central Anglo-American idea around which to group the doctrinal analysis of the tortious liability of employers, masters, principals, and corporations for the acts of their servants, agents, and officers, although the old maxims continue to be cited periodically, despite generally being regarded as useless.

The challenge posed to basing liability on the maxims was particularly acute where the act or omission was fraudulent, and it was in a line of fraud cases that the terminology of vicarious liability first came into regular use by the courts. This culminated in *Lloyd v. Grace, Smith & Co* (1912), where it was held that a master might be liable even if an agent's fraudulent act was for the agent's own benefit, and the master had not profited from it.

In 1916 Thomas Baty's polemical *Vicarious Liability* set out an attack on the trend of the cases since the late seventeenth century that had culminated in *Lloyd* (describing the apparent "luxuriant growth" of employer liability as based upon "a tissue of misapprehensions"). The debate continued for several decades at least, seeking to reconcile High Victorian individualist principles of common law with the social and economic realities of the industrial age. There was a continuing sense that vicarious liability was unnatural and only defensible, if at all, on grounds of policy or expediency, and the pejorative tone of the terminological usage only gradually fell away over the course of the first half of the twentieth century, once the basic idea of employers' strict enterprise liability became generally conceded and the debate had moved on to points of detail such as concerning the effect on the employer's liability of some special defense available to the servant or agent, or the analysis of issues concerning contributory negligence. The American scholar (and later Supreme Court justice) William O. Douglas had adopted a realist analysis of employer liability in 1929, and in the latter part of the twentieth century this approach triumphed. Conceding that the old test of "course of employment" would exclude employer liability for sexual abuse committed by employees put in a position of trust, the courts substituted a wider, policy-driven test of mere "close connection" informed by risk internalization and efficiency considerations.

[*See also* Company Law, *subentry on* English Common Law; Employment and Labor Law, *subentry on* English Common Law; Negligence; *and* Tort, *subentries on* English Common Law *and* Tort, Negligence, and Delict.]

BIBLIOGRAPHY

Atiyah, Patrick S. *Vicarious Liability in the Law of Torts*. London: Butterworths, 1967.

Baty, Thomas. *Vicarious Liability: A Short History of the Liability of Employers, Principals, Partners, Associations, and Trade-Union Members, with a Chapter on the Laws of Scotland and Foreign States*. Oxford, U.K.: Clarendon Press, 1916.

Douglas, William O. "Vicarious Liability and Administration of Risk." *Yale Law Journal* 38 (1929): 584–604.

Ibbetson, David. "The Tort of Negligence in the Common Law in the Nineteenth and Twentieth Centuries." In *Negligence: The Comparative Legal History of the Law of Torts*. Edited by Eljto J. H. Schrage. pp. 229, 248–252. Berlin: Duncker & Humblot, 2001.

Isaacs, Nathan. "Fault and Liability: Two Views of Legal Development." *Harvard Law Review* 31 (1918): 954–979.

Mark C. McGaw

Medieval and Post-Medieval Roman Law

The archetype of vicarious liability in Europe was the Roman noxal liability: when slaves or minor children had committed a delict, the *paterfamilias* could either surrender the wrongdoer or pay a fixed penalty. Roman law recognized other instances of liability for the acts of others without, however, developing a general principle. Some of these instances survived through the period of the *ius commune* and had a strong impact on the development of vicarious liability in post-medieval times. In the case of the *actio de deiectis vel effusis* a householder was held responsible if something was thrown out or poured down from his dwelling; it did not matter whether he himself, a member of his household, or any other person within had actually committed the wrong. Sea carriers, innkeepers, and stable keepers (*nautae, caupones, stabularii*) were liable if their customers' property were damaged or stolen by one of their employees. Tax farmers (*publicani*) were held responsible for acts of their family, and "family" was in the course of time understood to include free servants employed in the collecting of taxes. The *actio exercitoria* lay against an *exercitor navis* (merchant shipowner) for commercial debts incurred within the terms of the so-called *praepositio* (appointment to command) of his *magister navis* (shipmaster), and the *actio institoria* was available against an employer for commercial debts incurred by an employee who had been put in charge of an inn or some similar business. Unlike the sources of noxal liability these (contractual) actions were not based on a status relationship, but rather on the function to which the wrongdoer had been appointed.

In medieval Germanic customary laws, concepts similar to noxal liability seem to have prevailed. If a servant committed a delict, the head of the household had to pay a fixed penalty, or could surrender the actual wrongdoer instead. The personal responsibility of the householder, however, seems to have diminished in the course of time. Accordingly, in Saxonian law, as it was set down between 1220 and 1227 in the *Sachsenspiegel* (Mirror of the Saxons), the master was liable for a delict, but only up to the amount of unpaid wages. This kind of wage liability was widespread, and was still reported by some Roman-Dutch authors during the seventeenth and eighteenth centuries.

Roman standards of liability for acts of others came to be known in medieval Europe through the works of the glossators, from the first half of the twelfth century, and were adopted (with modifications) through the following process of reception of Roman law. This applies to the *actio de deiectis vel effusis*, to the liability of *nautae*, *caupones*, and *stabularii*, and to the responsibility of the tax farmer for the acts of members of his family, as well as to the *actiones exercitoria* and *institoria* and other cases of liability for others. Further regional provisions dealt with liabilities such as that of an owner for fire set in his house by a servant or a member of his family that caused damage to his neighbor. With the abolition of slavery in Europe, however, Roman noxal liability fell into disuse. A controversy arose among civil-law writers on how to fill the gaps in the system establishing liability for the acts of others. While some, such as Hugo Grotius, advocated wage liability, others, under the influence of natural law, argued in favor of the master's *culpa* (fault, broadly defined) as a general requirement of liability for the acts of his servants. This was the position adopted in the Prussian Code of 1794 and favored by nineteenth-century pandectist writers such as Bernhard Windscheid. The most influential approach, though, was the concept of strict functional liability, which in its basic structure corresponded to the view of vicarious liability that prevails in modern European law: the master was responsible for wrongs committed by his servants in the course of performing the functions to which they were appointed. This form of liability can in its general structure be traced back to a commentary by the fourteenth-century postglossator Bartolus. In the second half of the eighteenth century Johannes Voet referred back to the Roman liability of *nautae*, *caupones*, and *stabularii* and the responsibility of the *publicanus*. A similar position was taken by the French author Robert Joseph Pothier in a passage that formed the basis of the later provision in article 1384 of the Napoleonic Code Civil. Pothier was influenced by the concept of the *praepositio* (appointment to command), as it was known from the Roman *actiones exercitoria* and *institoria*. To illustrate the principle he referred to the Roman liability of the *publicanus*. This demonstrates how the modern principle of vicarious liability was developed during the period of *ius commune* by a collective process of generalizing special instances of liability for others derived from Roman law. Article 2049 of the Italian Codice Civile is almost identical to the French law.

The position in section 831 of the German Civil Code, in contrast, was influenced by the pandectist doctrine of "no liability without fault," which prevailed in the period of liberalism during the second half of the nineteenth century. Under this, a person who employs another to do any work is liable for any damage the other unlawfully causes to a third party in the course of performance. If the employer, however, can show that he has exercised the necessary care in the selection or supervision of the employee, the duty to compensate does not arise. A similar approach is also followed in Swiss law.

The development of vicarious liability in English law reveals parallels to, and influence by, developments on the Continent. Sources from the Anglo-Saxon period indicate that, as with noxal liability, a master was responsible to pay a penalty for the wrong of a servant, but could surrender the wrongdoer instead. Furthermore, from records of manorial courts it appears that after the Norman Conquest a strict form of liability of the householder for wrongs committed by members of his household continued to prevail. From the reign of Edward I (1272–1307) until preindustrial times, however, the king's courts followed a more restrictive approach, under which the master was liable only if the servant acted at his command or with his assent. The harshness of this view, though, was tempered by a number of exceptions where strict liability for others obtained. The modern doctrine of vicarious liability was finally developed in two judgments by Lord Holt, who had profound knowledge of civil and commercial law. In the first decision, *Boson v. Sandford* (1691), Holt was probably influenced by the liability of the *nauta* and by the *actio exercitoria*, as they were received through the *lex mercatoria* (mercantile law). In the second, *Turberville v. Stampe* (1698), he referred to the *actio de deiectis vel effusis*: "But if my servant throws dirt into the highway, I am indictable." According to the headnote of this decision "a master is responsible for all acts done by his servant in the course of his employment, though without particular directions." Essentially, this corresponds to the modern strict and functional liability for others, as it was formulated in the Netherlands by Johannes Voet or in France by Pothier. Lord Holt may therefore be regarded as the leading English representative in the European process of developing modern vicarious liability by generalizing special instances of liability derived from Roman law.

[*See also* Agency; Bartolus of Saxoferrato; *Pandektenwissenschaft*; Pothier, Robert Joseph; Prussian Allgemeines Landrecht; *and* Windscheid, Bernhard.]

BIBLIOGRAPHY

Barlow, Trafford B. *The South African Law of Vicarious Liability in Delict and a Comparison of the Principles of other Legal Systems*. Cape Town: Juta, 1939.

Johnston, David. "Limiting Liability: Roman Law and the Civil Law Tradition." *Chicago Kent Law Review* 70 (1995): 1515.

Wicke, Hartmut. *Respondeat Superior—Haftung für Verrichtungsgehilfen im römischen, römisch-holländischen, englischen und südafrikanischen Recht*. Berlin: Duncker & Humblot, 2000.

Zimmermann, Reinhard. *The Law of Obligations—Roman Foundations of the Civilian Tradition*. Cape Town: Juta, 1990.

Hartmut Wicke

VIETNAM. From 111 B.C.E. to 939 C.E., Vietnam was almost continuously under Chinese control and legal principles were imported from China. China's Tang code (first compiled in 624 C.E.) integrated Confucian conceptions into the legalist framework and was influential throughout Southeast Asia. The Ngo Dynasty (939–965 C.E.) started nine centuries of self-rule in Vietnam, while China remained a threat to sovereignty and influenced Vietnamese legal thought.

The Le Code. The earliest surviving Vietnamese legal text, probably from 1428, is the penal code of the Le dynasty (the Le code), operative until 1788. Some 200 of the Le code's 722 articles, particularly those addressing criminal, administrative, and military matters, originated from the Tang code. Although both codes adopted Confucianism, the Le code introduced many civil-law innovations protecting private interests. It imposed heavy penalties for coercion in sale contracts, instituted formality requirements for contracts, and extended civil liability to cases of bodily harm. Women could in certain circumstances inherit property and obtain divorce based on emotional and sexual neglect.

The Gia Long Code. The subsequent Gia Long code of the Nguyen Dynasty (1802–1945), Vietnam's last traditional code, marked a formal return to Chinese legal principles. The Gia Long code virtually replicated China's Qing code, adopting its 397 principal articles, 30 supplementary articles, and most of its substatutes, and abandoning only 39 articles. The Gia Long code was principally concerned with criminal sanctions, ignoring areas of social conduct such as marriage and inheritance. Hence, civil norms of the earlier Le code filled the lacunae, together with village customs, reflected in the Vietnamese proverb *"phep vua thua le lang"* ("the laws of the emperor bow before village customs").

French Influence. The Nguyen Dynasty eventually experienced the increasing influence of the French, who established a colony in Cochin China (in 1875) and two protectorates over Tonkin and Annam (1883). French rhetoric rationalized the colonization of Vietnam based on "the civilizing mission." The French enacted significant reforms, varying in substance and effect according to region. In Cochin China, a French lieutenant-governor was appointed under the governor-general of Indochina. By 1900 he was assisted by a *conseil privé* comprising colonial officials and two Vietnamese members and a *conseil colonial* of sixteen members: six French citizens elected by the French, six Vietnamese elected by the Vietnamese, and four members of the Chamber of Commerce of Saigon. In Tonkin, a *résident supérieur* was appointed, and local mandarins were made accountable to him. A *résident supérieur* was similarly established in Annam, where the Annamite Imperial Court continued to govern, its edicts subject to endorsement of the *résident supérieur* and approval of the governor-general.

However, the Gia Long code continued to operate unless a French provision repealed or replaced it. Sometimes, the Le code was applied in place of the Gia Long code because it contained more comprehensive prescriptions. The French treated the Le code as customary law. Where precedents on a particular question did not exist in the indigenous codes or Vietnamese custom, French principles were applied. For this reason, French commercial law was received throughout Vietnam. Where it was uncertain whether French or Vietnamese principles were applicable, jurists considered the parties' nationality. If all were Vietnamese, the French would apply Vietnamese law; if one party was French, French law applied.

Vietnamese law became more closely aligned with French legal principles; the French also reformed many areas of Vietnamese law directly, enacting revised codes. The criminal law was perceived by the French as callous, and in Cochin China the entire criminal code was revised (1880). Substantial debate continues on Vietnam's French legal inheritance, with differing views on the depth of impact and on whether French legal reform was intended to improve Vietnamese law or was simply an instrument of colonial power.

The Rise of Communism. By the mid-twentieth century, French law faced embittered Vietnamese rhetoric and condemnation of French "justice." Strong nationalist undertones helped validate and empower revolutionaries who argued that the Vietnamese needed to construct their own institutions, including dispute-resolution mechanisms, and demanded the destruction of Western law and the establishment of socialism. On September 2, 1945, Ho Chi Minh declared Vietnam's independence in Hanoi. The First Indochina War concluded in 1954, when the Viet Minh defeated the French at Dien Bien Phu. On July 21, 1954, the Geneva Conference provisionally divided the country, the North becoming the Viet Minh–controlled Democratic Republic of Vietnam, the South the State of Vietnam under Emperor Bao Dai. The Geneva Conference provided for Vietnam's reunification after an internationally supervised election, but this election was never held because of fears that Ho Chi Minh would prevail. The Second Indochina War, the Vietnam War, lasted over thirty years, first against the French and then against the American-led allies, until Vietnam was reunified as the Socialist Republic of Vietnam in 1976.

The war period prevented endogenous legal development. Vietnam relied on Socialist models from the Soviet Union and China, which assisted with land reforms in the 1950s. Law as party control dominated Vietnam's legal thinking, but Vietnam never sought to completely abandon law, presumably because Ho Chi Minh recognized the failure of this approach in the Soviet Union. As in China, the Communist Party of Vietnam fostered "virtue rule" and Socialist morality, privileging moral education over a formal legal system.

Legal Reforms of the 1980s and 1990s. Market-oriented reforms introduced in 1986 (*doi moi*, meaning "renovation") under Nguyen Van Linh (1986) generated substantial legal reform, including the introduction of laws enabling the establishment of business entities and investment; the adoption of new civil and criminal codes; the radical reform of the courts; and the implementation of governance reforms to make the law more accessible and the government more accountable. However, the party-state retains tight control. The primary objective of strictly controlled economic liberalization has been stimulation of economic development.

Vietnam's fourth Constitution, adopted in 1992, embedded substantial legal reforms agreed to at the Seventh Party Congress in 1991. Most importantly, the doctrine of *nha nuoc phap quyen* (law-based state) was adopted, signaling a new determination to see economic relationships regulated by law rather than by bureaucratic discretion. The 1992 Constitution provides in theory that party organizations must "operate within the framework of the Constitution and the law," but the party-state retains its position of primacy. Socialist morality, Confucian practices, long-standing distrust of state legal institutions, and legal insecurity combine to produce uneven and generally low engagement with the formal legal system.

[*See also* Chinese Law, History of.]

BIBLIOGRAPHY

Gillespie, John. *Transplanting Commercial Law Reform: Developing a "Rule of Law" in Vietnam*. Aldershot, U.K. and Burlington, Vt.: Ashgate, 2006. A compelling analysis of Socialist commercial laws in transition, using discourse theory.

Gillespie, John, and Pip Nicholson, eds. *Asian Socialism and Legal Change: The Dynamics of Vietnamese and Chinese Reform*. Canberra, Australia: Asia Pacific Press, 2005. Chronicling contemporary legal change in Vietnam, this covers Socialist law, legal education, Vietnamese jurisprudence, lawyering in Vietnam, state-owned enterprises, and the role of international law and Catholicism in Vietnam.

Hooker, M. B. *A Concise Legal History of South-East Asia*. Oxford, U.K.: Clarendon Press; New York: Oxford University Press, 1978. An authoritative and meticulously researched account of indigenous and colonial laws in Southeast Asia.

Nguyen Ngoc Huy, and Ta Van Tai. *The Le Code: Law in Traditional Vietnam*. Athens: Ohio University Press, 1987. Text and expert analysis of the features and idiosyncrasies of the Le code.

Nicholson, Penelope (Pip). *Borrowing Court Systems: The Experience of Socialist Vietnam*. Leiden, Netherlands, and Boston: Martinus Nijhoff, 2007. History of Socialist Vietnamese court development from 1945 to 2007, focusing on the extent to which Vietnamese Socialist courts mirrored their Soviet counterparts.

Woodside, Alexander Barton. *Vietnam and the Chinese Model: A Comparative Study of Nguyen and Ch'ing Civil Government in the First Half of the Nineteenth Century*. Cambridge, Mass.: Harvard University Press, 1971. Wide-ranging analysis of precolonial government and law in China and Vietnam, including coverage of village-level governance in Vietnam.

Vietnam Update Series. Singapore: Institute of Southeast Asian Studies. Not strictly about law, this series is an invaluable source of Vietnam-related scholarship relevant to legal research, publishing scholarly contributions to the Vietnam Update Conference held annually in either Canberra or Singapore. For example, see Benedict J. Tria Kerkvliet and David Marr, eds., *Beyond Hanoi: Local Government in Vietnam* (Singapore: Institute of Southeast Asian Studies, 2004).

Penelope (Pip) Nicholson

VILLEINAGE. In medieval English law, the term "villeinage" had two distinct, if not entirely unrelated, meanings. On the one hand, it was a status: villeins (also called "neifs"—those in the legal state of villeinage or neifty) were individuals who were personally "unfree," often referred to as servile. Villeinage, however, was also a form of land tenure; land might be held of a lord in villeinage. The dual meaning of "villein" and "villeinage," embracing both personal status and land tenure, is unfortunate, because it produces a description of villeinage that seems replete with logical inconsistencies. In the first place, the personal status of those in villeinage was relative; thus a villein was servile as against his own lord, but not with respect to others, and was therefore able to hold free tenements of another lord; likewise, a freeman might hold land of a lord in villeinage tenure, and not be in servile status. Indeed, that a person held land in villeinage was not regarded in law to be evidence of villein status. Moreover, villeins did not need to hold land of their lord in villein tenure to be in servile status. In reality, however, most villeins probably did at some time in their lives hold land in villeinage tenure; and most villein tenure was likely held by those in villein status. What distinguished freehold land from land held in villein tenure was that rights to land held in villeinage could not be enforced in the king's court, even by a freeman. Although one might transfer land held in villeinage, villein status was accorded to individuals by birth through their fathers, and could only be shed by seigneurial manumission.

Development of Villeinage Rights. While legal disabilities attached to villein status and villeins were indeed unfree, they should not be regarded as slaves, akin to the Roman *servus*, though contemporary legal characterizations sometimes equate the two. The story of villein status is more nuanced. Anglo-Saxon England was a socially stratified society. By 1066, the legal status of individuals who lived on the land was layered. Many individuals were of free status. But the Domesday Book enumerated serfs living on the land described, indicating that slavery in some form did exist in Anglo-Saxon England. Whatever the constraints visited upon serfs by their status, serfdom, not villeinage, is more properly equated with slavery, but serfdom appears to have disappeared soon after the Norman Conquest. Other individuals, however, were bound to the land, and "villein" eventually came to be associated with the legal status of all those peasants who were tied to a lord.

During the course of the Middle Ages, villeinage as a status was transformed dramatically both by the common law and by evolving notions of customary law. As the legal rights of freeholders were defined at common law, the common law of villeinage also developed in the twelfth and thirteenth centuries in the royal courts. Commentators such as the authors of *Glanvill* and *Bracton* were intrigued by the law of villeinage, and the latter explored its doctrine in considerable detail. The common law of villeinage served to determine which members of the peasant class were free rather than servile, and then carried on to regulate and to limit the exactions that lords could demand of their unfree tenants. At the same time, customary law also governed seigneurial relations, as well as other areas of servile life. Such overlapping legal orders were not uncommon in medieval English law.

One indicator of the legal nature of villein status was whether the villein might in fact own personal property free of the claims of his lord. If villeins were the property of their lords, it follows that any personal property that they acquired during their lives in that status would likewise be the chattels of their lord. Similarly, if one regards the villein as the lord's chattel, it might also follow that lords held the power of life and death over their villeins. In both cases, the property law analysis is insufficiently nuanced and fails to explain the complexities of villein status. While lords could physically discipline their villeins without fear of civil actions brought by the neif in trespass, the criminal law protected villeins as well as it did the freeman. More-over, with respect to chattels that the villein possessed, villein rights were recognized and protected in the manorial courts to which the villeins owed suit. The manor court was a forum, usually presided over by the lord's steward, in which land transfers were recorded, seigneurial rights defended, and civil matters between members of the manorial community resolved. Manor courts, for example, probated the wills of personal property of villeins, including, but not limited to devises (bequests) of their personal and household effects. In many manors, villeins produced crops for a broader market in return for cash payments. They also undertook by-employment such as brewing. These activities yielded money, and cash bequests can also be found in probated wills recorded in the court rolls. Moreover, the manorial economy required an active credit market; and the manor court records (called court rolls) demonstrate that the court enforced wide-ranging creditor-debtor relationships between villeins, including mortgages of land in villein tenure. In substance, then, villeins dealt freely with their personal property.

Moreover, if villein tenure was held subject to arbitrary demands exacted from its holder by his lord, the lord should have been able to transfer rights in land held in villein tenure from one villein to another freely. Likewise, the lord might arbitrarily determine labor services due and assess a variety of tenurial incidences. Once again the manor courts tell a different story about land held in villeinage. While villein land was held "subject to the will of the lord," tenure in villeinage was also held "according to the custom of the manor." Land in villeinage tenure was generally freely alienable by its holder. While the form of transfer supported the underlying notion of seigneurial control of rights in land (because the land in question was not directly transferred from tenant to tenant but surrendered to the lord by the vendor and regranted by the lord to the vendee), the court rolls nevertheless illuminate an active market in villein land. In addition, manor courts recognized inheritance rights in kin and the widow's right to free bench (i.e., holding her late husband's land until she remarried—villein tenure's analogue to common-law dower). Some manorial court rolls even record complex intergenerational family settlements of land held in villein tenure by will. Customary dues, or heriots (usually the best beast of a deceased tenant), paid by the heirs upon entrance into land held in villeinage by an ancestor, were largely fixed; and merchets (cash payments demanded for giving a daughter in marriage, on the grounds that she might leave the manor to live elsewhere with her husband) were determined, though there were instances of dispute between the lord's steward and the manorial court jurors on the amount of the payment owed.

The balance in the servile relationship is underscored by the fact that the lord did not always prevail in disputes with his villeins over tenurial obligations; the custom of the manor, if it could be demonstrated by reference to entries in the court rolls, was the driving force that informed the seigneurial relationship. Finally, the court rolls also indicate that by the thirteenth century the labor services owed by villeins to the lord were largely fixed, although again there are instances of disputes between the stewards of manorial lords and members of the servile community over their extent.

Burdens and Objections. One should not, however, paint a portrait of seigneurial relations as conflict free or as dealings based on equality. There was a distinct hierarchy in rural medieval England; villeins were near the bottom, and villein status remained a burden. But the relationship between lord and villeins was not unaffected by economic trends. To some extent, the lord's ability to exact services and monetary payments based upon villein status or villein tenure was not unrelated to land and labor scarcity. When the population rose in the early fourteenth century, a lord might have been more able to demand services and payments from his villeins in return for their landholding. But after the Black Death (1348–1350), when land was relatively plentiful, both villein status and seigneurial exactions waned. Regardless of the balance, the lord's excessive exactions were limited by the very real need to retain and propagate a productive workforce. As the medieval economy matured, those who continued to hold in villeinage were more likely to have their services commuted into cash payments to their lord. Likewise, political events such as the Peasants' Revolt of 1381 should not be ignored; disquiet also influenced the legal nature of the servile relationship, as well as its economic reality.

Not surprisingly the burdens of servile status led some villeins to flee, particularly when economic conditions allowed a fresh start elsewhere, free of the bond of servile status. Should that occur, and the neif be located, the lord could bring an action *de nativo habendo* to recover the absconding villein. The lord procured a writ that directed the sheriff to return the alleged villein to the lord, unless he had taken refuge on the ancient (royal) demesne. If the individual claimed to be free, and gave the sheriff security, he could obtain a writ *de liberate probanda* in which the issue of villeinage was brought before the king's justices. Why the king's court intervened in these matters (particularly since it had no interest in land held in villein tenure even by freemen) is perplexing given the limitations of royal justice during the period after the Black Death. Personal liberty was, as Bracton noted, "inestimable," and perhaps it was believed that the issue of neifty should be tried in the highest of tribunals. As the action proceeded, the lord asserted in his count that the villein was "possessed" by him, and he was required to produce two male relatives who were of the same blood, and who would swear to the runaway's servile status. Judge and jury were the ultimate arbiters of villein status in neifty actions, and their views might be guided by their position on whether the underlying institution should continue given current economic and social conditions. Judges had to fashion the law of villeinage within the theoretical constructs of a burgeoning common law. The jury, on the other hand, with its members' own social status perhaps less than demonstrable, probably became less willing to condemn others to servile status.

Disappearance. The burdens of villein status became more fixed over the course of the thirteenth and fourteenth centuries. At the same time, the law increasingly provided mechanisms for terminating villein status. Action by lords, voluntary manumissions, could transform their villeins into freeman. Various principles of family law had an effect on those in servile status. Consistent with coverture, the legal doctrine that considered the property of a married woman to be held by her husband, the marriage of a servile woman to a freeman terminated her villein status during the marriage.

Illegitimacy also had an effect. Because an illegitimate child had no inheritance rights from parents, he was deemed free, villein status being inherited through the father. In a society with considerable migration, and before the advent of parish registers, questions of pedigree were difficult to prove or dispute.

By the fifteenth century, villeinage as a status had all but disappeared. At the same time, villein tenure was transformed into copyhold—tenure of land according to the custom of the manor, as recorded in the manor court. Even in the earlier period, villeins had a large degree of security of tenure because their right to land was recorded in the manor court rolls, a process that gave holders rights against the lord's arbitrary dispossession and protected them against the encroachment of others. The transition to copyhold expressed both the decline of the villein status and the reality that villein land tenure was in fact secure. Chancery, and then the common-law courts, eventually allowed actions to be brought based upon land held in copyhold, and the legal peculiarity of villein status and tenure in villeinage was no more.

[*See also* Feudal Law; Land, *subentry on* Land Registration in English Common Law; Servitude in Real Estate; Slavery, *subentry on* English Common Law; Succession, *subentry on* English Common Law; *and* Tenure, Doctrine of.]

BIBLIOGRAPHY

Baker, John Hamilton. *An Introduction to English Legal History.* 4th ed. London: Butterworths; Dayton, Ohio: LexisNexis, 2002.

Hyams, Paul R. *King, Lords, and Peasants: The Common Law of Villeinage in the Twelfth and Thirteenth Centuries.* Oxford, U.K.: Clarendon Press, 1980.

Maitland, Frederic William. *Equity; also, The Forms of Action at Common Law.* Cambridge, U.K.: The University Press, 1910.

Milsom, Stroud F. C. *The Legal Framework of English Feudalism.* Cambridge, U.K., and New York: Cambridge University Press, 1976.

Poos, L. R., and Lloyd Bonfield. *Select Cases in Manorial Courts, 1250–1550: Property and Family Law.* Selden Society, Vol. 114. London: Selden Society, 1998.

Vinogradoff, Sir Paul. *Villeinage in England.* Oxford, U.K.: Clarendon Press, 1892.

Lloyd Bonfield

VINDICATIO. *See* Property, *subentry on* Roman Law.

VYAVAHĀRA. Besides being an ancient Indian juridical term, *vyavahāra* (from Sanskrit *vi-ava-hri* "to transpose, exchange, have intercourse with") is first an expression generally denoting interaction or contextualized practice, a form of interpersonal negotiation, and second a designation of activity ruled by social convention, referring to both the inherent rules of custom and common sense and the activities themselves, thereby denoting ordinary life rather than specific formal legal contexts.

The term first occurs in its Middle Indic form *viyohāla-samatā* in the third century B.C.E. on Emperor Aśoka's Delhi-Topra Pillar Edict. One of the earliest Buddhist texts from roughly the same period, the *Vinaya* (1:74 and 2:158), mentions a ministerial post connected with the type of dispute settlement called *vohārikamahāmatta*. The term *vyavahāra* acquired great importance during the late classical period (first and second centuries C.E.) in juridical contexts, especially in the *dharmaśāstras*, particularly the *Manusmriti* (8:1ff.) and *Yājñavalkyasmriti* (2:1ff.), which are part of the *smriti* ("remembered" as the opposed to "revealed") literature, but also in political treatises such as the *Arthaśāstra* (3:1.58). Its meaning here is generally connected with the more formal legal transaction of settling a dispute. The eminent Indian scholar Pandurang Vaman Kane in his groundbreaking *History of Dharmaśāstra* distinguishes three meanings: (1) a dispute, a lawsuit, (2) the legal capacity to enter into transactions, and (3) the means of deciding a matter, but then reduces it to the first. Although there is much in favor of seeing in *vyavahāra* a concept that helps deal with dharma in ways that are not reducible to religion, lawyers' common translations of *vyavahāra* as "civil law" positivistically transpose Western legal ideas into South Asian terminology and thus fail to capture the whole range of possible meanings. Taking into account that *vyavahāra* must be viewed both from the perspective of historical practice and from that of indigenous conceptualizations, recent interpretations therefore propose "interpersonal negotiation," "dispute resolution settlement," or "litigation process."

According to *Nāradasmriti* 1:1–2 and *Brihaspatismriti* 1:1, *vyavahāra* became necessary because of the decline of dharma among humans. A perceived decline in the efficacy of the self-control mechanisms of late classical South Asian law as well as a strengthening of the juridical administration may have been the reason for this view. Regarding the definition of *vyavahāra* in traditional Indian legal thought one can differentiate two strands, one discursive, the other practice-oriented. The traditions exist side by side in a definition that goes back to the third-century B.C.E. scholar Kātyāyana, referred to in Kullūka's commentary on *Manusmriti* 6:1 (see also *Parāśara Mādhacīya* III), where *vyavahāra* is defined twice, first, as an intellectual enterprise to remove doubt, etymologically interpreted as "various" (*vi-*), "doubt" (*-ava-*), and "removing" (*-hāra*), and second as a pragmatic attempt to settle a dispute. The author Hārīta defines *vyavahāra* as the procedure by which "the attainment of one's wealth (taken away by another) and the avoidance of the *dharmas* of others (such as those of heretics) are secured with the help of the means of proof" (*Smriticandrikā* II). Elsewhere *vyavahāra* is described as the "removal of doubts" (*Nāradasmriti* 1:3.17; *Manusmriti* 8:12), supporting the term's development in a more theoretical direction and linking it to textual authority in support of Kātyāyana's view that *vyavahāra* requires recourse to *smriti* rules. In contrast *Nāradasmriti* 1:11 states that *vyavahāra* "rests on the statements of witnesses." Mitramiśra's commentary on *Yājñavalkyasmriti* 2:1 calls *vyavahāra* "the averment (about a matter) as related to oneself in opposition to another." This practice-oriented notion of *vyavahāra* is also supported by the seventeenth-century author Nīlakantha in his *Vyavahāramayūkha*: "*Vyavahāra* is an action or operation that facilitates the exposure of the wrong that is not known . . . and that pertains to one out of the several persons that have a dispute . . . : or it is an operation in which the plaintiff and the defendant are the agents . . . and which helps the establishment (of truth) in the midst of conflicting alternatives." Such definitions appear to include both formal and informal dispute settlement processes.

Within the Jaina tradition, Hemācārya's *Arhannīti* (twelfth–fourteenth centuries) presents a different approach, defining *vyavahāra* as "pronouncement, utterance" (*vacana*) placing it in the realm of speech rather than cognition or action, a view related to that of the Brahman Mitramiśra (*Vīramitrodaya* 7:2–3) who called *vyavahāra* "narrative" (*kathā*). For Hemācārya *vyavahāra* is a pronouncement in a certain constellation where there is an object (*vastu*) and there are two mutually opposed claims or lines of action regarding an object (*dharma*). One of the two is eventually approved and the other discarded. Here *vyavahāra* is the discursive process leading up to the decision of approval or dismissal. Claim and disclaim as integral parts of *vyavahāra* are not supposed to represent irreconcilable opposites, rather subsequent stages in a process represented by the disputants, leading to the complete articulation of a verbally conceived disputed matter.

Vyavahāra is furthermore used when denoting a particular case of dispute or litigation (*vyavahāra-pāda* or *-viṣaya*), defined in the *Yājñavalkyasmriti* 2.5 as the plaintiff's act of informing the ruler about an action in opposition to dharma texts. *Manusmriti* 8:8 mentions eighteen categories under which *vyavahāra-pāda*s are traditionally subsumed; the number varies in other texts. The role of the Hindu king in dispute settlement as well as in law making is still under discussion, but was certainly less overruling and more engrained in processes of negotiation and delegation than previously thought. In a variant meaning of *vyavahāra-pāda*s, referring to steps of dispute settlement, the texts list four: namely dharma; *vyavahāra*, here to be translated as the transaction of the dispute itself; (evidence of) custom (*caritra*); and royal decree (*rājaśāsana*), each representing a step to be taken once the preceding proves insufficient (*Arthaśāstra*, 3:1.39; *Nāradasmriti* 1:10).

The elaboration and development of the concept of *vyavahāra* may be directly connected with attempts of textual experts to increase their role in dispute settlement by prescribing reference to Shastric texts, preparing for the gradual bureaucratization of legal transactions, rather than representing the common practice which the term itself seems to denote, and which remained informal and thus largely inaccessible to formal legal analysis.

[*See also* Aśoka; Dharma; *and* Jaina Law.]

BIBLIOGRAPHY

Derrett, J. D. M. *Religion, Law, and State in India*. London: Faber & Faber, 1968. Classic historical analysis of Hindu law through the ages.

Derrett, J. D. M. "Hemācārya's Arhannīti: An Original Jaina Juridical Work of the Middle Ages." *Annals of the Bhandarkar Oriental Research Institute* 57 (1976): 1–21. Specialist study on Jaina law.

Hultzsch, E. *Corpus Inscriptionum Indicarum*. Vol. 1, *Inscriptions of Asoka*. Oxford, U.K.: Clarendon Press for the Government of India, 1925. Specialist study of the stone-pillar edicts of Ashoka.

Kane, P. V. *History of Dharmaśāstra*. Vol. 3. 3d ed. Poona: Bhandarkar Oriental Research Institute, 1993. The most detailed traditional analysis of Hindu law.

Kuppuswami, Alladi, ed. *Mayne's Treatise on Hindu Law and Usage*. 12th ed. New Delhi: Bharat Law House, 1986. Standard lawyer's text.

May, Reinhard. *Law & Society, East and West: Dharma, Li, and Nomos: Their Contribution to Thought and to Life*. Stuttgart, Germany: F. Steiner Wiesbaden, 1985. Excellent comparative analysis.

Menski, Werner. *Hindu Law. Beyond Tradition and Modernity*. New Delhi and Oxford: Oxford University Press, 2003. A new analysis of traditional and modern Hindu law.

Christoph Emmrich

WAGER OF LAW (COMPURGATION). See Compurgation.

WANSHARISI, AHMAD IBN YAHYA AL-TILIMSANI AL- (A.H. 834/1430 C.E.–A.H. 914/1508 C.E.). Ahmad ibn Yahya ibn Muhammad ibn 'Abd al-Wahid al-Wansharisi was a Berber Muslim jurist, born in the Oursenis (Arabic Wansharis, hence his name), a mountain massif in northern Algeria approximately twenty-five miles (forty kilometers) south of the towns of Ténès and Cherchell. Al-Wansharisi spent his formative years in Tlemcen, where he studied Maliki substantive law and jurisprudence under the tutelage of a dozen or so distinguished scholars. In 1469, following a confrontation with the reigning sultan, al-Wansharisi's house was sacked and he fled to Fez, where he was appointed to several teaching posts, including professor of Maliki law at the Misbahiyya madrasa.

Known for his command of classical Arabic, eloquence, and mastery of substantive law and jurisprudence, al-Wansharisi composed at least twenty-eight treatises, of which ten are available in printed editions and five in lithograph. He is best known as the compiler of *Al-m'yar al-mu'rib wa-l-jami' al-mughrib* (The Clear Measure and the Extraordinary Collection), a massive compilation of approximately five thousand to six thousand fatwas (expert judicial opinions) issued by the greatest jurists of Ifriqiya, the Maghrib, and Andalusia, including many of al-Wansharisi's teachers. The fatwas included in the *Mi'yar* were composed between 1000 and 1500, and the longest and richest opinions were issued during the second half of this period. Begun around 1485 and completed in 1496, the *Mi'yar* is a treasure trove of information that has been used by historians to shed light on the social, economic, and legal history of the Islamic West. The eleven-volume lithograph edition produced in Fez in 1897–1898 served as the basis of the twelve-volume printed edition of the text published in Rabat between 1981 and 1983.

[See also Islamic Schools of Sacred Law, subentry on Sunni Schools: The Maliki School of Law, Part 1.]

BIBLIOGRAPHY

PRIMARY WORKS

Wansharisi, Ahmad al-. *Al-mi'yar al-mu'rib wa-l-jami' al-mughrib 'an fatawi 'ulama' Ifriqiya wa-l-Andalus wa-l-Maghrib*. Edited by Ahmad al-Bu'azzawi. 11 vols. Fez, Morocco, 1896–1897 (lithograph).

Wansharisi, Ahmad al-. *Al-mi'yar al-mu'rib wa-l-jami' al-mughrib 'an fatawi 'ulama' Ifriqiya wa-l-Andalus wa-l-Maghrib*. Edited by M. Hajji, 12 vols., Rabat, Morocco: Wizarat al-Awqaf wa-l-Shu'un al-Islamiyah lil-Mamlakah al-Maghribiyah, 1981–1983.

SECONDARY WORKS

Lagardère, Vincent. *Histoire et société en occident musulman au Moyen Âge: Analyse du Mi'yar d'al-Wansarisi*. Madrid: Casa de Velázquez, 1995.

Powers, David S. *Law, Society, and Culture in the Maghrib, 1300–1500*. Cambridge, U.K., and New York: Cambridge University Press, 2002.

Vidal Castro, Francisco. "Ahmad al-Wansarisi (m. 914/1508): Principales aspectos de su vida." *Al-Qantara* 12 (1991): 315–352.

Vidal Castro, Francisco. "Las obras de Ahmad al-Wansarisi (m. 914/1508): Inventario analítico." *Anaquel de Estudios Árabes* 3 (1992): 73–112.

Vidal Castro, Francisco. "El *Mi'yar* de al-Wansarisi (m. 914/1508), I. Fuentes, manuscritos, ediciones, traducciones." *Miscelánea de Estudio Árabes y Hebráicos* 42–43 (1993–94): 317–361.

Vidal Castro, Francisco. "El *Mi'yar* de al-Wansarisi (m. 914/1508), II. Contenido." *Miscelánea de Estudio Árabes y Hebráicos* 44 (1995): 213–246.

DAVID POWERS

WAR AND PEACE IN ISLAMIC LAW. War is the normal relationship between Muslim states and non-Muslim political entities according to the classical legal discussions. In the Qur'an, warfare, expressed by the term *qitāl* (fighting), is licit (9:111), is enjoined (2:116), and has the support of God (33:21). In the hadith (Prophetic tradition) literature the term "jihad" (struggle, endeavor) or the phrase *fī sabīl Allāh* (in the path of God) is used and has a spiritual but anonymous (cf. Qur'an 61:6) and salvific aspect. The process of warfare is for the purpose of lifting the Word of God to the highest (Qur'an 9:41; Bukhari, iv, 272, no. 2810) in the broadest sense.

The duty of warfare is incumbent upon the community at all times in a collective sense (*farḍ kifāya*, fulfilled as long as someone in the community is undertaking it), and in a personal, individual sense (*farḍ 'ayn*) when Muslim territory is under attack by an invader. It is incumbent upon any person who fulfills the following criteria: Muslim, male, free, able-bodied, sane, and adult. It is not necessarily incumbent upon women, although some contemporary scholars have challenged that prohibition. There is some amount of debate as to whether non-Muslims can participate in a jihad or fight alongside the Muslims against a Muslim enemy. The dominant classical view is that they cannot (although the Hanafi school allows for it), but during the past century several prominent examples can be cited of jihads in which non-Muslims played a prominent role (World War I with the Ottomans and the Germans; the Gulf War of 1991 with the Saudis and the United States). These examples are supported by fatwas issued by the highest legal authorities.

Justifications for War. Muslim warfare (jihad) is comparable to the Christian doctrine of just warfare in that it is a specialized type of warfare with a large number of regulations governing its practice. Classical Muslim scholars divided the world into two categories: the *dār al-Islām*, the territory in which the norms of Islam and the shari'a (the divine law of Islam) are paramount and in which peace reigns, and the *dār al-Ḥarb*, the territory of war. There is a third, optional territorial designation, the *dār al-Ṣulḥ*, referring to territories with which the Muslim states are at peace or have treaty obligations. Jihad begins when the rightfully designated leader of the Muslim state, ideally a caliph or an imam but more often the 'ulama' (religious leadership), calls upon the non-Muslim state to choose one of three things: to convert to Islam, to submit and pay the *jizya* tax (the poll tax levied upon non-Muslims), or to fight. This call can be omitted if the Muslim leader knows that it has been made in the past, if the situation is obvious to the non-Muslims (because of a state of continual warfare), or if making it would destroy the success of the war because of the loss of secrecy.

The Muslim state (or groups of Muslims) can wage jihad for the following reasons: to fight apostates (*ahl al-ridda*); to defend territory, possessions, and honor; to defend the holy places; to fight an unjust ruler; to combat *fitna* (temptation, sedition from the religion); to fight rebellious *dhimmīs* (Jews, Christians, Sabaeans, and others under the protection of Muslims); as a preemptive strike against a likely enemy; to establish a Muslim state; or to insure Muslim unity. From a historical point of view, although the jurisprudents do not dismiss the prospect of offensive jihad, most jihad is seen as defensive, and the obligation to join in a defensive jihad is very strong. Most jurists would distinguish jihad, however, from *ḥarb al-bughāt* (war against heretics) with regard to questions of property rights and the right to freedom. In principle, jihad is war against non-Muslims, whether it is offensive or defensive.

Waging the War. Once fighting has begun, according to the jurisprudents only combatants can be killed, and non-combatants, such as women, children, the elderly, and monks, cannot be harmed. However, both women and children can be taken into captivity. It is the prerogative of the Muslim commander to decide what to do with the non-Muslim captives: they can be killed, held for ransom, sold into slavery, or freed, as he sees fit. Tactics of jihad are varied. In offensive warfare it is forbidden to use excessive devices, such as wanton destruction of agriculture (despite Qur'an 59:5), surprise or night attacks, assassinations, or other such methods. But in defensive jihad all of these tactics are legitimate, and the tradition "war is deception" is often cited to cover these situations.

Non-Muslims either living or sojourning in the lands of Islam are covered by an elaborate set of protective rules. Those living in Muslim territory are considered *dhimmīs*, which means that, if they are Jews or Christians, they fall under the terms of the Pact of 'Umar, a ninth-century document in the name of the caliph 'Umar (r. 634–644) that delineates an agreement between the Christians of Syria and the caliph. If they belong to other religions, such as Zoroastrianism or Hinduism, they are given protection similar to that of the Pact according to some scholars.

Arab polytheists were not accorded protection under most circumstances; however, certain schools allow them to be considered *dhimmīs*. Non-Muslim travelers or merchants received an *amān*, safe-conduct, which would be revoked if they were caught spying or aiding the enemies of the Muslims. This was also true of the *dhimmīs*. A Muslim who harmed any of these groups without offense was committing a sin. All of the rules for *dhimmīs* and non-Muslims traveling with an *amān* are listed under the rules of jihad, which makes it clear that classical Muslim jurisprudents viewed all of these groups as one.

In general, Muslims do not have the right to settle in non-Muslim lands. In the classical sources, when a territory falls under the control of non-Muslims it is assumed that Muslims will emigrate from it. Dispensations are given for embassies or merchants, but those who remain for a long period are usually said, even today, to be in danger of losing their Islam. Exceptions were made for Muslim spies in the jihad literature. However, according to numerous discussions on the issue of Muslims sojourning in non-Muslim countries, it is clear that the Muslims are not to be considered to have exactly the same status as non-Muslims, and receive some protection in the event of a Muslim attack.

Results of War. Spoils in jihad are governed by the provisions in Qur'an 8:41: "And know whatever booty you take, the fifth thereof is for Allah, the Apostle, the near of kin, the orphan, and the wayfarer." In effect, the fifth was given in Sunni Islam to the caliph to distribute to these needy ones, while in Shi'i Islam the fifth went to the family of the Prophet Muhammad. Anyone caught stealing from the spoils before they are properly divided is committing a mortal sin.

The dead in jihad battles are either Muslims or non-Muslims. If they are Muslims, they are considered martyrs (*shuhadā'*) and are buried without being washed (unlike all other Muslim dead) in the clothing in which they were killed. If they are non-Muslims, their bodies are also to be buried, without mutilation or cremation.

Jihad in the classical literature can be concluded in a number of different ways. If the jihad campaign has been to the Muslims' advantage, they can sign a truce (usually for the ten-year period attested by Muhammad's treaty of Hudaybiyya in 628), or continue campaigning at a later time. This is at the discretion of the military commander and is usually called either a *hudna* (truce) or a *muwāda'a* (cease-fire). If the campaign has been to the Muslims' disadvantage, then a truce gaining the best terms possible for the Muslims should be signed. It is permitted for Muslims to surrender themselves or their countries to the enemy if they can hope to be saved from death by doing so.

Modern Interpretations. At the beginning of the colonial period, especially in India, doctrine concerning jihad began to be reassessed, and Muslim apologists began to emphasize the defensive and spiritual aspects of it more than the offensive militant ones. However, although this tendency has developed in Muslim literature in western languages, since the 1970s there has been a revival of classical jihad theory among Salafi Muslims. Salafis fiercely oppose any form of apologetics with regard to jihad and place it in its classical context of proclamation (*da'wa*) and "commanding the right and forbidding the wrong" (*al-amr bi-l-ma'rūf wa-l-nahī 'an al-munkar*). Since very few Muslim states (if any) actually use the laws of jihad today, most of the laws discussed above remain theoretical, except among Salafi radicals who attempt to recreate a Muslim state according to the classical definitions.

[*See also* Non-Muslims in Islamic Law *and* Territorial Concepts in Islamic Law.]

BIBLIOGRAPHY

Abou El Fadl, Khaled. "The Rules of Killing at War: An Inquiry into Classical Sources." *Muslim World* 89 (1999): 144–157.

Bonner, Michael David. *Jihad in Islamic History: Doctrines and Practice*. Princeton, N.J.: Princeton University Press, 2006.

Burzuli, Abu al-Qasim. *Fatawa al-Burzuli*. 7 vols. Beirut: Dar al-Gharb al-Islami, 2002.

Cook, David. *Understanding Jihad*. Berkeley: University of California Press, 2005.

Cook, David. "Women Fighting in Jihad?" *Studies in Conflict and Terrorism* 38 (2005): 375–384.

Fakhry, Majid, trans. *The Qur'an: A Modern English Version*. Reading, U.K.: Garnet Press, 1996.

Friedmann, Yohanan. *Tolerance and Coercion in Islam: Interfaith Relations in the Muslim Tradition*. Cambridge, U.K., and New York: Cambridge University Press, 2003.

Hasani, 'Abd al-'Aziz bin Muhammad bin Siddiq al-. *Hukm al-iqamah bi-bilad al-kuffar*. Tangier, Morocco: Matabi' al-Bughaz, 1996.

Haykal, Muhammad Khayr. *Al-jihad wa-l-qital fi al-siyasa al-shar'iyya*. 3 vols. Beirut: Dar al-Barayiq, 1993.

Ibn Hajar al-Haythami, Ahmad ibn Muhammad. *Al-Zawajir 'an iktiraf al-kaba'ir*. 2 vols. Beirut: Dar al-Ma'rifa, 1998.

Johnson, James Turner. *The Holy War Idea in Western and Islamic Traditions*. University Park: Pennsylvania State University Press, 2002.

Ibn Baz, 'Abd al-'Aziz ibn 'Abd Allah. *Fatawa Islamiya: Islamic Verdicts*. 8 vols. Riyadh, Saudi Arabia: Darussalam, 2002.

Khadduri, Majid. *War and Peace in the Law of Islam*. Baltimore, Md.: Johns Hopkins University Press, 1955.

Noth, Albrecht. *Heiliger Krieg und Heiliger Kampf in Islam und Christentum: Beiträge zur Vorgeschichte und Geschichte der Kreuzzüge*. Bonn, Germany: Röhrscheid, 1966.

Sarakhsi, Muhammad ibn Ahmad. *Kitab al-mabsut*. 15 vols. Beirut: Dar al-Fikr, 2000.

Wansharisi, Ahmad ibn Yahya. *Al-mi'yar al-mu'rib wa-al-jami' al-mughrib*. 13 vols. Beirut: Dar al-Gharb al-Islami, 1981.

DAVID COOK

WAR POWER. Nestled within some eighteen provisions of congressional authority specified in Article I, Section 8 of the U.S. Constitution is the power "to declare war." These three words need to be understood in terms of context and sequence. The context is what the framers considered and confronted as they drafted their new fundamental law. They had seen war; they had successfully fought against one of the greatest powers in Europe. In its aftermath, they witnessed what they perceived to be weaknesses of the new fledgling central government established under the Articles of Confederation. They were well familiar with the role of force, be it exercised by Parliament or the British monarchy. They were also cognizant of the compelling necessity for their new government to be strong enough to prevent war, yet also powerful enough to undertake it, if necessary, in order to confront both domestic and external challenges. In short, while they accepted the need for power, they were well aware of the perils concerning its application.

The context in which the framers did their work is also linked to the sequence of powers in Section 8. Immediately following the power to declare war are listed the powers to raise and support armies, to provide and maintain a navy, to make rules for the government and regulation of the armed forces, and to call out the militia. What is conspicuous by its absence is any congressional authority to command the military. Such an important omission was, of course, no accident. The framers gave the powers of the commander in chief to the president. Reflecting their concern with a balanced allocation of authority throughout the entire Constitution, they empowered the chief executive to command. But at the same time, they placed what they considered to be stringent limitations on his powers as commander in chief. Congress would determine the size of his forces, as well retain authority to clothe, house, arm, govern, and pay them. Further, both houses of Congress had to concur in these actions. Although the president could commission new officers, the Senate had to approve them. Although Congress could appropriate money for the military, such legislation had to be renewed after two years. Finally, only Congress could declare war, although an unwritten tradition (still observed) has placed such action solely as a response to a specific request from the president. In short, the framers conceived of a military establishment over which no single branch of government had total control and which could not threaten civilian supremacy.

Evolution of the War Power. Such may well have been their intent in 1787. Yet more than two hundred years have elapsed since their document became fundamental law. Modern technological, industrial, economic, and communication innovations have transformed American society, including, of course, the armed services. Such dramatic changes have also affected the nuanced balance of powers the framers envisaged, and the evolution, if not erosion, of the war-power provision affords an excellent example of this fact. Although the provision remains a part of our fundamental law, its effectiveness and relevance represent matters of ongoing debate and ambivalence—almost invariably couched in a political context as well.

It is easy to forget the great extent to which the military has affected our history. No generation has been spared war since the Revolutionary era. But very few of these wars have involved the congressional exercise of the war-power provision. Indeed, thus far in our history only on five occasions has Congress actually declared war—the War of 1812, the Mexican War, the Spanish-American War, and World Wars I and II—and each time it was in response to a presidential request. Notably missing from the five are two of America's bloodiest military conflicts: the Civil War and the protracted battles in Vietnam—to say nothing of the various "police actions" or "interventions" that have occurred throughout our history.

On the other hand, American legal history indicates that major constitutional changes occur without formal amendment. Although the Constitution has been amended on multiple occasions, nothing concerning the military has ever been added. What appears deceptively simple in fact conceals critical constitutional issues. There is, for example, no doubt that the war power belongs to Congress, just as there is no doubt that the president exercises military authority as the commander in chief. But important questions immediately arise.

Is his request to declare war subject to congressional rejection? Is, on the other hand, a declaration of war that is unsolicited by the president subject to a presidential veto and possible congressional override? What if Congress declares war in defiance of the president's wishes, and in response he declines to order the military into action? What if the war is fought without a congressional declaration? Are these political or legal questions? This particular query represents much more than mere semantics. Historically, courts have tended to avoid intervention in disputes between Congress and the chief executive concerning military authority, taking refuge in the claim that such a dispute represents a political question—and thus would be beyond the ken of judicial cognizance. Thus, the fact that our legal history offers limited answers to these questions, at best, may explain why with increasing frequency since 1941, American presidents have not found it necessary or desirable to ask Congress for a formal declaration of war. This seemingly modern alternative, however, was not unique to the twentieth century.

Even before Congress first exercised its power to declare war, which it did in the War of 1812, it had enacted at least ten specific authorizations of force against the Barbary powers. In none of these had Congress declared war, although by 1804, it had recognized a state of war but stopped short of actually declaring it. Long forgotten, the efforts of the United States against the Barbary "pirates" were recently revisited during the legal controversy over the use of American military force since September 2001, when the United States argued that "only wars between sovereign nations" qualified for a declaration of war. The government's underlying assumption was that since the War on Terror involved conflict with nebulous groups rather than a clearly identifiable nation, a congressional declaration of war was neither necessary nor appropriate. Be that as it may, the overwhelming majority of the more than one hundred American military interventions that have occurred since 1800—whether based upon congressional authorization or simply by "unilateral executive action"—have not involved formal declarations of war.

Aside from Congress, what restraints limit the president's options concerning the war power? The historical record indicates that there seem to be very few. When, for example, the Confederacy opened fire on Fort Sumter, thus beginning the military phase of the Civil War, Congress stood in recess. Lincoln responded by calling that body back for a special session in July, but between April 12 and July 4, 1861, he acted alone. He suspended the writ of habeas corpus, called up and augmented the state militias, and ordered a naval blockade against Southern ports. Without specific congressional authorization, did the presidential prerogative extend to the imposition of a blockade?

Although it took almost two years for the cases to reach the Supreme Court, in March 1863, with the outcome of the war far from certain, the justices answered this question. Their decision came at a crucial time, as the Union had not yet gained military supremacy. The naval blockade in the South, however, became more effective with each passing month. The Confederacy faced a serious threat of economic strangulation if the blockade was upheld, and thus the legal opponents of the blockade zeroed in on the war power. The blockade was truly an act of war and only Congress could declare it. This had not happened, even though the legislature had in fact authorized such a blockade—but only months after Lincoln first proclaimed it. How could such action make lawful what had clearly been unlawful when it occurred?

Lawyers for the government avoided constitutional rhetoric and focused more on the contemporary realities of armed conflict. Lincoln had sought to put down an actual insurrection, and the absence of a formal declaration of war was totally irrelevant to this fact. With a bare majority of five, the high court agreed. Calling the current conflict "the worst civil war in history" and implying thereby that the Court could take judicial notice of the conflict's scope, the Court found no justification to "paralyze" the government by "subtle definitions and ingenious sophisms." It also refused to declare that Lincoln had usurped a power possessed by Congress (Prize Cases, 67 U.S. 635 [1863]).

Lincoln was very much aware that his actions concerning the blockade and suspension of habeas corpus were of questionable legality. But he considered endorsement by Congress—which he ultimately received, albeit after he had acted—a sufficient answer to claims that his exercise of the war power was unconstitutional. Later, and possibly with these events in mind, he reminded Congress that the "dogmas of the quiet past are inadequate to the stormy present . . . As our case is new, so we must think anew and act anew." Whether or not he so intended, his comments surely could be applied to the traditional roles of Congress and the chief executive vis-à-vis the war power. But Lincoln consistently recognized Congress as the plenary source of the war power. On the other hand, authorizing the use of such power was one thing; exercise of it was quite another. It may be noted that Lincoln's famous Emancipation Proclamation was based on his authority as commander in chief. Further, he always assumed that such authority was finite, not open ended. He never asserted some inherent right, by virtue of his office, that authorized him to act. As will be seen, it is that assumption that separates Lincoln from a number of his successors.

While Lincoln lived, the high court never blocked his war measures. During the next century, by relying more on concrete realities rather than constitutional niceties, the justices also avoided any definitive ruling on whether a state of war could exist without a congressional declaration. In an 1889 decision, they noted as dicta that "the war making power of the United States was not vested in the president but in Congress" (The Chinese Exclusion Case 130 U.S. 581 [1889]). It might be noted that here the Court specifically mentioned the war-making power rather than just the power to declare war. Yet historically, and for very understandable reasons, the Court has tried to evade involvement in disputes between Congress and the president over the war power. In this resulting vacuum, Congress and the chief executive, for the most part, have had to delineate for themselves their perimeters of authority over the military.

During World War I, for example, President Woodrow Wilson sought to arm American merchant ships and asked for congressional approval. He added, however, "No doubt I already possess that authority without special warrant of law, by the plain implication of my constitutional duties and powers."

When the Senate blocked the measure, Wilson denounced the conduct of "a small group of willful men" and ordered the arming to proceed, but only for the "sole purpose of defense." In 1950, President Harry Truman sent American forces into action in Korea without seeking the approval of Congress, although he did inform its leadership—but only after he had initiated military intervention. Since the Korean War, many more examples of executive military action could be cited—for example, the invasion of the Dominican Republic, the rescue of the SS *Mayaguez*, the attempted rescue of U.S. hostages in Iran, the invasion of Grenada, the bombing of targets in Libya, the protection of oil tankers in the Persian Gulf, and the overthrow of Manuel Noriega. With one exception, Congress has ultimately acquiesced, either by silence or approval—even though as Justice Robert Jackson aptly observed, "only Congress itself can prevent power from slipping through its fingers." The inability of Congress to do just that is one of the more intriguing aspects of our national character.

The War Powers Act of 1973. Indeed, Justice Jackson's point might be kept in mind when one considers the War Powers Act of 1973, a statute passed by Congress toward the end of what is probably the most controversial and divisive war in American history. Louis Fisher is correct to describe this law as more than just the reaction of Congress

The Gulf of Tonkin Resolution. President Lyndon B. Johnson signing the Gulf of Tonkin resolution, August 1964. LYNDON BAINES JOHNSON LIBRARY

to the palpable public opposition to the Vietnam catastrophe and the unfolding Watergate scandal. It was, in reality, a result of "almost four decades of bipartisan effort to recapture legislative authority" concerning the war power; authority that somehow had "drifted to the President" (Fisher, p. 128). Passed over a presidential veto and criticized by every president ever since, the War Powers Act has never been considered by the Supreme Court and thus remains good law. Nevertheless, in a real sense the War Powers Act might well be described as too little and too late. In 1973, how could Congress claim to possess what in reality it had never been able to exercise: equal standing with the chief executive in terms of waging war?

As is so often the case in American constitutional history, when Congress drafted the War Powers Act, essential principles collided with the politics of expediency. The act's goal, "to ensure the collective judgment" of both Congress and the president when military actions are undertaken, remains legitimate. But the use of phrases such as "necessary and appropriate retaliatory actions," "endangered citizens," and "imminent threat" invite conflicting interpretation. Moreover, the statute mandates that congressional consultation occur "in every possible instance." Again, while the scope for differing interpretations is dramatic, the statute makes clear that consultation is to be undertaken when a military action is pending, not proceeding. Also, the law sets forth three conditions under which the president might order troops into combat: (1) in response to a congressional declaration of war; (2) when Congress specifically authorizes military action; or (3) when there occurs "a national emergency created by attack upon the United States, its territories, or its armed forces."

If only because the statute exists, one can state that it has been relatively effective. For better or worse, all chief executives since Nixon have followed its mandate at least to some extent, even as they object to its requirements. But the War Powers Act has not been very successful in regaining congressional equity in terms of war making. Time, technology, and the built-in tensions between executive and legislative branches have rendered the war-power provision less than meaningful. Unless and until Congress is inclined to enact and support legislation to correct this issue, probably contrary to the wishes of the president, the situation will remain as it now stands.

Effective application of the war power, then, has become increasingly problematic, in that for more than half a century, American forces have fought without formal mention or even application of the provision. If history is the guide, the framers probably assumed some sort of joint war-making authority exercised by both Congress and the president. But our history also reveals a consistent expansion of presidential authority in times of military conflict—an expansion either ignored or silently acquiesced in by Congress.

The War Power in the Twenty-First Century. The presumption of a dual war-making role appears to have been eclipsed since 2001, during which time it has been argued by some that the president stands supreme in his war-making capacity as commander in chief and that he has no obligation to share such power with Congress. This view assumes that the president has all the requisite and necessary authority to order whatever he deems necessary in terms of military operations and that Congress can claim only the power to declare war; the resulting operational conduct is strictly a presidential prerogative. Opponents of this interpretation point to all the additional powers dealing with the military that are vested in Congress.

In the aftermath of 9/11, Congress passed a resolution authorizing the use of military force, and President Bush created special military tribunals and ordered the detainment of certain prisoners, including some American citizens, without access to the traditional forms of due process. He justified his actions on the grounds of a terrorist threat unlike anything thus far confronted by American society. In establishing these tribunals, Bush limited procedural safeguards, completely ignored Congress, and insisted that the presidential prerogative as commander in chief justified his actions. He based his policy on Franklin Roosevelt's proclamation in 1942 setting up a special military tribunal to try the alleged Nazi saboteurs. To be sure, the Supreme Court unanimously upheld Roosevelt's action, even though its decision in *Exparte Quirin* (317 U.S. 1 [1942]) has been severely criticized. But 2002 is far from 1942, and what unites the two proclamations is essentially the striking aspect of unilateral executive decision making they reflected. FDR's tribunal dealt with fewer than a dozen individuals. Bush's more restrictive proclamation could apply to at least seventeen million people worldwide.

If Congress has done little about the Bush special tribunals, the same cannot be said for the high court. In two decisions, dominated by justices drawn from Bush's own party, the Supreme Court handed down significant restrictions on the presidential war power. In *Hamdi v. Rumsfeld*, 542 U.S. 507 (2004), the Court held that an American citizen classified as an enemy combatant must be given a meaningful opportunity to argue that classification before some neutral decision maker, although the Court did not specify who that might be. In *Hamdan v. Rumsfeld*, 548 U.S. 557 (2006), the Court ruled that the military tribunals established by the administration were ultra vires (beyond the scope of legal power or authority). The procedures for their operation not only violated federal law and the Uniform Code of Military Justice but also contravened the Geneva Conventions. One of the provisions common to all four of them prohibits the passing of sentences on defendants without previous consideration by a "regularly constituted court affording all the judicial guarantees recognized as indispensable by civilized peoples." The majority opinion in *Hamdan* emphasized that regardless of the supposed criminal nature of the defendant, "the Executive nevertheless must comply with the prevailing rule of law."

The Court's various opinions reflect the tension between traditional American forms of due process and the awareness that the current War on Terror has an amorphous character, which makes it unlike any previous war in our history. It is the fact that the ultimate outcome is not clear, nor even in sight, that makes this conflict so different from that faced by Lincoln and Roosevelt.

Neither Lincoln nor Roosevelt lived to see the final outcome of the wars they led, but both died confident in the knowledge of what the outcome would be. The current generation of Americans may well lack such confidence, even as they reaffirm traditional norms of due process.

Such a fear has led some who object to the Supreme Court's decisions in *Hamdan* and *Hamdi* to invoke the famous Latin maxim *inter arma silent leges* (in time of war, the law is silent). It surely has been cited on numerous occasions throughout our history. It has been employed to justify judicial avoidance of critical constitutional issues, as well as to limit judicial action concerning matters related to the conduct of war. Perhaps it is nothing more than judicial abnegation or a tacit acceptance of contemporary reality—an excuse for not exercising power when it would be most appropriate to do so. Whatever its origins, the concept comes into play only when intentionally acted upon by policymakers—be they judicial or executive in character.

The argument might be made that it is one thing to employ the maxim as justification for certain executive actions, but quite another thing for courts to employ it as a principle of constitutional law. When the executive claims virtually open-ended war powers, the maxim loses whatever limited credibility it may possess, and indeed it becomes imperative that the law not be silent; rather judicial intervention, legislative scrutiny, and public debate concerning executive actions all must come into play. The framers probably did not anticipate Congress's inability to make the exercise of the war power a meaningful part of governmental policy.

Assessment. This failure can only interest historians. It has been noted on numerous occasions that constitutional provisions and safeguards are supposedly unending. They do not wax and wane with the ebb and flow of historical events. They do not exist only in time of peace. Indeed, it is in the time of armed conflict involving Americans, of deep challenge to the traditional forms of due process, that the need for their continued if not expanded function becomes most urgent. The transformation of both congressional and executive exercise of the war power to what it has become need not be considered inevitable nor permanent. All too often, it is that which simply is not attempted that becomes unattainable. That may be the ultimate lesson to be learned from an examination of the war power since 1865.

[*See also* Constitution of the United States, *subentry on* The Constitution.]

BIBLIOGRAPHY

Belknap, Michal. "A Putrid Pedigree: The Bush Administration's Military Tribunals in Historical Perspective." *California Western Law Review* 38 (2002): 433–480. An excellent analysis that justifies the title of this article.

Ely, John Hart. *War and Responsibility: Constitutional Lessons of Vietnam and Its Aftermath*. Princeton, N.J.: Princeton University Press, 1993.

Fisher, Louis. *Military Tribunals and Presidential Power: American Revolution to the War on Terrorism*. Lawrence: University Press of Kansas, 2005. A thorough overview and a very appropriate source with which to begin exploring the war power.

Fisher, Louis. *Nazi Saboteurs on Trial: A Military Tribunal and American Law*. 2d ed. Lawrence: University Press of Kansas, 2005. A critical analysis of a controversial episode that continues to figure in the debate over the war power.

Friedman, Leon, and Burt Neuborne. *Unquestioning Obedience to the President: the ACLU Case Against the Illegal War in Vietnam*. New York: W. W. Norton and Company, 1972. A thought-provoking work that advocates a particular point of view.

Glennon, Michael J. *Constitutional Diplomacy*. Princeton, N.J.: Princeton University Press, 1990.

Keynes, Edward. *Undeclared War: Twilight Zone of Constitutional Power*. University Park: Pennsylvania State University Press, 1982.

Kohn, Richard H. *Eagle and Sword: The Federalists and the Creation of the Military Establishment in America, 1783–1802*. New York: Free Press, 1975. An outstanding historical analysis of the war power as conceived by the founding generation.

May, Ernest R., ed. *The Ultimate Decision: The President as Commander in Chief*. New York: G. Braziller, 1960. Long considered a standard source on presidential authority and the war power.

Rehnquist, William H. *All the Laws but One: Civil Liberties in Wartime*. New York: Alfred A. Knopf, 1998. A controversial analysis by the late chief justice of the United States, which many—including this author—will find unpersuasive.

Schlesinger, Arthur M., Jr. *War and the American Presidency*. New York: W. W. Norton and Company, 2004. A penetrating historical overview that substitutes insights for invective and thus is all the more persuasive.

Turner, Robert F. "War and the Forgotten Executive Power Clause of the Constitution: A Review Essay of John Hart Ely's *War and Responsibility*." *Virginia Journal of International Law* 34 (1994): 903–979. An essay that should be considered along with Ely's book cited above. It underscores the fact that the war power remains a source of ongoing scholarly controversy.

JONATHAN LURIE

WELFARE. At the federal level, the U.S. welfare system incorporates Social Security pensions, Medicare, Disability Insurance, Supplemental Security Insurance, the Earned Income Tax Credit (EITC), and food stamps, plus a wide range of other programs (housing vouchers, child care subsidies, etc.). At the state level, there are also many programs. The most prominent here are Temporary Assistance for Needy Families (TANF)—formerly Aid to Families with Dependent Children—and Medicaid. TANF is most commonly administered at the county level. Unemployment Insurance has federal requirements but is administered at the state level. General Relief, the program for childless non-aged adults, is administered at the county, and sometimes the municipal, level.

In the United States, the word "welfare" was originally associated with the broad array of government programs designed to ensure basic security for all citizens. Today, it has lost this positive meaning. Instead, welfare has become synonymous with TANF, the cash program for single mothers and their children. The stereotyped recipient has become a young inner-city African-American woman with substance abuse problems who bears more children in order to stay on welfare. In short, "welfare" connotes the underclass in the United States. In some respects, the intense political controversies surrounding this program are anomalous. At its height, in 1996, TANF (then AFDC) cost about $23 billion (state and federal share) annually, whereas in 1996 Social Security cost $300 billion. The EITC, which supplements low-wage earnings, is currently our most effective antipoverty mechanism, and costs considerably more than AFDC ever did, but is not popularly considered a welfare program. The reason is that a distinction between the "deserving" and "undeserving" poor lies at the core of U.S. welfare policy. Different programs are created based on the perceived status of recipients. Social insurance programs were created for the "deserving poor." They are entitlement programs administered by the federal government; anyone who meets eligibility requirements will get benefits, regardless of income or assets. Social Security is the prime example: benefits are tied to employment in covered occupations, and employees and employers pay taxes into the fund. Although the goal of Social Security is to provide support for the retired aged, fixed benefits are paid regardless of need. In contrast, public assistance programs are for the "undeserving" poor; these are usually administered and funded, at least partially, by state and local governments, and eligibility requirements and benefit levels vary from state to state. The stigma associated with welfare attaches to public assistance recipients, to whom are most often ascribed the moral faults once associated with paupers. The goal of public assistance is to help recipients survive, not to lift them out of poverty. While social insurance programs are closely protected by middle-class Americans who benefit from them, public assistance programs are under constant attack on grounds of "waste, fraud, and abuse."

This article will briefly outline the evolution of the U.S. welfare state, focusing on the distinction between "deserving" poor and "undeserving poor" programs, and will trace how the legal rights movement shaped and influenced the provision of welfare services in the United States.

Aid to Single Mothers and Their Children. During the Colonial period and early-nineteenth century, the principal concern of relief (public and private) was to control pauperism—the failure of the able-bodied to support themselves and their families by working. Pauperism was considered a moral failure, associated with other forms of deviant behavior such as intemperance, vice, criminality, sexual promiscuity, and illegitimacy. To discourage pauperism, local governments would deny aid to the able-bodied, forcing them into the labor market. Those who still could not find work were sent to poorhouses; outdoor relief (public works) was discouraged. In the mid-nineteenth

Mothers' Pensions. A National Child Labor Committee poster advertises mothers' pensions, c. 1914. PHOTOGRAPH BY LEWIS WICKES HINE. PRINTS AND PHOTOGRAPHS DIVISION, LIBRARY OF CONGRESS

century, states began to recognize that some categories of the poor could not support themselves; these were considered "deserving." Separate state institutions were therefore created for the blind, deaf, and insane. Then, following the Civil War, aid programs were established for war orphans, and pensions for veterans. They too were "deserving."

Poor single mothers and their children presented a dilemma. For most of welfare history, both were considered "undeserving." The mothers were tainted with suspicion of sexual promiscuity, child neglect, and—especially the Irish, Catholics, Italians, Jews, and others from southern Europe—being improper role models. Their children, however, were innocent; social reformers, alarmed at the number of immigrant children growing up in urban slums, expanded the definition of child neglect and removed many of these children to foster care, orphanages, and to be put up for adoption. Eventually, a number of social reformers known as the Child Savers claimed that if a mother was poor, but otherwise "fit and proper," the family should be supported in their own home. Starting in 1911, states quickly enacted Aid to Dependent Children programs, commonly called "mothers' pensions," aid provided under the supervision of the state (typically, of juvenile courts, which had jurisdiction over delinquent, dependent, and neglected children). Although statutes were broadly drafted, aid was, in practice, given primarily to white widows. All others, as well as divorced, deserted, and unmarried women, were excluded, considered not "fit and proper," and expected to enter the labor market. Mothers' pensions illustrate a characteristic of programs for the "undeserving poor" that has been called myth and ceremony. The myth was that poor mothers would be allowed to stay home and care for their children; the ceremony supporting it was the small number of white widows receiving aid. In reality, most single mothers were forced to work and became further stigmatized by not receiving mothers' pension aid.

The New Deal made few changes to ADC, which, along with old-age assistance and aid to the blind, became a grant-in-aid program under the Social Security Act of 1935. This received half its funding from the federal government, but the states retained administrative control. In 1939, widows and children of workers in covered employment were folded into Social Security. ADC became more a program for never-married, divorced, or deserted women. During the 1930s, state governments enacted a series of laws designed to change the morals of women left on the welfare rolls. For example, "man in the house" rules terminated or reduced a family's benefits if a recipient was cohabiting with a man who was not her spouse. States also developed "suitable home" and "fit parent" requirements to determine eligibility; these were disproportionately used to exclude African-American families.

Still, ADC remained small, and largely unnoticed. Then, starting in the late 1950s, the composition of ADC (subsequently called Aid to Families with Dependent Children, or AFDC) changed radically. With the mechanization of agriculture, there was a large migration of African Americans from the South into Northern urban centers where they sought jobs but were faced with poverty, unemployment, and a shortage of affordable housing. This was also a time of civil-rights activism, including the start of the legal-rights and welfare-rights movement. Welfare was redefined by the courts as a "right" (*Goldberg v. Kelly*, 397 U.S. 254 [1970]). State bars to benefits were breached, and poor mothers who had previously been excluded streamed in. Thus began the "welfare crisis." Over the next three decades, the rolls increased from 2 million recipients in the 1950s to approximately 13 million by the end of the 1980s.

The new entrants brought with them their "undeserving" status. In 1967, the first federal work requirement was enacted—the Work Incentive Program (WIN). At first, only conservatives supported work requirements. Asserting that welfare recipients were morally different from mothers who were either man-dependent or self-sufficient, they conjured up the image of the "welfare queen," a young African-American mother who bears children in order to stay on welfare. She fails to properly socialize her children, who grow up and repeat the same patterns. In other words, providing welfare without requiring work was creating a new underclass. Liberals at first countered that work requirements were unfair and punitive. Then, in the late 1980s, they too began to support them. They gave two reasons: first, since the majority of non-welfare mothers were now in the labor force, it was only reasonable to expect welfare mothers to work as well. Second, research was starting to show that families are materially and socially better off when mothers are gainfully employed, instead of on welfare.

Political controversy over AFDC heightened during the 1990s. Democratic presidential candidate Bill Clinton pledged to "end welfare as we know it." In 1996, as president, with the support of a strongly conservative, Republican-controlled Congress, he signed the Personal Responsibility and Work Opportunity Reconciliation Act into law. Under the new legislation, usually referred to simply as welfare reform, AFDC was replaced with TANF. Instead of an open-ended grant-in-aid to cover each family included, TANF provides block grants to the states based on past number of recipients. Strict work requirements and time limits were enacted: recipients could no longer receive aid for more than two consecutive years, and there was a five-year lifetime limit. States were required to move an increasing proportion of their recipients into the workforce or into work-related activities within six years. If recipients did not comply with work requirements, states were required to reduce their benefits; this was called a sanction.

Although the legislation gave states broad discretion in deciding how to reach their employment goals, most local governments adopted a "work first" strategy that emphasized taking any job, even a low-paying one, over education and training. The argument for this strategy was: (1) there are plenty of jobs for recipients who want to work; (2) by taking and sticking with any job, even an entry-level job, a person will move up the economic ladder; (3) welfare recipients do not otherwise have the motivation or incentives to leave welfare for the labor market; and (4) state demonstration programs have shown they can be moved from welfare to work.

In addition to work requirements, there were "family values" provisions in the legislation. For example, states were given the authority to deny welfare for children conceived while the mother was receiving welfare (this was called a family cap) and to limit or deny cash assistance to teenage mothers who do not reside with their parents or a responsible adult, or do not attend school. The federal government also required states to reduce a family's grant by 25 percent if they failed to cooperate (without good cause) with efforts to establish the paternity of their children. States might also choose to deny cash assistance for life to persons convicted of a felony, including the possession of even a small amount of marijuana.

TANF thus continued the long tradition of "undeserving poor" public assistance programs. Poverty was seen as caused by individual behavior. Welfare encouraged dependency with all its attendant ills for both adults and children. As in the earlier case of paupers, the intent of welfare reform was to ensure that able-bodied, morally suspect recipients worked and became independent. It was assumed that recipients were too lazy or otherwise unmotivated to find stable work without incentive to do so. Welfare recipients showed many of the moral failures attributed to paupers, including substance abuse, criminality, sexual promiscuity, and producing illegitimate children. Welfare reform strengthened social controls.

TANF also contributed, in fact, to strengthened local control. "Undeserving" programs are administered at the state and local level. The most morally suspect program—General Relief for non-aged, childless adults—is also the most local of all. Local governments set many of the rules of their programs, including benefit levels. The passage of welfare reform strengthened their control over the program by blocking grants, eliminating federal requirements that applications had to be acted on within 30 days, and allowing diversion. Although TANF set new federal work requirements, states were given broad discretion in designing programs to meet those goals. Block grants significantly increased this. Welfare benefits set by the states are always far below the federal poverty line; the goal of public assistance is not to lift recipients out of poverty, simply to help them survive. It costs less to support a family at a minimum level than to break up the home and place children in foster care or group homes. A foster parent has to be paid approximately $1,000 per child per month.

The Role of the Legal Rights Movement. One of the reasons for the rapid expansion of the welfare rolls in the 1960s and 1970s was the legal rights movement. During this time, Legal Services agencies were able to convince the courts to overturn many of the discriminatory restrictions used to keep poor families off welfare. Before the early 1960s, legal-aid offices were mostly concerned with representing individual clients in landlord-tenant, consumer, and family matters. Heavily influenced by the NAACP and its Legal Defense Fund's successful civil rights cases, Legal Services shifted its emphasis and became an integral part of President Johnson's War on Poverty. The overarching strategy became "community action," through which the poor would help themselves. Legal Services would empower them through the establishment of legal rights.

The specific model for Legal Services was the Ford Foundation's Gray Areas program, where community-based services, along with grass-roots activism, were seen as tools needed for the pro-active self-assertion of the poor and disfranchised. Legal Services addressed a wide range of concerns, including education, employment, welfare, health and mental health, individual problems, and community development. The dominating approach was litigating test cases to confirm individual rights and the rule of law in dealing with administrative agencies. The most important legal needs of the poor were assumed to be those concerning their relations with public programs such as welfare and housing.

While many ideas and organizations contributed to the development of Legal Services, three stand out. One was an article by Charles Reich, then a professor at the Yale Law School, who argued that relationships with government should have the same status and enjoy the same protection as traditional property rights. Reich coined the term the "new property." Another was an article published by Jean and Edgar Cahn, which presented the case for neighborhood, activist legal aid offices. The third was support for Legal Services from the American Bar Association, which became crucial not only in contests with local bar associations, but also against increasing conservative attacks on Legal Services.

From the mid-1960s to mid-1970s, Legal Services lawyers and their allies won a significant number of cases in a variety of areas. In *King v. Smith*, 392 U.S. 309 (1968), the U.S. Supreme Court held that welfare could not be denied simply because a mother cohabited with an unrelated male (the "man in the house" rule), and in *Shapiro v. Thompson*, 394 U.S. 618 (1969), that a state could not withhold welfare or provide lower benefits to poor people who migrated from another state. The most significant welfare case was *Goldberg v. Kelly*, in which the Court held that welfare was a statutory entitlement and that before it could be terminated the client had a due process right to a trial-type hearing at the administrative level, with the further right to judicial review of a determination made there. During this period storefront offices would advise welfare clients of their rights, both statutory and administrative. Clients were emboldened to confront welfare department staff, and, in certain parts of the country, to organize demonstrations and sit-ins at local offices. Welfare activists won significant victories in both federal and state courts. For example, persons were entitled to a due-process hearing to contest repossession of property or eviction from public housing (*Fuentes v. Shevin*, 407 U.S. 67 [1972]; *Thorpe v. Housing Authority of City of Durham*, 393 U.S. 268 [1969]); the mentally disabled had the right to be represented by an attorney in commitment hearings (*Lessard v. Schmidt*, 414 U.S. 473 [1974], reinstated 413 F. Supp. 1318 [E.D. Wis. 1976]); if confined to an institution, the mentally ill had a "right to treatment" (*Rouse v. Cameron*, 373 F.2d 451 [D.C. Cir. 1966]; *Wyatt v. Stickney*, 344 F. Supp. 373 [M.D. Ala. 1972]). In addition, new legislation—for example, the Voting Rights Act (1965), Americans with Disabilities Act (1990), and Education for All Handicapped Children Act (1975)—sought, among other things, to guarantee parent participation in special-education decisions.

Goldberg v. Kelly was the high-water mark in this period. Legal Services lawyers tried to establish that the right to a basic income was fundamental and deserved the same protection as other fundamental rights, such as speech, religion, and freedom from racial discrimination. But the Supreme Court almost immediately took back what it had given in *Goldberg*, holding in *Dandridge v. Williams*, 397 U.S. 471 (1970), that welfare was similar to other economic and social matters and could be regulated according to lower, more reasonable standards. Subsequent cases such as *Jefferson v. Hackney*, 406 U.S. 535 (1972), applied the "reasonable regulation" standard in upholding grant maximums regardless of family size; reductions in AFDC grants higher in percentage than those to for the aged, blind, and disabled; lower amounts of school funding in poorer districts; and unannounced caseworker visits, which were said not to violate the constitutional ban on unreasonable searches and seizure.

As a reaction to the activism of the 1960s began to take hold, its successes against government agencies aroused the hostility of state and local political leaders. Legal Services earned the undying enmity of Ronald Reagan, then (1967–1969) governor of California, when one office frustrated his attempts to cut back on welfare and health care for the poor. From time to time, governors attempted to prevent Legal Services offices from bringing suits against government agencies or on behalf of particular clients (such as migrant workers). After Reagan took office as president in 1981, he proposed no funds for Legal Services in seven straight budgets. The program survived, but funding cuts forced significant reductions in staff. Consequently, groups of cases (such as bankruptcies and disability-benefits disputes) had to be dropped by many offices. The Nixon administration had earlier tried to abolish Legal Services and distribute its funds to the states; when that failed, the compromise was to create an independent corporation, the Legal Services Corporation (1974). For the first time, restrictions on the kinds of cases that Legal Services could handle had been imposed. On the other hand, the corporation's budget had increased dramatically, from $71 million in 1975 to $321.3 million in 1981. Then the cuts started. After 1994 the Republican-controlled Congress made deep funding cuts (from $400 to $278 million annually) as part of a three-year plan to abolish Legal Services altogether, and added the most severe restrictions to date—prohibiting all class actions; eliminating the collection of attorneys' fees; and prohibiting participation in administrative rule making, lobbying, litigation on behalf of prisoners, representation of clients in drug-related public housing evictions, representation of certain categories of immigrants, or challenges to state welfare-reform laws, even if they violated the U.S. Constitution or federal laws.

These restrictions went into effect in August 1996, and Legal Services was forced to withdraw from more than 600 class-action lawsuits across the country. In 1997, its programs employed about 3,500 attorneys, assisted by about 59,000 private attorneys, mostly on a pro bono basis. The program closed 1.2 million cases and provided services for 1.9 million clients. In 1998, the budget for Legal Services was actually $21 million less than in 1980. The American Bar Association has estimated that only about 20 percent of the legal needs of the poor are being met. Thus, at a time when there is growing inequality and poverty, when more than 40 million Americans lack health care, when there is a growing shortage of affordable housing, and when the poor face some of the harshest welfare reforms in recent history, they are also being denied effective legal assistance.

Social Insurance Programs: Social Security. In contrast to aid for single mothers and their families stands aid to the aged. The beneficiaries of social insurance programs are the "deserving poor." They have worked hard and played by the rules, which entitles them to receive certain government benefits. Although the elderly (and subsequently, the disabled and blind) are the clearest example of the deserving poor, this was not always the case. The transformation of the dependent aged from morally ambivalent to clearly deserving illustrates the changes in the structural characteristics of the programs.

In the nineteenth century, elderly people had four alternatives to living in poverty: live on savings, move in with children, survive by relying on meager handouts from private and public charity, or keep working. When the Civil War pension program was abolished in 1917, pressure mounted for a new form of old-age assistance. States started creating their own programs in the 1920s. These were not widespread, and benefits were small. There was no universally agreed on age of retirement. There were many conditions imposed to make sure programs did not undermine the work ethic and family responsibility. For example, applicants who had failed to support their families or who had been vagrant were ineligible for benefits. There were also restrictions on disposing of property in order to qualify for relief. The politics of helping the aged changed, though, with the Great Depression, when middle-class families (and their parents) suddenly faced poverty. There was a shift in the moral categorization of the dependent aged. Political movements, such as that promoting the Townsend Plan, urged uniform and relatively condition-free "pensions" for the aged poor. The Roosevelt administration believed that if it did not come up with an alternative to the Townsend movement, the plan would be adopted and might bankrupt the country. On the other hand, Roosevelt was opposed to "welfare."

In response to these pressures, including removing those sixty-five and older from the competition for jobs, Roosevelt proposed the Social Security pension system. This was to be self-funding, and resembled a private insurance program. As long as one worked and paid taxes into the fund, one could receive benefits. To distinguish Social Security from welfare, it was to be available to only those workers who made sufficient contributions. To help the vast majority of the elderly poor who would not be covered, the federal government would provide matching grants-in-aid to state Old Age Assistance programs (along with matching grants to ADC and Aid to the Blind). Thus, one of the paramount goals of the Roosevelt administration was not to relieve need among the dependent aged through a form of welfare, rather to set up a slowly maturing insurance system that, among other things, would exclude the dependent aged. The administration did not want the stigma of the morally problematic poor to taint Social Security. Thus, in addition to requiring a period of work and contributions, the Social Security program, as originally devised, did not cover several categories of low-wage jobs. The exclusion of agricultural and domestic work, primarily filled by African Americans, was forced by Southern members of Congress.

Over time, the Social Security program has expanded to cover more people. In 1935, amendments allowed survivors otherwise not eligible to receive benefits. In 1956, disability insurance was added to the program. During this period, the program expanded to cover even many of the

Social Security. Unemployed workers signing up for unemployment benefits following passage of the Social Security Act, c. 1935. FRANKLIN D. ROOSEVELT PRESIDENTIAL LIBRARY AND MUSEUM

aged whose contributions did not equal what they received in benefits. By the years after World War II, the aged had clearly become the deserving poor; very few are now not covered. Thus Social Security, although originally designed for the nonpoor, has had redistributive effects, and poverty among the aged has been significantly reduced. For the relatively small number of the aged who were still not covered by the pension program, existing old-age assistance programs were folded into the Supplemental Security Income (SSI) program in 1972. Thus all of the aged, regardless of work histories and insurance contribution (or moral behavior), now receive most of their public support from a completely federally financed and federally administered program.

The goal of Social Security is to ensure that all elderly people have a decent standard of living; in other words, it tries to lift the elderly out of poverty. Most important, beneficiaries are considered "deserving." In contrast to TANF, the program does not try to change behavior: there are no work or "family values" provisions built in. And until recently, Social Security has been considered "the third rail of government": to try to reform it would be to jeopardize one's political career.

Health Care. The government's provision of health care also distinguishes between the deserving and undeserving poor. Unlike other industrialized Western nations, the United States does not have a national health system. Instead, private businesses are expected to provide health insurance for full-time employees. Relying on the private sector, however, leaves many uninsured, including many of the elderly, the disabled, the unemployed, people receiving public assistance, and, increasingly, low-wage workers. There are two government health insurance programs designed to provide at least minimal health insurance to these populations—Medicare and Medicaid, both enacted in 1965. These are radically different. Medicare is a social insurance program run by the federal government and designed to provide the elderly and disabled with prepaid hospital insurance and supplemental medical insurance. In 2001, the government paid $246.8 billion for Medicare payments and provided coverage to 40.6 million people. Medicaid was designed for the poor, including TANF and SSI recipients. To receive Medicaid, one must have earnings below a certain level. The federal and state governments jointly fund Medicaid, but states administer the program. In 2002, the federal government made $139.2 billion in Medicaid payments, not including money given to the states to administer the program. There were approximately 39.9 million Medicaid enrollees that year.

Costs for the Medicare and Medicaid programs grew substantially from the 1990s into the 2000s. Despite the increasing costs of Medicare, the federal government in 2004 added prescription drug coverage to the program. This was expected to add from $395 to $534 billion in expenditures in 2004–2013. In contrast, Medicaid tends to be cut by states when they face budget crises. In 2003 eighteen states said they would restrict Medicaid eligibility (as by postponing planned expansions or instituting measures that can make it more difficult to become or stay enrolled); fifteen said they would reduce benefits; fifteen would increase co-payments; forty would adopt cost containment strategies for prescription drugs; and twenty-nine would freeze or reduce payments to health care providers. Despite Medicare, Medicaid, and employer-purchased health insurance, there are serious gaps. At present, over 40 million Americans are without health insurance and have to rely on hospital emergency rooms for basic health care needs.

Summary. A central feature of the U.S. welfare state from its inception has been the distinction between the "deserving" and "undeserving" poor. Programs for the "deserving" are relatively condition-free, are federally administered, and have the goal of lifting recipients out of poverty. Social Security is only one example; others include Medicare, SSI, and EITC. Public assistance programs—"welfare"—are locally administered, vary widely, offer meager benefits, and have an underlying goal of changing the moral character of "undeserving" recipients. Public assistance programs include TANF, food stamps, and General Relief. Other programs are morally ambiguous; an example is Unemployment Insurance, which is state-administered (with federal requirements) and presently covers only about one-third of the unemployed. While public assistance programs—which carry the heaviest "moral" charge—are usually a central part of welfare debates, they represent only a small part of the welfare state. At its height, in 1996, AFDC cost $23 billion (both federal and state) annually. In 1996, Social Security cost $300 billion and the EITC $34 billion.

It is not just funding differences that distinguish public assistance programs from forms of social insurance. The goal of public assistance is not only to provide aid to the needy but to act as an agent of social control— to teach recipients proper values. In contrast, social insurance is given regardless of moral character. The fact that recipients worked hard and paid into the system is enough. One way in which the differences in assumptions can be seen is by examining who is labeled "dependent." One of the primary reasons for welfare reform was the assumption that recipients had become dependent on aid. Welfare offices were told to make these women learn the value of work. In contrast, no one criticizes social insurance recipients as dependent, even if Social Security keeps them out of poverty, and there are no attempts to control their behavior. As long as this distinction exists, there will always be two classes of public aid recipients.

[*See also* Elderlaw *and* Poverty.]

BIBLIOGRAPHY

Abramovitz, Mimi. *Regulating the Lives of Women: Social Welfare Policy from Colonial Times to the Present*. Boston, Mass.: South End Press, 1988.

Cahn, Edgar S., and Jean C. Cahn. "The War on Poverty: A Civilian Perspective." *Yale Law Journal* 73 (1964): 1317–1352.

Ellwood, David. *Poor Support: Poverty in the American Family*. New York: Basic Books, 1988.

Garfinkel, Irwin, and Sara S. McLanahan. *Single Mothers and Their Children: A New American Dilemma*. Washington, D.C.: Urban Institute Press, 1986.

Gordon, Linda. *Heroes of Their Own Lives: The Politics and History of Family Violence, Boston, 1880–1960*. New York: Viking, 1988.

Handler, Joel F. *Social Citizenship and Workfare in the United States and Western Europe: The Paradox of Inclusion*. Cambridge, U.K.: Cambridge University Press, 2004.

Kaiser Family Foundation. *The New Medicare Prescription Drug Law: Issues for Dual Eligibles with Disabilities and Serious Conditions*. http://www.kff.org/medicaid/7119.cfm (accessed December 1, 2008).

Katz, Michael B. *In the Shadow of the Poorhouse: A Social History of Welfare in America*. New York: Basic Books, 1986.

Katz, Michael B. *The Price of Citizenship: Redefining the American Welfare State*. New York: Metropolitan Books, 2001.

Ku, Leighton, and Matthew Broaddus. *Why Are States' Medicaid Expenditures Rising?* Center on Budget and Policy Priorities. http://www.cbpp.org/1-13-03health.htm (accessed December 1, 2008).

Mink, Gwendolyn. *Welfare's End*. Ithaca, N.Y.: Cornell University Press, 1998.

Piven, Frances Fox, and Richard A. Cloward. *Poor People's Movements: Why They Succeed, How They Fail*. New York: Pantheon, 1977.

Reich, Charles A. "The New Property." *Yale Law Journal* 73 (1964): 733–787.

Skocpol, Theda. *Protecting Soldiers and Mothers: The Political Origins of Social Policy in the United States*. Cambridge, Mass.: Belknap Press of the Harvard University Press, 1992.

U.S. Department of Health and Human Services. *2003 CMS Statistics*. http://www.cms.hhs.gov/CapMarketUpdates/Downloads/03CMSstats.pdf. (accessed December 1, 2008)

Weaver, R. Kent. *Ending Welfare as We Know It*. Washington, D.C.: Brookings Institution Press, 2000.

JOEL F. HANDLER

AMANDA SHEELY

WELSH LAW. The eastern boundary of the country which is modern Wales was not established until the sixteenth century, when the union legislation divided the border country into shires. Wales had, however, been a distinct entity in the preceding centuries, as the people who lived there were of a different ethnic origin and spoke a language different from that of their English neighbors. The Welsh as a people were descended from the native British who had been forced westwards by the Anglo-Saxon invasions. They maintained their view of themselves as British until the twelfth century.

The Roman Period. The native British had inhabited the British Isles before the coming of the Romans, but as they had no written tradition, it is very difficult to account for their law and governance. Under Roman rule, the free population attained Roman citizenship by virtue of the *Constitutio Antoniniana* in 212 C.E., but although they would have been governed by Roman public law, it is likely that in private law matters they continued to follow their own native customs. It is however known that some Roman practices were adopted; artisans, for example, are known to have formed Roman *societates* (associations) to pursue their trade and calling. When the Romans left Wales at the end of the fourth century, the native British clung to many elements of their Roman heritage, most notably the Christian faith. They also continued to use the Latin language, maintained Roman settlements, and adopted the dragon flag of the legions. It is not unlikely, therefore, that they retained some memory of Roman law in their own customary practices. These elements were all fostered by continued contact with parts of Gaul and the continent where Roman vulgar law held its place, although influence from Ireland, particularly in the west, also played a significant part in the development of the native Welsh laws. Nor should the presence of biblical precedents for some customs be discounted among so passionately Christian a people.

The Native Laws. The first firm evidence for the native laws of Wales concerns the society of the native princes from the tenth century on. Wales was at this time an amalgam of kingdoms, three of which were to rise to prominence: Gwynedd in the northwest, Deheubarth in the southwest, and Powys along the eastern frontier with England. In the first half of the tenth century, Hywel Dda, the ruler of Deheubarth, is said to have convened an assembly at Whitland to which he summoned representatives of all the Welsh kingdoms, for the moment largely united under his rule. At this assembly, he caused the laws of the various parts of Wales to be written down, amended so as to remove outdated elements, and harmonized, so as to achieve a legal unity within his realms. It is said that he then took the end-product to Rome where it was accorded the Pope's blessing. The story is unverified, but there was certainly thereafter a tradition that Hywel was Wales's law-giver, and the native customs came to be known as the Law of Hywel.

Hywel's was a written law, and its interpretation and application fell on a class of jurists, men learned in the laws of Wales, who in the northern kingdom served as judges in the law courts, while in the south they advised the lay judges. The momentary unity achieved by Hywel did not survive his death, as his kingdoms had to be shared among his sons. The several kingdoms therefore maintained their separate identities: within each a peculiar legal tradition emerged within the larger tradition of the law of Hywel and law books were produced, recording the local law and often bearing the name of a jurist or compiler associated with or honored in the locality. In Deheubarth, it was Blegywryd, said by some to have been archdeacon of Llandaff who acted as scribe to Hywel's assembly; in Gwynedd it was Iorwerth, a member of a family of distinguished jurists; in Powys, or possibly the southeast, Cyfnerth. *Llyfr Blegywryd*, *Llyfr Iorwerth*, and *Llyfr Cyfnerth*—llyfr, from Latin *liber*, means "book" in Welsh—represent the three great traditions of the native laws, living traditions which give their names to bodies of laws that grew organically and were constantly revised, unlike the static law of the Irish traditions to the west.

The three legal traditions are known from manuscripts written in either Welsh or Latin in which the customs are recorded. There are five main Latin texts, known today by the first five letters of the English alphabet. Latin A corresponds to the *Cyfnerth* tradition; B, C, and E to that of *Iorwerth*; and Latin D is very similar to *Blegywryd*. Among the Welsh traditions, there is also an abbreviated version of *Iorwerth*, known as *Llyfr Colan*, and there are also books of instances known as *Damweiniau* bearing Colan's name. The manuscripts are extant from the later twelfth century and continued to be produced, and updated, throughout the Middle Ages.

The laws recorded in them are distinctive in several ways. The Welsh laws deal extensively with the laws of the king's court, and often these sections contain elements supportive of the claims of a particular kingdom to hegemony over the others. Sections are also devoted to the law of wild and tame, dealing with property in animals, and to the three columns of the law, dealing with the most serious wrongs of theft, homicide, and arson. Homicide in the Welsh laws is treated as an occasion for compensation, to be paid by the family of the killer to that of the victim. There are elaborate rules for calculating the manner in which this payment, called *galanas*, is to be collected from and distributed to a wide range of relatives. Fixed compensation payments were also due for harms to a person's body and injuries, called *sarhad*, to his dignity; the payments for the latter varied with status. The procedure of the law courts is also described, and there appears to have been no trial by ordeal according to the native Welsh customs.

Property rights inhered in the family and the kin group rather than individuals. With land, for instance, there was generally no freedom of alienation during life or at death. A freeman's lands descended to his sons in equal shares, and when the last son died, it was shared out equally once more among the first person's grandsons. Daughters inherited movable property but not the family land. Marriage was based on consent, and divorce was possible, a feature of the Welsh laws which scandalized the Catholic clergy of the post-Norman period. Controversial also in their eyes was the fact that no stigma was attached to birth outside of wedlock; all of a man's sons, whether legitimate or illegitimate in the eyes of the Church, inherited from him. There were thus elaborate rules relating to affiliation.

As all extant manuscripts come from the period after some Norman incursion had occurred in Wales, it is likely that the story of ecclesiastical involvement in the laws' compilation may reflect a perceived need to meet clerical criticism. The manuscripts also bear witness to the influence of feudalism upon some of the native customs, particularly in the south. Thus, one sees the lord, or *arglwydd*, playing a part in social affairs that would earlier have been allotted to the *pencenedl*, the head of a kinship group, and there are numerous instances in which the feudal lord's claims to what had previously been ownerless property available to the first taker, such as fish and game, result in a compromise solution being given by the laws. English influence can also be seen in the importation of procedures, such as the jury of neighbors, *rhaith*, replacing that of kin, *rhaith cenedl*.

English Law and Medieval Wales. During the first half of the thirteenth century, the princes of Gwynedd were clearly preeminent among the Welsh rulers. On several occasions, they attempted with varying success to claim the homage of their fellow rulers, reserving to themselves alone the right to swear allegiance to the English king. Such subservience was not controversial because during centuries since the Roman withdrawal, the Welsh princes had acknowledged the primacy of the king in London, perhaps reflecting a memory of the position in later Roman times. Henry III and Edward I, however, were unhappy with Gwynedd's claims to the homage of the other Welsh princes, and the success with which the claim was advanced varied with the political and military vicissitudes suffered by both the Welsh and the English rulers. Edward I eventually tired of Llywelyn ap Gruffydd's resorts to rebellion, and after Llywelyn was killed in 1282,

Welsh Assembly. Alun Michael, leader of the Labor Party, addresses the Welsh Assembly during the Assembly's first sitting in nearly 600 years, Cardiff, May 1999. PHOTOGRAPH BY BARRY BATCHELOR. AP PHOTO

Edward annexed the lands of Gwynedd to the English crown as the principality of north Wales, while the shires of Cardigan and Carmarthen in the southwest formed the principality of the south.

Within the Principality, as the crown lands in Wales became known, English law was introduced by the Statute of Rhuddlan, also called the Statute of Wales. In both south and north, there were to be Justiciars, and courts similar to those of common law in England were introduced. The procedure within the courts, where the jurisdiction of the common pleas and the king's bench were not distinguished as at Westminster, was modeled on the writ system of the English common law, and the writs to be used were given in the statute. Opportunity was taken to remedy some of the inconveniences and defects of the English system when it was introduced into the Principality, so that the statute is a useful source for discovering royal policy and intentions with regard to legal development generally. Edward also advanced the cause of English settlement in Wales by establishing boroughs around the defensive castles he built. These boroughs had their own customs, modeled on those of such communities in England and France, and the native Welsh were often prohibited from settling in them, intermarrying with the burgesses, and trading within their walls. After the Glyn Dwr revolt at the start of the fifteenth century, such restrictions were often tightened with a vengeance.

Those parts of Wales that were outside of the Principality were known collectively as the March, a term which strictly should be confined to the border country. Nevertheless, other non-crown lordships, such as Pembroke and Glamorgan are usually called marcher lordships. These lordships were under the authority of the local Marcher lord, whose family had often come to control them by conquest. The king of England's writ, therefore, did not run in the March. The law was that of the Marcher lord, who was virtually a lord palatine within his lands. The people of the Marcher lordships lived according to the local law, although there were often separate customs for those of English and Welsh provenance in the Englishry and the Welshry respectively. The law of the March, never a homogeneous entity despite the description, was itself an amalgam of native Welsh and imported English practices. In particular, the native Welsh modes of landholding and family organization retained a strong hold. The fact, however, that wrongdoers could only with difficulty be extradited from one lordship to another to face justice contributed to the Marches' reputation for lawlessness and disorder.

Another abuse that contributed to the lawless character of the March was the custom of redeeming the sessions. The sessions were judicial sittings with general jurisdiction, whose timing and duration were regularly, perhaps deliberately, inconvenient to the local population. As a consequence, they paid sums of money to the lord in lieu of the holding of sessions either in whole or in part. The lords profited, but justice was left undone. As a result of escheats and forfeitures during the fifteenth century, however, more and more Marcher lordships came into the hands of the crown, and the Yorkist and Tudor kings set about restoring law and order in the area. One of the prime instruments in this effort was the Prince of Wales's Council in the marches of Wales, which came to be based at Ludlow. Under a series of energetic presidents, sometimes acting with ruthless determination, greater order was restored. Meanwhile, Welshmen who cooperated with the English crown were often rewarded with the grant of denizen status, that is, the rights of Englishmen within Wales and in particular within the Welsh boroughs. Such grants were sometimes given to whole communities.

The Union of Wales and England. With the accession to the English throne of a dynasty perceived to be Welsh, the Tudors, many felt that the problems of law and order within Wales would best be solved by uniting the two countries. This was done by the acts of union in 1536 and 1542. Under the provisions of these statutes, the Principality and the Marches were divided into shires. Some areas were allotted to neighboring English counties, while Wales itself was divided into thirteen. For the first time, these shires and the boroughs within them were permitted to send representatives to the parliament at Westminster. Likewise, members of the county gentry became qualified to sit as justices of the peace in the local petty sessions. For the middle classes of Tudor Wales, these opportunities afforded a path to civic and national status, and they were eagerly grasped. The sons of these men began to frequent the universities and the Inns of Court, and not a few served with distinction in the service of the civil law in the Admiralty court and before the ecclesiastical tribunals.

The thirteen Welsh counties were, for the purposes of administering justice, grouped into four circuits, each of three shires, Monmouthshire—as the closest county to London—being placed in a neighboring English circuit. The old Principality of north Wales became the shires of Anglesey, Caernarfon, and Merioneth; in the northeast, Flint, Denbigh, and Montgomeryshire formed the Chester circuit; in the southeast, Radnorshire, Brecknock, and Glamorgan formed the Brecknock circuit; while in the southwest, the old principality counties of Cardigan and Carmarthen were merged with the lordship of Pembroke to form the Carmarthen circuit. Within each, courts of Great Sessions were to be held for six days twice each year. These courts were to have the same jurisdiction as the common law courts at Westminster, with no distinction between King's Bench and Common Pleas. They were also to try serious crimes in the manner of the county assizes in England. While it is debated whether the

Sessions had, prior to the abolition of the Council at Ludlow at the close of the seventeenth century, an equitable jurisdiction to provide remedies where either the common law did not so provide or where its remedies were inadequate, they certainly acquired one thereafter. The Council itself, while it lasted, had not only an equitable jurisdiction similar to that of the Court of Chancery, but also the prerogative powers exercised in England by courts such as Star Chamber, the High Commission, and the Court of Requests. Each of the circuits was staffed by the end of the sixteenth century with a chief justice and a puisne (that is, subordinate, inferior) judge. There was also a range of court officers.

The Sessions were Wales's own courts of law. They were not, however, without their defects. They sat in each county for only six days each year, and the judges who staffed them had practices at the bar in London for the remainder of the year and tended to organize the sittings to their own convenience. Nothing came of the excellent suggestion that the judges should sit permanently at Ludlow when not in the counties. Questions were also asked about the standards of the lawyers who practiced before the courts.

During the eighteenth century, the Court of King's Bench at Westminster began to claim concurrent competence with the Sessions so as to give litigants the choice of whether to sue in their own county or in London. The Westminster courts were open for a greater part of the year. When concurrent competence was found to exist, other than for small claims, the fate of the Sessions was virtually assured. Edmund Burke challenged their cost-effectiveness, and a campaign began for their abolition. They were seen almost immediately in Wales as a focus of national identity. They were nevertheless abolished in 1830.

Devolution. The reform of the judicial system was but one feature of the wider reforms taking place in Britain, reforms that widened the franchise and increased pressure for legal solutions to Welsh problems of a singularly Welsh hue. One of the chief bones of contention was the payment of tithes by the Nonconformist Welsh majority to support what was seen as the alien Church of England. A campaign began to disestablish the church. The argument that legislation for Wales alone was not possible, as it was not a separate law district, foundered after the Sunday Closing Act in 1881 provided for the shutting of public houses in Wales on the Sabbath. The Welsh Church Act 1914 disestablished the Church of England in Wales, and when it came into force and effect in 1920, Wales had another national institution, the Church in Wales, to place alongside the University, the National Museum, and the National Library. Much disaffection also revolved around failures to give Wales control over its own education system. Throughout the twentieth century, the feeling grew that Wales ought to have its own secretary of state and a

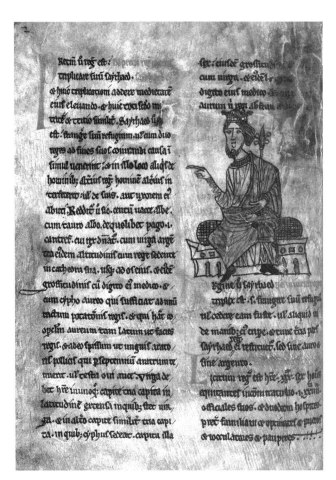

The Law of Hywel. Page from Peniarth MS 28, an early Welsh lawbook, thirteenth century. BY PERMISSION OF LLYFRGELL GENEDLAETHOL CYMRU/THE NATIONAL LIBRARY OF WALES

Welsh Office to oversee its administrative affairs. A secretary of state was appointed in 1964, and a Welsh office established in Cardiff shortly thereafter, Cardiff having been designated the national capital in 1955.

As devolved regional government, that is, the granting by the central state government of legislative, administrative, and sometimes judical power to more local national or regional governments, became a facet of the European legal scene, so the argument for a measure of devolution for Wales, along with Scotland, gained ground. Proposals to provide a devolved tier of government were rejected in a popular referendum in 1979. In the years that followed, however, there was increased dissatisfaction with the powers exercised by unelected bodies appointed by governments at Westminster which were largely unrepresentative of Wales. When, therefore, a fresh opportunity was given to vote on devolution in 1997, the proposal was accepted by the narrowest of margins, and in 1999, Wales obtained a democratically elected National Assembly with powers to frame secondary legislation for its people.

BIBLIOGRAPHY

Charles-Edwards, T. M. *The Welsh Laws*. Cardiff: University of Wales Press, 1989. Readable introductory account to the native Welsh legal texts.

Hywel Dda. Translated and edited by Dafydd Jenkins. *The Law of Hywel Dda: Law Texts of Medieval Wales*. Llandysul, U.K.: Gomer, 1986. A modern translation into English of the native Welsh laws.

Jenkins, Dafydd. *Cyfraith Hywel*. Llandysul, U.K.: Gomer, 1970. An examination of the main features of Welsh native law, written in Welsh.

Morgan, Kenneth O. *Rebirth of a Nation: Wales 1880-1980*. Oxford: Oxford University Press, and Cardiff: University of Wales Press, 1981. Principal narrative account of modern Welsh history containing a thorough overview of the development of devolved government and distinctive legislation for Wales.

Watkin, T. G. *The Legal History of Wales*. Cardiff: University of Wales Press, 2007. Overview of the legal history of Wales from the Romans to Devolution.

THOMAS GLYN WATKIN

WEST AFRICA. *See* African Law, Sub-Saharan, *subentry on* The Precolonial Period.

WESTERN CANON LAW. *See* Canon Law.

WILLS. [*This entry contains two subentries, on wills in English common law and in Islamic law. For discussion of wills in ancient Greek law, see Inheritance, subentry on Ancient Greek Law. For wills in Chinese law and United States law, see Succession.*]

English Common Law

The history of wills and testaments reflects the jurisdictional conflicts that existed between the royal and ecclesiastical authorities over the control of the disposition of property upon death. The common law, church, and chancery courts each gained control over different aspects of succession, leaving a complex body of law.

The division between land and chattels has been characterized as "the most fundamental dividing line of the medieval common law" (Holdsworth, p. 412). This division, the characterization of property as either land or chattel, mostly settled by around 1500, determined the treatment of the property for both testate and intestate estates. In the absence of a will, land was subject to precise rules of inheritance that operated by law to pass the property to the heir or heirs. The disposition of chattels, in the absence of a testament, was subject to local custom and the individual discretion of the ecclesiastic administering the estate. Wherever land was concerned, ecclesiastical courts were prohibited from acting. Indeed, the nature of the document or act controlling the disposition of property was determined by the type of property.

A "testament" dealing with chattels was proved in the ecclesiastical courts that had general testamentary jurisdiction over goods. The common law required fewer formalities, and thus a "last will," when recognized by the royal courts, could dispose of land. The terms were eventually brought together, and the term "will" encompasses the term "testament" in the Wills Act of 1837.

At the highest level of testamentary jurisdiction were the archiepiscopal provinces of York and Canterbury, each with a special probate court for estates with goods in more than one diocese or estates with values exceeding certain amounts. On the lower, diocesan level, there was substantial variation in the distribution of probate work between the archdeacon, commissary, and bishop. Probate, the proving of the testament by the executor, was conducted in either common or solemn form. Common form invoked the noncontentious jurisdiction of the ecclesiastical court where witnesses testified orally as to the testator's will. Solemn form required the witnesses to be examined by written articles and interrogatories. The church handled probate of wills in England until 1858, when the Principal Probate Registry provided a centralized structure in London with district registries in other cities.

Chancery gained a substantial jurisdiction in contentious suits over wills and testaments with the ecclesiastical courts maintaining noncontentious jurisdiction over probate of wills of personalty, the granting of administrations, and the appointing of executors. Although chancery could not decide cases concerning devises of land, actions against heirs, or the validity of a will, it did handle suits for legacies, accountings, the distributions of the residue of estates, the return of assets by a legatee, and the apportionment of debts.

Intestacy. Individuals near death were encouraged by attending priests to put both their spiritual and worldly affairs in order, and instructions included leaving a testament for the disposition of goods. Testaments often began with formulaic religious language, followed by pious bequests to the church. Despite such clerical and social encouragement, intestacy, or dying without a valid will, was a common occurrence throughout English history. Without a will, there were no instructions for the care of the deceased's soul, the distribution of lands and goods, the payment of debts, the provision of family members, the appointment of guardians, and the overseeing of these functions. Thus, intestacy was, in theory, to be avoided; in practice, it was common.

In the absence of a will, land passed automatically on the death of the owner. Under common-law primogeniture, land passed to the heir as determined through a parentelic scheme. A group of potential takers from the deceased's descendants (or descendants of the father or grandfather, if necessary) was selected. Males excluded females, and the eldest son was preferred to younger sons. Even the surviving son of a deceased eldest son was preferred to a younger surviving son of the deceased father. In families without a son, daughters took equally. If land came from the mother's side, the heir was determined from the mother's male line. There were also some notable regional variations; in Wales and Kent, for example, the customary practice was equal division of land among sons. These general principles were in effect until 1926.

Heirs were not bound by debts of the decedent that were charged against the decedent's chattels. By statute in 1833, land became available more generally for the payment of the debts of the decedent.

Chattels, unlike land, did not pass automatically by operation of the common law. With jurisdiction over the distribution of chattels at death, the church applied local customary and ecclesiastical law to this process through an administrator appointed by the ordinary. Along with the church's jurisdiction came the idea that a portion of the chattels should be applied for the good of the decedent's soul, and in many areas, especially in the north of England, the custom was to impose a tripartite division of property. One-third was given the surviving spouse, one-third to children, and one-third for religious or pious purposes. Under a statutory distribution scheme of 1670, the widow received one-third and the children two-thirds. If there were no children, the widow received one-half and the next of kin of the decedent received one-half. If there were no widow or children, the next of kin took all.

Wills and Testaments. In theory and at common law, land could not be devised by will; it was to descend to the heir in the scheme of primogeniture. Nonetheless land became, in practice, devisable through the mechanism of the use. The use separated the equitable from the legal ownership of the land. Feoffors (grantors) of land could transfer land to feoffees who held the land to the use of a third person called a "cestuy que use." The "use" was a bundle of benefits in the land the cestuy-que-use enjoyed without being the legal holder of the land. The cestuy-que-use could declare his will as to how his use of the land was to pass after his death. The will devised the use of the land, not the land itself.

By placing legal title in a group of feoffees, the owner of land not only created an interest that could be devised by will, but also sidestepped the imposition of feudal dues which were usually assessed on the death of the legal holder of the property. The use provided, in modern parlance, good tax planning. With fiscal considerations at the forefront in the mid-sixteenth century, the crown began an assault on the use, and with it, on wills of land. After the Commons had rebuffed a plan by Henry VIII to reimpose feudal dues on one-third of the applicable land, a test case was tried in 1535. The case was interpreted to say that any will of land, through a use or not, was invalid.

Because vast amounts, if not the majority, of land in England had been placed into uses and perhaps devised by will, this case called into question the title to all land in England. The Crown was now better positioned to effect legislation restoring its feudal incidents, and the statute bringing this about, the Statute of Uses (1536), contained a savings clause for devises of land before the date of the statute.

The Statute of Uses transferred legal ownership of the land from the feoffees to the cestuy-que-use who would then die seised of the land, resulting in the land passing to his heir. Feudal incidents then attached on his death. The effect of the statute was to prohibit the devise of land by will and to impose primogeniture on most of the land in England. Facing new techniques around the statute and perhaps influenced by its unpopularity, Henry VIII shifted away from its application.

In 1540, the Statute of Wills permitted landowners to devise land within certain limits. Generally, two-thirds of the applicable land could be devised, with the remaining one-third passing to the heir by descent and subject to feudal incidents. All socage land (land not held by knight service) could be devised, but the crown reserved various incidents to be paid by the devisee or heir. The statute's general permissive language, giving the testator the power to devise the applicable land at his "free will and pleasure" led to certain ambiguities, such as the age of testamentary capacity, which were addressed in a subsequent statute, the Explanation of the Statute of Wills (1542). The broad sweep of this language also permitted testators to create new types of future interests in land that had been substantially limited by the common law. Furthermore, land was often given during lifetime in elaborate settlements for family members.

This scheme applied for most land in England until the abolition of military tenures in 1660. Nonetheless, there were other lands in England that were devisable by local or regional custom and were not subject to the Statute of Uses. Copyhold land, land within certain manors, was devisable by the custom of the manor, and some land within cities, notably London, and certain boroughs was also devisable by the custom of the place. These lands were later addressed in the Statute of Frauds (1677) and the Wills Act of 1837.

Thus, before the Statute of Wills (1540), a will of land usually was a direction to feoffees to uses, and the land must have been conveyed to feoffees before the will. After the Statute of Wills, this general aspect continued; the will took effect on death and addressed only the land in possession of the testator when the will was executed and subsequently when the testator died. Each devise of land was a specific devise to the devisee, so that when a devise of land failed, it was the heir and not the residuary devisee who received the land. The Wills Act of 1837 abrogated these harsh rules that often ran counter to the testator's intent.

Chattels were not inherited, but were distributed by the executor appointed in the will or testament according to its provisions. Money, intangible property, and interests of or created from a term of years in real property could also be transferred this way. Following the tripartite divisions of chattels for the administration of testate estates, similar restrictions were placed on the decedent's testamentary freedom in wills. Under this principle of *legitim* (a portion of the testator's property that passed automatically to children), for much of the period, the testator could bequeath his one-third interest. The customary practices in York were somewhat different, but reflected the same ideas of permitting the testator to bequeath only a certain portion when survived by a wife or child. These restrictions gradually disappeared in England. In the south, they were gone by around 1400, and over the next hundred years, testamentary freedom became the norm with some important regional variations. In the seventeenth and eighteenth centuries, testamentary freedom was confirmed by statute on testators in York and London.

Other mechanisms, such as a doctrine of inofficious wills to protect family members, did not develop in England, and family members might be given a small bequest in a will—"cut off with a shilling"—to avoid any possible application of such rules. Surviving spouses were afforded some protection by the common-law rules of dower and curtesy. The crown, through mortmain legislation, restricted gifts of land to the church, ensuring that such property would go to the heir or devisee.

English law was not as exacting in its requirements for a valid will or testament as the civil law, with the testator's intent as the guiding principle of interpretation. Effective wills could be oral (nuncupative) or written, or both. Nuncupative testaments were created when the testator named an executor and declared his will by word of mouth. It could be later reduced to writing, was proved by two witnesses had equal force with a written testament, except for dispositions of land. Wealthier testators usually resorted to written wills, but nuncupative wills were useful when the testator was very ill, often on his deathbed, and the Statute of Frauds (1677) provided for deathbed nuncupative wills.

A will could be written by the testator or at the direction of the testator. It might be signed and sealed by the testator. Clergy (especially before the Reformation often attending the testator's deathbed), scriveners, and, later, lawyers were the primary drafters of written wills. Testators were given significant latitude in the choice of materials, language, and hand, with the comprehensibility of the document and the testator's intent as essential considerations. The Statute of Wills (1540) required that wills of land be in writing, but did not require the testator's signature.

A will dictated to another was valid under the statute. The Statute of Frauds (1677) required a writing signed by the testator (or by direction of the testator) and attested to by three or four witnesses. The Wills Act of 1837 required every will to be in writing and signed by two witnesses present.

The common law imposed restrictions on testamentary capacity that were not present under the ecclesiastical law. For example, under common law, villeins and married women were prohibited from making wills. While villein status had disappeared by 1600, the inability of married women to devise land was repeated in the Explanation of the Statute of Wills (1542). Chancery extended greater legal powers to married women, and by the mid-eighteenth century, the court recognized many independent rights, including the right to leave property by will.

Witnesses were competent when they met the requirements for being a witness by law, and judges exercised discretion in determining competency. Women and poor people were competent. For nuncupative wills exceeding £30 after 1705, the competency requirement was the same as that required for trials at law. According to Swinburne, legatees were competent except as to their own legacies. Under the Statute of Frauds (1677), a witness who was to receive a bequest through the will was not a credible witness, and many wills were declared void. By statute in 1752 and under the Wills Act of 1837, a legatee could be a witness, but his legacy was void.

Wills could be amended by codicil, or revoked. A later valid will could revoke a prior will and a nuncupative will could revoke a written one. Revocation by canceling or defacing the writing was possible whether done to a written will or a nuncupative will later reduced to writing. Becoming a criminal, marrying, or having children could trigger a revocation, as could an unsuccessful attempt to make a new will. The Wills Act of 1837 provided that marriage operates as a revocation.

Until the law relating to wills, testaments, and probate was substantially reformed during the mid-nineteenth century, the succession of property was subject to various sets of laws and jurisdictions. The intergenerational transfer of wealth through wills and testaments was influenced by contemporary ideas about religion, family, and death, as well as by legal considerations such as tax and the use of inter vivos transfers.

[*See also* Succession, *subentry on* English Common Law.]

BIBLIOGRAPHY

Baker, John. *1483–1558*. Vol. 6, *The Oxford History of the Laws of England*, edited by John Baker. Oxford: Oxford University Press, 2003. Chapter 35 presents recent research on uses and wills.

Bean, J. M. W. *The Decline of English Feudalism, 1215–1540*. Manchester, U.K.: Manchester University Press, 1968. Standard work on feudal incidents, uses, and the royal legislations addressing them.

Bonfield, Lloyd. *Marriage Settlements, 1601–1740: The Adoption of the Strict Settlement*. Cambridge, U.K.: Cambridge University Press, 1983. Inter vivos transfers of land.

Bonfield, Lloyd, ed. *Marriage, Property, and Succession*. Berlin: Duncker & Humblot, 1992. Several useful essays including Bonfield on settlements, Helmholz on English wills and the *ius commune*, and Sheehan on bequests of land.

Helmholz, R. H. "*Legitim* and English Legal History." *University of Illinois Law Review* (1984): 659–674. *Legitim* in ecclesiastical courts.

Helmholz, R. H. *The Canon Law and Ecclesiastical Jurisdiction from 597 to the 1640s*. Vol. 1, *The Oxford History of the Laws of England*, edited by John Baker. Oxford: Oxford University Press, 2004. Chapter 7 addresses testamentary law and probate jurisdiction.

Holdsworth, W. S. *A History of English Law*. 3d ed. London: Methuen & Co., 1945. Volume 4, chapter 2, addresses uses and trusts in the sixteenth and seventeenth centuries.

Houlbrooke, Ralph A. *Church Courts and the People During the English Reformation*, 1520–1570. Oxford: Oxford University Press, 1979. Ecclesiastical courts and probate.

Houlbrooke, Ralph A. *Death, Religion, and the Family in England*, 1480–1750. Oxford, U.K.: Clarendon Press, 1998. Describes changes in will making and content resulting from the Reformation.

Marchant, Ronald A. *The Church under the Law: Justice, Administration, and Discipline in the Diocese of York*, 1560–1640. London: Cambridge University Press, 1969. Ecclesiastical courts and probate.

Mirow, M. C. "Last Wills and Testaments in England 1500–1800." Recueils de la Société Jean Bodin pour l'Histoire *Comparative des Institutions* 60 (1993): 47–83. Survey of common-law and ecclesiastical-law principles and institutions.

Mirow, M. C. "Monks and Married Women: The Use of the Yearbooks in Defining Testamentary Capacity in Sixteenth- and Seventeenth-Century Readings on Wills." *Tijdschrift voor Rechtsgeschiedenis* 65 (1997): 19–39. Common-law testamentary capacity.

Sheehan, Michael M. *The Will in Medieval England: From the Conversion of the Anglo-Saxons to the End of the Thirteenth Century*. Toronto, Canada: Pontifical Institute of Medieval Studies, 1963. Standard work on wills in the medieval period.

Swinburne, Henry. *A Briefe Treatise of Testaments and Last Wills*. 2d ed. London: Company of Stationers, 1635. General treatise on ecclesiastical law of testaments, first published in 1590 and followed by numerous subsequent editions.

Wunderli, Richard M. *London Church Courts and Society on the Eve of the Reformation*. Cambridge, Mass.: Medieval Academy of America, 1981. London ecclesiastical courts.

Yale, D. E. C. "Witnessing Wills and Losing Legacies." *Law Quarterly Review* 100 (1984): 453–467. Discussion of the rule from 1677 to recent times.

M. C. Mirow

Testamentary Disposition in Islamic Law

A legacy (*waṣiyya*) is a transfer, from one person to another, of a substance or a usufruct, bequeathed for no consideration, which will be effective after the testator's death. The person entitled to make a legacy also has the right to revoke it. The revocation can be partial or total; the freeing of slaves, however, is irrevocable to the extent that the value of the slaves falls within the one-third of the estate that is not assigned by law and of which the testator can dispose freely. A testator can revoke a legacy at any time, even on his deathbed, either expressly or tacitly. The legacy, however, like any other gift, cannot be acquired until the legatee, following the testator's death, accepts it either expressly or by implication, whether he takes actual possession of it or not. Acceptance is not required if the legacy is in favor of an undetermined beneficiary (such as the poor) or when it regards the emancipation of a slave, because the slave cannot refuse to be freed. The legal effect of a bequest is to create a property right of the legatee, as is the case for a gift.

The *waṣiyya* can also concern dispositions imposing certain burdens on some heirs, like the fulfillment of a pilgrimage in the place of the testator, the freeing of a slave, the institution of a waqf, or the acknowledgment of a debt or a deposit which cannot be otherwise proved. It may also entrust to a person the task of paying debts, acknowledging a child, or taking guardianship of the children of the deceased. In these respects, the *waṣiyya* is not to be confused with the Roman testament through which an heir is instituted.

Elements of a Valid Will. There are four basic elements required for a *waṣiyya*. These are a testator (*mūṣī*), a legatee (*mūṣā lahu*), an object (*mūṣā bihi*), and the expression of the will (*ṣīgha*).

Testator. The testator must possess the legal capacity to make a disposition for no consideration, and be the owner of what he bequeaths at the time the *waṣiyya* is made. This implies that he must be free, adult, of sound mind, and acting on his own free will. An apostate or a slave, unless authorized by his or her master, cannot create a *waṣiyya* because such persons lack the juridical capacity. Persons who are insane, drunk, underage, insolvent, or lacking discernment because of illness are also unable to do it because they lack their capacity of contracting. Making a will is highly recommended to a person who is seriously ill (Qur'an 2:180; 5:106) as a means of giving a part of the estate to poorer relatives who would otherwise be excluded from inheritance.

Legatee. The legatee or beneficiary must be competent to receive a bequest at the time when the legacy is made; this means that he must be alive, even if he is underage or an unborn child. A slave is also capable of personally receiving a *waṣiyya* if this was the mind of the testator; otherwise the legacy will be acquired by his master. The beneficiary may be a natural person (an individual, or a more or less defined group of persons) or an institution having a charitable object (such as a mosque or a public school); in the latter case, it need not exist at the time the bequest is made. In such cases the legacy is presumed to be used for the necessities of that institution and for the benefit of the poor assisted by it. If there is more than one beneficiary, the whole bequest goes to the surviving beneficiaries if one or more died before the testator, unless each beneficiary was allotted a definite part of the bequest. A Muslim may lawfully make a bequest to a *dhimmī* or to a *musta'min* (a permanent or a temporary non-Muslim resident in Muslim territory), and vice versa, but a bequest to someone outside the community or to an enemy combatant is not lawful.

Apostates, persons who premeditatedly or intentionally killed the testator, and those who are heirs at the time of the testator's death cannot receive a legacy. (In the Muslim legal sense, an "heir" is a person who is automatically entitled to receive a portion of the testator's property without being specifically mentioned in the will.) The Zahiris, and some Malikis, Shafi'is, and Hanbalis, rule that a bequest to an heir is utterly void, but the Imamis and Zaydis accept it as valid up to one-third of the net estate without requiring the consent of the other heirs. According to a middle course, maintained by Hanafis, Hanbalis, Shafi'is, and the majority of Malikis, a bequest to an heir is subject to the consent of the other heirs. A ratification given only by some of them applies only to them.

Bequeathed object. A bequest must be something capable of being inherited or transferred after the testator's death, whether or not it existed at the time the will was made, but it must exist at the time of his death and be owned by the testator. It may be movable or immovable property, rights in property, or usufructs (for life or for a definite period). However, it is a condition for the validity of a will that the object of the bequest must be licit according to the shari'a. Thus, objects that cannot legally be sold (animals not ritually slaughtered, wine, blood, pigs) cannot be bequeathed. The same applies to things excluded from ownership (air, water, rivers, public roads). Moreover, the legacy must have a licit purpose: it must not be contrary to the ethical, religious, and juridical rules of Islam. A *wasiyya* is void, for instance, if intended for the construction of a church or a synagogue, or for other benefit of a non-Muslim denomination; if it is intended to compensate for a foul or criminal act; or if it implies an offense to the principles of the Islamic religion and law (building a mausoleum for a dead person, or placing a candelabra near a *walī*'s grave). On the other hand, a legacy intended for a charitable purpose, such as building or supporting a hospice, orphanage, or hospital, is valid.

If a Muslim leaves heirs, the bequests to persons other than the heirs may not exceed one-third of the estate. "Estate" is defined as everything left by a deceased that has to be devolved on heirs, including property, usufruct, or any other right related to property. The disposable third is reckoned upon the estate after the deduction, first, of specified goods which third persons can claim, and second, of the payment of reasonable funerary expenses and debts. Debts have priority on a will; thus, no will over an estate exhausted by debts is effective, unless the creditors allow it.

Expression of will. The *wasiyya* is usually recommended in case of serious illness. According to the prevalent doctrine, in such cases the legacy exceeding the one-third is not void *ab initio* but depends on the course of the illness. If the testator survives, the will is considered valid but in the nature of a donation. If the testator dies, any bequest exceeding the one-third, according to some jurists, is completely void, even if ratified by the heirs; but according to the prevalent doctrine (Malikis, Shafi'is, Hanafis), it may be validated by the assent of the heirs, expressly or by implication, after the testator's death. When only some of them consent, the bequest is payable to the beneficiary only from the shares of the consenting heirs in proportion of their shares. In the absence of any heir, the testator can bequeath the totality of his property, and this does not require any assent.

Emancipation, donations, waqf, and other transactions performed by a sick person on his deathbed that diminish the size of the estate are considered to be legacies, and operate only against a third of his property.

The *wasiyya* does not require a special form. Any expression clearly indicating the mind of the testator and the object of the legacy is admitted. A will can be made by spoken word, in writing, or by an intelligible gesture. The most customary form is in writing, attested by two fit witnesses, who ought to be Muslim but can also be Jews or Christians (Qur'an 2:181–182; 5:106–107). A will, under certain conditions, is also valid if it is holographic and unwitnessed. Moreover, a *wasiyya* is valid if written in the presence of a qadi, whose attestation suffices. If a *wasiyya* is made orally, especially when the testator is on his deathbed or it is impossible for him to write, it is valid if made in the presence of two fit male witnesses, preferably relatives.

A will can be subjected to conditions prescribed by the testator. A licit condition must be honored. If an illicit condition is stated, the condition itself is void, but the *wasiyya* remains valid.

Executor. The executor (*wasī, mūsā ilayhi*) is a trustee (*amīn*) appointed by the testator to superintend, protect, and care for his property and children after his death. His office (*wisāya*) is to be exercised by him personally; another person cannot take his place without lawful reasons. He is entrusted to pay debts, return deposits, deliver legacies, exercise guardianship of minor children, and serve as the agent of absent heirs. The *wasī* must be Muslim, of age, and legally competent (*rasīd*), having the reputation of being a good and upright administrator. The executor can refuse his office, and such refusal is irrevocable. An executor who accepts the office can revoke his acceptance only before the testator's death; after that, he can revoke it only on the basis of lawful reasons.

If the executor's powers are not specifically stated, he is deemed to hold a general mandate to settle all the testator's affairs. If his powers are determined, he can perform only what is specified in his mandate. If there are two or more executors, they cannot act separately, unless so authorized by the testator.

The executor's execution of duties is supervised by the qadi, to whom he must render account of his mandate; in particular, he must give proof of having performed the tasks entrusted to him in the way prescribed by the testator. If he proves unfit for his office, the judge must revoke his mandate. If he was also named as guardian, he must render account of this charge according to the usual rules for guardianship.

Grandchildren as Heirs. Some contemporary law codes provide for grandchildren whose parents have predeceased the grandparents, and who would otherwise be excluded from inheritance when the grandparents die on the principle that the closest heir excludes the most distant. There are two mechanisms for this: the obligatory bequest (*waṣiyya wāghiba*) and the right of representation (*tanzīl*). Both of these provide for an obligatory bequest in the grandchildren's favor, if they would otherwise not be entitled to inherit. The amount of such bequest is determined by what the predeceased parent would have received had he lived, provided always that this does not exceed the bequeathable third. The obligatory bequest in favor of the grandchildren should take priority, within the bequeathable third, over any other disposition, and this entitlement should be divided among the grandchildren according to the principle of a double share to males.

The device of the obligatory bequest is in force in Egypt (law no. 71, enacted on June 24, 1946, arts. 76–79), Syria (law no. 34 of December 31, 1975, art. 257), Tunisia (law enacted on August 13, 1956, arts. 191–192), Kuwait (law no. 51, enacted on July 7, 1984, art. 291.3), Yemen (law no. 20, enacted on March 29, 1992, arts. 259–260), and Morocco (law no. 70-03, enacted on February 3, 2004, arts. 369–372). The right of representation is in use in Algeria (law no. 84-11 of June 9, 1984, arts. 169–172). In the Moroccan Mudawwana (arts. 315–320) the term *tanzīl* expresses a completely different idea: the appointment of an heir, a principle of western juridical doctrine completely unknown to the Islamic law of inheritance.

[*See also* Inheritance, *subentry on* Islamic Law; *and* Personal Status Law, *subentry on* Personal Status Law in Islamic Countries.]

BIBLIOGRAPHY

Baillie, Neil B. E. *A Digest of Moohummdan Law: Compiled and Translated from Authorities in the Original Arabic with an Introduction and Explanatory Notes*. 4th ed. Lahore, Pakistan: Premier Book House, 1965.

Cilardo, Agostino. "On Some Recent Laws on the Islamic Law of Inheritance." In *Proceedings of the Arabic and Islamic Sections of the 35th International Congress of Asian and North African Studies (ICANAS) (Budapest, 1–7 July 1997)*, Part II, edited by Alexander Fodor. *The Arabist: Budapest Studies in Arabic* 21–22 (1999): 193–204.

Cilardo, Agostino. "La rappresentazione nel diritto ereditario musulmano." In *Atti del Congresso Internazionale su: Gli interscambi culturali e socio-economici fra l'Africa Settentrionale e l'Europa Mediterranea (Amalfi, 5–8 dicembre 1983)*, Vol. 2, pp. 931–941, Naples, Italy, 1986.

Gaziri, ʿAbd al-Rahman al-. *Kitab al-fiqh ʿala al-madahib al-arbaʿa*. 7th ed. 5 vols. Beirut, 1986. See especially Vol. 3.

Nasir, Jamal J. *The Islamic Law of Personal Status*. London and Gaithersburg, Md.: Graham and Trotman, 1986.

Santillana, David. *Istituzioni di diritto musulmano malichita con riguardo anche al sistema sciafiita*. 2 vols. Rome: Anonima Romana Editoriales, 1938. See especially Vol. 2.

Agostino Cilardo

WINDSCHEID, BERNHARD

(1817–1892). German jurist and pandectist. Born in Düsseldorf, Windscheid studied law in Bonn and Berlin. After receiving his doctorate and *Habilitation* (second advanced degree) in Bonn in 1838 and 1840, in 1847 he accepted his first professorship in Basel, Switzerland. From 1852 to 1874 he taught Roman law in Greifswald, Munich, Heidelberg, and Leipzig, declining professorships in Berlin. He considered himself a member of the middle class and therefore refused to use the title that the king of Saxony had bestowed upon him in 1868.

Windscheid was one of the most important representatives of the science of pandects and a pioneer of modern civil law. His textbook—the three-volume *Lehrbuch des Pandektenrechts* (Textbook of Pandect Law, 1862, 1865/66, and 1870)—and his activities with the first commission for the civil law code (1873–1886) brought him fame. His book *Die actio des römischen Civilrechts vom Standpunkte des heutigen Rechts* (The Claim in Roman Civil Law as Seen from the Standpoint of Present-day Law, 1856) created the concept of claim in present-day German civil law. His work *Die Lehre des römischen Rechts von der Voraussetzung* (Teachings of Roman Law on Prerequisites, 1850) is equally important. It clearly shows the dogmatic tendency that is common to all his writings, the attempt to "make the judge's indispensable freedom of action generally acknowledged" (translated from *Lehrbuch des Pandektenrechts*, Vol. 1, § 28, footnote 4). Here he showed himself as a pioneer in the development of twentieth-century law.

Windscheid's textbook went through seven editions during his lifetime; after his death two further editions appeared (1900–1901 and 1906), and it was translated into several languages. The text presented legal situations with masterly precision and formal clarity. Copious footnotes verified the Roman sources, offering concise dogmatic derivations and numerous references for legal decisions and teachings, often with Windscheid's own critical comments. For research into the history of dogma, the work remains invaluable.

Windscheid's ambiguous phrase about the limited role of the "jurist as such" is notorious. This phrase was the standard quotation used by his critics, who made him a symbolic figure of conceptual jurisprudence and legal positivism. Supposedly Windscheid separated jurisprudence from social reality and restricted judgment to a logical act of correct subsumption. This skewed image of Windscheid's views long remained uncontested, even though it overlooked the fact that in the passage containing the phrase he spoke exclusively of the jurist's role in legislation. The phrase specifically did not extend to the judge's decision or his teachings of law. That the phrase did not so extend is evident from each sentence in the context. As a member of a legislative commission the jurist should contribute his knowledge, but the political responsibility for the underlying contents of the law code should be left to the actual lawmaker—that is, in the case of the civil-law code, the German Reichstag, the first German parliament—representing voters equal before the law, exercising their rights freely in general elections. For Windscheid the parliamentary lawgiver as defined in the constitution was the authority to whom the basic ethical, political, and economic decisions are reserved. This point of view was rooted in the principle of the division of powers and has not been superseded in the German constitutional state, even in the twenty-first century.

[*See also* Pandektenwissenschaft.]

BIBLIOGRAPHY

Falk, Ulrich. *Ein Gelehrter wie Windscheid: Erkundungen auf den Feldern der sogenannten Begriffsjurisprudenz.* Frankfurt am Main, Germany: V. Klostermann, 1989. 2d ed., 1999.

Falk, Ulrich. "Der wahre Jurist und der Jurist als solcher." *Rechtshistorisches Journal* 12 (1993): 598–633.

ULRICH FALK AND ANNETTE KEILMANN
Translated from the German by Alexa Nieschlag

WITCHCRAFT IN CHINESE LAW. *See* Offenses against the State in Chinese Law, *subentry on* Offenses Threatening the Life or Well-Being of the Emperor *and* Poison (*Gu*).

WITCH TRIALS. The term "witch trial" refers to the criminal prosecution during the late Middle Ages and early modern times of those suspected of being in league with the devil, of participating in the witches' Sabbath, and of casting evil spells. The earliest evidence for the belief in the existence of such human beings goes back to the final quarter of the fourteenth century. The earliest trials are documented in the southern parts of Switzerland in the early fifteenth century. There is literary evidence from around 1300 for the German term *Hexe*, the equivalent of the Old English term *wicca*, or witch, referring to beings that could fly, that worshipped demons, and that addled the senses. One root of the persecution of witches goes back to the heresy discourse of the Middle Ages, according to which only Christians could be persecuted as witches. The overrepresentation of women among those prosecuted as witches—about 80 percent—can be explained by the medieval stereotype of the heretic, which held that women, as the weaker sex, succumbed to the temptations of the devil more easily than men did. The other root lies in the superstitious belief that magic could be used to damage people, animals, and crops. The image of female demons sucking out the blood of children, dismembering them, and eating them is found the world over.

The compounding of these elements to make witchcraft the sensational crime of early modern times took place in the fifteenth century, mainly at the hands of Dominican inquisitors. The German Dominicans Johannes Nider and Heinrich Kramer (also known by the Latinized name Heinrich Institoris) focused on evil spells as the centerpiece of their persecutions, whereas Francophone inquisition judges like Claude Tholosan concentrated on the witches' Sabbath. Article 109 of the Constitutio Criminalis Carolina, the criminal code ratified by the Holy Roman emperor Charles V in 1532, lists the casting of evil spells as the main element of the crime of sorcery. Both the casting of spells and participation in the witches' Sabbath were amalgamated into one complex crime at the turn of the fifteenth to the sixteenth century, forming the basis for the waves of witch hunts beginning in 1561. The early persecution in the fifteenth century took a greater toll than was once thought, with several thousands of victims. The normal penalty was burning at the stake; the main legal prerequisite was a trial by the inquisition, using torture to force confessions. The abatement of persecution at the beginning of the sixteenth century is as yet unexplained.

Although the *Malleus maleficarum* (Hammer of Witches, 1487) by Institoris did not have official legal authority, it was of prime importance for the historical development of witch hunting and trials. One of its main achievements was to declare obsolete the *canon episcopi* of canon law (Decretum Gratiani C. 26 q. 5 c. 12), which made the belief in flying, demon-worshipping females anathema and thus presented an obstacle to the persecution of witches. The total number of victims is hard to assess because of the large number of undocumented cases. The upper limit for all of Europe can be estimated at about one hundred thousand victims executed, plus the same number of victims who were not executed.

The center of the persecution of witches was the Holy Roman Empire, which accounted for more than half of the European victims. The persecution spread in various waves, beginning in southwestern Germany and spreading to the north and east, where it began later and accordingly ended only in the eighteenth century. In the south the last great wave of persecution took place after 1660. The height of the persecution was reached from the 1590s to the 1630s. During this time span, each wave of persecution claimed a death toll of a few thousand. During the more "legal" series of trials, up to half of the victims failed to confess and could not be executed despite torture or other faulty procedures. Thus they were set free, but they remained socially stigmatized. Up to 10 percent died from the consequences of torture or from the conditions of their imprisonment.

Midelfort's thesis—that the number of witch trials by Protestant authorities declined after 1600, while those by Catholics increased—is true only for the southwestern region of Germany and cannot be generalized, given the research on the Protestant territories of Thuringia and Mecklenburg, both of which had above-average numbers of victims—1,500 and 1,000 death sentences, respectively. Saxony, with 300 death sentences, and the even larger Bavaria, with fewer than a thousand, were both regions with a low rate of persecution, while the rate was high in southwestern Germany (3,300 death sentences) and Lorraine and Trier (1,500). The Catholic archbishoprics of Bamberg and Würzburg were particular strongholds of persecution.

The main theorists of witch persecution in the seventeenth century were the Jesuit Martin Delrio on the Catholic side and on the Protestant side the Saxonian jurist Johann Benedict Carpzov—who was not, however, a fanatic persecutor. The Jesuit Friedrich Spee von Langenfeld was the most important opponent of the persecution, unsparingly pointing out the weaknesses of the witch trials in his book *Cautio criminalis* (Precautions for Prosecutors, 1631)—pointing out, for instance, the prejudice of the inquisitors and the absurd precondition for the use of torture.

Outside the Holy Roman Empire, witches were prosecuted in Hungary and Yugoslavia—where shamanistic practices also came under the scrutiny of the persecutors—a large-scale children's trial was held in Sweden, and there were trials in Salem, Massachusetts. The extent of the persecution in Poland and Bohemia still awaits thorough evaluation and might affect the balance of victim numbers among the European countries. England, where the inquisition trials did not take hold, remained free of the Continental mass persecution but nevertheless had some instances of witch hunting. Ultimately, the persecution was reduced not so much by the relatively enlightened criticism of the so-called witch madness, but rather by increased requirements for evidence by higher

Witch Trial. Woodcut of a suspected witch being ducked in a mill stream, c. 1600. MARY EVANS PICTURE LIBRARY

authorities—for instance, by the university law faculties and by the Reichskammergericht (Court of the Imperial Chamber).

[*See also* Carpzov, Benedict; Evidence, *subentry on* Medieval and Post-Medieval Roman Law; *and* Reichskammergericht.]

BIBLIOGRAPHY

Ankarloo, Bengt, and Gustav Henningsen, eds. *Early Modern European Witchcraft: Centres and Peripheries*. Oxford, U.K.: Clarendon Press, 1990.

Broedel, Hans Peter. *The Malleus maleficarum and the Construction of Witchcraft: Theology and Popular Belief*. Manchester, U.K.: Manchester University Press, 2003.

Institoris, Heinrich. *Der Hexenhammer: Malleus maleficarum*. 3d ed. Translated and edited by Günter Jerouschek, Wolfgang Behringer, and Werner Tschacher. Munich, Germany: DTV, 2000. New translation into modern German with an introduction.

Institoris, Heinrich. *The Malleus maleficarum*. Edited and translated by P. G. Maxwell-Stuart. Manchester, U.K.: Manchester University Press, 2007.

Institoris, Heinrich. *Malleus maleficarum 1487*. Edited by Günter Jerouschek. Hildesheim, Germany: Georg Olms Verlag, 1992. A reprint of the Latin first edition of 1487.

Jerouschek, Günter. "Friedrich von Spee als Justizkritiker." In *Friedrich Spee zum 400. Geburtstag: Kolloquium der Friedrich-Spee-Gesellschaft Trier*, edited by Gunther Franz, pp. 115–136. Paderborn, Germany: Bonifatius, 1995.

Levack, Brian P. *The Witch-Hunt in Early Modern Europe*. 3d ed. Harlow, U.K.: Pearson Longman, 2006.

Midelfort, H. C. Erik. *Witch Hunting in Southwestern Germany, 1562–1684: The Social and Intellectual Foundations*. Stanford, Calif.: Stanford University Press, 1972.

Wilde, Manfred. *Die Zauberei- und Hexenprozesse in Kursachsen*. Cologne, Germany: Böhlau, 2003.

GÜNTER JEROUSCHEK
Translated from the German by Alexa Nieschlag

WITNESSES. For discussion of witnesses in Chinese law, *see* Procedure, *subentry on* Parties and Witnesses in Chinese Law. For witnesses in Islamic law, see Enforcement in Islamic Law; Judiciary, *subentry on* Islamic Law, Classical Period; *and* Procedure, *subentry on* Proof and Procedure in Islamic Law.

WITNESSES IN ANCIENT ATHENS. Witnesses (*martyres*) appeared in the Athenian courts to confirm statements of fact made by litigants. What they actually said, or what testimony of theirs was read out, however, is usually indicated only by a note in the texts indicating "witnesses," or "witness testimony" (*martyria*). We must thus infer what they said from the use the speakers make of the testimony. The witnesses could only report what they knew directly, not what they claimed to know by hearsay (Demosthenes 57.4). They were called by the litigants and so took a somewhat partisan role, but they were individually responsible for the truth of their statements—whether or not the litigant who called them won the case—and could be prosecuted subsequently in a suit for false testimony (*dikē pseudomartyriōn*). Three convictions for false testimony resulted in a loss of citizen rights (Hyperides 2.12). A litigant could also legally oblige a witness to appear by making a summons (*klēteusis*), the witness's only escape being an oath (*exōmosia*) in which he swore that he did not know about the matter in question. Only in homicide cases were witnesses obliged to swear an oath concomitant with their testimony, and then they swore not only to the truth of the litigant's specific statement but also to the guilt or innocence of the accused killer (Antiphon 5.12; Lysias 4.4).

Status. Though no law ordaining such a restriction is known, there is no evidence that anyone other than free, adult males appeared as a witness in the Athenian courts. Slaves' evidence could be elicited only as "information" (*mēnysis*), which had to be checked through further enquiry (Antiphon 5.38; Lysias 5.4), or through the mechanism of the torture challenge (*proklēsis eis basanon*). Women's evidence could be elicited only by the similar mechanism of the oath challenge (*prokleēsis eis horkon*). In neither case would this evidence properly be referred to as *martyria*. Evidence from a refused challenge is often employed where the two sides present conflicting witness testimony and must bolster it (Demosthenes 47.5, 8; Lycurgus 1.28). Both metics (resident foreigners) and free foreigners (*xenoi*) could give testimony as witnesses (Demosthenes 35.14, 20, 23, 33–4; Aeschines 2.155).

Terminology. Several terms are derived from the word *martyria* to describe the different functions served by witnesses. The *diamartyria* was a formal evidentiary statement declaring, for example, that an estate of a deceased man was not transferable by a will because there was a natural heir to it. Legal dispute over such an estate took the form of a suit for false testimony (*dikē pseudomartyriōn*) against the man making the *diamartyria* (Isaeus 2, 3, 6; Isocrates 18.11, 15; Demosthenes 44.57–60). It was announced by a formal objection (*episkēpsis*), which suspended any action being taken on the basis of the *diamartyria* until the suit for false testimony was settled. In Lysias 26.13–14, the *diamartyria* was used to make a formal declaration that a man was not a Plataean: he objected in the form of an *episkēpsis* but did not then pursue a suit for false testimony and had an award made against him in absentia. The suit brought against a litigant for recruiting false witnesses to his side was called a *dikē kakotechniōn* (Demosthenes 45.2, 52; 47.1, 56). The *ekmartyria* formed an exception to the hearsay rule: where a witness could not appear in court, men of good reputation could stand in for the jury and formally witness what he said and report on it in court (Isaeus 17.20–21). The *dikē lipomartyriou* was a suit against a witness for nonappearance (Demosthenes 49.19).

Procedure. In situations in which a litigant had to make a formal summons of an opponent, he took along witnesses called *proskltēres*, or simply *klētēres* (Demosthenes 40.28; Isaeus 3.19). In fact, the Athenians took care to have witnesses attend almost any formal act that might result in legal dispute, whether a wedding, a funeral, a child's naming ceremony—all activities that signaled a person's identity—or the paying of money. They served as a sort of living communal archive. Curiously, transactions with bankers are said not to have been witnessed (Demosthenes 52.7; Isocrates 17.2, 53; 21.7). In the preliminary stages of judicial disputes, witnesses took formal notice of the litigants' maneuverings and of the attempts to elicit binding admissions (*homologiai*) from their opponents (Demosthenes 27.10, 24, 34, 39, 42–43; 42.12, 28; 43.38). Accidental witnesses are summoned to crime scenes much as the police are summoned in modern contexts, a motif used often in comedies (Aristophanes, *Acharnians* 926; *Birds* 1031; *Clouds* 495, 1297; *Peace* 1119; *Wasps* 1436–1439; Demosthenes 47.38; 53.16, 18).

Written Testimony. Until the 370s, witnesses appear to have given testimony orally in court, although they may often only have said something as simple as "what he [the litigant speaking] said is true." But they may in some cases have faced interrogation by the opponent (Andocides 1.16). From the 370s on, it appears that the witnesses' presence in court was all that was required of them. Instead of speaking, the witness only listened as his statement—which had been recorded during a question-and-answer session (*anakrisis*) before a magistrate or during a hearing before a public arbitrator—was read aloud by a court secretary. In his testimony the witness identified himself by name and deme affiliation and said specifically what information he was attesting to. This change did not substantially alter the role of witnesses, but it led to greater accountability for their testimony (Demosthenes 45.44; 46.6; 47.8). By the same token, it seems likely that it was in many cases the litigant who formulated the witness's statement; the witness had only to confirm it.

Issues in Scholarship. Recent scholarly debate over witnesses has turned on the roles of their status and partisanship. Humphreys has argued the importance of their status as a mark of credibility, and Todd has noted the risk the witnesses took on behalf of the litigant for whom they testified. Scafuro has noted their role as a living, communal archive, and Mirhady has argued against Humphreys and Todd that the witnesses were relatively anonymous, indicating the limited importance of their status beyond their being free adult males, and that their risk was independent of the risk to the litigant. Rubinstein has sought to identify different hierarchies of credibility in public and private disputes.

Witness testimony seems to have been a nearly essential part of a litigant's presentation (Aristophanes, *Clouds* 776–780). Without it his account of the facts of the case had little credibility. With it, he was likely to win over the judges on that point of fact (Demosthenes 46.4; 47.3; 57.17, 36; Lycurgus 1.23). The enormous use made of witnesses, like the large juries empaneled to decide cases in Athens, testifies to the breadth of the judicial activity of Athens.

BIBLIOGRAPHY

Bonner, Robert J. *Evidence in Athenian Courts*. Chicago: University of Chicago Press, 1905.

Gernet, L. "La diamartyrie, procédure archaique du droit athènien (Diamartyria: An Archaic Procedure of Athenian Law)." *Legal History Review* 6 (1927): 5–24.

Humphreys, S. H. "Social Relations on Stage: Witnesses in Classical Athens." *History and Anthropology* 1 (1985): 313–369.

Leisi, E. *Der Zeuge im attischen Recht* (The Witness in Attic Law). Frauenfeld, Switzerland: Huber, 1907.

Mirhady, D. C. "Athens' Democratic Witnesses." *Phoenix* 56 (2002): 255–274.

Pringsheim, Fritz. "The Transition from Witnessed to Written Transactions in Athens." In Fritz Pringsheim, *Gesammelte Abhandlungen* (Collected Papers), vol. 2, pp. 401–420. Heidelberg, Germany: C. Winter, 1961. First published in *Aequitas und Bona Fides: Festgabe für A. Simonius* (Aequitas [Equity] and Bona Fides [Good Faith]: Celebratory Gift for A. Simonius), edited by A. Amiaud, et al., pp. 287–297, Basel, Switzerland: Helbing & Lichtenhahn, 1955.

Rubinstein, Lene. "Dangerous Liaisons? Litigants and Witnesses in the Athenian Courts." In *Symposion 2001*, edited by R. W. Wallace and M. Gagarin. Vienna: Verlag der Österreichischen Akademie der Wissenschaften, 2005.

Scafuro, Adele C. "Witnessing and False-Witnessing: Proving Citizenship and Kin Identity in Fourth-Century Athens." In *Athenian Identity and Civic Ideology*, edited by Alan L. Boegehold and Adele C. Scafuro, pp. 156–198. Baltimore, Md.: Johns Hopkins University Press, 1994.

Todd, S. C. "The Purpose of Evidence in Athenian Courts." In *Nomos: Essays in Athenian Law, Politics and Society*, edited by Paul Cartledge, Paul Millet, and Stephen Todd, pp. 19–39. Cambridge, U.K.: Cambridge University Press, 1990.

David Mirhady

WOLFF, CHRISTIAN VON

WOLFF, CHRISTIAN VON (1679–1754). After Hugo Grotius, Samuel von Pufendorf, and Christian Thomasius, Wolff was the last of the great natural law professors of the seventeenth and eighteenth centuries. Wolff was born in Breslau on January 1, 1679, and his parents determined that he would become a minister in the Lutheran church. Although he matriculated into the University of Jena with this goal as a student of theology, he heard mathematical and philosophical lectures that left him particularly awed by Grotius and Pufendorf's works of natural law.

Following his *Habilitation* (a postgraduate degree specific to the German-speaking world) in 1703, Wolff began giving lectures in mathematics and philosophy as a privatdozent in Leipzig. Ultimately, theology became a part of Wolff's program of study, but he resigned from his position as minister when in 1706, through the offices of Samuel Stryk and Gottfried Wil-helm Leibniz, he became professor of mathematics at the University of Halle, where, up until 1723, he spent his most fruitful years as a scholar. In those years he laid the groundwork for his entire philosophical system, in which he treated all fields of study with the same method. His reputation, though, stems above all from his success as a mathematician.

In this period, Wolff enjoyed great success as a teacher, and was overwhelmed by offers of academic positions. With this came membership in various academies. But in 1723, the Prussian king Friedrich Wilhelm I removed him from his professorship with the admonition that he was teaching determinism, which could justify the desertion of soldiers. His ejection from Prussia made Wolff a martyr to princely despotism. In 1740, Frederick the Great called him back in triumph to a chaired professorship in natural law, international law, and mathematics. At the height of his renown, Wolff was named a baron of the Empire. Though once more in Halle, he never succeeded in replicating his earlier great successes as a professor of law. Wolff died in Halle on April 9, 1754.

From early in his career, Wolff gave himself over to the problem of finding a mathematical, "demonstrative" method for proofs in answer to philosophical and juridical questions. His method was, in essence, based on the idea that all proofs must employ syllogisms. For Wolff, the syllogism really served as a medium of knowledge. Also important for Wolff, however, was the "continuity of coherence" [*der beständiger Zusammenhang*] of all of his doctrines, which he assured through a thorough system of references to already clarified points of debate. Wolff followed these methodological principles in his treatment of all the great fields of study, from logic through ontology and on to mathematics.

Particularly concerning law, Wolff was convinced that, through the mathematical method, his argumentation proved full agreement between the "natural" laws that were based on human nature and the "positive" laws that emerged in the totality of civil law doctrine. This meant, in Wolff's conviction, that only the truth as mediated by mathematical argumentation could guarantee justice. The essence of justice for Wolff, however, lay in the idea that each one is obliged to render to each his own. That meant that to be just was to fulfill one's duty. The fulfillment of duty, according to Wolff, guaranteed the felicity (*felicitas*) of human society. Because of this, Wolff presented his natural law as an obligatory doctrine, which—in contrast to the teachings of Christian Thomasius—recognized no sharp separation between law and morality. It was through this doctrine that Wolff had his greatest effect on Catholic doctrines of natural law.

Wolff's most significant work for legal studies is contained in his eight-volume *Ius naturae methodo scientifico pertractatum* (Law of nature treated in a scientific method, 1740–1748), in the *Ius gentium* (1749), and in a précis of all these teachings that was published in 1750 in Latin as *Institutiones juris naturae et gentium* and in 1754 in German as *Grundsätze des Natur- und Völckerrechts* (Principles of the law of nature and international law).

[*See also* Grotius, Hugo; International Law, *subentry on* Roman Law; Leibniz, Gottfried Wilhelm; Natural Law, *subentry on* Medieval and Post-Medieval Roman Law; Pufendorf, Samuel von; *and* Thomasius, Christian.]

BIBLIOGRAPHY

Carpintero, Francisco, and José Justo Megías Quirós. "Christian Wolff." In *Juristas universales*, edited by Rafael Domingo, Vol. 2, *Juristas modernos*, pp. 514–519. Madrid and Barcelona: Marcial Pons, 2004.

Frängsmyr, Tore. "Christian Wolff's Mathematical Method and Its Impact on the Eighteenth Century." *Journal of the History of Ideas* 36 (1975): 653–668.

Luig, Klaus. "Die Pflichtenlehre des Privatrechts in der Naturrechtsphilosophie von Christian Wolff." In *Rechtsdogmatik und praktische Vernunft: Symposion zum 80. Geburtstag von Franz Wieacker*, edited by Okko Behrends, Malte Diesselhorst, and Ralf Dreier, pp. 209–261. Göttingen, Germany: Vandenhoeck & Ruprecht, 1990.

Thomann, Marcel. "Christian Wolff (1679 – 1754)." In *Staatsdenker in der frühen Neuzeit*, edited by Michael Stolleis, pp. 257–283. 3d ed. Munich, Germany: Beck, 1995.

Wolff, Christian. *Jus naturae methodo scientifico pertractatum*. 8 vols. Leipzig, Germany: Prostat in Officina Libraria Rengeriana, 1741–1748. Wolff's main work, abridged as *Institutiones juris naturae et gentium: In quibus ex ipsa hominis natura continuo nexu omnes obligationes et jura omnia deducuntur* (Halle and Magdeburg, Germany, 1750). Available in German as *Grundsätze des Natur- und Völkerrechts: Worin alle Verbindlichkeiten und alle Rechte aus der Natur des Menschen in einem beständigen Zusammenhange hergeleitet werden* (Halle, Germany, 1754).

Klaus Luig
Translated from the German by Ira Allen

WOMEN. [*This entry contains six subentries, on women in ancient Greek law, in ancient Rome, in English common law, in Islamic law, in Hindu law, and in United States law. For discussion of women in Chinese law, see Marriage, subentry on Chinese Law and Punishment and Status in Chinese Law, subentry on Women.*]

Ancient Greek Law

Women's social and legal condition was different according to the region of ancient Greece and the organization of the community in which they lived. As usual, the majority of our information comes from Athens, the only city-state whose customs and rules may be reconstructed in considerable detail.

Athens. Athenian women, in their relation to the city, are denoted with the words *astē* (the feminine form of *astos*) and *politis* (the feminine form of *politēs*). As *astos* and *politēs* indicate the aspects of participation in civic life, this shows that women were considered citizens.

However, as in every other ancient culture, they were excluded from participation in political life: in other words, they had only the status, not the rights or functions, of citizens. After a decree passed in 450 B.C.E. by Pericles their status as citizens (as *astai*) became a condition for the citizenship of their children. Up to that moment citizenship had descended only through the male line.

Private law. In the field of private law, an Athenian woman was considered incapable of making competent and rational decisions and was submitted all her life to a *kyrios*, a man who had power and authority over her. The *kyrios* was her father; if the father was dead it was a brother by the same father; if the woman had no brothers it was the paternal grandfather or the uncle. Upon marriage her husband became the *kyrios*; if the husband died, the son of the widow became her *kyrios*. In case of dissolution of the marriage, the rights of the former *kyrios* revived. Among the powers of a *kyrios* was the right to decide on the terms of the woman's marriage. The only *kyrios* who did not have this power in his lifetime was the husband, but he could choose his future widow's husband in his testament.

In order to understand women's marital status and condition, it is necessary to recall that in Athens marriage was monogamous, but that while wives were bound to the strictest sexual fidelity, husbands were allowed to have sexual encounters and more or less stable relations with more than one woman (as well as the possibility of a relation with a boy). As stated in a famous passage of a speech attributed to Demosthenes, an Athenian man might have three kinds of women: a wife (*damar*) "for the production of legitimate children"; a concubine (*pallakē*) "for the care of the body" (an ambiguous expression usually interpreted as referring to the possibility of having regular if not daily sexual relations); and a "companion" (*hetaira*) "for pleasure." To understand the meaning of this last word we must recall that *hetairai* were women paid to accompany men on social occasions such as the famous banquets (*symposia*), where wives were not allowed, and where Athenian men discussed philosophy, politics, justice, love, and other issues, and had with *hetairai* sexual encounters not merely occasional, albeit usually not stable.

To give a full account of the possible heterosexual encounters of Athenian men, we must include the *pornai* (prostitutes), not mentioned by Demosthenes because they were only occasional partners in an act that did not involve a relationship.

The status of wife, as well as the legitimacy of children, depended on the celebration of a ceremony called *eggyē* (from *eggyēsis* "betrothed"), followed by a rite called *ekdosis*, "giving away." In principle, husband and wife both could dissolve the marriage. Divorce initiated by the husband was called *apopempsis* (repudiation); divorce

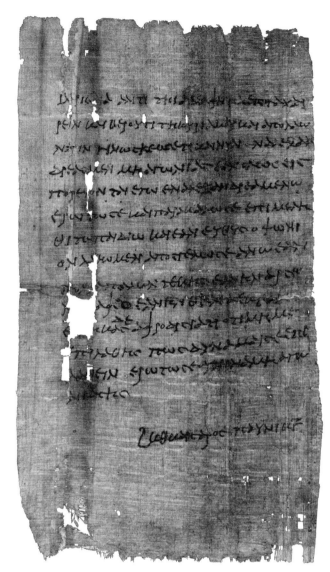

Greek Letter. From Hilarion to his wife Alis telling her "if you bear a child and it is male, let it be; if it is female, cast it out," 17 June 1 B.C.E. COURTESY OF THE THOMAS FISHER RARE BOOK LIBRARY, UNIVERSITY OF TORONTO

initiated by the wife was called *apoleipsis* (abandonment [by the woman] of the conjugal roof). Women, however, were legally and socially strongly disadvantaged, if they decided to interrupt their marriage. Legally, a wife who wanted to abandon the conjugal roof had to address the archon, accompanied by her *kyrios*, and record the act in the magistrate's office. Concerning social attitudes toward women who decided to divorce, suffice it to quote Medea's famous complaint in Euripides' tragedy: a woman cannot decide when and whom to marry; her father decides it, and she becomes a slave of a man who has been given an amount of money to accept her as a wife. The husband, though, does not lose his freedom: if and when he is tired of staying home, he simply goes out with a friend; but a woman, if her marriage is unhappy and she decides to divorce her husband, acquires a bad reputation.

In Athens the dissolution of a marriage could also be the consequence of the decision of a third person, usually the father of the wife, who did not need to obtain the assent of the daughter.

As far as love and sexuality are concerned, scholars debate their presence, quality, and intensity in marriages, and they compare conjugal Eros with different types of sexual relations, namely pederasty, the relation between an adult man and a youth. Some scholars maintain that while these relations were asymmetrical, in the sense that only one of the partners (the adult) felt sexual desire, marriage was the appropriate venue for reciprocal sexual desire. But this idea is unconvincing. Of course, Eros was not totally absent from marriages; reproduction requires at least a minimum of it. Certainly in some marriages a strong reciprocal sexual desire was felt. But if so, this was a happy coincidence. In Athens (as well as in the rest of the classical world) marriage can hardly be considered to have been the most appropriate venue for Eros. It was, instead, the institution that society and law had designed for the ordered procreation of citizens.

Economic rights and inheritance. At their father's death, if he had sired male offspring, Athenian women did not participate in the division of the family estate. A daughter (called an "heiress," *epiklēros*) inherited only in the absence of sons, even if according to special rules. The dowry received at the moment of marriage was considered her share of inheritance. Its value depended on the economic status of the family, ranging from 5 percent to 25 percent of the father's property.

The dowry only rarely included land; it usually consisted of money and other movable goods. Dowries were not administered by women, but by their husbands, who when the marriage ended were bound to give back the dowry to the original *kyrios* of their former wife. The penalty for a husband who failed to do this was the payment of interest, which could reach 18 percent a year.

Even if excluded from the division of their father's estate, Athenian women had some property of their own. Albeit only in the absence of brothers, male cousins, or uncles, they could inherit as sisters, cousins, or aunts. They could inherit under a will; they could receive gifts, and they owned personally the so-called paraphernalia, movable goods that they were given at marriage but were not part of the dowry. However, they could not make a will, and they did not control the management of their own property. In one of his speeches, the orator Isaeus says that "the law explicitly forbids a child or a woman to contract for the disposal of anything of a value above one *medimnos* of barley." Even if one *medimnos* of barley had a certain value (probably enough to feed a family for one week), this limit prevented women from engaging in major transactions. However, the law was not always respected; the consequences of its violation are uncertain, but it seems probable that such transactions were not invalid per se, but could be declared void if the *kyrios* challenged them in court.

Finally, it seems that while a woman needed the assent of her *kyrios* to make any major act of disposition, her *kyrios* did not need her consent to do so. How women felt about this limitation is suggested by some lines in *Ekklēsiazousai* (Women at the Assembly), where Aristophanes imagines that women, having taken political power, pass a law that imposes on men the limit of one *medimnos*.

Were Athenian women secluded? Until recently, scholars shared the belief that Athenian women who were not yet married were secluded in the inner apartments (*gynaikēnitis*) of the house, and that even after marriage they were allowed to cross the threshold of it only exceptionally. This hypothesis, however, has been more recently challenged by archaeologists and classicists. The archaeologists have debated at length the existence of quarters of the house where women and children would have been physically segregated. From the late 8th century B.C.E. to 4th, according to their research, house plans included a male space (a public room, the *andron*), where visitors were allowed, and a private, inner part of the house, where women lived. This inner space, symbolically feminine, was accessible only through male space and through a door guarded by the *kyrios*; the men of the family, however, were allowed to enter it. In the opinion of some scholars this design might suggest a hardening of the gender relation, compared with the previous historical period. Starting in the late eighth century B.C.E., the plan of the house suggests the existence of a strong gender distinction but not a social system that really and totally secluded women.

In addition, a new interpretation of literary sources leads some scholars to exclude the possibility that Athenian women were secluded and isolated. Even if on permission of the head of the household, women, according to their social and economical status, went out in the streets on different occasions and for different purposes: women who needed to earn their living went out to sell ribbon or bread, or to work in the fields; women who belonged to the higher class exchanged visits with friends and followed the funerals of the relatives. Recent scholarship believes that they even attended theatrical performances, and that women of every class participated in religious festivals.

Athenian women, then, were not denied any social life. However, at least if they belonged to the high classes, they were strictly controlled by men; if they possessed slaves they were accompanied by them in the streets. In short, they were not physically secluded, but certainly socially controlled. Moreover, in spite of the possibility of leaving their houses and taking part in public events they were not, unless they were *hetairai*, admitted to the best-known cultural functions in Athenian life, the famous banquets (*symposia*). Participation in such meetings, accompanied by drinking, singing, and dancing, would have been not only unbecoming but also embarrassing for "honest" women, who had never received an education. The maternal role, in Athens, did not require a woman to be educated. Once she had borne a child, her maternal function was accomplished. The education of sons was a matter for men. Whether this was because women did not receive an education, or because they were denied education because they would never need it, is a long-debated question, whose answer is tied up with the equally controversial question of the cultural and pedagogical role of pederasty.

As is well known, young Athenians of the elite class were not taught to become good citizens by their father, but by a "lover." This was due perhaps to the overwhelmingly public nature of Athenian men's lives, demanding the identification of an educator with the public, not the private, realm. What is certain is that Athenian women did not contribute to their children's education. Their role was purely biological.

Feminine sexual crimes. In Athens any sexual relation between a woman (unless she was his wife or concubine) and a man was a crime defined as *moicheia*. The criminalization of these kinds of sexual intercourse was the consequence of a law enacted in 621–620 B.C.E. by Draco, aimed at reducing the incidence of private revenge. This law stated that a person accused of homicide must undergo a judicial trial and suffer a penalty. There were, however, some special cases, in which a person could kill with impunity—among them, the case of the man who killed another (defined as *moichos*) caught "next to" his wife, mother, daughter, sister, or his free concubine.

Although often translated as "adultery," then, *moicheia* does not correspond with adultery in the modern sense. According to traditional and the great majority of contemporary scholarship, *moicheia* included also sexual intercourse with women not yet married or widowed—that is to say, to all the acts that allowed an Athenian citizen to kill with impunity a man caught in flagrante in his house.

As to the penalty for women who had committed *moicheia*, a law recorded in pseudo-Demosthenes establishes that "if a man surprises his wife with a *moichos*, he is not permitted to keep the woman as a wife, and if he does so, he shall be *atimos* [dishonored]. And the woman with whom the adulterer has been surprised shall not be permitted to appear at public cult ceremonies and, if she does, she shall suffer whatever may happen to her, apart from death."

What would happen to a woman repudiated for *moicheia* may be easily imagined: if reaccepted in the family of her father, she would probably spend a retired, not to say de facto, segregated life; even if no law explicitly prohibited marrying an adulteress, such an occurrence seems highly improbable. If the adulteress were not reaccepted in the family house, in the best of cases she would find a man (or a series of men) who would support her; in the worst, she would become a prostitute.

Doric Cities: Sparta and Gortyn. The information concerning Doric cities, particularly Sparta and Gortyn, poses methodological problems. As is well known, Sparta was the bitter enemy and rival of Athens. The two cities—both poleis (city-states)—had diametrically opposed concepts of the individual's relationship to the state, and we owe our information on Sparta to Athenian authors, either anti-Spartan like Aristotle or admirers of the Spartan system, like Xenophon and Plutarch. Therefore, the sources on Sparta are strongly biased and require careful and critical interpretation. The information related to Gortyn is, on the other hand, indigenous, and consists of a series of legal inscriptions dating from the end of the seventh century to the mid-fourth century. The main and most famous of these, known as the Code of Gortyn, consists of a list of the rules governing the city. They are therefore highly reliable, but by definition—being only rules—insufficient to allow us to know the reality of social life. In order to know whether and to what degree such rules were observed, we should be able to read other documents (historical works, literature, philosophical works, private letters), but unfortunately legal documents are practically the only indigenous material coming from Gortyn. This means that we do not have information about Gortynian individuals, their mentality, or their private life; in other words, we can reconstruct only the system that the Gortynian lawgivers wanted to impose, not the real relationships among the city's inhabitants.

Sparta. For the reasons already suggested, information on Sparta must be handled very carefully. Some information about Spartan marriage, albeit contradictory, comes from Plutarch and Aristotle, as well as that about women's education. According to Aristotle, Lycurgus was not able to educate women to the proper principles of modesty and restraint because they were too accustomed to the greatest license and power, which they enjoyed as a consequence of the long expeditions abroad of Spartan men. But Plutarch challenges this opinion. Lycurgus did pay the greatest attention to women's education; from the time they were very young, he wanted them to be strong and healthy, in order to struggle successfully with the difficulties of childbirth and produce strong citizens. For this reason women exercised their bodies in running, wrestling, and hurling the javelin.

Marriage was highly praised, but according to Plutarch, Lycurgus taught Spartan men that they had to be free from selfish jealousy, because the main purpose of marriage was to beget children. He also taught that men—especially husbands too old to procreate—must share their wives with other men worthy to beget children, and scorned those who might regard such privileges as intolerable and might resort to murder and war rather than grant them.

Plutarch, an admirer of the Spartan system, also recounts some famous anecdotes, such as that regarding the encounter between Gorgo, the wife of Leonidas, and a foreign woman, who tells her, "You Spartan women are the only ones who rule their men." The answer is, "Yes, we are the only ones who give birth to men."

Gortyn. The reading of the Gortynian law codes shows that between Athenian and Doric law there were many differences, within the frame of a common set of ethical and legal basic principles. From this law we know that in Gortyn the father of the bride was not allowed to thwart her marriage; that an heiress had some possibility of refusing a husband she did not want; and that in cases of divorce all women benefited from economic arrangements better than the ones they would be given in Athens, and might even be offered the possibility of raising a child their former husband had refused to accept. As it seems reasonable to interpret these rules as the expression of a culture diffused throughout the Doric area, the Code of Gortyn seems to confirm that in Dorian cities women were accorded more rights than their Athenian counterparts.

Given the difficulty of extracting historical reality from narrations and commentaries of these kinds, the discovery and publication of the Gortynian inscriptions, and particularly of their law code, was a very important event for scholars interested in the Spartan world. With caveats, the Gortynian law has come to be an additional subsidiary source for the reconstruction of Spartan law.

The Hellenistic period. The profound changes in political, philosophical, and scientific vision that characterized the Hellenistic period had inevitable important consequences for family structures and the condition of women. Women benefited from growing respect, greater chances for participation in social life, and a perceptible expansion of their legal capacities.

The Egyptian papyri, a great number of which preserve private documents, reveal profound transformations also. Even Greek women, traditionally subordinate to the power of a guardian, bought and sold goods and properties, mortgaged their own goods, and made wills. Women concluded their own marriage contracts, albeit rarely. At times, the mother appeared in marriage contracts, together with the father, as giving away the daughter in marriage. Subordination to male power still existed, however. We know for certain that the choice between raising and abandoning a newborn child still belonged to the father: in the first century B.C.E., in Oxyrhynchus (near the Nile), an absent husband wrote to his pregnant wife, giving her instruction:"if the new born will be a male, raise it: if it will be a female, abandon it." The tone of the letter reveals that its content was not abnormal.

The father still had the power to block his daughter's marriage, but in the second century, again at Oxyrynchus, a woman named Dionysia petitioned the local magistrate, claiming that her father wanted to separate her from her husband, and maintaining that "no law permits taking daughters away from their husband against their will." Even if illiteracy was still more frequent among women than men, female education was generally on the increase. An inscription at Theos informs us that a coeducational school existed. Alexandria, in particular, was a privileged city, where women were educated and enjoyed relative freedom. In sum, we can say that the Hellenistic period was a good time for women.

[*See also* Adultery in Ancient Greek Law; Divorce, *subentry on* Ancient Greek Law; Family, *subentry on* Ancient Greek Law; Inheritance, *subentry on* Ancient Greek Law; Marriage, *subentry on* Ancient Greek Law; *and* Prostitution in Ancient Greek Law.]

BIBLIOGRAPHY

Blundell, Sue. *Women in Ancient Greece*. Cambridge, Mass.: Harvard University Press, 1995.

Bremen, Riet van. "Family Structures." In *A Companion to the Hellenistic World*, edited by Andrew Erskine. Oxford and Malden, Mass.: Blackwell, 2003.

Calame, Claude. *L'Éros dans la Grèce antique*. Paris: Éditions Belin, 1996.

Cantarella, Eva. "A proposito di C. Calame, L'Éros dans la Grèce antique." *Annales E.S.C.* 54, No. 5 (1998): 1200–1203.

Cantarella, Eva. *Bisexuality in the Ancient World*. 2d ed. New Haven, Conn.: Yale University Press, 2002.

Cantarella, Eva. "La 'eggue' nel diritto matrimoniale attico." *Rend. Ist. Lombardo Scienze e Lettere* 98 (1964): 121–161.

Cantarella, Eva. "Gender, Sexuality, and Law." In *The Cambridge Companion to Ancient Greek Law*, edited by Michael Gagarin and David Cohen. Cambridge, U.K., and New York: Cambridge University Press, 2005.

Cantarella, Eva. "Moicheia, Reconsidering a Problem." In *Symposion 1990: Papers on Greek and Hellenistic Legal History*, edited by Michael Gagarin, pp. 289–296. Cologne: Böhlau, 1991.

Cantarella, Eva. *Pandora's Daughters: The Role and Status of Women in Greek and Roman Antiquity*. Baltimore, Md.: Johns Hopkins University Press, 1987.

Carey, C. "Rape and Adultery in Athenian Law." *The Classical Quarterly* 45, no. 2 (1995): 407–417.

Cohen, David. "The Athenian Law of Adultery." *Revue Internationale des Droits de l'Antiquité* 31 (1984): 147–165.

Cohen, David. "Seclusion, Separation and the Status of Women in Classical Athens." In *Women in Antiquity*, edited by Ian McAuslan and Peter Walcot. London: Oxford University Press, 1996.

Foxhall, Lin "Household, Gender, and Property in Classical Athens." *Classical Quarterly* 39, no. 1 (1989): 22–44.

Goldhill, Simon. "Representing Democracy: Women at the Great Dionysia." *Ritual, Finance, Politics: Athenian Democratic Accounts Presented to David Lewis*, edited by Robin Osborne and Simon Hornblower. New York: Oxford University Press, 1994.

Just, Roger. *Women in Athenian Law and Life*. London and New York: Routledge, 1989.

Leduc, C. "Comment la donner en marriage?" In *Histoire des femmes en Occident: L' antiquité*. Paris: Plon, 1991.

Mélèze Modrzejewski, Joseph. "Greek Law in the Hellenistic Period: Family and Marriage." In *The Cambridge Companion to Greek Law*, edited by Michael Gagarin and David Cohen, pp. 343–354. Cambridge, U.K., and New York: Cambridge University Press, 2005.

Morris, Ian. "Gender Relations in the Classical Greek Household: The Archaeological Evidence." *Annual of the British School at Athens* 90 (1995): 363–381.

Morris, Ian. "Household Archaeology and Gender Ideology in Archaic Greece." In *Transactions of the American Philological Association* 129 (1999): 305–317.

Nevett, Lisa C. "Separation or Seclusion: Toward an Archaeological Approach to Investigating Women in the Greek Household in the Fifth to Third Century B.C.E." In *Architecture and Order: Approaches to Social Spaces*, edited by Michael Parker Pearson and Colin Richards. London and New York: Routledge, 1994.

Nevett, Lisa C. *House and Society in the Ancient Greek World*. Cambridge, U.K., and New York: Cambridge University Press, 1999.

Ogden, Daniel. *Greek Bastardy in the Classical and Hellenistic Periods*. Oxford: Clarendon Press; New York: Oxford University Press, 1996.

Ogden, Daniel. "Rape, Adultery, and the Protection of Bloodlines in Classical Athens." In *Rape in Antiquity: Sexual Violence in the Greek and Roman Worlds*, edited by Susan Deacy and Karen Pierce. London: Duckworth, 1997.

Omitowoju, Rosanna. "Regulating Rape: Soap Operas and Self-interest in the Athenian Courts." In *Rape in Antiquity: Sexual Violence in the Greek and Roman Worlds*, edited by Susan Deacy and Karen Pierce. London: Duckworth, 1997.

Pomeroy, Sarah B. "The Education of Women in the Fourth Century and in the Hellenistic Period." *American Journal of Ancient History* 2 (1977): 51–68.

Pomeroy, Sarah B. *Women in Hellenistic Egypt: From Alexander to Cleopatra*. New York: Schocken, 1984.

Preaux, C. "Le statut des femmes à l'époque hellénistique, principalement en Egypte." *Recueils de la Société Jean Bodin* 11 (1959): 127–175.

Schaps, David M. *Economic Rights of Women in Ancient Greece*. Edinburgh: Edinburgh University Press, 1979.

Vatin, C, *Recherches sur le mariage et la condition de la femme mariée à l'époque hellénistique*. Paris: Ed. De Boccard, 1970.

EVA CANTARELLA

The Position of Women and Equality in Ancient Rome

The Roman jurist Papinian (d. 212 C.E.) remarked (*Digest* 1.5.9), "In many articles of our law the position of females is worse than that of males." However, in many areas of private law Roman women were not, in fact, worse off than men. Public life was closed to them (as to women in most societies and times until relatively recently), because they could not elect, legislate, or hold office. In private life, however, they enjoyed a high degree of independence and self-determination—once, that is, they were free of paternal control (*patria potestas*) and legally independent (*sui iuris*).

Patria Potestas. Sons and daughters were equally under the legal control and were the legal responsibility of the *paterfamilias* (head of household) during his lifetime, or until he released them (emancipation). They were incapable of independent legal action or ownership of property. In early Rome, a woman might also be brought at marriage into the *potestas* (in this instance known as *manus*) of her husband or his *paterfamilias*, and became a member of his descent group (*familia*). This effectively prolonged her period *in potestate*, which would end with the death of her husband rather than of her father. *Manus* was created for reasons concerned with the eventual rights of intestate inheritance to the woman herself, and had become virtually obsolete by the early empire (Treggiari, pp. 30–34; Gardner, *Family and* Familia, pp. 40–41). For practical purposes, therefore, *manus* is ignored in classical law.

Patria potestas had two aspects: power over free persons in the *familia*, and power over property. A man acquired both once released from *potestas*; a woman acquired control only over property. From this distinction spring most of the restrictions on the legal capacity of Roman women; it is also the basis of much of the social discrimination to which they were subjected (Gardner, *Roman Citizen*, pp. 85–109).

Power over persons. This legal asymmetry is evident in Roman marriage. Spouses owned property separately and independently, and dowry was returnable; sorting such matters out at the end of a marriage was mainly a matter of establishing relevant facts. However, children were under the legal authority of the father, as head of the *familia*, not of the mother. Both legal and literary sources indicate, nevertheless, that mothers were commonly influential in decision-making within the family (an influence probably enhanced by a wife's personal wealth and the size of her dowry). The father's authority covered not only custody and discipline, but also decisions on, for example, education and marriage. At his death, children who were still minors required a male *tutor*, or guardian (an agnate, that is, a close relative in the male line, or someone nominated by the *paterfamilias* or by a magistrate), to manage their property; women were not eligible to do this. Though some women do seem to have managed their children's affairs without resort to guardians, their lack of legal right to do so could give rise to problems in establishing liability (Gardner, *Family and* Familia, pp. 40–41). They could be prosecuted under the general heading of "unauthorised administration of affairs" (*actio negotiorum gestorum*; *Digest* 3.5.3, Buckland, pp. 537–538), which applied both to women and to men, or possibly the more specific charge of "unauthorised exercise of guardianship" (*actio protutelae*, *Digest* 27.5, Buckland, p. 545).

Wives and husbands were equally free to divorce, although if the wife initiated the divorce, the husband was entitled to retain part of the dowry if there were children of the marriage. Divorce did not affect the father's *potestas* or his right to custody of the children, although for practical reasons they might sometimes remain with the mother. From the time of Antoninus Pius, appeal might be made to a magistrate for a mother to have physical custody of the child, on the grounds of a father's bad character. Nevertheless, the father's *potestas* was unaffected.

Women could not have *potestas* as head of a *familia*, and therefore could not adopt. From the time of Diocletian, there was one limited concession. A woman who had lost her own children might be allowed to "adopt" someone; this fictitious legal relationship consisted only in giving the chosen person the same priority of claim to her intestate succession that since 178 C.E. her children would have had (*senatusconsultum Orphitianum*: *Digest* 38.17). Since only those with *potestas* could preserve the agnatic line, women were probably less often adopted than men. Until the imperial period, women who were already independent could not be adopted at all, because the necessary procedure (adrogation) involved a voting assembly, the *comitia curiata*, to which women did not have access. The obsolescence of the *comitia* removed this obstacle, and in the course of the second century C.E. adrogation of women by imperial rescript made its appearance.

Power over property. Adult women's control over their property was limited by the requirement to have a *tutor* (guardian), who did not manage the property, but whose authorization was required for certain transactions likely to affect it. In early Rome, the *tutor* was normally her nearest male agnate, who would also have been her intestate heir, and the purpose of the institution was to resist depletion of property and secure its transmission within the *familia*. With the decline of *manus*-marriage and the development of the praetorian rules of succession—in response, perhaps, to difficulty in maintaining agnate succession—the importance of the *tutor* diminished. Under Claudius, agnates ceased to be the "default" tutors, and Hadrian abolished the requirement of *coemptio* (a formal procedure breaking previous agnatic connections: Gaius *Institutes* 1.115–115a) for women to make a will. Augustus had already exempted mothers of three (or four for freedwomen) legitimate children from tutelage by the grant of *ius liberorum*, the "right of children" (Buckland, pp. 165–167; Gardner, *Women in Roman Law*, pp. 14–22; Gardner, *Roman Citizen*, pp. 89–100; Evans Grubbs, pp. 23–46).

Tutelage of women persisted until at latest 410 C.E. (Codex Theodosianus 8.17.3), when the *ius liberorum* was abolished, but may have already lapsed by the end of the third century (Evans Grubbs, pp. 43–46). However, literary, legal, and epigraphic evidence indicates that for women in the classical period it was little more than a formality, and for many types of transaction it was not required at all. By the second century C.E. its original purpose had so far been forgotten that its need was commonly ascribed to women's supposed irresponsibility and lack of judgment (Gaius *Institutes* 1.190).

Legal Capacity. Broadly speaking, women were excluded, except in matters where their own personal interests were concerned, from activities that might affect the *caput* (legal status), or indeed the property, of other citizens. In many criminal or civil actions, the condemned person incurred some loss of legal capacity (*infamia*), and in most, some loss of property was involved. Women could not be judges. A woman could not appear on behalf of others, on either side of a lawsuit, and she had the right to bring prosecutions, civil or criminal, only in cases in which she had a direct personal interest. (This did not include her husband's adultery, which was regarded, under a law introduced by the emperor Augustus, as an offense against the other woman's husband.) Indeed, the consent of a *tutor* was required to bring a lawsuit at all, presumably because of danger to the woman's property if she lost.

Exceptionally, in a joint rescript the emperor Septimius Severus and emperor-designate (198–211 C.E.) Antoninus "Caracalla" allowed women to make charges concerning offenses relating to the *annona* (state-subsidized grain ration). However, as a jurist of the same period tells us, they were forbidden by imperial constitutions from making denunciations concerning the *fiscus* (imperial treasury). Why the distinction? In the former instance, offenders were presumably taking from the state something to which they were not entitled; informing against them was, the emperors declared, in the public interest. The offenses against the *fiscus*, however, mainly involve individuals withholding or concealing private monies due to the treasury from such sources as forfeit inheritances, illegal trusts, taxes, etc. "Self-denunciation" (like the modern British "self-assessment" of income tax) was encouraged, for both sexes; however, informing against others (*delatio*) was generally considered dishonorable, even though "career" informers were encouraged and rewarded by the state. The alleged grounds on which certain categories of people were forbidden to inform in fiscal matters (*Digest* 49.14.18) include their status, honorable (veterans, soldiers, and, presumably, senators) or dishonored (condemned criminals); women, however, are excluded "because of the weakness of their sex." This sort of social prejudice will be discussed further below.

Besides litigation, women were also unable to participate freely in various legal transactions. For instance, the legal procedure of *mancipatio*, used in the making of wills and for immediate conveyance of legal ownership over certain kinds of property, required tutorial consent. In property deals, this was not too much of an impediment, because full legal ownership could be acquired after a period of possession. Tutorial control over will-making also diminished, except for freedwomen. However, only holders of *patria potestas*—that is, men—could provide the necessary witnesses to such transactions. Women were also legally unacceptable as guarantors for the debts of others (*senatusconsultum Velleianum*: *Digest* 16.2).

Social Discrimination. It is evident that women were legally excluded from participation not only in public affairs, but also from many routine transactions taking place in public in Roman daily life; they were therefore normally absent from the daily business of the forum. Unfortunately, this absence, especially when its original reason had been forgotten, came to be justified on grounds of propriety, or of women's mental incapacity and unfitness, or simply on the grounds that certain activities were the prerogative of men (Gardner, *Roman Citizen*, pp. 97–107). Thus, tutelage of women was justified by women's weakness, their incapacity to be tutors on the grounds that this was "men's business." Women were excluded from public office, or from judging, by "custom," because that was "received practice." Propriety also was a powerful justification. There were indeed hazards for women in the streets, and already in the Republic the praetor's edict prescribed penalties for attempted molestation of women appearing in public (*Digest* 47.10.15)—though the penalties were, significantly, less if the women's dress indicated that they were prostitutes or slaves. Unsurprisingly, for women to appear in public at all was therefore regarded as somewhat improper behavior.

Though unable to litigate on behalf of others, women were perfectly entitled to bring civil cases on their own account. There was, however, strong prejudice against their doing so. Valerius Maximus, writing in the reign of the emperor Tiberius (14–37 C.E.), says of a notoriously litigious female called Afrania (or possibly Carfania), "Of such a monster it is the date of its death rather than its birth that deserves record." Afrania was doing merely what was her legal right, that is, to litigate personally over her own concerns. The jurist Ulpian (d. 223/4 C.E.) goes so far as to attribute the origin of the ban on women involving themselves in the lawsuits of others and so undertaking "men's work" to Carfania's constant pestering of the praetor's court. Valerius, however, says of her and others that their natural condition (i.e., being women) and the modesty befitting the *stola* (the garb of respectable matrons) should have kept them out of the courts—and indeed out of the public eye altogether.

For both legal and social reasons, the visibility of Roman women is much reduced (see Gardner, "Gender-Role Assumptions" and "Women in Business Life"), both in legal texts and in private documents concerning business. There is extensive overlap between the legal capacity of Roman women and men, and where sex is irrelevant legal writers habitually use masculine forms, even to the extent of using *paterfamilias* merely to denote a person who is legally independent, or one who owns property. The husband is typically presented as the sole provider and householder of the family home, even though it is clear from texts concerning their separate property that both husbands and wives could and did commonly contribute to the needs of the household.

Three collections survive of wooden tablets, recording various business transactions in the towns of Pompeii, Herculaneum, and Puteoli, around the Bay of Naples in the first century C.E. The tablets are not themselves legal documents, but private records, sealed and witnessed, attesting that certain legally necessary verbal declarations have been made.

These tablets strikingly illustrate both the active engagement of women in business and their marginalization both in law and in practice. Women are found conducting a variety of business matters in much the same way as men, often necessarily personally present, and without the *tutor* seeming to offer any particular hindrance. However, there are certain striking features. Women are found both as debtors, receiving loans, and as creditors, receiving repayments of loans. In no document, however, does the woman herself write that she has made the necessary verbal declaration; a man writes that she has done so. We should not assume female illiteracy; rather, the man is likely to be her *tutor*, whose authorization was legally necessary both for undertaking an obligation and for releasing someone else from one. Here, there is an obvious legal explanation.

Much more surprising is the almost total absence of women among the witnesses who appended their seals to these tablets, even where the list of signatories appears complete. Only one example is known, that of the creditor herself. There is no legal reason preventing women from witnessing these purely private documents. However, women, even if physically present in the forum, would perhaps tend to be overlooked or even thought unsuitable as potential witnesses, because they were for legal reasons unable to render other small services through which men routinely networked in business life. They could not be witnesses to wills, or to transfers of ownership by *mancipatio*, nor were they acceptable as guarantors for the debts of others.

Women under the Law. Under Roman law, women enjoyed great economic and social independence, subject only to relatively minor restraints. The extent to which they were in practice able to avail themselves of this freedom would naturally vary. Some women, the evidence shows, did competently and confidently run their own affairs. However, social attitudes restricted many (perhaps most) women's opportunities to acquire the skills and knowledge available to men, making them dependent upon men for help and advice, and reinforcing the view that women were simply not up to tackling "men's business." Roman women were certainly not oppressed, but they were not regarded as the equals of men.

[*See also* Persons, *subentry on* Roman Law; Roman Law, *subentries* 27 B.C.E.–250 C.E. *and* 250–527 C.E.; *and* Succession, *subentry on* Roman Law.]

BIBLIOGRAPHY

Buckland, William W. *A Text-Book of Roman Law*. 3d ed. Revised by Peter Stein. Cambridge, U.K.: Cambridge University Press, 1963. The main English work of reference on Roman law.

Evans Grubbs, Judith. *Women and the Law in the Roman Empire: A Sourcebook on Marriage, Divorce, and Widowhood*. London and New York: Routledge, 2002. An excellent collection of mainly legal sources, with commentary and detailed notes and bibliography.

Gardner, Jane F. *Being a Roman Citizen*. London and New York: Routledge, 1993. See especially chapter 4, concerning limitations on women's legal capacity.

Gardner, Jane F. *Family and Familia in Roman Law and Life*. Oxford, U.K.: Clarendon Press, 1998. Discusses the relationship between family law and actual practice in Roman society.

Gardner, Jane, F. "Gender-Role Assumptions in Roman Law." *Échos du Monde Classique / Classical Views* 14 (1995): 377–400.

Gardner, Jane F. "Women in Business Life: Some Evidence from Puteoli." In *Female Networks and the Public Sphere in Roman Society*, edited by Päivi Setälä and Liisa Savunen, pp. 11–27. Rome: Institutum Romanum Finlandiae, 1999. Discusses the texts of some of the wooden tablets from Pompeii, Puteoli, and Herculaneum.

Gardner, Jane F. *Women in Roman Law and Society*. London: Croom Helm, 1986. A detailed survey of Roman law as it affected women.

Treggiari, Susan. *Roman Marriage: Iusti Coniuges from the Time of Cicero to the Time of Ulpian*. Oxford, U.K.: Clarendon Press, 1991. The best survey of social and legal aspects of Roman marriage.

JANE F. GARDNER

English Common Law

Before the end of the nineteenth century, English women cannot be discussed as a single group for most legal purposes. In the medieval period there were circumstances that determined a woman's position at law: her free or servile condition, her religious or lay status, and above all, her marital status—single, married, or widowed. The first of these determinants became largely unimportant in the fifteenth century, the second after the Reformation. But the third remained vital at least until the Married Women's Property Act of 1882, 45/46 Victoria c. 75 and for some purposes into the twentieth century. This note deals almost entirely with free laywomen; it does not discuss unfree women since, except with regard to crime, issues concerning them were generally handled in manor courts operating under the custom of a particular manor. Nor is it concerned with religious women, since as individuals they did not enter into contracts, litigate about torts, hold land, or—at least in theory—possess personal property.

Criminal Law. The area in which men and women were treated most alike—without regard to these life circumstances—was the criminal law. Both men and women could be, and were, tried for theft, arson, murder, and other felonies; the procedure did not vary according to the sex of the defendant, although theoretically a woman could not *appeal* a man—bring a private criminal accusation—except for her own rape or for the death of her husband under certain circumstances. The limitation became less significant as appeal fell into disuse before the end of the Middle Ages. Women were accused of crime less frequently than men, and several studies of fourteenth-, seventeenth-, and eighteenth-century records have shown an apparent lower conviction rate for women (Hanawalt, 1976; Herrup, 1987). Moreover, if convicted of most crimes women were less likely to be sentenced to death. In the later Middle Ages the crimes most frequently committed by women were larceny, burglary, and receiving thieves or stolen goods; in the early modern period women tended to be tried for theft, larceny, and infanticide. (Witchcraft, which involved women almost exclusively, was prosecuted infrequently). Infanticide, seen as a woman's crime, became the subject of frequent prosecution, in part because of a statute of 1623–1624 (21 James I c. 27) that made even concealment of a stillbirth a capital offense. This law was repealed in 1803 by another statute (43 George III c. 58).

Women were at a particular disadvantage in two areas. First, since not capable of being ordained, a woman could not have benefit of clergy until a seventeenth-century statute (21 James I c. 6, 1623–1624) provided that a woman should not suffer death for an offense for which "a man might have his clergie" but should be branded and whipped or imprisoned for up to a year. This statute was amended by 3 William and Mary c. 9 (1691), which narrowed the scope of the benefit but provided that where a man could still demand his clergy, a woman convicted of a similar offense would be punished as the man would have been. Second, a woman who murdered her husband was held to have committed petty treason—unlike a man who murdered his wife—and was executed by being burned to death. (Petty treason was abolished in 1828, when the sentence of burning had not been carried out since 1784.) Women did have the privilege of "benefit of belly," whereby a convicted pregnant woman was not executed until she had delivered her child; the sentence was sometimes permanently avoided or, by the seventeenth century, commuted to transportation abroad. Moreover, it was held that a married woman could not steal from her husband; was not obliged to divulge a crime he committed; and was under some circumstances held not liable for a criminal act committed in her husband's company, because it was presumed she had acted under his coercion—this last presumption, however, could be rebutted and in practice was steadily narrowed.

Marriage and Coverture. Criminal proceedings did not affect most women's lives and did not often interest the jurists who wrote on law. Treatise writers were concerned primarily with relations between husband and wife, with real and personal property, and to a lesser extent

Suffragist. A policeman and plainclothes officer arrest a suffragist, October 1913. PHOTOGRAPH BY BAIN NEWS SERVICE. GEORGE GRANTHAM BAIN COLLECTION/PRINTS AND PHOTOGRAPHS DIVISION, LIBRARY OF CONGRESS

with civil liability. In all these areas, status and gender intersected to determine a woman's rights and liabilities. Marital status, in particular, determined the ability of a woman to hold land or chattels, to make binding contracts, and to be responsible for her own torts. The formation and validity of marriage were governed by the canon law, but the results flowing from the marriage, such as the legitimacy of children or the right to dower, were the common law's to determine. From the late-twelfth century onward, the church took the position that mutual consent expressed in words *de praesenti* was sufficient to make a binding, but irregular, marriage. Both ecclesiastical and secular authorities tried to limit clandestine marriage; for instance, a widow who had married irregularly was not entitled to dower at common law. But clandestine marriages were declared invalid only in 1753, with Lord Hardwicke's Act (The Clandestine Marriages Act), 26 George II c. 33. The church's law on marriage was not simple; rules on precontract and consanguinity or affinity made it possible for people to be uncertain whether they were husband and wife, and consistory courts were kept busy with such issues through the early modern period.

Divorce was equally complicated, since it was really a decree of nullity based on want of consent or capability to marry.

At common law, nullity of a marriage resulted in the illegitimacy of any children of that marriage, but a decree of nullity restored a woman to the status she had held before the attempted marriage. The canon law also provided for what was in effect a legal separation, permitting the parties to live apart. That did not, however, change a woman's status at common law. Divorce per se came to England only slowly after the Reformation; after 1670 it was achieved through parliamentary procedure, was extremely expensive, and was available only on grounds of adultery (and effectively only for men). Real reform began in 1858 with the founding of the Court for Divorce and Matrimonial Causes authorized by an 1857 statute (20/21 Victoria c. 85) opening divorce to women, although even then, while men had only to prove adultery, women needed also to show incest, cruelty, or desertion. Further reforms in the twentieth century eventually produced the Divorce Reform Act (1969), c. 55 allowing divorce for the irretrievable breakdown of a marriage.

Assuming that the marriage was valid, the effects of *coverture* prevailed. Under the theory of coverture, husband and wife were one person in the eyes of the law: "[T]hat is," says Blackstone in his *Commentaries*, "the very being or legal existence of the woman is suspended during the marriage. . . ." The wife was said to be under the wing or protection of her husband: he was the head of the wife; she was within his power. F. W. Maitland suggested an analogy to guardian and ward to explain something of a husband's position, and that seems apt; a 1632 treatise explains that "Every feme covert is *quodammodo* [in a way] an infant" since she loses her power "even in that which is most her owne." (T.E., 1632) Married women, like infants or lunatics, were not *sui juris*; at common law, they were not free to make decisions about their activities or their property—ramifications of that position lasted, albeit with gradually decreasing importance, into the twentieth century.

Women and the Law of Real Property. One area significantly affected by coverture was landholding. Land was the measure of wealth for almost everyone outside medieval cities, and the rules affecting landholding were extensively developed. Villein women, like villein men, held their unfree tenements by the custom of the manor they lived on; they could not sue or be sued for land in the king's courts, and issues concerning their tenements were decided in the courts of individual lords. The common-law rules as to women's inheritance, acquisition, and conveyance of freehold tenements grew up in the twelfth and thirteenth centuries and remained law at least in part until the twentieth. Primogeniture was established firmly in the thirteenth century; its effect was to bar younger sons and all daughters from a share of freehold land, in favor of the oldest son. In the absence of sons, daughters inherited equally in partible shares as coparceners (joint heirs). A son of a second marriage would take in preference to a daughter of the first; daughters of different marriages took as coparceners.

An unmarried or widowed woman's rights in freehold land, if she acquired it, were essentially the same as a man's, although she did not perform some services in person. Marriage altered those rights significantly. While they might not be entitled to land by inheritance, women frequently received it from a father or other relative on marriage, as a *maritagium*. Such land was said to be held by the new husband in right of his wife; he was empowered to manage it—he could lease it out or mortgage it—but could not alienate it without her consent. If he died before his wife, the land returned to her; if she died first, the land descended to her heirs, although until 1285 it was subject to curtesy, the husband's life interest if there had been a child of the marriage. Similar conditions prevailed as to land the wife had bought before marriage or received by gift or inheritance before or during the marriage; curtesy continued to exist in such cases. If the husband alienated the land without his wife's consent, she could bring an action called *cui in vita* upon his death, alleging that the husband, who in life she could not contradict, had sold the land against her will. Ascertaining the wife's consent to a husband's alienation was the subject of judicial concern, resulting in a married woman's separate examination by the judge before whom she appeared to "levy a fine" with her husband, the only way her interest could be conveyed. The effectiveness of the procedure has been questioned, since a woman withholding her consent on examination had then to go home with her husband.

When the marriage ended with the husband's death, his widow was entitled to dower, an interest in his land. In the twelfth century, the bridegroom frequently stated at the church door what the dower would be, but in the thirteenth century such "nominated" dower became uncommon, and after some hesitation it was decided that a widow was entitled to a life estate in any land the husband had held in fee at any time during the marriage and which he had not alienated with her consent. A widow who had not received any or all of her dower could bring a writ of dower to the king's court, and widows enjoyed a high rate of success in the action.

Late-Medieval and Early Modern Developments. Women's position as landholders declined in the later Middle Ages and in the early modern period as a result of several developments. One was the rise of the *fee tail male* after 1285 as a result of the statute De Donis Conditionalibus (Statute of Westminster II c. 1), whereby land—often that granted as *maritagium*—was entailed: granted with the condition that it could not be alienated and could descend only to a male descendant of the grantee. This had the effect of preventing even women without brothers from becoming heirs; on the tenant's death, the tenement in question would go to the appropriate male relative, who became his heir at law. Another development was the transformation of the *maritagium* into the *marriage portion*: the gift of land to the young couple became a gift of money or movables that became the husband's sole property upon the marriage and did not return to the widow upon his death unless he bequeathed it to her. A third was the increased employment of the *use*—the ancestor of the trust—a device whereby before his marriage a landholder devised all or some of his land to trusted friends for his own benefit and, after his death, delivery to a named person. The named person could, of course, be the settlor's wife: the use could be written to provide for one's widow. But often enough it was used to keep land out of the dower pool, because it was held that a widow did not take dower on land in which her husband had held only a beneficial interest.

As a result, in the fourteenth century careful fathers of brides began negotiating for a *jointure*: this was a property given, usually by the bridegroom's family, to husband and wife with the right of survivorship, but expressed as a guaranteed yearly income, based on revenue from the property, to be paid to the widow. Originally it was a life interest, but it could be, and in the eighteenth century often was, limited to widowhood—again, unlike common-law dower. The jointure was almost always considerably less than dower, but it was secure; it usually formed the *res* of a trust, enforceable in equity but not at common law. Its value usually bore some relation to the marriage portion the bride brought to her husband; it has been calculated that in the early 1600s, the ratio of jointure to portion was one to five and later it declined to one to ten.

In the early modern period and into the nineteenth century, marriage settlements became an important feature of planning. The settlement could be a *strict settlement* involving entails, used by aristocratic and gentry families in the seventeenth century and thereafter to ensure the passage of real property to an appropriate male from generation to generation. But it could also be used to safeguard a bride's interest by setting up a trust as her sole and separate estate. The separate estate probably came into use late in the reign of Elizabeth I. Before she married, a woman could put assets into a trust for her sole and separate estate (although there was some opinion that to do so without his consent would be a fraud on the husband-to-be); a trust of property could also be established by a third party on the same terms, either before or after her marriage. While enforceable only in equity, this preserved a woman's right to the *res* of the trust during marriage. A marriage settlement—much like a modern prenuptial agreement—could also be used to secure benefits to a wife or widow that would not have been hers at common law. It could provide for pin money, an annual allowance from husband to wife; it could provide that the wife would be allowed to make a will up to a certain value in case she predeceased the husband; it could be used to secure the rights of children from a woman's previous marriage; or it could oblige a husband to leave his wife a given amount should he predecease her.

Married Women and Personal Property. The arrangements described above were essential because at common law a woman lost all rights to any personal property upon marriage: it became her husband's absolutely, nor did it return to her upon his death. In the twelfth and thirteenth centuries there had been a custom whereby a man making a will was obliged to leave his widow one-third of his personalty, and there was a common-law writ enabling both widow and children to claim their shares. However, this custom seems to have gradually fallen into disuse in the province of Canterbury (except in London); the province of York—the northern part of the country—retained it until 1692, when it was abolished by statute (4 William & Mary c. 2). The custom was ended in London by statute (11 George I c. 18 §17) in 1724. If a man died intestate, the ecclesiastical courts, which both probated wills and settled intestate estates, awarded the widow a third if there were children, the entire estate if there were not. That arrangement was ended in 1670 by the Statute of Distributions (22 & 23 Charles II c. 10), which established a fixed system of distribution that among other things limited the widow to a third even where there was no issue.

The disuse of the custom of thirds in the populous southern part of England meant that a testator was free to will personal property as he chose—although it was common for a man's will to provide for a percentage of his personal property (usually a third) to go to his widow or for the return to her of the things she had brought to him at their marriage. In theory, since a married woman had nothing she could bequeath, she could not make a will. In fact, during the thirteenth and fourteenth centuries married women did occasionally make wills, but the numbers were small and grew smaller during the fifteenth century and thereafter. Such a will could be made only with the consent of the husband, consent he could revoke after the wife's death but before probate unless some prohibiting circumstance—such as a provision in a marriage settlement—existed.

The husband's ownership of the personal property that had been his wife's, or which came to her during the marriage, had not been as significant in the medieval centuries—when personal property consisted chiefly of furnishings and clothing—as it became in the early modern period and thereafter when leases, bills, bonds, and other financial instruments (all considered *chattels real*) could be important components of the assets a woman brought to her husband. A well-to-do woman, or her family, could set up arrangements for her separate estate as described above, but a less-wealthy or less-sophisticated woman might find her financial security entirely dependent on her late husband's good will. The only exception was what was termed her *paraphernalia*, those things so peculiarly hers that if her husband had not alienated them during his lifetime he could not will them away from her. Originally, paraphernalia was said to comprise one set of clothing, but apparently it often included a bed and a chest as well as items such as rosaries and elaborate girdles. By the late-sixteenth century the category had expanded to include jewelry, and most of the later cases deal with the quality and quantity to be allowed.

With the 1833 Dower Act (Statute 3 & 4 William IV c. 105), which allowed a husband to bar dower either by alienating his real estate during his lifetime without his wife's assent or by devising it in his will, a widow could find herself with only the clothing on her back. After a vigorous campaign by reformers, limitations on married women's property ownership were removed by statutes, the most significant being the Married Women's Property Act of 1882, which provided that a married woman could hold and dispose of both real and personal property independently of her husband.

Guardianship and Custody of Children. Given all of the above, it is not surprising that into the nineteenth century a mother had no right to be the guardian of a child when its father died. When a medieval father held land by knight tenure, the wardship of his underage heir belonged to his lord, who might sell the wardship to the highest bidder. Wardships were economically valuable: the guardian was entitled to the proceeds of the child's property until his or her majority or marriage, and could arrange the child's marriage, for which the guardian might receive a considerable sum. Guardianship of the person and guardianship of the property were divisible, and a mother might purchase the former if not the latter. If a father had held in socage tenure, the wardship of the heir belonged to the nearest male member of the child's kin who could not inherit from him or her, and any profits from the ward's marriage belonged to the child. But the mother still had no legal right to be the guardian, although a surviving wife usually was given the nurturing of younger children.

When tenure by knight service ended in 1660, land so held fell into socage tenure, and socage wardship rules prevailed. By a 1660 statute (12 Charles II c. 24 §8), a father was given the right to appoint a guardian for his children by writing under seal during his lifetime or by will; the mother had no corresponding right and could not claim guardianship on the death of her husband. That remained the law until 1886 when, by statute (49 & 50 Victoria c. 27), the mother was made guardian on the death of a father if he had appointed none, and joint guardian if he had. In the absence of such appointment, the court could name a guardian to act with the mother. If a mother dying first had appointed a guardian to act with her husband the appointment could not take effect unless confirmed by a court that found the father unfit.

At common law, so long as a marriage existed, the father had the absolute right to the custody of his legitimate children, a right that continued well into the nineteenth century. On separation or divorce of parents, the father was entitled to custody of legitimate children and could deny the wife access to them; that was altered in 1873 by statute (36 & 37 Victoria c. 12), when a wife was enabled to apply for custody of or access to an infant child and a judge of the Chancery Division was empowered to award her either access or custody to the age of sixteen, the father also having access to the child in the latter case.

Contract and Tort. So far as transactions with third parties are concerned, a single woman—unmarried or widowed—had the same competence to enter into contracts as a man. A married woman could not enter into a binding contract; if she contracted a debt, it could not, with certain exceptions, be enforced against her, and her husband was a necessary party to any lawsuit. On the other hand, a husband was liable for debts and obligations his wife had entered into before their marriage. By the custom of certain cities, including London, a wife could become a *feme sole* and be registered as such, presumably with the consent of her husband. The effect was to enable her to conduct a trade in her own name and to sue or be sued for debts arising from trade. Less exceptionally, she could at common law act as the agent of her husband; the issue in many cases was whether she had been authorized to act, or whether her action had only later been ratified by her husband. The latter situation was not always clear. It was suggested in a 1505 case that even goods consumed by the household might not be chargeable to a husband who had not authorized their purchase. However, exceptions grew up: a husband was bound to maintain his wife and was liable for debts she incurred for necessaries—as she might do if deserted, as in *James v.* Warren Holt KB 104, 90 ER 956 (1707). A number of cases in the eighteenth and nineteenth centuries held that a married woman's separate estate could be liable for her debts under some circumstances; in *Hulme v Tennant* I Br Ch Ca 16; 28 ER 958 (1778) it was held that a separate estate was liable to satisfy her engagements in writing, if it appeared that she meant to bind it. The various Married Women's Property Acts, most significantly that of 1882, removed most contract disabilities, but some vestiges lingered into the twentieth century. For example, until the 1935 Law Reform (Married Women and Tortfeasors) Act, (25 & 26 George V c. 30 §2.2), a woman could not anticipate or alienate her interest in property settled for her separate use. The final restrictions were lifted in 1949 by the Married Women (Restraint upon Anticipation) Act (12, 13 & 14 George VI c. 78 §1).

As for torts, a single woman could sue or be sued for a civil wrong, but at common law a married woman could not, without her husband being joined as a party. As a plaintiff, any damages were his. As a defendant, it was not suggested that she was incapable of committing a tort; it was simply that as she had no property she could not pay damages. A husband's financial liability for his wife's torts ended finally in 1935 with the passage of the Married Women and Tortfeasors Act (25 & 26 George V c. 30).

[*See also* Divorce, *subentry on* English Common Law; Dower in English Common Law; Family, *subentry on* English Common Law; *and* Rape, *subentry on* English Common Law.]

BIBLIOGRAPHY

Baker, John Hamilton. *An Introduction to English Legal History*. 4th ed. London and Dayton, Ohio: Butterworths/LexisNexis, 2002. An excellent concise commentary on various issues affecting women. See especially chs. 26, 27, 28, and 30 on economic torts, status of persons, marriage and its consequences, and the substantive criminal law.

Beattie, John M. "The Criminality of Women in Eighteenth-Century England." *Journal of Social History* 8 (1975): 80–116. Analyzes women's crime in two counties, rural Sussex and more urban Surrey, and concludes that the different rates and types of crime reflect differences in women's work and lives in two settings.

Blackstone, Sir William. *Commentaries on the Laws of England in Four Books*. (1765). Many editions. Probably the treatise most influential on eighteenth- and nineteenth-century English and American legal thinking: see especially Bk. I, ch. 15, III.

Erickson, Amy Louise. *Women and Property in Early Modern England*. London and New York: Routledge, 1993. A significant work dealing with both legal theory and actual practice between the late-sixteenth and early-eighteenth centuries.

Hanawalt, Barbara A. "The Female Felon in Fourteenth-Century England." In *Women in Medieval Society*, edited by Susan Mosher Stuard. Philadelphia: University of Pennsylvania Press, 1976. Analyzes crime patterns for women in three counties, showing that the ratio of women to men accused of felony was 1:9 and suggesting that courts treated women more leniently.

Herrup, Cynthia B. *The Common Peace: Participation and the Criminal Law in Seventeenth-Century England*. Cambridge, U.K. and New York: Cambridge University Press, 1987. A well-researched book fitting women into the general picture of crime in England in the seventeenth century.

Kermode, Jenny and Garthine Walker, eds. *Women, Crime and the Courts in Early Modern England*. Chapel Hill: University of North Carolina Press, 1994. An excellent collection of essays; Garthine Walker deals with women and theft; other essays cover slander litigation, the legal process for handling witchcraft, and litigation over pensions for mid-seventeenth-century war widows, among other topics.

Loengard, Janet Senderowitz. "'Legal History and the Medieval Englishwoman' Revisited: Some New Directions." In *Medieval Women and the Sources of Medieval History*, edited by Joel T. Rosenthal. Athens: University of Georgia Press, 1990. A bibliographic essay with entries through 1988.

Lord, Hazel D. "Husband and Wife: English Marriage Law from 1750: A Bibliographic Essay." *Southern California Review of Law & Women's Studies* 11(1) (2001): 1–89. A thorough and thoughtful bibliographic essay.

Pollock, Sir Frederick and Frederic William Maitland. *The History of English Law before the Time of Edward I*. 2 vols. Cambridge, U.K., 1895; reissued with new introduction and bibliography by S. F. C. Milsom. London and Cambridge: Cambridge University Press, 1968. The ur-text in the modern discipline of English legal history; see especially Bk. II, chs. II, § 11; VI, §§ 2–4; and VII, § 2 on status, marriage, and husband and wife.

Sheehan, Michael M. *Marriage, Family, and Law in Medieval Europe*. Edited by James K. Farge. Toronto and Buffalo, N.Y.: University of Toronto Press, 1996. A collection of important essays, several showing the effect of canon law on issues such as the stability of marriage and women's property rights.

Spring, Eileen. *Law, Land, and Family: Aristocratic Inheritance in England, 1300 to 1800*. Chapel Hill: University of North Carolina Press, 1993. A provocative account arguing for a decline in the woman's position relative to real property over the period.

Staves, Susan. *Married Women's Separate Property in England, 1660–1833*. Cambridge, Mass.: Harvard University Press, 1990. An excellent account of the changing laws over the period, suggesting that laws and their interpretation by judges—often based on political ideology—actually circumscribed women's property rights rather than enhancing them, as has often been suggested.

Stretton, Tim. *Women Waging Law in Elizabethan England*. Cambridge, U.K. and New York: Cambridge University Press, 1998. Discusses how women used the law and explores their litigation, particularly in the Court of Requests.

Thomas, Edgar. *The Lawes Resolutions of Womens Rights*. London, 1632; reprinted by Walter J. Johnson, Inc. Theatrum Orbis Terrarum, Ltd., Amsterdam and Norwood, N.J., 1979 (No. 922 in *The English Experience: Its Record in Early Printed Books Published in Facsimile*). A well-known and often quoted treatise, not unsympathetic to women.

Waddams, S. M. "English Matrimonial Law on the Eve of Reform (1828–57)." *Journal of Legal History* 21(2) (2000): 59–82. A detailed account of a short but important period in the reform of matrimonial law.

Wright, Danaya C. "DeManneville v. DeManneville: Rethinking the Birth of Custody Law under Patriarchy." *Law and History Review* 17(2) (1999): 247–307. A careful account of a celebrated 1804 case, concluding that it was a "willful reaffirmation of strict patriarchal power within the private sphere" leaving a legacy of the near erasure of maternal rights.

JANET S. LOENGARD

Islamic Law

Islamic law has shaped the lives of Muslim women through the interplay of the doctrinal tradition (*fiqh*), the historical development of legal institutions and practices, and engagement in the legal process on the part of individuals, communities, and state powers. Although gender issues arise in many different aspects of the law, those arguably most central to women's lives include marriage and divorce, property rights, legal capacity, and the regulation of space and sexuality.

Fiqh. The Islamic legal tradition lived with a certain tension between gender equality/sameness and gender inequality/difference: works of Islamic jurisprudence (*fiqh*) assigned women and men distinct social roles and made some, but not all, rights and obligations contingent upon gender identity. Gender difference was one of the significant distinctions of the Islamic legal system, but certain aspects of the law took a gender-neutral position. Jurists from different Sunni and Shi'i schools of law, and even jurists within the same school, often disagreed on the exact nature of gendered rights and obligations, so a wide range of opinion can be found.

Marriage and divorce. Gender difference was embedded in the laws pertaining to marriage and divorce, including the areas of contracting a marriage, the rights and obligations of husbands and wives once married, and their ability to obtain a divorce. The contract of marriage or *nikāḥ* is one of equality between two consenting adults that enables them to engage in sexual activity with each other, and most jurists agreed that the consent of both parties was essential to the contract. Some Shafi'is, however, held that the virginal bride might be married off without her consent and against her will. If a girl were still in her legal minority, jurists of all schools agreed that she could be married off by her natural guardian—her father—without her consent. In the case of a marriage arranged by anyone other than the father or paternal grandfather, however, a girl could exercise her "option of puberty" (*khīyār al-bulūgh*) as soon as she came of age and request an annulment of the marriage from the court.

Most legal schools and jurists held that a mature woman required a guardian for the purposes of marriage. Hanafi jurists defended the right of a woman to choose her own spouse, but they subjected that choice to review by the woman's natural guardian: if a guardian thought that the groom was not suitable in any way, he could ask a judge to annul the marriage. *Kafā'a* (suitability) was a one-way street in the sense that the requirement that a groom be the bride's match in terms of social status and wealth could be applied only to a groom. A marriage contract also entailed the payment of a dower (*mahr*), in an amount appropriate to her station and personal qualities, by the groom to the bride. Most of the earlier jurists assumed that the entire *mahr* would be paid upon agreement to the marriage contract and that failing the receipt of the full *mahr* as specified, a bride could refuse consummation of the marriage. By the twelfth century, Hanafi jurists were condoning a system whereby the husband paid in two installments: a prompt portion (the *mu'ajjal*) to be paid at the signing of the contract and a deferred portion (the *mu'ajjal*) due to the woman at the time of her husband's death or upon repudiation.

The jurists also held out the possibility of including voluntary conditions, or stipulations, in the marriage contract. Hanbalis, who devoted the most attention to the subject, accepted stipulations prohibiting the husband

Jordanian Election. Officials check the identity of voters before they cast their votes at a polling station in Amman, November 2007. PHOTOGRAPH BY NADER DAOUD. AP PHOTO

from taking a second wife or a concubine, preventing him from removing his wife from her native city or even from her own house, and requiring him to accept to house and maintain his wife's children from a previous marriage. The contract could also give the bride a "right of option," that is, a right delegated by her husband to divorce him should he violate any stipulations. Alternately, she could go to court and request a judicial decree of divorce from the judge, who could then decide if the case warranted a divorce.

The rights and duties of a husband and wife within a marriage are contained, in large part, in the twin doctrines of *nafaqa* (maintenance) and *nushūz* (disobedience). The jurists agreed on the major components of the maintenance owed by a husband to his wife—namely, food, clothing, lodging, and other necessities of life, commensurate with her social background. Although *nushūz*, disobedience or rebelliousness, might in theory be applied to behavior on the part of either husband or wife that violated the rights of the other spouse, most jurists discussed *nushūz* exclusively in relation to a wife's responsibilities to her husband, what she must or must not do in order to retain her rights to maintenance. A husband who did not provide maintenance for his wife had no right to her sexual services, and some legal schools also allowed her to seek divorce. A wife who did not obey her husband's legitimate demands, primarily to be available for a sexual relationship, forfeited her maintenance. The jurists further underscored men's rights to sexual companionship by affirming the legality of polygyny for men and monogamy for women, permitting a man to marry up to four wives concurrently, though a woman was restricted to one husband.

The jurists developed rules for a number of different types of divorce, but the most common were *ṭalāq*, *tafrīq*, and *khul'*. The standard "man's divorce," *ṭalāq*, is a unilateral repudiation of a wife by her husband; in its baldest form, a man could end his marriage simply by pronouncing a formula of divorce, after which his wife must wait a statutory period (*'idda*) before the divorce is automatically finalized. There was no role for the court, no possibility of contest by the wife, and only limited obligations imposed on the husband for payment of any dower he owed and for temporary support of his wife while she waited for the divorce to be finalized. A woman did not have a reciprocal right of unilateral divorce; she could acquire the ability to choose divorce only if her husband delegated his power of *ṭalāq* to her.

A judge might step in to annul a marriage at the request of a woman or her family under certain circumstances. This annulment or *tafrīq* was a court procedure whereby a wife, her family, or according to some schools a husband could request that a defective marriage be annulled. The jurists differed as to what precisely constituted defects in a marriage severe enough to warrant annulment. A husband's impotence was the one condition that all jurists seemed to accept as grounds for annulment, but some jurists also included a husband's insanity or communicable disease as grounds. The jurists were also of different minds in the case of a husband who had gone missing, with neither his whereabouts nor whether he was dead or alive known (a *mafqūd*). The Malikis established a clear procedure for a wife who wished to be released from such a marriage within four years. So far as the Hanafi school was concerned, a woman remained the wife of her husband until she received reliable notice of his death or until he could be presumed dead under Hanafi rules—that is, after some period of time defined variously as 99 years, 120 years, or until all members of his peer group were dead.

Khul' was another type of "woman's divorce" of arguably lesser benefit to women. The basic meaning of *khul'* is that of a divorce desired by the wife in return for compensation paid to her husband. The most common opinion across schools was that a husband should not take more than the amount of either the dower or the dower plus any presents of such items as jewelry and clothing. Later Hanafi jurists added that the wife could also waive rights to maintenance during her waiting period, as well as her rights to receive maintenance for her children by her divorced husband. The wife was in effect buying her husband's marital right to her, so her husband was an essential—and necessarily willing—party to the sale. Either the husband or the wife could make an offer of *khul'*, and acceptance by the other party gave the divorce effect.

In brief, marriage and divorce, as described in the legal canon, conferred rights and duties in a highly gendered fashion. Husbands and wives, though subject to similar moral exhortations to support and cherish each other, were assigned distinct responsibilities, privileges, and rights before, during, and after a marriage.

Property rights and legal capacity. As to property rights and legal capacity, the jurists made little distinction between males and females. An adult, so long as she or he were of legal age, was a legal subject fully empowered to enter into contracts and exercise sole control over the property that he or she owned. Marital status held no ramifications for legal capacity, and the property that a woman acquired by way of her own efforts, dower payments, or inheritance was hers alone to manage and dispose of. Most jurists agreed that once a girl attained her legal majority, as signified by puberty and/or reaching the age of fifteen, she assumed full and unfettered control of both her person and her property so long as she had attained mental maturity. The Maliki school, however, developed a distinct position on this issue. Not only were mature females subject to their guardians' control in the matter of the marriage contract, but their property could also continue to be managed by their guardians for an extended period after their marriage, regardless of their physical or mental maturity. Females who had reached maturity could be retained under interdiction by their fathers until they married and four witnesses stepped forward to attest to their abilities to manage their own property.

Inheritance law did discriminate against females. It is particularly important to note two key aspects of the Sunni laws on inheritance: namely, that most female heirs, including wives, mothers, and daughters, were to inherit one-half of the share of the corresponding male relation, and that, should a man or woman die without sons, certain other male heirs on the paternal side enjoyed inheritance rights that could greatly reduce the shares of closer female relatives and indeed all relatives on the maternal side. Under Shi'i jurisprudence, the 2:1 ratio held for many male and female shares, but unlike under Sunni law, more distant male relatives on the paternal side had no special claims on inheritance and did not dilute the rights of closer female heirs.

The jurists' position that women were legal subjects with legal capacities little differentiated from those of men was also clouded by the view of female disability in the area of legal testimony. In general the jurists accepted women as witnesses in property matters, but they considered the testimony of two women to be equivalent to that of one man and preferred that at least one man be present as a witness in a court case. The majority of jurists barred women from testimony in criminal matters. The jurists recognized that there were certain facts with implications for inheritance and other legal claims that were likely to be known only by women, such as establishing the paternity of a child by fixing the date of its birth or ascertaining whether a baby had been stillborn, and in these cases the jurists acknowledged that female testimony alone provided sufficient evidence.

Regulation of space and sexuality. The regulation of space and sexuality was a final area of gendered law. The jurists identified the sexual drives of both men and women as threatening *fitna* (social disorder), and therefore the law concerned itself with the separation of the sexes on the one hand, and the punishment of illicit sexual intercourse (*zinā'*) on the other—with the punishment to be doled out without regard for gender difference. This principle of equality came to be transgressed in the process of elaboration of legal rules that assigned women the greatest responsibility, both actual and symbolic, for the dress and comportment that would minimize sexual attraction. The jurists highlighted biological difference, most dramatically in their discussion of the covering of female and male *'awras* (the sexually stimulating parts of the body) in such a way as to impose much greater restrictions in dress and comportment on women than on men. And although *zinā'* was, in principle, an equal-opportunity crime, Maliki doctrine held that out-of-wedlock pregnancy constituted proof of unlawful intercourse on the part of the pregnant woman but not on the part of her partner, who could opt to deny paternity. This position relaxed the strict standards of evidence for proving *zinā'*—four witnesses to the act or freely given confessions—for women only.

Historical Practices. Although reports of rulings according to Islamic law date back to the time of the Prophet and a formal system of judges and courts can be found as early as the Umayyad period in the eighth century, there are few extant records of legal practice before the sixteenth century. Much of what we know about subsequent legal practices in the early modern and modern period before the twentieth century derives from the legal records of the Ottoman Empire.

The Ottoman Empire instituted Hanafi law as the dominant school, and so, for instance, mature Muslim women might be expected to be empowered to arrange their own marriages. In 1544, however, the Ottoman sultan, exercising his prerogative as "Lord of the Caliphate" to interpret the shari'a, issued a decree forbidding women to marry without the express permission of their guardians and instructing judges not to accept a marriage unless the bride's guardian had given his consent. Despite the sultan's intervention, many women, particularly if they had been previously married, continued to arrange their marriages. In seventeenth- and eighteenth-century Syria and Palestine, for example, jurists invariably took the dominant Hanafi position that an adult woman could not be compelled to rely on, or even consult, her guardian.

Adult women also took advantage of the right to insert stipulations into the marriage contract, always with the agreement of the groom. By Mamluk times (thirteenth to fifteenth centuries), a variety of stipulations had become commonplace, such as allowing a wife to opt for divorce should her husband drink wine or fail to house and support her children from a previous marriage. In the Ottoman era the technique of expanding a bride's rights through contractual stipulation continued apace: a woman might insert clauses into the contract that gave her the right of divorce if the husband did any number of things, including taking a second wife, changing their residence against her will, traveling more than once a year, moving permanently to a distant location, or beating her with enough force to leave marks.

Women were also active in the defense of their rights to maintenance in marriage and to divorce payments. In eighteenth-century Syria and Palestine, women frequently came to court to ask the judge to assign them a fixed amount of maintenance from their husbands who, whether from absence or inability, were failing to support them properly. The judge imposed an appropriate level of maintenance—calculated to supply the necessary provisions for a woman of her status—on the husband, authorized the wife to borrow the money if her husband were not forthcoming, and held the husband responsible for any debts that his wife so incurred. There are also many examples of litigation in which a divorced wife claims that her ex-husband failed to deliver what he owed, including the balance of her dower, the costs of her maintenance, and perhaps the outstanding amount of a loan that she made to him or personal property that she had left behind. Women flooded into the Ottoman-period courts to sue for money and goods owed them by their former husbands, and they seem often to have met with success, particularly in their claims for payment of the balance of the dower.

Women also initiated many divorce actions. Given the very limited grounds for a judicial annulment in Hanafi *fiqh*, it might be expected that few such cases would be found in the Ottoman records. Surprisingly, however, at least some of the Ottoman-period jurists and courts were willing to entertain expanded grounds for *tafrīq*, most notably in the cases of a husband's blasphemy or desertion. Blasphemy became accepted grounds for *tafrīq* because it was interpreted by Ottoman jurists to denote apostasy on the part of the husband, an act that automatically dissolves the marriage. In addition, many women went to court to obtain annulments when they had been deserted by their husbands, at least in Ottoman Syria and Palestine, and the courts neatly sidestepped the problem of Hanafi doctrine by allowing assistant judges from the Shafi'i or Hanbali schools to preside over these cases. In at least a few instances, this liberalization of the grounds for annulment even extended to cases where the husband was physically present but was failing in his duty to maintain his wife properly.

Khul' was even more commonplace. The majority of divorces in Mamluk society were apparently *khul'* divorces, and this trend seems to have continued during Ottoman times. In Istanbul, Sofia, Cairo, Jerusalem, Nablus, and Damascus, *khul'* was the type of divorce most frequently encountered in court. Compensation varied in this period, but typically it entailed waiving the balance of the dower and maintenance during the waiting period; sometimes the compensation included additional payments such as the return of goods that formed part of the prompt dower and even an additional sum of money and the wife's agreement to assume child support. Although the practices of the Ottoman period certainly fell within broad doctrinal guidelines on *khul'*, they restricted a woman's ability to use *khul'* to her advantage: the husband was allowed to collect excessive compensation, his agreement was usually required, and the judge often seems to have limited the role of the court to notarial functions unless there was an egregious violation of a woman's rights.

Women do seem to have retained legal rights to inheritance shares and dowers that allowed some of them to come into possession of significant amounts of property in the Ottoman period. Some women chose to sell the real estate they received in order to acquire more liquid forms of property, but others were active in the real estate market, both selling and buying urban properties in ways and amounts little different from those of their male counterparts, as has been shown to be the case in many of the larger urban real estate markets.

Further legal recognition of the female capacity to manage property is found in the realm of guardianship. In the Ottoman period the jurists' view that a woman, if properly appointed, could act as a guardian for her child or other minor had strong resonance in legal practice. Indeed, in the event of the death of a child's or children's father—their natural guardian—there often seems to have been a bias toward appointing the mother as guardian. In a study of the period from 1818 to 1839 in Aleppo, for example, Meriwether found that women, usually the mothers, were designated the guardians for fatherless children more than half the time. Mothers were routinely favored as guardians over paternal uncles or older brothers, even though natural guardianship devolved to male relatives on the paternal side in the absence of any formal designation of a different guardian. These female guardians oversaw sales and purchases of property for their wards, collected the income owed to them from rents, and settled any debts they had inherited. In light of the extensive discourse in Islamic law about the importance of safeguarding the person and property of the orphaned child—who was fatherless but not necessarily motherless under Islamic law—the courts were apparently comfortable with entrusting women with this weighty responsibility.

There is less evidence, however, that women played much of a role as personnel or witnesses in Ottoman Islamic courts. No evidence exists that women were ever judges, assistant judges, or scribes. Although women appeared in court for all kinds of notarial purposes and as plaintiffs and defendants in litigation, they were far more likely than men to be represented by agents that they had appointed for the purpose of doing their business in the court. Nor did women often appear in court as witnesses. Peirce notes in her extensive study of Aintab in Anatolia from 1540–1541 that what was nearly a ban on women's testimony complicated and weakened many of the cases involving women because it was difficult to find appropriate male witnesses in many instances. So although adult women were, in principle, fully qualified to act on their own behalf and even to represent the interests of minors, they often resorted to the use of male agents, and their legal testimonies on these and related matters were not often welcome in court.

Ottoman courts viewed the regulation of space and sexuality as within the reach of the law, but they did not prove vigorous in the enforcement of legal norms in either area. The legal system seemed often to function passively, listening to complaints about local violations of the rules for male and female interactions and prescribing punishment, but also standing ready to accept interactions that made sense to the ongoing conduct of social and economic business in a community. Before the late nineteenth century, for example, women's comportment and dress were not matters that much engaged the attention of Islamic jurists and courts. Women (and men) no doubt dressed modestly, at least in large parts of the Islamic heartland, but a wide range of degrees of covering, reflecting differences in class and setting, appears to have been the norm. Urban women of the elite might lead a secluded life in which they ventured outside their homes only in full cover, but dress was an issue that most jurists and courts were content to leave in the hands of local custom and individual choice.

Modern Reform and Islamization. In the course of the later nineteenth and early to mid-twentieth centuries, a process of legal codification reached into matters of what came to be called personal status—marriage, divorce, inheritance, and so on—not only in the Ottoman Empire but in Egypt, Sudan, areas of sub-Saharan Africa, Iran, and parts of South and Southeast Asia. The first of what was to prove to be a long series of such state reforms was the Ottoman Law of Family Rights (OLFR) of 1917, a codified law regulating marriage and divorce. The framers of the OLFR employed the method of *takhayyur* whereby they studied both majority and minority opinions in the Hanafi school, or dominant doctrines in any Sunni school, to choose the rule on any given issue that seemed to suit modern circumstances best. The successor states of the Ottoman Empire and others later followed a similar course when they promulgated personal status laws. Algeria, Egypt, Indonesia, Iraq, Jordan, Kuwait, Lebanon, Libya, Malaysia, Morocco, Pakistan, Syria, Tunisia, and Yemen, among others, have all produced distinct personal status codes, and periodically reformed them, from the 1920s onward.

Many legal reforms—instituting a minimum age for marriage, reducing the power of the guardian, regulating polygyny, limiting men's powers of *ṭalāq*, and expanding women's powers of divorce through *faskh* (voiding the marriage) and *khulʿ*—have been oriented toward the incremental increase of a wife's rights vis-à-vis her husband, with the goal of achieving eventual equality. This piecemeal approach to attacking discrimination in marriage has proceeded slowly, and many of the basic elements of discrimination are still intact in twenty-first-century laws and practices. Although in many countries the issue of female testimony has been rendered marginal by changes in court procedure, there have been few reforms of inheritance law, and women remain disadvantaged. Most reformed codes do not include specific prescriptions for female dress and public behavior, so that issues of space and sexuality are left largely to the dictates of custom, the arguments of religious leaders, and the lifestyle choices made by Muslim women and men.

In the late twentieth century another brand of reform arose with the so-called Islamization of legal systems. As a number of political regimes faced crises of legitimacy as a result of failing social and economic policies, their strategies of modernization and Westernization were called into question. In Iran, for example, the overthrow of the Shah and the triumph of the Islamic Revolution in 1979 entailed a rejection of Western models and an attempt to institute a new Islamic order. In Pakistan the military regime of Muhammad Zia al-Haq emerged in the same period and embarked on a campaign to "restore" Islamic society.

Programs of Islamization inevitably took a critical look at prior legal reforms that seemed to be implicated in the overall project of Westernization, but they have not usually addressed all aspects of the legal system in equal measure: there has been a distinct tendency to focus on the showier—and easier, in that they were less disruptive to basic economic and political interests—areas of penal law and personal status law. The introduction of "Islamic" penalties of stoning for unlawful sexual intercourse in Pakistan (1979), Sudan (1983), and northern Nigerian states (by 2002) allows the state to display cultural legitimacy and punitive power at the same time, while the introduction of dress codes and other kinds of restrictions on women have the virtues of high visibility and minimum threat of serious opposition (because they tend to have the greatest impact on poorer females). In all instances the Islamization of law appears to have been tied to bids by central or provincial governments to lay claim to the mantle of Islam, to present themselves as the protectors and promoters of Islamic identity as a legitimating strategy.

Official state projects were not the only late twentieth-century developments in Islamic law. The popular engagement with Islam as both a religious and a cultural identity that modern regimes are trying to exploit has also found expression in nonofficial circles. The legal writings, including fatwas, of present-day religious leaders are an increasingly popular genre: in many instances they discuss current political issues but also matters of personal behavior, such as dress, comportment, and ritual. These fatwas are particularly prevalent in Shi'i communities, where the seeking of guidance from qualified 'ulama' is a basis of religious observance. Ayatollah Khomeini's fatwas have been hugely popular for the past forty years or so, as are those of Shaykh Fadlallah of Lebanon in the twenty-first century. Even among Sunnis there has been considerable interest in the legal guidance of prominent Islamic thinkers, whose books and radio and television shows are popular. Muslims who live in predominantly non-Muslim societies have also been taking advantage of the many Internet "fatwa sites," where individuals can obtain answers to questions about living a good Muslim life. Many legal issues of primary concern to women are thus being shaped in the twenty-first century by discussions among jurists and laypeople in extrajudicial settings.

[*See also* Body in Islamic Law; Children, *subentry on* Islamic Law; Contract, *subentry on* Contracts and Unilateral Acts in Islamic Law; Divorce, *subentry on* Consensual Divorce (*Khul'*) in Islamic Law; Family, *subentry on* Family and Kinship in Islamic Law; Fetus in Islamic Law; Inheritance, *subentry on* Islamic Law; Marriage, *subentry on* Islamic Law; Personal Status Law, *subentry on* Personal Status Law in Islamic Countries; *and* Purity and Impurity in Islamic Law.]

BIBLIOGRAPHY

PRIMARY SOURCES

Ibn al-Mutahhar al-Hilli, al-Hasan ibn Yusuf. *Mukhtalaf al-Shi'ah fi ahkam al-shari'a* (Shi'a Differences of Opinion on Shari'a Rules). 10 vols. Qom, Iran: Mu'assasat al-Nashr al-Islami, 1991–1999. A canonical collection of Shi'i jurisprudence.

Ibn Taymiyya, Taqi al-Din Ahmad ibn 'Abd al-Halim. *Fatawa al-Nisa'* (Women's Fatwas). 3d ed. Riyadh, Saudi Arabia: Dar al-Riyad lil-Nashr, 1987. A collection of fatwas related to women's affairs by a fourteenth-century Hanbali jurist.

Khalil ibn Ishaq, ibn Musa al-Jundi. *Abrégé de la loi Musulmane selon le rite de l'imam Malek* (A Short Guide to Islamic Law of the Maliki School). Translated by G. H. Bousquet. 4 vols. Algiers: Éditions Algérienne en-Nahdha, 1956–1962. An abridged edition of a key Maliki work of jurisprudence.

Marghinani, 'Ali ibn Abi-Bakr. *Al-hidayah = The Guidance: A Translation of "Al-hidayah fi sharh bidayat al-mubtadi," a Classical Manual of Hanafi Law*. Translated by Imran Ahsan Khan Nyazee. Bristol, U.K.: Amal Press, 2006. An English translation of the canonical compendium of Hanafi jurisprudence, with commentary on other Sunni schools as well.

Ramli, Khayr al-Din ibn Ahmad al-. *Kitab al-fatawa al-kubra li-naf' al-birriya* (The Book of Greater Fatwas for the Benefit of Righteousness). 2 vols. Cairo, 1856–1857.

SECONDARY SOURCES

Meriwether, Margaret L. "The Rights of Children and the Responsibilities of Women: Women as *Wasi*s in Ottoman Aleppo, 1770–1840." In *Women, the Family, and Divorce Laws in Islamic History*, edited by Amira El Azhary Sonbol, pp. 227–234. Syracuse, N.Y.: Syracuse University Press, 1996.

Mir-Hosseini, Ziba. *Marriage on Trial: Islamic Family Law in Iran and Morocco*. Rev. ed. London: I. B. Tauris, 2000.

Peirce, Leslie. *Morality Tales: Law and Gender in the Ottoman Court of Aintab*. Berkeley: University of California Press, 2003. An in-depth study of women and gender in a sixteenth-century town in Anatolia.

Peters, Rudolph. *Crime and Punishment in Islamic Law: Theory and Practice from the Sixteenth to the Twenty-First Century*. Cambridge, U.K.: Cambridge University Press, 2005. Includes discussion of recent Islamization projects.

Rapoport, Yossef. *Marriage, Money, and Divorce in Medieval Islamic Society*. Cambridge, U.K.: Cambridge University Press, 2005. The doctrines and practices of Islamic marriage and divorce in late medieval Cairo, Damascus, and Jerusalem.

Tucker, Judith E. *In the House of the Law: Gender and Islamic Law in Ottoman Syria and Palestine*. Berkeley: University of California Press, 1998. A study of jurisprudence and court practices in seventeenth- and eighteenth-century Syria and Palestine.

JUDITH E. TUCKER

Hindu Law

Hindu women's rights in the Indian subcontinent partly derived from ancient Hindu *dharmaśāstras*, first evolved orally within pastoral and agrarian communities roughly two thousand years ago, when property was primarily agricultural land held jointly by four generations of male members. But the denial of rights within the Hindu joint family property system cannot be construed to mean that women were deprived of all property rights and were awarded a low status. One of the most widely known Hindu textual authorities, the *Manusmriti*, described an institution of property owned by females, known as *strīdhan* or *strīdhanam* ("woman's property"), and laid down comprehensive rules regarding its character and devolution. Within patriarchal contexts, women also had the right to be maintained from the joint family property as daughters, wives, and widows.

Women's Status under the Dharma Texts. The dharma texts described marriage as an essential *saṃskāra* or religious obligation and awarded a ritually high status to the Hindu wife, termed *dharmapatnī* ("spouse in dharma," denoting a sacred union) and also referred to as *ardhāṅginī* (half of her husband). Without a wife, the Hindu male householder was not complete.

Chastity of women was exalted by the dharma texts. But until the Hindu Marriage Act in 1955, strict codes of sexual purity were applicable only to women, and Hindu marriages were not monogamous. Since progeny was of utmost importance, a husband could procure numerous wives. Children could also be begotten through concubines, mistresses, and slaves. The sacrosanct marital bond was said to be indissoluble and eternal—but more so for women. The lower castes, however, were not governed by the strict scriptural codes of sexual purity, and among many castes divorce and remarriage of women were permitted.

Nineteenth-Century Legal Reform. But over time, the status of women within Hindu society deteriorated. As child marriages became an accepted norm, the plight of millions of child widows turned worse. The practice of burning widows (*satī*) on the husband's funeral pyre became so frequent in Bengal and Rajasthan that it caused considerable concern under colonial rule. During the nineteenth century, women's low status became a matter of urgency for various Indian social reformers, who initiated campaigns for statutory enactments to enhance the legal status of Hindu women. In Bengal, the Sati Regulation of 1829 abolished the practice of *satī*. The Hindu Widows' Remarriage Act of 1856 granted upper-caste widows the right of remarriage, but led to the loss of inheritance rights. Revised regulations concerning the age of consent under criminal law adopted in 1872 and 1896, which prescribed the mandatory minimum age of consent for sexual intercourse and sought to raise the age of marriage, were important measures meant to protect the basic human rights of young Hindu women.

Property. Despite such positive enactments, women suffered serious setbacks in relation to *strīdhan* property. The scope of *strīdhan* became extremely constrained because of erroneous interpretations of this right by British judges during the latter half of the nineteenth century. To undo the harm caused by these decisions, in 1937 the Hindu Women's Right to Property Act was enacted, giving improved rights of inheritance to widows. Widows received a "life estate" in such inherited property, which reverted on the widow's death to the joint family. Later, through the enactment of the 1956 Hindu Succession Act, daughters were granted equal rights to a share in their father's separate property, and—very controversially—property inherited by widows became their absolute property. More or less complete gender equality in Hindu joint family property law was achieved only in 2005, through an amendment to the Hindu Succession Act.

The Hindu Marriage Act of 1955. After Christian marriage had been transformed from a sacrament to a contract under English law in 1857, social reformers waged a sustained campaign to transform Hindu marriage in a similar manner, culminating in the Hindu Marriage Act of 1955, through which upper-caste Hindu women acquired an equal right of divorce on the same footing as their husbands. Though the act retained the sacramental aspects and ritualistic solemnization of Hindu marriage, it rendered Hindu marriages more contractual and made marriage a dissoluble union between two consenting adults. Capacity to marry (section 5) and customary ceremonies of marriage (section 7) became necessary ingredients of a valid Hindu marriage. A marriage that did not meet these requirements could be declared void (section 11) or voidable (section 12). Hindu marriages could now be dissolved by divorce (section 13) under certain specific conditions based on fault grounds, clear departures from the traditional Hindu marriage regime.

Despite these gains, the legal reforms proved to be far from satisfactory, as they contained serious lacunae and were based on a false premise of equality, causing serious loss of rights to women. Although the Hindu Marriage Act of 1955 introduced the concept of equality between husband and wife, presuming that this notion of equality would enhance the status of women, marriages continued to be based on unequal status between the spouses. One concrete indication of this unequal status was the phenomenon of dowry, which a girl's parents were expected to provide at the time of marriage. Another indication was that men found it much easier to use the new provisions for divorce than did women.

However, within the notion of formal equality, the spouses were deemed to have equal rights and obligations

Women's Reservation Bill. All India Democratic Women's Association (AIDWA) activists stage a demonstration for the passage of the Women's Reservation Bill, Chennai, May 2005. PHOTOGRAPH BY M. KARUNAKARAN. THE HINDU IMAGES

toward each other. Although basic inequalities between men and women persisted, because the notion of Hindu undivided family (HUF) property was retained, women were denied rights to ancestral property as daughters. But under a perverse logic of equality, Hindu women were put under a legal obligation in section 25 of the Hindu Marriage Act to maintain their husbands. This concept did not exist under any type of marriage known in the Indian context—whether in Hindu law, either scriptural or customary, or Muslim law, or even in the modern and secular Special Marriage Act of 1954.

At the same time, the 1955 marriage act did not initially grant Hindu women the right of divorce by mutual consent, which had been introduced under the Special Marriage Act in 1954 but was considered too radical for the conservative Hindu society. Divorce by mutual consent was introduced under Hindu law only in 1976.

Gender imbalances are also evident in relation to the restitution of conjugal rights and the "lord and master" concept. Ironically, Hindu women were burdened with the responsibility of maintaining their husbands, but the courts continued to undermine a woman's right to retain a job against her husband's wishes under the ancient notion of the "lord and master" and for a long time granted husbands alone the privilege of determining the choice of matrimonial home. If a woman was employed at a place away from the matrimonial home, her husband could claim restitution of conjugal rights against the wife under section 9 of the Hindu Marriage Act.

For decades after the enactment of the marriage act, the courts held that Hindu marriage is a sacrament and that it is the sacred duty of the Hindu wife to follow her husband and reside with him wherever he chooses to live. In all such cases, the women were working and supporting the family. The husbands had approached the courts to restore conjugality, often just to spite their wives. The courts staunchly upheld the husbands' rights and granted them decrees of restitution.

In *Ram Prakash v. Savitri Devi* (1958), the court held that "according to Hindu Law, marriage is a holy union for the performance of marital duties with her husband where he may choose to reside and to fulfill her duties in her husband's home." In *Gaya Prasad v. Bhagwat* (1966), the court held that "a wife's first duty to her husband is to submit herself obediently to his authority and to remain under his roof and protection." The Punjab and Haryana High Court held in *Surinder Kaur v. Gardeep Singh* (1973), held that "the Hindu law imposes on the wife the duty of attendance, obedience to and veneration for the husband to live with him wherever he chooses to reside." Such north Indian cases virtually presumed a wife was the property of her husband's family.

In *Kailash Wati v. Ayodhia Parkash* (1977), the court reaffirmed that the wife's refusal to resign her job amounted to a withdrawal from her husband's society and granted a decree in favor of the husband. Although under the modern concept of equality husbands had the right to be maintained by their wives, the concept of sacramental marriage allowed men to restrain wives from gainful employment.

Only after 1975 did the courts begin to recognize a woman's right to hold a job away from her husband's residence. The leading case upholding this right was pronounced by the Delhi High Court in *Swaraj Garg v. R. M. Garg* (1978). The court held that "in the absence of a premarital agreement between the parties, it cannot be said that the wife who had a permanent job with good income had to live at a place determined by the husband when the husband did not earn enough to maintain the family." Providing constitutional validity to the wife's right to hold a job, the court ruled that giving an exclusive right to the husband to decide the matrimonial home would violate the constitutional provisions of equality.

The Hindu Marriage Act of 1955 also introduced the Christian concept of monogamy into modern Hindu marriage, ostensibly to elevate the status of Hindu women. The act transformed a Hindu marriage from a traditional status relationship into a dissoluble contract, but the form of solemnizing the contract remained Brahmanic and scriptural, with the *saptapadī* (the ritual of seven steps) and the *vivāha homa* (the sacred fire as witness) as essential features. But within a pluralistic society, the act also had to validate diverse customary practices, as prescribed by sections 7(1) and 7(2) of the Hindu Marriage Act of 1955. This mingling of Brahmanic rituals at one end and customary practices at the other has resulted in absurd and ridiculous rulings regarding the validity of Hindu marriages; women have been the main victims of such legal absurdities.

In particular, the resulting ambiguities have provided a Hindu male ample scope to contract bigamous marriages. Since modern Hindu law recognizes only monogamous marriages as legally valid, women in polygamous relationships are placed in a vulnerable situation. In the absence of any clear proof, the man has the choice of admitting either his first or a subsequent relationship as a valid marriage and may escape financial responsibility toward the other woman or women. When such a man refuses to validate the marriage, a woman not only loses her legal right to maintenance but also faces humiliation and social stigma as a mistress.

The flip side of this predicament in maintenance proceedings is the dilemma faced by women in criminal proceedings in cases of bigamy. Here, years of litigation failed to end in conviction for the errant male because the courts adopted a rigid precedent-based view that *saptapadī* and *vivāha homa* are essential for solemnizing a legally valid Hindu marriage, rather than applying presumptions of marriage to protect women's rights. If the Sanskritic ceremonies could not be proved by the first wife in respect of her husband's first or subsequent marriage, her husband could escape conviction, even though he had cohabited with a second wife (and might have admitted being married to her), the community had accepted the man and the second wife as husband and wife, or he had fathered children through the second wife. Only later did Indian courts become alert to such systematic abuses and apply stronger presumptions of marriage.

Although the reforms in Hindu law during the 1950s and 1970s have been partly beneficial to women, the impact of some provisions that were meant to empower women has actually proved to be detrimental to their rights.

[*See also* Custom, *subentry on* South Asian Law; Divorce, *subentry on* Hindu Law; Dowry, *subentry on* Hindu Law; Family, *subentry on* Indian Family Law; Marriage, *subentry on* Hindu Law; Property, *subentry on* Hindu Law; *and* Succession, *subentry on* Hindu Law.]

BIBLIOGRAPHY

Agnes, Flavia. *Law and Gender Inequality: The Politics of Women's Rights in India*. New Delhi and New York: Oxford University Press, 1999. Critical analysis of the legal position of Hindu women.

Bhattacharjee, A. M. *Hindu Law and the Constitution*. 2d ed. Calcutta, India: Eastern Law House, 1994. Examines the codified Hindu law against constitutional provisions.

Derrett, J. Duncan M. *Hindu Law, Past and Present*. Calcutta, India: A. Mukherjee, 1957. A standard book of legal history.

Desai, S. T., ed. *Mulla's Principles of Hindu Law*. 18th ed. New Delhi: LexisNexis. A standard law textbook for practitioners.

Diwan, Paras, and Peeyushi Diwan. *Law of Marriage and Divorce*. Delhi, India: Universal Law, 1997. A standard but now slightly outdated law textbook for practitioners.

Menski, Werner. *Modern Indian Family Law*. Richmond, U.K.: Curzon Press, 2001. Detailed analysis of Hindu family law.

Menski, Werner. *Hindu Law: Beyond Tradition and Modernity*. New Delhi and New York: Oxford University Press, 2003. Contains analyses of new developments in Hindu family law.

Flavia Agnes

United States Law

Not surprisingly, the history of "women" as a social and legal category became the subject of intense scholarly inquiry at a time when the content and contours of that category were undergoing rapid and often unsettling change. Since the 1970s, the legal history of American women, once an academic backwater, has become a vibrant area of interdisciplinary scholarship. Several themes emerge from this rich body of literature. First, the history of "women" as a social and legal category features a longstanding tension between women's roles as family members and caregivers—as daughters, wives, mothers, homemakers, and caretakers—and women's status as individuals, as workers, and as citizens of a polity. Second, this history finds women repeatedly attempting to reshape their relationship to family, work, and citizenship, sometimes claiming rights and obligations on the basis of essential similarities between men and women, and at other times emphasizing women's unique qualities and contributions to family and society. Third, attempts to redefine women's rights and duties frequently encountered resistance from historical actors who sought to preserve traditional conceptions of women's roles and relationships, resistance that influenced the nature and scope of changes to women's legal and social status. Finally, the formal definitions and ideologies that constructed "women" as a subject and object of the law often, if not always, obscured a complex social reality in which law on the books did not necessarily reflect social practice and, moreover, in which the category "women" comprised persons with various social, cultural, and economic statuses and experiences.

Coverture and Citizenship in the Early Republic. From the founding, white women were citizens of the new republic, but they did not possess the civil and political rights granted propertied male citizens—for instance, they could not vote, hold public office, or serve on juries. If they married, white women lost many of their remaining legal rights. Under coverture, the common law of husband-wife relations, a married woman was a *feme covert*, as opposed to a *feme sole*. A *feme covert*'s legal identity figuratively was covered by that of her husband. Married women lost their independent legal identities and could not hold property, make contracts, or sue in their own names. Nor was a married woman liable for a wide range of crimes committed in her husband's presence. The laws of marriage enforced a household economy in which wives owed husbands domestic and personal services, including housekeeping, childrearing, and sexual intercourse; in exchange, the law required husbands to provide economic support to their wives and other dependents. The exclusion of white women from the political realm went virtually unchallenged, since their interests presumptively were represented by their husbands, fathers, and brothers. These women's sanctioned contributions to the republic occurred in the domestic sphere, where they were to serve the polity by raising male citizens to participate virtuously in public life.

The legal fiction of marital unity and a theory of political representation in which male heads of households cast votes on behalf of dependent wives obscured a social reality in which the interests of married women and men were not always harmonious and in which some women and men remained unmarried or outside the boundaries of citizenship altogether. Despite formal constraints on divorce, nineteenth-century couples resorted to various legal and extralegal separation procedures and sometimes to bigamy and informal nonmarital relationships. Though subsumed in her husband's legal identity and dependent on him for protection, a married woman could, to some extent, assert her dominion over household management and the rearing of children: the ideology of separate spheres confined women to the domestic realm but invested them with moral authority in matters of home and hearth. Wives also used coverture strategically, with mixed success, to enforce their marital right to economic support.

Of course, not all women were married, and not all women were citizens. Free women who did not marry retained and widows regained—at least formally—control over property and the ability to make contracts, though they still could not vote or hold public office. At the same time, neither legal marriage nor the cult of domesticity was available to enslaved women, who by definition could not make contracts or own property and lacked the protective benefits of marriage, including the most basic—the ability to keep their families together. Although slaves often consecrated their partnerships informally, they had no legal recourse against owners who abused or sold their family members. Enslaved women could neither seek refuge in male protection nor escape hard physical labor by virtue of their sex; further, they were at the mercy of masters who owned their bodies and their sexual services.

Slavery, Abolition, and the Nineteenth-Century Women's Rights Struggle. Slavery's friends and foes alike believed the fates of slavery and marriage to be intimately connected. A developing rhetoric of women's rights compared marriage to slavery, charging that coverture gave husbands tyrannical power over their wives. Defenders of slavery warned that abolitionism led inexorably to the eradication of another sacred domestic institution, marriage. Notwithstanding the wide gulf between the lives of privileged white women and those of enslaved African Americans, and despite resistance from some male abolitionists, the movements to abolish slavery and to reform women's legal status grew in tandem. In the 1830s, women like Maria Stewart and Angelina Grimke attracted threats of violent retribution for daring to make abolitionist speeches before mixed public audiences; by 1840 the "woman question" had split the American Anti-Slavery Society. In 1848, the first large-scale women's rights meeting, convened by Elizabeth Cady Stanton in upstate New York, produced the Seneca Falls Declaration. Modeled on the Declaration of Independence, the document protested a long list of injustices, including women's loss of legal identity in marriage, their vulnerability under divorce and guardianship laws that favored husbands, their inability to earn and keep wages, and, perhaps most controversially, their political disenfranchisement.

Advocates for women saw the Northern victory in the Civil War, and the subsequent abolition of slavery by the Thirteenth Amendment (1865), as an unprecedented opportunity to enshrine the equality of the sexes, as well as the races, in the federal Constitution. Women, they argued, deserved the vote because as rights-bearing individuals they were worthy of participating in the polity alongside men. Some, like the formerly enslaved Sojourner Truth, also emphasized that African Americans would not be truly free if half of their number remained disenfranchised. But although the hard-won Fourteenth (1868) and Fifteenth (1870) Amendments granted the rights of national citizenship and the vote to freedmen, albeit with no guarantee of their enforcement, free and freed women would struggle for another half century to obtain the suffrage.

The next stage in the struggle for women's suffrage emphasized activism and litigation as tools for obtaining favorable interpretations of the new constitutional provisions. The "New Departure" strategy, pioneered by a Missouri couple, Francis and Virginia Minor, located a woman's right to vote among the "privileges and immunities" of citizenship guaranteed by the Fourteenth Amendment. The Minors encouraged women to seize the right to vote themselves by going to the polls, and many did, including Susan B. Anthony, who was arrested for "criminal voting" in 1872. New Departure activism did not find a sympathetic audience at the Supreme Court, however. In *Bradwell v. Illinois* (1873), the Court rejected Myra Bradwell's challenge to the Illinois bar's exclusion of women, and in *Minor v. Happersett* (1874), Virginia Minor's suit against the Missouri election official who disallowed her ballot, the justices unanimously held that the Constitution "does not confer the right of suffrage upon any one." These rulings not only stymied women's efforts at electoral participation but also, in conjunction with other contemporaneous decisions, weakened the Fourteenth Amendment's capacity to enforce the rights of freedmen.

Unable to secure women's legal rights through creative interpretation of the Reconstruction Amendments, suffragists began a long struggle to amend the Constitution. Though some suffrage advocates, particularly African Americans, continued to justify women's enfranchisement as an individual right grounded in universal human freedom, others turned to more expedient rationales that emphasized women's differences from men. On this view, women's votes would cleanse the corrupt political sphere with the moral superiority and feminine virtue nurtured in the domestic realm. Some white suffragists also appealed, explicitly or implicitly, to racist and nativist sentiments, positing women's enfranchisement as an antidote to the votes of men who were black, foreign-born, poor, or uneducated. Advocates of women's suffrage faced formidable opposition, but eventually prevailed upon President Woodrow Wilson to vocally support their cause as a reward for women's service in World War I. After a

Ratification Banner. Alice Paul unfurls a ratification banner from the balcony of the National Woman's Party headquarters following Tennessee's ratification of the Nineteenth Amendment, 18 August 1920. PHOTOGRAPH FROM *THE SUFFRAGIST*, VOL. 8, NO. 8, SEPTEMBER 1920. RECORDS OF THE NATIONAL WOMAN'S PARTY/MANUSCRIPT DIVISION, LIBRARY OF CONGRESS

spirited battle in the states, the Nineteenth Amendment to the Constitution was ratified in August 1920.

Beyond Suffrage. Although we remember the battle over women's suffrage primarily as a contest over the scope of voting rights, much more was at stake for the combatants than the casting of ballots. To many opponents of suffrage, enfranchising women meant dismantling the entire system of household government and endangering the institution of marriage itself. Well before women won the right to vote, they challenged both coverture and their exclusion from public life. As a result, by the late nineteenth century, coverture had begun, if not to erode, at least to change form. Women played crucial roles in many of these legal reforms, although their lack of formal political power and the competing visions of other legal actors often limited their success. For instance, the early women's rights movement claimed for wives a joint property right in family assets, on the ground that wives' household labor substantially contributed to the accumulation of family wealth. Some states also enacted earnings statutes that allowed wives to keep wages they received for "separate" or "personal" labor. Beginning in the 1840s, many states passed Married Women's Property Acts, which variously granted wives the right to hold property, make contracts, and sue in their own name. Courts frequently undermined these incursions on coverture, however, by reaffirming that the marriage contract required wives to provide personal and domestic services to husbands. Thus when married women claimed a property right in domestic labor such as keeping boarders, taking in laundry or piecework, housekeeping, and nursing, judges often declared these activities part of a wife's marital duties, for which she was not entitled to wages.

In the mid- to late nineteenth century, changes in family law reconfigured legal motherhood and fatherhood in ways that alleviated some forms of paternal domination but maintained clear sex roles in parenting and reinforced hierarchies based on class. Traditional common-law doctrines that granted fathers guardianship and custody of children in the event of divorce gave way to the "tender years presumption," which regarded mothers as the most appropriate caretakers of young children, and to a "best interests of the child" standard, which often favored maternal care over paternal prerogatives and sometimes allowed illegitimate children to inherit property. Nevertheless, these changes primarily benefited women who conformed to judicial conceptions of good motherhood; judges and family reformers also used the child-centered standard to separate poor children from both parents, and few illegitimate children stood to inherit from their mothers.

Women also exercised political influence through voluntary activities and government service even before they won the right to vote. Indeed, suffrage was just one of a panoply of causes that politically active women like Florence Kelley and many others advanced at the local, state, and national levels in the 1910s, including consumer protections, anticorruption measures, public-health improvements, temperance laws, maternal and child-health measures, and employment regulations. Opponents of Progressive reforms accused these women and their male allies of advancing a Socialist conspiracy, but historians have recognized the importance of this "maternalist" agenda in expanding and shaping the direction of the modern American state.

Progressives' promotion of protective labor legislation, in particular, had several profound and lasting effects on American constitutional law. First, a legal climate inhospitable to government interference in the employment relationship channeled reformers' efforts toward the protection of women qua women, creating a sex-specific regulatory regime. State laws that shielded workers from long hours and low wages frequently fell victim to the doctrine of freedom of contract associated with *Lochner v. New York* (1905), a doctrine that insisted on the individual right of each employee to bargain with his employer free from legal restrictions on wages or hours. But advocates for working women succeeded in convincing the Supreme Court that women's physical vulnerabilities and maternal duties warranted the regulation of their terms of employment, even if men's employment could not be so constrained. In *Muller v. Oregon* (1908), Josephine Goldmark and Louis Brandeis successfully defended Oregon's maximum-hours law for women with a lengthy brief containing detailed social science evidence to support the contention that women's health required legal protections. Thus the defense of protective labor legislation for women spurred the invention of a new litigation tool, the "Brandeis brief," which would later play a crucial role in dismantling racial segregation.

Finally, Progressive women's strong commitment to sex-specific protective labor legislation divided them from women who sought further legal guarantees of equality. In the early 1920s, Alice Paul, the founder of the National Woman's Party, drafted an Equal Rights Amendment (ERA) that proclaimed, "Men and women shall have equal rights throughout the United States and every place subject to its jurisdiction," and granted Congress "power to enforce this article by appropriate legislation." Many women's advocates opposed the ERA on the grounds that it would invalidate the protective labor laws that they had worked so hard to obtain. Business and professional women's groups were more inclined to support the amendment, causing their opponents to charge that they disdained the concerns of working-class women. ERA supporters retorted that sex-specific protective labor laws hurt working women by placing them at a competitive disadvantage in the workplace: if laws made employing women more costly, employers would refuse to hire them for more lucrative and desirable jobs. The Supreme Court's ruling in *Adkins v. Children's Hospital* (1923) appeared to validate labor advocates' fear that enshrining formal equality in the Constitution would undermine protective legislation. In *Adkins*, the Court struck down a minimum-wage regulation, citing the Nineteenth Amendment's elevation of women to the status of rights-bearing individuals—including the right to freedom of contract. Although a series of Supreme Court decisions in the mid- to late-1930s sustained New Deal legislation and removed the constitutional impediment to protective labor laws for both men and women, sex-specific employment laws and the antagonism between labor-oriented reformers and ERA supporters persisted into the 1960s.

Women as Workers and as Citizens. Reconciling women's traditional role as family caretakers dependent on husbands for economic support with their persistent engagement in various kinds of indispensable work—paid and unpaid, inside and outside the home—continued to befuddle policymakers and reformers throughout the twentieth century and beyond. As the welfare-state apparatus grew, social policies often developed along two tracks, tracks that assumed that the ideal family structure included a male breadwinner and a dependent female homemaker. For instance, widows' pensions and mothers' aid laws, passed by almost all states in the 1910s and 1920s to help women who lost their husbands to death or disability, assumed that women's economic insecurity resulted primarily from the lack of a male breadwinner. New Deal welfare programs such as Aid to Dependent Children, the precursor to Aid to Families of Dependent Children, served and often stigmatized impoverished women, whereas policymakers designed contribution-based social-insurance programs like Social Security with a worthy middle-class male breadwinner in mind. Public and private employment policies also reflected the assumption that married women should engage in paid work only as a last resort: skyrocketing unemployment rates led to explicit policies barring married women from jobs if their husbands were gainfully employed, and between 1932 and 1937 the government permitted only one member of a married couple to work in the civil service. At the same time, New Deal social policies designed to ease the impact of the Depression excluded large swaths of female and male workers: to garner the support of conservative southern Democrats in Congress, most New Deal legislation, including laws governing working conditions, excluded domestic and agricultural laborers, the vast majority of whom were people of color, and many of whom were women.

The assumption that homemaking and family caretaking constituted women's primary mission did not go unchallenged prior to the 1960s emergence of "second-wave" feminism. Though employment, social insurance, and tax policies assumed a male breadwinner–female homemaker model, women workers fought not only for better working conditions but also for greater pay equity and for entrance into traditionally male occupations in the 1930s, 1940s, and 1950s. The number of women in the paid workforce steadily increased during these years, and during World Wars I and II women demonstrated their ability to perform traditionally male jobs in place of men who had gone to war. Although the labor force remained, for the most part, rigidly segregated by sex (and in many sectors, by race), by the early 1960s advocates for women, and for African Americans, were making considerable headway in casting policies and practices that were once perceived to be commonsensical as wrongful discrimination. The Committee on Civil and Political Rights of the President's Commission on the Status of Women, convened from 1961 to 1962, produced a legal strategy conceived by civil-rights attorney Pauli Murray and designed to move women's advocates beyond their impasse over the ERA and toward greater legal rights under the Fourteenth Amendment.

The transformative moment came in 1964, when Title VII of the Civil Rights Act of 1964 prohibited, for the first time, employment discrimination on the basis of sex as well as race, color, religion, or national origin. The passage of Title VII had important and lasting effects not only on women's employment opportunities but also on the resurgence of women's activism. Ironically, it was the Equal Employment Opportunity Commission's (EEOC's) initial failure to enforce the sex-discrimination provision of Title VII that prompted feminists to found the National Organization for Women (NOW) in 1966. By listing sex alongside race as a prohibited category of discrimination, Title VII also linked women's rights to the cause of African-American civil rights, severing old opportunistic alliances between ERA advocates and racial segregationists and creating opportunities for both coalition and competition between white women, women of color, and men of color.

Title VII enabled significant changes in the nature and scope of women's employment opportunities. In the near term, the law set the stage for a successful campaign against job advertisements that specified the desired sex of the employee. No longer could employers legally state a preference for female secretaries or male truck drivers. In *Phillips v. Martin-Marietta* (1971), the Supreme Court interpreted Title VII to preclude policies that excluded women with young children from employment opportunities available to similarly situated men. That same year, in *Griggs v. Duke Power Company*, the Court ruled that facially neutral employment policies that had a disproportionately negative impact on certain groups of workers could be challenged under Title VII. Amendments to the Civil Rights Act in 1972 expanded the reach of Title VII to public employment and Title IX prohibited sex discrimination by publicly funded educational institutions. In the longer term, feminists won broader administrative, judicial, and legislative interpretations of Title VII's sex-discrimination ban than lawmakers originally had contemplated. After the Court ruled in *Gilbert v. General Electric* (1976) that Title VII did not prohibit discrimination based on pregnancy, feminists won congressional passage of the Pregnancy Discrimination Act of 1978. Feminists persuaded the EEOC and the courts to interpret discrimination "on the basis of sex" to include what the scholar and activist Catharine MacKinnon dubbed the "sexual harassment of working women." Affirmative-action employment programs, both public and private, often included women alongside ethnic minorities.

Further, by prohibiting differentiation between women and men in employment opportunities, Title VII triggered the demise of sex-specific labor laws, allowing advocates for women to move beyond their often bitter disagreement over the ERA and formulate a unified strategy for legal and constitutional change. By 1970, feminists had resolved to pursue the ERA, litigation under the Fourteenth Amendment, and legislative change simultaneously. In *Reed v. Reed* (1971), the Supreme Court ruled, for the first time, that a law differentiating between men and women—a state preference for male estate administrators—violated the equal protection clause. In 1972, Congress passed the ERA and sent it to the states for ratification. In *Frontiero v. Richardson* (1973), feminist lawyers, led by Ruth Bader Ginsburg, then a law professor and attorney for the American Civil Liberties Union (ACLU), came within one vote of persuading the Court to apply to sex-based legal classifications the same "strict scrutiny" to which racial classifications were subjected.

These early legislative and court victories belied the strength of resistance that feminists would face in seeking ratification of the ERA. Phyllis Schlafly, a longtime conservative political activist, successfully mobilized women who opposed the overthrow of the traditional male breadwinner–female homemaker model in the Stop ERA movement. After pitched battles in several borderline states and an extension of the ratification deadline until 1982, the ERA failed. By the end of the 1970s, though, court decisions arguably had accomplished most, though not all, of what ERA advocates sought. Laws that explicitly distinguished between men and women for purposes of military benefits, Social Security, alimony, age of majority, and even ability to purchase alcohol fell under the Court's newly established "intermediate scrutiny" standard, which required that sex-based classifications be "substantially related" to an "important governmental objective." In part, women's ability to achieve substantial judicial enactment of equal rights reflected how feminists had narrowed their constitutional change agenda in response to critics who charged, often hyperbolically, that the amendment would destroy the family, promote homosexuality and abortion, abolish single-sex toilets, and draft women into the military.

The question of whether the ERA—or, for that matter, the equal protection clause of the Fourteenth Amendment—would require women to be conscripted into military service on the same basis as men was only the latest installment of a long-standing debate over the relationship between women's rights claims and the affirmative duties and obligations of citizenship. Jury service was a particularly important context in which this discussion occurred, both because the right to trial by a jury of one's peers was central to the American legal system and because jury service exemplified the republican ideal of male citizens exercising virtue and intelligence in the public sphere. Since female citizens' civic obligations could be discharged through the office of republican motherhood, and since exposure to the rough world of criminal and civil disputes seemed to violate the ideal of feminine purity, through most of the nineteenth century the notion of women jurors seemed to many to be an oxymoron.

As women gained the right to vote in several, mostly western, states in the late nineteenth and early twentieth centuries, jury service sometimes, but not always, followed. In states where statutes defined jurors as "all qualified electors," the Nineteenth Amendment granted jury service to women, but in most states, new statutes were required to qualify women as competent jurors. Significantly, though, even in states where women were permitted to serve on juries, they were not required to do so: exemptions were available on the ground that women's family responsibilities were paramount and that women should not be required to abandon their domestic duties in order to serve. The Supreme Court upheld this justification for women's exemption from jury service as late as 1961, when, in *Hoyt v. Florida*, Justice John Marshall Harlan declared that a "woman is still regarded as the center of home and family life." By the 1960s, women's quest for equality in jury service had intersected with African-Americans' battle to fulfill the promise of *Strauder v. West Virginia* (1880), which established that the Fourteenth Amendment required access to jury service for African-American men but failed to alter the reality of all-white jury rolls. Working with the ACLU and the U.S. Department of Justice, Pauli Murray joined the longtime women's jury-service advocate Dorothy Kenyon in a brief on behalf of Gardenia White and other African-American women who were excluded from an all-white, all-male Alabama jury that had acquitted the accused murderers of two civil-rights workers. When their brief in *White v. Crook* (1966) helped persuade a three-judge federal district court to invalidate an Alabama law prohibiting women from serving on juries, two other states, Louisiana and Mississippi,

Jury Duty. Three women register for jury duty in the Hall of Records, New York City, 1937.
NEW YORK WORLD-TELEGRAM AND THE SUN NEWSPAPER PHOTOGRAPH COLLECTION/PRINTS AND PHOTOGRAPHS DIVISION, LIBRARY OF CONGRESS

had similar exclusions. Exemptions from mandatory jury service survived in many states until the late 1970s, when the Supreme Court invalidated such laws in *Duren v. Missouri* (1979). It was not until 1994 that the Court declared the use of sex-based peremptory challenges by the government unconstitutional, in *J.E.B. v. Alabama*.

Arguments for and against women's jury service alternated between an emphasis on women's and men's sameness, and gender difference. Sameness arguments for jury service stressed women's equal ability and right to serve in an important democratic institution; rationales that emphasized difference variously stressed women's alleged superiority in terms of fairness, disinterestedness, compassion, and conscientiousness. Foes of women's jury service responded that if women were similar to men, then the gender composition of a jury was irrelevant to defendants' rights, and that if the sexes differed, then women's supposed delicacy, emotional reasoning, and domestic responsibilities stood in the way of discharging a juror's duties.

In the context of military service, a more unambiguously masculine enterprise, women who sought greater equality with men gained relatively little from stressing sex differences. More so than jury service, the issue of military conscription deeply divided twentieth-century feminists, some of whom believed that women should not seek admittance to an institution defined by violence. However they may have felt about the draft, however, in the twentieth century women increasingly sought to enlist in the nation's armed forces. Women served in various capacities in World Wars I and II, in Korea and Vietnam, and in subsequent wartime and peacetime military missions. In the mid-1970s, women won admission to the U.S. service academies for the first time on a quota-limited basis. Military service afforded women both tangible benefits in the form of employment and government benefits and intangible rewards associated with fulfilling what had long been defined as the most basic obligation of citizenship. The 1979 Supreme Court case *Personnel Administrator v. Feeney* dramatized the long-term consequences of women's exclusion from most military occupations: in *Feeney*, the Court ruled that Massachusetts's absolute preference for veterans in allocating certain civil-service jobs did not violate the equal protection clause, despite the disproportionate negative impact on women.

Though women increasingly performed extensive and dangerous military service, their status as soldiers remained tenuous. In 1981, the Supreme Court ruled in *Rostker v. Goldberg* that exempting women from Selective Service registration, the basis for the draft, was not unconstitutional sex discrimination. In the 1980s and 1990s, women trained for various combat-related roles, and military service became an increasingly attractive career path for women and men of color seeking greater economic opportunity. At the same time, gender and sexuality remained hotly contested issues in the military, with high-profile sexual-assault accusations against male cadets, enlisted men, and officers and controversies over the prohibition on openly gay service members frequently making headlines. As women took on increasingly dangerous assignments in the Persian Gulf and Iraq wars, Americans again debated the proper balance between women's family responsibilities and their rights and obligations as citizens.

Women and Reproduction. Antifeminists of the 1970s may have overstated the extent to which the ERA would have wrought havoc on traditional family structures, but their sense of embattlement certainly was not without foundation in reality. Soaring divorce rates, increases in out-of-wedlock births, growing economic insecurity, liberalized sexual norms, and the influx of women into the labor force profoundly threatened the male breadwinner–female homemaker ideal that many traditionalist Americans believed was both divinely ordained and the foundation of a well-ordered society. It is hardly surprising, then, that laws pertaining to marriage, family, sexuality, and reproduction became cultural battlegrounds in the latter half of the twentieth century.

These conflicts, of course, had a long history. Although truly reliable methods of contraception remained elusive until the introduction of "the Pill" in the early 1960s, women had long sought to exercise control over their reproductive lives. Until the mid-nineteenth century, such efforts remained largely outside the public realm, with information about contraceptive methods—scientific and otherwise—passed on through informal channels. At common law, abortion was not a crime unless performed after "quickening"—the point at which fetal movement could be perceived, usually around the end of the fourth month of pregnancy. During the second half of the nineteenth century, however, states increasingly began to enact legislation restricting abortion, as well as the advertisement and distribution of contraceptive devices.

The political impetus for abortion restriction came largely from physicians, who presented a variety of medical, ethical, and social arguments against the termination of pregnancies. Doctors attacked the doctrine of "quickening," arguing that fetal life began at conception. Moreover, they contended that abortion interfered with the primary purpose of marriage and of womanhood itself: procreation. As abortion and contraception increasingly were perceived to be middle-class practices rather than the province of poor women, opponents of abortion claimed that birth control threatened the very future of civilization.

Physicians' anticontraception impulse stemmed not only from ideology but also from instrumental concerns, as (male) doctors formed professional associations that sought to limit the provision of medical services, including obstetrics, abortion, and contraception, by traditionally female lay practitioners. Moral reformers also targeted birth control as undermining marriage and promoting sexual disorder; their efforts culminated in the passage and enforcement of the Comstock Act in 1873. Named for its most fervent proponent and enforcer, Anthony Comstock, this federal statute prohibited the distribution of all sexually explicit material, including not only erotica but also birth-control devices and information, through the mails.

In contrast, nineteenth-century feminists endorsed a concept called "voluntary motherhood," which espoused women's ownership of their bodies and their labor, rejecting the notion that wives owed their husbands unlimited sexual access and that women's social duties included bearing children they did not want or could not afford to raise. Accordingly, although they usually did not explicitly promote the use of contraceptive devices or the practice of abortion as a means of birth control, advocates of "voluntary motherhood" asserted a woman's right to refuse sexual intercourse with her husband, to become a mother by choice rather than by force. These claims were consonant with feminists' larger effort, discussed above, to jettison coverture's assumption that husbands owned their wives' labor and personal services.

Although advocates of voluntary motherhood focused primarily on women's right to abstain from sexual intercourse rather than on their prerogative to participate in nonprocreative sexual activities, their notion that women were entitled to bodily and reproductive self-ownership resurfaced in the birth-control movement that emerged in the late nineteenth and early twentieth centuries. Supporters of birth control, like their opponents, drew on a variety of arguments and interpretations of the role of family limitation in the larger political economy. For some radical and Socialist proponents of contraception, like the labor leader Emma Goldman, birth control was essential to liberate poor and working-class women from the economic desperation that afflicted large families with few resources. Activists like Goldman and Margaret Sanger deliberately broke federal and state laws, illegally mailing information about contraception and opening birth-control clinics during the 1910s. In the wake of the Red Scare following World War I, the birth-control movement took on a more restrained, elite tenor. Influenced by the eugenic tradition, which sought to remove "undesirable" elements from the gene pool, reformers, including Sanger, increasingly emphasized population-control arguments for family planning. Birth control, in this view, could selectively lower the birth rate, reducing the number of physically, mentally, and economically "unfit" offspring by encouraging poor women to have fewer children. Patronage from corporations and philanthropists encouraged the movement's increasingly middle- and upper-class orientation.

Never entirely divorced from feminist concerns, the issues of contraception and abortion reform regained a prominent place on the women's rights agenda in the 1960s and 1970s. The campaign against anticontraception laws, still on the books in some states, laid the legal groundwork for a challenge to stringent abortion restrictions. After many attempts at legislative reform—vociferously opposed by the Catholic Church—Estelle Griswold, the executive director of the Planned Parenthood League of Connecticut, with the help of Yale law professors, persuaded the Supreme Court to invalidate Connecticut's ban on the use of contraceptives by married couples. *Griswold v. Connecticut* (1965) established a constitutional right to privacy that advocates immediately understood could open the door to abortion-law challenges. Although women of means had been able to obtain abortions clandestinely through the 1930s, the 1940s and 1950s saw increased repression of abortion provision, causing some physicians and lawyers to join in the quest for reform. Harrowing stories of couples seeking to avoid the fetal abnormalities caused by thalidomide and rubella put a sympathetic face on the costs of criminalizing abortion, but by 1967 reformers had succeeded in legalizing therapeutic abortions in only three states, and by 1969 advocates decided to litigate for the repeal of abortion restrictions rather than seek piecemeal legislative reform. In *Eisenstadt v. Baird* (1972), the Court invalidated a Massachusetts ban on the distribution of contraceptives to unmarried individuals, with Justice Brennan writing for the majority, "If the right of privacy means anything, it is the right of the individual, married or single, to be free from unwarranted intrusion into matters so fundamentally affecting a person as the decision whether to bear or beget a child." In *Roe v. Wade* (1973), the Court extended the right of privacy to include terminating a pregnancy, laying out a trimester-based framework for assessing the legality of restrictions on abortion.

Roe's impact extended far beyond the invalidation of state abortion restrictions, affecting the agendas not only of feminist lawyers and their immediate antagonists but also of interest groups, political parties, and the judicial appointments process. *Roe* galvanized an antiabortion movement and helped fuel broader anti-ERA, antifeminist, and conservative religious political mobilizations. Antiabortion protests disrupted clinics offering reproductive health care and occasionally turned violent. *Roe*'s reasoning came under attack even from those who agreed with its result, with some feminists arguing that reproductive rights were best justified as a matter of equal protection of the laws rather than privacy or physicians' prerogatives. On the other hand, the substantive due-process rationale advanced in *Griswold* and *Roe* formed the basis of arguments for other rights, such as the "right to die," and the right to choose sexual partners of the same sex. Although abortion became a "litmus test" issue for judicial appointments by presidents of both parties, with Democrats advancing the pro-choice banner and the Republican Party platform supporting a constitutional amendment banning abortion, once on the bench judges' positions on abortion proved less than predictable. Although the Supreme Court upheld some restrictions on abortion, including a twenty-four-hour waiting period and a "gag rule" preventing doctors from discussing abortion with their patients, in *Planned Parenthood of Southeastern Pennsylvania v. Casey* (1992) a majority of the justices upheld the core holding of *Roe*. In an unusual opinion authored by three justices, the Court abandoned *Roe*'s trimester framework, adopting Justice Sandra Day O'Connor's more lenient "undue burden" test but acknowledging the centrality of reproductive freedom to women's ability to control their lives and destinies.

The changing composition of the Court in the early years of the twenty-first century gave antiabortion activists reason to hope. In *Gonzales v. Carhart* (2007), the Court upheld the Partial-Birth Abortion Act of 2003, which proscribed a particular method of abortion—intact dilation and extraction—despite the statute's failure to exempt procedures necessary to preserve a woman's health. A vehement dissent from the Court's only remaining female Justice, Ruth Bader Ginsburg, assailed the five-justice majority for disregarding the integral role of reproductive choice in preserving "woman's autonomy to determine her life's course, and thus to enjoy equal citizenship stature," and for accepting dubious pseudoscientific evidence of the purported psychological harm of abortion to women.

Meanwhile, access to reproductive health care remained dependent on socioeconomic status throughout this period. Advocates for reproductive choice had limited success in securing access to abortion for poor women, as Supreme Court decisions in *Maher v. Roe* (1977) and *Harris v. McRae* (1980) upheld restrictions on government funding of abortions for indigent women. And impoverished and disabled women had historically faced restrictions on their freedom to bear children. Eugenic sterilization laws targeting those perceived as unfit—including, in some cases, welfare recipients—proliferated at the state level in the early twentieth century, although their enforcement was somewhat haphazard. Their association with Nazi extermination policies stymied eugenic laws by the late 1940s, but beginning in the late 1950s, a changing welfare caseload inspired a resurgence in proposals for coercive sterilization. Earlier, public relief had been the province of mostly white widows, perceived as deserving women who had fallen on hard times, whereas by 1961 unmarried women of all races constituted the majority of Aid to Dependent Children recipients, and an increasing proportion were women of color. Some politicians blamed rising rates of illegitimacy on black women's receipt of welfare benefits, and although efforts to legislate punitive sterilization for unwed mothers failed, some states and localities maintained de facto policies subjecting poor women of color to nonconsensual sterilization or conditioning the receipt of medical care upon sterilization. In the 1970s, activists of color fought to place the right to bear children on the agenda of the women's movement and to detach reproductive rights from their partial roots in eugenic population control.

Women and the Modern Family. The twentieth century saw sweeping changes in family law, as well as in the law's conception of women's place within and without the family. Among the most profound and controversial transformations came in the law of marital dissolution. Americans had argued about the nature of the marriage bond and the appropriate grounds, if any, for divorce since the early days of the republic, when for the most part divorces were available only through legislative decree. Beginning in the late eighteenth century, in most states, courts assumed jurisdiction over divorce. Grounds for divorce varied significantly by state; in New York, adultery was the sole ground, whereas other states allowed divorce on grounds including drunkenness, bigamy, extreme cruelty, and long-term desertion. In the 1850s and 1860s, women's rights advocates like Elizabeth Cady Stanton and Susan B. Anthony promoted the liberalization of divorce laws, while compatriots like Antoinette Brown Blackwell defended marriage's indissolubility. In the half century after the Civil War, conservatives condemned what they saw as "easy divorce" and lobbied, mostly unsuccessfully, for greater state uniformity in what had become increasingly diverse and complicated divorce grounds and procedures. During this period, the woman's movement increasingly focused less on reforming divorce law and more on obtaining the vote. After the passage of the Nineteenth Amendment, a few feminist lawyers, like Burnita Shelton Matthews and Blanche Crozier, chronicled and criticized the inequities of marriage law, but the reformation of family law remained low on the women's rights agenda at mid-century. When divorce-law reform regained momentum at the national level following World War II, the organized women's movement initially did not play a prominent role in shaping the debate.

The impulse toward divorce reform in the mid-twentieth century stemmed from a variety of concerns, including the dishonesty, collusion, and recriminations encouraged by the fault system; the desire to take a less adversarial and more therapeutic approach to divorce; and the effort to unify jurisdiction over the incidents of marital dissolution, including property distribution, alimony, child custody, and child support. Observers disagreed about the effects of the new model that emerged in the early 1970s, no-fault divorce. Some studies in the 1980s and 1990s suggested that no-fault worsened the economic situation of women and children; others attributed the impoverishment of women and children following divorce to factors other than the shift to no-fault. Feminists too disagreed over the economic effects of no-fault, but most agreed that women's continuing disproportionate responsibility for the tasks of homemaking and family caregiving meant that making family law formally sex neutral—for instance, providing that spouses have a duty of mutual support and removing the automatic preference for maternal custody—did not, in practice, eradicate the gender inequities of life after divorce or, for that matter, during marriage. As long as inequalities in family responsibilities and employment opportunities for men and women persisted, allocating property, spousal and child support, and child-custody obligations in a fair and equitable manner remained a complicated challenge with no easy solution.

In the decades after 1970, advocates for women renewed their challenge to other traditional assumptions underlying family law, most prominently the law's tolerance for intrafamily violence against women. At common law, husbands were entitled to physically chastise their wives, so long as they did not inflict permanent injury. Nineteenth-century women's rights agitation helped undercut the right of chastisement, but legal decision makers frequently substituted the doctrine of marital privacy for a husband's common-law prerogative to discipline his wife. Under this view, judges and law-enforcement officers should not probe intramarital conflict too deeply, lest they undermine family cohesion. This reluctance to intervene spanned the criminal and civil law, as many husbands—particularly those in the middle and upper classes—escaped prosecution for wife beating, and interspousal tort immunity prevented wives from recovering damages for injuries caused by their husbands. Over the vehement objections of women's rights advocates who questioned husbands' unlimited right to demand sexual access to their wives, rape laws exempted married couples from sanctions. The common-law justification for marital rape exemptions held that when a woman consented to marriage, she made herself unconditionally available to her husband for sexual as well other domestic services. Although states mitigated other aspects of coverture in the second half of the nineteenth century, they nevertheless refused to prosecute husbands for rape. Resistance to acknowledge that some instances of marital intercourse not only might be nonconsensual but also should be subject to criminal penalties or civil liability, remained robust throughout much of the twentieth century, as many states continued to provide lesser penalties and higher standards of proof in marital rape cases.

As it had been in earlier eras of women's rights advocacy, challenging the law's tolerance of domestic abuse became an important plank in the late-twentieth-century feminist platform. Women used public-education campaigns to resist cultural norms that relegated family violence to a private sphere untouched by societal or governmental intervention; they founded battered-women's shelters and legal-service organizations to provide women and children with alternatives to remaining in the homes of their abusers; and they sought to alter formal and informal law-enforcement policies of nonintervention in domestic disputes. By the 1990s, feminists sought to frame violence against women as a civil-rights issue, comparing rape and domestic violence to hate crimes against people of color. The 1994 Violence Against Women Act, which passed Congress with bipartisan support, provided federal funding for support services for battered women and created a federal civil remedy for "gender-motivated violence." In the search for legal remedies, anti-domestic-violence advocates confronted not only cultural norms about family privacy but also legal doctrines that limited the state's ability to intervene in intrafamily violence. Principles of federalism derailed the Violence Against Women Act's civil-rights remedy, which the Supreme Court, in *United States v. Morrison* (2000), found to be outside the scope of congressional power under the commerce clause and the Fourteenth Amendment. The state-action requirement foiled many attempts to hold police departments responsible for enforcement failures, most famously in *Town of Castle Rock v. Gonzales* (2005). Nevertheless, foes of domestic abuse had made significant strides in creating the political will to combat violence against women using the tools of the state.

In the final decades of the twentieth century, women and men challenged perhaps the most basic assumption underlying family law and structure: the notion that the family unit is composed of a male husband, a female wife, and their dependent children. Although alternative family arrangements had always existed at the margins of American society, public challenges to normative heterosexuality accelerated dramatically in the latter half of the twentieth century. The movement for recognition and rights for lesbians and gay men grew up alongside and in a complicated relationship to late-twentieth-century feminism. Some in the women's movement, perhaps fearing the labels of man-hater or lesbian often attached to feminists, initially distanced themselves from increasingly assertive campaigners for gay rights. Other feminists, gay and heterosexual alike, viewed restrictions on the freedom to choose one's sexual and life partners as imposing prescriptive norms of masculinity and femininity that constrained human flourishing and helped create social inequality. Under this view, laws that prohibited homosexual conduct, same-sex marriage, or the custody or adoption of children by gay parents, or that condoned discrimination in employment or government benefits against gay individuals or partners, reflected an injustice not unlike that suffered by women who wished to enter traditionally male occupations or who lost employment opportunities because of an insufficiently feminine appearance or demeanor or whose families lost out on government benefits because they and not their husbands were the primary breadwinners. Faced with these arguments, traditionalist conservatives, some of whom had anticipated that "homosexual rights" would grow naturally out of feminism, saw their prediction of family destruction as one step closer to fulfillment.

Women as Legal Professionals. For women, entering the American legal profession entailed a conflict similar to the one they faced in making the case for women's suffrage, military service, jury service, and equal employment opportunity. If women's primary role was as "the center of home and family life," then the rough, adversarial world of nineteenth-century legal practice—characterized by historians as well as contemporaries as quintessentially masculine—seemed an improper and even dangerous place for female presence, much less female achievement. These cultural assumptions about women's proper role as wives and mothers in the domestic sphere translated into formidable structural barriers to entry. For instance, when Myra Bradwell, the founder and publisher of the *Chicago Legal News*, was denied admission to the Illinois bar because of her sex, she appealed all the way to the Supreme Court, which in *Bradwell v. Illinois* (1873) affirmed the state's right to exclude women from legal practice. Justice Joseph P. Bradley's concurring opinion famously declared, "The paramount destiny and mission of woman are to fulfill the noble and benign offices of wife and mother. This is the law of the Creator." When women did win admission to the bar in the nineteenth century—largely through arduous attempts to persuade legislators to include women in licensing statutes—they often apprenticed and practiced with husbands or other male relatives. Resistance to women appearing in court as trial lawyers meant that many were confined to office practice in areas like domestic-relations law, probate, and real-estate conveyances.

There were significant exceptions to this rule. Clara Shortridge Foltz, who became California's first woman attorney in 1878, was instrumental in inventing a key institution in criminal law, the public defender; in adding a women's rights section to the California Constitution, and in other legal reforms. Belva Lockwood, a formidable politician and legal advocate, secured for women the right to practice before the federal courts and herself won admission to the Supreme Court bar in 1879. These prominent pioneers and lesser-known women lawyers struggled at the local and state levels for women's suffrage and for professional recognition, establishing interstate networks through organizations like the Equity Club, founded in the mid-1880s by women law students in Michigan. By 1920 the Nineteenth Amendment had mooted the argument that women should not be admitted to the bar because to do so would effectively admit their suitability for the suffrage, and in 1923 Delaware became the last state in the union to lift its ban on women licensed attorneys.

As the apprenticeship model of legal learning slowly began to give way to law-school education around the turn of the century, women sought admission to these institutions, generally facing lower barriers in western states and territories than in the South or the Northeast. Howard University Law School became, in 1869, the first law school to admit students regardless of race or sex, although early women students faced resistance from some faculty and only nine women graduated from Howard before 1900. Although a few law schools admitted more than an occasional woman (including the University of Michigan, which began admitting women in 1870 and graduated more women than any other law school in the following two decades; New York University School of Law, which began admitting women in 1890; Washington College of Law, founded in 1898; and Portia Law School for women, founded in Boston in 1908), the number of women law students remained minuscule in the late nineteenth and early twentieth centuries. The most prestigious law schools were often the last to open their doors to women, though their exclusionary policies did not go unchallenged: for instance, in 1944 Pauli Murray enlisted the help of Eleanor Roosevelt and President Franklin D. Roosevelt in her ultimately unsuccessful bid to gain admission to Harvard Law School's graduate program, a privilege traditionally granted to Howard Law School's top graduate; Harvard did not admit women to its law school until 1950.

The percentage of American lawyers who were women increased relatively little between 1930 (2.1 percent) and 1960 (3.6 percent), but a small coterie of women attorneys ascended the ranks of the profession. A smattering of women judges were appointed or elected to the bench before 1960, primarily though not exclusively in lower state courts; the 1935 appointment of federal district court judge Sarah T. Hughes, who would later administer the oath of office to President Lyndon B. Johnson, was a rarity. The small but growing African-American women's bar cultivated attorneys like the University of Pennsylvania Law School graduate and PhD economist Sadie T. M. Alexander, who, like many early white women lawyers, teamed up with her husband in private law practice and, like many well-to-do women of both races, performed significant work for community organizations. Others, like the Yale Law School graduate Jane M. Bolin, who would become the nation's first African-American woman judge at age thirty-one, launched their careers with low-level government work.

In seeking admission to the profession, early women lawyers used arguments familiar from the suffrage context: most often, they claimed the right to practice law because they possessed the same abilities and had acquired the same knowledge and skills as men. At times, they also advanced the expedient rationale that women's uniquely feminine attributes would help them better serve women clients, resolve family-related disputes, and mitigate the harsher aspects of the adversary system. This simultaneous assertion of equality and difference would resurface in the 1970s, as the number of women in law schools underwent an unprecedented and dramatic increase. Between 1947 and 1967, the percentage of women in law school remained a fairly constant 4 or 5 percent. By 1974, the proportion had skyrocketed to 20 percent; by the late 1980s, 40 percent, and at the turn of the twenty-first century, women represented approximately half of the law-student population.

Just as early women lawyers attempted to balance the demands of work and family and to overcome assumptions about their ability to compete in a "masculine" profession, so too did their successors. As their numbers increased, women confronted the existing structure of legal education and the legal profession with a complicated combination of conformity and challenge. Even as they sought to participate on the same terms as men, many hoped that the entrance of a critical mass of women would inspire reforms to the format and content of legal education and to the structure and goals of the bar and bench. On both fronts—participation and transformation—women enjoyed significant though ultimately limited success in the late twentieth century. The number of women judges, government officials, and law faculty increased significantly in the last quarter of the twentieth century. For example, in 1975, women made up less than 2 percent of the federal judiciary and 7 percent of tenure-track law faculty; by 2000, they held about one-fifth of federal judgeships and full professorships. Courses on women and the law and feminist jurisprudence appeared in law-school curricula, and some credited (or blamed) women for the modification of the traditional "Socratic method" as a staple of law-school pedagogy. Even the most prestigious private law firms added women partners to their rosters. Women attained prominence in public-interest law careers, including but not limited to positions in organizations devoted to the vindication of women's legal rights, such as the Women's Equity Action League (founded 1968), the ACLU Women's Rights Project (founded 1972), the ACLU Reproductive Freedom Project (founded 1974), and the NOW Legal Defense and Education Fund (founded 1970; renamed Legal Momentum in 2004). Judicial gender-bias task forces sought to rid the federal and state courts of practices harmful to women lawyers and litigants.

Equal Rights. Bella Abzug (*center with hat*) holds up an Equal Rights Amendment (ERA) sign as she participates in a pro-equal rights demonstration, New York City, August 1980. AP PHOTO

Nevertheless, many women reported, and empirical evidence suggested, that formal barriers to entering and flourishing within the legal profession had given way to more informal, but nevertheless formidable, obstacles. Women law students, despite entering law school with credentials as good as or better than those of their male counterparts, nevertheless graduated, as a group, with fewer academic and professional honors. Moreover, many reported that they found legal education demoralizing and that their law-school experiences diminished their initial desire to pursue public-interest law careers. Despite a large and increasingly diverse pool of entering associates, prestigious private law firms promoted very few women to partner, and attrition rates remained high, especially for women. Though rising, the percentage of women faculty at highly ranked law schools remained below 25 percent. Perhaps most strikingly, women and men who sought to balance a legal career with family caregiving responsibilities still found the long hours and rigid promotion track of law-firm life decidedly inhospitable.

"Women" at the Turn of the Twenty-first Century. By the time the new millennium began, the legal category "women" had undergone profound transformations. Marriage no longer submerged a woman's legal identity beneath her husband's; white male heads of households no longer were presumed to represent the political interests of their wives and other dependents; instead of a presumption of reasonableness, laws classifying individuals on the basis of sex were subject to heightened judicial scrutiny; employers no longer could denominate certain job categories as male or female with impunity; educational institutions receiving public funding no longer could exclude female students; victims of domestic violence increasingly could call on their communities and on law enforcement to assert their right not to be abused; and increasing numbers of women served in high-level positions in government and in the private sector. The historical legacy of "women" as a legal and social category remained potent, however. The tension between women's roles as family caregivers and as workers and citizens remained a defining element of American economic and social life. Balancing work and family obligations, establishing a place in traditionally male occupations, gaining control over sexual fulfillment and childbearing, overcoming physical domination and violence, redefining the structure and function of the modern family—all were as pressing dilemmas as they had been at any time in the American past.

In some ways, late-twentieth-century developments made "women" seem less useful as a social and legal category. Differences among women—social, political, religious, ethnic, racial, economic, and sexual—undermined efforts to speak of "women" as a cohesive group with definable interests. As the law increasingly ceased to explicitly designate "women" as a separate or special category of human beings, many saw continuing substantive inequalities beneath a veneer of formal legal equality. If the law assumed that women and men were similarly situated when in fact they continued to shoulder different burdens and responsibilities of family membership and of political and economic citizenship, then legal reform seemed a necessary, but hardly sufficient, ingredient for women's advancement.

[*See also* Family, *subentry on* United States Law, *and* Feminist Legal Theory.]

BIBLIOGRAPHY

Baer, Judith A. *Women in American Law: The Struggle toward Equality from the New Deal to the Present*. 2d ed. New York: Holmes & Meier, 1996.

Basch, Norma. *Framing American Divorce: From the Revolutionary Generation to the Victorians*. Berkeley: University of California Press, 1999.

Cott, Nancy F. *The Grounding of Modern Feminism*. New Haven, Conn.: Yale University Press, 1987.

Cott, Nancy F. *Public Vows: A History of Marriage and the Nation*. Cambridge, Mass.: Harvard University Press, 2000.

D'Emilio, John, and Estelle B. Freedman. *Intimate Matters: A History of Sexuality in America*. New York: Harper & Row, 1988.

Drachman, Virginia G. *Sisters in Law: Women Lawyers in Modern American History*. Cambridge, Mass.: Harvard University Press, 1998.

DuBois, Ellen Carol. *Feminism and Suffrage: The Emergence of an Independent Women's Movement in America, 1848–1869*. Ithaca, N.Y.: Cornell University Press, 1978.

DuBois, Ellen Carol. *Woman Suffrage and Women's Rights*. New York: New York University Press, 1998.

Garrow, David J. *Liberty and Sexuality: The Right to Privacy and the Making of* Roe v. Wade. New York: Macmillan, 1994.

Gordon, Linda. *The Moral Property of Women: A History of Birth Control Politics in America*. 3d ed. Urbana and Chicago: University of Illinois Press, 2002.

Gordon, Linda. *Pitied but Not Entitled: Single Mothers and the History of Welfare, 1890–1935*. New York: Free Press, 1994.

Grossberg, Michael. *Governing the Hearth: Law and the Family in Nineteenth-Century America*. Chapel Hill: University of North Carolina Press, 1985.

Grossberg, Michael, "Institutionalizing Masculinity: The Law as a Masculine Profession." In *Meanings for Manhood: Constructions of Masculinity in Victorian America*, edited by Mark C. Carnes and Clyde Griffen, pp. 133–151. Chicago: University of Chicago Press, 1990.

Harrison, Cynthia. *On Account of Sex: The Politics of Women's Issues, 1945–1968*. Berkeley: University of California Press, 1988.

Hartog, Hendrik. *Man and Wife in America: A History*. Cambridge, Mass.: Harvard University Press, 2000.

Jones, Jacqueline. *Labor of Love, Labor of Sorrow: Black Women, Work, and the Family from Slavery to the Present*. New York: Basic Books, 1985.

Kay, Herma Hill. "From the Second Sex to the Joint Venture: An Overview of Women's Rights and Family Law in the United States during the Twentieth Century." *California Law Review* 88 (2000): 2017–2093.

Kerber, Linda K. *No Constitutional Right to Be Ladies: Women and the Obligations of Citizenship*. New York: Hill and Wang, 1998.

Kerber, Linda K. *Women of the Republic: Intellect and Ideology in Revolutionary America*. Chapel Hill: University of North Carolina Press, 1980.

Kessler-Harris, Alice. *Out to Work: A History of Wage-Earning Women in the United States*. New York: Oxford University Press, 1982.

Kessler-Harris, Alice. *In Pursuit of Equity: Women, Men, and the Quest for Economic Citizenship in Twentieth-Century America*. Oxford and New York: Oxford University Press, 2001.

Mathews, Donald G., and Jane Sherron De Hart. *Sex, Gender, and the Politics of ERA: A State and the Nation*. New York: Oxford University Press, 1990.

Mohr, James C. *Abortion in America: The Origins and Evolution of National Policy, 1800–1900*. New York: Oxford University Press, 1978.

Pleck, Elizabeth. *Domestic Tyranny: The Making of Social Policy against Family Violence from Colonial Times to the Present*. New York: Oxford University Press, 1987.

Reagan, Leslie J. *When Abortion Was a Crime: Women, Medicine, and Law in the United States, 1867–1973*. Berkeley: University of California Press, 1997.

Siegel, Reva B. "Home as Work: The First Woman's Rights Claims Concerning Wives' Household Labor, 1850–1880." *Yale Law Journal* 103 (1994): 1073–1217.

Siegel, Reva B. "The Modernization of Marital Status Law: Adjudicating Wives' Right to Earnings, 1860–1930." *Georgetown Law Journal* 82 (1994): 2127–2211.

Siegel, Reva B. "'The Rule of Love': Wife Beating as Prerogative and Privacy." *Yale Law Journal* 105 (1996): 2117–2206.

Smith, J. Clay, Jr., ed. *Rebels in Law: Voices in History of Black Women Lawyers*. Ann Arbor: University of Michigan Press, 1998.

Terborg-Penn, Rosalyn. *African-American Women in the Struggle for the Vote, 1850–1920*. Bloomington: Indiana University Press, 1998.

Welke, Barbara Young. *Recasting American Liberty: Gender, Race, Law, and the Railroad Revolution, 1865–1920*. Cambridge, U.K., and New York: Cambridge University Press, 2001.

Zimmerman, Joan G. "The Jurisprudence of Equality: The Women's Minimum Wage, the First Equal Rights Amendment, and *Adkins v. Children's Hospital*, 1905–1923." *Journal of American History* 78 (1991): 188–225.

SERENA MAYERI

WORSHIP IN ISLAMIC LAW. In the conventional structure of Islamic legal works, acts of worship (*'ibādāt*) represent a category defined in distinction to (and in precedence over) *mu 'āmalāt*, or interpersonal transactions. Legal compendia traditionally begin with the rules for the major and minor ablutions (as preliminaries to worship), followed by prayer, fasting, alms tax, and the hajj (pilgrimage to Mecca). Jihad is also categorized as an *'ibāda* by legal scholars, although rules for warfare are not generally treated in the opening sections of legal manuals. Because it is primarily concerned with activities such as prayer, fasting, and pilgrimage, the category of *'ibādāt* roughly corresponds to that of religious ritual. However, it includes acts (such as jihad and the payment of alms tax) that would not conventionally be characterized as involving ritual or worship. The most important *'ibādāt* are the five "pillars of Islam," which are the confession of faith (the *shahāda*, "there is no god but God and Muhammad is the messenger of God"), the five daily canonical prayers, fasting during the daylight hours in Ramadan, the payment of mandatory alms (zakat), and the hajj. These are enumerated in a well-authenticated and widely cited hadith report.

The term *'ibādāt* (singular *'ibāda*) is derived from an Arabic root referring to the concept of servitude and means "obedience" or "submissiveness." Jurists generally agree that in technical legal terminology as well, the core meaning of the term *'ibāda* is "obedience." Some jurists further specify the category of obedience by adding the concept of seeking closeness to God (*taqarrub*, *qurba*). Others emphasize that acts of worship serve to combat and subdue the passions, requiring that the believer act in contradiction to personal whims or fundamental desires. Thus, for instance, the significance of mandatory almsgiving is widely understood to lie in the disciplining of acquisitiveness and greed. Viewed in this light, acts of worship are understood as tests or trials imposed by God. For other scholars, the element of glorification or veneration (*ta'ẓīm*) is decisive; the Hanafi scholar Abu 'l-Baqa' al-Kafawi (d. 1683) argues that while all acts performed in compliance with the divine command constitute obedience (*ṭā'a*), worship (*'ibāda*) involves "glorifying God to the utmost extent" (*al-Kulliyat*, p. 583).

Acts of worship are defined primarily in terms of obedience to the divine command rather than of symbolic or expressive action. Most acts of worship are understood in terms of *ta'abbud*, another concept derived from the Arabic root referring to servanthood or submission. An act that is *ta'abbudī* does not have any rationale that is discernible to the human intellect. Because such an act's function and objectives are unknown, its performance is grounded in pure obedience to God. The Shafi'i jurist and Sufi mystic al-Ghazali (d. 1111) argues that certain acts of worship frustrate the human desire for comprehension precisely so that they will be performed in a spirit of absolute subjection to the divine command (*Ihya'*, 1:315). In general, jurists refrain from analyzing the rationales for acts of worship or elaborating symbolic interpretations of their components. However, such analyses are not completely absent from Islamic legal texts. For instance, the Hanafi scholar Ibn Amir al-Hajj (d. 1474) emphasizes the expressive aspect of worship by analyzing each of the physical postures and verbal utterances of the canonical prayers as an expression of glorification (*ta'ẓīm*) of God (*al-Taqrir wā-l-tahbir*, 2:102). Jurists do not agree that all acts of worship are *ta'abbudī*, and in many cases debate whether individual acts of worship have discernible rationales or not.

Jurists of the Hanafi school define *'ibādāt* as acts of obedience that require *niyya*, or intent. This gives rise to a typology of acts of obedience. *Ṭā'a* (obedience) is quite simply compliance with the divine command, also defined as an action for which one will be rewarded (in the afterlife). *Qurba* (drawing close) is an act of obedience performed in the knowledge of the One Whom one approaches by means of it (i.e., of God). An *'ibāda* is an act of obedience that requires intent (*niyya*) for its validity. These categories are overlapping. Thus, acts of worship such as the five canonical prayers, fasting, mandatory almsgiving, and the pilgrimage to Mecca are simultaneously obedience (*ṭā'a*), "drawing close" (*qurba*), and *'ibāda*. Voluntary acts of piety such as Qur'anic recitation, the establishment of pious endowments (*waqf*), the manumission of slaves,

Reading the Qur'an. Afghan Muslim men read the Qur'an after Friday prayers at the Pul-e-Khashty mosque, Kabul, October 2005. PHOTOGRAPH BY MUSADEQ SADEQ. AP PHOTO

and supererogatory almsgiving are categorized in this schema as "drawing close" to God (*qurba*) and as obedience (*ṭāʿa*), but not as acts of worship (*ʿibāda*). Applying their rule that acts of worship are defined by the requirement of appropriate intent, the Hanafis argue that the minor ablutions (washing the extremities, face and head in preparation for prayer) do not require *niyya* and thus do not constitute an act of worship. A person who performs them without the appropriate intent will have performed valid ablutions, and will achieve the state of ritual purity required for prayer, but will not receive the reward for performing an act of worship. If the person performs the ablutions with the appropriate intent, in contrast, the ablutions will constitute an act of worship and will carry divine reward. Jurists of other schools take a more expansive approach to the category of *ʿibāda*, collapsing the distinctions among *ʿibāda*, *ṭāʿa*, and *qurba*.

Acts of worship are primarily understood as actions performed exclusively for the sake of adherence to the divine command or pursuit of otherworldly reward. Insofar as the act is performed (or omitted) for some other objective, it ceases to be *ʿibāda*. However, not all acts can be rendered *ʿibādāt* by the appropriate motivation. *ʿIbādāt* are sometimes contrasted with divinely commanded actions that have instrumental value on the level of this-worldly human existence, although many acts of worship are also recognized to have utilitarian value in this life. *ʿIbādāt* are understood as being performed in view of benefits that will occur after death, and not before. Repaying debts, financially supporting one's family, and the like are all acts of obedience to God, but they are not *ʿibādāt*; the objective of these actions (and of all transactions among human beings, *muʿāmalāt*) is benefit to other humans.

Scholars distinguish among the rules of the shariʿa that are the exclusive right (*ḥaqq*) of God, those that are exclusive rights of human beings, and those that partake of both. The exclusive rights of God include (in what most scholars recognized as descending order of precedence) faith in God and the major *ʿibādāt*: the mandatory prayers (*ṣalāt*), fasting, zakat, the hajj, jihad, and prayer retreats in mosques (*iʿtikāf*). After the exclusive rights of God come *ʿibādāt* that also involve an element of aid (*maʿūna*) to fellow human beings, such as the alms given at the end of the Ramadan fast. There is also a category of legal rules that combine elements of worship and of punishment; this category is exemplified by acts of expiation (*kaffārāt*). Acts whose exclusive objective is the alleviation of human suffering or the deterrence of crime do not fall into the category of acts of worship.

Although Hanafis give a distinctive role to *niyya* (intent) in defining the category of *ʿibādāt*, all scholars insist on its importance in the performance of a given act of worship. *Niyya* has sometimes been treated by non-Muslim scholars as the element of sincerity or "spirituality" in Islamic worship; however, Paul Powers has recently demonstrated that this is a misreading of the juristic tradition. The primary function of *niyya* is to distinguish acts of worship from profane activities that are formally identical; for instance, a person washing himself with water might be cleansing or cooling himself, or might be performing ritual ablutions; a person refraining from food and drink might be doing so for the sake of his health, or might be fasting. Second, *niyya* functions to distinguish among the varieties or degrees of a given act of worship; for instance, it distinguishes between obligatory and supererogatory prayers. *Niyya* involves no more than the mental resolution that, for instance, "I am performing the obligatory noontime prayer"; this intention constitutes the act of worship as such, and is necessary for its validity. Unlike profane activities, whose external forms inherently fulfill their objectives (for instance, the repayment of a debt), acts of worship can achieve their objective—which is the glorification of God—only by means of the actor's intent. *Niyya* is not identical with motivation; for instance, a person might pray for the sake of hypocritical show, but still have a valid *niyya* to perform a given prayer.

Islamic jurists do deal with issues of mental focus and emotional commitment, although not primarily in connection with the concept of intent. Most jurists categorize reverence (*khushūʿ*) as a desirable component (*sunna*) in prayer, although usually not a requirement for its technical validity. Some Shafiʿis, such as al-Ghazali, argue that reverence is a mandatory element of prayer. Reverence is understood not exclusively as an interior attitude, but as a combination of mental concentration and physical composure. The *khushūʿ* of the heart consists in awareness of God to the exclusion of all other preoccupations; the *khushūʿ* of the body consists of physical calm and restraint, and is negated (for instance) by unnecessary movements or rearrangement of one's clothing.

The discipline of Islamic law is concerned with the validity (*ṣiḥḥa*) of acts of worship, which designates their performance in conformity with God's commandment, fulfilling all the required elements (*wājibāt*) and free of any incompatible element. A valid act of worship is one that discharges the person's obligation to perform the act in question. The concept of validity is thus closely related to the concept of legal responsibility; acts of worship are incumbent only upon persons who have legal competency (*ahliyya*) and are subject to obligation (*mukallaf*) under the law. Exempted are children, the insane, and (according to some scholars) persons who are unconscious or mentally impaired as a result of illness or treatment with a licit drug. A prophetic hadith instructs that a child should be taught to perform *ṣalāt* at the age of seven, and disciplined for neglecting it from the age of ten. Most jurists argue that prayer becomes technically obligatory only upon reaching puberty, although valid prayers can be performed by a child who is capable of comprehending them. Fasting and the payment of zakat similarly become obligatory upon an individual upon reaching majority. The hajj is obligatory only on condition of physical and financial ability to make the journey. Jihad, although treated as an *'ibāda*, is ordinarily regarded as a group rather than an individual obligation; that is, it can be performed by a limited group on behalf of the community.

Obligatory acts of worship take precedence over voluntary or supererogatory acts, and are considered to be more meritorious. The issue of the legal validity of an act of worship is understood to be distinct from that of its religious merit. The validity of an act of worship does not necessarily entail divine reward (*thawāb*); the act may be valid, relieving the actor of legal obligation, but there is no reward. Divine reward is understood to be intimately connected with the issue of intent; however, a technically valid *niyya* for a given act of worship does not necessarily indicate appropriate religious motivation. The Hanafi jurist Ibn 'Abidin (d. 1836) remarks that sincerity (*ikhlāṣ*) is a condition for reward, not for validity. For instance, if someone were to say to a person, "Pray, and I will give you a dinar" and he prayed with that objective, the prayer would fulfill his obligation (*Hashiyat radd al-muhtar*, 1:415).

Nonbelievers cannot perform valid acts of worship. There is a difference of opinion among the jurists concerning their obligation to perform the *'ibādāt*; some scholars argue that nonbelievers cannot be obligated to comply with commands that they cannot validly fulfill, while others argue that they are obligated to perform the *'ibādāt* (and will be punished in the afterlife for their omission) because the necessary precondition (conversion to Islam) is within their power. The Shafi'is and Hanbalis hold that nonbelievers are not obligated to perform the *'ibādāt* in this life, but will nevertheless be punished for their omission in the next.

In respect to the validity of acts of worship and the obligation to perform them, scholars distinguish between bodily acts of worship (*al-'ibādāt al-badaniyya*) and financial acts of worship (*al-'ibādāt al-māliyya*). Some acts of worship, such as *ṣalāt*, fasting, and the ritual ablutions, are considered purely bodily; others, like zakat, are purely financial; and yet others, such as the hajj, combine both elements. In general, purely bodily acts of worship can be performed only by the individual subject to the obligation. This rule is subject to exceptions; for instance, it is textually established that the Prophet instructed a woman to fast on behalf of her deceased mother. Purely financial acts of worship, such as the payment of obligatory alms, can be delegated to an agent. The hajj, which is held to combine bodily and financial elements, can be delegated to an agent if one is permanently incapacitated from performing it; it can also be performed on behalf of the dead.

With some exceptions, acts of worship are treated as individual obligations whose nonperformance has consequences exclusively between the believer and God. However, mandatory alms (zakat) can also partake of the nature of a tax. Early authorities debated whether zakat could validly be paid to the government; in many premodern Islamic societies, however, the collection of zakat as a tax became standard. Jurists held that the agents of the government could forcibly collect "visible" assets, but that the payment of "concealed" assets was left to the conscience of the individual. Hanafis hold that the Friday congregational prayers must be led by the ruler or his appointed representative; the other schools of law deny that these prayers must be performed under the auspices of the authorities.

The canonical prayers are treated both as potential indicators of the boundaries of the faith community and as a matter of public order. Numerous hadith reports equate prayer with faith, and the failure to pray with unbelief. Failure to perform the obligatory prayers is, at least in theory, considered to be subject to criminal penalties. Those who fail to pray fall into two categories. The first category consists of those who deny the obligation to pray; this constitutes denial of the faith. Recent converts, or Muslims who grew up in remote and uncivilized areas, may claim ignorance and be instructed in the obligation to pray without further penalty. The second category comprises those who do not deny the obligation to pray, but fail to do so out of laziness or indifference. According to the jurists, such a person should be threatened with the death penalty. If he or she does not resume prayer (according to some jurists, after missing three prayers, or after three days), three out of the four Sunni schools of law hold that the death penalty should be imposed. The Hanafi school, in contrast, cites statements by the Prophet suggesting that only explicit apostasy can incur execution. Among those jurists who advocate the death penalty, it is debated whether failure to pray constitutes apostasy (in which case the offender would not be buried as a Muslim, and Muslim relatives would not inherit) or whether the execution is a *ḥadd* penalty analogous (for instance) to the penalty for adultery. The Hanbali jurist Ibn Qudama (d. 1223) points out that in reality, there are many Muslims who fail to pray; in practice, they are not separated from their Muslim spouses (as would be necessary if they were held to be apostates), nor are their Muslim heirs denied shares in their estates (*al-Mughni*, 3:357).

Manuals for market inspectors (*muḥtasib*s) indicate that such officials might exhort and pressure individuals to perform public prayer regularly and in an approved manner and to punish offenders. Public officials, however, are not entitled to enquire into the private ritual activities of individuals or to demand oaths affirming their performance. Authorities are not empowered to enforce any specific interpretation of the rite of prayer or any other ritual; individuals are entitled to select their own modes of worship, within the boundaries of the accepted schools of law. The Maliki legal theorist al-Qarafi (d. 1285) states that judicial verdicts (*ḥukm*) do not apply to the category of acts of worship. No judge has the authority to rule that a given prayer is valid or invalid; any statement that he makes to this effect would have the status of a fatwa, or a nonbinding legal opinion. Similarly, if a Shafi'i judge follows the doctrine of his school by accepting the testimony of a single witness on the sighting of the new moon of Ramadan, an individual Maliki has no obligation to follow his ruling and begin to fast (*Kitab al-furuq*, 4:1180).

BIBLIOGRAPHY

Denny, Frederick M. "Islamic Ritual: Perspectives and Theories." In *Approaches to Islam in Religious Studies*, edited by Richard S. Martin, pp. 63–77. Tucson: University of Arizona Press, 1985. Surveys different approaches to the interpretation of Islamic ritual.

Ghazali, Muhammad ibn Muhammad al-. *Ihya' 'ulum al-Din*. 5 vols. Beirut, 1994.

Graham, William A. "Islam in the Mirror of Ritual." In *Islam's Understanding of Itself*, edited by Richard G. Hovannisian and Speros Vryonis, Jr., pp. 53–71. Malibu, Calif.: Undena Publications, 1983. Argues that Islamic ritual is distinctively defined by the element of obedience to divine fiat, rather than symbolic significance or sacramental efficacy.

Ibn Abi Shayba, 'Abd Allah ibn Muhammad. *Kitab al-Musannaf fi al-ahadith wa'l-athar*. 9 vols. Beirut, 1995.

Ibn 'Abidin, Muhammad. *Hashiyat radd al-muhtar*. 8 vols. Cairo, 1966.

Ibn Amir al-Hajj, Muhammad ibn Muhammad. *Al-Taqrir wa 'l-tahbir*. 3 vols. Beirut: Dar al Kutub al-'Ilmiyya, 1983.

Ibn Qudama, 'Abd Allah ibn Ahmad. *Al-Mughni*. Edited by 'Abd Allah al-Turki. 15 vols. Cairo: Hajr, 1986–1990.

Jurjani, 'Ali ibn Muhammad al-. *Kitab al-Ta'rifat*. Beirut, 1983.

Kafawi, Abu'l-Baqa' al-. *Al-kulliyat*. Beirut: Al-Risala, 1992.

Katz, Marion H. "The Study of Islamic Ritual and the Meaning of *Wudū'*." *Der Islam* 82 (2005): 106–145. Discusses Islamic jurists' debates over whether Islamic ritual ablutions have a comprehensible meaning or symbolic significance.

Powers, Paul R. "Interiors, Intentions, and the 'Spirituality' of Islamic Ritual Practice." *Journal of the American Academy of Religion* 72 (2004): 425–459. Discusses the significance of the concept of *niyya* (intent) in juristic interpretations of Islamic ritual.

Qarafi, Ahmad ibn Idris al-. *Kitab al-Furuq*. 4 vols. Cairo: Dar al-Salam, 2001.

Sulami, 'Abd-'Aziz ibn 'Abd al-Salam al-. *Qawa'id al-ahkam fi masalih al-anam*. 2 vols. in one. Beirut, 1990.

Zarkashi, Muhammad ibn Bahadur al-. *Al-Bahr al-muhit fi usul al-fiqh*. 4 vols. Beirut: Dar al-Kutub al-'Ilmiyya, 2000.

MARION HOLMES KATZ

WOUNDING IN CHINESE LAW. The law of wounding throughout the imperial period was characterized by two essential features. First, liability was graded according to both the implement by which the wound was inflicted and the place or nature of the injury, and, second, liability on account of wounding was increased to liability on account of homicide should the victim die from the wound within a certain time. In Tang (618–907 C.E.) and pre-Tang law a distinction is further drawn between wounds inflicted in the course of a fight and those deliberately inflicted, but this distinction is not present in Ming (1368–1644 C.E.) and Qing (1644–1911) law. The reason for the change was perhaps the consideration that there was still an intention to wound in a fight. Hence, the law saw no need to maintain a category of "deliberate wounding" as distinct from one of "wounding in a fight." The distinction remained of importance only in the case where the victim died from the wound and liability for killing came into question.

Definition and Punishment of the Offense. These features are already apparent in the Qin laws of the third century B.C.E. (see Hulsewé [1985], D 65–66, 68, 70–71) and the Han code of 186 B.C.E. The latter contains articles (*Ernian lüling* slips 21, 25, 27–28, 31) which provide:

(i) that there is to be no liability if a wound is inflicted accidentally (*guoshi*) or in the course of a game (*xi*);
(ii) that where a person deliberately (*zei*) wounds another, the punishment is to be tattooing and the most severe form of hard labor;
(iii) that where in a fight one uses a sword, spear, lance, or cudgel and inflicts a wound, in all cases the punishment is to be the most severe form of hard labor without tattooing;
(iv) that where such weapons are not used but a person is blinded in one eye or has a limb, tooth, or finger broken or his nose or ear torn or cut, the punishment is to be hard labor;
(v) that where no wound has been inflicted but a person has been struck (*ou*), a fine of two ounces of gold is to be imposed, increased to four ounces should the victim be of higher rank;
(vi) that where the "wound" consists merely of a bruise or welt, a fine of four ounces of gold is to be imposed; and
(vii) that where a woman is struck in a fight and suffers a miscarriage, the punishment is to be hard labor.

By the end of the first century B.C.E. the code contained a more general formulation, providing that where a person was wounded with a cutting weapon in a fight the punishment is to be four years' hard labor, increased by one degree to five years if the wound was deliberately (*zei*) inflicted (Hulsewé (1955), p. 254).

The code of the Tang Dynasty (618–907 C.E.) distinguishes between beating or striking (*ou*) and wounding (*shang*). Article 302 provides that if someone strikes another with his hands or feet, the punishment is forty blows with the light stick, increased to sixty blows with the heavy stick if he inflicted a (light) wound, defined here as the drawing of blood, or used some other weapon for the beating. Article 303 specifies that if a tooth is broken, an ear or the nose injured, the sight of one eye damaged, a finger or toe broken, a bone fractured, or a wound inflicted by means of hot liquid or fire, the punishment is penal servitude for one year, increased to one and a half years where two or more teeth, fingers, or toes were broken or the victim became bald. Article 304, dealing with swords and the like, specifies that the mere use of such a weapon in a fight entails a punishment of one hundred blows with the heavy stick, even if no wound is inflicted. If a wound of any kind is inflicted, or if (otherwise) the victim has two ribs broken or the sight of both eyes damaged, or, if a woman, suffers a miscarriage, the punishment is two years of penal servitude. For the infliction of more serious injuries, such as the removal of the tongue, the punishment is to be exile to a distance of three thousand *li*, approximately one thousand miles (Article 305).

The Ming and Qing codes are broadly similar, with slight variations in the punishments (Ming art. 325; Qing art. 302). However, two important differences from the Tang law should be noted. All codes allow redemption for accidental wounding, but otherwise they differ in the relevance they attach to the "source" of the wound. The later codes treat wounds inflicted in the course of a game in the same way as those inflicted in a fight, while the Tang imposes a lesser punishment. The Tang code also provides that the punishment for deliberately inflicted wounds should be one degree more than that for wounds inflicted in a fight, but this distinction is suppressed in the Ming and Qing codes (Tang arts. 306, 338, 339; Ming art. 315; Qing art. 292). The second difference is that the later codes, following Mongolian practice that had been incorporated into the law of the Yuan Dynasty (1276–1368 C.E.), provided that where the injury led to permanent incapacity, half the property of the offender was to be given to the victim for his maintenance.

The *Baogu* System: Death Resulting from Wound. Should the victim die from his wounds, a set of rules known as *baogu* came into play. These rules determined the period of time within which the victim must die if the offense was to be one of wounding and not homicide. The Han code of 186 B.C.E. provided that, where the victim died from the wound within twenty days, the offender was to be held liable for killing (*Ernian lüling*, slip 24). The Tang code has a fully elaborated system, establishing the length of the relevant periods by reference to the nature of the weapon and gravity of the wound. For example, where the wound was inflicted only by hands or feet, the period was to be ten days; if by "another object," twenty days; and if by knives and the like, thirty days. If a limb was maimed or dislocated or a bone broken, irrespective of the nature of the implement, the period was to be fifty days (Article 307). If death in any of the above cases have resulted within the prescribed period, the circumstances in which the wound was inflicted determined the applicable category of homicide.

The Ming (art. 326) and Qing (art. 303) codes incorporated the Tang rules but made substantial changes. The ten-day period was changed to twenty, and the victim was to be entrusted to the care of the offender, upon whom was placed the responsibility of undertaking the cure. A Ming substatute introduced the concept of "the extra limit," by which each of the periods of time specified in the article of the code was to be extended (the twenty- or thirty-day periods by ten days and the fifty-day period by twenty days). If the victim died from the wound within the "extra limit," a petition to the throne was allowed, with the expectation that the emperor would commute the capital punishment to exile. Qing substatutes, enacted in the eighteenth century, provided that where the death resulted from "wind" introduced through the wound (evidenced principally where the victim died from a stroke), the punishment might be reduced to exile or penal servitude, depending upon the circumstances. Where the original wound had been inflicted in the course of an attempt to kill, irrespective of the time between wounding and death, the offender was to be sentenced on the ground of intentional killing or plotting to kill.

Self-Defense. Self-defense was accorded limited recognition as a ground of mitigation where wounds were inflicted in the course of a fight. The Tang code provides that if one party is in the right when returning a blow—acting purely in self defense—the punishment for inflicting the wound is two degrees less than that provided by the code (art. 310). The Ming (art. 325) and Qing (art. 302) codes broadly followed the Tang rule.

Status. The kinship relationship between the offender and victim profoundly affected the gravity of the offense and so the severity of the punishment. It was a much more serious offense for a junior relative (including a wife) to wound a senior relative (including a husband) than vice versa.

[*See also* Homicide, *subentry on* Chinese Law; Punishment, *subentry on* Chinese Law; *and* Punishment and Status in Chinese Law.]

BIBLIOGRAPHY

PRIMARY WORKS

Hulsewé, A. F. P. *Remnants of Ch'in Law: An Annotated Translation of the Ch'in Legal and Administrative Rules of the 3rd Century B.C. Discovered in Yün-meng Prefecture, Hu-pei Province, in 1975.* Leiden, Netherlands: E. J. Brill, 1985.

Hulsewé, A. F. P. *Remnants of Han Law*. Leiden, Netherlands: E. J. Brill, 1955–.

Johnson, Wallace, trans. *The T'ang Code*. 2 vols. Princeton, N.J.: Princeton University Press, 1979–1997.

Jones, William C. *The Great Qing Code*. With the assistance of Tianquan Cheng and Yongling Jiang. Oxford, U.K.: Clarendon Press; New York: Oxford University Press, 1994.

Jiang Yonglin. *The Great Ming Code / Da Ming lü*. Seattle: University of Washington Press, 2005. The is the first translation of the Ming code into a Western language. It omits the substatutes and commentary.

Zhangjiashan Hanmu zhujian. Beijing: Wen wu che ban she, 2001. Contains the recently discovered *Ernian lüling* (statutes and ordinances of 186 B.C.E.).

SECONDARY WORKS

MacCormack, Geoffrey. "The *Pao ku* System of Traditional Chinese Law." *Chinese Culture* 35, no. 4 (1994): 23–48.

GEOFFREY MACCORMACK

WRONGFUL JUDGMENT IN CHINESE LAW.

The general rule respecting wrongful judgment is that the same punishment which the judge wrongly imposed or failed to impose should be imposed on the judge himself. This is termed "reciprocal punishment." The application of this rule in particular cases depends upon the circumstances of the wrongful judgment. The main criteria are:

1. Criminal intent. The rule of reciprocal punishment applies generally to intentional acts of wrongful judgment, whereas accidental misjudgment is subject to penal mitigation.
2. Character of wrongfulness.
   a. Chinese law distinguishes wholly and partially wrongful judgments, that is, full acquittal of an actual offender, or conviction of an innocent person on the one hand, and too lenient or too severe sentencing for the offense in question on the other. Wholly wrongful judgments are subject to the rule of reciprocal punishment, whereas in cases of partial wrongfulness, the degree of wrongfulness is to be measured by a sort of subtraction of a recognized proper sentence from the actual improper conviction. The latter causes great technical difficulties and is resolved in different fashions at different times.
   b. There are periods in Chinese history in which improper acquittal or mitigation is handled with more leniency than improper conviction or aggravation.
3. Time of discovery. The rule of reciprocal punishment generally applies to wrongful judgments which have already been executed. In other words, wrongful punishment, not wrongful judgment, is the main subject of regulation. Therefore, wrongful judgment that is discovered and modified before execution—no matter how or by whom it was discovered—is often subject to substantial mitigation.

The Essential Idea of the Concept. Criteria 1. and 2.a. constitute the main framework of the Chinese concept of wrongful judgment, which mainly reflects the rule of reciprocal punishment from the point of view of two other essential features of the traditional law, that is, the distinction between criminal intent and negligence, and the subordination of judicial sentencing to an objective, quantitative scale of punishment. These two features, like the reciprocal punishment rule, can be traced back to the oldest known positive law of China, the Statutes of the Qin in the late Warring States period (third century B.C.E.). The rule of reciprocal punishment also applies to false accusation with a similar adjustment according to essentially identical criteria. In this sense, the concepts of wrongful judgment and false accusation can be understood as protections against improper prosecution, the former giving protection against acts of public agents and the latter against acts of private agents. Criterion 2.2 seems to arise from considerations of criminal policy, combined with efforts to give the regulation a more humanitarian aspect.

Continuity of Judgment and Execution. As to criterion 3, Chinese traditional law does not distinguish clearly between judicial judgment and the execution of punishment imposed by judicial judgment. There is no procedural element that marks an end to judicial judgment and the beginning of a separate procedure of execution of the sentence. In general, traditional statutes concerning execution merely require that the crime has been properly investigated with clear results, and that there is no suspicion of false charges. Hence, the burden of liability for wrongful judgment is not imposed on a single judge who issued the sentence in question. Instead, almost every person officially involved in a criminal case, from initial prosecution up to the execution of the sentence, incurs liability should the investigation at any intermediate stage prove to be improper.

This situation did not change materially with the construction of complex systems of judicial review in some historical periods. Even an imperial order for execution is made subject to three or five revisions and can be overturned if new doubts arise concerning the charges. Therefore, the whole process of punishing criminals, from initial prosecution through execution of the sentence, may be better understood as a single administrative procedure, distributed over two or more offices. Legislation concerning wrongful judgment provides protection against improper punitive actions by administrative agents and is in fact a regulation of wrongful punishment.

Historical Outline of Legislation Concerning Wrongful Judgment.

Qin. Legislation imposing liability for wrongful judgment can be traced back to the late Warring States period. Bamboo strips excavated from a tomb in Shuihudi in Hu-pei Province prove that the statutes of the Qin state, the forerunner of the first imperial dynasty (Qin, 221–206 B.C.E.), already divided wrong judgment into several types by use of the aforesaid criteria 1 and 2.

1. Wrongful judgment with intent.
   a. Improper acquittal, called *zongqiu* (illicit release of a suspect), or *guzong* (intentional illicit release).
   b. Improper conviction or intentional partially wrongful judgment, called *buzhi* (unjust, not straight).
2. Wrongful judgment without intent, called *shi* (mistake in judgment as to the degree of punishment). In this case, no distinction is drawn between whole and partial wrongfulness, or improper acquittal and conviction.

Han and Jin. With regard to the following Han Dynasty (206 B.C.E.–220 C.E.), the provision concerning wrongful judgment has been almost completely restored from materials unearthed in Zhangjiashan in Hubei Province. Its design follows the rules of the Qin statutes, and reciprocal punishment is imposed in cases 1.a. and 1.b., whereas case 2 is subject to mitigation by redemption by fine or labor. Furthermore, intentional wrongful judgment under the influence of bribery will be reciprocally punished with an increase of two degrees.

For the time between the Han and the Tang (618–907 C.E.), remnants of statutory law are too fragmentary to allow a detailed analysis of legislation concerning wrongful judgment. The publication of the statutes of the Western Jin (265–317 C.E.) written on wooden boards unearthed at Yumen in Gansu Province, will perhaps fill in the blank in the near future.

Tang and Song. The Tang legislation invented a new terminology. It distinguishes:

1. Improper conviction (*ru ren zui*, impose guilt on someone) and acquittal (*chu ren zui*, acquit someone).
2. Criminal intent (*gu*) and mistake (*shi*). In the case of mistake, punishment is mitigated by three degrees for improper conviction (*shi ru ren zui*, unintentionally convict someone) and five degrees for improper acquittal (*shi chu ren zui*, acquit someone by negligence), whereas Vcriminal intent is subject to reciprocal punishment.

There are very detailed rules for the calculation of liability in partial wrongful judgments, but no distinction is drawn in the terminology between complete and partial wrongfulness. Three further points with respect to liability for wrongful judgment may be made. First, liability occurs only in cases in which wrongful judgment makes a difference in punishment, whereas in cases in which, for instance, wrongful findings led to punishment of the same degree as would have a proper finding, the investigators go free. Secondly, if wrongful judgment has not yet resulted in improper punishment or release, or if the improperly released person is captured again or in the meantime has died, the liability of officials involved is mitigated by one degree. Third, if punishment following wrongful judgment is subject to mitigation caused by rank or other personal limitations of criminal liability, as age or physical disabilities, equal mitigation is granted to the persons liable for the judgment.

Corresponding legislation in the Song (960–1279 C.E.) and following dynasties basically follows the Tang Code. Rules for the calculation of liability in partial wrongful judgments were altered slightly and adjusted to changes in the penal system.

[*See also* Collective Liability; Corruption in Chinese Law; Intention in Chinese Law; Sentence in Chinese Law; *and* Zang.]

BIBLIOGRAPHY

Hulsewé, A. F. P. *Remnants of Ch'in Law: An Annotated Translation of the Ch'in Legal and Administrative Rules of the 3rd Century B.C. Discovered in Yün-meng Prefecture, Hu-pei Province, in 1975.* Leiden, Netherlands: E. J. Brill, 1985.

Hulsewé, A. F. P. *Remnants of Han Law.* Leiden, Netherlands: E. J. Brill, 1955.

Johnson, Wallace, trans. *The Tang Code.* 2 vols. Princeton: Princeton University Press, 1979–97. A translation of the Tang Code with commentary (*Tanglü shuyi*).

Momiyama, Akira. "Shin no Saibanseidō no Fukugen (Reconstruction of the Trial-System in Qin)." In Hayashi Inao, *Sengokujidai Shutudobunbutsu no Kenkyū.* Kyoto: Kyoto University Institute for Research in Humanities, 1985. See pp. 529–573. Revised in Momiyama Akira, *Chūgoku Kodai Soshōseidō no Kenkyū.* Kyoto, Kyoto University Press, 2006. See pp. 53–124. Contains explanation of *buzhi*, etc.

Shuihudi Qin mu zhu jian zhenglixiaozu. *Shuihudi Qin mu zhu jian.* Beijing, 1990. A report on the bamboo strips unearthed from a Qin grave in Shuihudi, by the editorial board of Shuihudi Qin mu zhu jian.

Sueyasu Ando (Arnd Helmut Hafner). "Shohyō: Momiyama Akira, 'Chūgoku Kodai Soshōseidō no Kenkyū,'" (Book Review of Momiyama Akira, *Research on Legal Proceedings in Ancient Chinese Law*). In Tōyōshikenkyū 66, no. 3 (2007). Contains a discussion on Continuity of Judgment and Execution, and the obstacles it raises for the correct understanding of traditional Chinese trial.

Zhangjiashan 247hao hanmu zhujian zhenglixiaozu. *Zhangjiashan Hanmu Zhujian.* Beijing, 2001. A report by the editorial board on the bamboo strips unearthed from Han grave No. 247 in Zhangjiashan.

ARND HELMUT HAFNER

Y

YEMEN. According to Islamic tradition, during his lifetime in the first century of the Muslim era (seventh century C.E.) the prophet Muhammad sent judges to Yemen. Most notable among those dispatched was the youthful 'Ali ibn Abi Talib, the future caliph and the Prophet's son-in-law. At the departure of a man named Mu'adh ibn Jabal, who was posted to Yemen (and also to the Hadramawt, part of the present-day Republic of Yemen), a famous interchange reportedly occurred. The Prophet asked, "On what basis will you judge?"

> Mu'adh: "According to the Book of God [the Qur'an]."
> Muhammad: "And if [the solution] is not found [there]?"
> Mu'adh: "According to the practice (Sunna) of the Prophet of God."
> Muhammad: "And if [the solution] is not found there?"
> Mu'adh: "I will exercise my own opinion."

Hearing these responses, the Prophet expressed confidence that he was sending "a man of knowledge" to Yemen as his judge. At the time, however, neither the judgeship itself nor the several schools of legal interpretation had been formalized.

The twelfth-century Yemeni jurist-historian Ibn Samura begins his account of the introduction of the Islamic legal regime into greater Yemen with mentions of these early events, but his main focus is the subsequent history of the Sunni school named after the prominent jurist Muhammad ibn Idris al-Shafi'i (d. 820). Ibn Samura states that the Hanafi and Maliki schools enjoyed initial popularity among Yemeni jurists but that from the fifth Muslim century (eleventh century C.E.) the Shafi'i school came to predominate in the southern part of the highlands, known as Lower Yemen, and also in Aden and its surrounding districts and in the Hadramawt. Ibn Samura's biographical history names individual jurists who traveled to centers of instruction such as Baghdad, as well as to nearby Mecca and Medina, and who then returned to Yemen to teach the new books of Shafi'i jurisprudence to their own students, some of whom later served as judges. These and many succeeding generations of Yemeni jurists formed part of the cosmopolitan Shafi'i school, which also had adherents in Egypt, the central Middle East, the Indian Ocean littoral, and in populous Southeast Asia. As in these other settings, authoritative texts by Abu Shuja', a resident of Basra active in the twelfth century, and by the Syrian Nawawi (d. 1277) became standards of instruction among the Shafi'is of Yemen. Before detailing the local dissemination of the Shafi'i school, however, Ibn Samura briefly mentions the earlier advent of two Shi'i movements, the Isma'ilis and the Zaydis, each of which would also have an enduring and mutually antagonistic presence in the highlands. For this Sunni author the appearances of these Shi'is on the scene represented instances of "discord" (*fitna*).

The Zaydis. Little is known of the legal aspects of the Isma'ili polities and societies that existed in Yemen, except for their reliance on a tenth-century law book, *Da'a'im al-Islam* (The Pillars of Islam), by al-Qadi al-Nu'man. A great deal is known, by contrast, about the Zaydis, who were dominant in the northern part of the highlands, or Upper Yemen, for more than a thousand years, down to the middle of the twentieth century. Zayd ibn 'Ali (d. 740), the eponym of the school, was a fifth-generation descendant of the Prophet whose name is associated with one of the earliest Muslim legal texts. Zaydi history began in Kufa, Iraq, and one branch later flourished in the Caspian region of Iran, but most of the school's juridical and related political history unfolded in Yemen. Unlike the situation of jurists in the Sunni schools, whose legal-religious authority generally stood apart from the temporal state authority of figures such as sultans and kings, the Zaydi polity was an imamate, a classical type of Islamic state in which legal-religious leadership and temporal leadership were unified in the rule of qualified shari'a interpreters known as imams. The Zaydi imams were unlike the Isma'ili imams in that the latter were considered infallible.

In the late ninth century, al-Hadi, the first Zaydi imam to establish himself in Yemen, was invited by tribes in the vicinity of the northern town of Sa'da to intervene in their conflicts. Although al-Hadi and the long line of Zaydi imams following him stood for the shari'a, from the outset their legal regime had to deal with the rules and the representatives of tribal custom. Located at the apex of shari'a justice, ruling imams appointed court judges and assessed their conduct, but they also remained key figures in major customary settlements. As opposed to the nomadic existence of the Arabian Bedouin, the tribes of Yemen were sedentary, village-residing cultivators. In addition to the central authority of the imam himself and the scholarship that occurred in town madrasas, small groups of Zaydis settled in numerous rural tribal districts of Upper Yemen in protected enclaves known as *hijra*s. As descendants of the Prophet and as jurists, they represented the shariʻa in the countryside while also specializing in the customary resolution of disputes.

Many of the ruling Zaydi imams over the centuries were prolific academic jurists whose scholarly books formed part of the accumulating doctrinal discussions of the school. Like that of the Ismaʻilis as set forth by al-Qadi al-Nuʻman, the Zaydi school—with notable exceptions, such as, for example, the rules concerning preemption—was relatively close to the four Sunni schools: Hanafi, Hanbali, Maliki, and Shafiʻi. Meanwhile the Zaydi school (similar to the Sunni) is classified among Shiʻi schools, along with the Ismaʻili and Imami schools, to the extent that it has sometimes been referred to as the fifth Shiʻi school. Al-Hadi, who left two major works, gave his name to the Hadawi mainstream of Zaydi school juridical thought. A later imam, al-Mahdi li-Din Allah Ahmad ibn Yahya al-Murtada (d. 1436), authored *Kitab al-Azhar* (The Book of Flowers), which became the mainstay of Zaydi-Hadawi law. This concise treatise not only served as the introductory text for all subsequent generations of Zaydi students but also generated the most important literary tradition in Zaydi jurisprudence, accumulating more than thirty commentaries. The first of these were by Imam al-Murtada himself and by his learned sister Dahmaʼ. The most authoritative is the fifteenth-century commentary by al-Murtada's student, ʻAbd Allah ibn Miftah (d. 1472), which, although it had a regular title, came to be known simply as *Sharh al-Azhar* (The Commentary on the Flowers).

In later centuries, beginning before and continuing after an interval of Ottoman rule (1538–1636), during which the Hanafi school was official in highland Yemen, there arose from the Zaydi mainstream a series of distinguished oppositional jurists known as "Sunnis" for their turn away from the standard Shiʻi sources to reliance upon Sunni works of hadith. The first of these was Muhammad ibn Ibrahim al-Wazir (d. 1436), and the last and most prominent was Muhammad ibn ʻAli al-Shawkani (d. 1834). Shawkani was also a staunch advocate of the continuing necessity of *ijtihād*, or independent legal reasoning, and now is recognized as one of the founders of Islamic modernism. He was a prolific author in law and other disciplines; he wrote a major biographical history of leading Muslim jurists, Yemeni and non-Yemeni. In addition to important works in *uṣūl*, the theory and method of the law, he also wrote in the applied *furūʻ* literature, including a scathing commentary on the classic Hadawi text *Kitab al-azhar*. Shawkani acted as a mufti issuing fatwas both momentous and minor—the former collected in book form, and the latter, which he said "could never be counted," leaving no archival trace—and he also served as the head shariʻa judge, the *qāḍī al-quḍāt*, in the Zaydi state of his time.

The Ottomans. When the Ottomans returned a second time to the highlands in the fifty-year period around the turn of the twentieth century, they introduced their newly drafted, shariʻa-derived civil-law code known as the Majalla or Mecelle, which a number of Yemenis studied, together with other new judicial institutions. Among these were new model courts, but these had only a brief history in the highlands as a parallel jurisdiction to the regular shariʻa courts. The Ottomans also brought an appeal court for the shariʻa jurisdictions, and this important institution continued to function in Yemen after the end of the empire in 1918. The Zaydi imam of the period, Yahya Hamid al-Din, who proclaimed himself in 1904, assumed control of both Upper and Lower Yemen in 1918 in an independent state. The shariʻa, according to the Zaydi school, was the law of the land. The imam himself appointed judges, ratified appeals, and was the final arbiter of the law.

During Imam Yahya's rule as king of Yemen (1918–1948), instruction in the law, with an emphasis on *Kitab al-azhar* and its major commentaries and also on the works of Shawkani and other leading "Sunnis," was instituted in a new-style madrasa opened in the capital, Sanaa (or Sanʻa), in 1924. Representing what may be the last commentary on *Kitab al-azhar*, and also the first written for printed publication, a four-volume work by Ahmad Qasim al-ʻAnsi appeared in the years 1938–1947. Earlier, another commentary and *Kitab al-azhar* itself appeared in printed editions. Like a number of their historical predecessors in the imamate, Imam Yahya and his son Imam Ahmad (r. 1948–1962) issued lists of doctrinal "choices" (*ikhtiyārāt*) on selected points of law. These were meant to guide court judges in their decisions and are referenced as such in judgments of that period. In the absence of Western colonial rule, which typically restricted the purview of Islamic law to matters of family law, the shariʻa courts of the twentieth-century imamate handled not only marriage, inheritance, and family endowment but also criminal cases, a variety of landed-property matters, and the occasional commercial dispute. Unlike many other historical settings—including much of the Ottoman heartlands, where there were contrasting systems of land tenure—in the Yemeni highlands the agrarian property relations prevailing on the ground were congruent with the system of individual ownership (known as *milk*) envisioned in shariʻa doctrine.

In Lower Yemen, with the return of Sunni rule by the Ottomans, the biographical histories report local adherents continuing to study the Shafiʻi texts. But with the end of the empire and the beginning of Zaydi rule some of the leading Shafiʻi jurists, by such gestures as commenting on the ruling imam's doctrinal "choices," adapted themselves to the new official school to make themselves eligible for appointments as judges. Further south and east, in Aden, the surrounding sultanates, and the Hadramawt, other Shafi'i jurists found themselves under the sway of the colonial British, who had seized Aden in 1839. English judges read their Nawawi in English translation, and because of the administrative connection with British India, there also was some influence in Aden of the hybrid Anglo-Muhammadan law. In addition to a variety of modern laws touching on the shari'a that were promulgated in the Crown Colony of Aden, on such topics as marriage and endowments, several of the surrounding sultanates also issued newly codified laws and, and some of these, in matters of leases and irrigation, also reflected the encroachment of the new cash economy. The Jews of Yemen, most of whom departed for Israel in the late 1940s, interacted both with Muslim courts and with the rural representatives of customary law. The history of their own jurisdictions and legal thought has yet to be written.

In the years after their respective revolutions in 1962 and 1967, the new nation-state republics in the former imamic north and in the former colonial south issued constitutions. That of the Yemen Arab Republic (YAR) in the north proclaimed in its Article 3, "The Islamic shari'a is the source of all laws." By contrast, in the southern regime known as the People's Democratic Republic of Yemen (PDRY), laws were adapted from Soviet-bloc socialist countries. The YAR embarked on a program of legislation, and many of the new laws, from bank codes to trademark laws, were not in any strict sense based on the shari'a. The modern university that opened in Sanaa in 1965 includes a College of Shari'a and Law that began to train modern lawyers. Shari'a-court judges began to receive formal training at the new High Judicial Institute. When the YAR and the PDRY were unified in 1990, the initial constitution of the new Republic of Yemen stated in its Article 3, "The Islamic shari'a is the main source of all laws," with the important added word "main" meant to reflect the different legal history of the southern regime. But after the southern socialists were vanquished in the civil war of 1994, Article 3 was amended to state, once again, "The Islamic shari'a is the source of all laws."

[*See also* Arab Countries, Islamic Law in; Islamic Schools of Sacred Law; Mahdi li-Din Allah Ahmad ibn Yahya al-Murtada, al-; Qadi al-Nu'man, Ibn Muhammad ibn Mansur, al-; *and* Zayd ibn 'Ali.]

BIBLIOGRAPHY

Anderson, J. N. D. *Islamic Law in Africa*. London: Frank Cass, 1970. Originally published in 1954.

Dresch, Paul. *Tribes, Government, and History in Yemen*. Oxford: Clarendon Press, 1989.

Haykel, Bernard. *Revival and Reform in Islam: The Legacy of Muhammad al-Shawkani*. Cambridge, U.K.: Cambridge University Press, 2003.

Ho, Engseng. *The Graves of Tarim: Genealogy and Mobility across the Indian Ocean*. Berkeley: University of California Press, 2006.

Hollander, Isaac. *Jews and Muslims in Lower Yemen: A Study in Protection and Restraint, 1918–1949*. Leiden, Netherlands: E. J. Brill, 2005.

Maktari, A. M. A. *Water Rights and Irrigation Practices in Lahj: A Study of the Application of Customary and Shari'a Law in South-west Arabia*. Cambridge, U.K.: Cambridge University Press, 1971.

Mermier, Franck. *Le cheikh de la nuit, Sanaa: Organisation des souks et socieéteé citadine*. Paris: Sinbad, 1997.

Messick, Brinkley. *The Calligraphic State: Textual Domination and History in a Muslim Society*. Berkeley: University of California Press, 1993.

Mundy, Martha. *Domestic Government: Kinship, Community, and Polity in North Yemen*. London: I. B. Tauris, 1995.

Weir, Shelagh. *A Tribal Order: Politics and Law in the Mountains of Yemen*. Austin: University of Texas Press, 2007.

Würth, Anna. *As-Sari'a fi Bab al-Yaman*. Berlin: Duncker und Humblot, 2000.

BRINKLEY MESSICK

ZAHIRI SCHOOL OF ISLAMIC LAW. *See* Islamic Schools of Sacred Law, *subentry on* Sunni Schools: The Zahiri School of Law.

ZAÏRE. *See* African Law, Sub-Saharan, *subentry on* After Independence.

ZAMBIA. *See* African Law, Sub-Saharan, *subentries on* The Colonial Period *and* After Independence.

ZANG. One of the most important concepts in the Chinese legal codes is that of *zang* (*tsang* in Wade-Giles transliteration), a term that may be translated broadly as "illicit goods." It underlies a large number of rules concerned with theft, corruption, misappropriation of property, and loss of or damage to goods. Although in all cases the punishment is graduated according to the value of the *zang*, the scale used for the determination of the punishment varies according to the gravity of the offense.

Types of Zang. Although *zang* is used in the Han Code of 186 B.C.E. to express the fact that liability (in different contexts) is to be based on the value of the goods forming the subject of the offense (*Ernian lüling*, slips 20, 58–60, 199), it is not until the code of the Tang Dynasty (618–907 C.E.) that we have detailed evidence of its critical role in the rules imposing liability for offenses connected with property. The code distinguishes six types of *zang*:

(1) goods taken by forcible theft,
(2) goods taken by ordinary theft,
(3) bribes taken to subvert the law,
(4) bribes taken without subversion of the law,
(5) property accepted by officials from persons under their jurisdiction, and
(6) goods underlying a variety of offenses where liability is expressed by the phrase *zuozang* (liability on account of illicit goods) (art. 33, commentary, in Johnson).

These six types can be regarded as expressing broad categories of offense, each category comprising a large number of distinct rules.

For each category, the punishment is determined according to a particular scale which correlates units of value with specific penalties. For example, the forcible theft of goods worth a piece of cloth one foot in length is punished with penal servitude for three years, and that of goods worth four hundred feet of cloth is punished by strangulation (art. 281). In the case of ordinary theft, the punishment for goods worth a piece of cloth one foot in length is sixty blows with the heavy stick, while that for stealing goods worth five hundred feet of cloth is exile with added labor (the maximum) (art. 282). This means that, in addition to exile, the offender is subjected to forced labor at the place of exile. In the case of the residual category called *zuozang*, the penalty starts with a beating of twenty blows with the light stick and progresses to a maximum of three years' penal servitude (art. 389).

Some changes occur in the codes of the Ming (1368–1644 C.E.) and Qing (1644–1911 C.E.) dynasties. The principal difference is that the Tang category of forcible theft is suppressed: the Ming and Qing codes punished all cases of forcible theft, irrespective of the value of what was taken, with beheading (Ming art. 289, in Jiang; Qing art. 266, in Jones) and replaced with the category of commoners stealing from the government. As in the Tang Code, the scale governing the allocation of punishment varies according to the category, though the unit of value is no longer length of cloth but weight of silver.

Multiple Offenses. The Tang Code provides that in the case of "repeated offenses," that is, where one person has committed several different offenses all involving *zang* or the same offense (as theft) against three or more persons, the offender is not to be sentenced separately in respect of each specific offense. Instead, the *zang* involved in all offenses are to be combined and the total halved, the half providing the basis for the sentence according to the most lenient of the applicable scales (art. 45, in Johnson).

Ming and Qing law assigns a much more restricted scope to this rule. The benefit of halving the total is not to be applied in cases where supervisory officials steal, where commoners steal from the government, where officials take bribes and subvert the law, or where there has been ordinary theft. In the first three cases, all the *zang* obtained are totaled and the offender sentenced on the basis of the final amount, while in the fourth case (ordinary theft) there is no totaling, and the offender is sentenced on the basis of the single most serious theft from the one owner.

The *zang* are to be totaled and the final amount halved only in cases of *zuozang* or where officials have accepted bribes without subverting the law. There is still a difference between these two cases. In the second, because no harm has been done, the offender is always to be sentenced on the basis of half the *zang*, even though there has been only one bribe.

Return of Zang. The earliest rule we have is that of the Han Code of 186 B.C.E., providing that stolen goods (the *zang*), if still in existence, were to be returned to the owner (slip 59). Later codes have more complex rules. The Tang Code provides that, where the offender still possessed the "original illicit goods" or other goods for which these had been exchanged, such goods were to be returned to the owner. In the case of theft, double the value was to be restored, as a further punishment for the offender's greed. If both the giver and receiver of illicit goods committed an offense, as in the case of the offer and acceptance of a bribe, or if a private person possessed prohibited goods such as military weapons, the illicit goods were not to be restored to the owner but confiscated by the government. If the illicit goods had already been consumed, the value was to be paid to the owner, provided the offender had not been sentenced to death or exile, an exception grounded in imperial benevolence (art. 33, in Johnson).

The Ming and Qing codes adopt these rules with certain modifications: there is no longer to be repayment of double the value in the case of theft, the value of illicit goods acquired by unauthorized use of labor or appropriation of rent is to be restored to the owner unless the offender has died, and the general obligation to pay the equivalent in value of expended illicit goods subsists unless the offender has died or been executed (Ming art. 23, in Jiang; Qing art. 24, in Jones).

[*See also* Corruption in Chinese Law; Deceit; Damage to Property in Chinese Law; *and* Theft, subentry on Chinese Law.]

BIBLIOGRAPHY

PRIMARY WORKS

Ernian lüling. This recently discovered collection of the statutes and ordinances of 186 B.C.E. is the earliest extant "code" to have survived in China. It is cited according to the edition published in *Zangjiashan Hanmu zhujian*, Peking, 2001. "Slip" refers to the number assigned to the bamboo fragments—from the Han Dynasty graves at Zhangjiashan—used in the reconstruction of the text.

Jiang Yonglin. *The Great Ming Code / Da Ming lü*. Seattle: University of Washington Press, 2005.

Johnson, Wallace, trans. *The T'ang Code*. 2 vols. Princeton: Princeton University Press, 1979–97. These volumes contain a complete translation of the Tang code, the most important source of Tang law, and of great significance for the later development of Chinese law.

Jones, William C., trans. *The Great Qing Code*. Oxford: Clarendon Press, 1994. This is the most authoritative translation into a Western language of the articles of the Qing penal code, but it omits the all-important substatutes and the commentaries.

Philastre, P. L. F. *Le code annamite*. 2 vols. 2d ed. Taipei: Ch'eng-wen, 1967. This work, first published in 1909, is a translation into French of the Vietnamese code of 1812, which closely followed the Qing code. It is invaluable for its translation of the substatutes and commentaries.

SECONDARY WORKS

MacCormack, Geoffrey. "The Concept of *Tsang* in the T'ang Code." *Revue internationale des droits de l'antiquité* 33 (1986), pp. 25–44.

MacCormack, Geoffrey. *Traditional Chinese Penal Law*. Edinburgh: University of Edinburgh Press, 1990. This contains a brief account of the nature of *zang* (*tsang*) and of the development of the relevant rules from the Tang to the Qing.

GEOFFREY MACCORMACK

ZANZIBAR. *See* African Law, Sub-Saharan, *subentries on* The Precolonial Period; The Colonial Period; *and* After Independence.

ZASIUS, ULRICH (1461–1535). Zasius was the first German jurist of international significance, and a great champion of humanistic jurisprudence. He studied first in Tübingen, worked after that as a recorder in the religious court in Konstanz, performed the office of city recorder in Freiburg in Breisgau starting in 1494, and there recommenced the study of law in 1499. He received his doctorate of jurisprudence in 1501 and finally, in 1506, attained to the rank of professor of law.

Zasius was the German jurist of the late Middle Ages who, through both teaching and practicing law, was responsible for focusing critical attention within the German legal world on the dominant Roman-canonical legal system, influenced as it was by Italy. He wanted to teach only "that which accords with the situation in Germany." From this stance, he developed the basis for a modern, self-contained German jurisprudence. In the legislative realm, he increased significantly the influence of Roman law through the introduction of a 1520 reform of Freiburg's city laws, but did so without thereby simply making Roman law primary. Zasius was also a highly sought attorney; his counsels were recorded in his *Opera omnia* (Complete works) which was published by a student of his—Joachim Mynsinger—and by his son J. U. Zasius in 1550–1551 and 1590. His many ties to European humanism, which had found its particular haven in nearby Basel, bred in Zasius a deep admiration for humanistically shaped jurisprudence. He promoted intensively the new, strongly philologically oriented legal methods, and sent some of his favorite students—among them Bonifacius Amerbach (1495–1562), later to become a printer and jurist in Basel—to study law at the University of Avignon. There, Andrea Alciati (1492–1550), the founder of humanistic legal studies and a man he deeply admired, taught. It was Zasius's authority, then, that opened the German legal sphere to humanistic jurisprudence. That said, from a scholarly perspective, Zasius himself cannot be properly said to have been a humanistically oriented jurist. His works could not meet the high philological standards of the humanists because of his lack of mastery of the ancient languages. Nonetheless, his best known works—*Lucubrationes* (Night musings, 1520) and *Intellectus singulares* (Individual essays on the law, 1526)—sought both in title and in style to align themselves with humanistic legal scholarship. These developed out of his activities as a teacher, and dealt with selected points from the Corpus Iuris Civilis. His enormous success as a teacher had to do with his fundamental position: that juridical exegesis needed to both be practicable and return the wording of the laws to the foreground. From this position, he spearheaded a general dissociation from Italy's juridical authority, a turning away from the scholastic method of teaching, and a movement toward a self-contained German legal scholarship.

[*See also* Alciati, Andrea; *and* Humanism.]

BIBLIOGRAPHY

Amerbach, Bonifacius. *Die Amerbachkorrespondenz*, edited and compiled by Alfred Hartmann; continued by B. R. Jenny. 10 vols. Basel, Switzerland: Verlag der Universitätsbibliothek, 1942–1995.

Juristas universales (zu ergänzen).

Ulrich Zasius (1461–1535). German Jurist. Engraving by Theodor de Brij, 1648. MARY EVANS PICTURE LIBRARY

Kleinheyer/Schröder 4.A. 1996, S. 455–459.

Rowan, Steven. *Ulrich Zasius:- A Jurist in the German Renaissance, 1461–1535*. Frankfurt am Main, Germany: V. Klostermann, 1987.

Zasius, Ulrich. *Opera omnia*. Lyon 1590, reprint Frankfurt am Main, Germany, 2006.

JOCHEN OTTO
Translated from the German by Ira Allen

ZAYD IBN ʿALI (A.H. 80/699 C.E.–A.H. 122/740 C.E.). A great-grandson of ʿAli ibn Abi Talib and Fatima, and the eponym of the Zaydiyya. He was born in Medina, where he received his religious training. He was involved in a revolt in Kufa against the Umayyads over legitimacy; it failed, and he lost his life on the battlefield. The Shiʿi debated the conduct of the caliphs Abu Bakr and ʿUmar. Some of them (Imami) radically rejected it, but Zayd took a moderate position, even while claiming that ʿAli and his successors had the pre-eminent right to power. This moderate position was reflected in the scholarly doctrine of his school.

Zayd is considered a *faqīh*, a commentator on the Qurʾan, an orator, and a gifted poet. It is doubtful, however, that he wrote the works attributed to him. For instance, the strong legitimistic tone of the *Risala ithbat wasiyyat amir al-Muʾminin* is hardly in accord with Zayd's generally attested political position. Moreover, the *Manasik al-hajj wa-ahkamuha*, transmitted from Abu Khalid al-Wasiti (d. 150/767), cannot be considered authentic. Griffini, however, regards it undoubtedly as such, which would make it one of the most ancient extant *fiqh* works. Doubts exist also over the authenticity of the *Tafsir gharib al-Qurʾan*, transmitted from Abu Khalid, with an anti-Qadari tone.

The question of the authenticity of Zayd's works involves the origin of Zaydi juridical science as well. The debate over *Majmuʿ al-fiqh* is paradigmatic. This work is presented by Griffini as the most ancient codification of Islamic jurisprudence, an opinion shared by Sezgin, who considers Zayd its true author. Both believe that it originated in a very ancient period before the time when divisions split the Islamic community, and that the juridical science and the related writings already existed in the first century A.H. A radical break between Sunni and Shiʿi occurred only in the second century. This is why many points of agreement exist between Sunni *fiqh* works and *al-Majmuʿ*: Iraq was the common cradle for all of them.

Santillana criticized Griffini's opinion severely, underlining some historical inconsistencies in the *Majmuʿ*, but above all stressing consistencies between its doctrine and Sunni (except Hanbali) law and its remarkable affinity with the Hanafi school. Santillana focused his criticism also on the transmitters, advancing many doubts about their reliability. Some case law has been examined by Cilardo, who reaches the conclusion that their solutions originated in a period following Zayd's death. *Al-Majmuʿ*

seems a very elementary compendium of law transmitting the most common Zaydi solution for each case, ignoring any scholarly debate.

Bergsträsser maintained that *Al-majmu'*'s rudimentary doctrines reproduce those of the Sunni *fiqh* of the second century, agreeing on many points with doctrines of the Iraqi jurists of that time. Also, its terminology is similar to that in use at the time in Iraq. The *Majmu'* seems to display a mere mechanical process of reception, however, failing to absorb any Iraqi juridical thought. It was presumably compiled by an Iraqi Shi'i scantily learned in juridical matters.

Strothmann, mainly on the base of "internal contradictions" between *Al-majmu'* and the Zaydi juridical literature, asserted that it originated in a period when doctrinal divergences between the upholders of 'Ali and the Sunni *fuqahā'* were minimal.

Schacht maintained that the authentic Zaydi juridical literature goes back no further than the third century. Particularly suspicious is the commonly used "family *isnād*" (Zayd transmitting from his father, from his grandfather, from 'Ali), a sign that the traditions are not authentic.

Madelung agrees with Bergsträsser and Strothmann that *Al-majmu'* cannot be directly attributed to Zayd, but he states that it must be considered essentially a work of the Kufan Abu Khalid al-Wasiti, who is said to have transmitted it from Zayd. Abu Khalid followed him to the various cities he visited, such as Mecca, Medina, and Kufa, from 118 to 122, when, at Zayd's death, only Abu Khalid escaped among his master's disciples. During these five years Abu Khalid learned many traditions directly from Zayd; other traditions were read to him by Zayd himself, using a copy he himself had compiled. It is likely that Abu Khalid transmitted Zayd's doctrines to his own disciples, and that one of these, Ibrahim ibn al-Zibriqan (d. 183/799), collected them.

The *Majmu'* does not play a significant role in the Zaydi legal tradition. As a matter of fact, some other later works are followed in the Zaydi school, such as the *Kitab Usul al-ahkam fi'l-halal wa-l-haram* by al-Mutawakkil 'Alallah Ahmad ibn Sulayman ibn al-Hadi ila-l-Haqq (d. 566/1170); *'Uyun al-azhar fi fiqh al-a'imma al-athar* and *Kitab al-bahr al-zakhkhar al-jami' li-madhahib 'ulama' al-amsar* by Ahmad ibn Yahya ibn al-Murtada (d. 840/1437); and *Al-rawd al-nadir* (a commentary, with glosses, on *Al-majmu'*) by al-Husayn ibn Ahmad al-Khaymi al-San'ani (d. 1221/1806).

[*See also* Islamic Schools of Sacred Law: Shi'i Schools, *subentry on* The Zaydi School of Law.]

BIBLIOGRAPHY

Bergsträsser, Gotthelf. "Review of *Majmu' al-Fiqh*, edited by E. Griffini." In *Orientalistische Literaturzeitung* 25 (1922): 114–124.

Cilardo, Agostino. *Teorie sulle origini del diritto Islamico*. Rome: Istituto per l'Oriente C. A. Nallino, 1990. See especially chapter 2, "Il 'Corpus Juris' di Zayd ibn 'Ali," pp. 19–35.

Griffini, Eugenio, ed. *"Corpus Iuris," la più antica raccolta di legislazione e di giurisprudenza Musulmana finora ritrovata*. Milan, Italy: U. Hoepli, 1919.

Ibn Hajar al-'Asqalani, Ahmad ibn 'Ali. *Kitab tahdhib al-tahdhib*. 12 vols. Hyderabad, India, 1325–1327/1907–1909; reprint, Beirut: Dar Sadir, 1968. See especially Vol. 3, pp. 419–420.

Madelung, Wilferd. *Der Imam al-Qasim ibn Ibrahim und die Glaubenslehre der Zaiditen*. Berlin: de Gruyter, 1965.

Santillana, David. "Il libro di diritto di Zayd b. 'Ali e il sistema zaydita." *Rivista degli Studi Orientali* 8 (1919–1920): 745–776.

Schacht, Joseph. *The Origins of Muhammadan Jurisprudence*. Oxford, U.K.: Clarendon Press, 1950.

Sezgin, Fuat. *Geschichte des Arabischen Schrifttums*. Leiden, Netherlands: E. J. Brill, 1967. See especially Vol. 1, pp. 556–560, no. 1.

Strothmann, Rudolf. "Die Literatur der Zaiditen." *Der Islam* 1 (1910): 354–368; 2 (1911): 49–78.

Strothmann, Rudolf. "Das Problem der literarischen Persönlichkeit Zaid b. 'Ali." *Der Islam* 13 (1923): 1–52.

Zirikli, Khayr al-Din al-. *Al-A'lam*. 2d ed. 10 vols. Cairo: Matba'at Kustatsumas, 1954–1959. See especially Vol. 3, pp. 98–99.

AGOSTINO CILADRO

ZAYDI SCHOOL OF ISLAMIC LAW. *See* Islamic Schools of Sacred Law, *subentry on* Shii Schools: The Zaydi School of Law.

ZEILLER, FRANZ VON (1751–1828). Austrian legal scholar. Born in Graz, Austria, on January 14, 1751, Franz Anton Felix von Zeiller studied philosophy there, earning his PhD on August 19, 1768. He then studied law in Vienna as a private student of Karl Anton von Martini and earned his JD on July 30, 1778, with the dissertation *De suspectis tutoribus*. The same year Zeiller was made an adjunct professor at the University of Vienna, and in 1782 he became a full professor as Martini's successor. In 1803, Zeiller served as the director of the university's law faculty, and in 1803 and 1807 he was the university's vice-chancellor. An instructor in law to several princes of the imperial house, Zeiller was ennobled in 1797, the same year that he served as honorary assessor of the Royal Commission on Legislation; two years later he served as assessor in the Royal Commission on Education. Zeiller died on August 23, 1828, in Hietzing, Vienna.

Zeiller was active in almost all fields of law: legislation, jurisdiction (at the supreme court), science, and the teaching of law—in civil and penal law. In 1793 he suggested reforms of the Josephinian Law Code (1787), and later he edited the first part of the *Gesetzbuch über Verbrechen und schwere Polizeiübertretungen* (Law Code on Crime and Severe Police Transgressions, September 3, 1803). He left his mark on the codification of civil law and made legal history as the editor in chief of the Allgemeines Bürgerliches Gesetzbuch (ABGB, or Austrian General Civil Code, 1811).

In 1801, Zeiller was a consultant to the Royal Commission for Legislation, and at a relatively late stage he initiated a renewed consultation on the draft of a civil-law code in three readings (1801–1810). He had great influence on the consultations, in which the principles of his work *Das natürliche Privatrecht* (Natural Private Law, 1802) were predominant and influenced the formulation of the legislation. Zeiller's activities were of great importance for the introduction of the ABGB, which became law on January 1, 1812.

Zeiller was the author of definitive commentaries: in 1809 he published "Probe eines Commentars für das neue Oesterreichische Bürgerliche Gesetzbuch" (Trial Commentary on the New Austrian Civil Code) in his journal *Jährlicher Beytrag* (Annual Contribution), and he published the four-volume *Commentar* (1811–1813), as well as the *Abhandlung über die Principien* (Essay on Principles, 1816–1820). He also defended the ABGB against attacks from German scholars of jurisprudence. Zeiller's activities as a teacher and university administrator were decisive for the positioning of the new civil code in law instruction, especially his legal-political curriculum that became effective in 1810. In this curriculum the historic subjects were deemphasized in favor of the systematic subjects, teachings on Roman law were reduced, and instruction in current law was emphasized with a view toward government service.

In penal law Zeiller introduced concepts of Paul Johann Anselm Feuerbach, especially in the drafts for the revision of penal law (1823 and 1825), and subsumed penal law to the state's goal of granting the individual the greatest possible freedom; he consistently demanded the separation of law and morality. Zeiller edited the journal *Jährlicher Beytrag zur Gesetzkunde und Rechtswissenschaft in den Oesterreichischen Erbstaaten* (Annual Contribution to the Teaching of Laws and Legal Science in the Austrian States, 1806–1809), the first law journal of the monarchy, and he also contributed to the publication edited by Carl Joseph Pratobevera, *Materalien für Gesetzkunde und Rechtspflege in den österreichischen Erbsstaaten* (Materials on Law and Jurisprudence in the Austrian States, 1814–1824), and to Vincenz August Wagner's *Zeitschrift für österreichische Rechtsgelehrsamkeit und politische Gesetzkunde* (Journal of Austrian Legal Scholarship and Political Law, 1825–1845). Because of his comprehensive activities in all fields of jurisprudence and his decisive influence on the codification of civil law and on its implementation, Zeiller is considered the most important Austrian jurist at the turn of the eighteenth to the nineteenth century.

[*See also* Austria.]

BIBLIOGRAPHY

PRIMARY WORKS

Abhandlung über die Principien des allgemeinen bürgerlichen Gesetzbuches für die gesammten deutschen Erbländer der österreichischen Monarchie. Edited by Wilhelm Brauneder. Vienna: Manz, 1986. Reprint essays originally published in *Materialien für Gesetzkunde und Rechtspflege in den österreichischen Staaten* in 1816–1820.

Commentar über das allgemeine bürgerliche Gesetzbuch für die gesammten deutschen Erbländer der österreichischen Monarchie. 4 vols. Vienna: Geistinger, 1811–1813.

Das natürliche Privatrecht. Vienna: Wappler and Beck, 1802. 3d ed., 1819.

SECONDARY WORKS

Kleinheyer, Gerd, and Jan Schröder. *Deutsche und europäische Juristen aus neun Jahrhunderten*. 4th ed. Heidelberg, Germany: C. F. Müller, 1996. See pp. 459–462.

Kohl, Gerald. "Franz von Zeiller." In *Juristen*, 2d ed., edited by Michael Stolleis, pp. 687–689. Munich, Germany: Beck, 2001.

Oberkofler, Gerhard. "Franz von Zeiller." In *Juristen in Österreich, 1200–1980*, edited by Wilhelm Brauneder. Vienna: Orac, 1987.

Selb, Walter, and Herbert Hofmeister, eds. *Forschungsband Franz von Zeiller (1751–1828): Beiträge zur Gesetzgebungs- und Wissenschaftsgeschichte*. Vienna: Böhlau, 1980.

Swoboda, Ernst. *Franz von Zeiller: Der grosse Pfadfinder der Kultur auf dem Gebiete des Rechts, und die Bedeutung seines Lebenswerkes für die Gegenwart*. Graz, Austria: Leuschner & Lubensky, 1931.

BARBARA DOLEMEYER
Translated from the German by Alexa Nieschlag

ZIMBABWE. *See* African Law, Sub-Saharan, *subentry on* The Colonial Period.

ZIVILGESETZBUCH. *See* Switzerland.

TOPICAL OUTLINE OF CONTENTS

The entries and subentries in *The Oxford International Encyclopedia of Legal History* are assembled according to the general conceptual categories listed in this topical outline. Entries in the Encyclopedia proper are organized alphabetically. The outline is organized as follows:

1. Ancient Greek Law
2. Ancient Roman Law
3. Chinese Law
4. English Common Law
5. Islamic Law
6. Medieval and Post-Medieval Roman Law
7. South Asian, African, and Latin American Law
8. United States Law
9. Overviews and Other Legal Traditions
10. Biographies

1. ANCIENT GREEK LAW

Adoption
    Ancient Greek Law
Adultery in Ancient Greek Law
Advocate
    Ancient Athens
Ancient Greek Law
    Overview and Historical Survey
    Sources
    The Origins of Ancient Greek Law
    The Archaic Period
    Hellenistic Law
    History of Scholarship
Anthropology and Ancient Greek Law
Arbitration in Ancient Athens
Athens
Codes and Codification
    Ancient Greek Law
Commercial Law
    Ancient Greek Law
Constitutional Law
    Ancient Greek Law
Contract
    Ancient Greek Law
Courts
    Ancient Greek: Courts and Magistrates in Ancient Athens
Criminal Law
    Ancient Athenian Law
Divorce
    Ancient Greek Law

Egypt
    Hellenistic Period
Evidence
    Ancient Athens
Family
    Ancient Greek Law
Gortyn
Graphē Paranomōn
Homicide
    Ancient Greek Law
Inheritance
    Ancient Greek Law
Judges
    Judges and Jurors in Ancient Greece
Legislation
    Ancient Greece
Literature and Law in Ancient Greece
Litigation in Ancient Athens
Logography
Maritime Law
    Ancient Greece
Marriage
    Ancient Greek Law
Oaths in Ancient Athens
Offenses against the State
    in Ancient Greece
Philosophy and Law, Ancient Greek
Prisons and Imprisonment
    Ancient Athens
Procedure
    Archaic Greek Law

Athens: An Overview
Trial Procedure in Ancient Athens
Property
Ancient Greek Law
Prostitution in Ancient Greek Law
Punishment
Ancient Athens
Rape
Ancient Greek Law
Religion
Religion and Law in Ancient Greece
Rhetoric in Ancient Greek Law
Sexual and Moral Regulation in Ancient Greece
Slavery
Ancient Greek Law
Sparta
Speech, Freedom of
Ancient Athens
Status
Ancient Greek Law
Theft
Ancient Greek Law
Torture
Ancient Athens
Witnesses in Ancient Athens
Women
Ancient Greek Law

2. ANCIENT ROMAN LAW

Business Law
Byzantium
Early Byzantium
Later Byzantium to 1453
Byzantine Legislation
Byzantine Jurists
Canon Law
Orthodox Churches
Celtic Law
Codes and Codification
Codifications in Ancient Roman Law
Cognitio and Imperial and Bureaucratic Courts
Consuetudo
Contract
Ancient Roman Law
Byzantine Law
Courts
Ancient Roman: Civil Courts
Ancient Roman: Criminal Courts in the Roman Republic and the Empire
Ancient Roman: Byzantium
Criminal Law
The Roman Republic
The Roman Empire
Byzantium

Delict
Roman Law
Byzantine Law
Education and Training
Ancient Rome
Egypt
Juristic Papyrology
Formula
Imperial Legislation
Institutional Writings
Ius
Jurists
Legal Reasoning
Legis Actiones
Legislative Assemblies
  (*Leges, Plebiscites*)
Lex
Lex Irnitana
Magistrates (Praetor, Aedile)
Persons
Roman Law
Byzantine Law
Praetorian Edict
Procedure
Byzantine Law
Property
Roman Law
Byzantine Law
Provincial Edicts and Government
Public Law
The Roman Republic
The Roman Empire
Byzantium
Religious Law
An Overview of Roman Religious Law
The Influence of the Adoption of Christianity on Roman Religious Law
Roman Citizenship and *Latinitas*
Roman Law
753–27 B.C.E.
27 B.C.E.–250 C.E.
250–527 C.E.
The Age of Justinian
Historiography
Senate, Roman
Slavery
Roman Law
Succession
Roman Law
Byzantine Law
Twelve Tables
Women
The Position of Women and Equality in Ancient Rome

3. CHINESE LAW

Accessory and Principal in Chinese Law
Adoption
    Chinese Law
Alcohol and Drugs
    Chinese Law
Amnesty in Chinese Law
Appeal
    Chinese Law
    Review in Chinese Law
Beating and Whipping in Chinese Law
Cangue, The
Capital Cases in Chinese Law
Capital Punishment
    Chinese Law
Chinese Law, History of
    Shang Dynasty (c. 16th–11th Century B.C.E.)
    Western Zhou Dynasty (c. 1045–771 B.C.E.)
    Eastern Zhou, Spring and Autumn (771–464 B.C.E.)
    Eastern Zhou, Warring States (464–221 B.C.E.), and Qin State and Empire (c. 350–206 B.C.E.)
    Han Empire (206 B.C.E.–220 C.E.)
    Three Kingdoms, Qin, and Southern Dynasties (220–589 C.E.)
    The Northern Dynasties (386–589 C.E.)
    Sui and Tang Dynasties (581–907 C.E.)
    Five Dynasties and Song Dynasty (907–1279 C.E.)
    Liao (937–1125 C.E.) and Qin (1115–1234 C.E.) Empires
    Yuan Dynasty (1279–1368 C.E.)
    Ming Dynasty (1368–1644 C.E.)
    Qing Dynasty (1644–1911 C.E.)
    The Republic, 1911–1949
    People's Republic of China
    Hong Kong and Macau
    Taiwan
Chinese Law, Sources of
    Administrative Codes or Regulations
    Penal Codes
    Classical (Ritual) Writings
    Judicial Precedent
    Custom
    Guilds
Collective Liability
Confession
    Chinese Law
    Confession and Acceptance of Sentence in Chinese Law
Contract
    Chinese Law
Corruption in Chinese Law
Courts
    Chinese: An Overview of Chinese Courts and Judicial Agencies
    Chinese: The Censorate
    Chinese: The Central Court
    Chinese: The Emperor
    Chinese: Local Courts
    Chinese: The Ministry of Justice (Board of Punishments)
Cursing
Damage to Property in Chinese Law
Deceit
Deposit
    Chinese Law
Doing What Ought Not to Be Done
Doubtful Cases
Ethnic Groups in Chinese Law
Exile in Chinese Law
Filial Piety, Lack of
Foreigners in Chinese Law
Gambling in Chinese Law
Hire in Chinese Law
Homicide
    Chinese Law
Homosexuality
    Chinese Law
Incest in Chinese Law
Intention in Chinese Law
Kidnapping
    Chinese Law
Land
    Title and Subordinate Interests in Chinese Law
Lawyers
    Chinese Law
Loan
    Chinese Law
Marriage
    Chinese Law
Mongolia
Mutilation in Chinese Law
Mutual Concealment
Offenses against the State in Chinese Law
    Overview
    Disrespect (Bujing)
    Heterodox Beliefs
    Offenses Damaging the Efficiency of Government
    Offenses Threatening the Life or Well-Being of the Emperor
    Offenses Threatening the Safety of the State or Dynasty
Offenses in Chinese Law, Classification of
Partnership
    Chinese Law
Penal Servitude in Chinese Law
Pledge
    Chinese Law
Poison (*Gu*)
Prisons and Imprisonment
    Chinese Law

168 TOPICAL OUTLINE OF CONTENTS

Procedure
  Criminal and Civil Procedure in Chinese Law
  Parties and Witnesses in Chinese Law
Punishment
  Chinese Law: Overview
  Chinese Law: Administrative Punishments
Punishment and Status in Chinese Law
  Overview
  Age
  Disability
  Officials
  Relatives
  Slaves
  Women
Rape
  Chinese Law
Redemption
Rule of Law
Sale
  Sale of Goods in Chinese Law
  Sale of Land in Chinese Law
Sentence in Chinese Law
Sexual Intercourse, Illicit in Chinese Law
Sexual Offenses in Chinese Law
Status
  Chinese Law
Succession
  Chinese Law
Sumptuary Laws in Chinese Law
Theft
  Chinese Law
Torture
  Chinese Law
Wounding in Chinese Law
Wrongful Judgment in Chinese Law
Zang

4. ENGLISH COMMON LAW

Adoption
  English Common Law
Agency
  English Common Law
Anglo-Saxon Law
Appeal
  English Common Law
Assault
Assizes
Australia
Bailment in English Common Law
Bankruptcy
  English Common Law
Banks and Banking
  English Common Law
Barristers
Bills of Exchange in English Common Law
Blackmail
Breach of Contract
  English Common Law
British Commonwealth
Burglary in English Common Law
Canada
  Canadian Law
  Native Peoples
Capital Punishment
  English Common Law
Censorship
  English Common Law
Central Government in English Common Law
Chancery
Charities
Children
  English Common Law
Church and State in English Common Law
Common Law
  English Common Law
Common Pleas
Company Law
  English Common Law
Competition
  English Common Law
Compurgation
Constitutional Law
  English Common Law
Consumer Protection
  English Common Law
Contract
  English Common Law
  Contracts in Favor of Third Parties in English Common Law
Conveyancing
Copyright in English Common Law
Courts
  English
Criminal Law
  English Common Law
Custom
  English Common Law
Divorce
  English Common Law
Doctors' Commons
Dower in English Common Law
Duress
  English Common Law
Easements
Ecclesiastical Law in English Common Law
Education and Training
  English Common Law

Employment and Labor Law
English Common Law
English Common Law, Historiography of
English Law
English Legal Treatises
Entails
Environmental Law
English Common Law
Equity
English Common Law
Error and Mistake
English Common Law
Estates, Doctrine of
European Union
Evidence
English Common Law
Exchequer
Family
English Common Law
Feudal Law
English Common Law
Final Process
Fraud
English Common Law
Guilds in English Common Law
Homicide
English Common Law
Inns of Court
Insanity
Insurance
English Common Law
Irish Law
Judiciary
English Common Law
Jury
English Common Law
Justices in Eyre
Justices of the Peace
Kidnapping
English Common Law
King's Bench
Land
Land Registration in English Common Law
Leases of Land in English Common Law
Law Merchant
English Common Law
Law Reform Movements
Law Reporting in English Common Law
Legal Literature in English Common Law
Legislation
Statute Law
Libel and Slander
Magna Carta

Marriage
English Common Law
Mesne Process
Monopolies
Mortgage
English Common Law
Mortmain
Nationality in English Common Law
Natural Law
English Common Law
Negligence
New Zealand
Nuisance in English Common Law
Obligations
English Common Law
Ordeal in English Common Law
Outlawry
Parliament
Petty Assizes
Pleading
Poor Laws in English Common Law
Possession
English Common Law
Precedent
Doctrine of Precedent
Procedure
Civil Procedure in English Common Law
Criminal Procedure in English Common Law
Property
Personal Property in English Common Law
Real Property in English Common Law
Public Law
English Common Law
Punishment
English Common Law
Rape
English Common Law
Real Actions
Restitution in English Common Law
Roman Law
Roman Law and English Common Law
Sale
English Common Law
Scotland
Serjeants at Law
Slavery
English Common Law
Solicitors
Sources of Law in English Common Law
Star Chamber
Strict Settlements
Subinfeudation and Substitution
Succession
English Common Law

Taxation
: *English Common Law*

Tenure, Doctrine of

Theft
: *English Common Law*

Tort
: *English Common Law*

Torture
: *English Common Law*

Treason

Trial by Battle

Trusts in English Common Law

Vicarious Liability
: *English Common Law*

Villeinage

Welsh Law

Wills
: *English Common Law*

Women
: *English Common Law*

5. ISLAMIC LAW

Abbasid Dynasty

Abrogation of Legal Norms (*Naskh*)

Acknowledgment (Avowal; *Iqrār*)

Administrative Decrees of the Political Authorities (*Qānūn*)
: *The Mamluk Period*
: *The Ottoman Period*

Adoption
: *Islamic Law*

Afghanistan, Islamic Law in

Agricultural Contracts and Sharecropping in Islamic Law

Alcohol and Drugs
: *Islamic Law*

Arab Countries, Islamic Law in
: *Overview*
: *Saudi Arabia*

Arabian Peninsula

Assignment (*Ḥawālah*)

Balkan Peninsula, Islamic Law in the

Banking and Finance in Islamic Law

Body in Islamic Law

Capacity (*Ahliyya*)

Capital (*Ra's al-mal*)

Capital Punishment
: *The Muslim World in the Twentieth Century*

Censorship
: *Islamic Law*

Children
: *Islamic Law*

China, Islamic Law in

Codes and Codification
: *Islamic Law*
: *Islamic Law in Africa*

Commercial Law
: *Islamic Law, Classical Period*
: *Islamic Law, Modern Period*

Commodity in Islamic Law

Compensation in Islamic Law

Constitutional Law
: *Constitutions and Constitutional Law in Islamic Law: Overview and The Arab Countries*
: *Constitutions and Constitutional Law in Islamic Law: Africa*
: *Constitutions and Constitutional Law in Islamic Law: Iran*
: *Constitutions and Constitutional Law in Islamic Law: Malaysia*
: *Constitutions and Constitutional Law in Islamic Law: Pakistan and Bangladesh*

Contract
: *Contracts and Unilateral Acts in Islamic Law*
: *Contract for Delivery with Prepayment (Salam) in Islamic Law*

Criminal Law
: *Crime and Punishment in Islamic Law*

Damage (*Darar*)

Deposit
: *Islamic Law*

Dissent (*Ikhtilāf*)

Divorce
: *Consensual Divorce (Khul') in Islamic Law*

Donation in Islamic Law

Duress
: Ikrāh

Duty (*Farḍ*)

Education and Training
: *Islamic Law*
: *Faculties of Islamic Law and Law Schools*

Egypt
: *Islamic Law in Egypt*

Enforcement in Islamic Law

Europe, Islamic Law in

Family
: *Family and Kinship in Islamic Law*

Fatwa

Fetus in Islamic Law

Forum, Exterior (*Ẓāhir*), and Interior Forum (*Bāṭin*)

Fungible Things (*Mithliyyat*)

Homosexuality
: *Islamic Law*

Individual Effort of Legal Reasoning (*Ijtihād*)

Inheritance
: *Islamic Law*

Insurance
  Islamic Law
International Law
  Islamic Public Law
Iran, Islamic Law in
Iraq, Islamic Law in
Islamic Law
  Overview
  Sources and Methodology of the Law
  Genres of Legal Literature
  Legal and Ethical Qualifications
  Spheres of the Law in the Fiqh
  Transmission and Authenticity of the Reports from the Prophet
Islamic Law and Its Political Geography
  Balkan Peninsula
  Southeast Asia
Islamic Schools of Sacred Law
  Shi'i Schools: The Imami School of Law
  Shi'i Schools: The Isma'ili School of Law
  Shi'i Schools: The Zaydi School of Law
  Sunni Schools: The Hanafi School of Law
  Sunni Schools: The Hanbali School of Law
  Sunni Schools: The Khariji School of Law
  Sunni Schools: The Maliki School of Law, Part 1
  Sunni Schools: The Maliki School of Law, Part 2
  Sunni Schools: The Shafi'i School of Law
  Sunni Schools: The Zahiri School of Law
Judicial Review in Islamic Law
  Classical Period
  Modern Period
Judiciary
  Islamic Law: Classical Period
  Islamic Law: Modern Period
Lawyers
  Islamic Law
Lease and Tenancy Contracts
  Islamic Law
Legal Acts and Legal Facts in Islamic Law
Legal Norms in Islamic Law, Production of
Legal Personality in Islamic Law
Legal Profession in Islamic Law, Part 1
Legal Profession in Islamic Law, Part 2
Loan
  Islamic Law
Maghrib and al-Andalus (Muslim Spain)
Marriage
  Islamic Law
Mufti
Non-Muslims in Islamic Law
Obligations
  Islamic Law
Option (*Khiyār*)
Ottoman Empire, Islamic Law in Asia Minor (Turkey) and the

Ownership (*Milk*)
Partnership
  Partnerships and Commercial Societies in Islamic Law
Personal Status Law
  Personal Status Law in Islamic Countries
  Personal Status Law in South and Southeast Asia
Persons
  Islamic Law
Pledge
  Rahn in Islamic Law
Political Dimension (*Siyāsa Shar'iyya*) of Islamic Law
Possession
  Yad in Islamic Law
Prisons and Imprisonment
  Islamic Law
Privacy
  Islamic Law
Procedure
  Proof and Procedure in Islamic Law
Profit in Islamic Law
Public Authority (Sultan) in Islamic Law
Public Law
  Public and Private Law in Islamic Law
Purity and Impurity in Islamic Law
Repudiation (*Talāq*)
Revealed Texts (*Nuṣūṣ*), Transmission of
Revelation, Forms of
Rights in Islamic Law
Sicily, Islamic Law in
Taxation
  Taxation and Religion in Islamic Law, Part 1
  Taxation and Religion in Islamic Law, Part 2
Territorial Concepts in Islamic Law
Torture
  Islamic Law
Turkey
  Islamic Law
Usurpation (*Ghaṣb*)
Usury
  Illicit Commercial Gain (Ribā) *in Islamic Law*
War and Peace in Islamic Law
Wills
  Testamentary Disposition in Islamic Law
Women
  Islamic Law
Worship in Islamic Law
Yemen

6. MEDIEVAL AND POST-MEDIEVAL ROMAN LAW

Absolutism
Administration, Public Law of
Admiralty
  Medieval and Post-Medieval Roman Law

Advocate
  Medieval and Post-Medieval Roman Law
Agency
  Medieval and Post-Medieval Roman Law
Assignment (Assignation)
Attempt
Austria
Baltic Nations
Banks and Banking
  Medieval and Post-Medieval Roman Law
Bishops and Archbishops
Breach of Contract
  Medieval and Post-Medieval Roman Law
Canon Law
  Protestant Churches
  The Codes of Canon Law (1917 and 1983)
  Courses and Classes
Church Councils and Conciliar Canons
Civil Law
  Medieval and Post-Medieval Roman Law
Codes and Codification
  Medieval and Post-Medieval Roman Law: Private Law
Company Law
  Medieval and Post-Medieval Roman Law
Competition
  Medieval and Post-Medieval Roman Law
Conflict of Laws
  Medieval and Post-Medieval Roman Law
Constitution
Consumer Protection
  Medieval and Post-Medieval Roman Law
Corpus Iuris Canonici
Courts
  Medieval and Post-Medieval Roman Law: Courts and Cases
  Medieval and Post-Medieval Roman Law: Faculties Acting as Courts
Credit in Medieval and Post-Medieval Roman Law
Crimes against Life and Body
Decretals and Decretal Collections
Delay
Denmark
Donation (Gift)
Duress
  Medieval and Post-Medieval Roman Law
Ecclesiastical Courts
Education and Training
  Faculties and Teaching Methods
Employment and Labor Law
  Medieval and Post-Medieval Roman Law
Enlightenment
Error and Mistake
  Medieval and Post-Medieval Roman Law
European Communities

European Union, Private Law in
Evidence
  Medieval and Post-Medieval Roman Law
Family
  Medieval and Post-Medieval Roman Law
Feudal Law
  Medieval and Post-Medieval Roman Law
Fideicommissum (*Familiae*)
France
Fraud
  Criminal Law in Medieval and Post-Medieval Roman Law
  Private Law in Medieval and Post-Medieval Roman Law
Germanic Provincial Administration
Germany
Guarantee
Guilt (*Schuld*)
Humanism
Hungary
Illegality and Immorality
Insolvency
Insurance
  Medieval and Post-Medieval Roman Law
Intellectual Property
  Medieval and Post-Medieval Roman Law
International Law
  Roman Law
Interpretation
Italy
Jewish Law
  Ashkenazi Jews
  Sephardic Jews
Judges
  Judges and Juries in Medieval and Post-Medieval Roman Law
Jurisprudence of Concepts
Late Scholasticism
Law Merchant
  Medieval and Post-Medieval Roman Law
Lease and Tenancy Contracts
  Medieval and Post-Medieval Roman Law
Legislation
  Medieval and Post-Medieval Roman Law
Maritime Law
  Medieval and Post-Medieval Roman Law
Mortgage
  Medieval and Post-Medieval Roman Law
National Socialist Law
Natural Law
  Medieval and Post-Medieval Roman Law
Negotiable Instruments (*Wertpapiere*)
Netherlands
Notary

Obligations
  Medieval and Post-Medieval Roman Law
Pandektenwissenschaft
Pledge
  Medieval and Post-Medieval Roman Law
Poland
Political Crimes
  Medieval and Post-Medieval Roman Law
Pope and Papacy
Possession
  Medieval and Post-Medieval Roman Law
Precedent
  Stare Decisis
Private Law, Concept of
Privileges
Procedure
  *Civil Procedure in Medieval and
    Post-Medieval Roman Law*
  *Criminal Procedure in Medieval and
    Post-Medieval Roman Law*
Property
  Medieval and Post-Medieval Roman Law
Prussian Allgemeines Landrecht
Punishment
  Medieval and Post-Medieval Roman Law
Punishment, Theories Regarding Purpose of
Reichskammergericht
Sale
  *Sale of Goods in Medieval and
    Post-Medieval Roman Law*
  *Sale of Land in Medieval and
    Post-Medieval Roman Law*
Servitude in Real Estate
Sexual Crimes in Medieval and
  Post-Medieval Roman Law
Social Security in Modern Europe
Spain
Succession
  Medieval and Post-Medieval Roman Law
Sweden
Switzerland
System and Systematization
Taxation
  Medieval and Post-Medieval Roman Law
Theft and Robbery
Tort
  Tort, Negligence, and Delict
Undue Influence in Medieval and
  Post-Medieval Roman Law
Universities
Unjust Enrichment in Medieval and
  Post-Medieval Roman Law
Usury
  Medieval and Post-Medieval Roman Law

Vicarious Liability
  Medieval and Post-Medieval Roman Law
Witch Trials

7. SOUTH ASIAN, AFRICAN, AND LATIN AMERICAN LAW

Aboriginal Law
Abortion in Hindu Law
Adat
Adoption
  Hindu Law
African Law, Sub-Saharan
  The Precolonial Period
  The Colonial Period
  After Independence
Argentina
Arthaśāstra
Ātmanastuṣṭi
Balinese Hindu Law
Bangladesh
Bermuda
Bhutan
Brazil
Burma
Cambodia
Caribbean Law
Central American Republics
Chile
Colombia
Comparative Law
Constitutional Law
  India
Consumer Protection
  Hindu Law
Criminal Law
  India
Custom
  South Asian Law
Dharma
Divorce
  Hindu Law
Dowry in Hindu Law
East Africa, South Asian Law in
East Timor
Environmental Law
  Indian Law
Ethiopia
Family
  Indian Family Law
Fiji
Folk Law
Fundamental Duties
Fundamental Rights
Guatemala

Guyana
Hindu Law
    Overview
    Vedic Law, 1500–800 B.C.E.
    The Formative Period, 400 B.C.E.–400 C.E.
    The Post-Formative Period, 400–1000 C.E.
    Medieval Hindu Law
    Anglo-Hindu Law
Hindu Nationalism
Homicide
    Hindu Law
Indian Subcontinent
    An Overview of Indian Law
    Christian Laws
Indonesia
Intellectual Property
    Southeast Asian Law
Jaina Law
Japan
Jewish Law
    India
Justice, Equity, and Good Conscience
Laos
Legal Anthropology
Liberia
Malaysia
Maldives
Manusmriti
Māori Law
Marriage
    Hindu Law
Marumakkathayam
Mauritius
Melanesia
Mexico
Mīmāṃsā
Naga Law
Nepal
Nītiśāstra
Pakistan, Secular Laws in
Pancasila
Papua New Guinea
Paraguay
Parsi Law
Peru
Philippines
Polynesia
Property
    Hindu Law
Public Interest Litigation in India
Punishment
    Hindu Law
Rājadharma
Rājaśāsana
Sadācāra

Secularism in Indian Law
Seychelles
Sikh Law
Singapore
Slavery
    South and Central America
Smriti
South Africa
    Overview
    Indian Law
South and Central America
    Overview
    Precolonial Laws
    Spanish Colonial Law
    Portuguese Colonial Law
    Other Colonial Laws
    Legal Pluralism
South Asian Law
    Buddhist Law
    Muslim Law
    South Asian Law in the United Kingdom
Southeast Asian Law
    Overview
    Buddhist Law
    Chinese Law
    Hindu Law
    Muslim Law
Sri Lanka
Śruti
Succession
    Hindu Law
Suriname
Thailand
Tibet
Trinidad and Tobago
Turkey
    Turkish Law
Uruguay
Venezuela
Vietnam
Vyavahāra
Women
    Hindu Law

8. UNITED STATES LAW

Academics
Administrative Agencies
Admiralty
    United States Law
Agency
    United States Civil Law
Alcohol and Drugs
    United States Law

TOPICAL OUTLINE OF CONTENTS

Alternative Dispute Resolution
Antitrust
Apportionment and Reapportionment
Arms, Right to Bear
Articles of Confederation
Bankruptcy
   United States Commercial Law
Business Organizations
Citizenship
Civil Law
   Colonial United States
Civil Rights and Civil Liberties in United States Law
Classical Legal Theory
Codes and Codification
   United States Law
Commerce Clause
Commercial Law
   United States
Common Law
   United States Law
Conflict of Laws
   United States Law
Constitution of the United States
   The Constitution
   Amendments to the Constitution
   Interpretation of the Constitution
Consumer Protection
   United States Law
Contract
   United States Civil Law
Contracts Clause
Courts
   United States Federal
Criminal Law
   Colonial United States
   United States Law
Critical Legal Studies
Critical Race Theory
Disability
Discrimination, Race and Sex
Due Process
Education and Training
   United States
Education Law
Elderlaw
Environmental Law
   United States Law
Equal Protection
Equity
   United States Law
Evidence
   United States Procedure
Executive Power
Family
   United States Law

Federalism
Feminist Legal Theory
Gay, Lesbian, Bisexual, and
   Transgender Theory
General Welfare Clause
Health
History, Uses of
Housing
Immigration
Inheritance
   United States Law
Intellectual Property
   United States Law
International Law
   Private Law in United States Law
   Public Law in United States Law
Judicial Power
Judiciary
   United States Law
Jury
   United States Law
Justice, Theories of
Juvenile Justice in United States Law
Labor and Employment Law
   United States Law
   Labor Arbitration in United States Law
Law and Economics
Law and Science
Law and Society
Lawyers
   United States Law
Legal Process
Legal Realism
Legislative Power
Local Government Law
Military Tribunals
Native American Law
Natural Law
   United States Law
Political Crimes
   United States Law
Political Parties and Elections
Positivism in United States Law
Postmodernism and Law
Poverty
Privacy
   United States Law
Procedure
   Civil Procedure in United States Law
   Criminal Procedure in United States Law
Property
   United States Law
   Protection of Property in United States Law
Punishment
   United States Law

Regulation
  Overview
  Agriculture Regulation
  Securities Regulation
  Telecommunications Regulation
  Transportation Regulation
Religion
  United States Law
Remedies
Search and Seizure
Separation of Powers
Slavery
  Slavery and Other Labor Systems in the Colonial United States
  United States Law
Social Science, Uses of
Speech, Freedom of
  Freedom of Speech and Press in the United States
State Law
  The Confederation Period
  State Constitutions
State Sovereignty
Statutory Interpretation and Legislation
Succession
  Family Law in the United States
Supremacy Clause
Takings Clause
Taxation
  United States Law
Tort
  United States Law
United States Law
  The Colonial Period: General Introduction and Historical Overview
  The Colonial Period: The Sources of Colonial Law
  The Colonial Period: The Colonies in the Empire
  The American Revolution
  The Nineteenth Century
  The Twentieth Century
War Power
Welfare
Women
  United States Law

9. OVERVIEWS AND OTHER LEGAL TRADITIONS

Ancient Near Eastern Law
International Law
  Modern Public International Law
Jewish Law
  Overview
  Law
Religion
  Religion and Law
Russia

10. BIOGRAPHIES

Abu Hanifa, al-Nuʿman ibn Thabit
Abu Yaʿla, Muhammad ibn al-Husayn ibn al-Farraʾ al-Baghdadi
Abu Yusuf, Yaʿqub ibn Ibrahim
Accursius, Franciscus
Alciati, Andrea
ʿAmili, Muhammad ibn Makki al-
ʿAmili, Zayn al-Din ibn ʿAli ibn Ahmad al-
Ansari, Murtada ibn Muhammad Amin al-
Aśoka
Austin, John
Azo
Baldus de Ubaldis, Petrus
Baqir al-Najafi, Muhammad Hasan ibn Muhammad
Bartolus of Saxoferrato
Basil I and the Macedonian Renaissance
Beccaria, Cesare
Bello, Andrés
Bentham, Jeremy
Bihbahani, Muhammad Baqir ibn Muhammad Akmal al-
Blackstone, William
Bracton, Henry de
Budé, Guillaume
Carpzov, Benedict
Carrara, Francesco
Celsus the Younger
Cicero
Coke, Edward
Colebrooke, H. T.
Cujas, Jacques
Daʾud al-Isbahani
De Luca, Giovanni Battista
Denning, Alfred Thompson
Domat, Jean
Donellus
Draco
Du Moulin, Charles
Faber, Antonius
Filangieri, Gaetano
Ghazali, Abu Hamid Muhammad
Gravina, Gian Vincenzo
Grotius, Hugo
Hadi ila l-Haqq Yahya ibn al-Husayn al-
Hastings, Warren
Hilli, Jaʿfar ibn al-Hasan al-
Hsueh Yun-Sheng (Xue Yunsheng)
Huber, Eugen
Ibn ʿAbidin, Muhammad Amin

Ibn al-Mutahhar, Hasan ibn Yusuf al-Hilli, known as al-'Allama
Ibn 'Aqil, Abu al-Wafa' 'Ali
Ibn Hanbal, Ahmad
Ibn Hazm, 'Ali ibn Ahmad ibn Sa'id
Ibn Qayyim al-Jawziyya, Muhammad ibn Abi Bakr
Ibn Qudama, Muwaffaq al-Din Abu Muhammad 'Abdallah
Ibn Rushd, Abu al-Walid Muhammad ibn Ahmad
Ibn Rushd, Abu al-Walid Muhammad ibn Ahmad ibn Muhammad
Ibn Surayj, Ahmad ibn 'Umar
Ibn Taymiyya, Taqi al-Din Ahmad ibn 'Abd al-Halim
Irnerius
Jhering, Rudolf von
Jones, William
Julian
Justinian
Juwayni, 'Abd al-Malik ibn Abi Muhammad, Imam al-Haramayn
Kalwadhani, Abu al-Khattab Mahfuz ibn Ahmad al-
Kane, P. V.
Kasani, Abu Bakr ibn Mas'ud
Khalil ibn Ishaq al-Jundi
Khallal, Abu Bakr Ahmad ibn Muhammad ibn Harun al-
Khiraqi, Abu 'Umar ibn al-Husayn ibn 'Abdallah al-
Kreittmayr, Wiguläus Xaver Aloys von
Labeo, Marcus Antistius
Leibniz, Gottfried Wilhelm
Mahdi li-Din Allah Ahmad ibn Yahya al-Murtada al-
Maine, Henry
Malik ibn Anas ibn al-Harith al-Asbahi
Mansfield, Lord
Mansur bi-llah 'Abd Allah ibn' al-
Muhammad Qadri Pasha al-Hanafi
Muzani, Abu Ibrahim Ism'il ibn Yahya al-
Noodt, Gerard

Oldendorp, Johann
Papinian
Paul
Pothier, Robert Joseph
Pufendorf, Samuel von
Qadi al-Nu'man, Ibn Muhammad ibn Mansur al-
Qaffal, Abu Bakr Muhammad ibn 'Ali ibn Isma'il al-Shashi
Qayrawani, Ibn Abi Zayd al-
Sabinus, Massurius
Sahnun, 'Abd al-Salam ibn Sa'id al-Tanukhi
Sarakhsi, Muhammad ibn Ahmad ibn Abi Sahl
Savigny, Friedrich Carl von
Servius Sulpicius Rufus
Shafi'i, Muhammad ibn Idris al-
Shaybani, Muhammad ibn al-Hasan
Shen Chia-Pen (Shen Jiaben)
Shirazi, Abu Ishaq Ibrahim ibn 'Ali
Solon
Stracca, Benvenuto
Subki, 'Abd al-Wahhab ibn 'Ali al-
Thomasius, Christian
Tiraquellus
Tribonian
Tusi, Muhammad ibn al-Hasan, al-, Shaykh al-Ta'ifa
Ulpian
Unger, Joseph
Vattel, Emer de
Wansharisi, Ahmad ibn Yahya al-Tilimsani al-
Windscheid, Bernhard
Wolff, Christian von
Zasius, Ulrich
Zayd ibn 'Ali
Zeiller, Franz von

DIRECTORY OF CONTRIBUTORS

Bina Agarwal
Institute of Economic Growth, University of Delhi, India
Succession: Hindu Law

Flavia Agnes
Majlis, Mumbai, India
Custom: South Asian Law; Jewish Law: India; Parsi Law; Women: Hindu Law

Ahmad Atif Ahmad
Department of Religious Studies, University of California, Santa Barbara
Divorce: Consensual Divorce (*Khul'*) in Islamic Law; Ibn 'Abidin, Muhammad Amin; Judicial Review in Islamic Law: Modern Period; Lawyers: Islamic Law

Engin Akarlı
Department of History, Brown University
Ottoman Empire: Islamic Law in Asia Minor and the Ottoman Empire

William P. Alford
Harvard Law School
Offenses against the State in Chinese Law: Overview

Daud Ali
Department of History, School of Oriental and African Studies, University of London
Nītiśāstra

J. W. F. Allison
Queens' College, Cambridge
Public Law: English Common Law

David A. Anderson
University of Texas Law School
Speech, Freedom of: Freedom of Speech and Press in the United States

Stuart Anderson
Faculty of Law, University of Otago, New Zealand
Land: Land Registration in English Common Law

Christoph Antons
Centre for Comparative Law and Development Studies in Asia and the Pacific, Faculty of Law, University of Wollongong, Australia
Indonesia; Intellectual Property: Southeast Asian Law; Philippines

Matthias Armgardt
Juristische Fakultät, Ruhr-Universität Bochum, Germany
Education and Training: Faculties and Teaching Methods; Hungary; Jewish Law: Sephardic Jews; Judges: Judges and Juries in Medieval and Post-Medieval Roman Law

Françoise Aubin
Center for Scientific Research, Paris, Emeritus
China, Islamic Law in; Mongolia

Martin Avenarius
Institut für Römisches Recht, Universität zu Köln, Germany
Roman Law: Historiography

Reuven S. Avi-Yonah
University of Michigan Law School
International Law: Private Law in United States Law

Hugh D. R. Baker
School of Oriental and African Studies, University of London, Emeritus
Punishment and Status in Chinese Law: Relatives

John Baker
St. Catharine's College, University of Cambridge
Inns of Court; Serjeants at Law

Edward J. Balleisen
Department of History, Duke University
Regulation: Overview

Kilian Bälz
Attorney at Law, Frankfurt am Main
Insurance: Islamic Law

Vikramjit Banerjee
Counsel, Supreme Court of India
Dharma

Randy E. Barnett
Georgetown University Law Center
Commerce Clause

Oscar Cruz Barney
Instituto de Investigaciones Jurídicas, UNAM, and Academia Mexicana de Jurisprudencia y Legislación
Mexico

Peter Bartlett
School of Law, University of Nottingham
Insanity

Friedrich Battenberg
Hessisches Staatsarchiv Darmstadt, Germany
Jewish Law: Ashkenazi Jews

Christoph Becker
Juristische Fakultät, Universität Augsburg, Germany
Agency: Medieval and Post-Medieval Roman Law; Credit in Medieval and Post-Medieval Roman Law; Mortgage: Medieval and Post-Medieval Roman Law; Pledge: Medieval

and Post-Medieval Roman Law; Usury: Medieval and Post-Medieval Roman Law

Ulrich Becker
Max-Planck-Institut für Ausländisches und Internationales Sozialrecht, Munich, Germany
Social Security in Modern Europe

Franz von Benda-Beckmann
Max Planck Institute for Social Anthropology, Halle, Germany
Adat

Keebet von Benda-Beckmann
Max Planck Institute for Social Anthropology, Halle, Germany
Legal Anthropology

Lutz Berger
University of Kiel, Germany
Alcohol and Drugs: Islamic Law

Jonathan P. Berkey
Department of History, Davidson College
Education and Training: Islamic Law

Jean A. Berlie
Centre of Asian Studies, University of Hong Kong
East Timor

Richard B. Bernstein
New York Law School
Constitution of the United States: The Constitution

Mary Frances Berry
Department of History, University of Pennsylvania
Discrimination, Race and Sex

Joseph Biancalana
University of Cincinnati College of Law
Dower in English Common Law; Entails; Petty Assizes; Real Actions

Mary Sarah Bilder
Boston College Law School
United States Law: The Colonial Period: The Sources of Colonial Law

Bettine Birge
Department of East Asian Languages and Cultures, University of Southern California
Chinese Law, History of: Yuan Dynasty (1279–1368 C.E.)

Italo Birocchi
Facoltà di Giurisprudenza, Università Degli Studi Roma Tre, Italy
Italy

Christiane Birr
Leopold-Wenger Institut für Rechtsgeschichte, Ludwig-Maximilians-Universität München, Germany
Attempt

Brian Bix
University of Minnesota Law School
Justice, Theories of

Barbara Aronstein Black
Columbia Law School, Emerita
Civil Law: Colonial United States; United States Law: The Colonial Period: General Introduction and Historical Overview

Peter Blanck
Burton Blatt Institute, Syracuse University
Disability

Lloyd Bonfield
New York Law School
Villeinage

Josef Bordat
Independent Scholar
Late Scholasticism

Rosabelle Boswell
Department of Anthropology, Rhodes University, South Africa
Mauritius

Bernard Botiveau
CNRS, Institut de Recherches et d'Études sur le Monde Arabe et Musulman, Aix-en-Provence, France
Adoption: Islamic Law; Education and Training: Faculties of Islamic Law and Law Schools; Egypt: Islamic Law in Egypt; Judiciary: Islamic Law: The Modern Period

David Bourchier
University of Western Australia
Pancasila

Jérôme Bourgon
IAO-CNRS, Université de Lyon, France
Chinese Law, History of: Qing Dynasty (1644–1911 C.E.); Chinese Law, Sources of: Custom; Contract: Chinese Law; Hsueh Yun-Sheng (Xue Yunsheng); Shen Chia-Pen (Shen Jiaben); Succession: Chinese Law

Allen D. Boyer
New York Stock Exchange
Coke, Edward

Gülnihal Bozkurt
Department of History of Law, Faculty of Law, Ankara University, Turkey
Turkey: Islamic Law

Oren Bracha
University of Texas School of Law
Monopolies

Paul Brand
All Souls College, University of Oxford
Bracton, Henry de; Judiciary: English Common Law; Justices in Eyre; Magna Carta; Mortmain

Wilhelm Brauneder
Universität Wien, Austria
Austria

David Brick
Department of Asian Studies, University of Texas, Austin
Smriti

DIRECTORY OF CONTRIBUTORS 181

Alfred L. Brophy
University of North Carolina–Chapel Hill School of Law
Contract: United States Civil Law

Jeremy Alexander Brown
School of Law, School of Oriental and African Studies, University of London
Aboriginal Law

Theodor Bühler
K & B Rechtsanwälte, Oberuzwil, Switzerland
Vattel, Emer de

Thomas M. Buoye
Department of History, University of Tulsa
Capital Cases in Chinese Law; Capital Punishment: Chinese Law; Pledge: Chinese Law

William Butler
Dickinson School of Law, Pennsylvania State University
Russia

John W. Cairns
University of Edinburgh
Scotland

Eva Cantarella
Department of Roman and Ancient Law, University of Milano, Italy
Adultery in Ancient Greek Law; Divorce: Ancient Greek Law; Homicide: Ancient Greek Law; Marriage: Ancient Greek Law; Prostitution in Ancient Greek Law; Sexual and Moral Regulation in Ancient Greece; Women: Ancient Greek Law

Pio Caroni
Universität Bern, Switzerland, Emeritus
Huber, Eugen; Switzerland

Paul D. Carrington
Duke University School of Law
Procedure: Civil Procedure in United States Law

Don Chalmers
Faculty of Law, University of Tasmania
Papua New Guinea

Pedro Chalmeta Gendron
Universidad Complutense of Madrid, Emeritus
Censorship: Islamic Law

Martha Chamallas
Moritz College of Law, Ohio State University
Feminist Legal Theory

Kevin Chambers
History Department, Gonzaga University
Paraguay

Sebastian Champappilly
Advocate, High Court of Kerala, India
Indian Subcontinent: Christian Laws; *Marumakkathayam*

Biswajit Chanda
School of Law, School of Oriental and African Studies, University of London; Department of Law and Justice, University of Rajshahi, Bangladesh
Bangladesh; South Asian Law: Islamic Law

Thomas Charles-Edwards
Jesus College, University of Oxford
Celtic Law

Lorie Charlesworth
Law School, Liverpool John Moores University, United Kingdom
Justices of the Peace; Poor Laws in English Common Law

Eric Chaumont
L'Institut Français du Proche-Orient, Aleppo, Syria
Abrogation of Legal Norms (*Naskh*)

Chiu-kun Chen
Institute of Taiwan History, Academia Sinica, Taiwan
Sale: Sale of Land in Chinese Law

Christian Chene
Faculté de Droit, Université Paris Descartes, France
Pothier, Robert Joseph

Pengsheng Chiu
Institute of History and Philology, Academia Sinica, Taiwan
Deposit: Chinese Law; Hire in Chinese Law; Loan: Chinese Law; Partnership: Chinese Law

Agostino Cilardo
Faculty of Arabic, Islamic and Mediterranean Studies, University of Naples "L'Orientale," Italy
Family: Family and Kinship in Islamic Law; Marriage: Islamic Law; Muhammad Qadri Pasha al-Hanafi; Personal Status Law: Personal Status Law in Islamic Countries; Wills: Testamentary Disposition in Islamic Law; Zayd ibn 'Ali

Duncan Cloud
School of Archaeology and Ancient History, University of Leicester, England
Courts, Ancient Roman: Civil Courts; Legislative Assemblies (*Leges*, *Plebiscites*); Magistrates (Praetor, Aedile)

Alison W. Conner
William S. Richardson School of Law, University of Hawai'i, Mānoa
Chinese Law, History of: The Republic, 1912–1949; Confession: Chinese Law; Confession: Confession and Acceptance of Sentence in Chinese Law; Lawyers: Chinese Law

Marianne Constable
Department of Rhetoric, University of California, Berkeley
Jury: United States Law

David Cook
Department of Religious Studies, Rice University
War and Peace in Islamic Law

Simon J. J. Corcoran
Department of History, University College London
Imperial Legislation

182 DIRECTORY OF CONTRIBUTORS

W. R. Cornish
Faculty of Law, University of Cambridge, Emeritus
Jury: English Common Law

Robert J. Cottrol
George Washington University Law School
Arms, Right to Bear; Slavery: South and Central America

Stephen Cretney
All Souls College, Oxford University, Emeritus
Adoption: English Common Law; Children: English Common Law; Divorce: English Common Law; Family: English Common Law

Jane E. Cross
Shepard Broad Law Center, Nova Southeastern University
Caribbean Law; South and Central America: Other Colonial Laws

Donald R. Davis, Jr.
Department of Languages and Cultures of Asia, University of Wisconsin-Madison
Arthaśāstra; Rājaśāsana

Meryll Dean
Department of Law, Oxford Brookes University, United Kingdom
Japan

Martina Deckert
Institut für Wirtschaftsrecht, Universität Kassel, Germany
European Union, Private Law in

Deborah A. DeMott
Duke University School of Law
Agency: United States Civil Law

Christine Desan
Harvard Law School
Legislative Power

Roshan de Silva Wijeyeratne
Griffith Law School, Griffith University, Australia
South Asian Law: Buddhist Law; Sri Lanka

Rajeev Dhavan
Public Interest Legal Support and Research Centre (PILSARC), New Delhi, India
Indian Subcontinent: An Overview of Indian Law

Anthony Dicks
School of Oriental and African Studies, University of London
Chinese Law, History of: Hong Kong and Macau; Ethnic Groups in Chinese Law; Foreigners in Chinese Law; Land: Title and Subordinate Interests in Chinese Law; Southeast Asian Law: Chinese Law

Frank Dikötter
Department of History, School of Oriental and African Studies, University of London
Prisons and Imprisonment: Chinese Law

Gerhard Dilcher
Johann Wolfgang Goethe-Universität Frankfurt am Main, Germany, Emeritus
Feudal Law: Medieval and Post-Medieval Roman Law

Barbara Dölemeyer
Max-Planck-Institut für Europäische Rechtsgeschichte, Frankfurt am Main, Germany
Codes and Codification: Medieval and Post-Medieval Roman Law: Private Law; Unger, Josef; Zeiller, Franz von

Franz Dorn
Universität Trier, Germany
Illegality and Immorality

Michael Dougan
Liverpool Law School, University of Liverpool
European Union

Gisela Drossbach
Leopold-Wenger-Institut für Rechtsgeschichte, Ludwig-Maximilians-Universität München, Germany
Sexual Crimes in Medieval and Post-Medieval Roman Law

Jacques E. du Plessis
University of Stellenbosch, South Africa
Duress: Medieval and Post-Medieval Roman Law; Fraud: Private Law in Medieval and Post-Medieval Roman Law; Undue Influence in Medieval and Post-Medieval Roman Law

Paul du Plessis
School of Law, Edinburgh University
Consuetudo; Contract: Ancient Roman Law; Ius; Persons: Roman Law; Property: Roman Law; Roman Law: The Age of Justinian; Servius Sulpicius Rufus

Thomas Duve
Facultad de Derecho Canónico, Pontificia Universidad Católica Argentina
Canon Law: The Codes of Canon Law (1917 and 1983); Church Councils and Conciliar Canons; Corpus Iuris Canonici

John C. Eastman
Chapman University School of Law
General Welfare Clause

Ahmed El Shamsy
Harvard University
Ibn Surayj, Ahmad ibn 'Umar; Islamic Schools of Sacred Law: Sunni Schools: The Shafi'i School of Law; Juwayni, 'Abd al-Malik ibn Abi Muhammad, Imam al-Haramayn; Muzani, Abu Ibrahim Ism'il ibn Yahya al-; Shirazi, Abu Ishaq Ibrahim ibn 'Ali

James W. Ely, Jr.
Vanderbilt University Law School
Property: Protection of Property in United States Law; Regulation: Transportation Regulation

Christoph Emmrich
Department and Centre for the Study of Religion, University of Toronto
Aśoka; Ātmanastuṣṭi; Bhutan; Sadācāra; Vyavahāra

Anver M. Emon
Faculty of Law, University of Toronto
Non-Muslims in Islamic Law

Daphna Ephrat
Department of History, Philosophy, and Judaic Studies, Open University of Israel
Kalwadhani, Abu al-Khattab Mahfuz ibn Ahmad al-; Legal Profession in Islamic Law, Part 1

William N. Eskridge, Jr.
Yale Law School
Gay, Lesbian, Bisexual, and Transgender Theory; Statutory Interpretation and Legislation

Mohammad Fadel
University of Toronto Faculty of Law
Forum, Exterior (*Ẓāhir*), and Interior Forum (*Bāṭin*); Procedure: Proof and Procedure in Islamic Law; Public Authority (Sultan) in Islamic Law; Public Law: Public and Private Law in Islamic Law; Torture: Islamic Law

Ulrich Falk
Universität Mannheim, Germany
Carpzov, Benedict; Jhering, Rudolf von; *Pandektenwissenschaft*; Windscheid, Bernhard

Daniel A. Farber
University of California, Berkeley
Environmental Law: United States Law

S. A. Farrar
Public Law Department, Ahmad Ibrahim Kulliyyah of Laws, International Islamic University Malaysia
Southeast Asian Law: Muslim Law

Celia Wasserstein Fassberg
Faculty of Law, The Hebrew University of Jerusalem, Israel
Conflict of Laws: United States Law

Stephen M. Feldman
University of Wyoming
Postmodernism and Law

Maribel Fierro
Instituto de Lenguas y Culturas del Mediterráneo y de Oriente Próximo, Consejo Superior de Investigaciones Científicas, Madrid, Spain
Maghrib and al-Andalus (Muslim Spain)

Paul Finkelman
Albany Law School
Slavery: United States Law; United States Law: The American Revolution; United States Law: The Nineteenth Century

Thomas Finkenauer
Juristische Fakultät, Universität Tübingen, Germany
Property: Medieval and Post-Medieval Roman Law

George Fisher
Stanford Law School
Alcohol and Drugs: United States Law

Martin S. Flaherty
Leitner Center for International Law and Justice, Fordham Law School
International Law: Modern Public International Law; International Law: Public Law in United States Law

James E. Fleming
Boston University School of Law
Natural Law: United States Law

Matthew L. M. Fletcher
Indigenous Law & Policy Center, Michigan State University College of Law
Native American Law

Peter Flügel
Department of the Study of Religions, School of Oriental and African Studies, University of London
Jaina Law

Wolfgang Forster
Justus-Liebig-Universität Gießen, Germany
Theft and Robbery

D. M. Fox
Faculty of Law, University of Cambridge
Possession: English Common Law; Property: Personal Property in English Common Law

Domenico Francavilla
Dipartimento di Scienze Giuridiche, Università di Torino, Italy
Mīmāṃsā

Ersilia Francesca
Facoltà di Studi Arabo-Islamici e del Mediterraneo, Università di Napoli l'Orientale, Italy
Acknowledgment (Avowal; *Iqrār*); Islamic Schools of Sacred Law: Sunni Schools: The Khariji School of Law; Loan: Islamic Law; Option (*Khiyār*); Possession: *Yad* in Islamic Law

Herbert Franke
University of Munich, Germany, Emeritus
Chinese Law, History of: Liao (937–1125 C.E.) and Qin (1115–1234 C.E.) Empires

Eric M. Freedman
Hofstra Law School
Articles of Confederation

Lawrence M. Friedman
Stanford Law School
Family: United States Law; United States Law: The Twentieth Century

Gerald E. Frug
Harvard Law School
Local Government Law

Lance Gable
Wayne State University Law School
Health

Marc Gaborieau
Centre National de la Recherche Scientifique, Paris; École des Hautes Études en Sciences Sociales, Paris
Constitutional Law: Constitutions and Constitutional Law in Islamic Law: Pakistan and Bangladesh

Michael Gagarin
Department of Classics, University of Texas at Austin
Ancient Greek Law: Overview and Historical Survey; Ancient Greek Law: Sources; Ancient Greek Law: The Origins of Ancient Greek Law; Ancient Greek Law: The Archaic Period; Ancient Greek Law: History of Scholarship; Anthropology and Ancient Greek Law; Athens; Draco; Literature and Law in Ancient Greece; Logography; Procedure: Archaic Greek Law; Rhetoric in Ancient Greek Law

Thomas P. Gallanis
University of Minnesota
Courts, English; Evidence: English Common Law; Ordeal in English Common Law; Trial by Battle

Jane F. Gardner
Department of Classics, University of Reading, U.K., Emerita
Roman Citizenship and *Latinitas*; Slavery: Roman Law; Women: The Position of Women and Equality in Ancient Rome

Bryant G. Garth
American Bar Foundation
Law and Society

Thomas Gergen
Universität des Saarlandes, Germany
Competition: Medieval and Post-Medieval Roman Law

Michael J. Gerhardt
University of North Carolina at Chapel Hill Law School
Executive Power; Federalism

Julius G. Getman
University of Texas School of Law
Labor and Employment Law: Labor Arbitration in United States Law

Joshua S. Getzler
St Hugh's College and Faculty of Law, University of Oxford; Faculty of Law, University of New South Wales
Company Law: English Common Law; Easements; Environmental Law: English Common Law

Tomasz Giaro
Faculty of Law and Administration, Warsaw University, Poland
Poland

Robert Gleave
Institute of Arab and Islamic Studies, University of Exeter
'Amili, Muhammad ibn Makki al-; 'Amili, Zayn al-Din ibn 'Ali ibn Ahmad al-; Ansari, Murtada ibn Muhammad Amin al-; Arab Countries, Islamic Law in: Saudi Arabia; Baqir al-Najafi, Muhammad Hasan ibn Muhammad; Bihbahani, Muhammad Baqir ibn Muhammad Akmal al-; Commercial Law: Islamic Law in the Classical Period; Commodity in Islamic Law; Da'ud al-Isbahani; Hilli, Ja'far ibn al-Hasan al-; Ibn al-Mutahhar, Hasan ibn Yusuf al-Hilli; Iran, Islamic Law in; Islamic Schools of Sacred Law: Shi'i Schools: The Imami School of Law; Islamic Schools of Sacred Law: Shi'i Schools: The Isma'ili School of Law; Qadi al-Nu'man, Ibn Muhammad ibn Mansur al-; Lease and Tenancy Contracts: Islamic Law; Partnership: Partnerships and Commercial Societies in Islamic Law; Subki, 'Abd al-Wahhab ibn 'Ali al-; Tusi, Muhammad ibn al-Hasan, al-, Shaykh al-Ta'ifa

Sarah Barringer Gordon
University of Pennsylvania Law School
Property: United States Law; Religion: United States Law

William M. Gordon
University of Glasgow, Emeritus
Delict: Roman Law

Arsha Gosine
Independent Scholar, London
Trinidad and Tobago

Lawrence O. Gostin
Georgetown University Law Center
Health

Mark A. Graber
University of Maryland School of Law
Procedure: Criminal Procedure in United States Law

Volker Grabowsky
Institut für Ethnologie, Westfälische Wihelms-Universität Münster, Germany
Laos

William Granara
Harvard University
Sicily, Islamic Law in

Athanasios Gromitsaris
Faculty of Law, Ludwig Maximilian University, Munich, Germany
Administration, Public Law of

Joanna Grossman
Hofstra University
Succession: Family Law in the United States

Lewis A. Grossman
Washington College of Law, American University
Codes and Codification: United States Law

R. Kent Guy
Department of History, University of Washington
Courts, Chinese: The Central Court

Hans-Peter Haferkamp
Institut für Neuere Privatrechtsgeschichte, University of Cologne, Germany
Guarantee; Jurisprudence of Concepts

Arnd Helmut Hafner
Research Institute for Languages and Cultures of Asia and Africa, Tokyo University of Foreign Studies
Accessory and Principal in Chinese Law; Doing What Ought Not to Be Done; Sentence in Chinese Law; Wrongful Judgment in Chinese Law

Jan Hallebeek
Department of Legal Theory and Legal History, Faculty of Law, Vu University, Amsterdam
Noodt, Gerard

Jean-Louis Halpérin
Ecole Normale Supérieure, Paris
France

Notker Hammerstein
Historisches Seminar, Johann Wolfgang Goethe-Universität, Frankfurt am Main, Germany
Universities

Haider Ala Hamoudi
University of Pittsburgh School of Law
Capital (*Ra's al-mal*)

Rishi Handa
Independent Scholar, Slough, U.K.
Sikh Law

Joel F. Handler
UCLA School of Law; School of Public Affairs, UCLA
Poverty; Welfare

Anders Hansson
Institute of Chinese Studies, Chinese University of Hong Kong
Punishment and Status in Chinese Law: Slaves; Status: Chinese Law

Jan Dirk Harke
Juristische Fakultät, Universität Würzburg, Germany
Delay; Error and Mistake: Medieval and Post-Medieval Roman Law

Jill Harries
School of Classics, University of St Andrews, Scotland, U.K.
Jurists; Religious Law: The Influence of the Adoption of Christianity on Roman Religious Law

Edward M. Harris
Department of Classics and Ancient History, Durham University, United Kingdom
Commercial Law: Ancient Greek Law; Contract: Ancient Greek Law; Criminal Law: Ancient Athenian Law; *Graphē Paranomōn*; Judges: Judges and Jurors in Ancient Greece; Maritime Law: Ancient Greece; Offenses against the State in Ancient Greece; Prisons and Imprisonment: Ancient Athens; Property: Ancient Greek Law; Punishment: Ancient Athens; Rape: Ancient Greek Law; Slavery: Ancient Greek Law; Solon

Ron Harris
School of Law, Tel Aviv University, Israel
Law and Economics

John F. Hart
Department of History, Duke University
Takings Clause

Christian Hattenhauer
Institut für Geschichtliche Rechtswissenschaft, Ruprecht-Karls-Universität Heidelberg, Germany
Assignment (Assignation)

Bernard Haykel
Department of Near Eastern Studies, Princeton University
Hadi ila l-Haqq Yahya ibn al-Husayn al-; Islamic Schools of Sacred Law: Shi'i Schools: The Zaydi School of Law; Mahdi li-Din Allah Ahmad ibn Yahya al-Murtada al-; Mansur bi-llah 'Abd Allah ibn' al-

Steve Hedley
Faculty of Law, University College, Cork, Ireland
Bankruptcy: English Common Law; Consumer Protection: English Common Law; Employment and Labor Law: English Common Law; Restitution in English Common Law

R. H. Helmholz
University of Chicago Law School
Compurgation; Ecclesiastical Law in English Common Law; Marriage: English Common Law

Thomas Henne
Law Faculty, University of Frankfurt am Main, Germany; Faculty of Law, University of Tokyo
Advocate: Medieval and Post-Medieval Roman Law

James A. Henretta
Department of History, University of Maryland
State Law: State Constitutions

Hans-Georg Hermann
Leopold-Wenger-Institut für Rechtsgeschichte, Ludwig-Maximilians-Universität München, Germany
Fideicommissum (*Familiae*)

Elizabeth L. Hillman
Rutgers University School of Law, Camden
Military Tribunals

Michael S. Hindus
Pillsbury Winthrop Shaw Pittman LLP
Punishment: United States Law

Adam J. Hirsch
Florida State University College of Law
Inheritance: United States Law

Mohammed Hocine Benkheira
EPHE, Section des Sciences Religieuses, Paris
Children: Islamic Law

Peter Charles Hoffer
Department of History, University of Georgia
Criminal Law: Colonial United States; Slavery: Slavery and Other Labor Systems in the Colonial United States

Livia Sorrentino Holden
Comparative Micro-Sociology of Criminal Procedures, Free University; Socio-Legal Research Centre, Griffith University
Divorce: Hindu Law; Marriage: Hindu Law

Ernst Holthöfer
Max-Planck-Institut für Europäische Rechtsgeschichte, Frankfurt am Main, Germany
Domat, Jean; Doneau, Hugues

Tony Honoré
All Souls College, Oxford University
Papinian; Paul; Ulpian

Herbert Hovenkamp
University of Iowa College of Law
Business Organizations

David Howlett
Independent Scholar, Hitchin, U.K.
Jones, William; Maine, Henry

John Hudson
Department of Mediaeval History, University of St Andrews, Scotland
Feudal Law: English Common Law

N. E. H. Hull
Rutgers School of Law, Camden
Elderlaw

Daniel J. Hulsebosch
New York University School of Law
United States Law: The Colonial Period: The Colonies in the Empire

Iza Hussin
Comparative Law and Society Studies Center, University of Washington
Personal Status Law: Personal Status Law in South and Southeast Asia

Andrew Huxley
School of Law, School of Oriental and African Studies, University of London
Burma; Southeast Asian Law: Buddhist Law

David Ibbetson
Faculty of Law, University of Cambridge, U.K.
Bailment in English Common Law; Breach of Contract: English Common Law; Business Law; Common Law: English Common Law; Contract: English Common Law; Contract: Contracts in Favor of Third Parties in English Common Law; Criminal Law: English Common Law; Custom: English Common Law; Duress: English Common Law; English Common Law, Historiography of English Law; Error and Mistake: English Common Law; Fraud: English Common Law; Insurance: English Common Law; Law Reporting in English Common Law; Legal Reasoning; Natural Law: English Common Law; Negligence; Obligations: English Common Law; Precedent: Doctrine of Precedent; Property: Real Property in English Common Law; Roman Law: Roman Law and English Common Law; Solicitors; Sources of Law in English Common Law; Tort: English Common Law

Colin Imber
University of Manchester, U.K.
Administrative Decrees of the Political Authorities (Qānūn): The Ottoman Period

Bernard S. Jackson
Centre for Jewish Studies, University of Manchester, U.K.
Jewish Law: Overview

Iván Jaksi
Stanford University
Bello, Andrés

Stephanie W. Jamison
University of California, Los Angeles
Hindu Law: Vedic Law, 1500–800 B.C.E.

Nishtha Jaswal
Department of Laws, Panjab University, India
Fundamental Duties

Paramjit S. Jaswal
Department of Laws, Panjab University, India
Fundamental Rights

Günter Jerouschek
Friedrich-Schiller-University Jena, Germany
Witch Trials

Yonglin Jiang
Department of History, Oklahoma State University
Chinese Law, History of: Ming Dynasty (1368–1644 C.E.)

Baber Johansen
Harvard University
Commercial Law: Islamic Law in the Classical Period; Commodity in Islamic Law; Contract: Contract for Delivery with Prepayment (*Salam*) in Islamic Law; Dissent (*Ikhtilāf*); Fungible Things (*Mithliyyat*); Islamic Law: Overview; Islamic Law: Genres of Legal Literature; Islamic Law: Legal and Ethical Qualifications; Islamic Law: Spheres of the Law in the *Fiqh*; Persons: Islamic Law; Taxation: Taxation and Religion in Islamic Law, Part 1; Territorial Concepts in Islamic Law

Wallace S. Johnson (Deceased)
Center for East Asian Studies, University of Kansas
Chinese Law, History of: Sui and Tang Dynasties (581–907 C.E.); Chinese Law, Sources of: Penal Codes; Doubtful Cases; Gambling in Chinese Law; Intention in Chinese Law; Offenses in Chinese Law, Classification of; Poison (*Gu*); Punishment and Status in Chinese Law: Overview; Punishment and Status in Chinese Law: Officials; Sumptuary Laws in Chinese Law

David Johnston
Axiom Advocates, Edinburgh
Succession: Roman Law

Bernie Jones
Department of Legal Studies, University of Massachusetts-Amherst
Critical Race Theory

Gareth Jones
Trinity College, Cambridge, Emeritus
Charities; Denning, Alfred Thompson

N. G. Jones
Faculty of Law, University of Cambridge
Chancery; Conveyancing; Equity: English Common Law; Land: Leases of Land in English Common Law; Strict Settlements; Trusts in English Common Law

C. C. Jones-Pauly
United States Institute of Peace, Washington, D.C.
Codes and Codification: Islamic Law; Codes and Codification: Islamic Law in Africa; Constitutional Law: Constitutions and Constitutional Law in Islamic Law: Africa

Vaijayanti Joshi
ILS Law College Pune, India
Kane, P. V.

Anita Jowitt
School of Law, University of the South Pacific, Vanuatu
Fiji; Melanesia; Polynesia

Craig Joyce
The University of Houston Law Center
Intellectual Property: United States Law

Cengiz Kallek
History Department, Fatih University, Turkey
Taxation: Taxation and Religion in Islamic Law, Part 2

Laura Kalman
Department of History, University of California, Santa Barbara
Legal Realism

Mohammad Hashim Kamali
International Institute of Advanced Islamic Studies (IAIS), Malaysia
Afghanistan, Islamic Law in; Banking and Finance in Islamic Law; Constitutional Law: Constitutions and Constitutional Law in Islamic Law: Malaysia; Islamic Law and Its Political Geography: Southeast Asia

Allen R. Kamp
John Marshall Law School, Chicago
Commercial Law: United States

Kenneth L. Karst
School of Law, University of California, Los Angeles, Emeritus
Equal Protection

Katrin Kastl
Juristische Fakultät, Universität München, Germany
Crimes against Life and Body; Political Crimes: Medieval and Post-Medieval Roman Law

Marion Holmes Katz
Department of Middle Eastern and Islamic Studies, New York University
Fetus in Islamic Law; Worship in Islamic Law

Ian R. C. Kawaley
Commercial Court Judge, Bermuda
Bermuda

Bruce Kercher
Macquarie University, Australia
Australia

Orin S. Kerr
The George Washington University Law School
Search and Seizure

Kishimoto Mio
Graduate School of Humanities and Sciences, Ochanomizu University, Japan
Sale: Sale of Goods in Chinese Law

Michael J. Klarman
University of Virginia School of Law
Civil Rights and Civil Liberties in United States Law

Daniel M. Klerman
University of Southern California
Rape: English Common Law

Fabian Klinck
Universität Passau, Germany
Possession: Medieval and Post-Medieval Roman Law

Viviana Kluger
Universidad de Buenos Aires
Argentina; South and Central America: Spanish Colonial Law

Birgit Krawietz
Asien-Orient-Institut, Universität Tübingen, Germany
Abu Ya'la, Muhammad ibn al-Husayn ibn al-Farra' al-Baghdadi; Ibn Qayyim al-Jawziyya, Muhammad ibn Abi Bakr; Ibn Qudama, Muwaffaq al-Din Abu Muhammad 'Abdallah

Leonard Van der Kuijp
Department of Sanskrit and Indian Studies, Harvard University
Tibet

Virendra Kumar
Faculty of Law, Punjab University, Chandigarh, India
Hindu Law: Overview

Kusum
New Delhi, India
Family: Indian Family Law

Alexandra D. Lahav
University of Connecticut School of Law
History, Uses of

Stephan Landsman
DePaul University College of Law
Social Science, Uses of

Christian Lange
University of Edinburgh
Homosexuality: Islamic Law; Privacy: Islamic Law

Donald C. Langevoort
Georgetown University Law Center
Regulation: Securities Regulation

Adriaan Lanni
Harvard Law School
Evidence: Ancient Athens; Litigation in Ancient Athens

Richard W. Lariviere
University of Kansas
Hindu Law: The Post-Formative Period, 400–1000 C.E.

188 DIRECTORY OF CONTRIBUTORS

Gerald James Larson
Indiana University, Emeritus; Religious Studies, University of California, Santa Barbara, Emeritus
Secularism in Indian Law

Nap-yin Lau
Institute of History and Philology, Academia Sinica, Taipei, Taiwan
Marriage: Chinese Law; Mutual Concealment

Douglas Laycock
University of Michigan Law School
Remedies

P. Leelakrishnan
School of Legal Studies, Cochin University of Science & Technology, India
Environmental Law: Indian Law

Susanne Lepsius
Institut für Rechtsgeschichte, Universität Frankfurt am Main, Germany
Company Law: Medieval and Post-Medieval Roman Law

Sanford Levinson
University of Texas School of Law and Department of Government
Constitution of the United States: Amendments to the Constitution

Andrew Lewis
Faculty of Laws, University College London
Bentham, Jeremy; Codes and Codification: Codifications in Ancient Roman Law; Germanic Provincial Administration; Institutional Writings; Julian; Praetorian Edict; Roman Law: 753–27 B.C.E.; Twelve Tables

Peter Leyland
London Metropolitan University
Thailand

José Reinaldo de Lima Lopes
Universidade de São Paulo Law School; Direito-GV (Fundação Getúlio Vargas) Law School
Brazil; South and Central America: Portuguese Colonial Law

Andrew Lintott
Worcester College, Oxford
Cicero; Lex

Michael Lobban
School of Law, Queen Mary, University of London
Austin, John; Education and Training: English Common Law; English Legal Treatises; Law Reform Movements; Legal Literature in English Common Law

Janet S. Loengard
Department of History, Moravian College, Emerita
Nuisance in English Common Law; Women: English Common Law

Rüdiger Lohlker
Institute of Oriental Studies, University of Vienna, Austria
Ibn Rushd, Abu al-Walid Muhammad ibn Ahmad ibn Muhammad; Islamic Schools of Sacred Law: Sunni Schools: The Maliki School of Law, Part 2; Khalil ibn Ishaq al-Jundi

J. H. A. Lokin
Rijksuniversiteit Groningen, Netherlands
Byzantium: Early Byzantium; Byzantium: Byzantine Legislation; Contract: Byzantine Law; Delict: Byzantine Law; Persons: Byzantine Law; Procedure: Byzantine Law; Property: Byzantine Law; Succession: Byzantine Law

Daniel H. Lowenstein
University of California, Los Angeles Law School
Political Parties and Elections

Joseph E. Lowry
University of Pennsylvania
Arabian Peninsula; Shafi'i, Muhammad ibn Idris al-

Richard Lufrano
The College of Staten Island, City University of New York
Chinese Law, Sources of: Guilds

Adam Lui
Department of History, the University of Hong Kong
Chinese Law, Sources of: Administrative Codes or Regulations; Corruption in Chinese Law; Courts, Chinese: An Overview of Chinese Courts and Judicial Agencies; Courts, Chinese: The Censorate; Courts, Chinese: The Emperor; Courts, Chinese: The Ministry of Justice (Board of Punishments)

Klaus Luig
Institut für Neuere Privatrechtsgeschichte, Universität zu Köln, Germany
Germany; Leibniz, Gottfried Wilhelm; National Socialist Law; Natural Law: Medieval and Post-Medieval Roman Law; Pufendorf, Samuel von; Thomasius, Christian; Wolff, Christian von

Jonathan Lurie
Department of History, Rutgers University
War Power

Marju Luts-Sootak
Faculty of Law, University of Tartu, Estonia
Baltic Nations

Ann Lyon
School of Law, University of Plymouth
Nationality in English Common Law; Treason

Melissa Macauley
Department of History, Northwestern University
Procedure: Criminal and Civil Procedure in Chinese Law; Procedure: Parties and Witnesses in Chinese Law

Geoffrey D. MacCormack
Faculty of Law, King's College, University of Aberdeen, Emeritus
Alcohol and Drugs: Chinese Law; Beating and Whipping in Chinese Law; Cangue, The; Collective Liability; Cursing; Damage to Property in Chinese Law; Deceit; Exile in Chinese

Law; Filial Piety, Lack of; Homicide: Chinese Law; Kidnapping: Chinese Law; Offenses against the State in Chinese Law: Disrespect (*Bujing*); Offenses against the State in Chinese Law: Heterodox Beliefs; Offenses against the State in Chinese Law: Offenses Damaging the Efficiency of Government; Offenses against the State in Chinese Law: Offenses Threatening the Life or Well-Being of the Emperor; Offenses against the State in Chinese Law: Offenses Threatening the Safety of the State or Dynasty; Penal Servitude in Chinese Law; Punishment: Chinese Law: Overview; Punishment: Chinese Law: Administrative Punishments; Redemption; Theft: Chinese Law; Torture: Chinese Law; Wounding in Chinese Law; *Zang*

Casey MacGregor
Department of Social Welfare, UCLA School of Public Affairs
Poverty

Alberto Maffi
Università degli Studi di Milano-Bicocca, Italy
Gortyn; Inheritance: Ancient Greek Law; Sparta

Ze'ev Maghen
The Begin-Sadat (BESA) Center for Strategic Studies, Bar-Ilan University, Israel
Purity and Impurity in Islamic Law

Sanjoy Mahajan
Massachusetts Institute of Technology
Censorship: English Common Law

Harald Maihold
Departement Rechtswissenschaften, Universität Basel, Switzerland
Guilt (*Schuld*)

Ayesha Malik
Pakistan College of Law
Pakistan, Secular Laws in

Chibli Mallat
S. J. Quinney College of Law, University of Utah; Campus Sciences Sociales, Université Saint-Joseph, Lebanon
Arab Countries, Islamic Law in: Overview; Commercial Law: Islamic Law in the Modern Period; Constitutional Law: Constitutions and Constitutional Law in Islamic Law: Overview and the Arab Countries; Contract: Contracts and Unilateral Acts in Islamic Law; International Law: Islamic Public Law

Dario Mantovani
Faculty of Law, University of Pavia, Italy
Justinian; Tribonian

Henry Mares
St. Hilda's College, University of Oxford
Star Chamber

P. J. Marshall
History Department, King's College London, Emeritus
Hastings, Warren

James May
Washington College of Law, American University
Antitrust

David von Mayenburg
Institut für Deutsche und Rheinische Rechtsgeschichte, University of Bonn, Germany
Fraud: Criminal Law in Medieval and Post-Medieval Roman Law

Serena Mayeri
University of Pennsylvania Law School
Women: United States Law

Aldo Mazzacane
Università degli Studi di Napoli Federico II, Italy
Carrara, Francesco; De Luca, Giovanni Battista; Filangieri, Gaetano; Gravina, Gian Vincenzo; Humanism

Mark C. McGaw
Solicitor, London, England
Agency: English Common Law; Final Process; Mesne Process; Outlawry; Pleading; Vicarious Liability: English Common Law

Brian E. McKnight
Department of East Asian Studies, University of Arizona, Emeritus
Amnesty in Chinese Law; Chinese Law, History of: Five Dynasties and Song Dynasty (907–1279 C.E.); Chinese Law, Sources of: Judicial Precedent

Christopher McNall
Barrister-at-Law, Manchester, U.K.
Assault; Assizes; Banks and Banking: English Common Law; Bills of Exchange in English Common Law; Blackmail; Burglary in English Common Law; Capital Punishment: English Common Law; Common Pleas; Exchequer; Homicide: English Common Law; Kidnapping: English Common Law; King's Bench; Law Merchant: English Common Law; Mortgage: English Common Law; Punishment: English Common Law; Theft: English Common Law; Torture: English Common Law

Stephan Meder
Faculty of Law, Leibniz Universität Hannover, Germany
Interpretation

Ajay K. Mehrotra
Law and History, Indiana University, Bloomington
Taxation: United States Law

Christopher Melchert
University of Oxford
Ibn Hanbal, Ahmad; Khallal, Abu Bakr Ahmad ibn Muhammad ibn Harun al-; Khiraqi, Abu 'Umar ibn al-Husayn ibn 'Abdallah al-

Joseph Mélèze Modrzejewski
Université de Paris I, Emeritus; École Pratique des Hautes Études, Paris
Ancient Greek Law: Hellenistic Law; Egypt: Hellenistic Period

Werner Menski
School of Law, School of Oriental and African Studies, University of London
Adoption: Hindu Law; Guyana; Hindu Nationalism; Justice, Equity, and Good Conscience; Maldives; Naga Law; Personal Law and General Law; Property: Hindu Law; *Rājadharma*; Seychelles; Suriname

Brinkley Messick
Department of Anthropology, Columbia University
Fatwa; Yemen

Ernest Metzger
University of Glasgow School of Law
Formula; Lex Irnitana

Rudolf Meyer-Pritzl
Rechtswissenschaftliche Fakultät, Christian-Albrechts-Universität zu Kiel, Germany
Prussian Allgemeines Landrecht

Axel Michaels
South Asia Institute, Heidelberg University, Germany
Nepal

David Mirhady
Department of Humanities, Simon Fraser University
Oaths in Ancient Athens; Religion: Religion and Law in Ancient Greece; Theft: Ancient Greek Law; Witnesses in Ancient Athens

M. C. Mirow
College of Law, Florida International University
South and Central America: Overview; Wills: English Common Law

Paul Mitchell
King's College London
Libel and Slander; Sale: English Common Law

Kjell Å Modéer
Faculty of Law, Lund University, Sweden, Emeritus
Sweden

Heinz Mohnhaupt
Max-Planck-Institut für Europäische Rechtsgeschichte, Germany
Privileges

Cosima Möller
Institut für Römische Rechtsgeschichte, Fachbereich Rechtswissenschaft, Freie Universität Berlin, Germany
Servitude in Real Estate

Najma Moosa
University of the Western Cape, Bellville, Cape Town, South Africa
South Africa: Indian Law

Rachel F. Moran
School of Law, University of California, Berkeley
Education Law

Jonathan Morgan
Christ's College, University of Cambridge
Central Government in English Common Law; Constitutional Law: English Common Law; Parliament

Robert P. Mosteller
Duke Law School
Evidence: United States Procedure

Harald Motzki
Department of Arabic and Islam, Radboud University of Nijmegen, Netherlands
Islamic Law: Transmission and Authenticity of the Reports from the Prophet

José Luis de los Mozos
Universidad de Valladolid, Spain, Emeritus
Budé, Guillaume

José Javier de los Mozos Touya
Facultad de Derecho, Universidad de Valladolid, Spain
Spain

Christian Müller
Institut de Recherche et d'Histoire des Textes, Centre National de la Recherche Scientifique, Paris
Enforcement in Islamic Law; Judiciary: Islamic Law, Classical Period; Legal Norms in Islamic Law, Production of

Miklos Muranyi
Siegburg, Germany
Islamic Schools of Sacred Law: Sunni Schools: The Maliki School of Law, Part 1; Malik ibn Anas ibn al-Harith al-Asbahi; Qayrawani, Ibn Abi Zayd al-; Sahnun, ʿAbd al-Salam ibn Saʿid al-Tanukhi

Ulrike Müßig
University of Passau, Germany
Absolutism; Precedent: Stare Decisis

Faizan Mustafa
Faculty of Law, Aligarh Muslim University, India
Criminal Law: India

Robert F. Nagel
University of Colorado School of Law
Judicial Power

Gerald L. Neuman
Harvard Law School
Immigration

Penelope (Pip) Nicholson
Asian Law Centre, School of Law, University of Melbourne
Vietnam

Knut Wolfgang Nörr
Juristische Fakultät, Universität Tübingen, Germany, Emeritus
Procedure: Civil Procedure in Medieval and Post-Medieval Roman Law

J. A. North
Department of History, University College London
Religious Law: An Overview of Roman Religious Law

Michael North
Ernst-Moritz-Arndt-Universität Greifswald, Germany
Banks and Banking: Medieval and Post-Medieval Roman Law

Bruce R. O'Brien
University of Mary Washington
Anglo-Saxon Law

Jonathan Ocko
Department of History, North Carolina State University; Duke University School of Law
Appeal: Chinese Law; Appeal: Review in Chinese Law

Peter Oestmann
Westfälische Wilhelms-Universität Münster, Germany
Courts, Medieval and Post-Medieval Roman Law: Courts and Cases; Courts, Medieval and Post-Medieval Roman Law: Faculties Acting as Courts; Lease and Tenancy Contracts: Medieval and Post-Medieval Roman Law; Legislation: Medieval and Post-Medieval Roman Law; Punishment: Medieval and Post-Medieval Roman Law; Reichskammergericht

Pontus S. J. Ohrstedt
Independent Scholar, London
Guatemala

Veena T. Oldenburg
Department of History, Baruch College, City University of New York
Dowry in Hindu Law

James C. Oldham
Georgetown University Law Center
Mansfield, Lord

Patrick Olivelle
Department of Asian Studies, University of Texas at Austin
Hindu Law: The Formative Period, 400 B.C.E.–400 C.E.; *Manusmriti*

Rosanna Omitowoju
Faculty of Classics and King's College, Cambridge
Literature and Law in Ancient Greece

Felicitas Opwis
Georgetown University
Ghazali, Abu Hamid Muhammad

John V. Orth
University of North Carolina School of Law
Due Process

Esin Örücü
School of Law, University of Glasgow, U.K., Emerita
Comparative Law

W. N. Osborough
School of Law, University College Dublin, Ireland
Irish Law

Jochen Otto
Universität zu Köln, Germany
Alciati, Andrea; Cujas, Jacques; Faber, Antonius; Oldendorp, Johann; Tiraquellus; Zasius, Ulrich

Sükrü Özen
Centre For Islamic Studies (ISAM), Istanbul, Turkey
Islamic Schools of Sacred Law: Sunni Schools: The Hanafi School of Law

Louis Pahlow
Universität Mannheim, Germany
Intellectual Property: Medieval and Post-Medieval Roman Law

Michael Palmer
Department of Law, School of Oriental and African Studies, University of London
Adoption: Chinese Law; Chinese Law, History of: People's Republic of China

David Ray Papke
Marquette University Law School
Political Crimes: United States Law

Rosemary Pattenden
Norwich Law School, East Anglia University, U.K.
Appeal: English Common Law

Cynthia B. Patterson
Department of History, Emory University
Family: Ancient Greek Law; Status: Ancient Greek Law

Walter Pauly
Faculty of Jurisprudence, Friedrich-Schiller-University of Jena, Germany
Constitution

Scott Pearce
Liberal Studies Department, Western Washington University
Chinese Law, History of: The Northern Dynasties (386–589 C.E.)

Rogelio Pérez Perdomo
Universidad Metropolitana, Caracas, Venezuela
Venezuela

Rudolph Peters
Faculty of Humanities, University of Amsterdam
Capacity (*Ahliyya*); Damage (*Darar*); Individual Effort of Legal Reasoning (*Ijtihād*)

Guido Pfeifer
Institut für Rechtsgeschichte, Johann Wolfgang Goethe-Universität Frankfurt am Main, Germany
Donation (Gift)

Richard H. Pildes
New York University School of Law
Apportionment and Reapportionment

James Gray Pope
Rutgers University School of Law - Newark
Labor and Employment Law: United States Law

David S. Powers
Department of Near Eastern Studies, Cornell University
Inheritance: Islamic Law; Judicial Review in Islamic Law: Classical Period; Wansharisi, Ahmad ibn Yahya al-Tilimsani al-

Wilfrid Prest
Law School and School of History and Politics, University of Adelaide, Australia
Barristers

Theodore N. Proferes
Department of the Study of Religions, School of Oriental and African Studies, University of London
Śruti

192 DIRECTORY OF CONTRIBUTORS

Josep Puig Montada
Universidad Complutense, Madrid, Spain
Ibn Hazm, 'Ali ibn Ahmad ibn Sa'id

Kurt A. Raaflaub
Department of Classics, Brown University
Constitutional Law: Ancient Greek Law

Intisar Rabb
Department of Near Eastern Studies, Princeton University
Administrative Decrees of the Political Authorities (Qānūn): The Mamluk Period

J. Michael Rainer
Universität Salzburg, Austria
Public Law: The Roman Republic

Jothie Rajah
Melbourne Law School, The University of Melbourne, Australia
Southeast Asian Law: Hindu Law

Susan E. Ramírez
Department of History, Texas Christian University
South and Central America: Precolonial Laws

Carlos Ramos Núñez
Pontificia Universidad Católica del Perú
Peru

Carolyn B. Ramsey
University of Colorado Law School
Criminal Law: United States Law

Martin Ramstedt
Max Planck Institute for Social Anthropology, Germany
Balinese Hindu Law

Yossef Rapoport
Department of History, Queen Mary, University of London
Ibn Taymiyya, Taqi al-Din Ahmad ibn 'Abd al-Halim; Political Dimension (Siyāsa Shar'iyya) of Islamic Law; Repudiation (Ṭalāq)

James S. Read
School of Oriental and African Studies, University of London
African Law, Sub-Saharan: The Precolonial Period; African Law, Sub-Saharan: The Colonial Period; African Law, Sub-Saharan: After Independence; Ethiopia; Liberia; South Africa: Overview

Bradly W. Reed
University of Virginia
Courts, Chinese: Local Courts

Tilman Repgen
Fakultät für Rechtswissenschaft, Universität Hamburg, Germany
Civil Law: Medieval and Post-Medieval Roman Law

Deborah L. Rhode
Stanford Law School
Lawyers: United States Law

Reinhard Richardi
Universität Regensburg, Germany
Negotiable Instruments (Wertpapiere)

John Richardson
Department of Classics, University of Edinburgh, Emeritus
Provincial Edicts and Government

Sebastián Ríos
Departamento de Derecho Privado, Facultad de Derecho, Universidad de Chile
Chile

David W. Robertson
University of Texas Law School
Admiralty: United States Law

O. F. Robinson
School of Law, University of Glasgow
Courts, Ancient Roman: Criminal Courts in the Roman Republic and the Empire; Criminal Law: The Roman Republic; Criminal Law: The Roman Empire

Ludo Rocher
Department of South Asia Studies, University of Pennsylvania, Emeritus
Colebrooke, H. T.; Hindu Law: Medieval Hindu Law; Hindu Law: Anglo-Hindu Law

Mathias Rohe
Institut für Bürgerliches Recht, Internationales Privatrecht und Rechtsvergleichung, Friedrich-Alexander-Universität Erlangen-Nürnberg, Germany
Europe, Islamic Law in

Andrea Romano
Facoltà di Scienze Politiche, Università degli Studi di Messina, Italy
Beccaria, Cesare; Stracca, Benvenuto

Lawrence Rosen
Department of Anthropology, Princeton University; Columbia Law School
Donation in Islamic Law

William G. Ross
Cumberland School of Law, Samford University
Equity: United States Law

Jane Rowlandson
Department of Classics, King's College London
Egypt: Juristic Papyrology

Lene Rubinstein
Department of Classics, Royal Holloway, University of London
Adoption: Ancient Greek Law; Advocate: Ancient Athens

Joachim Rückert
Institut für Rechtsgeschichte, Goethe-Universität Frankfurt am Main, Germany
Employment and Labor Law: Medieval and Post-Medieval Roman Law; Private Law, Concept of; Savigny, Friedrich Carl von

DIRECTORY OF CONTRIBUTORS 193

Yasmin Safian
Islamic Science University of Malaysia
Commodity in Islamic Law

Michael J. Saks
Sandra Day O'Connor College of Law, Arizona State University
Law and Science

Nabil Saleh
Law Consultant (Arab and Islamic Laws)
Usury: Illicit Commercial Gain (*Ribā*) in Islamic Law

Peter W. Salsich, Jr.
Saint Louis University School of Law
Housing

Jane Samson
Department of History and Classics, University of Alberta
British Commonwealth

Saud Al-Sarhan
University of Exeter, U.K.
Arab Countries, Islamic Law in: Saudi Arabia; Daʾud al-Isbahani; Subki, ʿAbd al-Wahhab ibn ʿAli al-

S. P. Sathe (Deceased)
Institute of Advanced Legal Studies, ILS Law College, Pune, India
Constitutional Law: India

Adele C. Scafuro
Department of Classics, Brown University
Arbitration in Ancient Athens

Sara Scalenghe
Indiana University
Body in Islamic Law

Martin J. Schermaier
Institute for Roman Law and Comparative Legal History, University of Bonn, Germany
Breach of Contract: Medieval and Post-Medieval Roman Law

Karl Otto Scherner
Universität Mannheim, Germany, Emeritus
Law Merchant: Medieval and Post-Medieval Roman Law; Maritime Law: Medieval and Post-Medieval Roman Law; Obligations: Medieval and Post-Medieval Roman Law; Sale: Sale of Goods in Medieval and Post-Medieval Roman Law; Sale: Sale of Land in Medieval and Post-Medieval Roman Law

Christoph M. Scheuren-Brandes
University of Bielefeld, Germany
Admiralty: Medieval and Post-Medieval Roman Law; Insurance: Medieval and Post-Medieval Roman Law

Reuel E. Schiller
Hastings College of the Law, University of California, San Francisco
Administrative Agencies

Asghar Schirazi
Middle East Section, Free University of Berlin
Constitutional Law: Constitutions and Constitutional Law in Islamic Law: Iran

Pierre Schlag
University of Colorado Law School
Critical Legal Studies

John Henry Schlegel
University at Buffalo Law School, State University of New York
Academics

Hans Schlosser
Universität Augsburg, Germany
Kreittmayr, Wiguläus Xaver Aloys von

Mathias Schmoeckel
Institut für Deutsche und Rheinische Rechtsgeschichte, Rheinische Friedrich-Wilhelms-Universität Bonn, Germany
Canon Law: Protestant Churches; Evidence: Medieval and Post-Medieval Roman Law; Procedure: Criminal Procedure in Medieval and Post-Medieval Roman Law

Irene Schneider
Seminar für Arabistik, Georg-August-Universität Göttingen, Germany
Prisons and Imprisonment: Islamic Law

Eltjo J. H. Schrage
Faculty of Law, University of Amsterdam
Unjust Enrichment in Medieval and Post-Medieval Roman Law

Jan Schröder
Eberhard-Karls-Universität Tübingen, Germany
System and Systematization

Werner Schroeder
Institute for European Law and Public International Law, University of Innsbruck, Austria
European Communities

Peter H. Schuck
Yale Law School
Citizenship

Eva Schumann
Institute of Legal History, Legal Philosophy and Comparative Law, Faculty of Law, Georg-August University Göttingen, Germany
Family: Medieval and Post-Medieval Roman Law

Gwen Seabourne
School of Law, Bristol University, U.K.
Competition: English Common Law; Guilds in English Common Law

Anthony J. Sebok
Brooklyn Law School
Positivism in United States Law

Brinderpal Singh Sehgal
University of Jammu, India
Abortion in Hindu Law

Theary C. Seng
The Center for Social Development, Phnom Penh, Cambodia
Cambodia

194 DIRECTORY OF CONTRIBUTORS

Delfina Serrano Ruano
Istituto de Lenguas y Culturas del Mediterráneo y del Próximo Oriente, Centro de Ciencias Humanas y Sociales (CSIC), Madrid, Spain
Ibn Rushd, Abu al-Walid Muhammad ibn Ahmad

Catherine A. Seville
Newnham College, Cambridge University, U.K.
Copyright in English Common Law

Prakash Shah
School of Law, Queen Mary, University of London
East Africa, South Asian Law in; South Asian Law: South Asian Law in the United Kingdom

Amir Shahruddin
Islamic Science University of Malaysia
Commercial Law: Islamic Law in the Classical Period; Lease and Tenancy Contracts: Islamic Law; Partnership: Partnerships and Commercial Societies in Islamic Law

Eran Shalev
Department of History, Haifa University, Israel
State Law: The Confederation Period

Amanda Sheely
Department of Social Welfare, UCLA School of Public Affairs
Welfare

Stephen A. Siegel
DePaul University College of Law
Contracts Clause

Norman Silber
Hofstra University School of Law
Consumer Protection: United States Law

Thomas Simon
Institut für Rechts- und Verfassungsgeschichte, Universität Wien, Austria
Enlightenment

Gurjeet Singh
The Rajiv Gandhi National University of Law, Punjab, India
Consumer Protection: Hindu Law; Public Interest Litigation in India

Boudewijn Sirks
All Souls College, University of Oxford
Cognitio and Imperial and Bureaucratic Courts; Public Law: The Roman Empire; Roman Law: 250–527 C.E.

David A. Skeel, Jr.
University of Pennsylvania Law School
Bankruptcy: United States Commercial Law

Laura A. Skosey
Department of East Asian Languages and Civilizations and the Law School, University of Chicago
Chinese Law, History of: Shang Dynasty (c. 16th–11th Century B.C.E.); Chinese Law, History of: Western Zhou Dynasty (c. 1045–771 B.C.E.); Chinese Law, History of: Eastern Zhou, Spring and Autumn (771–464 B.C.E.)

Billy K. L. So
Department of History, The Chinese University of Hong Kong
Punishment and Status in Chinese Law: Age; Punishment and Status in Chinese Law: Disability; Punishment and Status in Chinese Law: Women

J. R. Spencer
Faculty of Law, University of Cambridge, U.K.
Procedure: Criminal Procedure in English Common Law

Clyde Spillenger
School of Law, University of California, Los Angeles
Judiciary: United States Law

Peter Spiller
University of Waikato, New Zealand; Principal Disputes Referee of New Zealand
Canada: Canadian Law; New Zealand

Federico Squarcini
Department of History, University of Florence, Italy; Faculty of Oriental Studies, University of Rome "La Sapienza"
Homicide: Hindu Law; Punishment: Hindu Law

Chantal Stebbings
University of Exeter, U.K.
Taxation: English Common Law

Michael Ashley Stein
Harvard Law School
Disability

Penelope J. S. Stein
Harvard Project on Disability
Disability

Peter G. Stein
Faculty of Law, University of Cambridge, Emeritus; Queens' College, Cambridge
Celsus the Younger; Education and Training: Ancient Rome; Labeo, Marcus Antistius; Sabinus, Masurius

Robert Stevens
Yale University; Pembroke College, University of Oxford
Education and Training: United States

Devin J. Stewart
Department of Middle Eastern and South Asian Studies, Emory University
Islamic Schools of Sacred Law: Sunni Schools: The Zahiri School of Law

Michael Stolleis
Max-Planck-Institut für Europäische Rechtsgeschichte, Germany
National Socialist Law

Bernard H. Stolte
Royal Netherlands Institute, Rome; Faculty of Law, University of Groningen, Netherlands
Basil I and the Macedonian Renaissance; Byzantium: Later Byzantium to 1453; Byzantium: Byzantine Jurists; Canon Law: Orthodox Churches; Courts, Ancient Roman: Byzantium; Criminal Law: Byzantium; Public Law: Byzantium

Katherine Stone
Cornell University Law School, Emerita
Alternative Dispute Resolution

Philippa Strum
Division of United States Studies, Woodrow Wilson International Center for Scholars, Washington, D.C.
Privacy: United States Law

Carl-Friedrich Stuckenberg
Institute of Criminal Law, University of Bonn, Germany
Punishment, Theories Regarding Purpose of

Michael F. Sturley
University of Texas Law School
Admiralty: United States Law

Fritz Sturm
Faculty of Law and Criminal Justice, University of Lausanne, Switzerland, Emeritus
Conflict of Laws: Medieval and Post-Medieval Roman Law

Warren M. Swain
School of Law, Durham University
Blackstone, William; Procedure: Civil Procedure in English Common Law

Merlin Swartz
Institute for the Study of Muslim Societies and Civilizations, Boston University
Ibn ʿAqil, Abu al-Wafaʾ ʿAli; Islamic Schools of Sacred Law: Sunni Schools: The Hanbali School of Law; Mufti

Richard J. A. Talbert
Department of History, University of North Carolina
Senate, Roman

Brian Z. Tamanaha
St. John's University School of Law
Law

Ditlev Tamm
Faculty of Law, University of Copenhagen, Denmark
Denmark

Kevin Y. L. Tan
Independent Scholar, Singapore
Malaysia; Singapore; Southeast Asian Law: Overview

David S. Tanenhaus
Department of History and William S. Boyd School of Law, University of Nevada, Las Vegas
Juvenile Justice in United States Law

Mauricio Tapia
Departamento de Derecho Privado, Facultad de Derecho, Universidad de Chile
Chile

Linda Te Aho
University of Waikato, New Zealand
Māori Law

Olga E. Tellegen-Couperus
Faculty of Law, Tilburg University, Netherlands
Legis Actiones

Silvia Tellenbach
Max Planck Institute for Foreign and International Criminal Law, Freiburg, Germany
Capital Punishment: The Muslim World in the Twentieth Century; Compensation in Islamic Law; Criminal Law: Crime and Punishment in Islamic Law; Duress: *Ikrāh*

Janet Theiss
Department of History, University of Utah
Homosexuality: Chinese Law; Incest in Chinese Law; Rape: Chinese Law; Sexual Intercourse, Illicit in Chinese Law; Sexual Offenses in Chinese Law

Andreas Thier
Faculty of Law, University of Zurich
Bishops and Archbishops; Canon Law: Courses and Classes; Decretals and Decretal Collections; Ecclesiastical Courts; Pope and Papacy; Taxation: Medieval and Post-Medieval Roman Law

Jean-Louis Thireau
Université Paris I (Sorbonne-Panthéon)
Du Moulin, Charles

J. Michael Thoms
History Department, Vancouver Island University, Powell River Campus
Canada: Native Peoples

Gerhard Thür
Roman Law and Ancient Legal History, University of Graz, Austria
Codes and Codification: Ancient Greek Law; Courts, Ancient Greek: Courts and Magistrates in Ancient Athens; Legislation: Ancient Greece; Procedure: Athens: An Overview; Procedure: Trial Procedure in Ancient Athens; Torture: Ancient Athens

Mathieu Tillier
Université de Provence, France
Abbasid Dynasty; Iraq, Islamic Law in

Nurit Tsafrir
Tel Aviv University, Israel
Abu Yusuf, Yaʿqub ibn Ibrahim; Kasani, Abu Bakr ibn Masʿud; Sarakhsi, Muhammad ibn Ahmad ibn Abi Sahl; Shaybani, Muhammad ibn al-Hasan

Judith E. Tucker
Georgetown University
Women: Islamic Law

Karen Gottschang Turner
Department of History, College of the Holy Cross; East Asian Legal Studies, Harvard Law School
Rule of Law

Mark Tushnet
Harvard Law School
Constitution of the United States: Interpretation of the Constitution

DIRECTORY OF CONTRIBUTORS

Wilhelm Uhlenbruck
Rechtswissenschaftliche Fakultät, Universität zu Köln, Germany
Insolvency

Victor M. Uribe-Uran
Department of History and College of Law, Florida International University
Colombia

George William Van Cleve
Department of History, University of Virginia
Slavery: English Common Law

Rena van den Bergh
Department of Jurisprudence, School of Law, University of South Africa
Roman Law: 27 B.C.E.–250 C.E.

Miloš Vec
Max-Planck-Institut für Europäische Rechtsgeschichte, Germany
Consumer Protection: Medieval and Post-Medieval Roman Law

Stephen I. Vladeck
American University Washington College of Law
Supremacy Clause

Christian Waldhoff
Kirchenrechtliches Institut - Lehrstuhl für Öffentliches Recht, Universität Bonn, Germany
Taxation: Medieval and Post-Medieval Roman Law

Robert W. Wallace
Northwestern University
Speech, Freedom of: Ancient Athens

Benjamin E. Wallacker
Department of East Asian Languages and Cultures, University of California, Davis, Emeritus
Chinese Law, History of: Three Kingdoms, Qin, and Southern Dynasties (220–589 C.E.); Chinese Law, Sources of: Classical (Ritual) Writings

Tay-sheng Wang
College of Law, National Taiwan University
Chinese Law, History of: Taiwan

Thomas Glyn Watkin
University of Wales, Bangor
Church and State in English Common Law; Doctors' Commons; Estates, Doctrine of; Legislation: Statute Law; Subinfeudation and Substitution; Succession: English Common Law; Tenure, Doctrine of; Welsh Law

Peter Weimar
Rechtswissenschaftliches Institut, Universität Zürich
Accursius, Franciscus; Azo; Baldus de Ubaldis, Petrus; Bartolus of Saxoferrato; Irnerius

Louise Weinberg
The University of Texas School of Law
Courts, United States Federal

Robert Weisberg
Stanford Law School
Legal Process

Bernard G. Weiss
Department of Languages and Literature, University of Utah
Islamic Law: Sources and Methodology of the Law; Revealed Texts (*Nuṣūṣ*), Transmission of; Revelation, Forms of

Stephan Wendehorst
Simon-Dubnow-Institut für Jüdische Geschichte und Kultur, Leipzig, Germany
Notary

Keith Werhan
Tulane Law School
Separation of Powers

Patrick S. Werner
Department of Social Science, Ave Maria University, Latin American Campus, San Marcos, Nicaragua
Central American Republics

Gunter Wesener
Institut für Römisches Recht, Antike Rechtsgeschichte und Neuere Privatrechtsgeschichte, Karl-Franzens-Universität Graz, Austria, Emeritus
Succession: Medieval and Post-Medieval Roman Law

Raymond Westbrook
Department of Near Eastern Studies, The Johns Hopkins University
Ancient Near Eastern Law

Brannon Wheeler
United States Naval Academy
Assignment (*Ḥawālah*)

Johannes Christian Wichard
Ornex, France
Legal Personality in Islamic Law; Obligations: Islamic Law; Ownership (*Milk*); Profit in Islamic Law

Hartmut Wicke
Notary Public, Munich, Germany
Vicarious Liability: Medieval and Post-Medieval Roman Law

William M. Wiecek
Syracuse University College of Law
Classical Legal Theory

Norman R. Williams
Willamette University College of Law
State Sovereignty

Bénédict Winiger
Department of History of Law, Law School, University of Geneva, Switzerland
Tort: Tort, Negligence, and Delict

Laurens Winkel
Erasmus University Rotterdam, Netherlands
Grotius, Hugo; Netherlands

Michael Winter
Department of Middle Eastern and African History, Tel Aviv University, Emeritus
Legal Profession in Islamic Law, Part 2

John Fabian Witt
Columbia Law School
Tort: United States Law

Victoria Saker Woeste
American Bar Foundation
Regulation: Agriculture Regulation

Antonio Carlos Wolkmer
Federal University of Santa Catarina Law School, Brazil
South and Central America: Legal Pluralism

Gordon R. Woodman
Birmingham Law School, University of Birmingham, U.K.
Folk Law

L. Kinvin Wroth
Vermont Law School
Common Law: United States Law

Tim Wu
Columbia Law School
Regulation: Telecommunications Regulation

Hiroyuki Yanagihashi
The University of Tokyo
Abu Hanifa, al-Nu'man ibn Thabit; Agricultural Contracts and Sharecropping in Islamic Law; Deposit: Islamic Law; Pledge: *Rahn* in Islamic Law; Usurpation (*Ghaṣb*)

Robin D. S. Yates
Department of East Asian Studies, McGill University
Chinese Law, History of: Eastern Zhou, Warring States (464–221 B.C.E.), and Qin State and Empire (c. 350–206 B.C.E.); Chinese Law, History of: Han Empire (206 B.C.E.–220 C.E.); Mutilation in Chinese Law

Robert A. Yelle
Department of History, University of Memphis
Religion: Religion and Law

Ihsan Yilmaz
Fatih University, Istanbul, Turkey
Turkey: Turkish Law

Joseph P. Younger
History Department, Princeton University
Uruguay

Harvey Yunis
Department of Classics, Rice University
Philosophy and Law, Ancient Greek

Selma Zecevic
Division of Humanities, York University
Balkan Peninsula, Islamic Law in the; Islamic Law and Its Political Geography: Balkan Peninsula

Karl-Heinz Ziegler
Fakultät für Rechtswissenschaft, Universität Hamburg, Emeritus
International Law: Roman Law

Aron Zysow
Department of Near Eastern Studies, Princeton University
Duty (*Farḍ*); Legal Acts and Legal Facts in Islamic Law; Qaffal, Abu Bakr Muhammad ibn 'Ali ibn Isma'il al-Shashi; Rights in Islamic Law

INDEX OF LEGAL CASES

AUSTRALIA

Attorney General v. Brown (1847) 1 Legge 312, **1**:246

Cook v. Cook (1986) 162 C.L.R. 376, **1**:243

Cooper v. Stuart (1889) 14 App. Cas. 286, **1**:246

Mabo v. Queensland (No. 2), 175 C.L.R. 1 (1992), **1**:3, 243

Parker v. R., (1963) 111 C.L.R. 610, **1**:243

R. v. Bon Jon (1841) S.Ct.N.S.W., unreported, **1**:239

R. v. Ballard (1829) S.Ct.N.S.W., unreported, **1**:239

R. v. Murrell (1836) 1 Legge 72, **1**:239

Trimble v Hill (1879) 5 App. Cas. 342, **1**:242

Viro v. R., (1978) 141 C.L.R. 88, **1**:243

Wik Peoples v. Queensland (1996) 187 CLR 1, **1**:3, 244

BANGLADESH

Masdar Hossain, (2000) 52 DLR (AD) 82, **1**:260

Muhammad Abu Baker Siddique v. S.M.A. Bakar & others (38 Dhaka Law Reports [AD] 1986), **4**:300

Nelly Zaman v. Giasuddin Khan (34 Dhaka Law Reports 221, 1982), **4**:300

BURMA

Hong Ku v. Ma Thin (1872–92) 5 J.R.L.B. 135, **5**:319

CANADA

Calder v. Attorney-General of British Columbia, (1973) S.C.R. 313, **1**:342

St. Catherine's Milling & Lumber Co. v. The Queen, (1888) 14 A.C. 46, **1**:342

Thorson v. Attorney General of Canada, (1975) 1 S.C.R. 138, **1**:340

CHINA

Bandhua Mukti Morcha (1984), **5**:6

Dai Qi (1826), **5**:46

Ding Qisan (1826), **5**:46

Li Jiuxian (1820), **5**:46

Macdonald v. Anderson (British S.Ct. for China, 1904), **3**:92

Zhang Liangbi (1812), **5**:46

Zhu Shenger (1796), **5**:46

ENGLAND (–1707)

Aldred's Case (1610), **2**:380, 449

Appleton v. Prior of Mottisfont (1268), **2**:86

Bates, **5**:426

Bodenham v. Halle (1456) 10 Sel. Soc. 137, **4**:188

Bole v. Horton (1673) Vaughan 360 at 380, **4**:378, 381

Bonham's Case (1610), **2**:56

Boson v. Sandford (1691), **6**:78

Bromwich v. Lloyd (1692), **1**:292; **4**:38

Broughton v. Prince (1590) 74 Eng. Rep. 656 (Q. B.), **1**:277

Burton v. Davy (1437), **1**:292

Bushell's Case (1670) 24 Eng. Rep. 1006 (C.P.), **1**:380; **3**:440

Butts v. Penny (1677), **6**:34

Calvin's Case (1608) 77 Eng. Rep. 377, **1**:313; **2**:55; **4**:214–215

Cantrel v. Church (1601) 78 Eng. Rep. 1072, **4**:239

Carrier's Case (1473) Y.B.13 Edw. IV, f. 9, pl. 5, **5**:462

Case of Commendams (1616), **2**:55

Case of Market Overt (1594), **5**:189

Case of Proclamations (1611), **4**:89, 284; **5**:277

Case of the Crown Jewels (1457), **5**:189

Cawdrey's Case (1591) 4 Rep. 1, **2**:129

Chudleigh's Case (1594), **2**:54

Claxton v. Lilburn (1638), **6**:7

Clerke v. Martin (1702) 2 L.R. 757 (K.B.), **1**:292; **4**:38

Coggs v. Barnard (1703) 92 Eng. Rep. 999, **1**:249

Colthirst v. Bejushin (1550) 1 Plow. 21, 75 Eng. Rep. 33, **5**:365

Cook v. Fountain (1676) 3 Swanst 585, **2**:469

Darcy v. Allen [Case of Monopolies] (1603) 77 Eng. Rep. 1260 (K.B.), **2**:88, 101–102

Dean and Chapter of Exeter v. Hamlyn (1521), **2**:379
Dean of St. Asaph's Case (1784), **3**:441
Dodwell v. Burford (1669) 1 Mod. Rep. 24, **1**:226
Dolphyn v. Barne (1540) KB 27/1116, **1**:292; **4**:38
Dr. Bonham's Case (1610) 77 Eng. Rep. 638, **4**:89, 215; **5**:277
Duncomb v. Duncomb (1695) 3 Lev. 437, 83 Eng. Rep. 770, **5**:365
Earl of Oxford's Case (1615) 1 Rep. Charles. 1, **2**:469
Emmanuel College v. Evans (1625) 1 Rep. Ch. 18, **4**:189
Felton's Case (1628) 3 How. St. Tr. 371, **5**:484
Gouriet v. Union of Post Office Workers, A.C. 435 (1978), **5**:16
Hales' Case (1569), **2**:449
How v. Vigures (1628) 1 Rep. Ch. 32, **4**:189
James v. Warren Holt (1707) 90 Eng. Rep. 956 (K.B.), **6**:124
John Dyer's Case (1414) 2 Hen. V, f5, pl. 26, **2**:101
Lord Dacre's Case (1535) 105 B. & M. 109, **6**:12
Lord Rea v. Ramsey (1631), **6**:7
Mathews v. Erbo (1698), **4**:271
Maynard v. Dyce (1542), **4**:38
Moses v. Macferlan (1760), **5**:130
Newcomb v. Bonham (1681) 1 Vern. 7, 23 Eng. Rep. 266, **4**:189
Paradine v. Jane (1647) 82 Eng. Rep 897 (K.B.), **1**:306
R. v. Crosby (1695) 88 Eng. Rep. 1171, **5**:3
R. v. Hampden (1637) 3 State Trails 1087, **2**:130; **5**:426
R. v. Preston (1691), **6**:3
Rogers v. Parrey (1413) 80 Eng. Rep. 1012 (K.B), **2**:101
Sandforth's Case (1584), **3**:271
Sarsfield v. Witherley (1689), **1**:292
Sheldon v. Hentley (1680) 33 Car. II; 2 Show. 160, **4**:38
Shelley's Case (1581) 1 Co. Rep. 93, 76 Eng. Rep. 206, **2**:54
Ship Money case (R. v. Hampden) (1637) 3 State Trials 1087, **2**:130; **5**:426
Slade's Case (1602) 76 Eng. Rep. 1074, **2**:54, 85–86, 196; **3**:472
Smith v. Brown and Cooper (1701), **6**:34
Smith v. Gould (1705), **6**:34
Smythe v. Bondelin (1458), **4**:37
Southern v. How (1618) 79 Eng. Rep. 1243 (K.B.), **1**:109
Spencer's Case (1583) 5 Coke Rep. 16a, **4**:12–13
Taltarum's Case (1472) Y.B., 12 Edward IV, **2**:213–214, 447–448
Thornbrough v. Baker (1676) 1 Ch. Ca. 284, **4**:189
Turberville v. Savage (1669) 1 Mod. Rep. 3, **1**:226
Turberville v. Stampe (1698) 91 Eng. Rep. 1072 (K.B.), **6**:78

Vynior's Case (1609) 77 Eng. Rep. 595 (K.B.), **1**:130
Waltham Carrier Case (1321) 86 SS 286 (Herle, C.J.), **2**:195

EUROPEAN UNION
Cassis de Dijon (1978) C-120/78, **2**:495
Costa v. Enel (1964) C-6/64, **2**:490
van Gend en Loos v. Netherlands Inland Revenue Administration (1963) ECR 1, **2**:490

FRANCE
Fruehauf Corp. v. Massardy, Ct. App. Paris, 14e ch., Gazette du Palais 1965, 2, pan. Jurisp. 86, trans. in 5 ILM 476 (1966), **3**:289

GREAT BRITAIN (1707–1800)
Bishop of London v. Ffytche (1783), **4**:378
Campbell v. Hall (1774) 98 Eng. Rep. 1045 (K.B.), **1**:312
Carter v. Boehm (1766), **3**:253
Casborne v. Scarfe (1738) 1 Atk 603; 26 Eng. Rep. 377, **4**:189
Constable v. Nichols (1726), **3**:4
Da Costa v. Jones (1778), **3**:252
Donaldson v. Beckett (1774) 4 Burr. 2408; 1 Eng. Rep. 837 (H.L.), **2**:216; **3**:266; **4**:143
Dormer v. Parkhurst (1740) 6 Bro. PC 351; 2 Eng. Rep. 1127, **5**:365
Edmondson v. Stevenson (1766), **4**:106
Entick v. Carrington (1765) 95 Eng. Rep. 807 (K.B.), **2**:130; **5**:203
Folkes v. Chadd (1782) 99 Eng. Rep. 589 (K.B.), **4**:29
Hulme v. Tennant (1778) 28 Eng. Rep. 958, **6**:124
Jones v. Randall (1774) Lofft 385; 98 Eng. Rep., **4**:142
Lewis v. Price (1761), **2**:381
Millar v. Taylor (1769) 4 Burr. 2303; 98 Eng. Rep. 201 (K.B.), **2**:216; **4**:143
Mitchell v. Allestry (1767), **6**:76
Perrin v. Blake (1770) 4 Burr. 2579, 1 W.Bl. 672 (K.B.), **4**:143
Pillans v. Van Mierop (1765) 3 Burr. 1663 (K.B.), **4**:143
R. v. Bazeley, (1799) 168 Eng. Rep. 517, **5**:462
R. v. Hensey (1758) 19 State Tr. 1341; 1 Burr. 642, **6**:3
R. v. Jones (1776), **1**:296
R. v. Journeyman Tailors of Cambridge (1721), **2**:101
R. v. Pear, (1779) 168 Eng. Rep. 208, **3**:101; **5**:462
R. v. Robinson (1796), **1**:296
Rann v. Hughes (1778) 101 Eng. Rep. 1014, **4**:143
Rex v. Shipley (1784) 4 Doug. 73, **4**:143
Reynolds v. Clarke (1725) 93 Eng. Rep. 747, **5**:469

INDEX OF LEGAL CASES 201

Ringstead v. Lady Lanesborough (1783) 3 Doug. 197, **4**:143
Robinson v. Raley (1757) 1 Burr. 316, **4**:324
Shelley's Case (1581) 1 Co. Rep. 93, 76 Eng. Rep. 206, **4**:143
Somerset case (1772) Lofft 1, 98 Eng. Rep. 499, 20 S.T. 1, **5**:250, 252
Somerset case (1772) Lofft. 1, 98 Eng. Rep. 499, 20 S.T. 1, **4**:143
Wilkes v. Wood (1763) 98 Eng. Rep. 489 (C.P.), **5**:203

HONG KONG

Ho Tsz Tsun v. Ho Au Shi and Others (1915) 10 HKLR 69, **1**:449

INDIA

A.I.I.M.S. Students Union, A.I.R. 2001 S.C. 3262, **3**:105
Anupama Pradhan, 1991 Criminal Law Journal 3216, **2**:308
Bal Patil v. Union of India, A.I.R. 2005 S.C. 3172, **3**:365
Bhagawandas Tejmal v. Rajmal, 10 Bom HC 241 (1873), **3**:364
Collector of Madura v. Mottoo Ramlinga, 12 Moore's Indian Appeals 397 (1868), **2**:307; **3**:147
Danial Latifi, 2001 (6)S.C.A.L.E. 537, **3**:50–51
Fertilizer Corporation Kamgar Union (1981), **5**:6
Fundamental Rights Case, A.I.R. 1973 S.C. 1461, **2**:146; **3**:106, 217, 221
Gasito, 1894 I.L.R. (Calcutta) 1499, **2**:307–308
Gateppa v. Eramma, A.I.R. Madras 228 (1927), **3**:364
Gaya Prasad v. Bhagwat, A.I.R. 1966 Madhya Pradesh 212, **6**:132
Hussainara Khatoon (1979), **5**:6
Jorden Diengdeh, A.I.R. 1985 SC 935 (1985), **2**:308
Kailash Wati v. Ayodhia Parkash, I.L.R. (1977) 1 Punjab and Haryana 642, **6**:132
Kalavagunta Venkata Kristnayya, 1908 I.L.R. 32 (Madras) 185, **2**:308
Kesavananda Bharati v. State of Kerala, A.I.R. 1973 S.C. 1461, **2**:146; **3**:106, 217, 221
Lakshmi Kant Pandey cases (1984, 1985, 1987, 2001), **1**:50; **3**:223
M. C. Mehta (1987), **5**:7
Madhu Kishwar v. State of Bihar (1996) 5 Supreme Court Cases 125 (1996), **2**:309
Maharaja Govind Nath Ray v. Gulab Chand, 5 Cal SDA Sel. Rep. 276 (1833), **3**:364
Mandal case (1992), **3**:219
Maneka Gandhi, A.I.R. 1978 Supreme Court 597, **3**:106
Mathura Naikin v. Esu Naikin, 1880 I.L.R. 4 (Bombay) 545, **2**:307
Mohd. Ahmed Khan v. Shah Bano Begum, A.I.R. 1985 S.D. 945, **3**:50–51; **5**:308
Mumbai Kamgar Sabha (1976), **5**:6
Olga Tellis (1986), **5**:6
People's Union for Democratic Rights (1982), **5**:7
Rachel Benjamin v. Benjamin Solomon Benjamin, 28 Bombay Law Reporter 328 (1925), **3**:398
Ram Prakash v. Savitri Devi, A.I.R. 1958 Punjab 87, **6**:132
Ratlam Municipality (1980), **5**:7
Rattan Devi, 1981 Criminal Law Journal 1422 (1981), **2**:308
S. P. Gupta (1982), **5**:6
Sasson v. Sasson, Appeal Cases 1007 (1924), **3**:398
Sheela Barse (1983), **5**:6
Sheosingh Rain v. Dakho, I.L.R. Allahabad 688 (1878), **3**:364
Solomon v. Solomon, 71 Bombay Law Reporter 578 (1968), **3**:399
Surinder Kaur v. Gardeep Singh, A.I.R. 1973 Punjab and Haryana 134, **6**:132
Swaraj Garg v. R. M. Garg, A.I.R. 1978 Delhi 296, **6**:133
Unni Krishnan, A.I.R. 1993 Supreme Court 2178, **3**:106
Upendra Baxi (1983), **5**:6
Vishaka v. State of Rajasthan, A.I.R. 1997 S.C. 3011, **3**:220; **5**:6

IRELAND

A.G. v. McCarthy (1911), **3**:312
Beamish v. Beamish, 9 HLC 274 (1861), **3**:312; **4**:379
Bell v. G.N.R., 26 LR Ir. 428, **3**:312
Gray v. R., 11 Cl. & F. 427 (1844), **3**:312
Murray v. Bateman, (1776) Wall. 181 (Ireland), **3**:310
O'Connell v. R. (1844) 11 Cl. & Fin. 155, **3**:312
O'Hanlon v. Logue (1906) 1 I.R. 247, **3**:313
O'Keeffe v. Cullen (1873) I.R. 7 C.L. 319, **3**:313
Plucke v. Digges, 2 H&B 1 (1832), **3**:312
R. v. Millis. 10 Cl & F 534 (1844), **3**:312
Ussher v. Ussher (1912) 2 I.R. 445, **3**:313

MALAYSIA

Kaliammal Sinnasamy v. Pengarah Jabatan Agama Islam Wilayah Persekutuan & Ors (2006), **4**:301
Lina Joy v. Majlis Agama Islam Wilayah Persekutuan & Ors (2005 and 2007), **4**:301

NETHERLANDS

Compagnie Européenne des Pétroles v. Sensor Nederlands, Dist, Ct. The Hague, 1982 Rechtspraal van de Week 167, 22 ILM 66 (1983), **3**:289

NEW ZEALAND

Baigent's Case [Simpson v. Attorney-General], [1994] 3 N.Z.L.R. 667, **4**:232

Invercargill City Council v Hamlin [1994] 3 N.Z.L.R. 513, **4**:232

Ngati Apa v. AG [2003] 3 N.Z.L.R. 643, **4**:147

Nireaha Tamaki v. Baker [1901] N.Z.P.C.C. 371, **4**:146

R. v. Symonds [1847] N.Z.P.C.C. 387, **4**:146

Te Runanganui o Te Ika Whenua Inc Soc v. A-G [1994] 2 N.Z.L.R. 20, **4**:146

Wi Parata v. Bishop of Wellington [1877] 3 N.Z. Jur [NS] 72, **4**:146

PAKISTAN

Allah Rakha v. Federation of Pakistan, PLD 2000 FSC 1, **5**:309

SCOTLAND

Donoghue v. Stevenson, (1932) A.C. 562, **4**:221

SINGAPORE

Sonia Chataram Aswami v. Haresh Jaikishin Buxani (1995) 3 Sing L.R. 627, **5**:321

SRI LANKA

Kodeeswaran v. Attorney General (1969) 72 NLR 337, **5**:341–342

UNITED KINGDOM (1800–)

Ashford v. Thornton (1818), **4**:423

Attorney-General v. HRH Prince Ernest Augustus of Hanover, (1957) A.C. 436, 1 All E.R. 49, **4**:206

Bamford v. Turnley (1862), **2**:449, 450

Barrington v. Lee (1972), **4**:381

Bell v. Lever Brothers (1932) A.C. 161 (H.L.), **2**:474

Bradford v. Pickles (1895), **2**:382

Bruton v. London & Quadrant Housing Trust, (2001) 1 A.C. 406, **4**:13

Cambridge Water Co. v. Eastern Counties Leather Plc (1994), **2**:452

Carlill v. Carbolic Smoke Ball Co. (1893), **2**:169

Chief Adjudication Officer v. Bath (2000) 1 F.L.R. 8, **3**:446

Clark v. University of Lincolnshire and Humberside (2000) 3 All E.R. 752, **5**:16

Cooper v. Wandsworth Board of Works (1863), **2**:451

Dalton v. Angus (1881), **2**:381

Davies v. Johnson (1979), **4**:381

Donoghue v. Stevenson, H.L.; All E.R. 1 (1932), **2**:169, 443; **5**:469

Gallie v. Lee (1969), **4**:381

Gillick v. West Norfolk and Wisbech Area Health Authority (1985) 3 All E.R. 402 (H.L.), **3**:34

Gray v. R. (1844) 11 Cl. & F. 427, **3**:312

Hadfield's Case, 27 State Trials 1281 (1800), **3**:247

Hadley v. Baxendale, (1854) 156 Eng. Rep. 145, **2**:76

Hochster v. De La Tour, (1853) 118 Eng. Rep. 922 (Q.B.), **2**:76

Hornby v. Close, (1867) L.R. 2 Q.B. 153, **2**:426

Hunter v. Canary Wharf (1997), **2**:382, 452

J. A. Pye (Oxford) Ltd. and J. A. Pye (Oxford) Land Ltd. v. United Kingdom (2005), **2**:381

J. v. C., (1969) 1 All E.R. 788 (H.L.), **1**:394

Keech v. Sandford, (1726) 25 Eng. Rep. 223, **6**:13

Krell v. Henry, (1903) 2 K.B. 740, **2**:76

Lloyd v. Grace, Smith & Co. (1912), **6**:77

London Street Tramways v. London County Council (1898), **4**:379

M'Naghten's Case, (1843) 8 Eng. Rep. 718, **3**:247

Mercury Communications Ltd v. Director General of Telecommunications, 1 W.L.R. 48 (1996), **5**:16

Miliangos v. George Frank Textiles (1975), **4**:379

Mirehouse v. Rennell, 1 Cl. & Fin.527 at 546 (1833), **4**:381

Newberry v. James, (1817) 35 Eng. Rep. 1011 (Ct. Ch.), **3**:273

Nottidge v. Ripley (Ex. Ch., 1849), **3**:246

O'Reilly v. Mackman (1982) 3 All ER 680 (CA), 1124 (HL), **5**:16

Pepper v. Hart (1993) A.C. 593, **4**:90

Pluck v. Digges (1832) 2 H. & B., **3**:312

Quinn v. Leatham, A.C. 495 (1901), **2**:426

Rangeley v. Midland Railway Co. (1868), **2**:380

R. v. Ahlers, 1 K.B. 616 (1915), **6**:3

R. v. Casement, 1 K.B. 98 (1917), **6**:3

R. v. Davis (1823), **1**:317

R. v. Day (1845), **1**:226

R. v. DeJager, A.C. (1907), **6**:3

R. v. Hensey (1758), **5**:441

R. v. Lynch, 1 K.B. 444 (1903), **6**:3

INDEX OF LEGAL CASES   203

Roy v. Kensington and Chelsea and Westminster Family Practitioner Committee (1992) 2 WLR 239, **5:**16
Rylands v. Fletcher (1865–1868), **2:**449
Salomon v. Salomon & Co. Ltd, (1897) A.C. 22 (H.L.), **2:**91
Santley v. Wilde, (1899) 2 Ch. 474, **4:**188
Sasson v. Sasson, Appeal Cases 1007 (1924), **3:**398
Solle v. Butcher, (1950) 1 K.B. 671, **2:**474
St. Helens' Smelting Co. v. Tipping (1865), **2:**449
Stephens v. Myers (1830) 172 Eng. Rep. 735, **1:**226
Taff Vale Railway Case, (1901) A.C. 426 (H.L.), **2:**426
Thoburn v. Sunderland City Council, E.W.H.C. 195 (2002), **2:**133
Thorley v. Lord Kerry, (1812) 128 Eng. Rep. 367, **4:**106
Tinline v. White Cross Insurance (1921), **3:**253
Toogood v. Spyring, (1834) 149 Eng. Rep. 1044 (H.L.), **4:**106
Town Investments v. Department of the Environment, AC 359 (1978), **5:**16
Tulk v. Moxhay (1848), **2:**450
Tweddle v. Atkinson, (1861) 121 Eng. Rep. 762, **2:**198
Vaughan v. Menlove, 3 Bing. NC 468 (1837), **4:**221
Velazquez Ltd. v. Inland Revenue Commissioners (1914), **4:**379
Weyland v. Elkins (1816), **6:**76
Williams v. Holland, (1833) 131 Eng. Rep. 848, **5:**469
Winterbottom v. Wright, (1842) 152 Eng. Rep. 402 (Ex.), **2:**169
Young v. Bristol Aeroplane Co. Ltd., (1944) K.B. 718, **4:**379
Young v. Bristol Aeroplane Co. Ltd., (1944) KB 718, **4:**381

UNITED STATES
Abington School District v. Schempp, 374 U.S. 203 (1963), **5:**118
Ableman v. Booth, 62 U.S. (21 How.) 506 (1859), **3:**60; **5:**263
Adair v. United States, 208 U.S. 161 (1908), **2:**25, 369
Adamson v. California, 332 U.S. 46 (1947), **3:**165; **4:**453
Adarand Constructors v. Pena, 515 U.S. 200 (1995), **2:**343
Adkins v. Children's Hospital, 261 U.S. 525 (1923), **2:**26; **3:**61; **4:**491; **6:**137
AFSCME v. Washington State, 770 F 2d 1401 (9th Cir., 1985), **2:**340
Akron v. Akron Center for Reproductive Health, 462 U.S. 416 (1983), **4:**389
Alcoa, United States v., 148 F.2d 416 (2d Cir. 1945), **1:**190; **3:**288

Alden v. Maine, 527 U.S. 706 (1999), **2:**259; **5:**354
Alexander v. Gardner-Denver Co., 415 U.S. 36 (1974), **3:**488, 489
Alexander v. Sandoval, 532 U.S. 275 (2001), **2:**344
Allgeyer v. Louisiana, 165 U.S. 578 (1897), **2:**25, 208, 369; **4:**490
American Banana Co. v. United Fruit Co., 213 U.S. 347 (1909), **3:**288
American Insurance Co. v. Canter, 26 U.S. (1 Pet.) 511 (1828), **2:**256
American Tobacco Co., United States v., 221 U.S. 106 (1911), **1:**189
Amistad, United States v., 40 U.S. (15 Pet.) 518 (1841), **3:**293; **5:**263
Andrews v. the State, 50 Tenn. 165 (1871), **1:**219
Antelope, The, 23 U.S. (10 Wheat.) 66 (1825), **5:**263
Ashcroft v. American Civil Liberties Union, 542 U.S. 656 (2004), **5:**335
Aspen Skiing v. Aspen Highlands Skiing Corp., 472 U.S. 585 (1985), **1:**192
Associated Press v. International News Service, 248 U.S. 215 (1918), **3:**272–273
Aymette v. State, 21 Tenn. 154 (1849), **1:**218
Babcock v. Jackson, 12 N.Y. 2d 473, 191 N.E. 2d 279 (1963), **2:**118
Baker v. Carr, 369 U.S. 186 (1962), **1:**201; **2:**261; **6:**59
Baker v. Selden, 101 U.S. 99 (1880), **3:**267
Ballew v. Georgia, 435 U.S. 223 (1978), **5:**268
Banco Nacional de Cuba v. Sabbatino, 376 U.S. 398 (1964), **3:**296
Bank of Augusta v. Earle, 38 U.S. (13 Pet.) 519 (1839), **6:**46
Barron v. Baltimore, 32 U.S. (7 Pet.) 243 (1833), **2:**155; **3:**60, 458; **4:**489
Bas v. Tingy, 4 U.S. (4 Dall.) 37 (1800), **3:**293
Basic Inc. v. Levinson, 485 U.S. 224 (1988), **5:**95
Batson v. Kentucky, 476 U.S. 79 (1986), **3:**444
Bellotti v. Baird, 443 U.S. 622 (1979), **4:**389
Belmont, United States v., 301 U.S. 324 (1937), **3:**22
Benedict v. Ratner, 268 U.S. 353 (1925), **2:**77
Berger v. New York, 388 U.S. 41 (1967), **4:**387; **5:**206
Berman v. Parker, 348 U.S. 26 (1954), **4:**484
Bernhard v. Harrahs Club, 16 Cal. 3d 313, 546 P.2d 719 (1976), **2:**118
Bethel School District No. 403 v. Fraser, 478 U.S. 675 (1986), **2:**409

Bigelow v. Virginia, 421 U.S. 809 (1975), **5:**336

Blakely v. Washington, 542 U.S. 296 (2004), **2:**293

Bleistein v. Donaldson, 188 U.S. 239 (1903), **3:**267

Block v. Hirsch, 256 U.S. 135 (1921), **2:**27

BMW of North America, Inc. v. Gore, 517 U.S. 559 (1996), **2:**371

Board of Education v. Rowley, 458 U.S. 176 (1982), **2:**335

Board of Trustees of the University of Alabama v. Garrett, 531 U.S. 356 (2001), **2:**336

Bob Jones University v. United States, 461 U.S. 54 (1983), **2:**343

Bobbs-Merrill v. Straus, 210 U.S. 339 (1908), **3:**267

Bolling v. Sharpe, 347 U.S. 497 (1954), **2:**371

Booker, United States v., 543 U.S. 220 (2005), **2:**293

Boston Water Power v. Boston & Worcester Railroad, 40 Mass. (23 Pick.) 360 (1839), **6:**46

Bowers v. Hardwick, 478 U.S. 186 (1986), **2:**292, 370, 464; **3:**63, 112, 166–167, 168; **4:**390

Boyd v. United States, 116 U.S. 616 (1886), **4:**386, 451; **5:**204, 205

Bradwell v. Illinois, 83 U.S. 130 (1873), **3:**480; **4:**218; **6:**135, 143

Brandenburg v. Ohio, 395 U.S. 444 (1969), **5:**334

Breed v. Jones, 421 U.S. 519 (1975), **3:**461

Bronson v. Kinzie, 42 U.S. (1 How.) 311 (1843), **4:**490

Brown v. Board of Education, 347 U.S. 483 (1954), **2:**19, 20, 21, 153, 258, 299, 300, 302, 341, 371, 410, 411, 460, 461, 473; **3:**62, 163, 165, 166, 410; **4:**68, 78, 363, 367; **5:**118, 268, 269, 412; **6:**57, 59

Brown v. Board of Education, 349 U.S. 294 (1955; Brown II), **2:**410

Brown v. Kendall, 60 Mass. (6 Cush.) 292 (1850), **5:**474

Buchanan v. Warley, 245 U.S. 60 (1917), **4:**491

Buck v. Bell, 274 U.S. 200 (1927), **2:**334

Buckley v. Valeo, 424 U.S. 1 (1976), **4:**340–341

Burrow-Giles v. Sarony, 111 U.S. 53 (1884), **3:**267

Bush v. Gore, 531 U.S. 98 (2000), **2:**258, 261, 473; **4:**339

Butler v. Boston & Savannah S.S. Co., 13 U.S. 527 (1889), **1:**39

Butler, United States v., 297 U.S. 1 (1936), **2:**27; **3:**61, 114; **4:**76; **5:**90

Calder v. Bull, 3 U.S. (3 Dall.) 386 (1798), **2:**24, 27, 160–161; **4:**218, 489; **5:**423

California Democratic Party v. Jones, 530 U.S. 567 (2000), **4:**343

California v. Ciraolo, 476 U.S. 207 (1986), **4:**387

California v. Greenwood, 486 U.S. 35 (1988), **4:**387

Callender, United States v., 25 Fed. Cas. 239 (1800), **4:**450

Calvert Cliffs Coordinating Committee v. AEC, 449 F.2d. 1109 (D.C. Cir., 1971), **2:**456

Campbell v. Acuff-Rose, 510 U.S. 569 (1994), **3:**268

Cantwell v. Connecticut, 310 U.S. 296 (1940), **5:**117

Carolene Products, United States v., 304 U.S. 144 (1938), **2:**370; **3:**409, 410; **4:**491

Carter v. Carter Coal Co., 298 U.S. 238 (1936), **2:**27; **3:**61; **5:**353

Central Bank of Denver v. First Interstate Bank of Denver, 511 U.S. 164 (1994), **5:**95

Central Hudson Gas & Electric Corp. v. Public Service Commission, 447 U.S. 557 (1980), **5:**336

Central Virginia Community College v. Katz, 546 U.S. 456 (2006), **3:**65

Chambers v. Florida, 309 U.S. 227 (1940), **2:**18

Champion v. Ames, 188 U.S. 321 (1903), **2:**65

Champion v. Casey, Cir. Ct. R.I. (1792), **4:**489

Charles River Bridge v. Warren Bridge, 36 U.S. 420 (1837), **2:**211; **3:**60; **4:**490; **6:**46

Chelentis v. Luckenbach S.S., 247 U.S. 372 (1918), **1:**39

Cherokee Nation v. Georgia, 30 U.S. 1 (1831), **2:**340; **4:**208; **6:**50

Chiarella v. United States, 445 U.S. 222 (1980), **5:**94

Chicago, Burlington, and Quincy Railroad Company v. Chicago, 166 U.S. 226 (1897), **2:**24; **4:**490

Chicago, Milwaukee & St. Paul Railway v. Minnesota, 134 U.S. 418 (1890), **2:**24; **4:**490; **5:**101

Chimel v. California, 395 U.S. 752 (1969), **4:**387

Chinese Exclusion Case (Chae Chan Ping v. United States) 130 U.S. 581 (1889), **3:**208; **6:**89

Chisholm v. Georgia, 2 U.S. (2 Dall.) 419 (1793), **2:**157, 259; **3:**59; **6:**40

City of Boerne v. Flores, 521 U.S. 507 (1997), **2:**261; **3:**64; **5:**119

City of Cleburne v. Cleburne Living Center, Inc., 473 U.S. 432 (1985), **2:**335, 462

City of Salina v. Blaksley, 72 Kan. 230, 231, 83 Pac. 619, 620 (1905), **1:**219

City of Sherrill v. Oneida Indian Nation, 544 U.S. 197 (2005), **4:**213

Civil Rights Cases, 109 U.S. 3 (1883), **2:**67, 340, 341, 460, 464; **3:**61; **6:**52
Claflin v. Claflin, 149 Mass. 19 (1889), **5:**407
Claflin v. Houseman, 93 U.S. 130 (1876), **2:**259
Clingman v. Beaver, 544 U.S. 581 (2005), **4:**343, 344
Clinton v. City of New York, 524 U.S. 417 (1998), **3:**22
Clinton v. Jones, 520 U.S. 681 (1997), **3:**23, 24
Cohens v. Virginia, 19 U.S. (6 Wheat.) 264 (1821), **3:**59; **5:**411; **6:**40–41, 45
Coker v. Georgia, 433 U.S. 584 (1977), **2:**18
Colegrove v. Green, 328 U.S. 549 (1946), **1:**201
Collyer Insulated Wire, 192 N.L.R.B. 837 (1971), **3:**488
Commonwealth v. Fisher, 213 Pa. 48, 62 A. 198 (1905), **3:**460
Commonwealth v. Hunt, 45 Mass. (4 Met.) 111 (1842), **3:**479; **6:**48
Commonwealth v. Porter, 51 Mass. 263 (1845), **4:**451
Commonwealth v. Pullis (Pa. 1806), **3:**479; **6:**48
Continental T.V., Inc. v. GTE Sylvania, Inc., 433 U.S. 36 (1977), **1:**191
Cooley v. Board of Wardens, 53 U.S. (12 How.) 299 (1851), **3:**60; **6:**46
Cooper v. Aaron, 358 U.S. 1 (1958), **5:**412
Coppage v. Kansas, 236 U.S. 1 (1915), **2:**25, 369–370
Cotton Petroleum Corp. v. New Mexico, 490 U.S. 163 (1989), **4:**213
County of Allegheny v. ACLU, 492 U.S. 573 (1989), **5:**119
County of McLean v. Humphreys, 104 Ill. 378 (1882), **3:**459
Covington and Lexington Turnpike Road Co. v. Sandford, 164 U.S. 578 (1896), **5:**101
Crawford v. Washington, 541 U.S. 36 (2004), **3:**14–15
Crowley v. Lewis, 239 N.Y. 264, 146 N.E. 374 (1925), **1:**114
Cruikshank, United States v., 92 U.S. 542 (1876), **1:**218
Cruzan v. Director, Missouri Department of Health, 497 U.S. 261 (1990), **4:**220, 390
Cunningham v. Neagle, 135 U.S. 1 (1890), **3:**20
Curtiss-Wright Export Corp., United States v., 299 U.S. 304 (1936), **3:**22
Cutter v Wilkinson, 544 U.S. 709 (2005), **5:**119
Dandridge v. Williams, 397 U.S. 471 (1970), **4:**371; **6:**95
Darby, United States v., 312 U.S. 100 (1941), **2:**66, 68

Dartmouth College v. Woodward, 17 U.S. (4 Wheat.) 518 (1819), **1:**321; **2:**207, 211; **4:**120, 489; **6:**40, 45
Daubert trilogy, **3:**12, 13–14; **4:**29
Daubert v. Merrill Dow Pharmaceuticals, 509 U.S. 579 (1993), **3:**13–14; **4:**29
Davidson v. New Orleans, 96 U.S. 97 (1878), **2:**369
Davis v. Bandemer, 478 U.S. 109 (1986), **1:**202
Davis v. Beason, 133 U.S. 333 (1890), **6:**51
Davis v. Washington, 547 U.S. 813 (2006), **3:**15
Davoll v. Brown, 7 F. 197 (Cir. Ct. D Mass.) (1845), **3:**265
Debs, United States v. (1894), **2:**261
Delancy v. Insurance Co., 52 N.H. 581 (1873), **2:**176
Delaware v. Prouse, 440 U.S. 648 (1979), **4:**387
DeLovio v. Boit, 7 Fed. Cas. 418 (C.C.D. Mass. 1815), **1:**38
Dennis v. United States, 341 U.S. 494 (1951), **5:**334
Denver Area Educational Telecommunications Consortium v. FCC, 518 U.S. 727 (1996), **5:**335
DeWitt, United States v., 76 U.S. (9 Wall.) 41 (1869), **2:**65
Diamond v. Chakrabarty, 447 U.S. 303 (1980), **3:**271; **5:**84
Diamond v. Diehr, 450 U.S. 175 (1981), **3:**271
Dillon v. Gloss, 256 U.S. 368 (1921), **2:**156
Dirks v. SEC, 463 U.S. 646 (1983), **5:**94
District of Columbia v. Heller, 554 U.S. (2008), **1:**216, 221–222
Dolan v. City of Tigard, 512 U.S. 374 (1994), **4:**492
Dred Scott v. Sandford, 60 U.S. (19 How.) 393 (1857), **1:**218; **2:**153, 260, 340, 369, 459; **3:**60, 209, 293, 408; **4:**482; **5:**263–264, 353; **6:**40, 52
Duncan v. Kahanamoku, 327 U.S. 304 (1946), **4:**180
Duncan v. Louisiana, 391 U.S. 145 (1968), **3:**443–444; **4:**453
Dunn v. Blumstein, 405 U.S. 330 (1972), **4:**339
Duren v. Missouri, 439 U.S. 357 (1979), **6:**139
Duro v. Reina, 495 U.S. 676 (1990), **4:**213
E. C. Knight Co., United States v., 156 U.S. 1 (1895), **1:**189; **2:**24, 65; **5:**79, 353; **6:**48
Eastman Kodak Co. v. Image Technical Services, Inc., 504 U.S. 451 (1992), **1:**192
EEOC v. Arabian American Oil Co., 499 U.S. 244 (1991), **3:**288

INDEX OF LEGAL CASES

Eisenstadt v. Baird, 405 U.S. 438 (1972), **2**:370; **6**:141
Eldred v. Ashcroft, 537 U.S. 186 (2003), **3**:268
Elk v. Wilkins, 112 U.S. 94 (1884), **6**:50
Emerson, United States v., 46 F. Supp. 2d 598 (2001), **1**:221
Employment Division v. Smith, 494 U.S. 872 (1990), **5**:119
Engel v. Vitale, 370 U.S. 421 (1962), **5**:118
Erie Railroad v. Tompkins, 304 U.S. 64 (1938), **1**:39; **2**:76, 258; **3**:273; **4**:444
Ernst & Ernst v. Hochfelder, 425 U.S. 185 (1976), **5**:94
Escott v. BarChris Construction Corp., 283 F. Supp. 643, S.D.N.Y. (1968), **5**:93
Eu v. San Francisco County Democratic Central Committee, 489 U.S. 214 (1989), **4**:343
Evans v. Eaton, 20 U.S. (7 Wheat.) 356 (1822), **3**:270
Everson v. Board of Education, 330 U.S. 1 (1947), **5**:118
Ex parte Bollman, 8 U.S. (4 Cranch) 75 (1807), **6**:45
Ex parte Crouse, 4 Whart. 9 (Pa. 1838), **3**:458–459, 460
Ex parte Crow Dog, 109 U.S. 556 (1883), **4**:209
Ex parte Jackson, 96 U.S. 727 (1878), **5**:333; **6**:51
Ex parte McCardle, 74 U.S. 506 (1869), **3**:408
Ex parte Milligan, 71 U.S. (4 Wall.) 2 (1866), **3**:24, 408; **4**:178, 180
Ex parte Quirin, 317 U.S. 1 (1942), **3**:24; **4**:179; **6**:90
Ex parte Vallandigham, 68 U.S. (1 Wall.) 243 (1863), **4**:178, 180
Ex parte Young, 209 U.S. 123 (1908), **2**:259–260; **5**:412
Exxon Corp. v. Central Gulf Lines, 500 U.S. 603 (1991), **1**:39
Exxon Shipping Co. v. Baker, 554 U.S. ___ (2008), **1**:39
Fairfax's Devisee v. Hunter's Lessee, 11 U.S. (7 Cranch) 603 (1813), **5**:411
Farrington v. Tokushige, 273 U.S. 284 (1927), **2**:409
Farwell v. Boston & Worcester Railroad, 45 Mass. (4 Met.) 49 (1842), **2**:207; **6**:48
FCC v. Brand X Internet Services, 545 U.S. 967 (2005), **5**:98
FCC v. Pacifica, 438 U.S. 726 (1978), **5**:335
FCC v. Wisconsin Right to Life, Inc., 127 S.Ct. 2652 (2007), **5**:337–338

Feist v. Rural Telephone, 499 U.S. 340 (1991), **3**:268
Ferguson v. Gies, 82 Mich. 358 (1890), **6**:52
Ferguson v. Skrupa, 372 U.S. 726 (1963), **2**:370
Fisher v. United States (1805), **5**:360
Fletcher v. Peck, 10 U.S. (6 Cranch) 87 (1810), **2**:207, 210–211; **3**:59; **4**:218, 489; **6**:45
Folsom v. Marsh, 9 F. 342 (Cir. Ct. O. Mass., 1841), **3**:267
Foster v. Neilson, 27 U.S. (2 Pet.) 253 (1829), **3**:293
Frank v. Mangum, 237 U.S. 309 (1915), **4**:452
Franklin Nat'l Bank v. New York, 347 U.S. 373, 378–79 (1954), **5**:412
Frontiero v. Richardson, 411 U.S. 677 (1973), **2**:337, 339; **6**:138
Frye v. United States, 293 F. 1013 (D.C. Cir. 1923), **3**:13; **4**:29
FTC v. Brown Shoe Co., 384 U.S. 316 (1966), **3**:288
FTC v. Ruberoid Co., 343 U.S. 470 (1952), **5**:220
Fuentes v. Shevin, 407 U.S. 67 (1972), **6**:95
Fullilove v. Klutznick, 448 U.S. 448 (1980), **2**:343
Furman v. Georgia, 408 U.S. 238 (1972), **2**:21, 293; **5**:40; **6**:60
Garcia v. San Antonio Metropolitan Transit Authority, 469 U.S. 528 (1985), **3**:63
Gebhart v. Belton, 33 Del. Ch. 144, 91 A.2d 137 (1952), **3**:165
Geduldig v. Aiello, 417 U.S. 484 (1974), **3**:67
General Dynamics Corp., United States v., 415 U.S. 486 (1974), **1**:191
General Electric Co. v. Joiner, 522 U.S. 136 (1997), **3**:13–14; **4**:29
Genesee Chief v. Fitzhugh, 53 U.S. 443 (1851), **1**:38–39
Georgia, United States v., 546 U.S. 151 (2006), **3**:65
Gibbons v. Ogden, 22 U.S. (9 Wheat.) 1 (1824), **1**:321; **2**:64–65; **3**:59–60, 142; **5**:76, 353, 411; **6**:46
Gideon v. Wainwright, 372 U.S. 335 (1963), **2**:18; **4**:51, 371, 447, 454
Gilbert v. General Electric (U.S., 1976), **6**:138
Gilmer v. Interstate/Johnson Lane Corp., 500 U.S. 20 (1991), **1**:131; **3**:488–489
Gitlow v. New York, 268 U.S. 652 (1925), **3**:409; **4**:386
Glass v. Sloop Betsey, 3 U.S. (3 Dall.) 6 (1794), **1**:38
Goldberg v. Kelly, 397 U.S. 254 (1970), **2**:368; **4**:371, 483, 492; **6**:93, 95
Gonzales v. Carhart (U.S., 2007), **6**:141
Gonzales v. Raich, 545 U.S. 1 (2005), **2**:68; **3**:65
Goodridge v. Department of Public Health, 440 Mass. 309, 798 N.E. 2d 941 (2003), **2**:371

INDEX OF LEGAL CASES 207

Graham v. John Deere Co., 383 U.S. 1 (1966), **3:**270

Granger Cases 94 U.S. 113 (1877), **5:**88

Green v. Biddle, 21 U.S. (8 Wheat.) 1 (1823), **2:**207

Greenman v. Yuba Power Products, 59 Cal. 2d 57 (1963), **2:**209

Griggs v. Duke Power, 401 U.S. 424 (1971), **2:**342; **3:**483; **6:**137

Griswold v. Connecticut, 381 U.S. 479 (1965), **2:**18, 164, 370; **4:**219, 363, 388; **6:**59, 141; **165–166**

Grove City College v. Bell, 465 U.S. 555 (1984), **2:**340

Groves v. Slaughter, 40 U.S. (15 Pet.) 449 (1841), **5:**263

Grutter v. Bollinger, 539 U.S. 306 (2003), **2:**462, 465

Guinn v. United States, 238 U.S. 347 (1915), **2:**341

Haelen Laboratories v. Topps Chewing Gum, 202 F. 2d 866 (2d Cir. 1953), **3:**274

Hague v. CIO, 307 U.S. 496 (1939), **5:**336–337

Hamdan v. Rumsfeld, 548 U.S. 557 (2006), **3:**24; **4:**448; **5:**219; **6:**90–91

Hamdi v. Rumsfeld, 542 U.S. 507 (2004), **3:**24; **4:**181, 448; **6:**90, 91

Hammer v. Dagenhart, 247 U.S. 251 (1918), **2:**65; **3:**61; **6:**58

Hans v. Louisiana, 134 U.S. 1 (1890), **2:**259; **5:**412

Harper v. Virginia Board of Elections, 383 U.S. 663 (1966), **2:**18

Harris v. McRae, 448 U.S. 297 (1980), **4:**389; **6:**141

Hartford Fire Insurance Co. v. California, 509 U.S. 764 (1993), **3:**288

Harvard College v. Amory, 26 Mass. 446 (1830), **5:**407

Hawaii Housing Authority v. Midkiff, 467 U.S. 229 (1984), **4:**492

Hazelwood School District v. Kuhlmeier, 484 U.S. 260 (1988), **2:**409

Heart of Atlanta Motel v. United States, 379 U.S. 241 (1964), **2:**67, 341; **3:**62

Hodel v. Irving, 481 U.S. 704 (1987), **5:**402

Hodges v. United States, 203 U.S. 1 (1906), **2:**340

Holden v. Hardy, 169 U.S. 366 (1898), **6:**49

Holy Trinity Church v. United States (1892), **5:**360–361

Home Building and Loan Association v. Blaisdell, 290 U.S. 398 (1934), **2:**27, 207, 211; **4:**491

Hopwood v. Texas, 78 F. 3d 932 (5th Cir., 1996), **2:**344

Hotchkiss v. Greenwood, 52 U.S. 248 (1850), **3:**270

Hoyt v. Florida (U.S., 1961), **6:**138

Huddleston v. United States, 458 U.S. 681 (1988), **3:**13

Hudson and Goodwin, United States v., 11 U.S. (7 Cranch) 32 (1812), **2:**283; **6:**51

Hunt v. Rousmanier's Administrators, 21 U.S. [8 Wheat.] 174 (1823), **1:**113

Hunter v. Pittsburgh, 207 U.S. 161 (1907), **4:**120

Hurtado v. California, 110 U.S. 516 (1884), **4:**451

Hush-a-Phone v. FCC, 283 F.2d. 266 (D.C. Cir., 1956), **5:**97

Icar v. Suares, 7 La. 517 (1835), **2:**207

ICC v. Alabama Midland Railway Co., 168 U.S. 144 (1897), **5:**101

ICC v. Cincinnati, New Orleans and Texas Pacific Railway Co., 167 U.S. 479 (1897), **5:**101

Illinois v. Gates, 462 U.S. 213 (1983), **5:**207

Immigration and Naturalization Service v. Chadha, 462 U.S. 919 (1983), **5:**218, 219

In re Baby M, 537 A.2d 1227, 109 N.J. 396 (1988), **3:**55

In re Debs, 158 U.S. 564 (1895), **2:**24; **3:**20; **6:**48

In re Ferrier, 103 Ill. 367 (1882), **3:**459, 460

In re Garnett, 141 U.S. 1 (1891), **1:**39

In re Gault, 387 U.S. 1 (1967), **3:**461

In re Jacobs, 98 N.Y. 98 (1885), **2:**24

In re Kemmler, 136 U.S. 436 (1890), **6:**50

In re Lynch, 8 Cal. 3d 410 (1972), **5:**41

In re Winship, 397 U.S. 358 (1970), **3:**461

In re Yamashita, 327 U.S. 1 (1946), **4:**180

Inhabitants of Worcester v. Western Railroad, 45 Mass. (4 Met.) 564 (1842), **6:**46

International Shoe Co. v. Washington, 326 U.S. 310 (1945), **4:**445

Ives v. South Buffalo Railway Co., 201 N.Y. 271, 94 N.E. 431 (1911), **2:**24, 370

J.E.B. v. Alabama ex rel T.B., 511 U.S. 127 (1994), **6:**139

Jacobsen, United States v., 466 U.S. 109 (1984), **5:**207

Jacobson v. Massachusetts, 197 U.S. 11 (1905), **3:**144

Japanese Immigrant Case (Yamataya v. Fisher), 189 U.S. 86 (1903), **3:**209

Javins v. First National Realty, 428 F.2d 1071, *cert.den.* 400 U.S. 925 (1970), **3:**163, 186; **4:**486

Jay Burns Baking Co. v. Bryan, 264 U.S. 504 (1924), **2:**26

Jefferson v. Hackney, 406 U.S. 535 (1972), **6:**95

Jerome B. Grubart, Inc. v. Great Lakes Dredge & Dock Co., 513 U.S. 527 (1995), **1:**39

Jew Ho v. Williamson, 103 F. 10 (C.C.N.D. Cal. 1900), **3:**143

John Doe v. Unocal (2003), **1:**318

John Peter Zenger libel trial (1735), **4:**447–448, 449, 450

Johnson v. Eisentrager, 339 U.S. 763 (1950), **4:**180

Johnson v. M'Intosh, 21 U.S. 543 (1823), **4:**208, 481; **6:**49

Johnson v. Southern Pacific Company, 196 U.S. 1 (1904), **5:**102

Johnson v. Transportation Agency of Santa Clara County, 480 U.S. 616 (1987), **2:**340

208 INDEX OF LEGAL CASES

Jones v. Alfred H. Mayer Co., 392 U.S. 409 (1968), **2**:461

Jones v. Crittenden, 4 N.C. 55 (1814), **4**:490

Jones v. Van Zandt, 46 U.S. (5 How.) 215 (1847), **5**:263

Jones v. West Side Buick, 93 S.W.2d 1083 (Mo. App. 1936), **2**:175

Kagama, United States v., 118 U.S. 375 (1886), **4**:209–210

Karcher v. Daggett, 462 U.S. 725 (1983), **1**:201

Katz v. United States, 389 U.S. 347 (1967), **4**:387, 388; **5**:206

Katzenbach v. McClung, 379 U.S. 294 (1964), **2**:67, 341; **3**:62

Kelo v. City of New London, 545 U.S. 469 (2005), **4**:484, 492

Kent v. United States, 383 U.S. 541 (1966), **3**:461

Kewanee Oil v. Bicron, 416 U.S. 470 (1974), **3**:273

Keyes v. School District No. 1 Denver, Colorado, 413 U.S. 189 (1973), **2**:342

King v. Smith, 392 U.S. 309 (1968), **4**:371; **6**:94

Korematsu v. United States, 323 U.S. 214 (1944), **2**:18, 341, 460; **3**:24

Kossick v. United Fruit Co., 365 U.S. 731 (1961), **1**:39

Kramer v. Union Free School District No. 15, 395 U.S. 621 (1969), **4**:339–340

KSR International v. Teleflex, 550 U.S. 398 (2007), **3**:270

Kumho Tire Co. v. Carmichael, 526 U.S. 137 (1999), **3**:13–14; **4**:29

Kyllo v. United States, 533 U.S. 27 (2001), **4**:391

Laidlaw v. Organ, 15 U.S. (2 Wheat.) 178 (1817), **2**:205

Lara, United States v., 541 U.S. 193 (2004), **4**:213

Late Corporation of the Church of Jesus Christ of Latter-Day Saints, The v. United States, 136 U.S. 1 (1890), **6**:51

Lau v. Nichols, 414 U.S. 563 (1974), **2**:342, 344

Lawrence v. Texas, 539 U.S. 558 (2003), **2**:18, 292, 371, 464, 465; **3**:63, 112, 167–168; **4**:380; **6**:59

League of United Latin American Citizens v. Perry, 548 U.S. 399 (2006), **1**:202

Lee v. Weisman, 505 U.S. 577 (1992), **5**:118

Legal Services Corp. v. Velazquez, 531 U.S. 533 (2001), **4**:373

Lemon v. Kurtzman, 403 U.S. 602 (1971), **5**:118–119

Leon, United States v., 468 U.S. 897 (1984), **5**:207

Lessard v. Schmidt, 414 U.S. 473 (1974), **6**:95

Lever Brothers v. United States, 981 F. 2d 1330 (D.C. Cir., 1989), **3**:272

Liggett Co. v. Lee, 288 U.S. 517 (1933), **1**:325

Lindsay v. Lindsay, 257 Ill. 328, 100 N.E. 892 (1913), **3**:460

Local 174, Teamsters v. Lucas Flour Co., 369 U.S. 95 (1962), **3**:487

Lochner v. New York, 198 U.S. 45 (1905), **1**:324; **2**:25, 208, 211, 259, 369; **3**:61, 144, 164, 408; **4**:218, 451, 491; **5**:79, 266, 267; **6**:49, 58, 136

Locke v. Davey, 540 U.S. 712 (2004), **5**:119

Lockhart v. McCree, 476 U.S. 162 (1986), **5**:269

Lone Wolf v. Hitchcock, 187 U.S. 553 (1903), **4**:210

Lopez, United States v., 514 U.S. 549 (1995), **2**:67, 68; **3**:63–64; **5**:353

Loretto v. Teleprompter Manhattan CATV Corp., 458 U.S. 419 (1982), **4**:492

Lottawanna, The, 88 U.S. 588 (1874), **1**:39

Loucks v. Standard Oil Co. of New York, 224 N.Y. 99, 120 N.E. 198 (1918), **2**:117

Louisiana ex. rel. Francis v. Resweber, 329 U.S. 459 (1947), **5**:40

Loving v. Virginia, 388 U.S. 1 (1967), **2**:342; **6**:57

Lucas v. South Carolina Coastal Council, 505 U.S. 1003 (1992), **4**:484, 492

Luther v. Borden, 48 U.S.1 (1849), **2**:260, 261

Lynch v. Donnelly, 465 U.S. 668 (1984), **5**:119

M.L.B. v. S.L.J., 519 U.S. 102 (1996), **2**:463

MacPherson v. Buick Motor Co., 217 N.Y. 382, 111 N.E.1050 (1916), **2**:176, 209; **5**:475; **6**:57

Madera v. Secretary of Executive Office, 636 N.E. 2d 1326 (Mass. 1994), **3**:186

Maher v. Roe, 432 U.S. 464 (1977), **4**:389; **6**:141

Mapp v. Ohio, 367 U.S. 643 (1961), **4**:386, 453, 454; **5**:205–206

Marbury v. Madison, 5 U.S. (1 Cranch) 137 (1803), **2**:153, 256, 257, 259, 260, 261; **3**:407, 408, 410; **4**:97, 450; **6**:40, 45

Martin v. Hunter's Lessee, 14 U.S. (1 Wheat.) 304 (1816), **2**:258; **3**:59; **5**:411; **6**:40, 45

Marvin v. Marvin, 18 Cal.3d 660 (1976), **3**:55

Maryland v. Wirtz, 392 U.S. 183 (1968), **3**:62–63, 63

Mathews v. Eldridge, 424 U.S. 319 (1976), **4**:371

Mayor of the City of New York v. Miln, 36 U.S. (11 Pet.) 102 (1837), **2**:65; **6**:46

Mazer v. Stein, 347 U.S. 401 (1954), **3**:267

McCleskey v. Kemp, 481 U.S. 279 (1987), **5**:269

McConnell v. Federal Election Commission, 540 U.S. 93 (2003), **4**:341; **5**:337–338

McCoy, United States v., 323 F.3d. 1114 (9th Cir. 2003), **2**:68

McCreary County v. ACLU, 545 U.S. 844 (2005), **5**:119

McCulloch v. Maryland, 17 U.S. (4 Wheat.) 316 (1819), **2**:160, 161; **3**:59; **5**:411, 441; **6**:40, 45, 46
McFarland v. Newman, 9 Watts 55 (Pa. 1839), **2**:206, 207
McKeiver v. Pennsylvania, 403 U.S. 528 (1971), **3**:461
McKim v. McKim, 12 R.I. 462 (1879), **6**:45
McLaurin v. Oklahoma State Regents for Higher Education, 339 U.S. 637 (1950), **2**:460
Meachum v. Fano, 427 U.S. 215 (1976), **4**:219–220
Metro Broadcasting v. FCC, 497 U.S. 547 (1990), **2**:343
Meyer v. Holley, 537 U.S. 280 (2003), **1**:114
Meyer v. Nebraska, 262 U.S. 390 (1923), **2**:370, 409
Michael H. v. Gerald D., 491 U.S. 110 (1989), **3**:164
Michigan Department of State Police v. Sitz, 496 U.S. 444 (1990), **4**:387–388
Miles v. Apex Marine, 489 U.S. 19 (1990), **1**:40
Miller v. California, 413 U.S. 14 (1973), **5**:335
Miller, United States v., 307 U.S. 174 (1939), **1**:219–220
Miller, United States v., 425 U.S. 435 (1976), **4**:387
Milliken v. Bradley, 418 U.S. 717 (1974), **2**:342
Minor v. Happersett, 88 U.S. (21 Wall.) 162 (1875), **6**:45, 135
Miranda v. Arizona, 384 U.S. 436 (1966), **2**:20, 258; **3**:62; **4**:453
Missouri v. Holland, 252 U.S. 416 (1920), **3**:294
Mitchell v. Helms, 530 U.S. 793 (2000), **5**:119
Mitsubishi Motors Corp. v. Soler Chrysler-Plymouth, 473 U.S. 614 (1985), **1**:131; **3**:488
Montana v. United States, 450 U.S. 544 (1981), **4**:213
Moore v. Dempsey, 261 U.S. 86 (1923), **4**:452–453
Moore v. Illinois, 55 U.S. (14 How.) 13 (1852), **5**:263
Morehead v. New York ex rel. Tipaldo, 298 U.S. 587 (1936), **2**:27; **3**:61
Morrison, United States v., 529 U.S. 598 (2000), **2**:67, 68, 464; **3**:64; **5**:353; **6**:143
Moses Taylor, The, 71 U.S. 411 (1866), **1**:38
Mulford v. Smith, 307 U.S. 38 (1939), **5**:90
Muller v. Oregon, 208 U.S. 412 (1908), **2**:26, 208; **3**:165; **5**:266, 267; **6**:136
Munn v. Illinois, 94 U.S. 113 (1877), **4**:490; **5**:88, 100; **6**:48
Murray v. The Charming Betsy, 6 U.S. (2 Cranch) 64 (1804), **3**:293
Myers v. United States, 272 U.S. 52 (1926), **3**:23
National Labor Relations Board v. Jones & Laughlin Steel, 301 U.S. 1 (1937), **2**:66, 67; **3**:62
National League of Cities v. Usery, 426 U.S. 833 (1976), **3**:63
Near v. Minnesota, 283 U.S. 697 (1931), **5**:335
Nebbia v. New York, 291 U.S. 502 (1934), **2**:27; **3**:409

Nebraska Press Association v. Stuart, 427 U.S. 539 (1976), **5**:335
Nevada Department of Human Resources v. Hibbs, 538 U.S. 721 (2003), **3**:65
Nevada v. Hicks, 533 U.S. 353 (2001), **4**:213
New Jersey v. T. L. O., 469 U.S. 325 (1985), **4**:387
New State Ice Co. v. Liebmann, 285 U.S. 262 (1932), **2**:26
New York Times Co. v. Sullivan, 376 U.S. 254 (1964), **5**:333, 336
New York v. United States, 505 U.S. 144 (1992), **3**:64; **5**:412
Nixon v. Fitzgerald, 457 U.S. 731 (1982), **3**:23
Nixon, United States v., 418 U.S. 683 (1974), **2**:153; **3**:22
Nollan v. California Coastal Commission, 483 U.S. 825 (1987), **4**:492
Nordyke v. King, 364 F. 3d 1025 9th Cir. (2004), **1**:221
Norfolk Southern Railway v. Kirby, 543 U.S. 14 (2004), **1**:39
Norris v. Alabama, 294 U.S. 587 (1935), **2**:341
Northern Pipeline Co. v. Marathon Pipe Line Co, 458 U.S. 50 (1982), **2**:256
O'Brien, United States v., 391 U.S. 367 (1968), **5**:337
O'Hagan, United States v., 521 U.S. 642 (1997), **5**:94
O'Hara v. People, 3 N.W. 161 (Mich. 1879), **4**:451
Ogden v. Saunders, 25 U.S. (2 Wheat.) 213 (1827), **2**:207; **3**:60
Ohio v. Roberts, 448 U.S. 56 (1980), **3**:15
Olin Corp., 268 N.L.R.B. 573 (1984), **3**:488
Oliphant v. Suquamish Indian Tribe, 435 U.S. 191 (1978), **4**:213
Oliver v. United States, 466 U.S. 696 (1984), **4**:387
Olmstead v. L.C. ex rel Zimring, 527 U.S. 581 (1999), **2**:336
Olmstead v. United States, 277 U.S. 438 (1928), **4**:386, 387
Ortiz, United States v., 422 U.S. 891 (1975), **4**:387
Osborn v. Bank of the United States, 22 U.S. (9 Wheat.) 738 (1824), **2**:256; **3**:60
Panama Railroad Co. v. Johnson, 264 U.S. 375 (1924), **1**:40
Paquete Habana, The, 175 U.S. 677 (1900), **3**:294, 296
Parmalee v. United States, 113 f.2d 729 [D.C. Cir. 1940], **5**:267
Passenger Cases, 48 U.S. (7 How.) 283 (1849), **2**:65; **3**:206
Pennoyer v. Neff, 95 U.S. 714 (1878), **4**:442, 445
Pennsylvania Coal Co. v. Mahon, 260 U.S. 393 (1922), **2**:26; **4**:484, 491; **5**:424

People v. Defore, 242 N.Y. 13 (1926), **5:**204
People v. Hall, 4 Cal. 399 (1854), **6:**51
People v. Ruggles, 8 Johns (N.Y.) 290 (1811), **5:**115–116
People v. Turner, 55 Ill. 280, 8 Am. R. 645 (1870), **3:**459
Permoli v. New Orleans, 44 U.S. (3 How.) 589 (1845), **5:**116
Perry Education Association v. Perry Local Educators' Association, 460 U.S. 37 (1983), **5:**337
Personnel Administrator v. Feeney, 442 U.S. 256 (1979), **6:**139
Phillips v. Martin-Marietta, 400 U.S. 542 (1971), **6:**137
Pierce v. Society of Sisters, 268 U.S. 510 (1925), **2:**370, 409
Place, United States v., 462 U.S. 696 (1983), **4:**387
Planned Parenthood Association of Kansas City v. Ashcroft, 462 U.S. 476 (1983), **4:**389
Planned Parenthood of Southeastern Pennsylvania v. Casey, 505 U.S. 833 (1992), **2:**339, 370, 464; **3:**63; **4:**389; **6:**141
Plessy v. Ferguson, 163 U.S. 537 (1896), **2:**18, 20, 153, 299, 340, 460; **3:**164; **4:**218; **6:**52–53, 57
Plyler v. Doe, 457 U.S. 202 (1982), **2:**18, 463–464; **3:**208
Plymouth, The, 70 U.S. 20 (1865), **1:**39
Poe v. Ullman, 367 U.S. 497 (1961), **1:**221
Police Department of Chicago v. Mosley, 408 U.S. 92 (1972), **5:**337
Pollock v. Farmers' Loan & Trust Co. II, 158 U.S. 601 (1895), **2:**24
Pollock v. Farmers' Loan & Trust Co., 157 U.S. 429 (1895), **3:**61; **4:**490, 491; **5:**443
Powell v. Alabama, 287 U.S. 45 (1932), **2:**341; **4:**452, 453
Powell v. McCormack, 395 U.S. 486 (1969), **2:**261
Presser v. Illinois, 116 U.S. 252 (1886), **1:**218–219
Prigg v. Pennsylvania, 41 U.S. (16 Pet.) 539 (1842), **3:**60, 293; **5:**263
Prince v. Prince, 18 S.C. Eq. (1 Rich. Eq.) 282 (1845), **6:**45
Printz v. United States, 521 U.S. 898 (1997), **1:**221; **2:**166; **3:**64
Prize Cases, 67 U.S. (2 Black) 635 (1863), **3:**20
ProCD, Inc. v. Zeidenberg, 86 F.3d 1447 (7th Cir. 1996), **2:**76
Providence Bank v. Billings, 29 U.S. (4 Pet.) 514 (1830), **4:**489
Pumpelly v. Green Bay Co., 80 U.S. (13 Wall.) 166 (1872), **4:**490
Rabinowitz, United States v., 339 U.S. 56 (1950), **4:**387

Raich v. Ashcroft, 352 F. 2d 1222 (9th Cir. 2003), **2:**68
Railroad Erie v. Tompkins, 304 U.S. 64 (1938), **3:**427
Rasul v. Bush, 542 U.S. 466 (2004), **4:**181
Reagan v. Farmers' Loan and Trust Co., 154 U.S. 362 (1894), **5:**101
Red Lion Broadcasting v. FCC, 395 U.S. 367 (1969), **5:**98, 335
Reed v. Reed, 404 U.S. 71 (1971), **2:**339; **6:**57, 138
Regents of the University of California v. Bakke, 438 U.S. 265 (1978), **2:**302, 343
Reid v. Covert, 354 U.S. 1 (1957), **3:**296
Reno v. American Civil Liberties Union, 521 U.S. 844 (1997), **5:**335
Reynolds v. Sims, 377 U.S. 533 (1964), **1:**201
Reynolds v. United States, 98 U.S. 145 (1879), **3:**52; **5:**117, 118; **6:**51
Richardson v. Ramirez, 418 U.S. 24 (1974), **4:**340
Richmond v. Croson, 488 U.S. 469 (1989), **2:**343
Roberts v. City of Boston, 59 Mass. (5 Cuth.) 198 (1850), **2:**340
Rochin v. California, 342 U.S. 165 (1952), **2:**371
Rodriguez de Quijas v. Shearson/American Express, Inc., 490 U.S. 477 (1989), **1:**131
Roe v. Wade, 410 U.S. 113 (1973), **2:**20, 21, 339, 370; **3:**63, 67; **4:**68, 363, 389, 390; **6:**59, 141
Romer v. Evans, 517 U.S. 620 (1996), **2:**462–463; **4:**390
Roper v. Simmons, 543 U.S. 551 (2005), **3:**462
Rostker v. Goldberg, 453 U.S. 57 (1981), **2:**339; **6:**139–140
Roth v. United States, 354 U.S. 476 (1957), **5:**335
Rouse v. Cameron, 373 F.2d 451 (D.C. Cir., 1966), **6:**95
Rust v. Sullivan, 500 U.S. 173 (1991), **4:**389
Rutgers v. Waddington [mayor's court, New York, 1784], **3:**291
Saenz v. Roe, 526 U.S. 489 (1999), **2:**464
San Antonio Independent School District v. Rodriguez, 411 U.S. 1 (1973), **2:**411, 463; **4:**471
Santa Clara County v. Southern Pacific Railroad, 118 U.S. 394 (1996), **2:**369; **6:**46
Santa Clara Pueblo v. Martinez, 436 U.S. 49 (1978), **4:**213
Santa Fe Independent School District v. Doe, 530 U.S. 290 (2000), **2:**464; **5:**118
Scenic Hudson Preservation Conference v. Federal Power Commission, 354 F 2d. 608 (2d. Cir., 1965), **2:**456–457
Schechter Poultry Corp. v. United States, 295 U.S. 495 (1935), **1:**190; **2:**27, 65; **3:**22, 61; **5:**80, 90, 353
Schenck v. United States, 249 U.S. 47 (1919), **5:**334

School Board of Nassau County v. Arline, 480 U.S. 273 (1987), **2**:335
SEC v. Ralston Purina Co., 346 U.S. 119 (1953), **5**:92
SEC v. Texas Gulf Sulphur Co., 446 F.2d 1301 (1971), **5**:93
SEC v. W. J. Howey & Co., 328 U.S. 293 (1946), **5**:92
Seixas v. Woods, 2 Cai., 48 (N.Y. Sup. Ct. 1804), **2**:206
Seminole Tribe of Florida v. Florida, 517 U.S. 44 (1996), **3**:64; **5**:354
Seymour v. Delancy, 3 Cow. 445 (N.Y. Sup. Ct.) (1824), **2**:205
Shapiro v. Thompson, 394 U.S. 618 (1969), **2**:464; **4**:371; **6**:94–95
Shaughnessy, United States ex rel. Knauff v., 338 U.S. 537 (1950), **3**:209
Shaw v. Reno, 509 U.S. 630 (1993), **1**:202
Shearson/American Express, Inc. v. McMahon, 482 U.S. 220 (1987), **1**:131
Shelley v. Kraemer, 334 U.S. 1 (1948), **2**:460; **4**:486
Shreveport Rate Cases, 234 U.S. 342 (1914), **5**:102
Skinner v. Oklahoma ex rel. Williamson, 316 U.S. 535 (1942), **4**:219
Slater v. Mexican National Railway, 194 U.S. 120 (1904), **2**:117
Slaughterhouse Cases, 83 U.S. 36 (1873), **1**:322; **2**:340, 369; **3**:61, 143; **4**:218; **6**:52
Smith v. Allwright, 321 U.S. 649 (1944), **2**:18, 19, 20, 341; **4**:342, 343
Smyth v. Ames, 169 U.S. 466 (1898), **5**:101–102
Snail Darter case (Tennessee Valley Authority v. Hill), 437 U.S. 153 (1979), **2**:457
Sony v. Universal City Studios, 464 U.S. 417 (1984), **3**:268
South Dakota v. Dole, 483 U.S. 203 (1987), **3**:65, 114–115
Southern Pacific Co. v. Jensen, 244 U.S. 205 (1917), **1**:39; **2**:258
Sparf and Hansen v. United States, 156 U.S. 51 (1895), **3**:444
Spies v. Illinois, 123 U.S. 131 (1887), **6**:51
Springer v. United States, 102 U.S. 586 (1881), **4**:490; **5**:441
Spur Industries v. Del E. Webb Development Co., 494 P.2d 700 (Ariz., 1972), **4**:485
Standard Oil Co. v. United States, 221 U.S. 1 (1911), **1**:189
Stanley v. Georgia, 394 U.S. 557 (1969), **4**:387
State Street Bank and Trust v. Signature Financial Group, 149 F. 3d 1368 (CAFC, 1998), **3**:271
State v. Felter, 25 Iowa 67 (1868), **6**:50

State v. Mann, 13 N.C. 263 (1829), **5**:261
Steelworkers Trilogy, **3**:487
Sterward Machine Co. v. Davis, 301 U.S. 459 (1937), **5**:267
Stewart, United States v., 348 F.3d 1132 (9th Cir. 2003), **2**:68
Stone v. Farmers' Loan and Trust Co., 116 U.S. 307 (1886), **5**:100
Stone v. Mississippi, 101 U.S. 814 (1880), **2**:211
Stone v. Powell, 428 U.S. 465 (1976), **4**:454
Strate v. A-1 Contractors, 520 U.S. 438 (1997), **4**:213
Strauder v. West Virginia, 100 U.S. 303 (1880), **3**:443; **6**:138
Stuart v. Laird, 5 U.S. 299 (1803), **2**:261
Sturges v. Crowninshield, 17 U.S. (4 Wheat.) 122 (1819), **2**:207; **6**:40, 45
Swann v. Charlotte-Mecklenburg Board of Education, 402 U.S. 1 (1971), **2**:342
Sweatt v. Painter, 339 U.S. 629 (1950), **2**:341, 460
Swift v. Tyson, 41 U.S. 1 (1842), **2**:75, 258; **4**:441, 444
Tahoe-Sierra Preservation Council v. Tahoe Regional Planning Agency, 535 U.S. 302 (2002), **4**:492
Tashjian v. Republican Party of Connecticut, 479 U.S. 208 (1986), **4**:342, 343, 344
Taylor v. Louisiana, 419 U.S. 522 (1975), **3**:444
Tennessee v. Lane, 541 U.S. 509 (2004), **2**:336; **3**:65
Terrett v. Taylor, 13 U.S. (9 Cranch) 43 (1815), **4**:489; **6**:45
Terry v. Ohio, 392 U.S. 1 (1968), **4**:387; **5**:206
Texas v. Johnson, 491 U.S. 397 (1989), **5**:337
Thomson v. Winchester, 36 Mass. [19 Pick.] 214 (1837), **3**:271
Thornburg v. Gingles, 478 U.S. 30 (1986), **1**:202
Thornburgh v. American College of Obstetricians and Gynecologists, 476 U.S. 747 (1986), **4**:389
Thorpe v. Housing Authority of City of Durham, 393 U.S. 268 (1969), **6**:95
Tinker v. Des Moines Independent School District, 393 U.S. 503 (1969), **2**:409
Town of Castle Rock v. Gonzales (U.S., 2005), **6**:142–143
Trade-Mark Cases, 100 U.S. 82 (1879), **3**:271
Troxel v. Granville, 530 U.S. 57 (2000), **2**:424
Tumey v. Ohio, 273 U.S. 510 (1927), **2**:368
Turner v. Williams, 194 U.S. 279 (1904), **5**:333–334
TVA v. Hill, 437 U.S. 153 (1978), **2**:457
Two Pesos v. Taco Cabana, 505 U.S. 763 (1992), **3**:272

U.S. Term Limits v. Thornton, 514 U.S. 779 (1995), **2**:166; **5**:353

United States ex rel. Knauff v. Shaughnessy, 338 U.S. 537 (1950), **3**:209

United States v. Alcoa, 148 F.2d 416 (2d Cir. 1945), **1**:190; **3**:288

United States v. American Tobacco Co., 221 U.S. 106 (1911), **1**:189

United States v. Belmont, 301 U.S. 324 (1937), **3**:22

United States v. Booker, 543 U.S. 220 (2005), **2**:293

United States v. Butler, 297 U.S. 1 (1936), **2**:27; **3**:61, 114; **4**:76; **5**:90

United States v. Callender, 25 Fed. Cas. 239 (1800), **4**:450

United States v. Carolene Products, 304 U.S. 144 (1938), **2**:370; **3**:409, 410; **4**:491

United States v. Cruikshank, 92 U.S. 542 (1876), **1**:218

United States v. Curtiss-Wright Export Corp., 299 U.S. 304 (1936), **3**:22

United States v. Darby, 312 U.S. 100 (1941), **2**:66, 68

United States v. Debs (1894), **2**:261

United States v. DeWitt, 76 U.S. (9 Wall.) 41 (1869), **2**:65

United States v. E. C. Knight Co., 156 U.S. 1 (1895), **1**:189; **2**:24, 65; **5**:79, 353; **6**:48

United States v. Emerson, 46 F. Supp. 2d 598 (2001), **1**:221

United States v. General Dynamics Corp., 415 U.S. 486 (1974), **1**:191

United States v. Georgia, 546 U.S. 151 (2006), **3**:65

United States v. Hudson and Goodwin, 11 U.S. (7 Cranch) 32 (1812), **2**:283; **6**:51

United States v. Jacobsen, 466 U.S. 109 (1984), **5**:207

United States v. Kagama, 118 U.S. 375 (1886), **4**:209–210

United States v. Lara, 541 U.S. 193 (2004), **4**:213

United States v. Leon, 468 U.S. 897 (1984), **5**:207

United States v. Lopez, 514 U.S. 549 (1995), **2**:67, 68; **3**:63–64; **5**:353

United States v. McCoy, 323 F.3d. 1114 (9th Cir. 2003), **2**:68

United States v. Miller, 307 U.S. 174 (1939), **1**:219–220

United States v. Miller, 425 U.S. 435 (1976), **4**:387

United States v. Morrison, 529 U.S. 598 (2000), **2**:67, 68, 464; **3**:64; **5**:353; **6**:143

United States v. Nixon, 418 U.S. 683 (1974), **2**:153; **3**:22

United States v. O'Brien, 391 U.S. 367 (1968), **5**:337

United States v. O'Hagan, 521 U.S. 642 (1997), **5**:94

United States v. Ortiz, 422 U.S. 891 (1975), **4**:387

United States v. Place, 462 U.S. 696 (1983), **4**:387

United States v. Rabinowitz, 339 U.S. 56 (1950), **4**:387

United States v. Stewart, 348 F.3d 1132 (9th Cir. 2003), **2**:68

United States v. The Amistad, 40 U.S. (15 Pet.) 518 (1841), **3**:293; **5**:263

United States v. Verdugo-Urquidez, 494 U.S. 259 (1990), **1**:221

United States v. Virginia, 518 U.S. 515 (1996), **2**:462

United States v. Wheeler, 435 U.S. 313 (1978), **4**:213

United States v. Wong Kim Ark, 169 U.S. 649 (1898), **3**:209; **6**:52

United Steelworkers of America v. American Mfg. Co., 363 U.S. 564 (1960), **3**:487

United Steelworkers of America v. Enterprise Wheel and Car Corp., 363 U.S. 593 (1960), **3**:487

United Steelworkers of America v. Warrior and Gulf Navigation Co., 363 U.S. 574 (1960), **3**:487

Vacco v. Quill, 521 U.S. 793 (1997), **4**:390

Van Orden v. Perry, 545 U.S. 677 (2005), **5**:119

Vanhorne's Lessee v. Dorrance, 2 U.S. (2 Dall.) 304 (1795), **4**:489; **5**:423

Vegelahn v. Guntner, 167 Mass. 92 (1896), **2**:26

Verdugo-Urquidez, United States v., 494 U.S. 259 (1990), **1**:221

Vernonia School District 47J v. Acton, 515 U.S. 646 (1995), **4**:388

Vickery v. Welch, 36 Mass. [19 Pick.] 523 (1837), **3**:273

Vieth v. Jubelirer, 541 U.S. 267 (2004), **1**:202

Village of Euclid v. Ambler Realty, 272 U.S. 365 (1926), **2**:27; **3**:182; **4**:484, 485, 491

Virginia, United States v., 518 U.S. 515 (1996), **2**:462

Wabash, St. Louis & Pacific Railway v. Illinois, 118 U.S. 557 (1886), **5**:101; **6**:48

Wallace v. Jaffree, 472 U.S. 38 (1985), **5:**118

Warden v. Hayden, 387 U.S. 294 (1967), **5:**206

Ware v. Hylton, 3 U.S. (3 Dall.) 199 (1796), **5:**411

Waring v. Clarke, 46 U.S. 441 (1847), **1:**38

Washington v. Glucksberg, 521 U.S. 702 (1997), **2:**370; **4:**220, 390

Weaver v. Palmer Bros. Co., 270 U.S. 402 (1926), **3:**144

Webster v. Reproductive Health Services, 492 U.S. 490 (1989), **4:**389

Weeks v. United States, 232 U.S. 383 (1914), **4:**386, 451; **5:**204

Weems v. United States, 217 U.S. 349 (1910), **5:**40

West Coast Hotel Co. v. Parrish, 300 U.S. 379 (1937), **2:**370; **3:**62, 409; **4:**483; **5:**81

West River Bridge Co. v. Dix, 47 U.S. (6 How.) 507 (1848), **2:**211; **3:**60

Weston v. City Council of Charleston, 27 U.S. (2 Pet.) 449 (1823), **5:**441

Whalen v. Roe, 429 U.S. 589 (1977), **2:**370

Wheaton v. Peters, 33 U.S. [8 Pet.] 591 (1834), **3:**267

Wheeler, United States v., 435 U.S. 313 (1978), **4:**213

White v. Crook, 251 F. Sup. 401 (DCMD Ala. 1966), **6:**138–139

Whitney v. California, 274 U.S. 357 (1927), **3:**409

Wickard v. Filburn, 317 U.S. 111 (1942), **2:**66–67, 68; **3:**62

Wilburn Boat Co. v. Fireman's Fund Insurance Co., 348 U.S. 310 (1955), **1:**39

Wilkinson v. Leland, 27 U.S. (2 Pet.) 627 (1829), **2:**368

Wilko v. Swan, 346 U.S. 427 (1953), **3:**486

Williams v. Florida, 399 U.S. 78 (1970), **5:**268, 269

Williams v. Lee, 358 U.S. 217 (1959), **4:**211

Williams v. Mississippi, 170 U.S. 213 (1898), **6:**44

Williams v. Walker-Thomas Furniture Co., 350 F.2d 445 (D.C. Cir. 1965), **2:**209–210

Willson v. Black Bird Creek Marsh Co., 27 U.S. (2 Pet.) 245 (1829), **2:**65

Winans v. Denmead, 56 U.S. 330 (1853), **3:**270

Wisconsin v. Yoder, 406 U.S. 205 (1972), **2:**409; **5:**119

Witherspoon v. Illinois, 391 U.S. 510 (1968), **5:**268–269

Wolf v. Colorado, 338 U.S. 25 (1949), **5:**205

Wong Kim Ark, United States v., 169 U.S. 649 (1898), **3:**209; **6:**52

Wong Wing v. United States, 163 U.S. 228 (1896), **3:**208

Wood v. Dummer, 3 Mason 308, Fed. Cas. No. 17, 944 (1824), **1:**326

Worcester v. Georgia, 31 U.S. (6 Pet.) 515 (1832), **4:**208, 209; **6:**50

Wyatt v. Stickney, 344 F. Supp. 373 (M.D. Ala., 1972), **6:**95

Wyman v. James, 400 U.S. 309 (1971), **4:**371

Wynehamer v. People, 13 N.Y. 378 (1856), **2:**24; **4:**490

Yick Wo v. Hopkins, 118 U.S. 356 (1886), **3:**208; **4:**219

Younger v. Harris, 401 U.S. 37 (1971), **2:**260

Youngstown Sheet & Tube Co. v. Sawyer, 343 U.S. 579 (1952), **3:**24; **5:**218–219

Zacchini v. Scripps-Howard Broadcasting, 433 U.S. 562 (1977), **3:**274

Zelman v. Simmons-Harris, 540, 536 U.S., 639 (2002), **5:**119

Zenger (1735), **4:**447–448, 449, 450

INDEX

Page numbers in boldface refer to the main entry on the subject. Page numbers in italics refer to illustrations.

A

AAA. *See* Agricultural Adjustment Act
AALS. *See* Association of American Law Schools
AARP, **2:**422
ABA. *See* American Bar Association
Abas, Tun Salleh, **4:**139
Abbasid dynasty, **1:1–2; 3:**418–419
   development of the *fiqh* under, **3:**315
   Hanbali school under, **3:**347
   Khariji revolts under, **3:**348
   legal professions in, **4:**71
   in Maghrib and al-Andalus, **4:**127
   muftis in, **4:**194
Abbott, Charles, **2:**89, 441
ʿAbd al-Barr, Abu ʿUmar ibn, **4:**128
ʿAbd Allah ibn Ibad, **3:**349
ʿAbd Allah ibn Miftah, **6:**156
ʿAbd al-Malik ibn Habib, **3:**350
ʿAbd al-Rahman, Rabiʿa ibn Abi
   influenced by Malik ibn Anas, **3:**350; **4:**140
   influence on Sahnun, ʿAbd al-Salam ibn Saʿid al-Tanukhi, **5:**182
abduction. *See* kidnapping
ʿAbduh, Muhammad, **6:**69
   on decline of Islamic society, **2:**421
   on life insurance, **2:**61
Abdülhamit II (Ottoman sultan), **4:**269
Abdurrahman (Afghanistan), **1:**59
ABF. *See* American Bar Foundation
ABGB. *See* Austrian Allgemeines Bürgerliches Gesetzbuch
Abhandlung über die Principien (Zeiller), **6:**163
Abhari, al-, **3:**350
Abidhamma Pittaka, **5:**302
ʿAbidir, Ibn, **6:**149
Abi Duʾad, Ahmad ibn, **1:**1
Abi Rabah, ʿAtaʾ ibn, **5:**182

ABN Amro, **1:**261
Abolition Act (Trinidad, 1834), **6:**9
abolitionism
   natural law and, **4:**218
   United States, **5:**259
   women in, **6:**134–136
aboriginal law, **1:2–4,** 239–240, 243–245. *See also* Maori law
   in British Commonwealth, **1:**315
   common-law doctrine on, **4:**146–147
   feminist legal theory on, **3:**67
Aborigines Protection Act (Australia, 1905), **1:**3
abortion
   England, **3:**178
   federalism and, **3:**63
   gender equality and, **2:**339–340
   Hindu law, **1:4–5**
   sex-selective in India, **2:**365
   United States, **6:**140–142
      case law, **6:**59
      constitutional right to, **3:**411, 412
      due process and, **2:**370–371
      equal protection, **2:**464
      privacy and, **4:**388–390
      Supreme Court, **2:**165
Abraham, **3:**389
Abrams, Kathryn, **3:**69
abrogation of legal norms (*naskh*), **1:5–6**
Absentee Ownership and Business Enterprise in Recent Times (Veblen), **1:**325
ʿAbsi, ʿAli ibn Ziyad Abu al-Hasan al-, **4:**140
absolute privilege defense, **4:**106
absolutism, **1:6–9**
   Denmark, **2:**328–329
   divorce and, **3:**44
   Enlightment views of, **1:**8; **2:**445
   guardianship and, **3:**47–48

marriage under, **3:**40
Napoleonic Code and, **3:**99–100
Abu ʿAbdallah al-Damaghani, **3:**465
Abu al-Fazl, **2:**282
Abu al-Khattab, Mahfuz ibn Ahmad al-Kalwadhani. *See* Kalwadhani, Abu al-Khattab Mahfuz ibn Ahmad al-
Abu al-Walid al-Baji, **3:**351
   on *fiqh*, **4:**128
Abubacer. *See* Ibn Tufayl
Abu Bakr. *See* Ibn Tufayl
Abu Bakr al-Khallal, **3:**305
Abu Bakr ibn al-ʿArabi, **3:**198
Abu Bakr Muhammad ibn Daʾud, **3:**354
Abu Hanifa, al-Nuʿman ibn Thabit, **1:**9–10. *See also* Hanafi school of Islamic law
   Hanafi school and, **1:**252
   on judicial review, **3:**413
   on option, **4:**262
   on partnership, **4:**289
   on possession, **4:**360
Abu Khalid al-Wasiti, **6:**161, 162
Abu Muhriz, **5:**239
Abu Shujaʿ, **5:**322; **6:**155
Abu ʿUthman, **3:**352
Abu Yaʿla, Muhammad ibn al-Husayn ibn al-Farraʾ al-Baghdadi, **1:**10; **3:**347
   Ibn ʿAqil, Abu al-Wafaʾ ʿAli, student of, **3:**196
Abu Yusuf, Yaʿqub ibn Ibrahim, **1:**10–11; **3:**181, 305, 343, 344
   Abbasids and, **1:**2
   as Grand Qadi, **1:**1
   influence on al-Shaybani, **5:**236
   on the legal bond, **5:**452
   on option, **4:**262
   on partnership, **4:**289
   on possession, **4:**360
Abzug, Bella, **6:***145*
academics, **1:**11–18
   on environmental law, **2:**452
   on Greek law, **1:**161–167
   legal treatises in, **2:**440–443
Academy of Arcadia (Rome), **3:**126
Academy of Sciences (Russia), **5:**171, 177
Ācāradinakara (Vardhamānasūri), **3:**364
Accademia dei Pugni (Milan), **1:**285
Accademia dei Trasformati (Milan), **1:**285

Accedemia degli Investiganti, **3:**126
accessory
   guarantee in Roman law, **3:**128–129
   and principal in Chinese law, **1:**18–19
Access to Justice (Woolf), **1:**199
Access to Justice Act (U.K., 1999), **1:**199
Accident Compensation Act (New Zealand, 1972), **4:**231
accident insurance, **3:**253
Accord on Strengthening Civil Society and the Role of the Army (Guatemala), **3:**131
Accord on the Identity and Rights of Indigenous People (Guatemala), **3:**131
accountability
   of administrative agencies, **1:**29
   Africa, **1:**97
   of children in medieval and post-medieval Roman law, **3:**44–45
   in education, **2:**412
   guilt and, **3:**135, 136
   of lawyers, **4:**54
Accounting and Auditing Organization for Islamic Financial Institutions (AAOIFI), **1:**262
Accursius, Franciscus, **1:**19; **3:**355. *See also Glossa ordinaria*
   on agency, **1:**111
   compared to
      Bartolus, **1:**281
      Cujas, Jacques, **2:**303
   on conflict of laws, **2:**111
   influenced by Azo, **1:**248
   on succession, **5:**386
   on unjust enrichment, **6:**65
acephalous societies
   advocates and, **1:**55
   precolonial Africa, **1:**64, 67
Acevedo, Eduardo, **6:**66
Acharonim, **3:**388, 392–393
Achilles, **4:**399
Ackerman, Bruce
   on 14th Amendment, **2:**158, 160
   in legal process, **4:**69
acknowledgment (avowal; *iqrār*), **1:**19–20
ACLU. *See* American Civil Liberties Union
ACLU Reproductive Freedom Project, **6:**144
ACLU Women's Rights Project, **6:**144
acquis communautaire, **2:**496

Acquis Group. *See* European Research
    Group on Existing EC Private
    Law (Acquis Group)
Acta Apostolica Sedis, **1:**353; **2:**319
"Act about the Casuall Killing of Slaves, An"
    (Virginia, 1669), **5:**258
Act concerninge matters of assurances, amonste
    merchantes (England, 1601), **3:**258
Act for the Better Relief of the Poor (England, 1601),
    4:347, 349
Act for the Modernization of the Law of Obligations
    (Germany, 2001), **4:**395
*Act for the Treatment and Control of Dependent,
    Neglected and Delinquent Children, An*
    (Illinois, U.S., 1899), **3:**459–460
actio de peculio, **5:**249
*Actio des römischen Civilrechts vom Standpunkte
    des heutigen Rechts, Die* (Windscheid),
    6:107
actio exercitoria, **5:**249
actio institoria, **5:**249
Action Plan (EU, 2003), **2:**496
actions
    action of debt on a conditional bond, **2:**197
    Gaius on, **3:**251
    at law, **2:**183
actio quod lussu, **5:**249
Act IX. *See* ParSee Immovable Property Act
Act of 1327 (England), **3:**452
Act of 1361 (England), **3:**452
Act of 1704 (England), **3:**311
Act of 1705 (England), **4:**206
Act of 1709 (Great Britain), **3:**311
Act of Abjuration (Netherlands, 1581), **4:**225
Act of Explanation (Ireland, 1665), **3:**311
Act of Parliament (England, 1531), **3:**176
Act of Settlement (England, 1701), **2:**132;
    3:416; **4:**89
Act of Settlement (Ireland, 1662), **3:**311
Act of Supremacy (England, 1534), **1:**350; **2:**129
Act of Uniformity (England, 1662), **1:**468
Act of Union (England and Scotland, 1707), **2:**132
Acton Burnell statute (1283, England), **4:**35
Act on the Protection and Promotion of Thai Traditional
    Medicine (Thailand, 1999), **3:**264
Act to Provide for the Transportation of Certain
    Juvenile Offenders to States under the
    Law of Which They Have Committed
    Offenses or Are Delinquent and for
    Other Purposes (U.S., 1932), **3:**461

actual malice test, **5:**336
Adams, Abigail, **2:**338
Adams, Charles Francis, **1:**326
Adams, Charles Francis, Jr., **5:**77
Adams, Henry Carter, **5:**79
Adams, John, **6:**38
    administrative agencies under, **1:**25
    Alien and Sedition Acts and, **6:**40, 50
    on colonial courts, **3:**424
    on education, **2:**408
    electoral votes of slave states in non-election
        of, **5:**260
    on federal juries, **4:**450
    on general welfare clause, **3:**114
    judicial power under, **3:**407
Adams, John Quincy, **3:**294
    electoral college and, **4:**339
    on general welfare clause, **3:**114
Adams, T. S., **3:**286–288
adat, **1:20–21**
    in Balinese law, **1:**251
    Hindu-Buddhist legal concepts as *adat* in Indonesia,
        3:225
    in legal anthropology, **4:**59
    Malaysia, **4:**137–138
    Singapore, **5:**241
    Southeast Asia, **5:**313, 314
        Islamic law and, **5:**322
Addams, Jane, **5:**79
Addington, Henry, **5:**428
Addison, C. G., **2:**442
Adelphia, **5:**95
Aden, influence of Anglo-Muhammadan law in,
    6:157
Adenauer, Konrad, **2:***485, 490*
ad exhibendum action
    Sabinus, Masurius, on, **5:**180
Ad Fletam Dissertatio (Selden), **2:**98
ADHGB. *See* Allegemeines Deutsches
    Handelsgesetzbuch
Adigama, **5:**321
Ādipurāṇa (Jinasena), **3:**364
adjudicatory jurisdiction. *See* conflict of laws
administration, public law of, **1:21–25**
Administration of Estates Act (U.K., 1925),
    3:88; **5:**384
Administration of Islamic Law Enactments (Malaysia),
    2:140; **3:**337
Administration of Justice Act (U.K., 1841), **3:**17
Administration of Justice Act (U.K., 1977), **4:**36

Administration of Justice from Homer to Aristotle, The (Smith), **1:**163
administration of justice in Chinese law
   under Song, **1:**425–426
   under Tang, **1:**423–424
Administration of Justice Regulation (India, 1781), **3:**446
Administration of Muslim Law Act (Singapore, 1966), **3:**339
Administration of Muslim Law Enactments (Malaysia, 1952), **4:**301
administrative agencies in the United States, **1:**25–33
   in antitrust, **1:**188
   environmental, **2:**456–458
   in labor arbitration, **3:**487–488
   law and science and, **4:**30
   legislative power of, **4:**99
   separation of powers and, **5:**220
   in statutory interpretation, **5:**361
   supremacy clause and, **5:**412
administrative decrees of the political authorities (*qānūn*), **1:**33–35
   Mamluk period, **1:**33–34
   Ottoman Empire, **1:**34–35; **4:**266–267
Administrative Dispute Resolution Act (U.S., 1990), **1:**131
Administrative Justice Act (Japan, 1890), **3:**380
administrative law. *See also* administrative agencies
   absolutism and, **1:**8
   Africa after independence, **1:**99
   ancient Near Eastern law, **1:**168–169
   Austria, **1:**246, 247
   Colombia, **2:**63
   English legal treatises on, **2:**443
   France, **3:**100
   Germany under National Socialists, **4:**203–204
   legal process on, **4:**67
   separation of powers and, **5:**220
   Spain, **5:**326
   state constitutions and, **5:**351
   in Sui and Tang codes, **1:**422
   Switzerland, **5:**418
   United States
      Articles of Confederation on, **1:**224
      rise of, **1:**30
Administrative Litigation Law (China, 1990), **1:**195, 446

Administrative Procedure Act (U.S., 1946), **1:**28–29; **3:**207; **5:**81
   judicial review and, **1:**31
administrative procedure in Qin dynasty, **1:**408
Administrative Reconsideration Law (China), **1:**195
admiralty, **1:**35–40
   medieval and post-medieval Roman law, **1:**35–37
   United States law, **1:**37–40
   Wales, **6:**100
Adnotationes in Pandectas (Budé), **3:**191
Adnotationes in tres posteriores libros Codicis Iustiniani (Alciato), **3:**191
adoption, **1:**40–50
   ancient Greece, **1:**40–43
      Athens, **1:**234
      Code of Gortyn, **1:**142; **3:**121, 123
      Hellenistic, **1:**159
      posthumous, **3:**231
   ancient Near East, **1:**172–173
   ancient Rome, **4:**303, 304, 305, 306, 308; **6:**118
      adoption of citizens, **4:**93
      slavery and, **5:**247
   Bangladesh, **4:**300
   Chinese law, **1:**43–46
      for succession, **5:**380
   by Chinese-speaking Muslims, **1:**400
   English common law, **1:**46–47
   Gaius on, **3:**251
   gay, **6:**143
   Hindu law, **1:**49–50
   India, **2:**307, 308; **3:**148, 149
      Christians, **3:**223
   Islamic law, **1:**47–49, 396
      abolished, **4:**164
   Kuwait, **4:**298
   medieval and post-medieval Roman law, **3:**46
   model law of the European Council, **2:**115
   Southeast Asia, **5:**318
   Tunisia, **4:**297
   United States, **3:**54–55
      interracial, **3:**55
Adoption and Children Act (U.K., 2002), **1:**47; **3:**36
Adoption Law (China, 1991), **1:**46
Adoption of Children Act (U.K., 1926), **1:**46–47
Adoption of Children (Regulation) Act (U.K., 1939), **1:**47
Adorno, Theodor, **2:**297

Ad Q. Mucium (Pomponius), **3:**434
Adulteration of Food and Drink Act (U.K., 1860), **2:**168
adultery
   Afghanistan, **1:**62
   Africa, **1:**102
   ancient Greece, **1:**50–53; **6:**115
      Code of Gortyn, **3:**120, 123
      divorce and, **2:**346
      rape and, **5:**65
   ancient Near East, **1:**175
   ancient Rome, **2:**269, 271, 273; **4:**306; **6:**118
   Aztec law, **5:**287, 288
   Carolina (German criminal code) on, **5:**230
   Cohen, David, on, **1:**51; **5:**358
   East Timor, **2:**384
   England
      divorce and, **2:**347–348, 349
      ecclesiastical law on, **2:**389
   Inca law, **5:**288–289
   India
      divorce, **2:**353
      punishment, **2:**280, 281, 283
   Islamic law
      paternity disownment and, **3:**37–38
      punishment for, **6:**130
      stoning for, **1:**6, 62
      women in, **6:**127
   Laos, **4:**14
   legitimacy of children from, **3:**46
   medieval and post-medieval Roman law, **5:**229–230
   United States
      colonial period, **2:**288–289
      as grounds for divorce, **3:**53
advertising, commercial speech in, **5:**336
advocate, **1:**53–58
   ancient Athens, **1:**53–55; **4:**113–115
      logography and, **4:**123–126
   medieval and post-medieval Roman law, **1:**55–58
Advysen over den Koophandel en Zeevaert, **4:**151
Aebutian law on *formula*, **3:**94
Aegidio, Alexander de Sancto, **1:**248
Aelius Paetus Catus, Sextus, **3:**434; **6:**20
Aemilius Macer, **3:**436
Aenmerckingen over de Zeerechten (Glins), **4:**151
Aeschines
   forensic speeches by, **1:**149
   on *graphē paranomōn*, **1:**141; **3:**124, 125
   on homosexual behavior, **5:**228
   on logographers, **4:**125
   on theft, **5:**457
   on witnesses, **6:**110
Aeschylus, **4:**399
   on adultery, **1:**50
   judicial scenes by, **1:**148
   law depictions by, **4:**108, 110–111
   on metics, **5:**357
Aethelberht (king of Kent), codification by, **1:**177; **2:**434; **3:**117
Aethelred I (England)
   ecclesiastical law under, **2:**387
   on feud, **1:**180
   on juries, **1:**182
   on wrongs, **1:**179
Aethelred II (England), **1:**385
   codification by, **1:**178
Aethelstan on theft, **1:**178
AFBF. *See* American Farm Bureau Federation
AFDC. *See* Aid to Families with Dependent Children
'Affan, 'Uthman ibn, **1:**33
affirmative action
   constitutional interpretation and, **2:**165
   in education, **2:**344
   gender-based, **2:**340
   India, **3:**219; **5:**208
   in labor and employment law, **3:**483
   in legal education, **1:**16
   Mauritius, **4:**172
   race-based, **2:**343–344
   sex discrimination and, **3:**484
   statutory interpretation in, **5:**362
Afghan Civil Law (Qanun-i Madani, 1355/1977), **1:**61–62
Afghani, Jamal al-Din al-
   on decline of Islamic society, **2:**421
Afghanistan
   codification, **2:**35–36
   conflict of laws, **2:**114
   constitutions, **2:**37; **3:**317
   courts, **1:**60, 61
   criminal law, **2:**279
   death penalty, **1:**368
   Islamic law, **1:**58–63
      non-Muslims in, **4:**235
Afonso I (Kongo), **1:**66, 79
Afrania/Carfania, lawsuits by, **6:**119
African Central Bank, **1:**107
African Charter on Human and Peoples' Rights, **1:**107

African Charter on the Rights and Welfare of the Child (1990), **1:**107
African Civil Aviation Commission, **1:**107
African Commission on Human and Peoples' Rights, **1:**107
African Convention on the Conservation of Nature and Natural Resources (1968), **1:**107
African Court of Justice, **1:**107
African Court on Human and Peoples' Rights, **1:**107
African Economic Community, **1:**107
African law, **1:63–108.** *See also specific countries*
    after independence, **1:96–108; 2:**43–45
    arbitration
        after independence, **1:**99–100
        precolonial law on, **1:**74
    British Commonwealth in, **1:**312, 313, 315
    codes and codification
        colonial period, **2:**42–43
        family law, **2:**38
        independence, **2:**43–45
    colonial period, **1:75–96**
        codes and codification, **2:**42–43
    constitutional law, **2:137–138**
    dual courts systems
        colonial period, **2:**42
        at independence, **2:**43
    legal education, **2:**398
    precolonial period, **1:63–75**
    South Asian law in, **2:**382–384
African Nuclear-Weapon-Free-Zone Treaty (1996), **1:**107
African Peer Review Mechanism, **1:**107
African Union, **1:**107
Afrique Équatoriale Française, **1:**89
Afrique Occidentale Française, **1:**89
Against Dionysodorus, **4:**149
Against Euxenippus (oration, Hyperides), **4:**246
Against Leocrates (Lycurgus), **3:**124, 125
Against Meidias (Demosthenes), **2:**266
Against Neaira (attr. Demosthenes), **4:**154
    on adultery, **1:**51, 52
    on Areopagus jurisdiction, **4:**247
Against Nicomachus (Lysias), **2:**30
Against Stephanus II (oration attr. Demosthenes), **3:**231
Agamemnon, **4:**399
AGB. *See* Allgemeine Gesetzbuch für die Preussischen Staaten
Age Discrimination Act (U.S., 1975), **2:**424

Age Discrimination in Employment Act (U.S., 1967)
    arbitration and, **1:**131
    elderlaw and, **2:**424
    on labor arbitration, **3:**488–489
agency, **1:108–116**
    ancient Greek law, **2:**71
    Anglo-Saxon law, **1:**181
    business law and, **1:**319–320
    English common law, **1:108–110**
        women, **6:**124
    medieval and post-medieval Roman law, **1:110–112**
    modern Islamic law, **2:**75
    of necessity, **3:**33
    partial, **3:**69
    partnership and, **1:**320
    of slaves in Roman law, **5:**248–249
    United States civil law, **1:112–116**
agō (competitive debate)
    Athens, **1:**234, 235
    literature depictions, **4:**108
    literature depictions of, **4:**109–111
Agobard of Lyon, **3:**8
agoranomoi (market controllers), **2:**69
agrarian policy
    China
        damage to property, **2:**312–313
        land leases, **4:**6–7
    Germany under National Socialist, **3:**110
    Islamic law (*See also* agricultural; agricultural contracts and sharecropping in Islamic law)
        on lease and tenancy, **4:**55, 56
    Roman law, **2:**321
    South and Central America
        colonial, **5:**298
        reform laws in Colombia, **2:**63
    United States agriculture regulation, **5:**86–92
Agreement on Trade-Related Aspects of Intellectual Property Rights (TRIPs), **3:**268, 271, 285
Agreement on Trade Related Investment Measures (TRIMs), **3:**285
Agricultural Act (U.S., 1970), **5:**90
Agricultural Adjustment Act (U.S., 1933), **2:**66–67; **3:**409; **5:**81, 89, 90
Agricultural Adjustment Administration, **2:**27
agricultural contracts and sharecropping in Islamic law, **1:116–118; 2:**73, 74
Agricultural Marketing Agreement Act (U.S., 1938), **5:**90
Aguesseau, Henri-François d', **2:**47; **3:**99; **4:**366
Agustín, Antonio, **5:**325
Ahkam al-kubra (Ibn Sahl), **3:**350

Ahmadiyya Muslims, codes for, **2:**39
Ahmed I (Ottoman Empire), **1:**35
Ahrens, Henri, **1:**303
AHRQ. *See* Agency for Healthcare Research and Quality
Aid to Dependent Children (ADC). *See also* Aid to Families with Dependent Children
    forced sterilization and, **6:**142
    grants-in-aid under, **4:**370
    New Deal changes to, **6:**93
    stigma of, **6:**137
Aid to Families with Dependent Children (AFDC), **6:**92
    cost of, **6:**92, 97
    deserving and undeserving poor in, **6:**93
    reform and replacement of, **4:**371–372
Aiginetikos (Isocrates), **2:**109
Aikokusha. *See* League for the Promotion of Parliament
AIM. *See* American Indian Movement
Air (Prevention and Control of Pollution) Act (India, 1981), **2:**453
Air Commerce Act (U.S., 1926), **5:**103
Airline Deregulation Act (U.S., 1978), **2:**178; **5:**104
airline regulation in the United States, **5:**103–104
Aischines, **1:**54; **2:**229
Akan, **1:**68
Akbar (Mughal emperor), **2:**36
Akham ahl al-Dhimma (Ibn Qayyim al-Jawziyya), **3:**199
Akham al-Qur'an (Jassas), **3:**328
Akham al-sultaniyya (al-Mawardi), **2:**36
Akhbariyya school of legal thought, **1:**291
Akihito (Japanese emperor), **3:**366
Akitoye (Lagos), **1:**86
Aksum, **1:**67; **2:**479
Aktiengesetz (Germany, 1937), **2:**96
'Ala al-Din al-Samarqandi, **3:**466
Alabama, CSS, **3:**294
Al-ahkam al-sultaniyya (Abu Yaaynla), **1:**10
Al-akham al-shar'iyya fi-l-ahwal al-shahsiyya (Muhammad Qadri Pasha al-Hanafi), **4:**195–196
Al-'amal al-Fasi (al-Fasi), **4:**129
Alanus Anglicus, decretal collection by, **2:**319
Alaric II (king of the Visigoths). *See* Lex Roman Visigothorum
Al-asl (Shaybani), **5:**236
al-Azhar University, **2:**398; **3:**422
Al-bahr al-zakhkhar (Ibn al-Murtada), **4:**136
Albania, Islamic law in, **1:**251; **3:**334
Alberdi, Juan Bautista, **1:**216

Albertine Statute (Italy, 1848), **3:**358
Alcatraz, Indian takeover of, **4:**212
Alchemy of Race and Rights: Diary of a Law Professor, The (Williams), **2:**301
Alciati, Andrea, **1:**118–119; **2:**7; **3:**356
    at University of Avignon, **6:**160
    at University of Bourges, **1:**316; **2:**400; **5:**467
Alciati, Francisco, **1:**118
Alciato, Milanese Andrea, **3:**191
Alciatus, Franciscus. *See* Alciati, Francisco
Alcibiades, **2:**346; **5:**113
alcohol and drugs, **1:**119–128
    Chinese law, **1:**119
    Islamic law, **1:**119–123
    United States law, **1:**123–128
Aleiniikoff, Alexander, **4:**69
Alekseev, N. N., **5:**178
Alekseev, S. S., **5:**178
Alemanic law on children, **3:**44
Alexander, Sadie T. M., **6:**144
Alexander III (pope)
    decretals by, **2:**221, 317; **4:**353
    ecclesiastical courts under, **2:**386
    on marriage, **2:**388; **4:**161
Alexander IV (pope), **2:**317
Alexander VI (pope), **5:**290, 299
Alexander I (Russia), **5:**172
Alexander I (Scotland), **5:**197
Alexander II (Scotland), **5:**197
Alexander III (Scotland), **5:**197, 198
Alexander Tartagnus, **2:**111
Alexander the Great
    dedication by, **1:***158*
    Greece unified by, **1:**136, 137
    Greek law under, **1:**135
    immigration under, **1:**157–158
Alexandro, Alexander ab, **5:**467
Alexis I Mikhailovich (Russian Tsar), **5:**170
Alexius I Comnenus, **4:**416
Alfenus, **4:**290
Alfonse X (Spain), **1:**384
Alfonso V (king of León), **3:**397
Alfonso VI (king of León and Castile), **3:**397
Alfonso X (the Wise, Spain)
    codification, **1:**215; **5:**325
    colonial law, **5:**298–299
    formalization of law, **5:**290
    Roman law under, **5:**253

Alfred (Anglo-Saxon king)
  codification by, **1:**177
  on injury, **1:**179
  on oath, **1:**181
  on rape, **5:**67–68
  treason under, **6:**1
Algeria
  adoption, **1:**48
  conflict of laws, **2:**114
  Constitution, **4:**298
  death penalty, **1:**368
  family law, **4:**130
  Ibadis in, **3:**349
  jurisdiction in, **1:***64*
  Maliki school of law in, **3:**351
  personal status law, **4:**297; **6:**129
  polygamy, **4:**297
  wills, **6:**107
Al-ghayth al-midrar (Ibn al-Murtada), **4:**136
ALI. *See* American Law Institute
'Ali, Muhammad
  legal education reforms by, **2:**398
  merchants councils by, **4:**47
Alien Act (U.S., 1798), **3:**206
Alien and Sedition Acts (U.S., 1798), **6:**40
alienation
  African German colonies, **1:**84–85
  ancient Near Eastern law, **1:**173
  China
    land law, **4:**1, 2, 3–4
    resistance to, **4:**5
  England
    dower and, **2:**362
    entails, **2:**446–448
    feudal law, **3:**74
    mortmain and, **4:**191
    subinfeudation and substitution, **5:**368–370
  in lease and tenancy contracts, **4:**57
Alien Enemies Act (U.S., 1798), **3:**206
Aliens Act (Britain, 1870)
  duty of allegiance, **6:**4
  on nationality, **4:**206
Aliens in Medieval Law: The Origins of Modern Citizenship (Kim), **4:**205
Alien Tort Claims Act (U.S., 1789), **3:**297
'Ali ibn Abi Talib
  as caliph, **1:**33
  on inheritance, **3:**233
  as judge in Yemen, **6:**155

  on non-Muslim *jizya*, **4:**233
  Yemen, **6:**155
alimentation. *See* maintenance
alimony
  England, adultery and, **2:**349
  medieval and post-medieval Roman law, **3:**43
  United States
    cohabitation and, **3:**55
    women in, **6:**138
al-Istidhkar fi sharh madhahib 'ulama' al-amsar (Ibn 'Abd al-Barr), **4:**141
Alito, Samuel A., Jr.
  on federalism, **3:**65
  on right to bear arms, **1:**222
Al-jami' al-kabir (Shaybani), **3:**343; **5:**236
Al-jami' al-saghir (Shaybani), **3:**343; **5:**236
Alkali Act (U.K., 1863), **2:**450
All-Africa Constitutional Conference (1970), **1:***96*
'Allama, al-. *See* Ibn al-Mutahhar, Hasan ibn Yusuf al-Hilli
'Allāma, al-, **3:**340
Allen, Christopher J. W., **3:**6
Allende, Salvador, **1:**398
Allgemeine Gesetzbuch für die Preussischen Staaten (AGB) (Prussia, 1792), **5:**1
Allgemeine Hypotheken-Ordnung (Prussian Mortgage Act) (Prussia, 1783), **5:**1
Allgemeines Bürgerliches Gesetzbuch (Austria, 1811), **2:**9, 47; **5:**1, 2
  on assignment, **1:**227
  on breach of contract, **1:**307, 308
  on civil liability, **5:**471
  common law, **4:**392
  on delay, **2:**320
  education on, **2:**400–401
  employment and labor law, **2:**428
  Enlightenment influences on, **2:**444
  on error and mistake, **2:**475–476
  on illegal transactions, **3:**203
  on immoral transactions, **3:**204
  influence on Hungarian law, **3:**194
  influences on, **1:**246
  on lease and tenancy contracts, **4:**57
  and *Pandektenwissenschaft*, **4:**278
  on profiteering contracts, **3:**204, 205
  on property, **4:**475, 478
  renewal of, **1:**247
  on sale of goods, **5:**192
  on succession, **5:**384, 385, 389, 394
  Zeiller, Franz von, editor in chief of, **6:**163

Allgemeines Deutsches Handelsgesetzbuch
(Germany, 1861), **4:**478; **5:**2
corporations in, **2:**95
Allgemeines Landrecht für die Preussischen Staaten
(1794), **2:**9, 47; **5:**1–3
agency in, **1:**110
on assignment, **1:**227
on breach of contract, **1:**307
on church, **1:**351
education on, **2:**400–401
Enlightenment influences on, **1:**8; **2:**444
on error and mistake, **2:**475
on *fideicommissum*, **3:**81
on illegal transactions, **3:**203
on immoral transactions, **3:**204
law merchant in, **4:**39
on lease and tenancy contracts, **4:**57
on mortgage, **4:**190
on precedents, **4:**380
private law, **4:**394
on profiteering contracts, **3:**205
on property, **4:**361, 475
on sale of goods, **5:**192
on sale of land, **5:**194
on social security, **5:**270–271
on taxation, **5:**437, 438
on vicarious liability, **6:**78
All India Democratic Women's Association
(AIDWA), **6:***132*
All-India Jain Association. *See* Young Jain Men's
Association
All India Women's Conference, **5:**397
Allott, Antony, **1:**88
Al-lumaʿ (Shirazi), **5:**238
Al-masaʾil al-muʿtabara (Muzani), **4:**200
Al-miʿyar al-muʿrib (Wansharisi), **4:**128
Almohad dynasty
Ibn Rushd and, **3:**200
in Maghrib and al-Andalus, **4:**128
Almoravid dynasty, **3:**200
al-Qaʿida, **3:**281
ALR. *See* Allgemeines Landrecht für die Preussischen
Staaten
Al-riʿaya fi ʿilm al-diraya (al-ʿAmili), **1:**132–133
Altan Khan, **4:**184
alternative dispute resolution, **1:128–132.** *See also*
arbitration; dispute resolution
Africa, **1:**100
grievance mediation, **3:**489–490
guilds in, **3:**131–132

Islamic in Europe, **2:**484
in Japan, **3:**383–384
legal process on, **4:**66
United States, **3:**68; **4:**446
Althusius, Johannes, **3:**193
on systematization, **5:**421
AMAA. *See* Agricultural Marketing Agreement Act
Āpastambadharmasūtra, **3:**179
Amanullah (Afghanistan), **1:**59
Amaral, Xavier do, **2:**385
Ambedkar, Bhimrao Ramji, **3:**220
Ambedkar, Dr., **5:**398
Amendments to the Clean Air Act (U.S., 1990),
2:457
Amerbach, Bonifacius, **3:**191; **6:**160
American Anti-Slavery Society, **6:**134
American Arbitration Association, **1:**129, 131
American Bankers Association, **1:**15–16
American Bar Association (ABA)
academics and, **1:**14
accreditation by, **1:**16
on civil procedure, **4:**444
code of ethics, **4:**50–51, 53
discrimination by, **2:**406
on elderlaw, **2:**422
Improvements in the Law of Evidence committee,
3:10
influence of, **4:**50
in law and society research, **4:**32
on law school admission standards, **6:**43
on legal education, **2:**404
on legal needs of the poor, **6:**95
Legal Services support by, **4:**370, 371; **6:**94
on profession, **4:**48
American Can trust, **1:**324
American Civil Liberties Union (ACLU), **4:**52
creation, **2:**17
enforcement of rights and, **2:**20
on sexual and gender variation, **3:**111
American Civil War. *See* Civil War (U.S.)
American Colonization Society, **4:**107
American Farm Bureau Federation (AFBF), **5:**89
American Federation of Labor, **3:**481
American Indian Movement (AIM), **4:**337
American Law and Economics Association, **4:**27
American Law Institute (ALI), **2:**84. *See also* entries
starting with *Restatement of*
on agency, **1:**113
creation, **2:**76
on evidence, **3:**11

Model Penal Code, **2:**291–292
   on sexual and gender variation, **3:**110
   restatement project, **2:**51, 84; **4:**75
   Uniform Commercial Code, **6:**61
American Law Register, **6:**43
American Medical Association, **4:**52
American Municipal Association, **4:**121
American Psychology-Law Society, **5:**268
American Revolution, **6:**36, *37,* 37–41, **37–41,** 42
   common law and, **2:**83–84
   criminal law and, **2:**287, 289
   Filangieri, Gaetano, on, **3:**84
   inheritance and, **3:**236
   property rights and, **4:**488
   rights and justice as justification for, **3:**447–448
   right to bear arms and, **1:**217, *217*
   state law on, **5:**348
   taxation and, **5:**440
   treason charges stemming from, **4:**335
American Samoa, **4:**346
American Slave Code in Theory and Practice (Goodell), **2:**207
Americans with Disabilities Act (U.S., 1990), **2:***335,* 335–337
   elderlaw and, **2:**424
   federalism in, **3:**65
   on job rights, **6:**57
   on special education, **6:**95
American Telephone and Telegraph Company (AT&T), **1:**192; **5:**96, 97, 98
American Tobacco Company, **1:**324; **5:**78
Ames, James Barr
   English common law historiography by, **2:**434
   on possession, **4:**358
   as teacher, **1:**13
Amherst Seminar, **4:**34
Amidi, al-, **3:**119–120
Amiens, Treaty of (1801), **5:**341
'Amili, Muhammad ibn Makki, al-, **1:**132
'Amili, Zayn al-Din ibn 'Ali ibn Ahmad al-, **1:**132–133
Amin, al-
   civil war by, **1:**1
Amistad, **3:**294
Amitagati, **3:**364
Ammi-Saduqa, edict of (Babylon), **1:**167, 174
amnesty in Chinese law, **1:**133–135
   imperial amnesties for capital cases, **1:**364

Amnesty International, **3:**461
Amos, Andrew, **2:**394, 395
amr bi-l-ma 'rūf, **1:**382
Amr bi-l-ma 'ruf wa-l-nahy 'an al-munkar (Khallal), **3:**467
Amsterdam, Treaty of (1997), **2:**487, 488, 492
   on private law, **2:**495
Amsterdamsche Wisselbank, **1:**275
analogy technique
   Chinese law, **5:**214
   in Islamic law (*See qiyās* (analogical reasoning))
   in Roman law, **3:**476; **4:**80
Analysis of the Law (Hale), **2:**394, 440
   influence on Blackstone, William, **1:**298
   legal theory in, **4:**61
Analysis of the Laws of England (Blackstone), **1:**297–298
Anand Marriage Act (India, 1908), **5:**241
Anastasius I (emperor)
   administrative policy under, **5:**14
   death and successor of, **3:**454
   on guarantee, **3:**129
   papacy and, **4:**352
Anatoli, Jacob, **3:**201
Anatolia. *See* ancient Near Eastern law
Anaximander, **1:**145
Anaximenes, **1:**149
Ancestral Worship Order (Sarawak, 1930), **5:**319
Ancher, Peder Kofod, **2:**328
Anchialos. *See* Michael II of Anchialos
anchisteia (head of household), family law and, **3:**27–28
ancient Greek law, **1:**135–167. *See also* Athens; Draco; Gortyn; Solon; Sparta
   overview and historical survey, **1:**135–146
   archaic period, **1:**153–157
      family law, **3:**28–29
      procedure, **4:**399–402
   Hellenistic law, **1:**157–161
   adoption, **1:**40–43
      posthumous, **3:**231
   adultery, **1:**50–53; **6:**115
      divorce and, **2:**346
      rape and, **5:**65
   agreements between cities for commerce, **2:**72
   anthropology and, **1:**184–187
   arbitration
      literary depictions, **1:**148
      oath challeng, **4:**242
      reconciliation and, **2:**233

banking and finance
  evidence in, **3:**2
  witnesses to transactions in, **6:**111
comparative inquiry, **2:**97
conflict of laws, **2:**109
debt
  arbitration, **1:**212
  enslavement for, **3:**30
  Solon on, **5:**274–275
definition of law, **4:**21
divorce, **1:**159; **2:**346–347
  in Egypt, **2:**412–416
evidence, oaths as, **4:**241–242
family, **2:**229; **3:27–32,** 29; **6:**116
  public actions to protect, **2:**268
freedom of speech, **4:**112; **5:329–331**
graphē paranomōn on, **3:**123–126
history of scholarship, **1:161–167**
homicide, **2:**228, 229, 232, 267–268; **3:169–171,**
    404; **4:**399–400; **5:**23, 65, 113
  Draco on, **1:**139, 154, 155; **2:**29–30, 366–367;
    5:227
  evidence in, **3:**2
  inscriptions on, **1:**147
  oaths in trials for, **4:**242
  of slaves, **5:**245
inheritance, **3:228–232,** 229
  adoption and, **1:**40–41
  divorce and, **2:**346–347
  inscriptions on, **1:**154
  marriage of heiresses, **4:**153, 155
  of slaves, **5:**244
  Sparta, **5:**328–329
  women in, **6:**114, 116
judges and juries, **3:**400–404
legislation, **4:84–87**
literature on, **4:**108–113
litigation, **1:**151; **4:**113–116
  anthropological perspective on, **1:**186
  oaths in, **4:**241–242
logography, **4:**123–126
maritime, **1:**35; **4:147–150,** 382
marriage, **4:***152,* 152–155; **6:**115–116, 116
  of adoptees, **1:**42
  adultery, **1:**50–53
  Athens, **1:**140
  divorce, **2:**346–347
  family and, **3:27–32,** 31
  foreigners in, **3:**31
  Gortyn, **1:**142

  Hellenistic, **1:**158–160
  offenses against the state and, **4:**247
  papyri on, **1:**147
  sexual and moral regulation of, **5:**226–227
  between siblings, **1:**159
  Sparta, **3:**29; **5:**328–329
  unity of Greek law and, **1:**136
offenses against the state, **4:246–248**
origins, **1:152–153**
prisons and imprisonment, **4:382–383;**
    5:23, 244
procedural law, **1:**136–137, 140
  anthropological perspective on, **1:**186–187
  Archaic, **1:**155–156
  Athenian influence in, **1:**143
  literature on, **1:**152–153
  in offenses against the state, **4:**247–248
  social importance of, **1:**144–145
  Solon on, **1:**155–156
property, **4:456–459**
  of foreigners, **5:**357
  inscriptions on, **1:**154
  marriage and, **4:**154
  military service and, **4:**247
  papyri on, **1:**147
  women and, **1:**159
prostitution, **4:493–495; 6:**113
  adultery and, **1:**51, 53
rape, **5:64–66**
  punishment for, **1:**52
  slavery and, **5:**355
religion and, **5:110–113**
rhetoric in, **5:134–136**
rule of law, **5:**164
sexual and moral regulation, **5:***226,*
    226–229
slaves and slavery, **5:243–247**
  enslavement of free citizens, **2:**267–268
  Gortyn, **1:**142
  Hellenistic, **1:**158, 160
  manumission, **1:**143, 158
  murder of slaves, **3:**404
  selling daughters into, **3:**31
  slaves as prison guards and executioners, **4:**382
  Solon on, **3:**30; **5:**275
  Sparta, **5:**327–328
  status of slaves, **5:**355–356
  testimony of slaves, **3:**1; **4:**406; **6:**110
  torture of slaves, **5:**479–481
sources, **1:146–152**

status in, **5:**354–358
theft, **5:456–457**
torture
  evidence gained through, **3:**2
  of slaves, **5:**245
women, **5:**64–66; **6:112–117**
  adoption of, **1:**41
  Athens, **1:**140, 234
  Bachofen, J. J., on, **1:**185
  in divorce, **2:**346–347
  Hellenistic, **1:**159
  homosexual behavior among, **5:**228–229
  legal status of, **5:**357–358
  oaths by, **4:**241–242
  property ownership rights, **4:**456–457
  prostitution, **4:**493–494, 495
  sexual and moral regulation of, **5:**226–227
  as slaves, **5:***243*, 244
  Sparta, **3:**29; **5:**328–329
ancient Greek philosophy and law, **4:**320–323
Ancient Law (Maine), **2:**98; **4:**137; **5:**108, 160
  anthropological perspective of, **1:**185
  on Greek law, **1:**162
Ancient Laws of Ireland (Brehon Law Commissioners), **3:**306
ancient Near Eastern law, **1:167–177**
ancient Rome. *See also* Roman law
  courts, **2:234–239**
    cognitio, **2:51–54**
    formula in, **3:**93–97
    magistrates in, **4:**131–132
    Senate as, **5:**212
  imperial legislation, **3:210–213**
  women, **6:117–120**
Andalus, al-
  Awzaʿi school of Islamic law, **4:**127
Andalus, al- (Muslim Spain), **4:127–130**
Andalusian Ibn Rushd, **5:**487
Anderson, Chief Justice, **1:**231
Anderson, John, **4:**344
Andocides, **2:**30
  forensic speeches by, **1:**149
  on *graphē paranomōn*, **3:**123, 124
  imprisonment of, **4:**382
  on Solon, **5:**274
  on torture, **5:**479
  on witnesses, **6:**111
André, John, **4:**177

Andreae, Johannes, **2:**223
Andrianampoinimerina (Madagascar), **1:**66
And We Are Not Saved: The Elusive Quest for Racial Justice (Bell), **2:**301
Angel Island (San Francisco Bay), **3:**207
Angell, Joseph K., **6:**46
Anglican Church. *See also* Church of England
  in Wales, **6:**101
Anglo-Burmese Wars, **1:**318
Anglo-Chinese Commercial Treaty (1902), **3:**93
Anglo-Chinese Treaty (1858), **3:**92
Anglo-Hindu law, **3:157–159**
Anglo-Indian Codes, **3:**215–216
  Burma, **1:**318
Anglo-Irish War (1919–1921), **3:**313
Anglo-Japanese Commercial Treaty (1899), **3:**375
Anglo-Muhammadan law
  in Aden, **6:**157
  in Burma, **3:**334
  in Malaysia, **3:**337
Anglo-Saxon Chronicle, **1:**178
Anglo-Saxon Dooms (Laws) of Ethelbert (England, 604), **5:**27
Anglo-Saxon law, **1:177–184**
  homicide, **3:**177
  legislation, **5:**276
  marriage, **4:**161
  ordeals, **4:**262–263
  outlawry, **4:**270–271
  provincial administration, **3:**117
  sale, **5:**189
  system of compensation, **1:**364
  torts, **5:**473, 474
  treason, **6:**1
Angola, decolonization of, **1:**93
Anguilla, **1:**369
Anmati, al-, **3:**201
Anmerkungen (Kreittmayr), **3:**474
Annapolis Convention (1786), **2:**149
Anne (queen of England)
  judiciary under, **3:**416
  Scotland under, **5:**200
Annotationes in Tres Posteriores Libros Codicis Iustiniani (Alciati), **1:**118
Annotationes in XXIV Pandectarum libros (Budé), **1:**316
"Announcement to Prince Kang," **1:**195–196
annuity for life, tontines and, **3:**258
Ansaldus de Ansaldis, **2:**93

Ansari, Murtada ibn Muhammad Amin al-, **1:184**; **3**:347
  influenced by
    Baqir al-Najafi, Muhammad Hasan ibn Muhammad, **1**:276
Anschütz, Gerhard, **2**:121
Ansegis, **3**:8
Anselm of Canterbury, **3**:133
'Ansi, Ahmad Qasim al-, **6**:156
Anson, William
  on academic law, **2**:443
  on contracts, **2**:442
Ansotegui, Juan Crisóstomo de, **5**:291
Anthony, Susan B.
  arrest and conviction for voting, **6**:45, 135
  on divorce, **6**:142
  in women's rights movement, **2**:338
anthropology and ancient Greek law, **1:184–187**
antichresis in ancient Near Eastern law, **1**:174
anticorruption legislation, **3**:289
Anti-Cybersquatting Consumer Protection Act (U.S., 1999), **3**:272
Anti-Federalists
  on Articles of Confederation, **1**:225
  on judicial power, **3**:406
  on judiciary, **3**:425
Antigua and Barbuda, **1**:369
Antinous, **1**:160–161
Antiochus Chuzon, **3**:437
Antiphon
  as advisor, **1**:232
  criticisms of, **4**:125
  forensic speeches by, **1**:149
  on law, **4**:320
  as logographer, **4**:123
  on *nomos*, **1**:145
  on punishment, **5**:22
  on torture of slaves, **5**:480
  on witnesses, **6**:110
Anti-Rightist Movement (People's Republic of China, 1957), **1**:443
Anti-Social Behaviour Order (U.K., 1998), **4**:426
Anti-Subversion Law (Indonesia, 1963), **3**:228
Anti-Tribonian (Coquille), **3**:191
Anti-Tribonian (Hotman), **2**:47; **6**:9
antitrust, United States law, **1:187–193**, 323–324; **5**:78, 79, 80, 82, 83, 84, 88, 89. *See also* Sherman Antitrust Act (U.S., 1890)
  administrative agencies in, **1**:26
  Chicago school on, **4**:23–24, 25–26
  extraterritorial application, **3**:288
  legal education suit in, **1**:16–17
  social sciences on, **5**:269
  strike breaking and, **1**:325
Antoninus Caracalla (Roman emperor)
  cosmopolitan outlook, **6**:23
  Papinian and, **4**:278–279
  Ulpian on, **6**:23
  on women, **6**:118
Antoninus Elagabal (Roman emperor), **6**:23
Antoninus Pius (Roman emperor)
  public courts under, **3**:436
  women under, **6**:118
Antonius, M., **2**:391
Aotearoa. *See* New Zealand
APA. *See* Administrative Procedure Act
apartheid, **5**:280–281
  end of, **1**:104, 106
Āpastamba, **3**:152, 156
  on *smriti*, **5**:264
Apel, Johannes, **3**:193
  on obligations, **4**:245
aphairesis, **2**:346
Apocrypha, **3**:390
apoleipsis, **2**:346
Apollodorus, **4**:457
  on adultery, **1**:51
  forensic speeches by, **1**:149
  as logographer, **4**:123
Apology (Plato), **1**:148
  on imprisonment, **5**:23
Apology for the Book on the Just Causes of War (Sepúlveda), **4**:16
apopempsis, **2**:346
apostasy in Islamic law
  capital punishment, **1**:367
  conviction of Abu Zayd, Nasr Hamid, **2**:421
  Hanafi school on, **2**:278–279
Apoukakos, John, **1**:330
appeal, **1:193–200**. *See also specific courts*
  ancient Greek law under Solon, **2**:228, 231
  Australia, **1**:240–241, 242, 243
  Chinese law, **1:193–195**; **2**:246–247
    doubtful cases, **2**:361
    Han dynasty, **1**:416
    Qing dynasty, **2**:246
    review, **1:195–198**

ecclesiastical courts, **2**:386, 388
English common law, **1:198–200**
 ecclesiastical law and, **2**:388
 tutorial, **2**:388
Germany under National Socialism, **4**:204
Native American, **4**:213
New Zealand, **4**:230–231, 232
Ottoman Empire, **4**:268
Roman law, **2**:238
 Institutes (Justinian) on, **2**:238
Scotland, **5**:200, 201
of search and seizure, **5**:204
Singapore, **5**:242
South Africa, **5**:280–281
Sweden, **5**:415
Appellate Jurisdiction Act (Great Britain, 1876), **1**:199
Appendix Concilii Lateranensis, **2**:318
Appius Claudius, **6**:20
Application of English Law Act (Singapore, 1994), **5**:242
apportionment and reapportionment, **1:200–204**
 equal protection and, **2**:463
apprenticeship
 English common law, **2**:425
  assault and, **1**:227
 in legal education, **1**:11, 12
  United States, **2**:401, 402; **4**:48–49
 Mauritius, **4**:171–172
 United States
  colonial, **5**:257
  for lawyers, **4**:48–49
appurtenancy in easements, **2**:380–381
'āqila, **3**:39
Aquino, Benito, **4**:319
Aquino, Corazón, **4**:319
Arab countries
 constitutional law in, **2:134–137**
 Islamic law in, **1:204–209**
  overview, **1:204–208**
  Saudi Arabia, **1:208–209**
Arab Gulf states
 Islamic insurance companies, **3**:256
Arabi, Abu Bakr ibn al-, **4**:128
Arabian Peninsula, **1:209–212**
 Shafi'i school of law in, **3**:352
Arangio-Ruiz, Vincenzo, **5**:161
Araucano, El (Chile, newspaper), **1**:286

arbitration, **1**:128. *See also* alternative dispute resolution
Africa
 after independence, **1**:99–100
 precolonial law on, **1**:74
ancient Greece
 Athens, **1**:141, **212–215**; **2**:233
 literary depictions of, **1**:148
 oath-challenge in, **4**:242
Bangladesh, **1**:260
collective bargaining and, **3**:489
company law and, **2**:96
Islamic law, **4**:429
Roman law, **5**:180–181
United States, **1**:130–131; **3**: 486, 487
 commercial, **2**:78
 labor arbitration, **3:486–490**
 Taft-Hartley Act on, **3**:483
Arbitration (Menander), **1**:148
Arcadius Charisius, **3**:213, 436
 compendia of, **5**:151
archaeology. *See also* papyrology
 Anglo-Saxon law and, **1**:178
Archbold, J. F., **2**:442
Archbold on Criminal Pleading, Evidence, and Practice (Archbold), **2**:442
archdeacons, **1**:295
Archer, Gleason, **2**:404
Archias, **5**:112
Architectural Barriers Act (U.S.), **2**:335
Arc of Instability, **4**:174
Arduum sane munus (Pius X, 1904), **1**:353
Arelatanus, Ioannes Nicolaus, **1**:118
Areopagus (Athens), **1**:141
 in homicide cases, **1**:232
 jurisdiction of, **1**:232
 religious jurisdiction of, **4**:247
 Solon on, **5**:273
Aretinus, Angelus, **3**:102
Argentina, **1:215–216**; **6**:66
 codification, **4**:281; **5**:286
  Civil Code, **1**:398
  Penal Code, **4**:282
 influence on Paraguay, **4**:281
 Jesuit reductions in, **5**:300
 slavery abolished in, **5**:255
Argentré, Bertrand d' (Argentraeus, Betrandus de), **5**:467
 on conflict of laws, **2**:111
Arhannīti (Hemācārya), **3**:364
Arhtaśāstra, **6**:83

Arifin, Bustanul, **3:**337
Aristenos (Alexios Aristenos), **1:**348
  on canon law, **1:**330
  information on, **1:**333
Aristogeiton, **5:**330
Aristophanes
  on advocates, **1:**54
  on arbitration, **1:**212
  on homosexual behavior, **5:**228
  on juries, **1:**151
  law depictions by, **1:**148; **4:**111–112
  on litigiousness of Athenians, **1:**232; **4:**115
  prosecuted for slander, **5:**330–331
  public figures ridiculed by, **4:**112
  on rape, **5:**65
  on rhetoric, **5:**134
  on Solon, **3:**30–31
  on theft, **5:**457
  on witnesses, **6:**111
  on women, **6:**114
Aristophon, **3:**125
Aristophon of Azenia, **1:**54
Aristotle. *See also* Athenian Constitution
  academic study of, **6:**62
  on adoption, **1:**40
  on adultery, **1:**51
  on arbitration, **1:**214
  commentaries by Ibn Rushd on works of, **3:**201
  on constitutional theory, **1:**162; **2:**125–126
  on courts, **2:**231
  on Cretan customs, **1:**142
  on definition of law, **4:**18, 19
  on equity, **2:**466, 468
  on evidence, **3:**1, 2; **4:**405
  on fairness, **3:**403
  on family, **3:**28, 31
  on freedom of speech, **5:**329
  on *graphē paranomōn*, **3:**123
  on guilt, **3:**134
  on homicide, **3:**170
  on *hybris*, **2:**267
  influence on Paul, **4:**291
  on justice, **3:**446–447; **5:**474
  on kings, **2:**414
  on logographers, **4:**124
  on oaths, **4:**242
  papyrology on, **2:**413
  philosophy of law, **4:**321–323
  on philosophy of law, **1:**149
  positivist approach by, **1:**145
  on punishment, **5:**24
  on rhetoric, **4:**112; **5:**135
  on rule of law, **5:**164, 165
  Russian translation of the works of, **5:**177
  on slavery, **5:**244
  on Solon, **5:**274
  on Sparta, **1:**142–143; **5:**327, 329; **6:**115
  on volunteers in public cases, **4:**113
  on women, **6:**115
arms, right to bear, **1:216–222**
Arms Act (India, 1988), **2:**283
arm's-length standard, **3:**287
Army Corps of Engineers, **2:**455
Arnesberg, Arndts von, **4:**277
Arnim, Achim von, **5:**195
Arnold, Thurman, **2:**297
  on antitrust, **1:**190
  in legal realism, **4:**74, 76
  in New Deal, **4:**78
Aśoka, **5:**35
Aronson, Arnold, **2:***342*
arrest, mesne process in, **4:**174–175
Arsinoe II, **1:**159
arson
  Chinese law, **2:**331
  English common law, **6:**120
  Welsh law, **6:**99
arthaśāstra, **1:**223; **3:**152–153, 179, 364
Arthaśāstra (Kautilya), **5:**63
  consumer protection, **2:**173
  on *nītiśāstra*, **4:**232–233
Articles of Confederation, **1:**223–225
Articles of Confederation (U.S.), **1:223–225,** *224*; **2:**148
  on admiralty, **1:**38
  adoption of, **6:**39
  commerce clause and replacement of, **2:**64
  on courts, **2:**256; **3:**406
  debtor-relief laws and, **2:**210
  on executive power, **3:**19
  full faith and credit clause, **1:**224
  on judiciary, **3:**425
  on Native Americans, **4:**207–208
  provisions of, **6:**39–40
  state law in, **5:**347
  taxation, **5:**440
Articles of Confederation and Perpetual Union (U.S.). *See* Articles of Confederation (U.S.)
Articles of the Barons, **4:**135

Articuli Henriciani of, **4**:330; **4**:1573
Articuli super cartas (England, 1300)
   on Exchequer, **3**:17
   on Magna Carta, **4**:135
Artigas, José Gervasio, **6**:66
Arusha, **1**:91
Arya Samaj movement, **3**:159
Asad ibn al-Furat, **4**:127
   influence on Sahnun, **5**:183
   on Sicily, **5**:239
Asadiyya, al- (Asad ibn al-Furat)
   influence on Sahnun, **5**:183
   syncretism in, **4**:127
Asamm, Abu Bakr al-, **4**:55
Asante, **1**:68
Ashanti, **1**:70, 75, 86
Ashʿari, Abu Musa al-, **3**:413
   influence in Maghrib and al-Andalus, **4**:128
Ashʿari theology, **3**:352
Ashcroft, John, **1**:221
Asher ben Yehiel ("Rosh," or Asheri), Rabbenu, **3**:392
Ashhurst, William, **2**:394
Ashkenazi Jews, **3**:388, 392, 393, 394–396
Ashmun, John, **2**:403
Asian crisis of 1997–1998, effect on Indonesia, **3**:227
Asili, al-, **4**:128
Askia Muhammad (Songhai), **1**:74
Aśoka, **1**:*225*, **225–226**; **3**:154, 155
   Delhi-Topra Pillar Edict, **6**:83
   Sri Lanka under, **5**:339
Aspasia, **5**:331
assault, **1:226–227**. *See also* sexual assault
   libel and slander as, **4**:105
Assecuranz- und Haverey-Ordnung (Hamburg, 1731), **3**:258
Assembly of Experts of Leadership (Iran), **2**:139
Assembly of Heads of State and Government, **1**:97, 107
Assembly of the People (Athens), **2**:232–233
Asser, Tobias M. C., **4**:226
assets by descent, **2**:447
Assicurazioni Generali, **3**:258
assignation. *See* assignment (assignation)
assignment (*ḥawālah*), **1**:229
assignment (assignation), **1:227–229**
   of negotiable instruments, **4**:222–223

assimilation
   Africa, **1**:78–79
      French colonies, **1**:89, 90
      Portuguese colonies, **1**:69
      Spanish colonies, **1**:80–81
   education's role in, **2**:408–409
   Native American, **4**:209, 211
   queer theory on, **3**:112
   Suriname, **5**:414
Assize of Bread and Ale (England), **1**:231
Assize of Clarendon (England, 1166), **1**:231
Assize of Northampton (1176), **4**:263
Assize of Novel Disseisin (England, 1166)
   on nuisance, **4**:239
assize of nuisance
   in environmental law, **2**:448
assizes, **1:229–231**
   Chinese
      amnesty in, **1**:134
   Egypt
      juristic papyrology on, **2**:418
   England
      estates doctrine and, **2**:477
      in legislation, **4**:87
   English common law
      evidence in, **3**:4
   nuisance in, **4**:239–240
   Scotland, **5**:197
Assizes of Clarendon (1166), **4**:423; **5**:28
   on juries, **1**:182
Assizes of Jerusalem
   maritime law in, **1**:36
Association internationale des sciences juridiques, **2**:99
Association of African Trade Promotion Organizations, **1**:107
Association of American Law Schools (AALS), **1**:14
   accreditation by, **1**:16
   on elderlaw, **2**:422
   standards by, **2**:404
assumpsit, action of, **3**:472
   breach of contract and, **1**:306
   contracts and, **2**:196–197
   equity and, **2**:469
   error and mistake in, **2**:474
   growth of, **2**:437
   King's Bench and, **2**:85
   in law merchant, **4**:38
astronomical studies as offense against the Chinese state, **4**:252

astynomoi (city controllers), **2**:69
asylum, European Union and, **2**:492
asylums for the insane, **3**:245, *245*
    United Kingdom, **3**:247–248
Atatürk, Mustafa Kemal, **6**:15
Ateius Capito, **3**:434, 436
At Faiyish, Muhammad Yusuf, **2**:41
Atharvaveda, **1**:4
Athenaeus
    on *graphē paranomōn*, **3**:125
    on prostitution, **4**:494
Athenaion politeia (Aristotle), **2**:125
Athenaion politeia (Pseudo-Xenophon), **2**:124
Athenian Constitution, **1**:231
    on arbitration, **1**:214
    Aristotle's influence on, **1**:149
    Beauchet, Ludovic, on, **1**:162
    history in, **1**:140, 148
    legal system in, **1**:232
    on offenses against the state, **4**:246
    papyri of, **1**:146, *148*, 162
    scholarship on, **1**:164
Athenogenes, **4**:126
Athens, **1**:231–236
    adoption, **1**:40, 41–42
    adultery, **1**:52–53
    advocates, **1**:53–55
    arbitration in, **1**:212–215; **2**:233
    archaeological evidence in, **1**:149, 164–165, *165*
    Areopagus, **1**:141
        in homicide cases, **1**:232
        jurisdiction, **1**:232; **4**:247
        Solon on, **5**:273
    codes and codification, **2**:29–30
    constitutional terminology, **2**:123–124
    constitution of, **4**:86
    courts and magistrates, **2**:228–234, **228–234**
        arbitration, **1**:211–214
        rise in use of, **1**:232
        Solon on, **5**:275
    criminal law, **2**:265–268
    custom, **1**:150
    demokratia, **2**:124
    evidence, **3**:1–3; **4**:405–406
        logographers on, **4**:124
        of slaves, **5**:355
    family law, **3**:30
    freedom of speech, **5:329–331**
    influence, **1**:143
    inheritance, **1**:140, 234; **3**:229–230; **4**:114
        heiress and, **3**:230
    interstate trade, **4**:149
    judicial procedure, **1**:136–137
    legal procedure, **4:402–411**
    legal system, **1**:140–142
    legislation, **4**:84–85
    literature on law in, **4**:109
    litigation, **1**:235; **4:113–116**, 409–410
        magistrates in, **1**:232
        rise in, **1**:232
    logography, **4**:123–126
    market, **2**:69
    oaths, **4:241–242**
    offenses against the state, **4**:246–248
    procedural law, **1**:233, 234–235; **4**:113–115
    procedure
        trial procedure, **4:411–416**
    punishment, **5:22–24**
    reforms by Draco (*See* Draco)
    reforms by Solon (*See* Solon)
    slaves and slavery, **5**:243
        gender and status in, **5**:358
        in litigation, **4**:114
        status of, **1**:234
    sources of law, **1**:148–149
    status, **5**:355–356, 356–357
    statutes, **1**:150
    torture, **5:478–482**
        free status and, **5**:356
        oath-challenge, **4**:242
        of slaves, **5**:355
    trial procedure, **4**:411–416
    witnesses in, **6:110–111**
    women, **6**:112–115
        legal status of, **5**:357–358
    written law, **1**:139
atimia, Code of Gortyn on, **3**:121
Atiyah, P. S., **2**:442
Atkyns Reports, **4**:142
Atlas Historique (Chatelain), **5**:*199*
Atmadja, Kusuma, **3**:*227*
ātmanastuṣṭi, **1**:236
Atomic Energy Commission, **1**:28
AT&T. *See* American Telephone and Telegraph Company
Atta, Ofori, **1**:73
attaint in Australia, **1**:240
attempt, **1:236–238**

Attic Nights (Gellius), **3:**435
Attic Orators, **1:**232
   on arbitration, **1:**214
Atticus, **4:**497
Attorney Act (Great Britain, 1729), **4:**41
attorney general, **1:**25
attorneys in England, **4:**41; **5:**272
attornment with homage, **3:**75
Aucoc, Léon, **1:**23
Auflösungsgesetzen on *fideicommissum*, **3:**80
Augsburg, Peace of (1555), **2:**120
Augustine (of Hippo), Saint
   on evidence, **3:**8, 9
   on goals of government, **4:**96
   on guilt, **3:**133
   on sexual crimes, **5:**229
   on torture, **5:**123
   on war, **4:**16
Augustus (Roman emperor)
   adoption of, **4:**93
   on adultery, **2:**269, 273; **6:**118
   as advocate, **1:**56
   army under, **5:**12
   courts under, **2:**236, 270
   criminal prosecutions under, **5:**145
   jurists and, **5:**147
   legis actiones abolished by, **4:**81
   legislation under, **3:**210–211
      consolidation statutes, **2:**32
      on formula, **3:**94
      Labeo, Marcus Antistius, on, **3:**475
      on marriage, **4:**307
   political power under, **5:**144
   powers of, **3:**210
   restoration of the Republic, **5:**11
   Senate and, **5:**210, 212
   slavery and, **4:**306; **5:**249
   social and moral change under, **5:**145
   on succession, **5:**375
Aulus Gellius. *See* Gellius, Aulus
Aulus Ofilius, **3:**434
Aung San Suu Kyi, **5:**314
Aurangzeb (Mughal emperor), **2:**36, 281; **5:**307
Austin, John, **1:**238–239
   on Blackstone, William, **1:**298
   on classical common law, **4:**355, 356
   definition of law, **4:**18, 19
   fascism and, **4:**356
   influenced by Bentham, Jeremy, **1:**287
   legal theory by, **4:**61
   legal treatises by, **2:**443
   at London University, **2:**395
   natural law and, **4:**215
   in reform movements, **4:**42
Australia, **1:**239–246. *See also* aboriginal law
   in British Commonwealth, **1:**313
   equity law, **2:**440
   federalism in, **5:**354
   land registration system in, **4:**7–8
   Myall Creek trials, **1:**239
   New Zealand law influenced by, **4:**231–232
   notaries in, **4:**237
Australia Acts (1986), **1:***244*
   on appellate power, **1:**243
Australian Courts Act (1828), **1:**239
Australian Journal of Legal History, **1:**245
Australian New Guinea Act (Papua New Guinea, 1920), **4:**280
Australian Papua New Guinea Independence Act (Papua New Guinea, 1975), **4:**280
Austria, **1:**246–248. *See also* Unger, Josef
   codification, **2:**48 (*See also* Allgemeines Bürgerliches Gesetzbuch (Austria, 1811))
      Civil Code of Procedure (1895), **4:**435
      Codex Theresianus (1766), **4:**380, 477
      Josephinian Law Code (1787), **2:**9; **4:**380, 394; **6:**162
   company law, **2:**96
   competition regulation, **2:**103
   conflict of laws, **2:**113
   constitutions
      Constitution of 1920, **2:**122
      May Constitution of 1934, **2:**122
   consumer protection, **2:**171
   Enlightenment in, **2:**444
   in European Union, **2:**491
   fideicommissum, **3:**80
   German law and, **6:**26
   guarantee, **3:**128, 129
   housing, **4:**58
   Islamic law, **1:**253
   procedure, **4:**435
   property law, **4:**476
   Protestant church in, **1:**351
   sale of land, **5:**193
   social security, **5:**271
   succession, **5:**387
   Theresiana, **4:**439
   tontines, **3:**258

Austrian Civil Code. *See* Allgemeines Bürgerliches Gesetzbuch
Austrian Law for a Reordering of the Legal Status of Illegitimate Children (1970), **5:**387
Austro-Hungary, Islamic law in, **3:**334
Authenticum, **1:**328; **3:**456
   in legal education, **2:**399
   medieval legal education and (*See Tres libri codicis*)
authority
   doctrines of actual and apparent, **1:**113
   parental, **1:**394
   paternal, **3:**45
   political, **1:**33
   political, Islamic law on, **1:**33
   public, Islamic law on, **5:**3–6
   royal, **2:**130
authors, rights of, definition, **3:**259
Autonomy Act (Philippines, 1916), **4:**318
Autumn Assizes (China), **1:**360, 361–362, 364
   under Qing dynasty, **1:**434, 436, 437
Avellaneda, Nicolás, **1:**216
Averroës. *See* Ibn Rushd, Abu al-Walid Muhammad ibn Ahmad bin Muhammad
Avicenna, **1:**34
avowal. *See* acknowledgment (avowal; *iqrār*)
'awras, **1:**299–300
   of women, **6:**127
Awzai, al-, **3:**343
Awzaʿi school of Islamic law, **4:**127
axōnes, **5:**274
Ayala, Balthazar, **3:**282
Ayliffe, John, **2:**441
Aymette, William, **1:**218
A-Yun, **1:**197
Azerbaijan, abolition of death penalty, **1:**367
Azhar Islamic Institute, al- (Cairo), **3:**281
ʿAziz, Ashab ibn ʿAbd al-, **3:**350; **5:**183
ʿAziz, ʿUmar b. ʿAbd al-
   on political authority, **1:**33
ʿAziz al-Halwaʾi, Muhammad ibn ʿAbd al-
   Sarakhsi, Muhammad ibn Ahmad al-, and, **5:**194
Azo, **1:**248; **3:**355; **6:**65
   on fraud, **3:**104
   influence on
      Accursius, Franciscus, **1:**19
      Bracton, Henry de, **4:**214
   influence on *Bracton*, **5:**157
   inluence on doctrine of precedent, **4:**377
   on possession, **4:**361
   and rule of *actor sequitur forum*, **2:**111
   on succession, **5:**386, 392
Azpilcueta, Martín de, **4:**15
Aztec law, **5:**287–288, 298

B

Babylonian Talmud, **3:**257
Baby M, **3:**55, *56*
Bacchylides, **2:**413
Bach, J. A.
   on Roman law, **5:**158
Bachof, Otto, **1:**23
Bachofen, Johann Jakob, **1:**185
Bacon, Francis, **3:**193
   acceptance of bribes, **3:**417
   on assizes, **1:**230
   as barrister, **1:**278
   Coke, Edward, and, **2:**56
   comparative law, **2:**98
   on definition of law, **4:**18
   influence on
      Russian law, **5:**173
      United States colonial law, **2:**284
   on law reform, **4:**41
   on law reporting, **4:**45
   on legal maxims, **4:**61
   as queen's counsel, **5:**222
   Roman law used by, **5:**157
Bacon, Matthew, **2:**441; **4:**61
Bacon, Nicholas, **1:**231
Bacon, Roger, **4:**21
Badaʾiʿ al-sanaʾiʿ fi tartib al-sharaʾiʿ (Kasani), **3:**466
Badawi, Abdullah Ahmad, **2:**140
Bagehot, Walter, **2:**133
Baghdad
   Hanbali school in, **3:**346
   Imāmi school in, **3:**340
   Shafiʿi school of law in, **3:**352
Baghdadi, Ibn Haydar al-, **1:**34; **3:**305
Bagshaw, Edward, **2:**440
Bahamas, **1:**369
Bahja, al- (al-Tasuli), **3:**351
Bähr, Otto, **1:**228
Bahrain
   banking and finance, **1:**262
   codification, **2:**40
   constitution, **3:**317
   family law, **3:**37
   non-Muslims in, **4:**234–235

shari'a as principal source of legislation in, **3**:317
zakat in, **5**:431
Bahr al-muhit, al- (al-Zarkashi), **3**:353
bailment in English common law, **1**:249–250; **3**:400
    mesne process in, **4**:174–175
Bainimarama, Frank, **3**:*83*
Baji, Sulaiman ibn Khalaf al-, **4**:141
Baker, John, **2**:85, 86
Baker, John Hamilton
    on law merchant, **4**:37
    on villeinage, **5**:250
Bakkar ibn Qutaybah
    Muzani, Abu Ibrahim Isma'il ibn Yahya al-, and, **4**:200
Baldassaroni, Ascanio
    on maritime law, **4**:151
Balduini, Jacobus, **2**:111
Balduinus. *See* Baudouin, François
Baldus de Ubaldis, Angelus, **1**:250
    on succession, **5**:393
Baldus de Ubaldis, Petrus, **1**:250–251; **2**:7, 92; **5**:470
    on conflict of laws, **2**:111
    influenced by Bartolus of Saxoferrato, **1**:280
    international private law and, **2**:110
Baldwin, Stanley, **1**:*314*
Balfour, Lord, **1**:*314*
Bali Agama, **5**:321
Balinese Hindu law, **1**:251; **5**:321
Balkan Peninsula, Islamic law in the, **1**:251–253; **3**:333–334
Balkh, **3**:343
Balkin, J. M., **4**:365
Ball, Harry, **4**:33
Ballow, Henry, **2**:441
    on contract law, **2**:194, 197; **4**:215
    on equity, **2**:470
Balsamon, Theodore
    on canon law, **1**:330
    commentary on the *Syntagma canonum*, **1**:348
    information on, **1**:333
    on interest, **2**:192
    on *sunegoroi*, **1**:333
Baltic Governorates' Provincial Law (1845), **1**:255
Baltic Nations, **1**:253–257
Baltic Private Law Act (1864), **1**:255
Baltimore, Lord (George Calvert), **6**:29, 31
Balugianskii, Mikhail A., **5**:172, 178
Banco della Piazza di Rialto (Venice), **1**:274, 275

Banco di Messina, **1**:274
Banco di Sant'Ambrogio (Milan), **1**:274
Bandaranaike, **5**:342
Bañez, Domingo, **4**:15
Bangladesh, **1**:257–260. *See also* South Asian law
    adoption, **1**:48; **4**:300
    Anglo-Hindu law, **3**:159
    constitutional law, **2**:141–143
    family law, **5**:308, 309
    Islamic law, **5**:306, 309
    legal education, **2**:398
    marriage, **3**:221
    personal status law, **4**:299, 300
    zakat, **5**:431
banishment. *See* exile
Bank Acts (U.K., 1844, 1846), **1**:275
Bank Charter Act (England, 1844), **1**:272
Bankhead-Jones Farm Tenant Act (U.S., 1937), **3**:183
Banking Act (U.K., 1987), **1**:273
banking and finance. *See also* banks and banking
    Africa, **1**:107
    agency in, **1**:111
    ancient Greek law
        evidence in, **3**:2
        witnesses to transactions in, **6**:111
    bankruptcy, **1**:266–270
    bills of exchange in, **1**:291–293
    business law and, **1**:319
    China, loans in, **4**:116–118
    currency exchange in, **4**:39
    Islamic law, **1**:260–266
        assignment (*ḥawālah*), **1**:229
        Europe, **2**:484
        on loans, **4**:118–119
        Malaysia, **3**:337
    in the Muslim world, **2**:75; **3**:255–256
    Noordt, Gerard, on, **4**:236
    Ottoman Empire, **4**:265
    United States, **1**:269
Banking and Financial Institutions Act (Malaysia, 1989), **3**:337
Bank Islam Malaysia Berhad (BIMB), **1**:261
Bank Muamalat, **1**:261
Bank Negara Malaysia (BNM), **1**:263
Bank of England, **1**:275
    foundation of, **1**:386
    South Sea Bubble and, **2**:88
Bank of England Act (1694), **1**:271
Bank of England Act (1708), **1**:272
Bank of England Act (1833), **1**:272

Bank of England Act (1946), **1**:272
Bank of England Act (1998), **1**:273
Bank Restriction Act (Great Britain, 1797), **1**:271
bankruptcy, **1:266–270**. *See also* insolvency
    England, **1**:272
        common law, **1:266–267**
            equity and, **2**:471
            reforms of, **4**:42
        international law, **3**:289
        multinational, **3**:289
        United States, **1:267–270**; **2**:76; **6**:61
            equitable receiverships, **2**:473
            federal bankruptcy law, **2**:76
            federalism and, **3**:65
            history of, **5**:77
Bankruptcy (Goudy), **5**:202
Bankruptcy Act (U.K., 1831), **1**:267
Bankruptcy Act (U.K., 1883), **1**:267
Bankruptcy Act (U.S., 1800), **5**:77
Bankruptcy Act (U.S., 1841), **5**:77
Bankruptcy Act (U.S., 1978), **1**:269–270; **2**:78
Bankruptcy Commission (U.S.), **1**:269
Bankruptcy Law (China, 1935), **1**:440
Bankruptcy Reform Act (U.S., 2005), **2**:78
Banks and Bankers Act (New Zealand, 1880), **4**:228
banks and banking, **1:270–276**
    English common law, **1:270–273**
    medieval and post-medieval Roman law, **1:273–276**
Banner system (China, Qing), **1**:435
banns, **4**:162
baogu, wounding and, **6**:150, 151
baojia (liability of neighbors in Chinese law), **2**:60–61
Bao Shu, **4**:287
Bao Zheng, **1**:194
Baqir al-Najafi, Muhammad Hasan ibn Muhammad, **1:276–277**; **3**:340
    influence on al-Ansari, **1**:184
Barbados reliance on British case law and principles, **1**:369
Barbahari-al, **3**:346, 468
Barbaros, Francesco, **5**:467
Barbary pirates, United States war with, **6**:88
Barbeyac, Jean
    influence on Blackstone, William, **1**:298
    translation of *De officio hominis et civis libri duo*, **5**:21
Barclays Bank (England), **1**:276

Bar Council, **1**:279
    on legal education, **2**:395
Baring Brothers & Co. (England), **1**:272
Barnardo's homes (U.K.), **3**:35
Barnes, Thomas G.
    on Star Chamber, **5**:345, 346
Baron, Eguinaire, **3**:192
    Doneau, Hugues, and, **2**:359
Baron, J., **4**:277
Barons' War, **4**:283
Barre, Siad, **1**:105
Barreto, Tobias
    on natural law, **1**:303
barristers, **1:277–280**, *279*
    serjeants at law compared with, **5**:222–223
barter
    Sabinus, Masurius, on, **5**:180
Bartholomaeus de Saliceto, **2**:111
Bartolism, **3**:356
    Du Moulin, Charles, on, **2**:373
    humanism and, **3**:190, 193
Bartolomé de Medina, **4**:15
Bartolus of Saxoferrato, **1:280–281**; **2**:7; **3**:189; **6**:25
    on conflict of laws, **2**:111
    on fraud, **3**:102
    influence on
        Baldus de Ubaldis, Petrus, **1**:250
    international private law and, **2**:110
    on interpretation, **3**:298
    on lease and tenancy contracts, **4**:57
    in legal education, **2**:399
    on property, **4**:475
    on succession, **5**:386
    on vicarious liability, **6**:78
    on war and reprisals, **3**:282
base clientship in Wales and Ireland, **1**:377–378
Basic Law on Judicial Power (Indonesia, 1970), **4**:301
Basic Law on Judiciary Power (Indonesia, 1970), **3**:227
Basil I (the Macedonian)
    legislation by, **1**:328–329
    and the Macedonian Renaissance, **1:281–283**
Basilica, **1**:282, 329
    compilation of, **5**:151
    on delict, **2**:325
    influence of, **1**:283
    on legal procedure, **4**:416
    scholia on, **1**:329–330, 332
    on succession, **5**:376, 377

Basilius. *See* Basil the Great
Basilius II, **4:**469
Basotho, **1:**72
Basran school of Islamic law, **3:**305; **4:**144
Bassiano, Giovanni, **3:**355
Bassianus, Johannes, **5:**156; **6:**65
   influence on
      Azo, **1:**248
   on possession, **4:**361
   on succession, **5:**392
Bastardy Law (Amendment) Act (U.K., 1872), **1:**394
Basutoland, **1:**86
   Anglo-Roman-Dutch law in, **1:**87
Batbie, Anselme, **1:**23
Batchelor, Barry, **6:***99*
Bateman, William
   in legal education, **2:**393
battery. *See* assault
Battle of Bosworth Field (1485), **6:**5
Battle of Lewes (1264), **6:**1
Battle of Tewksbury (1471), **6:**4
Battle y Ordóñez, José, **6:**66–67
Baty, Thomas, **6:**77
Baudhāyana, **3:**152, 155
   on *smriti*, **5:**264
Baudouin, François, **3:**192
    Doneau, Hugues, and, **2:**359
    at University of Bourges, **2:**400
Baudouin, François
    Cujas, Jacques and, **2:**303
Bauman, Richard A., **3:**431
Bavaria
   codification in, **2:**47
Bavarian Civil Code of 1756 *(Codex Juris Bavarici Civilis)*, **3:**473, 474
Bavarian Code of Civil Procedure of 1753 *(Codex Juris Bavarici Judiciarii)*, **2:**47; **3:**473, 474
Bavarian Criminal Code of 1751 *(Codex Juris Bavarici Criminalis)*, **2:**47; **3:**473–474
Baxter, William F.
   on conflict of laws, **2:**118
bay' al-'īna (sell and buy back), **1:**264
bay' al-mu'ajjal (BM, deferred-payment sale), **1:**263, 264
Bayan wa-l-tahsil, al- (IBn Rushd), **3:**200, 350, 351
Baydawi, al-, **5:**370
Bayezid II (Ottoman Empire)
   administrative decrees codified by, **1:**34–35
   legal education under, **4:**72

Bayley, John, **2:**441
   on bills of exchange, **1:**293
BCRA. *See* Bipartisian Campaign Reform Act
Beale, Joseph H.
   on conflict of laws, **1:**15; **2:**117
   legal realism on, **4:**75–76
   Restatements of the Law of Conflict of Laws, **2:**113
beating and whipping in Chinese law, **1:**283–285
   for deceit, **2:**315
   exile and, **3:**25
   of parent, lack of filial piety in, **3:**85
   sentencing and, **5:**213
   wounding and, **6:**150–151
Beattle, J. M., **1:**364
Beauchet, Ludovic
   on ancient Greek law, **1:**162
Beaumanoir, Philippe de
   on customary law, **3:**78
Beaumont, Gustave de, **3:**457, 458
Be blaserum, **1:**178
Beccaria, Cesare, **1:**285–286; **2:**289; **3:**358; **4:**439; **5:**172
   law reforms based on, **4:**41
   on punishment, **4:**92
   on torture, **3:**9
Bech, Joseph, **2:***485, 490*
Bechuanaland, **1:**86
   Anglo-Roman-Dutch law in, **1:**87
Beck, Adolf, **1:**199
Beckenstein, Johann Simon, **5:**171
Becker, Gary
   on law and economics, **4:**24
   Nobel Prize to, **4:**25
Becket, Thomas. *See* Thomas à Becket
Bede
   Aethelberht's laws, **3:**117
   on ecclesiastical history, **1:**178
Bede (property levy), **5:**435–436
Beecher, Henry Ward, **3:**428
Beecher, Lyman, **5:**115
   on alcohol, **1:**124
Beeching, Richard
   on assizes, **1:**230
Begriffsjurisprudenz. *See* jurisprudence of concepts
Behrends, Okko, **5:**162
Belarus
   conflict of laws, **2:**113

Belfote, Petrus
    influenced by
        Baldus de Ubaldis, Petrus, **1:**250
Belgium
    African colonies, **1:**82–83
        decolonization of, **1:**93
    African law studies in, **1:**91
    assignment in, **1:**228
    conflict of laws, **2:**113
    constitution of 1831, **2:**120–121
    property law, **4:**476
Belize, **5:**296–297
Bell, Derrick, **2:**299, 300, 301, 302; **4:**365
Bellamy, John G.
    on treason, **6:**1
Bello, Andres
    codification by, **5:**286
Bello, Andrés, **1:286,** 398
    Chilean Civil Code and, **1:**384
    codification by, **1:**216
Bellot, Pierre-François, **4:**434
Beltrán, Gonzálo Aquirre, **5:**254
Benavot, Aaron, **2:**408
Benedictus Levita, **5:**230
Benedict XIII (antipope), **3:**398
Benedict XIV (pope), **1:**353
Benedict XV (pope), **4:**354
benefices, ecclesiastical, **2:**389, 390
beneficium competentiae, **5:**180
benefit of clergy
    secular court and, **1:**467
benefit of clergy, capital punishment and, **1:**364
benefit of the belly, capital punishment and, **1:**364
Benin, **1:**68, *68*, 70
    national conference in, **1:**104–105
Benjamin, J. P.
    on property sales, **2:**442
Benjamin, Walter, **2:**297
Bennett, John, **1:**245
Benston, George
    on securities laws, **5:**94
Bent, Ellis, **1:**240
Bentham, Jeremy, **1:286–288,** *287,* 387
    Austin, John, on, **1:**238–239
    on Blackstone, William, **1:**279, 298
    on civil liberties, **3:**450
    on classical common law, **4:**355
    codification concept, **2:**9, 46; **5:**109
    in evidence law reform, **3:**6
    fascism and, **4:**356
    on gender and sexual variation, **3:**110
    influence on
        Maine, Henry, **4:**137
    influence on Russian law, **5:**173
    influence penal code for British India, **2:**283
    on justice, **3:**447
    on law and economics, **4:**23
    law of nations and, **3:**276–277
    law reforms based on, **4:**41, 42
    on legal institutions, **1:**279; **4:**422
    on legal theory, **4:**61
    model prison of, **5:**29
    religious law and, **5:**108
    Russian translation of the works of, **5:**172
    secularization of law and, **5:**110
    and term codification, **2:**31
    on workhouses, **4:**349
Bentham Project, The, **1:**288
Bereford, William
    on equity, **2:**466
    on interpretation of legislation, **5:**276
    on law merchant, **4:**37
    on statute law, **4:**88
Berger, Raoul, **3:**23
Bergh, G. C. J. J. van den, **4:**226
Bergmann, Fridericus, **4:**434
Bergsträsser, Gotthelf, **6:**162
Berkeley Village Law Project, **4:**33
Berle, Adolph
    on corporations, **1:**325–326
Berlich, Mathias
    on guarantee, **3:**128
Berlin Act (1908), **1:**77; **2:**217
    Congo Free State in, **1:**82
Berlin Conference (1884–1885), **1:**75, 76–77
    Congo Free State in, **1:**82
Berman, H., **3:**79
Bermuda, **1:288–289**
Bernard of Pavia
    decretal collection by, **2:**319
Bernard of Pavia (Bernardus Papiensis)
    decretal collection by, **2:**319
Bern Convention Implementation Act (U.S., 1988), **3:**268
Berne Convention for the Protection of Literary and Artistic Works (1886), **2:**217, 218; **3:**262, 265, 267

Bernold of Constance
    on decretals, **2:**317
Berò, Agostino, **5:**364
Berry, Chuck, **2:**292
Beseler, Georg
    on systematization, **5:**421
Beseler, Gerhard von, **5:**161
Bestes, Theodore
    on canon law, **1:**330
    revision of the *Nomocanon,* **1:**347
Bethlehem Hospital (Bedlam, London), **3:**245, *245*
Betraying the Young: Human Rights Violations against Children in the U.S. Justice System (Amnesty International), **3:**461
betrothal
    ancient Greece, **4:**153
    China, **4:**157
Beven, Thomas, **2:**442
Bever, Thomas, **2:**393
Beveringk, Hieronymus van, **4:**235
Bevilaqua, Clóvis, **1:**304
Beza, Theodor, **1:**349
Bhadrabāhu Samhitā, **3:**364
Bhadrabāhu Samhitā (translation) (Jaini), **3:**364
Bhagavadgītā, **5:**35
    ātmanustuṣhṭi in, **1:**236
Bhagwati, P. N., **5:**7
Bhartrihari, **5:**344
Bhaṭṭa, Kumārila, **4:**182
Bhoras, **2:**43
Bhutan, **1:289–291**
Bhutto, Benazir, **2:**142
Bhutto, Zulfikar Ali, **2:**142
Biafra, **1:**97
Bible. *See also* Leviticus
    academic study of, **6:**62
    Apocrypha, **3:**390
    Greek translation, **3:**390
    Hebrew, **3:**388–389
    justice in, **3:**446
    King James version, **1:**468
    New Testament, **3:**390
    Old Testament
        on capital punishment, **5:**31
    Pentateuch, **3:**389, 390
    Torah, **3:**387, 388, 390, 398, 399
Bickel, Alexander, **2:**164
    on American citizenship, **2:**1
    on legal process, **4:**65
Bidayat al-mujtahid (Ibn Rushd), **3:**201; **4:**128

Bielfeld, J. F. von, **5:**172
bifu (analogy), **5:**214
bigamy, **3:**52
    India, **2:**308
Bigelow, Melville
    as teacher, **1:**14
Bihbahani, Muhammad Baqir ibn Muhammad Akmal, al-, **1:291**
    influence on
        Baqir al-Najafi, Muhammad Hasan ibn Muhammad, **1:**276
Bijnkershoek, Cornelis van
    Noodt, Gerard, compared with, **4:**235
bilateral investment treaties (BITs), **3:**285
Bill of Middlesex (England, 1531), **3:**472
bill of Middlesex, fictional
    King's Bench and, **2:**85
Bill of Rights (Britain, 1689), **5:**29–30
    on right to bear arms, **1:**217
Bill of Rights (Canada, 1960), **1:**342
Bill of Rights (England, 1689), **2:**132
Bill of Rights (U.S.), **2:***157*
    applicability to state and local government, **3:**408, 409–410, 458
    applicability to states, **2:**260; **3:**60, 62
    on church and state, **5:**114
    common-law protections of the individual in, **2:**84
    on due process, **2:**368–372
    incorporation of, **5:**205–206
    influence on state laws, **4:**489
    on judicial power, **3:**407
    jury trails, **3:**442–443
    natural rights and social-contract tradition and, **3:**448
    on privacy, **2:**370; **4:**388
    on rights of criminal suspects, **4:**447, 449, 450
    on right to bear arms, **1:**216–222
    on search and seizure, **5:**203–208
Bill of Rights Act (New Zealand, 1990), **4:**232
bills of exchange
    business law, **1:**319
    Islamic law
        loans and, **4:**119
    Italy, **1:**273
    in law merchant, **4:**38
Bills of Exchange Act (U.K., 1882), **1:**291, 293
bills of exchange in English common law, **1:291–293**
bills of lading, **1:**36
Bills of Sale Act (U.K., 1878), **2:**169

Billy Budd (Melville), **4:**108
Binchy, D. A., **3:**306
Binder, Julius
   on jurisprudence of concepts, **3:**432
Binding, Karl
   on guilt, **3:**135
Bingham, Jonathan
   on right to bear arms, **1:**218
Bingham, Lord, **2:**330
Bipartisan Campaign Reform Act (2002), **4:**341; **5:**337–338
Birds, The (Aristophanes), **3:**30–31
bi regulations under Han, **1:**454
Birkenhead, Lord, **1:***314*
Birks, Peter, **5:**130–131
   legal treatises by, **2:**443
birth control. *See* contraceptives
Biscardi, Arna do, **1:**164
   in Symposion, **1:**165
bishops and archbishops, **1:293–296**
   decretals on, **2:**316–317
   ecclesiastical courts, **2:**385–386
Bismarck, Otto von
   on concept of constitution, **2:**121
   influence on private law, **4:**394
   social security under, **5:**271
   taxation under, **5:**438
Bituminous Coal Conservation Act (U.S.), **3:**409
Björnståhl, Jacob Jonas, **3:**83
bKa'chrims, **1:**289–290
Black, Donald, **4:**18
Black, Hugo, **3:**165
   on apportionment and reapportionment, **1:**201
   on criminal procedure, **4:**453
   on natural law, **4:**219
   on New Deal, **3:**62
   on privacy, **4:**387, 388
   on separation of powers, **5:**218–219
Black Assizes (England, 1577), **1:**230
Black Book of the Admiralty, **1:**36–37
Blackburn, Colin, **2:**441–442
Blackburn, Lord, **2:**381
Black Code (Barbados, 1661)
   Mauritius in, **4:**171
   United States slave law based on, **5:**257
Black Codes (U.S.), **1:**218–219; **2:**291
Black Death, **2:**436
blackmail, **1:296–297**
Blackmun, Harry, **3:**167
   on abortion, **4:**389, 390

   on homosexual activity, **4:**390
   retirement of, **3:**63
   on social sciences, **5:**268
Blackstone, William, **1:***297*, **297–298**; **5:**171, 172
   on agency, **1:**108
   on assault and battery, **1:**226
   Bentham, Jeremy, on, **1:**287
   on blasphemy, **5:**115
   classical common-law theory of, **4:**355
   on contracts, **2:**204
   on coverture, **6:**121
   on due process, **2:**368
   on duress, **2:**374
   on easements, **2:**379, 381
   educational reforms by, **2:**393, 394
   education and, **1:**279; **2:**395
   on equity, **2:**470
   influenced by natural law, **2:**437
   influence on legal literature, **2:**441
   influence on United States property law, **4:**486
   on judicial law making, **5:**277
   on juries, **3:**440
   on legal theory, **4:**61
   on Parliament's power, **6:**36
   on property, **2:**449
   on right to bear arms, **1:**217
   on sources of law, **4:**87
   on sovereignty, **5:**352
   on statutory interpretation, **5:**360
   on torts, **5:**474
Blackstone's Commentaries (Tucker), **6:**38, 41
Blackwell, Antoinette Brown, **6:**142
Blake, William, **2:***388*
blasphemous libel, **1:**380
blasphemy
   Blackstone, William, on, **5:**115
   in Pakistan, **2:**142
Blastares, **1:**347–348
Blastares, Matthew, **1:**330
Bleak House (Dickens), **2:**250
Blegywryd, **6:**98
Block, Marc, **3:**77
block grants in welfare, **6:**93, 94
Blodwell, Richard, **2:**354
blood feuds
   Aeschylus on, **4:**111
   Islam, **3:**39
blood money. *See diya* (blood money)

blood-price, **3**:169–170
Blood Protection Law (Germany, 1935), **4**:204
Bloody Code, **1**:364
Bluebell, HMS, **6**:3
Bluhme, Friedrich, **5**:153, 159; **6**:8
Bluntschli, Johann Caspar, **3**:283–284
Board of Punishment (China), **2**:240, 241, 242, 243, 246, **247–249**; **5**:214
    on illicit sexual intercourse, **5**:232
    Qing dynasty, **1**:434, 435–436, 437, 438
    Shen Chia-Pen (Shen Jiaben) on, **5**:237–238
    Song dynasty, **1**:426
Bochove, Thomas van, **1**:281
Böcking, Eduard, **5**:162–163
Bodde, Derk, **5**:46
Bodenhamer, David, **4**:449
bodily harm
    crimes against life and body, **2**:264–265
    Welsh law, **6**:99
Bodin, Jean, **1**:350; **3**:190
    on absolutism, **1**:6–7, 9
    on Cujas, Jacques, **2**:303
    doctrine of sovereignty of, **2**:252
    on sovereignty, **5**:352
    on state sovereignty, **3**:79, 282
    on systematization, **5**:421
body in Islamic law, **1**:298–301
Body of Liberties (Massachusetts, 1641), **2**:286, 288
Boegehold, Alan L., **1**:149
Boeotian Confederacy, **4**:86
Boer War, **1**:272
Boesky, Ivan, **5**:94
Bohannan, Paul, **4**:18
Bohemond, **3**:*40*
Böhmer, Johann Samuel Friedrich von, **3**:134
Böhmer, Justus Henning, **2**:219, 224
Bohu tong, **3**:91
Boissonade, Gustave, **3**:374, 375
Bok, Derek, **2**:298
Boleyn, Ann, **1**:366
Bolin, Jane M., **6**:144
Bolívar, Simon, **4**:314
    on colonial law, **5**:285
    on slavery, **5**:255
Bolivian Civil Code (1830), **1**:384
Bologna, law school of, **3**:314
Bolognin, Zalterio, **5**:158
Bombay Hindu Divorce Act (India, 1947), **2**:353

Bombay Parsi Panchayat, **4**:287
Bonaire, **1**:369
Bonaparte, Napoleon, **3**:99–100
Boncompagni, Ugo, **5**:364
Boniface VIII (pope). *See also Liber Sextus*
    decretals of, **2**:222–223; **4**:433
    decretals of, in legal education, **2**:399
    homosexuality accusation, **5**:230
    on papal power, **4**:353
    pontificates of, **2**:223
    on taxation of clergy, **5**:436
Bonn Agreement of the Afghan Interim Authority (2001), **1**:60
Bonner, Robert J.
    on ancient Greek law, **1**:163
    anthropological perspective of, **1**:185
Bonnie, Richard, **1**:126
Bonnot de Mably, Gabriel, **3**:283
bonorum possessio, **5**:373
Book of Bounty (England, 1610), **4**:187
Book of Changes, **1**:402, 403
Book of Common Prayer, **1**:468
Book of Documents, **1**:402; **2**:361
    distinction between offenses with or without intent, **1**:459
Book of Documents (Shujing), **1**:455
Book of Han (Han shu), **1**:404
Book of Lord Shang, **1**:404, 408, 460
Book of Odes, **1**:402
Book of Rites, **4**:157–158
Book of Rites (Liji), **5**:48
Book of Sale (Kisani), **3**:329
Book of the Eparch, **5**:14
Book of the Pilot. See Kormchaia kniga (Russia)
Books of Penal Law/Punishments (Zi Chan), **1**:404
Books of Rites (Zhou dynasty), **1**:361
Booth, John Wilkes, **4**:178–179, 335
Boothby, Benjamin, **1**:241
Bork, Robert, **2**:*163*; **3**:166
    on Microsoft antitrust case, **1**:*192*
    on natural law, **4**:219
    nomination to Supreme Court, **2**:165–166
    rejection of, **3**:63
Bosnia, Islamic law in, **1**:253
Bosnia and Herzegovina, Islamic law in, **3**:334
Bossuet, Jacques-Bénigne, **1**:8
Boston University Law School, **1**:14
Bosworth Field, Battle of (1485), **6**:5
bot, **1**:182

Botswana
  constitution in, **1**:98
  independence of, **1**:93
bottomry, contract of, **3**:258
Bouhier, Jean, **2**:112
Boullenois, Louis, **2**:112
Bourdieu, Pierre, **1**:55
Bourjons, François, **4**:477
Bousquet, Georges, **3**:373–374, 374
Boutard, L. P., **4**:*248*
Brachylogus (Böcking), **5**:163
Bracton
  on attornment with homage, **3**:75
  on bailment, **1**:249
  on conveyancing, **2**:212
  on easements, **2**:379, 380, 381
  on environmental harms, **2**:449
  on equity, **2**:466
  on judicial decisions, **2**:439
  on land leases, **4**:11
  on law merchant, **4**:37
  on legal theory, **4**:61
  on mortgage, **4**:188
  on obligations, **4**:242
  on rape, **5**:68
  revised by Bracton, Henry de, **1**:301
  Roman law in, **5**:157
  on villeinage, **6**:81, 82
Bracton, Henry de, **1**:301–302; **3**:395
  on abolutism, **1**:7
  on abortion, **3**:178
  on common law, **2**:436
  on natural law, **4**:214
  on petty assizes, **4**:315
  on power of the king, **2**:128
  on sale, **5**:189
  on sources of law, **4**:87
  on theft, **5**:461
  on torture, **5**:484
Bracton's Note Book (Maitland), **1**:301
Bradley, Joseph P.
  on due process, **2**:369
  on equal protection, **2**:460
  on federal government subpoena power, **4**:451
  on natural law, **4**:218
  on privacy, **4**:386
  on women in the legal profession, **3**:480; **6**:143
  on women's role, **2**:338

Bradwell, Myra, **2**:338; **6**:135, 143
Bramwell, Baron, **2**:449, 450
Bramwell, George, **2**:90
Brandeis, Louis D., **2**:77; **3**:164–165
  classical legal theory and, **2**:26
  on federal court jurisdiction, **2**:258
  on freedom of speech, **3**:409
  on full disclosure, **5**:92
  Hurst, James, Willard, clerkship with, **4**:33
  in legal realism, **4**:74
  on privacy, **4**:386–387, 391
  on privacy right, **3**:273
  regulation and, **5**:79
  on social science, **5**:266, 269
  on women's labor laws, **6**:136
Brandeis brief, **2**:26
Bṛaspatismṛti, **6**:83
Bratton. *See* Bracton
Bratus, Sergei N., **5**:178
Brazil, **1**:302–305; **6**:66
  Civil Code
    modeled after Chilean Civil Code, **1**:398
  codification in, **1**:216; **5**:286
  colonial law in, **5**:292–294, 300–301
  courts, **5**:294
  Governo Geral in, **5**:298
  Jesuit reductions in, **5**:300, 301
  private law in, **4**:392
  slavery abolished in, **5**:253, 255–256
breach of contract, **1**:*305*, 305–310
  English common law, **1**:305–306
    obligations and, **4**:243
  guilds and, **3**:132
  Islamic law, **2**:201
  medieval and post-medieval Roman law, **1**:306–310
  United States doctrine on, **2**:76
Bréard-Neuville, Abbot, **4**:367
Breda, Treaty of (1667), **5**:296
Brehon Law, **3**:308
  influence on English common law, **3**:308–309
Brenkman, Henrik, **4**:226
Brennan, T. Corey, **4**:82
Brennan, William J., **3**:164
  on contraceptives, **6**:141
  on due process, **2**:370
  on gender-based affirmative action, **2**:340
  on general welfare clause, **3**:115
  on the political question doctrine, **2**:261

on sex discrimination, **2**:337
on statutory interpretation, **5**:361, 362
Brennan, William J., Jr., **5**:350
Brentano, Clemens von, **5**:195
Bretone, Mario, **5**:161
Brevia placitata, **4**:61
Breviarium Alaricianum. See Lex Romana Visigothorum
Breviarium Extravagantium (Bernard of Pavia), **2**:319
Breviarum Romanum (1568), **2**:224
Breviary of Alaric. *See* Lex Romana Visigothorum
Breyer, Stephen
 appointment of, **3**:63
 on right to bear arms, **1**:222
bribery in ancient Greece, **4**:246
Bricker Amendment, **3**:296
brieves in Scotland, **5**:197
Brihaspati, **3**:155
British Commonwealth, **1**:310–316. *See also* Australia; New Zealand
 African states in, **1**:93, 106
 Bermuda in, **1**:288–289
 Caribbean law, **1**:369
 Fiji in, **3**:82
 on folk law, **3**:90
 Guyana in, **3**:138
 Maldives, **4**:139–140
 Mauritius, **4**:171–172
 notaries in, **4**:237
 Seychelles in, **5**:234–235
 South Africa in, **5**:279
British East India Company
 as administrator in India, **5**:209
 in Bangladesh, **1**:257
 Chinese law under, **5**:318
 on dowry, **2**:364
 in India, **4**:273
 Singapore under, **5**:241
 in Sri Lanka, **5**:341
British Guiana. *See* Guyana
British Guiana Act (1928), **5**:295
British Honduras. *See* Belize
British law
 court system, **3**:405
 Hindu law and, **3**:400
 justice, equity, and good conscience, **3**:445–446
British Nationality Act (1948), **4**:206
 on India and Pakistan, **4**:206

British Nationality and Status of Aliens Act (1914)
 on naturalization, **4**:206
British North America Act (1867), **1**:338
 on criminal law and procedure, **1**:341
 renamed Constitution Act of 1967, **1**:339
British North Borneo, **3**:261–262
British Settlement Act (1843), **1**:312
British South Africa Company, **1**:86, 88
British Virgin Islands, **1**:369
Britton
 on fraud, **3**:101
 on land leases, **4**:11
Brockway, Zebulon, **5**:41
Broke, Serjeant Richard, **4**:471
Bronchorst, Everard, **2**:360
Brooke, James, **4**:138; **5**:313
Brooke, Robert, **4**:381
 abridgements by, **4**:61
Broom, Herbert, **4**:61
Brougham, Henry
 on bankruptcy, **1**:267
 on court reform, **2**:437
 on final process, **3**:88
 influenced by
  Bentham, Jeremy, **1**:288
 in reform movements, **4**:42
 reform under, **1**:280
 speech on the Motion to Enquire into the Education of the Poor, **1**:392
Brown, John, **4**:336
Brownrigg, Robert, **5**:341
Bruce, Robert, **3**:76
Bruce, S. M., **1**:*314*
Brunei, **5**:315. *See also* Southeast Asian law
 Chinese law in, **5**:319
 independence of, **5**:314
 intellectual property, **3**:264
 Islamic law in, **3**:334–335, 338–339; **5**:323, 324
Brunner, Heinrich, **4**:223
Bruns, **5**:161
Brussels Act (1890), **1**:76
Brussels Convention on Jurisdiction and Enforcement of Judgments in Civil and Commercial Matters (1968), **2**:114
Brutus, Marcus Junius, **3**:475
 on legal reasoning, **4**:79
Bryan, William Jennings, **5**:442
Bryan CJ, **2**:213
Bubble Act. *See* Royal Exchange and London Assurance Corporation Act (1720)

Bucer, Martin, **1:**350
Buchanan, James
   on general welfare clause, **3:**114
   on regulations, **5:**83
Buck, Carrie, sterilization of, **2:**334
Buckland, William Warwick, **5:**248
Budapest Treaty on the International Recognition of the Deposit of Micro-Organisms for the Purpose of Patent Procedure (1981), **3:**263
Buddhadhamma, **5:**302, 304
Buddhagosa, **5:**303
Buddhist law
   Aśoka on, **1:**226
   Bhutan, **1:**289–290
   Burma, **1:**317–318
   dharma in, **2:**332–334
   elements in Cambodian law, **1:**335
   on filial piety, **3:**84
   Laos, **4:**14
   Malaysia, **4:**137
   Maldives, **4:**139
   Mongolia, **4:**184
   South Asia, **5:**302–306
   Southeast Asia, **5:**315–317
   Sri Lanka, **5:**339, 342–344
   Tibet, **5:**465
Buddhist Temporalities Ordinance (Sri Lanka, 1889), **5:**304
Budé, Guillaume, **1:**316
   Alciati, Andrea, on, **1:**118
   humanist jurisprudence of, **1:**118
Bueno, José Pimenta, **1:**302
Buganda, **1:**68–69
   indigenous rights in, **1:**88
Bugenhagen, Johannes, **1:**349
   university reorganization by, **2:**328
Bugnet, Jean Joseph, **4:**367
bujing (disrespect), **4:**250–252
Bukhara, **3:**343
Bukhari, Muhammad ibn Isma'il al-, **2:**358
Bula Inter Caetera (Alexander VI), **5:**299
Bulgaria
   accession into European Union, **2:**492
   constitution, **2:**122
   Islamic law in, **1:**251–253; **3:**333
Bulgarus, **3:**314
Buller, Francis, **4:**143
   in King's Bench, **4:**144
   on negligence, **4:**221
   as teacher, **2:**394
Bulletin des Jurisdictions Indigènes et du Droit Coutumier Congolais, **1:**91
Bumiller, Kristin, **4:**34
Burdwan, Maharajah of, **1:***314*
bureaucracy, Chinese
   civil service exam in Song dynasty, **1:***426*
   collective liability of officials, **2:**59–60
   under Tang, **1:**423
Bureau for International Narcotics and Law Enforcement Affairs, **1:**122
Bureau of Immigration (U.S.), **3:**207
Bureau of Indian Affairs, **4:**211
Bureaux Internationaux Réunis pour la Protection de la Propriété Intellectuelle (BIRPI), **3:**265
Burge, William, **2:**98
Burger, Warren E., **3:**166
   alternative dispute resolution and, **4:**446
   on bankruptcy, **1:**269
   on caseloads, **1:**130
   civil rights deregulation under, **2:**461–462
   on right to bear arms, **1:**220
   on school-desegregation, **2:**260
   on separation of powers, **5:**218
   on social sciences, **5:**268
Bürgerliches Gesetzbuch Deutschland (German Civil Code), **2:**10; **3:**432
   apex of idea of national codification, **2:**28
   on assignment, **1:**228
   Baltic nations under, **1:**255
   on breach of contract, **1:**307–308
   on delay, **2:**320
   on donation, **2:**357–358
   education on, **2:**401
   employment and labor law, **2:**428
   Greek law influenced by, **1:**330
   influence by Roman law, **5:**163
   influence on
      Hungarian law, **3:**194
   on negotiable instruments, **4:**223
   on obligations, **4:**245
   on possession, **4:**362
   private law and, **4:**392, 395, 396
   on profiteering contracts, **3:**204
   on property, **4:**475, 476, 477, 478
   ratification of, **4:**277
   Roman law and, **5:**160
   on sale of goods, **5:**192
   on sale of land, **5:**193, 194

on succession, **5:**385, 386, 389, 394
on unjust enrichment, **6:**65
on vicarious liability, **6:**78
Bürgerliches Gesetzbuch für das Deutsche Reich (Civil Code for the German Empireü 1896–1900), **2:**48
Burgerlijk Wetboek (Netherlands)
on breach of contract, **1:**308
on illegal transactions, **3:**203
on sale of goods, **5:**192
on sale of land, **5:**193
burglary in English common law, **1:316–317**
Burgundus, Nicolaus
on conflict of laws, **2:**112
Burhan, al- (al-Juwayni), **3:**463
Burke, Edmund, **6:**36
on American legal process, **3:**406
British rule in India and, **3:**141
on justices of the peace, **3:**454
on the Sessions, **6:**101
Burke, Thomas, **5:**477
Burkina Faso
age for marriage, **2:**44
constitution, **2:**137
National Assizes, **1:**105
Burlamaqui, Jean Jacques, **3:**291
Burma, **1:317–318.** *See also* Southeast Asian law
under British rule
application of Anglo-Muhammadan law of British India, **3:**334
merging of Muslims and Buddhist principles in family law, **3:**334
Buddhist law in, **5:**315–316
Chinese law in, **5:**319
Hindu law in, **5:**320
intellectual property, **3:**264
Islamic law in, **3:**334
post-colonial, **5:**314
Burma Muslim Dissolution of Marriages Act (Burma, 1953), **3:**334
Burn, Richard
justice of the peace manual by, **4:**61
Burnaby's Code (Belize, 1765), **5:**296
Burnet, John, **5:***381*
Burnett, H. L., **4:***178*
Burnham, Forbes, **3:**138
Burnside, Ambrose, **4:**178
Burr, Aaron, **4:**339
Burrow, James
law reporting by, **4:**45, 60

Bursa Malaysia, **1:**262
Burt, Robert
in legal process, **4:**69
Burundi, **1:**63–64
Bush, George H. W., **3:***286*
administrative agencies under, **1:**30
Americans with Disabilities Act, **2:***335*
executive power under, **3:**24
judicial appointments, **2:**343
race neutral approach of, **2:**343
regulatory system under, **5:**83–84
Bush, George W.
administrative agencies under, **1:**30
election of, **4:**339
judicial appointments, **2:**344
military tribunals under, **4:**180–181
regulatory system under, **5:**85
separation of powers and, **5:**219
war power under, **6:**90–91
business law, **1:319–320.** *See also* antitrust
ancient Rome
women in, **6:**119
Austria, **1:**247–248
monopolies, **4:**186–187
South and Central America, **5:**286–287
United States, **6:**60–61
business organizations, **1:320–327**
business purpose clauses, **1:**323
Business Registration Ordinance (Hong Kong, 1952), **1:**450
Business Roundtable, **5:**84
Busxbaum, David C., **2:**193
Buti, Saʿid Ramadan al-, **3:**281
Butler, Judith
on sexual and gender variation, **3:**112
Butler, Pierce, **2:**27
Buttrigarius, Jacobus
influence on
Bartolus of Saxoferrato, **1:**280
Buwayti, Abu Yaʿqub al-, **3:**352
on Shafiʿi, Muhammad ibn Idris al-, **5:**235–236
buxiao (not filial child), **3:**85–86; **4:**259
Buyid dynasty (Persia)
Hanbali school and, **3:**346–347
Imāmi school under, **3:**340
Zahiri school of law under, **3:**354
Byles, J. B.
on bills of exchange, **1:**293
legal treatises by, **2:**441
Bynkershoek, Cornelis van, **3:**283; **4:**226

Byzantine Orthodox Church
  canon law and, **1:**346
Byzantium, **1:327–334**
  under Basil I, **1:**281–283
  contract law, **2:191–192**
  courts in, **2:239–240**
  criminal law, **2:**275–276
  delict in, **2:**324–326
  early Byzantium, **1:**327–329
  Greek and Roman culture in, **1:**137
  influence on Russian law, **5:**166, 167, 170
  jurists, **1:332–334**
  later Byzantium to 1453, **1:**329–331
  legal procedure, **4:416–417**
  legislation, **1:331–332; 5:**163
  Ottoman Empire as inheritor of, **4:**264
  persons in, **4:309–310**
  property law, **4:468–470**
  public law in, **5:14–15**
  succession in, **5:376–377**

C

Caecilius of Calacte
  on *eisangelia*, **4:**246
Caelius Sabinus, **3:**435
Caesar (Roman ruler)
  courts under, **2:**234
  criminal penalties under, **2:**271
Caesar, Julius, **3:**434, 435
  assassination of, **5:**8, 144
  codification proposal, **2:**32
  Gaius Octavius adopted by, **4:**93
  provincial jurisdiction under, **4:**496
  on the Senate, **5:**210, 211
  Senate under, **5:**212
  Servius Sulpicius Rufus pardoned by, **5:**225
Cahn, Edgar, **4:**371; **6:**94
Cahn, Jean, **4:**371; **6:**94
Cai Fadu, **1:**419
Cain, Patricia, **3:**69
Cairns, Lord
  on land registration, **4:**8, 9
Cakobau, Ratu Seru, **3:**82
Calabresi, Guido
  on constitutional review, **4:**68
  in Court of Appeals, **4:**27
  on judicial interpretation of statutes, **4:**69
  on law and economics, **4:**24
  on statutory interpretation, **5:**362
Calasso, Francesco, **5:**163

Calder, N.
  on Abu Yusuf, **1:**10
Calder, Norman
  on Shaybani, Muhammad ibn al-Hasan, **5:**236
Calendars of the Justiciary Rolls, **3:**307
Calhoun, George
  on ancient Greek law, **1:**163
California
  code of civil procedure, **2:**50
Callimachus
  on logographers, **4:**124
Callistratus, **3:**251, 436; **5:**13
Calonius, Matthias
  law of reason and, **2:**8
Caloprese, Gregorio
  influence on
    Gravina, Gian Vincenzo, **3:**126
Calvert, George (Lord Baltimore), **6:**29, 31
Calvin, John, **1:**349
Calvinism
  Grotius, Hugo, on, **3:**127
Cambacérès, Jean-Jacques-Régis de
  civil code projects, **3:**99
Cambodia, **1:335–336.** *See also* Southeast
      Asian law
  Buddhist law in, **5:**316–317
  Chinese law in, **5:**320
  Hindu law in, **5:**320–321
  intellectual property, **3:**264
  post-colonial, **5:**314
Cambridge Essays
  Maine, Henry, in, **4:**137
Cambridge University
  Cambridge ritualists at, **1:**185
  educational reforms at, **2:**395–396
  legal education at, **2:**393–394
  mortmain and, **4:**192, 193
Camden, Lord
  on search and seizure, **5:**203
Cameroon
  courts in, **1:**84
  French law in, **1:**63
  indigenous rights in, **1:**88
  land law, **1:**84–85
  law reform in, **1:**100
  official languages in, **1:**99
Cammillus, **2:**269
campaign finance reform, **5:337–338**
Campanella, Thomas
  on property, **4:**475

Campbells Bank (England), **1:**271
Campos, Francisco, **1:**304
Canada, **1:336–345**
   in British Commonwealth, **1:**312, 313
   Canadian law, **1:336–343**
      New Zealand law influenced by, **4:**229, 231–232
   Charter of Justice, **4:**232
   federalism in, **5:**354
   federal *versus* provincial powers, **1:**339
   land registration in, **4:**9
   Lower Canada legislative assembly, **1:***339*
   native peoples, **1:**342, **343–345**
      reserved hunting grounds by royal proclamation of 1763, **1:***338*
   notaries in, **4:**237
   Nova Scotia and Cape Breton's oath of allegiance to King George II, **1:***338*
   Statute of Westminster on, **1:**242–243
Canada Act (1982), **1:**339
Canadian Charter of Rights and Freedoms (1982), **5:**282
cangue, **1:***345*, **345–346**, 403
Cannegieter, Hermann, **5:**158
Cano, Melchor, **4:**15
Canones urbicani, **2:**318
canon law, **1:346–357**. See also administrative decrees of the political authorities *(qānūn)*; Corpus Iuris Canonici
   Africa, **1:**65
   alternative dispute resolution in, **1:**129
   Anglo-Saxon, **1:**178
   Austria, **1:**246
   Baltic nations, **1:**255
   bishops and archbishops in, **1:**293–296
   Brazil
      colonial, **5:**293
   Byzantine, **1:**327, 328, 330
   codes of canon law (1917 and 1983), **1:**293, **352–355**
   on concubinage, **3:**46–47
   courses and classes, **1:355–357**
   decretals, **2:**316–319
   Denmark, **2:**328
   development of, **1:**33
   on engagement, **3:**41
   England, **2:**387–391
      Chancery and, **2:**467
      on divorce, **2:**347–348
      Doctors' Commons in, **2:**353–355
      evidence in, **3:**5–6
      family and, **3:**32–33
      on marriage, **4:**160–163; **6:**121
      on succession, **5:**383–384
   France, **3:**98
   guilt in, **3:**133–134
   in legal education, **2:**399
   on marriage
      clandestine, **3:**41
   medieval and post-medieval Roman law
      on divorce, **3:**43
      on evidence, **3:**8
      on marital sex, **5:**230
   negotiable instruments and, **4:**223
   Orthodox churches, **1:346–348**
   procedure
      civil, **4:**431–435
      criminal, **4:**435–440
   Protestant churches, **1:348–352**
   Roman law scholarship in, **1:**162
   Russia, **5:**167
   Scotland, **5:**197, 199
   Spain, **5:**324–325
   Sweden, **5:**414
   Wales, **6:**99
   on witches, **6:**108
Canon of Laws (Fa Jing), **1:**407
Canons of the Kings (325)
   in Ethiopia, **2:**479
Canute (king of England)
   on burglary, **1:**317
   codification by, **1:**178
   on feud, **1:**180
   on strangers, **1:**182
   on wrongs, **1:**179
Cao Cao, **1:**418
capacity *(ahliyya)*, **1:357–359**
   in acknowledgement, **1:**20
   legal acts and facts and, **4:**58
   legal personality and, **4:**65
Cape Verde islands
   Portuguese colonies in, **1:**79
capias ad satisfaciendum, writ of, **3:**88–89
capital *(ra's al-mal)*, **1:359–360**
capital cases in Chinese law
   for putting spells on the emperor, **4:**255–256
   review of, **1:195–198**
   for Ten Abominations, **4:**259–260
capital gains tax
   England, **5:**429

capital punishment, **1:362–368**
  abolition of
    Carrara, Francesco, and, **1**:372
    Africa
      after independence, **1**:101
      German colonies, **1**:84
      precolonial, **1**:72
  ancient Athens, **2**:267–268; **3**:402; **4**:382; **5**:23–24, 479
  ancient Greece
    slaves in, **5**:244
  Anglo-Saxon law, **1**:178, 182
  Australia, **1**:240
  Beccaria, Cesare, on, **1**:285
  children and
    in U.K., **1**:394
  China, **5**:213
    amnesty from, **1**:133–135
    for illicit sexual intercourse, **5**:231–232
    mutual concealment and, **4**:198, 199
    sentencing and, **5**:214
    Shen Chia-Pen (Shen Jiaben) on, **5**:237
  Chinese law, **1:360–362, 362–364,** *363;* **4**:383; **5**:459, 460
    courts for, **2**:240–241
    for deceit, **2**:315
    Easter Zhou, Spring and Autumn period, **1**:405
    emperor's pardons, **2**:243
    execution types, **5**:25
    under Han, **1**:417
    for incest, **3**:213
    for lack of filial piety, **3**:86
    Ming, **1**:430–431, 431, 432
    offences eligible for, **5**:25
    Qing dynasty, **1**:434–435
    rape, **5**:66–67
    seasons and, **1**:424
    under Song, **1**:426
    under Tang, **1**:424
    torture and, **2**:108–109
    trial procedure, **4**:417
    under Western Zhou dynasty, **1**:403
    Yuan empire, **1**:429
  Colombia, **2**:63
  criticism of, **4**:439
  English common law, **1:364–367**
    application of, **5**:27
    capital crimes, **2**:276
    early 19 century, **4**:425–426
    for heresy, **2**:390
    mitigating factors, **2**:276
    rape, **5**:69
    reforms of, **4**:41–42
    robbery, **5**:462
    women in, **6**:120
  English law
    abolition of, **3**:179
  Hindu law, **5**:35
  Inca law, **5**:289
  India, **2**:280, 281–282, 283
  Iran, **2**:279
  Islamic law, **3**:325
    sodomy, **3**:181
  of juveniles, **3**:462
  Laos, **4**:14
  medieval and post-medieval Roman law
    for sexual crimes, **5**:230
  methods of execution
    in Chinese law, **1**:362–364
    Chinese Shang dynasty, **1**:401
    England, **1**:364, 365–367
  Mongolia, **4**:184–185
  in Mughal Empire, **2**:36
  Muslim world in the twentieth century, **1:367–368**
  Native American law, **4**:207
  Pakistan, **2**:142
  Peru, **4**:314
  reform since the 18th Century, **5**:34
  Roman law, **2**:237, 268–269, 269, 270–271; **5**:9, 31, 32–33
  Southeast Asia, **5**:315
  suppression in Venezuela, **6**:74
  for theft, **5**:463
  Tibet, **5**:465
  for treason, **6**:1
  United States, **2**:290, 291, 293; **5**:38, 39–41, 42; **6**:50
    colonial law, **6**:30, 31
    colonial period, **2**:285, 286, 288, 289
    law, **6**:60
    social science research on, **5**:268–269
Capito, Gaius Ateius
  rivalry with Labeo, Marcus Antistius, **3**:475
  Sabinus, Masurius, and, **5**:179
  teachings of, **5**:147
Capitulaciones de Santa Fe (1492)
  in colonial law, **5**:290, 297–298
capitulações, **5**:299
Capitulare Missorum speciale (Charlemagne), **1**:356

capitulations, **3**:281
Capper-Volstead Act (U.S., 1922), **5**:89
Caracalla (Roman emperor)
   citizenship extended by, **1**:161; **3**:115; **4**:497; **5**:139, 250
   on guardianship of women, **2**:420
   legislation under, **3**:211
   Paul and, **4**:290
   on property, **4**:464–465
   on slavery, **5**:248, 250
   universal enfranchisement by, **2**:419
Caracciolo, Carafa
   De Luca, Giovanni Battista, and, **2**:326
Caracciolo, Innico
   De Luca, Giovanni Battista, and, **2**:326
Carbado, Devon, **3**:70
Cardozo, Benjamin N., **2**:26; **3**:429; **4**:452; **6**:57
   on agency, **1**:114
   on consumer protection, **2**:176
   on contracts, **2**:209
   on vested rights, **2**:117
Cardozo, Benjamin Nathan
   in legal realism, **4**:74
   on search and seizure, **5**:204
   on statutory interpretation, **5**:361
Caribbean Court of Justice, **1**:369
Caribbean law, **1:368–371**
Carlin, George, **5**:335
Carlin, Jerome
   on law and society, **4**:32
Carlisle, Abraham
   treason of, **4**:335
Carl XIV Johan (Sweden), **5**:416
Carmer, Heinrich Casimir von, **5**:1
Carnegie Endowment for the Advancement of Teaching
   on medical education, **2**:404
Carolina (German criminal code)
   on adultery, **5**:230
Carolus de Tocco
   on conflict of laws, **2**:111
Carpzov, Benedict, **1:371–372**; **4**:333
   on fraud, **3**:103
   on guilt, **3**:134
   influenced by
      Faber, Antonius, **3**:27
   on marriage, **3**:41
   opinions of, **2**:254
   positions held by, **2**:254
   on theft, **5**:463

Carrara, Francesco, **1:372**
Carriage of Goods by Sea Act (U.S., 1936), **1**:40
Carrick, John de, **5**:198
Carrington, Paul, **2**:298
Carson, Edward, **3**:308
Carson, Rachel, **2**:455; **5**:82
Carta del lavoro (Italy), **4**:204
Carta mercatoria (England)
   on foreign merchants, **4**:35
cartels, **1**:189
   prohibitions of, **2**:103
Carter, James Coolidge
   affirmative action under, **2**:343
   opposition to codification, **2**:50
Carter, Jimmy
   regulatory system under, **5**:83
Cartier, Jacques, **1**:337
Cary, William, **5**:93
Casa de Contratación, **5**:285, 298
Casa de Suplicação (Portugal), **5**:301
Casa di San Giogio (Italy), **1**:274
Casas, Bartolomeo de las, **4**:393
Cas des nobles hommes et femmes, Des, **2**:*429*
casebooks, **1**:15, 16
   under the Ming, **1**:462
   under the Qing, **1**:462
case law
   English common law, **5**:277–278
   France, **3**:100
   legal realism on, **4**:77
   United States
      on inheritance, **3**:239
Casement, Roger, **6**:3–4
case method, **1**:14–15; **2**:84
   in advocate training, **1**:57–58
   first case book on contracts, **2**:208
   at Harvard, **2**:403–404
Case of the Army Truly Stated, The, **2**:130
Cases on Sales of Personal Property (Langdell), **5**:190
cash payments in lieu of penalties
   in Chinese law, **1**:417
Cassander
   Athens under, **3**:31
Cassiodorus
   on Edictum Theodorici, **3**:116
Cassius Deo, **4**:278
Cassius Longinus, **3**:435
Cassius Longinus, C., **3**:435

caste
  Bali, **1:**251
  Bangladesh, **1:**257
  East Africa, **2:**383
  India
    adoption and, **1:**49
    dharma and, **2:**333
    fundamental rights on, **3:**106
    in Sikh law, **5:**240
  Nepal, **4:**224, 225
  South and Central America
    slavery and, **5:**254
  Sri Lanka, **5:**341
Caste Disabilities Removal Act (India, 1850), **3:**158
caste system
  Sri Linka, **5:**303
Castle Chamber (Ireland), **3:**310
Castles, Alex, **1:**245
castration
  Shang dynasty, **1:**401
Castro, Alfonso de
  on guilt, **3:**134
  in Scholasticism, **4:**15, 16
Castro, Manuel Antonio de, **1:**216
Castro, Paulus de, **3:**189
  influenced by Baldus de Ubaldis, Petrus, **1:**250
Casus codicis (Accursius), **1:**19
Casus digesti novi (Accursius), **1:**19
Casus institutionum (Accursius), **1:**19
Cateau-Cambrésis, Peace of (1559), **3:**357
Catechismus Romanus (1566), **2:**224
Catherine II (Catherine the Great, Russia), **5:**171, 172, 173, 178
  enlightened absolutism under, **1:**8; **2:**445
Catherine of Lancaster, **6:**2
Catherine the Great (Russia)
  Baltic nations under, **1:**255
Catholic Church. *See* Roman Catholic Church
Catholic Queen Mary, the. *See* Mary I (England)
Catholic University of America, **2:**404
Cato (Anti-Federalist)
  on executive power, **3:**20
Cato Uticensis, **1:**56
causa and guilt, **3:**134
cautio (written account of a debt), **2:**186, 187
Cave, L. W., **2:**442
Cavers, David F.
  on conflict of laws, **2:**111, 113, 118
  on law and society, **4:**31
  law and society research by, **4:**32

Cayman Islands, **1:**369
CDBG. *See* Community Development Block Grant
CDC. *See* Centers for Disease Control and Prevention
Código Civil (Portugal, 1867), **4:**475
Cecil, William, **2:**129
  collaboration with Coke, Edward, on finance, **2:**55
Cecil, William (Lord Burghley), **1:**386
Cediminas (Grand Duke of Lithuania), **1:**254
Celestial Masters (China), **4:**2–3
Celestine I (pope)
  decretals by, **2:**316
  on knowledge of canon law, **1:**356
Celsus the Younger (Publius Juventius Celsus), **1:**372–374
  on legal reasoning, **4:**81
  on unjust enrichment, **6:**64
Celtic law, **1:**374–378
Celts, Irish law and, **3:**306–307
Censorate (China), **1:**423, 432; **2:**241–242
censorship, **1:**378–384
  China
    heterodox beliefs and, **4:**252–253
  English common law, **1:**378–382
  freedom of speech and, **5:**329
  Islamic law, **1:**382–384
  United States
    freedom of speech and, **5:**332–338
    pornography and, **3:**68
Center for the Study of Law and Society (University of California, Berkeley), **4:**32–33, 33–34
Centers for Disease Control and Prevention (CDC)
  creation of, **3:**144
  mission of, **3:**145
Central American republics, **1:**384–385
central government in English common law, **1:**385–387
Central People's Government (People's Republic of China), **1:**442
Cephalus
  on *graphē paranomōn*, **3:**125
c.e. RCLA. *See* Comprehensive Environmental Response, Compensation, and Liability Act (U.S., 1980)
Ceremoniale Episcoporum (1600), **2:**224
Cervidius Scaevola, Quintus, **3:**435
Cesare, Oscar Edward, **5:***216*
cessio in iure, **2:**182, 184
cestuy-que-use, **6:**103
Ceylon (Sri Lanka), **5:**157
Ceylon National Congress (CNC), **5:**342

Chabrias
   graphē paranomōn against, **3**:125
Chadwick, Edwin, **2**:450
   civil war in, **1**:105
   constitution, **2**:137
Chafee, Zechariah, **6**:30
Chafee, Zechariah, Jr., **5**:334
Chaisangsukkul, Pitinai, **5**:316
challenges
   ancient Athens
      evidence gained through, **3**:2
Chalmers, Mackenzie
   on bills of exchange, **1**:293
   on sale of goods, **5**:190–191
Chamberlain, Joseph
   on appellate power, **1**:242
Chambers, Robert, **2**:394
Champlain, Samuel de, **1**:337
Chancellor of the Exchequer, **1**:385
Chancery, **1**:385, **387–390**, *388*, 389–390; **2**:249, 250, *438*
   appeal in, **1**:197
   Bermuda, **1**:289
   charitable gifts and, **1**:392
   common law and, **2**:436
   conscience in, **2**:466–467
   contractual jurisdiction, **2**:196, 197, 198
   on duress, **2**:373–374
   ecclesiastical law *vs*., **2**:389
   English side *versus* Latin side, **1**:388
   equity and, **2**:471, 472
   on error and mistake, **2**:473–474
   evidence in, **3**:5–6
   on fraud, **3**:101–102
   insanity cases and, **3**:245
   in Ireland, **3**:307
   jurisdiction of, **2**:437, 467–468
   on land leases, **4**:12
   on land registration, **4**:8
   litigation on insurance contracts, **3**:252
   Mansfield, Lord, in, **4**:142
   on mortgage, **4**:188–189
   on obligations, **4**:243
   origins of, **1**:388; **2**:82; **4**:422
   petitions about charities in testaments, **1**:390
   quarrel with King's Bench
      Coke, Edward, and, **2**:55
   reform of, **2**:437; **4**:41
   solicitors in, **5**:272
   Wales, **6**:101
   on women and wills, **6**:104
Chandler Act (U.S., 1938), **2**:78
   on bankruptcy, **1**:269
Chansonnette, Claude. *See* Cantiuncula
Chappuis, Jean, **2**:219, 223
Chapter 11. *See* Bankruptcy Act (U.S., 1978)
Charitable and Religious Endowments Act (India, 1890), **3**:216
charities
   England
      mortmain and, **4**:191–193; **5**:369
   Southeast Asia, **5**:318
   succession and, **5**:388–389
   trusts, **5**:407–408
Charities Act (U.K., 1960)
   on mortmain, **4**:193
charities in England, **1**:**390–393**
Charlemagne
   feudal grants by, **3**:78
   on knowledge of canon law, **1**:356
   legislation by, **4**:90
   papacy and, **4**:352
Charles I (England), **2**:130
   Coke, Edward, and, **2**:56
   execution, **1**:366
   execution of, **4**:96
   gold of seized, **1**:271
   judiciary under, **3**:416
   law reform after, **4**:41
   legislation under, **4**:89
   parliament and, **4**:284
   Star Chamber under, **5**:346
Charles II (England), **2**:131; **6**:35
   control of printing under, **2**:216
   on corporate status of cities, **4**:119
   Declaration of Indulgence, **1**:468
   judiciary under, **3**:416
   juries under, **3**:438, 440
   on king's counsel, **5**:222
Charles II (Spain), **1**:384
Charles IV (Holy Roman emperor), **1**:*293*
   Bartolus of Saxoferrato as ambassador to, **1**:280
Charles River Bridge (36 U.S. 420) (1837)
   on corporations, **1**:321–322
Charles V (Holy Roman Emperor)
   on attempt, **1**:237
   on guilt, **3**:133
   Jews under, **3**:396
   on punishment, **5**:32

on theft, **5:**463
witch trials under, **6:**108
Charles V (Spain)
on colonial law, **5:**291
Charles VII (France)
codification by, **3:**98
Charles XI (Sweden), **5:**415
Baltic nations under, **1:**255
Charlottetown Accord (Canada, 1992), **1:**339
Charondas, **2:**30
written law by, **1:**154
Charondas Le Caron, Louis, **3:**99
charter
corporate, **1:**320–321
monopolies and, **4:**186–187
chartered foreign trading companies, **2:**88
Charter Oath of Five Articles (Japan), **3:**373
Charter of Dvina Land (Russia, 1397), **5:**168
Charter of Fundamental Rights (Europe), **2:**488, 493
Charter of Rights and Freedoms (Canada, 1982), **1:**342
Charter of the City of Novgorod (Russia, 1471), **5:**168
Charter of the Organization of African Unity (OAU), **1:**106–107
Chase, Samuel, **2:**23, 27
on constitutional limitations, **2:**161
impeachment of, **4:**336, 450
on supremacy clause, **5:**411
on takings, **4:**489; **5:**423
chastisement, **3:**328
Chatelain, Henri Abraham, **5:***199*
chattel real
English common law
land leases, **4:**11
Chaudhry, Mahendra, **3:***83*
Chaumont, Éric, **3:**316, 321
Chávez, Hugo, **6:**74, *75*
Cheatham, Elliott E.
on conflict of laws, **2:**118
check law. *See also* bills of exchange
on negotiable instruments, **4:**223
checks and balances
separation of powers compared with, **5:**217
in state constitutions, **5:**350
Chehata, Chafik, **2:**199
Chen Banghuai, **1:**401
Chen Code (China), **5:**72, 74
Chenghua (Chinese emperor), **2:**225
Chernyshevskii, Nikolay G., **5:**178
Chevron doctrine, **1:**31
Chhotanagpur Tenancy Act (1908), **2:**309

chi (imperial edicts)
under Song dynasty, **1:**457
Chicago Jury Project, **5:**268
Chicago Legal News, **6:**143
Chicago school of economics, **4:**23–26
on ancient Greek law, **1:**163
anthropological perspective in, **1:**185
on antitrust, **1:**190
Chicherin, B. N., **5:**178
child abuse, **3:**34
Child & Co. (England), **1:**271
Childebert I (Salian king), **3:**117
child marriage
Afghanistan, **1:**61
India
divorce from, **2:**353
Hindu law, **6:**131
Child Marriage Restraint Act (India, 1929), **3:**49; **4:**299, 300
in Bangladesh, **1:**259
children, **1:393–397.** *See also* adoption; child marriage
Afghanistan, **1:**61
Africa
after independence, **1:**102–103
Charter on the Rights and Welfare of the Child, **1:**107
Alemanic law, **3:**44
ancient Greek law
family and, **3:**29–32
burglary, **1:**317
Chinese law
filial piety of, **3:**84–86
parental obligations to, **4:**158
competency of as heirs, **5:**388
custody of
gay, lesbian family, **3:**69
Islamic law, **1:**397
delinquent
England, **3:**35–36
divorce and
England, **2:**349
Islamic law, **2:**352
emancipation of
medieval and post-medieval Roman law, **3:**45
employment and labor law
England, **2:**426
medieval and post-medieval Roman, **2:**430
England
common law, **1:**393–396
employment and labor law, **2:**426

rights of, **3**:34
women's custody of, **6**:123–124
evidence by, **3**:16
in feudal law, **3**:74
grandparent-visitation statutes, **2**:424
India
custody and quardianship, **3**:51
fundamental rights on, **3**:106
Islamic law, **1**:*396*, **396–397**
acts of worship by, **6**:148–149
the body, **1**:299–300
custody, **3**:37
legal personality of, **4**:65
marriage and annulment, **6**:125
paternity of, **3**:36–38
Islamic law on
legal personality of, **4**:58
jihad, **6**:86
legitimacy
in England, **1**:392–393
legitimacy of
ancient Greece, **3**:30–31; **4**:154; **6**:113
England, **3**:34–35; **4**:162; **6**:121
India, **3**:50, 51
Islamic law, **3**:37–38
medieval and post-medieval Roman law, **3**:46–47
succession and, **5**:387
United States, **3**:54–55
medieval and post-medieval Roman law, **3**:44–47
Ottoman Empire, **6**:129
in poverty, **4**:368–370
recovered memories in, **3**:16
South and Central America, **5**:286
support and maintenance of
England, **1**:394; **3**:34
in Islamic law, **1**:397
surrogate parenthood and, **3**:55, *56*
trafficking in
Africa, **1**:76
United States
custody of, **3**:54–55
in divorce, **3**:54
labor laws, **6**:49
succession by, **5**:405–406
women's custody of, **6**:136, 142
Children Act (England, 1908), **1**:394

Children Act (England, 1908, 1948, 1989), **3**:35
on dispute resolution, **3**:36
Children Act (U.K., 1908, 1948, 1989)
on adopted children's parents, **1**:47
Children Act (U.K., 1975)
on adoption, **1**:47
Children Act (U.K., 1989), **1**:392, 395
Children Act (U.K., 2004), **3**:34
Children and Young Persons Act (U.K., 1933), **1**:394
Children and Young Persons Act (U.K., 1933, 1969), **3**:35
on delinquency, **3**:35–36
Child Savers, **4**:369; **6**:93
Child Support Act (U.K., 1991), **3**:34
Child Support Agency (U.K.), **3**:34
Chile, **1**:397–399
Bello, Andrés, in, **1**:286
codification in, **5**:286
slavery abolished in, **5**:254
Chilean Civil Code (1855), **1**:384
chilling effect, on free speech, **5**:338
Chilperic I (Salian king), **3**:117
China. *See also* Tibet
Cochin, French law in, **5**:313
disrespect *(bujing)*, **4**:250–252
effect of missionaries on legal system, **1**:438
judicial structure and procedure
under Ming, **1**:431–432
Mongolia, **4**:183–186
Tibet invaded by, **5**:305
treaties, **3**:372
China, Islamic law in, **1**:399, **399–400**
China law
private law, **4**:392
Chinese Chops Order (Sarawak, 1930), **5**:319
Chinese Exclusion Act (U.S., 1882), **6**:52
Chinese exclusion laws (U.S.), **3**:207–208
Chinese Family and Commercial Law (Jamieson), **1**:450
Chinese in Indonesia
application of European law to, **3**:226
Chinese law. *See also* Chinese law, history of; Hsueh Yun-Sheng
accessory and principal in, **1**:18–19
on adoption, **1**:43–46
on alcohol and drugs, **1**:119
amnesty in, **1**:133–135, 364
appeal in, **1**:193–195
collective liability, **2**:57–62

concept of *zang,* **6:**159
confession, **2:106–109**
   and acceptance of sentence, **2:107–109**
      recantation of, **1:**195–196
contracts, **2:192–194**
corruption in the, **2:**225–227
courts and judicial agencies, **2:**240–249
damage to property, **2:**311–313
debt, gambling and, **3:**109
deceit, **2:**314–316
deposit, **2:330–332**
disability, **5:**47–48
doing what ought not to be done, **2:355–356**
doubtful cases, **2:**361
ethnic groups in, **2:**481–483
exile in, **3:**25–26
five punishments in, **1:**362
   Ming dynasty, **1:**431
   Qing, **1:**433–434
   during Shang dynasty, **1:**401
   under Song, **1:**426
   in Yuan law, **1:**429
foreigners in, **3:**91–93
gambling, **3:109**
hire in, **3:160–163**
homicide, **3:171–176**
   accessory and principal in, **1:**18
   parricide, **3:**84–85
   paument of funeral expenses in Yuan law, **1:**429
   wounding and, **6:**150, 151
   wrongful accusation, **2:**315
homosexuality, **3:**180, **180**
on illicit sexual intercourse, **5:231–232**
incest, **3:213–215; 4:**259
   family and political order and, **5:**232
   as illicit sexual intercourse, **5:**232
   lack of filial piety and, **3:**86
   levirate marriage as, **4:**160
   Tang code on, **5:**233
influence on Japanese law, **3:**366, 367, 369
inheritance
   adoption and, **1:**43–46
   land law, **4:**3, 4
   sale of land and, **5:**187
   Song dynasty, **1:**425
insanity, **3:**175
intention, **3:275–276**
judicial review, **1:**195–198
   on doing what ought not to be done, **2:**355–356

doubtful cases, **2:**361
   in wrongful judgment, **6:**152
on lack of filial piety, **3:**84–87
lawyers in, **4:45–47**
liability (*See also* collective liability in Chinese law)
   accessorial, **1:**18
   for deceit, **2:**315
   for endangering the emperor, **4:**256
   for lack of filial piety, **3:**85
   for offenses against the state, **4:**257–258
   reciprocal, **2:**315
   in wrongful judgment, **6:**152, 153
on loans, **4:116–118**
marriage, **4:155–160,** *156*; **5:**54
   status and, **5:**358
   succession and, **5:**378–380
military service
   land tenure based on, **4:**4
   offenses against the state in, **4:**251
mutilation in, **4:196–197**
on mutual concealment, **4:**197–199
offenses, classification of, **4:259–260**
offenses against the state
   overview, **4:249–250**
   damaging the efficiency of government, **4:253–255**
   disrespect *(bujing),* **4:250–252**
   heterodox beliefs, **4:252–253**
   threatening the life or well-being of the emperor, **4:255–256**
   threatening the safety of the state or dynasty, **4:256–258**
parties and witnesses, **4:418–419**
partnerships, **4:287–288**
penal servitude, **4:292–293**
pledge, **4:325–327**
prisons and imprisonment, **4:**383, **383**
procedure, **4:417–418**
property
   damage to, **2:**311–312
   mutual concealment and, **4:**199
   obtaining through deceit, **2:**314–315
   People's Republic, **1:**443
   transfer, **1:**417
prostitution
   adoption for, **1:**45–46
   as illicit sexual intercourse, **5:**232
   sexual offenses in, **5:**233
punishment
   abolition of cruel punishments, **1:**439
   accessory and principal in, **1:**18

administrative punishments, **5:26–27**
amnesty in, **1:**133–135
beating and whipping, **1:**283–285
Board of Punishments, **2:**240, 241, 242, 243, 246, **247–249**
collective, **4:**259–260
for corruption, **2:**226–227
for cursing, **2:**304
damaging efficiency of government, **4:**253–254
for damaging efficiency of government, **4:**253–254, 255
death penalty, **2:**240–241, 243
for deceit, **2:**315
for disrespect *(bujing)*, **4:**251
for doing what ought not to be done, **2:**355–356
doubtful cases, **2:**361
exile, **3:**25–26
five punishments in, **5:**213–214
Han dynasty, **1:**417
imprisonment, **4:**383
for lack of filial piety, **3:**84–86
levels of, **2:**246
in Liao empire, **1:**427
mutilation, **4:**196–197
for offenses against the state, **4:**249, 259–260
overview, **5:24–26**
penal servitude, **4:**292–293
for plotting rebellion, **4:**257–258
prisons and imprisonment, **4:**383
reciprocal, **6:**152
redemption, **5:**72–75
reeducation through labor in People's Republic, **1:**443, 446
review and, **1:**196–197
sentence in, **5:213–215**
social status and, **4:**259
sumptuary laws, **5:**410
voluntary surrender and, **2:**106
for wounding, **6:**150–151
punishment and status
age, **5:**45, **45–47**
disability, **5:47–48**
officials, **5:**44–45, **48–51**
overview, **5:44–45**
relatives, **5:**44, 50, **51–54**
slaves, **5:**44, 45, **54–56**
women, **5:56–57**
rape, **3:**180; **5:66–67**
redemption, **5:72–75**

registration penalty, **1:**426
revenge, **3:**175
role of emperor in capital cases, **1:**360
rule of law, **5:**164–166
sale
of goods, **5:183–185**
of land, **5:185–189**
sentence, **5:213–215**
review and, **1:**196–197
under Wester Zhou dynasty, **1:**403
sentence in, **5:213–215**
sexual offenses, **5:232–234**
disrespect *(bujing)* in, **4:**250
mutual concealment and, **4:**199
sexual offenses in, **5:232–234**
slaves and slavery, **5:**44, 45
illicit sexual intercourse in, **5:**231
punishment, **5:**54–56
rape, **5:**66, 67
sexual offenses in, **5:**233
Southeast Asia, **5:**313, **317–320**
status in, **5:358–359**
on succession, **5:377–381**
suicide, **3:**175
sumptuary laws, **5:409–410**
taxation
amnesty from, **1:**135
land service tenure, **4:**4
land transfer tax, **4:**3, 6
in sale of land, **5:**186, 187, 188
Ten Abominations, **3:**84, 214; **4:**249
disrespect *(bujing)*, **4:**250–252
endangering the emperor, **4:**256
in Heqing code, **1:**421
plotting rebellion *(moufan)*, **4:**257
punishments for, **4:**259–260
sedition *(dani)*, **4:**257
sexual offenses in, **5:**233
status and, **5:**359
treason *(pan)*, **4:**257–258
theft, **5:457–461**
accessory and principal in, **1:**18
deceit as, **2:**314–316
as disrespect *(bujing)*, **4:**250
mutilation for, **4:**197
torture, **5:**482, **482–484**
abolition, **1:**439
importance of confession and, **2:**107, 108
under Jin, **1:**419–420

Shen Chia-Pen (Shen Jiaben) on, **5:**237
  under Tang, **1:**424
witnesses, **4:**418
women
  adoption of, **1:**45–46
  exile of, **3:**25, 26
  punishment, **5:**56–57
  rape, **5:**66–67
  redemption, **5:**73–74
  in succession, **5:**378
  wounding, **6:**150
  under Yuan empire, **1:**429
wounding in, **6:**150–152
wrongful judgment in, **6:**152–153
Chinese law, history of
  Shang dynasty (c. 16th–11th Century B.C.E.), **1:**400–402
  Western Zhou dynasty (c. 1045–771 B.C.E.), **1:**402–404
  Eastern Zhou, Spring and Autumn (771–464 B.C.E.), **1:**404–406
  Eastern Zhou, Warring States (464–221 B.C.E.), and Qin State and Empire (c. 350–206 B.C.E.), **1:**406–412
  Han Empire (206 B.C.E.–220 C.E.), **1:**412–418
  Three Kingdoms, Qin, and Southern Dynasties (220–589 C.E.), **1:**418–420
  Northern Dynasties (386–589 C.E.), **1:**420–421
  Sui and Tang dynasties (581–907 C.E.), **1:**421–425, *422*
  Five Dynasties and Song dynasty (907–1279 C.E.), **1:**425–427
  Liao (937–1125 C.E.) and Qin (1115–1234 C.E.) Empires, **1:**427–428
  Yuan dynasty (1279–1368 C.E.), **1:**428–430
  Ming dynasty (1368–1644 C.E.), **1:**430–433
  Qing dynasty (1644–1911 C.E.), **1:**433–439
  Republic, 1912–1949, **1:**439–441
  People's Republic of China, **1:**441–447, *444, 445*
  Hong Kong and Macau, **1:**447–451
  Taiwan, **1:**451–453
Chinese law, sources of, **1:**453–465
  administrative codes or regulations, **1:**453–455
  classical (ritual) writings, **1:**459–460
  custom, **1:**462–464
  doing what ought not to be done, **2:**355–356
  guilds, **1:**464–465

judicial precedent, **1:**460–462
penal codes, **1:**455–459
of Song law, **1:**426–427
Yuan dynasty, **1:**428–429
Chinese Nationalist Party. *See* Kuomintang
Chinese Partnerships Ordinance (Hong Kong, 1911), **1:**450
Chinese People's Political Consultative Conference (People's Republic of China), **1:**442
Chipman, Daniel, **2:**204
chirographum (written account of a debt), **2:**186, 187
Chitty, Joseph, **4:**324
  on bills of exchange, **1:**293
  on contracts, **2:**204
  legal treatises by, **2:**441, 442
Chitty on Contracts, **2:**442
Chlotar I (Salian king), **3:**117
C. Hoare & Co (England), **1:**271
Cholmondeley, Earl of
  on gin, **1:**124
Chomatenos of Ohrid, Demetrios, **1:**333, 348
Chongjun tiaoli (Regulations concerning military exile), **1:**431
Choppin, René
  on civil law, **3:**99
chorepiscopus (rural bishop), **1:**295
Chosrgyal, bsTan 'dzin, **1:**289
Christ, Matthew, **4:**113
Christian, Edward, **2:**394
Christian III (Denmark), **2:**328
Christianity
  on alcohol and drugs, **1:**124
  British Commonwealth
    legal superiority of, **1:**313
  conversion to, and freedom from slavery, **5:**258
  ecclesiastical courts, **2:**385–386
  Ethiopia, **2:**479
  influence on Roman Religious law, **5:**122–125
  Naga law and, **4:**201
  precolonial Africa, **1:**67, 69
  in Scholasticism, **4:**15
  on sexual and gender variation, **3:**110
Christian Marriage Act (Bangladesh, 1872), **1:**259
Christian V (Denmark), **2:**328
Christina (Sweden), **1:**255
Christoffer (Sweden), **5:**415
Christoph of Württemberg, **1:**349
Chronique d'Ernoul et de Bernard le Trésorier, **3:**40
chthonic law. *See* folk law

Chu, state of, **1**:411–412
Chulalongkorn (Rama V) (Thailand), **5**:315, 455
Chulkov, M. D., **5**:172
church and state in English common law, **1**:465–469
church councils and conciliar canons, **1**:469–472. *See also* ecumenical councils
    Council of Elvira (306), **1**:471
    Council of Toledo (633), **1**:471
        on canon law, **1**:356
    Hagia Sophia Council (876), **1**:347
    Quinisextum Council (692)
        and canon law, **1**:328, 346–347
Churchill, Winston, **1**:*314*
    on European Communities, **2**:485
Church of England
    on divorce, **2**:348–349
    ecclesiastical courts, **2**:385, 386
    ecclesiastical law, **2**:388–391
    General Synod, **1**:469
    Henry VIII and, **4**:284
    marriage requirements of, **3**:33
Church of Jesus Christ of Latter-Day Saints
    polygamy in, **3**:52; **5**:116–117
chu ren zui (acquit someone), **6**:153
Chu Yuanzhang (Chinese emperor), **1**:458
Cibber, Theophilus, **4**:142
Cicero, Marcus Tullius, **1**:472–475, *474*
    as advocate, **1**:56
    on courts, **4**:132
    on custom as a source of law, **2**:167
    on definition of law, **4**:18
    on formula, **3**:94
    historical information provided by, **5**:158
    house of, **5**:121
    influence, **3**:192
        on Pomponius, **5**:158
    on legislative assemblies, **4**:94, 95
    on magistrates, **4**:132
    on Manilius, **3**:434, 435
    on notaries, **2**:391
    on the pontificate, **5**:121
    on provincial edits, **4**:497
    on religious law, **5**:120
    on Roman citizenship, **5**:139
    on Roman jurists, **5**:146
    Servius Sulpicius Rufus and, **5**:224–225
    as source for Roman law, **5**:143
    systematization by, **5**:420
    on the Twelve Tables, **6**:20
    use of term *ius*, **3**:360
Cieza de León, Pedro, **4**:16
Cigarette Labeling Act (U.S., 1966), **2**:178
Cilardo, Agostino, **6**:161
Cinus de Sighibuldis (Cino da Pistoia), **1**:280
circumspecte agatis (1285), **2**:436
Citations Act (Roman, 426), **5**:153, 154
Cité Antique, La (Fustel de Coulanges), **1**:185
Citibank in Muslim countries, **1**:261
citizenship. *See also* naturalization
    Africa
        colonial, **1**:79
        in French colonies, **1**:89–90
    ancient Greece
        oaths in, **4**:241
        offenses against the state and, **4**:247
        Sparta, **5**:327
    ancient Greek law
        in arbitration, **1**:213
        Athen, **1**:233
        Athens, **1**:234
        family in, **3**:31
        Hellenistic, **1**:158
    ancient Near Eastern law, **1**:170–171
    Egypt juristic papyrology on, **2**:419–420
    European Union, **2**:491
    India
        fundamental duties of, **3**:104–105
        secularism in, **5**:208–209
    Islamic law, adoption and, **1**:48–49
    lex Irnitana on, **4**:102
    Malaysia, **4**:138
    nationality and, **4**:205–206
    natural law on, **4**:216–217
    plural, **2**:2–3
    proclamation of in Ireland, **3**:310
    Roman law, **5**:137–140, 150
        extended by Caracalla, **1**:161
        formula in, **3**:94
        manumission of slaves, **5**:249
        statutes on, **4**:101
    Sri Lanka, **5**:342
    United States, **2**:1–4
        class, **2**:*2*
        federal employment and, **2**:3
        women, **6**:137–140, *138*
    Wales, **6**:98

women
    ancient Greece, **6:**112–113
    United States, **6:**137–140, 138
Citizenship Act (Bhutan, 1977, 1985), **1:**290
city managers, **4:**121
civic-virtue theories on gay, lesbian, bisexual, and transgender, **3:**110
Civil Aeronautics Act (1938), **5:**104
Civil Aeronautics Administration, **1:**29
Civil Aeronautics Board, **5:**104
Civil Code (Chile), **1:**398
    Bello, Andrés, and, **1:**286
Civil Code (China, 1929–1931), **1:**440
Civil Code (Colombia, 1873–1876), **2:**63
Civil Code (Egypt, 1948), **2:**35; **3:**422
    on contracts, **2:**202
    on insurance, **2:**61
    Syrian adoption of, **2:**398
Civil Code (France, 1804), **4:**328, 362, 366, 367, 381, 392, 394, 398, 475; **5:**1, 2
    influence of, **2:**49
    Pothier, Robert Joseph influence on, **4:**366–367
    Russian translation, **5:**172
Civil Code (Germany, 1975), **4:**395
Civil Code (Iran, 1931), **4:**296
Civil Code (Italy, 1865), **4:**392, 475
Civil Code (Japan, 1890), **3:**375, 376–377
Civil Code (Jordan, 1976), **3:**256
Civil Code (Paraguay), **4:**281
Civil Code (Peru, 1852), **4:**314
Civil Code (Peru, 1854), **4:**314
Civil Code (Philippines, 1889), **4:**318
Civil Code (Poland, 1964), **4:**331
Civil Code (Poland, 2003), **4:**332
Civil Code (Quebec, 1994), **1:**341
civil Code (Switzerland), **4:**295, 392, 476, 478
Civil Code (Turkey, 1926), **4:**295
Civil Code (Turkey, 2001), **6:**18
Civil Code (Portugal, 1867), applicable in Macau, **1:**448
Civil Code for Galicia (1797), **1:**246
Civil Code of Procedure (Austria, 1895), **4:**435
Civil Code of the Republic of China (1931), **5:**54
"Civil Justice and the Poor" (Carlin, Messinger, and Howard), **4:**32
Civil Justice Committee (India), **3:**216
Civil Justice Reform Act (1990), **4:**446
civil law, **2:**1–15. *See also ius commune*
    adoption of Western style, in China, **1:**439
    Austria, **1:**247

Bangladesh, **1:**260
Bentham, Jeremy, on, **1:**287
China
    procedure, **4:**417–418
Chinese law
    appeal in, **1:**193–195
    Shen Chia-Pen on, **5:**237–238
colonial United States, **2:**11–15
De Luca, Giovanni Battista, on, **2:**326
Egypt
    Egyptianization of, **1:**205–206
England
    Doctors' Commons in, **2:**353–355
    evidence in, **3:**3–7
    reforms of, **4:**42–43
English common law
    procedure, **4:**419–423
European Union, **2:**496
France, **3:**99
Germany
    under National Socialism, **4:**204
    National Socialist Law, **3:**110
history
    England, **6:**27
    United States, **6:**27
India
    secularism in, **5:**208–209
Islamic law
    in Arab countries, **1:**205–206
    Europe, **2:**483–484
medieval and post-medieval Roman law, **2:**1–11
    on duress, **2:**376
    law merchant in, **4:**35–40
    on obligations, **4:**245
natural law in, **4:**216
Quebec
    infuence of common-law, **1:**341
Roman
    formula in, **3:**95
    legis actiones in, **4:**81–84
    Sabinus, Masurius, on, **5:**179
Roman law
    procedure, **4:**431–435
Savigny, Friedrich Carl von, on, **5:**195
Scholasticism on, **4:**16
South and Central America, **5:**286
Spain, **5:**324–325, 326
Suriname, **5:**296
Switzerland, **5:**419–420

United States
  arbitration in, **1:**130–131
  procedure, **4:**440–447
Civil Law in its Natural Order, The (Domat)
  English translations of, **2:**440–441
Civil Law *(ius civile)* (Roman), **6:**23
civil law traditions
  Cambodia, **1:**335
  Caribbean law, **1:**369–370
civil liability. *See* tort
Civil Partnership Act (U.K., 2004), **3:**33, 35
  adoption and, **1:**47
civil procedure
  in colonial United States, **2:**12
Civil Procedure Act (U.S., 1792), **4:**442
Civil Procedure Acts Repeal Act (U.K., 1879), **4:**271
Civil Procedure Code (India, 1859, 1908), **4:**273
Civil Procedure Code (Philippines, 1853), **4:**318
Civil Procedure Law (People's Republic of China, 1991), **1:**446
Civil Procedure Rules (U.K.), **4:**422; **5:**16
  on appeals, **1:**199
Civil Procedure (Amendment No. 4) Rules (U.K., 2000), **5:**16
Civilprozessordnung (Civil Code of Procedure) (Austria, 1895), **4:**435
civil rights
  absolutism and, **1:**7
  administrative law in, **1:**22
  Africa
    in French colonies, **1:**89–90
  Australia, **1:**245
  England, **2:**438–439
  India
    secularism in, **5:**208–209
  Mauritius, **4:**172
  Nigeria, **1:**93
  South Africa, **5:**281–282
  Suriname, **5:**414
Civil Rights Act (U.S., 1866)
  on discrimination in contracts, **2:**340
  equal protection in, **2:**459
  statutory interpretation of, **5:**362
Civil Rights Act (U.S., 1871), **2:**260; **3:**409–410
  supremacy clause and, **5:**412
Civil Rights Act (U.S., 1875)
  invalidation of, **2:**460
Civil Rights Act (U.S., 1964)
  on affirmative action, **2:**343
  amendments to, **6:**137–138
  commerce regulation in, **2:**341; **3:**62
  desegregation under, **2:**342
  on employment discrimination, **3:**483
  interstate commerce in, **2:**461
  on labor arbitration, **3:**487–488
  Reagan, Ronald, on, **2:**343
  on sex discrimination, **3:**484
  on sexual harassment, **2:**340
  state sovereignty and, **5:**353–354
  Title II justified by commerce clause, **2:**67
  Title IX, **2:**340
    feminist legal theory on, **3:**66–67
  Title VII, **2:**339; **6:**137–138
  on women, **2:**339, 340; **6:**57, 137–138
Civil Rights Act (U.S., 1968)
  Indian rights in, **2:**340
Civil Rights Act (U.S., 1991)
  affirmative action and, **3:**483
civil rights and civil liberties in United States law, **2:15–22**
  administrative agencies in, **1:**28
  desegregation at Little Rock Central High School, **2:***19*
  disability in, **2:**334–337
  due process in, **2:**367–368, 370–372
  equal protection and, **2:**458–465
  equity and, **2:**472–473
  legal services and, **4:**52–53
  legislative power and, **4:**97
  Native Americans in, **4:**212–213
  racial profiling, **2:**344
  right to bear arms, **1:**216–222
  separation of powers and, **5:**219
  slavery and, **5:**257
  state constitutions and, **5:**351
  state sovereignty and, **5:**353–354
  unenumerated, **2:**368–370
  violence against women and, **6:**142–143
  Warren Court on, **3:**62–63
  welfare and, **6:**93–95
Civil Rights Commission (U.S.)
  on 2000 election, **2:**344
  under Reagan, Ronald, **2:**343
civil rights movement (U.S.), **2:**341–342
  international law and, **3:**296
  law and society influenced by, **4:**32
  legal education and, **2:**406–407
Civil Rights Restoration Act (U.S., 1987), **2:**340
Civil War (U.S.)
  bonds, **5:**88

effect on civil procedure, **4**:442
effect on contract law, **2**:208
expansion of rights as result of, **2**:16
federalism and, **3**:60–61
international law and, **3**:294
martial law in, **4**:180
military tribunals in, **4**:177–178
nationality and, **4**:206
pensions abolished, **6**:96
property law and, **4**:490
rethinking of the Constitution, **2**:154–155
state sovereignty in, **5**:353, 354
taxation and, **5**:441–442
treason charges as a result of, **4**:335
war power in, **6**:88–89
Claflin doctrine, **5**:407
Claim of Right (Scotland), **5**:200
Clandestine Marriages Act (Great Britain, 1753), **3**:32–33; **6**:121
Clarendon Code (1661–1665), **1**:468
Clarity Act (Canada, 2000), **1**:339
Clark, Charles E.
   on law and society, **4**:31
   in legal realism, **1**:15; **4**:74, 75
Clark, Mark, **4**:337
Clarke, Ellis, **6**:11
Claro, Giulio (Julius Clarus), **1**:371
   on attempt, **1**:237
   on theft, **5**:463
class-action litigation, **4**:52
classical legal theory, **2**:22–28
Classic of Filial Piety, The (Xiao jing), **1**:422
Classified Law Paragraphs of the Qing-Yuan period, **1**:426
Classified Rules of the Ministry of Personnel, **1**:426
Claudius (Roman emperor)
   on succession, **5**:375
   women under, **6**:118
Claudius I (Roman emperor), **3**:211
Claudius Saturninus, **3**:436
Claudius Tryphoninus, **3**:435
Clayton Act (1914), **1**:188
   on antitrust, **1**:189, 190
Clayton Act (U.S., 1914), **6**:61
   federal oversight of railroad rates under, **5**:78
   on labor disputes, **1**:325
Clean Air Act (U.S., 1963, 1970), **2**:454–455, 456
   cost of, **2**:457
Clean Water Act (U.S., 1972), **2**:456
   sovereign immunity and, **5**:354

clear and present danger, **5**:334
clearing banks medieval, **1**:274–275
Cleary, Edward, **3**:11–12
Cleirac, Estienne, **4**:151
Cleisthenes, **5**:111
   Council of Five Hundred created by, **5**:275
   political reforms by, **1**:232
   reforms by, **1**:141; **2**:123
Clement I (pope), **4**:351
Clementinae, **1**:356, 471
   in legal education, **2**:6, 399
Clement IV (pope), **2**:317
Clement V (pope), **2**:223; **4**:432–433
Clement VII (pope)
   on College of Justice, **5**:199
   decretals by, **2**:317–318
Clendemin, C. R., **4**:*178*
Cleon, **5**:330
Cleveland, Grover, **4**:336
clientship in Irish law, **3**:306
climate change, European Union on, **2**:493
Clinton, Bill
   administrative agencies under, **1**:30
   affirmative action under, **2**:344
   environmental law under, **2**:457
   executive power under, **3**:22
   impeachment, **3**:23–24
   judicial appointments by, **3**:63
   judicial diversity under, **2**:343–344
   on legal services, **4**:373
   regulatory system under, **5**:84
   securities regulation under, **5**:95
   sex discrimination under, **2**:340
   trade policy under, **5**:84
   welfare reform by, **4**:372; **6**:93–94
Clodius, Publius, **1**:473
   consecration of Cicero's house, **5**:121
Clontarf, battle of (Ireland, 1014), **3**:307
close corporation, **1**:326
Closer Economic Relations Trade Agreement (New Zealand, 1983), **4**:231–232
Clouds (Aristophanes), **5**:228
Clovis (Salian king), **3**:116–117
ClS. *See* critical legal studies
Coase, Ronald, **4**:485
   on law and economics, **4**:24
   on regulations, **5**:83
Coast Theorem, **4**:24
Coates, J. G., **1**:*314*
Cobb, Thomas R. R., **5**:261, 262

Cocceji, Heinrich von, **2:**112
Cocceji, Samuel von, **2:**47; **5:**1
Cochin Christian Civil Marriage Act (1921), **3:**222
Cockburn, J. S., **1:**230
    on assizes, **1:**231
Code Civil (1583), **4:**476
Code Civil (France, 1804), **2:**9, 47; **3:***99;* **4:**362; **5:**471; **6:**65
    on adoption, **3:**46
    applicable to Renoncents of Pondicherry (India) in matters of marriage, **3:**223
    on assignment, **1:**227
    on breach of contract, **1:**307
    on cause illicite, **3:**203
    on delay, **2:**320
    on donation, **2:**357, 358
    education on, **2:**400–401
    in Egypt, **2:**421
    employment and labor law, **2:**428
    on engagement, **3:**41
    on error and mistake, **2:**475
    French Revolution influences on, **3:**99–100
    on guarantee, **3:**129
    on guardianship, **3:**48
    on immoral transactions, **3:**204
    on lease and tenancy contracts, **4:**57
    on legitimacy of children, **3:**47
    on profiteering contracts, **3:**205
    Russian translation of, **5:**172
    on sale of goods, **5:**192
    on succession, **5:**384, 385, 386
    on vicarious liability, **6:**78
Code Civil du Bas-Canada (1866), **1:**337
Code de Commerce (France, 1807)
    on bankruptcy, **3:**249
    corporations in, **2:**95
Code de Commerce (France, 1808), **4:**40
Code de la Nationalité (Morocco, 1958), **4:**297
Code de la Nationalité (Morocco, 1993), **4:**297
Code de Procedure Civile (France, 1806), **4:**362
Code de Procédure Civile (France, 1806)
    influences on, **3:**100; **4:**434
Code de Procédure Pénal (France, 1808), **4:**439
Code des Obligations Suisse (Switzerland, 1911), **5:**471
Code d'Indigénat, **4:**173
Code Européen des Contrats
    on breach of contract, **1:**309
Code Morand, **4:**129
Code Napoléon. *See* Code Civil (France, 1804)

Code of 101 Articles (Madagascar, 1868), **1:**71
Code of Alfred (England)
    rape, **5:**67–68
Code of Chinese Usages and Customs (Macau, 1909), **1:**448
Code of Civil Law (Quebec, 1866–1867), **1:**341
Code of Civil Procedure (China, 1929), **1:**440
Code of Civil Procedure (France, 1806). *See* Code de Procédure Civile (France, 1806)
Code of Civil Procedure (France, 1819), **4:**434
Code of Civil Procedure (Germany, 1877), **3:**375
Code of Civil Procedure (India, 1859), **3:**216
Code of Civil Procedure (India, 1908), **3:**148, 216
    environmental law in, **2:**452–453
Code of Civil Procedure (Japan, 1890), **3:**375, 376–377
Code of Civil Procedure (N.Y., 1848), **2:**49; **4:**442, 443
Code of Civil Procedure (Poland, 1930), **4:**331
Code of Civil Procedure (Quebec, 1866–1867), **1:**341
Code of Civil Procedure (U.K., 1806), **4:**434
Code of Civil Trasnactions of the United Arab Emirates (1985), **3:**256
Code of Criminal Instruction (Japan, 1880), **3:**374
Code of Criminal Procedure (China, 1928), **1:**440
Code of Criminal Procedure (Colombia, 2004), **2:**63
Code of Criminal Procedure (France, 1808)
    influences on, **3:**100
Code of Criminal Procedure (India, 1861, 1898, 1973), **3:**216
    environmental law in, **2:**453
    on maintenance, **3:**50
Code of Criminal Procedure (India, 1973)
    on dowry death, **2:**365
Code of Criminal Procedure (Japan, 1922), **3:**374, 376–377
Code of Criminal Procedure (Amendment) Act (India, 2001), **3:**149
Code of Eshnunna, **1:**168
Code of Euric, **2:**33
    on provincial administration, **3:**116
Code of Gentoo Laws (Halhed), **3:**157
Code of Gortyn (Great Code). *See* Gortyn
Code of Hammurabi, **1:**167, 168, *168;* **5:**473
    on justice and equity, **1:**169
    maritime law in, **1:**35
Code of Justinian. *See* Codex Justinianus
Code of Lipit-Ishtar, **1:**168
Code of Muslim Personal Law of the Philippines (1977), **3:**338

Code of Obligations (Poland, 1933), **4:**331
Code of Personal Status (Majalla) (Tunisia, 1957), **4:**296
Code of Procedure for Shariʿa Courts (Egypt, 1931), **4:**295
Code of Professional Responsibility (ABA), **4:**53
Code of Ranavalona I (Madagascar), **1:**71
Code of Steppe Laws of the Nomadic Peoples of Eastern Siberia, **5:**174
Code of the Ma'dhunun (Egypt, 1955), **4:**295
Code of Theodoric, **2:**33
Code of Ur-Nammu, **1:**168
code pleading, **1:**15
codes and codification, **2:**28–51
  Africa
    indigenous law, **1:**91–92
    precolonial, **1:**71–72
  ancient Greek law, **2:**28–31; **4:**84
    impetus for, **3:**28
  ancient Near Eastern law, **1:**167–168
  ancient Roman law, **2:**31–34
  Anglo-Saxon law, **1:**177
  in Arab countries, **1:**205, 207–208
  Argentina, **1:**216
  Austria, **1:**246
  Betham, Jeremy, and term codification, **2:**31, 46
  in Central American nationa, **1:**384
  China
    by Shen Chia-Pen (Shen Jiaben), **5:**237
    in Chinese Republic during Nanjing Decade, **1:**440
  civil law
    medieval and post-medieval Roman law, **2:**9
  colonial rule and, **2:**42–43
  comparative law and, **2:**98
  conflict of laws and, **2:**113–114
  consumer protection development out of, **2:**170
  Egypt
    Hellenistic period, **2:**414
    under Nasser, **2:**421
  under enlightened absolutism, **1:**8–9
  Enlightenment on, **2:**444
  Ethiopia, **2:**479–480
  India
    by Maine, Henry, **4:**137
    secularism and, **5:**208–209
  Islamic law, **2:**34–40, 397; **3:**317
    administrative decrees in, **1:**33–35
    in Africa, **2:**40–46
  Italy
    under Napoleon, **3:**358

  Laos, **4:**13–14
  legislation and, **4:**92
  Leibniz, Gottfried Wilhelm, in, **4:**100
  maritime law, **1:**36
  medieval and post-medieval Roman law: private law, **2:**46–50
    Icelandic law code, **2:**46
  Mexico, **4:**176
  Ottoman Empire, **4:**268–269
  Roman law
    lex in, **4:**101–102
  Savigny, Friedrich Carl von, on, **5:**195
  Scotland, **5:**200, 202
  South and Central America, **5:**285–286
  Southeast Asian law, **5:**313
  Spain, **5:**325–326
  Sweden, **5:**415–416
  Switzerland, **5:**419–420
  translations, **2:**99
  United States law, **2:**50–51
    evidence rules, **3:**11–14
Code Santillana, **4:**129
Codes et Lois du Cameroun (1956), **1:**89
Codes of Criminal Procedure of 1859 (India), **3:**148
Codex
  in legal education, **2:**399
  meaning of, **2:**31
  medieval law instruction and, **2:**6
Codex (Justinian), **2:**5
  on agency, **1:**110
  use in medieval teaching of law, **2:**6
Codex Canonum Ecclesiarum (Caode of Canons of the Eastern Churches) (1991), **1:**352, 470
Codex Euricianus, **5:**150
Codex Euricianus (475), **2:**110
Codex Fabrianus definitionum forensium (Faber), **3:**27
Codex Florentinus. See Littera Florentina
Codex Gregorianus (291–292), **1:**327; **2:**32–33; **3:**213, 456; **5:**149
Codex Hermogenianus (295), **1:**327; **2:**32; **3:**213, 456; **5:**149
Codex Iuris Bavarici Criminalis (1751), **4:**439
Codex Iuris Canonici, **4:**351
Codex Iuris Canonici (1917), **1:**352–354
  on bishops and archbishops, **1:**293
Codex Iuris Canonici (1917, 1983)
  on bishops and archbishops, **4:**354

Codex Iuris Canonici (1983), **1**:354–355; **4**:399
   on bishops and archbishops, **1**:293
Codex Iustinianus, **3**:456. *See* Codex Justinianus
Codex Juris Bavarici Criminalis (Bavarian criminal code) (1752), **5**:33
Codex Juris Bavarici Judicarii (Bavaria, 1753)
   on insolvency, **3**:249
Codex Justinianus, **1**:327–328; **4**:361
   on administrative policy, **5**:13
   aim of, **5**:152–153
   Baldus de Ubaldis, Petrus, on, **1**:250
   Bartolus of Saxoferrato on, **1**:280
   Christianity's influence on, **5**:122–125
   on church matters, **1**:346
   Codex Gregorianus included in, **2**:32
   Codex Hermogenianus included in, **2**:32
   on contracts, **2**:188–190
   historiography of, **5**:158
   imperial rescripts, **3**:436
   on legal procedure, **2**:236; **4**:416
   on pledge, **4**:328
   on possession, **4**:361
   on property, **4**:468, 476
   purpose of, **3**:437
   on slavery, **5**:253
   Tribonian and, **6**:7–9
Codex Leopoldinus, **4**:100
Codex Maximilianeus Bavaricus Civilis (1756)
   on succession, **5**:386, 391, 393
Codex Maximilianeus Bavaricus Civilis (Bavaria, 1756), **2**:47, 400
   civil law codification and, **2**:9
   on guarantee, **3**:129
   on immoral transactions, **3**:204
   on precedent, **4**:380
   private law, **4**:394
   protection of possession, **4**:361–362
Codex Maximilianeus Juris Bavarici (Bavaria, 1756), **2**:47; **3**:473
Codex of 438, **1**:327
Codex Repetitiae Praelectionis, **1**:328; **5**:154. *See* Constitutio Cordi
Codex Theodosianus (429–438), **1**:327; **2**:33, 187; **3**:190, 437, 456; **5**:148, 149
   on administrative policy, **5**:13
   Christianity's influence on, **5**:122–125
   final edition of, **5**:160
   historiography, **5**:160
   influence on, **5**:152
   legal studies, **5**:148
   Visigothic law, **3**:116
   on jurists, **5**:151, 153
   on possession, **4**:361
   promugation of, **5**:149
   on women's education, **6**:118
Codex Theresianus (Austria, 1766), **4**:380, 477
Codice Civile (1376), **4**:476
Codice Civile (Italy, 1865)
   in African colonies, **1**:81–82
   on assignment, **1**:228
   on breach of contract, **1**:308
   on delay, **2**:320
   on donation, **2**:357
   on error and mistake, **2**:475
   French influence on, **2**:49
   law merchant in, **4**:40
   on profiteering contracts, **3**:205
   on sale of goods, **5**:192
   on vicarious liability, **6**:78
Codice Civile (Italy, 1942), **2**:96; **4**:395; **5**:471
Codice di Commercio (Italy, 1865), **2**:95
Codice di Commercio (Italy, 1882), **2**:95, 96
Codice di Procedura Civile (Code of Civil Procedure) (Italy, 1865), **4**:434–435
codicils
   England, **6**:104
   medieval and post-medieval Roman law on, **5**:389–390
codification à droit constant, **2**:49
Codification Bureay (China, Qing), **1**:436
Codification Proposal to All Nations Professing Liberal Opinions (Bentham), **2**:46
Código Bustamante (1928), **2**:114
Código Civil (Portugal, 1867)
   on error and mistake, **2**:476
   French influence on, **2**:49
Código Civil (Portugal, 1966)
   Africa under, **1**:80
Código Civil (Spain)
   on sale of goods, **5**:192
Código Civil (Spain, 1889)
   on assignment, **1**:228
   on children's accountability, **3**:44–45
   on error and mistake, **2**:475
   French influence on, **2**:49
Código das Siete Partidas (1256), **5**:298–299
Código de Comercio (Spain)
   admiralty law in, **1**:36

Código Negro (Spain)
    on slaves, **5**:253–254
Código Sustantivo del Trabajo (Colombia, 1951), **2**:63
cognitio in ancient Roman law, **2**:51–54
    Gaius on, **3**:251
Cohen, David, **4**:403, 409, 410; **5**:456
    on adultery, **1**:51; **5**:358
    anthropological studies by, **1**:186
    on litigation in ancient Athens, **4**:113
    in Symposion, **1**:165
Cohen, Edward, **1**:165
    in Symposion, **1**:165
Cohen, Felix, **2**:297
    in legal realism, **4**:74, 75
    on Native American law, **4**:211
Cohen, Morris, **4**:355
coinage
    Athens, **2**:70, *70*
Coing, Helmut, **5**:163
    on succession, **5**:387
Coke, Edward, **2**:54–56, *55*; **3**:176, 178; **4**:324
    on abolutism, **1**:7
    on arbitration, **1**:130
    on barristers, **1**:278
    on burglary, **1**:316
    in Court of Common Pleas, **2**:86
    on Court of Common Pleas, **2**:85
    on courts deriving from King'd Bench, **3**:471
    on court types in England, **2**:249
    on customary law, **2**:305
    on due process, **2**:367
    on easements, **2**:380, 381
    on English common law, **6**:33
    on entails, **2**:448
    on Exchequer, **3**:17
    on final process, **3**:87
    in House of Commons, **2**:130
    influence on
        Blackstone, William, **1**:298
    on Inns of Court, **3**:240
    and James I, **2**:129–130
    on judicial law making, **5**:277
    on jurisdiction of King's Bench, **3**:472
    on land leases, **4**:11–12
    on larceny, **5**:462
    law reporting by, **4**:44, 60
    in legal education, **2**:394
    on legal theory, **4**:61
    on Littleton, Thomas, **2**:440; **4**:61
    on Magna Carta, **4**:135
    on monopolies granted by the Crown, **2**:88
    on precedent, **4**:378
    on property, **4**:487
    on punishment, **5**:30–31
    as source of law, **5**:278
    in Star Chamber, **5**:345
    on statute law, **4**:89
    on theft, **5**:461
    on torture, **5**:484
Coke on Littleton. See *Commentary upon Littleton* (Coke)
Coke upon Littleton. See *Institutes of the Laws of England* (Coke)
    influence in the British North American colonies, **2**:83
Colan, **6**:98
Colbert, Jean-Baptiste, **2**:92; **5**:325
Colebrooke, Henry Thomas, **2**:56–57, 442; **3**:158
Colebrooke-Cameron Commission (1832), **5**:341
Coler, Martin
    on maintenance, **3**:46
collateral transactions rule, **1**:323
collateral warranty
    entails and, **2**:447
Collationes (Innocent IV)
    decretals in, **2**:319
Collected Date for a Continuation of the Comprehensive Mirror for Aid in Government, **1**:426
Collectio Avellana, **2**:318
Collectio Bambergensis, **2**:318–319
Collectio Britannica, **2**:318
Collectio Corbeiensis, **2**:318
Collectio Dionysiana, **2**:318
Collectio Dionysio-Hadriana, **2**:318
Collectio Francofurtana, **2**:318
Collectio Gilberti, **2**:319
Collectio Hispana (conciliar canons), **1**:470
Collectio librorum iuris anteiustinianei (Mommsen), **5**:160
Collectio L titulorum
    on canon law, **1**:328
Collection of Enlightened Judgments, **1**:461–462
Collection of Some Principall Rules and Maximes of the Common Law (Bacon), **4**:61
Collectio Parisiensis II, **2**:318
Collectio Pithouensis, **2**:318
Collectio tripartita (part of *Nomocanon*), **1**:328
Collectio Wigorniensis II, **2**:318
collective bargaining
    arbitration and, **3**:489

English common law, **2:**426
Germany
National Socialist law, **4:**204
United States
arbitration and, **3:**486–487
decline of, **3:**484–485
Taft-Hartley Act on, **3:**483
collective liability in Chinese law, **2:57–62**
in offenses against the state, **4:**257–258
in wrongful judgment, **6:**152, 153
collective rights
right to bear arms as, **1:**219–220
collegantia partnership, **2:**94
Collège des Lecteurs Royaux
Budé, Guillaume, in, **1:**316
College of Advocates and Doctors of Law
Doctors' Commons and, **2:**354–355
College of Justice (Scotland), **5:**199
College of William and Mary (Williamsburg, Va.), **1:**12
Collier, John
as commissioner of Indian affairs, **4:**211; **6:**58
Collins, Hugh
on contracts, **2:**442
Colombia, **2:62–63**
adoption of Chilean Civil Code, **1:**398
slavery abolished in, **5:**254–255
Colonial Act (East Timor, 1930), **2:**384
colonialism
Africa, **1:**75–96
codification, **2:**42–43
Portuguese, **1:**69
scramble for, **1:**76–77, 78
Argentina, **1:**215–216
Australia
Aboriginal law and, **1:**2–3
constitutions and, **2:**135
definition of law and, **4:**19
indirect rule in, **1:**78–79
insurance in Islamic countries under, **2:**60–61
in Laos, **4:**13, 14
legal anthropology on, **4:**59–60
in Liberia, **4:**107
in Maghrib and al-Andalus, **4:**129
Malaysia, **4:**137–138
Maldives, **4:**139
Maori law and, **4:**145–147
Mauritius, **4:**171
Scholasticism on, **4:**15–17
South and Central America, **5:**284–285, 297–298

Southeast Asia, **5:**322–323
influence of Western laws on Muslim law, **3:**334
protection of intellectual property, **3:**261
Sri Lanka, **5:**339–342
Colonial Laws Validity Act (1865)
on Australia, **1:**241, 242–243
on Canada, **1:**338
Columbia College, **2:**403
legal realism at, **1:**15; **4:**75
Columbus, Christopher, **5:**290, 298
Trinidad and, **6:**9
Combination Act (1799, 1800)
guilds in, **3:**132
Combination Act (U.K., 1799, 1800), **2:**425–426
Comité d'Études du Haut Congo, **1:**82
comitia centuriata, **4:**93, 94
comitia curiata, **4:**93
comitia populi tributa, **4:**93–94
comitia tributa, **4:**93–94
comity, theory of
conflict of laws and, **2:**117
commenda, **2:**87, 94
as insurance, **3:**258
Commentaire sur le traité des délits et des peines (Voltaire), **1:**285
Commentar (Zeiller), **6:**163
Commentaria ad pandectas (Commentaries on the Digest) (Voet), **4:**226
Commentaries (Plowden), **4:**44, 60, 324
Commentaries on American Law (Kent), **2:**206; **6:**41, 46
on conflict of laws, **2:**117
on international law, **3:**293
in legal education, **1:**12
on public corporations, **4:**120
commentaries on Chinese law
on Tang code, **1:**457
Commentaries on Colonial and Foreign Laws (Burge), **2:**98
Commentaries on Equity Jurisprudence (Story), **2:**205
Commentaries on the Conflict of Laws (Story), **2:**112
Commentaries on the Law of Agency as a Branch of Commercial and Maritime Jurisprudence (Story), **1:**108, 113
Commentaries on the Laws of England (Blackstone), **1:**297–298; **3:**252, 440; **5:**474
on agency, **1:**108
in barrister education, **1:**279
Bentham, Jeremy, on, **1:**287
on capital punishment, **1:**364
on contracts, **2:**204

on coverture, **6:**121
on customary law, **2:**305
on easements, **2:**379
on equity, **2:**470
influence in the Colonies, **2:**83
influence on
   legal education, **2:**394
   legal literature, **2:**441
legal theory in, **4:**61
natural law in, **2:**437
on right to bear arms, **1:**217
Russian translation, **5:**172
on sources of law, **4:**87
on sovereignty, **5:**352
on statutory interpretation, **5:**360
Commentarii (Celsus the Younger), **1:**373
Commentarii (Connan), **3:**190, 192
Commentarii ad Rescripta Principum (Alciati), **1:**118
Commentarii de iure civili (Doneau), **2:**360; **3:**192
   systematization in, **5:**421
Commentarii de utroque retractu et municipali et conventionaliex integris in Pictonum consuetudines commentariis (Tiraquellus), **5:**467
Commentarii iuris civilis (Connan)
   systematization in, **5:**421
Commentarii linguae Graecae (Budé), **1:**316
Commentariorum sive recitationum ad librum quartum Codicis Justiniani paralipomena (Doneau), **2:**360
Commentary of Master Zuo (Zuo zhuan), **1:**404, 405
Commentary upon Littleton (Coke), **2:**56; **4:**324
commentators of civil law, **2:**7
Comment on the Commentaries, A (Bentham), **1:**287
commerce clause, **2:64–68,** 154
   antitrust law and, **1:**189
   federalism and, **3:**60, 62, 63–64
   Native Americans under, **4:**206–207
   railroads and, **6:**48
commerce power, **3:**292
commercial arbitration
   in the United States, **2:**78
Commercial Code (Colombia, 1853), **2:**63
Commercial Code (Colombia, 1971), **2:**63
Commercial Code (Japan, 1898), **3:**375, 376–377
Commercial Code (Philippines, 1885), **4:**318
Commercial Code (Poland, 1934), **4:**331
commercial courts, **2:**96
commercial exchange
   Islamic law, **3:**324

commercial law, **2:68–79.** *See* agency; banks and banking; business law; maritime law
   ancient Greek law, **2:69–72**
      Athens, **1:**140, 234
      maritime, **4:**147–149
   Argentina, **1:**216
   assignment in, **1:**227–228
   Austria, **1:**247
   bankruptcy, **1:**266–270
   Brazil, **1:**304
   China
      deposit, **2:**331
      guilds and regulations, **1:**464–465
      on sale of goods, **5:**183–185
   Chinese Republic, **1:**440
   Contract Law (People's Republic of China, 1999), **1:**446
   definition of law and, **4:**19
   Denmark, **2:**328
   England
      bills of exchange, **1:**291–293
      law merchant in, **4:**35–38
      Magna Carta on, **4:**134
   Ethiopia, **2:**480
   European Union, **2:**496
   freedom of speech and, **5:**336
   guarantee in, **3:**129
   insolvency and, **3:**248
   in Iran, **3:**304
   Islamic law, **3:**328–329
      in Arab countries, **1:**205–206
   Islamic law, classical period, **2:72–74**
   Islamic law, modern period, **2:74–75**
   legal education in, **2:**400
   medieval and post-medieval Roman law
      agency in, **1:**110–112
      law merchant, **4:**38–40
   Netherlands, **4:**226
   New Zealand, **4:**228
   Ottoman Empire, **4:**267
   People's Republic of China
      law on Chinese-foreign joint ventures, **1:**445
   Roman
      slaves in, **5:**248–249
   Scotland, **5:**201–202
   South and Central America
      colonial, **5:**285, 298
   Spain, **5:**325, 326
   Switzerland, **5:**420

United States, **2:**75–79
   agency in, **1:**112–116
   alternative dispute resolution in, **1:**129–130
   antitrust, **1:**187–193
Commercial Law of the World (Levi), **2:**98
commercial speech, **5:**336
Commission on Civil Rights (U.S.)
   on comparable worth, **2:**340
Commission on Fok Law and Legal Pluralism, **3:**90
Commission on Legal Problems of the Elderly, **2:**422
Commission on the Status of Women, **3:**70
Committee on Civil and Political Rights (U.S.), **6:**137
Committee on Fundamental Rights (India), **3:**105–106
Committee on Legal Education
   standards by, **2:**404–405
Committee on Legal Education and Training (Japan), **3:**386
commodatum (loan for use), **2:**184, 186, 187, 189
commodity in Islamic law, **2:**79–80
Commodus (Roman emperor)
   Paul and, **4:**290
Common Bench. *See* Common Pleas, Court of
common carriers, **1:**321
Common Cause (New Delhi), **2:**174
common employment, doctrine of, **4:**30; **6:**76
Common Foreign and Security Policy
   reforms to, **2:**486–487, 491, 493
Common Frame of Reference (EU), **2:**496
Commonhold and Leasehold Reform Act (U.K., 2002)
   estates doctrine in, **2:**479
common law, **2:**80–85. *See also* English common law
   abolutism and, **1:**7
   Africa
     colonial, **1:**79
   alternative dispute resolution in, **1:**129
   ancient Greece, **1:**136, 157–158
   antitrust, **1:**188–189
   Bangladesh, **1:**257
   Canada, **1:**337
   Denning, Alfred Thompson, on, **2:**329–330
   on donation, **2:**357–358
   fideicommissum in, **3:**80–81
   on fraud, **3:**102–103
   legal process on, **4:**67
   medieval and post-medieval Roman
     in sale of land, **5:**193
   Melanesia, **4:**174
   New Zealand, **4:**227
   origins, **2:**80–81, 82
   partnership in, **1:**320
   real actions, **5:**69–72
   Scotland, **5:**198
   South African, **1:**87
   Sri Lanka, **5:**341–342
   United States law, **2:**82–85
   villeinage and, **6:**81
Common Law, The (Holmes), **2:**25
   on agency, **1:**108
   on contracts, **2:**204
   on social science, **5:**266
Common Law and the Case Method in American University Law Schools, The (Redlich), **2:**403
Common Law Procedure Act (Brit., 1852)
   on equity, **2:**471
   on outlawry, **4:**271
   on writs of execution, **3:**87
Common Law Procedure Act (Brit., 1854), **4:**472
Common Law Procedure Act (U.K., 1854), **4:**325
   on fraud, **3:**101–102
   on pleading, **4:**325
Common Market. *See* European Economic Community
Common Pleas, Court of, **2:**85–86
   barristers in, **1:**277, 278
   Coke, Edward, chief of justice of, **2:**55
   decline of, **2:**436
   on entails, **2:**447–448
   in environmental law, **2:**449
   history of, **2:**249
   King's Bench and, **3:**472
   law merchant in, **4:**37
   origin of, **2:**80, 435; **3:**471
   restrictions of other tribunals by, **2:**55
   serjeants at law before, **5:**221
Common Program (People's Republic of China), **1:**441, 442–443
common right
   easements and, **2:**380
commons
   easements and enclosure of, **2:**381–382
   in environmental law, **2:**450
   wrongful enclosure of as nuisance, **4:**239
Commons, John R., **5:**79
   on law and economics, **4:**23
common Sense (Paine), **3:**447–448

Commonwealth and Colonial Law (Wray), **1:**310
Commonwealth Fund
   on national evidence law, **3:**10
Commonwealth Papua Act (Papua New Guinea, 1905), **4:**280
Communications Act (U.S., 1934), **5:**97, 98
Communiqué of the Third Plenum of the Eleventh Central Party Committee (People's Republic of China, 1978), **1:**445
communism
   Albania, **1:**253
   Bali, **1:**251
   Germany
     under National Socialist law, **3:**110
   Laos, **4:**13, 14
   Malaysia, **4:**138
   notaries in, **4:**237
   United States
     labor law on, **3:**483
Community Development Block Grant, **3:**185, 186
community property, **5:**404–405
Comnenus. *See* Manuel I Comnenus
Comnenus, Manuel I, **4:**416
Comoros
   constitution, **2:**137
Compagnie des Cent Associés, **1:**337
Companies Act (U.K., 1862), **2:**90
Companies Act (U.K., 2006), **2:**91
Companies Clauses Consolidation Act (U.K., 1845), **2:**89
company law, **2:86–97**
   English common law, **2:87–92**
   medieval and post-medieval Roman law, **2:92–97**
Company Law (China, 1929), **1:**440
comparative impairment, theory of, **2:**118
comparative law, **2:97–100**
   anthropology in, **1:**185–187
   establishment of term, **2:**99
Compendium Codocis Bavarici—Grundriss der gemain- und bayrischen Privatrechtsgelehrsamkeit (Kreittmayr), **3:**473
compensation
   China
     for damage to property, **2:**312, 313
   in Islamic law, **2:100–101**
     kinship and, **3:**39
   Naga law, **4:**201
   Roman law
     delict, **2:**321

Compensation Act, Criminal Law. *See* Criminal Law Compensation Act
competition, **2:101–104**
   antitrust and, **1:**187–193
   Byzantine law on, **1:**329
   corporations and, **1:**322–327
   English common law, **2:101–102**
   medieval and post-medieval Roman law, **2:102–104**
   monopolies and, **4:**186–187
Compilationes antiquae, **1:**356; **2:**319
Compilation of Islamic Law in Indonesia (Kompilasi Hukum Islam di Indonesia) (1991), **3:**336, 337
Compilation of Laws of the Kingdoms of the Indies (1680), **4:**176
Compilation of the Laws of Indies. See Recopilación de Leyes de las Indias (1680)
Compilatio Prima (Bernard of Pavia), **2:**319
Compilatio Tertia, **2:**319
Compleat Body of Conveyancing, A (Wood), **2:**441
Complete System of Pleading, A (Wentworth), **4:**324
Comprehensive Encyclopedia (Tong dian), **1:**422
Comprehensive Environmental Response, Compensation, and Liability Act (U.S., 1980), **2:**456
Comprehensive Hindu Code project (India), **5:**398
Compromise of 1850 (U.S.), **5:**262
Compromise of 1877 (U.S.), **2:**460
compurgation, **2:104–106,** 388
   England, **2:**196; **3:**3–4
Comstock, Anthony
   on sexual and gender variation, **3:**110
Comstock Act (U.S., 1873), **6:**51
   on contraceptives, **6:**140
   freedom of speech and, **5:**333
Comte, Auguste
   influence on
     Brazilian law, **1:**303
Comunidad Andina, **2:**115
Comyn, Samuel
   on contracts, **2:**204
Comyns, John
   abridgements by, **4:**61
Concept of Law, The (Hart), **4:**357
Concept Plan of Redress (Guyana), **5:**295
Concession of the West Jersey Proprietors (1677), **2:**286
conciliation, **1:**128
Conclusiones de statutes et consuetudinibus localibus (Du Moulin), **2:**111–112

Concordat of Worms (1122)
  on bishops, **1:**295
  feudal law and, **3:**79
Concordia discordantium canonum. *See* Decretum Gratiani
Concordia discordantium canonum. See Decretum of Gratian; Decretum of Gratian
Concordia Discordantium Canonum (Gratian), **1:**356
concubinage
  ancient Greece, **4:**153
  China, **4:**158
    lack of filial piety and, **3:**86
  legitimacy of children from, **3:**46–47
condemnatio (condemnation)
  in formula, **3:**96–97
condictio furtiva (claim relating to theft), **2:**321
Confederation of Kilkenny (Ireland), **3:**309
Confederation of the Rhine
  constitution, **2:**120
Confessio Belgica (1561), **1:**350
confession
  in Chinese law, **2:106–109**
    and acceptance of sentence, **2:107–109**
    recantation of, **1:**195–196
  under duress, **2:**375
  Islamic law
    threats, beating, torture for, **2:**432
  medieval and post-medieval Roman law
    as evidence, **3:**8
  ordeals and, **4:**262–263
Confession Augustana (Melanchthon), **1:**349
Confirmation of the Magna Carta (1297), **2:**128
Confiscation Act (U.S., 1862), **4:**490
Confiscation Acts (U.S., 1861 and 1862), **6:**52
Conflict of Law Complementary Statute (Germany, 1999), **2:**113
Conflict of Law Reform Act (Germany, 1986), **2:**113
conflict of laws, **2:109–119**
  medieval and post-medieval Roman law, **2:109–116**
  United States law, **2:116–119**
Conflict of the Orders, **4:**93
Conformity Act (U.S., 1872), **4:**442
Confrontation Clause
  evidence and, **3:**14–15
Confucianism
  and moralization of law, **1:**460
Confucious
  heterodox beliefs and, **4:**252
Confucius
  on adoption, **1:**43
  on amnesty, **1:**133, 134
  on criminal law, **1:**459
  on disability, **5:**47
  on doing what ought not to be done, **2:**356
  on filial piety, **3:**84
  on land, **4:**1
  on law, **3:**366
  on mutual concealment, **4:**198
  on penal codes, **1:**455
  on punishment, **5:**45, 48
  on women, **5:**56–57
Congo
  constitution of, **1:**106
  decolonization of, **1:**93
  independence of, **1:**98
  law reform in, **1:**100
  slavery in, **1:**76
Congo Free State, **1:**82–83
Congressional Government (Wilson)
  on executive power, **3:**20
Congressional Office of Technology Assessment (OTA), **4:**30
Congress of Vienna
  German Confederation formed in, **1:**246
Coniecturae iuris civilis (Faber), **3:**27
Connan, François, **3:**192
  on systematization, **5:**421
Connecticut Compromise, **2:**149
Connecticut Planned Parenthood League, **4:**388
Conrad II (Holy Roman Emperor), **2:**110
  on feudal law, **3:**79
Conrat (Cohn), Max, **5:**158, 162
Conrings, Hermann, **2:**8
Conseil d'État, **3:**100
Conseil d'Etat (France), **1:**21–22
Conseils de Prudhommes (industrial tribunal, France), **2:**430
Conseil Souverain of New France, **1:**337
consensual contracts in Roman law, **2:**184, 186, 187–188
  under Justinian, **2:**189
consensual divorce in Islamic law, **2:**37
consensualism
  Du Moulin, Charles, on, **2:**373
  legal process on, **4:**67–68
consideration, rules of, **2:**198
consignment
  medieval and post-medieval Roman law
    agency and, **1:**111
consilia (advisers), **2:**392

consistory (Protestant ecclesiastical court), **1:**349
conspiracy
   England
      employment and labor law, **2:**425–426
      strike breaking and, **1:**325
   United States
      labor law, **3:**478–479
Constance, Peace of (1183)
   Baldus de Ubaldis, Petrus, on, **1:**250
Constant, Benjamin, **1:**302
   antimajoritarian devices by, **1:**302
   on Filangieri, Gaetano, **3:**84
Constantine (emperor)
   on slavery, **5:**247
Constantine (Roman emperor)
   accepted body of law under, **5:**149
   and church councils, **1:**471
   executive structure of Empire under, **5:**13
   marriage law under, **4:**307
   papacy and, **4:**352
   paternal power under, **4:**305
   Paul's works under, **4:**290
   religious law under, **5:**123, 124
   written evidence under, **2:**189
Constantine IX Monomachos (emperor)
   on legal education, **1:**330, 333
Constantine V (Byzantine emperor)
   on purpose of law, **1:**330
Constantine VII (Byzantine emperor)
   on Basil I, **1:**281
   on legal procedure, **4:**416
   on property, **4:**469
Constantine VII Porphyrogenitus, **4:**469
Constantinople
   law school at, **2:**392
Constantius II (Roman emperor), **3:**455
   religious law under, **5:**123
"Constant Laws" (Zhao Xuanzi), **1:**404
Constitutio Antoniniana (Rome, 212), **2:**110; **3:**211; **6:**24
   Wales under, **6:**98
Constitutio Criminalis Carolina, **4:**91
Constitutio Criminalis Carolina (1532), **2:**47; **4:**438
   on attempt, **1:**237
   on case-forwarding, **2:**254
   on fraud, **3:**102
   on punishment, **5:**32, 43
   witch trials under, **6:**108

constitution, **2:119–122**
   origin of term, **2:**119
Constitution (Cambodia, 1947), **1:**335
Constitution (Chinese Republic, 1946), **1:**440
Constitution Act (Canada, 1982), **1:**339
   status and rights of Natice peoples in, **1:**342
Constitution (42nd Amendment) Act (India, 1976)
   on environmental law, **2:**454
Constitutional Code (Bentham), **1:**287
Constitutional Convention (U.S., 1787)
   on copyright law, **3:**266
   on executive power, **3:**19–20, 22–23
   on general welfare clause, **3:**113
   Hamilton, Alexander on self-interest, **4:**481
   on patents, **3:**269
   on slavery, **5:**260
   on state sovereignty, **5:**352
   on supremacy clause, **5:**411
Constitutional Council (Cambodia), **1:**335
constitutional law, **2:122–147.** *See also* constitutions and constitutional law in Islamic law
   in administration, public law of, **1:**23–24
   Afghanistan, **1:**59–61
   Africa
      after independence, **1:**97–98
      British colonies, **1:**86
      colonial, **1:**79
      Congo, **1:**83
      decolonization and, **1:**92–93
      French colonies, **1:**89
      post-independence, **1:***96,* 104–106
   ancient Greek law, **2:**122–127
      inscriptions on, **1:**154
      philosophy of, **1:**162
   ancient Near Eastern law, **1:**168–169
   Arab countries, **1:**206–207
   Argentina, **1:**216
   Australia, **1:**245
      Aboriginal law and, **1:**3
   Austria, **1:**246–247
   Bangladesh, **1:**259, 260
   Bermuda, **1:**289
   Brazil, **1:**302, 303–304
   classical legal theory on, **2:**23
   England
      on legislative power, **4:**96
      Magna Carta in, **4:**135–136
   English common law, **2:127–134,** 438
   Enlightment views of, **2:**445
   Ethiopia, **2:**479

European Communities, **2:**488
Fiji, **3:**82
France, **3:**100
Germany
   in National Socialist Law, **3:**110
Guyana, **5:**295–296
India, **2:143–147**
   on civil code, **5:**308
   Sikh law under, **5:**241
   on succession, **5:**399
Islamic, **1:**209–210
Laos, **4:**14
legal process on, **4:**68–69
on legislation, **4:**92
Malaysia, **4:**138, 139
Maldives, **4:**139
Mauritius, **4:**172
Mexico, **4:**176
Nepal, **4:**225
New Zealand, **4:**228
   on Maori law, **4:**146–147
Ottoman Empire, **4:**269–270
Pakistan, **5:**308–309
Roman law
   lex in, **4:**101–102
Seychelles, **5:**234–235
South Africa, **5:**280, 281–282
South and Central America, **5:**285
Spain, **5:**326
Sri Lanka, **5:**342–343
Suriname, **5:**413–414
Sweden, **5:**416, 417
Thailand, **5:**315
United States
   on apportionment and reapportionment, **1:**201
   state, **5:**348, 349–351
constitutional review in Islamic countries, **2:**135–136
"Constitutional Right to Keep and Bear Arms, The" (Emery), **1:**219
Constitutional Treaty. *See* Treaty Establishing a Constitution for Europe
Constitution Criminalis Carolina
   on guilt, **3:**133
Constitutiones Clementinae (Clement V), **2:**223
Constitutiones Livoniae (Livonian Ordinances) (1582), **1:**255
Constitution for Europe (2004), **2:**493
Constitution of Algeria, **4:**298
Constitution of Cuba (1976), **1:**370
Constitution of France (1791), **4:**398
Constitution of Germany, **4:**396
Constitution of India
   on customary law, **2:**308
   on environmental law, **2:**453–454
   on equality, **2:**309
   on family, **3:**48
   on fundamental duties, **3:**104–105
   on fundamental rights, **3:**105–107
   on public interest litigation, **5:**7
   on uniform civil code, **4:**294
Constitution of Indonesia, **4:**302
Constitution of Japan (1946), **3:**378–380
Constitution of Malaysia, **4:**301
Constitution of Mauritania, **4:**298
Constitution of Morocco, **4:**298
Constitution of North Carolina (U.S., 1776), **4:**488
Constitution of Pakistan, **4:**273–274, 299–300
Constitution of Poland, **4:**331–332
Constitution of the Athenians (attr. Aristotle), **2:**123; **4:**403–404, 411, 456
   on courts and magistrates, **2:**228
   on evidence relevance, **3:**2
   on market regulation, **2:**69
   papyrology on, **2:**413
   on Solon, **5:**273
Constitution of the Athenians (attr. Xenophon), **2:**123
Constitution of the Empire of Japan, The, **3:**375–377
Constitution of the People's Republic of China (1954), **1:**443
Constitution of the People's Republic of China (1975), **1:**444
Constitution of the People's Republic of China (1978), **1:**445
Constitution of the People's Republic of China (1982), **1:**445, 446
Constitution of the People's Republic of China (1993), **1:**446
Constitution of the Philippines, **4:**319
Constitution of the Roman Empire, **5:**11–12, 13–14
Constitution of the Roman Republic, **5:**8
Constitution of the United States, **2:147–156.** *See also* admiralty clause; bankruptcy clause; commerce clause; contracts clause; general welfare clause; takings clause
   academics on, **1:**13
   on admiralty law, **1:**39
   change, **2:**152–154
      through custom and usage, **2:**153–154

common law and, **2**:84; **6**:38
on Congressional representation, **6**:38
Contracts Clause
   takings clause and, **5**:424
on copyright, **3**:266
corporations in, **1**:324
courts, **3**:423
on courts, **2**:256–257, 261
critical period before, **1**:223–224
critical race theory and, **2**:300
on due process, **2**:367–372
due process clause, **3**:408; **5**:79, 117
due process clauses
   property protection, **2**:211
on education, **2**:408, 409
on elections, **4**:339
on equal protection, **2**:458–465
Equal Rights Amendment, **2**:338; **6**:136–137
establishment clause, **5**:114–116
on evidence, **3**:14–15
on executive power, **3**:19–25
federalism and, **3**:59–66
on freedom of speech and press, **5**:332–338
free speech, **3**:409
general welfare clause, **3**:113–115
influence on constitutionalization in France, **2**:120
influence on Philippine Constitution, **4**:319
insurrections clause, **5**:260
international law and, **3**:292–293
interpretation, **2**:160–167
on involuntary servitude, **3**:479
on judicial power, **3**:406–408
on jury trials, **3**:441–442, 442–443
on legal representation, **4**:51
on legislative power, **4**:97, 98, 99
on martial law, **4**:180
on the military, **6**:88
on Native Americans, **4**:206–207, 208
on naturalization, **3**:206
natural law and, **4**:217–220
new textualism and, **5**:363
original intent, **3**:166
on privacy, **4**:386–391
on property, **4**:480–482, 488
rights enumerated in, **2**:15
   enforcement of, **2**:20
right to a jury trial, **4**:440
on right to bear arms, **1**:216–222
on search and seizure, **5**:203–208
on separation of powers, **5**:215–221

signing of, **2**:*148*
on slavery, **2**:340; **3**:450; **5**:258, 260, 264
on state sovereignty, **5**:352–353
strict construction, **3**:59
supremacy clause, **2**:258, 259; **5**:408–413, 410–413
on taxation, **5**:440
on treason, **4**:335
on war power, **6**:87–91
women's rights in, **2**:338–339; **6**:134–136
Constitution of the United States, amendments to,
   2:156–160. *See also* Bill of Rights (U.S.)
1st Amendment, establishment clause, **4**:342, 388
3rd Amendment, **4**:386
4th Amendment (*See* search and seizure:
   United States)
5th Amendment, **4**:386, 388, 482, 484, 488
   (*See* takings clause)
6th Amendment, **3**:443–444; **4**:453
7th Amendment, **3**:443, 444
9th Amendment, **4**:388, 389
10th Amendment, **2**:258
11th Amendment, **2**:157, 259
   ratification of, **6**:40
12th Amendment, **2**:157
13th Amendment, **2**:157, 299; **6**:43, 52
14th Amendment, **2**:1, 157–158, 259, 260; **4**:340, 342,
   389, 390, 442, 445, 447, 451, 482
   citizenship for black men, **6**:44
   citizenship for native-born, **6**:52
   and jury trials, **3**:443
   Native Americans under, **6**:50
   as precedent, **3**:165–166
   privileges or immunities clause, **6**:52
   religion clauses, **5**:117
   sex discrimination, **6**:57
   slavery, **6**:43
   takings clause and, **5**:423, 424
15th Amendment, **4**:339, 342; **6**:43, 44, *44*, 52
   and jury trials, **3**:443
16th Amendment, **2**:159; **5**:443
17th Amendment, **2**:159
18th Amendment (*See* Prohibition)
19th Amendment, **2**:*158*, 159; **4**:339
20th Amendment, **2**:159
21st Amendment, **2**:159
22nd Amendment, **2**:159
23rd Amendment, **2**:159
24th Amendment, **2**:159
25th Amendment, **2**:159
26th Amendment, **2**:159

27th Amendment, **2:**156
amendment process, **2:**152, 156–157
Bill of Rights
ratification of, **6:**40
states and, **6:**38
time limit on ratification, **2:**156
Constitution of the U.S.S.R., **5:**176
Constitution of Tunisia, **4:**298
constitutions and constitutional law in Islamic law, **2:**36–37; **3:**317
overview and Arab countries, **2:134–137**
Africa, **2:137–138**
Bangladesh, **2:141–143**
Iran, **2:138–140**
Malaysia, **2:140–141**; **3:**337
Pakistan, **2:141–143**
constitutions of Chile, **1:**397–398
Constitutions of Clarendon (1164), **1:**467; **4:**315
on ecclesiastical benefices, **2:**389
constitutions of Colombia, **2:**62–62
Constitutions of Melfi, **4:**91
Constitutio Omnem (Justinian)
on jurists, **1:**332
Constitutio Omnen
on legal studies, **2:**392
Constitutive Act of the African Union, **1:**107
consuetudo, **2:167–168**
Consular Courts (Fiji), **3:**82
Consulate of the Sea
maritime law in, **1:**36
Consultatio veteris cuiusdam iurisconsulti, **5:**151
Consumer Cable Communications Law (U.S., 1993), **2:**178
consumer credit
in United Kingdom, **2:**169
in United States, **2:**176
Consumer Credit Act (U.K., 1974), **2:**169
Consumer Disputes Redressal Mechanism (India), **2:**174
Consumer Education and Research Centre (Ahmedabad, India), **2:**174
consumer groups in India, **2:**174
Consumer Guidance Society of India, **2:**174
consumer law reports (India), **2:**174
consumer movement (United States), **2:**177
Consumer Product Safety Commission, **1:**29
creation of, **5:**82
consumer protection, **2:168–178**
Austria, **1:**247
definition, **2:**169, 174–175
English common law, **2:168–169**
Hindu law, **2:***173*, **173–174**
lease law and, **4:**58
medieval and post-medieval Roman law, **2:169–173**
in sale of goods, **5:**192
United States law, **2:174–178**; **4:**445
Consumer Protection Act (India, 1986, 1993, 2002), **2:**173, 174; **5:**7
Consumer Protection Act (U.K., 1987), **2:**169
Consumer Unity and Trust Society (India), **2:**174
Conte, Antoine Le, **3:**192
contempt of court
equitable remedies and, **2:**472
Continental Congress (U.S., 1776)
and Articles of Confederation, **2:**148
on copyright law, **3:**266
court function of, **2:**256
international law and, **3:**291
on Native Americans, **4:**207
Contingent Remainders (Fearne), **2:**441
continuity of coherence
Wolff, Christian von, on, **6:**112
Contius, Antonius. *See* Le Conte, Antoine
contraceptives
natural law on, **4:**219
United States, **6:**140–142
due process and, **2:**370–371
Contract Act (U.K., 1872), **4:**273
Contract as Promise: A Theory of Contractual Obligation (Fried), **2:**210
Contract Clause, **2:**207
private agreement protection, **4:**490
property rights and, **4:**488
state laws and the, **4:**489, 492
Contract Law (Germany, 1957), **4:**395
Contract Law (People's Republic of China, 1999), **1:**446
Contract Law in America: A Social and Economic Case Study (Friedman), **2:**209; **4:**33
Contractors and Workmens Liens Act (New Zealand, 1892), **4:**229
contracts, **2:179–210**. *See also* business law
admiralty law, **1:**38
agency and, **1:**109, 114
ancient Greek law, **2:***179*, **179–181**
on arbitration, **1:**212
in Athens litigation, **4:**114
evidence on, **3:**2

in maritime law, **4:**148
   papyri on, **1:**147
ancient Near Eastern law, **1:**173–174
ancient Roman law, **2:181–191,** *188*; **5:**143, 144
   legal reasoning on, **4:**80–81
antitrust law and, **1:**188–189
assignment in, **1:**228
Austria, **1:**246
bailment, **1:**249
bills of exchange and, **1:**291–293
breach of, **1:**305–310
Byzantine law, **2:191–192**
children in, **3:**44
China
   land, **4:**6–7
   loan, **4:**116–117
   in sale of land, **5:**186, 188
Chinese law, **2:192–194**
   deposit, **2:**331
Code of Gortyn on, **3:**123
in colonial United States, **2:**14
contracts and unilateral acts in Islamic law
   on fungible things, **3:**107–108
delay and, **2:**319–320
donation as, **2:**357–358
   Islamic law, **2:**359
duress in, **2:**373–374, 375
Egypt, **2:***413*
   juristic papyrology on, **2:**418, 419, 420
employment and labor law
   medieval and post-medieval Roman law, **2:**428–431
England
   actions in, **2:**437
   law merchant on, **4:**37–38
   Mansfield, Lord, on, **4:**143
   women in, **3:**34; **6:**124
English common law, **2:194–197,** *195*
   contract as abstract legal category, **2:**198
   contracts in favor of third parties, **2:198–199**
   employment and labor, **2:**425–428
   error and mistake in, **2:**473–474
   formal contracts, **2:**195–196, 198
   fraud in, **3:**101–102
   informal contracts, **2:**196, 198
   land leases, **4:**10–13
   obligations and, **4:**242–243
   in sale, **5:**189–190
European Union, **2:**496

France
   Du Moulin, Charles, on, **2:**372, 373
guarantee in, **3:**129
guilds in, **3:**131
in Islamic banking and finance, **1:**262–265
in Islamic commercial exchange, **2:**73–74
Islamic law, **2:199–202; 3:**324
   agricultural, **1:**116–118
   Arab countries, **1:**205
   deposit, **2:**332
   distinction between commercial contracts and others, **3:**329
   duress in, **2:**375
   insurance and, **3:**255
   lease and tenancy, **4:**55–56
   loans, **4:**118–119
   marriage as, **3:**329; **4:**164–167
   nullity, **2:**74
   object of commercial contract, **2:**79
   obligations and, **4:**244
   option in, **4:**261–262
   ownership *(milk)* and, **4:**272
   salam (delivery with prepayment), **2:202–203**
legal realism on, **4:**76
marriage as, **3:**40
medieval and post-medieval Roman law
   agency in, **1:**110
   error and mistake in, **2:**475–476
   on fraud, **3:**104
   lease and tenancy, **4:**56–58
   on sale of goods, **5:**192
   of succession, **5:**393
   women, **3:**42
Native American law, **4:**207
natural law on, **4:**215, 216–217
negotiable instruments, **4:**222–223
rescission of, **1:**308–309
Roman law
   Labeo, Marcus Antistius, on, **3:**475–476
   Sabinus, Masurius, on, **5:**180
   slaves in, **5:**249
South and Central America
   slaves in, **5:**254
Sri Lanka, **5:**339
United States, **2:204–210**
   arbitration in, **1:**130
   discrimination in, **2:**340
   due process and, **2:**369–370, 371
   federalism and, **3:**61

freedom of, labor laws and, **6:**136–137
indentured labor, **3:**477–478
slaves in, **5:**262
standardization, **2:**76
yellow dog, **3:**480
in Welsh and Irish laws, **1:**377
Contracts (Rights of Third Parties) Act (U.K., 1999), **2:**198–199
Contracts Clause, **2:210–212**
on corporate charters, **1:**321
on federalism, **3:**59
legislative power and, **4:**97
Contracts of Employment Act (U.K., 1963)
notice periods in, **2:**427
Contraloria General de la Republica (Chile), **1:**398
Contrat social (Rousseau), **5:**418
Contra Vitam Monasticam ad Bernardum Mattium Epistola (Alciati), **1:**119
Controlled Substances Act (U.S., 1970), **3:**65
on medicinal marijuana, **1:**127
contumelia (insult)
Labeo, Marcus Antistius, on, **3:**475
Conventicle Act (England), **1:**468
Convention for the Protection of Human Rights and Fundamental Freedoms (1953)
conflicts with statute laws, **4:**89
Convention Governing the Specific Aspects of Refugee Problems in Africa (1969), **1:**107
Convention of Peking (Beijing) (1898), **1:**450
Convention on the Civil Aspects of International Child Abduction (1980), **2:**114
Convention on the Elimination of All Forms of Discrimination against Women
Maldives acceptance of, **4:**140
Convention on the Law Applicable on Surname and Forename (1980), **2:**114
Convention on the Recognition and Enforcement of Foreign Arbitral Awards (New York Convention)
Arab countries in, **2:**74
conversion actions
in bailment, **1:**249
England
equity and, **2:**470
conveyancing, **2:212–216**
England
deeds in, **4:**7–10
entails, **2:**446–448
in sale, **5:**189–190
strict settlements, **5:**364–368

Conveyancing and Law of Property Act (U.K., 1881), **2:**215; **6:**14
convict burials (China), **1:**405–406
convict labor
United States, **5:**256
Cook, Walter Wheeler
on law and society, **4:**31
in legal realism, **4:**74, 75
Cooley, Thomas M.
on right to bear arms, **1:**219
as teacher, **1:**13, 14
Cooper, John Gilbert, **4:***248*
Co-operative Republic of Guyana. *See* Guyana
Coote on Mortgages, **4:**189
copyhold land, **2:**214–215; **6:**103
copyright
Cambodia, **3:**264
England, **3:**265–266
in English common law, **2:216–218**
first French law, **3:**259
Germany, **3:**260
Indonesia, **3:**263
Malaysia, **3:**262, 263
in Malay states, **3:**261
Philippins, **3:**262
in Spain, **3:**260
Thailand, **3:**262, 264
United States, **3:**265–268
Copyright Office, **3:***266*
Copyright, Designs and Patents Act (U.K., 1988), **2:**217
Copyright Act (Great Britain, 1709), **2:**217–218
Copyright Act (Philippines, 1879), **3:**261
Copyright Act (U.K., 1814), **2:**218
Copyright Act (U.K., 1842), **2:**216, 217
Copyright Act (U.K., 1911), **2:**217, 218
Copyright Act (U.S., 1976), **3:**267–268
Copyright Act of 1709. *See* Statute of Anne (Great Britain, 1709)
Copyright Term Extension Act (U.S., 1998), **3:**268
Coquille, Guy, **3:**191
on civil law, **3:**99
on conflict of laws, **2:**112
Coras, Jean, **3:**192
humanist instruction by, **2:**359
Corbin, Arthur, **2:**209
on contracts, **1:**16
Corcoran, Thomas, **5:**92
Cormenin, Louis de, **1:**22
Cornell, Tim J., **5:**138

Cornwallis, Charles
  on Indian courts, **1**:312
  on Indian criminal law, **2**:282
Coronation Charter (England, 1100), **4**:135
corporal punishment
  Africa
    after independence, **1**:101
    German colonies, **1**:84
  ancient Athens
    free status and, **5**:356
  Chinese law
    Shen Chia-Pen (Shen Jiaben) on, **5**:237
  Islamic law
    Europe, **2**:483
  Mongolia, **4**:184
  Suriname, **5**:414
corporate charters, **4**:119–120
corporate law
  on bankruptcy, **1**:268–269
  China
    extraterritoriality in, **3**:92
  close corporation, **1**:326
  early history of, **1**:320–321
  Islamic law
    ownership *(milk)* and, **4**:272
  municipal, **4**:119–123
  natural law on, **4**:215
  public *vs.* private corporations, **4**:120
  United States, **1**:321–327; **6**:46, 48–49
    agency in, **1**:112
    federalism and, **3**:62
    national, **1**:326–327
    twentieth century, **6**:60–61
corporate personality, **2**:87
  not recognized in Islamic law, **1**:357
corporation, commercial
  definition, **2**:87
  in the Middle Ages, **2**:93–94
corporation, early, **2**:87–88
Corporation Act (England), **1**:468, 469
corporations
  De portibus maris (Hale) on, **1**:321
Corpus inscriptionum Latinarum, **5**:160
Corpus iuris, **3**:457
  Azo on, **1**:248
  Bartolus of Saxoferrato in, **1**:281
  feudal law and, **3**:78
  influence on Western law, **3**:454
  Mommsen, Theodor edition of, **5**:160
  rediscovery of in Bologna, **1**:282

Corpus Iuris (Justinian), **3**:189, 190, 191
Corpus Iuris Canonici, **2**:47, **218–225**, *220*, *221*.
    See also canon law
  on bishops, **1**:296
  civil law and scientific treatment of, **2**:5
  council resolutions in, **1**:470
  on decretals, **2**:317, 319
  ecclesiastical courts in, **2**:385–386
  England, **2**:388
  in Italy, **3**:356
  in legal education, **2**:399
  Nomocanon of the Fourteen Titles compared to, **1**:347
  resolutions of papal councils in, **1**:471
Corpus Iuris Civilis, **4**:380
  Accursius, Franciscus, on, **1**:19
  on assignment, **1**:227
  Baldus de Ubaldis, Petrus, on, **1**:250
  Basilica on, **1**:282
  civil law and scientific treatment of, **2**:5
  on crime, **2**:271
  Doneau, Hugues, on, **2**:360
  on evidence, **3**:7
  Faber, Antonius, on, **3**:27
  and immorality, **3**:203–204
  influence of, **5**:155, 469–470
  jurists and, **3**:437
  on kings, **2**:251
  Noordt, Gerard, on, **4**:236
  on obligations, **4**:245
  on offices of the state, **5**:14
  overview of, **5**:154
  rediscovery of, **3**:355
  Scholastic method and, **2**:6
  study of, **4**:276
  translations of, **5**:162
Corpus Iuris Fridericianum, **4**:434
Corpus Iuris Hibernici (Binchy), **3**:306
Corpus Juris Fridericiani (Germany, 1748), **4**:380
Corpus Juris Fridericianum (1782), **5**:1
Corpus Juris Fridericianum (1783)
  on insolvency, **3**:249
Correctores Romani (1566), **2**:224
corruption in Chinese law, **2:225–227**
  wrongful judgment, **6**:152–153
Cortés, Hernando
  Nahua cooperation with, **4**:*208*
Corwin, Edward S.
  on allocation of powers in foreign afffairs, **3**:292
  classical legal theory and, **2**:23, 26
  on executive power, **3**:22

Corwin Amendment (U.S., 1861), **2:**157
Cory, Donald Webster
   on sexual and gender variation, **3:**111
Costa Rica
   Civil Code, **1:**384
   slavery abolished in, **5:**254
Costs of Accidents, The (Calabresi), **4:**25
Costumen van Antwerpen, **4:**150
Cottrell, Leonard "Slats," **4:**32
Coughlin, Charles E.
   on wealth redistribution, **5:**445
Council for Fair Business Practices (Bombay, India), **2:**174
Council for Legal Education (U.K.), **2:**395
Council for Public Interest Law, **4:**52–53
Council of Ankyra (314), **1:**471
Council of Charles, **1:**470
Council of Constantinople (691–692). *See* church councils: Quinisextum Council
Council of Europe
   on conflict of laws, **2:**114
   law standardization, **2:**115
Council of Five Hundred (Athens), **1:**233; **2:**124, 229, 231, 232–233
   advocates and, **1:**54
   creation of, **5:**275
   eligibility to serve on, **1:**141
Council of Five Thousand (Athens), **2:**125
Council of Four Hundred (Athens), **2:**125
Council of Indonesian Ulama, **3:**335
Council of Islamic Ideology (Pakistan), **2:**141–142
Council of Islamic Religion (Malaysia), **2:**140
Council of Law Reporting (U.K.), **4:**45
Council of Legal Education (Great Britain), **2:**395; **3:**243
Council of Oxford (1222)
   on defamation, **2:**389
Council of Serdica (342)
   on bishops and archbishops, **1:**294; **4:**351
Council of Six Hundred (Athens)
   prevention of counterfeit weights and measures, **2:**69
Council of the Areopagus (Athens), **2:**232–233; **4:**399
   Aeschylus on, **4:**111
Council of the Indies, **1:**215–216
Council of Trent. *See under* ecumenical councils
Council on Legal Education for Professional Responsibility, **2:**406
councils, ecumenical. *See* ecumenical councils

councils of the Catholic Church. *See under* church councils and conciliar canons
counterfeiting
   Chinese law, **2:**314
Countil of Trent
   Scholasticism in, **4:**15
Countrey Justice, The (Dalton), **2:**284
Country Bankers' Act (U.K., 1826), **1:**272
Country Justice (Dalton), **4:**61
Courland, Duchy of, **1:**255
Courland Statutes (1617), **1:**255
Court for Crown Cases Reserved, **3:**312
Court for Crown Cases Reserved (England and Ireland)
   appeal in, **1:**199
Court for Divorce and Matrimonial Causes (Britain), **3:**33; **6:**121
   jurisdiction of, **2:**347
   Restitution of Conjugal Rights and, **3:**34
Court for Matrimonial Causes (Ireland), **3:**312
Court for the Marches administration (China, Qing), **1:**435
Court Leete, et Court Baron, Le (Kitchin), **4:**324
Court Martial Appeal Court of Canada, **1:**340
Court of Admiralty (England)
   on agency, **1:**109
   common law and, **2:**436
   Doctors' Commons in, **2:**353–355
   jurisdiction of, **1:**36–37
   law merchant in, **4:**36
   litigation on insurance contracts, **3:**252
   reform of, **2:**437
Court of Admiralty (Ireland), **3:**310, 312
Court of Appeal (England)
   Denning, Alfred Thompson, in, **2:**330
   precedent in, **5:**277–278
Court of Appeal in Chancery (Ireland), **3:**312
Court of Appeals in Cases of Capture (U.S.), **1:**38
Court of Chancery (Ireland)
   in Ireland, **3:**308
Court of Common Pleas in Fifteenth Century England, The (Hastings), **2:**86
Court of Criminal Appeal (U.K.)
   retrials and, **1:**199
Court of Delegates (England)
   ecclesiastical law and, **2:**388
Court of Ecclesiastical Causes (United Kingdom), **2:**385

Court of Errors
　Bermuda, **1:**289
Court of Exchequer Chamber
　appeal in, **1:**197
　on environmental law, **2:**449
Court of General Assize
　Bermuda, **1:**289
Court of High Commission (England)
　enforcement of the Reformation settlement, **1:**468
Court of Industrial Relations (Kansas, U.S.), **3:**428
Court of Judicature and Revisions (China), **1:**428
Court of Judicial Review (China), **1:**423, 432
Court of King's Bench
　on land leases, **4:**11
　Star Chamber subsumed by, **5:**347
Court of Prerogative and Faculties (Irish ecclesiastical court), **3:**310
Court of Record (England)
　for divorce, **2:**347
Court of Requests (Britain)
　Wales, **6:**101
Court of the Arches (London)
　in legal education, **2:**354
Court of the Lord High Admiral (England), **1:**37
Court of the Master of the Rolls (Ireland), **3:**312
Court of Wards and Liveries
　on land leases, **4:**13
Court of Wards and Liveries (England), **1:**393
court-ordered arbitration, **1:**128
Court Organization Law (Japan, 1890), **3:**377, 380
courts, **2:228–262,** *231, 234, 240, 244, 253, 255*. *See also* administration, public law of; judges; judiciary; Supreme Courts
　Afghanistan, **1:**60, 61
　ancient Athens, **2:228–234**
　　in arbitration, **1:**211–214
　　rise in use of, **1:**232
　　Solon on, **5:**275
　ancient Near East, **1:**169
　ancient Rome
　　cognitio, **2:51–54**
　　formula in, **3:**93–97
　　magistrates in, **4:**131–132
　　Senate as, **5:**212
　Australia, **1:**239–240, 243
　Brazil, **5:**294
　British Commonwealth, **1:**312
　Byzantium, **2:239–240**
　Canada, **1:**340–341
　Denmark, **2:***327,* 328
　dual systems
　　in colonial Islamic Africa, **2:**42
　　in Dutch Indonesia, **3:**225
　　in independent African countries, **2:**43–44
　East Africa, **2:**383
　Egypt, **2:**421–422
　Ethiopia, **2:**480
　European Union, **2:**486, 492, 493
　Fiji, **3:**82
　France, **3:**100
　India, **2:**147
　　British India, **3:**215
　　fundamental rights and, **3:**105
　Indonesia, **3:**337
　　under British, **3:**226
　　dual system under Dutch, **3:**225, 226
　Iran under Safavids, **3:**302–303
　Ireland, **3:**310, 312
　　modeled after England, **3:**307
　Irish Free State, **3:**313
　Islamic law and, **2:**432–433
　Italy, **3:**356–357
　law merchant, **4:**39
　Macau, **1:**448
　Maghrib and al-Andalus, **4:**129
　Malaysia, **2:**140; **4:**139
　Melanesia, **4:**174
　Netherlands East Indies, **3:**335
　New Zealand, **4:**230
　19th and 20th century Europe, **2:**252–253
　Ottoman Empire, **2:**397–398; **4:**264–265, 266, 267
　　market courts, **2:**35
　　mazalim courts, **2:**35
　　reorganization of, **4:**267–268
　Pakistan
　　constitutional court, **2:**136
　　Shariat Federal Court, **2:**142
　People's Republic of China, **1:**442, 445, 446
　Roman
　　ancient, **2:234–237**
　　medieval and post-medieval, **2:251–255**
　　Roman Empire, **2:**53–54
　　Roman Republic and the Empire, **2:237–239**
　Saudi Arabia, **1:**208–209

Scotland, **5:**197, 199–200
Singapore, **5:**241–242
South and Central America
 colonial, **5:**285
 slaves in, **5:**254
transnational, **3:**279
United Kingdom, **2:**82
courts, Chinese
 overview, **2:240–241**
 Censorate, **1:**423, 432; **2:241–242**
 Central Court, **2:242–243**
 Chinese Republic, **1:**440
 Emperor, **2:243–244**
 local courts, **2:244–247**
 Ministry of Justice (Board of Punishments)
  review in, **1:**197
 review in, **1:195–198**
courts, English, **2:249–251**, 435–436. *See also* Chancery, Court of; Common Pleas, Court of; King's Bench; Star Chamber
 Anglo-Saxon, **1:**180–182
 assizes, **1:**229–231
 divorce, **2:**355
 ecclesiastical, **2:**387–388
 equity, **2:**468–472
 historiography, **2:**434
 industrial, **2:**427
 legal professions in, **5:**272–273
 outlawry and, **4:**270–271
 piepowder, **4:**36
 probate, **2:**355
 reforms of, **4:**42–43
 seigneurial, **3:**73, 74
 substantive law by, **2:**437
courts, medieval and post-medieval Roman law
 manor courts and villeinage, **6:**81
courts, United States
 colonial
  inheritance and, **3:**235
 Court of Appeals for the Federal Circuit (CAFC), **3:**270
 enforcement of rights, **2:**17–19
  and resistance to, **2:**20–21
  types of rights, **2:**21–22
  unpredictable consequences of, **2:**21
 federal, **2:255–262**
  on commerce clause, **2:**68
  enforcement of civil rights, **2:**18–19
  on patents, **3:**270

state courts
 and development of common law, **2:**84
Supreme Court, **6:**45–46
 activist nature of, **6:**58–59
 anti-Progressive decisions, **2:**162
 circuit riding, **2:**257
 commerce power and, **2:**64–68
 constitutional creation of, **3:**425
 constitutional establishment of, **2:**256
 and constitutional interpretation, **2:**164–166
 controversial social policy and politics, **2:**260–261
 on copyright, **3:**267, 268
 within court system, **3:**423–424
 enforcement of rights, **2:**19
 on federalism, **3:**59–66
 on federal judicial power, **3:**427
 on immigration, **3:**206, 208–209
 on international law, **3:**293
 judicial review, **3:**429
 jurisdiction of, **2:**256–257; **3:**425
 patent appeals, **3:**270
 power of, **4:**365
 power over state courts, **2:**258
 on trademark law, **3:**271–272
 use of precedents, **3:**165–166
Courts Act (U.K., 1971), **3:**453
 on assizes, **1:**229, 230
courts-martial, **4:**177, 179–180
Courts of Indian Offenses, **4:**209
Courts of the Staple, **4:**36, 37
Cousin, Victor, **1:**303
Coustumes pour les Asseurances d'Amsterdam (1598), **3:**258
Coutts & Co. (England), **1:**271
Coutume de Beauvaisis (Beaumanoir), **3:**78
Coutume de Bretagne (d'Argentré), **2:**112
Coutume de Paris followed in New France, **1:**337
Coutumes du pays et comté de Nivernais (Coquille), **2:**112
Covarrubias y Leyva, Diego de, **2:**7; **5:**325
 on guilt, **3:**134
 in Scholasticism, **4:**15, 16
covenant. *See* writ of covenant
Covenant Code (Jewish law), **1:**168; **3:**389
Cover, Robert, **4:**69
coverture
 in colonial United States, **2:**13–14
 English law, **6:**121–122
 United States, **6:**134

Cowell, John, **2:**393; **5:**157
Cowper, Henry, **4:**45
Cox, Archibald, **3:**487; **4:**363
Craanen, The odoor
   on Cartesianism, **4:**236
   influence on Noodt, Gerard, **4:**235
Craig, Thomas, **2:**441; **5:**200
Crandall, Reuben, **6:**51
Cranmer, Thomas, **1:**366
Cranworth, Lord, **4:**7
Crawford, M. H., **6:**19, 20, 21
Crawford, T. Hamilton, **1:**297
credit. *See also* creditors
   consumer
      United Kingdom, **2:**169
      United States, **2:**176
   and loans in Islamic law, **4:**118–119
credit in medieval and post-medieval Roman law, **2:262–264**
   agency and, **1:**111
   negotiable instruments in, **4:**223
   pawnbrokers in, **1:**274
   in sale of goods, **5:**192
Crédit Mobilier (France), **1:**276
creditors
   in bankruptcy, **1:**266, 267, 268
   goldsmiths as, **1:**275
   principle of equal treatment of, **3:**248
Creel, Herrlee G., **1:**408
Crenshaw, Kimberlé
   Bell, Derrick, and, **2:**301
   on gender, **2:**301
   on intersectionality, **3:**69
   on race, **2:**300, 301
Crime and Disorder Act (U.K., 1998), **1:**395
   on treason, **6:**1
crimes
   gu (intentional), **3:**275
   insanity and, **3:**246–247
   against life and body, **2:264–265**
      attempt in, **1:**237–238
      Native peoples in Canada and, **1:**344
      reporting in Chinese law, **1:**423
      U.S. immigration and, **3:**207
Criminal Appeal Act (U.K., 1907), **1:**199
Criminal Cases Review Commission (U.K.), **1:**199
Criminal Code (Austria, 1787), **5:**43
Criminal Code (Bavaria, 1813), **5:**34
Criminal Code (Canada, 1892), **1:**341

Criminal Code (China, 1928), **1:**440
Criminal Code (Colombia, 1837), **2:**63
Criminal Code (Colombia, 2001), **2:**63
Criminal Code (Cuba, 1979), **1:**370
Criminal Code (Germany, 1871), **4:**395
Criminal Code (Iran, 1982, 9183, 1991, 1996), **2:**279
Criminal Code (Japan, 1880), **3:**374, 376–377
Criminal Code (People's Republic of China, 1979), **1:**445
Criminal Code (Philippines, 1870), **4:**318
Criminal Code (Switzerland, 1937–1942), **5:**34
Criminal Code (Tuscany, 1786), **5:**43
Criminal Code Act (Bermuda, 1907), **1:**289
Criminal Code Act (Papua New Guinea, 1974), **4:**281
Criminal Code of Procedure, **4:**282
Criminal Justice Act (U.K., 2003), **1:**199
Criminal Justice Administration Act (U.K., 1914), **1:**297
Criminal Justice in Cleveland (Pound and Frankfurter), **3:**428
criminal law, **2:265–295**, *266, 274, 278, 282, 292*
   Africa, **1:**100–101
   ancient Greece, **1:**139–140
      Athens, **1:**234; **2:265–268**
      inscriptions on, **1:**154
   ancient Near East, **1:**175–176
   ancient Rome, **3:**436
      delict, **2:**321
      magistrates in, **4:**131–132
      procedure, **4:**435–440
      Roman Empire, **2:271–275**
         criminal courts, **2:**237–239
      Roman Republic, **2:268–271**
         criminal courts, **2:**237–239
   Arab countries, **1:**206–207
   attempt in, **1:**236–238
   Austria, **1:**247
   Bangladesh, **1:**258, 260
   Bentham, Jeremy, on, **1:**287
   Brazil, **1:**302
   Byzantium, **2:**239, **275–276**
   Canada, **1:**341
   Chinese law
      appeal in, **1:**193–195
      mutual concealment and, **4:**197–199
      procedure, **4:**417–418
      Shen Chia-Pen on, **5:**237–238
      status and, **5:**358

England, **2**:439–440
  reform movements, **4**:41–42
English common law, **2:276–277; 3**:438
  on appeals, **1**:199
  assault, **1**:226–227
  assizes in, **1**:230–231
  duress and, **2**:374–375
  evidence in, **3**:4
  on fraud, **3**:100–101
  on outlawry, **4**:270–271
  procedure, **4**:423–427
  women in, **6**:120
English legal treatises on, **2**:443
Ethiopia, **2**:480
Germany, **3**:118
  under National Socialism, **4**:204
  National Socialist Law, **3**:110
guilt in, **3**:133, 134
Guyana, **3**:137
India, **2:280–284**
  Islamic, **5**:307–308
  secularism and, **5**:208–209
Islamic law
  crime and punishment, **2:277–280**
  duress in, **2**:375
legal education in, **2**:400
libel and slander in, **4**:105–106
medieval and post-medieval Roman
  on fraud, **3**:102–103
natural law in, **4**:216
ordeals in, **4**:262–263
Ottoman Empire, **4**:266, 267–268
Pakistan, **4**:274–275
protection of villeins in, **6**:81
Scholasticism on, **4**:16
Seychelles, **5**:235
South Africa, **5**:279
South and Central America, **5**:287
Southeast Asia, **5**:318
Spain, **5**:326
in Sui and Tang codes, **1**:422
Suriname, **5**:296
Thailand, **5**:315
United States, colonial era, **2:284–287,** 287–289
United States law, **2:287–295**
  indentured labor in, **3**:478
  individual rights in, **3**:62
  justice and, **3**:449
  procedure, **4**:447–454
  on search and seizure, **5**:203–208
  twentieth century, **6**:59–60
Criminal Law Act (U.K., 1967), **3**:470
Criminal Law and Procedure (Ireland) Act (U.K., 1887), **3**:312
Criminal Law Commission (U.K.), **4**:41–42
Criminal Law Compensation Act (Papua New Guinea, 1991), **4**:281
Criminal Law Consolidation Act (U.K., 1861), **1**:365
Criminal Law Order (1877, Germany), **3**:10
Criminal Procedure Act (South Africa, 1917), **5**:280
Criminal Procedure Code (Bhutan), **1**:290
Criminal Procedure Code (India, 1973), **2**:365
Criminal Procedure Code (Indonesia, 1981), **3**:227
Criminal Procedure Code (Pakistan, 1898), **4**:275
Criminal Procedure Code (Philippines, 1882), **4**:318
Criminal-procedure law (People's Republic of China, 1979), **1**:445
critical legal studies, **2:295–299**
  critical race theory and, **2**:298, 300
  on evidence, **3**:16
  law and society in, **4**:34
  legal process and, **4**:68, 69
  as opposition to Richard Posner, **4**:26
  United States, **2**:407
critical race theory, **2:299–303**
  critical legal studies and, **2**:298, 300
  feminist theory and, **3**:71
Critiques (Kant), **1**:8
Crito (Plato), **1**:148, 149; **4**:321
Croatia
  in European Union, **2**:493
  Islamic law in, **1**:253
Cromwell, Oliver, **2**:130, 131, *131*
Cromwell, Richard, **2**:131
Cromwell, Thomas, **1**:386; **2**:129; **5**:272
cross-dressing, United States laws on, **3**:110
Crouse, Mary Ann, **3**:458
Crow Dog, **4**:207, 209
Crown Lands Ordinance (New Zealand, 1849), **4**:228
Crown Porceedings Act (U.K., 1948), **2**:132
Crozier, Blanche, **6**:142
Cruelty to Women (Deterrent Punishment) Ordinance (Bangladesh, 1983), **1**:259; **4**:300

Ctesiphon, **3:**125
Cuba, **1:**370
  slavery, **5:**253, 255
Cuffy, slave revolt by, **3:**137
cui in vita action, **6:**122
Cujas, Jacques (Cujacius), **2:**7, **303–304**; **3:**192
  Doneau, Hugues, and, **2:**359
  humanism and, **2:**360
  on possession, **4:**361
  on Roman law, **3:**98–99
  at University of Bourges, **2:**400; **5:**467
Cullavagga, **5:**303
culpa (fault)
  in breach of contract, **1:**307, 309
  in contrahendo, **1:**309
  legal reasoning on, **4:**81
cultural feminism, **3:**68
Cumberbatch, Claire, **5:***267*
Cumberland Gap road, **3:**113
Cum pro munere (Gregory XIII), **2:**224
Cum Universi (papal bull), **5:**197
Curaçao, **1:**369
Curia Filípica (Hevia Bolaños), **1:**215–216; **5:**291
currency exchange
  in law merchant, **4:**39
  negotiable instruments in, **4:**222–223
Currie, Brainerd, **2:**113, 118, 119
cursing in Chinese law, **2:304–305**
Curso de Derecho Mercantil (Tejedor), **1:**216
curtesy in colonial United States, **3:**235
curule aediles, **4:**132
  on slave sales, **5:**248
Custody of Children Act (U.K., 1839, 1891), **1:**394; **3:**35
custom, **2:305–309.** See also *consuetudo;*
    folk law
  Africa, **1:**63, 91–92
    after independence, **1:**99
  ancient Greece
    as source of law, **1:**150–151
    written law compared with, **1:**156
  Austria, **1:**246
  Brazil
    Portuguese law in, **5:**293
  China
    of ethnic groups, **2:**481–482
  Chinese law
    Shen Chia-Pen (Shen Jiaben) on, **5:**237
    common law *vs.*, **1:**7

England, **2:**435–436
English common law, **2:305–307**
  as source of law, **5:**276
  in feudal law, **3:**78
Fiji, **3:**82
Guatemala, **3:**129–131
Hindu law
  sadācāra in, **5:**181–182
India
  in Sikh law, **5:**240
Islamic law
  adat, **1:**20–21
Laos, **4:**13–14
legal anthropology on, **4:**59–60
legal process on, **4:**66
lex compared with, **4:**101
Maghrib and al-Andalus, **4:**129
Malaysia, **4:**137–138
Maori, **4:**145–147
Melanesia, **4:**174
Mongolia, **4:**185
Native American, **4:**207
Nepal, **4:**224–225
Ottoman Empire, **4:**266–267
Roman law
  in legal reasoning, **4:**80
  on sale of land, **5:**192, 193
  as source of Chinese law, **1:462–464**
South Asia, **5:**307
South Asian law, **2:307–309**
  Naga law, **4:**201
Southeast Asia, **5:**313
Spain, **5:**324
Sri Lanka, **5:**340, 341
of tribes in Yemen, **6:**155
villeinage and, **6:**81
customary dues
  England, **2:**389
Cyfnerth, **6:**98
Cylon, **2:**366; **5:**111
cy-près doctrine, **1:**392; **5:**407–408
Cyprian of Carthage, **1:**294; **4:**351
Cyprus, **2:**492
Cyrene Edicts (23 B.C.E.), **3:**210
Cyril, **2:**392
Czechoslovakia, constitution of 1918–1920, **2:**122
Czech Republic
  accession into European Union, **2:**492
  constitution, **2:**122
Czolgosz, Leon, **4:**335

D

Daʿāʾim al-islam (al-Qadi al-Nuʿman), **4:**127; **5:**60
    Yemen, **6:**155
Dabb ʿan madhhab Malik ibn Anas, al- (Ibn Abi Zaid), **5:**61
Dacey, Norman, **3:**239
Daendels, Herman Willem, **3:**226
Dafydd ap Gruffydd, **6:**2
Da Gama, Vasco, **1:**79
Daggett, David, **2:**402
dahef. *See* dowry in Hindu law
Dahomey, **1:**68, 75, 88
Dáil courts, **3:**313
dain. *See* obligations: Islamic law
Dai Sheng, **4:**157–158
Dalai Lama, **5:**305–306, 466
Dalrymple, James, Viscount of Stair, **3:**252
    comparative law, **2:**98
    on law of Scotland, **5:**200
Dalsh, Amr, **1:***207*
Dalton, Clare, **2:**298
Dalton, Michael, **2:**284
    justice of the peace manual by, **4:**61
damage (*ḍarar*), **2:**311
damage (*ḍarar*)
    breach of contract and, **1:**309
damage to property
    Byzantine law
        delict, **2:**325–326
    Chinese law, **2:**311–313
        deposit in, **2:**331
    Roman law
        delict, **2:**320–321
Damaghani, Abu al-Hasan al-, **3:**344
D'Amato, Anthony, **4:**364
Da Ming huidian (Collected Statutes of the Great Ming), **1:**454
Da Ming ling (Great Ming Commandment, 1368), **1:**430, 454
Da Ming lü (Great Ming Code), **1:**430, 454, 458
Da Ming lü fuli jianshhi (Commentary to the great Ming code with regulations) (Wang qiao and Wang Kentang), **1:**433, 458
Da Ming lü jijie fuli jianshi (Ming Code with Notes and Explanations) (Wang Kentang), **1:**436
Da Ming Lüling (Ming Statutes and Commands) (China, 1368), **1:**430
Dammartin, Stephen, **3:**74
Damweiniau, **6:**98
Danaeus, Lambertus, **1:**349

Danby, Earl of (Thomas Osborne). *See* Osborne, Thomas
D'Andrea, Francesco, **3:**126
Dane, Nathan, **2:**205
Dan Fodio, Usman, **1:**68; **2:**41, 42
Dangerous Drugs Act (India, 1930), **2:**173
Danilevskii, Nikolai Ia, **5:**178
Danish Code (1683), **2:**327, 328
Danquah, J. B., **1:**65
Da Qing huidian, **2:**248, 249
Da Qing huidian shili, **1:**455; **2:**331
Da Qing huidian zeli/shili, **1:**455
Da Qing lü ji jie fu li (Shen Zhiqi), **4:**117
Da Qing lü jizhu (Shen Zhiqi), **1:**436
Da Qing Lüli. *See* Qing code (China)
dār al-Ḥarb
    in Islamic division of the world, **3:**280
    justification for war based on, **6:**86
dār al-Islām
    in Islamic division of the world, **3:**280
    justification for war based on, **6:**86
dār al-silm, **3:**280
dār al-Ṣulḥ, **6:**86
Dareius, **4:**149
Dareste, R. B., **1:**163
Darius I (Persia), **2:**414
Darling, Charles John, **6:**3
darrein presentment, **4:**317–318
Dart, Justin, **2:***335*
Dasch, George, **4:**179
Datini, Francesco di Marco, **1:**273
Daʾud ʿAli al-Isbahani, **2:**313–314
Daʾud B. ʿAli al-Isbahani, **3:**353
Daughters of Bilitis, **3:**111
Daumier, Honoré, **1:***56*
David, René, **2:**480
David I (Scotland), **5:**197
    Anglo-French lords under, **3:**76
    feudal law under, **5:**202
David II (Scotland), **5:**197
Davies, John, **3:**310
Davis, Kenneth Culp
    on administrative law, **1:**16
    on social sciences, **5:**267
Dawes Act. *See* General Allotment Act (U.S., 1887)
Dawson, John, **3:**437
Dawudi, Abu Jaʿfar al-, **5:**239–240
Day, William Rufus, **2:**65

Dāyabhāga (Jimutavāhana), **3:**156, 158
   Bangladesh, **1:**257
   on succession, **5:**394–395, 398–400
   translation by Colebrooke, **2:**57
Dayanand Saraswati, **3:**159
Da Yuan shengzheng guochao dianzhang, **5:**188
dBang po, Mi pham, **1:**289
Dead Sea Scrolls, **3:**389, 390, 391
De alimentis libri tres (Coler), **3:**46
De aliumentis (Bartolus of Saxoferrato), **1:**281
De apostato capiendo writ (England), **2:**390
De Asse (Budé), **1:**316; **3:**191
De Assecurationibus Tractatus (Stracca), **5:**364
Death on the High Seas Act (U.S., 1920), **1:**40
death penalty. *See* capital punishment
De bannitis (Bartolus of Saxoferrato), **1:**280
Debs, Eugene V., **4:**335, 337
   on antitrust, **1:**189
   conviction of, **6:**48
debt
   African indigenous laws on, **1:**73
   agency and, **1:**109
   ancient Greece
      on arbitration, **1:**212
      Code of Gortyn on, **3:**123
      enslavement for, **3:**30
      Hellenistic, **1:**158, 160
      Solon on, **5:**274–275
   ancient Near Eastern law, **1:**171, 174
   assignment in, **1:**228
   bankruptcy and, **1:**266–270
   bills of exchange in settling, **1:**291–293
   breach of contract and, **1:**305
   Chinese law
      gambling and, **3:**109
      loans, **4:**116–118
   delay and, **2:**319–320
   England
      equity and, **2:**469
      evidence in, **3:**3–4
      final process in, **3:**87–89
      law merchant on, **4:**35–38
      Magna Carta on, **4:**134
      obligations and, **4:**243
      of women, **6:**124
   guarantee and, **3:**128–129
   guilds on, **3:**131
   Islamic law
      on assignment (*ḥawālah*), **1:**229
      banking and finance, **1:**262
      loans and, **4:**118–119
      obligations and, **4:**244
      wills, **6:**106
   medieval and post-medieval Roman law
      on obligations, **4:**245
   New Zealand, **4:**229
   Roman law
      legis actiones in, **4:**83–84
      slaves as security for, **5:**248
      written account of, **2:**186
   United States
      colonial period, **2:**14
      indentured labor, **3:**477–478
      lawyers in collection of, **4:**48
   wills and, **6:**103
debt-adjustment, **2:**77
Debtors Act (U.K., 1869)
   on final process, **3:**89
   imprisonment and, **4:**422
   on mesne process, **4:**175
deceit, 2:314–316
Decent Home, A (President's Committee on Urban Housing), **3:**182
Deciani, Tiberio, **3:**134
Decius (Roman emperor), **3:**212
Decius, Philippus, **2:**111
De civitate Dei (Augustine), **3:**9
Déclaration des droits de l'homme et du citoyen (France, 1789), **2:**120; **4:**475; **5:**438
Declaration of Independence (U.S., 1776), **6:**37–38, 42
   on citizen rights, **3:**448
   critical period after, **1:**223–224
   critical race theory and, **2:**300
   on due process, **2:**368
   on equality, **2:**459
   natural law in, **4:**217–218, 219
   on privacy, **4:**386
Declaration of Indulgence (England, 1672), **1:**468
Declaration of the Rights of Man and Citizen (France, 1789). *See Déclaration des droits de l'homme et du citoyen* (France, 1789)
Declarations of Local Customary Laws (Tanganyika, 1963), **1:**101–102
Declaratory Act (or Dependency of Ireland on Great Britain Act) (Great Britain, 1719), **3:**307, 309
Decline and Fall of the Roman Empire (Gibbon), **5:**159
decodification, **2:**49
   consumer protection and, **2:**171
De collisione legum (Hert), **2:**109

decolonization
    in Africa, **1**:92–94
    British Commonwealth, **1**:313–315
De conflictu legum (Huber), **2**:117
De copia verborum (Oldendorp), **4**:261
De cosibus perplexis (Leibniz), **4**:100
Decree Law 25 (Egypt, 1929), **4**:295
Decree Law 44 (Egypt, 1979), **4**:295
decrees
    ancient Greece, **4**:85
    graphē paranomōn on, **3**:123
    Hellenistic period in Egypt, **2**:414, 415
    as legislation, **4**:86
Decretales (Gregory IX). *See Liber Extra*
Decretales Extravagantes, **2**:318
decretals and decretal collections, **2**:316–319
    in legal education, **2**:399
    as legislation, **4**:91
    Scotland, **5**:197
Decretos de Nueva Planta (Spain, 1707–1716), **5**:325
Decretum Gratiani, **2**:47, *317*; **4**:333, 353
    overview, **2**:219–221, 223
    academic instruction and, **2**:6
    on bishops and archbishops, **1**:294
    on compurgation, **2**:104
    on decretals, **2**:317, 318
    in Law of Jutland, **2**:327
    Roman-canon and, **4**:433, 437
    Scotland and, **5**:197
    Teutonicus, Johannes, on, **2**:317
    on witches, **6**:108
De cura rei publicae et sorte principantis (Philip of Leiden), **4**:225
De Donis (England)
    on dower, **2**:362
    on entails, **2**:446
De Donis Conditionalibus (England)
    on entail, **4**:88
    on fee tail, **2**:478
    women in, **6**:122
"De duobus fratribus" (Petrus de Ulbaldis), **2**:92
deed-of-settlement company, **2**:88–89
defamation
    civil, **4**:106
    England
        ecclesiastical law on, **2**:389
        jurisdiction of church courts, **1**:467
        libel and slander as, **4**:105
        Star Chamber in, **5**:346
    guilds on, **3**:131

Defense Lawyer, The (Daumier), **1**:56
Defense of Marriage Act (U.S., 1996), **3**:55
defenses
    duress, **2**:373–376
    formulae in Roman law, **3**:96–97
    guilt and intent in, **3**:134
    against libel and slander, **4**:106
    against negligence, **4**:220–221
De fideicommissis et signater ex prohibita alienatione resultantibus (Petra), **3**:80
De fideicommissis praesertim universalibus tractatus (Pellegrini), **3**:80–81
De Finibus Levatis (England, 1299), **2**:213
definition of law, **1**:373; **4**:18, 19, 20, 21
    Islamic, **1**:206–207
    public international, **3**:276
Definitions (Plato), **3**:123
De fluminibus (Bartolus of Saxoferrato), **1**:281
defraud, bankruptcy and, **1**:266
Deganawida, **1**:345
De Guelphis et Ghibellinis (Bartolus of Saxoferrato), **1**:280
De heretico comburendo statute (England, 1401), **2**:390
De hispanorum primogeniorum origine ac natura libri quatuor (Molina), **3**:81
Dei delitti e delle pene (On Crimes and Punishments) (Beccaria), **1**:285; **4**:439
    on torture, **3**:9
Dei difetti della giurisprudenza (Muratori), **3**:358
De Indis (Vitoria), **4**:16–17
De insigniis et armis (On Signs and Arms) (Bartolus of Saxoferrato), **1**:280
Deioces (Medes king), **4**:399
De iure belli (Vitoria), **4**:16–17
De iure belli ac pacis libri tres (Grotius), **3**:127, 283; **5**:470
    influence on German law, **3**:118
    on natural law, **4**:215, 216–217
De iure belli libri tres (Gentili), **2**:393; **3**:283
De iure civili (Massurius Sabinus), **3**:434
De iure civili diffi cultate ac docendi methodo (Pace), **3**:191
De iure civitatis (Huber), **4**:226
De iure et aequitate forensis disputatio (Oldendorp), **4**:261
De iure et officiis bellicis et disciplina militari libri tres (Ayala), **3**:282
De iure fisci et populi (Callistratus), **5**:13
De iure naturae et gentium libri octo (von Pufendorf), **3**:276, 283; **5**:21

on absolutism, **1:**8
English translations of, **2:**440–441
influence on German law, **3:**118
on natural law, **4:**215
on negligence, **4:**221
on paternal authority, **3:**45
De Iure Praedae (Grotius), **3:**127
De Laudibus Legum Angliae (Fortescue), **4:**214
delay, **2:**319–320
in breach of contract, **1:**308
Del disordine e de' rimedi delle monete nello Stato di Milano (Beccaria), **1:**285
De legationibus libri tres (Gentili), **3:**282–283
De legibus (Cicero), **5:**120, 121
De legibus abrogatis (Groenewegen van der Made), **4:**226
De legibus et consuetudinibus Angliae (Bracton), **3:**395
De legibus et consuetudinibus regni Anglie (Glanvill). *See Glanvill*
De l'esprit des lois (Montesquieu), **2:**98
on absolutism, **1:**9
on separation of powers, **5:**215
Delgado, Richard, **2:**301; **4:**365
Delhi Sultanate (India), **5:**307
criminal law, **2:**280–281
Delian League, **4:**85–86
De libellis famosis (England, 1606), **1:**379
de liberate probanda writ, **6:**82
delict, **2:**320–326
ancient Near Eastern law, **1:**175–176
Byzantine law, **2:**324–326
Gortyn, **1:**142
Roman law, **2:**320–324
Della pubblica felicità (Muratori), **3:**358
Dello stile legale (De Luca), **2:**326
Delrio, Martin, **6:**109
De Luca, Giovanni Battista, **2:**326; **3:**356
Demaratus, **1:**150–151
De Martino, Francesco, **5:**161
De Mercatura Decisiones et Tractatus (Stracca), **5:**364
De Mercatura seu Mercatore Tractatus (Stracca), **5:**364
De methodo ac ratione studendi in iure (Gribaldi Mofa), **3:**190
Demetrius Chomatenos, **1:**348
on canon law, **1:**330
Demetrius of Phalerum, **3:**31

democracy
Africa
precolonial, **1:**70–71
South Africa, **1:**106
ancient Greek law, **2:**125
Athens, **1:**140–141
Demosthenes on, **5:**331
Baltic states, **1:**255, 256
Europe
European Communities, **2:**488
Islamic law and, **2:**483
expansion through amendments to U.S. Constitution, **2:**152
freedom of speech in, **5:**330
natural law and, **3:**118; **4:**216
proportional representation in, **1:**204
Switzerland, **5:**418, 419
Democratic Kampuchea, **1:**335
Demonax, **2:**30
demonstratio (declaration), **3:**96
Demosthenes, **2:**71
on adoption, **1:**41, 42
on adultery, **1:**51
on advocates, **1:**53, 55
on arbitration, **1:**212, 213
on democracy, **5:**331
forensic speeches by, **1:**149
on freedom of speech, **5:**329
on *graphē paranomōn*, **1:**141; **3:**124, 125
on heliastic oath, **4:**241
on *hybris*, **2:**267
on impiety, **5:**112
on judges, **3:**403
as logographer, **4:**123
on logographers, **4:**125
on maritime law, **4:**148, 149
on public actions for crimes against individuals, **2:**265–266
on public debtors, **3:**402
on punishment, **5:**22
Russian translation of the works of, **5:**177
on slavery, **5:**244–245
on Solon, **3:**30
suit against guardians, **4:**400–401
on theft, **5:**456, 457
on torture of slaves, **5:**479
on treason, **4:**382
on types of women, **6:**113
on witnesses, **6:**110, 111

Demotic Casebook, **2:**414–415
   translated into Greek, **2:**416
Demotic Chronicle (Egypt), **2:**414
De muneribus (On Civil Obligations)
   (Charisius), **5:**151
De Natis Ultra Mare, **4:**205
Deng Xi, **1:**404
Deng Xiaoping, **1:**446
Denman, George, **2:**86
Denman, Thomas, **1:**288
Denmark, **2:**326–329. *See also* Scandinavia
   accession into European Union, **2:**490
   currency of, **2:**491
   maritime law of Karl V, **4:**150
   Protestant church in, **1:**351
   state church in, **1:**350
   tontines, **3:**258
Denmark Vesey conspiracy, **5:**261
Denning, Alfred Thompson, **2:329–330,** 442
   on error and mistake, **2:**474
   on judicial review procedure, **5:**17
   on precedent, **4:**379; **5:**278
De officio hominis et civis libri duo (von Pufendorf), **5:**21, 171
De officio praefecti praetorio (Charisius), **5:**151
De Oratore (Cicero), **5:**158
De origine iuris germanici (Conrings), **2:**8
Department for Environment, Food, and Rural Affairs (Defra, U.K.), **2:**452
Department of the Environment (U.K.), **2:**452
Dependency of Ireland on Great Britain Act. *See* Declaratory Act (1719)
De philologia (Budé), **1:**316
De portibus maris (Hale), **1:**321
deposit, **2:330–332**
   ancient Greek law, **2:**180
   ancient Roman law, **2:**184, 187, 189
      of fungibel things, **2:**186
   Chinese law, **2:330–332**
   Islamic law, **2:**332
deposit banks, medieval, **1:**273–274, 274–275
depositum (deposit), **2:**184
De Praesumptionibus (Alciati), **1:**118
depravity, Chinese law on, **4:**259
De Prerogative Regis (England, 1324), **3:**244
De privilegiis piae causae (Tiraquellus), **5:**467
De Proxenetis et proxeneticis Tractatus (Stracca), **5:**364
De Quinque Pedum Praescriptione (Alciati), **1:**118
de rationalibus divisis, writ of, **3:**307

Der Beruf Unserer Zeit für Gesetzgebung und Rechtswissenschaft (Savigny), **5:**195
Derecho Criminal (Tejedor), **1:**216
Derecho Indiano, **1:**215–216; **5:**290–291
Derecho Público Eclesiástico (Sársfield), **1:**216
De regimine civitatis (Bartolus of Saxoferrato), **1:**280
De repressaliis (On Reprisals) (Bartolus of Saxoferrato), **1:**280
De re publica (Cicero), **4:**94
De re uxoria (Barbaros), **5:**467
derivative action, **2:**91
Dermot MacMurrough (king), **3:**307
Dernburg, Heinrich, **4:**277; **5:**2
   commentary on the pandects, **2:**10
Derrett, J. Duncan, **5:**108
Derrida, Jacques, **2:**297; **4:**364
Descartes, René, **3:**193
   definition of law by, **4:**21
   natural law based on, **2:**400
   on systematization, **5:**421
Description of England (Harrison), **5:**251
De sine assensu capituli writ (England), **2:**390
Desnitskii, S. E., **5:**171–172, 177
De specialibus legibus (Philo), **3:**390
De statu imperii Germanici (Pufendorf), **5:**20
De suspectis tutoribus (Zeiller), **6:**162
De Synodo Diocesiana (Lambertini), **1:**357
Detainee Treatment Act (U.S., 2005), **4:**181
De testibus (Bartolus of Saxoferrato), **1:**281
De testibus (Charisius), **5:**151
detinue
   bailment and, **1:**249, 250
   evidence and, **3:**3–4
De transitu Hellenismi ad Christianismum (Budé), **1:**316
De tyrannia (On Tyranny) (Bartolus of Saxoferrato), **1:**280
Deuteronomic Code, **1:**168; **3:**389
Devanampiyatissa (Sri Lanka), **5:**303
Devanter, Willis Van, **2:**27
De verborum significatione (Alciati), **1:**118; **3:**189
Devereux, Robert, earl of Essex, **2:**54
De vi laica removenda writ (England), **2:**390
De Viris Religiosis. *See* Statute of Mortmain (1279)
devises, **1:**392
devises of land, **6:**103
Devlin, Patrick (Lord Devlin), **3:**440
Dewing, Arthur Stone, **1:**326
Dhahabi, al-, **3:**467
Dhaka University (Bangladesh), **2:**398
dhamma. See dharma
dhammasat, **5:**315–316

dhammasat (Burma), **1:**318
dhammathats, **5:**303, 304, 320
    in Sri Lanka, **5:**339
Dhammavilasa, **1:**318
dharma, **2:**332–334; **5:**63
    Aśoka on, **1:**225–226
    ātmanustuṣhṭi and, **1:**236
    dharmaśāstra jurisprudence and, **3:**215
    environmental law and, **2:**452
    Hindu law, **3:**146–148, 151–157; **5:**36, 63
    Jaina law, **3:**363, 364
    mīmāṃsā and, **4:**182–183
    Nepal law, **4:**224
    sadācāra and, **5:**181
    Sikh law on, **5:**240
    śruti and, **5:**344–345
dharmaśāstras, **3:**150, 153–158; **4:**224; **6:**83
    on abortion, **1:**4
    Arthaśāstra in, **1:**223
    in Burma, **5:**320
    on custom, **2:**307
    as guidebook *vs.* legal code, **2:**333
    Manusmriti in, **4:**144–145
    nītiśāstra and, **4:**232–233
    smriti in, **5:**264–265
    in Sri Lanka, **5:**339
    study by Kane, **3:**465–466
    on succession, **5:**394
    on women, **6:**131
Dharmashastra (Manu), **2:**363
dharmasūtras, **3:**150–152, 156–158
    on adoption, **1:**49
Dhayl 'ala Tabaqat al-Hanabila (Ibn Rajab), **3:**347
dhimma, ahl al- (protected non-Muslims), **3:**280–281
dhimmīs (non-Muslims), **1:**358; **4:**233, 234
    bequests to, **6:**106
    in jihad, **6:**86
    legal personality of, **4:**64
Diagoras, **5:**112
diagrammata (decrees). *See* decrees
Diallo, Amadou, **2:**302
Dialogi de iuris interpretibus (Gentili), **3:**191
Dialogus de fundamentis legum Anglie et de conscientia (St. German). *See Doctor and Student* (St. German)
Dialogus de Scaccario, **1:**385; **3:**17
diamartyria, **1:**42; **6:**110
Diamond, Arthur S., **5:**108, 109
dian (antichresis), **4:**6–7
Diary of Coercion (Harrington), **3:**312
Dias, Paolo, **1:**79
Dicaeologica (Althusius), **5:**421
Dicey, Albert Venn, **5:**15–16, 17–18
    on academic law, **2:**443
    on English constitutional law, **2:**133
    on environmental law, **2:**451
    influence on Beale, Joseph, **2:**117
    at Oxford, **2:**395
    on sources of law, **5:**277
Dickens, Charles, **2:**250
Dictata ad ius hodiernum (Lessons on the law of today) (Voorda), **4:**226
dictatorships
    Venezuela, **6:**74
Dictatus Papae (Gregory VII), **4:**352–353
Dictum of Kenilworth (1266)
    on treason, **6:**1
Diderot, Denis, **5:**172
Dies geniales: Semestria in genialumdierum libri VI (Alexandro), **5:**467
Diet of Roncaglia (1158), **3:**314
Diet of Worms, **4:**91
Dietze, H. H., **4:**204
Difesa della lingua italiana (De Luca), **2:**326
difference theory, **3:**67
Difficult Man (Menander), **5:**65
Digambara All-India Jaina Mahāsabhā, **3:**364
Digest (Justianian). *See* Pandects (Pandectae)
Digest (Papinian), **3:**95, 97
Digesta (Julian), **3:**430, 431–432
    on custom as a source of law, **2:**167
Digesta (Justinian), **3:**251
Digesta (Scaevola), **3:**436
Digest of Hindu Law, on Contracts and Successions (Colebrooke), **2:**57; **3:**158
Digest of the Criminal Law (Stephen), **5:**484
    on blackmail, **1:**296
Digest of the Law of Bills of Exchange, Promissory Notes, and Cheques (Chalmers), **1:**293
Digestorum (Azo), **1:**248
Digests (Justianian), **2:**5
    use in medieval teaching of law, **2:**6
Digestum novum
    in legal education, **2:**399, 400
    medieval law instruction and, **2:**6
Digestum vetus
    in legal education, **2:**399
    medieval law instruction and, **2:**6

Diggers, **1:**380
Digital Millennium Copyright Act (U.S., 1998), **3:**268, 274
dihairetic method of systematization, **5:**420, 421
dikasterion, **3:**121
dikastic oath, **4:**241
Dike (journal), **1:**166
dikê (suit), **1:**235
dilapidations, law of, **2:**389
Dilemma of Democracy, The (Hailsham), **2:**133
Dillon, John F.
    on municipal corporations, **4:**120, 121
    as teacher, **1:**13, 14
Dillon's rule, **4:**120
Dilthey, P. H., **5:**171, 172
Dinarchus
    forensic speeches by, **1:**149
    as logographer, **1:**232; **4:**123
Ding procedure (Frankish and Saxon procedure), **2:**5
Dio Chrysostom, **5:**244
Diocletian (Roman emperor), **2:**32
    codification under, **3:**436, 456
    edicts by, **2:***419*
    executive structure of the Empire under, **5:**12, 13
    jurists under, **3:**434
    legislation under, **3:**212, 213
    paternal power, **4:**306
    property law, **4:**465
    provincial structure, **2:**238–239
    religious law, **5:**123
    women, **6:**118
Diodorus, **3:**124
Diodorus Siculus, **5:**113
    on history of Rome, **4:**130
Dionysius, **4:**456
Dionysius Exiguus
    on canon law, **1:**327
    on decretals, **2:**318
Dionysius Gothofredus. *See* Godefroy, Denis
Dionysius of Halicarnassus, **5:**141
    historical information provided by, **5:**158
    on history of Rome, **4:**130
Dionysodorus, **3:**403
Diósdi, György, **2:**187
Dipavamsa, **5:**303
diplomacy
    agency and, **1:**109
    ancient Near Eastern law, **1:**176–177
    nītiśāstra on, **4:**232–233
    in precolonial Africa, **1:**74
    Senate and, in ancient Rome, **5:**212
    separation of powers and, **5:**217–218
    state sovereignty and, **5:**352
direct effect of European Union law, **2:**487
Direction or Preparative to the Study of the Law (Fulbeck), **2:**394
Director, Aaron
    on antitrust, **1:**190
    in Chicago school of economics, **4:**23–24
Directorate of Education (China), **1:**423
Direito das coisas (Pereira), **1:**302
Direito de família (Pereira), **1:**302
Direito público brasileiro (Bueno), **1:**302
Diritto greco antico (Biscardi), **1:**164
Dirksen, Heinrich Eduard, **5:**159
disability, **2:334–337**
    2000 election disfranchisement based on, **2:**344
    Chinese law, **5:**47–49
    educational equal opportunity and, **2:**410–411
    feminist legal theory on, **3:**67
    U.S. insurance programs, **6:**96
Disability Insurance (U.S.), **6:**91. *See also* welfare
Discourses of the States (*Guoyu*), **1:**404
discovery in employment discrimination, **3:**489
discrimination, **2:337–344**
    Aboriginal law and, **1:**3
    disability and, **2:**335, 336–337
    elderlaw and, **2:**423–424
    England
        of nonconformist dissenters, **1:**468, 469
        of Roman Catholics, **1:**468, 469
    equal protection and, **2:**458–462
    feminist legal theory on, **3:**68–69
    gay, lesbian, bisexual, and transgender theory and, **3:**110–112
    hate speech and, **5:**337
    India
        child custody, **3:**51
        dowry, **2:**363–366
        fundamental rights and, **3:**105
        secularism and, **5:**208–209
    Mauritius, **4:**172
    against non-Muslims in Islamic law, **4:**233–235
    United States
        anti-Semitism, **2:**406
        in apportionment and reapportionment, **1:**201–204
        commerce and, **3:**62
        in education, **2:**409–412, *410*
        in employment, **6:**137–138

federalism and, **3:**61, 65
immigration policy, **3:**208
in labor unions, **3:**481–482
in legal education, **2:**404, 405, 406; **4:**49
in legal profession, **4:**53–54
in legal services, **4:**51–53
suffrage, **2:**20, 340–341
Title VII on, **3:**484
disease, U.S. immigration and, **3:**207
disparate impact test, **3:**483
for sex discrimination, **3:**484
Dispunctiones (Alciati), **1:**118
Disputationes (Ulpian), **6:**24
on conflict of laws, **2:**109–110
Disputationes metaphysicae (Suárez), **4:**15, 17
dispute resolution. *See also* alternative dispute resolution; arbitration
  Africa
    after independence, **1:**97
    precolonial, **1:**65, 66, 70
  ancient Greece, **1:**136, 137–138; **4:**399
  in Japan, **3:**370, 383–384
dissent *(ikhtilāf)*, **2:**345; **3:**316
Dissertations on Early Law and Custom (Maine), **4:**137
anthropological perspective of, **1:**185
Dissertation sur les raisons d'établir ou d'abroger les lois (Friedrich II), **3:**9
Dissolution of Muslim Marriages Act (India, 1939)
  in Bangladesh, **1:**259
  in Bangladesh and Pakistan, **4:**299, 300
  on women, **3:**49; **5:**308
distraint, **3:**74
Distribution Enactment (Malaysia, 1929), **5:**319
distributive justice, **3:**448–449
Dithyrambs (Bacchylides), **2:**413
diversity clause, **1:**324
divorce, **2:**345–353. *See also* marriage
  Afghanistan, **1:**61–62
  Africa
    East Africa, **2:**383
    Egypt, Islamic law and, **2:**421–422
    precolonial, **1:**66
  ancient Greek law, **2:**346–347
    Code of Gortyn, **3:**120–121, 122
    Hellenistic, **1:**159
  ancient Near Eastern law, **1:**172
  ancient Roman law, **6:**117–118
  Australia, **1:**242
  Austria, **1:**247
  Aztec law, **5:**288

Bangladesh, **1:**259
Byzantine law, **4:**310
China, **4:**158–159
England
  canon law on, **3:**32; **4:**162
  common law, **2:**347–349; **4:**161, 163
  ecclesiastical law on, **2:**388–389
  property division in, **3:**33
  reforms of, **4:**43
  women in, **6:**121, 124
Hindu law, **2:**352–353
  marumakkathayam in, **4:**171
  women in, **6:**131, 132
Hong Kong, **1:**449
India, **3:**49–50, 149, 398
  dowry in, **2:**365
  secularism in, **5:**208–209
Indonesia, **3:**336
Islamic law, **4:**167–168; **5:**127–129, 428 (*See khul'* (divorce))
  consensual divorce (*See khul'*)
  damage in, **2:**311
  Europe, **2:**484
  maintenance in, **3:**50–51
  on non-Muslim, **4:**234
  ṭalāq, **2:**44; **6:**126
  waiting period, **5:**20
  women in, **6:**125–127, 129
Jewish law, **3:**392, 393, 398
Maldives, **5:**310
medieval and post-medieval Roman law, **3:**42–43, 43–44
migratory, **3:**53
no-fault, **3:**53–54
Parsi law, **4:**286, 287
South and Central America, **5:**286
South Asia, United Kingdom and, **5:**311
South Asian law and United Kingdom, **5:**312
Southeast Asia, **5:**319
  Hindu law, **5:**322
Sri Lanka, **5:**341
Suriname, **5:**414
United States, **3:**52–54; **6:**45
  no-fault, **6:**59
  women in, **6:**134, 136, 142
Welsh law, **6:**99
women and
  ancient Greece, **6:**113–114
  Ottoman Empire, **6:**128
  United States, **6:**134, 136, 142

Divorce Act (Bangladesh, 1869), **1:**259
Divorce Act (India, 1869), **3:**223
Divorce Reform Act (Brit., 1969), **6:**121
    grounds for divorce in, **4:**163
    on irretrievable breakdown, **2:**348–349
Dixon, Owen, **1:**242, 243
diya (blood money), **2:**100; **3:**39
    Afghanistan, **1:**62
    Africa, **1:**72
    enforcement, **2:**432
Diyat Ordinance (Pakistan, 1990), **2:**142
djabr. *See* compensation: in Islamic law
Djibouti, **2:**137
Docemo (Lagos), **1:**86
Doctor and Student (St. German)
    on bailment, **1:**249
    on conscience, **2:**468
    on natural law, **4:**214
    theory of judicial lawmaking, **4:**377–378
Doctors' Commons, **2:**353–355
Doctrina Placitandi (Euer), **4:**324
Dodd, Samuel, **1:**323
Dodderidge, John
    on logic, **4:**61
    Roman law used by, **5:**157
Doe, Charles, **2:**176
Dohm, Christian Wilhelm, **3:**396
doing what ought not to be done, **2:**355–356
Dole, Robert, **2:***163*
Dollfuss, Engelbert, **2:**122
dolus (fraud), **3:**103–104
    Labeo, Marcus Antistius, on, **3:**475
Domat, Jean, **2:**356–357
    English translations of, **2:**440–441
    influence on Blackstone, William, **1:**298
    on Justinian organization, **2:**400
    law of reason and, **2:**8
    on lease and tenancy contracts, **4:**57
    on Roman law, **3:**99
    on systematization, **5:**421
Domesday Book (1086), **1:**178, 385
    compiling of, **3:**437
    on land distribution, **3:**73
    on mortgage, **4:**188
    on rape, **5:**68
    reason for, **5:**425
domestic violence
    Native American punishments for, **4:**207
    United States
        equitable remedies for, **2:**473
        evidence of, **3:**15
Domestic Violence and Matrimonial Proceedings Act (U.K., 1976), **3:**35
Domini 400 Social Index, **1:**262
Dominica, **1:**369
Dominican Republic, **1:**370
Domitius Ulpianus. *See* Ulpian
Domna, Julia, **2:**392
donation (gift), **2:**357–358
    England, **2:**362, 478
    France, **3:**99
    Islamic law, **2:**201, **358–359**
    in marriage, **3:**42–43
    Roman law, **2:**187, 189–190
Donatists, **5:**123
Doneau, Hughes (Hugo Donellus), **2:**7, 303, *359*, **359–361**; **3:**192
    on servitude in real estate, **5:**224
    on systematization, **5:**421
    on torts, **5:**470
    at University of Bourges, **2:**400
    at University of Leiden, **4:**226
Donellus enucleatus (Doneau), **2:**360
Dong Kang, **1:**439
Dong Zhongshu, **1:**363; **3:**275
Donoughmore Constitution (Sri Lanka, 1931), **5:**342
Doppelurkunde (duplication of written documents), **2:**415
Dorna, Bernardus, **1:**248
Dorotheus
    Digesta translated by, **1:**328
    Justinian's *Institutes* and, **3:**252; **6:**8
dos (dowry). *See* dowry
Dos escuelas del derecho, Las (Avellaneda), **1:**216
Dottore volgare, Il (De Luca), **2:**326
double-voucher recovery, **2:**448
doubtful cases, **2:361**
Douglas, Sylvester, **4:**45
Douglas, William O., **2:**3
    on bankruptcy, **1:**269
    on commerce clause, **2:**67
    employer liability analysis, **6:**77
    on labor arbitration, **3:**487
    on law and society, **4:**31
    in legal realism, **1:**15; **4:**74, 75
    on marital privacy, **4:**388
    on natural law, **4:**219
    in New Deal, **4:**78

on regulations, **5:**81
securities, **5:**92
on right to bear arms, **1:**220–221
doulos, Code of Gortyn on, **3:**121
Dove, Richard, **2:**219
Dover, K., **4:**495
Dover, K. J., **4:**124
Dove's Necklace, The (Ibn Hazm), **3:**197
Dowager Empress Cixi (China), **3:**187
dower
   English common law, **2:**361–363
     entails and, **2:**447–448
   Hindu law, **2:**363–366
   United States, **3:**236
     colonial period, **2:**13; **3:**235
Dower Act (U.K., 1833), **6:**123
Dow Jones Islamic Index (JDII), **1:**262
dowry
   Africa
     precolonial, **1:**72–73
   ancient Greek law, **4:**152–153; **6:**114
     Athens, **1:**234
     in divorce, **2:**346, 347
     Hellenistic, **1:**159
     Plutarch on, **4:**154–155
     Sparta, **5:**329
   ancient Near Eastern law, **1:**172, 173
   ancient Roman law, **6:**117
   Bangladesh, **4:**300
   Byzantine law, **4:**309, 310
   Chinese law
     adoption to avoid, **1:**46
     in succession, **5:**378
   Egypt, **4:**296
     Hellenistic period, **2:**415
     juristic papyrology on, **2:**420
   England, **4:**161; **6:**122
     dower and, **2:**361–363
     strict settlements and, **5:**365–366
     succession and, **5:**383
   Hindu law, **2:**363–366
     selective abortion to avoid, **1:**5
   India
     selective abortion to avoid, **1:**5
     in succession, **5:**397, 398, 401
   Islamic law
     in consensual divorce, **2:**350, 351
     marital seclusion and, **4:**428
     women in, **6:**125, 127
   medieval and post-medieval Roman law, **3:**42–43, 45–46

   Ottoman Empire
     women in, **6:**128–129
   property and
     English common law, **2:**362–363
     Hindu law, **2:**363–366
     Roman law, **4:**304, 305, 306, 307, 308
Dowry Prohibition Act (Bangladesh, 1980), **1:**259; **4:**300
Dowry Prohibition Act (India, 1961), **2:**364–365
Draco, **1:**231; **2:**366–367
   on adultery, **1:**51, 53
   on family, **3:**30
   on homicide, **1:**154, 155; **2:**232; **3:**169–170; **4:**399–400
   law on homicide, **2:**29–30
   legal code by, **1:**150
   on legal procedure, **3:**401
   on oaths, **2:**228
   on private revenge, **5:**227
   scholarship on, **1:**164
   on sexual crimes, **6:**115
   written law by, **1:**139, 147, 154
Draft of Documents Pertaining to Matters of State in the Song Dynasty, **1:**426
Drakon. *See* Draco
Dramatic Copyright Act (U.K., 1833), **2:**216
Dreros law inscriptions, **1:**154
drinking age, general welfare clause and, **3:**114–115
Droit des gens, ou principes de la loi naturelle, appliqués à la conduite et aux affaires des nations et des souverains, Le (Vattel), **3:**276, 283, 291; **6:**73
"Droit et Prédroit" (Gernet), **1:**186
Droit français on sale of goods, **5:**192
Droit musulman (Chehata), **2:**199
Droit musulman-algérien, **4:**129
Droit public, Le (Domat), **2:**357
Droit public de l'Europe, fondé sur les traités, Le (Bonnot de Mably), **3:**283
Droysen, Johann Gustav, **1:**157
drugs. *See* alcohol and drugs
Drugs and Cosmetics Act (India, 1940), **2:**173
drug trafficking, **1:**127
   Islamic law on, **1:**122
Duaren, Francoid, **5:**467
Duarenus. *See* François le Douaren
Dubai Islamic Bank, **1:**261
Dublin
   charter of, **3:**307
   Four Courts, **3:***308*
Ducrocq, Théophile, **1:**23

due process
　English common law, **2:**367–368
　　equity and, **2:**467
　　in Star Chamber, **5:**346
　India, **3:**107
　United States, **2:367–372**
　　abortion and, **6:**141
　　administrative agencies and, **1:**31
　　balancing test, **4:**483–484
　　criminal proceedings and, **4:**452–453
　　economic rights and, **4:**488
　　federalism and, **3:**61, 63
　　as guarantee of property rights, **4:**490
　　juvenile justice and, **3:**459, 460
　　monopolies and, **1:**322
　　Native American, **4:**213
　　natural law on, **4:**218
　　prior notice of adverse judicial action, **4:**445
　　privacy and, **4:**388
　　regulation and, **5:**79
　　in search and seizure, **5:**205
　　slavery and, **4:**482
　　state constitutions and, **2:**24
　　state law and, **5:**350
　　state power, limites on, **2:**155
　　state regulation and, **2:**259
　　Supreme Court and, **2:**24
　　in War on Terror, **6:**91
　　work rules and, **4:**451
Dufour, Gabriel, **1:**23
Duguit, Léon
　on administrative law, **1:**23
　on public law, **3:**100
Duke Dao, **1:**404
Duke of Norfolk (3rd), **6:**5
Duke Ping, **1:**404
Duli cunyi (Xue Yunsheng), **1:**436; **3:**187
Dulles, John Foster, **3:**293
Du lü suoyan (Lei Menglin), **1:**433
Dumas, Roland, **1:***336*
Du Moulin, Charles, **2:372–373; 3:**191; **5:**467
　on civil law, **3:**99
　on conflict of laws, **2:**111–112
Duncombe, Giles, **3:**5
Dunsaete, **1:**178
Dupin, André Marie Jean Jacques, **4:**367
Duranti, Guilelmus
　Baldus de Ubaldis, Petrus, on, **1:**250
　on legal procedure, **4:**434, 437

duress, **2:373–376**
　English common law, **2:373–375**
　　obligations and, **4:**243
　ikrāh, **2:375**
　medieval and post-medieval Roman law, **2:**376
Durkheim, Émile, **5:**108
　on administrative law, **1:**23
　on profession, **4:**48
Dutch Civil Code, **6:**64
Dutch colonies. *See also* Netherlands East Indies
　Caribbean and, **1:**369
Dutch East India Company (VOC)
　African colonies, **1:**81
　in Ambon, **5:**313
　Chinese law under, **5:**317
　Grotius, Hugo, and, **3:**126–127
　Indonesia, **3:**225
　Mauritius, **4:**171
　Sri Lanka, **5:**340
　Taiwan, **1:**452–453
Dutch Elegant School, **4:**235–236
Dutch law. *See* Netherlands
Dutch Wetboek
　Brazil, **5:**292
　Guyana, **5:**295
Dutch Wetboek
　on children's accountability, **3:**44–45
Duties of Christian Masters, The, **5:**262
Duttabaung, **5:**315
duty *(farḍ)*, **2:376–377**
duty of care
　negligence and, **4:**221–222
　New Zealand, **4:**232
Duty of Clergymen in Relation to the Marriage of Slaves, **5:**262
Duxbury, Neil, **4:**74
Du Yu, **1:**405
Dworkin, Andrea, **3:**67–68
Dworkin, Ronald
　on constitutional interpretation, **2:**164
　critical legal studies, **2:**407
　judicial influence of, **2:**443
　on law and economics, **4:**26
　on legal positivism, **4:**357
　on legal process, **4:**67–68
　on statutory interpretation, **5:**362
Dyer, James
　on assizes, **1:**230
　law reporting by, **4:**44
Dyophysites, **3:**456

E

Early Greek Law (Gagarin), **1:**164, 186
Earned Income Tax Credit (U.S., 1975), **6:**91. *See also* welfare
  cost of, **6:**92, 97
earnest money, English common law on, **5:**189–190
easements, **2:**379–382
  in environmental law, **2:**450
  nuisance and, **4:**240
  servitude in real estate and, **5:**224
East Africa
  courts, **2:**383
  land registration in, **4:**9
  South Asian law in, **2:**382–384
East African Community, **1:**107
Easterbrook, Frank
  in Court of Appeals, **4:**27
  on statutory interpretation, **5:**362
Easter Depot (palace eunuch agency, China), **1:**432
Eastern Caribbean Supreme Court, **1:**369
Easter Rising (Dublin, 1916), **6:**3
East India. *See* Guyana
East India Company, **2:**88; **3:**215
  Burma, **1:**318
  Colebrooke, Henry Thomas, and, **2:**56–57
  courts of, **1:**312
  language of, **3:**400
  Parsi law and, **4:**286
East Pakistan. *See* Bangladesh
East Timor, **2:**384–385; **5:**313. *See also* Southeast Asian law
Ebüssu'ud, codification by, **1:**35
Eccius, Max Ernst, **5:**2
ecclesiastical courts, **2:**385–387
  consistory (Protestant), **1:**349
  contractual jurisdiction, **2:**196
  Denmark, **2:**328
  England, **1:**467; **2:**81
    divorce by, **3:**33
    history of, **2:**250
    inefficiency of, **2:**437
    jurisdiction boundaries of, **2:**436
    on libel and slander, **4:**105
    reforms of, **4:**42
    on spousal duty to live together, **3:**34
    on wills, **6:**102, 103, 104
  Ethiopia, **2:**480
  Gregorian reforms and, **1:**466
  Ireland, **3:**307, 310, 312
  jurisdiction over testament of personalty, **1:**390
  Scotland, **5:**197, 199
ecclesiastical law
  Buddhist, **5:**304
  English common law, **2:**387–391
    Doctors' Commons in, **2:**353–355
Ecclesiastical Licenses Act (England, 1533), **4:**237
Eckhard, Christian Heinrich, **3:**297
Ecloga
  on contract, **2:**192
  on delict, **2:**325
  on legal procedure, **4:**416
  on property, **4:**468
  on succession, **5:**376, 377
Ecloga aucta, **1:**328
  on purpose of law, **1:**330
Ecloga basilicorum, **1:**328, 330
Ecloga legum, **3:**431
Ecloga privata aucta, **1:**328
  on contract, **2:**191
Ecole de l'Exégèse, Dutch jurisprudence and, **4:**226
econometrics, **4:**27
Economic, Social, and Cultural Council (Africa), **1:**107
Economic Analysis of Law (Posner), **4:**26
economic development
  Africa after independence, **1:**100
  environmental law and
    England, **2:**449–450
  Laos, **4:**14
  legal anthropology on, **4:**59–60
  legislative power and, **4:**98
  Scholasticism on, **4:**15–16
  South and Central America, **5:**286
  Trubek, David, on, **4:**34
Economic Growth and Tax Relief Reconciliation Act (2001), **5:**408
economics and law, **4:**23–28. *See also* Chicago school of economics
  on antitrust, **1:**190–191
  law and society influenced by, **4:**32
  legal process and, **4:**68
  South and Central America, **5:**285
  U.S. state regulations, **5:**348
Economics Institute for Law Professors, **4:**26
ECSC Treaty. *See* European Coal and Steel Community
Ecuador, **1:**398
ecumenical councils
  Byzantium, **1:**327
  Council of Basel-Ferrara-Florence-Rome (1431–1445), **1:**470; **2:**224; **4:**353

Council of Chalcedon (451), **1**:327; **3**:456; **4**:351
Council of Constance (1414–1418), **1**:470; **2**:224; **4**:353
Council of Constantinople I (381), **1**:327, 470
Council of Constantinople II (553), **1**:470
Council of Constantinople III (680–681), **1**:470
Council of Constantinople IV (869–870), **1**:470
Council of Ephesus (431), **1**:470
Council of Lyon I (1245), **1**:470
Council of Lyon II (1274), **1**:470
Council of Nicaea I (325), **1**:327, 470
  Canons of the Kings by, **2**:479
  on the metropolitan, **1**:294
Council of Nicaea II (787), **1**:347, 470
Council of Trent (1545–1563), **1**:470; **4**:353
  on bishops, **1**:296
  decrees of, **2**:224
  Du Moulin, Charles, on, **2**:373
  on ecclesiastical courts, **2**:386
  on evidence, **3**:8
  on marriage, **2**:389; **3**:41; **4**:162
  unification of Catholic texts, **2**:224
Council of Vienne (1311–1312), **1**:470; **2**:223
Lateran Council I (1123), **1**:470
Lateran Council II (1139), **1**:470
Lateran Council III (1179), **1**:470; **4**:317
  decretal collections on, **2**:318
  on homosexuality, **5**:230
  papal elections and, **4**:352
  resolutions of, **2**:221
Lateran Council IV (1215), **1**:161, 470; **4**:263, 432
  on charities, **1**:390
  on clerical participation in ordeals, **3**:4
  on consanguinity and affinity, **4**:161–162
  on evidence, **3**:8
  on incest, **5**:230
  on ordeals, **4**:263
  resolutions of, **2**:221
Lateran Council V (1512–1517), **1**:470; **2**:224; **4**:353
Vatican I (1869–1870), **1**:353, 470; **4**:354
Vatican II (1962–1965), **1**:470; **4**:354
  on bishops, **1**:296
  Codex Iuris Canonic (1983) and, **1**:354
  on ecclesiastical courts, **2**:386
Edalji, George, **1**:199
Edgar (Scotland), **5**:197
edict. *See also* praetorian edict
  definition in Roman law, **3**:116
  papal, **2**:316
  Sabinus, Masurius, on, **5**:179

Edict, Praetor's. *See* Praetorian Edict
Edict of Caracalla (212 c.e.), **5**:249
Edict of Rothari (643), **3**:117
edicts in Imperial Rome, **3**:211
Edictum Theodorici
  on provincial administration, **3**:116
Edison, Thomas, **5**:40
Editio Romana (1582), **2**:219, 224
Edmund (England, r. 959–975), **1**:178
Edmund, Earl of Kent, execution of, **6**:2
Edmunds Act (U.S., 1882), **6**:51
Edmunds-Tucker Act (U.S., 1887), **6**:51
education. *See also* legal education
  administrative agencies in, **1**:26
  affirmative action, **2**:344
  Africa, **1**:65
  discrimination in, **2**:337, 340–341
    due process and, **2**:371
  Enlightenment views of, **2**:444
  funding, **4**:122
  guilds in, **3**:132
  India, **3**:219
    fundamental right to, **3**:105, 106, 107
  Islamic in the Philippines, **3**:338
  in Maghrib and al-Andalus, **4**:129
  Native Americans, **4**:209, 211
  Ottoman Empire, **4**:268
  segregation in, **2**:341, 342–343
  Spain, **5**:324–325
  special, **6**:95
  Sri Lanka, **5**:343
  United States
    desegregation, **2**:20
    equal protection in, **2**:463–464
    law, **2:408–412**
  women
    in ancient Greece, **6**:115, 116
    in ancient Rome, **6**:118
Education Amendments (U.S., 1972)
  on sex discrimination, **2**:339
education and training. *See* legal education
Education for All Handicapped Children Act (U.S., 1975), **2**:335
  on parent participation, **6**:95
Edward I (England), **3**:177
  on appeal, **1**:197
  on banking, **1**:270–271
  beginning of parliament and, **2**:128
  conveyancing under, **2**:213
  on Exchequer, **3**:17

feudal law under, **3:**75–76
financing of Scottish campaigns, **1:**385
homosexuality accusation, **5:**230
imprisonment of, **6:**1
legal education under, **2:**436
legislative reforms under, **4:**87–88, 283
Magna Carta reissued by, **4:**133, 135
mortmain and, **4:**191; **5:**369–370
pleading principles under, **4:**324
trade growth under, **4:**35
treason against, **6:**1–2
Wales under, **6:**99–100
Edward II (England), **2:**128; **3:**179
financial extravagance, **1:**385
law reporting under, **4:**44
Magna Carta reissued by, **4:**135
treason under, **6:**2
Edward III (England)
courts under, **2:**250
debt nonpayment by, **1:**273
justices in eyre under, **3:**451
treason under, **6:**2
Edward IV (England)
bills of exchange under, **1:**292
on mortgage, **4:**188
Edward the Confessor
cut farthing issued by, **1:***271*
legal treatises on, **1:**183
records on, **1:**178
Edward VI (England), **1:**468; **2:**129, 130
Edward VII (England), **1:**272
EEC. *See* European Economic Community
EEOC. *See* Equal Employment Opportunity Commission
effects doctrine in antitrust, **3:**288
Effenterre, Henri van, **4:**84
Egerton, Thomas (Baron Ellesmere)
Coke, Edward, and, **2:**55
on equity, **2:**469
Egistus Painter, **5:***243*
Egypt, **2:**412–422. *See also* ancient Near Eastern law; Arab countries, Islamic law in
administrative decrees, **1:**33–34
adoption, **1:**49
banking and finance, **1:**261
civil law, **1:**205–206
codification, **2:**35
conquest by Alexander the Great, **1:**137
constitution, **3:**317
courts, **2:**421–422
Supreme Constitutional Court, **2:**135, 136

divorce
damage, **2:**311
grounds for, **2:**350
women's rights in, **2:**351
dowry, **4:**296
Hellenistic period, **2:**415
juristic papyrology on, **2:**420
Fatimids in, **4:**127
Greek law in, **1:**135–136, 143–144
papyri on, **1:**147–148
Hellenistic period, **2:412–417**
loans, **1:**160
inheritance law, **2:**38
insurance, **2:**60
Islamic law, **2:421–422; 3:**414
mosque and madrasa of Sultan Hassan, **3:***346*
Muhammad Qadri Pasha al-Hanafi in, **4:**195–196
judiciary, **3:**420, 421–423
juristic papyrology, **2:417–421**
lawyers, **4:**47
legal education, **2:**397, 398
legal sources, **1:**167
maritime law, **4:**148
military regime, **2:**135
Muslim Brotherhood, **1:**207
Napoleon's occupation of, **1:**204
non-Muslims in, **4:**234–235
Nubia, **1:**67
obligatory bequests, **6:**107
papyrology in, **1:**157
personal status laws, **4:**295–296; **6:**129
property ownership, **4:**457
Roman citizenship, **5:**150
Shafi'i, Muhammad ibn Idris al-, in, **5:**235–236
Shafi'i school of law in, **3:**352
shari'a as principal source of legislation in, **3:**317
sibling marriage, **1:**159
Tulunids in, **1:**1
in U.N. Convention on Contracts for the International Sale of Goods, **2:**74
women in ancient, **6:**116
Ehrenzweig, Albert A., **2:**113
Ehrenzweig, Armin, **5:**386
Ehrlich, Eugene, **4:**18, 19, 20
Eike von Repgow, **5:**436
Einkindschaft, **3:**46. *See also* adoption
Eisagog
on contract, **2:**192
on succession, **5:**376, 377

Eisagōgē (Photius), **1:**328; **2:**239
   on delict, **2:**325
      Macedonian Renaissance and, **1:**281–282
      on offices of the state, **5:**14
      on purpose of law, **1:**330
Eisagoge iuris naturalis (Oldendorp), **4:**261
eisangelia, **4:**246
Eisenhower, Dwight D.
   creation of the Department of Health, Education, and Welfare, **3:**144
   defeat of Bricker Amendment and, **3:**296
   equal protection under, **2:**460
   regulatory oversight under, **5:**82
EITC. *See* Earned Income Tax Credit
ejectment, action of, **2:**437
Ekklēsiazousai (Women at the Assembly) (Aristophanes), **6:**114
Elagabal. *See* Antoninus Elagabal (Roman emperor)
Elara of Anuradhapura, **5:**303
Elaya Kyemin Pyatton, **5:**303
El Bierzo edicts (15 B.C.E.), **3:**210
elderlaw, **2:422–425**
   equal protection and, **2:**462–463
   social security and, **6:**95–96
Elder Law Journal, **2:**422
ElderLaw Report, **2:**422
Eldon, Lord. *See* Scott, John
Eleanor of Aquitaine, **4:**36
elections. *See also* political parties and elections
   apportionment and reapportionment and, **1:**200–204
   campaign finance reform, **5:**337–338
   city, **4:**121
   United States, **5:**348
Electoral College, **4:**339
Elegabal, **4:**290
Elegantiae latinae linguae (Valla), **3:**189
elegit, writ of, **3:**88
Elementa Iuris Cambialis (Heineccius), **4:**222
Elementa jurisprudentiae universalis (Pufendorf), **5:**20
Elementi di economia pubblica (Beccaria), **1:**285
Elements of International Law: With a Sketch of the History of the Science (Wheaton), **3:**293
Elements of the Law of Contracts (Leake), **2:**442
Eleven Mon Dhammasat Texts (Hla), **1:**318
Elias, T. Olawale, **1:**65
Elijah ben Solomon Zalman of Vilnius, Rabbi, **3:**393
Eliot, Charles William, **2:**403

Elizabeth I (England)
   bills of exchange under, **1:**292
   law in Ireland under, **3:**310
   monopolies under, **4:**186–187
   religion under, **2:**129
   religious settlement, **1:**468
   Ridolfi Plot against, **6:**5
   separate estates under, **6:**122–123
Elizabeth II (England), **1:***244*
   African states under, **1:**93, 98
   assault on, **6:**6
Elkins Act (U.S., 1903), **5:**78
Ellenborough, Lord. *See* Law, Edward
Ellesmere, Lord Chancellor (Thomas Egerton). *See* Egerton, Thomas (Baron Ellesmere)
Elliott, Charles, **1:**449
Ellis, Havelock, **3:**110
Ellis, Ruth, **1:**365
Ellis, Thomas Flowers, **2:**442
Ellis Island (New York), **3:***207*
Ellsworth, Oliver, **2:**257
Elon, Menachem, **3:**388
El Salvador
   abolition of slavery, **5:**254
   adoption of Chilean Civil Code in 1859, **1:**384, 398
Ely, John Hart
   on constitutional interpretation, **2:**164
   on representation reinforcement, **4:**68
Ely, Richard T., **5:**79
   on monopolies, **1:**325
   on property, **4:**483
Elyot, Thomas, **3:**243
Emancipation Proclamation (1863), **2:**459
   based on war power, **6:**89
   importance of, **6:**52
"Embarrassing Second Amendment, The" (Levinson), **1:**221
embezzlement
   ancient Greece, **4:**246
   Chinese law
      deposit and, **2:**331
      government property, **5:**459
   English common law
      fraud and, **3:**100
      servants, **5:**462
Emblemata (Alciati), **1:**118
Embu, **1:**71
Emérigon, Balthazar-Marie, **4:**151
Emery, Lucilius A., **1:**219

eminent domain (United States)
  federalism and, **3:**60
  takings clause, **4:**488–489
Employed Laborer Law (China, 1588), **3:**162–163
Employee Retirement Income Security Act
    (U.S., 1974), **3:**484
Employers and Servants Ordinance (Guyana, 1853),
    3:137
Employers and Workmen Act (U.K., 1875), **2:**426
Employers' Liability Act (U.K., 1880), **3:**254
employment and labor law. *See* labor and
    employment law
Enabling Act (Germany, 1933), **3:**110
Enantiophanes, **1:**328, 333
encomienda, **5:**291, 298
  Guatemala, **3:**130
  rebellions against, **5:**300
Encyclopédie (Diderot), **5:**172
Endangered Species Act (U.S., 1973), **2:**456, 457
En Dansk Lov-historie (Ancher), **2:**328
endowment in medieval and post-medieval Roman law,
    3:45–46
enforcement
  of international law, **3:**279
  in Islamic law, **2:431–434**
Enforcement of Shari'h Act (Pakistan, 1991),
    4:299–300
Engels, Friedrich
  influence on private law, **4:**394
  on matriarchy, **1:**185
England. *See also* Anglo-Saxon law; English common
    law; English law
  absolutism in, **1:**7
  African colonies
    decolonization of, **1:**92–93
  alternative dispute resolution in, **1:**129
  antitrust law, **1:**188–189
  banking in, **1:**275–276
  bishops in, **1:**296
  church and state in, **1:**465–469
  colonization of Canada, **1:**337
  compurgation, **2:**105; **3:**3–4
  convict labor from, **5:**256
  copyright, **3:**265–266
  coronation, liturgy of, **1:**465, *466*
  courts in, **2:**249–251
  debt
    equity and, **2:**469
    evidence in, **3:**3–4
    final process in, **3:**87–89
  law merchant on, **4:**35–38
  Magna Carta on, **4:**134
  obligations and, **4:**243
  of women, **6:**124
divorce
  canon law on, **3:**32; **4:**162
  common law, **2:347–349; 4:**161, 163
  ecclesiastical law on, **2:**388–389
  property division in, **3:**33
  reforms of, **4:**43
  women in, **6:**121, 124
Enlightenment in, **2:**444, 445
fideicommissum in, **3:**80
first documented contract of insurance, **3:**258
formation of the secular nation, Inns of Court and,
    3:242–243
freedom of speech in, **5:**332
inheritance, **2:**13; **6:**30
  on adoption, **1:**46–47
  custom in, **5:**276
  disinheritance of wives, **3:**33
  dower, **2:**361–363
  ecclesiastical courts in, **2:**81, 436
  ecclesiastical law on, **2:**389
  entails, **2:**446–448
  estates doctrine, **2:**476–479
  by illegitimate children, **4:**161
  real and personal property, **4:**470
  strict settlements, **5:**364–368
  taxation, **5:**426–427
  women in, **6:**121–122
interpretation, **3:**299
juries, **2:**82, 439–440; **5:**276
  assizes, **1:**229–231
  Courts of the Staple, **4:**36
  decline of use, **3:**6
  evidence and, **3:**4–5
  on libel and slander, **4:**105–106
  mesne process for, **4:**174
justices in eyre, **3:**450–452
law reform movements, **4:**41–43
legislative power in, **4:**95–96
local government law in, **4:**119–120
mixed government theory in, **5:**215
Parliament, **4:**282–286
positivism in, **4:**355
procedural law, **2:**435–436
  environmental law and, **2:**450
  evidence in, **3:**6
  Henry II on, **4:**87

outlawry in, **4:**270–271
reform of, **2:**437
Star Chamber in, **5:**346–347
religious discrimination, **1:**468–469
rent control in, **4:**58
Roman law scholarship in, **1:**162
Singapore under, **5:**241–242
state church in, **1:**350
state sovereignty in, **5:**352
taxation in, **5:**435–436, 436, 438
tensions between ecclesiastical and secular courts, **1:**466
wills in, **5:**403
witch trials, **6:**109
England's Balme (Sheppard), **4:**41
English Civil War (1642–1648), **1:**271
English common law, **2:80–82.** *See also* equity
abortion, **3:**178
adoption, **1:46–47**
advocates in, **1:**57
in Africa, **1:**63, 100
in African British colonies, **1:**86–87
agency in, **1:108–110**
on alcohol and drugs, **1:**123–124
alternative dispute resolution in, **1:**129, 130
on appeal, **1:198–200**
on assault, **1:**226–227
bailment in, **1:**249–250
bankruptcy, **1:266–267**
banks and banking, **1:270–273**
benefit of clergy, **3:**178; **5:**27–28
Bentham, Jeremy, on, **1:**287
bills of exchange in, **1:291–293**
breach of contract in, **1:305–306**
burglary in, **1:**316–317
capital punishment, **1:364–367**
censorship, **1:378–382**
central government, **1:385–387**
chance-medley, **3:**178
children, **1:393–396**
church and state in, **1:465–469**
in the Commonwealth, **1:**310
competition, **2:101–102**
constitutional law, **2:127–134**
consumer protection, **2:168–169**
contracts, **2:194–197**
conveyancing, **2:**212–216
copyright, **2:216–218**
criminal, **2:276–277**
custom, **2:305–307**

Denning, Alfred Thompson, on, **2:**329–330
divorce, **2:347–349; 4:**161, 163
duress, **2:373–375**
ecclesiastical law in, **2:387–391**
employment and labor, **2:425–428**
entails, **2:446–448**
environmental law in, **2:448–452**
error and mistake in, **2:473–475**
evidence in, **3:**3–7
exportability of, **2:**440
family, **3:32–36**
feudal law, **3:72–77**
final process, **3:**88–89
fraud, **3:100–102**
guilds in, **3:131–133**
hearsay, **4:**421
homicide, **3:176–179; 5:**27
infant death, **3:**178
influenced by Roman law
theft, **5:**461–462
influence on American trial by jury right, **4:**440
influence on United States law, **3:**426 (*See also* United States law, colonial period)
insurance, **3:252–254**
in Ireland, **3:**308–309
judiciary, **3:415–418,** 424
barristers and, **1:**277–280
education of, **2:**439–440
in legislation, **4:**88
mesne process in, **4:**174–175
power of, **2:**437–438
as source of law, **5:**277–278
jury, **3:**437–441
labor and employment, **2:425–428**
Black Death and, **2:**436
land, **2:**12 (*See also* conveyancing)
dower, **2:**361–363
estates doctrine, **2:**476–479
fee tail holding, **2:**362
feudal, **3:**72–77
inheritance of land, **5:**381–382
land registration, **2:**379–382; **3:**73; **4:7–10**
lease, **4:10–13**
leases of land, **3:**72; **4:10–13**
registration, **4:**7–10
on sale of land, **5:**189–191
strict settlements, **5:**364–368
subinfeudation, **2:**436; **5:**368–370
substitution, **5:**368–370

wills, **6:**102–104
women in, **6:**121–122
law merchant, **4:35–38**
law reporting, **2:**436; **4:43–45,** 60
legal treatises on, **2:**442
law reporting in, **4:43–45**
legal education, **2:393–396,** 439
Blackstone, William, in, **1:**297–298
common-law, **1:**297–298; **2:**436
Doctors' Commons, **2:**354–355
legal treatises in, **2:**441–442
reforms of, **2:**437
legal literature in, **4:60–62**
on libel and slander, **4:**104–107
Magna Carta in, **4:**133–136
Mansfield, Lord, on, **4:**142–143
manslaughter, **3:**177–178, 179
marriage, **3:**35; **4:160–163**
divorce and, **2:**347–348
dower, **2:**361–363
ecclesiastical courts in, **2:**81, 355, 436
ecclesiastical law on, **2:**388–389, 390–391
entails and, **2:**446–447
family based on, **3:**32–33
jurisdiction of church courts, **1:**467
women in, **6:**120–121, 122
mesne process in, **4:**174–175
monopolies, **4:**186–187
mortgage, **4:188–189**
mortmain, **4:**191–193
murder, **3:**176–178
nationality in, **4:205–206**
natural law, **4:214–215**
notaries in, **4:**237
nuisance, **4:239–240**
oaths
evidence in, **3:**4
as *judicium Dei*, **4:**262, 263
religious opposition to, **3:**6
serjeants at law, **5:**222
in Star Chamber, **5:**346
obligations, **4:242–243**
ordeal, **4:***262,* 262–263
evidence in, **3:**4
outlawry, **4:**270–271
overview of, **6:**26–27
pardons, **3:**179
poisoning, **3:**176
poor laws, **4:347–351**
possession, **4:358–359**

private law, **4:**393–394
procedure
civil, **4:419–423**
criminal, **4:423–427**
property
personal, **4:470–473**
real, **4:473–474**
public law, **5:15–19**
punishment, **3:**178–179; **5:27–31**
rape, **5:67–69,** 569
reform movements, **4:**41
restitution, **5:129–131**
on right to bear arms, **1:**216–217
roman law and, **5:155–157**
sale, **5:189–191**
on search and seizure, **5:**203
in Seychelles, **5:**235
in Singapore, **5:**241–242
slavery, **5:***250,* **250–253,** 258
sodomy, **3:**167
sources of law in, **5:276–278**
in South Africa, **5:**279
in Southeast Asia, **5:**313, 318
succession, **5:***381,* **381–384**
taxation, **5:425–429,** *427*
theft, **5:461–463**
fraud and, **3:**101
women in, **6:**120
tort, **5:467–469,** 471–472, 473
assault, **1:**226–227
environmental law, **2:**449–450
on fraud, **3:**101
on obligations, **4:**243
torture, **5:484–486,** *485*
trusts, **6:11–14**
vicarious liability, **6:75–77**
Wales under, **6:**100
wills, **6:102–105**
witchcraft, **3:**176
women, **6:120–125**
dower, **2:**361–363
punishment, **5:**30
rape, **5:**67–69
in succession, **5:**383
English common law, historiography of, **2:434**
English Constitution, The (Bagehot), **2:**133
English law, **2:434–440.** *See also* United States law: colonial period
abortion, **3:**178
civil law system history, **6:**27

divorce, **2:**347–349
donation, **2:**358
on donation, **2:**358
on family, **3:**32–36
guarantee in, **3:**128, 129
guilds in, **3:131–133**
influenced by Jewish law, **3:**393
influenced by Roman law
   treason, **6:**1
influence on
   Pakistan, **4:**273
influence on Russian law, **5:**166, 173
insanity defense in, **3:**135
justice, equity, and good conscience
   in, **3:**446
in Malaysia, **4:**138
natural law in, **4:**214–215
negligence, **4:**220–222
North American colonies and, **2:**11
precedent, **4:**381
privileges, **4:**398
remedies, **5:**125, 126
restitution, **5:**131
as a source of United States colonial law,
   6:33–34
treason, **6:**1–6, *3*
English Laws Act (New Zealand, 1858), **4:**227
English legal treatises, **2:440–443**
   Anglo-Saxon law, **1:**183
   on evidence, **3:**5
   as source of law, **5:**278
English Matrimonial Causes Act
   (1837), **4:**286
English-Siamese Treaty (1909), **4:**138
English Society of Comparative Legislation, **2:**99
Enlightened Judgments, The, **1:**426; **3:**109
Enlightenment, **2:444–446**
   Bartolus of Saxoferrato in, **1:**281
   on children, **3:**44
   codification and, **2:**46, 47
   definition of law and, **4:**21
   on feudal law, **3:**77
   Filangieri, Gaetano, in, **3:**84
   on guardianship, **3:**48
   influence on U.S. Constitution, **2:**150–151
   on the jury system, **3:**441
   legal education in, **2:**400
   on marriage and divorce, **3:**43–44
   Napoleonic code and, **3:**99–100
   natural law in, **3:**118; **4:**216

Roman law and the, **5:**158–159
on slavery, **5:**255
Spain, **5:**325–326
Sweden, **5:**416
tax equality, **5:**437
Enneccerus, Ludwig, **4:**277
Enquiry into the Effects of Spirituous Liquors (Rush),
   1:124
Enrico da Susa (Ostiense), **3:**356
Enron, **5:**85
Ensaio de direito administrativo (Souza), **1:**303
entails, **2:446–448**
   England
      estates doctrine in, **2:**477–478
      strict settlements, **5:**365
   fideicommissum, **3:**80–81
   United States
      abolition after Revolution, **3:**236
      colonial period, **2:**13; **3:**235
Entgeldliche Verträge über Dienstleistungen
   (Nongratuitous Contracts for Services,
   Austria), **2:**428
entireties, rule of, **3:**478
entitlement, **4:**24
entry, **1:**317. *See also* burglary in English
   common law
Entwurf eines bürgerlichen Gesetzbuches für das
   Königreich Sachsen mit bes. Rücksicht auf das
   Österreichische Allgemeine Bürgerliche
   Gesetzbuch, Der (Unger), **6:**25
Environment (Protection) Act (India, 1986), **2:**453
Environmental Decade (1969–1981), **2:**455–456
Environmental Defense Fund, **2:**455
environmental law, **2:448–458**
   Aboriginal law, **1:**3
   African contributions to, **1:**107
   Calabresi, Guido, on, **4:**25
   English common law, **2:448–452,** *451*
   Indian law, **2:452–454**
   science and, **4:**29–30
   United States law, **2:454–458; 6:**55
      structural injunctions in, **2:**473
Environmental Protection Act (U.K., 1990), **2:**452
Environmental Protection Agency, **1:**29; **2:**456
   scientific research under, **4:**30
Environmental Protection Agency (EPA)
   creation of, **5:**82
EPA. *See* Environmental Protection Agency
Epagathus, **6:**23
Epanagoge. See Eisagōgē (Photius)

Eparchikon biblion (book of the prefect), **1:**282, 329
EPC. *See* European Political Community
Ephialtes
  institutional reforms, **2:**124
  on jurisdiction, **1:**232
Epicurus, **5:**177
epidikasia (adjudication of inheritance), **1:**41
epigraphy, **1:**163
Epikteta, will of, **3:**231
Epinicians (Bacchylides), **2:**413
Episcopal Church of Scotland, **1:**468
Epistolae decretales, **2:**318
Epistulae (Celsus the Younger), **1:**373
Epistula in Bartoli de insigniis et armis libellum, **3:**189
Epitadeus, **5:**329
Epitome (Apollodorus), **1:**51
Epitome canonum (Harmenopoulos), **1:**330
Epitome iuris (under the name Gaius), **5:**151
Epitome legum, **1:**329
Epitome of Law (Hermogenian), **3:**213
Epitrepontes (Menander), **4:**111
Equal Employment Act (U.S., 1972), **2:**339
Equal Employment Opportunity Commission (U.S.)
  arbitration in, **1:**131
  under Bush, George H. W., **2:**343
  creation of, **5:**82
  elderlaw and, **2:**424
  on race discrimination, **3:**483
  on sex discrimination, **6:**137
equality and democracy in ancient Greek law, **2:**125
Equal Pay Act (U.S., 1963), **2:**339
equal protection, **2:458–465**
  abortion and, **2:**339
  monopolies and, **1:**322
  segregation and, **2:**341
Equal Rights Amendment (U.S.), **2:**156–157, 339; **6:**136–137, 138, *145*
Equitable Life Assurance Society, **3:**253
equity, **2:**81–82, **466–473**
  African courts of, **1:**77
  English common law, **2:**438–439, **466–472**; **6:**27
    appeal in, **1:**197
    on error and mistake, **2:**474
    Exchequer of Please, **3:**17
    interpretation and, **3:**297
    ius commune and, **2:**10
  legal reasoning on, in ancient Rome, **4:**81
  Mauritius, **4:**172
  on mortgage, **4:**188–189
  regulation of competition and, **2:**101
  United States law, **2:472–473**; **6:**27
    colonial period, **2:**12
    incorporation in the law, **2:**84
equity receivership, **1:**269
  United States, **2:**76
Erasmus, **1:**119
Erbrecht in weltgeschichtlicher Entwicklung, Das (Gans), **2:**98
Erfolgsstrafrecht
  guilt and, **3:**133
Eritrea, **1:**81–82
  Ethiopia conflict with, **1:**105; **2:**480
  indigenous law, **1:**65, 71, 101
Ermächtigungsgesetz (Enabling Act) (Germany), **2:**122
Ernian lüling
  on damage to property, **2:**311, 312
  on deceit, **2:**314, 315
  on lack of filial piety, **3:**85
  on parricide, **3:**84
  on wounding, **6:**150, 151
Ernst, Morris, **1:**381
Ernst August (Hanover), **4:**91
error and mistake, **2:473–476**
  English common law, **2:473–475**
  medieval and post-medieval Roman law, **2:475–476**
Ershad, Hossain Mohammad, **2:**143
Erskine, Thomas, **3:**441
  influenced by Ashhurst, William, **2:**394
Ervin, Sam, **4:**211
Esbozo (Freitas), **1:**216
Escarra, Jean, **1:**462
escheat, **3:**74; **5:**450
Eskridge, William, **4:**69–70
Esmein, Adhémar, **3:**100
Espéculo, **1:**215; **5:**290
Espinasse, Isaac, **4:**45
espionage, military tribunals on, **4:**177
Espionage Act (U.S., 1917), **3:**409; **5:**333–334
  restriction of rights, **2:**16
"Essay on the Action for Money Had and Received, An" (Evans), **5:**130
Essay on the Doctrine of Contracts (Verplanck), **2:**204
Essay on the Law of Bailments (Jones), **1:**249; **2:**441
  on negligence, **4:**221

Essay on the Law of Contracts (Chipman), **2:**204
Essay on the Learning of Contingent Remainders (Fearne), **2:**441
Essay upon Contracts and Agreements (Powell), **2:**194
Essay upon the Law of Contracts and Agreements (Powell), **2:**441
Essential Commodities Act (India, 1955), **2:**173
Essential Documents of the Song Dynasty (Songhuiyao), **1:**457
Estado Novo (Brazil), **1:**303
estates, doctrine of, **2:476–479**
  China
    antichresis sale, **4:**6–7
    land law, **4:**4–5
  England
    equity and, **2:**470
    strict settlements, **5:**364–368
  entails, **2:**446–448
  in succession, **5:**381–382
estate tax, United States, **3:**238, 239
Estatutos de Limpieza de Sangre (Statues on Blood Purity) (city of Toledo, Spain, 1449), **3:**398
Estländisches Ritter-und Landrecht (Estonian Noble and Common Law, 1650), **1:**254
Estonia. *See also* Baltic nations
  in European Union, **2:**492
  as republic, **1:**255
Ethelbert. *See* Aethelberht
Ethelred. *See* Aethelred II
Ethical Investment Research Service, **1:**262
ethics
  as distinguished from Islamic law, **3:**323
  U.S. codes of legal, **4:**50–51
Ethics (Aristotle), **3:**403
Ethiopia, **2:479–481**
  canon law in, **1:**65
  Islam in, **1:**69
  Italian invasion of, **1:**78, 82
  prohibition of polygamy, **2:**37
Ethiopian Orthodox Church, **1:**67
ethnic discrimination, U.S. immigration policy and, **3:**208
ethnic groups in Chinese law, **2:481–483.** *See also* foreigners in Chinese law
ethnicity, principle of
  in Qing dynasty, **1:**435
  in Yuan law, **1:**428–429
ethnicity, principle of (China)
  in legal system of the Liao, **1:**427
Eto, Shinpei, **3:**373

Etymologiae (Isidore of Seville), **2:**5
  on Visigothic law, **3:**116
Eucrates, **4:***85*
Euer, Samson, **4:**324
eugenics
  birth control and, **6:**140–141
  disability and, **2:**333
  forced sterilization, **6:**141–142
  gay, lesbian, bisexual, and transgender theory and, **3:**110
  Germany under National Socialist law, **4:**204
  in immigration policies, **4:**29
  marriage restriction and, **3:**52
  natural law on, **4:**219
Eugenius IV (pope), **2:**386; **4:**353
Euler, Leonhard, **3:**258
Eumenides (Aeschylus), **4:**399, 401
  judicial scenes in, **1:**148
  law depictions in, **4:***110,* 110–111
  on metics, **5:**357
  on oaths, **4:**402
Eunus, Gaius Novius, **5:**249
Euphiletus, **1:**52
Euratom. *See* European Atomic Energy Community
Euric (king of the Visigoths), **3:**116
Euripides
  on divorce, **2:**346; **6:**113–114
  on finding the middle, **2:**125
  on freedom of speech, **5:**329
  on judicial processes, **1:**140
  law depictions by, **4:**109–110
  on rape, **5:**64–65
  on written law, **1:**156
Europäisches Privatrecht (Coing), **5:**163
Europäisches Privatrecht II (Coing), **5:**387
Europe. *See also* European Communities; European Union
  Islamic law in, **2:483–485**
  social security in, **5:270–272**
European Agreement on the Adoption of Children (1967), **3:**46
European Association of Law and Economics, **4:**27
European Atomic Energy Community (EAEC), **2:**486, 489
European Central Bank, **2:**486
European Civil Code, **2:**428
European Coal and Steel Community, **2:**486, 488–489
European Commission, **2:**486, 489
European Committee of the Regions, **2:**486

European Communities, **2:485–488**
  administration, public law of, **1**:24
  European Union compared with, **2**:493
  guilt in, **3**:136
  on judges, **3**:406
  legal supremacy of, **4**:89
  legal system standardization in, **3**:119
  social security in, **5**:271
  source of law in, **5**:277
  Spain in, **5**:326
  Sweden in, **5**:417
European Communities Act (1972), **2**:133
European Convention on Human Rights, **1**:365; **3**:279, 406
  in Africa, **1**:93, 106
  Dennins, Alfred Thompson, on, **2**:330
  on freedom of religion, **2**:483
  on freedom of speech, **4**:106–107
  incorporated into English domestic law, **2**:437–438
  on legitimacy of children, **3**:47
  in Mauritius law, **4**:172
  as natural law, **4**:215
  in Sweden, **5**:417
  treason and, **6**:6
European Council, **2**:486, 489–490
  conflict of laws and, **2**:114
  model law on Adoption in the Convention on the Adoption of Children (1967), **2**:115
European Council of Ministers, **2**:489
  decision-making power of, **2**:491
  voting in, **2**:492
European Court, **2**:253
European Court of Auditors, **2**:486
European Court of Human Rights, **2**:253
  on conflicts with statute laws, **4**:89
  on easements, **2**:381
European Court of Justice, **2**:486, 489; **3**:279
  administrative law, **1**:24
  European Union development and, **2**:490
  jurisdiction, **2**:492
  supranationalism, **2**:487
  supremacy doctrine, **2**:495
European Defence Community, **2**:486, 489
European Economic and Social Committee, **2**:486
European Economic Community (EEC), **2**:486, 489
European Economic Interest Grouping, **2**:93
European Parliament, **2**:486, 489
  decision-making power of, **2**:491, 492
  influence of, **2**:493

European Political Community, **2**:486, 489
European Research Group on Existing EC Private Law (Acquis Group), **2**:496
European Union (EU), **2:488–494**. *See also* European Communities
  antitrust legislation, **3**:288
  Austria in, **1**:248
  Baltic states in, **1**:256
  British constitutional law and membership in, **2**:133
  commercial law unification, **4**:40
  consumer protection, **2**:169, 172
  copyright and, **2**:217, 218
  corporations, new types of, **2**:93
  Denmark in, **2**:328
  development of, **2**:486–487
  disability law, **2**:337
  Guyane and, **5**:296
  integration of laws on competition, **2**:103
  law standardization, **2**:115
  private law in, **2:494–496**
  on sale of goods, **5**:191
  Scotland in, **5**:202
  standardization of law, **2**:114
  state sovereignty and, **5**:354
  Turkey and, **6**:18
European Union, Treaty on (1648), **2**:491
European Union Defective Products Directive, **2**:169
Eustathios Rhomaios, **1**:330
  cases adjudicated by, **2**:239
  information on, **1**:333
Euthydemus (Plato), **4**:456
Euthyphro (Plato), **1**:148, 149
  on slavery, **5**:245
Evander of Thespiae, **4**:149
Evans, W. D., **2**:442
Evans, William, **5**:130
Everaerts, Nicolaas, **4**:225
Everyday Matters (Res cottidianae) (Gaius), **3**:251
eviction, **4**:57–58
evidence, **3:1–16**
  ancient Athens, **3**:1–3; **4**:405–406
    logographers on, **4**:124
    of slaves, **5**:355
  ancient Greece
    oaths as, **4**:241–242
  ancient Near Eastern law, **1**:170
  Anglo-Saxon law, **1**:177, 181

Bentham, Jeremy, on, **1:**287
English common law, **3:3–7,** 438
India
    Islamic law, **5:**307–308
    medieval and post-medieval Roman law, **3:7–10**
in military tribunals, **4:**180
Nepal, **4:**224
New Zealand, **4:**228
Oldendorp, Johann, on, **4:**261
scientific expert, **4:**28–29
South Africa, **5:**279
United States procedure, **3:10–17,** *14*
    social sciences as, **5:**266–270
witch trials, **6:**109–110
Evidence Act (India, 1872), **3:**216; **4:**299
    on dowry death, **2:**365
Evidence Act (New Zealand, 1871), **4:**228
Evidence Act (Pakistan, 1872), **5:**308–309
Ewald, Paul, **2:**316
Ewiger Landfriede (Eternal Public Peace, 1495), **2:**120
ex ante analysis, **4:**27–28
exceptio (affirmative defense), **3:**96–97
exchange in Islamic banking and finance, **1:**263–265
Exchequer, **1:**385; **2:**250; **3:17–19**
Exchequer (Ireland), **3:**308
exclusionary rule in search and seizure, **5:**204
excommunication, **2:**390
Execution Act (England, 1844), **3:**89
executive power, **3:19–25.** *See also* separation of powers
    of administrative agencies, **1:**24
    Africa
        after independence, **1:**97
    Australia, **1:**240
    legal process on, **4:**66
    military tribunals and, **4:**180
    presidential power in the United States
        war-making power, **2:**153
    privilege and, **3:**11–12
    South and Central America, **5:**286
        colonial, **5:**298
    Suriname, **5:**413–414
    United States
        state, **5:**348
        war power, **2:**155
exegesis, school of
    Dutch jurisprudence and, **4:**226
    in Italy, **3:**358–359

exigent-circumstances exception, **5:**207
exigibility, final process and, **3:**87, 88
Exiguus, Dionysius, **2:**318
exile
    ancient Greece, **1:**155
        Draco on, **2:**366–367
    Chinese law, **1:**403; **3:25–26**
        for deceit, **2:**315
        under Han, **1:**417
        under Ming dymasty, **1:**431
        for parricide, **3:**84–85
        review of, **1:**196
        sentencing and, **5:**213
Eximiae Devotionis (Alexander VI), **5:**290
Expatriation Act (U.S., 1907), **3:**209
Expediency Council (Iran), **2:**139
Explanation of the Statute of Wills (England, 1542), **6:**103
    on women, **6:**104
Exposicion of the Kinges Prerogatiue, An (Staunford), **2:**440
ex post analysis, **4:**27–28
Extradition Act (Canada, 1985, 1999), **1:**341
Extraordinary Chamber in the Courts of Cambodia, **1:**336
extraterritoriality
    British Commonwealth, **1:**312–313
    China
        ethnic groups and, **2:**481
        foreigners in, **3:**92–93
    U.S. antitrust law, **3:**288
Extravagantes Communes, **2:**223
Extravagantes Johannis XXII, **2:**223, 224
Eyffinger, A., **3:**127
Ezekiel Landau, Rabbi, **3:**393
Ezra, **3:**389, 390

F

FAA. *See* Federal Aviation Agency
FAA (Federal Aviation Agency), **5:**104
Faber, Antonius, **3:27**
    influence of, **2:**356
    on succession, **5:**389
Fabricius, Ernst, **2:**28
fact-finding, **1:**128
Factories Act (U.K., 1833, 1844)
    on child labor, **2:**426
    on women, **2:**426
Factory Inspectorate (U.K.), **2:**426
Faculty of Advocates (Scotland), **5:**200, 202

Fadlallah, Shaykh, **6:**130
FAIR. *See* Federal Agricultural Improvement and Reform Act
fair comment defense, **4:**106
Fair Credit Opportunity Act (U.S., 1974), **2:**178
Fair Credit Reporting Act (U.S., 1970), **2:**178
Fair Debt Collection Practices Act (U.S., 1978), **2:**178
Fair Employment Practices Committee, **2:**341
Fair Housing Act (U.S., 1968), **3:**185–186
    Reagan, Ronald, on, **2:**343
Fair Housing Agency (U.S.), **2:**344
Fair Housing Amendments Act (U.S., 1988)
    on disability, **2:**335
Fair Labor Standards Act (U.S., 1938), **3:**409
    federalism and, **3:**62–63
    hourly wage in, **3:**484
    sovereign immunity and, **5:**354
    upheld by Supreme Court, **2:**66
Fairman, Charles, **3:**165
fairness doctrine, **5:**97, 98, 335–336
Fair Packaging and Labeling Act (U.S., 1965), **2:**178
fairs
    banking and, **1:**275
    law merchant in, **4:**35–36, 39
fair trading, law of, **2:**102
Faisal Islamic Banks, **1:**261
Fakhr al-Din al-Razi, **3:**119–120
Falkland Islands, **1:**312
false testimony. *See also* witnesses
    ancient Athens, **3:**2; **6:**110
    Chinese law, appeal and, **1:**194
    Islamic law
        enforcement and, **2:**431
        in forum, external and internal, **3:**98
falsum, **3:**102, 103
Falü dawen, **4:**116–117
family, **3:**27–57. *See also* juvenile justice in United States law; personal status law
    Afghanistan, **1:**61
    Africa, **1:**102–104
        after independence, **1:**99; **2:**44
        precolonial, **1:**65, 66, 72–73
    ancient Greek law, **2:**229; **3:**27–32, *29*; **6:**116
        Athens, **1:**234; **2:**229
        Code of Gortyn on, **3:**121–123
        Hellenistic, **1:**158–160
        inscriptions on, **1:**154
        public actions to protect, **2:**268
        Sparta, **5:**328–329
    ancient Near Eastern law, **1:**171–173
    Austria, **1:**247
    Balkan peninsula, **1:**253
    Bangladesh, **1:**258, 259; **5:**308
    Brazil, **1:**304
    Chinese law, **5:**52–54
        on adoption, **1:**43–46
        gambling, **3:**109
        lack of filial piety, **3:84–87**
        under Liao empire, **1:**427
        on mutual concealment, **4:**197–199
        Qin code, **1:**428
        sexual offenses in, **5:**232
        status and crimes against, **5:**359
        on succession, **5:**378–380
    Denmark, **2:**328
    divorce and
        England, **2:**348–349
        Islamic law, **2:**351
    Egypt
        Hellenistic period, **2:**416
        Islamic, **2:**421–422
    English common law, **3:***32,* 32–36
    Ethiopia, **2:**480
    evolution in Islamic law, **3:**317
    feminist legal theory on, **3:**66, 67
    fideicommissum, **3:**80–81
    Germany under National Socialism, **4:**204
    Hindu law, **3:**219
        on abortion, **1:**4–5
        dowry, **2:**363–366
        marumakkathayam in, **4:**170–171
    India, **3:48–51,** 216; **4:**294
        Christian law, **3:**221–222
        Islamic law, **3:**219
        secularism in, **5:**208–209
    Indonesia, **3:**337
    Islamic law, **3:36–39,** 329–330; **5:**127–129
        acknowledgement in, **1:**19–20
        adoption and, **1:**47–49
        in Arab countries, **1:**207–208
        codes and codification, **2:**37–38
        colonialism and, **2:**43
        in Europe, **2:**483, 484
        in Maghrib and al-Andalus, **4:**129–130
        for non-Muslims, **4:**234
        obligations and, **4:**244
        option in, **4:**261–262
        reforms, **2:**38–39
        slaves, **1:**358

South Asia, **5:**307
tribalism *vs.*, **4:**164
Westernization of, **1:**204
Malaysia, **3:**337
Maldives, **5:**309
medieval and post-medieval Roman law, **3:***40,*
40–48
Mongolia, **4:**185
Naga law, **4:**201
New Zealand, **4:**230
Ottoman Empire, **4:**267
Pakistan, **5:**309
Roman, **5:**124–125
Scotland, **5:**202
of slaves
Islamic law, **1:**358
Roman law, **5:**247
United States law, **5:**262
South and Central America, **5:**293
South Asian law and United Kingdom,
5:311–312
Southeast Asia, **5:**317
Sri Lanka, **5:**340
United States law, **3:**51–57
on cohabitation, **3:**55
due process in, **2:**370–371
education and, **2:**409
parental rights, **3:**164
pre-Revolutionary, **3:**477
reproductive rights, **6:**140–142
of slaves, **5:**262
on succession, **5:**402–409
women in, **6:**136, 142–143
values in welfare programs, **6:**94
villein status and, **6:**82
Wales, **6:**99, 100
World War I disruption of, **2:**348
Family Act (Maldives, 2000), **5:**310
Family Act (Yemen, 1974), **4:**298
Family Affairs Law (Japan, 1947), **3:**381
Family and Medical Leave Act (U.S., 1993),
2:340
Family Code (Germany, 1965), **4:**395
Family Courts Act (India, 1984), **3:**398
Family Courts Ordinance (Bangladesh, 1985),
1:259; **4:**300
Family Division of the High Court (England), **3:**32
Family Homes Protection Act (New Zealand, 1895), **4:**229
Family Law Act (Iran, 1967), **3:**303
repeal after Islamic Revolution, **3:**304

Family Law Reform Act (England, 1987, 1989), **3:**35
Family Medical Leave Act (U.S., 1993), **3:**65
Family Protection Act (Iran, 1967, 1975), **4:**296
Fa Ngum (Laos), **4:**13
Fang Xuanling, **1:**456
Fannie Mae. *See* Federal National Mortgage
Association
Fan Quan, **1:**420
Fanti states, **1:**68
Fan Wuzi, **1:**404
Fan Xuanzi, **1:**404
Fara 'id al-usul (Ansari), **1:**184
Farber, Daniel, **2:**302
farḍ. See duty *(farḍ)*
Farewell to the Assizes: The Sixty-one Towns
(Nield), **1:**230
Farinacci, Prospero, **5:**463
Farmers' Alliance, **5:**88
Farmers Home Administration, **3:**183
Farra', Abu Ya'la ibn al-, **1:**10
Fasi, 'Abd al-Rahman al-
on judicial practice, **4:**129
on legal methodology, **4:**128
Fasl al-maqal (Ibn Rushd), **3:**201
Fatawa 'Alamgiriyya, **2:**36
Fatawa-i-Alamgiri, **1:**257; **5:**307
Fatawa-i Hindiyya, **2:**36
Fatawa of Qadi Khan, **2:**35–36
Fatimid caliphate
in Maghrib and al-Andalus, **4:**127
in Sicily, **5:**239
fatwas, **3:***57,* **57–59**, 320–321
by al-Wansharisi, **3:**58; **4:**128
by 'Amili, Muhammad ibn Makki al-, **1:**132
enforcement and, **2:**431
of Idn Rushd, **3:**200
in Maghrib and al-Andalus, **4:**128, 129
Malaysia, **2:**140; **3:**337
Mansur bi-llah 'Abd Allah ibn Hamza, al-,
on, **4:**144
muftis and, **4:**193–195
on permissibility of insurance transactions,
3:255
popularity of, **6:**130
Songhai, **1:**74
South Asia, **5:**307
Fatwa Secretariat (Amanat al-Fatwa, Damascus),
3:195
Faure, Maurice, **2:***490*
Faustus, Gaius Sulpicius, **5:**249

Fawkes, Guy, **5:**484
Fäwse Mänfäsawi (Ethiopia, c. 1450), **2:**479
FBI (Federal Bureau of Investigation), **6:**59
FCC. *See* Federal Communications Commission
Fearne, Charles, **2:**441
Febronius. *See* Hontheim, Nikolaus von
FECA. *See* Federal Election Campaign Act
Federal Advisory Committee Act (U.S., 1972), **5:**83
Federal Agricultural Improvement and Reform Act (U.S., 1996), **5:**91
Federal Arbitration Act (U.S., 1925), **1:**130; **3:**488–489; **4:**446
Federal Aviation Agency (FAA), **5:**104
Federal Bureau of Investigation (FBI), **6:**59
Federal Communications Commission (FCC), **5:**79, 83, 97, 98
Federal Constitutional Court (Germany), **3:**119
Federal Court of Canada, **1:**340
Federal Election Campaign Act (U.S., 1971), **4:**340
Federal Election Campaign Act Amendments (1974), **4:**340
Federal Emergency Relief Administration (U.S.), **1:**27
Federal Employees Liability Act (U.S., 1908), **6:**57
Federal Farm Board, **5:**89
Federal Farm Loan Act (U.S., 1916), **5:**88
Federal Foods and Drugs Act (U.S., 1906), **5:**78
Federal Home Loan Bank Act (U.S., 1932), **3:**182
Federal Home Loan Bank Board (U.S.), **3:**182
Federal Home Loan Mortgage Corporation (Freddie Mac), **3:**183
Federal Home Loan Mortgage Corporation Act (U.S., 1970), **3:**183
Federal Housing Administration (FHA), **3:**182
Federal Islamic Republic of the Comoros, **1:**102, 105
federalism
  Germany under National Socialism, **3:**111
  India, **2:**145
  in Islamic countries, **2:**136
  in state constitutions, **5:**350
  state sovereignty and, **5:**352–354
  United States, **3:59–66**
    in Articles of Confederation, **1:**224–225
    in Constitution, **2:**149–150
    influence on law of conflict of laws, **2:**116
    labor law and, **3:**485

Federalist Papers, **2:**151
  on copyright law, **3:**266
  on executive power, **3:**19–20, 22–23
  on federalism, **3:**59
  on judicial power, **3:**406
  on judicial review, **2:**152–153
  on judiciary, **3:**425
  on Native Americans, **4:**208
  on observance of international law, **3:**290
  on right to bear arms, **1:**217–218
  on separation of powers, **5:**215, 217
Federal National Mortgage Association (Fannie Mae), **3:**183
Federal Power Commission, **1:**27, 29
federal preemption, **5:**412
Federal Prison Reform Act (U.S., 1984), **5:**41
Federal Radio Commission, **1:**27; **5:**79, 97; **6:**55
Federal Railroad Administration, **5:**103
Federal Republic of Germany. *See* Germany
Federal Reserve Board, **1:**27; **2:**76; **5:**79
Federal Rules of Appellate Procedure (U.S., 1967), **4:**445
Federal Rules of Civil Procedure (U.S.), **2:**50; **4:**444, 446
  on admiralty law, **1:**39
  on equity, **2:**472
Federal Rules of Evidence (U.S.), **3:**12; **4:**445
  class bias in, **3:**16
  on social sciences, **5:**267
  state adoption of, **3:**14
Federal Trade Commission, **5:**79, 92; **6:**60
  in antitrust, **1:**188
  revised antitrust guidelines, **1:**191
Federal Trade Commission Act (U.S., 1914), **1:**188; **2:**177; **5:**78; **6:**54
Federal Water Pollution Control Act Amendments (U.S., 1972), **2:**456
Federated Malay States, **3:**261
Federation of Malaya, **5:**242
  Chinese law in, **5:**319
  intellectual property, **3:**262–263
Feenstra, Robert, **3:**127
fee tail holding
  dower and, **2:**362
  estates doctrine and, **2:**478
fee tail male, **6:**122
Feinstein, Moses (Moshe), Rabbi, **3:**393
Felix III (pope), **4:**351
fellow-servant rule. *See* common employment, doctrine of

feminist legal theory, **3:**66–71
   critical legal studies and, **2:**298, 407
   on evidence, **3:**16
Feng Huan, **4:**116
Fenus nauticum (loan for a voyage), **2:**186
feoffments, **1:**392
Ferdinand (Spain), **1:**384
   Jews under, **3:**398
Ferdinand VII (Spain), **5:**326
Fernando of Aragón, **5:**290, 325
Fernando Po, **1:**79
Festus
   historical information provided by, **5:**158
   on magistrates, **4:**131
Fetha Negest (Ethiopia), **2:**479, 480
fetus
   in Islamic law, **1:**358; **3:**71–72
   in Roman law, **3:**44
feudal law, **3:**72–80, 73
   ancient Near Eastern law, **1:**173
   Anglo-Saxon, **1:**183
   Austria, **1:**246
   Baltic nations, **1:**254
   China
      abolished, **4:**1
      tenure forms, **4:**2–3
   Craig, Thomas, on, **5:**200
   English common law, **3:**72–77
      chattel real in, **4:**11
      on easements, **2:**379, 381
      estates doctrine, **2:**477
      introduction of, **2:**435
      on land leases, **4:**13
      subinfeudation and substitution, **5:**368–370
      succession and, **5:**383
   final process in, **3:**88
   France, **3:**99
   Japan, **3:**366, 367, 368, 369–372, 373
   medieval and post-medieval Roman law, **3:**77–80
   nationality and, **4:**205
   Scotland, **5:**197, 200, 202
   servitude in real estate and, **5:**224
   Spain, **5:**325
   as system of landholding, **2:**127–128
   on treason, **6:**1–2
   uses and, **6:**12
   Wales, **6:**99, 100
feuds
   ancient Greek law, **1:**186
   Anglo-Saxon law, **1:**180–182

Feuerbach, Paul Johann Anselm von
   concepts introduced by Franz von Zeiller, **6:**163
   on guilt, **3:**135
   influence on Ørsted, Anders Sandøe, **2:**328
   on punishment, **5:**34, 43
Feuerkontrakte (Hamburg), **3:**257
FHA. *See* Federal Housing Administration
Fichte, Johann Gottlieb
   on enlightened absolutism, **1:**8
   neoidealism of, **4:**204
fideicommissum (familiae), **3:**80–81
   bequests and, **5:**390–391
   succession and, **5:**374–375, 385
fiducia, **2:**183, 184
fiduciaries, agents as, **1:**113
Field, Barry, **3:**462
Field, David Dudley, **4:**442
   and New York Code of Civil Procedure, **2:**50
Field, Stephen J., **5:**443
   on due process, **2:**369
   on natural law, **4:**218
   on property, **4:**490
Field Code. *See* Code of Civil Procedure (N.Y., 1848)
Fiennes, Thomas, Lord Dacre of the South, **6:**12
fieri facias, writ of, **3:**88
Fifoot, C. H. S., **4:**143
Fiji, **3:**81–83. *See also* Melanesia
   independence, **4:**174
   land registration, **4:**9
Filangieri, Gaetano, **3:**83–84, 358
filial piety, lack of, in Chinese law, **3:**84–87
   marriage and, **4:**157–158
   mutual concealment and, **4:**198–199
filiation, patrilineal, **1:**396
Filiation Reform Act (Germany, 1997), **2:**113
Fillmore, Millard, **3:**371
final process, **3:**87–89
Financial Industry Regulatory Authority, **5:**81
Financial Services and Markets Act (U.K., 2000), **1:**273
Financial Times Islamic Markets Index, **1:**262
Finch, Henry, **2:**394
Findlay, Vera, **3:**32
Fine Arts Copyright Act (U.K., 1862), **2:**216
Fines and Recoveries Act (U.K., 1833), **2:**215
fines in Chinese law, **1:**403

Fineux, John, **2:**196
fingerprints, **3:**14, *14*
Finland. *See also* Scandinavia
    in European Union, **2:**491
    under Sweden, **5:**416
Finley, Moses
    on bride-purchase, **4:**152
    on unity of Greek law, **1:**136, 163–164
fiqh, **3:**315
    administrative decrees of political authorities, **1:**33–35
    Afghanistan, **1:**59, 61
    ʿAmili, Muhammad ibn Makki al-, on, **1:**132
    Asili, al-, **4:**128
    casuistry structure around legal principles, **3:**326
    categories of, **3:**322–323
    commercial law in, **2:**72–73
    contract of sale, **2:**199
    definition, **3:**320
    dissent in, **2:**345
    as distinguished from *shariʿa*, **3:**317
    in education, **2:**396–397, 398
    in Europe, **2:**484–485
    hierarchy of norms in, **2:**37
    Ibn Hazm concept of, **3:**198
    insurance, **3:**254
    legal norms in, **4:**62–64
    Malik ibn Anas and, **4:**140–141
    non-Muslims in, **4:**234
    Sahnun, ʿAbd al-Salam ibn Saʿid al-Tanukhi, on, **5:**182–183
    spheres of the law in the, **3:326–330**
    women in, **6:**125–127
    on worship as set of legal obligations, **3:**323–324
Fiqh ʿala al-Madhabib al-arbaʿah (al-Rahman al-Jaziri), **2:**44
Firearms Owners Protection Act (U.S., 1986), **1:**221
fire insurance, **3:**253, 257
Firoz Tughlaq (India), **2:**281
First and Second Confiscation Acts (U.S., 1861, 1862), **5:**262, 264
First Charter of Justice (South Africa, 1827), **5:**279
First Judiciary Act. *See* Judiciary of of 1789
First Letter of Clement (Clement), **4:**351
Fischer, David Hackett, **2:**422
Fisher, John, Bishop, **3:**440
Fisher, Louis, **6:**89–90
Fisher and Lightwood on the Law of Mortgages, **4:**189

Fiss, Owen, **4:**68
Fitting, Hermann, **5:**162
Fitzgerald, F. Scott, **1:**270
Fitzgibbon, Gerald, **3:**312
Fitzherbert, Anthony, **4:**61, 381
Fitzjames-Stephen, James, **1:**296
Five Directorates (China), **1:**423
Five Listenings (China), **1:**420
Five-Mile Act (England), **1:**468
Flacius Marcianus. *See* Marcian (emperor)
Flade, P. J., **1:**285
flag burning, **5:**337
Flammable Fabrics Act (U.S., 1953), **2:**177
Flavius the Scribe (Gnaeus Flavius), **3:**434
Fleet, the. *See* London Prison
Fleet Prison marriages, **4:**162
Fleet Street Inn, **5:**222
Fleiner, Fritz, **5:**418
Fleta, **4:**283
Fletcher, Alice, **4:***210*
Fletcher, Arthur, **2:**343
Fletcher, George, **5:**462
Flexner Report (1910), **2:**404
Florentinus, **3:**251
Florum Sparsio ad Jus Justinianeum (Grotius), **3:**127
Flos ultimarum voluntatum (Passagerii), **4:**237
Flower, Lucy, **3:**459
Foelix, Jean Jacques Gaspard, **2:**98
Fögen, M., **5:**161
Fögen, Marie Theres, **1:**282
folk law, **3:89–91**
Foltz, Clara Shortridge, **6:**143
Food, Drug, and Cosmetic Act (U.S., 1938), **2:**177; **3:**144
    Food Additives Amendments (1958), **2:**177
food, right to, in India, **3:**220
Food and Drug Administration (U.S.), **4:**30; **5:**84
Food and Drugs Act (U.S., 1906), **2:**177; **6:**54
    Amendments (U.S., 1962), **5:**82
food safety, administrative agencies and, **1:**26
food stamps, **6:**91
    moral judgement about, **6:**97
Foraker Act (U.S., 1900), **1:**370
Forbes, Francis, **1:**240
force and fraud, **3:**100
Force Bill (U.S., 1833), **5:**411–410

Forchhammer, Emil, **5**:316
Ford, Gerald, **2**:*163*
Ford, Henry Jones, **3**:20
Ford Foundation
    Gray Areas program, **4**:370–371; **6**:94
    in law and society research, **4**:31–32
    in legal education, **2**:406
    on social sciences, **5**:268
foreclosure, **4**:189
foreign commerce, Native Americans and, **4**:208
Foreign Corrupt Practices Act (U.S., 1977), **3**:289; **5**:94
foreign direct investment, United States and, **3**:285
foreigners in Chinese law, **3**:91–93
foreign judgments, law of, **2**:116
Foreign Jurisdiction Act (U.K., 1890), **1**:313
    Africa under, **1**:85
Foreign Lawyers' Law (Japan, 1986), **3**:385
Foreign Sovereign Immunities Act (U.S., 1976), **3**:296–297
foreign tax credit rules, **3**:287
forensic evidence, **3**:13–14
Foreshore and Seabed Act (New Zealand, 2004), **4**:147
Forest (Conservation) Act (India, 1980), **2**:453
forestalling, prohibition of, **2**:101
Forest Charter (England, ca. 1217), **4**:134, 135
    Magna Carta and, **4**:133
forgery
    ancient Greek law, **3**:2
    Chinese law, **2**:314
    medieval and post-medieval Roman law, **3**:102–103
Formey, Jean-Henri-Samuel, **6**:73
formula in ancient Roman law, **2**:51, 183; **3**:93–97
    compared to *cognitio*, **2**:52
    Gaius on, **3**:251
    legis actiones, **4**:81, 82
Formula secundam quam debetur sancta synodus in Dei nomine fieri, **1**:471
Förster, Franz, **5**:2
Forsthoff, Ernst, **1**:23
Fortas, Abe
    legal realism and, **4**:74
    New Deal and, **4**:78
Fortescue, John, **2**:128–129
    on absolutism, **1**:7
    comparative law, **2**:98

    on customary law, **2**:305, 306
    on Inns of Chancery, **3**:243
    on Inns of Court, **3**:242
    on legal theory, **4**:61
    on natural law, **4**:214
Fort Laramie, Treaty of (1868), **4**:209
forum, exterior *(ẓāhir)*, and interior forum *(bāṭin)*, **3**:97–98
Foster, Robert S., **4**:*178*
Foster, William Z(ebulon), **4**:336
Foucault, Michel
    on homosexuality, **3**:112
    on power, **4**:365
Fourteen Titles. See *Nomocanon*
Fourth World Conference on Women (Beijing, 1995), **3**:71
Fox, Charles James, **1**:380; **3**:441; **4**:143
Fox, Fowler and Company (England), **1**:272
Foxhall, Lin, **1**:186
Fragmenta Vaticana, **5**:151, 159
Fragment on Government, A (Bentham), **1**:287
Fragmento preliminar al estudio del derecho (Alberdi), **1**:216
Frames of Government of Pennsylvania (1681, 1683), **2**:286
Framework Agreement on Intellectual Property Cooperation (ASEAN, 1995), **3**:264
Framework Directive on Employment (European Union), **2**:337
France, **3**:98–100
    administrative law, **1**:21–22, 24
    adoption, **3**:46
    advocates in, **1**:57
    African colonies, **1**:78, *84*, 88–90
        decolonization of, **1**:92
        liberty villages, **1**:76
    anthropological perspective in, **1**:185–186
    attempt, **1**:237
    breach of contract, **1**:306–307
    Canada and, **1**:337
    children
        accountability of, **3**:44–45
    codes and codification, **2**:47, 48
        company law and, **2**:92
    company law, **2**:96
    conflict of laws, **2**:113
    constitutions, **2**:120, 121, 122
        constitution of 1791, **2**:120
    consumer protection, **2**:171–172
    courts, **2**:252, 253, 254; **3**:405, 406

supreme court, **3:**100
Enlightenment, **2:**444
feudal law, **3:**77
fideicommissum in, **3:**81
guarantee, **3:**128
housing, **4:**58
influence on
   Islamic law, **3:**421
   Japanese law, **3:**366, 373, 374, 375
   Russian law, **5:**166, 172
   Vietnamese law, **6:**79
insolvency law, **3:**249
insurance, **3:**258
interpretation, **3:**299, 300
Islamic symbols regulated in, **2:**483
Japan, treaty with, **3:**365, 372
judiciary in, **3:**422
Laos annexed by, **4:**13
law merchant, **4:**38
legal education, **2:**400
legislation in, **4:**91–92
maritime law, **4:**150
Ottoman Empire and, **3:**283
patent law, **3:**259
possession, **4:**362
precedent, **4:**381
private law, **4:**393, 394
privileges, **4:**398
procedure, **4:**434–435, 439
property law, **4:**476
public law, **5:**17
revolution of 1848, **2:**121
sale of land, **5:**193
servitude in real estate, **5:**224
Seychelles annexed by, **5:**234
social security, **5:**271
taxation, **5:**435, 436, 437, 438
United States colonies and, **6:**26, 32–33
franchise taxes, **1:**326
Francis, Richard, **4:**61
Franciscans in banking, **1:**274
Francisci, Pietro de, **5:**161
Francis I (France), **3:**191
   agreement with Süleiman, **3:**281
   Budé, Guillaume, and, **1:**316
Franco, Francisco, **2:**122; **5:**326
François I (France). *See* Francis I (France)
François le Douaren, **3:**192, 193
   Cujas, Jacques and, **2:**303
   Doneau, Hugues, and, **2:**359

Frank, Jerome
   on law and society, **4:**31
   on legal education, **4:**77
   in legal realism, **4:**74, 75
   in New Deal, **4:**78
Frank, Leo, **4:**452
Frank, Reinhard, **3:**136
Frankenstein, Incorporated (Wormser), **1:**325
Frankfurter, Felix, **3:**165, 428; **5:**92
   on administrative agencies, **1:**31
   on apportionment and reapportionment, **1:**201
   Hurst, James, Willard, clerkship with, **4:**33
   influence on Houston, Charles Hamilton, **2:**299
   in legal realism, **4:**74
   on search and seizure, **4:**387
   on statutory interpretation, **5:**361
Franklin, Benjamin, **1:**124
   Filangieri, Gaetano, and, **3:**84
   on poor people, **4:**368
   on University of Pennsylvania, **2:**402
Fraser, Simon
   act of attainder against, **6:**5
   execution, **1:**366
Fratres Militiae Christi, **1:**254
fraud, **3:**100–104
   bankruptcy and, **1:**266
   criminal law in medieval and post-medieval Roman law, **3:**102–103
   duress in, **2:**376
   England
      common law, **3:**100–102
      equity and, **2:**468, 470–471
   Islamic law
      banking and finance, **1:**262, 265
      in forum, external and internal, **3:**98
      obligations and, **4:**244
      option in, **4:**261
   New Zealand land registration, **4:**9
   private law in medieval and post-medieval Roman law, **3:**103–104
   Roman law
      delict, **2:**322–323
      formula in, **3:**95
      Labeo, Marcus Antistius, on, **3:**475
Fraud Act (U.K., 2006), **3:**101
Fraunce, Abraham, **4:**61

Frederick I Barbarossa (Holy Roman emperor), **4**:438; **5**:32
    feudal law under, **3**:78
    law school of Bologna and, **3**:314
    legislation by, **4**:91
    universities under, **6**:61
Frederick III (Palatinate), **2**:359
Frederick II the Great (Prussia), **2**:252
    enlightened absolutism under, **1**:8
    procedural law under, **4**:434
    promulgation of laws under, **5**:1
    on torture, **3**:9
    Wolff, Christian von, and, **6**:112
Frederick II (Sicily), **3**:395
    codification under, **2**:327
    courts under, **2**:251
    legislation by, **4**:91
    taxation under, **5**:436
Frederick Augustus II (king of Poland and elector of Saxony), **6**:73
Frederick William the Great Elector (Brandenburg), **3**:396
Frederick William I (Prussia), **5**:1
    on witchcraft, **2**:444–445
    Wolff, Christian von, and, **6**:112
Frederick William III (Prussia)
    unification of Protestant churches, **1**:351
Freedman's Bureau Act (U.S., 1867), **1**:218
Freedom of Information Act (U.S., 1966), **1**:29; **5**:83
    PATRIOT Act and, **5**:338
freedom of speech. *See* speech, freedom of
freedom of the press. *See* press, freedom of the
Freeman, S., **1**:*287*
Free Papua Movement, **4**:173
Free Speech League, **5**:333
free will and guilt, **3**:135
Freige, Johann Thomas, **3**:193
Freisler, Roland, **3**:*111*
Freitas, Augusto Teixeira de, **1**:302
    codification by, **1**:216; **5**:286
French Civil Code. *See* Code Civil (France, 1804)
French East India Company, **4**:171
French Guiana. *See* Guyane
French law. *See* France
French Law School (Cairo), **2**:398
French Polynesia. *See* Polynesia

French Revolution, **3**:396
    codification and, **2**:48
    effect on protection of intellectual property, **3**:259
Frescobaldi family, **1**:271
Freud, Sigmund, **3**:110
Freund, Ernst, **2**:26
Frickey, Philip
    on legal process, **4**:69
    on statutory interpretation, **5**:362
Fried, Charles, **2**:210
Friedan, Betty, **2**:339
Friedberg, Emil, **2**:219
Friedman, Lawrence, **3**:427; **4**:481; **5**:476
    on contracts, **2**:209
    on law and society, **4**:33, 35
    on state constitutions, **5**:350
Friedman, Mordechai Akiva, **3**:391
Friendly, Fred, **2**:155
Friendly, Henry, **5**:93
Frolik, Lawrence, **2**:423
"from status to contract" process, **2**:429–430
Fry, Elizabeth, **4**:41
Fuero Real (1252–1255), **1**:215; **5**:290, 298
Fueros Municipales, **5**:298, 299
Fuggers family, **1**:273
Fugitive Slave Act (U.S., 1793), **5**:263; **6**:39
    federalism and, **3**:60
Fugitive Slave Act (U.S., 1850), **5**:260
    federalism and, **3**:60
Fuhrman, Mark, **2**:302
Fulani, **1**:68, 73
Fulbeck, William, **2**:394
    on logic, **4**:61
Fuller, Lon
    on definition of law, **4**:18
    on legal positivism, **4**:356, 357
    on legal process, **4**:65
    on legal realism, **4**:356
    on natural law, **4**:219
Fuller, Melville W., **4**:490; **5**:443
full faith and credit
    in Articles of Confederation, **1**:224
    and law of foreign judgements, **2**:116
Fulvius Centumalus, **2**:269
Fundamenta juris naturae et gentium (Thomasius), **5**:464
    on absolutism, **1**:8
fundamental duties, **3**:104–105

fundamental interests, equal protection and, **2:**462, 463
Fundamental Principles of Civil Legislation (Russia, 1991), **5:**177
fundamental rights, **3:105–107**
   environmental law, **2:**453–454
   European Communities, **2:**488
   European Union, **2:**487
   family law, **3:**48
   Indian Constitution, **2:**145
funerary ritual
   ancient Greece, **3:**28
   China, **3:**86
      Chinese-speaking Muslims, **1:**399–400
fungible things *(mithliyyat)*, **2:**79; **3:107–108**
   loans of, **4:**118–119
   obligations and, **4:**244
   salam and, **2:**203
fuqahāayn (expert in legal sciences), **4:**71
furnace land (China), **4:**4
Fürsprecher (intercessor), **1:**56
furū' al-fiqh, **3:**320–321
Fustel de Coulanges, Numa Denis, **1:**185
Fyneux, John, **3:**472

G
Gabon, **1:**105
Gabriel's conspiracy, **5:**260
Gadamer, Hans-Georg, **4:**363, 364
Gagarin, Michael
   anthropological perspective of, **1:**186
   on Draco, **1:**164–165
   on oaths, **4:**402
   on torture, **5:**481
   on unity of Greek law, **1:**164
Gaill, Andreas, **2:**112; **5:**106
Gaius. *See also Institutes* (Gaius)
   on the areas of Roman law, **4:**459–460
   on conflict of laws, **2:**109
   didactic programs, **3:**456
   on employment and labor law, **2:**430
   on formula, **3:**94, 95–96
   historigraphic work of, **5:**158
   influence on
      Paul, **4:**290
      Tribonian, **6:**8
   on inheritance, **3:**435
   on jurists, **3:**434
   Labeo, Marcus Antistius, on, **3:**475
   on the law of persons, **4:**302
   on legal procedure, **5:**142
   on *legis actiones*, **3:**94; **4:**82, 83–84
   on obligations, **4:**243
   on ownership, **4:**462
   on partnership, **1:**319
   on the procedural system, **4:**375, 376
   on property, **4:**462, 464, 465
   on the provincial edict, **3:**431
   on reason, **4:**17
   on religious law, **5:**120
   on ritual search, **2:**323
   on Rufus, Servius Sulpicius, **4:**79
   on schools of jurists, **2:**392
   systematization by, **5:**420
   on the Twelve Tables, **6:**20
   on unjust enrichment, **6:**65
   on wills, **5:**372
   women under, **6:**118
Gaius Octavius. *See also* Augustus (Roman emperor)
Galanter, Marc, **4:**33, 34
Gale, Charles, **2:**379
Gale, Charles James, **5:**157
Galen (Galenus), **5:**420; **6:**62
Galileo, Galilei, **3:**193
Gallanis, Thomas P., **3:**5
Gallen, Saint, **5:**31
Gallus, C. Aquillius, **3:**434
Gama, Vasco de, **5:**234
Gambia
   British rule, **1:**85–86
   constitution, **2:**137
   independence of, **1:**93
gambling
   Chinese law, **3:109**
   Islamic law, **1:**260, 262
Gandhi, Indira, **5:**208
   use of Emergence Powers, **2:**146
Gandhi, Mohandas K., **3:**216; **5:**283, *283*, 284
Gandius, Albertus, **4:**437; **5:**32
Gandoni, Matteo, **2:**399
Ganerbschaft, **3:**80
Gans, Eduard, **6:**25
   comparative law and, **2:**98
Gao Zu (Han emperor), **1:**456
   on amnesty, **1:**133
   review under, **1:**196
gap research, **4:**33
García Fernández (count of Castile), **3:**397
Gardella, Robert, **2:**193

Gardiner, Lord, **4**:42
Gardner, Jane F., **6**:117, 119
Garfield, James A., **4**:335
Garofalo, Luigi, **5**:163
Garo Hills (Christian Marriage) Act (India, 1954), **3**:223
Garrison, Lloyd K.
    Hurst, James Willard, and, **4**:33
    on law and society, **4**:31
Garrison, William Lloyd, **4**:336
Gasparri, Pietro, **1**:353
GATS. *See* General Agreement on Trade in Services
GATT. *See* General Agreement on Tariffs and Trade
Gaulle, Charles de, **1**:92
Gautama, **3**:152, 155, 156
    on *smriti*, **5**:264
Gautamadharmasūtra, **5**:35–37
gavelking, **2**:81
gay, lesbian, bisexual, and transgender theory, **3:109–112**
    equal protection and, **2**:462–463
    family law and, **6**:143
    feminist legal theory and, **3**:68–69
    same-sex marriage and
        England, **3**:33, 35
        United States, **3**:55–56
Gayoom, Maumoon Abdul, **4**:139–140
gay rights
    adoption in the United Kingdom, **1**:47
    United States
        equal protection in, **2**:464
        legal profession participation, **4**:53
Gazeta de Caracas (Venezuela, newspaper), **1**:286
ge
    under Song dynasty, **1**:454, 457
    in Sui and Tang law, **1**:454
Geist des römischen Rechts, Der (Jhering), **3**:399; **5**:160
Gelasius I (pope), **2**:318; **4**:351–352
Geldart, James, **2**:394
Gellius, Aulus, **3**:435
    historical information provided by, **5**:158
    on jurists, **2**:391
    on Labeo, Marcus Antistius, **3**:476
    on magistrates, **4**:132
gender
    Bangladesh, **1**:258, 259
    in Canadian Supreme Court, **1**:340
        gay, lesbian, bisexual, and transgender theory on, **3**:109–112

    Imāmī school and, **3**:340
    in Indonesia, **3**:335–336
    inheritance law and, **3**:238
    naturalization law and, **3**:209
    natural law on, **4**:218
    parental authority and, **1**:394
General Abridgement and Digest of American Law, A (Dane), **2**:205
general acceptance test, **3**:13
General Agreement on Tariffs and Trade (GATT)
    United States and, **3**:284–285
    Uruguay Round, **3**:285
General Agreement on Trade in Services (GATS), **3**:285
General Allotment Act (U.S., 1887), **4**:210; **6**:50
General Board of Health (U.K.), **2**:451
General Clauses Act (India, 1868, 1897), **3**:216
General Council of the Bar (U.K.), **4**:42
general law and personal law. *See* personal law and general law
"General Provisions for Legilsation in the Netherlands East Indies," **3**:226
General Relief (U.S.), **6**:94
    moral judgement about, **6**:97
General Strike (U.K., 1926), **2**:427
General Terms and Conditions Act (Germany), **4**:395
general welfare clause, **3:113–115**
generation-skipping transfer tax (U.S., 1986), **3**:238
Geneva Agreements (1954), **5**:314
Geneva Convention (1864), **3**:283
Geneva Convention on the International Recognition of Rights in Aircraft (1948), **2**:114
Geneva Convention Relating to the Status of Refugees (1951–1967), **2**:114
Geneva Convention Relating to the Status of Stateless Persons (1954), **2**:114
Genghis Khan, **4**:183
genital mutilation
    Africa, **1**:71, 73
    feminist legal theory on, **3**:71
genos (birth), **3**:27
Genovesi, Antonio, **3**:83
Gentili, Alberico, **3**:191; **5**:156
    on international law, **3**:282–283
    at Oxford University, **2**:393
Gentili, Scipione, **3**:192
    Hugues, Doneau, and, **2**:360
Gentlemen's Agreement for voluntary restriction of immigration from Japan (1907), **3**:208

Gény, François
 on judges, **4:**226
 on private law, **3:**100
Genzmer, Erich, **5:**163
Geographical Indications Act (Malaysia, 2000), **3:**263
Geonim, **3:**388, 391
George, David Lloyd, **4:**90
George, Duke of Clarence, **6:**5
George, Henry, **5:**442
George, Lloyd, **5:**429
George I (England), **2:**132
George II (England), **2:**132
 barristers under, **1:**279
 Mansfield appointed by, **4:**142
George III (England), **4:**386
 United States colonies and, **6:**32
George V (England), **2:**132
George VI (England)
 treason under, **6:**5
George Taufa'ahau Tupou I (Tonga king), **4:**345
Georgetown University, **2:**404
George Washington University, **2:**404
Georgia, codification in, **2:**50
Geradas, **1:**53
Gérando, Marie-Joseph de, **1:**23
Gerber, Carl Friedrich von, **1:**23
German Act to Modernize the Laws of Obligations (2001), **3:**119
German Civil Code. *See* Bürgerliches Gesetzbuch Deutschland
German Code of Commerce (1861–1865), **4:**222
German Democratic Republic, **3:**119. *See also* Germany
 constitutions, **2:**122
Germania (Tacitus), **6:**1
Germanic customary laws, medieval
 on adoption, **3:**46
 advocates in, **1:**56–58
 on children, **3:**44
  property rights, **3:**45–46
 on guardianship, **3:**47–48
 on legitimacy of children, **3:**47
 on marriage, **3:**41–42
 on sexual crimes, **5:**229–230
 vicarious liability and, **6:**77
Germanic provincial administration, **3:**115–117
German Illegitimacy Act (1969), **5:**387
German National Socialist Workers Party, **6:**71

Germany, **3:117–119.** *See also* German Democratic Republic; National Socialist law
 absolutism, **1:**7–8
 accession into European Union, **2:**491–492
 administrative law, **1:**22
 African colonies, **1:**83–85
  on citizenship, **1:**79
  decolonization of, **1:**93–94
  liberty villages, **1:**76
 African law studies, **1:**91
 alternative dispute resolution, **1:**129
 anthropological perspective on, **1:**186–187
 assignment, **1:**228
 attempt, **1:**237
 Austrian law and, **6:**26
 Baltic states occupied by, **1:**256
 banking, **1:**275
 bishops, **1:**296
 company law, **2:**96
 competition regulation, **2:**102–103
 conflict of laws, **2:**113
 constitutions, **2:**120, 121, 122
 consumer protection, **2:**171
 courts, **2:**252, 253, 254
  ecclesiastical, **2:**385
 Enlightenment, **2:**445
 federalism, **5:**354
 feudal law, **3:**77
 fideicommissum, **3:**80
 fraud, **3:**103
 guarantee, **3:**128
 guilt, **3:**133, 135, 136
 humanism, **2:**400
 influence on
  Japanese law, **3:**375
  Russian law, **5:**166, 170
 insolvency law, **3:**248, 249, 250
 insurance, **3:**258
 intellectual property, **3:**260
 interpretation, **3:**299–300
 judges, **3:**405–406
 jurisprudence of concepts, **3:**432–433
 law merchant, **4:**40
 legislation, **4:**91, 92
 medieval and post-medieval Roman law
  on evidence, **3:**7–8, 9, 10
 negotiable instruments, **4:**222, 223
 New Guinea annexed by, **4:**173
 positivism, **4:**355
 precedent, **4:**380–381

private law, **4**:393–396
procedure, **4**:435, 438, 439
property law, **4**:476, 477
restitution, **5**:131
revolution of 1848, **2**:121
Roman law and, **4**:276–278; **5**:158, 162
servitude in real estate, **5**:224
social security in, **5**:271
taxation, **5**:436, 437, 438–439
theft and robbery, **5**:463
treason and World War I, **6**:3–4
undue influence, **6**:25
witch trials, **6**:108–109
Gernet, Louis
   on ancient Greek law, **1**:163
   anthropological perspective of, **1**:185–186
Gerry, Ellbridge, **1**:202
gerrymandering, **1**:201, 202, *203*
Gerson, Jean, **5**:230
   on equity, **2**:468
Geschichte der Quellen und Literatur (Corat), **5**:158
Geschichte des römischen Rechts im Mittelalter (Savigny), **5**:159, 162, 195
Gesetzbuch über Verbrechen und schwere Polizeiübertretungen (Law code on Crime and Severe Police Transgressions, Austria, 1803), **6**:162
Geta, **4**:279
Ghana
   in British Commonwealth, **1**:315
   constitution, **1**:105
   diplomacy, **1**:74
   empire of, **1**:67
   family law, **1**:103, 104
   independence, **1**:93
   indigenous law, **1**:65
   inheritance, **2**:38
   judicial system, **1**:99
gharar. *See* fraud: Islamic law
Ghazali, Abu Hamid Muhammad al-, **3:119–120**, 352
   on *amr bi-l-ma 'rūf*, **1**:382
   in spiritual renewal, **4**:128
   on worship, **6**:147, 148
Ghita', Muhammad Kashif al-, **1**:205
Ghiyath al-umam (al-Juwayni), **3**:463
Gia Long code (Vietnam), **6**:79
Giannelli, Paul, **3**:13
Giannini, Massimo Severo, **1**:23
Gibbon, Edward, **5**:159, 160
G.I. Bill (U.S., 1944), **2**:405; **3**:183

GI Bill of Rights (U.S.), **6**:54
Gibsons, John, **2**:206
Gideon, Clarence, **4**:454
Gideon's Trumpet, **4**:454
Gierke, Otto von, **4**:394
   on systematization, **5**:421
gift. *See* donation (gift)
Gilbert, Jeffray, **2**:441
   on equity, **2**:470
   on evidence, **3**:5
Gilbert's Act (Great Britain, 1782), **4**:349
Gilfix, Michael, **2**:422
Gilligan, Carol, **3**:68
Gilmore, Grant
   on "death of contract," **2**:209
   on pre-UCC commercial law, **2**:76
   on Uniform Commercial Code, **2**:77
Ginnie Mae. *See* Government National Mortgage Agency
Ginsburg, Ruth Bader
   on abortion, **2**:339
   appointment of, **2**:344
   feminist legal theory of, **3**:66
   on reproductive rights, **6**:141
   on right to bear arms, **1**:222
   on sex discrimination, **2**:339; **6**:138
Giolla na Naomh mac Aodhagaín, **3**:309
Giovanni d'Andrea, **3**:356
Giphanius, Hubert, **2**:360
Gira Sandesaya, **5**:303
Gitlow, Benjamin, **3**:409
Giuntini, Vincenzo, **1**:285
Giurisprudenza mercantile, **4**:40
Gladstone, William, **2**:90; **5**:429
Glanvill, **3**:177
   agreements under seal distinguished from informal contracts, **2**:195–196
   on contractual remedies, **2**:194
   on conveyancing, **2**:213
   on equity, **2**:466
   on grant of land, **4**:317
   influence on Scottish law, **5**:198
   on obligations, **4**:243
   on punishment, **5**:27
   on rape, **5**:68
   Roman law in, **5**:157
   on royal supervision of land, **3**:75
   on writs, **2**:80; **4**:419, 420
Glanvill, Ranulf de, **3**:177
   on bailment, **1**:249

influence on Blackstone, William, **1:**298
   on mortgage, **4:**188
   on sale, **5:**189
   treatise by, **2:**435
   on writs, **4:**419
Glaser, Julius, **6:**26
gleaning, right of, **2:**381
Gleeson, Murray, **1:**244–245
Glenelg, Charles Grant Lord, **1:**239
Glins, Taco van, **4:**151
Global Crossing, **5:**95
globalization
   legal anthropology on, **4:**60
   in public law of administration, **1:**23–24
   Southeast Asia in, **5:**316
Glorious Revolution (1688), **1:**386; **4:**282; **6:**31, 36
Glossa ordinaria (Accursius), **1:**19, 248; **2:**6, 303; **3:**355
   on conflict of laws, **2:**111
   on succession, **5:**385, 392
Glossa ordinaria (Johannes Teutonicus), **2:**220–221, 317
glossators of civil law, **2:**6–7; **3:**297, 355
Glotz, Gustave, **1:**185
Gluckman, Max
   in legal anthropology, **4:**59
   on Lozi judges, **1:**91
Gnomon of the Idios Logos, **2:**417–418
   on inheritance, **1:**159–160
Gobierno del Perú (Matienzo), **1:**215–216; **5:**291
Godefroy, Denis, **2:**356; **3:**190
Godefroy, Jacques, **2:**356; **3:**190; **6:**20
Goebbels, Joseph, **3:**110
Goebel, Julius, **6:**30
Goethe, Johann Wolfgang von
   as advocate, **1:**57
   on Filangieri, Gaetano, **3:**84
Goff, Robert, **2:**443; **5:**130
Goitein, Samuel, **2:**74
Goldberg, Stephen, **3:**489
Gold Coast Colony, **1:**86
Golden Bull (1356), **1:***293*; **2:**120; **3:**395
   on age of majority, **3:**45
Golden Pali Text, **5:**315
Golden Yoke, **5:**305
Goldman, Emma, **6:**140
Goldmark, Josephine
   on social science, **5:**266
   on women's labor laws, **6:**136

Goldschmidt, Levin
   comparative law, **2:**99
   on negotiable instruments, **4:**223
goldsmiths in English banking, **1:**271
Goldziher, Ignaz, **3:**198
Gómez, Juan Vicente, **6:**74
Goodell, William, **2:**207
good faith
   Islamic law, **3:**98
   Roman law, **5:**144
      contract, **1:**319
   in search and seizure, **5:**206
Goodhart, Arthur L., **4:**379–380
Gorbachev, Nikolai, **4:**14
Gordian III (emperor), **3:**211–212
Gordley, James, **2:**208
Gordon, George, **6:**3
Gordon, William E., **2:**442
Gorgias (Plato), **4:**321; **5:**23
   on forensic oratory, **4:**112
   on *nomos*, **1:**145
Goriushkin, Z. A., **5:**172
Gortyn, **1:**142; **2:**28–29; **3:**120–123, **120–123**; **4:**401
   adoption, **1:**40, 42
   adultery, **1:**51–52
   divorce, **2:**346
   family law, **3:**30
   free persons, **5:**356
   inheritance, **1:**142; **3:**30, 120–121, 122–123, 229
      heiress, **3:**230
   inscriptions in, **1:**147
   judges, **1:**154
   judicial procedure, **1:**136–137
   legal procedure, **4:**400, 401
   marriage, **4:**155
   oaths, **1:**153; **4:**402
   procedural law, **1:**142
   rape, **5:**65–66
   scholarship on, **1:**163
   Second Code, **1:**142
   slavery, **5:**245, 246
   status, **5:**355
   women, **6:**115, 116
   as written law, **1:**139, 154
Goseibai Shikimoku (Institutes of Justice) (Japan, 1232), **3:**368
Gothofredus. *See* Godefroy, Denis; Godefroy, Jacques
Goulart, Simon, **1:**349
Gould, James, **1:**12

Gould, Jay, **1:**268–269
Gouriet, John, **2:**330
government. *See also* absolutism; military governments
    Augustine, Saint, on goals of, **4:**96
    Chinese law
        offenses damaging the efficiency of government, **4:253–255**
        structure under Tang, **1:**422–423
    due process as restraint on, **2:**367–368
    England
        cabinet government, **1:**386; **2:**132
        central government, **1:385–387**
        mixed government theory, **5:**215
    legitimacy
        Africa, **1:**98–99
        British Commonwealth, **1:**310, *311*, 312, 313
        Islamization and, **6:**129–130
    local government law, **4:119–123**
    subjected to the norms of the shari'a, **3:**318
    United States, growth of, **6:**53–55
Government National Mortgage Agency (Ginnie Mae), **3:**183
Government of India Act (1935), **1:**313–314; **2:**143–144; **3:**216
    on succession, **5:**398
Government of Ireland Act (1920), **3:**313
Govinda, **1:**236
Gowon, Yakubu, **1:***96*
Gozzadini, Ludovico di Gozzadino de', **5:**364
Grabar, V. E., **5:**178
Gracchus, Tiberius Sempronius, **4:**94
Gradenwitz, Otto, **5:**161
Graebner, William, **2:**423
Grammar of the Spanish Language (Bello), **1:**286
Gramsci, Antonio, **2:**297
Gran Colombia, Republic de, **2:**62
Grand Assize (England), **3:**75
Grandes Ordonnances of Louis XIV (France), **2:**47
Grand Pronouncements (case law code, Ming), **1:**430
Granger laws, **5:**100–101
Grangers, **5:**77, 88
Grant, Ulysses S., **6:**51
Grant Duff, M. E., **4:**137
Grantees of Reversions Act (England, 1540), **4:**13
graphē paranomōn, **3:123–126**
    Athens, **1:**141
    for magistrates, **1:**234
    prevalence of, **1:**143

Gratian (monk), **4:**433
Gratian (Roman emperor). *See also Decretum Gratiani*
    decretals under, **5:**197
    religious law under, **5:**123
    on sexual crimes, **5:**229
Gratius, **5:**230
Grattan's parliament (Ireland, 1782), **3:**309
Gravina, Gian Vincenzo, **3:126,** 357
Gray, John Chipman, **2:**26
    on property, **1:**13
    on trusts, **5:**407
Gray's Inn. *See* Inns of Court
Great Act of Grace (China, 729), **1:**134–135
Great Britain. *See also* England
    African colonies of, **1:**78, 85–88
    and Indonesia, **3:**226
    insolvency law, **3:**249–250
    jurisdiction over inheritance, **3:**235
    Seychelles annexed by, **5:**234–235
    treaty with Japan, **3:**365, 372
    trusts in, **3:**237
Great Chronicles (Sri Lanka), **5:**303, 304
Great Code. *See* Code of Gortyn
Great Compromise. *See* Connecticut Compromise
Great Council of Chiefs (Fiji), **3:**82
Great Council of Malines, **4:**225
Great Depression
    administrative agencies in, **1:**27–28
    bankruptcy during, **1:**269
    executive power in, **3:**22
    federalism during, **3:**61–62
    housing, **3:**182–183
    judicial power and the, **3:**409
    labor and employment law, **3:**480–481
    legal education in, **2:**405
    property rights and the, **4:**491
    regulation during the, **5:**80, 81
    taxation and, **5:**444–446
    welfare programs, **6:**96
Great Leap Forward (People's Republic of China, 1958), **1:**444
Great Ming Code. *See* Ming code (China)
Great Nordic War (1700–1718), **5:**415
Great Principles of the Civil Law (People's Republic of China, 1985–1986), **1:**446
Great Proletarian Cultural Revolution (People's Republic of China, 1966–1976), **1:**444

Great Qing Code with Collected Commentaries and Appended Substatutes *(Da Qinglüjijiefuli)* (1646), **1:**459, 461
Great Reform Act (Britain, 1832), **2:**132
Great Reform Act (England, 1832), **4:**285
Great Rhetra (Sparta), **5:**327, 328
Great Sessions (Wales), **6:**100–101
Great Society (U.S.), **5:**82, 83
    administrative agencies in, **1:**29
    legal aid in, **4:**51–52
    legal education and, **2:**406
Great Yuan Complete Regulations *(Da Yuantongchi)* (1321), **1:**458
Great Yuan Statutes and Precedents *(Da Yuandianzhang)* (1322), **1:**458
Great Zimbabwe, **1:**69
Greece, modern
    accession into European Union, **2:**490
    civil code of, **1:**330
    conflict of laws, **2:**113
    guarantee in, **3:**129
    Islamic law in, **3:**333
Greek Law of Sale, The (Pringsheim), **1:**163
Green, Leon, **4:**74, 77
Greene, Nathanael, **4:**177
Greenleaf, Simon, **1:**12; **6:**46
Greenstein, Fred, **3:**22
Gregorian Code. *See Codex Gregorianus* (291–292)
Gregorius, **3:**436
Gregory I (pope)
    decretals by, **2:**316
    on evidence, **3:**8
    papacy of, **4:**352
Gregory VII (pope)
    bishops and archbishops under, **1:**295
    decretals by, **2:**317
    papal power under, **4:**352–353
    reforms under, **1:**466
Gregory VIII (pope), **2:**317
Gregory IX (pope)
    Baldus de Ubaldis, Petrus, on, **1:**250
    on charities, **1:**390
    codification under, **2:**327
    decretals of, **2:**221–222, 399; **4:**433
Gregory X (pope), **2:**223
Gregory XIII (pope)
    decretals, **2:***317*
    papal bulls of, **2:**224
Gregory of Tours, **5:**31

Grenada
    reliance on British case law and principles, **1:**369
    U.S. invasion of, **6:**89
Gresham, Thomas, **1:**292
Gretna Green marriages, **4:**162–163, *163*
Greve, Petrus de, **4:**235
Grey, Jane, **1:**366
Gribaldi Mofa, Matteo, **3:**190
grievances
    against lawyers, **4:**50–51
    mediation and, **3:**489–490
    Saudi Arabia, **1:**208
    Taft-Hartley Act on, **3:**483
Griffini, Eugenio, **6:**161
Griffith, Walter Hussey, **2:**442
Grimke, Angelina, **6:**134
Grimm, Jakob, **2:**254
Griquas, **1:**70
Griswold, Estelle, **6:**141
Groenewegen van der Made, Simon, **4:**226
Grogger, Jeffrey, **4:**373
Groot, Huig de, **3:**193. *See* Grotius, Hugo
Gross, Charles, **4:**36
Grossman, Joel, **4:**33
Grotius, Hugo, **3:**126–128, 291; **5:**438
    on breach of contract, **1:**307, 309
    on civil liability, **5:**470
    on error and mistake, **2:**475
    on illegality and invalidity, **3:**203
    influenced by
        Descartes, René, **2:**400
        Doneau, Hugues, **2:**360; **4:**226
    influence on
        German law, **3:**118
        Pufendorf, Samuel von on, **5:**21
        Scottish law, **5:**200
        Thomasius, Christian, **5:**464
        Wolff, Christian von, **6:**111
    on international law, **3:**283; **4:**16
    on natural law, **4:**215, 216–217; **5:**43
    on ownership, **4:**476
    on punishment, **3:**134
    on servitude in real estate, **5:**224
    on succession, **5:**384
    on systematization, **5:**421
    on unjust enrichment, **6:**65
    on war and peace, **3:**276
Growing Old in America (Fischer), **2:**422

Growth of Criminal Law in Ancient Greece, The (Calhoun), **1:**163
Growth of the Law, The (Cardozo), **2:**26
Gruffydd, Dafydd ap, **4:**205
Grundgesetz für die Bundesrepublik Deutschland (Basic Constitutional Law for the Federal Republic of Germany) (1949), **2:**122
Grundriss des allgemeinen, deutschen und bayrischen Staatsrechtes (Kreittmayr), **3:**473
Grundsätze des Natur- und Völckerrechts. See *Institutiones juris naturae et gentium* (Wolff)
Guadeloupe, **1:**369
Guandong leased territory, **1:**451
Guangzhouwan, French territory of, **1:**451
Guanshilü (Code on Customs-Stations and Markets), **5:**183–184
Guantanamo Bay, **4:**180–181
Guanxingtong. See Song code (China)
Guan Zhong, **4:**287
Guanzi, **5:**165
Guaranítica Wars (1754–1756), **5:**300
guarantee, **3:128–129**
Guardian Council (Iran), **2:**139
Guardians and Wards Act (India, 1890), **3:**51, 223; **4:**299
  on adoption, **1:**49
  in Bangladesh, **4:**300
Guardians and Wards Act (Pakistan, 1890), **4:**275
guardianship
  ancient Greece, **4:**153
  Byzantine law, **4:**309
  elderlaw on, **2:**424, 425
  England, **1:**393
    equity and, **2:**470
  French Code Civil on, **3:**48
  India, **3:**51
  Islamic law, **4:**165–166
  Italy, **3:**48
  in Libya, **4:**297
  medieval and post-medieval Roman law, **3:**47–48
  in Pakistan, **4:**275
  Roman law, **2:**420; **4:**304, 305, 306, 307, 308
Guardianship Act (U.K., 1973), **1:**394
Guardianship of Infants Act (U.K., 1886, 1925), **1:**393; **3:**34
  on mothers' rights, **1:**394
Guarino, Antonio, **5:**161
Guarnerius. See Irnerius
Guatemala, **3:129–131**
  adoption of Peruvian Civil Code, **1:**384
  slavery abolished in, **5:**254

Gui, Bernardo, **4:**438
Guidon de la Mer, **1:**36
guilds
  Chinese law, **1:464–465**
    contracts and, **2:**193
    sale of goods, **5:**185
  as early corporations, **2:**88
  English common law, **3:131–133**
    alternative dispute resolution in, **1:**129
  mutual support in, **5:**270–271
guilt *(Schuld)*, **3:133–137**
Guinea-Bissau
  constitution, **2:**137
  decolonization, **1:**93
  formation, **1:**79
Guiteau, Charles, **4:**335
Guizot, François-Pierre-Guillaume, **1:**302
Gulati, Mitu, **3:**70
Gulf of Tonkin resolution (U.S., 1964), **6:**89
Gun Control Act (U.S., 1968), **1:**220
gun-control movement, **1:**220–222
Gundebad, **3:**116
Gun-Free School Zones Act (1990), **3:**63–64
Gunpowder Plotters, **6:**3
Gurney, Baron, **1:**231
Gusfield, Joseph
  on alcohol use, **1:**125
  on drinking and driving, **1:**127
Gusmão, Xanana, **2:**385
Gustavus II Adolphus (Sweden), **5:**415
Gustavus III (Sweden), **5:**416
  enlightened absolutism under, **1:**8
Guttridge, H. C., **2:**99
Guy, J. A., **5:**345, 346
Guy, Thomas, **4:**193
Guyana, **3:137–138**
  colonial law, **5:**295–296
Guyana Independence Act (1966), **3:**138
Guyane, **5:**296

H

habeas corpus, **4:**69
Habeas Corpus Act (England, 1641), **5:**347
Habibie, **3:**227–228
Habibullah (Afghanistan), **1:**59
Habilitation (Wolff), **6:**111
Habitat Conservation Plans, **2:**457
Hadawiyya, al-, **3:**341
ḥadd crimes, **1:**367, 368

Hadi ila-l-Haqq, ʿAlallah Ahmad ibn Sulayman bin al-, **6:**162
Hadi ila l-Haqq Yahya ibn al-Husayn, al-, **3:**139, 341; **4:**144; **6:**155, 156
hadiths, **3:***332*
    Abu Hanifa on, **1:**9–10
    on alcohol and drugs, **1:**120
    authenticity of, **3:**331
    censorship and, **1:**382
    collection by Ibn Hanbal, **3:**196
    Ibn Hazm and, **3:**198
    on lease and tenancy, **4:**56
    in legal education, **2:**396–397
    Malik ibn Anas on, **4:**140
    muftis on, **4:**194
    Sahnun, ʿAbd al-Salam ibn Saʿid al-Tanukhi, on, **5:**182–183
    Shafiʿi, Muhammad ibn Idris al-, on, **5:**236
    transmitters of, **4:**71
    Western scholars on authenticity of, **3:**333
Hadrami, Ba-Fadl al-, **2:**41
Hadrian (Roman emperor), **3:**211
    Celsus the Younger in advisory legal council of, **1:**373
    decretal collection by, **2:**318
    on formula, **3:**95
    Hellenistic law under, **1:**160–161
    Julian and, **3:**430–431
    jurists under, **3:**435
    legal procedure under, **2:**235
    on magistrates, **4:**132
    praetorian edict consolidation, **2:**32; **3:**430–431; **4:**464; **5:**146
    women under, **6:**118
Hadza, **1:**71
Haenel, Gustavus, **5:**159
Hägerström, Axel, **5:**417
Hague Conference (1964), **5:**192
Hague Conference on Private International Law (1893), **2:**114
Hague Peace Conferences (1899 and 1907), **3:**283
Hahn, Heinrich, **5:**384
Hai Gaon, Rav, **3:**391
Hailey, Lord, **1:**65
Hailsham, Lord, **2:**133
Haiti, **1:**370
    slave rebellions in, **5:**259
Haitian Codes (1825), **1:**370
Hajj, Ibn Amir al-, **6:**147

hajr (restriction of capacity to act and contract), **1:**359
Halabi, Ibrahim al, **4:***264*
Halbherr, Federico, **2:**28
Hale, Matthew, **1:**387; **2:**284; **3:**178, 247
    on bills of exchange, **1:**292
    on burglary, **1:**317
    on corporations, **1:**321
    on duress, **2:**374
    English common law and, **6:**33
    on English law and Christianity, **5:**109
    influence on Blackstone, William, **1:**298
    on inland bills, **4:**38
    on judicial law making, **5:**277
    in law reform, **4:**41
    in legal education, **2:**394
    on legal theory, **4:**61
    on precedent, **4:**378
    on rape, **5:**68
    on structure of law, **2:**440
    on torture, **5:**485
    on treason, **6:**2
Hale, Nathan, **4:**177
Hale, Robert, **2:**297
    on law and economics, **4:**23
    in legal realism, **4:**74, 75, 76
Hales, Justice, **5:**461
Halévy, Élie, **3:**437
Halhed, Nathaniel Brassey, **3:**157
Hall, Radclyffe, **1:**381
Hallaj, al-Husayn ibn Mansur al-, **3:**196
Hallaq, Wael, **4:**194
Haller, Berchtold, **1:**350
Halley, Janet, **3:**70
Hallifax, Samuel, **2:**393–394
Hallstein, Walter, **2:***490;* **4:**395
Halsbury, Lord (Hardinge Stanley Giffard), **4:**9–10
Hamas, **1:**207
Hamdan, Salim Ahmed, **4:**181
Hamilton, Alexander, **4:**97. *See also Federalist Papers*
    Annapolis Convention and, **2:**149
    on bankruptcy, **1:**267
    on commerce clause, **2:**64
    defense of John Peter Zenger, **3:**442
    on executive power, **3:**19–20, 22–23
    on general welfare clause, **3:**113, 114
    on judicial power, **3:**406
    on judicial review, **2:**152–153
    on judiciary, **3:**425

on oppressive laws, **4**:454
on property, **4**:483
on right to bear arms, **1**:217–218
on self-interest, **4**:481
on taxation, **5**:440
Whiskey Rebellion and, **6**:40
Hamilton, Walton H.
   in legal realism, **4**:74, 76
Hammurabi (Babylonian king), **3**:389; **5**:273. *See also* Code of Hammurabi
Hampton, Fred, **4**:337
Hamza, Abu, **3**:348
Hanafi school of Islamic law, **3:342–345**; **6**:155. *See also* Abu Yusuf, Yaʻqub ibn Ibrahim; Ibn ʻAbidin, Muhammad Amin; Kasani, Abu Bakr ibn Masʻud; Muhammad Qadri Pasha al-Hanafi; Muzani, Abu Ibrahim Ismaʻil ibn Yahya al-; Sarakhsi, Muhammad ibn Ahmad ibn Abi Sahl; Shaybani, Muhammad ibn al-Hasan al-; Zufar ibn al-Hudhail
   under Abbasid dynasty, **1**:2
   acknowledgement, **1**:20
   alcohol and drug use, **1**:121, 122
   apostasy, **2**:278–279
   the body, **1**:299
   books on legal devices by, **3**:321
   child support, **1**:397
   codifications by, **2**:397
   commercial law, **2**:73
   concept of law, **5**:451
   consensual divorce, **2**:350
   contracts, **2**:74, 199
      agricultural, **1**:116–117
      object of commercial, **2**:79
   custody rights, **1**:397
   custom, **4**:266
   damage, **2**:311
   deposit, **2**:332
   distinction between religious duty and legal obligation, **3**:322
   donation, **2**:359
   duress, **2**:375
   duty, **2**:376–377
   education in, **4**:71
   enforcement, **2**:431
   father-child relations, **3**:37
   fungible things, **3**:108
   geographical presence
      Afghanistan, **1**:59, 60
      Balkan peninsula, **1**:252
      Bangladesh, **1**:257
      China, **2**:482
      Iran, **3**:301
      Iraq, **3**:305
      Maghrib and al-Andalus, **4**:127–128
      Ottoman Empire, **4**:73, 264–270; **6**:128
      Pakistan, **4**:275
      South Asia, **5**:307
      Yemen, **6**:155
   guardianship, **4**:166
   imprisonment, **4**:384
   impurity of dead bodies, **5**:59
   influence on Ottoman civil code, **2**:35
   inheritance, **3**:39
   lease and tenancy, **4**:56
   legal norms, **4**:62
   legal reasoning, **4**:63, 64
   marriage, **4**:165, 166
      repudiation of, **4**:168
   non-Muslims, **3**:316
   partnership, **4**:289
   persons, **4**:311–312
   pledge, **4**:327
   possession, **4**:360
   public law, **5**:19
   punishment, **4**:431
   relatives proximity, **3**:38
   retaliation, **2**:279
   rights, **5**:136–137
   Shafiʻi school and, **3**:352
   sodomy, **3**:181
   territorial concepts, **5**:451, 452–454
   trade, **2**:73
   usurpation, **6**:67–68
   usury, **6**:69
   war, **6**:86
   women, **6**:125, 127
   worship, **6**:147–148
   zakat and taxation, **5**:430
Hanbali school of Islamic law, **3:345–348**. *See also* Abu Yaʻla, Muhammad ibn al-Husayn ibn al-Farraʼ al-Baghdadi; Ibn ʻAqil, Abu al-Wafaʼ ʻAli; Ibn Hanbal, Ahmad; Ibn Qayyim al-Jawziyya, Muhammad ibn Abi Bakr; Ibn Qudama, Muwaffaq al-Din Abu Muhammad ʻAbdallah; Ibn Taymiyya, Taqi al-Din Ahmad ibn ʻAbd al-Halim; Kalwadhani, Abu al-Khattab Mahfuz ibn Ahmad al-; Khallal, Abu Bakr Ahmad ibn Muhammad ibn Harun, al-; Khiraqi, Abu ʻUmar ibn al-Husayn ibn ʻAbdallah, al-

acknowledgement, **1:**20
alcohol and drug use, **1:**121
the body, **1:**299
children
    child support, **1:**397
    custody rights, **1:**397
compared to Maliki and Shafi'i schools, **3:**468
contracts
    agricultural, **1:**116
    object of commercial, **2:**79
deposit, **2:**332
duty, **2:**376
education in, **4:**71
geographical presence
    Iraq, **3:**305–306
    Saudi Arabia, **1:**209
guardianship, **4:**166
inheritance, **3:**39
legal norms, **4:**62
maintenance, **3:**38
marriage, **4:**165, 166
non-Muslims, **3:**316
option, **4:**261
partnership, **4:**289
persons, **4:**312
pledge, **4:**327
on political dimension of Islamic law, **4:**338
possession, **4:**360
trade, **2:**73
trial based on suspicion, **2:**432
wills, **6:**106
women, **6:**125–126
worship, **6:**149
Han code (China, 186 B.C.E.)
    abduction *(lue)*, **3:**468
    accessory and principal in, **1:**18
    appeal, **1:**193–194
    beating and whipping, **1:**283
    collective liability, **2:**58, 59, 60
    cursing, **2:**304
        the emperor, **4:**255
    damage to property, **2:**311, 312–313
    damaging efficiency of government, **4:**253
    deceit, **2:**314
    disrespect *(bujing)*, **4:**250–251
    endangering the emperor, **4:**256
    enticement (you), **3:**469
    foreigners, **3:**91
    homicide, **3:**171, 172–173, 175
    illicit sexual intercourse, **5:**231
    incest, **3:**213
    lack of filial piety, **3:**84, 85
    land, **4:**1
    mistaken judgments, **4:**254
    mistaken recommendations, **4:**254–255
    mutilation, **4:**197
    mutual concealment, **4:**198
    offenses against the state, **4:**249
    parricide, **3:**84
    penal servitude, **4:**292
    plotting rebellion, **4:**257
    rape, **5:**66
    redemption, **5:**72
    review, **1:**197
    sale of a free person by consent, **3:**469
    sale of land, **5:**186
    seizing a free person for ransom (jie), **3:**469
    succession, **5:**377
    theft, **5:**458, 459, 460
    wounding, **6:**150
    wrongful judgment, **6:**153
    zang, **6:**159, 160
Hand, Learned, **2:**22
    international antitrust law, **3:**288
    on statutory interpretation, **5:**360–361
Handbook (Enchiridion) (Pomponius), **3:**251
Handbuch der Quellen und Literatur der neueren europäischen Privatrechtsgeschichte (Coing), **5:**163
Handler, Joel F., **4:**33
    on law and society, **4:**34
Han dynasty (China). *See also* Han code (China, 186 B.C.E.)
    confession, **2:**107
    Confucianism and, **5:**51–52
    corruption in the, **2:**225, 227
    disability, **5:**47
    judicial precedent, **1:**460
    partnership contracts, **4:**287
    penal codes, **1:**456
    prohibited books, **4:**252
    punishment, **5:**48
    role of emperor in capital cases, **1:**360
    rule of law, **5:**165
    sentencing, **5:**214
    slavery, **5:**55
    types of legislation under, **1:**413–415
        administrative codes and regulations, **1:**454
    use of *gu* poison during, **4:**329
    voluntary surrender and confession, **2:**106

Han Fei, **1:**407–408; **3:**160
Han Fei Zi (Han Fei), **1:**404
Hanifa, Abu, **3:**342
   on agricultural contracts, **1:**117
   on duty, **2:**377
   influence on
      Abbasid dynasty, **1:**2
      Shaybani, Muhammad ibn al-Hasan al-, **5:**236
   on usurpation, **6:**67
Hanseatic League, **1:**254
   maritime law in, **1:**36, 37
   maritime partnerships in, **2:**95
Hansen, Mogens Herman, **1:**164; **2:**229, 233; **5:**329
Hansische Seerecht (Hanseatic sea law), **1:**37
Hanü jicun (Xue), **3:**187
haqq. See obligations: Islamic law
Harahap, Yahya, **3:**337
Harangues (Domat), **2:**357
ḥarbīs, **4:**233
Harcourt, William, **5:**429
Harding, Warren G.
   Roberts, Owen, appointed by, **3:**62
   and time limits on ratification to constitutional amendment, **2:**156
hard labor
   in Chinese law, **1:**417
   Stephen, James Fitzjames, on, **5:**29
hard-look review, **1:**31
Hardres' Reports, **3:**17
Hardwicke, Lord (Philip Yorke), **1:**468; **6:**13
   on clandestine mariage, **2:**389
   on Fleet marriages, **4:**162
   on idea of formed opposition, **2:**132
   on mortgage redemption, **4:**189
   on precedent, **2:**470
   on slavery, **5:**251–252
Hargobind, **5:**240
Hārīta, **6:**83
Harlan, John Marshall, **6:**53
   classical legal theory and, **2:**25
   on due process, **4:**388
   on equal protection, **2:**460
   on privacy, **4:**387
   on right to bear arms, **1:**220–221
   on search and seizure, **5:**206
   on social science, **5:**266
   on statutory interpretation, **5:**361
   on women on juries, **6:**138
Harmenopoulos, **1:**330

Harmodius, **5:**330
Harpalos, **2:**233
Harpocration, Valerius, **4:**246
Harrington, Christine, **4:**34
Harrington, Michael, **2:**423–424
Harrington, Timothy, **3:**312
Harris, Angela P., **3:**69
Harris, Katherine, **4:**339
Harris, Ron, **2:**88
Harrison, A. R. W., **1:**164; **4:**403
Harrison, William, **5:**251
Harrison Narcotics Act (U.S., 1914)
   on opium and cocaine, **1:**123
   racism in, **1:**126–127
Hart, Henry M.
   on legal process, **4:**65, 66–68, 69
   on statutory interpretation, **5:**361, 362, 363
Hart, H. L. A.
   on Austin, John, **1:**238–239
   critical legal studies and, **2:**407
   on definition of law, **4:**18, 19
   Fuller, Lon, on, **4:**219
   on legal positivism, **4:**356–357
   on legal theory, **4:**61
Harter Act (U.S., 1893), **1:**40
Harurites. *See* Khariji school of Islamic law
Harvard Civil Rights–Civil Liberties Law Review, **2:**300
Harvard Law School, **2:**401, 403
   case method at, **2:**76, 403–404
   instruction at, **1:**12
   legal process at, **4:**65, 66
   legal realism at, **4:**74, 75
   process approach at, **2:**407
Harvey, C. P., **2:**442
Hashiyat radd al-muhtar ('Abidir), **6:**149
Haskins, Charles Homer, **2:**6
Haskins, George, **2:**12
Haslam, John, **3:**247
Hassanali, Noor, **6:**11
Hassoulier, Th., **1:**163
Hastings, Margaret, **2:**85, 86
Hastings, Warren, **3:**140–141, 147, 157
   Bangladesh under, **1:**257
   criminal law by, **5:**209
   on Islamic law, **5:**307
   legislation under, **2:**36
   on personal law in India, **3:**222
Hastings Plan (Great Britain, 1772), **4:**299

Hatch Act (U.S., 1887), **5:**88
hate speech, **5:**337
Hathth 'ala al-tijara (Khallal), **3:**467
Hatti-Hümayun (Ottoman legal decree, 1856), **6:**15, 16
Hatti-Şerif of Gülhane (Ottoman legal decree, 1856), **6:**15
Haudenosaunee Confederacy (Iroquois), **1:**345
Haur, Bhagwan, **5:**241
Hauriou, Maurice
 on administrative law, **1:**23
 on public law, **3:**100
Hausa, **1:**67–68
Haustürwiderrufsgesetz (Germany, 1986), **2:**171
Haw-Haw, Lord. *See* Joyce, William
Hawke, Bob, **1:***244*
Hawkins, William, **2:**284, 441
Hawley-Smoot. *See* Smoot-Hawley
Hayek, F. A., **5:**164
Hayes, Rutherford B., **5:**96
 electoral college and, **4:**339
 Reconstruction under, **2:**460
Haymarket Square (Chicago), **4:**336–337; **6:**51
Haywood, William "Big Bill," **4:**337
Hazardous Substances Labeling Act (U.S., 1960), **2:**177
Headlam, J. W., **5:**481
health, **3:**141–146
 advance directives, **2:**424
 Africa, precolonial, **1:**66
 in consensual divorce, **2:**350
 elderlaw and, **2:**423, 424
 environmental law and, **2:**450–451
  United States, **2:**454–455, 456
 Germany under National Socialism, **4:**204
 India, **3:**220
  abortion and, **1:**4–5
  fundamental right to, **3:**107
 Islamic law, alcohol and drug use and, **1:**121, 122
 law and science in, **4:**29–30
 race discrimination in, **2:**344
 services in Canada, **1:**339
 United States
  alcohol, **1:**124
  marijuana, **1:**127
  opium, **1:**126
  welfare programs, **6:**97
Health Insurance Portability and Accountability Act (U.S., 1996), **2:**178
Health Insurance Portability and Accountability Act (HIPAA) (U.S., 1996), **4:**391

Health Resources Fund Act (Canada, 1966), **1:**339
hearsay
 ancient Athens, **3:**1; **6:**110
 English common law, **3:**5; **4:**421
 Islamic law, **4:**428
 United States, **3:**15
Heath, Robert, **4:**324
Heck, Philipp, **3:**432
Hedaya (compilation of fatwas), **1:**257
Hedendaagse Regsgeleerdheid (Jurisprudence of my time) (Huber), **4:**226
Hegel, Georg Wilhelm Friedrich
 comparative law, **2:**98
 on enlightened absolutism, **1:**8
 on guilt, **3:**135
 influence on Rudolf von Jhering, **3:**399
 jurisprudence of concepts and, **3:**433
 National Socialist law based on, **4:**204
 on punishment, **5:**43
 on social state, **5:**271
He Guang, **1:**432
Heiliges Recht (Latte), **1:**186
Heine, Heinrich, **5:**163
Heineccius, Johann Gottlieb
 on Cujas, Jacques, **2:**304
 on negotiable instruments, **4:**222
 in paratitle style, **2:**400
 on Roman law, **5:**158
 on succession, **5:**393
Heinrichs, Wolfhart, **3:**322
Heinz, John P., **2:**405
Heise, Georg Arnold, **2:**48
 on systematization, **5:**421
heliastic oath, **4:**241
Hellenika (Xenophon), **3:**124
Heller, Dick Anthony, **1:**221–222
Heller, Hermann, **2:**121
Helmholz, Richard H.
 on councils of the medieval papal church, **1:**471, 472
 on self-incrimination, **3:**6
Helots, **5:**245, 327–328
Helper, Hinton Rowan, **6:**51
Helsinki Watch, **3:**297
Hemacandra, **3:**364
Hemācārya, **3:**364; **6:**83
Hengham, Chief Justice, **4:**284
Hengham, Ralph de
 on statute law, **4:**88
Henkin, Louis, **3:**279, 297

Henry, Jabez, **2:**117
Henry I (England), **3:**178
    Anglo-Saxon law under, **1:**182
    civil wars after death of, **2:**477
    Coronation Charter, **4:**135
    courts under, **1:**182; **2:**85
    David I and, **5:**197
    feudal law under, **3:**73, 74, 76
    justices in eyre under, **3:**450–451
    legal treatises on, **1:**183
    statute law under, **4:**87
    succession to the crown of, **5:**382
    upholding laws of Edward the Confessor, **2:**127
Henry II (England)
    assizes
        grand assize, **1:**231; **3:**4
        of mort d'ancestor, **5:**368, 381
        petty assizes, **4:**315
    capital punishment under, **1:**364
    courts under, **2:**249
    creation of precursor of the Court of Common Pleas, **3:**471
    criminal procedure under, **4:**423
    on ecclesiastical benefices, **2:**389
    ecclesiastical law under, **2:**387
    estates doctrine under, **2:**477–478
    Exchequer under, **1:**385
    feudal law under, **3:**74–75
    imprisonment under, **5:**28
    intensification of royal government under, **4:**135
    in Ireland, **3:**307
    judiciary, **3:**415
    juries, **3:**437
    justices in eyre, **3:**451
    land claims, **6:**7
    Magna Carta on redress for wrongs by, **4:**134
    on mortgage, **4:**188
    novel disseisin under, **4:**315–316
    on nuisance, **4:**239
    on ordeals, **4:**263
    organization of law, **2:**80
    property disputes under, **4:**419, 473
    punishment under, **5:**27
    real actions, **5:**69, 70
    reforms by, **2:**436
    returnable writs by, **2:**435
    Roman Catholic Church and, **1:**466–467
    statute law under, **4:**87
    succession to the crown of, **5:**382
Henry Bolingbroke. *See* Henry IV (England)

Henry III (England)
    courts under, **2:**249
    justices in eyre under, **3:**451
    legislation under, **4:**87–88
    Magna Carta reissued by, **4:**133, 135
    papacy and, **4:**352
    Parliament and, **4:**283
    rebellion against, **6:**1
    on religious corporations, **5:**369
    succession to the crown of, **5:**382
    trade growth under, **4:**35
    Wales under, **6:**99
Henry IV (England), **2:**128
    Investiture Controversy and, **4:**353
    judiciary under, **3:**415
    legislation under, **4:**88
Henry VI (England)
    corporate charter granted by, **4:**119
    on mortgage, **4:**188
Henry VII (England), **2:**129
    law merchant under, **4:**36
    parliamentary bills under, **4:**284
    Star Chamber under, **5:**345
    treason under, **6:**4, 5
Henry VIII (England), **2:**129
    attainder under, **6:**5
    on banking, **1:**271
    barristers increased under, **1:**277
    control of printing under, **2:**216
    court jurisdiction under, **2:**250
    executions under, **1:**364; **6:**5
    juries under, **3:**440
    legal education under, **2:**393
    legislation under, **4:**88
    licensing system of printed material, **1:**379
    and Reformation, **1:**468
    Roman law studies under, **5:**156
    supremacy over the Church of England, **4:**284
    torture under, **5:**484, 485
Henry VII (Holy Roman Emperor), **1:**281
Henry Plantagenet. *See* Henry II (England)
Henry Tudor. *See* Henry VII (England)
Hepburn Act (U.S., 1906), **5:**78, 102, 104
Heqing code (564), **1:**421
Heracleitus. *See* Heraclitus
Heraclides Lembos, **4:**456
Heraclitus, **5:**355
Heraclius, **1:**347; **4:**320
Herculaneum, **5:**139
Herero, **1:**70

heriots, **6:**81
Herle, William, **2:**195
Hermeneutica iuris (Eckhard), **3:**297
hermeneutics, definition, **3:**297
Hermippus, **4:**154
Hermogenian, **2:**32; **3:**213, 436; **5:**149, 151
   on custom, **2:**167–168
Hermogenian Code. *See Codex Hermogenianus* (295)
Herodas, **2:**413
Herodotus
   on adoption, **1:**40
   on advocates, **1:**54
   Constitutional Debate, **2:**126
   on dispute resolution, **4:**399
   law depictions by, **1:**148
   on marriage, **4:**155
   on procedure, **1:**153
   Russian translation of the works of, **5:**177
   on Sparta, **5:**327, 328
Herschell, Farrer, Lord, **4:**10
Hert, Nikolaus, **2:**109
   on conflict of laws, **2:**112
Herzegovina, Islamic law in, **1:**253
Herzen, Alexander, **5:**178
Herzog, J. B., **1:***314*
Hesiod
   on adultery, **1:**51
   on dispute resolution, **1:**136, 137–138; **4:**399
   on inheritance, **3:**228
   on judges, **3:**401
   on law, **1:**148; **4:**109, 320
   on loan payment, **5:**275
   on oaths, **4:**402
   on procedure, **1:**152
   on property, **4:**456
   on punishment, **5:**22
   on slavery, **5:**243
   on theft, **5:**457
   on theology of law, **5:**110–111
   on witnesses, **4:**401
hetairia
   ancient Greek law, **6:**114, 115
   Code of Gortyn on, **3:**121
Hetch Hetchy Valley dam, **2:**455
Hevia Bolaños, Juan de, **1:**215–216; **5:**291
Hevia de Bolaños, **4:**151
HEW. *See* U.S. Department of Health, Education, and Welfare
Hewart, Lord Chief Justice, **5:**17

Hexabiblos (Harmenopoulos), **1:**330
   on delict, **2:**325
   on succession, **5:**376
Heyland, Anna Christine, **5:**464
HHS. *See* U.S. Department of Health and Human Services
Hiawatha, **1:**345
hiba. See donation (gift): Islamic law
Hicks, David, **4:**181
Hidaya (al-Kalwadhani), **3:**347
Hidaya, al-, **2:**36; **5:**307
Hideyoshi, Toyotomi, **3:**368–369
Higginbotham, A. Leon, Jr., **2:**300
High Council of the Netherlands, **1:**369
High Court (Ireland), **3:**312
High Court of Admiralty (Britain)
   jurisdiction of, **1:**38
   outlawry and, **4:**271
High Court of Justice (China, Song), **1:**426
High Court of Justice (U.K.)
   Exchequer Division, **3:**19
   Queen's Bench Division, **3:**473
Hilarion, **6:***113*
Hilarion of Kiev, **5:**177
Hilary rules of 1843, **4:**325
Hildebrandine reform. *See under* Gregory VII (pope)
Hill-Burton Act (U.S., 1946), **4:**31
Hilli, al-'Allāma, al-, **3:**146
   'Amili, Zayn al-Din ibn 'Ali ibn Ahmad al-, on, **1:**132
Hilli, Ja'far ibn al-Hasan, al-, **3:146**
   al-'Allama and, **3:**195
   Baqir al-Najafi on, **1:**276
Hilliard, Francis, **5:**474
Hilliger, Oswald, **2:**360
Hills, Carla, **3:***286*
Himerius of Tarragona, **2:**316
Hinckley, John, **3:**12
Hindu Adoptions and Maintenance Act (India, 1956), **1:**49; **3:**148
   gender discrimination in, **1:**49–50
   on maintenance, **3:**50
   marumakkathayam in, **4:**171
"Hindu Courts of Justice" (Colebrooke), **2:**57
Hindu Endowments Act (Singapore, 1970), **5:**321
Hindu Lagnavicccheda Nibandha (India, 1931), **2:**353

Hindu law, **3:146–159**. *See also arthaśāstra;* dharma; *Manusmriti*
- overview, **3:146–150**
- abortion, **1:4–5**
- adoption, **1:49–50**
- Anglo-Hindu law, **3:157–159**
- British law and, **3:**400
- consumer protection, **2:***173*, **173–174**
- custom, **2:**307, 308
- dharma in, **2:**332–334; **5:**63
- divorce, **2:**352–353
  - *marumakkathayam* in, **4:**171
  - women in, **6:**131, 132
- dowry, **2:**363–366
- environmental law, **2:**452–454
- geographical presence
  - Africa, **1:**63
  - Bali, **1:**251
  - East Africa, **2:**383
  - Indian subcontinent, **3:**215
  - Indonesia, **3:**225
  - Malaysia, **4:**137
  - Nepal, **4:**224–225
  - Singapore, **5:**241
  - South Africa, **5:**283–284
  - Southeast Asia, **5:**312–313, **320–322**
  - Sri Lanka, **5:**339
  - Suriname, **5:**414
  - United Kingdom, **5:**311–312
- history
  - formative period, 400 B.C.E.–400 C.E., **3:151–155**
  - medieval Hindu law, **3:156–157**
  - post-formative period, 400–1000 C.E., **3:155–156**
  - Vedic law, 1500–800 B.C.E., **3:150–151**
- homicide, **3:179–180**
- Indian criminal law, **2:**280
- influence on Indian public interest litigation, **5:**6
- inheritance
  - ancient texts, **3:**158–159
  - dowry, **2:**362–366
  - *marumakkathayam* in, **4:**170–171
- Jaina law and, **3:**364–365
- legal tradition, **5:**108–109
- marriage, **3:**48–50; **4:169–170,** *170* (See also Hindu Marriage Act (India, 1955))
  - dowry, **2:**363–366
  - *sadācāra* in, **5:**181
  - women in, **6:**131
- *mīmāṃsā* in, **4:**182–183
- murder, **3:**179
- property, **4:479–480**
- punishment, **5:35–37**
- *rājadharma,* **5:**63
- *rājaśāsana,* **5:**63–64
- *sadācāra* in, **3:**215; **4:**182; **5:181–182**
- secularism and, **5:**208–209
- secularization of, **5:**109
- Sikh law and, **5:**240, 241
- *smriti* in, **5:**264–265
- *śruti,* **5:344–345**
- on succession, **5:396–402**
- women, **4:**479; **6:131–133**
  - adoption of, **1:**49–50

Hindu Marriage Act (India, 1955), **3:**48–49, 148, 149, 222; **4:**287; **6:131–133**
- on abortion, **1:**4
- amendments to, **2:**353
- on customs, **2:**308
- customs *vs.* norms in, **4:**169
- on divorce, **2:**353
- divorce grounds in, **3:**50
- on maintenance, **3:**50
- *marumakkathayam* in, **4:**171

Hindu Marriage and Divorce Ordinance (Kenya, 1960), **2:**383

Hindu Marriage and Divorce Ordinance (Uganda, 1961), **2:**383

Hindu Married Women's Right to Separate Residence and Maintenance Act (India, 1946), **2:**353

Hindu Minority and Guardianship Act (India, 1956), **3:**51, 148

Hindu nationalism, **3:159–160**

Hindu Nibandha Act (India, 1937), **2:**353

Hindu Succession Act (India, 1956), **3:**148; **5:396–400; 6:**131
- British modification of, **4:**479
- on dowry, **2:**364

Hindu Succession (Amendment) Act (India, 2005), **4:**479; **5:401–402**

Hindutva (Savarkar), **3:**159–160

Hindu Widows' Remarriage Act (India, 1856), **2:**307; **3:**158; **6:**131

Hindu Women's Right to Property Act (India, 1937), **4:**479; **5:**397; **6:**131
- in Bangladesh, **1:**259
- on succession, **5:**397

Hine, Lewis Wickes, **6:***92*

Hinschius, Paul, **2:**219
Hintze, Otto, **3:**77
HIPAA. *See* Health Insurance Portability and Accountability Act
Hipparete, **2:**346
Hippias, **5:**275
Hippodamus of Miletus, **2:**124
Hippolytus (Euripides), **5:**64–65
hire in Chinese law, **3:160–163**
Hire Purchase Act (India, 1972), **2:**174
hire-purchase contract, **2:**169
Hirohito (Japanese emperor), **3:**366
Hirst, John, **1:**240
Hispanus, Vincentius, **3:**9
Hiss, Alger, **4:**337
Historia Augusta, **3:**431
Historia ecclesiastica gentis Anglorum
(Bede), **1:**178
Historia Gothorum, Vandalorum et Langobardorum
(Grotius), **3:**127
"Historical Foundations of the Law of Evidence"
(Langbein), **3:**5
Historical Records (Sima Qian), **1:**404, 411
on gambling law, **3:**109
"Preface of the Grand Historian," **1:**413
Historical School (Germany),
2:9–10, 48
comparative law and, **2:**98
influenced by Montesquieu, **2:**98
Histories (Herodotus), **2:**124
historiography of Roman law,
5:157–164
History (Thucydides), **2:**124
on constitutional law, **2:**126
on *nomos,* **1:**145
history, uses of, **3:163–168**
notary records in, **4:**238
History and Anthropology (journal), **1:**186
History of Dharmaśāstra (Kane), **3:**465–466
History of English Assizes, 1558–1714 (Cockburn),
1:230, 231
History of English Law (Holdsworth), **2:**434
History of Private Law (Wieacker), **5:**2
*History of Retirement, A: The Meaning and Function of
an American Institution, 1885–1978* (Graebner),
2:423
History of Roman Legal Science (Schulz), **5:**161
History of Sexuality, The (Foucault), **3:**112
History of the Common Law of England
(Hale), **2:**440

History of the Criminal Law of England
(Stephen), **1:**365
History of the Former Han Dynasty, **1:**456
History of the Koryo Dynasty (Koryo sa), **1:**424
History of the Law of the South, **1:**289–290
History of the Pleas of the Crown
(Hale), **5:**68–69
History of the Wars (Procopius), **3:**454
Hitler, Adolf. *See also* National Socialist law
assassination attempts on, **3:***111*
law under, **3:**119
religious dissenters and, **5:**118
Hittite law, **1:**168
ḥiyal (books of legal devices), **3:**321
Hlothere, code of, **1:**181
Hoare, Richard, **1:**271
Hobbes, Thomas
on absolutism, **1:**7
on definition of law, **4:**18
on governance, **4:**96
influence on Pufendorf, Samuel von,
4:217; **5:**21
on justice, **3:**447
law of reason and, **2:**8
Leibniz, Gottfried Wilhelm,
on, **4:**100
on social contract, **4:**216
on sovereignty, **5:**352
on systematization, **5:**421
on war, **2:**445
Ho Chi Minh, **6:**79
Hock, Lim Yew, **5:**242
Hogarth, William, **1:**365, *366*
Hogg, James Edward, **4:**9
Hohfeld, Wesley, **2:**26
holding companies, trusts and,
1:323–324
Holdsworth, William, **2:**85, 434
on Coke, Edward, **2:**56
on outlawry, **4:**271
Holiness Code of Leviticus, **3:**389
Holinshed, Raphael, **5:**484
Holland, John (Duke of Exeter), **5:**484
Holmes, Hugh, **3:**312
Holmes, Oliver Wendell, Jr., **2:**25, 26;
3:164; **4:***74*
on agency, **1:**108, 113
on contracts, **2:**204
on copyright, **3:**267
due process, **4:**452–453

on economic policy, **4:**491
on freedom of contract, **2:**371
on freedom of speech, **3:**409; **5:**334
influence on development of law, **6:**46
on international law, **3:**294
on involuntary sterilization, **2:**334
on judge-made law, **2:**257, 258
on organic logical concept of law, **3:**432
on property, **4:**484
as realist, **4:**74
on social science, **5:**266
on statutory interpretation, **5:**360
on takings, **5:**424
on torts, **2:**442; **5:**474, 475, 476
on vested rights, **2:**117

Holt, John
on bailment, **1:**249
on bills of exchange, **1:**292
judgements on vicarious liability, **6:**78
on slaves and writ of trover, **5:**251

Holt, Joseph, **4:***178*

Holy Roman Empire
Austria in, **1:**246
banking, **1:**274
bishops and archbishops in, **1:**295
codification, **2:**47
dissolution of, **3:**118–119
end of reception of Roman law in, **2:**7
feudal law in, **3:**78–79
German Confederation as successor to, **1:**247
on guilt, **3:**133
Jews in the, **3:**395
legislation in, **4:**91
Netherlands in, **4:**225, 226
witch trials, **6:**108–109

Homan, Johannes Linthorst, **2:***490*

Homer, **3:**169. *See also Iliad; Odyssey*
on adultery, **1:**50–51
on barter, **5:**180
on dispute resolution, **1:**136, 137–138; **4:**399
on exile, **1:**155
on family, **3:**28
on feminine character, **5:**227
on heterosexual morals, **5:**226
on inheritance, **3:**228
on judges, **3:**401
law depictions by, **1:**148; **4:**108–109
on loan payment, **5:**275
on oaths, **4:**242
on political structures and relations, **2:**123
on procedure, **1:**152
on property, **4:**456
on punishment, **5:**22
Russian translation of the works of, **5:**177
on seizure-marriage, **4:**152
on slavery, **5:**243–244, 355
on social and urban life, **1:**137
theology of law, **5:**111

home rule, **4:**121

Homestead Act (U.S., 1862), **5:**86

homicide, **3:168–180**
Afghanistan, **1:**62
Africa, **1:**102
precolonial laws, **1:**73
ancient Greek law, **2:**228, 229, 232, 267–268; **3:169–171**, 404; **4:**399–400; **5:**23, 65, 113
Athens, **1:**232, 234
Draco and, **1:**139, 154, 155; **2:**29–30, 366–367; **5:**227
evidence in, **3:**2
Gortyn, **1:**142
inscriptions on, **1:**147
oaths in trials for, **4:**242
of slaves, **5:**245
ancient Near Eastern law, **1:**175
Anglo-Saxon laws, **1:**182; **3:**177
Australia among Aborigines, **1:**239
Aztec law, **5:**287
Chinese law, **3:171–176**
accessory and principal in, **1:**18
parricide, **3:**84–85
paument of funeral expenses in Yuan law, **1:**429
wounding and, **6:**150, 151
wrongful accusation, **2:**315
duress defense for, **2:**374, 375
English common law, **3:176–178**, **176–179**; **5:**27
women in, **6:**120
Hindu law, **3:**179, **179–180**
Inca law, **5:**288
India
bride burning, **2:**364–365
dowry-motivated, **2:**364
feticide and infanticide, **3:**105
Laos, **4:**14
Native American punishments for, **4:**207
punishment for, **2:**265

Roman law, **2:**269, 271
of slaves in the United States, **5:**258–259, 261
Welsh law, **6:**99
witnesses to, in ancient Athens, **6:**110
Homicide Act (U.K., 1957), **1:**365; **3:**179, 247
Hommel, K. F., **1:**285
homophile theory, **3:**111
Homosexual in America, The (Cory), **3:**111
homosexuality, **3:180–182**
ancient Greece, **5:**227–228
among women, **5:**228–229
Chinese law, **3:**180
as sexual offense, **5:**234
Iranian law, **2:**279
Islamic law, **3:181–182**
medieval and post-medieval Roman law, **5:**230
Roman law, **2:**271, 273
United States law, **2:**292; **3:**166–168; **4:**390
Honduras
Civil Code, **1:**384, 398
slavery abolished in, **5:**254
Hong Kong
Chinese law in, **1:**448–451
New Territories, **1:**450
Hongwu (Chinese emperor), **2:**225
Honoré, Tony, **6:**8
on Roman imperial legislation, **3:**212–213
Honorius III (pope), **4:**263
Hontheim, Nikolaus von, **1:**295–296; **4:**354
Hooker, Evelyn, **3:**111
Hoover, Herbert
agricultural policy, **5:**89
on antitrust, **1:**190
on federalism, **3:**61
regulation under, **5:**79–80, 89
on taxation, **5:**444
telecommunications policy, **5:**96
Hoover, John, **5:**261
Hopewell, Treaty of, **4:**209
Hopkins, Samuel, **5:**78
Horem-Heb, edicts of, **1:**167
Horkheimer, Max, **2:**297
hornbooks, **1:**15
Horta, José Ramos, **2:**385
Horten, Johann Bernhard, **5:**386
Horwitz, Morton J.
on contracts, **2:**205, 206
on law and economics, **4:**26
on legal realism, **4:**76

Hostiensis (Henricus de Segusio), **6:**65
on didactical analysis of legal text, **1:**356
Hotman, François, **2:**47; **3:**191
Cujas, Jacques and, **2:**303
Doneau, Hugues, and, **2:**359
on the *Pandects (Pandectae)*, **6:**9
at University of Bourges, **2:**400
Hou Hon shu, **2:**225
Hours of Service Act (U.S., 1907), **5:**102
housebreaking, **1:**317. *See also* burglary in English common law
House Concurrent Resolution 108 (1953), **4:**211
Houseman, Alan, **4:**370
housing, **3:182–187**
England
environmental law and, **2:**451
land leases in, **4:**13
lease and tenancy contracts in, **4:**57–58
United States
equal protection in, **2:**462
race discrimination in, **2:**342, 343
welfare programs, **6:**95
Housing Act. *See* National Housing Act
Housing and Community Development Act (U.S., 1974), **3:**184, 185
Housing and Urban Development Act (U.S., 1968), **3:**183
Houston, Charles Hamilton
legal liberalism and, **2:**299
in NAACP Legal Defense Fund, **2:**341
Howard, Catherine, **1:**366
Howard, Ebenezer, **4:**485
Howard, Henry, Earl of Surrey, **6:**5
Howard, Jacob, **1:**218
Howard, Jan, **4:**32, 33
Howard, John, **5:**28–29, 33
on prison reform, **4:**41
Howard, Thomas, **6:**5
Howard University, **1:***11*; **2:***402*
law school, **4:**49
Howe, Samuel, **2:**403
Howe, William, **4:**177
How to Avoid Probate! (Dacey), **3:**239
Hozumi, Nobushige, **3:**374, 375
Hsueh Yun-Sheng (Xue Yunsheng), **1:**436, 438, 439, 459; **3:187**
influence on Shen Chia-Pen (Shen Jiaben), **5:**237
Huang Gan, **5:**379
Huang Kan, **1:**462

Huang-Lao (the Yellow Emperor and Lozi [Lao Tzu]), **1**:408
Huber, Eugen, **3**:188; **5**:420
Huber, Ulrich, **2**:7, 109; **4**:226
   on conflict of laws, **2**:112, 117
   Noodt, Gerard, and, **4**:235
HUD. *See* U.S. Department of Housing and Urban Development
Hudaybiyya, Treaty of, **3**:281; **4**:233
Huddleston, John, **3**:19
Hudood Ordinances (Pakistan, 1979), **2**:142; **4**:274–275, 300
Hudson's Bay Company, **1**:337
ḥudūd, **3**:327
hue and cry, **3**:309
Huejotzingo Codex, **4**:*208*
Hughes, Charles Evans, **2**:27
   on federalism, **3**:61
Hughes, Sarah T., **6**:144
Hugh of Pisa. *See* Huguccio
Hugo, Gustav, **5**:159, 160
   on systematization, **5**:421
Hugo de Porta Ravennate, **3**:314
Hugolinus, **2**:111
Hugonis Donelli ... Opera omnia ... cum notis Osvaldi Hilligeri (Doneau), **2**:360
Hugucciao of Pisa, **4**:333
Huguccio, **4**:263
Hui (Chinese-speaking Muslims). *See* China, Islamic law in
Huidian (Qing dynasty), **1**:434, 454–455
Hujja 'ala Ahl al-Madina, al- (al-Shaybani), **3**:343
ḥukm (judgment)
   in enforcement, **2**:431
   fatwas compared with, **3**:57
Hull, Cordell, **5**:443
Hulsewé, A. F. P.
   on damage to property, **2**:312, 313
   on disrespect *(bujing)*, **4**:250
   on Han law, **1**:413, 414
   on lack of filial piety, **3**:85
   on Qin state, **1**:408, 409, 411
   on wounding, **6**:150
humanism, **3**:188–193
   Alciati, Andrea, in, **1**:118
   Bartolus of Saxoferrato and, **1**:281
   on breach of contract, **1**:309
   Budé, Guillaume, and, **1**:316
   civil law and, **2**:7
   comparative law and, **2**:98
   Doneau, Hugues, and, **2**:359–361
   Doneau, Hugues and, **2**:359–361
   Du Moulin, Charles, and, **2**:373
   Dutch Elegant School, **4**:235–236
   Faber, Antonius, and, **3**:27
   France, **3**:98–99
   German, **3**:118
   Grotius, Hugo, and, **3**:126–127
   on guilt, **3**:134
   international law and, **3**:282, 283
   in legal education, **2**:399–400
   Netherlands, **4**:226
   on obligations, **4**:245
   Oldendorp, Johann, in, **4**:261
   Roman law and, **5**:158
   in Scholasticism, **4**:15
   on servitude in real estate, **5**:223–224
   Spain, **5**:325
   on systematization, **5**:421
   Zasius, Ulrich, and, **6**:160
humanitarian law of armed conflict. *See* laws of war
human liberty, classical legal theory on, **2**:23
human rights. *See also* Human Rights Act (U.K., 1998); Universal Declaration of Human Rights (1948)
   abuses
      Bangladesh, **1**:258
      Venezuela, **6**:74
   Afghanistan, **1**:60
   Africa
      after independence, **1**:107
      indigenous laws on, **1**:73
   Denmark, **2**:328
   dharma in, **2**:333
   European Communities, **2**:488
   India
      fundamental duties and, **3**:104–105
      fundamental rights and, **3**:105–107
      secularism and, **5**:308
   international law and, **3**:278–279, 295–296
   Islamic law in Europe, **2**:483
   Mexico, **4**:176
   Mongolia, **4**:185
   South and Central America, **5**:286
   in Taiwan under Kuomintang, **1**:453
   women's rights as, **3**:71

Human Rights Act (U.K., 1998), **1:**365; **2:**133; **6:**6
    on children, **3:**34
    on conflict with statute laws, **4:**89
    on freedom of speech, **4:**106–107
Human Rights First, **3:**297
Human rights Watch, **3:**297
human trafficking
    children in Africa, **1:**76
    Indian fundamental rights on, **3:**106
Humble Petition and Advice, The (England, 1657), **2:**131
Humboldt, Wilhelm von, **6:**63
Hume, David, **1:**378–379
    law of reason and, **2:**8
Humphreys, Sally C., **3:**2
Humphreys, S. H., **6:**111
    anthropological perspective of, **1:**186
Hundred Flowers Campaign (People's Republic of China, 1956), **1:**443
Hundred Years War, taxation as a result of, **5:**435
Hunernome (Lokman), **1:***252*
Hungary, **3:**193–194
    constitution, **2:**122
    in European Union, **2:**492
    feudal law, **3:**79
    Islamic law, **1:**253
    separation from Austria, **1:**246–247
    witch trials, **6:**109
hunting rights, easements and, **2:**381
Hurgronje, Snouck, **1:**21
Hurst, James Willard
    on contracts, **2:**209
    on law and society, **4:**31, 33, 35
    on statutory interpretation, **5:**362
Huschke, Philip E., **5:**159; **6:**8
Hush-a-Phone, **5:**97
Hussein, Sultan, **5:**241, 323
Hutchins, Robert Maynard
    in legal realism, **4:**74, 75
    at Yale, **2:**405
Hutchinson, Anne, **3:**428; **4:**334
Hutton, Richard
    on King's Bench at Westminster Hall, **3:**472
    on Westminster Hall, **2:**86
ḥwāshiī (glosses), **3:**320
hybris, **5:**245–246
Hydra mistica (Gravina), **3:**126
Hyman, Harold, **2:**459

Hymn to Hermes (Homer), **4:**399; **5:**111
Hyperides
    on advocates, **1:**55
    on *eisangelia*, **4:**246
    on false testimony, **6:**110
    forensic speeches by, **1:**149
    on *graphē paranomōn*, **3:**124
    graphē paranomōn against, **3:**124–125
    as logographer, **4:**123, 126
    on slavery, **5:**246
hypotheca (security), **1:**320
    in mortgage, **4:**189–190
Hypotheken- und Concursordnung (Mortgage and Bankruptcy Law) (Prussia, 1722), **3:**249
Hywel Dda (Welsh king), **1:**375, *375*
    Law of, **6:**98, *101*

I

Iacobus de Porta Ravennate, **3:**314
Iashchenko, A. S., **5:**178
Iavolenus Priscus, **3:**435
'ibādāt (acts of worship), **6:**146–150
aynibādāt (relations between God and humans), **2:**483
Ibadi school of Islamic law, **3:**348, 349
    influence in Africa, **2:**41
    on inheritance, **3:**39
Ibbetson, David, **5:**189, 190
IBM (International Business Machines Corporation), **1:**192
Ibn 'Abbas, **1:**210, 211; **5:**59; **6:**69
Ibn 'Abd al-Barr, **3:**351
    on Malik ibn Anas, **4:**141
Ibn 'Abd al-Hakam, 'Abd Allah, **3:**350
Ibn 'Abd al-Rahman, Shabatun Ziyad, **3:**350
Ibn Abi al-Dam, **1:**382
Ibn Abi al-Dhi'b, **3:**350
Ibn 'Abidin, Muhammad Amin, **3:**195; **4:**431
    on insurance, **3:**254
Ibn Abi Sulayman, Hammad, **3:**342
    Abu Hanifa and, **1:**9
Ibn Abi Zayd al-Qayrawani. *See* Qayrawani, Ibn Abi Zayd al-
Ibn al-'Attar, **3:**351
Ibn al-Hadrami, Ala, **5:**432
Ibn al-Hajib
    influenced by al-Ghazali, **3:**119–120
    Subki, 'Abd al-Wahhab ibn 'Ali al-, on, **5:**370

Ibn al-Jawzi, Abu al-Faraj, **3:**347
   teacher of Ibn Qudama, **3:**199
Ibn al-Mughallis, **3:**354
Ibn al-Muna, **3:**199
Ibn al-Mutahhar, Hasan ibn Yusuf al-Hilli (al-ʿAllama), **3:195–196**
Ibn al-Rami, **4:**129
Ibn al-Sabbagh, **5:**238
Ibn ʿAqil, Abu al-Wafaʾ ʿAli, **3:196,** 347
Ibn ʿArafa, **4:**128
Ibn ʿAsim, **3:**351
Ibn Batta, **3:**347
Ibn Battuta, **2:**280
   on Maldives, **4:**139
   on Mali, **1:**67
Ibn Farhun, **5:**487
Ibn Hamadi Buhiry, Ali, **2:**42
Ibn Hamid, **1:**10; **3:**347
Ibn Hanbal, Ahmad, **3:196–197,** 305, 345
   on constitutional law, **2:**135
   on duty, **2:**377
Ibn Hazm, ʿAli ibn Ahmad ibn Saʿid, **3:197–199,** 354
   on *amr bi-l-maʿrūf,* **1:**382
   on Maliki interpretations, **4:**128
   in Zahirism, **4:**128
Ibn ʿIsa ibn Kinana, ʿUthman, **3:**350
ibn Ishaq al-Jundi, Khalil, **2:**41
Ibn Khaldun, **3:**316, 321
Ibn Mada, **3:**354
Ibn Muflih, **3:**347
Ibn Nujaym, **5:**370
Ibn Qayyim al-Jawziyya, Muhammad ibn Abi Bakr, **3:199,** 347; **6:**69
   on political dimension of Islamic law, **4:**338
Ibn Qudama, ʿAbdallah ibn Ahmad, **3:**413
Ibn Qudama, Muwaffaq al-Din Abu Muhammad ʿAbdallah, **3:199–200,** 347
   on Abu Yaʿla, **1:**10
   called "the judge," **1:**10
   influenced by al-Ghazali, **3:**119–120
   on lease and tenancy, **4:**55
   on partnership, **4:**289
   on persons, **4:**312
   on worship, **6:**149
Ibn Rajab, **3:**347
Ibn Rushd, Abu al-Walid Muhammad ibn Ahmad, **3:200**
Ibn Rushd, Abu al-Walid Muhammad ibn Ahmad ibn Muhammad ibn Rushd (Averroës), **3:200–201,** *201,* 350, 351

Ibn Rushd al-Jadd, **4:**128
Ibn Sahl, **3:**350
Ibn Samura, **6:**155
Ibn Sirin, **5:**59
Ibn Surayj, Ahmad ibn ʿUmar, **3:201–202**
   on Shafiʿi, Muhammad ibn Idris al-, **5:**236
Ibn Taymiyya, Taqi al-Din Ahmad ibn ʿAbd al-Halim, **3:202,** 347
   on aims of law, **4:**64
   on alcohol and drugs, **1:**122
   on al-Ghazali, **3:**120
   on chastisement, **2:**279
   Ibn Qayyim al-Jawziyya disciple of, **3:**199
   on political dimension of Islamic law, **3:**318; **4:**338
Ibn Tufayl, **1:**210
   Ibn Rushd and, **3:**200
   on *zakat* and taxation, **5:**430
Ibn Tumart, Muhammad, **1:**382
   radicalism of, **4:**128
   religious reforms of, **3:**200–201
ibn ʿUmar Shatti, Hasan, **3:**347
ibn Ziyad al-Luʾlui, Hasan, **3:**343
Ibrahim ibn Jabir, **3:**354
ICC. *See* International Criminal Court; Interstate Commerce Commission
Iceland, Icelandic law code, **2:***46*
ICJ. *See* International Court of Justice
Ickes, Harold L., **4:**211
identity performance, **3:**69–70
"Idle Prentice Executed at Tyburn, The" (Hogarth), **1:**365, *366*
Idris I, **4:**127
Idrisid dynasty (Morocco), **4:**127
Ieng Sary, **1:**335
Igbo societies, **1:**70–71
Ighathat al-lahfan min masayid al-Shaytan (Ibn Qayyim), **3:**199
Ihya al-sunna wa ikhmad al-bidʿa (Usman dan Fodio), **2:**41
ijāza (license)
   al-ʿAmili on, **1:**132–133
   in legal education, **2:**397
ijmā (consensus), **3:**319, 346
ijra certificates, **1:**264, 265
ijtihād (independent legal reasoning), **3:224–225,** 319; **6:**156
   Afghanistan, **1:**61
   effect of codification on, **2:**43
   in forum, exterior and interior, **3:**97

Ibn Hazm and, **3**:198
Imāmī school and, **3**:195, 340
legal norms and, **4**:62–63
in Maghrib and al-Andalus, **4**:129
muftis in, **3**:57; **4**:194
neo-Hanbali school and, **3**:199
reform of family law and, **2**:38
Saudi Arabia, **1**:209
use by Akbar, **2**:36
in Zaydi school of law, **3**:342
Ikham fi usul al-ahkam, al (Ibn Hazm), **3**:354
ikhtilāf. See dissent *(ikhtilāf)*
Ikhtilaf usul al-Madhahib (Qadi al-Nu'man), **5**:59
I'lam al-muwaqqi'in 'an Rabb al-'Alamin (Ibn Qayyim), **3**:199
Île de France, British rule in, **1**:86
Iliad (Homer), **3**:169
   on adultery, **1**:50–51
   on communal order, **2**:123
   on conflict resolution, **4**:399
   on dispute resolution, **1**:137–138
   on family, **3**:28
   on heterosexual morals, **5**:226
   on judges and trials, **3**:401
   law depictions in, **4**:108–109
   on oaths, **4**:242, 401
   on procedure, **1**:152–153
   on social and urban life, **1**:137
Ilin, I. A., **5**:178
'illa (cause), in alcohol and drug use, **1**:120–121
illegality and immorality, **3**:203–205
ILO. *See* International Labor Organization
Imāmī school of Islamic law, **3**:340–341
   child support, **1**:397
   custody rights, **1**:397
   inheritance law, **3**:233
Imami Shi'ism, **1**:132. *See also* Ansari, Murtada ibn Muhammad Amin al-
immigration. *See also* immigration to the United States
   ancient Greece, **1**:157–158
   Australia, **1**:241, 242
   Chinese to Taiwan, **1**:451, 452
   East Africa from India, **2**:383
   England, **2**:330
   eugenics and, **4**:29
   European Union, **2**:492
   folk law and, **3**:90
   Madagascar, **1**:70

   nationality and, **4**:206
   New Zealand, **4**:227
Immigration Act (U.S., 1990), **2**:3
Immigration and Nationality Act (U.S., 1952), **2**:1; **3**:207, 208
Immigration and Nationality Act Amendments (U.S., 1965), **2**:1, 2
Immigration and Naturalization Service (INS), **3**:207
Immigration Reform and Control Act (U.S., 1986), **3**:208
immigration to the United States, **3**:206–210
   constitution questions and, **2**:155
   education and socialization and, **2**:408–409
   El Paso immigration station, **3**:*209*
   federal statutes, **3**:206
   labor and employment law, **3**:481
   legal education and, **2**:403, 404
   opium use and, **1**:126
   Prohibition and, **1**:125
   reform in 1965, **3**:208
   religion and, **6**:51–52
   restrictions on, **6**:52
   welfare and, **6**:93
impeachment, **3**:20
   ancient Greece, **1**:54
     Athens, **1**:233, 235
   Clinton, Bill, **3**:23–24
   Nixon, Richard, **3**:22–23
Impending Crisis of the South, The (Helper), **6**:51
Imperator Caesar Flavius Iustinianus Augustus. *See* Justinian
Imperatoriam (Justinian), **1**:331
Imperial Bodyguard (China), **1**:432
Imperial Chamber of Justice. *See Reichskammergericht* (Imperial Chamber of Justice)
Imperial Conference (London, 1926), **1**:*314*
Imperial Copyright Act (U.K., 1911), **3**:261, 262
Imperial Criminal Code (Germany, 1871), **1**:238
Imperial Diet (Japan), **3**:376, 379
Imperial Edicts (Antwerp, 1537, 1541), **1**:275
Imperial Laws Application Act (New Zealand, 1988), **4**:227
imperial legislation (Roman empire), **3**:210–213
Imperial Notary Act (1512), **5**:388, 389
impersonation in Chinese law, **2**:314
impressment, **3**:470
Improvements in the Law of Evidence Committee (U.S.), **3**:10

Imwinkelried, Edward, **3**:13
In a Different Voice (Gilligan), **3**:68
In Aymonis Cravettae Responsa Annotationes (Stracca), **5**:364
Inca law, **5**:288–289, 298
incest
    among slaves in Roman law, **5**:247
    ancient Near Eastern law, **1**:175
    Aztec law, **5**:288
    Chinese law, **3**:213–215; **4**:259
        family and political order and, **5**:232
        as illicit sexual intercourse, **5**:232
        lack of filial piety and, **3**:86
        levirate marriage as, **4**:160
        Tang code on, **5**:233
    Egypt, juristic papyrology on, **2**:420
    Islamic law
        consensual divorce, **2**:350
    legitimacy of children from, **3**:46
    medieval and post-medieval Roman law, **5**:230
    Mongolia, **4**:185
Inc Fund. *See* NAACP-LDF
in claris formula, **3**:299
Incorporated Council of Law Reporting (U.K., 1865), **4**:60, 378
Incorporated Law Society, **4**:42
    education by, **2**:395
incorporeal hereditaments, **2**:379
indecent speech, **5**:335–336
indefeasibility in English common law, **4**:9, 10
indentured labor
    Guyana, **3**:137
    Mauritius, **4**:172
    Suriname, **5**:413
    United States, colonial, **2**:14–15; **3**:477–478; **5**:256–257
India, **3:215–224**. *See also* Hindu law; Parsi law; South Asian law
    overview of Indian law, **3:215–221**
    Anglo-Indian law, **1**:87
    under Aśoka, **1**:225–226
    in British Commonwealth, **1**:312
    British law in, **3**:140–141, 147, 154, 157–159, 445
    British nationality and, **4**:206
    British rule in, **3**:215–216
        Colebrooke, Henry Thomas, and, **2**:57
    Christian laws, **3:221–224**
    codification, **2**:36
    conquest by Alexander the Great, **1**:137

Constituent Assembly, **2**:*144*, 144–145
Constitution, **2:143–147**; **3**:216–217
    amendments, **2**:146
    dharma and, **2**:333
    on Naga law, **4**:201
    courts, **2**:147
        under British rule, **3**:215, 216
        fundamental rights and, **3**:105
    criminal law, **2**:280–284
    Danlal Latifi (2001), **5**:308
    discrimination
        child custody, **3**:51
        dowry, **2**:363–366
        fundamental rights and, **3**:105
        secularism and, **5**:208–209
    divorce, **3**:49–50, 398
        consensual, **2**:352
        dowry in, **2**:365
        secularism in, **5**:208–209
    dowry, **2**:362–366, 363–366
    environmental law, **2:452–454**
    family law, **3:48–51**, 216; **4**:294
        Christian law, **3**:221–222
        Islamic law, **3**:219
        secularism in, **5**:208–209
    on fundamental duties, **3**:104–105
    Hindu nationalism, **3**:159–160
    homicide
        bride burning, **2**:364–365
        dowry-motivated, **2**:364
        feticide and infanticide, **3**:105
    independence, **1**:313–314
    inheritance, **2**:307, 309
        Hastings, Warren, on, **5**:209
        Sikh, **5**:241
    Islamic law, **1**:315; **3**:140, 419; **5**:306
        colonial, **5**:307–308
        dharma and, **2**:333
        on divorce, **3**:49
        Hindus and, **3**:157
        on marriage, **3**:49–50
        Naga law and, **4**:201
        secularism *vs.*, **5**:208–209
    Jaina law, **3**:363–365
    Jewish law, **3**:398–399
    jihad doctrine, **6**:87
    judicial review, **3**:218
        dharma and, **2**:333
        fundamental rights on, **3**:106

justice, equity, and good conscience in, **3:**446
legal profession, **1:**58
Maine, Henry, on law of, **4:**137
marriage, **2:**308–309; **3:**398; **4:***170*
   child, **2:**353; **3:**49
   of Christians, **3:**222–223
   Christians in British India, **3:**222
   custom, **2:**307, 308
   Hindu law, **2:**363–366; **3:**48–50; **4:**169–170, *170*; **5:**181; **6:**131
   sadācāra in, **5:**182
   secularism in, **5:**208–209
   Sikh law, **5:**241
   sources of law, **3:**148, 150
   in succession, **5:**400
Naga law, **4:**201
nītiśāstra in, **4:**232
personal law in, **4:**294
public interest litigation in, **5:**6–8
Rājasśaāsana, **5:**63–64
religion
   as fundamental right, **3:**48
   fundamental rights on, **3:**106
   secularism in, **5:**208–209
   separation of state and, **2:**333
secularism, **2:**145; **5:**208–209, 308
   dharma and, **2:**333
sex ratio in, **2:**364
Sikh law in, **5:**240–241
women
   adoption, **2:**307, 308
   bride burning, **2:**364–365
   bride price, **2:**308
   inheritance, **2:**307
   Islamic law on, **5:**308
   marriage, **2:**308–309
   as prisoners, **2:**283
   prostitution, **2:**307
   selective abortion and, **1:**5
   in succession, **5:**396–402
   widows, **2:**307
India Independence Act (1947), **4:**273
Indian Act (Canada, 1876), **1:**342
Indian Administrative Service. *See* Civil Justice Committee (India)
Indian Bill of Rights. *See* Indian Civil Rights Act
Indian Child Welfare Act (1978), **4:**213
Indian Christian Marriage Act (1872), **3:**49, 222
Indian Civil Rights Act (1968), **4:**211

Indian Civil Service (ICS). *See* Civil Justice Committee (India)
Indian Companies Act (1866), **3:**216
Indian Constitution and codified law, **3:**148–149, 160
Indian Contract Act (1872), **3:**216
Indian Divorce Act (1869), **3:**216, 222
   grounds in, **3:**50
   on maintenance, **3:**50
Indian Divorce (Amendment) Act (2001), **3:**149, 222, 223
Indian Evidence Act (India, 1872), **2:**281, 307; **3:**148
Indian Financing Act (1974), **4:**213
Indian Foreign Service. *See* Civil Justice Committee (India)
Indian Gaming Regulatory Act (U.S., 1988), **4:**213
Indian Independence Act (1947), **2:**144
Indian Law Commission, **3:**222; **5:**401
Indian Major Crimes Act (U.S., 1885), **6:**50
Indian Marriage Law (Trinidad, 1890), **6:**10
Indian National Congress, **2:**143
Indian Penal Code (India, 1860), **3:**148, 216
   on abortion, **1:**4
   in Africa, **1:**86, 87, 93
   on dowry death, **2:**365
   environmental law in, **2:**452–453
   on evidence, **5:**307–308
Indian Reorganization Act, **4:**211–212
Indian Standards Institution (Certification of Marks) Act (India, 1956), **2:**173
Indian subcontinent. *See* Bangladesh; India; Pakistan
Indian Succession Act (1865, 1925), **3:**216, 222, 399; **4:**286, 287
   Amendment Act (1939), **4:**287
Indian Tribal Governmental Tax Status Act (1982), **4:**213
Indian Trusts Act (1882), **3:**216
Indies Law (Derecho Indiano), **4:**314
indigenous law. *See also* folk law
   Africa, **1:**65–66
      after independence, **1:**96–97, 101–102
      Belgian colonies, **1:**82–83
      British colonies, **1:**87, 88
      under colonial rule, **1:**91–92
      Dutch colonies, **1:**82
      French colonies, **1:**89
      German colonies, **1:**84

Portuguese colonies, **1:**80
precolonial, **1:**71–72
Argentina, **1:**215–216
Australia, **1:**2–4, 239–240, 243–245
Baltic nations, **1:**255
British Commonwealth, **1:**312, 313
Egypt, **2:**413
Ethiopia, **2:**479
Guatemala, **3:**129–131
Mexico, **4:**175–176
South Africa, **5:**282
South and Central America, **5:**284, 285
   Aztec, **5:**287–288
   colonial, **5:**298–299
   in colonial law, **5:**291
   Inca, **5:**288–289
   Portuguese colonies, **5:**301
Sri Lanka, **5:**339
Wales, **6:**98–99
indigenous people, protection of in East Timor, **2:**384
Indigenous Peoples Rights Act (Philippines, 1997), **3:**264
indirect rule, **1:**91
  in Africa, **1:**78–79
  in Liberia, **4:**107
  Southeast Asia, **5:**317–318
Indische Staatsregeling (1925), **3:**226
individual effort of legal reasoning. *See ijtihād*
individuals, international law and, **3:**290
Individuals with Disabilities Education Act (U.S., 1997), **2:**335
Individuals with Disabilities Education Improvement Act (U.S., 2004), **2:**335
Indochina
  Chinese law in, **5:**319–320
  intellectual property, **3:**262
Indochina War, First, **6:**79
Indochina War, Second. *See* Vietnam War
Indonesia, **3:225–228.** *See also Pancasila*
  adat in, **1:**20–21
  annexation of, **5:**313
  constitution, **3:**335–337
  Constitution (1945), **3:**228
  courts, **3:**337
    under British, **3:**226
    dual system under Dutch, **3:**225, 226
  intellectual property, **3:**262, 263
  Islamic law in, **3:**334, 335–337
  legal education in, **2:**398

personal status laws, **4:**301–302; **6:**129
post-colonial, **5:**314
Shafiʿi school of law in, **3:**353
zakat in, **5:**431
Indonesian Muslim Intellectuals' Association (ICMI), **3:**336
in dubio pro reo principle, **3:**10
industrialization
  administrative agencies and regulation in, **1:**25, 26
  consumer protection and, **2:**170
  Sweden, **5:**416–417
Industrial Relations Act (U.K., 1971), **2:**427
Industrial Revolution
  banking and, **1:**271–272
  government power and, **3:**372
Industrial Workers of the World, **4:**337
In egregii I.C. Aymonis Cravettae Responsa Annotationes (Stracca), **5:**364
in factum conceptae formula, **3:**95
infallibilism, doctrine of, **3:**341
infamia, **2:**183
infancy (nonage), legal concept of, **1:**393
infant death, English common law and, **3:**178
infanticide
  English common law, **6:**120
  India, **4:**169
    dowry and, **2:**364
Infant Life (Preservation) Act (U.K., 1929), **3:**178
Infants Relief Act (U.K., 1874), **1:**395
Infants Settlements Acts (U.K., 1855), **1:**395
informal law. *See* folk law
Infortiatum
  in legal education, **2:**399
  medieval law instruction and, **2:**6
inheritance, **3:228–240.** *See also* intestacy; succession; wills
  Africa
    after independence, **2:**44–45
    Dutch colonies, **1:**82
  ancient Greek law, **3:228–232,** *229*
    adoption and, **1:**40–41
    Athens, **1:**140, 234
    in Athens litigation, **4:**114
    divorce and, **2:**346–347
    Gortyn, **1:**142; **3:**30, 120–121, 122–123
    inscriptions on, **1:**154
    marriage of heiresses, **4:**153, 155
    of slaves, **5:**244
    Sparta, **5:**328–329
    women in, **6:**114, 116

ancient Near Eastern law, **1:**171, 173
ancient Roman law, **6:**117
Balinese Hindu law, **1:**251
Chinese law
    adoption and, **1:**43–46
    land law, **4:**3, 4
    sale of land and, **5:**187
    Song dynasty, **1:**425
donation and, **2:**358
Egypt, juristic papyrology on, **2:**417–418
elderlaw and, **2:**423, 424
England, **2:**13; **6:**30
    on adoption, **1:**46–47
    custom in, **5:**276
    disinheritance of wives, **3:**33
    dower, **2:**361–363
    ecclesiastical courts in, **2:**81, 436
    ecclesiastical law on, **2:**389
    entails, **2:**446–448
    estates doctrine, **2:**476–479
    by illegitimate children, **4:**161
    real and personal property, **4:**470
    strict settlements, **5:**364–368
    taxation, **5:**426–427
    women in, **6:**121–122
feudal law, **3:**74, 79
fideicommissum, **3:**80–81
Hindu law
    ancient texts, **3:**158–159
    dowry, **2:**362–366
    marumakkathayam in, **4:**170–171
Imāmī school and, **3:**340
India, **2:**307, 309
    Hastings, Warren, on, **5:**209
    Sikh, **5:**241
Indonesia, **3:**337
Irish laws, **1:**377
Islamic law, **3:**232–235, *234*
    acknowledgement in, **1:**19–20
    adoption and, **1:**48–49
    colonialism and, **2:**43
    enforcement in, **2:**431
    Europe, **2:**483–484
    family and, **3:**39
    by fetus, **3:**71–72
    marriage and, **4:**167
    non-Muslims, **4:**234
    reforms, **2:**38
    wills, **6:**105–107
    women in, **6:**127

    in lease and tenancy contracts, **4:**57
    medieval and post-medieval Roman law
        disinheritance, **5:**391–392
        marriage and, **3:**42
    Mongolia, **4:**183, 185
    mortmain and, **4:**191–193
    nationality and, **4:**205
    Native American, **4:**211
    New Zealand, **4:**229
    Ottoman Empire
        women in, **6:**128–129
    Parsi law, **4:**287
    primogeniture
        England, **6:**121–122
    rights of villeins, **6:**81
    Roman law
        Sabinus, Masurius, on, **5:**180
    Saudi Arabia, **1:**208–209
    of slaves in Dutch African colonies, **1:**81
    South and Central America, colonial, **5:**285
    Southeast Asia, **5:**318
    United States, **3:**235–240; **6:**30, 34
        colonial period, **2:**13
        by illegitimate children, **3:**55
        of slave status, **5:**258
    Welsh law, **1:**377; **6:**99
iniuria
    in delict, **2:**321, 322, 323, 325–326
    Labeo, Marcus Antistius, on, **3:**475
injunction
    in antitrust, **1:**188
    England, equity and, **2:**469
    United States
        as equitable remedy, **2:**472, 473
        in labor and employment law, **3:**480, 481, 483
        structural, **2:**473
Inleidinge tot de Hollandsche Rechts-geleerdheid (Grotius), **2:**360; **3:**127, 252; **4:**226
    systematization in, **5:**421
In materiam fideicommisarium epitome (Marzari), **3:**80
Inner Temple. *See* Inns of Court
Innocent I (pope), **2:**385
Innocent III (pope)
    on consanguinity and affinity, **4:**161–162
    creation and promulgation of laws by, **4:**353

decretals by, **2:**317, 319; **4:**333
ecclesiastical courts under, **2:**386
Fourth Lateran Council and, **4:**432
on inquiry, **4:**263
inquisition procedure under, **4:**437
on Magna Carta, **4:**135
on ownership, **4:**477
Innocent IV (pope)
creation and promulgation of laws by, **4:**353
decretals by, **2:**223, 319
on evidence, **3:**9
lawgiving activity of, **2:**223
procedural practices under, **4:**438
Innocent VIII (pope), **4:**438
Innocent XI (pope), **2:**326
Innocent XII (pope), **3:**126
Innocentius, **2:**33
innominate contracts, **2:**187, 188, 189
Inns of Chancery, **3:**240, 243
barristers in, **1:**277
education in, **2:**354
legal professionals in, **2:**393
Inns of Court, **3:**240–244. *See also* Lincoln's Inn
American students in, **2:**401; **4:**48
barristers in, **1:**277
curriculum of, **2:**439
education in, **1:**278, 297; **2:**354, 436
law reporting in, **4:**44
legal treatises in, **2:**441
Maine, Henry, in, **4:**137
Middle Temple, **3:***241*
Middle Temple Hall, **3:***241*
rise and decline of, **2:**393
university centered on, **2:**395
Inns of Court Commission, **2:**394–395
Inns of Court Law School, **1:**280
Inoue, Kowashi, **3:**374, 376
in personam action, **2:**466
Inquiry into the Law of Negro Slavery in the United States of America, An (Cobb), **5:**261
Inquisition
Brazil, **5:**293
ecclesiastical courts and, **2:**386
Holy Office and, **4:**353
Jews and the, **3:**398
procedure for cases of public scandal, **4:**437
witch trials by, **6:**108

insanity
Chinese law, **3:**175
as a defense, **6:**50
in English law, **3:244–248**
guardianship and
medieval and post-medieval Roman law, **3:**47
guilt and, **3:**134, 135
inscriptions in ancient Greek law, **1:**146–147, *147*
insolvency, **3:248–250**. *See also* bankruptcy
Insolvency Act (U.K., 1986), **4:**175
Institoris, Heinrich, **4:**438
Institut de droit comparé, **2:**99
Institute for Juvenile Research. *See* Juvenile Psychopathic Institute
Institute for the Unification of Law (Unidroit), **2:**115
Institute of the Laws of England (Wood), **2:**394, 441; **3:**252
legal theory in, **4:**61
Institutes (Callistratus), **3:**251
Institutes (Florentinus), **3:**251
Institutes (Gaius), **3:250–251**
on the areas of Roman law, **4:**459–460
classification of contracts, **2:**181
on conflict of laws, **2:**109
on delict, **2:**324
Egyptian law and, **2:**419
as evidence for classical law, **5:**147
on *formula*, **3:**94, 95–96, 97
historiography in, **5:**158
influence on *Institutes* (Justinian), **5:**154
Labeo, Marcus Antistius, on, **3:**475
legal education and, **2:**392
on *legis actiones*, **4:**82, 83–84
on literal contract, **2:**184
on marriage, **4:**303
on ownership, **4:**462
on the procedural system, **4:**375
on property, **4:**462, 464, 465
systematization in, **5:**420
on unjust enrichment, **6:**65
use of, **5:**151
Veronese manuscript, **5:**160
on women, **6:**118
Institutes (Justinian), **1:**330; **2:**5; **3:**251, 252
on agency, **1:**110
on appeals, **2:**238
on appurtenancy, **2:**380

Azo on, **1**:248
on bailment, **1**:249
on contracts, **2**:182, 188
Cujas, Jacques on, **2**:303, 304
in Danish education, **2**:328
on delict, **2**:324, 325
Dorotheus and, **6**:8
educational aims, **5**:153–154
on employment and labor law, **2**:430
influence on
 Blackstone, William, **1**:298
 English common law, **5**:156
 Grotius, Hugo, **3**:127
 Hale, Matthew, **2**:440
 humanism, **3**:193
influence on English common law,
 5:157
on law of persons, **4**:302
in legal education, **2**:399, 400
on legal reasoning, **4**:81
legal studies and, **2**:6, 392
on obligations, **4**:242, 245
on property, **4**:466–467
publication of, **3**:456
on purpose of law, **1**:331
on treason, **6**:1
Tribonian and, **6**:7–9
Vinnius, Arnold, commentary on, **4**:226
Institutes (Loisel), **2**:357
Institutes (Marcian), **3**:251
Institutes (Paul), **3**:251
Institutes (Ulpian), **3**:251
Institutes coutumières (Loisel), **3**:98
*Institutes of Hindu Law; or, The Ordinances of Menu...
 Comprising the Indian System of Duties,
 Religious and Civil; Verbally Translated from
 the Original Sanscrit* (Jones), **3**:157
Institutes of Oratory (Quintilian), **3**:250
Institutes of the Laws of England (Coke), **2**:56, 440;
 3:176; **5**:461
 on burglary, **1**:316
 on courts, **2**:249
 legal education and, **2**:394
 on property, **4**:487
 as source of law, **5**:278
institutional writings, **3:250–252**
Institutiones (Ulpian), **6**:24
Institutiones iuris canonici (Lancelotti), **1**:357; **2**:224
Institutiones iurisprudentiae divinae (Thomasius),
 5:464

Institutiones juris Anglicani (Cowell), **5**:157
Institutiones juris naturae et gentium (Wolff), **6**:112
Institutions of the Law of Scotland (Dalrymple), **2**:98;
 3:252; **5**:200
Institutionum (Azo), **1**:248
Instruções, **5**:299
Instructions for the Government of the Armies of the
 United States in the Field. *See* Lieber Code
Instrument of Government (England), **2**:130
insurance, **3:252–259**
 English common law, **3:252–254**
 guarantee as, **3**:128–129
 health, U.S. welfare programs, **6**:97
 Islamic law, **3:254–257**, 337
 law merchant on, **4**:40
 marine, **1**:36
 Mansfield, Lord, on, **4**:142
 medieval and post-medieval Roman law,
 3:257–259
 maritime, **4**:147
 social security, **5**:270–271
Insurance Law (China, 1929), **1**:440
Insurance Supervision Law (Saudi Arabia, 2003),
 3:256
intellectual property, **3:259–275**
 copyright in English common law,
 2:216–218
 definition, **3**:265
 medieval and post-medieval Roman law,
 3:259–260
 Southeast Asian law, **3:260–265**
 United States law, **3:265–275**; **5**:84
Intellectus singulares (Zasius), **6**:161
intent
 Anglo-Saxon law, **1**:180
 in attempt, **1**:236–238
 Chinese law, **3:275–276**
 accessory and principal in, **1**:18
 in wrongful judgment, **6**:152
 donation and, **2**:359
 duress and, **2**:374–375
 guilt and, **3**:134, 135
 in Islamic worship law, **6**:146–150
 Roman law, **2**:323
intentio (charge) in *formula*, **3**:96
Inter-American Academy of International and
 Comparative Law, **2**:99
Inter-American Court of Human Rights, **3**:279
Interamerican Specialised Conference on Private
 International Law, **2**:115

interest groups, administrative agencies and, **1**:29
intermediate scrutiny standard, women in, **6**:138
Internal Revenue Code (United States), **6**:55
International Academy of Comparative Law (The Hague), **2**:99
International African Association, **1**:82
international agreements as source of international law, **3**:277
International and Comparative Law Quarterly, **2**:99
international antitrust law, **3**:288–289
International Commission of Civil Status, **2**:114
International Commission of Jurists, **4**:42
International Court of Justice (ICJ), **3**:279
   African judges in, **1**:106
   on South African mandate, **1**:93–94
International Covenant on Civil and Political Rights, **3**:296
   on folk law, **3**:90
   international law and, **3**:278
   People's Republic of China and, **1**:447
International Covenant on Civil and Political Rights and the Convention against Torture, **3**:461
International Covenant on Economic, Social, and Cultural Rights, **3**:296
   international law and, **3**:278–279
   People's Republic of China and, **1**:447
International Criminal Court (ICC), **3**:279
   founding of, **2**:253
   on sexual and gener violations, **3**:71
International Criminal Tribunal (Rwanda), **1**:107
international custom as source of international law, **3**:277–278
International Encyclopedia of Comparative Law, **2**:99
Internationale Vereinigung für vergleichende Rechtswissenschaft und Volkswirtschaftslehre, **2**:99
International Exchange Law Conference (1930), **4**:223
International Faculty for the Teaching of Comparative Law (Strasbourg), **2**:99
International Islamic Financial Market (IIFM), **1**:262
International Islamic Rating Agency (IIRA), **1**:262
International Labor Organization (ILO)
   on international labor law, **3**:484–485
   on social security, **5**:270

international law, **3:276–297**. *See also* public international law
   Africa in, **1**:106–107
   ancient Near Eastern, **1**:176–177
   colonialism and, **1**:77–78
   definition of law and, **4**:18–19
   definition of public international law, **3**:276
   Du Moulin, Charles, on, **2**:373
   European Communities, **2**:487
   Grotius, Hugo, on, **3**:127
   on insolvency, **3**:249
   Islamic law
      Europe, **2**:483–484
      public law, **3:280–282**
   private law in United States law, **3:284–290**
   Roman law, **3:282–284**
   Savigny, Friedrich Carl von, on, **5**:195
   Scholasticism on, **4**:16–17
   term coined by Jeremy Bentham, **3**:276–277
   Vattel, Emer de, and, **6**:73
International Law: A Treatise (Oppenheim), **3**:284
International law of armed conflicts. *See* laws of war
international sanctions, **3**:289
International Specialised Conference on Private International Law, **2**:114
international tax law, United States and, **3**:286–288
International Union of Anthropological and Ethnological Sciences, **3**:90
Internet
   fatwa sites, **6**:130
   regulation of, **3**:274; **5**:98–99
   trademark and, **3**:272
Internet Corporation for Assigned Names and Numbers (1998), **3**:272, 274
interpretation, **3:297–301**
   of wills, **5**:404
Interregnum (England, 1649–1660), **2**:130–131
   intellectual freedom in, **1**:380
interrogatio, **5**:211, 212
intersectionality, **3**:69
Intersexes, The (Prime-Stevenson), **3**:111
interstate commerce (U.S.)
   equal protection and, **2**:461
   Native Americans and, **4**:208
   state sovereignty in, **5**:353
Interstate Commerce Act (U.S., 1887), **1**:26; **5**:101

Interstate Commerce Commission (ICC), **1**:26
  abolished, **1**:29
  creation of, **5**:77
  elimination of, **5**:104
  New Deal and, **5**:79
  telecommunications regulation, **5**:96
  transportation regulation, **5**:78, 101
intestacy
  England, **2**:13; **6**:102–103
  Hong Kong, **1**:449
  United States, **3**:236
    blended families and, **3**:238
    colonial period, **2**:13; **3**:235
    rights of surviving spouse, **3**:237
intime conviction (deep-seated conviction),
    3:9–10
Introduction of Convicts Prevention Act (New Zealand,
    1867), **4**:228
Introduction to American Law (Walker), **2**:204
*Introduction to the History and Sources of Jewish Law,
    An* (Hecht), **3**:388
Introduction to the Law of Restitution, An (Birks),
    2:443; **5**:130
Introduction to the Law of Tenures (Wright), **2**:441
Introduction to the Law Relative to Trials at Nisi Prius
    (Buller), **4**:221
*Introduction to the Principles of Morals and Legislation,
    An* (Bentham), **1**:287
invalidity of a transaction
  illegality and, **3**:203
  immorality and, **3**:204
Invective Ageinst Glotony and Dronkennes, An,
    1:123
Inventions Enactment of the Federation of Malay
    States (1914), **3**:261
Investiture Contest, **1**:295
Investiture Controversy, **4**:353
Investment Bank and Monetary Fund, **1**:107
invisible hand, Berle and Means on, **1**:325–326
Ioffe, Olimpiad S., **5**:178
Iorweth, **6**:98
iparrhēsia (free speech), **5**:329–330
iqrār. *See* acknowledgment (avowal; *iqrār*)
Iran
  alcohol and drugs, **1**:121, 123
  ancient law, **3**:150
  capital punishment of juveniles in, **3**:462
  civil law, **1**:205
  codes and codification
    Islamic penal law, **2**:39

constitution, **2**:135, **138–140**
constitutional court, **2**:136
Constitutional Revolution (1905–1911),
    2:135, 138
criminal law, **2**:279
death penalty, **1**:368
duress, **2**:375
Islamic law in, **3:301–304**
  banking and finance, **1**:260, 262, 263
  non-Muslims in, **4**:234–235
Islamic Revolution, **3**:340
Islamization in, **1**:206–207; **6**:130
judiciary, **3**:419, 420
legal education, **2**:398
Parliament, **2**:*139*
personal status law, **4**:296
temporary marriage, **4**:167
U.S. hostage rescue, **6**:89
Iranian Penal Code (1991), **3**:181–182
Iraq. *See also* Baghdad
  conflict of laws, **2**:114
  constitution of 2005, **2**:136
  death penalty, **1**:368
  Islamic law in, **3:304–306**
    personal status laws, **6**:129
    Shafiʻi, Muhammad ibn Idris al-, in,
        5:235
    Shafiʻi school of law, **3**:352
  judiciary in, **3**:422
  Mecelle civil code in, **2**:35
  military regime in, **2**:135
  in U.N. Convention on Contracts for the International
      Sale of Goods, **2**:74
Iredell, James
  on constitutional limitations, **2**:161
  on natural law, **4**:218
Ireland
  courts, **3**:307, 310, 312
  in European Union, **2**:490
Irene (Empress), **2**:191
Irigoyen, Hipólito, **1**:*215*
Irikagina (king in Sumer)
  on cult of Baba, **1**:169
  edicts of, **1**:167
Irish Free State, **3**:313
Irish law, **3:306–314**
Irish Republic, **3**:313
Irnerius (Guarnerius, Wernerius),
    3:314, 355
  on lease and tenancy contracts, **4**:57

Irti, Natalino, **2:**49
Isaac ben Jacob Alfasi ("Rif"), Rabbi, **3:**392
Isaac ben Sheshet Perfet ("Ribash"), Rabbi, **3:**392
Isaacsz, Claas, **5:**339
Isabella (Spain), **1:**384; **5:**290, 325
   Jews under, **3:**398
   treason under, **6:**2
Isaeus
   on arbitration, **1:**213
   forensic speeches by, **1:**149
   as logographer, **4:**123, 124
   on witnesses, **6:**110
   Wyse, William, on, **1:**163
Isaurian Ecloga, **2:**275
isēgoria (free speech), **5:**329–330
Isidore of Seville, **1:**470
   citations of Roman jurists by, **2:**5
   in Danish law, **2:**327
   on Visigothic law, **3:**116
Iskandar Shah (Malaysia), **4:**137; **5:**322
Islahat Decree (Ottoman legal decree, 1856), **6:**15
Islam Hadhari (Malaysia, 2004), **2:**140–141
Islamic Banking Act (Malaysia, 1983), **3:**337
Islamic Bank of Brunei, **1:**261
Islamic Development Bank, **1:**261
Islamic Family Law (Federal Territories) (Amendment) Bill (Malaysia, 2005), **4:**301
Islamic Family Law Enactments (Malaysia, 1983), **4:**301
Islamic financial institutions, **3:**256
Islamic Financial Services Board (IFSB), **1:**262
Islamic law, **3:315–333**. *See* fatwas; *fiqh*; hadiths; *ijtihād* (independent legal reasoning); mufti
   overview, **3:315–318**
   abrogation of legal norms *(naskh)* in, **1:**5–6
   acknowledgement in, **1:**19–20
   administrative decrees of political authorities in, **1:**33–35
   on adoption, **1:47–49**
   Africa, **1:**64
      after independence, **1:**96–97, 99, 102
      East Africa, **2:**383
      indigenized, **1:**65, 67
      precolonial, **1:**65, 66, 67–68, 69
      on slavery, **1:**75
      spread of, **1:**73–74
   agricultural contracts, **1:**116–118
   on alcohol and drugs, **1:**119–123
   al-Ghazali in, **3:**119–120
   Arab countries, **1:**201–209
   arbitration, **4:**429
   Balkan peninsula, **1:**251–253
   Bangladesh, **1:**257–260
   banking and finance, **1:260–266**
      assignment *(ḥawālah)*, **1:**229
      Europe, **2:**484
      on loans, **4:**118–119
      Malaysia, **3:**337
   beginnings of, **1:**209–210
   on the body, **1:**298–301
   Brunei, **5:**315
   capital punishment, **1:367–368**; **3:**181
   censorship, **1:382–384**
   children, **1:***396*, **396–397**
   China
      ethnic groups, **2:**482
      on foreigners, **3:**91–92
   claims of God *versus* claims of men, **3:**325, 327
   contracts, **2:199–202**
   courts, **2:**432–433
   crime and punishment, **2:**277–280
   debt
      on assignment *(ḥawālah)*, **1:**229
      banking and finance, **1:**262
      obligations and, **4:**244
      wills, **6:**106
   definitions of, **1:**206–207
   deposit, **2:**332, **332**
   development of, **2:**396
   dissent in, **2:**345
   divorce, **4:**167–168, 428; **5:**127–129 (*See khulʿ* (divorce))
      consensual divorce (*See khulʿ*)
      damage in, **2:**311
      Europe, **2:**484
      maintenance in, **3:**50–51
      mubaraat, **3:**50
      on non-Muslim, **4:**234
      ṭalāq, **2:**44, 126
      waiting period, **5:**20
      women in, **6:**125–127, 129
   donation, **2:**201, **358–359**
   duress, **2:**375
   duty, **2:**376–377
   Egypt, **2:**421–422

enforcement in, **2:431–434**
Ethiopia, **2:**479, 480
Europe, **2:483–485**
family, **3:36–39,** 329–330; **5:**127–129
   acknowledgement in, **1:**19–20
   adoption and, **1:**47–49
   in Arab countries, **1:**207–208
   codes and codification, **2:**37–38
   colonialism and, **2:**43
   in Europe, **2:**483, 484
   in Maghrib and al-Andalus, **4:**129–130
   for non-Muslims, **4:**234
   obligations and, **4:**244
   option in, **4:**261–262
   reforms, **2:**38–39
   slaves, **1:**358
   South Asia, **5:**307
   tribalism *vs.*, **4:**164
   Westernization of, **1:**204
fetus in, **3:**71–72
forum, exterior *(ẓāhir)* and interior *(bāṭin),* **3:**97–98
foundational texts of, **5:**131–132
fungible things *(Mithliyyat),* **3:**107–108, *108*
hearsay, **4:**428
homosexuality, **3:181–182**
India, **1:**315; **3:**140, 419; **5:**306
   colonial, **5:**307–308
   dharma and, **2:**333
   on divorce, **3:**49
   Hindus and, **3:**157
   on marriage, **3:**49–50
   Naga law and, **4:**201
   secularism *vs.*, **5:**208–209
inheritance, **3:232–235,** *234*
   acknowledgement in, **1:**19–20
   adoption and, **1:**48–49
   colonialism and, **2:**43
   enforcement in, **2:**431
   Europe, **2:**483–484
   family and, **3:**39
   by fetus, **3:**71–72
   marriage and, **4:**167
   non-Muslims, **4:**234
   reforms, **2:**38
   wills, **6:**105–107
   women in, **6:**127
insurance, **3:254–257,** 337
judicial review, **3:413–415**

judiciary, **3:**315
   Abbasid dynasty, **1:**1
   Abu Hanifa on, **1:**9
   classical period, **3:418–421**
   dissent in, **2:**345
   modern period, **3:421–423**
lease and tenancy contracts, **4:55–56**
legal acts and facts in, **4:58–59**
legal and ethical qualifications, **3:322–326**
legal education, **2:**396–397; **3:**421–422; **4:**70–72
   Arabian peninsula, **1:**33
   faculties and law schools, **2:397–399; 4:**72
   lawyers, **4:**47–48
legal literature genres, **3:320–322**
legal personality, **4:64–65**
   in acknowledgement, **1:**20
   legal acts and, **4:**58
   obligations and, **4:**244
   in ownership *(milk),* **4:**272
legal profession, **4:70–73**
   lawyers, **4:**47–48
loans, **4:118–119**
Malaysia, **4:137–139**
Maldives, **4:139–140**
marriage, **2:**201; **3:**324–325, 329–330, **466;** **4:163–169; 5:**127–129
   on the body, **1:**299
   children in, annulment and, **1:**300
   colonialism and, **2:**43
   consensual divorce, **2:**350–352
   duress in, **2:**375
   in Europe, **2:**484
   option in, **4:**261
   public law regarding, **5:**20
   women in, **6:**125–127, 129
Nepal, **4:**225
Nigeria, **1:**93
non-Muslims in, **4:233–235**
obligations, **4:244**
Ottoman Empire, **4:**263–270, *264*
on ownership, **4:**272
partnerships, **4:288–290**
personal status law, **4:295–302**
persons in, **4:311–313**
pledge *(rahn),* **4:327–328**
political dimension *(siyāsa Sharʿiyya),* **4:337–338**
principles imported through codification, **2:**43
prisons and imprisonment, **4:383–385**
privacy, **4:385**

production of legal norms, **4:62–64**
profit in, **4:454–455**
proof and procedure in, **4:427–431**
property, **5:**19
public and private, **5:**19–20
public authority, **5:3–6**
punishment, **3:**325, 328, 330
   for adultery, **6:**130
   for alcohol or drug use, **1:**120, 121, 122
   crimes according to penalties, **2:**277–278
   enforcement of, **2:**431–434
   prisons and imprisonment, **4:**383–384
   stoning for fornication, **1:**6, 62
   types of penalties, **2:**278–280
purity and impurity in, **5:57–59**
revelation in, **5:132–134**
rights in, **5:136–137**
in Sicily, **5:**239–240
slaves and slavery
   abolishment of, **1:**300
   the body in, **1:**299
   legal bond and slaves, **5:**452, 454
   legal personality of, **4:**58, 64, 65
   manumission of, **2:**375
   option in, **4:**261
   taxes, **5:**430, 431, 432
   wills, **6:**105
sodomy laws, **3:**181
sources and methodology of the law, **3:318–320**
South Africa, **5:**283–284
South Asian, **5:306–311**
Southeast Asia, **5:**312–313, **322–324**
spheres of the law in the *fiqh*, **3:326–330**
Sri Lanka, **5:**339–340
Suriname, **5:**414
taxation, **5:430–435**
territorial concepts, **5:451–454**
on testamentary disposition, **6:105–107**
torture, **5:486–488**
transmission and authenticity of the reports from the prophet, **3:330–333**
Turkey, **6:14–15**, 16
United Kingdom, **5:**311–312
on war and peace, **6:85–87**
women, **6:125–130**
   in Arab countries, **1:**207–208
   the body in, **1:**299; **4:**385
   crime and punishment of, **2:**277
   Europe, **2:**484
   in legal education, **2:**397
   legal personality of, **4:**64
   obligations to children, **3:**37
   on worship, **6:146–150**
yad (possession), **4:359–360**
Islamic law, political geography of. *See* Afghanistan: Islamic law in; Arab countries: Islamic law in; Balkan Peninsula, Islamic law in; China, Islamic law; Egypt: Islamic law; Europe, Islamic law in; Iran, Islamic law in; Iraq, Islamic law in; Ottoman Empire: Islamic law in; Saudi Arabia; Sicily, Islamic law in; Southeast Asia, Islamic law in
Islamic Law of Nations, The (Khadduri), **5:**451
Islamic mutual insurance schemes, **3:**256
Islamic Religious Council (Malaysia), **3:**337
Islamic schools of sacred law, **3:**315–316
   ijtihād and, **3:**224
   Shiʻi schools, **3:**315, **340–342** (*See* Imāmī school of law; Ismaʻili school of law; Zaydi school of law)
      on possession, **4:**360
      on repudiation, **5:**128
      on revelation, **5:**133
   Sunni schools, **3:**315–316, **342–352** (*See also* Hanafi school of law; Hanbali school of law; Khariji school of law; Maliki school of law, Part 1; Maliki school of law, Part 2; Shafiʻi school of law; Zahiri school of law)
      on the body, **1:**299
      on divorce, **5:**128
      on proof and evidence, **4:**337–338
      on repudiation, **5:**127, 128
      on revelation, **5:**133
      sources of law in, **3:**330–331
      Zaydi school close to, **6:**156
Islamization
   codes and, **2:**39
   in Iran under Khomeini, **3:**304
Ismaʻilis
   codes for communities of, **2:**38
   internal tribunals, **2:**43
   Yemen, **6:**155
Ismaʻili school of Islamic law, **3:341**
   in Maghrib and al-Andalus, **4:**127, 128
Isocrates, **2:**109
   on adoption, **1:**40
   on freedom of speech, **5:**329
   litigation speeches by, **1:**140, 149
   as logographer, **4:**123
   on witnesses, **6:**110, 111

isonomia (equal access to law), **3**:31
Israel, **2**:35; **3**:393
Istibsar, al- (al-Tusi), **6**:18
istidlāl, concept of, **3**:353
istihsān (juridical preference)
    Abu Hanifa on, **1**:9
istisn' (contract of sale of goods), **1**:265, 359; **2**:73, 200
Italian style. *See* Bartolism
Italienische Reise (Goethe), **3**:84
Italy, **3**:354–359
    administrative law, **1**:24
    advocates in, **1**:57
    African colonies, **1**:81–82
    attempt, **1**:237
    banking, **1**:273, *274*, 274–275
    codes and codification, **2**:48
        company law and, **2**:92
    company law, **2**:92–93
    constitutions, **2**:121, 122; **3**:359
    Ethiopian occupation by, **2**:479
    fideicommissum, **3**:80–81
    guarantee, **3**:128
    guardianship, **3**:48
    housing, **4**:58
    influence on Russian law, **5**:166
    insolvency law, **3**:250
    insurance, **3**:258
    intellectual property, **3**:259
    judges, **2**:254
    law merchant, **4**:38, 39
    legislation, **4**:91
    Libyan occupation by, **4**:129
    Lombard law, **3**:117
    procedure, **4**:435
    property law, **4**:476
    revolution of 1848, **2**:121
    Roman law and, **5**:162
    social security, **5**:271
    sources of law, **3**:355–356
Ito, Hirobumi, **3**:374, 376
Ito, Miyojo, **3**:376
Ituri, **1**:71
Iuliani epitome Latina novellarum, **3**:456
Iulius Paulus. *See* Paul
iuris consultus. *See* advocate
Iuris et iudicii fecialis, sive iuris inter gentes, et quaestionum de eodem explicatio (Zouche), **3**:283
Iuris universi distributio (Bodin), **5**:421

Iuris utriusque methodica traditio (Lagus), **5**:421
ius, **1**:327; **3:360–361**
Ius canonicum universum (Zeger van Espen), **1**:357
ius commune. *See also* civil law
    adaptation of, **2**:5
    bodily injury, **2**:264
    children and property rights, **3**:45–46
    compurgation, **2**:104–105
    Derecho Indiano in, **5**:291
    employment and labor law, **2**:430
    Enlightenment on, **2**:444
    entire legal system as subject of, **2**:5
    European Union, **2**:494–495
    evidence, **3**:8–9
    German Historical School and, **2**:9–10
    humanist criticism of and codification, **2**:46
    justification of the basis of the law, **2**:5
    Mexico, **4**:176
    procedure, **4**:437
    Spain, **5**:324–325
    succession, **5**:386
Ius gentium methodo scientifica pertractatum (Wolff), **3**:283; **6**:112
Ius naturae methodo scientifico pertractatum (Wolff), **4**:217; **6**:112
ius novum, **1**:471
ius publicum ecclesiasticum, **1**:353
Ius Romanum medii aevi, **5**:163
Iuventius Celsus, **3**:431, 435
Ivan IV (Russia)
    legal theory, **5**:177
    Livonia invaded by, **1**:254
    nobility under, **5**:169
Ivory Coast
    law reform in, **1**:100
    political parties in, **1**:106

J

Jackson, Andrew
    administrative agencies under, **1**:25–26
    on corporations, **1**:322
    election of judges under, **4**:441
    electoral college and, **4**:339
    on equal protection, **2**:459
    on executive power, **3**:20
    on general welfare clause, **3**:114
    military tribunals by, **4**:177
    military tribunals under, **4**:180
    Native Americans under, **4**:208

Jackson, Bernard, **5**:108
Jackson, R. M., **2**:443
Jackson, Robert
    on patents, **3**:270
    on religious dissention, **5**:118
Jackson, Robert H.
    on executive power, **3**:24
    on right to bear arms, **1**:219–220
    on separation of powers, **5**:218
    on war power, **6**:89
Jacob, Giles, **2**:441
Jacob, H., **1**:76
Jacob, Herbert, **4**:33
Jacob ben Asher, Rabbi, **3**:392
Jacob ben Meir ("Rabbenu Tam"), Rabbi, **3**:392
Jacob Emden, Rabbi, **3**:393
Jacobi, Ernst, **4**:223
Jacobs, Giles, **2**:394
Jacobus de Ardizone, **1**:248
Ja'far al-Ṣādiq, **3**:340, 341
Ja'fari school of law
    on consensual divorce, **2**:350
    on the Mecelle, **1**:205
Jaffé, Philippe, **2**:316
Jagan, Cheddi, **3**:137–138
Jagan, Janet, **3**:138
Jagdeo, Bharrat, **3**:138
Jagiello, Baltic nations under, **1**:254
Jährlicher Beytrag zur Gesetzkunde und Rechtswissenschaft in den Oesterreichischen Erbstaatan (Zeiller, ed.), **6**:163
Jaimini, **4**:182
Jain, C. R., **3**:364
Jaina law, **3**:363–365
    dharma in, **2**:332
    vyavahāra in, **6**:83
Jaina Law (Jain), **3**:364
Jaini, J. L., **3**:364
Jakarta Charter *(Piagam Jakarta)*, **3**:335
Jakob (Duke of Courland), **1**:255
Jakobs, Günther, **3**:136
Jalaluddin Khilji (India), **2**:281
Jama'a Islamiyya (Pakistan), **3**:281
Jama'at-i-Islami, **2**:141
Jamaica
    in British Commonwealth, **1**:314
    reliance on British case law and principles, **1**:369

Jamali, Hasan, **3**:37
Jam' al-Jawami' (al-Subki), **3**:353
James I (England) and VI (Scotland), **2**:129
    Coke, Edward, and, **2**:55
    court intervention by, **2**:437
    judiciary under, **3**:416
    jury trials in colonial America and, **3**:442
    law in Ireland under, **3**:310
    law reporting under, **4**:45
    monopolies under, **4**:187
    parliament and, **4**:284
    Scotland under, **5**:200
    Star Chamber under, **5**:346, 347
    support for the doctrine of tracts in Ireland, **3**:309
    torture under, **5**:484
    women under, **6**:120
James II (England), **2**:131
    on Bermuda, **1**:289
    on corporate status of cities, **4**:119
    in Ireland, **3**:311
    Irish parliament of, **3**:309
    judiciary under, **3**:416
    juries under, **3**:440
    parliament and, **4**:285
James V (Scotland)
    College of Justice founded by, **5**:199
James VI (Scotland). *See* James I (England)
James Stuart. *See* James I (England)
James, Duke of Monmouth, **6**:5
James, Duke of York, **6**:35
James, Thomas, **2**:408
Jami' alahkam fi al-halal wa-l-haram (Al Hadi), **3**:139
Jam'i al-Jawami' (al-Subki), **5**:370
Jamieson, G., **1**:450
Jami' li-'ulum Ahmad ibn Hanbal, al- (Abu Bakr al-Khallal), **3**:305, 467
Japan, **3**:365–387, *367, 369, 372, 377, 378, 380*
    constitutions
        Constitution of 1946, **3**:378–380
        Meiji, **3**:375–376
    court system, **3**:380–382
    extraterritoriality, **3**:93
    influence of Tang code, **1**:424
    legal profession, **3**:384–386
    litigation and alternative dispute resolution, **3**:383–384
    Meiji period, **3**:372–376, 382

occupation of
  Indonesia, **3:**226
  Malaya, **4:**138
  Singapore, **5:**242
  Taiwan, **1:**451, 453
overview of legal history, **3:**365–369
private law, **4:**392
Six Codes of, **3:**376–377
Taisho period, **3:**366, 367, 377–378, 383
Tokugawa period, **3:**366, 367, 369–372, 383
Japanese Americans, internment during World War II, **2:**16, *17*; **3:**24; **6:**58
Japan Federation of Bar Associations, **3:**385
Jardine, John, **5:**316
Jariri school of Islamic law, **3:**353
Jarnsida (Iceland), **4:**91
Jassas, **3:**328
Java, Hindu law in, **5:**321
Java War (1825–1830), **3:**226
Javolenus, **3:**430
  on Labeo, Marcus Antistius, **3:**475
Jay, John, **2:**151
  on observance of international law, **3:**290
Jbir ibn Zayd, **3:**349
Jefferson, John Jay, **4:**480
Jefferson, Thomas
  Alien Acts and, **6:**40
  on bankruptcy, **1:**267, 268
  on the Bill of Rights, **5:**114
  Chase, Samuel, impeachment and, **4:**450
  on colonial courts, **3:**424
  courts under, **2:**259
  on due process, **2:**368
  on education, **2:**408
  electoral college and, **4:**339
  electoral votes of slave states in election of, **5:**260
  on executive power, **3:**20
  on general welfare clause, **3:**113, 114
  on natural law, **4:**217–218
  political crimes under, **4:**336
  on property, **4:**480
  prosecution of critics of, **6:**50–51
  on punishment, **2:**289
  on religion and law, **5:**115
  Sedition Act and, **5:**333
  on separation of powers, **5:**220
  slavery and, **2:**459; **3:**448; **5:**262
  Virginia state laws and, **6:**39
Jeffreys, George "Hanging Judge Jeffreys," **1:**365

JEGC. *See* justice, equity, and good conscience
Jehovah's Witnesses, **5:**117–118
Jekyll, Joseph, **4:**193
Jenkins, Leoline, **2:**355
Jesuits. *See* Society of Jesus
Jewish law, **3:387–399,** *388, 392.*
  See also Jews; Judaism
  overview, **3:387–394**
  Ashkenazi Jews, **3:394–396**
  early law, **5:**108
  India, **3:398–399**
  overview, **3:387–394**
  Sephardic Jews, **3:396–398**
Jewish Marriage in Palestine: A Cairo Geniza Study (Friedman), **3:**391
Jews. *See also* Jewish law; Judaism
  ancient Greece
    citizenship of, **1:**158
  Ashkenazi, **3:**388, 392, 394–396
  in banking, English common law and, **1:**270
  barred from being advocates, **1:**57
  as pawnbrokers, **1:**274
  Sephardic, **3:**388, 392, 396–398
  in U.S. legal education, **2:**406
  in Yemen, **6:**157
Jhering, Rudolf von, **3:**399; **3:399–400; 4:**226
  on breach of contract, **1:**309
  commentary on the pandects, **2:**10
  influence on Danish law, **2:**328
  on jurisprudence of concepts, **3:**432
  on Roman law, **5:**160, 163
Jiang Qing, **1:***445*
Jiao'ao (Kiaochoa), German leased territory of, **1:**451
Jiaqing emperor (China), **1:**195
Jia Yi, **1:**407
Jie (Chinese king), **5:**57
jihad, **3:**280. *See also* war and peace in Islamic law
  in Africa
    precolonial, **1:**68
    Tukulor Empire, **1:**88
  Ibn Taymiyya and, **3:**202
  legal reasoning on, **4:**63–64
  non-Muslims in, **6:**85–86
  in Sicily, **5:**239
  as worship, **6:**146
Jihan's Law (Egypt), **2:**421–422
Jimutavāhana, **3:**156, 158
Jina Samhitā (Vasunandi Indranandi), **3:**364

Jinasena, **3**:364

Jinbulü (Code on Moneys), **5**:183–184

Jin code (China), **5**:72, 73

Jin dynasty (China)
    accessory and principal in, **1**:18
    appeal in, **1**:194
    on astronomical studies, **4**:252
    on ethnic groups, **2**:481
    on theft, **5**:458
    on wrongful judgment, **6**:153

Jing Junjian, **5**:359

Jingshi dadian (Great Institutions of Statecraft), **1**:428

Jin History, **1**:455–456

Jin shu (History of Qin Dynasty), **1**:413

Jiu ming qi yuan (Wu), **1**:195

Jiyi wencun (Shen), **5**:238

jizya (poll tax)
    jihad and, **6**:86
    on non-Muslims, **4**:233

Joerges, Christian, **2**:496

Jogaila. *See* Jagiello

Johannes Apokaukos. *See* Apoukakos, John

Johannes Teutonicus, **2**:7
    on decretals, **2**:317
    influenced by Azo, **1**:248

Johannes Teutonnicus
    on decretals, **2**:220–221

Johansen, Baber, **4**:194

John XXII (pope), **2**:223
    ecclesiastical courts under, **2**:386

John I (king of Castile), **3**:397

John (England)
    appointment of Stephen Langton as Archbishop of Canterbury, **1**:467
    courts under, **2**:249
    on due process, **2**:367
    Magna Carta, **4**:133–136
    nationality under, **4**:205
    succession to the crown of, **5**:382

John M. Olin Foundation, **4**:26–27

John of Cobham, **2**:85

John of Salisbury, **2**:220
    on power of the king, **2**:128

John Paul II (pope)
    on Corpus Iuris Canonici, **1**:355
    Sacra disciplinae leges (1983), **1**:354

John Peckham, **4**:191

Johns Hopkins University, **2**:405
    legal realism at, **1**:15; **4**:75

Johnson, Andrew
    equal protection under, **2**:459
    impeachment of, **3**:23
    understanding of the Civil War, **2**:157

Johnson, Lyndon B., **3**:185
    administrative agencies, **1**:29
    antidiscrimination legislation, **2**:341–342
    elderlaw, **2**:424
    Great Society programs, **3**:62; **4**:370; **5**:82, 83
    law students drafted under, **1**:16
    legal education and, **2**:406
    legislation passed under, **6**:57
    regulatory system under, **5**:82, 83
    war power under, **6**:89

Johnson, Samuel, **2**:64, 368; **3**:448
    on Mansfield, Lord, **4**:141

Johnson, William, **4**:218

Johnson-Sirleaf, Ellen, **4**:107

Johnstone, Alexander, **5**:339, 340, 341

Johnstone, Steven, **4**:403

John the Scholastic, **1**:328

joint and several liability, rule of, **2**:87

Joint Commission on Accreditation of Hospitals, **5**:82

Joint Hindu Family System (Abolition) Act (India, 1975)
    marumakkathayam in, **4**:171
    on succession, **5**:400

joint-stock companies, **2**:87, 88
    agency and, **1**:109
    banking and, **1**:272, 275
    bankruptcy and, **1**:267

Joint Stock Companies Act (U.K., 1844), **2**:90
    amended in 1855, **2**:90
    on banks, **1**:272

joint-stock corporations, **2**:95–96

jointure
    England, **6**:122
    in strict settlements, **5**:366

Jolof empire, **1**:68

Jolowicz, H. F., **5**:161

Jonas, Hans, **3**:136

Jones, Artemus, **6**:4

Jones, Gareth, **5**:130

Jones, G. H., **2**:443

Jones, Mother, **4**:179

Jones, William, **2**:441; **3**:157–158, **400**; **4**:143
    on agency, **1**:109
    on bailment, **1**:249

on Blackstone, William, **1**:298
influence on Maine, Henry, **4**:137
on negligence, **4**:221
on Pothier, Robert-Joseph, **2**:442
Jones Act (U.S., 1920), **1**:40
Jones-Shafroth Act (Jones Act), **1**:370
Jonsbok (Iceland), **4**:91
Jordan
conflict of laws, **2**:114
judiciary, **3**:422
Mecelle civil code, **2**:35
personal status laws, **6**:129
zakat in, **5**:431
Jörs, Paul, **5**:161
Joseph II (Holy Roman emperor), **3**:194
enlightened absolutism under, **1**:8
Josephinian Law Code (Austria, 1787), **2**:9; **4**:380, 394
Zeiller, Franz von, and, **6**:162
Joseph of Volokolamsk, **5**:177
Josephus, Flavius, **3**:390
Joshua, **3**:389
Josiah (Judaean king), **3**:389
Jospin, Lionel, **4**:*173*
Jouannet, Emmanuelle, **3**:283
Journal of African Law, **1**:88
Journal of Juristic Papyrology, **2**:413
Journal of Law and Economics, **4**:23, 24
Journeymen Tailor's Union, London, **2**:425
Joyce, James, **3**:165
Joyce, William, **6**:3
duty of allegiance, **6**:4–5
JRC. *See* Judicial Reform Council (JRC) (Japan)
Juan Carlos I (Spain), **5**:326
Judaism. *See also* Jewish law; Jews
in ancient Near Eastern law, **1**:167, 168
on debt release, **1**:174
judges, **3:400–406**, *405. See also* courts; judiciary
advocates as, **1**:57
ancient Greece, **1**:154; **3:400–404**
China
mistaken judgements by, **4**:254
England
ecclesiastical law and, **2**:388
education of, **2**:439
Exchequer, **3**:17, 18
legal professions under, **5**:272
legislative interpretation by, **4**:88–90

Islamic law, **5**:4–5
as guarantors of rule of law, **2**:135
Japan, **3**:381
legal realism on, **4**:74, 76–77
Maldives, **4**:140
medieval and post-medieval Roman law, **3:404–406**
evidence evaluation by, **3**:7, 9–10
Ottoman Empire, **4**:264–265, 267
Roman law, *Lex Irnitana* on, **4**:103
Saudi Arabia, **1**:208–209
United States
as evidence gatekeepers, **3**:13–14
mistrust of, **4**:440–441
as teachers, **1**:12–13
Judgments Act (U.K., 1838)
on final process, **3**:88, 89
on mesne process, **4**:175
Judgments Act (U.K., 1864), **3**:88
Judgments of Damme, **1**:36
Judicature Act (New Zealand, 1908), **4**:230–231
Judicature Act (U.K., 1873), **1**:390; **2**:82; **4**:472–473
abolition of the Court of Common Pleas, **2**:86
Exchequer abolished by, **3**:19
on land leases, **4**:12
reforms in, **2**:437
Judicature Act (U.K., 1875), **4**:472–473
on serjeants at law, **5**:221, 223
Judicature Acts (U.K., 1870s), **4**:422, 472–473; **6**:14
on appeal, **1**:197–198
Judicial Branch of the Navajo Nation, **4**:*212*
Judicial Charter of the City of Pskov (Russia, 139–1467), **5**:168
Judicial Committee of the Privy Council
Australia and, **1**:241, 242
Caribbean nations and, **1**:369
as court of last appeal for Canada, **1**:340
ecclesiastical courts under, **2**:385
Singapore under, **5**:242
Judicial Conference of the United States, **3**:11–12
judicial decisions as source of international law, **3**:278
judicial power, **3:406–413**, *411. See also* separation of powers
of administrative agencies, **1**:24
Afghanistan, **1**:60
over administrative agencies, **1**:30–32

Sparta, **5:**328
Suriname, **5:**414
Judicial Reform Council (JRC) (Japan), **3:**380, 381, 382, 383–384, 385–386
judicial review
    administrative agencies and, **1:**30–31
    Austria, **1:**247
    Brazil, **1:**302
    China, **1:**195–198
        on doing what ought not to be done, **2:**355–356
        doubtful cases, **2:**361
        in wrongful judgment, **6:**152
    classical legal theory and, **2:**22–23
    England, **2:**437–438
    France, **3:**99
    Germany under National Socialism, **3:**111
    India, **3:**218
        dharma and, **2:**333
        fundamental rights on, **3:**106
    Islamic law, **3:413–415**
        classical period, **3:413–414**
        modern period, **3:414–415**
    legal process on, **4:**68–69
    legislative power and, **4:**97–99
    People's Republic of China, **1:**446–447
    United States, **2:**152–153
        distinction between federal-federal and federal-state, **2:**153
        on equal protection, **2:**462–463
judiciary, **3:415–430,** *417, 419, 425. See also* judges
    Africa
        after independence, **1:**99–100
        Belgian colonies, **1:**83
        British colonies, **1:**87
        Dutch colonies, **1:**81
        French colonies, **1:**90
        German colonies, **1:**83–84
        Italian colonies, **1:**81–82
        precolonial, **1:**66, 73–74
    ancient Greece, **1:**135
        assessment of, **1:**153
        Athenian influence in, **1:**143
        authority of, **1:**140
        Gortyn, **1:**142
        social importance of, **1:**144–145
    ancient Near Eastern, **1:**169
    ancient Rome, **4:**131–132
    Anglo-Saxon law, **1:**180–181
    in Arab countries, **1:**205

Australia, **1:**240
    activism of, **1:**244–245
Aztec, **5:**288
Balkan peninsula, **1:**252–253
Baltic nations, **1:**255
Bangladesh, **1:**257, 259–260
Bermuda, **1:**288–289
Bhutan, **1:**290
Brazil, **1:**303–304
Cambodia, **1:**335
Chile, **1:**398
China
    on foreigners, **3:**92
    under Qing dynasty, **1:**434
    Shen Chia-Pen on, **5:**237–238
church
    bishops and archbishops in, **1:**295
church, bishops and archbishops in, **1:**294
Denmark, **2:**328
Egypt
    Hellenistic period, **2:**415–416
    Islamic law and, **2:**421–422
    juristic papyrology on, **2:**418–420
English common law, **3:415–418,** 424
    barristers and, **1:**277–280
    education of, **2:**439–440
    in legislation, **4:**88
    mesne process in, **4:**174–175
    power of, **2:**437–438
    as source of law, **5:**277–278
Germany, **3:**118, 119
    activism, **3:**119
    National Socialist, **4:**202–204
of guilds, **3:**131
India, **3:**217–218
    dharma in, **2:**333
    Naga law and, **4:**201
Indonesia under Dutch, **3:**225
Islamic law, **3:**315
    Abbasid dynasty, **1:**1
    Abu Hanifa on, **1:**9
    classical period, **3:418–421**
    dissent in, **2:**345
    modern period, **3:421–423**
Laos, **4:**14
legal process on, **4:**66, 67, 68–70
Malaysia, **4:**139
Native American, **4:**209, *212,* 213
Nepal, **4:**224

Netherlands, **4:**225
New Zealand, **4:**230–232
Ottoman Empire, **4:**73, 264–265, 267–268
 education of, **4:**72
 reform by, **4:**40
Seychelles, **5:**235
South Africa, **5:**280–281, 282
 Indian law and, **5:**284
South and Central America, **5:**286
 colonial, **5:**300–301
 in Jesuit reductions, **5:**300
statutory interpretation and, **5:**360–363
Sweden, **5:**414, 416
Switzerland, **5:**418
United States, **3:**423–430 (*See also* Judiciary Act)
 administrative agency oversight by, **1:**28–29
 bar association on independence of, **4:**51
 equal access to, **2:**463
 immigration role, **3:**207
 labor law and, **3:**484, 485
 law and economics influence in, **4:**27
 legislative power and, **4:**97–99
 racial diversity in, **2:**343–344
 social science use in, **5:**266–270
 state, **5:**349
 women in, **6:**144
 Wales, **6:**100
Judiciary Act (Philippines, 1901), **4:**318
Judiciary Act (U.S., 1789), **3:**407, 425; **6:**40
 on admiralty law, **1:**38
 federalism under, **3:**59
 overview, **2:**257–258
 on removal of state cases to federal court, **2:**260
 on suits against a state, **2:**259
 supremacy clause and, **5:**411
judicium Dei, ordeals in, **4:***262*, 262–263
Judicium Pillorie. *See* Statute of the Pillory
Judikatenbuch (Germany, 1854), **4:**380
Juenger, Friedrich K., **2:**111, 113
Julian (Roman emperor), **5:**124
Julian (Salvius Julianus), **3:**298, **430–432**; **4:**497; **5:**162; **6:**24
 on custom as a source of law, **2:**167
 on formula, **3:**95
 on legal procedure, **2:**235
 legislation under Hadrien, **3:**211
 on magistrates, **4:**132

Paul on, **4:**290
 praetorian edict and, **2:**32; **4:**376
Juliani epitome Latina novellarum Justiniani, **1:**328
Julian Law on Adulteries. *See* Lex Iulia de Adulteris
Julian law on formula, **3:**94
Julius Caesar. *See* Caesar, Julius
Juridiskt Arkif, **5:**416
juries, **3:437–445,** *439*
 ancient Greece, **3:400–404**
  Athens, **1:**141, 233
  in Athens, **4:**115
  composition of, **1:**151
  evidence evaluation by, **3:**3
  oaths by, **1:**233
  size of, **4:**109
 ancient Rome, **1:**473
 Anglo-Saxon, **1:**182
 England, **2:**82, 439–440; **5:**276
  assizes, **1:**229–231
  Courts of the Staple, **4:**36
  decline of use, **3:**6
  evidence and, **3:**4–5
  on libel and slander, **4:**105–106
  mesne process for, **4:**174
 English common law, **3:437–441,** 453
 Japanese law, **3:**381
 medieval and post-medieval Roman law, **3:404–406**
 merchants for insurance cases, **3:**253
 psychological studies of, **4:**35
 United States, **3:441–445; 5:**135
  citizenship and, **2:**3
  equity and, **2:**472
  evidence presentation to, **3:**16
  right to a jury trial, **4:**440
  women, **6:**138–139, *139*
 Wales, **6:**99
Juries Act (U.K., 1825), **3:**440
Juries Ordinance (New Zealand, 1841), **4:**230
jurisdiction
 in abolutism, **1:**7
 Africa, consular, **1:**77
 Athens, **1:**141
 under enlightened absolutism, **1:**8–9
 in feudal law, **3:**79
 France, **3:**100

positivism in, **5:**351
Roman law
  lex Irnitana on, **4:**103–104
jurisprudence
  Chinese under Qing, **1:**437
  consumer protection and, **2:**170
  German, **6:**160
  reformation theology and, **1:**349
Jurisprudence and Social Policy (JSP), **4:**33
jurisprudence of concepts, **3:432–433**
Jurisprudentia contracta (Vinnius), **4:**226
Jurisprudentia Ecclesiastica seu Consistorialis (Caprzov)
  on marriage, **3:**41
Jurisprudentia ecclesiastica seu consistorialis (Carpzov), **1:**371
Jurisprudentia forensis (Carpzov), **1:**371
juristic papyrology, **2:**413, 417–421
jurists, **3:433–437**
  administrative law developed by, **1:**22–23
  Byzantine, **1:**332–334
  China under Qing dynasty, **1:**435–436
  English treatises by, **2:**440–443
  German, **3:**118
  German Idealist, **3:**135
  Islamic, **1:**33
  Roman law, **1:**149; **2:**391–392; **5:**146–147, 153
    on formula, **3:**94–95
    legal reasoning of, **4:**78–81
  Windscheid, Bernhard, on, **6:**108
Jury Law (Japan, 1923), **3:**375, 377, 381
Jury Selection Act (U.S., 1879), **3:**443
Jus canonicum generale distributum in articulos (Pillet), **1:**353
jus cogens, **3:**278
Jus Feudale (Craig), **2:**441; **5:**200
jus hodiernum (modern law), **2:**8, 400
jus modernum (modern law), **2:**400
Jus Naturae (Wolff), **5:**470
jus sanguini, citizenship and, **2:**2
jus soli, citizenship and, **2:**1
Justi, J. H. G. von, **5:**172
justice, equity, and good conscience, **3:445–446**
  in definition of law, **4:**20–21
  dharma on, **2:**333
  enforcement and, **2:**432, 433
  in natural law, **4:**217
  Wolff, Christian von, on, **6:**112
justice, restorative, **1:**70, 72, 101

justice, theories of, **3:446–450**, *447*
  administrative law in, **1:**22
Justice and the Poor (Smith), **4:**51
Justice of the Peace, The (Burn), **4:**61
justices in eyre, **3:450–452**
justices of the peace, **3:452–454**
  Wales, **6:**100
Justice Staff and Operating Regulations (Japan, 1872), **3:**384
Justin I (Roman emperor), **3:**454
Justinian, **1:**327–328; **3:**454–457, **454–457**, *455*
  Accursius, Franciscus, on, **1:**19
  on agency, **1:**110
  Alciati, Andrea, on, **1:**118
  on appurtenancy, **2:**380
  on assignment, **1:**227
  on attempt, **1:**237
  on bailment, **1:**249
  Baldus de Ubaldis, Petrus, on, **1:**250
  Bartolus of Saxoferrato on, **1:**280, 281
  classification of contracts, **2:**191
  codification by, **2:**28, 31, 33
  on concubinage, **3:**47
  on credit, **2:**262
  on delict, **2:**324, 325
  on disinheritance, **5:**373
  Domat, Jean, on, **2:**356–357
  on donation, **2:**357, 358
  Doneau, Hugues, on, **2:**360
  Dutch commentaries on, **4:**226
  Empire reunification by, **5:**12
  on engagement, **3:**41
  on error and mistake, **2:**475
  Faber, Antonius, on, **3:**27
  on *fideicommissum*, **3:**81
  on formula, **3:**95
  on freedom of testament, **5:**391
  on guarantee, **3:**128, 129
  on illegitimate children, **3:**46, 47
  influenced by
    Jewish law, **3:**393
    Sabinus, Masurius, **5:**179
  influence on
    Blackstone, William, **1:**298
    Grotius, Hugo, **3:**127
    Hale, Matthew, **2:**440
    humanism, **3:**189, 193
    Macedonian Renaissance, **1:**281–282

insolvency, **3**:249
on jurists, **1**:332
law of contract, **2**:182
law of persons, **4**:307–309
legal education, **2**:392
on legal reasoning, **4**:79, 81
on *legis actiones*, **4**:81–82
legislation in matters of church, **1**:346
on liability of heirs, **5**:393–394
on maritime law, **1**:35; **4**:151
on mortgage, **4**:189
Noodt, Gerard, on, **4**:235–236
on notaries, **1**:333
on obligations, **4**:242, 245
overview of works, **5**:152–155
on Papinian, **4**:280
on personal identity, **5**:384
prohibition of interpretation and commentary, **3**:297
on purpose of law, **1**:331
rediscovery of Justinianic law in Italy, **3**:355
on servitude, **5**:223
on Servius Sulpicius Rufus, **5**:225
on sexual crimes, **5**:230
on succession, **5**:372, 374, 375, 376
    intestate, **5**:385–386
systematization by, **5**:421
Vinnius, Arnold, on, **4**:226
Justinianic Code. *See* Codex Justinianus
Justin II (emperor), **1**:282; **3**:454
Juvenile Justice (Care and Protection of Children) Act (India, 2000), **3**:223
    on adoption, **1**:50
Juvenile Justice and Delinquency Prevention Act (U.S., 1974), **3**:461
juvenile justice in United States law, **3**:428, **457–462**, *458*
    poverty and, **4**:369, 370
Juvenile Law (Japan, 1922), **3**:377
Juvenile Law (Japan, 1948), **3**:381–382
Juvenile Law (Japan, 2000), **3**:382
Juvenile Psychopathic Institute, **3**:460
Juwayni, ʿAbd al-Malik ibn Abi Muhammad, Imam al-Haramayn, **3**:352, **462–463**
Jyske Lov (Law of Jutland), **2**:327, *327*

K

Kāamandaka
    on *arthaśāstra*, **1**:223
    on *nītiśāstra*, **4**:233

Kabaka Mutesa I, **1**:68; **2**:42
Kabila, Laurent-Desiré, **1**:106
kafāla, **1**:48. *See also* adoption
Kafawi, Abu ʾl-Baqaʿ al-, **6**:147
Kafiya, al- (al-Juwayni), **3**:463
Kafka, Franz, **4**:108
Kahn, Alfred E., **5**:83
Kaishung code (China, 583), **1**:421
Kaitei Ritsurei (Japan, 1873), **3**:372–373
Kaltenbrunner, Ferdinand, **2**:316
Kalven, Harry, Jr.
    law and society research by, **4**:32
    on social sciences, **5**:270
Kalwadhani, Abu al-Khattab Mahfuz ibn Ahmad al-, **3**:347, **465**
Kameny, Franklin, **3**:111, 112
Kampf ums Recht, Der (Jhering), **3**:399
Kanagawa, Treaty of (1854), **3**:365, 371
Kandyan Convention (1815), **5**:341
Kane, P. V. (Pandurang Vaman), **3**:465–466
    History of Dharmaśāstra, **6**:83
Kaneko, Kentaro, **3**:376
Kang Gao, **1**:360
Kang Shu Feng, **1**:402
Kangxi (China), **4**:184
Kano Law School (Islamic law), **2**:398
Kansas-Nebraska Act (U.S., 1854), **5**:262
Kant, Immanuel
    on autonomy, **1**:8
    on definition of law, **4**:18
    on guilt, **3**:135, 136
    influence on
        Dutch jurisprudence, **4**:226
        private law, **4**:393
        property law, **4**:475
        jurisprudence of concepts and, **3**:433
    on justice, **3**:447
    on natural law, **4**:217
    on punishment, **5**:34, 43
    on systematization, **5**:422
Kantorowicz, Hermann
    on guilt, **3**:136
    on rediscovery of Roman Law, **2**:6
    on Roman law, **5**:162
ḵānūn (dynastic law), **1**:252
Kargl, Walter, **3**:136
Kari Keiritsu (Japan, 1870), **3**:372

Karim-Hassan, Zaydan Abu al-, **6**:69
Karkhi, al-, **3**:343
Karl V (Denmark), **4**:150
Karl Theodor (Palatinate), **3**:473
karma, dharma linked to, **2**:332–333
Karo, Joseph ben Ephraim, **3**:388, 392
Karoly, Lynn, **4**:373
Karpov, Fedor, **5**:177
Karrāmiyya movement, **3**:301
Karzai, Hamid, **1**:*60*
Kasani, Abu Bakr ibn Mas'ud al-, **2**:201; **3**:329, **466**
  on imprisonment, **4**:384
Kasavubu, Joseph, **1**:98
Kaser, Max, **2**:167, 168
  on term *ius*, **3**:360
Kashf al-ghita' 'an hukm sama' al-ghina' (Ibn Qayyim al-Jawziyya), **3**:199
Katherine of Aragon, **1**:468
Katikavata (Burma), **5**:304
Kātyāyana, **3**:152, 155; **6**:83
Katz, Michael, **4**:368
Katzenbach, Nicholas, **2**:*411*
Kaufmann, Arthur, **3**:136
Kaufmann, Erich, **2**:121
Kautilya
  Artha'sāstra, **1**:223
  on forest management, **2**:452
  on *nītiśāstra*, **4**:232–233
Kavelin, Konstantin, D., **5**:178
Kazakhstan
  adoption in, **1**:48
  conflict of laws, **2**:113
Kazimierz the Great (Poland), **4**:330
Keating, H. S., **2**:442
Keener, William
  New York Law School founded by, **2**:403
  on quasi-contracts, **2**:443
Kefauver-Harris Drug Amendments (U.S., 1962), **2**:177
Keller, F. von, **5**:160
Kelley, Florence, **6**:136
Kellogg-Briand Pact, **3**:278, 295. *See* Pact of Paris
Kelly, Fitzroy, **2**:394–395
  in Exchequer, **3**:19
Kelsen, Hans, **2**:121
Kelsey, Francis, **3**:127

Kemble, E. W., **1**:*323*
  influence on Maine, Henry, **4**:137
Kemp, Evan, **2**:*335*
kencogus, **3**:309
Kennan, George F., **3**:293
Kennedy, Anthony, **3**:168
  on abortion, **4**:389–390
  on affirmative action, **2**:343
  appointment of, **3**:63
  on privacy for homosexuals, **4**:390
  on right to bear arms, **1**:222
  on state sovereignty, **5**:353
Kennedy, Charles Rann, **1**:280
Kennedy, Duncan, **2**:296, 297
  on law and economics, **4**:26
Kennedy, John F.
  assassination of, **1**:220; **4**:335
  consumers' legal rights and, **2**:177
  legal education and, **2**:406
  on Native American termination, **4**:211
  poverty policy, **2**:423–424; **4**:371
  on race discrimination, **2**:341
  regulatory system under, **5**:82
  securities policy under, **5**:93
Kennedy, Joseph, **1**:269
Kennedy, Randall, **2**:302
Kennedy, Robert F., **1**:220
Kent, James, **2**:205–206; **5**:115; **6**:41, 46
  apprenticeship of, **2**:402
  on comparative law, **2**:98
  on conflict of laws, **2**:117
  on easements, **2**:379
  on public corporations, **4**:120
  as teacher, **1**:12
Kent, Thomas, **2**:354
Kenya
  age-sets in, **1**:71
  British rule, **1**:85, 86
  constitution, **2**:138
  decolonization, **1**:93
  family law reform, **1**:103
  independence, **1**:93
  indigenous law, **1**:91, 102
  inheritance, **2**:38, 44–45
  Mau Mau rebellion, **1**:88, 93
  political parties, **1**:104
    one-party system, **1**:98
  racist land law, **1**:88
  South Asian law in, **2**:382–384
Kenyon, Dorothy, **6**:138–139

Ker, Charles Henry Bellenden, **2:**90
Kercher, Bruce, **1:**242
ke regulations under Han, **1:**454
Kerner Commission, **3:**185, 186
Kerr, John, **1:**243
Key, Francis Scott, **6:**51
Khadduri, Majid, **5:**451
Khadr, Omar, **4:**181
Khalil ibn Ishaq (ibn Musa) al-Jundi, **3:**351, **467**; **5:**3
Khalkha jirum, **4:**184
Khallal, Abu Bakr Ahmad ibn Muhammad ibn Harun, al-, **3:**345–346, **467**
   teacher of al-Khiraqi, **3:**468
Khalsa Dharamshastar, **5:**241
Khalsa Sudhar Taru, **5:**241
Khamhi Phathammasat Luang (Laos), **4:**14
Khan, Ayub, **2:**141, 142
   reform by, **5:**309
Khan, Gushri, **5:**305
Khan, Yahya, **2:**141
Khandhaka, **5:**302
Khariji school of Islamic law, **3:**348–350
   in Maghrib and al-Andalus, **4:**127
Khassaf, Ahmad Abu Bakr al-, **3:**413
Khattab, Abu al-, **3:**348
Khattab, ʿUmar b. ʿAbd al-, **4:**384
   as caliph, **1:**33
   on political authority, **1:**33
Khedival School of Law, **4:**47
   founding of, **2:**398
Khiraqi, Abu ʿUmar ibn al-Husayn ibn ʿAbdallah, al-, **3:**346, **468**
   influence on Abu Yaʿla, **1:**10
khiyār. See option *(khiyār)*
Khmer Republic, **1:**335
Khmer Rouge movement (Cambodia), **1:**335
Khmer Rouge Tribunal, **1:**336
Khoe, **1:**69, 81
Khojas, **2:**38
   internal tribunals, **2:**43
Khomeini, Ayatollah Ruholla, **3:***303,* 303–304
   fatwas by, **6:**130
   influenced by al-Ansari, **1:**184
   leadership of the jurist doctrine, **3:**146
   libel against, **2:**280
Khubilai Khan, **1:**428; **4:**184

khulʿ (divorce), **2:350–352**; **6:**126, 127
   Afghanistan, **1:**61–62
   Ottoman Empire, **6:**128
khushūʿ (reverence), **6:**148
kidnapping, **3:468–471**
   Chinese law, **3:**468–470
   English common law, **3:**470–471
Kikuyu, **1:**71
Kimball, Bruce A., **2:**403
King, Martin Luther, Jr., **3:**185
   arrest of, **4:**336
   assassination, **1:**220; **2:**342; **4:**336
   "I have a dream" speech, **3:**448
King, Rodney, **2:**302
King, W. L. Mackenzie, **1:***314*
Kingdom of Kandy. *See* Sri Lanka
Kingdom of Tonga, **4:**345
King's Bench, **3:***471,* **471–473**
   appeal in, **1:**197
   on assault, **1:**226
   barristers in, **1:**278
   Common Pleas subordinate to, **2:**85
   decline of, **2:**436
   history of, **2:**249–250
   law reports, **4:**45, 60
   on libel and slander, **4:**105–106
   litigation on insurance contracts, **3:**252, 253
   Mansfield, Lord, as chief justice in, **4:**142–144
   nuisances before, **4:**240
   organization of, **5:**16
   origins of, **2:**81
   quarrel with Chancery, **2:**55
   records, **3:**472–473
   restrictions of other tribunals by, **2:**55
   resurgence of, **2:**436–437
   serjeants at law before, **5:**221, 222
   Wales, **6:**101
Kingsbury Commitment (1914), **5:**96, 97
King's counsel (England), **5:**222–223
kingship in Welsh and Irish law, **1:**376
King's Inns, **3:**308, 310
King's Remembrancer, **3:**17
King Wuwang, **3:**275
Kinsey, Alfred, **3:**111
kinship laws
   Islamic law
      compensation, **3:**39
      wet nurses and, **1:**396

of Native peoples in Canada, **1:**345
   in Wales and Ireland, **1:**377
Kirschenbaum, Aaron, **5:**249
Kirti Sri Rajasinha (Sri Lanka), **5:**340
Kissinger, Henry, **3:**293
Kistiakovskii, B. A., **5:**178
Kitab al-ahkam (al-Hadi), **3:**341
Kitab al-amwal (Dawudi), **5:**239–240
Kitab al-ashbah wa-l-naza'ir (al-Subki), **5:**370
Kitab al-athar (Abu Yusuf), **3:**343
Kitab al-azhar (al-Murtada), **3:**341; **6:**156
Kitab al-azharfi fiqh al-a 'imma al-athar (Ibn al-Murtada), **4:**136
Kitab al-bahr al-zakhkhar al-jami'li-madhabib 'ulama' al-amsar (Murtada), **6:**162
Kitab al-bay' (Khomeini), **1:**184
Kitab al-farq bayn wilayat ahl al-islam wa bayn wilayat ahl al-kufr (Usman dan Fodio), **2:**41
Kitab al-funun (Ibn 'Aqil), **3:**196
Kitab al-fusal fi al-milal wa-l-ahwā' wa-l-nihal (Ibn Hazm), **3:**198
Kitab al-ikham li-usul al-ahkam (Ibn Hazm), **3:**198
Kitab al-i-'lan bi-ahkam al-bunyan (Ibn al-Rami), **4:**129
Kitab al-kharaj (Abu Yusuf), **1:**2, 10; **3:**305, 343
Kitab al-mabsut (al-Sarakhsi), **5:**194
Kitab al-makasib (Ansari), **1:**184
Kitab al-muntakhab (Al-Hadi), **3:**139
Kitab al-nawadir wa-l-Ziyadat (al-Qayrawani), **3:**351
Kitab al-radd 'ala al-nuhah (Ibn Mada), **3:**354
Kitab al-Shafi (Mansur), **4:**144
Kitab alsiyaral-kabir (Shaybani), **5:**451
Kitab al-tahrir (al-Husayn), **3:**139
Kitab al-umm (al-Shafi'i), **5:**236
Kitab al-wadih fi usul al-fiqh (Ibn 'Aqil), **3:**196
Kitab al-watha'iq (ibn al-'Attar), **3:**351
Kitab ikhtilaf al-Fuqahahamza (al-Tabari), **4:**56
Kitab Tahrim al-Nazar fi Kutub Ahl al-Kalam (Ibn Qudama), **3:**199
Kitab Usul al-ahkam fi'l-halal wa-l-haram (Hadi ila-l-Haqq, al-), **6:**162
Kitchin, John, **4:**324
klaros, Code of Gortyn on, **3:**122
Klein, Ernst Ferdinand, **5:**1
Klerman, Daniel, **3:**4
Klerman, Jacob, **4:**373

Knatchbull's Act (Great Britain, 1723), **4:**349
Knight, Frank, **4:**23
knight service, **3:**73, 78
Knights of Columbus, **2:**404
Knights of Labor, **5:**77
Knipschildt, Philipp, **3:**81
Koch, Christian Friedrich, **5:**2
Koehler, U., **3:**170
Koerner, Reinhard, **4:**84
Kohler, Josef, **3:**260
   African law codification by, **1:**91
   comparative law, **2:**99
Köhler, Michael, **3:**136
koine. *See* common law:ancient Greece
Koller, Carl, **1:**126
Konbaung empire (Burma), **1:**317–318
Kongo, **1:**69, 79
Kong Yingda, **1:**404
Konsumentenschutzgesetz (Austria, 1979), **2:**171
Korean War
   executive military action in, **6:**89
   influence of Tang code, **1:**424
Korkunov, Nikolai M., **5:**178
Kormchaia kniga (Russia), **5:**167, 168, 170
Korovin, Evgenii A., **5:**178
Koschacker, Paul, **5:**163
kosmoi, Code of Gortyn on, **1:**154; **3:**121
Kotliarevskii, S. A., **5:**178
Kotmai Phosarat (Laos), **4:**14
Kotmai Tra Sam Duang (Thailand, 1805), **5:**320
Kovalevskii, M. M., **5:**178
Koxinga government in Taiwan, **1:**452
Krafft-Ebing, Richard von, **3:**110
Kramer, Heinrich, **6:**108
Krause, Christian, **1:**303
Kreitner, Roy, **2:**208–209
Kreittmayr, Wiguläus Xaverius Aloysius von, **2:**9, 47; **3:**473–474
Kriechbaum, M., **5:**163
Krishna Iyer, V. R., **5:**7
Križanić, Juraj, **5:**177
Kronman, Anthony, **4:**26
Kropotkin, Pyotr A., **5:**178
Krüger, Paul, **5:**161
Krypteia, **5:**245
Kuala Lumpur, banking and finance in, **1:**262

Kublai Khan, **1:**458
Kübler, Bernhard, **5:**161
Kudriavtsev, V. N., **5:**178
Kufan school of Islamic law, **3:**305, 342
Kuhn, Thomas, **4:**363, 364
Kujikata Osadamegaki (Japan, 1742), **3:**371
Kulliyat, al- (al-Karawi), **6:**147
Kullūka
   on *ātmanustuṣṭi,* **1:**236
   commentary of *Manusmṛti,* **6:**83
Kumar, K. Murali, **3:***49*
Kumārapāla (king Cālukya dynasty), **3:**364
Kumaratunga, Chandrika, **5:***343*
Kunkel, Wolfgang, **2:**237, 238; **5:**161
Kuntze, Johannes Emil, **4:**277
Kuomintang, **1:**452
Kurbskii, Andrei M., **5:**177
Kurhessische Oberappellationsgerichtsordnung (Germany, 1746), **4:**380
Kush, **1:**67
Kutara Manawa, **3:**225
Kuttner, Stephan, **1:**354; **2:**222
Kuwait
   adoption, **4:**298
   banking and finance, **1:***261,* 263
   conflict of laws, **2:**114
   constitution, **3:**317
   Maliki school of law in, **3:**351
   Mecelle civil code, **2:**35
   obligatory bequests, **6:**107
   personal status laws, **4:**298; **6:**129
   shari'a as principal source of legislation, **3:**317
   zakat, **5:**431
Kuwait Finance House, **1:**261, *261*
Kwartierlijke Academie (Nijmegen, Netherlands), **4:**235
Kyd, Stewart, **1:**293
Kyrgyzstan, **2:**113

L

Laband, Paul, **2:**121
Labeo, **4:**290, 291
Labeo, **1:**166
Labeo, Antistius, **3:**435
Labeo, Domitius, **1:**373
Labeo, Marcus Antistius, **3:475–477**
   influence of, **1:**333
   on legal reasoning, **4:**80
   Sabinus, Masurius, on, **5:**179–181
   teachings of, **5:**147
   on the Twelve Tables, **6:**20
Labeo, Pacuvius, **3:**475
labor and employment law
   agency in, **1:**114, 115
   alternative dispute resolution in, **1:**129–130
   Bhutan, **1:**290
   Brazil, **1:**304
   China, common tenure and, **4:**3
   classical legal thought and, **2:**23
   corporate law and, **1:**325
   elder law and, **2:**423
   English common law, **2:425–428**
      Black Death and, **2:**436
   feminist legal theory on, **3:**70
   Germany under National Socialism, **4:**204
   guilds in, **3:**131–133
   India
      fundamental rights on, **3:**106
      women in, **6:**132–133
   Islamic law, **4:**56
   medieval and post-medieval Roman law, **2:428–431**
   Native American, **4:**211
   social security exclusions, **6:**96
   Spain, **5:**326
   unions, **6:**42
   United States, **3:477–486**
      alternative dispute resolution in, **1:**130
      colonial period, **2:**14–15
      on disability, **2:**334, 336
      due process and, **2:**369–370
      equal protection in, **2:**462
      equity and, **2:**472
      federal court jurisdiction in, **2:**261
      federalism and, **3:**61, 62–63
      feminist theory on, **3:**68
      labor arbitration, **3:486–490**
      picket line, **2:***23*
      progressive era, **5:**78, 79
      race discrimination in, **2:**342
      safety, **6:**48–49
      unions, **6:**42, 48
      women in, **2:**339, 340; **6:**136–137, 137–138, 138, 145
      working conditions, **6:**49
Labor Relations Act (U.S., 1935), **6:**54
Labyrintho del comercio terrestre y naval, **5:**291

Labyrinthus creditorum concurrentium ad litem per debitorem communem inter illos causatam (Samoza), **3**:249
Lachmann, Karl, **5**:160
Laden, Osama bin, **4**:181
Lady Chatterleys' Lover, The (Lawrence), **1**:381
laesio enormis, **3**:205
Laferrière, Edouard, **1**:23
Lafleur, Jacques, **4**:*173*
Lagos, British rule in, **1**:86
Lagus, Conrad, **3**:193
  on systematization, **5**:421
lāhamzaḥ, **1**:34. See also administrative decrees of the political authorities *(qānūn)*
Lakedaimonion politeia (attr. Xenophon), **5**:327
Lambda Legal Defense and Education Fund, **3**:111
Lambert, Edouard, **2**:99
Lambertini, Prospero, **1**:357. See also Benedict XIV (pope)
  canonical work of, **1**:352
Lancaster Banking Company, **1**:272
Lancelotti, Giovanni Paolo, **1**:353; **2**:224
Lancelotti, Paolo, **1**:357
land, **4:1–13**. See also lease and tenancy contracts
  Africa
    after independence, **1**:99; **2**:45
    Belgian colonies, **1**:83
    British colonies, **1**:87–88
    colonial, **1**:79
    Dutch colonies, **1**:81
    French colonies, **1**:90
    German colonies, **1**:84–85
    indigenous, **1**:92
    Italian colonies, **1**:82
    precolonial, **1**:71
  ancient Greece
    adoption and, **1**:40–41
    Hellenistic, **1**:160
    lease, **2**:69
    Sparta, **3**:29; **5**:327–328, 329
    women in, **6**:114
  ancient Near Eastern law, **1**:173–174, *174*
  Anglo-Saxon, **1**:178, 179, 183
  Australia, **1**:241
    Aboriginal, **1**:3, 239, 243–244
  Bali, **1**:251
  British Commonwealth, **1**:310, *311*, 312
  China
    on sale of land, **5**:185–189
  Chinese law
    title and subordinate interests, **4:1–7**
  copyhold, **6**:82
  East Timor, **2**:385
  Egypt, Greek law on, **1**:144
  England
    tenancy at will, **4**:12
  English common law, **2**:12 (See also conveyancing)
    dower, **2**:361–363
    estates doctrine, **2**:476–479
    fee tail holding, **2**:362
    feudal, **3**:72–77
    inheritance of land, **5**:381–382
    land registration, **2**:379–382; **3**:73; **4:7–10**
    leases of land, **3**:72; **4:10–13**
    on sale of land, **5**:189–191
    strict settlements, **5**:364–368
    on subinfeudation, **2**:436
    subinfeudation and substitution, **5**:368–370
    wills, **6**:102–104
    women in, **6**:121–122
  entails, **2**:446–448
  feudal, **3**:72–80, 73–74
  Fiji, **3**:81
  guilds on, **3**:132
  Hong Kong, **1**:450
  India
    dowry, **2**:363–366
    in succession, **5**:399–400, 401
  Ireland, **1**:376; **3**:312
    discrimination against Catholics, **3**:311
  Islamic law
    administrative decrees on, **1**:34–35
  Islamic law, agricultural contracts, **1**:116–118
  Maori, **4**:145–147
  medieval and post-medieval Roman
    on sale of land, **5**:193–194
  Mongolia, **4**:185
  mortgage, **4**:187–191
  mortmain, **4**:191–193
  Native American, **4**:208, 209, 210–211
  New Zealand, **4**:228, 229–230
  nuisance in, **4**:239–240
  Ottoman Empire, **4**:266, 269
  redistribution in Colombia, **2**:63
  reform in Islamic countries, **2**:37

Scotland, **5:**200, 202
  feu-farm, **3:**76
  seigniorial system in French
    Canada, **1:**337
  servitude in real estate, **5:**223–224
  Sicily, **5:**239–240
  South and Central America, **5:**286
    Portuguese colonial, **5:**292
  Sri Lanka, **5:**340
  United States, **6:**31
    colonial period, **2:**12–13, 13
    conservation in, **2:**455–456
    due process and, **2:**371
    Indian land, **6:**49–50
    takings clause, **5:**424
  villeinage, **6:**80
  Wales, **1:**376; **6:**100
Land Acquisition Act (Pakistan, 1894), **4:**275
Land Act (Bhutan, 1991), **1:**290
Land Apportionment Act (Southern
    Rhodesia, 1930), **1:**88
Land Claims Ordinance (New Zealand, 1841),
    4:228
Landis, James, **5:**81, 92
Lando, Ole, **2:**496
Landownership (Rankine), **5:**202
Land Reform Law (People's Republic
    of China, 1950), **1:**442
Land Reform Legislation (1961, Bali), **1:**251
Land Registration Act (Papua New Guinea, 1889),
    4:281
Land Registration Act (Papua New Guinea, 1924),
    4:281
Land Registration Act (U.K., 1925),
    2:215; **4:**10
Land Registration Act (U.K., 2002), **4:**10
Landslag (Sweden), **4:**91
Landslög (Norway), **4:**91
Land Tax Reform Law (Japan, 1873),
    3:373
land tenure. *See* land
Land Transfer Act (1897), **4:**470
Land Transfer Act (New Zealand, 1870),
    4:229–230
Land Transfer Act (U.K., 1862)
  on land registration, **5:**190
Land Transfer Act (U.K., 1875), **4:**8
Land Transfer Act (U.K., 1897), **5:**190
Lanfranc, archbishop of Canterbury,
    1:466

Langbein, John, **5:**484
  on evidence, **3:**5
  on jury trials, **3:**4
  on Litchfield Law School, **2:**402
Langdell, Christopher Columbus, **2:**208; **4:***65*,
    355–356
  case method of, **2:**24, 405
  education reform by, **1:**57–58
  at Harvard Law, **1:**13
  Holmes, Oliver Wendell, Jr., on, **4:**74
  jurisprudence of, **2:**76
  lecture-and-quiz method of, **2:**403
  on legal process, **4:**65
  legal realism on, **4:**75, 77
  on sale, **5:**190
Langdellism
  critical legal studies on, **4:**68
  on legal process, **4:**65, 66
Lange, Hermann, **5:**163
Langer, Karl H., **5:**171, 172
Langobards, **4:**90
Langton, Stephen, **1:**467; **4:**135
Lanham Act (U.S., 1946, 1962, 1996),
    3:272
Lao People's Revolutionary Party
    (LPRP), **4:**14
Laos, **4:13–15.** *See also* Southeast Asian law
  Buddhist law in, **5:**316–317
  intellectual property, **3:**264
  post-colonial, **5:**314
Laoust, Henri, **3:**345
LaPiana, William P., **2:**403
Laptev, V. V., **5:**178
La Ramée, Pierre de, **3:**193; **4:**61
  on systematization, **5:**421
larceny. *See* theft
Larceny Act (U.K., 1861), **5:**462
  on blackmail, **1:**297
  on burglary, **1:**317
Larceny Act (U.K., 1916), **3:**101
Larenz, Karl, **3:**432
LaSalle, Ferdinand, **4:**394
Las Casas, Bartolomé de
  on colonialism, **4:**17
  on colonial law, **5:**291, 299–300
  in Scholasticism, **4:**15, 16
Laskin, Bora, **1:**340
Lateran councils. *See under* ecumenical
    councils
late Scholasticism, **4:15–17**

Lathrop, Julia, **3:**459
Latimer, Hugh, **1:**366
Latinitas, **5:137–140**
Latte, Kurt, **1:**163
  anthropological perspective of, **1:**186
Latvia. *See also* Baltic nations
  accession into European Union, **2:**492
  as republic, **1:**255
Laudensis, Martinus Garatus, **3:**282
Laumann, Edward O., **2:**405
law, **4:17–23**
  ancient Greece
    creation of, **4:**85
    written, **1:**139–140, 146–147, 154
  autonomy of, **4:**66, 67
  European Communities, **2:**487–488
  as evidence, **3:**1
  legal process on, **4:**66, 67
Law, Edward (Lord Ellenborough), **2:**89
  influence on contract and commercial law, **4:**421
Law, Society, and Industrial Justice (Selznick, Nonet, and Vollmer), **4:**32
Law, Sylvia, **3:**67
Law, Violence, and Community in Classical Athens (Cohen), **4:**113
Law Amendment Society, **4:**42
  on education, **2:**395
  on land registration, **4:**7
law and economics, **4:23–28**. *See also* Chicago school of economics
  on antitrust, **1:**190–191
  law and society influenced by, **4:**32
  legal process and, **4:**68
  South and Central America, **5:**285
  U.S. state regulations, **5:**348
Law and History Conference, **1:**245
law and science, **4:28–31**
law and society, **4:31–35**
  effects of science on, **4:**30–31
Law and Society Association, **4:**31, 34–35; **5:**268
law-and-society movement, **2:**407
  anthropology and, **1:**186
Law and the Behavioral Sciences (Friedman and Macaulay), **4:**33
Law Commission (U.K.), **4:**10
Law Enforcement Assistance Act (U.S., 1965), **6:**60
Lawes, **4:** 324

Law for the Prevention of Genetically Diseases Offspring (Germany, 1933), **4:**204
Law for the Punishment of Corruption (People's Republic of China, 1952), **1:**442
Law for the Punishment of Counterrevolutionaries (People's Republic of China, 1951), **1:**442
Lawiers Logike (Fraunce), **4:**61
law-in-action approach, **1:**186
Law Magazine, **4:**62
law merchant, **4:35–40**
  English common law, **4:35–38**
  medieval and post-medieval Roman law, **4:38–40**
"Law Merchant and the Common Law before 1700, The" (Baker), **4:**37
Law of Arbitration (U.K.), **4:**273
Law of Citations, **4:**291
Law of Contracts (Parsons), **2:**208
Law of Contracts and Promises (Comyn), **2:**204
Law of Evidence (Gilbert), **3:**5
Law of Evidence (Nelson), **3:**5
Law of Hywel (Wales), **6:**98, *101*
law of nations, **3:**276, 290
Law of Nations, The; or, Principles of the Law of Nature (Vattel). *See Droit des gens, ou principes de la loi naturelle, appliqués à la conduite et aux affaires des nations et des souverains, Le* (Vattel)
Law of Nicophon (Athens, 375/274), **2:**70
Law of Peace and Justice (Colombia, 2005), **2:**63
Law of Procedure Before Shari'a Courts (Egypt, 2000), **1:**208
Law of Property Act (U.K., 1922), **2:**215
  on mortgage, **4:**189
Law of Property Act (U.K., 1925), **1:**395; **2:**215
Law of Property (Miscellaneous Provisions) Act (1989), **4:**189
Law of Restitution, The (Goff and Jones), **2:**443; **5:**130
Law of the Constitution (Dicey), **5:**15, 17
"Law of the [Palace's] Reed Gate" (China), **1:**405
Law of the Sea Convention (1982), **1:**106
"Law of Those Fleeing Battle" (State of Chu, China), **1:**405
Law of Torts, or Private Wrongs, The (Hilliard), **5:**474
Law of Torts, The (Pollock), **2:**442
Law of War and Peace, The (Grotius). *See De Iure Belli ac Pacis* (Grotius)
Law on Religious Courts (Indonesia, 1989), **3:**336, 337; **4:**302

Law on the Organization of National Labor (Germany, 1934), **4:**204
Law Quarterly Review, **4:**62
Law Reform (Enforcement of Contracts) Act (U.K., 1954), **5:**190
Law Reform (Married Women and Tortfeasors) Act (1935), **3:**34; **6:**124
Law Reform Committee (U.K.), **4:**42
law reform movements, **4:**40–43
    England on assizes, **1:**230–231
Lawrence, D. H., **1:**381
law reporting
    English common law, **2:**436; **4:**43–45, 60
        legal treatises on, **2:**442
    South Africa, **5:**279
law reviews, **1:**15, 16
Law Revision Committee (U.K.), **4:**42
Laws (Plato), **1:**140, 148, 149, 162; **4:**321
    comparative law in, **2:**97
    constitutional law and, **2:**123, 124, 125
    on *nomos*, **1:**145
    on status, **5:**357
    on wills, **3:**231
Laws (Theophrastus), **1:**149
Laws, The (Theophrastus), **4:**246
Laws and Liberties (Massachusetts, 1648), **2:**286
Law School Admission Council, **1:**15–16
Law Society, **5:**273
Law & Society Review, **4:**33
Laws of Beilu (China, 621 B.C.E.), **4:**196
Laws of Burgos (Spain, 1512), **5:**291
Laws of Edward the Confessor, **1:**178
Laws of Eric, **2:**326
Laws of Henry I, **1:**178
Laws of Khun Bulom (Borom) (Laos), **4:**13–14
Laws of Lerotholi (Lesotho), **1:**72
Laws of Manu, **3:**179
    on *smriti*, **5:**265
Laws of Manu (Hindu), **3:**153; **5:**108, 109, 110
Laws of Pilu (China), **1:**404
Laws of the Akan, **1:**65
Laws of the Indies, **1:**215–216
Laws of the Six Officials (China), **1:**404
Laws of Toro (Spain, 1505), **1:**215
Laws of Valdemar, **2:**326
Laws of Visby, **1:**37
laws of war, **3:**276, 278. *See also* war and peace in Islamic law
    influence of Lieber Code on, **3:**294

"Laws on Hiding Fugitives, The" (State of Chu, China), **1:**405
Law Tracts (Blackstone), **1:**298
lawyers, **4:**45–55. *See also* legal profession
    academics, **1:**11–17
    Byzantine, **1:**333
    Chinese law, **4:**45–47
    Islamic law, **4:**47–48
    in People's Republic of China, **1:**443
    United States law, **4:**48–55
Lawyers and Litigants in Ancient Athens (Bonner), **1:**163
Lawyers' Committee for Civil Rights under Law, **4:**52
Lawyers Committee for Human Rights, **3:**297
Lawyers' Ethics (Carlin), **4:**32
Lawyers Law (Japan, 1893), **3:**384
Lawyers Law (Japan, 1949), **3:**385
Lawyers on Their Own (Carlin), **4:**32
Layout-Designs of Integrated Circuits Act (Malaysia, 2000), **3:**263
Layti, Yahya ibn Yahya al-, **4:**140
LCS. *See* Legal Services Corporation
Leach, John A., **1:***125*
Leadership Conference on Civil Rights, **2:**340
League for the Promotion of Parliament, **3:**376
League of Arab States, **3:**281
League of Nations, **3:**284, 294–295, *295*
    influenced by Grotius, Hugo, **3:**127
    mandates, **1:**314–315
    protectorates, **1:**313
    U.S. failure to ratify, **3:**21
Leake, S. M., **2:**442
lease and tenancy contracts, **4:**55–58
    ancient Greek law, **2:**180
        Hellenistic, **1:**160
        maritime law, **4:**148
    case law on, **3:**163
    Chinese law, **4:**6
    England
        in estates doctrine, **2:**478–479
        land, **4:**10–13
        land registration and, **4:**10
        in strict settlements, **5:**367
    Islamic law, **4:**55–56
    lease of agricultural land, **2:**187
    long term lease of public land, **2:**187
    medieval and post-medieval Roman law, **4:**56–58
    subinfeudation and substitution, **5:**368–370

Leasehold Reform Act (U.K., 1968), **2**:478–479
Lebanon
   Imāmi school in, **3**:340
   Mecelle civil code in, **2**:35
   personal status laws, **6**:129
   zakat in, **5**:431
Lebensversicherungsbank für Deutschland zu Gotha, **3**:258
Leclère, Adhémard, **5**:316
Lê Code (Vietnam, 1428), **6**:79
Le Conte, Antoine, **2**:359
Lectura (Baldus de Ubaldis), **2**:111
Lectura Autentici (Bartolus of Saxoferrato), **1**:281
Lectures Introductory (Dicey), **2**:133
Lectures on Equity (Maitland), **4**:188
Lectures on Jurisprudence (Austin), **1**:238
Lectures on the Early History of Institutions (Maine), **4**:137
Le Douaren. *See* François le Douaren
Lê dynasty (Vietnam), **1**:424
Lee, Richard Henry, **1**:223
Lee, R. W., **3**:127
Leeuwen, Simon van, **4**:226; **5**:340
Le Ferron, Arnoul, **2**:359
Leflar, Robert A., **2**:111, 113, 118, 119
legal acts and legal facts in Islamic law, **4**:58–59
legal aid
   U.K., **4**:43
   United States, **4**:51–52
Legal Aid Board (U.K.), **4**:43
Legal Aid Movement, **5**:6
Legal and Political Hermeneutics (Lieber), **2**:161
legal anthropology, **4**:59–60
   on African indigenous law, **1**:91–92
   on definition of law, **4**:19
   in law and society, **4**:33, 35
   Nader, Laura, on, **4**:33
legal capacity. *See also* capacity *(ahliyya)*
   of children in the United Kingdom, **1**:394–395
   Labeo, Marcus Antistius, on, **3**:476
Legal Code of Hermopolis West (Egypt), **2**:414
Legal Decree of the Glorious 'Brug pa Rin po che, the Mighty Ngag gi dBang po, The Discourse, Victorious in All Directions, The, **1**:289–290
Legal Defense Fund. *See* NAACP Legal Defense Fund

legal education, **2**:391–408. *See also* Inns of Court
   of advocates, **1**:56, 57–58
   African British colonies, **1**:88
   ancient Rome, **2**:391–392
   Balkan peninsula, **1**:252–253
   of barristers, **1**:277, 278, 279, 280
   Brazil, **1**:303
   Burma, **1**:318
   Byzantine, **1**:330, 332, 333
   canonical law, **1**:355–357
   China, **4**:45–47
   Chinese Republic, **1**:440
   Denmark, **2**:328
   East Timor, **2**:384
   on elderlaw, **2**:422, 424
   English common law, **2**:393–396, 439
      Blackstone, William, in, **1**:297–298
      common-law, **1**:297–298; **2**:436
      Doctors' Commons, **2**:354–355
      legal treatises in, **2**:441–442
      reforms of, **2**:437
   European Union, **2**:496
   faculties and teaching methods, **2**:399–401
   feminist legal theory in, **3**:66
   France, **3**:100
   Iraq, **3**:306
   Ireland, **3**:308
   Islamic law, **2**:396–397; **3**:421–422; **4**:70–72
      Arabian peninsula, **1**:33
      faculties and law schools, **2**:397–399; **4**:72
      lawyers, **4**:47–48
   Japan, **3**:374
   Laos, **4**:14
   law and economics in, **4**:27–28
   law and science in, **4**:35
   legal process on, **4**:66
   legal realism on, **4**:77
   Maghrib and al-Andalus, **4**:129–130
   Maine, Henry, on, **4**:137
   Netherlands, **4**:225, 226
   of notaries, **4**:237
   Oldendorp, Johann, on, **4**:261
   Ottoman Empire, **4**:264, 265–266
   Quebec, **1**:342
   Scotland, **5**:198, 199–200, 201

South and Central America, **5:**286
  Brazil, **5:**294
Spain, **5:**324–325, 325–326
Sweden, **5:**414, 415, 416
Switzerland, **5:**418
United States, **2:401–408**
  lawyers, **4:**48–49
  women in, **6:**143–145
legal formalism, legal realism on, **4:**74–75
legal history
  Australia, **1:**245
  law and society on, **4:**35
  legal anthropology on, **4:**59–60
  on obligations, **4:**243
  reliability of Roman, **4:**130
legalist philosophers (China), **1:**407, 456
legal justice. *See* justice, theories of
legal liberalism, critical race theory and, **2:**299–300
legal literature
  in English common law, **4:60–62**
    historiography, **2:**434
  in Qing dynasty, **1:**436–437
legal majority. *See* majority
Legal Momentum, **6:**144
legal norms in Islamic law, production of, **4:62–64**
Legal Observer (journal), **4:**62
legal orthodoxy. *See* classical legal theory
legal personality
  first corporations with, **2:**95
  in Islamic law, **4:64–65**
    in acknowledgement, **1:**20
    legal acts and, **4:**58
    obligations and, **4:**244
    in ownership *(milk)*, **4:**272
  non existent in ancient Greek law, **2:**70
legal process, **4:65–70**
  under Han dynasty, **1:**415–417
  on statutory interpretation, **5:**361–362
Legal Process, The: Basic Problems in the Making and Application of Law (Hart and Sacks), **4:**65–67
  on statutory interpretation, **5:**361
legal profession. *See also* barristers; judges; lawyers; logography; mufti; notary
  African British colonies, **1:**88
  ancient Greek, **4:**113
    advocates, **1:**53–58
    in Athens litigation, **4:**113–115

    jurists, **1:**149
    logographers, **4:**123–126
  ancient Rome, **2:**391–393
  Anglo-Saxon law, **1:**180–181
  Brazil, **5:**293
  Burma, **1:**318
  Byzantine, **1:**332–334
  Canada, **1:**340
  China
    Chinese Republic, **1:**440
    litigation masters, **1:**195
  in elderlaw, **2:**422, 423
  England
    agency and, **1:**109
    beginning of, **2:**81
    monopoly of, **2:**435
    reform of, **4:**41
    serjeants at law, **5:***221*, 221–223
    solicitors, **5:272–273**
  Ireland, **3:**307, 310–311
  Islamic law, **4:70–72**
  Japan, **3:**384–386
  Ottoman Empire, **4:72–73**, 265–266
    women in, **6:**129
  Roman, **4:**79
  Scotland, **5:**201
  shortage in Cambodia, **1:**335
  South and Central America, **5:**285
  Sweden, **5:**414, 416
  United States, **6:**43, 55–56
    academics in, **1:**11–18
    women in, **6:**143–145
legal realism, **3:**164–165; **4:74–79**
  of academics, **1:**15
  on classical legal theory, **2:**26
  influence on U.S. law of conflict of laws, **2:**116
  law and economics, **4:**23, 26
  legal education, **2:**405
  South and Central America, **5:**286
  study of law and society, **4:**31
legal reasoning, **4:79–81**
  Islamic law (*See ijtihād* (independent legal reasoning))
  legal process on, **4:**65–70
Legal Research and Training Institute (Japan), **3:**385
Legal Services (U.S.). *See also* Legal Services Corporation (LSC)
  legal education and, **2:**406
  Reagan on, **4:**373; **6:**95
  welfare and, **6:**94–95

Legal Services Corporation, **4**:52; **6**:95
   in legal education, **2**:406
Legal Training and Research Institute, **3**:386
Leges Edwardi Confessoris (England), **1**:183
Leges Francorum, **3**:98
leges fundamentales, **2**:120
Leges Henrici Primi (England, 1115), **1**:183, 364; **3**:178; **5**:27
Leges Juliae, **2**:32; **4**:375
Leges Langobardorum, **3**:117
Leges Liciniae Sextiae, **5**:142
Leges Porciae. *See* Lex Porcia
Leggi e constituzioni de Sua Maestà (Laws and Constitutions of Our Savoyard Majesty) (Sardinia, 1723), **3**:358
legis actiones, **4**:81–84; **5**:143
   formula and, **3**:94
legislation, **4**:84–92
   abolutism and, **1**:7
   Africa, precolonial, **1**:66
   ancient Greece, **1**:155–156; **4**:84–87
      written, **1**:156–157
   Australia, **1**:240–241
   Brazil, colonial, **5**:293
   Byzantine, **1**:327, 328–329
   comparative law in, **2**:98
   England
      Mansfield, Lord, on, **4**:142–143
      as source of law, **5**:276–277
   under enlightened absolutism, **1**:8–9
   European Union, **2**:495
   Germany in National Socialist Law, **3**:110
   medieval and post-medieval Roman law, **4**:90–92
   New Zealand, **4**:228
   Ottoman Empire, **4**:268
   ripper, **4**:121
   in Roman law, **1**:327
   statute law, **4**:87–90
   statutory interpretation and, **5**:360–363
Legislation on Decentralization and Regional Autonomy (Bali, 1999 and 2004), **1**:251
legislative assemblies *(Leges, plebiscites)*, **4**:92–95
legislative histories, **3**:163–164
legislative power, **4**:95–100. *See also* separation of powers
   of administrative agencies, **1**:24
   in admiralty law, **1**:39–40
   Africa, **1**:97
      after independence, **1**:107
   executive power as balance to, **3**:21–23

Islamic law, **4**:195
   legal process on, **4**:66, 67, 69–70
   Maldives, **4**:140
   of Roman Senate, **5**:212
   Scotland, **5**:202
   South Africa, **5**:279
   Suriname, **5**:296, 413
   Sweden, **5**:417
   United States
      in apportionment and reapportionment and, **1**:200–204
      state, **5**:348, 350–351
   veto power in, **5**:218, 219
legislators, interpretation and, **3**:299
legitimacy, government
   Africa, **1**:98–99
   British Commonwealth, **1**:310, *311*, 312, 313
   Islamization and, **6**:129–130
Legitimacy Act (U.K., 1926), **1**:392
legitime, **5**:376–377
Legum delectus (Domat), **2**:357
Lehnrecht. *See* feudal law: medieval and post-medieval law
Lehrbuch des Pandektenrechts (Windscheid), **4**:276; **6**:107
   systematization in, **5**:421
Lehre des römischen Rechts von der Voraussetzung, Die (Windscheid), **6**:107
Leibgeding, **3**:42
Leibniz, Gottfried Wilhelm, **4**:100–101
   on codification, **2**:47
   comparative law, **2**:98
   on definition of law, **4**:18
   influenced by Suárez, Francisco, **4**:17
   on Justinian organization, **2**:400
   Wolff, Christian von, and, **6**:111
Leibzucht, **3**:42
Lei da Boa Razão (Brazil, 1769), **5**:294
Lei de Toro (1505), **5**:298–299
Lei dos Índios (1570), **5**:301
Lei Menglin, **1**:433
Leis de Burgos (1512), **5**:299
Leis Novas (1542), **5**:299, 300
Leis Willhelme (England), **1**:178, 183
Lenel, Otto, **5**:160, 161
Lenger, Marie-Thérèse, **4**:86
Lenin, Vladimir Ilich, **5**:173
Leo (Roman emperor), **2**:187

Leo I (pope)
   on bishops and archbishops, **1**:294; **4**:351
   decretals by, **2**:316
   highest judicial authority claimed by, **2**:385
Leo IV (pope)
   decretals by, **2**:318
Leo XIII (pope), **1**:353
Leocrates, **4**:246
Leo III the Isaurian
   Iconoclasts and, **1**:328
   on purpose of law, **1**:331
Leon Pinelo, Antonio de, **1**:215–216; **5**:291
Leontev, Konstantin N., **5**:178
Leopard Associations, **1**:71
Leopold (Grand Duke), **3**:358
Leopold, Nathan Freudenthal, Jr., **3**:428
Leopold II (Belgium), **1**:76
   Congo under, **1**:77, 82
Leo the Wise (Roman emperor), **2**:192; **4**:469
Leo VI the Wise (Byzantine emperor)
   Basilica under, **1**:282
   legislation by, **1**:281
   Novellae by, **1**:329
   on purpose of law, **1**:331–332
   on succession, **5**:376
Lesotho, **1**:63–64
   independence of, **1**:93
   indigenous law, **1**:72
Lessa, Pedro, **1**:304
letters patent, **3**:269
letting and hiring
   ancient Roman law, **2**:188, 189
   contract in Roman law, **2**:184, 185, 186
Leuenberg Concord (1973), **1**:352
levari facias, writ of, **3**:88
Levelers, **1**:380
Levellers (England), **4**:41
Levi, Leone, **2**:98
Leviathan (Hobbes)
   on absolutism, **1**:7
   on sovereignty, **5**:352
Levine, Dennis, **5**:94
Levinson, Sanford, **1**:221
levirate
   ethnic practice in Liao empire (China), **1**:427
   Yuan law (China), **1**:429

Lévi-Strauss, Claude, **2**:297
Leviticus, **5**:108, 110
Leviticus Code. *See* Holiness Code of Leviticus
Levy, Ernst, **2**:168
Lévy-Ullmann, Henri, **2**:99
Lewandowski, Herve, **1**:*168*
Lewes, Battle of (1264), **6**:1
Lewis, Anthony, **4**:454
Lewis, David M., **4**:85
lex, **4**:101–102
Lex Aebutia, **2**:32
   and the procedural system, **4**:375
Lex Aelia Sentia (4 C.E.), **3**:210–211
   on manumission, **4**:306
   on Roman citizenship, **5**:138
   on slavery, **5**:249
Lex Aquilia
   on damage to property, **4**:375
   on delict, **2**:322, 324, 325
   Labeo, Marcus Antistius, on, **3**:475
   on legal reasoning, **4**:80
   Sabinus, Masurius, on, **5**:179
Lex Atilia
   on minors, **4**:305
Lex Atinia, **4**:461
Lex Aurelia (70 B.C.E.), **2**:238
Lex Calpurnia (149 B.C.E.), **2**:270
Lex Citandi, **1**:327; **5**:149, 151
Lex Cornelia (81 B.C.E.)
   on delict, **2**:322
   on fraud, **3**:102
Lex Dei, **5**:151
Lex Dei (Collatio Legum Mosaicarum et Romanorum), **2**:97–98
Lex de Imperio Vespasiani, **5**:12
Lex Domitia (104 B.C.E.), **5**:121
Lex Falcidia (40 B.C.E.), **5**:374
   on succession, **5**:391
Lex Flavia (municipalis), **5**:139
lex fori in ancient Greece, **2**:109
Lex Fufia Caninia, **5**:374
   on manumission, **4**:306
   on slavery, **5**:249
Lex Fufia Caninia (2 B.C.E.), **3**:210
Lex Hortensia (287 B.C.E.), **5**:10, 142
Lex Irnitana (91 C.E.), **4**:102–104, 497; **5**:139, 140

Lex Iulia (18 B.C.E.)
    on dowry, **4:**306
    Egyptian law and, **2:**420
    on paternal power, **4:**305, 306
Lex Iulia de Adulteriis (17 B.C.E.), **4:**306
Lex Iulia de Maritandis Ordinibus (18 B.C.E.), **3:**210
Lex Iulia iudiciorum publicorum (17 B.C.E.), **2:**238, 273–274
Lex Julia (49 B.C.E.), **2:**110
Lex Julia (Rome, 9 B.C.E.), **5:**209
Lex Junia Norbana, **5:**249
Lex Laetoria (200 B.C.E.), **4:**305
lex mercatoria, **2:**93; **4:**36–37
Lex Ogulnia (300 B.C.E.), **5:**121
Lex Ovinia (312 B.C.E.), **5:**11
    on the Senate, **5:**210
Lex Poetelia, **2:**269
    on slavery, **5:**247
Lex Porcia, **2:**237
Lex Quisquis, **4:**332
    on political crimes, **4:**333
Lex Regia (1665)
    on absolutism, **2:**328
    Bodin, Jean, on, **1:**7
Lex Remnia, **2:**238
Lex Rhodia de Iactu, **1:**35; **3:**257
Lex Ribuaria, **3:**117
    on political crimes, **4:**333
Lex Romana Burgundionum, **3:**116
    on Germanic provinicial administration, **3:**116
Lex Romana Visigothorum, **2:**33, 110
    on fraud, **3:**102
    Haenel's edition of, **5:**163
    influenced by Codex Theodosianus, **2:**33; **3:**116
    influence on Roman law, **5:**162
    Jewry law, **3:**397
    on law merchant, **4:**38
    on succession, **5:**388
Lex Roscia (49 B.C.E.), **2:**110
Lex Rupilia, **4:**496
Lex Sempronia (122 B.C.E.), **2:**238
Lex Servilia Caepionis (106), **2:**238
Lex Servilia Glauciae (104), **2:**238
Lex Visigothorum, **3:**116. *See also* Lex Romana Visigothorum
Ley de enjuiciamiento civil (Spain, 1881), **5:**326

Ley de enjuiciamiento criminal (Spain, 1882), **5:**326
Ley de las siete partidas (Spain, 1265), **5:**325
    in colonial law, **5:**290
    on slavery, **5:**253, 254
    South and Central America under, **5:**285
Leyes de Indias, **5:**299
Leyes de Toro (Spain, 1505), **5:**325
Leyes Fundamentales del Reino (Spain), **2:**122
Ley orgánica del poder judicial (Spain, 1870), **5:**326
Leyser, Augustin
    on fraud, **3:**103
    on succession, **5:**393
L'Hommeau, Pierre de, **3:**99
L'Hospital, Michel de, **2:**359
li
    in Ming dynasty, **1:**461
    under Song dynasty, **1:**457
liability. *See also* noxal liability
    agency and, **1:**109–110
    ancient Roman law
        of seller in contract of sale, **2:**184
        women and, **6:**117
    bailment and, **1:**249
    breach of contract and, **1:**306, 307
    of children in tort, **1:**395
    Chinese law (*See also* collective liability in Chinese law)
        accessorial, **1:**18
        for deceit, **2:**315
        for endangering the emperor, **4:**256
        for lack of filial piety, **3:**85
        for offenses against the state, **4:**257–258
        reciprocal, **2:**315
        in wrongful judgment, **6:**152, 153
    corporate, **1:**322
    in delay, **2:**319–320
    employment and labor law
        medieval and post-medieval Roman, **2:**429
    in error and mistake, **2:**474
    guarantee and, **3:**128–129
    guilt and, **3:**136
    of heirs in succession, **5:**393–395
    Islamic law
        banking and finance, **1:**264
        in deposit, **2:**332
        ownership *(milk)* and, **4:**272

joint and several, **1**:320
    Du Moulin, Charles, on, **2**:373
    Islamic law, **3**:39
  in libel and slander, **4**:105
  limited, bankruptcy and, **1**:267
  maritime law, **1**:35–36
  medieval and post-medieval Roman law
    agency in, **1**:110–111
  natural law and, **4**:215
  negligence and, **4**:220–222
  products evidence in, **3**:14
  on Roman business law, **1**:319–320
  United States law, **6**:56–57
  watered stock and, **1**:326
liability insurance, **3**:254
li'ān (sworn allegation of adultery)
  paternity disownment by, **3**:37–38
Liang code (China), **1**:420
  on beating and whipping, **1**:283
  on enticement (you), **3**:469
  on redemption, **5**:73–74
Liang Zhiping, **1**:463
Liao dynasty (China), **2**:481
Libel Act (Great Britain, 1792), **1**:380; **3**:441;
    4:106, 143
Libel Act (Japan, 1875), **3**:376
libel and slander, **4**:104–107
  Afghanistan, **1**:62
  England
    Star Chamber in, **5**:346
    free speech and, **5**:336
libel and treason, law of (England), **1**:380
libellus process, **2**:53
Liber albus (London, 1221), **4**:36
Liberal Revolution (1871, Guatemala), **3**:130
liberal theory on sexual and gender variation, **3**:110, 111–112
Liberation Tigers of Tamil Eelam (Sri Lanka), **5**:343
Liberator, The, **5**:*253*
Liber Augustalis, **4**:91, 333
Liber Constitutionum (Frederick II, 1231), **3**:355
Liber Constitutionum (Papirius Justus), **3**:213
Liber constitutionum Siciliae, **4**:91
Liber Extra (Gregory IX), **1**:356, 471; **4**:353
  Baldus de Ubaldis, Petrus, on, **1**:250
  on compurgation, **2**:104
  decretals in, **2**:319; **4**:433
  initiative behind, **2**:327
  in legal education, **2**:399
  overview, **2**:221–222, 224
Liber Extra (Innocent IV), **3**:9
Liber feudorum, **1**:19
liber horon (book of definitions), **4**:79
Liberia, **4**:107
  Glebo society, **1**:70
Liberian Code of Law (1956–1958), **4**:107
Liber iudiciorum (654), **2**:110
Liber Iudiciorum (Recceswinth), **3**:397
Liber judiciorum, **5**:324
Liber lexis Scaniae (Sunesen), **2**:327
Liber minoricarum decisionum (Bartolus of Saxoferrato), **1**:281
Liber pauperum (Vacarius), **2**:393
Liber Sextus, **1**:356, 471; **4**:353
  decretals in, **4**:433
  in legal education, **2**:399
  overview, **2**:222–223, 224
  use in law education, **4**:333
Liber Singularis Regularum, **5**:158
libertarians, **2**:15
  on gay, lesbian, bisexual, and transgender, **3**:110
liberty
  democracy and in ancient Greek law, **2**:125
  due process and, in United States, **2**:368–369
Liberty Fund, **4**:26
Liber XXIV (Cujas), **2**:303
Liber XXVIII (Cujas), **2**:303
Library of Congress, Copyright Office, **3**:*266, 267, 268*
Libre del Consolat de Mar (Spain, 1345), **4**:150; **5**:325
Libri feudorum, **3**:72, 78
  on evidence, **3**:8
  in legal education, **2**:399
  use in medieval teaching of law, **2**:6
  use in Scotland, **3**:76
Libro de las leyes, El (Spain), **5**:325
Libu Tiaoli (Regulations for the Ministry of Personnel) (China, 1498), **1**:454
Libya
  conflict of laws, **2**:114
  criminal law, **2**:279
  death penalty, **1**:368
  divorce law, **2**:351, 352
  personal status laws, **4**:297; **6**:129

U.S. executive military action in, **6**:89
zakat in, **5**:431
licenses
   guilds and, **3**:132
   mortmain and, **4**:191
   United States
      discrimination in, **3**:479–480
      National Industrial Recovery Act on, **3**:482
Licensing Act (England, 1662), **1**:380
Li Chunyou, **1**:44
Lidai xingfa kao (Shen), **5**:238
Lidai xingguan kao (Shen), **5**:238
Lieber, Francis, **2**:403; **3**:294
   on constitutional interpretation, **2**:161, 162
Lieber Code (U.S., 1863), **3**:294
liens
   in mortgage, **4**:190
   New Zealand, **4**:229
Li Fan Yuan (Bureau of Colonial Affairs, China), **2**:482
Lifanyuan zeli (Mongolia, 1815–1817), **4**:184
Life Assurance Companies Acts (U.K., 1970 and 1872), **3**:253
life insurance, **3**:253, 258
Life of Basil (Constantine VII), **1**:281
Life of Lycurgus (Plutarch), **5**:327
Life of Socrates, The (Cooper), **4**:*248*
Ligesse, **3**:78
Lignago, Johannes de, **3**:282
Liji
   on land, **4**:1
   on sale, **5**:183
   on succession, **5**:379
Lilburne, John, **1**:379
Lilly, John, **4**:61
Limerick, Treaty of (1691), **3**:311
Limitation Act (India, 1859, 1908, 1963), **3**:216
Limitation Act (India, 1908), **4**:273
Limitation Act (U.S., 1851), **1**:40
Limited Liability Act (U.K., 1855), **2**:90
limited liability partnership, **2**:87
Linant de Bellefonds, Y., **3**:327
Lincoln, Abraham
   assassination of, **4**:*178*, 178–179, 335
   bar exam conducted by, **4**:49
   the Civil War and, **6**:52
   Civil War war powers of, **3**:408; **4**:335; **6**:88–89
   on *Dred Scott*, **5**:264
   equal protection under, **2**:459
   executive power under, **3**:20
   on federalism, **3**:60
   on judicial power, **3**:412
   martial law under, **4**:180
   on religious discrimination, **6**:51
   state sovereignty under, **5**:353
   taxation under, **5**:441
Lincoln's Inn, **2**:*395;* **3**:241. *See also* Inns of Court
   barristers in, **1**:277
   Denning, Alfred Thompson, in, **2**:330
   Mansfield, Lord, at, **4**:141
Lindley, Nathaniel, **5**:223
   last appointed to the Common Pleas, **2**:86
   on mortgage, **4**:188
Linear B tablets, **5**:243
Line Item Veto Act (U.S., 1966), **3**:22
ling
   under Han, **1**:414, 454
   under Song dynasty, **1**:454, 457
   in Sui and Tang law, **1**:454
Lingiari, Vincent, **1**:3
Lipit-Ishtar, **5**:273
Lipsius, **4**:403
Lipsius, Justus Herman, **1**:162
Liquidity Management Centre (LMC), **1**:262
Lisan al-'Arab, **3**:328
Lisbon, Treaty of/Reform Treaty (2007), **2**:487, 488, 493–494
Li Si, **1**:407, 410
   impact on Qin law, **1**:409
Liszt, Franz von
   on criminal codes, **4**:92
   on evidence, **3**:10
   on guilt, **3**:135
   on punishment, **5**:34
Litchfield Law School, **1**:11–12; **2**:402
literal contract in Roman law, **2**:184, 186, 187
   under Justinian, **2**:189
literature and law in ancient Greece, **4**:108–113
Lithuania. *See also* Baltic nations; Poland
   accession into European Union, **2**:492
   influence on Russian law, **5**:166, 170
   in Russian empire, **1**:255
litigation
   Africa
      addiction to, **1**:72
      precolonial, **1**:66

alternative dispute resolution and, **1:**128–129
ancient Greek law, **1:**151
    anthropological perspective on, **1:**186
    oaths in, **4:**241–242
ancient Near Eastern, **1:**169–170
ancient Rome, **2:**234–237
    formulae in, **3:**94–95
    legis actiones, **4:**81–84
    lex Irnitana on, **4:**104
Athens, **1:**235; **4:**113–116, 409–410
    magistrates in, **1:**232
    rise in, **1:**232
India, **5:**6–8
Japan, **3:**383–384
Litigious Athenian, The (Christ), **4:**113
litis denuntiatio process (Roman Empire), **2:**53
Litovskii Statut (Lithuanian Code, 1588), **5:**170
Littera Florentina
    Cujas, Jacques use of, **2:**303
    Noodt, Gerard, on, **4:**235–236
Littleton, Thomas, **2:**440; **4:**324
    on easements, **2:**380, 381
    on land leases, **4:**11
    as source of law, **5:**278
    on substantive law, **4:**60–61
Lituanian Statutes (1529, 1566, 1588), **4:**330
Liu Bang, **1:**412, 413
Liu Song dynasty, **5:**458
Liu Wenqing, **1:**456
Livermore, Samuel, **1:**108, 109
Livermore, Saul, **2:**117
living law. *See* folk law
Livingston, Edward, **2:**50, 291
living trusts, **3:**239
Livonian Confederation, **1:**254
Livro de Ordens, **5:**300
Livy, **6:**19, 20
    on the cult of Bacchus, **2:**269
    on the death penalty, **2:**270
    historical information provided by, **5:**158
    on history of Rome, **4:**130
    on homicide, **2:**269
    on *legis actiones*, **4:**82
    on magistrates, **4:**131
    on Roman citizenship, **5:**138
    on treason, **2:**269

Llerena, Baldomero, **1:**216
Llewellyn, Karl
    influence on U.S. private law, **2:**78
    legal process on, **4:**67
    in legal realism, **4:**74, 75
    on Native American law, **4:**207
    on pre-UCC commercial law, **2:**76
    and Uniform Commercial Code, **2:**51
Lloyds Bank, **1:**272, 276
Llyfr Blegywryd (Wales), **6:**98
Llyfr Colan (Wales), **6:**98
Llyfr Cyfnerth (Wales), **6:**98
Llyfr Iorwerth (Wales), **6:**98
Llywelyn ap Gruffydd, **6:**2, 99
loans, **4:**116–119
    ancient Greek law, **2:**180
        Hellenistic, **1:**160
        maritime, **4:**148–149
        Solon on, **5:**274–275
    ancient Near Eastern law, **1:**173–174
    in ancient Roman law, **2:**183
    Chinese law, **4:**116–118
        deposit in, **2:**331
    as insurance for transportation, **3:**257–258
    Islamic law, **4:**118–119
    mortgage, **4:**187–191
    Roman business law on, **1:**320
Local Government Act (U.K., 1929), **4:**350
Local Government Board (U.K.). *See also* General Board of Health (U.K.)
    in environmental law, **2:**451
local government law, **4:**119–123
Local Law Theory, **2:**117
locatio conductio contracts, **1:**319
    employment and labor law on, **2:**430
    estates doctrine and, **2:**478
    lease and tenancy as, **4:**55, 56–57
Loccenius, Johannes, **4:**151
Lochnerism, **5:**79
Locke, John
    on definition of law, **4:**18
    on due process, **2:**368
    on justice, **3:**447
    on land rights, **1:**312; **4:**480
    law of reason and, **2:**8
    on legislation, **4:**92
    on natural rights, **3:**448
    on prejudices, **4:**439
    social compact, **4:**487
Lockwood, Belva, **6:**143

Locri Epizephirii, **1:**52
locus standi in Indian law
    consumer protection and, **2:**174
    environmental law, **2:**452, 453
Loeb, Richard A., **3:**428
logography, **1:**151; **4:**112, **123–126,** *125*
    in Athens, **4:**115
    duration of, **1:**232
Loh, Wallace, **5:**268
Loi-Cadre (France, 1956), **1:**92
Loi Fondamentale (Belgium), **1:**93, 98
Loi Lamine Gueye (Senegal, 1946), **1:**90
Lois civiles dans leur ordre natural, Les (Domat), **2:**356
    on Roman law, **3:**99
Loisel, Antoine, **2:**357; **3:**98
lois fondamentales, **2:**120
Lokman, **1:***252*
Lombard law, **3:**117
    on attempt, **1:**237
Lombroso, Cesare
    on guilt, **3:**135
    on punishment, **5:**34
London
    banking in, **1:**275
    Great Smog of 1952, **2:***451*
    guilds in, **3:**131, 132
    Killer Fog, **2:**454
    public nuisances in, **4:**240
London and Westminster Bank, **1:**276
London Court of Arbitration, **1:**129–130
Long, Huey, **5:**445
Longinus, Cassius, **5:**179
Long Parliament (England, 1640–1653), **1:**379
Longshore and Harbor Workers' Compensation Act (1927), **1:**40
Lon Nol, **1:**335
Loomis, W. T., **2:**180
López de Gómara, Francisco, **4:**16
Lord Brougham's Act (U.K., 1856), **4:**163
Lord Cairns' Act (U.K., 1858), **2:**471
Lord Chancellor's Office (U.K.), **4:**42
Lord Hardwicke's Act. *See* Clandestine Marriages Act (1753)
Lord High Admiral (England), **2:**354
Lords Auditors of Causes and Complaints (Scotland), **5:**198–199
Lords of Council (Scotland), **5:***199*

Loss, Louis, **5:**93
    on securities law, **1:**16
Lothmar, P., **4:**277
Louima, Abner, **2:**302
Louis, Saint. *See* Louis IX (France)
Louis VI (France), **2:**359
Louis IX (France), **3:**98; **5:**32
    courts under, **2:**251
Louis XII (France), **1:**316
Louis XIV (France), **1:**7
    civil procedure under, **4:**92
    codification, **2:**47
    ordinances ob, **3:**99
    papal power under, **4:**353–354
Louis the Pious (Holy Roman emperor), **1:**295; **3:**395
Louis Eugene of Württemberg, **1:**285
Louis of Hungary, **4:**330
Louisiana
    codification of international private law in, **2:**113
    Louisiana Civil Code (1825), **2:**50
Lovat, Lord. *See* Fraser, Simon (Lord Lovat the 11th)
Lowe, Robert, **2:**90
Lowewnfeld, Samuel, **2:**316
Lowi, Theodore, **3:**22
Lozi empire, **1:**69, 70
    judges in, **1:**91
lü
    definition under Qing dynasty, **1:**433
    on doing what ought not to be done, **2:**355, 356
    under Han, **1:**414, 454
    under Song dynasty, **1:**454
    in Sui and Tang law, **1:**454
Luba empire, **1:**69
Lübisches Recht, **1:**37
Lublin Union (1569), **1:**254
Lucius Crassus, **1:**473
Luckhoo, Joseph Alexander, **3:**138
Lucretia, **5:**141
Lucubrationes (Zasius), **3:**191; **6:**161
Ludovisi, Niccolò, **2:**326
Ludwig, Karl, **4:**277
Lugano Convention with regard to Switzerland and Members of the European Free Trade Association (1988), **2:**114
Luhmann, Niklas
    on definition of law, **4:**18
    on guilt, **3:**136
Luig, Klaus, **2:**8

Lui Zhi, **1:**400
Lüjie bianyi (Code with commentariews and explication of questions), **1:**432
Lukács, György, **2:**297
Lüli jianshi (Wang Kentang), **2:**331
Lüling zhijie (The code and commandment directly explained), **1:**432
Lüli tongkao (General Collation of the Statutes and Substatutes) (Wu Tan), **1:**436
Lum'a al-Dimashqiyya, al (al-'Amili), **1:**132
  al-'Amili on, **1:**132–133
Lunacy Act (U.K., 1890), **3:**246
Lunda empire, **1:**69
Lundström, Vilhelm, **5:**417
Luns, Joseph, **2:***490*
Luther, Martin
  burning of the Corpus Iuris anonici, **1:**348
  on divorce, **3:**43
  on marriage, **3:**41
Lutz, Donald, **2:**159–160
Luwaran, **5:**323
Lycinus, **3:**124–125
Lycurgus
  code of, **3:**28
  on *eisangelia*, **4:**246
  forensic speeches by, **1:**149
  Gortyn's influence on, **3:**30
  on *graphē paranomōn*, **3:**124, 125
  laws in Sparta, **2:**30
  pronouncements by, **1:**156
  on Spartan children, **3:**29
  in Spartan law, **5:**328–329
  Spartan law and, **5:**327
  on witnesses, **6:**110
  on women, **6:**115
  written law by, **1:**154
Lykourgos, **1:**54
Lysias, **2:**30
  on adultery, **1:**51, 52
  on advocates, **1:**55
  on enforcement of religious piety, **5:**113
  forensic oratory, **1:**149; **4:**112
  on freedom of speech, **5:**330
  as logographer, **4:**123, 124
  on Pericles, **5:**112
  on priesthood, **5:**112
  on rape, **5:**65
  on slavery, **5:**244
  on torture, **5:**479
  on witnesses, **6:**110

M

Maarif, Ahmad Syafi'i, **3:**336
Maasai, **1:**71, 73, 78
Maastricht, Treaty of. *See* Treaty Establishing the European Union (1992)
Mabadi' al-usul (Ibn al-Mutahhar), **3:**195
Mabāsammata, **4:**145
Mabsut, al- (al-Tusi), **6:**18
Macao, foreigners in, **3:**92
Macarel, Louis, **1:**22
MacArthur, Douglas, **3:**378
Macartney, George, **5:**173
Macau, **1:**447–448
Macaulay, Stewart
  on contracts, **2:**209
  on law and society, **4:**33, 34
  on legal realism, **4:**78
Macaulay, Thomas Babington, **2:**218
  penal code for India, **2:**283
Macclesfield, Lord (Thomas Parker), **4:**41
McCormack, Ellen, **5:***332*
McCormick, Charles Tilford, **3:**11
Macdonald, Alexander, **3:**76
MacDonald, John, **1:**341
MacDowell, Douglas M., **1:**164, 165; **4:**403; **5:**65
  on marriage, **4:**155
Macedonia
  in European Union, **2:**493
  Macedonian Renaissance, **1:281–283**
Machado, José Olegario, **1:**216
Machiavelli, Niccolò, **3:**282, 357
Mack, Julian, **3:**460
Mackenzie, George, **5:**200
McKinley, William
  on bankruptcy, **1:**268
  executive power under, **3:**20
MacKinnon, Catharine
  on dominance feminism, **3:**67–68
  on sexual harassment, **6:**138
Mackintosh, James, **4:**41
MacLean, Arthur, **2:**404
MacMichael, Harold, **4:**138
McReynolds, James, **1:**220
Madagascar, **1:**63–64
  codification, **1:**71–72
  Indonesian immigration to, **1:**70
  law reform, **1:**100
Madelung, Wilferd, **3:**341
  on Zaydi juridical literature, **6:**162

Madison, James. *See also Federalist Papers*
   Annapolis Convention and, **2:**149
   Bill of Rights and, **5:**114
   on civic virtue, **5:**440
   on commerce clause, **2:**64
   on copyright law, **3:**266
   on due process, **2:**368
   on education, **2:**408
   on freedom of speech, **5:**333
   on general welfare clause, **3:**113, 114
   on Native Americans, **4:**208
   official conduct under, **2:**259
   on patents, **3:**269
   on property, **4:**488
   on right to bear arms, **1:**217–218
   on separation of powers, **5:**215, 217, 350
   on state law, **5:**349
   on state sovereignty, **5:**353
   on supremacy clause, **5:**411
   on takings clause, **5:**423
   "Vices of the Political Systems of the United States," **3:**291–292
madrasas
   development of legal, **4:**71–72
   in legal education, **2:**396–397
   Philippines, **3:**338
Madrid Agreement (Concerning the International Registration of Marks, 1891), **3:**272
Madrid Agreement on Origins and Trademarks (1891), **2:**103
Madrid Protocol, **3:**272
Magdeburg Law, **1:**254
Magellan, Ferdinand, **5:**313
Maghili, Muhammad ibn 'Abd al-Karim al-, **1:**74; **2:**41
Maghrib. *See also* Morocco; Tunisia
   Awza'i school of Islamic law, **4:**127
   as part of Muslim Spain, **4:**127–130
magistrates
   Athens, **1:**233
      scrutiny of, **1:**234
      Solon on, **5:**275
   Rome (*praetor, aedile*), **4:**101, 102, 130–133
      formula use by, **3:**93–94, 95
      in legislative assemblies, **4:**93
      lex Irnitana on, **4:**103, 104
      offenses against the state by, **4:**246–247
   in the Senate, **5:**210–211
   succession, **5:**371–372
   Sparta, **5:**328
Magistrates Courts (New Zealand), **4:**230
Magna Carta (1215), **1:**385; **2:**80, 128–129; **4:***133*, 133–136
   on alienation of land, **5:**369
   on assizes, **1:**231
   on citizen rights, **3:**447
   on common pleas, **2:**249, 435
   Court of Common Pleas and, **2:**85
   on dower, **2:**362
   due process in, **2:**367
   on giving of aids, **5:**450
   impact of, **2:**436, 438
   on juries, **3:**442
   on justice, **3:**447
   legislation and, **4:**87, 91
   liberty of the English Church and, **1:**467
   limits on royal power, **2:**128
   on praecipe writs, **5:**69–70
   on restriction of royal lordship, **3:**75
   on taxation, **4:**487; **5:**436
   on torture, **5:**484
Magna glossa (Accursius). *See Glossa ordinaria* (Accursius)
Magnum Bullarium, **2:**319
Magnus Eriksson (Sweden), **4:**91; **5:***415*
Magnus Erlingsson (Norway), **5:**32
Magnus Hakonarson (Norway), **4:**91
Magnus II Eriksson (Sweden), **5:***192*
Magnuson-Moss Warranty Act (U.S., 1975), **2:**178
Magnus VII Eriksson (Sweden), **5:**230
Maguires, Molly, **4:**336
Mahābhārata, **3:**364; **5:**35
   on kingship, **4:**232
   on *smriti*, **5:**265
Mahanama, **5:**303
Mahasin al-shari'a (al-Qaffal), **5:**60
Mahavamsa (Mahanama), **5:**303, 339
Mahāvīra, **3:**363
Mahdi, li-Din Allah Ahmad ibn Yahya al-Murtada al-, **3:**420; **4:**136; **6:**156, 162
   in Abbasid dynasty, **1:**2
Mahmud II (Ottoman Empire)
   court reform by, **4:**268
   martial law under, **4:**267
Mahomed, Ismail, **5:**280

Mahomedan Marriage Ordinance (Malaysia, 1880), **3:**334–335
mahr (nuptial gift), **4:**165, 166–167
Mail Fraud Act (U.S., 1872), **2:**176
Maine, Henry (James Sumner), **2:**10, 23; **4:137;** **5:**108, 156, 160
   on ancient Roman law, **2:**31
   anthropological perspective of, **1:**185
   on Austin, John, **1:**238
   comparative law, **2:**99
   on contracts, **2:**208
   on Greek law, **1:**162
   influenced by Montesquieu, **2:**98
   legal treatises by, **2:**443
   at Oxford, **2:**395
   on statute law, **4:**87
   on succession, **5:**371
Maine Laws, **1:**124–125. *See also* Prohibition amendment
Maino, Giason del, **3:**190
maintenance
   England, **3:**33–34, 35
     adultery and, **2:**349
   India, **2:**353; **3:**50–51; **4:**170
     Islamic law on, **5:**308
   Islamic law
     consensual divorce and, **2:**350
     divorce and, **3:**37
     in marriage contracts, **4:**167
     proximity and, **3:**38
   medieval and post-medieval Roman law, **3:**43, 46
Maintenance of Internal Security Act (India, 1971), **2:**174
Mainz, Peace of (1235), **4:**333; **5:**32
Maitland, Frederic William, **1:**386
   on assault, **1:**227
   on *Bracton*, **1:**301
   on criminal procedure, **4:**423
   English common law historiography by, **2:**434
   on English company law, **2:**90
   on equity, **2:**471
   on Exchequer, **3:**17
   on feudal law, **2:**128; **3:**72
   on Henry VIII, **4:**284
   on law merchant, **4:**37
   on law of incorporeal things, **2:**379–382
   on mortgage, **4:**188
   on possession, **4:**358
   on royal authority, **2:**130
   on unincorporated associations, **2:**89

Majalla (Mecelle). *See also* Ottoman Civil Code (Majalla or Mecelle) (1877)
   Afghanistan influenced by, **1:**59
   in Iraq, **1:**205
   reforms in, **4:**269
   in Yemen, **6:**156
Majishun, al-, **3:**350
Majithia, Dyal Singh, **5:**241
Majmu' (Zayd ibn 'Ali), **3:**341
Majmu' al-fiqh, **6:**161–162
Major Crimes Act (U.S.), **4:**209–210
Majorian (Roman emperor), **5:**124
majority
   in England, **1:**393
   Golden Bull on, **3:**45
   Islamic law on, **1:**300
Majul, Cesar Adib, **5:**323
Makdisi, George, **3:**345
Malacca Sultanate, **4:**137; **5:**322
Malawi
   constitution, **1:**105
   independence, **1:**93
Malaya, **4:**9
Malayan Union, **5:**242
Malaysia, **4:137–139**
  adat, **1:**20–21
  adoption, **1:**48
  banking and finance, **1:**261, 262, 263
  in British Commonwealth, **1:**315
  constitution, **2:140–141**
  courts, **2:**140; **4:**139
  Hindu law, **5:**321–322
  intellectual property, **3:**263
  Islamic insurance companies, **3:**256
  Islamic law, **3:**334–335, 337–338; **5:**322, 323, 324
    Shafi'i school of law, **3:**353
  legal education, **2:**398
  personal status laws, **4:**300–301; **6:**129
  post-colonial, **5:**314
  zakat in, **5:**431
Malaysian Government Investment Certificates (MGICs), **1:**263
Malcolm III (Scotland), **5:**196
Malcolm IV (Scotland), **5:**197
Maldives, **4:139–140**
  Islamic laws in, **2:**40; **5:**306, 309–310
Mali, **1:**67, 74
  age for marriage, **2:**44

constitution, **2**:137
inheritance, **2**:44–45
law reform in, **1**:100
Malik ibn Anas ibn ibn al-Harith al-Asbahi, **3**:350,
     351; **4**:140–141; **5**:3, 59, 487
  Egyptian students of, **4**:127–128
  influence on
     Sahnun, ʿAbd al-Salam ibn Saʿid al-Tanukhi,
        5:182
     Shafiʿi, Muhammad ibn Idris al-, **5**:235
  on judicial review, **3**:413
  on lease and tenancy, **4**:56
  in Medinese tradition, **1**:210–211
  on possession, **4**:360
  and scholarly codifications, **2**:45
Maliki school of Islamic law, **3**:350–352. *See also* Ibn
     Rushd, Abu al-Walid Muhammad ibn Ahmad;
     Khalil ibn Ishaq (ibn Musa) al-Jundi; Malik ibn
     Anas ibn al-Harith al-Asbahi; Qayrawani, Ibn
     Abi Zayd, al-; Sahnun; Sahnun, ʿAbd al-Salam
     ibn Saʿid al-Tanukhi; Wansharisi, Ahmad ibn
     Yahya al-Tilimsani
  in Abbasid dynasty, **1**:2
  alcohol and drug use, **1**:121
  arbitration, **4**:429
  the body, **1**:299
  children
     child support, **1**:397
     father-child relations, **3**:37
  concept of law, **5**:451
  consensual divorce, **2**:350
  contracts
     agricultural, **1**:116, 117
     object of commercial, **2**:79
  custody rights, **1**:397
  damage, **2**:311
  deposit, **2**:332
  donation, **2**:359
  duress, **2**:375
  duty, **2**:376
  education in, **4**:71
  family, **3**:38–39
  geographical presence
     Africa, **1**:73–74, 90, 102; **2**:41
     in Arab countries, **1**:205
     Arabian peninsula, **1**:211
     in Maghrib and al-Andalus, **4**:127–128,
        128–129
     Sicily, **5**:239–240
     Yemen, **6**:155

  guardianship, **4**:166
  lease and tenancy, **4**:55
  legal norms, **4**:62
  legal reasoning, **4**:62
  maintenance, **3**:38–39
  marriage, **4**:165, 166
     dissolution of, **5**:128
  non-Muslims, **3**:316
  option, **4**:261
  partnership, **4**:289
  persons, **4**:311, 312
  pledge, **4**:327
  possession, **4**:360
  rights, **5**:137
  rules of evidence, **4**:428, 429
  taxation, **5**:433, 434
  torture, **5**:487
  wills, **6**:106
  women, **6**:127
  worship, **6**:150
Malinowski, Bronisław Kasper
  anthropological studies of, **1**:185
  on definition of law, **4**:18, 19
  in legal anthropology, **4**:59
Malleus maleficarum (Kramer and Sprenger),
     4:438; **6**:108
Malta, **2**:492
Malveisin, William, **5**:197
Mamluks
  courts under, **4**:338
  formal equality of the Sunni schools
     under, **3**:352
  Hanafi school under, **3**:344
  judiciary under, **3**:419
Maʾmun, al-, **3**:420
  Ibn Hanbal and, **2**:135
Mahamzamun, al-, **1**:1
Manasik al-hajj wa-ahkamuha (attr. Zayd ibn ʿAli),
     6:161
Mānava-Dharmaśāstra. *See* Laws of Manu
Mancham, James, **5**:235
Manchester & Liverpool District Banking Co.,
     1:272
Manchester & Salford Bank, **1**:272
Mancini, Pasquale, **1**:372
Mancini, Pasquale Stanislao, **2**:112
mancipatio, **2**:182, 184
  for women, **6**:118–119
mandates
  agency in, **1**:110

Roman law
    contract, **2:**184, 185, 186
    Sabinus, Masurius, on, **5:**180
Mande culture, **1:**67
Mandela, Nelson, **1:**104
Manhaj (al-ʿUlaymi), **3:**347
Manilius, **3:**435
Manilius, Manius, **4:**79
Mann, Bruce, **2:**206
Mann, Bruce H., **2:**14
Mann Act (U.S., 1910), **2:**292
Manne, Henry
    on corporations, **4:**26
    judiciary training by, **4:**27
Mann-Elkins Act (U.S., 1910), **5:**96, 102
Manning, William, **5:**342
Mansa Musa, **1:**74
Mansfield, Lord (William Murray), **4:***141,*
        141–144
    on commercial law, **2:**437
    on conflict of laws, **2:**117
    on custom and trade, **2:**306
    Dennins, Alfred Thompson, compared with,
        2:330
    on equity, **2:**470
    on error and mistake, **2:**474
    on indigenous people, **1:**312
    influence on contract and commercial law,
        4:421
    insurance law, **3:**252, 253
    on judicial law making, **5:**277
    law reporting by, **4:**45, 60
    maritime law by, **1:**36
    on precedent, **4:**378, 380
    on slavery, **5:**250, 252
    on social science, **5:**266
    use of juries, **3:**440
manslaughter. *See also* homicide
    English common law, **3:**177–178, 179
    punishment for, **2:**265
Mansur, Ismaʿil al-
    al-Qadi al-Nuʿman and, **5:**59
    Baghdad as new capital under, **1:**1
Mansur bi-llah ʿAbd Allah ibn Hamza, al-,
        4:144
Manu, **3:**153, 155; **5:**265. *See also* Laws of Manu
    on dowry, **2:**363
    on *smriti*, **5:**264
Manual for Courts-Martial, **4:**177
Manu Bhāshya (Medhātithi), **3:**146

Manuel I (Portugal)
    African assimilation under, **1:**69
Manuel I Comnenus (emperor), **1:**348
Manusmriti (Code of Hindu law), **3:**156, 364, 400;
        4:144–145; 6:83
    ātmanustuṣhṭi in, **1:**236
    consumer protection, **2:**173
    on procreation, **1:**4
    on *sadācāra*, **5:**181
    on *smriti*, **5:**265
    on women, **6:**131
Māori Land Court, **4:**145, *146,* 147
Maori law, **4:145–147**
    appeal in, **4:**231
    courts in, **4:**230
    Treaty of Waitangi on, **4:**227,
        227, 231
Mao Zedong, **1:**441, *441,* 444
    mass line party leadership, **1:**441–442
    Pro-Mao rally, **1:***444*
    theory of contradictions, **1:**442
Maqrizi, al-, **4:**384
Marcellinus, Ammianus, **5:**212
Marcellus, Marcus Claudius, **5:**225
March on Washington for Jobs and Freedom (1963),
        2:341
Marcian (emperor), **3:**251
Marcianus, Aelius, **3:**436
Marcos, Ferdinand, **4:**319
Marcus Antistius Labeo. *See* Labeo,
        Marcus Antistius
Marcus Antonius, **1:**473
Marcus Aurelius (Roman emperor), **3:**435
    guardianship of minors under, **4:**306
    Paul and, **4:**290
Marcus Aurelius Antoninus. *See* Caracalla
        (Roman emperor)
Marcuse, Herbert, **2:**297
Marcus Flavius, **2:**269
Marcus Manlius, **2:**269
Mardawi, al-, **1:**10
Mare Liberum (Grotius), **3:**127
Margarine Act (New Zealand, 1895), **4:**228
marginalist value conceptions, **1:**326
Maria Theresa (Archduchess of Austria), **2:**9
Marihuana Tax Act (U.S., 1937), **1:**123, 127
Marine Insurance Act (U.K., 1906), **3:**253
marine insurance in English common law,
        3:252–253
maritagium (dower), **2:**361–362

Maritime Commercial Code (Colombia, 1870), **2**:63
maritime law, **4**:147–152. *See also* admiralty
   ancient Greek law, **1**:35; **4**:147–150, 382
      Athens, **1**:234
         contracts in Athens, **2**:179
      definition of, **1**:37
   Denmark, **2**:328
   England, **4**:142
   Ethiopia, **2**:480
   medieval and post-medieval Roman law, **4**:150–152
   pseudo-Rhodian collection of laws, **3**:257
   Spain, **5**:325
Maritime Law (China, 1929), **1**:440
market
   and enforcement of emerging rights in the United States, **2**:21
   regulation of commodities prices in English common law, **2**:101
   Rome, **2**:*185*
   rules in ancient Greek law, **2**:69
   supervision in Islamic law, **1**:382–383
market overt rule, **5**:189
marketplace of ideas, **5**:335
marketplace test, **4**:29
Marnius, Claudius, **2**:303
Marquard, Johannes, **2**:95
   on law merchant, **4**:39
   on maritime law, **4**:151
Marquess of Reading, **6**:3
marriage, **4**:152–170. *See also* child marriage; divorce; family; personal status law; persons
   Afghanistan, **1**:59, 61–62
   Africa
      after independence, **1**:102–103
      indigenous law on, **1**:91–92
      Islamic law, **1**:102
      precolonial, **1**:66, 72–73
   age for
      in Africa, **2**:44
      medieval and post-medieval Roman law, **3**:41
   ancient Greek law, **4**:152–155; **6**:115–116, 116
      of adoptees, **1**:42
      adultery, **1**:50–53
      Athens, **1**:140
      Code of Gortyn, **3**:120–121, 122, 123
      divorce, **2**:346–347
      family and, **3**:27–32, 31
      foreigners in, **3**:31
      Gortyn, **1**:142
      Hellenistic, **1**:158–160
      offenses against the state and, **4**:247
      papyri on, **1**:147
      sexual and moral regulation of, **5**:226–227
      between siblings, **1**:159
      Sparta, **3**:29; **5**:328–329
      unity of Greek law and, **1**:136
   ancient Near Eastern law, **1**:171–173
   annulments
      ecclesiastical courts in, **2**:386
      England, **3**:32
      Islamic law on, **1**:300; **6**:125
      United States, **3**:53
   Australian Aboriginal law, **1**:2
   Austria, **1**:247
   Aztec law, **5**:288
   Baltic nations, **1**:255
   Bangladesh, **1**:259
   Byzantine law, **4**:309–310
   Chinese law, **4**:155–160; **5**:54
      status and, **5**:358
      succession and, **5**:378–380
   civil, **3**:41
      in Venezuela, **6**:74
   clandestine, **3**:41
   covenant, **3**:54
   Denmark, **2**:328
   duress in, **2**:374
   East Africa, **2**:383
   East Timor, **2**:384
   ecclesiastical courts on, **2**:386
   Egypt
      Greek law on, **1**:144
      Islamic law and, **2**:421–422
      juristic papyrology on, **2**:417–418, 420
   engagement and, **3**:41
   English common law, **3**:35; **4**:160–163
      divorce and, **2**:347–348
      dower, **2**:361–363
      ecclesiastical courts in, **2**:81, 355, 436
      ecclesiastical law on, **2**:388–389, 390–391
      entails and, **2**:446–447
      family based on, **3**:32–33
      jurisdiction of church courts, **1**:467
      women in, **6**:120–121, 122
   Ethiopia, **2**:480

feminist legal theory on, **3**:66
France, **3**:98
Gaius on, **3**:251
Germany under National Socialism, **4**:204
Hindu law, **3**:48–50; **4:169–170**
    dowry, **2**:363–366
    sadācāra in, **5**:181
    women in, **6**:131
Hong Kong, **1**:449, 450
inchoate, **1**:172
India, **3**:398
    child, **2**:353; **3**:49
    of Christians, **3**:222–223
    Christians in British India, **3**:222
    custom, **2**:307, 308
    sadācāra in, **5**:182
    secularism in, **5**:208–209
    Sikh law, **5**:241
    sources of law, **3**:148, 150
    in succession, **5**:400
Islamic law, **2**:201; **3**:324–325, 329–330, 466; **4:163–169**; **5**:127–129
    on the body, **1**:299
    children in, annulment and, **1**:300
    colonialism and, **2**:43
    consensual divorce, **2**:350–352
    duress in, **2**:375
    in Europe, **2**:484
    option in, **4**:261
    public law regarding, **5**:20
    women in, **6**:125–127, 129
Jewish law, **3**:382, 389, 392, 393, 398
legitimation of children in, **3**:47
Madagascar, **1**:71–72, 72
medieval and post-medieval Roman law, **3**:40–48
Mongolia, **4**:185
Pakistan, **4**:275
Parsi law, **4**:286, 287
Peru law, **4**:314
registration in Islamic countries, **2**:37
rites of Chinese-speaking Muslims, **1**:400
Roman law, **3**:40–44; **5**:143
    among slaves, **5**:253
same sex, **3**:*111*, 112; **6**:143
    due process and, **2**:371
    England, **3**:33, 35
    United States, **3**:55–56
between siblings
    ancient Greece, **1**:161

South Africa, **5**:280, 284
South Asian law in United Kingdom, **5**:311
Southeast Asia, **5**:318, 319
    Hindu law, **5**:321, 322
Sri Lanka, **5**:339, 341
surviving spouses and estate plans, **3**:240
United Kingdom
    South Asian law and, **5**:312
United States, **3**:51–52
    common-law, **3**:52
    equal protection, **2**:465
    polygamy, **5**:117
    rights of surviving spouse, **3**:236–237
    slaves, **5**:262
    succession, **5**:404–405
    women's rights, **6**:134, 136, 145
Visigothic era, **3**:397
Welsh law, **6**:99
women
    ancient Greece, **6**:113–114
    ancient Roman law, **6**:117–118
    Ottoman Empire, **6**:128
    United States, **6**:134, 136, 145
Marriage Act (Austria, 1938), **1**:247
Marriage Act (Great Britain, 1753, 1823), **1**:468
    on clandestine marriage, **2**:389
    on Fleet marriages, **4**:162
    procedures approved in, **3**:33
Marriage and Divorce (Muslim) Act (Sri Lanka, 1951), **5**:309
marriage-gift, **3**:42, 43
Marriage Law (Indonesia, 1974), **3**:227; **4**:301
Marriage Law (People's Republic of China, 1950), **1**:442
Marriage Law of the People's Republic of China, The (China, 1950), **5**:54
Marriage Laws (Amendment) Bill (India, 1981), **2**:353
Marriage Ordinance (Hong Kong, 1875), **1**:449
Marriage Ordinance for Asiatics (Suriname, 1907), **5**:414
Married Woman Statute (Brazil, 1962), **1**:304
Married Women (Restraint upon Anticipation) Act (U.K., 1949), **6**:124
Married Women and Tortfeasors Act (U.K., 1935), **6**:124
Married Women's Property Act (U.K., 1870), **4**:42

Married Women's Property Act (U.K., 1882), **3:**33; **6:**120, 123
    on contracts, **6:**124
    on legal personality, **3:**34
Married Women's Property Act (U.S.), **2:**338; **5:**403
Marshal, William, **4:**135
Marshall, Alfred, **4:**23
Marshall, David, **5:**242
Marshall, John
    on agency, **1:**113
    on commerce clause, **2:**64
    on constitutional interpretation, **2:**161, 162, 166
    on contracts, **2:**207
    on courts, **2:**256
    establishment of the opinion of the court, **4:**441
    on federal commerce power, **2:**154
    on federalism, **3:**59–60
    on Indian tribes, **6:**49
    on international law, **3:**293
    on the judicial branch, **2:**257
    on judicial power, **3:**407
    on judicial review, **2:**153
    on Native American land ownership, **4:**481
    on natural law, **4:**218
    petty assizes, **4:**316
    on political question doctrine, **2:**260
    on property, **4:**489
    on rights and liberties, **2:**155
    on slavery, **5:**262, 263
    on statutory interpretation, **5:**360
    on supremacy clause, **5:**411
    Supreme Court power and, **6:**40, 45–46
    on taxation, **6:**46
    on unconstitutional laws, **2:**259
Marshall, Leon Carroll, **1:**15; **4:**75
Marshall, Thurgood, **3:**165
    in NAACP-LEF, **2:**341
    on tiers of judicial scrutiny, **2:**463–464
Martens, Georg Friedrich von, **3:**283
martial law
    Indian fundamental rights on, **3:**106
    United States, **4:**180
Martin, David, **2:**1
Martini, Karl Anton von, **6:**162
    on succession, **5:**393
Martinique, **1:**369
Martino, Gaetano, **2:***490*
Martin of Littlebury, **2:**85
Martin of Pattishall, **1:**301

Martinus Gosia, **3:**297, 314; **6:**65
marumakkathayam, **4:170–171**
Marvin, Lee, **3:**55
Marvin, Michele Triola, **3:**55
Marwan II, **1:**1
Marwazi, Abu Ishaq al-, **3:**201
Marwood, William, **1:**366
Marx, Karl, **6:**71
    influence on private law, **4:**394
    on law and economics, **4:**23
    scientific socialism of, **4:**475
Mary, Queen of Scots. *See* Mary Stuart
Mary I (England), **2:**129; **6:**2
    charter of Stationers' Company, **1:**379
    control of printing under, **2:**216
Mary II (England)
    Parliament and, **4:**285
    women under, **6:**120
Mary Stuart
    execution, **2:**129
    religion under, **1:**468
    Ridolfi Plot and, **6:**5
Marzari, Francesco, **3:**80
Masa'il (Ibn Hanbal), **3:**345
Masalik al-Afham (al-'Amili), **1:**132
Masao, H. T., **5:**316
Maschi, C. A., **5:**158
maṣlaḥa, **3:**120
Massachusetts
    Constitution on separation of powers, **5:**216–217
    General Court, **2:**12
    rights of widows in, **2:**13
Massachusetts Railroad Commission, **5:**77
Massignon, Louis, **3:**354
Master and Servant Act (U.K., 1867), **2:**426
Masters, John, **4:**206
master-servant law
    agency in, **1:**115
    United States, **3:**478, 482–483
master's liability for servant's wrongs
    beginning of cases on, **6:**76
masturbation, medieval and post-medieval Roman law, **5:**230
Mashamzaudi, al, **1:**70
Masurius Sabinus. *See* Sabinus, Massurius
matchmakers in China, **4:**157
Materialien für Gesetzkunde und Rechtspflege in den österreichischen Erbsstaaten (Pratobevera, ed.), **6:**163

maternity pay, **2:**427
Mather, Increase, **1:**123
Matienzo, Juan de, **1:**215–216; **4:**314; **5:**291
Matiti, al-, **5:**487
Matrimonial Causes Act (U.K., 1857)
    on divorce, **2:**347–348; **4:**163
    ecclesiastical jurisdiction undermined by, **4:**161, 163
Matrimonial Causes Act (U.K., 1973), **3:**33
Matsuhito (Japanese emperor), **3:**366
Mattachine Society, **3:**111
Mattarellis, Nicolaus de, **3:**9
Matthews, Burnita Shelton, **6:**142
Matthias I Corvinus (Hungary), **3:**194
Maturidi, Abu Mansur al-, **3:**343
Mau Mau rebellion (Kenya), **1:**88, 93
Mauritania
    abolition of slavery, **1:**76
    constitution, **2:**137; **3:**317
    court system, **2:**44
    death penalty, **1:**368
    Maliki school of law, **3:**351
    penal code, **2:**45
    shariʿa as principal source of legislation, **3:**317
    waqf property, **2:**45
Mauritius, **4:**171–172
    constitution, **1:**98
    English law in, **1:**87
    French law in, **1:**63
    independence, **1:**93
    Seychelles as dependency of, **5:**234
Mauryan empire, **1:**225–226
Mauss, Marcel, **4:**152
Mawardi, Abu al-Hasan al-, **3:**352
    on enforcement, **2:**432–433
    manual of good governance by, **2:**36
    on political authority, **1:**33
Mawsili, al-, **3:**343
Maximes générales du droit François (L'Hommeau), **3:**99
Maximilian I (Holy Roman emperor)
    notaries under, **4:**237
    taxation under, **5:**436
Maximilian II Emanuel (Bavaria), **3:**473
Maximilian III Joseph (Bavaria), **2:**47; **3:**473
Maxims and Rules of Pleading (Heath), **4:**324
Maxims of Equity (Francis), **4:**61
Maximus the Greek, **5:**177
Ma Xiwu, **1:**442

Max Planck Institute for Foreign and International Private Law, **2:**99
Mayan law in Guatemala, **3:**130
Mayer, Otto, **1:**23
mayhem, **1:**226. *See also* assault
Maylis Ugama Islam Singapore (MUIS), **5:**323
Mayne, John D., **3:**146
Mayno, Jason de, **1:**118
Mazari, al-, **4:**128
Mazzini, Giuseppe, **1:**372
McAdoo, William G., **5:**443
MCI (Microphone Communications Inc.), **5:**97
McIntosh, Mary, **3:**112
McKinley, William
    assassination of, **4:**335
    Philippines and, **4:**318
McLachlin, Beverly, **1:**340
McNealy, Scott, **4:**391
McReynolds, James, **2:**27
Means, Gardiner, **1:**325–326
Meat Inspection Act (U.S., 1904), **2:**176–177
Meat Inspection Act (U.S., 1906), **5:**78
Meat Packers trust, **1:**324
Mecelle, the. *See* Majalla
Mecelle-i Ahkam-i Adliye (Compendium of Rules of Justice, Ottoman), **3:**421
Mecham, Floyd, **1:**113
med-arb, **1:**128
Medea (Euripedes), **2:**346
Medhāthiti, **3:**147
    on *ātmanustuṣhṭi*, **1:**236
    on *mīmāṃsā*, **4:**182
media
    executive power and, **3:**22
    freedom of speech and, **5:**335–336
    freedom of the press in the United States, **5:**332–338; **6:**51
    on miscarriage of justice in China, **1:**197
mediation, **1:**128
    grievance mediation, **3:**389–390
    in People's Republic of China, **1:**442, 443, 446
Medicaid, **6:**54, 97
    for abortions, **4:**389
    creation of, **3:**144
    elderlaw and, **2:**424
Medical Jurisprudence, as It Relates to Insanity, according to the Law of England (Haslam), **3:**247

Medical Termination of Pregnancy Act (India, 1971), **1**:4
Medicare, **6**:54, 91, 97. *See also* welfare
    American Medical Association opposition to, **4**:52
    creation of, **3**:144
    elderlaw and, **2**:424
    regulation of hospitals under, **5**:82
Medici Bank, **1**:273
medicine
    earliest manual on forensic, **1**:426
    on gay, lesbian, bisexual, and transgender, **3**:110–111
    tradition, **3**:264
Medicine Lodge Treaty (1867), **4**:210
medieval and post-medieval Roman law
    admiralty, **1**:35–37
    adoption, **3**:46
    adultery, **5**:229–230
    advocate, **1**:55–58
    agency, **1**:110–112
    agency and consignment, **1**:111
    alimony, **3**:43
    banks and banking, **1**:273–276
    breach of contract, **1**:306–310
    canon law
        on divorce, **3**:43
        on evidence, **3**:8
        on marital sex, **5**:230
    capital punishment
        for sexual crimes, **5**:230
    children, **3**:44–47
        accountability of, **3**:44–45
        emancipation of, **3**:45
        employment and, **2**:430
        legitimacy, **3**:46–47
    civil law, **2**:1–11
        on duress, **2**:376
        law merchant in, **4**:35–40
        on obligations, **4**:245
    codes and codification, **2**:46–50
        Icelandic law code, **2**:*46*
    codicils, **5**:389–390
    commercial law
        agency in, **1**:110–112
        law merchant, **4**:38–40
    company law, **2**:92–97
    competition, **2**:102–104
    conflict of laws, **2**:109–116

    consumer protection, **2**:169–173
        in sale of goods, **5**:192
    contracts
        agency in, **1**:110
        error and mistake in, **2**:475–476
        on fraud, **3**:104
        lease and tenancy, **4**:56–58
        on sale of goods, **5**:192
        of succession, **5**:393
        women, **3**:42
    courts, **2**:251–255
        manor courts and villeinage, **6**:81
    credit, **2**:262–264
        agency and, **1**:111
        negotiable instruments in, **4**:223
        pawnbrokers in, **1**:274
        in sale of goods, **5**:192
    criminal law, **3**:102–103
    debt on obligations, **4**:245
    divorce, **3**:42–43, 43–44
    dowry, **3**:42–43, 45–46
    duress, **2**:376
    endowment, **3**:45–46
    error and mistake, **2**:475–476
    evidence, **3**:7–10
        torture and, **3**:7, 8
    family, **3**:*40*, **40–48**
    feudal law, **3**:77–80
    forgery, **3**:102–103
    fraud, **3**:103–104, **103–104**
    guardianship, **3**:47–48
    homosexuality, **5**:230
    incest, **5**:230
    inheritance
        disinheritance, **5**:391–392
        marriage and, **3**:42
    insanity, **3**:47
    insurance, **3**:257–259
        maritime, **4**:147
    intellectual property, **3**:259–260
    judges, **3**:404–406
        evidence evaluation by, **3**:7, 9–10
    juries, **3**:404–406
    labor and employment law, **2**:428–431
    law merchant, **4**:38–40
    lease and tenancy contracts, **4**:56–58
    legislation, **4**:90–92
    liability
        agency in, **1**:110–111
    liability and employment and labor law, **2**:429

maintenance, **3:**43, 46
maritime law, **4:150–152**
marriage, **3:**40–48
　age for, **3:**41
　husband's right to punishment, **3:**41
masturbation, **5:**230
mortgage, **4:189–191**
natural law, **4:216–217**
notaries, **5:**193
obligations, **4:245**
paraphernalia, **3:**43
partnerships, **1:**111
patria potestas, **3:**45
pledge, **4:328–329**
　in mortgage, **4:**189–190
political crimes, **4:332–334**
possession, **4:360–362**
procedure
　civil procedure, **4:431–435**
　criminal procedure, **4:435–440**
property, **3:**42–43; **4:474–479**
　of children, **3:**45–46
　family and, **3:**40–41
　marriage and, **3:**41–42
　personal property of villeins, **6:**81
　sale of land, **5:**193–194
punishment, **5:31–35**
rape, **5:**229, 230
sale
　sale of goods, **5:191–193**
　sale of land, **5:193–194**
sale of land, **5:**193–194
sexual crimes, **5:229–231**
succession, **5:384–396**
taxation, **5:435–439**, 437
theft, **3:**7–8
trusts, **3:**48
undue influence, **6:**25
　duress and, **2:**373, 376
　women and guarantee in, **3:**129
unjust enrichment, **6:64–66**
usury, **6:70–72**
vicarious liability, **6:77–78**
witnesses, **3:**8
women
　employment, **2:**430
　sexual crimes, **5:**229–231
medieval law
　Hindu, **3:**156–157
　on sale of goods, **5:**191–193

　on sexual crimes, **5:**229–231
　Spain, **5:**324–325
　on succession, **5:**384–396
Mediterranean Society, A (Friedman), **3:**391
Meech Lake Accot (Canada, 1987), **1:**339
Meerman, Gerard, **5:**158
Meese, Edwin, **2:**164
Megenberg, Konrad von, **5:**229, 230
Mehmed Ali, **3:**344
Mehmed II
　administrative decrees by, **1:**34
　Balkan peninsula under, **1:**251
　legal education under, **4:**72
Meier, M. H. E., **1:**162
Meijers, Eduard Maurits, **4:**226
Meir of Rothenberg ("Maharam"),
　　Rabbi, **3:**392
Melamed, A. Douglas, **4:**25
Melanchthon, Philip
　influence on Danish education,
　　2:328
　on ius divinum, **1:**348–349
Melanesia, **4:172–174**
Melchert, Christopher, **3:**345
Meletus, **4:**415; **5:**23
　on impiety of Scorates, **5:**112
　on religious offenses, **4:**247
Mello, Sebastião José de Carvalho e,
　　5:294
Mello, Sergio de, **2:**384
Mellon, Andrew, **5:**444, 445
Melville, Herman, **4:**108
Menander
　on family, **3:**31
　on law, **1:**148; **4:**111
　on rape, **5:**65
Mencius
　on adoption, **1:**43
　on ideal of not punishing the guiltless,
　　1:460
Mendoza, Don Antonio de, **4:**176
Menelik II (Ethiopia), **2:**479
　Italian treaties with, **1:**81
Mengchang, **4:**116
Menger, Anton, **4:**394
Menggu lüli (Mongolia, 1789), **4:**184
Menippus of Caria, **4:**149
Menkel-Meadow, Carrie, **3:**68
Menocchio, Jacopo, **1:**371
Mental Capacity Act (U.K., 2005), **3:**245

Mental Deficiency Acts (U.K., 1913, 1927), **3:**246
mental health, welfare programs and, **6:**95
Mental Health Act (U.K., 1959), **3:**245, 246
mental illness. *See* insanity
Mentschikoff, Sonia, **4:**32
Menzies, William, **5:**279
Mercado, Thomás de, **4:**15
Mercantile Amendment Act (1856), **3:**89
Mercantile Court (Fiji), **3:**82
mercanzia (juridiction in company-law matters), **2:**96
Mercator, Isidorus, **2:**318
Merchant Assurances Act (England, 1601), **3:**252
merchant banks, medieval, **1:**273
Merchant Shipping Act (U.K.), **4:**7
Merchants statute (1285, England), **4:**35
merchnets, **6:**81
MERCOSUR, **2:**115
Meredith, James, **2:**341
"Mergers and the Market for Corporate Control" (Manne), **4:**26
Merger Treaty (EEC, 1965), **2:**489
Meriam Report, **4:**211
Merilo pravednoe (Just Measure) (Russia), **5:**168
Merina Kingdom, **1:**70
Merkel, Adolf, **3:**103
Merlin, **4:**367
Merry, Sally Engle, **4:**34
Merryman, John, **3:**408; **4:**335
Meru, **1:**71
Meschin, Ranulf, **3:**76
mesne process, **4:174–175**
    imprisonment on, **3:**89
Mesopotamia. *See also* ancient Near Eastern law
    envelope tablet in, **2:**415
Messinger, Sheldon, **4:**32
Metastasio, Pietro, **3:**126
metics, **5:**356–357
metronomoi (controllers of measures), **2:**69
Metropolitan District Commission, **4:**122
Metropolitan Law Society, **5:**273
Metternich, Klemens von, **2:**120
Mettius Rufus, **2:**419
Mevius, David, **2:**112
Mexican War (1846–1848), **6:**88
Mexico, **4:175–177**
    abolition of slavery, **5:**254
    federalism, **5:**354
    racial classification, **5:**254

Meyer, Walter E., **4:**32
Meyer Institute. *See* Walter E. Meyer Research Institute of Law
MFLO. *See* Muslim Family Law Ordinance
Miagh, Thomas, **5:**485
Michael, Alun, **6:***99*
Michael Attaliates. *See* Attaliates
Michael II of Anchialos, **1:**348
Michael VII Doukas, **4:**416
Michel, James, **5:**235
Michelman, Frank, **4:**69
Microphone Communications Inc. (MCI), **5:**97
Microsoft Corporation antitrust case, **1:***192*, 192–193
Middle Ages. *See also* medieval and post-medieval Roman law
    canon-law ban on interest, **3:**204
    central government in English Common Law, **1:**385–386
    codes and codification during, **2:**46–47
    company law, **2:**92
    comparative law in, **2:**98
    compurgation during, **2:**104
    consumer protection, **2:**170
    development of science of law in universities, **2:**6
    insanity and crime in, **3:**247
    insolvency, **3:**249
    Italy, **3:**354–355
    origins of the modern international state system, **3:**282
    partnerships during, **2:**93
        land-based businesses, **2:**95
        in maritime business, **2:**94–95
    regulation of competition
        in English common law, **2:**101
        in Roman law, **2:**102
Middle Assyrian laws, **1:**168
Middle East, Shafi'i school of law in, **3:**353
Middle Temple. *See* Inns of Court
Midelfort, H. C. Erik, **6:**109
Midland Bank (England), **1:**276
Mielnik Privilege of, **4:**330; **4:**1501
Mieszko I (Poland), **4:**330
Miftah, 'Abd Allah ibn, **4:**136
Military Commission Act (U.S., 2006), **4:**181
military governments
    and constitutions in Arab countries, **2:**135
    Ottoman Empire, **4:**266–267
    Pakistan, **2:**141
    Suriname, **5:**413

Military Reconstruction Acts (U.S., 1875), **2:**257
military service
   African French colonies, **1:**90
   ancient Athens
      foreigners in, **5:**357
      offenses against the state and, **4:**247–248
   Brazil, **5:**294
   Chinese law
      land tenure based on, **4:**4
      offenses against the state in, **4:**251
   feudal law on, **3:**78
      estates doctrine and, **2:**477
   Islamic law, **1:**33–34, 34–35
   military tribunals and, **4:**177–182
   nationality and, **4:**205
   Ottoman Empire, **4:**266–267
   sex discrimination in, **2:**339
   Sri Lanka, **5:**343
   United States
      discrimination in, **2:**340, 341
      effects of on history, **6:**88
      right to bear arms and, **1:**216–220
      women in, **6:**138, 139–140
Military Statute (Russia, 1716), **5:**170
military tribunals, **4:177–182**
   separation of powers and, **5:**219
Militia Act (U.S., 1792), **1:**218
milk. See ownership *(milk)*
Mill, John Stuart, **3:**239
   on civil liberties, **3:**450
   on evidence, **1:**287
   on sexual and gender variation, **3:**110
Millar, Fergus, **5:**140
Millat wa-al-Din, Siraj al-, **1:**59
Miller, Jack, **1:**219–220
Miller, Samuel F., **2:**369
Milligan, Spike, **4:**206
Milsom, S. F. C.
   English common law historiography by, **2:**434
   on evidence, **3:**5
Miltiades, **1:**54
mīmāṃsā, **4:182–183**
Mimes, The (Herodas), **2:**413
Minangkabau, **1:**20
Mindaugas (grand duke of Lithuania), **1:**254
Mines Regulation Act (U.K., 1844), **2:**426
Ming code (China), **1:**430, 454, 458; **5:**26
   abduction *(lue)*, **3:**468

   amnesty, **1:**134
   appeal, **1:**194
   astronomical studies, **4:**252
   censorship, **4:**252
   collective liability, **2:**58, 59, 60
   corruption, **2:**226, 227
   cursing, **2:**304, 305
   damage to property, **2:**312, 313
   damaging efficiency of government, **4:**254
   deceit, **2:**314, 315
   deposit, **2:**331
   disrespect *(bujing)*, **4:**250, 251
   doubtful cases, **2:**361
   endangering the emperor, **4:**256
   enticement *(you)*, **3:**469
   errors in official documents, **4:**254
   exile, **3:**25–26
   foreigners, **3:**91–92
   homicide, **3:**171–172, 173, 174–175
   homosexuality, **3:**180
   illicit sexual intercourse, **5:**231
   incest, **3:**214
   lack of filial piety, **3:**84, 85, 86
   land, **4:**2
   litigation masters, **4:**46
   magic and sorcery, **4:**253
   marriage, **4:**156, 157
      remarriage, **4:**160
   mistaken judgments, **4:**254
   mistaken recommendations, **4:**255
   mutual concealment, **4:**199
   offenses against the state, **4:**249
   parricide, **3:**84
   penal servitude, **4:**293
   persons as security, **4:**326
   plotting rebellion, **4:**257
   punishments, **5:**25, 26–27
      beating and whipping, **1:**283–284
      five punishments, **1:**362; **5:**213
   rape, **5:**66–67
   redemption, **5:**72, 73, 74
   review, **1:**196–197, 197
   sale
      of a free person by consent, **3:**469
      of goods, **5:**185
      of land, **5:**185, 187–188
      of relatives, **3:**469
   sexual offenses, **5:**233
      sodomy, **5:**234

slavery, **5:**55, 56
status, **5:**359
succession, **5:**380
sumptuary laws, **5:**410
Ten Abominations, **4:**260
theft, **5:**458–459, 460, 461
torture, **5:**482–483
treason, **4:**258
wounding, **6:**150, 151
zang, **6:**159, 160
Ming dynasty (China, 1361–1644)
    administrative codes and regulations, **1:**454
    bureaucracy and capital punishment, **1:**360
    corruption in the, **2:**225–226
    courts in the, **2:**241, 242, 245, 248
    emperor's power during the, **2:**243
    guilds during, **1:**464
    judicial precedent, **1:**461
    Mongols and, **4:**183–184
    penal code organization, **1:**458
Ming gong shupan qingming ji, **5:**186
Minglü, **1:**434
Minhaj al-Talibin (al-Nawawi), **2:**41, 44
Minhaj al-wusul (Ibn al-Murtada), **4:**136
Minicius, **3:**430
mining in Athens, **2:**71–72
Ministry of Justice (China), **1:**423, 432
Ministry of Justice Law School. *See* Tokyo Imperial University Department of Law
Ministry of Religion (Indonesia), **3:**335
mini-trials, **1:**128
Minnesänger, **5:**195
Minor, Frances, **6:**135
Minor, Virginia, **6:**135
minority in Islamic law, **1:**359
Minors Contracts Acts (U.K., 1987), **1:**395
Minos (Plato), **4:**17, 21
Minow, Martha, **3:**69
mintian (common tenure), **4:**3–4
Miranda, Pontes de, **1:**304
Mirhady, David C., **5:**481
mirror for princes literature. *See Sachsenspiegel; Schwabenspiegel*
misappropriation, tort of, **3:**272
Mishnah, the, **3:**390, 391
Mishneh Torah (Maimonides), **3:**392
Miśra, Prabhākara, **4:**182
Missale Romanum (1570), **2:**224

Mission of Friar William of Rubruck, The, **4:**183
Missouri Compromise (U.S., 1820), **5:**260, 262, 263; **6:**52
mistake. *See* error and mistake
Mitākshara (Vijñāneśvara), **3:**156, 158
    on succession, **5:**396, 397, 398–400
    translation by Colebrooke, **2:**57
Mitchell, Billy, **4:**179
Mitchell, Richard E., **4:**82
mithliyyat. See fungible things
Mitramiśra, **6:**83
Mitsukuri, Rinsho, **3:**373
Mitteis, Heinrich, **3:**79
Mitteis, Ludwig, **5:**150
    on ancient Greek law, **1:**163
    on juristic papyrology, **2:**417
    in papyrology, **2:**413
Mittelmaier, Carl Joseph Anton, **2:**98
mixed government theory, **5:**215
Mi'yar al-'uqul fi'ilm al-usul (Ibn al-Murtada), **4:**136
M'Naghten, Daniel, **3:**247
Mobilization Law (Japan, 1939), **3:**377
Mobutu, Joseph, **1:***98*
Mobutu Sésé Séko, **1:***98*
Model Business Corporation Act (U.S., 1950), **1:**324
Model Code of Evidence, **3:**10–11
Model Penal Code (American Law Institute, 1962), **2:**51
    influence of, **2:**293
    on sexual and gender variation, **3:**110
Model Rules of Professional Conduct (ABA), **4:**53
Modern Corporation and Private Property, The (Berle and Means), **1:**325–326
Modern Entries (Lilly), **4:**61
Moderne Völkerrecht der civilisirten Staaten als Rechtsbuch dargestellt, Das (Bluntschli), **3:**283–284
modernism, **3:**165
    classical legal theory and, **2:**25
Modestinus, **3:**435, 436
Modrzejewski, Joseph, **1:**165
Mohamad, Mahathir bin, **2:**140
Mohammad bin Qasim of Sindh, **4:**273
Mohammad Reza Shah, **3:**303
Mohammedan Marriage Ordinance (Malaysia, 1880), **4:**301
moicheia. See adultery

Molina, Louis de
    on *fideicommissum*, **3:**81
    in Scholasticism, **4:**15
Molinaeus, Carolus. *See* Du Moulin, Charles
Mommsen, Theodor, **2:**237; **5:**159, 160, 162
    on Alciati, Andrea, **1:**118
Monachus, Johannes, **2:**223
Monahan, John, **5:**266
monarchy
    absolutism, **1:**6–9
    administrative law and judiciary, **1:**21–22
    Africa, precolonial, **1:**70, 71
    ancient Near Eastern law, **1:**168–169, 176
    ancient Rome, **4:**130
    Anglo-Saxon law, **1:**179
    British Commonwealth, **1:**313
    Buddhist models of, **5:**303, 304
    Denmark, **2:**328
    Egypt, **2:**413–414
    England
        Magna Carta on, **4:**133–136
        as source of law, **5:**277
        succession in, **5:**382–383
    Enlightenment views of, **2:**445
    in feudal law, **3:**72–80
    guilds and, **3:**132
    Hindu law, **1:**223
    local government law and, **4:**119–120
    Malaysia, **4:**138, 139
    Nepal, **4:**224, 225
    nītiśāstra on, **4:**232–233
    Protestant churches and, **1:**349–350
    Saudi Arabia, **1:**209
    Scotland, **5:**197, 200
    Spain, **5:**325–326
    Sparta, **5:**328
moneychangers, **1:**273–274
Moneylenders Act (U.K., 1900), **2:**169
Mongolia, **4:183–186**
    conflict of laws, **2:**113
Mongol-Oïrat code, **4:**184
Mongols in Iran, **3:**302
Monier, Raymond, **5:**161
Monnet, Jean, **2:**486
    functionalist approach of, **2:**495
monopolies, **4:186–187**. *See also* antitrust
    banking, **1:**275
    corporations and, **1:**321–322
    domestic, **2:**88

granting of monopoly rights
    in English common law, **2:**101–102
Monopolies and Restrictive Trade Practices Act
    (India, 1969), **2:**173–174
Monopolies and Trusts (Ely), **1:**325
Monroe, James
    Bill of Rights and, **5:**114
    on executive power, **3:**23
    on general welfare clause, **3:**113
Monroe, W. S., **1:***314*
Montagu, Edward, **1:**292; **4:**38
Montague-Chelmsford Reform (India, 1919), **2:**143
Montaigne, Michel de
    on procedural law, **4:**439
    on torture, **3:**9
Monte di Pietà, **1:**273, 274
Montenegro, Islamic law in, **1:**253; **3:**333
Montesinos, Antonio de
    on colonial law, **4:**16; **5:**291
    in Scholasticism, **4:**16
montes pietatis, **3:**258
Montesquieu, Charles-Louis de Secondat, Baron
        de la Brède et de, **2:**9; **5:**160, 172
    comparative law, **2:**98
    on enlightened absolutism, **1:**8–9
    on legislation, **4:**92
    on separation of powers, **5:**215
    theory of separation of powers
        influence on French constitution of 1791, **2:**120
Montevideo, Treaties of (1889), **2:**114
Montfort, Simon de
    influence of, **6:**1
    Parliament and, **4:**283
Montserrat, **1:**369
Monzambano, Severinus de. *See* Pufendorf, Samuel von
Mooney, Tom, **4:**337
Moore, Francis, **1:**390
Moore, James William, **1:**16
Moore, Sally Falk, **4:**59
Moore, Underhill
    on law and society, **4:**31
    in legal realism, **1:**15; **4:**74, 75
moot courts in English legal education, **2:**393
Mootz, Francis J., **4:**365
Moralia (Plutarch), **3:**124

More, Thomas, **1:**389
   as barrister, **1:**278
   in Chancery, **2:**468
   on procedural law, **4:**439
   on property, **4:**475
Morellet, André, **1:**285
Morgan, Edmund M.
   on evidence, **3:**5, 11
   on national evidence law, **3:**10
Morgan, J. P. (John Pierpont), **4:**482; **5:**445
Morgenthau, Henry, **5:**445, 446
Morley Minto Reform (India, 1909), **2:**143
mormaers, **5:**196
morning gift, **3:**42, 43
Morocco. *See also* Maghrib
   adoption in, **1:**48
   civil law, **1:**205
   conflict of laws, **2:**114
   inheritance law, **2:**38
   Maliki school of law in, **3:**351
   obligatory bequests in, **6:**107
   personal status laws, **4:**130, 297; **6:**129
Morrill Land Grant Act (U.S., 1862), **5:**86, 88; **6:**51
Morris, Clarence, **5:**46
Morris, Gouverneur, **5:**411
Morris, Ian, **4:**152–153
Morse, Allen B., **6:**52
mort d'ancestor, writ of, **3:**75, 76; **4:**316–317; **5:**70
   in England, **4:**87
   in Ireland, **3:**307
mortgage, **4:187–191**
   China, **4:**2, 6–7
   England
     equity and, **2:**470
   English common law, **3:**394; **4:188–189**
   in Ireland, **3:**309
   Islamic law, **2:**484
   medieval and post-medieval Roman law, **4:189–191**
   United States, **3:**182–183, 184
     recording in colonial period, **2:**13
Mortimer, Roger de, **6:**2
mortis causa donation
   in ancient Greek law, **3:**231
mortmain, **4:191–193**
   guilds on, **3:**132
   subinfeudation and, **5:**369–370
Mortmain Act (Great Britain, 1736), **1:**392; **4:**192–193
Moscow Lomonosov State University, **5:**177

Moses, **3:**389
Moses ben Israel Isserles, Rabbi, **3:**392
Moses ben Maimon (Moses Maimonides, or "Rambam"), Rabbi, **3:**388, 392
Moses ben Nahman (Nahmanides, or "Ramban"), Rabbi, **3:**392
Mos gallicus in legal education, **2:**399–400
Moshoeshoe, **1:**70, 72, 86
Mos italicus
   Bartolus of Saxoferrato in, **1:**281
   Budé, Guillaume, on, **1:**316
   in legal education, **2:**399–400
Mothers Against Drunk Driving (MADD), **1:**127
mother's pensions, **6:***92*, 93, 137
Motion Picture Patents monopoly, **1:**324
Motion to Enquire into the Education of the Poor (speech, Brougham), **1:**392
Motor Carrier Act (U.S., 1935), **5:**103
Motor Carrier Act (U.S., 1980), **5:**104
motor vehicle regulation (U.S.), **5:**103–104
mou fan (plotting rebellion, China), **4:**257
Mount Vernon Conference (1785), **2:**149
Mozambique
   decolonization of, **1:**93
   Portuguese colony, **1:**80
Mozi (Mo Tzu), **1:**412
Mu'adh ibn Jabal, **6:**155
muaynāmalāt (relations between humans), **2:**483
Muaturidism, **3:**343
Mu'ayyad Ahmad ibn al-Husayn, al-, **3:**139
mubaraat (divorce by mutual consent), **3:**50
Mubarak, Hosni, **4:**47
Mucius Scaevola, Quintus, **4:**375
   on legal reasoning, **4:**79
muḍāraba (commenda), **1:**261
   in banking and finance, **1:**262
Mudawana (Moroccan law code) (Morocco, 1957 and 1958), **4:**297
Mudawwana (Malik), **5:**487
Mudawwana, al- (Sahnun), **5:**239, 240
Mudawwana al-Kubra (Muhammad Yusuf at Faiyish), **2:**41
Mudawwana al-kubra (Sahnun), **3:**351; **4:**127–128; **5:**182–183, 487
   commentary by Ibn Rushd, **3:**200
   on Malik ibn Anas, **4:**140
Mufriha, Ibn, **1:**10
mufti, **4:***193*, **193–195**
   in Balkan peninsula, **1:**252–253
   education of, **4:**72

in enforcement, **2**:431
fatwas by, **3**:57–58
Ottoman Empire, **4**:73, 265
qualification for, **3**:57
treatises on, **3**:58
Mughal Empire
codification, **2**:36
consumer protection, **2**:173
criminal law, **2**:281–282
Mughni, al- (Qudama), **3**:347
on worship, **6**:149
Mughni ʿala Mukhtasar al-Khiraqi, Al- (Ibn Qudama), **3**:199
Muhadhdhab, al- (Shirazi), **5**:238
Muhadhdhab fi-l-fatawa, al- (Mansur), **4**:144
Muhakkima. *See* Khariji school of Islamic law
Muhalla, al- (Ibn Hazm), **3**:354
Muhalla bi-l-athar fi sharh al-mujalla, al- (Ibn Hazm), **3**:198
Muhammad
abrogation of legal norms and, **1**:5–6
on adoption, **1**:48
on agricultural contracts, **1**:116
on assignment (*ḥawālah*), **1**:229
Companions of the Prophet, **1**:210, 211
on donation, **2**:358
hijra of, **1**:209–210
on imprisonment, **4**:384
judicial role of, **4**:70
purification procedures performed by, **5**:59
revelation of Qurʾan to, **5**:133
Treaty of Hudaybiyya, **4**:233
Muhammad ʿAlaʾ al-Din, **3**:195
Muhammad Hasan al-Najafi. *See* Baqir al-Najafi, Muhammad Hasan ibn Muhammad
Muhammadiyyah (Indonesia), **3**:336
Muhammad Qadri Pasha al-Hanafi, **4:195–196**
Muhammedan Code (Sri Lanka), **5**:340
Muhammedan Marriages Act (India, 1876), **4**:299
Muḥbaqqiq al-Awwal, al. *See* Hilli, Jaʿfar ibn al-Hasan, al-
Mühlenbruch, Christian Friedrich, **4**:277
Mühlenbruch, Friedrich, **1**:228
Muhtalita, **5**:183
muhzirs (summons officers), **4**:73
Muʿid al-niʿam wa-mubid al-niqam (al-Subki), **5**:370
Muir, John, **2**:455
Mui Tsai Enactment (Brunei, 1933), **5**:319
Muʿizz li-Din Allah, **5**:59

mujtahid, **3**:224, 319
al-Bihbahani on, **1**:291
al-Mahdi as, **4**:136
Imāmī school and, **3**:340
muftis as, **4**:194–195
mukalʾaf (moral agent), **3**:97
Mukhasat al-kabir, al- (Ibn ʿAbd al-Hakam), **3**:350
Mukhtar, al- (al-Mawsili), **3**:343
Mukhtasar (ʿAbd Allah ibn ʿAbd al-Hakam), **3**:468
influence on Abu Yaʿla, **1**:10
Mukhtasar (Abu Musʿab al-Zhuri), **3**:468
Mukhtasar (al-Buwayti), **3**:468
Mukhtasar (al-Muzani), **3**:352, 468; **4**:200
Mukhtasar (al-Subki), **5**:370
Mukhtasar (ibn ʿUmar Shatti), **3**:347
Mukhtasar (Khalil ibn Ishaq), **2**:41, 42; **3**:351, 467
Mukhtasar, al- (al-Karkhi), **3**:343
Mukhtasar, al- (al-Khiraqi), **3**:346, 467, 468
commentary by Ibn Qudama, **3**:199
Mukhtasar, al- (al-Quduri), **3**:343
Mukhtasar, al- (al-Tahawi), **3**:343
Mukhtasar al-mudawwana wa-l-mukhtalita (Ibn Abi Zayd), **5**:61
Mukhtasar al-Nāfiʿ, al- (Al-Hilli), **3**:146
Mulk, Nizam al-, **3**:352
Shirazi, Abu Ishaq Ibrahim ibn ʿAli, and, **5**:238
system of Nizamiyya madrasas, **3**:344
Müller-Arnold trial, **2**:252
Mulroney, Brian, **3**:*286*
multilateral agreement on investment (MAI), **3**:285
multilinguality
of Qin empire, **1**:428
in Qing dynasty, **1**:435
multiple listing service (MLS), **1**:114
Mulukimacron Ain, **4**:224–225
Muluki Ain (Nepal), **5**:182
munāẓara (disputation), **2**:397
Munhumutapa, **1**:69
municipal law, **4**:119–123
lex Irnitana, **4**:102–104
Muqaddamat (Ibn Rushd), **3**:200
Muqaddimat al-hadramiyya (al-Hadrami), **2**:41
Muqaffaayn, Ibn
on political authority, **1**:33
Muratori, Lodovico Antonio, **3**:358
Muravʾyov, Nikita, **5**:178
murbaḥa (sale), **1**:263–264, 359
murder. *See* homicide
Murder (Abolition of the Death Penalty) Act (U.K., 1965), **1**:365

Murena, L(ucius) Licinius, **5:**225
Muromtsev, Sergei A., **5:**178
Murray, Pauli
  on jury duty, **6:**138–139
    in National Organization for Women, **2:**339
    Roosevelt, Eleanor, and, **6:**144
    on women's rights, **6:**137
Murray, William. *See* Mansfield, Lord
Murshid al-Hayran (Qadri Pasha), **2:**35
Murshid al-hayran ila ma'rifat ahwal al-insan (al-Hanafi), **4:**195
Murtada, Ahmad ibn Yahya ibn al-. *See* Mahdi, Li-Din Allah Ahmad ibn Yahya al-Murtada al-
Mus'ab, Abu, **4:**140
mushāraka (partnership)
  in banking and finance, **1:**262, 263, 264
Musharraf, Pervez, **2:**141, 142
Muslim, Abu, **1:**1
Muslim Brotherhood, **1:**207; **3:**281
Muslim Divorce Registration Act (Bangladesh, 1876), **5:**308
Muslim Family Law Ordinance (Pakistan, 1961), **2:**38, 142; **4:**299
Muslim Family Laws Ordinance (Bangladesh, 1961), **1:**259; **4:**300; **5:**309
Muslim Intestate Succession Ordinance (Sri Lanka, 1931), **5:**310
Muslim League, **2:**143–144
Muslim Marriage and Divorce Act (Trinidad, 1964), **6:**10
Muslim Marriage and Divorce Registration Law (Indonesia, 1946), **4:**301
Muslim Marriage and Divorce Registration Ordinance (Sri Lanka, 1929), **5:**310
Muslim Marriages and Divorces (Registration) Act (Bangladesh, 1974), **1:**259; **4:**300; **5:**308
Muslim Mosques and Charitable Trusts and Waqfs Act (Sri Lanka, 1956), **5:**310
Muslim Personal Law (Shariat) Application Act (India, 1937), **5:**308
  in Bangladesh, **1:**259
  in Bangladesh and Pakistan, **4:**275, 299, 300
  on marriage, **3:**49
Muslim Women (Protection of Rights on Divorce) Act (India, 1986), **3:**50
Musnad (Ibn Hanbal), **3:**197, 345
Mussalman Wakf Validating Act (India, 1913 and 1930), **5:**308
Mustakhraja, al- (al-'Utbi), **3:**350

musta'min, **4:**233
  bequests to, **6:**106
Musto, David, **1:**126
Mutarrifiyya, **4:**144
Mutawakkil, al-, **3:**196
Mu'tazili school of Islamic theology, **3:**352
  Hanafi school and, **3:**343
  Ibn 'Aqil, Abu al-Wafa' 'Ali, and, **3:**196
  Khariji school and, **3:**348
  in Maghrib and al-Andalus, **4:**127, 128
  methods opposed by Ibn Qudama, **3:**199
mutilation
  in Chinese law, **1:**408; **4:196–197**; **5:**214
    exile with, **3:**25, 26
    under Han, **1:**417
    under Western Zhou dynasty, **1:**403
  genital, **3:**71
    Africa, **1:**71, 73
  in Islamic law, **3:**325
Mutterrecht, Das (Bachofen), **1:**185
mutual concealment, **4:197–199**
  marriage and, **4:**158
mutual surveillance. *See* collective liability in Chinese law
mutuum (loan for consumption), **2:**184, 186, 187, 189
Muwatta (Malik), **3:**350, 351; **4:**140–141
  commentaries on, **3:**351
  edition by Yahya ibn Yahya, **3:**351
  Yahya ibn Yahya on, **4:**128
Muwatta', al- (Malik), **1:**211; **5:**235
Muyart de Vouglans, Pierre-François, **3:**103
muyou (legal secretaries), **4:**46
Muzadi, Hasyim, **3:**336
Muzani, Abu Ibrahim Isma'il ibn Yahya al-, **3:**352; **4:200**
  Da'ud 'Ali al-Isbahani dispute with, **2:**313
  influenced by al-Shafi'i, **5:**236
Myanmar. *See* Burma
m'yar al-mu'rib wa-l-jami' al-mughrib, Al- (al-Wansharisi, comp.), **6:**85
Mynsinger, Joachim
  on conflict of laws, **2:**112
  publisher of Zaius's *Opera omnia,* **6:**160
  as *Reichskammergericht* assessor, **5:**106
Mzilikazi, **1:**70

N

naẓ (gaze), women and, **1:**299
NAACP. *See* National Association for the Advancement of Colored People

NAACP Legal Defense Fund
  legal services by, **4:**52, 367, 370
  Marshall, Thurgood, in, **2:**341
Nader, Laura
  on law and society, **4:**33
  in legal anthropology, **4:**59
Nader, Ralph, **5:**83
Nadir, Muhammad, **1:**59
Nadir Shah (Persia), **3:**400
NAFTA. *See* North American Free Trade
      Agreement
Nafzawi, al-. *See* Qayrawani, Ibn Abi Zayd, al-
Naga law, **4:201**
Nahdatul 'Ulama' (Indonesia), **3:**336
Nahrawan, Battle of (658), **3:**348
Nahua law, **4:***208*
naifty, writ of, **3:**307
Nai Pan Hla, **1:**318
Namibia
  decolonization of, **1:**93–94
  indigenous law, **1:**101
Nanak, Guru, **5:**240
Nandana, **1:**236
Nandi, **1:**71
Nanjing, Treaty of (China, 1842)
  on extraterritoriality, **3:**92
  Hong Kong and, **1:**448
Nanking, Treaty of. *See* Nanjing, Treaty of
      (China, 1842)
Nan Yuquan, **1:**414
Napoleonic Code (1810), **3:**98; **4:**281, 318, 330; **6:**16.
      See also Code Civil (France, 1804)
  in Africa, **1:**79
  in African French colonies, **1:**89
  in Argentina, **1:**216
  commentators on, **3:**100
  education on, **2:**401
  in Egypt, **3:**421
  Enlightenment influences on, **2:**444
  in Germany, **3:**118
  in Laos, **4:**14
  in Seychelles, **5:**235
  stare decisis, **3:**406
Napoleonic Code Pénal, **5:**34
Napoleonic Loi 25 Ventôse année XI (France, 1803),
      4:237
Napoleonic Wars
  banking and, **1:**271, 272
  effects of, **4:**349
  papal power and, **4:**354

Nārada, **3:**153, 155, 156
Nāradasmriti, **3:**179; **4:**224; **6:**83
Narayan, Rudy, **2:**330
Nārāyana, **1:**236
Narcotic Control Act (Canada, 1985), **1:**341
Narcotic Drugs and Psychotrophic Substances Act
      (India, 1988), **2:**283
Nari O Shishu Nirjatan (Bishesh Bidhan) Ain
      (Bangladesh, 1995), **1:**259
Nari O Shishu Nirjatan Daman Ain
      (Bangladesh, 2000), **1:**259
Narvaja, Tristán, **6:**66
NASD. *See* National Association of Securities
      Dealers
naskh. *See* abrogation of legal norms *(naskh)*
Nasser, Gamal Abdel
  Board of the Bar Association dissolved by, **4:**47
  codification under, **2:**421
Natal, Anglo-Roman-Dutch law in, **1:**87
National Academy of Elder Law Attorneys (NAELA),
      2:422
National Academy of Sciences, **4:**30
National and Provincial Bank (England), **1:**276
National Association for the Advancement of
      Colored People (NAACP), **2:**299; **3:**165; **4:**336,
      367, 370
  and enforcement of rights, **2:**20
  Parade for Victory, **2:***461*
National Association of Manufacturers, **5:**84
National Association of Real Estate Boards,
      3:183
National Association of Securities Dealers
      (NASD), **5:**81
National Child Labor Committee (U.S.), **6:**92
National Commission of Minorities Act (India, 1992),
      3:365
National Commission on the Review of the Constitution
      (India), **3:**105
National Conference of Commissioners on Uniform
      State Laws (1892), **2:**51, 76, 115; **3:**273; **5:**402
  on evidence, **3:**11
National Conference of the Active Forces of the Nation
      (Benin, 1990), **1:**104–105
National Conscription Act (U.S.), **4:**336
National Council of Women in India, **5:**397
National Environmental Policy Act (U.S., 1969),
      2:456
National Firearms Act (U.S., 1934), **1:**219–220
National Grange of the Order of Patrons of
      Husbandry. *See* Grangers

National Health Service, provisions for the insane, **3**:246
National Health Service Act (U.K., 1946), **4**:350
National Highway Traffic Safety Administration, **5**:82
National Housing Act (U.S., 1934), **3**:182
National Housing Act (U.S., 1937), **3**:183–184, 186
    on agency, **1**:114
National Housing Act Amendments of 1938 (United States), **3**:183
National Industrial Recovery Act (U.S., 1933), **3**:481–482
    antitrust and, **1**:190
    executive power and, **3**:22
National Industrial Relations Court (U.K.), **2**:427
nationalism
    Baltic states, **1**:256
    Hindu, **3**:159–160
    Islamic legal education influenced by, **2**:398
nationality in English common law, **4**:205–206
National Labor Relations Act (U.S., 1935), **1**:325; **3**:409, 481–482
    commerce clause and, **3**:62
    on labor arbitration, **3**:487, 488
    upheld by Supreme Court, **2**:66
National Labor Relations Board, **1**:28, 325; **3**:482; **5**:80
    in labor arbitration, **3**:488
National Law Examination Law (Japan, 1949), **3**:385
National Lawyers Guild, **4**:52
National Organization for Women (NOW), **6**:137
    on Title VII, **2**:339
National Parks and Access to the Countryside Act (U.K., 1949), **2**:451
National Prohibition Act (U.S., 1919), **2**:292
National Prohibition Act (U.S., 1928), **4**:386
National Provinicial Bank of England, **1**:272
National Recovery Administration, **1**:28
    Supreme Court and, **2**:27
National Recovery Administration (NRA), **5**:80
National Reporter System (West), **6**:46
National Resistance Movement (Uganda), **1**:99
National Rifle Association (NRA), **1**:220
National Science Foundation
    on law and society, **4**:32
    on social sciences, **5**:267–268
National Senior Citizens Law Center, **2**:422
National Socialist law, **3**:119; **4**:201–205
    jurisprudence of concepts, **3**:432
    natural law and, **4**:219
    partnerships in, **2**:94
    taxation, **5**:439
National Student Marketing Corporation, **5**:94
National Traffic and Motor Vehicle Safety Act (U.S., 1966), **2**:178
National Trust (U.K.), **2**:451
National University School of Law, **2**:404
National Voter Registration Act (U.S., 1993), **2**:344; **4**:339
National Wilderness Preservation System, **2**:455
National Women's Party, **2**:339; **6**:136
Natiq Abu Talib Yahya ibn al-Husayn, al-, **3**:139
Native Administration Act (South Africa, 1927), **5**:280
Native American law, **4**:206–214
    Civil Rights Act of 1968, **2**:340
    military tribunals and, **4**:178
    nineteenth century, **6**:49–50
    twentieth century, **6**:57–58
Native Converts' Marriage Dissolution Act (India, 1866), **2**:353
Native Land Trust Board (Fiji), **3**:82
native law. *See* folk law
Native Resettlement Act (South Africa, 1954), **5**:*281*
NATO. *See* North Atlantic Treaty Organization
Natronai Gaon, Rav, **3**:391
Naturalisation Act (U.K., 1870), **4**:206
naturalism, international law and, **3**:283
naturalization
    nationality and, **4**:205–206
    United States, **2**:2; **3**:209–210
        discrimination in, **2**:344
natural law, **4**:214–220
    absolutism and, **1**:8
    on agency, **1**:109
    ancient Greek law, **1**:145
    on assignment, **1**:227
    Bentham, Jeremy, on, **1**:288
    Brazil, **1**:303
    on breach of contract, **1**:307, 308, 309
    on children, **3**:44
        paternal authority over, **3**:45
    on colonialism, **5**:299
    comparative law and, **2**:98
    definition of law in, **4**:20, 21
    on delay, **2**:320
    Denmark, **2**:328
    dharma compared with, **2**:333
    Domat, Jean, on, **2**:356–357
    English common law, **2**:437; **4**:214–215

on error and mistake, **2:**475
France, **3:**99
on gay, lesbian, bisexual, and transgender, **3:**110
German, **3:**118
on guilt, **3:**134
international law and, **3:**283
law of reason and, **2:**8
on lease and tenancy contracts, **4:**57
in legal education, **2:**400
legal education in, **2:**400
Leibniz, Gottfried Wilhelm, on, **4:**100
medieval and post-medieval Roman law, **4:**216–217
on negligence, **4:**221
Netherlands, **4:**226
Noordt, Gerard, on, **4:**236
on obligations, **4:**245
Oldendorp, Johann, on, **4:**261
on ownership, **4:**465, 467, 475
private law and, **4:**393
Pufendorf, Samuel von on, **5:**21
on punishment, **5:**43
Scholasticism and, **4:**15–17
in Scotland, **5:**200
on servitude in real estate, **5:**223–224
Spain, **5:**325–326
on succession, **5:**385, 388, 393, 394
on systematization, **5:**421
Thomasius, Christian on, **5:**464–465
United States law, **4:**217–220
unjust enrichment, **6:**64
Wolff, Christian von, on, **6:**111–112
Nature and Sources of the Law, The (Gray), **2:**26
"Nature of the Firm, The" (Coase), **4:**24
Nature of the Judicial Process, The (Cardozo), **2:**26
Natürliche Privatrecht, Das (Zeiller), **6:**163
Nausimakhos, **1:**213
Naval Statute (Russia, 1720), **5:**170
Navigation Acts (England), **1:**36
    U.S. colonial courts and, **2:**255
Nawadir wa-l-ziyadat 'ala ma fi al-Mudawwana min ghayriha min al-ummahat (Qayrawani), **3:**250; **5:**61
Nawawi, Abu Zakaria Mohiuddin Yahya bin Sharaf al-, **2:**41; **3:**352; **6:**155
    on judicial review, **3:**414
    on muftiship, **3:**58
Nazione, La (newspaper), **1:**372

Nazi Party. *See* German National Socialist Workers Party
Nazzam, al-, **3:**354
Ndebele kingdom, **1:**70
negligence, **4:**220–222
    bailment and, **1:**250
    breach of contract and, **1:**307
    Chinese law
        deposit, **2:**331
        in wrongful judgment, **6:**152
    consumer protection and, **2:**169
    English common law
        in fraud, **3:**101
        legal treatises on, **2:**442–443
    guilds on, **3:**132
    guilt and, **3:**134, 135
    New Zealand, **4:**232
    science and, **4:**30–31
    Scotland, **5:**201
negotiable instruments, **4:**222–224
    bills of exchange, **1:**292–293
    in colonial United States, **2:**14
Negotiable Instruments Act (U.K., 1881), **4:**273
Negotiable Instruments Law (China, 1929), **1:**440
negotiorum gestio (management of another's affirs without instruction), **2:**185–186
Negro Seaman's Act (S.C., 1822), **3:**294
Nehrman, David, **5:**416
Nehru, Jawaharlal, **2:**143–144; **3:**218–219
    in Constituent Assembly, **2:**144
    on succession, **5:**398
    on uniform civil code, **5:**209
Nehru, Motilal, **2:**145
neifs. *See* villeinage
Neighbors and Strangers (Mann), **2:**206
Nellen, H. J. M., **3:**127
Nelson, William, **3:**5
Nene, Tamati Waka, **4:**227
neoclassical economics, **4:**23
Neo-Confucianism
    on filial piety, **3:**84
    on succession, **5:**379, 380
Nepal, **4:**224–225
    Islamic law in, **5:**306–307, 310
    sadācāra in, **5:**182
Neratius, **4:**290
Neratius Priscus, Lucius, **3:**431, 435
Nerva (Roman emperor), **3:**211

Netherlands, **4:225–227**
  African colonization, **1**:81
  assignment, **1**:228
  banking, **1**:275
  civil marriage, **3**:41
  conflict of laws, **2**:113
  Constitution (1848)
    effect on Indonesia, **3**:226
  fideicommisum, **3**:80
  guarantee, **3**:129
  influence on Russian law, **5**:166
  insurance, **3**:258
  in South Africa, **5**:279
  in Sri Lanka, **5**:340–341
  treaty with Japan, **3**:365, 372
  undue influence, **6**:25
  United States colonies and, **6**:32, 33
Netherlands East Indies
  intellectual property, **3**:261, 262
  Islamic law in, **3**:335
  Napoleon and, **3**:226
  types of law in, **3**:336–337
Nettelbladt, Daniel, **5**:172
  on Justinian organization, **2**:400
Neudong Code (Tibet), **5**:305
Neue Fallitenordnung (New Bankruptcy Law
  (Hamburg, 1753), **3**:249
Neustadt, Richard, **3**:22
New Abridgment (Bacon), **2**:441
New Caledonia, **4**:173. *See also* Melanesia
New Code of the Wei dynasty, **2**:314
New Compilation (Spain, 1567), **1**:215
New Deal
  administrative agencies in, **1**:27–28, 30–31
  agriculture policy, **5**:89–90
  antitrust law, **1**:189–190
  on bankruptcy, **1**:269, 270
  on corporations, **1**:325–326
  environmental law in, **2**:455
  executive power in, **3**:22
  federalism in, **3**:61–62
  judicial power and the, **3**:409, 412
  judicial review in, **1**:30–31
  labor and employment law, **3**:480–481
  on labor disputes, **1**:325
  legal realism in, **4**:77–78
  legislative power in, **4**:98–99
  positivism and, **4**:356
  property rights and, **4**:491–492
  protective labor laws, **6**:137

  public health law, **3**:144–145
  reasons for the, **4**:483
  regulations and, **5**:79–82, 84, 89–90
  scope of, **6**:54
  statutory interpretation in, **5**:361
  Supreme Court and, **2**:27, 260
  tax policy, **5**:444–446
  welfare programs, **6**:93
  women in, **6**:137
New Departure strategy, **6**:135
Newgate, or Tyburn, Calendars (Malefactors'
  Bloody Register), **1**:365
New Guinea, **4**:173
Ne Win, **5**:314
New Institute of the Imperial or Civil Law, A (Wood),
  2:441
New Law Dictionary (Jacob), **2**:441
New Model army (England), **2**:130
New Natura Brevium (Fitzherbert), **4**:61
New Pandect of Roman Civil Law (Ayliffe), **2**:441
New Programme for African Development (NEPAD),
  1:107
New Republic, The (magazine), **2**:302
New River Company, **2**:89
New South Wales. *See* Australia
New South Wales Act (1823), **1**:240
New Tang History, The (Xin Tan shu), **1**:422
new textualism, **5**:362–363
Newton, Isaac, **4**:21
New York Arbitration Act (1920), **1**:130
New York City
  creation of, **4**:121
  municipal government, **4**:122–123
New York City bar association. *See* Association
  of the Bar of the City of New York
New York City Cotton Textile Merchants, **1**:129–130
New York Convention on the Recognition and
  Enforcement of Foreign Arbitral Awards
  (1956), **2**:114
New York House of Refuge, **3**:457
New York Law School, **1**:14; **2**:403
New York State Code of Civil Procedure (1848), **2**:50;
  4:442, 443
New York State Commissioners of Public
  Charities, **4**:368
New York Stock Exchange (NYSE), **5**:81, 94
New York Times Magazine, **2**:299
New Zealand, **4**:227, **227–232**, 345–346
  in British Commonwealth, **1**:313
  land registration in, **4**:7–8

Maori law, **4:**145–147
notaries in, **4:**237
New Zealand Constitution Act (1852), **4:**228
nexum, **2:**183, 184
Nezahualcoyotl of Texcoco, **5:**288
Nguyen Van Linh, **6:**80
Nicaragua
  abolition of slavery, **5:**254
  Civil Code, **1:**384, 398
Niccoló Tedschi (Panormitano), **3:**356
Nice, Treaty of (2001), **2:**487, 492
  rejections of, **2:**493
Nice Agreement on International Classification for Purposes of Registration of Marks (1957), **2:**103
Nicephorus II Phocas, **4:**469
Nicholas I (pope), **3:**8
Nicholas III (pope), **2:**223
Nicholas I (Russian Tsar), **5:**172
Nicholas II (Russian Tsar), **5:**174
Nichomachean Ethics (Aristotle), **3:**123
Nicolai, H., **4:**204
Nider, Johannes, **6:**108
Niebuhr, Barthold Georg, **5:**159
  discovery of Gaius's *Institutes,* **3:**251
Niebuhr, Reinhold, **5:**477
Nield, Basil, **1:**230
Nietzsche, Friedrich, **3:**450
Nigel, Richard fitz, **3:**17
Niger
  abolition of slavery, **1:**76
  age for marriage, **2:**44
  constitution, **2:**137
  divorce, **2:**44
  penal code, **2:**45
Niger Coast Protectorate, **1:**86
Nigeria
  alcohol and drugs, **1:**123
  in British Commonwealth, **1:**315
  British rule in, **1:**86
  capital punishment of juveniles in, **3:**462
  codification, **2:**36
  constitution, **1:**105–106; **2:**137
  criminal law, **2:**279
  death penalty, **1:**368
  dual court system, **2:**43
  ethnic rivalries, **1:**97
  independence, **1:**93
  Indian Penal Code in, **1:**87
  Islamic law in, **1:**102; **2:**39

  land law, **1:**92
  law reform, **1:**100
  legal education, **2:**398
  Nok culture, **1:**67
  official languages, **1:**99
Nihaya, al- (al-Tusi), **6:**18
Nihayat al-matlab (al-Juwayni), **3:**463
Niida Noboru, **1:**463; **2:**193
Nikon (Patriarch), **5:**170
Nīlakantha, **6:**83
NIMBY (not in my back yard), **4:**122
Nimmer, Melville B., **3:**274
Nine Courts (China), **1:**423
"Nine Dignitaires" tribunal (China), **1:**360–361
Ninety-Nine Laws of Perak, **4:**137–138
Nine Years' War (Ireland), **3:**310
Nishapur, **3:**344
Nītasāra (Kāmandaka), **1:**223
Niti Nighanduva, **5:**303
  in Sri Lanka, **5:**339
nītiśāstra, **4:**232–233
Nitisera (Kamandaki), **4:**233
Nitivakyamrtam (Somadevasuri), **4:**233
Nītivāmṛta (Somadevasuri), **1:**223
Nixon, Richard M., **2:**164
  creation of the Environmental Protection Agency, **6:**55
  discrimination under, **2:**342–343
  environmental law under, **2:**456
  executive power under, **3:**22–23
  on federalism, **3:**63
  impeachment of, **3:**410
  on judicial power, **3:**412
  Legal Services, **4:**373; **6:**95
  on Native Americans, **4:**212–213
  Pentagon Papers and, **5:**335
  regulatory system under, **5:**82
niẓām, **1:**34. *See also* administrative decrees of the political authorities *(qānūn)*
Nóbrega, Manoel de, **5:**301
Nok culture, **1:**67
Nol, Lon, **1:**335
Nomocanon of the Fourteen Titles, **1:**328, 347
  Balsamon on, **1:**333; **2:**192, 348
  revision by Bestes, **1:**330
  revision by Photius, **1:**329, 347
Nomoi (Plato). *See Laws* (Plato)

Nomos Georgikos, **1:**328
   on delict, **2:**325
   on property, **4:**468–469
Nomos Rhodiōn Nautikos, **1:**328
Nomos Stratiotikos, **1:**328
Nomotechnia (Finch), **2:**394
nomothetai, **2:**29, 30
Nomothetai (Athens), **1:**232
Nonet, Philippe, **4:**32
nongovernmental organizations
   enforcement of international law and, **3:**279
   international rule of law and, **3:**297
non-Muslims in Islamic law, **4:233–235**
   in jihad, **6:**85–86
   legal capacity, **1:**358
   residency and, **1:**358
non-state. *See* folk law
Noodt, Gerard, **2:**7; **4:**226, **235–236**
Nordic Convention for Jurists, **5:**416
Noriega, Manuel, **6:**89
normalization, queer theory on, **3:**112
Normans
   chancery under, **1:**388
   Irish law and, **3:**307
   system of compensation, **1:**364
normative concept of guilt, **3:**136
Norodom Sihanouk (Cambodia), **1:**335, *336*
Nörr, Dieter, **5:**158
Norris-LaGuardia Anti-Injunction Act
      (U.S., 1932), **2:**261
   equity and, **2:**472
   on injunctions, **3:**483
   on strikes, **3:**481
North American Free Trade Agreement (NAFTA),
      3:285, *286*
   copyright and, **3:**268
North American Review, **1:**326
North Atlantic Treaty Organization (NATO), **3:**278
North Borneo Company, **5:**313, 319
Northcote-Trevelyan Report (1855, implemented 1870),
      1:387
Northern Chi dynasty (China), **2:**242
Northern Ireland, devolution of powers to, **2:**133
Northern Qi, **1:**421
Northern Qi code (China, 564), **5:**72, 73
Northern Rhodesia, **1:**92
Northern Securities merger, **1:**324
Northern Wei code (504), **1:**420–421
   abduction *(lue),* **3:**468
   divorce, **4:**159
   lack of filial piety, **3:**86
   land, **4:**1
   marriage, **4:**156
   sale
      of a free person by consent, **3:**469
      of land, **5:**186
      of relatives, **3:**469
   status, **5:**358
   theft, **5:**458
Northern Wei dynasty
   collective liability, **2:**58, 59, 61
   partnerships, **4:**287
   use of the cangue, **1:**345
Northern Zhou, **1:**421
North Frederic, **5:**341
North German Confederation, **2:**121
Northwest Ordinance (U.S., 1787), **1:**224; **3:**427;
      4:488; **6:**39
   on slavery, **5:**259–260, 262
Norway. *See also* Scandinavia
   legislation in, **4:**91
   union with Sweden, **5:**416, 417
Norwegian Code (1687), **2:**328
Notae Pauli, **5:**149
Notae solemnes (Du Moulin), **2:**372
Notae Ulpiani, **5:**149
notaries, **4:236–239,** *237*
   ancient Rome, **2:**391
   Byzantine, **1:**333
   in Chinese Republic, **1:**440
   Egypt
      Greek law on, **1:**144
      Hellenistic period, **2:**414
   Islamic law, **4:**73
   on law merchant, **4:**38
   medieval and post-medieval Roman,
      5:193
   in Quebec, **1:**342
Notes on the State of Virginia (Jefferson),
      5:262
Nottingham, Heneage Finch, Earl of, **6:**13
   on equity and conscience, **2:**469–470
   on mortgage redemption, **4:**189
Noumea Accord (New Caledonia, 1998),
      4:173, *173*
Nourse, Timothy, **5:**30
Nova methodas discendae docendaeque jurisprudentiae
      (Leibniz), **4:**100
Novel (Constantine IX), **1:**333
Novel (Irene), **4:**416

novel disseisin, writ of, **3:**75; **4:**11, 87, 315–316; **5:**70, 71
    estates doctrine and, **2:**477
    in Ireland, **3:**307
Novellae (Constitutiones) (laws of Justinian)
    Accursius, Franciscus, on, **1:**19
    by Justin II, **1:**282
    by Leo VI, **1:**282
    Macedonian Renaissance on, **1:**282
    by Tiberius, **1:**282
    use in medieval teaching of law, **2:**6
Novellae posttheodosianae (post-Theodosian Novels), **1:**327
novels *(novellae constitutiones)*, **3:**212
Novgorodtsev, P. I., **5:**178
Novikov, Nikolay I., **5:**172
Novísima Compilation (Spain, 1804), **1:**215
    applicability in Spanish Chile, **1:**397
Novísima recopilación (Spain, 1805), **5:**326
NOW. *See* National Organization for Women
NOW Legal Defense and Education Fund, **6:**144
noxal liability
    in Byzantine law, **2:**325
        in delict, **2:**325
    in Roman law, **6:**77
        in delict, **2:**323, 324
NRA. *See* National Recovery Administration
Nri kingdom, **1:**70
Nītivākyāmrtam (Somadeva Sūri), **3:**364
nuclear power
    African contributions to policy on, **1:**107
    tort liability in, **4:**31
Nueva Recopilación de las Leyes Destos Reynos (Spain, 1567), **1:**384; **5:**325
    Philippines under, **5:**313
    South and Central America under, **5:**285
Nuevas Leyes de Indias (1542), **5:**291
    in Guatemala, **3:**130
Nuevas leyes Destos Reynos de las Indias, La (Spain, 1680), **1:**384
nuisance
    in English common law, **4:239–240**
        in easements, **2:**380, 381
        in environmental law, **2:**448, 449–450
    in environmental law
        India, **2:**452–453
        United States, **2:**454–455
numerus clausus
    easements and, **2:**381–382
Nur al-Din Mahmad, **3:**466

Nussbaum, Arthur, **3:**283
Nutrition Labeling and Education Act (U.S., 1990), **2:**178
Nyasaland, **1:**315
Nyāyavikāsinī, **4:**224
NYSE. *See* New York Stock Exchange
Nytt Juridiskt Arkif, **5:**416
Nzinga Mbemba, **1:**69, 79, *80*

O

oaths
    ancient Greece
        anthropological perspective on, **1:**186–187
        in Gortyn code, **1:**153
        by juries, **1:**233
    ancient Near Eastern law, **1:**170, 173
    Anglo-Saxon law, **1:**181
    Athens, **4:241–242**, 401–402
        evidence gained through, **3:**2
        jurors', **3:**3
        by witnesses, **3:**1
    canonical, **3:**8
    English common law
        evidence in, **3:**4
        as *judicium Dei*, **4:**262, 263
        religious opposition to, **3:**6
        serjeants at law, **5:**222
        in Star Chamber, **5:**346
    Roman law, **4:**83
Objectives Resolution (Pakistan, 1949), **5:**308
obligatio, **2:**186, 188
Obligationenrecht (Switzerland, 1911)
    on breach of contract, **1:**308, 309
    on error and mistake, **2:**476
obligations, **4:242–245**
    Baius on, **3:**251
    in easements, **2:**380
    English common law, **4:242–243**
        in land leases, **4:**12
    French law, **3:**98
    Islamic law, **4:244**
        duty, **2:**376–377
        legal personality and, **4:**64
    medieval and post-medieval Roman law, **4:245**
    Roman law, **2:**181
        school disputes over, **3:**476–477
Obligationsrecht (Savigny), **5:**195
Obscene Publications Act (U.K., 1857), **1:**381

Obscene Publications Act (U.K., 1959), **1**:381
obscenity
    freedom of speech and, **5**:333, 335
    regulation of in the United Kingdom, **1**:380–381
Observationes (Cujas), **2**:303
Observationes et emendationes (Cujas), **2**:303
Observationes tumultuariae (Bynkershoek), **4**:226
Observationes tumultuariae novae (Pauw), **4**:226
Ocakutta, Samana Manaskara, **3**:49
occupational choice, freedom of, **2**:428–429
Occupational Safety and Health Act (U.S., 1970), **3**:484
Occupational Safety and Health Administration (OSHA), **3**:484
    creation of, **1**:29; **5**:82
    scientific research under, **4**:30
Ocko, Jonathan K., **2**:193
O'Connor, Sandra Day, **3**:268
    on abortion, **4**:389–390; **6**:141
    on affirmative action, **2**:343, 344
    on federalism, **3**:64, 65
    on gender-based affirmative action, **2**:340
    on general welfare clause, **3**:115
    Supreme Court appointment of, **6**:55
Odovacar. *See* Ottokar (Ostrogoth ruler)
Odyssey (Homer)
    on adultery, **1**:50–51
    on communal order, **2**:123
    on family, **3**:28
    on heterosexual morals, **5**:226
    on inheritance, **3**:228
    on judges and trials, **3**:401
    on marriage, **4**:152
    on procedure, **1**:152
    on slavery, **5**:243–244, 244, 355
    on social and urban life, **1**:137
    on theology of law, **5**:111
OECD, anticorruption legislation and, **3**:289
Oedipus at Colonus (Sophocles), **4**:242
Oekolampadius, Johannes, **1**:350
OEO. *See* Office of Economic Opportunity
Oertmann, Paul, **4**:277
Oeuvres complètes (Domat), **2**:357
Oeuvres de Pothier (Bugnet), **4**:367
Offa, codification by, **1**:177

Offence of Zina (Enforcement of Hudood) Ordinance (Pakistan, 1979), **2**:279; **4**:299
Offences against the Person Act (U.K., 1861), **3**:178
    on assault, **1**:227
    on kidnapping and abduction, **3**:470
offenses against the state, **4**:246–260
    in ancient Greece, **4**:246–248
    in Chinese law
        overview, **4**:249–250
        damaging the efficiency of government, **4**:253–255
        disrespect *(bujing)*, **4**:250–252
        heterodox beliefs, **4**:252–253
        threatening the life or well-being of the emperor, **4**:255–256
        threatening the safety of the state or dynasty, **4**:256–258
offenses in Chinese law, classification of, **4**:259–260
Office of Economic Opportunity (OEO), **1**:29
    legal-services programs, **4**:52, 370, 371
Office of Management and Budget (OMB)
    administrative agency review by, **1**:30
    environmental law and, **2**:457
Office of Price Administration, **1**:28
official secret, notion of, **1**:381
Officium (ecclesiastical court), **2**:386
Of the Law of Nature and Nations (von Pufendorf). *See De iure naturae et gentium libri octo* (von Pufendorf)
Ohlin, Lloyd, **4**:32
oikeus, Code of Gortyn on, **3**:121
Oikonomikos (Xenophon), **3**:31
oikos (household), **3**:27, 28
    legitimate children in, **3**:30, 31
    Solon on, **3**:30
Oil Rivers Protectorate, **1**:86
Okamatsu, Santaro, **1**:45
Old Age Assistance (U.S.), **6**:96
Oldenbarnevelt, Johan van
    Grotius, Hugo, and, **3**:127
Oldendorp, Johann, **4**:260–261
Older Americans Act, **2**:424
Older and Younger Anonymus. *See* Enantiophanes
oligarchy in ancient Greece, **2**:125; **4**:86
Oliphant, Herman, **1**:15; **4**:74, 75
Olivecrona, Karl, **5**:417
Ollennu, N. A., **1**:73

Omani sultanate, **2:**42
   constitution, **3:**317
   Ibadis in, **3:**348, 349
   shari'a as principal source of legislation in, **3:**317
Omar (caliph, d. 644), **1:**120
ombudsman, **1:**128
   Sweden, **5:**416
On Behalf of Euxenippus (Hyperides), **1:**55, 475
On Buildings (Procopius), **3:**454
On Crimes and Punishments (Beccaria), **2:**289
On Laws (Cicero), **1:**475
On Liberty (Mill), **3:**110
"On Paederasty" (Bentham), **3:**110
"On the Crown" (Demosthenes), **1:**141; **3:**125
On the Different Forms of Insanity in Relation to Jurisprudence (Prichard), **3:**247
On the Law of Nature and of Nations (von Pufendorf). *See De iure naturae et gentium libri octo* (von Pufendorf)
On the Laws and Customs of England (attr. Bracton)
   common law character in, **2:**436
   on customary law, **2:**305
   on natural law, **4:**214
On the Laws and Customs of the Realm of England (Glanville), **3:**177
On the Murder of Eratosthenes (Lysias), **4:**112
On the Mysteries (Andocides), **2:**30
   on *graphē paranomōn*, **3:**123
On the Orators (Cicero), **1:**475
On Truth (Antiphon), **5:**22
Opera, quae de jure fecit in hunc usque diem (Cujas), **2:**303
Opera omnia (Amerbach), **3:**191
Opera omnia (Cujas), **2:**303
Opera omnia (Zasius), **6:**160
Opera posteriora (Cujas), **2:**303
Opera postuma Cuiacii (Cujas), **2:**303
Opera priora (Cujas), **2:**303
Opiniones (under the name Ulpian), **5:**151
opium, Chinese law on, **1:**119
Opium Wars, **3:**92
Oppenheim, Lawrence, **3:**284
Oppression of Women and Children (Special Enactment) Act (Bangladesh, 1995), **4:**300
Optatus, Aristius, **2:***419*
option *(khiyār)*, **4:261–262**
Opuscoli di diritto criminale (Carrara), **1:**372
Opuscula (Gravina), **3:**126

Opus tripartitumiuris consuetudinarii (von Werböczy), **3:**194
Orange Free State, **1:**86
Oration against Timarchus (Aeschines)
   on homosexual behavior, **5:**228
Orationes (Gravina), **3:**126
orationes in Imperial Rome, **3:**211
orators, in ancient Roman courts, **2:**391–392
Ordal, **1:**178
ordeal
   Africa, precolonial, **1:**66
   Agobard of Lyon on, **3:**8
   ancient Greece, **1:**186–187
   ancient Near Eastern law, **1:**170
   Anglo-Saxon law, **1:**178, 181–182
   English common law, **2:**435; **4:262–263**
      evidence in, **3:**4
   evidence from, **3:**4, 9
   Inca law, **5:**289
   Ireland, **3:**307
   Nepal, **4:**224
Ordenações (Portugal), **1:**302
Ordenações Alfonsinas (Portugal, 1446), **5:**301
Ordenações de Reino (Portugal), **5:**301
Ordenações Filipinas (Portugal)
   on slaves, **5:**254
   South and Central America under, **5:**285, 293
Ordenações Manuelinas (Portugal, 1521), **5:**301
Ordenações Reais (Portugal), **5:**301
Ordenamiento de Alcalá de Henares (Spain, 1348)
   in colonial law, **5:**290, 298
   on royal law, **5:**325
Ordenamiento de Alcalá de Nehares (Spain, 1348), **1:**215
Ordenanzas de Bilbao (Spain, 1737), **5:**325
Ordenanzas Reales de Castilla (Spain, 1484), **5:**290
Order of the Coif. *See* serjeants at law
Ordinance of 1311 (England), **1:**386
Ordinance of Labourers. *See* Statute of Labourers (England, 1349–1351)
Ordinance of Montils-lès-Tours (France, 1454), **3:**98
Ordinance of Vâsteras (Sweden, 1527), **1:**349–350
Ordinances of the Jews (England, 1194), **1:**270
Ordinationes Livoniae (Livonian Regulations) (1589, 1598, 1609), **1:**255

Ordin-Nashchokin, Afanasii L., **5:**177
"Ordnung eines gemeinen Kastens" (Luther), **1:**349
Ordo digestorum, **2:**304
Ordo iudiciarius, **4:**433
Ordonance de la Marine (Spain, 1681), **5:**325
Ordonance du Commerce (Colbert), **5:**325
Ordonanzas von Bilbao (1737), **4:**150–151
Ordonnance civile of Louis XIV (France, 1667), **4:**362
Ordonnance Civile touchant la Réformation de la Justice (France, 1667), **2:**47; **4:**92, 434
Ordonnance concernant les Substitutions (France, 1747), **2:**47
Ordonnance concernant les Testaments (France, 1735), **2:**47
Ordonnance Criminelle (France, 1670), **2:**47
Ordonnance de la Marine (France, 1681), **1:**36; **2:**47; **3:**258
Ordonnance du Commerce (France, 1673), **2:**47, 92
Ordonnance of St. Germain-en-Laye (1670), **4:**439
Ordonnances
   commentaries on, **4:**39–40
   legislation and, **4:**91–92
Ordonnances sur les Donations (France, 1731), **2:**47
Oresteia (Aeschylus)
   on adultery, **1:**50
   on law, **4:**111
Organic Act (U.S. Virgin Islands, 1936), **1:**370
Organic Charter of the Portuguese Colonial Empire (1933), **2:**384
Organic Law (Portugal, 1953), **1:**80
Organisation for Economic Cooperation and Development (OECD), **3:**289
Organization for the Harmonization of Business Law in Africa (OHBLA), **2:**115
Organization of the Islamic Conference, **3:**281
Oriental Republic of Uruguay. *See* Uruguay
originalism, conservative, **2:**164–165, 165
   Bork, Robert, and, **2:**165–166
Origines (Gravina), **3:**126
Originum iuris civilis libri tres (Gravina), **3:**126
Orlando, Vittorio Emanuele, **1:**23
Ormonde, first duke of (James Butler), **3:**310–311
Ørsted, Anders Sandøe, **2:**328
Ortiz, Tomás, **4:**16
Orto, Obertus de, **3:**78
Osadamegaki (Japan), **3:**371
Osborne, Thomas (Lord Danby), **1:**386

Oscar I (Sweden), **5:**416
Ose Tutu, **1:**68
OSHA. *See* Occupational Safety and Health Administration
Osman, **4:**263, 264
Ostrogoths
   end of rule by, **3:**117
   Germanic provincial administration under, **3:**115
Oswald, Lee Harvey, **4:**335
Other America, The (Harrington), **2:**423–424
Otis, James, **3:**424, 447
   on writs of assistance, **5:**203
Ottokar (Ostrogoth ruler), **4:**351
Ottoman Civil Code (Majalla or Mecelle) (1877), **2:**397; **3:**344; **6:**16
   on breach of contract, **2:**201
   definition of contract, **2:**202
   on duress, **2:**375
   use in twentieth century in Arab countries, **2:**35
Ottoman Commercial Code (1850), **2:**74; **6:**16
Ottoman Criminal Code (1911), **6:**17
Ottoman Empire (1453–1922)
   administrative decrees in, **1:**34–35
   Balkan peninsula in, **1:**251–253
   codification under, **2:**34–36 (*See also specific codes*)
   constitutions, **2:**36, 135
   courts, **2:**397–398; **3:**414; **4:**264–265, 266, 267
      market courts, **2:**35
      mazalim courts, **2:**35
      reorganization of, **4:**267–268
   enforcement in, **2:**433
   France and, **3:**283
   Hanafi school in, **3:**344
   Islamic law in, **4:263–270; 6:**14–15, 16, 17
   Islamic taxation, **5:**435
      millet system, **4:**234
   judiciary, **3:**419–420, 421, 422; **4:**73, 264–265, 267–268
      education of, **4:**72
   legal education, **2:**397–398
   legal professions, **4:72–73**
   modern commercial law, **2:**74–75
   Muallimhane-i nüvvab la school, **3:**344
   muftis in, **3:**58
   non-Muslims in, **4:**234
   personal status law, **4:**293, 295
   recognition as member of the society of nations, **3:**283

Tanzimat reforms and codification, **2**:34
women in, **6**:128–129
Ottoman Family Laws Ordinance (1917), **6**:17
Ottoman Land Code (1858), **6**:16
Ottoman Law of Family Rights (1917), **3**:344; **5**:129; **6**:16, 129
Ottoman Maritime Code (1863), **6**:16
Ottoman Penal Code (1840), **6**:16
Ottoman Penal Code (1858), **6**:16
Ottoman Reform Rescript of 1856, **5**:435
Ottomans in Yemen, **6**:156–157
outlawry, **4**:270–272, 420
Outlines of Historical Jurisprudence (Vinogradoff), **1**:185
ouvidor, **5**:300–301
Overend, Gurney crash (1866), **1**:267, 272
Oviedo, Gonzalo Fernández de, **4**:16
ownership *(milk)*, **4**:272
Oxford University
educational reforms at, **2**:395–396
legal education at, **2**:393–394
mortmain and, **4**:192, 193
Oxyrhynchus papyrus, **2**:414
Oyo empire, **1**:68, 75

P

Pace, Giulio, **3**:191
Pacific Islanders Protection Acts (1872, 1875), **4**:173
Pact of ʿUmar, **4**:234; **6**:86
pacts, recognition of in Roman law, **2**:187, 189
Pactus Legis Salicae, **3**:117
Pacuvius Labeo. *See* Labeo, Pacuvius
Padoux, Georges, **5**:315
Pagan empire (Burma), **1**:317, 318
Pahlavi Civil Code (Iran, 1979), **4**:296
Paine, Thomas, **3**:447–448
Pakistan. *See also* Parsi law; South Asian law
alcohol and drugs, **1**:123
Anglo-Hindu law, **3**:159
Bangladesh as province of, **1**:257–258
banking and finance, **1**:260, 262
British law in, **3**:445
British nationality and, **4**:206
capital punishment of juveniles, **3**:462
codes and codification, **2**:38
Islamic penal law, **2**:39
Islamization, **2**:39
constitutional law, **2**:141–143; **3**:317
courts
constitutional court, **2**:136
Shariat Federal Court, **2**:142
criminal law, **2**:279
death penalty, **1**:368
divorce, **2**:352
family law reform, **2**:38
Imāmī school in, **3**:340
inheritance law, **2**:38
Islamic law, **5**:306, 308–309
shariʿa as principal source of legislation in, **3**:317
Islamization, **6**:130
legal education, **2**:398
military regime, **2**:135
non-Muslims in, **4**:234–235
partition, **1**:314
personal status laws, **4**:299–300; **6**:129
secular laws, **4**:273–275
zakat in, **5**:431
Palestine. *See also* ancient Near Eastern law
adoption in, **1**:48
Hamas in, **1**:207
Paley, William, **1**:108
on agency, **1**:109
Pali Chronicles, **5**:338
Palingenesia iuris civilis (Lenel), **5**:160
Palles, Christopher, **3**:312
Palmer, A. Mitchell, **4**:337
Palmer Raids (1919–1920), **3**:208
Pan-African Parliament, **1**:107
Panama, **1**:398
Pancasila, **4**:275–276
panchayat
in India, **2**:146
Nepal, **4**:225
Panday, Basdeo, **6**:11
Pandectae Justinianae in novum ordinem digestae (Pothier), **4**:366
Pandectes du droit Français (Charondas), **3**:99
Pandectists. *See also* Dernburg, Heinrich; Jhering, Rudolf von; *Pandektenwissenschaft*; Puchta, Georg Friedrich; Windscheid, Bernhard
on assignment, **1**:228
Brazilian law and, **1**:304
on breach of contract, **1**:307, 308
on delay, **2**:320–321
Denmark, **2**:328
on error and mistake, **2**:475–476
influence in Italy, **3**:359

Jhering on, **3:**399
  on liability, **6:**78
  on succession, **5:**391, 394
  on systematization, **5:**421–422
Pandects (Pandectae)
  on agency, **1:**110
  on appurtenancy, **2:**380
  Azo on, **1:**248
  Baldus de Ubaldis, Petrus, on, **1:**250
  Bartolus of Saxoferrato on, **1:**280, 281
  Christianity in, **5:**125
  commentary on Praetorian Edict, **3:**430
  content of, **6:**24
  on credit, **2:**262
  historiographic work in, **5:**158
  on legal reasoning, **4:**79
  Macedonian Renaissance on, **1:**282
  on maritime law, **1:**35
  Mommsen, Theodor edition of, **5:**160
  Noodt, Gerard, on, **4:**235–236
  Paul's influence on, **4:**290, 291
  pledge rulings in, **4:**328
  Pothier, Robert Joseph on, **4:**366
  publication of, **3:**456
  on purpose of law, **1:**330
  Roman law differences in, **5:**162
  Sabinus, Masurius, in, **5:**179
  on Servius Sulpicius Rufus, **5:**225
  source of, **6:**23
  on the source of law, **1:**328
  study of, **4:**276–278
  Theophilus and, **6:**8
  Tribonian and, **6:**7–9
  on unjust enrichment, **6:**64
  on usury, **6:**70
  Voet, Johannes, commentary on, **4:**226
Pandektenwissenschaft, **2:**9, 10; **3:**118; **4:276–278.** *See also* Pandectists
  codification and, **2:**48
  Windscheid, Bernhard, in, **6:**107–108
Pang Juan, **4:**196–197
Pangkor, Treaty of (1874), **4:**138; **5:**323
Paniagua, Fernando Jiménez, **5:**291
Panopticon, **1:**287
Pantainetos, **4:**415
pao chia. *See* collective liability
papacy. *See* pope and papacy
Papal Curia, **1:**466
Papal Register, **2:**316
Papers Relative to Codification (Bentham), **2:**46

Papinian (Aemilius Papinianus), **3:**212, 435, 436; **4:278–280; 6:**23
  on agency, **1:**319
  on formula, **3:**95
  influence of, **1:**333
  on legal reasoning, **4:**81
  Paul and, **4:**290
  on women, **6:**117
Papirius, **5:**141
Papirius Iustus, **3:**213
Pappadakis bronze, **3:**229
Papua and New Guinea Act (Papua New Guinea, 1949), **4:**280
Papua New Guinea, **4:280–281.** *See also* Melanesia
  independence of, **4:**174
papyrology, **1:**144; **2:**412–413, 417–421
  on ancient Near Eastern law, **1:**167
  anthropology and, **1:**186
  on Hellenistic law, **1:**157
  in scholarship, **1:**162
  scholarship on, **1:**165
  on sources of Greek law, **1:**146, 147–148
Paradoxa (Alciati), **1:**118
Paraguay, **4:281, 281–282**
  Civil Code, **1:**398
  Jesuit reductions in, **5:**300
Parakramabahu I (Burma), **5:**304
Parallelon Rerum Publicarum de Moribus Ingenioque Populorum Atheniensium, Romanorum, Batavorum (Grotius), **3:**127
Parameswara, **4:**137
paraphernalia, **6:**123
  Egypt Hellenistic period, **2:**415
  medieval and post-medieval Roman law, **3:**43
Parāśara, **3:**156
Paratitla in L libros digestorum (Cujas), **2:**304
paratitle style, **2:**400
pardon. *See also* amnesty in Chinese law
  Draco on, **2:**366
  English common law, **3:**179
parental authority in United Kingdom, **1:**394
Paris, Treaty of (1783), **2:**148; **3:292**
  British colonies in, **1:**86
  French colonies in, **1:**88
  supremacy clause and, **5:**411
  United States and, **3:**291
Paris, Treaty of (1951), **2:485**
Paris Convention (1989), **3:**263
Paris Convention for the Protection of Industrial Property (1883), **3:**265, 271

Paris Convention on Means of Protection against Unfair Commercial Use of Goods and Services (1883), **2:**103
Parisio, Pietro Paolo, **5:**364
Paris Peace Agreement (1991), **1:**335, *336*
Paris Peace Treaty of 1856, **3:**283
Parivara, **5:**302
Park, James, **2:**441
Park, James Allan, **3:**253
Parker, Isaac, **1:**12
Parker, Thomas (Lord Macclesfield), **4:**41
Parks, Rosa, **2:**341
Parlement of Paris, **2:**7
Parliament (Australia), **1:**240–241, *241*, 242–243
Parliament (England), **4:**282–286, *283*
   appellate jurisdiction, **1:**197–198
   beginning of as separate institution, **2:**128
   Coke, Edward, and, **2:**55–56
   and direct taxation, **2:**129
   legislation under, **4:**87–90
     as source of law, **5:**276–277
   legislative power of, **4:**96
   Long Parliament, **2:**131
   on monopolies, **4:**187
   Reformation Parliament of 1529–1536, **2:**129
   Rump Parliament, **2:**130
   Scotland, **5:**198–199, *199*, 201
Parliament (Ireland), **3:**309–310
   abolition of, **3:**311
Parliament (Maldives), **4:**140
Parliament Act (U.K., 1911, 1949), **2:**132; **4:**285
   on legislation rejection, **4:**90
parliamentary systems
   in Canada, **1:**338–339
   Germany under National Socialist law, **3:**110
Parmensis, Bernardus, **2:**222
parricide
   Chinese law, **3:**84–85
   Roman law, **2:**271
Parrino, Sandra, **2:***335*
Parsee Immovable Property Act (Act IX) (1837), **4:**286
Parsee Intestate Succession Act (1865), **4:**286
Parsee Marriage and Divorce Act (1865), **4:**286
Parsi law, **4:**286–287
Parsi Marriage and Divorce Act (India, 1865), **4:**287

Parsi Marriage and Divorce Act (India, 1936), **3:**49; **4:**287
Parsi Marriage and Divorce (Amendment) Act (India, 1988, 1998), **4:**287
Parsons, Talcott, **4:**48
Parsons, Theophilus, **2:**205, 208
Part B States (Laws) Act (India, 1951), **3:**222
Partial-Birth Abortion Act (U.S., 2003), **6:**141
Partnership Act (India, 1932), **3:**216
Partnership Act (U.K., 1890)
   on agency, **1:**115
partnerships, **1:**320; **4:**287–290
   ancient Greek law, **2:**71, 180
   Brazil, **1:**304
   Chinese law, **4:**287–288
   common-law, **1:**320
   English law merchant on, **4:**36
   Gaius on, **2:**183
   Islamic law, **1:**262–263
     commercial societies in, **4:**288–290
     legal personality in, **4:**64–65
     loans and, **4:**119
     obligations and, **4:**244
     silent partnership, **2:**73
   limited liability, **1:**115
   medieval and post-medieval Roman law, **1:**111
   Middle Ages, **2:**93
     land-based businesses, **2:**95
     in maritime business, **2:**94–95
   one-partner private limited-liability company, **2:**96
   precursor of corporation, **2:**87
   Roman law, **1:**319; **2:**184, 185, 186
     under Justinian, **2:**189
     Labeo, Marcus Antistius, on, **3:**475–476
     lex Irnitana on, **4:**104
     Sabinus, Masurius, on, **5:**180
   sleeping partners, **2:**87
   United States, **1:**112
     agency in, **1:**114–115
Party Processions Act (Ireland, 1832), **3:**313
Pascal, Blaise, **2:**356
Pashtunwa, **1:**59
Pashukanis, Evgenii B., **5:**178
Pasicles, **4:**457
Pasion, **4:**457
Passagerii, Rolandinus, **4:**237–238
Patanjali, **3:**152
Patel, Vallabhbhai, **5:**398

Patent Act (U.S., 1952), **3:**270
Patent and Trademark Office, **3:**269, 270
Patent Cooperation Treaty (1970), **3:**263, 271
patent law
    Burma, **3:**264
    in France, **3:**259
    Germany, **3:**260
    Indonesia, **3:**263
    Laos, **3:**264
    Malaysia, **3:**263
    monopolies and, **4:**187
    in Philippines, **3:**261
    Philippins, **3:**262
    in Southeast Asia, **3:**261–262
    Thailand, **3:**264
    United States, **4:**30
    United States law, **3:**268–271
        history of, **5:**77
Patent Office. *See* Patent and Trademark Office
Patents Act (New Zealand, 1870), **4:**228
paterfamilias
    in family, **3:**40
    guardianship and, **3:**47
Paterson, William
    on banking, **1:**271
    on property, **4:**489
    on takings, **5:**423
"Path of Law, The" (Holmes), **2:**25–26
patria potestas, **6:**117–118
    medieval and post-medieval Roman law, **3:**45
    wilāa as, **3:**37
patriarch of Constantinople, **1:**347
Patricius, **2:**392
Patterson, Dennis, **4:**365
Paul (Iulius Paulus), **3:**251, 435, 436; **4:**290–292
    on custom, **2:**167
    decreta, **3:**212
    on delict, **2:**324
    on duress, **2:**376
    on fetuses, **3:**44
    on fraud, **3:**102
    on Labeo, Marcus Antistius, **3:**475
    on legal reasoning, **4:**79, 81
    on maritime law, **4:**148
    on Sabinus, Masurius, **5:**179
Paul, Alice, **6:***135*
Paula, Julia Cornelia, **4:**290
Paul III (Pope), **5:**300
Paul IV (Pope), **5:**364

Paulus, Christoph G., **3:**250
Paulus, Iulius. *See* Paul
Paulus de Castro, **2:**111
Paul VI (pope), **1:**354
Pausanias
    on Helots, **5:**245
    on religious offenses, **4:**247
Pauw, Wilhelmus, **4:**226
pawn banks, **1:**273
    African indigenous laws on, **1:**73
    ancient Near Eastern law, **1:**174
    China, **2:**331
pawnbrokers
    China
        loans from, **4:**118
        in sale of land, **5:**186, 187
    medieval, **1:**274
"pay on death" designations, **3:**239
Peace, Amity, and Commerce, Treaties of (Japan, 1858), **3:**365, 372, 373
Peace of God movement, **5:**31, 32
Peace Preservation Law (Japan, 1925), **3:**377
Peacock, Barnes, **2:**283
peasant laws in Baltic nations, **1:**254
Peblis, John de, **5:**198
Peck, Pieter, **4:**151
Peckham, John. *See* John Peckham
Peckham, Rufus W.
    on antitrust, **1:**189
    classical legal theory and, **2:**25
    on due process, **2:**259
peculium, **1:**320
    slaves and, **5:**248–249
Peddler, John, **1:**240
pederasty, ancient Greek law, **5:**228; **6:**114
Pedro de Córdoba, **4:**16
Pedro I (Brazil)
    independence under, **1:**302
Pedro II (Brazil), **5:***292*
Peel, Robert
    on banking, **1:**272
    on capital punishment, **4:**41
    on income tax, **5:**428
    on jury service, **3:**439–440
Peinliche Halsgerichtsordnung (Penal Capital Court Ordinance) (Holy Roman Empire, 1532)
    on bodily injury, **2:**264
    on guilt, **3:**133
Peinlicher sächsischer Inquisitions- und Achtsprocess (Carpzov), **1:**371

Peira (Eustathios), **1:**333
 on contract, **2:**192
 on delict, **2:**325–326
 on succession, **5:**376
Peirce, Leslie, **6:**129
Peisistratus, **5:**275
"Pei tian qiyue" (Compensation-for-Land Contracts), **5:**188
Pelagius I (pope), **2:**318
Pellegrini, Bartolomeo Francesco, **2:**360
Pellegrini, Marcantonio, **3:**80–81
Peloponnesian War (431–404), **1:**137, 232
 Helots in, **5:**328
Peltzman, Sam, **5:**83
Peñaforte, Raimundus de, **2:**222
"Penal Books" (Fan Xuanzi), **1:**404
Penal Code (Afghanistan, 1976), **1:**62
Penal Code (Argentina, 1883), **4:**282
Penal Code (Colombia, 1890, 1936), **2:**63
Penal Code (Ethiopia, 1930), **2:**479
Penal Code (Ethiopia, 1957), **2:**480
Penal Code (France, 1810), **3:**100
 on attempt, **1:**238
 on fraud, **3:**103
 on punishment, **5:**34
Penal Code (France, 1840), **3:**421
Penal Code (India, 1860), **2:**283
Penal Code (India, 1947), **2:**283
Penal Code (Japan, 1882), **3:**373
Penal Code (Pakistan, 1860), **4:**274–275
Penal Code (Pakistan, 1947), **2:**283
Penal Code (Paraguay, 1914), **4:**282
Penal Code (Peru, 1862), **4:**314
Penal Code (Poland, 1928), **4:**331
Penal Code (Poland, 1932), **4:**331
Penal Code (Poland, 1998), **4:**332
Penal Code (Amendment) Act (India, 1992), **2:**283–284
penal codes
 in Africa
  after independence, **2:**45
 in China, **1:**455–459
 Denmark, **2:**328
 United States, **6:**59–60
penal law
 adoption of Western style, in China, **1:**439
 Bentham, Jeremy, on, **1:**287
 Enlightenment on, **2:**444–445
 Islamic, Islamization and, **2:**39
 Ottoman Empire, **2:**35

 Sweden, **5:**416–417
 United States, **2:**84
 Zeiller, Franz von, and, **6:**163
"Penal Laws/Punishments Written on Bamboo Slips" (Deng Xi), **1:**404
penal law *versus* administrative law in China, **1:**408–409
penal servitude in Chinese law, **4:292–293**
 under Ming, **1:**431
 under Song, **1:**426
 under Tang, **1:**424
Penance of Jane Shore in St. Paul's Church, The (Blake), **2:***388*
Penitentiary Act (Great Britain, 1779), **5:**29
Penn, William, **2:**286
Pennsylvania Hospital for the Sick Poor, **4:**368
Pension Benefit Guaranty Corporation, **3:**484
pensions
 United States
  disabled veteran, **2:**334
  elderlaw and, **2:**423
Pentagon Papers, **3:**411
Pentateuch, **3:**389, 390
People's Code (Germany, 1942), **4:**395
People's Court (Athens), **1:**213
People's Democratic Republic of Yemen (PDRY), **6:**157
people's law. *See* folk law
People's National Congress (PNC, Guyana), **3:**138
People's Progressive Party (PPP, Guyana), **3:**137–138
People's Republic of China, **1:441–447**
 on counterrevolution as offense against the state, **4:**249–250
 notaries in, **4:**237
People's Republic of Kampuchea, **1:**335
Pepin, **4:**352
Peraldus, Guilelmus, **5:**230
Percy Commission. *See* Royal Commission on the Law relating to Mental Illness and Mental Deficiency
Pereira, Lafayette Rodrigues, **1:**302
Peresvetov, Ivan S., **5:**177
Pereyra, Juan de Solórzano, **1:**215–216; **5:**291
Pérez de Cuéllar, Javier, **1:***336*
Performers' Protection Acts (U.K.), **2:**217
Pericles
 on Areopagus jurisdiction, **1:**232

on citizenship, **3**:31; **4**:154, 247; **5**:356
on freedom of speech, **5**:330
on impiety, **5**:112
institutional reforms, **2**:124
as statesman, **5**:112
on women as citizens, **6**:113
Perioikoi (Sparta), **5**:327, 328
perjury
    ancient Near Eastern law, **1**:175
    Anglo-Saxon law, **1**:181
Perle, Linda, **4**:370
Perot, Ross, **4**:344
perpetuatio obligationis, **2**:319–320
perpetuities, rule against, **3**:238–239
Perry, Matthew, **3**:371
Persian Wars (490–479), **1**:137
personae–res–actiones (persons–objects–actions), **4**:245
personal *infamie*, **3**:248
personal injury
    Anglo-Saxon law, **1**:179
    Byzantine law, **2**:325–326
personality, principle of, **2**:109–110
    in Islamic law, **2**:136
personal law and general law, **4**:293–295
    Africa, **1**:102–104
    Bangladesh, **1**:259
    India
        codification of, **3**:148–149
        family law and, **3**:48
        Islamic, **5**:308
        reform, **3**:219
        secularism in, **5**:208–209
        Sikh, **5**:241
    Islamic
        India, **5**:308
        South Asia, **5**:307
    New Zealand, **4**:231
    Philippines, **5**:323
    Roman, **3**:96
Personal Responsibility and Work Opportunity Reconciliation Act (U.S., 1996), **4**:372; **6**:93–94
personal security contract, **2**:180
personal status law, **4**:295–302. *See also* repudiation (*Ṭalāq*); status
    Africa, precolonial, **1**:72
    ancient Near Eastern law, **1**:170–171
    codification in Egypt, **2**:35
    divorce and, **2**:352

    Islamic countries, **4**:295–299
    lawyers and, **4**:47
    in Maghrib and al-Andalus, **4**:130
    Muhammad Qadri Pasha al-Hanafi on, **4**:195
    Ottoman Empire, **4**:268–269
    South Africa, **5**:284
    South and Southeast Asia, **4**:299–302
    Southeast Asia, **5**:321
    women in, **6**:129
persons, **4**:302–313, *303, 307, 311*
    Byzantine law, **4**:309–310
    Gaius on, **3**:251
    Islamic law, **4**:311–313
    Roman law, **4**:302–309
Peru, **4**:*313*, 313–315
    slavery abolished in, **5**:255
Peruvian Civil Code, **1**:384
Pestel, Pavel I., **5**:178
Peter I the Great (Russia), **5**:170–171, 172, 173
    Leibniz, Gottfried Wilhelm, and, **4**:100
Petersdorff, Charles
    legal treatises by, **2**:441
    on mesne process, **4**:174
"Petition of Dionysia" (Egypt), **2**:420
Petition of Right (England, 1628), **2**:56, 130
    on legislative power, **4**:96
Petition of the Barons (1258), **4**:192
Petra, Pietro Antonio de
    on *fideicommissum*, **3**:80
Petrovsky-Sitnianovich, Samuil. *See* Polotskii, Simeon
Petrucci, Federicus, **1**:250
Petrus de Ancharano, **1**:250
pettifoggers, **4**:49
    China, **1**:195
petty assizes, **4**:315–318
Pfaff, Christoph Matthäus, **1**:351
Phaleas of Chalcedon, **2**:124
Pheidias, **5**:112
Philadelphia Convention. *See* Constitutional Convention (U.S.)
Philadelphia House of Refuge, **3**:458
Philip Augustus (Philip II) (France)
    on fiefs, **3**:98
    nationality under, **4**:205
Philip IV (France), **4**:353; **5**:32
Philip II (Spain), **6**:2
    and Central America, **1**:384
    law compilation under, **5**:291
    maritime law by, **4**:150

Philip III (Spain), **5:**293
Philip V (Spain), **5:**325
Philip (Filips) of Leiden, **4:**225
Philip of Macedon, **1:**136, 137
Philipp II (Hessian landgrave)
    Oldendorp, Johann, and, **4:**260–261
Philippine Independence Act (1934), **4:**319
Philippine Law of 1902, **4:**318
Philippines, **4:**318–320, *319*. *See also* Southeast Asian law
    Chinese law in, **5:**317–318
    colonial law in, **5:**313
    independence of, **5:**313
    intellectual property, **3:**261, 262, 263
    Islamic law in, **3:**338; **5:**323
    protection of traditional knowledge, **3:**264
Phillips, George, **1:**357
Philocrates, **3:**124–125
philoi (friends), **3:**27
Philo Judaeus, **3:**390
Philosophical Origins of Modern Contract Doctrine, The (Gordley), **2:**208
philosophy and law, ancient Greek, **4:**320–323, *322*
Philotheus, **5:**177
Phocas (Byzantine ruler), **4:**352
Phormion, **1:**54
Photios (Byzantine patriarch), **4:**352
Photius
    Eisagōgē and, **1:**282, 329
    on judicial organization, **2:**239
    on purpose of law, **1:**330, 331
Physiocrats on enlightened absolutism, **1:**8
Pickering, John, **4:**336
piepowder courts (England), **4:**36
Piermont, Strube de, **5:**172
Pierre de Belleperche (Petrus de Bella Pertica), **2:**111
Pierrepoint, Albert, **1:**366
Pietism, **1:**351
Pignatelli, Cardinal Antonio, **3:**126
pignus (pledge), **1:**320
    in mortgage, **4:**189–190
Pillet, Albert, **1:**353
Pillii, Tancredi, Gratiae libri de iudiciorum ordine, Göttingen (Bergmann), **4:**434
Piłsudski, Józef, **4:**331
Pinakes (Callimachus), **4:**124
Pinchot, Gifford, **2:**455
Pinckney, Charles, **3:**269
Pinckney, Charles Cotesworth, **5:**260
Pindar, **4:**494
Pineau, Christian, **2:***490*
Pinochet, Augusta, **1:**398
Piperata, Thomas de, **3:**9
piracy, British Commonwealth and, **1:**313
Pirhing, Ehrenreich, **1:**357
Pirus, Jan, **5:**339
Pisanelli, Giuseppe, **1:**372
Pithana (Labeo), **4:**290, 291
Pitman, Mary, **5:***406*
Pitney, Mahlon, **2:**25
Pitt, William (the Younger), **5:**428
Pittakus, **2:**30
Pius V (pope), **2:**224
Pius IX (pope), **1:**353
Pius X (pope), **4:**354
    Arduum sane munus (1904), **1:**353
    ecclesiastical courts under, **2:**386
Placcaten (Sri Lanka), **5:**340
Placentinus
    Azo compared with, **1:**248
    on possession, **4:**361
plain view exception, **5:**207
Plan for the Civil Government of Liberia (1824), **4:**107
Planned Parenthood League, **4:**388
Plant Varieties Act (Malaysia, 2004), **3:**263
Plant Varieties Act (Thailand, 1999), **3:**264
Planum Tabulare (Hungary), **3:**194
Plato. *See also Laws* (Plato); *Republic, The* (Plato)
    on adoption, **1:**40
    definition of law by, **4:**17, 21
    on family, **3:**31
    on forensic oratory, **4:**112
    on *graphē paranomōn*, **3:**123
    on guilt, **3:**134
    on Helots, **5:**245
    on homosexual behavior, **5:**228
    ideal law code by, **1:**162
    influence of Athenian law on, **1:**140
    influence on Philo Judaeus, **3:**390
    on justice, **3:**450
    on *nomos*, **1:**145
    on philosophy of law, **1:**148–149; **4:**321
    on property, **4:**456
    on punishment, **5:**22, 23, 42
    on rhetoric, **5:**134, 135
    on rule of law, **5:**164

Russian translation of the works of, **5**:177
on slavery, **5**:245
on Socrates, **5**:331
on sovereignty, **5**:352
on status, **5**:357
Platt, Anthony, **3**:460
Plautianus, **4**:278
Plautius, **4**:290; **5**:65
pleading, **4**:323–325. *See also* procedure
   ancient Greek law, **1**:151
   code, **1**:15
   England
      mesne process in, **4**:174–175
      paper, **2**:437
      serjeants at law in, **5**:221–222
      special, **2**:439
Pleas of the Crown (Hale), **2**:284, 440; **3**:178; **6**:2
Pleas of the Crown (Hawkins), **2**:284
pledge, **4**:325–329
   Chinese law, **4**:325–327
      land lease, **4**:6–7
      in loans, **4**:117–118
   contract of, **2**:186, 187, 189
   Islamic law *(rahn)*, **4**:327–328
   medieval and post-medieval Roman law, **4**:328–329
   in mortgage, **4**:189–190
   Roman law
      legis actiones in, **4**:83–84
Plees del Coron, Les (Staunford), **2**:440
Pliny the Younger, **2**:274; **3**:435
   as advocate, **1**:56
Plowden, Edmund, **4**:324
   law reporting by, **4**:44, 60
pluralism
   Africa, **1**:96–97
   definition of law and, **4**:19
   Egypt Hellenistic period, **2**:415
   in law and economics, **4**:27
   legal anthropology on, **4**:59–60
   South and Central America, **5**:297–302
   Sweden, **5**:414
Plutarch
   on adultery, **1**:52
   on dowry, **4**:154–155
   on family, **3**:29
   on *graphē paranomōn*, **3**:124
   on history of Rome, **4**:130
   on marriage, **4**:154
   on pronouncement by Lycurgus, **1**:156

on property, **4**:456
Russian translation of the works of, **5**:177
on Solon, **1**:148; **3**:30, 31; **5**:273, 275
on Sparta, **1**:143; **5**:327, 328, 329; **6**:115, 116
on volunteers in public cases, **4**:113
Pobedonostsev, Konstantin P., **5**:178
Poder Moderador (Brazil), **1**:302, 303
Podio, Orlandino de, **1**:271
poena extraordinaria, **3**:9
Poindexter, Joseph, **4**:180
Poinsett, Joel Robert, **1**:397
poison *(gu)*, **2**:59; **4**:329, **329–330**
poisoning in English common law, **3**:176
Pokora, Timoteus, **1**:407
Poland, **4**:330–332
   accession into European Union, **2**:492
   Baltic nations under, **1**:254–255
   constitution of 1791, **2**:120
   constitution of 1921, **2**:122
   constitutions of 1992 and 1997, **2**:122
   courts in, **2**:254
   feudal law in, **3**:79
   influence on Russian law, **5**:166
   witch trials, **6**:109
Polemon, **5**:274
Police and Criminal Evidence Act (U.K., 1984), **4**:424
Police and Judicial Co-operation in Criminal Matters, **2**:486–487
police powers
   Australia Aboriginal, **1**:3
   Germany, **4**:91
      under National Socialism, **4**:204
   identification procedures, **3**:16
   Islamic law, **2**:432, 433
   South Africa, **5**:281
   United States
      right to bear arms and, **1**:219
      in search and seizure, **5**:203–208
      state, **5**:351
Policing and Punishment in London, 1660–1750 (Beattle), **1**:364
Polish Civil Code, **1**:255
Politian (Angelo Ambrogini/Poliziano), **5**:158
Política Indiana (Pereyra), **1**:215–216; **5**:291
Political Constitutional Ordinance (Guyana, 1891), **5**:295

political crimes, **4:332–337**, *334*
   Roman law, medieval and post-medieval, **4:332–334**
   United States law, **4:334–337**
political dimension *(siyāsa Sharʿiyya)* of Islamic law, **4:337–338**
Political Ordinance (Holland, 1580), **1:**81
political parties and elections. *See also* elections
   Africa, **1:**98
      sub-Saharan, **1:**104
   in apportionment and reapportionment and, **1:**200–204
   Guyana, **5:**295
   Maldives, **4:**140
   Ottoman Empire, **4:**269
   United States, **4:338–345**, *340*, *341*
      state law on, **5:**350
Politics (Aristotle), **4:**321–323, 456
   on adoption, **1:**40
   comparative law in, **2:**97
   and constitutional law, **2:**123, 124
   critical of Plato, **2:**126
   on Greek city legal systems, **1:**149
   on kings, **2:**414
   positivist approach in, **1:**145
   on Sparta, **1:**142–143
Politique tirée de l'Écriture Sainte (Bossuet), **1:**8
Poliziano, Angelo, **3:**189. *See* Politician
Polk, James K.
   executive power under, **3:**20
   on general welfare clause, **3:**114
Pollock, Frederick (1783–1870)
   on academic law, **2:**443
   on contracts, **2:**442
   at Oxford, **2:**395
   on torts, **2:**442
Pollock, Frederick (1845–1937), **4:**358, 423; **5:**108
   on criminal procedure, **4:**423
   at International Congress of Comparative Law, **2:**99
   on sale, **5:**190
poll taxes
   equal protection and, **2:**463
   on non-Muslims, **4:**233
      in Mughal Empire, **2:**36
pollution. *See also* environmental law
   nuisance on, **4:**240
Pollution Control Boards (India), **2:**453
Polotskii, Simeon, **5:**177
Pol Pot, **1:**335; **5:**314

Polybius, **2:**126, 270–271
   on military history of Rome, **4:**130
polygamy
   Afghanistan, **1:**61
   Africa
      Ashanti, **1:**70
      indigenous law on, **1:**91–92
   Algeria, **4:**297
   ancient Near Eastern law, **1:**172
   Bangladesh, **4:**300
   East Timor, **2:**384
   India, **4:**170
      abolished, **3:**49
      divorce and, **2:**353
      Hindu law, **6:**133
   Indonesia, **4:**301
   Islamic law, **4:**164; **6:**126
   Jewish law, **3:**392
   Libya, **4:**297
   Madagascar, **1:**72
   Maldives, **5:**310
   Morocco, **4:**297
   Pakistan, **4:**299
   prohibition in modern codes, **2:**37
   Southeast Asia, **5:**318
   Syria, **4:**296
   Tunisia, **4:**296
   United States, **3:**52; **5:**116–117; **6:**44, 51
   Yemen, **4:**298
Polynesia, **4:345–347**
Pomeroy, John Norton
   code interpretation method, **2:**50
   as teacher, **1:**13
Pompey, **5:**225
Pomponius, Sextus, **5:**141; **6:**19–20, *20*
   historiographic work of, **5:**157–158
   on jurists, **3:**434, 436
   on Labeo, Marcus Antistius, **3:**475
   on legal reasoning, **4:**79, 81
   on Sabinus, Masurius, **5:**179
   unjust enrichment, **6:**64
Ponderationi sopra la contrattatione maritime (Targa), **4:**151
Ponte, Oldradus de, **5:**389
Pontiac cooperation of with British, **4:**207
pontiffs, **4:**79
Pontificale Romanum (1596), **2:**224
Poor Law (U.K., 1832), **4:**349
Poor Law Act (U.K., 1834), **4:**349
Poor Law Act (U.K., 1927), **4:**350

Poor Law Act (U.K., 1934), **4:**350
Poor Law Amendment Act (U.K., 1834), **4:**350
   on illegitimate children, **3:**35
poor laws in English common law, **4:**347–351, *350*
   illegitimate child and, **1:**394
Poor People's Campaign, **4:**337
Poor Relief Act (England, 1662), **4:**249, 348
poor-relief statutes (England), **1:**390
Poor Removal Act (Great Britain, 1795), **4:**349
Poor Removal Act (U.K., 1846), **4:**350
Pope, Alexander, **2:**131
   Mansfield, Lord, and, **4:**141
pope and papacy, **4:**351–355, *354*
   authority of, **5:**299
   bishops and archbishops under, **1:**294–296
   decretals, **2:**316–319
   ecclesiastical courts, **2:**385–386
   English ecclesiastical courts and, **2:**354
   on evidence, **3:**8
   legislation by, **4:**91
   Magna Carta and, **4:**135
   notary appointment by, **4:**238
   papal revolution and, **3:**79
   state sovereignty and, **5:**352
Popular Government (Maine), **4:**137
popular sovereignty
   due process and, **2:**368
   freedom of speech and, **5:**333
Populists, **5:**77, 88
Porius, Azo. *See* Azo
pornography
   censorship
      China, **4:**252
      United States, **3:**68
   feminist legal theory on, **3:**67–68
Portales, Diego, **1:**398
Porteous, Captain (John), **4:**142
Portia Law School, **2:**404
Portugal
   accession into European Union, **2:**490
   administrative law, **1:**24
   colonies, **5:**292–294
      African, **1:**69, 79–80
      East Timor, **2:**384
      Macau, **1:**447–448
      South and Central America, **5:**300–301
   community of shippers, **3:**257
   conflict of laws, **2:**113
   decolonization of African colonies, **1:**93–94
   Jews in, **3:**396–398
   on slavery, **5:**253–254
   slave trade abolished, **1:**75–76
positive law, **1:**238–239
positive morality. *See* folk law
positivism
   Austin, John, on, **1:**238–239
   Bentham, Jeremy, and, **1:**287
   Brazil, **1:**304
   classical legal theory and, **2:**24
   definition of law in, **4:**18–19
   international law and, **3:**283
   law of nations and, **3:**276–277
   on legislative power, **4:**99
   Maori law and, **4:**146
   South and Central America, **5:**286
   United States law, **4:**355–358
      business practices, **4:**452
      natural law and, **4:**215, 219
      natural law compared with, **4:**218
   Windscheid, Bernhard, in, **6:**108
Posner, Richard
   in Court of Appeals, **4:**27
   on Japanese internment, **3:**24
   on law and economics, **4:**25–26
   on regulations, **5:**83
   on statutory interpretation, **5:**362
Pososhkov, Ivan T., **5:**177
possession, **4:**358–362
   English common law, **4:**358–359
   Roman law, Medieval and post-medieval, **4:**360–362
   yad in Islamic law, **4:**359–360
   deposit and, **2:**332
Postan, M. M., **1:**291, 292
postmaster general, **1:**25
postmodernism and law, **4:**362–366, *364*
Post Office Savings Bank (England), **1:**272
Pothier, Robert Joseph, **2:**197; **4:**366–367; **5:**471; **6:**65
   on ancient law, **2:**357
   on fraud, **3:**104
   on joint liability, **2:**373
   on Roman law, **3:**99
   treatises by, **2:**442
   on vicarious liability, **6:**78
   on will theory, **2:**474
potlaches, **1:**344

Potthast, August, **2**:316
Pound, Ezra, **4**:335
Pound, Roscoe, **2**:26; **3**:428; **4**:355, 446
    comparative law, **2**:99
    on definition of law, **4**:18
    at Harvard, **1**:15
    in legal realism, **4**:74, 75
    on organic logical concept of law, **3**:432
    on social science, **5**:266
    on sociological jurisprudence, **2**:405
    on statutory interpretation, **5**:360, 361
poverty
    administrative agencies and, **1**:26
    birth control and, **6**:141–142
    "deserving" and "undeserving" poor, **6**:92–93, 95–96, 97
    elderlaw and, **2**:423–424
    feminist legal theory on, **3**:70–71
    legal aid and, **4**:51–52
    Native American, **4**:211
    social security and, **5**:270–271
    United States, **4**:367–374, *369*
        (*See also* welfare)
        health care and, **6**:97
        immigration and, **3**:207
    welfare and, **6**:91–98
Powell, Edward, **3**:4
Powell, J. J., **2**:441
Powell, Joseph, **2**:194
Powell, Lewis F., Jr.
    on the exclusionary rule, **4**:454
    on federalism, **3**:63
    on right to bear arms, **1**:220–221
    on social sciences, **5**:268
Powell, Thomas Reed, **4**:75
power of attorney
    agency and, **1**:113–114
    elderlaw and, **2**:424
Power of Attorney Act (U.K., 1882), **4**:273
Powers, Paul, **6**:148
Poynings, Edward, **3**:309
Practica (attr. Baldus), **1**:250
Practica actionum forensium (Oldendorp), **4**:261
Practical Treatise of the Law of Evidence (Starkie), **3**:5
Practical Treatise on the Law of Contracts (Chitty), **2**:204
Practica nova Imperialis Saxonica rerum criminalium (Carpzov), **1**:371
Practica offi cii inquisitionis (Gui), **4**:438

Practicks (Sinclair), **5**:199
praedial principle, **2**:381
Praetermissa (Alciati), **1**:118
praetor, office of, **2**:183
    in *legis actiones*, **4**:82
        Sabinus, Masurius, on, **5**:179, 180–181
    in the Senate, **5**:210–211
praetorian edict, **2**:183; **3**:211, 430–431; **4**:374–376, 464
    consolidation of, **2**:32
    on contracts, **2**:191
pragmatikoi (scribes), **2**:391
Prasad, Rajendra, **3**:*217*; **5**:398
Pratobevera, Carl Joseph, **6**:163
precedent, **4**:377–382
    Bangladesh, **1**:260
    Chinese law, **1**:460–462
        deposit, **2**:331
        Ming legal case collections, **1**:433
        under Song dynasty, **1**:457
        under Yuan dynasty, **1**:429
    doctrine of, **3**:163; **4**:377–380
    England
        common law, **5**:277–278
        equity and, **2**:469
    law reporting and, **4**:45
    Mansfield, Lord, on, **4**:142
    natural law and, **4**:214
    Nepal, **4**:225
    New Zealand, **4**:228
    originalism and U.S. constitution interpretation, **2**:165
    South Africa, **5**:279
    stare decisis, **4**:378–379, **380–382**
    in statutory interpretation, **5**:361
    use of doctrine in Quebec, **1**:341
Précis du droit des gens modernes de l'Europe fondé sur les traités et l'usage (Martens), **3**:283
predial servitude, **5**:223–224
Preemption Act (U.S., 1841), **5**:86
Pregnancy Discrimination Act (U.S., 1978), **2**:339; **6**:138
Prenatal Diagnostic Technique (Regulation and Prevention of Misuse) Act (India, 1994), **1**:5
Prescription Act (Great Britain, 1832), **2**:381
Presidential Commission on Competitiveness, **4**:446
President's Commission on the Status of Women, **6**:137
President's Committee on Urban Housing, **3**:182

press, freedom of the
    Brazil, **1:**302
    United States, **5:332–338; 6:**51
Press Act (Japan, 1875), **3:**376
press-ganging. *See* impressment
Prest, Wilfrid, **1:**58
Prevention of Cruelty to and Protection
    of Children Act (U.K., 1889), **3:**35
Prevention of Food Adulteration Act (India,
    1954), **2:**173
Prevention of Repression against Women and
    Children Act (Bangladesh, 2000),
    4:300
Price-Anderson Act (U.S., 1957), **4:**31
Prices Edict (Rome, 301), **3:**213
Prichard, James Cowles, **3:**247
Priests Courts (Indonesia), **3:**335, 336
Primero de Rivera, Miguel, **2:**122
Prime-Stevenson, Edward, **3:**111
Primitive Law (Diamond), **5:**108
Primo de Rivera, Miguel, **5:**326
primogeniture, **5:**382
    England, **2:**81
    feudal law, **3:**74
    United States, **5:**405
        in southern colonies, **3:**235
Primosecunda council (861), **1:**347
Prince of Wales's Council, **6:**100
Princess Sophia's Naturalisation Act. *See* Act
    of 1705 (England)
Principal Probate Registry (England), **6:**102
Principate (Rome), **5:**211
Príncipe, Portuguese colonies in, **1:**79
Principios de Derecho Civil (Somellera), **1:**216
Principles of European Contract Law, **2:**496
    on breach of contract, **1:**309
    on delay, **2:**320
    on donation, **2:**358
    on error and mistake, **2:**475
Principles of International Law (Bello),
    1:286
principles of law recognized by civilized nations as
    source of international law, **3:**278
Pringsheim, F., **2:**180
prior restraint, **5:**335
Priscus, Neratius, **1:**373
Prison Discipline Society, **4:**41
Prisons Act (U.K., 1877), **5:**29
prisons and imprisonment, **4:382–385**. *See also*
    punishment

    ancient Greece
        Athens, **4:382–383; 5:**23
        slaves in, **5:**244
    ancient Near Eastern law, **1:**175
    Chinese law, **4:383; 5:**49
    England, **5:**28–29
        as final process, **3:**88–89
    Europe, **5:**33–34
    India
        British India, **2:**283
        Delhi Sultanate, **2:**281
        fundamental rights in, **3:**107
        Mughal dynasty, **2:**282
    Islamic law, **4:383–385**
    reform movements on, **4:**41
    United States, **5:**38–39; **6:**50, 60
Prisot, John, **4:**377, 380
Pritchard, Thomas, **3:**82
Prithivinārāyana Śāha, **4:**224
privacy, **4:385–391**, *388*
    contraception and, **6:**141
    Indian fundamental right to, **3:**107
    Islamic law, **4:**385
    natural law on, **4:**219
    search and seizure and, **5:**206–207
    United States law, **3:**273–274; **4:385–391**
        due process and, **2:**369, 370, 371–372
        right to bear arms and, **1:**221
private government. *See* folk law
private international law
    history, **2:**109–115
    United States and, **3:284–290**
private justice. *See* folk law
private law, **4:391–397**
    administrative law compared with, **1:**22
    Baltic states, **1:**255, 256
    Bartolus of Saxoferrato on, **1:**281
    Brazil, **1:**302, 304
    classical legal theory on, **2:**23
    in Code of Gortyn, **3:**120–121
    Du Moulin, Charles, on, **2:**373
    England, **2:**438
    European union, **2:**493–496
    France, **3:**98
    Germany, **3:**118, 119
        under National Socialist law, **3:**110
    insolvency and, **3:**248
    Islamic law, **5:**19–20
        Europe, **2:**483–484
    legal realism on, **4:**76

medieval and post-medieval Roman
  on fraud, **3:**103–104
 South and Central America, **5:**286
 Sparta, **5:**328–329
 systematization into, **5:**421–422
 women in ancient Greece, **6:**113–114
private limited liability companies, **2:**94
Private Securities Litigation Reform Act
  (1995), **5:**95
privileges, **4:397–399**
 executive power and, **3:**22–23
 as protection of intellectual property in early modern
   period, **3:**259
 Watergate scandal and, **3:**11–12
Privileges and Immunities clause
 in Articles of Confederation, **1:**224
privilegium fori (privilege of jurisdiction)
 on bishops and archbishops, **1:**294
 ecclesiastical courts, **2:**385
Privilegium Sigismundi Augusti (Privilege of
  Sigismund August) (1561), **1:**254
Privy Council (Britain), **1:**386. *See also* Judicial
  Committee of the Privy Council
 Coke, Edward, and, **2:**55
 under Elizabeth I, **2:**129
 in Ireland, **3:**310
 jurisdiction of, **5:**15
 oversight of colonial judicial decisions, **2:**83
 Star Chamber and, **5:**345
probable cause, **5:**205
probate
 common *versus* solemn form, **6:**102
 England, **6:**102
  abolition of, **5:**429
  court created, **2:**355
  ecclesiastical law on, **2:**389
  introduction of, **5:**426–427
  jurisdiction of church courts, **1:**467
 United States, **3:**239; **5:**406, *406*
"Probe eines Commentars für das neue
  Oesterreichische bürgerliche
  Gesetzbuch" (Zeiller), **6:**163
"Problem of Social Cost, The" (Coase), **4:**24–25
"Problem of Unity of Greek Law, The" (Finley),
  1:163
pro bono service, **4:**53
procedure, **4:399–454,** *405, 409, 413, 421, 425, 443, 448, 452*
 administrative agencies in, **1:**28
 admiralty, **1:**39

Africa, **1:**100–101
ancient Greek law, **1:**136–137, 140
 anthropological perspective on, **1:**186–187
 Archaic, **1:**155–156
 archaic, **4:399–402**
 Athenian influence in, **1:**143
 Gortyn, **1:**142
 literature on, **1:**152–153
 in offenses against the state, **4:**247–248
 social importance of, **1:**144–145
 Solon on, **1:**155–156
in ancient Rome (*See cognitio* in ancient Roman law;
  formula in ancient Roman law)
 for contracts, **2:**182
Athens, **1:**233, 234–235; **4:**113–115
 no requirement for contracts, **2:**179
 overview, **4:402–411**
 trial procedure, **4:411–416**
Austria, **1:**246
Byzantine law, **4:416–417**
Chancery and, **1:**389
Chinese law
 appeal, **1:**193–195
 criminal and civil procedure, **4:417–418**
 parties and witnesses, **4:418–419**
 Western Zhou dynasty, **1:**402–403
Egypt
 Greek law in, **1:**144
 juristic papyrology on, **2:**418–419
England, **2:**435–436
 environmental law and, **2:**450
 evidence in, **3:**6
 Henry II on, **4:**87
 outlawry in, **4:**270–271
 reform of, **2:**437
 Star Chamber in, **5:**346–347
English common law
 civil procedure, **4:419–423**
 criminal procedure, **4:423–427**
Ethiopia, **2:**480
final process, **3:**87–89
Gaius on, **3:**251
Germany, **3:**118
Hindu law, **1:**223
India
 codification of, **5:**209
 Islamic, **5:**307–308
Islamic law, **4:427–431**
 acknowledgement in, **1:**19–20
 enforcement in, **2:**431, 432

forum, external and internal, **3**:97–98
    obligations and, **4**:244
legal education in, **2**:400
legal process on, **4**:66–67
medieval and post-medieval Roman law
    civil procedure, **4:431–435**
    criminal procedure, **4:435–440**
natural law in, **4**:216
Ottoman Empire, **4**:266, 267–268
Roman, **2**:273–274
Roman law
    in legislative assemblies, **4**:*94*, 94–95
    in *lex Irnitana*, **4**:103
Scotland, **5**:198
Sweden, **5**:417
United States
    administrative agencies and, **1**:31
    alternative dispute resolution, **1**:128–129
    civil procedure, **4:440–447**
    criminal procedure, **4:447–454**
Processus juris in foro Saxonico (Carpzov), **1**:371
Prochiron, **1**:281–282, 329
    on contract, **2**:192
    on delict, **2**:325
    on succession, **5**:376, 377
Proclamation of 1763 (Great Britain), **1**:315
Proclamation of Emergency (India, 1975), **2**:146
Procopius, **3**:454
proctors, **2**:388
Proculian school of jurists, **2**:392
    Celsus the Younger last known head of, **1**:373
    Labeo, Marcus Antistius, in, **3**:475, 476–477
    on legal reasoning, **4**:80
Proculus, **5**:179
products liability, **2**:177
profit
    England, **2**:380, 381
    in Islamic law, **4:454–455**
profiteering contracts. *See* usury
Programma del corso di diritto criminale (Carrara), **1**:372
Progressivism
    agricultural policy and, **5**:88–89
    business practices and, **4**:451
    on civil procedure, **4**:444–445
    and constitutional amendments, **2**:159
    consumer protection and, **2**:176
    courts and, **3**:428
    on criminal procedure, **4**:452
    on education, **2**:408–409
    on evidence, **3**:10–11
    federalism in, **3**:61
    on governmental involvement in the economy, **4**:491
    juvenile justice, **3**:459–461
    on labor unions, **1**:325
    on law and economics, **4**:23
    legislative power in, **4**:98
    on the New York Stock Exchange, **5**:94
    police power in, **5**:351
    on property, **4**:483
    regulation and, **5**:77–79, 81
    on social science, **5**:266–267
    state constitutions in, **5**:350
    women's rights and, **6**:136
Prohibition, **1**:123; **2**:159, 292; **5**:79; **6**:59
    administrative agencies with, **1**:27
    due process and, **2**:369
    rise of gangs under, **1**:219
    search and seizure under, **5**:204–205, *205*
    temperance movement and, **1**:124–126
Prohibition of Child Marriage Act (India, 2006), **3**:49
Prohibitions del roy (Coke), **1**:7
Prokudin-Gorskii, Sergei Mikhailovich, **3**:*108*
prolocutor, **1**:56
promissory notes
    as bills of exchange, **1**:291
    Islamic law, **4**:119
Promissory Notes Act (England, 1704), **1**:292; **4**:38
Promotion of Unity and Reconciliation Act (South Africa, 1995), **5**:282
Promptuarium universorum operum Cuiacii (Cujas), **2**:303
Prontuario de Práctica Forense (Castro), **1**:216
property, **4:456–493**, *458, 460, 491*. *See also* damage to property; possession; private law, concept of; slavery; succession
    African indigenous laws on, **1**:73
    ancient Greek law, **4:456–459**
        Athens, **1**:140, 234
        of foreigners, **5**:357
        Gortyn, **3**:30
        inscriptions on, **1**:154
        marriage and, **4**:154
        military service and, **4**:247
        papyri on, **1**:147
        on women, **1**:159

ancient Near Eastern law, **1:**171, 173
Australia, **1:**242
Brazil, **1:**302
Byzantine law, **4:468–470**
of children
    legitimacy and, **3:**47
    medieval and post-medieval Roman law, **3:**45–46
Chinese law
    damage to, **2:**311–312
    mutual concealment and, **4:**199
    obtaining through deceit, **2:**314–315
    People's Republic, **1:**443
    transfer, **1:**417
donations, **2:**357–358
    Islamic law, **2:**358–359
dowry
    English common law, **2:**362–363
    Hindu law, **2:**363–366
Egypt, **2:**419
England
    easements, **2:**379–382
    equity in, **2:**470
    serjeants at law in, **5:**221
    Star Chamber in, **5:**346
    tenure and estates in, **2:**438
    trusts in, **2:**437
    of women, **6:**121–122
English common law
    duress and, **2:**374
    equity in, **2:**468–469
    error and mistake in, **2:**473–474
    family in, **3:**33
    personal property, **4:470–473**
    real property, **4:**239–240, **473–474**
    succession of, **5:**383–384
English common law, real property
    mortgage and, **4:**188–189
    mortmain in, **4:**191–193
in environmental law
    English common law, **2:**449–450
    India, **2:**453
    United States, **2:**457, 458
feudal law and, **3:**79
final process and, **3:**87, 88
Gaius on, **3:**251
guilds on, **3:**132
Hindu law, **4:479–480**
    adoption and, **1:**49–50
    undivided family, **6:**132

Islamic law, **3:**324
    marriage contracts and, **4:**165–167
    obligations and, **4:**244
    on ownership *(milk)*, **4:**272
    private rights, **5:**19
    women, **6:**127
law and economics on, **4:**24
legal education in, **2:**400
Libri feudorum on, **2:**399
Malaysia, **3:**337
medieval and post-medieval Roman law, **3:**42–43; **4:474–479**
    family and, **3:**40–41
    marriage and, **3:**41–42
    personal property of villeins, **6:**81
    sale of land, **5:**193–194
Mongolia, **4:**185
Native American law, **4:**207, 209
Native law in Canada, **1:**344
natural law on, **4:**216
numerus clausus and, **2:**381–382
Ottoman Empire
    women in, **6:**128–129
partnership and, **1:**320
Roman law, **4:459–468**
    Roman Empire, **2:**273
    women and, **6:**117, 118
Scotland, **5:**202
sex discrimination in, **2:**338
South and Central America, **5:**286
South Asia
    Buddhist law, **5:**304
Southeast Asia, **5:**317
Sri Lanka, **5:**339
Suriname, **5:**296
United States, **4:480–486** (*See also* Contracts Clause)
    due process and, **2:**368–369
    English common law influence on, **4:**484–485
    indentured laborers as, **3:**477–478
    marriage and, **3:**52, 54
    protection of property, **4:486–493**
    search and seizure of, **5:**203–208
    takings clause, **5:**423–425
    women's rights, **6:**134, 136
Welsh law, **6:**99
women
    ancient Greek law, **1:**159
    in colonial United States, **2:**14

Islamic law, **6:**127
Ottoman Empire, **6:**128–129
United States, **6:**134, 136
"Property Rules, Liability Rules, and Inalienability: One View of the Cathedral" (Calabresi and Melamed), **4:**25
Prophet's House *(ahl al-bayt)*, **3:**139
Prosecution of Offences Act (U.K., 1985), **4:**424
Prosperous Justice Party (Indoensia), **3:***336*
prostagmata (ordinances). *See* ordinances
prostitution
　ancient Greek law, **4:493–495; 6:**113
　　adultery and, **1:**51, 53
　Chinese law
　　adoption for, **1:**45–46
　　as illicit sexual intercourse, **5:**232
　　sexual offenses in, **5:**233
Protagoras, **4:**320; **5:**331
　constitution for Thurii, **2:**124
　on punishment, **5:**22–23
Protection of Civil Rights Act (India, 1976), **3:**219
Protection of Telegrams Act (New Zealand, 1882), **4:**228
Protection of Women (Criminal Laws Amendment) Act (Pakistan, 2006), **2:**142; **4:**300
Protection of Women from Domestic Violence Act (India, 2005), **3:**105
protectorates in British Commonwealth, **1:**312–313
Protestant churches, canon law in, **1:**348–352
Protestant Reformation. *See* Reformation
Proverbia: legem servare hoc est regnare (Wipo), **4:**90
Providentissima Mater Ecclesia (apostolic constitution, 1917), **1:**352
Province of Jurisprudence Determined, The (Austin), **1:**238
Provincial Edict, The (Gaius), **3:**431
provincial edicts and government, **4:495–498**
Provisional Criminal Code (China, 1912), **1:**440
Provisions of Oxford (England, 1258), **1:**385–386; **4:**87–88, 283
Provisions of Westminster (England, 1259), **4:**87–88
　on land leases, **4:**12
　on mortmain, **4:**192
proxies, agency and, **1:**111–112
prudent investor rule, **5:**407
Prussia. *See also* Allgemeines Landrecht für die Preussischen Staaten (1794)
　administrative law, **1:**22
　Austrian rivalry with, **1:**247
　codification in, **2:**48
　constitution of 1850, **2:**121
　ecclesiastical courts in, **2:**386
　influence on Japanese law, **3:**366, 373, 374, 376
　maritime law, **4:**151
　Protestant church in, **1:**351
Prussian Allgemeines Landrecht. *See* Allgemeines Landrecht für die Preussischen Staaten (ALR) (1794)
Prussian Code of 1794. *See* Allgemeine Landrecht für die Preussischen Staaten
Prussian Criminal Code (1851)
　on attempt, **1:**238
　on fraud, **3:**103
Prussian Kabinettsorder (Germany, 1836), **4:**380
Prynne, William, **1:**379
Pseudo-Demosthenes, **4:**493
　on adultery, **1:**52
pseudo-Isidoric Decretal Collection, **2:**318; **4:**352
Psistratus, **1:**232
psychology
　on guilt, **3:**134–135
　on sexual and gender variation, **3:**110–111
Psychopathia Sexualis (Krafft-Ebbing), **3:**110
Ptolemy I, **1:**161
Ptolemy II Philadelphus
　judiciary system under, **2:**415–416
　marriage of, **1:**159
public accommodation
　disability and, **2:**336–337
　United States, federalism and, **3:**61
public assistance programs, **6:**92
public authority *(sulṭān)* in Islamic law, **5:3–6**
public choice economics, **4:**27
public choice theory, **4:**69–70
public defenders, **6:**143
Public Health Act (U.K., 1848), **2:**450
public housing, **3:**184–185
public-interest law firms, **2:**341
public interest litigation
　India, **2:**147; **5:6–8**
　　dharma in, **2:**333
　　fundamental duties in, **3:**105
　Islamic law, **4:**63
　United States, **4:**52–53
public international law
　definition, **3:**276, 290
　Islamic law and, **3:280–282**
　modern, **3:276–280**

origins of, **3:**276–277, 282–283, 291
sources, **3:**277–278
United States and, **3:290–297**
publicity, right of, **3:**274
public law, **5:8–20,** *15*
  ancient Greece, **1:**139–140
    Athens, **1:**233–234
  Bartolus of Saxoferrato on, **1:**280–281
  Byzantium, **5:14–15**
  English common law, **5:15–19**
  Germany, **3:**118
    under National Socialist law, **3:**110
  Islamic law, public and private, **5:19–20**
  Islamic law enforcement of, **2:**432–433
  legal education in, **2:**400
  legal realism on, **4:**76
  Ottoman Empire, **4:**266
  Roman Empire, **5:11–14**
  Roman Republic, **5:8–11**
  Savigny, Friedrich Carl von, on, **5:**195
  Switzerland, **5:**419
  systematization into, **5:**421–422
  United Kingdom, **2:**437–438
public limited-responsibility companies, **2:**94
Public Security Organs (People's Republic of China), **1:**442, 443, 444
public trust doctrine, **2:**453
public use, takings clause and, **5:**423–424
public utilities, administrative agencies and, **1:**26
Publius. *See* Quintus Mucius Scaevola
Publius Rupilius, **4:**496
Puche, Jaime Serra, **3:***286*
Puchta, Georg Friedrich, **4:**277
  commentary on thepandects, **2:**10
  influence on private law, **4:**396
  influence on Rudolf von Jhering, **3:**399
  jurisprudence of concepts and, **3:**433
Puerto Rico, **1:**370
  slavery in, **5:**255
Pufendorf, Samuel von, **3:**291; **5:20–22,** 171, 172, 471
  on absolutism, **1:**7, 8
  English translations of, **2:**440–441
  on error and mistake, **2:**475
  on illegality and invalidity, **3:**203
  influenced by
    Descartes, René, **2:**400
    Grotius, Hugo, **3:**127
  influence on
    Blackstone, William, **1:**298

German law, **3:**118
  Thomasius, Christian, **5:**464
  Wolff, Christian von, **6:**111
on law of nations, **3:**276
Leibniz, Gottfried Wilhelm, on, **4:**100
on natural law, **4:**215, 217; **5:**43
on negligence, **4:**221
on obligations, **4:**245
on paternal authority, **3:**45
in Sweden, **5:**415
on systematization, **5:**421
Pullman, George, **4:**336
punishment, **5:22–42,** *29, 33, 38, 40. See also* prisons and imprisonment
  Afghanistan, **1:**62
  ancient Athens, **4:**382–383, 411; **5:22–24**
    for adultery, **1:**52–53
  ancient Greece
    Draco on, **2:**366–367
    slavery as, **5:**244
  ancient Near Eastern law, **1:**175
  Anglo-Saxon, **1:**182
  Aztec law, **5:**288
  Brazil, **1:**302
  Byzantium, **2:**275
  Chinese law (*See also* punishment and status in Chinese law)
    abolition of cruel punishments, **1:**439
    accessory and principal in, **1:**18
    administrative punishments, **5:26–27**
    amnesty in, **1:**133–135
    beating and whipping, **1:**283–285
    Board of Punishments, **2:**240, 241, 242, 243, 246, **247–249**
    collective, **4:**259–260
    for corruption, **2:**226–227
    for cursing, **2:**304
    damaging efficiency of government, **4:**253–254
    for damaging efficiency of government, **4:**253–254, 255
    for deceit, **2:**315
    for disrespect *(bujing)*, **4:**251
    for doing what ought not to be done, **2:**355–356
    doubtful cases, **2:**361
    exile, **3:**25–26
    five punishments in, **5:**213–214
    Han dynasty, **1:**417
    imprisonment, **4:**383
    for lack of filial piety, **3:**84–86

levels of, **2**:246
in Liao empire, **1**:427
mutilation, **4**:196–197
for offenses against the state, **4**:249, 259–260
overview, **5:24–26**
penal servitude, **4**:292–293
for plotting rebellion, **4**:257–258
prisons and imprisonment, **4**:383
reciprocal, **6**:152
redemption, **5**:72–75
reeducation through labor in People's Republic, **1**:443, 446
review and, **1**:196–197
sentence in, **5:213–215**
social status and, **4**:259
sumptuary laws, **5**:410
voluntary surrender and, **2**:106
for wounding, **6**:150–151
corporal
England, **3**:34
parental right of, **3**:45
for deceit, **2**:315
England common law
in Star Chamber, **5**:346–347
English common law, **3**:178–179; **5:27–31**
outlawry, **4**:270–271
Germany under National Socialism, **4**:204
guilt and, **3**:133–136
Hindu law, **5:35–37**
husband's right to
medieval and post-medieval Roman law, **3**:41
Inca law, **5**:*288*, 289
India, **2**:283–284
Islamic law, **3**:325, 328, 330
for adultery, **6**:130
for alcohol or drug use, **1**:120, 121, 122
crimes according to penalties, **2**:277–278
enforcement of, **2**:431–434
prisons and imprisonment, **4**:383–384
stoning for fornication, **1**:6, 62
types of penalties, **2**:278–280
by Native Americans, **4**:207
Nepal, **4**:224
no punishment without law, **4**:92
in Pakistan, **2**:142
for prevention, **3**:134
restitution and, **3**:134

Roman law
delict, **2**:321
Roman Empire, **2**:274–275
Roman Republic, **2**:268–269
Roman law, medieval and post-medieval, **5:31–35**
United States, **5:37–42**; **6**:50
colonial period, **2**:285–286, 288–289, 289
for drug crimes, **1**:127
reform, **2**:291
of slaves, **5**:258–259
punishment, theories regarding purpose of, **5:42–44**
punishment and status in Chinese law, **5:44–57**, 358–359
age, **5**:45, **45–47**
disability, **5:47–48**
in illicit sexual intercourse, **5**:231
officials, **5**:44–45, **48–51**
overview, **5:44–45**
relatives, **5**:44, 50, **51–54**
marriage and, **4**:158–160
in sexual offenses, **5**:232–234
slaves, **5**:44, 45, **54–56**
women, **5:56–57**
Punishment of Deat Act (U.K., 1832), **1**:365
Punjab Land Alienation Act (Pakistan, 1900), **4**:275
Punjab Land Revenue Act (Pakistan, 1871), **4**:3
Punjab Tenance Act (Pakistan, 1887), **4**:275
Pure Food and Drug Act. *See* Food and Drugs Act
purity and impurity
Hindu law, **6**:131
Islamic law, **5:57–59**, *58*
alcohol and drugs and, **1**:119–123
body in, **1**:298–301
pyattons, **5**:303
Pyrard, François, **4**:139
Pyu King's Dhammasat, **5**:315

Q

Qabisi, al-, **4**:128
Qadi Abu al-Yaʻla, Al, **3**:465
Qadi al-Nuʻman, Ibn Muhammad ibn Mansur al-, **3**:341; **4**:127; **5:59–60**
on Sicily, **5**:239
Qadi ʻIyad, **5**:182
Qadir al-Jilani, ʻAbd al-, **3**:347

qadis, **3:**315
  Afghanistan, **1:**61
  Africa, **2:**41–42
    private, **2:**43, 44
  Arab countries, **1:**205
  dissent in, **2:**345
  education of, **2:**397; **4:**70–71
  enforcement by, **2:**431–432, *432*
  fatwas by, **3:**57–58
  Grand Qadi in Abbasid dynasty, **1:**1
  Ibn Taymiyya on, **3:**202
  interpretation of codes in Ottoman Empire, **2:**35
  Iran, **3:**302
  Iraq, **3:**305
  Malaysia, **2:**140
  Ottoman, **4:**72
    salaries of, **4:**73
  Tanzania, **2:**44
  Zanzibar, **1:**74
Qadri Basha, Muhammad, **1:**205
Qadri Pasha, Muhammad, **3:**415
Qaffal, Abu Bakr Muhammad ibn ʿAli ibn Ismaʿil al-Shashi al-, **5:**60
Qaffal al-Marwazi, Abu Bakr ʿAbd Allah ibn Ahmad al-, **5:**60
Qaffal the Elder, al-. *See* Qaffal, Abu Bakr Muhammad ibn ʿAli ibn Ismaʿil al-Shashi al-
Qaffal the Younger, al-. *See* Qaffal al-Marwazi, Abu Bakr ʿAbd Allah ibn Ahmad al-
qānūn (codified law), **1:**33–35
  in Syria, **2:**398
Qanun-e-Shahadat (Law of Evidence) Order (Pakistan, 1984), **4:**299
Qarafi, Shihab al-Din al-, **4:**430
  on alcohol and drug use, **1:**121
  influenced by al-Ghazali, **3:**120
  on rights, **5:**137
  on worship, **6:**150
qarḍ ḥasan (benevolent loan), **1:**263; **4:**118–119
Qari, ʿAbdallah al-, **1:**206
qasāma (accusation), **3:**39
Qasim, Mohammad ibn, **5:**307
Qasim ibn Ibrahim, Hasanid al-, **3:**341
Qatar
  constitution, **3:**317
  shariʿa as principal source of legislation in, **3:**317
qawāʿid (principles of the *fiqh*), **3:**321–322

Qayrawani, Ibn Abi Zayd al-, **3:**250, 351; **5:**60–61
  on legal methodology, **4:**128
Qianlong (Chinese emperor), **1:**434
  censorship by, **4:**252
Qin, state of
  collective liability, **2:**58
  crime, distinction between intentional and accidental, **3:**275
Qin code (China), **1:**428
  accessory and principal in, **1:**18
  on alcohol and drugs, **1:**119
  on appeal, **1:**193–194
  on beating and whipping, **1:**283, 284
  on damage to property, **2:**311
  on homicide, **3:**171, 173
  on illicit sexual intercourse, **5:**231
  on incest, **3:**213
  influence on Sui and Tang codes, **1:**421
  on lack of filial piety, **3:**85
  on land, **4:**1
  on loans, **4:**116–117
  on mutilation, **4:**197
  on mutual concealment, **4:**198
  on offenses against the state, **4:**249
  on penal servitude, **4:**292
  on prisons and imprisonment, **4:**383
  on punishment, **5:**26
  on rape, **5:**66
  on review, **1:**196
  on sale, **5:**183–184
  on succession, **5:**377
  on theft, **5:**458, 459, 460, 461
  on wounding, **6:**150
  on wrongful judgment, **6:**152–153
Qindin lü gao tiaolo (Imperially approved regulation of the code with pronouncements), **1:**430
Qin dynasty (China 221–206 B.C.E.)
  collective liability, **2:**58
  corruption in the, **2:**225
  judicial precedent, **1:**460
  laws of, **1:**453–455
  pledging of goods during, **4:**326–327
  rule of law, **5:**165
Qin empire (1115–1234 C.E.), **1:**427–428
Qing code (China), **1:**434, 436
  abduction *(lue),* **3:**468
  accessory and principal in, **1:**18
  adoption, **1:**43, 44, 45
  amnesty, **1:**134

appeal, **1:**194–195
astronomical studies, **4:**252
censorship, **4:**252
collective liability, **2:**58, 59, 60
confession, **2:**107–108
corruption, **2:**226, 227
cursing, **2:**304, 305
damage to property, **2:**312, 313
damaging efficiency of government, **4:**254
deceit, **2:**314, 315
deposit, **2:**331
disrespect *(bujing)*, **4:**250, 251
doubtful cases, **2:**361
drugs, **1:**119
endangering the emperor, **4:**256
enticement, **3:**469
errors in official documents, **4:**254
ethnic groups, **2:**481–482
exile, **3:**25–26
foreigners, **3:**92
gambling, **3:**109
gu poison, **4:**329
homicide, **3:**171–172, 173, 174–175
homosexuality, **3:**180
illicit sexual intercourse, **5:**231–232
incest, **3:**214
influence on Gia Long Code, **6:**79
lack of filial piety, **3:**84, 85, 86
land, **4:**2
    alienability, **4:**3–4
    sales, **5:**185–**186**, 188
lawyers, **4:**46
magic and sorcery, **4:**253
marriage, **4:**156, 157
    remarriage, **4:**160
mistaken judgments, **4:**254
mistaken recommendations, **4:**255
in Mongolia, **4:**184
mutual concealment, **4:**199
offenses against the state, **4:**249
parricide, **3:**84
penal servitude, **4:**293
persons as security, **4:**326
plotting rebellion, **4:**257
prisons and imprisonment, **4:**383
punishment, **1:**362; **5:**25, 26–27, 52
    beating and whipping, **1:**283, 284
    Board of Punishments, **2:**249
    capital punishment, **1:**362
    five punishments, **5:**213
    of women, **5:**57
rape, **5:**67
redemption, **5:**72, 73, 74
review, **1:**197
sale
    of a free person by consent, **3:**469
    of land, **5:**185–186, 188
    of relatives, **3:**469
secret societies, **4:**258
sexual offenses, **5:**233–234
slavery, **5:**55
status, **5:**359
succession, **5:**380
sumptuary laws, **5:**410
Ten Abominations, **4:**260
theft, **5:**458–459, 460
torture, **2:**108; **5:**482–483
treason, **4:**258
voluntary surrender, **2:**106
wounding, **6:**150, 151
zang, **6:**159, 160
Qing dynasty (China, 1644–1911), **1:**433–439
    administrative codes or regulations, **1:**454–455
    appeal in the, **2:**246
    Boxers, **1:***434*
    bureaucracy and capital punishment, **1:**360
    collective liability, **2:**61
    corruption in the, **2:**226, 227
    courts in the, **2:**241, 242, 243, 244, 245, 246, 247–248
    diffusion of Chinese legal culture in Taiwan, **1:**452
    emperor's power during the, **2:**243
    guilds during, **1:**464
    penal codes, **1:**459
    rule of law, **5:**166
    use of the cangue, **1:**345
Qin legislation
    collective liability, **2:**59, 60, 61
    in Shuihudi documents, **1:**406
    types of, **1:**410–411
Qin Shi Huang Di (Chines emperor), **5:**51
qiṣāṣ (right to retaliation), **1:**367, 368; **2:**100; **3:**327–328
    in Pakistan, **2:**142
qitāl (fighting), **6:**85

qiyās (analogical reasoning), **3:**224
   on alcohol and drugs, **1:**120–121
   Hanbali school and, **3:**346
   in legal reasoning, **4:**63
   Muzani, Abu Ibrahim Ismaʿil ibn Yahya al-, on, **4:**200
quaestio (literary form), **3:**355
Quaestiones (Azo), **1:**248
Quaestiones (Celsus the Younger), **1:**373
Quaestiones (Papinian), **4:**279; **5:**149
Quaestiones (Paul), **4:**291
Quaid-e-Azam University (Islamabad, Pakistan), **2:**398
quality control, consumer protection and, **2:**168
Quanun-e-Shahadat Order (Pakistan, 1984), **4:**3; **5:**308–309
quasi-contracts, **2:**185–186, 188, 189
Quduri, al-, **3:**343
Quebec
   codes, **1:**341–342
     codification of international private law, **2:**113
Quebec Act (Canada, 1774), **1:**312, 337
Queen's Bench (U.K.), appeal in, **1:**199
Queensbury, Marquis of, **4:**106
Queensland Criminal Code (Papua New Guinea), **4:**281
queer theory, **3:**110, 112
Quezon, Manuel, **4:**319
Quia Emptores (England, 1290), **6:**33
   on conveyancing, **2:**212
     estates doctrine and, **2:**478
   on landholding, **3:**75–76; **4:**473; **5:**370
   on subinfeudation, **2:**436; **4:**88
qui facit per alium facit per se, **6:**76
Quinctius, Kaeso, **4:**95
Quinlan, Karen Ann, **2:**424
Quinquaginta decisiones (Justinian), **6:**7
Quinque compilationes antiquae, **2:**221
Quintilian, **3:**435
Quintus Mucius Scaevola. *See* Scaevola, Quintus Mucius
quod permittat action
   in easements, **2:**380
   in environmental law, **2:**448
   for nuisance, **4:**239
Quoniam Attachiamenta (Scotland), **5:**198
Qur'an
   on abrogation of legal norms, **1:**6
   on adoption, **1:**47–48

   on alcohol and drugs, **1:**120
   censorship and, **1:**382
   on crime penalties, **2:**277, 278
   on divorce, **5:**129
   as foundational text for Islamic law, **5:**131–132
   on impurity, **5:**57, 59
   on inheritance, **3:**232
   interpretation of, **6:**18
   Jews subject to the, **3:**394
   on judicial review, **3:**413
   legal content of, **1:**210
   muftis on, **4:**194
   Philippine law and, **4:**318
   on pledge (*rahn*), **4:**327
   on privacy, **4:**385
   on punishment, **4:**384
   revelation in, **5:**132–133
   rights in, **5:**136
   Shafiʿi, Muhammad ibn Idris al-, on, **5:**236
   on sodomy, **3:**181
   as source of Islamic law, **3:**319, *319*
   on taxation, **5:**431–432, 433
   use in Pakistan laws, **4:**274
   on usurpation, **6:**67
   on usury, **6:**69, 70
   on *zakat* (obligatory alms), **5:**430
qurba (drawing close), **6:**147–148

R
Raad van Justitie, **5:**279
Rabel, Ernst, **2:**99
Rabiʿ, al-, **5:**236
Rabin, Robert, **5:**475
race, naturalization and, **3:**209
Racial Discrimination Act (Australia, 1975), **1:**3
racial profiling, **2:**344
racism
   Becker, Gary, on, **4:**24
   British Commonwealth, **1:**314–315
   in colonial Africa, **1:**79, 88
   England, **2:**330
   Guyana, **3:**138
   natural law on, **4:**218
   South Africa, **5:**280–281
   United States
     in alcohol and drug laws, **1:**125, 126–127
     in apportionment and reapportionment, **1:**201–204
     civil rights activism, **2:**299–300

labor law, **3:**479–480
    marriage restrictions based on, **3:**52
    welfare and, **6:**92
Racketeer Influenced and Corrupt Organizations Act (RICO), **2:**293
    arbitration and, **1:**131
Radbruch, Gustav, **3:**135
Radd al-Muhtar (Ibn ʿAbidin), **3:**195
    on insurance, **3:**254
Radin, Max, **4:**74
Radio Act (U.S., 1927), **5:**96, 97
Radishchev, Aleksandr N., **5:**177–178
Radzinowicz, Leon, **1:**364–365
Rafʿ al-hahib (al-Subki), **5:**370
Raffles, Thomas Stamford, **5:**241, 323
    lieutenant-governor of Indonesia, **3:**226
Ragion poetica (Gravina), **3:**126
Rahitnamas, **5:**240
Rahman, Mujibur, **1:**258, *258*
Rahman, Temenggong Abdul, **5:**241
Rahman, Tunku Abdul, **4:**138; **5:**242
Rahman, Ziaur, **1:**258; **2:**143
Rahman al-Jaziri, ʿAbd, **2:**44
Railroad Retirement Act (U.S.), **3:**409
railroads
    administrative agencies and, **1:**26
    bankruptcies, **1:**268–269
    bill of lading, **2:**76
    company law and, **2:**89
    corporate charters, **1:**321
    regulation of, **2:**259
    trusts, **1:**324
    United States, **6:**46, 48
        regulations and case law, **5:**100–105
Railway Clauses Consolidation Act (U.K., 1845), **2:**89
Rainerius de Arisendis, **1:**280
Raiser, Ludwig, **4:**395
rājadharma, **5:**63
    Arthaśāstra in, **1:**223
Rajaki, Harry, **3:**249
rājamaṇḍala, **4:**232–233
rājaśāsana, **5:**63–64
rajasat, **5:**315–316
Rajasat (Ayutthyan), **5:**455
rajathats, **5:**303, 304
Rakove, Jack, **2:**151–152
Raleigh, Walter
    Guyana explorations by, **3:**137
    prosecution by Edward Coke, **2:**54
Ram, Sevak, **5:**307

Rama I, **5:**455
Rāma Śāha of Gorkha, **4:**224
Rāmāyaṇ, **5:**265
Rambam. *See* Maimonides, Moses
Ramus. *See* La Ramée, Pierre de
Rāṇā, Janga Bahādura, **4:**224–225
Ranavalona I (Madagascar), **1:**71
Ranavalona II (Madagascar), **1:**71
Randolph, A. Philip, **2:***342*
Ŕankara, Advaitin, **5:**344
Rankin Committee (India). *See* Civil Justice Committee (India)
Ranters, **1:**379
rape, **5:64–69**
    ancient Greek law, **5:64–66**
        punishment for, **1:**52
        slavery and, **5:**355
    ancient Near Eastern law, **1:**170, 176
    Aztec law, **5:**288
    Chinese law, **3:**180; **5:66–67**
        as illicit sexual intercourse, **5:**232
        and incest, **3:**214
    Code of Gortyn on, **3:**120, 123
    English common law, **5:67–69**
    feminist legal theory on, **3:**67, 69, 71
    Inca law, **5:**289
    India, **2:**283
    Islamic law on duress, **2:**375
    medieval and post-medieval Roman law, **5:**229, 230
    Roman law, **2:**271
    United States
        marital, **6:**142–143
        shield law, **3:**12
    of slaves, **2:**337; **5:**261
rasāʾil (treatises), **3:**321
Rashid, Harun al-, **3:**344
    Abu Yusuf appointed by, **1:**10
    Grand Qadi created by, **1:**1
    judges under, **4:**70
    legal literature commissioned by, **1:**2
    Shaybani, Muhammad ibn al-Hasan al-, and, **5:**236
Rasselas (Johnson), **2:**368
Ratio Fundamentalis Institutionis Sacerdotalis (Congregation for Formation), **1:**357
rational-basis test, sex discrimination and, **2:**339
Rationale of Judicial Evidence (Bentham), **1:**287
Rationalia in Pandectas (Faber), **3:**27
rationes (research method), **3:**355

Rattray, R. W., **1:**65
Rau Committee (India), **5:**397, 398
Rawda al-Bahiyya, al- (al-ʿAmili), **1:**132
Rawd al-nadir, Al- (Sanʿani), **6:**162
Rawdat al-nazir wa-jannat al-munazir (Ibn Qudama), **3:**199
Rawls, John, **3:**449–450
Ray, Isaac, **3:**247
Ray, James Earl, **4:**336
ra'y (personal judgement), **3:**350
Raymond, Robert, **3:**4
Raz, Joseph, **4:**21
RBOCs. *See* Regional Bell Operating Companies
Reading, Lord, **6:**4
Reading on the Statute (Moore), **1:**390
Reagan, Ronald
   assassination attempt on, **3:**12
   on civil rights, **2:**300
   deregulation under, **1:**29–30
   environmental law under, **2:**457
   on federalism, **3:**63
   international trade under, **3:**285
   on Japanese internment, **3:**24
   judicial appointments, **2:**343
   on Legal Services, **4:**373; **6:**95
   race neutral approach of, **2:**343
   regulatory system under, **5:**83–84
   securities policy under, **5:**94
   sex discrimination under, **2:**340
   tax policy, **5:**447–448
   on welfare, **4:**367
real actions, **5:69–72**
Reale, Miguel, **1:**304
real estate law
   agency in, **1:**114
   lease contracts in, **4:**58
"Realistic Jurisprudence, A—The Next Step" (Llewellyn), **4:**75
Real Property Act (U.K., 1833), **2:**215; **4:**359
Real Property Act (U.K., 1845), **4:**12
Real Property Act (U.K., 1858), **4:**7
Real Property Commissioners, **2:**215; **4:**7
real security contract in ancient Greek law, **2:**180–181
Reapportionment Act (U.S., 1842), **1:**200
reason
   ius commune and, **2:**8–9
   in legal education, **2:**400
   Leibniz, Gottfried Wilhelm, on, **4:**100
   natural law and, **4:**214–215, 216, 217
   Sabinus, Masurius, on, **5:**180
   Scholasticism and, **4:**15–17
reasonable accommodation for disability, **2:**336–337
reasonable care, negligence and, **4:**221
reasonableness test in environmental law, **2:**449
"reasonable regulation" standard in welfare programs, **6:**95
Reccared (King of the Visigoths), **3:**397
Recceswinth (King of the Visigoths), **2:**110; **3:**397
receptionists (Ottoman Empire), **4:**268, 269
Recht des Besitzes, Das (Savigny), **5:**195
Rechtsbücher, **4:**91
Rechtweiser (legal adviser), **1:**56
reciprocal punishment, **6:**152
Reconstruction, **2:**154
   14th Amendment and, **2:**158
   civil rights laws in, **2:**460
   effect on civil procedure, **4:**442
   federalism and, **3:**60–61, 63
   legislative power in, **4:**98
Recopilación de Leyes de las Indias (1680), **5:**291, 325
   South and Central America under, **5:**285, 299
Recueil des inscriptions juridiques grecques (Dareste, Hassoullier, and Reinach), **1:**163
Recueil Martens, **3:**283
redemption *(shu)*, **5:72–75**
   in land sales, **4:**5–6; **5:**188
   sentence conversion and, **5:**214
Red Guards, **1:**444
Redlich, Joseph, **2:**403
Reed, Alfred Z., **2:**404–405
Reed Report. *See Training for the Public Profession of the Law* (Reed)
Reese, Willis L. M.
   on conflict of laws, **2:**118
   Restatements of the Law of Conflict of Laws, **2:**114
Reeve, Tapping, **6:**43
   law school of, **1:**12
   Litchfield Law School under, **2:**402
Reflections on the Natural and Acquired Endowments Requisite for the Study of the Law (Simpson), **2:**394

Reform Acts (Scotland, 1832), **5**:201
Reformation
    Budé, Guillaume, on, **1**:316
    canon law after, **2**:354
    Denmark, **2**:328
    divorce after, **3**:43
    Du Moulin, Charles, on, **2**:373
    in England, **1**:468
    guilds and, **3**:132
    humanism and, **3**:189
    legal education and, **2**:400
    on marriage, **3**:40, 41
    natural law in, **4**:216
    Sweden, **5**:415
    on "true" religion, **5**:109
Reform Bill (Ottoman Empire, 1856), **4**:268, 269–270
Reform Rescript (Ottoman Empire, 1839), **4**:267
Refugee Act (U.S., 1980), **3**:208
refugee law, African contributions to, **1**:107
refugees, **3**:208
Regelsberger, Ferdinand, **4**:277
Regerings Reglement (Indonesia, 1854), **3**:226
Regestum Practicale (Stiles), **4**:324
Regiam majestatem (Scotland), **5**:198, 200
Régime féodal, **3**:77
Regional Bell Operating Companies (RBOCs), **5**:97–98, 99
regionalism, in local government, **4**:121–122
Register Act (U.S., 1792–1793), **1**:36
Register of Sasines (Scotland), **5**:200, 202
Registration Act (U.K., 1908), **4**:273
Registration of Muhammadan Marriages and Divorces Orders (Malaysia, 1885), **4**:301
Registration of Muslim Marriages Ordinance (Sri Lanka, 1896), **5**:310
Reglamento de Imprentas (Spain, 1834), **3**:260
regrating, prohibition of, **2**:101
regula
    Labeo, Marcus Antistius, on, **3**:476; **5**:181
    Sabinus, Masurius, on, **5**:181
Regulae (Ulpian), **5**:151
Regulae (under the name Gaius), **5**:151
regulation. *See also* administrative agencies; antitrust
    of corporations, **1**:321–327
    England, environmental law, **2**:451–452
    guilds in, **3**:131, 132
    Islamic banking and finance, **1**:262
    in Ming dynasty, **1**:431

    telecommunications regulation
        free speech in, **5**:335–336, 337–338
    United States, **5**:75–105, *78, 87, 99*
        agency forcing provisions in, **1**:29
        agriculture, **5**:86–92
        agriculture regulation, **5**:80
        bar association in, **4**:51
        deregulation, **1**:29–30
        environmental law, **2**:457
        judicial review in, **1**:30–31
        legislative power of, **4**:98–99
        overview, **5**:75–86
        science and, **4**:30–31
        securities, **5**:92–95
        telecommunications, **5**:95–99
        transportation regulation, **5**:99–105
Regulations for the Procuracy for Chinese Affairs (Macau, 1862), **1**:448
regulatory takings, doctrine of, **2**:26–27
Rehabilitation Act (U.S., 1973), **2**:335
Rehnquist, William, **2**:67
    on abortion, **4**:390
    civil rights deregulation under, **2**:461–462
    on federalism, **3**:63–65
    on Japanese internment, **3**:24
    on the political question doctrine, **2**:261
    on property rights, **4**:492
    racial neutrality doctrine of, **2**:461–462
    on right to bear arms, **1**:221
    on the right to die, **4**:390
    on social sciences, **5**:268, 269
    on statutory interpretation, **5**:362
Reich, Charles
    on law and society, **4**:33, 34
    on new property, **4**:371, 483; **6**:94
Reich Ministry for Public Enlightenment and Propaganda (Germany), **3**:110
Reichsabschiede, **4**:91
Reichscivilprozessordnung (Imperial Civil Procedural Code) (Germany, 1877), **4**:435
Reichskammergericht (Imperial Chamber of Justice), **5**:105–107
    civil law and, **2**:7
Reichstag (Assembly) of Roncaglia (1158), **2**:251
Reichstag under National Socialist law, **3**:110
Reichtskammergerichtsordnung (Code of the Imperial Chamber Court) (1495)
    usus modernus and, **2**:8
Reid, David, **1**:*244*
Reid, John P., **3**:427

Reign of Queen Victoria, The (Ward), **4:**137
Reinach, Th., **1:**163
Reinkingk, Theodor, **1:**350
Rei vindicatio formula, **3:**95
relational feminism, **3:**68
religion, **5:***107,* **107–120,** *111, 116*
    African indigenous law and, **1:**65–66
    in ancient Greece, **5:110–113**
    ancient Near Eastern law on offenses against, **1:**176
    ancient Rome, Senate on, **5:**212
    Athens, offenses against, **1:**234; **4:**247
    effect on punishment in Islamic law, **3:**325
    Egypt Hellenistic law, **2:**414
    England
        in assizes, **1:**230
        divorce and, **2:**348–349
        kingship and, **2:**129
        mortmain and, **4:**191–193
    Enlightenment views of, **2:**444–445
    folk law and, **3:**90–91
    freedom of
        Balkan peninsula, **1:**253
        Europe, **2:**483–484
    Germany under National Socialist law, **3:**110
    guilds and, **3:**132
    guilt in, **3:**133–134
    Guyana, **3:**137
    India
        as fundamental right, **3:**48
        fundamental rights on, **3:**106
        secularism in, **5:**208–209
        separation of state and, **2:**333
    law and science and, **4:**28
    marriage law influenced by, **3:**51–52
    Native American, **4:**209
    natural law and, **4:**216
    Near Eastern law on, **1:**169, 175
    Netherlands, **4:**225–226
    for non-Muslims in Islamic law, **4:**234–235
    Noordt, Gerard, on freedom of, **4:**236
    in oaths and evidence, **3:**6
    Roman law
        regulations in, **4:**96
    slavery and, **5:**258, 259
    Sweden, **5:**417
    United States law, **5:114–120; 6:**30, 51
        education and, **2:**408, 409
        equal protection in, **2:**464
        religious freedom cases, **2:**261

Religious Councils, State Custom, and Kathis Court Enactment (Brunei, 1955), **3:**338–339
religious freedom
    Indian jurisprudence and, **3:**218
    South Africa, **5:**284
Religious Freedom Restoration Act (U.S., 1993), **2:**261; **3:**64; **5:**119
Religious Land Use and Institutionalized Persons Act (RLUIPA) (U.S., 2000), **5:**119
religious law, **5:120–125**
    influence of the adoption of Christianity on Roman religious law, **5:122–125**
    overview of Roman religious law, **5:120–122**
religious toleration, **4:**143
remedies, **5:125–127**
    equitable, **2:**472–473
Remington, Frank J., **4:**32
remissio mercedis, **2:**185
Remy, Joseph, **2:**357
Renaissance
    German, **3:**118
    humanism and, **3:**189
    justice theories, **3:**447
    Macedonian, **1:**281–283
    Scholasticism and, **4:**15
Rendel, George, **5:**242
René, Albert, **5:**235
renvoi, **2:**118
Reorganization Committee (U.S.), **1:**269
Repetitio (Baldus de Ubaldis), **2:**111
Repgow, Eike von, **3:***117*
    on feudal law, **3:**78
replicatio, **3:**97
Report of the Committee for Gender Equality in Land Devolution in Tenurial Laws, The, **5:**401
Report on Manufactures (Hamilton), **3:**113
Reports (Coke), **2:**56; **4:**44, 60
Reports (Dyer), **4:**44
Reports of the Surveys on Customs in Civil and Commercial Matters *(Minshang shi xiguan diaocha baogao lu),* **1:**463
reproductive rights in the United States, **4:**388–390; **6:**140–142
Republic, The (Plato), **3:**450
    on constitutional law, **2:**123, 124
    on family, **3:**31
    on ideal constitution, **2:**126
    on law, **4:**321
    on *nomos,* **1:**145
    on sovereignty, **5:**352

republican motherhood, **6:**138
Republic of China, 1912–1949, **1:439–441**
   laws implemented in Taiwan, **1:**452
   voluntary surrender and, **2:**107
République (Bodin), **3:**190
repudiation *(Ṭalāq)*, **2:**37; **4:**167; **5:127–129**. *See also* personal status law
repugnancy
   Afghanistan, **1:**60–61
   Australia, **1:**240, 241, 243
   British Commonwealth law on, **1:**313
   folk law and, **3:**90
Requerimento, **5:**301
Requerimento (Rubios), **5:**299
Rerum Patriae Libri IV (Alciati), **1:**118
rescission of contract, **1:**308–309
   delay and, **2:**320
Res cottidianae sive aurea (under the name Gaius), **5:**151
rescripts, imperial (Rome), **2:**53
Resource Management Act (New Zealand, 1991)
   on Maori law, **4:**145
respondeat superior, **6:**76
   agency and, **1:**115
Responsa (Papinian), **3:**436; **4:**279
Responsa (Paul), **4:**291
Responsa Juris (Alciati), **1:**118
Restatement of African Law project, **1:**88
Restatement of Agency, **1:**113, 115
Restatement of Contracts (1932), **2:**76
Restatement (Second) of Contracts (1981), **2:**78
Restatement of Foreign Relations Law of the U.S., **3:**288
Restatement (First) of Restitution (1937), **5:**130
Restatement of the Foreign Relations Law of the United States (1986), **3:**297
Restatement of the Law of the Conflict of Laws, **2:**113, 117, 118–119
Restatement of Torts (1939), **3:**273
Restatement (Second) of Torts (1978)
   consumer protection and, **2:**177
   right of privacy, **3:**273–274
   trade secrets, **3:**273
Restatement (Third) of Unfair Competition, **3:**273, 274
restitution
   English common law, **2:**473–474; **5:129–131**
   English legal treatises on, **2:**443
   guilt and, **3:**134
   obligations and, **4:**245

Restitution of Conjugal Rights (England), **3:**34
Restoration Settlement (England, 1660), **2:**131; **4:**285
restorative justicve, **1:**344
restraint of trade
   guilds and, **3:**132
   medieval rules against, **2:**101
retribution
   Anaximander on, **1:**145
   Mongolia, **4:**184
Reuchlin, Johannes, **3:**395–396
Reuther, Walter P., **2:***342*
revealed texts *(nuṣūṣ)*, transmission of, **5:131–132**
revelation, forms of, in Islamic law, **5:132–134**
revenge in Chinese law, **3:**175
Revenue Act (U.S., 1916), **5:**443
Revenue Act (U.S., 1932), **5:**444
Revenue Act (U.S., 1934), **5:**445
Revenue Act (U.S., 1935), **5:**445
Revenue Act (U.S., 1936), **5:**445
Revenue Act (U.S., 1942), **5:**447
reverse-Erie doctrine, **1:**39
Révigny, Jacques de
   on conflict of laws, **2:**111
   on Justinian, **1:**281
Revised Organic Act (U.S. Virgin Islands, 1954), **1:**370
revocability in alternative dispute resolution, **1:**130
revocable inter vivos trust (RIVT), **5:**408
Revolutionary War (American). *See* American Revolution
Revue historique de droit français et étranger, **1:**166
Revue internationale de droit comparé, **2:**99
Revue internationale des droits de l'antiquité, **1:**166
Revue Juridique du Congo Belge, **1:**91
Rex pacificus (papal bull, 1234), **2:**222
Reynolds, Susan, **3:**78
Reza Khan, **3:**303
Reza Shah Pahlavi, **3:**303
RFRA. *See* Religious Freedom Restoration Act
rhetoric
   in ancient Greek law, **5:134–136**
   in ancient Roman law, **2:**391
Rhetoric (Aristotle), **5:**135, 480
   Athenian law influenced by, **1:**149

on evidence, **3:**1
law as literature and, **4:**112
on oaths, **4:**242
positivist approach in, **1:**145
on slavery, **5:**244
Rhetorica ad Herennium, **2:**391
Rhetoric to Alexander (Anaximenes), **1:**149
Rhodes, Cecil, **1:**78
Rhodes, Peter J., **4:**85
ribā (interest), **1:**262, 359; **2:**75
obligations and, **4:**244
Riccardi family, **1:**271
Rich, Giles S., **3:**270
Richard, Earl of Cornwall and King of the Romans, **6:**1
Richard de Clare, earl of Pembroke (Strongbow), **3:**307
Richard I (England)
justices of the peace under, **3:**452
legal history beginning with, **4:**87
Magna Carta on redress for wrongs by, **4:**134
succession to the crown of, **5:**382
Richard II (England), **2:**128
on mortmain, **4:**192
on nuisance, **4:**239
parliament and, **4:**284
Richard III (England), **4:**44
Richter, Emil Ludwig, **2:**219
RICO. *See* Racketeer Influenced and Corrupt Organizations Act
Ricoeur, Paul, **3:**133
Riḍa, ʿAli al-, **3:**340
Ridley, Nicholas, **1:**366
Ridolfi Plot (1570), **6:**5
Riflessioni politiche su l'ultima legge del sovrano, che riguarda la riforma dell'amministrazione della Giustizia (Filangieri), **3:**83
Riforme del codice, **1:**285
Rigaud, Hyacinthe, **1:**7
right, writ of, **3:**307; **5:**69–70
"Right of Publicity, The" (Nimmer), **3:**274
right-of-way, easements, **2:**379
rights, definitions of, **2:**15
positive and negative conceptions of, **2:**15–16
rights in Islamic law, **5:136–137**
acknowledgement of, **1:**19–20
Rights of Man and the Citizen, **3:**99
Rights of the Crown of England, The (Bagshaw), **2:**440
Rights of War and Peace, The (Grotius), **3:**276

right to bear arms, **1:216–222**
Rigveda, **5:**344
ripper legislation, **4:**121
Risala (al-Shafiʿi), **5:**236
Risala (Ibn Abi Zayd al-Qayrawani), **2:**41; **3:**351
basis for Nigerian codification, **2:**36
Risāla (Shafiʿi), **3:**316
Risala fi talab al-ʿilm (Ibn Abi Zayd), **5:**61
Risālah (al-Qayrawani), **3:**250
Risala ithbat wasiyyat amir al-Muʾminin (attr. Zayd), **6:**161
"Rise of Modern Evidence Law" (Gallanis), **3:**5
Rise of the City, 1878–1898 (Schlesinger), **4:**121
Rishonim, **3:**388, 392
rita (cosmic order), **3:**215
Ritchu, Sarup, **5:**316
Rites of Zhou (Confucius), **1:**459–460; **5:**47
Rituale Romanum (1614), **2:**224
Rivers and Harbors Act (U.S., 1899), **2:**454–455
RLUIPA. *See* Religious Land Use and Institutionalized Persons Act
robbery
ancient Greek law, **2:**267–268
delict and, **2:**325
English common law, **5:**462
German law, **5:**463
punishment for, **5:**463
Roman law, **5:**463
versus theft, **5:**463
Robert Bruce. *See* Robert I (Scotland)
Robert I (Scotland), **5:**197–198
Robert II (Scotland), **5:**197
Roberts, John
on federalism, **3:**65
on right to bear arms, **1:**222
treason of, **4:**335
Roberts, Owen, **2:**27
on federalism, **3:**62
on general welfare clause, **3:**114
T-square rule of, **4:**76
Robertson, George, **1:**12
Robertson, Thomas E., **3:***269*
Robinson, A. N. R., **6:**11
Robinson, Jackie, **4:**179
Robson, William, **5:**17
ROC. *See* Republic of China
Rocco, Francesco, **4:**151
Rockefeller, John D., **4:**482
Rodenburg, Christian, **2:**109
on conflict of laws, **2:**112

Roesler, Hermann, **3**:374, 375
Roffredus de Epiphanio, **1**:248
rogator (one who asks), **4**:95
Roger II (Sicily), **4**:91
Rogerius, **4**:361
Roger of Seaton, **2**:85
Roman Catholic Church. *See also* pope and papacy
   appointment of prelates, **1**:467
   in Baltic nations, **1**:254
   on bishops and archbishops, **1**:293–296
   Brazil, **1**:303
   on contraception, **6**:141
   ecclesiastical courts, **2**:385–386
   England
      dissolution of monastic orders, **2**:129
      legislation discriminating against, **3**:311
   Gregorian Reforms, **1**:466, 471
   in Irish law, **3**:313
   Netherlands, **4**:225–226
   notaries in, **4**:237–238
   in ordeals, **4**:262–263
   principles of international law handed fown by, **3**:282
   on slavery, **5**:253–254
   South and Central America, **5**:299
   Sweden, **5**:414
Roman citizenship and Latinitas, **5**:137–140
   nationality and, **4**:205–206
Roman-Dutch Law (Leeuwen), **5**:340
Roman Empire
   conflict of laws in, **2**:110
   division of, **1**:137
Romania
   accession into European Union, **2**:492
   Islamic law in, **1**:253; **3**:333
Romanistische Abteilung, **1**:166
Roman jurists, **3**:433–437
Roman law, **5**:140–164, *142, 145, 150, 159*. *See also* ancient Rome; Justinian; Paul; praetorian edict; Ulpian
   27 B.C.E.–250 C.E., **5:144–148**
   250–527 C.E., **5:148–152**
   753–27 B.C.E., **5:140–144**
   adoption, **4**:303, 304, 305, 306, 308
   on advocates, **1**:55–58
   Africa, **1**:63
      in Dutch colonies, **1**:81
   agency, **1**:108, 110–112
   the Age of Justinian, **5:152–155**
   alternative dispute resolution in, **1**:129
   arbitration, **5**:180–181
   on assignment, **1**:227
   on attempt, **1**:236–237
   Austria, **1**:246
   on banking, **1**:273–274
   under Basil I, **1**:282
   on breach of contract, **1**:307, 308–309
   business law, **1**:319–320
   Byzantium, **1**:327–334
   on children, **3**:44
   citizenship, **5**:137–140, 150
   codification in ancient, **2:31–34**
   conflict of laws, **2**:109
   courts, **2**:234–239, 251–255
   credit, **2**:262–264
   criminal, **2**:268–275
      courts, **2**:237–239
   critiques of, **2**:357
   debt
      legis actiones in, **4**:83–84
      slaves as security for, **5**:248
      written account of, **2**:186
   on delay, **2**:319–320
   on delict, **2:320–324**
   Domat, Jean, on, **2**:356–357
   on donation, **2**:357–358
   Doneau, Hugues, on, **2**:360
   dowry, **4**:304, 305, 306, 307, 308
   Du Moulin, Charles, on, **2**:372
   on easements, **2**:379, 380
   Egypt
      juristic papyrology on, **2**:417–421
   on engagement, **3**:41
   England, **2**:436, 439
      reception of, **2**:439
   English common law and, **5:155–157**
   Enlightenment on, **2**:444
   on equity, **2**:466
   error and mistake in, **2**:475–476
   evidence in, **3**:5–6
   family, **3**:40–48; **5**:124–125 (*See also* persons, Roman law)
   fideicommissum in, **3**:81
   first act of codification of, **3**:211
   foreigner self-rule under, **3**:115–116
   formula in, **3**:93–97
   on fraud, **3**:102–103

Germany, **3:**117–118
  provincial administration and, **3:**115–117
Gravina, Gian Vincenzo, on, **3:**126
guarantee in, **3:**128–129
on guardianship/curatorship, **3:**47–48
guilt in, **3:**133
Hellenistic law in, **1:**160–161
Hindu law and, **3:**148
historiography, **5:157–164**
humanisim and, **3:**188–189, 190, 191–192
illegality in, **3:**203
influenced by
  Christianity, **5:**122–125
  Jewish law, **3:**393
influence on
  Danish law, **2:**328
  English law, **5:**461–462; **6:**1
  French law, **3:**98–99
  liability law, **5:**469–472
  Russian law, **5:**166
insolvency law, **3:**248–249
ius in, **1:**327
Jewry law, **3:**395–396
judges and juries, **3:**404–406
justice, equity, and good conscience, **3:**445
legal education in, **2:**391–393, 400
legal reasoning in, **4:**79–81
legis in, **1:**327
legislative assemblies in, **4:**92–95
on legitimacy of children, **3:**46–47
Leibniz, Gottfried Wilhelm, on, **4:**100
lex in, **4:**101–102
Macedonian Renaissance, **1:**283
Maine, Henry, on, **4:**137
maritime, **1:**35
natural law in, **4:**216–217
Noordt, Gerard, on, **4:**236
notaries in, **4:**237
organization of codes based on, **2:**48
perpetuatio obligationis, **2:**319–320
personal status, **4:**293
persons in, **4:302–309**
pledge, **4:**328–329
political crimes, **4:**332–334
possession, **4:**358, 360–362
on predial servitude, **5:**223–224
private law, **4:**392–393

privileges, **4:**397–398
procedure
  civil, **4:**431–435
  criminal, **4:**435–440
property, **3:**79; **4:459–468,** 474–479
provincial edicts and government, **4:**495–498
public law
  Roman Empire, **5:11–14**
  Roman Republic, **5:8–11**
punishment, **5:**31–35
reception of, **5:**223–224
rediscovery of, **2:**5–6
religious law, **5:**120–125
Savigny, Friedrich Carl von, on, **5:**195
scholarship on, **1:**162
on slavery, **5:***247,* **247–250**
  manumission, **5:**246
in South Africa, **5:**279
Spain, **5:**325
spread of, **2:**440
study of, **4:**276–278
on succession, **5:370–376,** *376*
systematization of, **5:**420–421
taxation, **5:**435–439, *437*
theft and robbery, **5:**463
Twelve Tables, **6:***19,* 19–21
undue influence, **6:**23–25
unjust enrichment, **6:**64–66
usury, **6:**70–72
vicarious liability in, **6:**77–78
Wales, **6:**98
women in, **6:**117–120
Roman law, medieval and post-medieval. *See* medieval and post-medieval Roman law
Romano, Santi, **1:**23
Roman schools of law. *See* Labeo, Marcus Antistius; Sabinus, Massurius; Servius Sulpicius Rufus
Roman Statutes (Crawford), **6:**21
Romanus I Lecapenus, **4:**469
Rome, Treaty of (1957), **2:**489, *490*
  on private law, **2:**495
Rome Convention for the Protection of Performers, Producers of Phonograms and Broadcasting Organizations (1984), **3:**263
Rome of the Twelve Tables (Watson), **6:**21
Romero, Silvio, **1:**303
Rome Treaties (1957), **2:**486

Romilly, Samuel
    on bankruptcy, **1:**267
    campaign against capital punishment, **1:**365
    on capital punishment, **4:**41
Römisches Staatrecht (Mommsen), **5:**159, 160
Romulus (Roman king), **5:**140
Romulus Augustulus, **2:**237, 268
Roncaglia, Peace of (1158), **4:**91
Roomsch Hollandsch Recht (Roman-Dutch law) (Leeuwen), **4:**226
Roosevelt, Eleanor, **3:**295
Roosevelt, Franklin D.
    administrative agencies under, **1:**27–28, 29
    agriculture policy under, **5:**89
    on antitrust, **1:**190
    on bankruptcy, **1:**269
    corporations under, **1:**325–326
    court-packing plan, **3:**61–62, 409, 482; **4:**483
    environmental law under, **2:**455
    executive power of, **3:**22, 24; **5:***216*
    federalism under, **3:**61–62
    international rule of law and, **3:**295
    on judicial power, **3:**412
    judicial review under, **1:**31
    labor and employment law, **3:**482
    legislative power of, **4:**98
    media and, **6:**54
    on military tribunals, **4:**179
    military tribunals under, **6:**90
    Native Americans under, **4:**211
    New Deal, **3:**144; **4:**483, 491–492; **5:**80
    poverty programs under, **4:**370
    public-works programs, **3:**182
    securities policy under, **5:**92
    social security, **6:**96
    tax policy, **5:**444–446, 446–447
    use of federal power over the economy, **2:**155
Roosevelt, Theodore
    on antitrust, **1:**189
    on bankruptcy, **1:**268
    on conservation, **2:**455
    corporations under, **5:**78
    executive power under, **3:**20, 21
    Native Americans under, **4:**210
    on taxation, **5:**443

Root, Elihu, **2:**404–405
Root, Jesse, **6:**38
Rorty, Richard, **4:**363, 364
Rosen, Jeffrey, **2:**302
Rosenberg, Ethel, **4:**335
Rosenberg, Julius, **4:**335
Rosenblum, Victor, **5:**267–268
Rostovtzeff, Michael, **1:**160
Rostow, Eugene, **2:**406
Rota Romana, **2:**7; **3:**356
Rothschild, Nathan Mayer, **1:**272
Rousseau, Jean-Jacques
    on capital punishment, **5:**34
    on democracy, **5:**418
    influence on French constitution of 1791, **2:**120
    on justice, **3:**447
Royal Asiatic Society of Great Britain and Ireland, **2:**57
Royal Commission on the Law relating to Mental Illness and Mental Deficiency (Percy Commission), **3:**246
Royal Exchange (England), **1:**292
Royal Exchange and London Assurance Corporation Act (1720), **2:**88, 89
royal grants, monopolies and, **4:**186–187
Royal Institute of Law and Administration (Laos), **4:**14
Royal Niger Company, **1:**86
Rubino, J., **5:**159
Rubinstein, Lene, **1:**165; **6:**111
Rubios, Palacios, **5:**299
Rudorff, A. A. Friedrich, **5:**160
Rudorff, Otto, **3:**374
Ruffin, Thomas, **5:**261
Rufus, Servius Sulpicius. *See* Servius Sulpicius Rufus
rule of law, **5:164–166**
    classical legal theory on, **2:**23
rule of reason on antitrust, **1:**191
Rules Enabling Act (U.S., 1934), **4:**444
    on evidence, **3:**11
rules of choice-of-law. *See* conflict of laws
Rules of Civil Procedure (U.S.), **4:**445
Rules of Oléron, **4:**150
    law merchant, **4:**36
    maritime law, **1:**36, 37
    Spain, **5:**325
Rumania, **2:**113
Rupert's Land, **1:**337

ru ren zui (impose guilt on someone), **6:**153
Ruschenbusch, Eberhard, **1:**164; **2:**30
Rush, Benjamin, **2:**289
   on alcohol, **1:**124
Rushdie, Salman, **1:**381; **2:**280
Russel, John, **4:**41–42
Russell, Karen, **3:***111*
Russell Sage Foundation, **4:**32
   law and society research by, **4:**34
Russia, **5:**166–178, *171, 174, 175. See also* Union of Soviet Socialist Republics (USSR)
   advocates in, **1:**58
   Baltic nations under, **1:**255
   enlightened absolutism in, **2:**445
   influenced by Roman law, **5:**163
   Kievan Rus, **5:**166–167, 177
   legal Doctrine, **5:**177–178
   Mongol Subjugation, 1240–1480, **5:**167–168
   Muscovite Law, 1480–1648, **5:**168–170
   private law, **1:**255
   Russian Empire, 1649–1917, **5:**170–174
   Soviet era, 1917–1991, **5:**174–177
   treaty with Japan, **3:**365, 372
Russian Federation, **2:**113
Russian Penal Code (1846), **1:**255
Russkaia Pravda (Russia), **5:**167
Rustamid dynasty, **3:**348
Rutherforth, Thomas, **1:**109
Rutilius Rufus, Publius, **4:**375
Ruzé, Françoise, **4:**84
Rwabugiri (Rwanda), **1:**69
Rwanda, **1:**63
   decolonization of, **1:**93
   official languages in, **1:**99
   precolonial kingdoms, **1:**69
Ryder, Dudley, **4:**142

S

Sá, Mem de, **5:**301
Saadia Gaon, Rav, **3:**391
Saba, **1:**369
Śabarasvāmin, **4:**182
Sabha, Tat Khalsa Singh, **5:**241
Sabinian school of jurists, **2:**392
   disputes with Proculian school, **3:**476–477
   Labeo, Marcus Antistius, and, **3:**475
   on legal reasoning, **4:**80
Sabinus, Masurius, **3:**434, 436; **5:179–181**
   civil law summary by, **2:**392
   legal education by, **2:**391–392
   Paul's commentary on, **4:**290
Sacco, Nicola, **4:**337
Sachs, Margaret, **5:**93
Sachsenspiegel, **1:**246; **3:***117*; **4:**91; **5:**436
   on feudal law, **3:**78
   on liability of master, **6:**77
   principle of personality, **2:**110
   on sexual crimes, **5:**230
   on succession, **5:**394
Sacks, Albert
   on legal process, **4:**65, 66–68, 69
   on statutory interpretation, **5:**361, 362, 363
Sacrae disciplinae leges (apostolic constitution, 1983), **1:**352, 354
Sacra Paenitentiaria, **2:**386
Sacra Rota Romana, **2:**386
Sacred Dukes (China), **4:**2
sadācāra, **3:**215; **5:181–182**
   mīmāṃsā and, **4:**182
Sadat, Anwar as-, **2:**421
Safavids dynasty (Iran), **3:**302
Safety Appliance Act (1893), **5:**102
Saffah, Abu al-'Abbas al-, **1:**1
Safwat al-ikhtiyar fi usul al-fiqh (al-Mansur), **4:**144
Sagha, Singh, **5:**241
Śāha, Surendra Vikrama, **4:**224–225
Sahnun, 'Abd al-Salam ibn Sa'id al-Tanukhi, **3:**351; **5:182–183,** 239, 240
   on Malik ibn Anas, **3:**350; **4:**140
   Maliki law compiled by, **4:**127–128
Sahnun, Abu 'Abdallah ibn, **3:**197
Said, Seyyid, **1:**69
Sa'id, Abu, **2:***351*
Saint Barthélemy, **1:**369
Saint Eustatius, **1:**369
Saint Kitts and Nevis, **1:**369
Saint Lucia, **1:**369
Saint Maarten, **1:**369
Saint Martin, **1:**369
Saint Vincent and the Grenadines, **1:**369
Saiyidi Maula, **2:**281
Salafi, **6:**87
salafiyya concept, **3:**202
salam (deferred-delivery sale), **1:**264–265, 359; **2:**73, 79, 200, **202–203**

Sala wa-hukm tarikiha, Al- (Ibn Qayyim al-Jawziyya), **3:**199
Salazar, António de Oliveira, **2:**384
sale, **5:**183–194
   ancient Roman law, **2:**184, 186, 187–188
      differentiated from barter, **2:**189
   Chinese law
      sale of goods, **5:**183–185
      sale of land, **4:**5–6; **5:**185–189
   contracts in Islamic law, **3:**324
   English common law, **5:**189–191
   in Islamic law, **2:**73–74, *200*
   medieval and post-medieval Roman law
      sale of goods, **5:**191–193
      sale of land, **5:**193–194
      Sabinus, Masurius, on, **5:**180
   of slaves in ancient Greece, **5:**244
Saleilles, Raymond
   comparative law, **2:**99
   on private law, **3:**100
Sale of Goods Act (India, 1930), **2:**173; **3:**216
Sale of Goods Act (U.K.), **4:**471; **5:**190–191
Sale of Goods (Amendment) Act (U.K., 1994), **5:**189
Salic law, **3:**116–117
Salinas, Carlos, **3:***286*
Salutati, Coluccio, **3:**189
Salvius Julianus. *See* Julian
Salvius Julianus, Publius, **5:**146
Samaʿ (Ibn al-Qasim), **5:**183
Samaʿ (al-Malik ibn Habib), **3:**350
Samarqand, **3:**343, 344
Sāmaveda, **5:**344
Sambourne, Edward Linley, **1:***78*
Samoa, **4:**346
Samoza, Salgado de, **3:**249
Sampson, William, **2:**50
San (Bushmen), **1:**71
Sanʿani, al-Husayn ibn Ahmad al-Khaymi al-, **6:**162
Sanches de Bustamante y Sirvén, Antonio /should be Sanchez/?, **2:**114
Sanger, Margaret, **6:**140
Sangkum Reastre Niyum Party (Cambodia), **1:**335
Sanhedrin, **3:**388
Sanhuri, ʿAbd al-Razzaq Ahmad al-, **3:**345
   administrative decrees by, **1:**34
   civil code by, **1:**205–206; **2:**35
   on contracts, **2:**199

   on insurance, **3:**255
   on public law in classical Islam, **2:**134
Sanhuri Code (Egypt), **2:**421
sanitary movement, **3:**143
Santander, Francisco de Paula, **2:**62, *62*
Santarém, Pedro de, **4:**151
Santerna, Pietro, **5:**364
Santillana, David, **4:**129
   on Zaydi juridical literature, **6:**161
São Tomé, **1:**79
Sapienza University, La, **3:**126
Sappho, **5:**228–229
Sarakhsi, Muhammad ibn Ahmad ibn Abi Sahl, **4:**289; **5:**194
   on agricultural contracts, **1:**116
   on constitutional law, **2:**134–135
   on contracts, **2:**199–200
   on public international law, **3:**280
   on sale, **3:**328
   territorial concepts, **5:**451, 453
   on torture, **5:**487
Sarat, Austin, **4:**34
Sarawak, **5:**319
Sarbah, J. M., **1:**65
Sarbanes-Oxley Act (U.S., 2002), **5:**85, 95
Sársfield, Dalmacio Vélez, **1:**216
   codification by, **5:**286
Sarsfield, Velez, **1:**302
Sartre, Jean-Paul, **2:**297
Sarwey, Otto von, **1:**23
Sassoferato, Bartolus de. *See* Bartolus of Saxoferrato
Sassoferrato, Bartolo da. *See* Bartolus of Saxoferrato
Satanic Verses, The (Rushdie), **1:**381
Śatapathabrāhmana, **3:**179
satī, **6:**131
Sati Regulation (Bengal, 1829), **6:**131
Satyagraha in South Africa (Gandhi), **5:**284
Saudi Arabia
   alcohol and drugs, **1:**122–123
   codification, **1:**206
   contract law following uncodified Islamic law, **3:**256
   courts for Islamic punishments, **1:**368
   criminal law in, **2:**279
   death penalty, **1:**368
      of juveniles, **3:**462
   Islamic law, **1:**208–209, **208–209**
   political dimension of Islamic law, **4:**338
   zakat, **5:**431

Saul (King of Israel), **3**:389
Sauser-Hall, Georges, **2**:99
Savarkar, Vinayak Damodar, **3**:159–160
Savigny, Friedrich Carl von, **2**:9–10; **4**:276, 277, 278; **5**:194–196; **6**:25
    on the ALR, **5**:2
    on assignment, **1**:228
    on breach of contract, **1**:307
    on codification, **2**:48; **5**:326
    on conflict of laws, **2**:112
    on definition of law, **4**:19–20
    on Doneau, Hugues, **2**:360
    on Dutch jurisprudence, **4**:226
    on error and mistake, **2**:475–476
    influence on
        historians, **5**:160
        Ørsted, Anders Sandøe, **2**:328
        private law, **4**:396
        Russia, **5**:172
        Unger, Josef, **6**:26
    on interpretation, **3**:299–300
    Jhering and, **3**:399
    on possession, **4**:358, 361
    on property, **4**:476
    on Roman law, **5**:159, 160, 162, 163
    on succession, **5**:391
    on systematization, **5**:421
savings clauses, British colonial law and, **1**:369
Savorgnan de Brazza, Pierre, **1**:88
Saxoferato, Bartolus de, **2**:254
Sayl al-jarrar, al- (Shawkani), **4**:136
Sayles, G. O., **3**:473
Sayrafi, Abu Bakr al-, **3**:201
Scaccia, Sigismondo, **4**:39
Scaevola, Cervidius, **4**:290
Scaevola, Publius Mucius, **5**:121
Scaevola, Q. Cervidius, **3**:436; **5**:375
Scaevola, Quintus Mucius, **4**:497; **5**:121
    on civil law, **5**:179
    on jurists, **3**:434
    on legal reasoning, **4**:79–80
    Servius Sulpicius Rufus and, **5**:225
Scafuro, Adele C., **4**:403; **6**:111
Scalia, Antonin, **2**:165; **3**:164, 166, 168
    on affirmative action, **2**:343
    on environmental law, **2**:458
    on federalism, **3**:65
    on the *Lemon* test, **5**:119
    on natural law, **4**:219–220
    on right to bear arms, **1**:222
    on standing, **2**:458
    on statutory interpretation, **5**:362
Scandalum Magnatum (England, 1275), **4**:105
Scandinavia. *See also* Denmark; Finland; Norway; Sweden
    bishops in, **1**:296
    feudal law in, **3**:79
    legislation in, **4**:91
    positivism in, **4**:355
    state church in, **1**:349–350
Scantinius, **2**:269
SCAP. *See* Supreme Commander for the Allied Powers
Schacht, Joseph, **3**:316, 326, 330, 349
    on judicial review, **3**:413
    on legal reasoning, **4**:63
    on option, **4**:261
    on Zaydi juridical literature, **6**:162
Schapera, Isaac, **1**:91
Scheduled Castes and Scheduled Tribes (Prevention of Atrocities) Act (India, 1989), **2**:283; **3**:219
Scheid, John, **5**:122
Schelling, F. W. J. von
    jurisprudence of concepts and, **3**:433
    neoidealism of, **4**:204
Scheuner, Ulrich, **1**:352
Schiffsordnung, maritime law in, **1**:36
Schiprecht (Hamburg, c. 1300), **4**:150
Schlafly, Phyllis, **6**:138
Schleiermacher, Friedrich, **6**:63
Schleiermacher, Friedrich Ernst Daniel, **1**:351
Schlesinger, Arthur M., Jr.
    on executive power, **3**:22
    on urbanization, **4**:121
Schlossman, Steven, **3**:458
Schminck, Andreas, **1**:281
Schmitt, Carl, **2**:121, 122
    on National Socialist law, **4**:204
Schneidewein, Nicolaus, **4**:245
Scholasticism. *See also* late Scholasticism
    Bartolus of Saxoferrato in, **1**:280–281
    on breach of contract, **1**:307
    and development of science of law, **2**:6
    on error and mistake, **2**:475
    humanism and, **3**:189–191

Irnerius and, **3**:314
in legal education, **2**:399–400
Scholia Sinaitica, **5**:151
Scholten, Paul, **4**:226
Schömann, G. F., **1**:162
Schreinsbücher (Cologne)
on mortgage, **4**:190
Schröder, Jan, **5**:163
Schulting, Anton, **5**:158
Schulting, Johan, **4**:235
Schulz, Fritz, **5**:161
on Roman jurist schools, **2**:392
Schuman, Robert, **2**:*485*
in European Coal and Steel Community founding, **2**:486, 488–489
Schuman Declaration (1950), **2**:488–489
Schürpf, Hieronymus, **1**:349
Schuster, Claud, **4**:42
Schwabenspiegel, **1**:246; **4**:91
on sexual crimes, **5**:230
on succession, **5**:394
Schwartz, Richard "Red," **4**:33
science of law, development of, **2**:6
"science of the shares" in Islamic law, **3**:232
Scientific Evidence (Giannelli and Imwinkelried), **3**:13
Scienza della legislazione (Filangieri), **3**:83–84
Scotch Reform (Bentham), **1**:287
Scotland, **5**:196–203
devolution of powers to, **2**:133, *133*
feudal law in, **3**:76
juries in, **3**:437
Roman law, **5**:157
state and church in, **1**:468
undue influence in Scottish law, **6**:25
Scott, John (Lord Eldon), **2**:89, *438*
on bankruptcy, **1**:267
on conscience, **2**:470
Scott, Winfield, **4**:177
Scottish Church, **1**:468
Scottsboro Boys, **4**:452
Scrope, Henry le, **4**:377
SC Turpillianum, **2**:274
scutage, **3**:73
Seagle, William, **1**:381
Sealey, Raphael, **1**:164, 165

search and seizure
Roman law
delict, **2**:321, 322, 323
ritual, **2**:322, 323
United States, **4**:386–387, 387, 388, 451; **5**:203–208
search incident to arrest exception, **5**:207
Sears, Roebuck and Co., **3**:68
Seavey, Warren, **1**:113
Sebastião, D., **5**:301
SEC. *See* Securities and Exchange Commission
secessionist movements in Canada, **1**:339
Second Charter of Justice (U.K., 1826), **5**:241–242
Second Restatement of Torts. *See* Restatement (Second) of Torts
Second Treatise of Civil Government (Locke), **4**:487
Secret History (Procopius), **3**:454
Secret History of the Mongols, The (Rachewiltz), **4**:183
secret societies in China, **4**:258
Section 8 certificates and vouchers, **3**:184–185
secularism in Indian law, **2**:145; **5**:208–209, 308
dharma and, **2**:333
secularization in Italy, **3**:357
Securities Act (U.S., 1933), **2**:177; **6**:59
on arbitration, **3**:486
Berle and Means influence on, **1**:326
on stock market trading, **5**:92
Securities and Exchange Act (U.S., 1934), **6**:59
Berle and Means influence on, **1**:326
Securities and Exchange Commission, **1**:28; **5**:81, 92–95
on bankruptcy, **1**:269, 270
Berle and Means influence on, **1**:326
scientific research under, **4**:30
Securities Exchange Act (U.S., 1934), **5**:92
securities regulation, United States, **5**:92–95
Sedgwick, Eve Kosovsky, **3**:112
sedition
ancient Near Eastern law, **1**:175
Aztec law, **5**:288
Chinese law, **4**:257, 259
Sedition Act (U.S., 1798), **4**:450; **6**:50
backlash to, **2**:17
freedom of speech and, **5**:333
Sedition Act (U.S., 1918)
restriction of rights, **2**:16
Sedition and Espionage Acts (U.S., 1917 and 1918)
creation of ACLU in reaction to, **2**:17

Segni, Antonio, **2:***490*
Segovia, Lisandro, **1:**216
segregation, **2:**340–341
    case law on, **3:**163–164, 165–166
    desegregation, **2:**342–343, 410
        equity in, **2:**473
    due process and, **2:**371
    education law on, **2:**409–412, *410*
    equal protection and, **2:**460, 461
    social science evidence on, **5:***267*, 268
Segu-Tukulor empire, **1:**68
seigneurial courts (England), **3:**73, 74
seisin. *See also* novel disseisin, writ of
    action of novel disseisin, **3:**76
    easements and, **2:**381
    final process for, **3:**88
    subinfeudation and, **5:**368
Selassie, Haile, **2:***480*
    codification by, **2:**479
Selden, John
    as barrister, **1:**278
    comparative law, **2:**98
    on torture, **5:**484
Select Case in the Court of King's Bench (Sayles, ed.), **3:**473
Select Committee on Noxious Vapours (U.K., 1862), **2:**450
Selection of Cases on the Law of Contracts, A (Langdell), **2:**208
Selection of Leading Cases in Various Branches of the Law, A (Smith), **2:**442
Selection of Legal Maxims, A (Broom), **4:**61
self-defense
    Chinese law, **6:**151
    England, **2:**439
    right to bear arms and, **1:**218
    Roman law, **2:**323
Seligman, Edwin, **3:**286
Selinous, **1:**54
Seljuq Turks, Hanafi school and, **3:**343–344
Selznick, Philip, **4:**32
    on law and society, **4:**33
Senanayake, D. S., **5:**342
Senate, Roman, **5:**11, **209–213,** *210*
Senatus Consultum Claudianum (Rome, 52 c.e.), **4:**305
    on slavery, **5:**247
Senatus Consultum Macedonianum, **2:**186
senatus consultum ultimum, **5:**212

Senchas Már Ancient Tradition (Irish law book), **1:**374
Seneca
    on guilt, **3:**134
    on punishment, **5:**42–43
Seneca Falls Convention, **6:**45
Seneca Falls Declaration, **6:**134
Senegal
    constitution, **1:**106; **2:**137
    court system, **2:**43
    French law in, **1:**89
    inheritance, **2:**38
    law reform, **1:**100
    political parties, **1:**104
sentence in Chinese law, **5:213–215**
    review and, **1:**196–197
    under Wester Zhou dynasty, **1:**403
Sententiae Pauli (Paul)
    on delict, **2:**324
    on fraud, **3:**102
    influence of, **5:**151
separate spheres ideology, **6:**134
    feminist legal theory on, **3:**66, 68
    in labor and employment law, **3:**480
separation of powers, **5:215–221**
    Brazil, **1:**302
    Denmark, **2:**328
    Germany under National Socialist law, **3:**110
    in Islamic countries, **2:**37
    United States
        in state constitutions, **5:**350
        state law, **5:**348, 349
Sephardic Jews, **3:**388, 392, 396–398
Septimius Severus (Roman emperor), **3:**213, 435
    jurists under, **3:**434
    marriage of, **6:**23
    money and administrative reform under, **3:**436
    Papinian and, **4:**278–279
    on property, **4:**464–465
    replies to petitions, **6:**23
    on women, **6:**118
Sepúlveda, Juan Ginés de, **4:**15
    in Scholasticism, **4:**16
Serbia, Islamic law in, **1:**251–253; **3:**333
Serbs, Croats, and Solvenes, Kingdom of, **3:**334

serfdom, **6**:80
    Baltic nations, **1**:255
serjeants at law, **5**:*221*, **221–223**
Serjeant's Inn, **5**:222, 223
Serrigny, Denis, **1**:23
Servicemen's Readjustment Act (U.S., 1944).
    See G.I. Bill
servitude in real estate, **5:223–224**
    easements and, **2**:379–380
Servius Alexander (Roman emperor), **4**:290
Servius Cornelius, **3**:431
Servius Cornelius Salvidienus Orfitus, **3**:431
Servius Sulpicius Rufus, **3**:434, 435; **5**:162,
    224–225
    on legal reasoning, **4**:79
    on theft, **5**:179
Servius Tullius (Roman king), **5**:10, 141
Setenario, **1**:215; **5**:290
Settled Land Act (U.K., 1882), **5**:367
Seven Expulsion Conditions (China), **4**:159
Seventy-first Report (1978) of the Indian Law
    Commission, **3**:50
Seven Years' War (1756–1763), **1**:337
    Quebec defeat in, **1**:312
Severus, Septimius, **2**:418
Severus Alexander (Roman emperor)
    death of, **5**:148
    on slavery, **5**:248
    on validity of wills, **2**:420
Seward, William, **2**:158
sexual and moral regulation in ancient Greece,
    5:226–229
    adultery, **1**:50–53
    anthropological perspective on, **1**:186
sexual assault
    duress in, **2**:375
    United States in the military, **6**:140
sexual crimes in medieval and post-medieval Roman law,
    5:229–231
sexual harrassment
    Chinese law, **5**:232, 234
    feminist legal theory on, **3**:67
    as Title VI violation, **2**:340
sexual intercourse
    illegal in Islamic law, **1**:367; **3**:325
    illicit in Chinese law, **4**:159; **5:231–232**
sexuality. *See also* gay, lesbian, bisexual, and
    transgender theory
    ancient Greece, **6**:114, 115
    China, lack of filial piety and, **3**:86

    feminist legal theory on, **3**:69, 70
    women
        in Hindu law, **6**:131
        in Islamic law, **6**:127–128
        in Ottoman Empire, **6**:129
sexual offenses
    ancient Near Eastern law, **1**:175
    Chinese law, **5:232–234**
        disrespect *(bujing)* in, **4**:250
        mutual concealment and, **4**:199
    England, ecclesiastical law on, **2**:389
    Islamic law, **4**:164
        abrogation of legal norms and, **1**:6
    United States, evidence on, **3**:12
Seychelles, **5:234–235**
    British colonies in, **1**:86
    English law in, **1**:87
    French law in, **1**:63
    official languages in, **1**:99
Sezgin, Fuat, **6**:161
Sforza, Carlo, **2**:*485*
sGam po, Srong btsan, **1**:290
Shafi'i, Muhammad ibn Idris al-, **3**:352; **5:235–236**;
    6:155
    on abrogation of legal norms, **1**:6
    on agricultural contracts, **1**:117
    Da'ud on, **3**:353
    Ibn Hanbal and, **3**:197
    on ijtihyā, **3**:224
    influence on
        Da'ud 'Ali al-Isbahani, **2**:313
        Muzani, Abu Ibrahim Isma'il ibn Yahya
            al-, **4**:200
    on lease and tenancy, **4**:56
    on legal reasoning, **4**:62
    in Meccan legal tradition, **1**:210
    on option, **4**:262
    on possession, **4**:360
    on taxation, **5**:432
Shafi'i school of Islamic law, **3:352–353**. *See also*
    'Amili, Muhammad ibn Makki al-; Ibn
    Surayj, Ahmad ibn 'Umar; Juwayni,
    'Abd al-Malik ibn Abi Muhammad, Imam
    al-Haramayn; Muzani, Abu Ibrahim Isma'il
    ibn Yahya al-; Qaffal, Abu Bakr Muhammad
    ibn 'Ali ibn Isma'il al-Shashi al-; Shirazi, Abu
    Ishaq Ibrahim ibn 'Ali
    abrogation of legal norms, **1**:6
    alcohol and drug use, **1**:121
    al-Ghazali in, **3**:119–120

the body, **1:**299
children
  child support, **1:**397
  custody rights, **1:**397
  father-child relations, **3:**37
competition with Hanafi school, **3:**343
concept of law, **5:**451
contracts
  agricultural, **1:**116, 117
  object of commercial, **2:**79
deposit, **2:**332
education in, **4:**71
geographical presence
  Africa, **1:**74; **2:**41
  Iran, **3:**301
  Malaysia, **2:**140
  Yemen, **6:**155
guardianship, **4:**166
lease and tenancy, **4:**55, 56
legal norms, **4:**62
legal reasoning, **4:**63
marriage, **4:**165, 166
  repudiation of, **4:**168
in Meccan legal tradition, **1:**210
non-Muslims, **3:**316
option, **4:**261
partnership, **4:**289
persons, **4:**312
pledge, **4:**327
profit, **4:**455
rules of evidence, **4:**428
sale of debts, **1:**264
taxation, **5:**432, 433
trade, **2:**73
usurpation, **6:**67–68
usury, **6:**69
wills, **6:**106
Shahid al-Awwal, al-. *See* 'Amili, Muhammad ibn Makki al-
Shahid al-Thani, al-. *See* 'Amili, Zayn al-Din ibn 'Ali ibn Ahmad al-
Shahid I, the First Martyr. *See* 'Amili, Muhammad ibn Makki al-
Shahid II, the Second Martyr. *See* 'Amili, Zayn al-Din ibn 'Ali ibn Ahmad al-
Shaibani, Muhammad ibn al-Hasan al-
  on Malik ibn Anas, **4:**140
Shaka, **1:**69–70
Shaltut, Mahmud, **3:**281

Shang, Lord. *See* Shang Yang
Shang dynasty (China), **5:**57
  corruption, **2:**225
  courts, **2:**241
  mutilation, **4:**196
Shanghai, extraterritoriality in, **3:**92
Shangshu, **2:**356
Shang Yang, **1:**407, 408, 410; **5:**165
  influence on Qin law, **1:**409
  on land, **4:**1
  legal changes influenced by, **1:**456
  liability of neighbors, **1:**415–417; **2:**60
  offenses against the state by, **4:**249
Shanu-Razah, Ahmed (Maldives), **4:**139
Shapiro, Barbara J., **3:**6
Shara'i 'al-Islam (al-Hilli)
  'Amili, Zayn al-Din ibn 'Ali ibn Ahmad al-, on, **1:**132
  Baqir al-Najafi on, **1:**276
Shara'i' al-Islām (al-Hilli), **3:**146
sharecropping. *See* agricultural contracts and sharecropping in Islamic law
shares, **2:**87
  preference share, **2:**89
  as rewards to managers, **2:**91
Sharh 'ala Amthilat al-Fara'id (Uthman al-Wakari), **3:**234
Sharh al-Azhar (The Commentary on the Flowers) ('Abd Allah ibn Miftah), **6:**156
  on Ibn al-Murtada, **4:**136
Sharh al-Luma' (Shirazi), **5:**238
Sharh kitab al-siyar al-kabir (al-Sarakhsi), **5:**194
Sharh minhaj al-usul (al-Subki), **5:**370
shari'a
  Afghanistan, **1:**58–59
  on alcohol and drug use, **1:**122
  Bangladesh, **1:**258
  constitutions citing it as principal source of legislation, **3:**317
  debate in Indonesia, **3:**336
  definitions of, **2:**483; **3:**318
  European, **2:**483–485
  on gambling, **1:**262
  Ghazali, Abu Hamid Muhammad, on, **3:**119–120
  insurance and, **2:**61
  judiciary and, **3:**422–423
  Maghrib and al-Andalus, **4:**129–130
  Ottoman Empire, **4:**267

Philippines, **3:**338
on taxes, **5:**432
on worship, **6:**146–150
Shariah Act (Pakistan, 1991), **4:**274
Shariat Act (India, 1937), **4:**171
Sharif, Nawaz, **2:**142
sharika in banking and finance, **1:**263
Shar kitab al-Nil (Muhammad Yusuf at Faiyish), **2:**41
Sharp, Granville, **4:**143
Shatibi, Abu Ishaq al-
on muftis, **4:**194
reasoning used by, **3:**120
Shaw, James, **1:***241*
Shaw, Lemuel, **3:**426; **5:**350
on criminal procedure, **4:**451
on torts, **5:**474
Shawkani, Muhammad ibn ʿAli al-, **3:**342; **6:**156
on Zaydi school, **4:**136
Shaybani, Muhammad ibn al-Hasan al-, **3:**181, 305; **5:236–237**
on Abu Hanifa, **1:**10
on agricultural contracts, **1:**117
on duty, **2:**377
influence on
Shafiʿi, Muhammad ibn Idris al-, **5:**235–236
on Islamic territorial concepts, **5:**451
legal literature by, **1:**2
on option, **4:**262
on public international law, **3:**280
Sarakhsi, Muhammad ibn Ahmad al-, on, **5:**194
Shaykh al-Islam, **4:**268
Shays, Daniel, **4:**335
Shays's Rebellion, **1:**224
Shen Buhai, **1:**407, 408
Shen Chia-Pen (Shen Jiaben), **1:**438, 439; **5:237–238**
shenming, **1:**457
Shen Zhiqi, **1:**436, 459
on loans, **4:**117
Shen Zong, **1:**425, 461
Sheppard, Sam, Dr., **3:**428
Sheppard, William, **4:**41
Sherira Gaon, Rav, **3:**391
Sherman Antitrust Act (U.S., 1890), **1:**188, 324; **5:**79. *See also* antitrust, United States law
arbitration and, **1:**131

creation of the Interstate Commerce Commission, **5:**77
horizontal agreements and, **1:**191
impact of, **6:**48
on strikes, **1:**325; **6:**48
upheld by Supreme Court, **2:**65
Sherman-White, A. N., **5:**138, 139
Sherry, Suzanna, **2:**302
Shershenevich, G. F., **5:**178
shi
under Song dynasty, **1:**454, 457
in Sui and Tang law, **1:**454
shi crimes (accidental crimes), **3:**275
Shiga Shūzō, **1:**463
Shih Chi-ching, **1:***452*
Shiʿi internationalism, **3:**281
Shiʿi Islam in Iran, **3:**302
Shiʿi law, **6:**18. *See also* Tusi, Muhammad ibn al-Hasan al-
Shiji (Sima), **4:**197
Shi jing (Confucious), **4:**1
Shinritsu Koryo (Japan, 1870), **3:**372, 373
Shipley, William Davies, **4:**143
Shirazi, Abu Ishaq Ibrahim ibn ʿAli, **3:**352; **5:238–239**
on Sahnun, ʿAbd al-Salam ibn Saʿid al-Tanukhi, **5:**182
translation by Éric Chaumont, **3:**316–317
Shi Wei, **1:**404
Shotoku Taishi (Japanese prince), **3:**367
Shromani Gurdwara Prabandhak Committee (SGPC, India), **5:**241
shuibudi Documents, **1:**406–407
Shujing (Book of documents), **3:**275
Shulhan Arukh (code of Joseph Karo), **3:**392
Shulman, Harry, **3:**486–487
shurūḥ (commentaries), **3:**320
Shurūt (handbooks for natories), **3:**321
Shu Xiang, **1:**455
Shuzui tiaoli (Regulation on redemption of Crimes), **1:**431
Siam. *See* Thailand
Sicily, Islamic law in, **5:239–240**
Sickles, Daniel, **3:**428
Sidney, Henry, **3:**310
Siegel, Reva, **3:**68
Sierra Leone
in British Commonwealth, **1:**315
British rule in, **1:***85*, 85–86
constitution, **2:**137

independence, **1:**93
inheritance, **2:**44–45
slavery abolished in, **1:**76
Sierra Leone Company, **1:**85–86
Siete Partidas (Spain, 1265), **1:**215, 384. *See Ley de las siete partidas* (Spain, 1265)
applicability in Spanish Chile, **1:**397
Sieyès, Emmanuel-Joseph, **2:**120
on privileges, **4:**397
Sigismund II Augustus (Poland)
Baltic nations under, **1:**254
on Courland, **1:**255
Signatura apostolica, **2:**386
Sihanouk, Norodom (Cambodia), **5:**314
Sikh law, **5:240–241**
dharma in, **2:**332
Sikh Rehat Maryada (India, 1936), **5:**241
Silbey, Susan S., **4:**34
Silent Spring (Carson), **5:**82
Sima Guang, **1:**197
on mutilation, **4:**197
Sima Qian, **1:**411
on gambling law, **3:**109
Simes, Lewis, **3:**236
Simon, Dieter, **1:**330
Simon, Johann Georg, **5:**464
Simon, John, **2:**451
Simon, William, **4:**26–27
Simonds, Viscount, **2:**330
Simonides, **4:**494
Simons, Lord, **4:**42
Simpson, A. W. Brian, **2:**206
on mortgage, **4:**188
Simpson, Joseph, **2:**394
Simpson, O. J., **2:**301–302; **3:**428; **5:**108
Sinclair, Upton, **5:**78
Singapore, **5:241–242**. *See also* Southeast Asian law
Hindu law in, **5:**321–322
independence of, **5:**314
intellectual property, **3:**263
Islamic law in, **3:**339; **5:**323
shari'a courts, **3:**338
Singh, Gobind, **5:**240
Singh, Maharaja Ramjit, **5:**240
Single European Act (1986), **2:**491
single-member districts, **1:**200, 204
Siraj al-akham, **1:**59
Siricius (pope), **2:**316; **4:**351

Sirmondian Constitution. *See* Constitution Sirmondianae
Sisebut (King of the Visigoths), **3:**397
sitophylakes (grain wardens), **2:**69, 71
Six Acts (U.K., 1819), **1:**380
Six livres de la République, Les (Bodin), **1:**6–7; **3:**282
Six Rites of Marriage (China), **4:**157
Sixteen Moral Principles (Tibet), **5:**305
Sixtus I (pope), **2:**386
Sixtus IV (pope), **2:**223
Sixtus V (pope), **4:**353
siyaāsa shar'iyya (civil policy in concordance with religious law), **3:**202
Siyar al-kabir, al- (Shaybani), **5:**236
Siyar al-saghir, al (Shaybani), **5:**236
Sjø-Lag (Sweden, 1667), **4:**150
Skene, John, **5:**200
Skevington, William, **5:**485
Skolnick, Jerome, **4:**32
Skowronek, Stephen, **3:**426
slander. *See also* libel and slander
Athens, **5:**330
slaves and slavery, **5:243–264**
abolition of slave trade, **1:**75–76
Africa
abrogation under colonial rule, **2:**42
colonialism in, **1:**75–76, 76
Dutch colonies, **1:**81
indigenous laws on, **1:**73
precolonial, **1:**66
African participants in, **1:**71
ancient Athens
gender and status in, **5:**358
in litigation, **4:**114
status of, **1:**234
ancient Greek law, **5:243–247**
enslavement of free citizens, **2:**267–268
Gortyn, **1:**142
Hellenistic, **1:**158, 160
manumission, **1:**143, 158
murder of slaves, **3:**404
selling daughters into, **3:**31
slaves as prison guards and executioners, **4:**382
Solon on, **3:**30; **5:**275
Sparta, **5:**327–328
status of slaves, **5:**355–356

testimony of slaves, **3:**1; **4:**406; **6:**110
torture of slaves, **5:**479–481
ancient Near Eastern law, **1:**170–171, 171
    in litigation, **1:**169
Anglo-Saxon law, **1:**180
for bad debt in Rome, **2:**183
Brazil, **1:**302
    Portuguese law in, **5:**293
British Commonwealth, **1:**313
    Brussels Act on, **1:**77
business law and agency, **1:**319–320
Byzantine law, **4:**309
Chinese law, **5:**44, 45
    illicit sexual intercourse in, **5:**231
    punishment, **5:**54–56
    rape, **5:**66, 67
    sexual offenses in, **5:**233
Code of Gortyn on, **3:**120, 122, 123
in commerce in Athens, **2:**71
contracts and, **2:**207
England
    Mansfield, Lord, on, **4:**143
English common law, **5:**250–253
family
    Islamic law, **1:**358
    Roman law, **5:**247
    United States law, **5:**262
Gaius on, **3:**251
Guatemala, **3:**130
Guyana, **3:**137
international law and, **3:**293–294
Islamic law
    abolishment of, **1:**300
    the body in, **1:**299
    legal bond and slaves, **5:**452, 454
    legal personality of, **4:**58, 64, 65
    manumission of, **2:**375
    option in, **4:**261
    taxes, **5:**430, 431, 432
    wills, **6:**105
jihad and, **3:**280
legal capacity in Islamic law, **1:**358
Liberia, **4:**107
Mauritius, **4:**171–172
natural law on, **4:**218
Peru, **4:**314
Portuguese trade in, **1:**79
and right to trade in Islamic law, **2:**73

Roman law, **2:**272; **5:**123, **247–250** (*See also* persons, Roman law)
    lex Irnitana on, **4:**103
of sailors, **1:**36
servitude in real estate compared with, **5:**223
sex discrimination in, **2:**337
South and Central America, **5:253–256**
    abolished, **5:**285
    colonial, **5:**298
and state migration policies, **3:**206
suppression in Venezuela, **6:**74
United States, **2:**15; **5:258–264**; **6:**28, 30–31, 34, 37, 38, 39, 41, 42, 43–44
    abolished, **2:**340
    ban on importation of slaves, **3:**206
    civic rituals, **3:**428
    colonial period, **2:**286–287, 289; **5:256–258**
    Constitution and, **2:**150
    Constitution on, **2:**154; **3:**448
    criminal law applied to slaves, **2:**290
    equal protection and, **2:**458–462
    federalism and, **3:**60
    free speech and, **6:**51
    marriage of, **6:**134
    natural rights and, **3:**448
    nineteenth century, **6:**52–53
    property law, **4:**482
    punishment of slaves, **5:**38
    religion and, **5:**115
    right to bear arms and, **1:**218–219
    slaves defined as property, **5:**75
    state sovereignty in, **5:**353
    taxes, **5:**440, 441
    territorial status and, **5:**116
villeinage distinguished from, **6:**80
slave trade
    ancient Greek law, **2:**180
    ancient Roman law, **2:**184
Sloan, Alfred P., **5:**445
Sloper, William, **4:**142
Slovakia, **2:**492
Slovak Republic constitution, **2:**122
Slovenia
    accession into European Union, **2:**492
    Islamic law in, **1:**253
Small, Albion, **2:**161

small claims courts
　　in alternative dispute resolution, **1:**128–129
　　New Zealand, **4:**230
Small Constitution (Poland), **4:**331–332
Smend, Rudolf, **2:**121
Smith, Adam, **5:**438
　　on law and economics, **4:**23
　　opposition to joint-stock capitalism, **2:**89
　　on succession, **5:**371
Smith, Arthur, **1:**45
Smith, Gertrude, **1:**163
Smith, J. C., **2:**443
Smith, John, **5:**463
Smith, Joseph, **5:**116
Smith, J. W., **2:**441, 442
Smith, Reginald Heber, **4:**51–52
Smith, Rogers M., **2:**1
Smith, Stanley Alexander de, **2:**443
Smith, Thomas, **3:**243; **5:**156
　　as Regius Professor, **2:**393
Smith Act (U.S.), **5:**334
Smith-Lever Act (U.S., 1914), **5:**88
Smiths of Nottingham, **1:**271–272
smriti, **5:264–265**
　　mīmāṃsā and, **4:**182
Snoy, Jean-Charles, **2:**490
Sobhuza, **1:**70
Sobornoe Ulozhenie (Russian legal code, 1649), **5:**172
socage tenure, **5:**368; **6:**123
Social Civil Code (Cuba, 1988), **1:**370
social-constructionist theory
　　on homosexuality, **3:**112
social contract, Enlightenment concept of, **2:**444
Social Darwinism, **4:**29
Social Defense Code (Cuba, 1936), **1:**370
Social Encyclical of 1891 (Leo XIII), **4:**395
socialism
　　Guyana, **3:**138
　　United States, **5:**78
social science, uses of, **5:266–270**
　　in definition of law, **4:**19–20, 21
　　in disability definitions, **2:**334–335
　　in evidence, **3:**16
　　folk law and, **3:**90
　　guilt definitions and, **3:**135
　　in law and economics, **4:**27
　　in legal process, **4:**65
　　in legal realism, **4:**76–77
　　in study of law and society, **4:**31–35
　　women's labor laws, **6:**136
Social Science Association, **4:**42
Social Science Methods in Legal Education (SSMILE), **4:**32
Social Security, **1:**27
social security. *See also* welfare
　　elderlaw and, **2:**423
　　Germany under National Socialism, **4:**204
　　in modern Europe, **5:270–272**
　　United States, **6:**91
　　　administrative agencies in, **1:**27, *27*
　　　cost of, **6:**92, 97
　　　deserving *vs.* undeserving poor in, **6:**95–96, 137
　　　disability, **2:**334
　　　sex discrimination in, **2:**339
　　　women in, **6:**138
Social Security Act (U.S., 1935), **3:**144; **4:**370, 371; **5:**445; **6:**54, *96*
　　administrative agencies in, **1:**27, 28
　　elderlaw and, **2:**424
　　on labor and employment pensions, **3:**484
　　pensions in, **2:**423
　　social service amendments, **4:**371
social structure
　　Africa
　　　age-set based, **1:**70–71
　　　precolonial, **1:**66–67
　　　stateless, **1:**70–71
　　ancient Athens, **4:**114
　　China
　　　adoption and, **1:**43
　　　sumptuary laws and, **5:**409–410
　　Enlightment views of, **2:**445
　　Fiji, **3:**81–82
　　Hindu law, **5:**182
　　Islamic law, **2:**432
　　Native American, **4:**207
　　natural law on, **4:**216–217
　　New Zealand, **4:**228
　　nītiśāstra on, **4:**232
　　non-Muslims in Islamic law on, **4:**234
　　United States, welfare and, **6:**92
societa maris/terrae partnership, **2:**94
Societas Europae, **2:**93
Société de législation comparée, **2:**98–99
　　International Congress of Comparative Law (Paris, 1900), **2:**99
Société Générale (Belgium), **1:**276

Societies Law (Indonesia, 1985), **4**:4
Society for Equitable Assurance on Lives and Survivorships, **3**:258
Society for Greek and Hellenistic Legal History, **1**:165
Society for the Prevention of Cruelty to Children, **4**:369
Society of Gentlemen Practisers, **5**:272, 273
Society of Jesus, **6**:63
   in South and Central America, **5**:300, 301
Socinus, Marianus, **6**:25
sociological jurisprudence, **2**:26, 405
Socondat, Charles-Louis de, **5**:172
Socrates
   definition of law by, **4**:17
   freedom of speech and, **5**:329, 331
   impiety and, **5**:112
   on imprisonment, **4**:382
   obligation to obey the law, **4**:321
   Plato on, **1**:148–149
   on punishment, **5**:23
   self-advocacy by, **1**:55–56
   trial for impiety of, **1**:234
   trial of, **4**:*248*
Socratic method, **1**:14, 15, 16
sodomy laws
   Chinese law
      as illicit sexual intercourse, **5**:232
      Ming code on, **5**:234
   Islamic law, **3**:181
   United States
      case law, **2**:292
      equal protection in, **2**:464
      federalism and, **3**:63
      history of, **3**:166–168
soft law, international law and, **3**:278
Sohm, Rudolf, **1**:352
Sokoto Caliphate, **1**:68
Soldanus, Azo. *See* Azo
sole proprietorship, **1**:320
solicitors, **5**:272–273
Solicitors Act (U.K., 1922), **2**:395
Solicitor's Journal, **4**:62
Solicitors' Remuneration Act (England, 1881), **2**:215
Solidarité de la famille dans le droit criminel en Gréce, La (Glotz), **1**:185
Solidarity, **4**:331
Solomon ben Abraham Adret ("Rashba"), Rabbi, **3**:392

Solomon ben Isaac ("Rashi"), Rabbi, **3**:392
Solomon Islands. *See also* Melanesia
   independence of, **4**:174
Solon, **1**:*155*; **2**:123; **4**:320; **5**:273–276, *274*
   on adoption, **1**:41
   appeal process under, **2**:228, 231
   courts under, **2**:231–232
   Draco's laws superseded by, **2**:366; **4**:400
   family law, **3**:30
   on freedom of speech, **5**:330
   on homicide, **2**:232
   influence of, **1**:154
   introduction of the will, **3**:230
   law against tyranny, **1**:233
   on legal procedure, **3**:401; **4**:400, 401
   legal reforms by, **1**:141; **2**:30, 123
   on marriage, **4**:154
   on oaths, **4**:401
   on finding the middle, **2**:125
   in origin of Athenian legal history, **1**:231
   Plutarch on, **1**:148
   on procedure, **1**:155
   property law, **4**:458
   prostitution under, **4**:493
   scholarship on, **1**:164
   on slavery, **5**:245, 355
   statutes by, **1**:150
   theory of constitutional change, **2**:126
   on volunteers in public cases, **4**:113
   written law by, **1**:139
Solon (Plutarch), **1**:52
Solórzano, **4**:314
Solov'yev, Vladimir S., **5**:178
Somadevasuri
   on *arthaśāstra*, **1**:223
   on *nītiśāstra*, **4**:233
Somadeva Sūri, **3**:364
Somalia, **1**:105
   conflict of laws, **2**:114
   Islamic law in, **1**:102
Somaliland, **1**:82
   as British protectorate, **1**:86
   constitution, **2**:137
Somellera, Pedro de, **1**:216
"Some Realism about Realism—Responding to Dean Pound" (Powell), **4**:75
Somers, George, **1**:288
Somerset, James, **4**:143; **5**:252
Somers Isles Company, **1**:288, 289

"Some Thoughts on Risk Distribution and the Law of Torts" (Calabresi), **4:**25
Song code (China)
　amnesty, **1:**133–134
　appeal, **1:**194
　confession, **2:**107
　corruption, **2:**226
　divorce, **4:**159
　ethnic groups, **2:**481
　exile, **3:**25
　five punishments, **1:**426
　homosexuality, **3:**180
　illicit sexual intercourse, **5:**231
　land, **4:**1–2
　marriage, **4:**156
　　remarriage, **4:**160
　mutual concealment, **4:**199
　offenses against the state, **4:**249
　review, **1:**196
　sale
　　of goods, **5:**185
　　of land, **5:**185, 186–187
　succession, **5:**378
Song dynasty (China)
　administratives codes and regulations, **1:**454
　corruption in the, **2:**225
　doubtful cases, **2:**361
　on filial piety, **3:**84
　on foreigners, **3:**91
　lawyers in, **4:**45–46
　penal codes use of precedent as law, **1:**457
　pledging of land during, **4:**326
　role of emperor in capital cases, **1:**360
　types of legislation under, **1:**425
　on wrongful judgment, **6:**153
Songhai, **1:**67, 74
Song Penal Repository (Song hsing-t'ung), **1:**425
songshi (litigation masters), **4:**46
Songtsen gampo, **5:**465
Songtsen Gampo (Tibet), **5:**305
Song xingtong, **5:**186
Sophocles
　on oaths, **4:**242
　on religious offenses, **4:**247
　religious offenses by, **4:**247
Søret (Denmark, 1561), **4:**150
Sorsky, Nil, **5:**177
Sotho kingdom, **1:**70

Soto, Domingo de
　on colonialism, **5:**299
　on guilt, **3:**134
Soulbury Commission (1945), **5:**342
sources of law
　admiralty, **1:**35–36
　ancient Greek law, **1:**146–152
　ancient Near Eastern law, **1:**167–168
　Egypt, **2:**413–414
　English common law, **5:**276–278
　European Communities, **2:**487–488
　Hindu law, **5:**264–265
　historical, **3:**163–168
　of international law, **3:**277–278, 290
　Islamic, **3:**318–319
　　abrogation of legal norms and, **1:**5–6
　　legal norms, **4:**62–64
　Roman-Dutch, **1:**81
　Scotland, **5:**201
　South and Central America, **5:**298–299
　South Asia, **5:**307
Sousa, Tomé de, **5:**301
Souter, David, **2:**166
　on abortion, **4:**389–390
　civil rights views of, **2:**343
　on right to bear arms, **1:**222
South Africa, **1:**87; **5:**279–284
　overview, **5:**279–283
　Anglo-Roman-Dutch law in, **1:**63
　apartheid ended in, **1:**104, 106
　in British Commonwealth, **1:**313, 314
　decolonization of, **1:**92–93, 94
　democracy in, **1:**106
　Indian law, **5:**283–284
　marriage law, **1:**92
　official languages in, **1:**99
　restorative justice in, **1:**72
　Roman law, **5:**157
　undue influence in South Africa law, **6:**25
South Africa Act (1877), **5:**279
South African Law Reform Commission, **5:**284
South African Truth and Reconciliation Commission, **5:**282
South and Central America, **5:**284–302. *See also specific countries*
　overview, **5:**284–287
　legal pluralism, **5:**297–302
　other colonial laws, **5:**294–297
　Portuguese colonial law, **5:**292–294

pre-colonial laws, **5**:287–290
slavery in, **5**:*253*, 253–256
Spanish colonial law, **5**:290–292
in Mexico, **4**:175–176
South Asian law, **5**:302–312
on *ātmanustuṣṭi*, **1**:236
Buddhist law, **5**:302–306
custom, **2**:307–309
East Africa, **2**:382–384
Islamic law, **5**:306–311
sadācāra in, **5**:181–182
in the United Kingdom, **5**:311–312
Southeast Asian law, **5**:312–324. *See also*
Indonesia; Malaysia; Singapore
overview, **5**:312–315
banking and finance, **1**:261
Buddhist law, **5**:315–317
Chinese law, **5**:317–320
Hindu law, **5**:320–322
intellectual property, **3**:260–265
Islamic law, **3**:334–340; **5**:322–324
adat in, **1**:20–21
Southern Qi Code (China), **5**:72
Southern Rhodesia
Anglo-Roman-Dutch law in, **1**:87
British rule in, **1**:85, 86, 88
decolonization of, **1**:93
South Sea Bubble (1720), **2**:88, *88;* **5**:92
South Sea Company, **2**:88
South West Africa, Anglo-Roman-Dutch law in, **1**:87
Southwest Ordinance (U.S.), **5**:260
Souvanna Phouma, **5**:314
Souza, Paulino Soares de, **1**:303
sovereign immunity, **5**:353–354
Spaak, Paul-Henri, **2**:489, *490*
Spain, **5**:324–327. *See also* Andalus, al-
accession into European Union, **2**:490
administrative law, **1**:24
African colonies, **1**:80–81
civil marriage in, **3**:41
colonial, **5**:284–285, 290–291, 298–300
conflict of laws, **2**:113
constitutions, **2**:120, 122
courts in, **2**:253
Enlightenment influences in, **5**:255
fideicommissum in, **3**:80
guardianship, **3**:48
Guatemala, **3**:129–130
Inquisition, **3**:134

intellectual property, **3**:259–260
Islamic law in, **2**:484
Italy and, **3**:357
Jews in, **3**:396–398
lex Irnitana, **4**:102–104
sale of land, **5**:193
slavery, **5**:253–254
taxation, **5**:436, 437
United States colonies and, **6**:26, 32–33
Venezuela, **6**:73
Spanish-American War
declaration of war in, **6**:88
military tribunals in, **4**:179
taxation and, **5**:442
Spanish Succession, War of the (1701–1714), **5**:325
Italy and, **3**:357
Sparta, **1**:142–143; **5**:327–329
adoption, **1**:40
adultery, **1**:53
constitution, **2**:123; **4**:86
constitutional terminology in, **2**:123–124
custom in laws of, **1**:150–151
family law, **3**:28–29
free persons, **5**:356
Helots, **5**:245
judicial procedure, **1**:136–137
laws in, **2**:30
marriage, **4**:154, 155
punishment, **5**:24
slavery, **5**:243, 245
status, **5**:355
women, **3**:29; **5**:328–329; **6**:115–116
Spartan Constitution (Aristotle), **1**:143
Spartiates, **5**:327–328
Special Court for the Chinese of Macau, **1**:448
Special Marriage Act (Bangladesh, 1872), **1**:259; **3**:221
Special Marriage Act (India, 1872), **2**:353
Special Marriage Act (India, 1954), **3**:49, 221, 222; **6**:132
Special Marriage Act (Pakistan, 1872), **3**:221
Special Measures Law (Japan, 1994), **3**:385
Specific Relief Act (India, 1877), **4**:273
Specific Relief Act (India, 1877, 1963), **3**:216
Specimen usus modernus pandectarum (Stryk), **2**:8; **4**:393
Speculum iudiciale (Duranti)
Baldus de Ubaldis, Petrus, on, **1**:250
on legal procedure, **4**:434, 437

speech, freedom of, **5:329–338**
   Athens, **4:**112; **5:329–331**
   education and, **2:**409
   in English parliament, **2:**132
   expansion in the United States, **2:**16
   libel and slander and, **4:**106–107
   national security and, **3:**409
   political process and, **3:**410
   United States, **6:**50–51
   in the United States, **5:332–338**
Speight, George, **3:**83
Spencer, Herbert, **1:**303, 304
Spenser, Edmund, **3:**309
Speranskii, Mikhail M., **5:**172–173, 178
Spinoza, Benedict (Baruch) de
   definition of law by, **4:**18, 21
   influenced by Suárez, Francisco, **4:**17
Spinsters Act (Zanzibar, 1985), **2:**45
Spirit of the Laws, The (Montesquieu). *See De l'esprit des lois* (Montesquieu)
Spotted Tail, **4:**207, 209
Spreng, Johannes, **1:**111
Sprenger, Jakob, **4:**438
Sprint, **5:**98
Spruchrepertorium (Germany, 1872), **4:**380
Sri Aurobindo, **3:**159
Sri Lanka, **5:338–344**. *See* Ceylon (Sri Lanka); South Asian law
   Buddhist law in, **5:**302–305
   Islamic law in, **5:**306, 309
Sri Wickrama Rajasinha (Sri Lanka), **5:**341
śruti, **5:344–345**
Ṣādiq, Jaʿfar al-, **3:**340
Staggers Rail Act (1980), **5:**104
Staines, Richard, **3:**473
Stalin, Joseph, **5:**176
Stammgut, **3:**80
Stammler, Rudolf, **4:**226
Stamp Act (Great Britain), **4:**335
Stamp Act (U.K., 1899), **4:**273
stamp tax, censorship and, **1:**380
Standard Oil, **1:**324; **5:**78
standing doctrine, administrative agencies and, **1:**31
Stanser Verkommnis (Switzerland, 1481), **5:**419
Stanton, Edwin M., **3:**23
Stanton, Elizabeth Cady
   on divorce, **6:**142
   Seneca Fall Declaration by, **6:**134
   in women's rights movement, **2:**338

Staples, Seth, **2:**402
Star Chamber, **5:345–347**
   campaign against solicitors in, **5:**272
   censorship and, **1:**379
   criminal procedure, **4:**423–424
   jurisdiction of, **5:**15
   on libel and slander, **4:**105
   origin of, **2:**250
   reform of, **4:**41
   royal proclamations and, **4:**89
   Wales, **6:**101
stare decisis, **4:380–382**
   arbitration and, **3:**486
Starkie, Thomas, **2:**394
   on evidence, **3:**5
   at Inner Temple, **2:**395
Starr, Kenneth, **3:**23–24
state law
   Afghanistan, **1:**59–60
   definition of law in, **4:**19, 20
   local government and, **4:**122–123
   state courts, **2:**258–259, 260, 262
state law, United States, **5:347–351**
   administrative agencies and, **1:**25–26
   Confederation period, **5:347–349**
   state constitutions, **5:349–351**
   supremacy clause and, **5:**408–413
State of Prisons in England and Wales (Howard), **5:**28–29, 33
State of the Prisons (Howard), **4:**41
state police power control by state judges, **2:**23
state sovereignty, **5:351–354**. *See also* federalism
   Articles of Confederation on, **1:**224
   European Communities, **2:**485
   feudal law and, **3:**79
Stationers' Company, **2:**216
   censorship and, **1:**379
Stationers' Guild, **3:**266
Statues of Charitable Uses (1597 and 1601), **1:**390
Stature of the Jewry (England, 1275), **1:**270
status, **5:354–359**. *See also* personal status law
   ancient Greek law, **5:354–358**
   Chinese law, **5:358–359**
   homocide sentences, **1:**362
   of villeins, **6:**80, 81–82
statute law
   England, **4:**87–90
      Mansfield, Lord, on, **4:**142–143

New Zealand, **4:**228
Roman law, **4:**101–102
Scotland, **5:**197
Statute of 5 Richard II, c. 7 (England, 1381), **5:**71
Statute of 8 Henry VI, c. 9 (England, 1429), **5:**71
Statute of 1330 (England), **4:**284
Statute of 1430 (England), **4:**285
Statute of 1484 (England), **2:**213
Statute of 1540 (England), **2:**213
Statute of 1576 (England), **5:**68
Statute of 1705 (England), **2:**215
Statute of Anne (England, 1705), **4:**324
Statute of Anne (Great Britain, 1709), **2:**216
Statute of Artificers (England, 1563), **2:**425
   on contract laborers, **5:**256–257
   guilds in, **3:**132
Statute of Distributions (1670), **5:**384
   women in, **6:**123
Statute of Edward III (England, 1362), **4:**324
Statute of Enrolments (England, 1536), **2:**214, 215
Statute of Frauds (England, 1677), **6:**33
   on agency, **1:**109
   on conveyancing, **2:**215
   on copyhold land, **6:**103
   on equity, **2:**470
   on final process, **3:**89
   on land leases, **4:**12
   on nuncupative wills, **6:**104
   on sale, **5:**190
   on succeession, **5:**403
Statute of George II (Great Britain, 1731, 1933), **4:**323
Statute of Gloucester (England, 1278), **4:**12
Statute of Hamburg (1603), **1:**36
Statute of Henry VIII c 30 (England, 1540), **4:**323
Statute of Jeofails (England, 1543), **3:**308
Statute of Labourers (England, 1349–1351), **2:**425, 436; **4:**347
   employment contracts and, **2:**196
   guilds in, **3:**132
Statute of Limitations (England, 1624), **2:**212
Statute of Marlborough (England, 1267), **3:**177
   on land leases, **4:**12
   on mortmain, **4:**192
   on uses, **6:**12

Statute of Marlborough (England, 1275), **4:**87–88
Statute of Merton (England, 1236), **1:**392; **4:**87
Statute of Monopolies (England, 1624), **2:**102; **3:**269; **4:**187
Statute of Mortmain (England, 1279), **4:**191; **5:**370
   on church grants, **3:**75
Statute of Rhuddlan (Wales), **6:**100
   on Exchequer, **3:**17
Statute of Sewers (England, 1532), **1:**277
Statute of the International Court of Justice, **3:**290
   source of international law codofied in, **3:**277
Statute of the Pillory (England, 1267), **5:**30
Statute of the Staple (England, 1353), **4:**36
Statute of Treasons (England, 1351–1352)
   attainder, **6:**5
   definition and scope of treason, **6:**2
   on nationality, **4:**205
   requirement of allegiance, **6:**4
   World War I use of, **6:**4
Statute of Uses (England, 1536), **4:**474
   on conveyancing, **2:**214
   on devises of land, **6:**103
   on dower, **2:**363
   equity in, **2:**469
   incidents of tenure, **5:**451
   on private trusts, **5:**406
   on strict settlements, **5:**365
   on trusts, **6:**11–13
Statute of Wales (1284), **3:**76
Statute of Westminster (England, 1382), **5:**68
Statute of Westminster (U.K., 1931)
   on Australian parliament, **1:**242–243
   on British Commonwealth, **1:**313
   on Canada, **1:**339
   on dower, **2:**362
Statute of Westminster Adoption Act (New Zealand, 1947), **4:**228
Statute of Westminster I (England, 1275), **5:**68, 462
   on torture, **5:**484–485
Statute of Westminster II (England, 1285)
   on conditional gifts, **2:**478
   on final process, **3:**87, 88
   on rape, **5:**68
   on writs of execution, **3:**87
Statute of Wills (England, 1540), **4:**470, 474; **6:**13
   on devises of land, **6:**103
   on land leases, **4:**11

Statute of Wills (England, 1542), **1**:395
Statute on Persons Firmly Established or Purely Resident (Switzerland, 1891), **2**:112
Statute on the Academy (Russia, 1540), **5**:171
Statutes and Precedents of the Yuan (Yuan Tien-chang), **1**:461
Statutes of Batavia, **3**:225; **5**:313
    Sri Lanka in, **5**:340
Statutes of Kilkenny (1366), **3**:308
Statutes of Tivoli (Roman, 1305), **5**:32
Statutes on the Composition of Judgements (Han), **1**:415–417
statutory interpretation and legislation, **5**:360–363
    legal process on, **4**:69–70
    United States, **4**:96–99
Staunford, William, **2**:440
Staunton, George, **1**:437
stay laws, bankruptcy and, **1**:268
Steel, Lewis M., **2**:299
Stefancic, Jean, **4**:365
Stein, Lorenz von
    comparative law, **2**:99
    on social state, **5**:271
stellionatus, **3**:102, 103
Stephani, Joachim, **1**:350
Stephanus
    on the Digesta, **1**:328
    information on available, **1**:333
Stephen (England), **3**:74
Stephen, Henry J., **4**:324
Stephen, James Fitzjames
    on Burma, **1**:318
    on hard labor, **5**:29
    Indian law codification by, **4**:137
    on retention of death penalty, **1**:365
    on sale, **5**:190
    on theft, **5**:461, 462
    on torture, **5**:484, 486
Stephen II (pope), **4**:352
Stephen of Tournai, **2**:317
sterilization, involuntary
    of disabled persons, **2**:334
    natural law on, **4**:219
Stern, Betsy, **3**:*56*
Stern, William, **3**:*56*
Steunenberg, Frank, **4**:337
Stevens, John Paul
    on apportionment and reapportionment, **1**:201
    on federalism, **3**:65
    on natural law, **4**:219–220
    on right to bear arms, **1**:222
Stevens, Robert, **4**:77
Stewart, Maria, **6**:134
Stewart, Potter
    on freedom of the press, **5**:332
    on privacy, **4**:387
St. German, Christopher
    on bailment, **1**:249
    on conscience, **2**:468
    on equity, **2**:468–469
    on kingship, **2**:129
    on legal theory, **4**:61
    on natural law, **4**:214
    on precedent, **5**:277
    on reason and precedent, **4**:377–378
Stigler, George, **4**:25
    on regulations, **5**:83
    on securities laws, **5**:94
Stikker, Dirk Uipko, **2**:*485*
Stiles, Ezra, **2**:402
Stiles, William, **4**:324
Stillington, Robert, **4**:214
stipulatio, **2**:182, 184, 186, 187, 191
    Egypt juristic papyrology on, **2**:420
    under Justinian law, **2**:188–189, 191
    legal reasoning on, **4**:81
    during the Republic, **2**:183
stipulation in law merchant, **4**:40
stock exchanges in the Muslim world, **2**:75
stock markets
    Islamic, **1**:262
    United States, **5**:89
Stokes, Whitley, **4**:137
Stone, Harlan Fiske
    classical legal theory and, **2**:26
    on consitutional interpretation, **2**:163
Stone, Lucy, **2**:338
stoning, **1**:6, 62
    in Islamic law, **1**:367; **3**:325
Stooss, Carl, **5**:34
Story, Joseph, **3**:294
    on agency, **1**:108, 109, 113
    on codification, **2**:50
    on common law, **6**:30
    comparative law, **2**:98
    on conflict of laws, **2**:112, 117
    on contracts, **2**:204, 205
    on copyright, **3**:267

on due process, **2**:368
on easements, **2**:379
at Harvard, **1**:12; **2**:403
at Harvard Law School, **6**:43
influence of, **6**:46
on international law, **3**:293
on marine insurance, **1**:38
on right to bear arms, **1**:218
on slavery, **5**:263
on supremacy clause, **5**:411
on Supreme Court power, **2**:258
on torts, **2**:442
trust fund doctrine of, **1**:326
Story, William Wetmore, **2**:204; **6**:46
Stowell, Baron. *See* Scott, William
Strabo
   on Helots, **5**:245
   on prostitution, **4**:494
   on provincial government, **4**:497
Stracca, Benvenuto, **2**:93; **5**:363–364
   on law merchant, **4**:39
Straccha, Benvenuto, **4**:151
Straits Settlements, **4**:138; **5**:241–242. *See also* Malacca; Penang; Singapore
   on caste, **5**:321
   on courts, **5**:313
   indirect rule under, **5**:318
   intellectual property legislation, **3**:261
strategoi in Egypt, **2**:418
Strato, **5**:227
Strickland, George, **1**:45
strict functional liability, concept of, **6**:78
strict scrutiny standard
   on affirmative action, **2**:343
   for equal protection, **2**:462
   for evidence, **3**:13, 14
strict settlements, **5**:364–368
stridhan (woman's wealth), **2**:363. *See also* dowry in Hindu law
Strothmann, Rudolph, **6**:162
Stroud, Ronald, **3**:170
   on ancient Greek legislation, **4**:85
   on Draco, **1**:164
Strube de Piermont, Friedrich Heinrich, **5**:171
Struck, Susan, **2**:339
Structure of Scientific Revolutions, The (Kuhn), **4**:363
Struve, Georg Adam
   comparative law, **2**:98
   on possession, **4**:361

Stryk, Samuel, **5**:464
   comparative law, **2**:98
   on private law, **4**:393
   usus modernus and, **2**:8
   Wolff, Christian von, and, **6**:111
Student's Companion, The (Jacob), **2**:394
Study Group on a European Civil Code, **2**:496
Study of the Doubtful Points of the Substatutes (Xue), **1**:459
Sturges, Wesley, **4**:74
Stutz, Ulrich, **1**:352; **2**:219
Stypmann, Franz, **4**:151
Suanjing (Zhang Qiujian), **4**:287
Suárez, Francisco, **3**:282
   in Scholasticism, **4**:15, 16
   on war, **4**:17
subinfeudation, **5**:368–370
   abolished, **5**:383
   succession and, **5**:390
Subki, 'Abd al-Wahhab ibn 'Ali al-, **3**:353; **5**:370
   on agricultural contracts, **1**:117
   on Da'ud 'Ali al-Isbahani, **2**:313
subscriptiones, **3**:211
substantive law, **4**:60
   ancient Athens, **1**:233–234
   ancient Greece, **1**:153, 154
Substatutes Presently in Force *(Xianxingceli)* (1679), **1**:459
substitution, **5**:368–370. *See* subinfeudation and substitution
Subversive Activities Control Board, **1**:28
succession, **5**:370–409. *See also* inheritance; intestacy; wills
   Africa
     after independence, **1**:103–104
     Islamic law, **1**:102
   ancient Greece
     Hellenistic, **1**:158–160
   ancient Near Eastern law, **1**:172–173, 173
   assignment and, **1**:228
   Baltic nations, **1**:255
   Byzantine law, **5**:376–377
   Chinese law, **5**:377–381
     adoption and, **1**:43–46
   Code of Gortyn on, **3**:122–123
   England, ecclesiastical law on, **2**:389
   English common law, **5**:381–384
     estates doctrine in, **2**:476–479
     wills in, **6**:102–104

entails and, **2**:446–448
Ethiopia, **2**:479
feudal law, **3**:74
fideicommissum, **3**:80–81
Gaius on, **3**:251
Hindu law, **5**:396–402
Hong Kong, **1**:449
India
   Christian laws, **3**:222
   Islamic law, **2**:484
   Jewish law, **3**:398
   medieval and post-medieval Roman law,
      5:384–396
   natural law on, **4**:216
   Roman law, **5**:370–376
      women, **6**:118
Scotland, **5**:202
South Asian Buddhist law, **5**:304–305
Southeast Asia, **5**:319
United States, **5**:402–409
Succession Law Amendment (Austria, 1989),
   5:387
Sudan
   banking and finance in, **1**:260
   as British protectorate, **1**:86
   civil war in, **1**:97
   conflict of laws, **2**:114
   constitution, **2**:137; **3**:317
   criminal law in, **2**:279
   death penalty in, **1**:368
   Indian Penal Code in, **1**:87
   Islamic law in, **1**:102
   Islamic penal law in, **2**:39
   shariʿa as principal source of legislation in,
      3:317
   zakat in, **5**:431
Sudebnik (Russian legal code, 1497
   1550), **5**:168, 169, 170
Suffolk Law School (Boston), **2**:404
suffrage
   ancient Greece, **1**:*138*
   in Britain, **2**:132
   Guyana, **5**:295
   Roman law, **4**:94, *94*
   United States, **6**:43–45
      citizenship and, **2**:3
suffrage, universal
   Africa
      in French colonies, **1**:90
   Australia, **1**:240, 242

   Denmark, **2**:328
   Fiji, **3**:82
   Guyana, **3**:137
   proportional representation and, **1**:204
   Sweden, **5**:417
   United States
      discrimination in, **2**:20, 340–341
      equal protection in, **2**:459–460, 463
      state law on, **5**:349–350
      women in, **2**:338; **6**:134–136
   Venezuela, **6**:74
Sufism, **3**:347
Sufrites, **3**:348
Suharto, **4**:276; **5**:314
   containment of Islam and shariʿa, **3**:335
   New Order in Indonesia, **3**:227
suicide
   assisted, **2**:424
   Aztec law, **5**:287
   Chinese law, **3**:175
      lack of filial piety driving parents to,
         3:85
   Chinese-speaking Muslims and, **1**:400
Sui code (China)
   on beating and whipping, **1**:283
   on exile, **3**:25
   on Jin code, **1**:419
   on offenses against the state, **4**:249
   on penal servitude, **4**:292
   on prohibited books, **4**:252
   on punishment, **5**:25
   on redemption, **5**:73
   on review, **1**:196
   on Ten Abominations, **4**:259–260
Sui dynasty (China), **1**:456
   administrative codes and regulations,
      1:454
   collective liability, **2**:61
   courts in the, **2**:241, 242, 247
Sui Wendi, **1**:421
Sukarno, **3**:227; **4**:276; **5**:314
   containment of Islam and shariʿa, **3**:335
   Guided Democracy concept, **3**:227
   Pancasila, **3**:226
Sukarnoputri, Megawati, **3**:228
Ṣukūk (bonds), **1**:265
Sulayman, al-Rabiʿ ibn, **2**:313
Sulayman the Magnificent, **3**:344
Süleiman I (Ottoman Empire)
   agreement with Francis I, **3**:281

Balkan peninsula under, **1**:251, *252*
colleges built by, **4**:265
Süleiman Kanuni (Ottoman Empire)
legal education under, **4**:72–73
Sulla, **1**:473
on magistrates, **4**:131
on the Senate, **5**:210
Sulla, Cornelius L.
courts under, **2**:270
Sulla, Cornelius L., **2**:238, 274; **4**:495, 496
Sullivan, Serjeant, **6**:4
Sullivan Law (New York), **1**:219, 220
Sulpicius Galba, **2**:270
summa (literary form), **3**:355
Summa autenticarium (Accursius), **1**:19
Summa codicis (Azo), **3**:355
summae (of Justinian law), **1**:328
Summae Codicis (Azo), **1**:248
Summa feudorum (Accursius), **1**:19
Summa in Titulos Decretalium, **5**:198
Summar artis notariae (Passagerii), **4**:237
Summary Jurisdiction Act (Great Britain, 1857)
on appeal, **1**:199
summary jury trials, **1**:128
Summa theologiae (Aquinas)
on evidence, **3**:8
on reason, **4**:216
Summit of Heads of State or Government, **1**:107
Sumner, William Graham, **2**:208
sumptuary laws
Chinese law, **5**:409–410
Hindu law, **2**:364
Sun Bin, **4**:196–197
Sunday Closing Act (Wales, 1881), **6**:101
Sunder, Madhavi, **3**:70
sunegoroi (barristers), **1**:333
Sunesen, Andreas, **2**:326
Sung dynasty (China)
judicial precedent, **1**:461
penal servitude, **4**:293
Sunna
as foundational text for Islamic law, **5**:131–132
revelation in, **5**:132–133
as source of Islamic law, **3**:319, 331–332
use in Pakistan laws, **4**:274
Sunnis
in Abbasid dynasty, **1**:1–2
internationalism, **3**:281

Sunni schools of Islamic law. *See* Islamic schools of sacred law; *specific schools*
Sunshine Act (U.S., 1976), **5**:83
Sunstein, Cass, **4**:69
Sun Wu, **4**:196
Superfund act. *See* Comprehensive Environmental Response, Compensation, and Liability Act (U.S., 1980)
Supplemental Security Income, **6**:91, 96. *See also* welfare
Supplementum Epigraphicum Gracum (Selinous), **1**:54
Suppliants, The (Euripides), **1**:156
Suppliant Women (Euripides), **2**:124
suppression remedy in search and seizure, **5**:204, 205, 206
supranationalism, **2**:487
supremacy clause, **5**:410–413
absolutism and, **1**:7
in Articles of Confederation, **1**:224
expansion of, **5**:350
international law and, **3**:292
Supreme Commander for the Allied Powers (SCAP), **3**:378
Supreme Constitutional Court (SCC, Egypt), **2**:421–422
Supreme Council of the Magistracy (Cambodia), **1**:335
Supreme Court Act (Bermuda, 1905), **1**:289
Supreme Court Judges Act (New Zealand, 1858), **4**:230
Supreme Court of Judicature (United Kingdom), **2**:86
equitable remedies in, **2**:471
evidence in, **3**:6
Supreme Court of Judicature (Ireland) Act (United Kingdom, 1877), **3**:312
supreme courts. *See also* courts
Canada, **1**:340–341
China, **2**:240–241, 248–249
England, **2**:250–251
Fiji, **3**:82
France, **3**:100
India, **3**:400
on fundamental rights, **3**:106
on public interest litigation, **5**:6–7
Japan, **3**:379, 382–383
New Zealand, **4**:230–231
United States, **6**:45–46
activist nature of, **6**:58–59

anti-Progressive decisions, **2:**162
circuit riding, **2:**257
commerce power and, **2:**64–68
constitutional creation of, **3:**425
constitutional establishment of, **2:**256
and constitutional interpretation, **2:**164–166
controversial social policy and politics, **2:**260–261
on copyright, **3:**267, 268
within court system, **3:**423–424
enforcement of rights, **2:**19
on federalism, **3:**59–66
on federal judicial power, **3:**427
on immigration, **3:**206, 208–209
on international law, **3:**293
judicial review, **3:**429
jurisdiction of, **2:**256–257; **3:**425
patent appeals, **3:**270
power of, **4:**365
power over state courts, **2:**258
on trademark law, **3:**271–272
use of precedents, **3:**165–166
Uruguay, **6:**66, 67
Supreme People's Court (Laos), **4:**14
suretyship in Irish law, **3:**306
Surface Transportation Board, **5:**104–105
Suriname, **5:**296, **413–414**
colonial law in, **5:**295
territorial disputes with Guyana, **3:**138
Surrey, Stanley, **3:**287
surrogate mothers, **3:**55, 56
Survey of the Administration of Criminal Justice (U.S.), **4:**32
suspect classification in equal protection, **2:**462–463
sustainable development
English law on, **2:**452
India, **2:**454
Sutherland, George, **2:**26, 27; **4:**484, 491
on commerce clause, **2:**65
Sutta Pittaka, **5:**302
Suttavibhanga, **5:**302
Suʿud, Abu al-, **3:**58
Suyuti, Jalal al-Din al-, **3:**225
svadharma, **2:**333
Svarez, Carl Gottlieb, **5:**1
Svod Zakonov Rossiiskoi Imperii (Digest of Laws of the Russian Empire, 1832), **5:**172
Swaine, Robert, **1:**269

Swazi kingdom, **1:**70
Swaziland, **1:**63–64
Anglo-Roman-Dutch law in, **1:**87
British protectorate in, **1:**86
independence of, **1:**93
Sweden, **5:414–417.** *See also* Scandinavia
accession into European Union, **2:**491
admiralty law in, **1:**37
Baltic nations under, **1:**254–255
influence on Russian law, **5:**166, 170
legislation in, **4:**91
maritime law, **4:**150
social security in, **5:**271
state church in, **1:**349–350
Swift, Zephaniah, **2:**206
Swinburne, Henry, **6:**104
Swiss Civil Code, **5:**420. *See* Zivilgesetzbuch (Civil Code, Zwitzerland)
Swiss Debt Prosecution and Bankruptcy Law, **3:**250
Swiss Law of Obligations (1881), **4:**56
Swiss Law of Obligations (1911), **2:**320
Switzerland, **5:418–420**
bishops in, **1:**296
codes and codification, **2:**48–49
company law, **2:**93
competition regulation, **2:**103
conflict of laws, **2:**113
ecclesiastical courts, **2:**385
guarantee in, **3:**129
housing in, **4:**58
property law, **4:**476
Protestant churches in, **1:**350
servitude in real estate in, **5:**224
taxation in, **5:**436, 437, 438
Syariah Criminal Offences (Federal Territories) Act (Malaysia, 1997), **4:**301
Syariah Index, **1:**262
sycophancy, **4:**115
syllogism, **6:**112
Sylvester I (pope), **4:**352
symbolic speech, **5:**337
Syme, **6:**24
Symposion, **1:**165
Symposium (Plato)
on homosexual behavior, **5:**228
syndikoi, **4:**85
synegoroi, **1:**54–55. *See also* advocate
synod court, **2:**385–386. *See also* ecclesiastical courts

Synod of Homberg, **1:**349
Synod of Sutre (1046), **4:**352
synods *versus* councils, **1:**470
Synopsis maior, **1:**330
Synopsis minor, **1:**330
Syntagma alphabeticum canonum (Blastares), **1:**330, 347–348
Syntagma canonum. *See Nomocanon* (Blastares)
Syntagma canonum (580), **1:**328
Syrakosios, **5:**331
Syria. *See also* ancient Near Eastern law
   conflict of laws, **2:**114
   constitution, **3:**317
   inheritance law, **2:**38
   judiciary in, **3:**422
   legal education in, **2:**397, 398
   Mecelle civil code in, **2:**35
   obligatory bequests in, **6:**107
   personal status laws, **4:**296; **6:**129
   Shafi'i school of law in, **3:**352
   shari'a as principal source of legislation in, **3:**317
   in U.N. Convention on Contracts for the International Sale of Goods, **2:**74
Syrian-Roman Law Book, **5:**151
system and systematization, **5:420–422**
Systematical View of the Laws of England (Wooddeson), **1:**108
System des Heutigen Römischen Rechts (Savigny), **5:**195, 421
System des heutigen römischen Rechts (Savigny), **4:**277
System of the Law of Marine Insurances (Park), **3:**253
System on the Laws of the State of Connecticut, A (Swift), **2:**206

T

Ṭāʿa (obedience), **6:**147–148
taʿabbud, **6:**147
tabanni. *See* adoption
Tabaqat, Al- (Khallal), **3:**467
Tabaqat al-Shafi'iyya (al-Subki), **5:**370
Tabari, Abu Ja'far Muhammad ibn Jarir al-, **3:**353
   on lease and tenancy, **4:**56
Tabari, Abu Tayyib al-, **5:**238
Tabari, al-
   on inheritance, **3:**233
   teachers of Al-Qaffal, **5:**60
Table Talk (Selden), **5:**484
Tablettes Albertini, **3:**116
taboullarioi (notaries), **1:**333

Tabsirat al-hukkam, **5:**487
Tabula Amalphitana, **1:**36
Tabula Contrebiensis, **3:**97; **4:**497
Tabula de Amalfa, **3:**257
Tacitus, **3:**435
   on punishment, **5:**31
tafrīq (annulment), **6:**126–127
   Ottoman Empire, **6:**128
Tafsir gharib al-Qur'an (attr. Zayd ibn 'Ali), **6:**161
Taft, William Howard, **2:**26; **4:**318
   on antitrust, **1:**189
   on discovery rules, **4:**444
   on executive power, **3:**23
   on privacy, **4:**386
   on property, **4:**482
   at University of Cincinnati, **1:**13
   writ of certiorari and, **4:**444
Taft-Hartley Act (U.S., 1947), **3:**483; **5:**82
   English law influenced by, **2:**427
Tagivetau, Inoke, **3:**83
Taha, Mahmud Muhammad, **1:**206, 368
Tahafut al-tahafut (Ibn Rushd), **3:**201
Tahawi, al-, **3:**343
Tahdhib, al- (al-Tusi), **6:**18
Tahfat al-fuqaha' (al-Samarqandi), **3:**466
Tahiti, **4:**347
Tahtawi, Rifa'a Rafi al-, **2:**398
Taiho code (China, 1202), **1:**427–428
Taiho ritsuryo (Japan, 701), **3:**367, 372
Taika Reform Edict (Japan, 646), **3:**366, 367
Taiwan, **1:451–453**
   codes of Chinese Republic applicable in, **1:**440–441, 452
Taiwan shih (Private Law of Taiwan), **1:**463
Taizu (Song emperor)
   on appeal, **1:**194
   review under, **1:**196–197
Taj al-Din. *See* Subki, 'Abd al-Wahhab ibn 'Ali al-
Taj al-Din fi ma yajibu 'ala al-muluk (al-Malik), **2:**41
taj al-mudhhab li-ahkam al-madhhab, al- (al-'Ansi), **4:**136
takāful (Islamic mutual insurance schemes), **3:**256
   in Malaysia, **3:**337
Takaful (Islamic Insurance) Act (Malaysia, 1984), **3:**337–338
takings clause, **5:423–425**
   due process and, **2:**371; **4:**484
   eminent domain and, **4:**488–489, 489
   environmental law and, **2:**458

property rights and, **4**:490, 491, 492
in succession, **5**:402
ṭalāq (divorce), **2**:44; **6**:126
Talbot, Charles, **5**:251
talfiq, **2**:44
Talfourd, Serjeant, **2**:218
Talib, 'Ali ibn Abi. *See* 'Ali ibn Abi Talib
Taliban, **1**:60, 62
talio (retaliation). *See also qiṣāṣ*
in delect, **2**:321
Islamic law legal reasoning on, **4**:64
tally sticks, **3**:*18*
Talmud, **3**:388, 391, 392
Tamassuk al-quddat amaniya, **1**:59
Tamworth Manifesto of, **4**:285; **4**:1834
Tanbig, al- (Shirazi), **5**:238
Tancred of Bologna, **4**:437
Tancredus, **4**:433
Taney, Roger B.
on Civil War secessionists, **4**:335
on corporations, **1**:322, 324; **6**:46
on due process, **2**:369
on federal commerce power, **2**:154
on federalism, **3**:60
on the guaranty clause, **2**:260–261
on property, **4**:489–490
on race, **2**:340
on the sectional controversy, **2**:260
on slavery, **2**:153, 459; **5**:262
on statutory interpretation, **5**:360
TANF. *See* Temporary Assistance for Needy Families)
Tanganyika
independence of, **1**:93, 97
indigenous law, **1**:91, 101–102
indigenous rights in, **1**:88
Tang code (China), **1**:456–457
abduction *(lue)*, **3**:468
accessory and principal in, **1**:18
alcohol and drugs, **1**:119
amnesty, **1**:133, 134–135
appeal, **1**:194
application in Vietnam, **6**:78–79
influence on Le Code, **6**:79
collective liability, **2**:58, 59, 60
compared to Ming code, **1**:458
confession, **2**:107
corruption, **2**:226–227
cursing, **2**:304–305
damage to property, **2**:312, 313
damaging efficiency of government, **4**:253

deceit, **2**:314, 315
deposit, **2**:330–332
disrespect *(bujing)*, **4**:250, 251
divorce, **4**:159
doing what ought not to be done, **2**:355
doubtful cases, **2**:361
endangering the emperor, **4**:256
enticement *(you)*, **3**:469
errors in official documents, **4**:254
ethnic groups, **2**:481
exile, **3**:25
foreigners, **3**:91
gambling, **3**:109
gu poison, **4**:329
homicide, **3**:171, 172–173, 173, 174–175
illicit sexual intercourse, **5**:231
incest, **3**:214
influence on Japanese law, **3**:367
intention, **3**:275
lack of filial piety, **3**:85, 86
land, **4**:1
litigation masters, **4**:46
loans, **4**:117
marriage, **4**:156
mistaken judgments, **4**:254
mistaken recommendations, **4**:255
mutual concealment, **4**:198–199
offenses against the state, **4**:249
parricide, **3**:84
persons as security, **4**:326
punishments, **5**:25, 44
age as redemption factor, **5**:45
beating and whipping, **1**:283–284
disability as redemption factor, **5**:47
five punishments, **1**:362; **5**:213
of officials, **5**:48, 50, 51
penal servitude, **4**:292
of women, **5**:57
putting spells on the emperor, **4**:255–256
rape, **5**:66
redemption, **5**:72, 73
review, **1**:196
sale
of a free person by consent, **3**:469
of goods, **5**:184–185
of land, **5**:186
of relatives, **3**:469
seizing a free person for ransom (jie), **3**:469
sexual offenses, **5**:232–233
slavery, **5**:54–55

status, **5:**358
succession, **5:**377, 378
sumptuary laws, **5:**409–410
theft, **5:**458, 459, 460, 461
treason, **4:**257–258
voluntary surrender and confession, **2:**106
wounding, **6:**150–151
wrongful judgment, **6:**153
zang, **6:**159, 160
Tang dynasty (China)
administrative codes and regulations, **1:**454
collection sof edicts assource of laws, **1:**460
collective liability, **2:**61
corruption in the, **2:**225
courts in the, **2:**241, 244, 247
distributed-field system in, **5:**186
lawyers in, **4:**45
partnerships, **4:**287
penal codes, **1:**456–457
pledging of goods during, **4:**325–326
role of emperor in capital cases, **1:**360
Tang liudian (Compendium of Administrative Law of the Six Divisions of the Tang Bureaucracy), **1:**454
Tanglü shuyi. See Tang code (China)
Tang Ming lü hebian (Joint edition of the Tang and Ming statutes) (Xue), **3:**187
Tannenbaum, Frank, **5:**253
Tantawi, Muhammad Sayyid, **6:**70
Tanucci, Bernardo, **3:**83
Tanzania
Arusha in, **1:**91
in British Commonwealth, **1:**315
constitution, **2:**137, 138
court system, **2:**43–44
family law reform, **1:**103; **2:**38
independence of, **1:**97
inheritance, **2:**45
law reform in, **1:**101
marriage, **2:**44
political parties, **1:**104
one-party system, **1:**98
South Asian law in, **2:**382–384
taqlīd (duty to follow an existing doctrine), **3:**198, 224–225, 342
in Africa, **2:**41
Taqrib li-hadd al-mantiq, al- (Ibn Hazm), **3:**197–198
Taqrir wa-l-tahbir, Al- (al-Hajj), **6:**147
Targa, Carlo, **4:**151

Tariff of Abominations (U.S., 1828), **5:**411–410
Tarquinius Superbus, **5:**141
expulsion of, **4:**130
Tasuli, al-, **3:**351
Tatar law, **5:**166
Tatbiq ma wujida fi'l-qanun al-madani muwafiqan li-madhhab Abi Hanifa (al-Hanafi), **4:**195–196
Tatishchev, Vasilii N., **5:**177
tattoo as punishment in Chinese law, **1:**403
under Han, **1:**417
under Song, **1:**426
Taubenschlag, Raphael, **2:**413
Tawshih al-tashih fi usul al-fiqh (al-Subki), **5:**370
Tawshih al-tashih was tarjih al-tashih (al-Subki), **5:**370
Tax Amending Law (Germany, 1934), **4:**204
taxation, **5:425–448**
African Belgian colonies, **1:**83
China, **2:**315
amnesty from, **1:**135
land service tenure, **4:**4
land transfer tax, **4:**3, 6
in sale of land, **5:**186, 187, 188
England
under Charles I, **2:**130
death taxes, **6:**103
English common law, **5:425–429,** *427*
geld, **3:**72
Germany under National Socialism, **4:**204
Islamic law, **5:430–435**
administrative decrees on, **1:**33, 35
as worship, **6:**146, 149
medieval and post-medieval Roman law, **5:435–439**
Roman law, medieval and post-medieval, **5:***437*
sex discrimination in, **2:**338
slamic law
assignment *(ḥawālah),* **1:**229
South and Central America, **5:**298
United States, **5:439–448,** *446*
general welfare clause, **3:**113–115
income, **3:**61
income tax, **6:**55
inheritance, **5:**408
state power in, **5:**348, 349
Tax Court of Canada, **1:**340
Tax Reform Act (U.S., 1986), **3:**185; **5:**447–448

taʿzīr (chastisement)
  in enforcement, **2:**431–432
taʿzīr crimes, **1:**367
Tea Act (Great Britain), **4:**335
Techow, Hermann, **3:**374, 375
Tejedor, Carlos, **1:**216
Telecommunications Act (1996), **5:**98
telecommunications regulation, United States, **5:95–99**
Telegraph Act (U.S., 1866), **5:**96
Telephone Consumer Protection Act (U.S., 1991), **2:**178
Temperance Movement, **1:**124. *See also* Prohibition amendment
Temple, Henry John (Lord Palmerston), **2:**90
Temporary Assistance for Needy Families (U.S., 1997), **4:**367, 372–373; **6:**92, 93–94. *See also* welfare
  moral judgement in, **6:**97
Ten Abominations (China), **3:**214; **4:**249
  disrespect *(bujing)*, **4:**250–252
  endangering the emperor, **4:**256
  in Heqing code, **1:**421
  plotting rebellion *(moufan)*, **4:**257
  punishments for, **4:**259–260
  sedition *(dani)*, **4:**257
  sexual offenses in, **5:**233
  status and, **5:**359
  treason *(pan)*, **4:**257–258
Tenantry Act (Ireland, 1780), **3:**310
Ten Commandments, Danish king as guardian of, **2:**328
tender years presumption, **6:**136
Ten Last Jatakas, **5:**303, 304
Ten Nonvirtuous Acts (Tibet), **5:**305
tenure, doctrine of, **5:448–451**. *See also* feudal law
  Chinese land law, **4:**1–7
  England, **2:**476–479
Tenure in Office Act (1867), **3:**23
Tenures (Littleton), **2:**440
  as source of law, **5:**278
  on substantive law, **4:**60–61
Tenures Abolition Act (England, 1660), **1:**393; **5:**451
Terence, **5:**65
terra nullius, **1:**239, 244, 245–246
  Aboriginal law and, **1:**3
  in Malaysia, **4:**138
  Singapore as, **5:**241
  Southeast Asia as, **5:**313
Terrestrial Commercial Code (Colombia, 1887), **2:**63

territorial concepts in Islamic law, **5:451–454**
  in war, **6:**86
territorial law, negotiable instruments in, **4:**223
terrorism, military tribunals on, **4:**177, 180–181
Tesawalamai, **5:**339, 340
Test Act (England, 1673), **1:**468
  repeal, **1:**469
Test Acts, **4:**285
Testator's Family Maintenance Act (New Zealand, 1900), **4:**229
testimonial approach, **3:**15
Testimoniurum (On Evidence) (Bartolus of Saxoferrato), **1:**281
testimony. *See* witnesses
Teubner, Gunther, **5:**18
Teutonic Order, **1:**254, 255
Tewksbury, Battle of (1471), **6:**4
Textes préparatoires (Sanhuri), **1:**205
Textus Roffensis, **1:**177
Thach, Charles C., Jr., **3:**21
Thailand, **5:**314–315, **454–456**. *See also* Southeast Asian law
  Chinese law in, **5:**319
  Hindu law in, **5:**320
  intellectual property, **3:**262, 264
  Islamic law in, **3:**338; **5:**323
  protection of traditional knowledge, **3:**264
Thalelaeus
  Codex commentary by, **1:**328
  information on available, **1:**333
Thaw, Harry K., **3:**428
Thawri, Sufyan al-, **3:**232
Thayer, James Bradley, **2:**26
  on evidence, **1:**13; **3:**5, 6
  on judicial restraint, **2:**163
Thayer, Webster, **4:**337
Theatrum veritatis et iustitiae (De Luca), **2:**326
Thebes, **4:**86
theft, **5:456–463**
  Afghanistan, **1:**62
  ancient Greek law, **5:**23, **456–457**
  ancient Near Eastern law, **1:**175, 176
  Anglo-Saxon law, **1:**179
    sale of land and, **5:**189
  Aztec law, **5:**287–288
  blackmail as, **1:**296
  burglary, **1:**316–317

Byzantine law
  delict, **2:**325
  on delict, **2:**325
Chinese law, **5:**457–461
  accessory and principal in, **1:**18
  deceit as, **2:**314–316
  as disrespect *(bujing)*, **4:**250
  mutilation for, **4:**197
English common law, **5:**461–463
  fraud and, **3:**101
  women in, **6:**120
fraud and, **3:**100
Inca law, **5:**289
Islamic law, **4:**272
Laos, **4:**14
medieval and post-medieval Roman law
  evidence of, **3:**7–8
robbery, **5:**463–464
Roman law
  delict, **2:**320, 321–323
  formula in, **3:**96
  lex Irnitana on, **4:**104
  manifest *vs.* nonmanifest, **2:**321, 322
Sabinus, Masurius, on, **5:**179, 180
Welsh law, **6:**99
Theft Act (U.K., 1968), **5:**463
  on blackmail, **1:**297
  on burglary, **1:**317
  on fraud, **3:**101
themistes (rules and customs), **1:**153
Theodora, **3:**454–455
Theodoric II (king of the Visigoths). *See also* Edictum Theodorici
  Germanic provincial administration under, **3:**116
Theodoric the Great (Ostrogothic king), **5:**149
  rule of Italy, **5:**14
Theodosian Code. *See Codex Theodosianus*
Theodosius I (Roman emperor)
  code compilation under, **2:**33
  marriage laws under, **4:**307
  religious law under, **5:**123
Theodosius II (Roman emperor), **2:**187
  jurists under, **3:**434
  law issued under, **3:**456
  legal studies under, **5:**148
  Lex Citandi, **1:**327
  praetorian edict and, **4:**376

  on succession, **5:**388
  universal code under, **3:**437
Theogony (Hesiod)
  on dispute resolution, **1:**138
  on procedure, **1:**152
Theophilus
  information on available, **1:**333
  on the *Institutes*, **1:**282, 328
  Institutes paraphrased by, **1:**332
  Justinian's *Institutes* and, **3:**252
  Pandects (Pandectae), **6:**8
Theophrastus, **1:**149; **2:**180; **4:**457
  on *eisangelia*, **4:**246
Theory of Justice, A (Rawls), **3:**449–450
thiasoi, **5:**228–229
Thibaut, Anton Friedrich Justus, **2:**48; **5:**2
Thibaut, Justus Friedrich
  on ownership, **4:**476
Thirty Tyrants, **1:**232; **2:**125
Thirty Years' War, **3:**396
  rise of nation-states in, **5:**352
Tholosan, Claude, **6:**108
Thoma, Richard, **2:**121
Thomas, Christopher, **6:**75
Thomas, Clarence
  on the *Lemon* test, **5:**119
  on natural law, **4:**219
  on right to bear arms, **1:**221, 222
Thomas, Kendall, **4:**365
Thomas à Becket, **1:**467; **4:**315, 316; **5:**27
  on ecclesiastical law, **2:**387
Thomas Aquinas, Saint, **5:**450
  on breach of contract, **1:**307
  on definition of law, **4:**18
  on evidence, **3:**8
  on guilt, **3:**134, 136
  influence on Vitória, Francisco de, **5:**299
  on natural law, **4:**214
  on property, **4:**475
  on reason, **4:**216, 217
  in Scholasticism, **4:**15
  on war, **4:**16
Thomasius, Christian, **1:**350–351; **5:**464–465
  on absolutism, **1:**7, 8
  constitutional work for Frederick William I, **5:**1
  on error and mistake, **2:**475, 476
  inluence of Pufendorf, Samuel von on, **5:**21

on interpretation, **3**:300
on Justinian organization, **2**:400
on natural law, **3**:118; **4**:217
on witch trials, **2**:444
Thorne, S. E., **1**:301
Thrasymachus the Sophist, **3**:450
Three Anti-expulsion Conditions (China), **4**:159
Three Seals Law (Thailand), **5**:455
Thucydides. *See also History* (Thucydides)
on Antiphon, **4**:123, 125
on Athens' litigiousness, **4**:115
on constitution of the Five Thousand, **2**:125
law depictions by, **1**:148
on maritime law, **4**:148
on *nomos*, **1**:145
on slavery, **5**:243
on Sparta, **5**:327, 329
Thun-Hohenstein, Leo Graf, **6**:25
Thür, Gerhard, **4**:403
anthropological perspective of, **1**:187
Thurii, **2**:124, 180
Thurnwald, Richard, **4**:59
Tianjin, Treaty of (China, 1858), **3**:92
Tiberius (Byzantine emperor)
legislative assemblies under, **4**:95
Novellae by, **1**:282
Tiberius Coruncanius, **3**:434
Tiberius II (Byzantine emperor)
on Sabinus, Masurius, **5**:179
treason under, **6**:1
Tiberius Julius Alexander, **2**:418
Tibet, **5**:465–467. *See also* South Asian law
autonomy of, **2**:482
Buddhist law in, **5**:305–306
Tidd, William, **2**:441
Tidskrift för lagskipning, lagstiftning och förvaltning, **5**:416
Tiedeman, Christopher G., **1**:13
Tikanga Māori, **4**:145–147
Tilden, Samuel, **5**:408
Tillman Act (1907), **4**:340
timetos, **3**:124
Timofeev, Ivan, **5**:177
Timoleon, **4**:456
Timotheus, **3**:125
Tipitaka, **5**:302
Tiraquellus, Andreas (André Tiraqueau), **5**:467
on conflict of laws, **2**:111
on punishment, **3**:134
tithes in England, **2**:389

Titius Aristo, **3**:435
Title VIII of the Fair Housing Act (U.S., 1968). *See* Fair Housing Act (U.S.,1968)
tobacco, Chinese law on, **1**:119
Tobago. *See* Trinidad and Tobago
Tocqueville, Alexis de, **5**:2
on American juvenile justice, **3**:457, 458
on American legal process, **3**:406
influence on Dicey, Albert Venn, **5**:17
on lawyers, **4**:48
Todd, S. C., **6**:111
Todd, Stephen
on Athenian law, **1**:164, 233
in Symposion, **1**:165
on witness testimony, **3**:2
Todd, Stephen C., **4**:403, 407
Togo, **1**:*84*
slavery in, **1**:76
Tokugawa Ieyasu, **3**:369
Tokyo Imperial University, **3**:374
Department of Law, **3**:384
Tokyo Law School. *See* Tokyo Imperial University
Tokyo Rose, **4**:335
Toleration Act (England, 1689), **1**:468
Tolpuddle martyrs (U.K.), **2**:426
Tongzhi tiaoge (Regulations from the Comprehensive Laws), **1**:429
tontines, **3**:258
Tooke, Andrew, **5**:21
Topornin, Boris N., **5**:178
Torah, Egyptian translation of, **2**:416
Tordesillas, Treaty of (1494), **5**:290
Torelli, Lelio, **3**:190
Torrens, Robert, **1**:241
land registration system by, **4**:8–9
Torres Strait Islands. *See also* Melanesia
Torrey, Jay, **1**:268
tort, **5**:467–478. *See also* delict; vicarious liability
agency in, **1**:111
ancient Greece
Gortyn, **1**:142
Calabresi, Guido, on, **4**:25
in colonial United States, **2**:14
England
legal treatises on, **2**:442–443
libel and slander, **4**:105
women in, **6**:124
English common law, **5**:467–469
assault, **1**:226–227
environmental law, **2**:449–450

on fraud, **3**:101
on obligations, **4**:243
Islamic law
obligations and, **4**:244
religion and, **3**:325
law and science in, **4**:30–31
Naga law, **4**:201
natural law on, **4**:215
negligence, **4**:221–222
tort, negligence, and delict, **5:469–472**
United States, **5:472–478**, *473*; **6**:42–43
admiralty, **1**:39
torture, **5:478–488**, *482, 485*
ancient Athens, **5:478–482**
free status and, **5**:356
oath-challenge, **4**:242
of slaves, **5**:355
ancient Greek law
evidence gained through, **3**:2
of slaves, **5**:245
Chinese law, **5**:*482*, **482–484**
abolition, **1**:439
importance of confession and, **2**:107, 108
under Jin, **1**:419–420
Shen Chia-Pen (Shen Jiaben) on, **5**:237
under Tang, **1**:424
De civitate Dei (Augustine) on, **3**:9
English common law, **5:484–486**, *485*
in Star Chamber, **5**:346
evidence and
ancient Greek law, **3**:2
medieval and post-medieval Roman law, **3**:7, 8
Inca law, **5**:289
Islamic law, **2**:375; **5:486–488**
in enforcement, **2**:432
Native American law, **4**:207
ordeals, **4**:262–263
South Africa, **5**:281
United States, Guantanamo Bay, **4**:181
totalitarianism
administrative, **1**:31
legal realism and, **4**:77, 78
Tottell, Richard, **4**:44
Toungoo empire (Burma), **1**:317
Town and Country Planning Act (U.K., 1949), **2**:451
Townsend, Francis, **5**:445
Townsend Plan (U.S.), **6**:96
Towns Improvement Clauses Act (U.K. 1847), **2**:450

Toy Safety Act (U.S., 1969), **2**:*177*, 178
Tractatus de Assecurationibus (Santerna), **5**:364
Tractatus de assecurationibus (Stracca), **5**:364
Tractatus de Assecurationibus, De Adiecto Tractatus (Stracca), **5**:364
Tractatus de bello, de represaliis et de duello (Lignano), **3**:282
Tractatus de fideicommissis familiarum nobilium (Knipschildt), **3**:81
Tractatus de legibus et consuetudinibus regni Angliae (attr. Glanvill), **2**:435
Tractatus de maleficiis (Gandius), **5**:32
Tractatus de notulis (Passagerii), **4**:237
Tractatus represaliarum (Bartolus of Saxoferrato), **3**:282
Tractatus Universi Iurus (Stracca), **5**:364
tracts, custom of, **3**:309
abolition, **3**:310
trade
ancient Greece, **2**:69
grain trade, **2**:71
international law and, **3**:278
United States and, **3**:284–286
risk-bearing communities
community of donkey drivers, **3**:257
shipowners, **3**:257
Trade and Intercourse Act (U.S., 1790), **4**:208
Trade Boards (U.K.), **2**:426
Trademark Counterfeiting Act (U.S., 1984), **3**:272
trademark law
British Borneo, **3**:262
Cambodia, **3**:264
Germany, **3**:260
Indonesia, **3**:262, 263
Laos, **3**:264
Malaysia, **3**:262, 263
Malay states, **3**:261
Philippines, **3**:261
Philippins, **3**:262
Thailand, **3**:262, 264
United States, **3**:271–272
Trade Regulation of 1869 (Germany), **2**:102–103
Trades Dispute Act (U.K., 1906), **2**:427
trade-secrecy law, **3**:273
Trade Union Act (U.K., 1871), **2**:426
Trade Union Law (People's Republic of China), **1**:442

trade unions. *See also* employment and labor law
  English common law on, **2:**425–428
  guilds as, **3:**132
traditio cartae (handing over of paper)
  medieval and post-medieval Roman
    in sale of land, **5:**193
Traditional and Alternative Medicine Act
    (Philippines, 1997), **3:**264
traditional knowledge, protection of, **3:**264
traditional law. *See* folk law
"trailbaston" juridiction of King's Bench,
    3:*471*
Trail of Tears, **4:**209
Trainin, A. N., **5:**178
Training for the Public Profession of the Law
    (Reed), **2:**404–405
Traité des délits et des peines (Morellet), **1:**285
Traité des lois (Domat), **2:**357
Traité des Obligations (Pothier), **2:**442
Traités (Pothier), **2:**357
Trajan (Roman emperor), **3:**435; **5:**12
Trano, Goffredus, **5:**198
  influenced by Azo, **1:**248
transaction in Islamic law, **3:**326
Transfer of Property Act (India, 1872), **3:**216
Transfer of Property Act (Pakistan, 1882), **4:**275
transfer pricing, **3:**287
Transformation of American Law, The (Horwitz), **2:**205
Trans-Missouri joint venture, **1:**324
transportation, insurance for, **3:**257–258
Transportation Act (Great Britain, 1718, 1720),
    5:28, 256
Transportation Act (U.S., 1920), **5:**103
transportation regulation, **5:99–105**
Transvaal, **1:**86
Transvaal Code (1903), **5:**280
Transylvania University (Kentucky), **1:**12
Tratado de confirmaciones reales, encomiendas,
    oficios y casos en que se requiren para las Indias
    (Pinelo), **1:**215–216; **5:**291
Travancore Christian Guardianship Act (India, 1941),
    3:223
Traynor, Roger, **2:**209; **3:**429
treason, **6:1–6**, *3*
  ancient Athens, **5:**479
  ancient Greece, **4:**246
    in military service, **4:**248
  ancient Near Eastern law, **1:**175
  Chinese law, **4:**249–250, 257–258, 259
    punishment for, **4:**260

  English law, **2:**276
    capital punishment and, **1:**366, 379
    nationality in, **4:**205–206
    women in, **6:**120
  Roman law, **2:**238, 268–269, 270, 272; **4:**333
  United States law, **4:**334–335
Treason Act (England, 1555), **6:**2
Treason Act (U.K., 1842), **6:**6
Treason Felony Act (U.K., 1848), **6:**6
treaties
  ancient Near Eastern law, **1:**176–177
  ancient Rome, **5:**212
  British Commonwealth, **1:**312
  encouragement for production of intellectual
    property, **3:**259
  European Union, **2:**487–488
  Islamic law on non-Muslims in, **4:**233
  protection from unfair competition and, **2:**103
  separation of powers and, **5:**217–218
  state sovereignty and, **5:**352
  United States
    with Native Americans, **4:**207–210, 213
    Supreme court on, **3:**293
Treatise of Equity (Ballow), **2:**194, 441
Treatise of the Pleas of the Crown (Hawkins), **2:**441
Treatise on Law of Master and Servant (Wood), **1:**115
Treatise on the Conflict of Laws (Beale), **2:**117
Treatise on the Conflict of Laws and the Limits of their
    Operation in Respect of Place and Time
    (Savigny), **2:**112
Treatise on the Effect of the Contract of Sale,
    A (Blackburn), **2:**441–442
Treatise on the Law of Contracts Not under Seal
    (Story), **2:**204–205
Treatise on the Law of Easements (Gale), **2:**379
Treatise on the Law of Quasi-Contracts (Keener),
    2:443
Treatise on the Law of Sale of Personal Property
    (Benjamin), **2:**442
Treatise on the Medical Jurisprudence of Insanity,
    A (Ray), **3:**247
Treatise on the System of Evidence in Trials at Common
    Law, A (Wigmore), **4:**443
Treaty Establishing a Constitution for Europe (2004),
    2:122
Treaty Establishing the European Community,
    2:486
Treaty Establishing the European Union (1992)
  rejections of, **2:**493
  on state sovereignty, **2:**485

Treaty on the Functioning of the Union (2007), **2:**487, 493
Trebatius
    influence of, **1:**333
    Labeo, Marcus Antistius, on, **3:**475
    as legal advisor to Caesar, **3:**434
Treby, George, **1:**292
Trent, Council of. *See under* ecumenical councils
Tres ancienne coutume de Normandie, **3:**78
Tres libri Codicis in legal education, **2:**6, 399
trespass
    agency and, **1:**109
    bailment and, **1:**250
    English law, **2:**437
        in assault, **1:**226, 227
        duress and, **2:**374
        in easements, **2:**380
        evidence in, **3:**4
        fraud and, **3:**101
        land leases, **4:**11
    in environmental law, **2:**449
    Islamic law, **4:**272
    mesne process in, **4:**175
    negligence in, **4:**220–221
    nuisance and, **4:**239, 240
Tretiakov, Ivan A., **5:**171, 172
Trial, The (Kafka), **4:**108
trial by battle, **6:**6, **6–7**
    English common law, **4:**262, 263
    estates doctrine and, **2:**477
"Trial of Satan" (Bartolus?), **1:**281
trial procedure. *See* procedure
trials
    in ancient Rome
        Cicero on, **1:**473, 474–475
    in early People's Republic of China, **1:**442
    England
        evidence in, **3:**3–7
tribal customs. *See also* folk law
    Afghanistan, **1:**59
    Yemen, **6:**155
Tribonian, **2:**33; **6:7–9**
    in Codex Justinianus commission, **1:**327–328; **3:**437
    as jurist, **1:**332
    Justinian's *Institutes* and, **3:**252
    on Papinian, **4:**280
    praetorian edict and, **4:**376
Tribunal and Inquiries Act (England, 1958), **5:**16
Tribunal des Conflits (France), **1:**22

tribunes
    in legislative assemblies, **4:**93
    veto power of, **4:**95
Triepel, Heinrich, **2:**121
Trinidad and Tobago, **6:9–11**, *10*
    reliance on British case law and principles, **1:**369
Tripartita (Aelius Paetus Catus), **6:**20
Triple Alliance War, **4:**282
TRIPS. *See* Agreement on Trade-Related Aspects of Intellectual Property Rights
Trojan Women (Euripides), **4:**109–110
Troje, Hans-Erich, **5:**163
trover, writ of, **5:**251–252
Trubek, David, **2:**298
    on law and society, **4:**34
Trubetskoi, E. N., **5:**178
Truck Act (U.K., 1831), **2:**425
Trudeau, Pierre, **1:**342
Trullanum Council. *See* church councils: Quinisextum Council (692)
Truman, Harry
    antidiscrimination agenda of, **2:**341
    segregation in the military and, **6:**57
    steel mills seized by, **5:**218–219
    war power under, **6:**89
Trustee Act (U.K.), **6:**14
trust fund doctrine, **1:**326
trusts
    agency and, **1:**109
    antitrust law and, **1:**187–193
    charitable
        in England, **1:**392
    England, **2:**436
        dower in, **2:**363
        equity and, **2:**470
        growth of, **2:**437
        land registration in, **4:**7
        women in, **6:**122–123
    English common law, **6:11–14**
        natural law on, **4:**215
    exemption form rule against perpetuities, **3:**239
    medieval and post-medieval Roman law, **3:**48
    prudent-investor standard, **3:**238
    revocable inter vivos, **5:**408
    Roman law, **5:**374–375
    United States, **1:**323–324
        charitable, **5:**407–408

equity and, **2:**472
inheritance and, **3:**237
in marriage, **3:**54
in succession, **5:**406–407
Trusts of Land and Appointment of Trustees Act (1996), **2:**478
Truth, **4:**320
Truth, Sojourner, **6:**134–135
Truth-in-Lending Act (U.S., 1968), **2:**78, 178
Tryals per Pais (Duncombe), **3:**5
Tryphoninus. *See* Claudius Tryphoninus
Tshombé, Moíse-Kapenda, **1:**98
T-square rule of decision making, **4:**76
Tthammasat (Ayutthyan), **5:**455
Tucker, St. George, **6:**38, 46
   on international law, **3:**293
   on right to bear arms, **1:**218
Tughlaq, Mohannad Bin, **2:**280–281
Tuhafat al-Hukkam (Ibn 'Asim), **3:**351
Tuhr, Andreas von, **4:**277
Tukulor empire, **1:**73–74, 88
Tulin, Leon, **4:**74
Tullius, Servius, **4:**93
Tullock, Gordon, **5:**83
Tulufan chutu wenshu, **5:**186
Tumanov, Vladimir A., **5:**178
Tun, Than, **5:**316
Tunisia. *See also* Maghrib
   adoption in, **1:**48; **4:**297
   civil law, **1:**205
   codification in, **2:**37
   conflict of laws, **2:**114
   death penalty in, **1:**368
   as French protectorate, **4:**129
   Ibadis in, **3:**349
   inheritance law, **2:**38
   obligatory bequests, **6:**107
   personal status laws, **4:**130, 296–297; **6:**129
Tunkin, Grigorii Ivanovich, **5:**178
tuntian (service tenure), **4:**4
Turin Codex, **5:**155
Turkestanskii al'bom: Chast' etnograficheskaia Tuzemnoe aselenie v Russkikh vladieniiakh Srednei Azii, **2:**432
Turkey, **6:**14–18
   abolition of death penalty, **1:**367
   abolition of *Mecelle*, **3:**344; **6:**16
   codification in, **2:**37
   conflict of laws, **2:**113

   constitution, **2:**36, 135
   in European Union, **2:**493
   Islamic law, **2:**483; **3:**414; **4:**263–270; **6:**14–15, 16, 17
     judiciary, **3:**419
   legal education in, **2:**398
   military regime in, **2:**135
   personal status law in, **4:**295
   private law in, **4:**392
   Turkish law, **6:**16–18
Turkish Civil Code (Turkey, 2002), **6:**15
Turkmenistan, **1:**367
Turks and Caicos Islands, **1:**369
Turner, Fredrerick Jackson, **4:**480
Turtushi, al-, **4:**128
Turuq al-hukmiyya, al- (Ibn Qayyim al-Jawziyya), **3:**199
Tuscan Leopoldina, **4:**439
Tusi, Muhammad ibn al-Hasan al-, Shaykh al-Ta'ifa, **6:**18–19
tutelage, **2:**185–186
Tuvalu, **4:**346
Twelver. *See* Imami
Twelve Tables (451–450 B.C.E.), **2:**31, 32; **5:**473; **6:***19*, 19–21
   on adoption, **4:**308
   contract and, **2:**182
   on contracts, **5:**143
   criminal law in, **2:**268, 269
   Danish king as guardian of, **2:**328
   on debt-bondage, **5:**275
   on delict, **2:**320–321, 322
   enactment of the, **5:**141
   formulae from, **3:**95
   on insolvency, **3:**248
   on intestate property, **5:**143
   on jurists, **3:**434
   Labeo, Marcus Antistius, on, **3:**475
   on *legis actiones*, **4:**83
   lex in, **4:**101
   on marriage, **4:**305
   Oldendorp, Johann, on, **4:**261
   on partnership, **2:**185
   on persons, **4:**303
   on property, **4:**460–462, 465
   public law in, **5:**9
   on religious law, **5:**120
   Sabinus, Masurius, on, **5:**179
   Servius Sulpicius Rufus on, **5:**225
   on slavery, **4:**302

on succession, **5:**370, 371, 372
on summons and legal procedure, **2:**234–235
Twin Cities Metropolitan Council, **4:**122
Two Treatises on the Hindu Law of Inheritance (Colebrooke), **2:**57; **3:**158
Tyack, David, **2:**408
Tyberiadis (Bartolus of Saxoferrato), **1:**281
Tyburn gallows (London), **1:**365
Tyco, **5:**95
Tyrone's Rebellion, **3:**310
Tyrtaeus, **5:**355

U

Ubaldis, Baldus de, **2:**254
Über den Entwicklungsgang der österreichischen Civiljurisprudenz (Unger), **6:**26
Über die Nothwendigkeit eines allgemeinen bürgerlichen Rechts für Deutschland (Thibaut), **2:**48
ubuntu-botho, **5:**282
UCC. *See* Uniform Commercial Code
Udaya I (Sri Lanka), **5:**303
aynudda fi usual al-fiqh, al- (Abu Yaaynla), **1:**10
Uganda
   in British Commonwealth, **1:**315
   as British protectorate, **1:**86
   colonial court system, **2:**42
   constitution, **2:**138
   expulsion of Asians from, **2:**384
   family law, **1:**104
   independence of, **1:**93
   indigenous rights in, **1:**88
   judicial system, **1:**99
   political parties in, **1:**104
   South Asian law in, **2:**382–384
Uighur Empire, **4:**183
Ukraine
   conflict of laws, **2:**113
   courts in, **2:**254
'ulama' (legal scholars)
   education of, **2:**397–398
   high status in Imami community, **3:**195
'Ulaymi, al-, **3:**347
Ulozhenie Code (Russia), **5:**170
Ulpian, **3:**212; **6:**23–24
   on Byzantine emperors and the law, **5:**14–15
   on conflict of laws, **2:**109
   on courts, **2:**238
   on custom, **2:**167
   on imperial grants, **3:**212

on legal reasoning, **4:**81
on natural law, **4:**216
on partnership, **1:**319
on public *vs.* private Roman law, **5:**17
on Sabinus, Masurius, **5:**179
under Septimius Severus, **3:**435
on women, **6:**119
Ulster Banking Co., **1:**272
Ulysses (Joyce), **3:**165
'Umar I (Caliph), **3:**304
'Umar ibn al-Khattab
   on inheritance, **3:**233
   on judicial review, **3:**413
   in Pact of 'Umar, **4:**234
   on taxation, **5:**430, 432
Umayyads
   Arabizing and centralizing efforts of, **5:**431
   Khariji movement under, **3:**348
   on legal reasoning, **4:**62
   Maliki school under in Andalusia, **3:**351
   muftis in, **4:**193–194
Una et eadem lex (English Royal ordinance, 1331), **3:**308
Unam sanctam (papal bull), **2:**223
UNCITRAL model law for international insolvency law, **3:**250
Uncle Tom's Cabin (Stowe), **6:**51
Undang-undang Laut Melaka, **4:**137–138
Undang-Undang Melaka, **4:**137–138; **5:**322
Underwood Tariff Act (U.S., 1913), **5:**443
undue influence in medieval and post-medieval Roman law, **6:**25
   duress and, **2:**373, 376
   women and guarantee in, **3:**129
Unemployment Act (U.K., 1934), **4:**350
unfair competition
   Lanham Act on, **3:**272
   treaties as protection from, **2:**103
   U.S. law, **3:**272–273
Unfederated Malay States, **3:**261
Unger, Josef, **6:**25–26
   comparative law, **2:**99
Unger, Roberto, **2:**296
U.N. Human Rights Commission, **3:**295
Unidad Revolucionaria Nacional Guatemalteca (URNG), **3:**130
UNIDROIT Principles of International Commercial Contracts (1994), **2:**115
   on donation, **2:**358

Unified Law for International Sale of Movable Items, **5:**192
Unified Law of International Contracts, **5:**192
Uniform Act. *See* Uniform Trade Secrets Act
Uniform Child Custody Jurisdiction and Enforcement Act, **2:**115
Uniform Civil Code (India), **4:**294
Uniform Code of Military Justice
    on military tribunals, **4:**179
    military tribunals and, **5:**219
uniform codes, **2:**51
Uniform Commercial Code (UCC), **2:**51, 76–78, 114, 115; **6:**61
    on agency, **1:**114
    assignment in, **1:**228
    contracts and, **2:**209
    on Native Americans, **4:**207
Uniform Interstate Family Support Act, **2:**115
uniform laws, conflict of laws and
    uniform choice of law, **2:**114
    uniform substantice law, **2:**114–115
Uniform Limited Partnership Act (U.S., 1916), **1:**115
Uniform Negotiable Instruments Law, **2:**76
Uniform Parentage Act, **2:**115
Uniform Partnership Act (U.S., 1914), **1:**115
Uniform Probate Code, **5:**402
Uniform Rules of Evidence (U.S., 1953), **3:**11
    state adoption of, **3:**12
Uniform Sales Act, **2:**76
Uniform Trade Secrets Act (1979), **3:**273
Union Act (Canada, 1840), **1:**337–338
Union Chargeability Act (U.K., 1865), **4:**350
Union of London & Smith's Bank (England), **1:**272
Union of Soviet Socialist Republics (USSR). *See also* Russia, Soviet era, 1917–1991
    Baltic states annexed by, **1:**256
    Cold War relations with U.S., **4:**335, 337
United Arab Emirates
    conflict of laws, **2:**114
    constitution, **3:**317
    constitutional court, **2:**136
    death penalty in, **1:**368
    shari'a as principal source of legislation in, **3:**317
    zakat in, **5:**431
United Irishmen, **3:**311
United Kingdom
    accession into European Union, **2:**490
    anthropological perspective in, **1:**186
    courts (*See* courts, English)
    currency of, **2:**491
    freedom of speech in, **5:**329
    indirect rule by, **1:**78
    Islamic law in, **5:**311–312
    Islamic marriage in, **2:**484
    Islamic symbols regulated in, **2:**483
    judiciary in, **3:**422
    positivism in, **4:**355
    social security in, **5:**271
    South Asian law in, **5:311–312**
United Malays National Organisation, **4:**138
United Nations, **3:**284; **5:**314
    Afghanistan reconstruction under, **1:**60
    Africa in, **1:**106
    African mandates under, **1:**85
    agreements unifying international private law, **2:**114
    Charter, **3:**295
    Guyana in, **3:**138
    India and, **3:**220
    Japan in, **3:**380
    Security Council and enforcement of international law, **3:**279, 295
    state sovereignty and, **5:**354
United Nations Commission on International Law (UNCITRAL), **2:**115
United Nations Convention on Contracts for the International Sale of Goods, **2:**115
    Arab countries in, **2:**74
    influence of Uniform Commercial Code on, **2:**78
United Nations Convention on the Rights of Children
    adoption of, **3:**461
    on legitimacy, **3:**47
United Nations Convention on the Rights of Persons with Disabilities, **2:**337
United Nations Educational, Scientific and Cultural Organization (UNESCO)
    on Eritrea, **1:**101
    Universal Copyright Convention, **3:**267
United Nations Guidelines for Consumer Protection (1985), **2:**174
United Nations Transitional Administration in East Timor (UNTAET), **2:**384
United Nations Transitional Authority in Cambodia (UNTAC), **1:**335
United Provinces of Central America, **1:**384
United Republic of the Seven Dutch Provinces, **4:**225, 226

United States, **6:26–61**. *See also* American Revolution; common law: United States law; due process; immigration to the United States; regulation, United States; United States, colonial period
   abortion, **6:140–142**
      case law, **6**:59
      constitutional right to, **3**:411, 412
      due process and, **2**:370–371
      equal protection, **2**:464
      privacy and, **4**:388–390
      Supreme Court, **2**:165
   academics, **1**:*11*, 11–18
   admiralty, **1**:37–40
   advocates, **1**:57–58
   agency, **1:112–116**
   alcohol and drugs, **1**:123–128
   antitrust, **1**:187–193, 323–324
   arbitration, **1**:130–131; **3**:486, 487
      commercial, **2**:78
      labor arbitration, **3:486–490**
      Taft-Hartley Act on, **3**:483
   bankruptcy, **1:267–270**
   capital punishment, **3**:462
   choice of law in interstate context, **2**:117–118
   commercial law, **2**:75–76
      federal jurisdiction, **2**:75
   common law, **2**:440
   conflict of laws, **2:116–119**, 1120113
   consumer protection, **2:174–178**
   contracts, **2:204–210**
   corporate, **1**:321–327
   courts, federal, **2**:255–262
   criminal, **2**:284–295
   debt
      indentured labor, **3**:477–478
      lawyers in collection of, **4**:48
   discrimination
      anti-Semitism, **2**:406
      in apportionment and reapportionment, **1**:201–204
      commerce and, **3**:62
      in education, **2**:409–412, *410*
      in employment, **6**:137–138
      federalism and, **3**:61, 65
      in labor unions, **3**:481–482
      in legal education, **2**:404, 405, 406; **4**:49
      in legal profession, **4**:53–54
      in legal services, **4**:51–53
      Title VII on, **3**:484
   divorce, **3**:52–54; **6**:45
      no-fault, **6**:59
      women in, **6**:134, 136, 142
   donation, **2**:358
   education, **2**:408–412
   environmental, **2:454–458**
   equity, **2:472–473**
   evidence, **3:10–17**
   executive power, **3**:19–25
   family, **3:51–57**
   federalism, **3**:59–66
      international law and, **3**:291
   freedom of speech in, **5**:329, **332–338**
   homosexuality, **3**:166–168; **4**:390
   housing, **3**:182–186
   idealist approach to international law, **3**:293
   influenced by Jewish law, **3**:393
   influence on New Zealand law, **4**:229
   inheritance, **3**:235–240; **6**:30, 34
      colonial period, **2**:13
      by illegitimate children, **3**:55
      of slave status, **5**:258
   intellectual property, **3:265–275**
   judicial review, **2**:152–153
      distinction between federal-federal and federal-state, **2**:153
      on equal protection, **2**:462–463
   judiciary, **3:423–430**
      administrative agency oversight by, **1**:28–29
      bar association on independence of, **4**:51
      equal access to, **2**:463
      immigration role, **3**:207
      labor law and, **3**:484, 485
      law and economics influence in, **4**:27
      legislative power and, **4**:97–99
      racial diversity in, **2**:343–344
      social science use in, **5**:266–270
      state, **5**:349
      women in, **6**:144
   judicicial power, **3**:406–413
   juries, **3:441–445**; **5**:135
      citizenship and, **2**:3
      equity and, **2**:472
      evidence presentation to, **3**:16
      right to a jury trial, **4**:440
      women, **6**:138–139, *139*
   juvenile justice, **3**:428, 457–462
   labor and employment, **3:477–486**; **6**:42, 48–49
      alternative dispute resolution in, **1**:130
      colonial period, **2**:14–15

on disability, **2:**334, 336
due process and, **2:**369–370
equal protection in, **2:**462
equity and, **2:**472
federal court jurisdiction in, **2:**261
federalism and, **3:**61, 62–63
feminist theory on, **3:**68
labor arbitration, **3:486–490**
picket line, **2:**23
progressive era, **5:**78, 79
race discrimination in, **2:**342
safety, **6:**48–49
unions, **6:**42, 48
women in, **2:**339, 340; **6:**136–137, 137–138, 138, 145
working conditions, **6:**49
land, **6:**31
conservation in, **2:**455–456
due process and, **2:**371
Indian land, **6:**49–50
takings clause, **5:**424
law and society in, **4:**31–35
lawful permanent residents *versus* citizens, **2:**3–4
lawyers in, **4:48–55**
legal education, **2:401–408**
lawyers, **4:**48–49
women in, **6:**143–145
legal profession, **6:**43, 55–56
academics in, **1:**11–18
women in, **6:**143–145
legislative power, **4:**96–99
limitation of mobility between states, **3:**206
local government, **4:**120–123
marriage, **3:**51–52
equal protection on, **2:**465
polygamy, **5:**117
of slaves, **5:**262
in succession, **5:**404–405
women's rights in, **6:**134, 136, 145
military service
discrimination in, **2:**340, 341
effects of on history, **6:**88
right to bear arms and, **1:**216–220
women in, **6:**138, 139–140
military tribunals, **4:**177–182
on Native Americans, **4:**206–214; **6:**49–50
natural law and, **4:217–220**
New Deal era public health law, **3:**144–145
nineteenth century, **6:41–53,** *44, 47, 49*
notaries in, **4:**237

political crimes, **4:334–337**
political parties and elections, **4:338–345**
positivism in, **4:355–358**
postmodernism and, **4:**362–366
privacy, **4:385–391**
private international law, **3:284–290**
private law, **4:**393, 396
procedure
administrative agencies and, **1:**31
alternative dispute resolution, **1:**128–129
civil, **4:440–447**
criminal, **4:447–454**
progressive era
public health law, **3:**143–144
regulation, **5:**77–79
property, **4:480–486**
protection of property, **4:486–493**
public health law in, **3:**141–146
public interest, **5:**6
public international law, **3:290–297**
punishment, **5:37–42; 6:**50
for drug crimes, **1:**127
reform, **2:**291
of slaves, **5:**258–259
realist approach to international law, **3:**293
regulation, **5:75–105,** *78, 87, 99*
agency forcing provisions in, **1:**29
agriculture, **5:**80, **86–92**
bar association in, **4:**51
deregulation, **1:**29–30
environmental law, **2:**457
judicial review in, **1:**30–31
legislative power of, **4:**98–99
overview, **5:75–86**
science and, **4:**30–31
securities, **5:92–95**
telecommunications, **5:95–99**
transportation, **5:99–105**
transportation regulation, **5:99–105**
religion, **5:114–120; 6:**30, 51
education and, **2:**408, 409
equal protection in, **2:**464
religious freedom cases, **2:**261
remedies, **5:**125, 126–127
reproductive rights, **4:**388–390
rhetoric in jury trials, **5:**135
right to die, **4:**390
science and, **4:**28–31
search and seizure, **4:**387; **5:**203–208

slaves and slavery, **5:258–264; 6:**28, 30–31, 34, 37, 38, 39, 41, 42, 43–44
   abolished, **2:**340
   ban on importation of slaves, **3:**206
   civic rituals, **3:**428
   colonial period, **2:**286–287, 289
   Constitution and, **2:**150
   Constitution on, **2:**154; **3:**448
   criminal law applied to slaves, **2:**290
   equal protection and, **2:**458–462
   federalism and, **3:**60
   free speech and, **6:**51
   marriage of, **6:**134
   natural rights and, **3:**448
   nineteenth century, **6:**52–53
   property law, **4:**482
   punishment of slaves, **5:**38
   religion and, **5:**115
   right to bear arms and, **1:**218–219
   slaves defined as property, **5:**75
   state sovereignty in, **5:**353
   taxes, **5:**440, 441
   territorial status and, **5:**116
sodomy laws, **3:**110
   case law, **2:**292
   equal protection in, **2:**464
   federalism and, **3:**63
   history of, **3:**166–168
state law
   in commerce, **2:**76
   confederation period, **5:**347–349
   conflict of laws and, **2:**116
succession, **5:402–409**
taxation, **5:439–448**, *446*
   general welfare clause, **3:**113–115
   income, **3:**61
   income tax, **6:**55
   inheritance, **5:**408
   state power in, **5:**348, 349
tort, **5:**471–472, **472–478**, *473*; **6:**42–43
   admiralty, **1:**39
treaty with Japan, **3:**365, 372
trusts, **1:**323–324
   charitable, **5:**407–408
   equity and, **2:**472
   marriage, **3:**54
   succession, **3:**237; **5:**406–407
twentieth century, **6:53–61**
welfare, **6:91–98**
witch trials, **6:**109

women, **6:**44–45, 45, **133–146**
   educational equal opportunity and, **2:**410–411
   equal protection, **2:**462–463
   labor law on, **3:**479–480
   as lawyers, **4:**49
   in legal profession, **4:**53–54
   punishment of, **2:**290
   suffrage, **4:**339
women in, **6:**44, 45, **133–146**
United States, colonial period
   overview, **6:26–32**
   colonies in the Empire, **6:34–36**
   consumer protection statutes, **2:**175
   debt, **2:**14
   inheritance, **3:**245–246
   land, **2:**12–13, 13
   public health law, **3:**142–143
   punishment, **2:**285–286, 288–289, 289
   reception of common law, **2:**82–83
   slavery, **5:256–258**
   sources of colonial law, **6:32–34**
   women, **2:**13–14, 289
United States Code on educational equal opportunity, **2:**410–411
United States Sentencing Commission, **1:**127
United States Steel, **5:**78
United Steelworkers, **3:**487
unity doctrine, **3:**34
   ancient Greek law, **1:**136, 163–164
   England, **3:**33
"Unity of Greek Law, The" (Finley), **1:**136
"Unity of Greek Law, The" (Gagarin), **1:**164
Universal Declaration of Human Rights (1948), **3:**295, 450
   India's fundamental rights influenced by, **3:**105–106
   international law and, **3:**278
   on social security, **5:**270
Universal (Male) Suffrage Law (Japan, 1925), **3:**377
universities, **6:61–64**
University College London, **1:**288
University of Alabama, **2:***411*
University of al-Azhar, **2:**421
University of Bologna, **2:**399, *399*
University of Bourges, **2:**7, 400
University of California, Berkeley, **4:**32–34
University of Copenhagen
   reforms at, **2:**328
   reorganization of, **2:**328

University of Halle, **6:**111–112
University of Leiden, **4:**225, 226
    Doneau, Hugues, in, **2:**359–360
University of London. *See* University College London
University of Notre Dame, **2:**404
University of Orléans, **4:**225
University of Pennsylvania Law Review, **6:**43
University of Wisconsin
    in law-and-society movement, **2:**407
    law and society program, **4:**33–34
unjust enrichment in medieval and post-medieval Roman law, **6:**64–66
unjustified enrichment in ancient Roman law, **2:**183, 186, 187, 188, 190
Unkovskii, Aleksei M., **5:**178
unlawful means and objectives test in labor law, **3:**479, 480
unlimited joint liability in medieval partnerships, **2:**93
unofficial. *See* folk law
Unterricht über die Gesetze für die Einwohner der preussischen Staaten (Carmer and Svarez), **5:**1
Untouchability (Offences) Act (India, 1955), **3:**219
U Nu, **5:**314
Upāsakādhyayana, **3:**363
UPC. *See* Uniform Probate Code
Upplandslagen (Sweden, 1296), **5:**414
Urban II (pope), **2:**318
Urban VI (pope), **1:**250
urbanization
    administrative agencies and regulation in, **1:**25, 26
    local government law and, **4:**121–122
    Maghrib and al-Andalus, **4:**129
    nuisance and, **4:**239–240
    Sweden, **5:**416–417
    United States
        apportionment and reapportionment and, **1:**201–204
Uriburu, José Félix, **1:***215*
Urseius Ferox, **3:**430
Uruguay, **6:**66–67
    Civil Code, **1:**398
Uruguay Round, **3:**285
ʿUrwa, Hisam ibn, **4:**140
U.S. Advisory Commission on Intergovernmental Relations, **4:**122
USA PATRIOT Act (U.S., 2001), **4:**391; **5:**338
U.S. Children's Bureau, **3:**459, 460
U.S. Constitution. *See* Constitution of the United States
U.S. Court of Appeals for the Armed Forces, **4:**179

USDA. *See* U.S. Department of Agriculture
U.S. Department of Agriculture (USDA), **1:**27, 28; **5:**80, 86, 88, 91
U.S. Department of Health, Education, and Welfare (HEW). *See* U.S. Department of Health and Human Services
U.S. Department of Health and Human Services
    air-quality standards by, **2:**454
    creation of, **3:**144
    mission of, **3:**145
U.S. Department of Housing and Urban Development (HUD), **1:**29; **3:**182, 183, 184, 186
    fair housing under, **2:**343
U.S. Department of Justice, **1:**27
U.S. Department of Justice
    antitrust actions, **5:**78, 80, 83
    originalism and, **3:**166
    revised antitrust guidelines, **1:**191
U.S. Department of Labor, **1:**131
U.S. Department of Transportation, **5:**103
U.S. Department of Veterans Affairs, **3:**183
Us et costumes de la mer (Cleirac), **4:**151
Usher, Stephan
    on logographers, **4:**124
U.S. Housing Authority. *See* Department of Housing and Urban Development (HUD)
U.S. Internal Revenue Service, **3:**185
Usman dan Fodio. *See* Dan Fodio, Usman
U.S. Public Health Service, **3:**144
U.S. Supreme Court. *See* supreme court: United States
U.S. Treasury Department, **1:**27
usufruct
    English common law, **4:**11
    Islamic law, **4:**55–56
uṣūl al-fiqh (legal theory), **3:**316–317, 321
    Hanbali school and, **3:**346
    Imāmi school and, **3:**340
    Qadi al-Nuʿman and, **5:**59
    Shafiʿi school of law and, **3:**352
Usul al-Sarakhsi (al-Sarakhsi), **5:**194
Usuli school of Isamic, **1:**291
usurpation *(ghaṣb)*, **6:**67–68
usury, **6:**68–72
    canon law doctrine on, **2:**93
    evolution of English common law, **2:**101
    in Germany law, **3:**204–205
    illicit commercial gain *(ribā)* in Islamic law, **6:**68–70
    medieval and post-medieval Roman law, **6:**70–72
    Pakistan, **5:**309
    repeal of usury laws in the U.K. in 1854, **2:**169

usus feudorum
  in legal education, **2:**399
usus modernus
  on emancipation of children, **3:**45
  on obligations, **4:**245
  on sale of goods, **5:**192
  Spain, **5:**325
usus modernus pandectarum (modern use of the pandects), **1:**371; **2:**7–8
U.S. Virgin Islands, **1:**370
'Utaqi, 'Abd al-Rahman ibn al-Qasim al-, **4:**127
  influence on Sahnun, **5:**182, 183
  on Malik ibn Anas, **3:**350; **4:**140
  on torture, **5:**487
'Utbi, al-, **3:**350
utilitarianism
  Bentham, Jeremy, in, **1:**287
  Brazil, **1:**302
  Islamic law, **1:**9
  in law and economics, **4:**68
  in law reform movements, **4:**41
utilities, impact on company law in Great Britain, **2:**89–90
uti possidetis principle, **1:**107
Utrecht, Treaty of (1579), **4:**225
utrum, **4:**315
Utrush, al-Nasir al-Hasan ibn 'Ali al-, **3:**341
  on duty, **2:**376
'Uyayna, Sufyan ibn, **5:**235
'Uyun al-azhar fi fiqh al-a'imma al-athar (Murtada), **6:**162
Uzbekistan
  abolition of death penalty, **1:**367
  conflict of laws, **2:**113

V

Vacarius, **5:**156
  in English common law education, **2:**393
Vagrancy Act (England, 1530), **5:**29
vagrancy laws, **3:**478
Vaines, Crossley, **4:**470
Valdemar II (Denmark), **2:**327
Valentinian I (Roman emperor), **5:**123, 124
Valentinian III (Roman emperor), **4:**280; **5:**388
  on bishops and archbishops, **4:**351
  Lex Citandi, **1:**327
  Paul's works under, **4:**290
Valeriae Horatiae (Valerian-Horatian laws, ca. 450 B.C.E.), **5:**9

Valerius Maximus
  on Afrania, **6:**119
  on women, **6:**119
Valin, René Josué, **4:**151
Valla, Lorenzo, **3:**189; **5:**158; **6:**9
Vallandigham, Clement L., **4:**180, 335
  trial of, **4:**178
Valuation Act (India, 1887), **4:**273
Vandals, **3:**115, 116
Vanderbilt, Cornelius, **4:**482
van der Linden, Joannes
  on Grotius, Hugo, **3:**127
Van der Sprenkel, Sybille, **1:**462
Van der Wee, H., **1:**275
Van Devanter, Willis, **3:**62
Van Diemen's Code (1642), **1:**81
Van Diemen's Land. *See* Tasmania
Vangerow, Karl Adolf von, **4:**277
Vansittart, Robert, **2:**393
Vanuatu, **4:**173–174. *See also* Melanesia
  independence of, **4:**174
Van Zeeland, Paul, **2:**485
Vanzetti, Bartolomeo, **4:**337
Vaqiaynat-i Baburi, **1:***117*
Vardhamāna Nāputra. *See* Mahāvīra
Vardhamānanīti (Amitagati), **3:**364
Vardhamānasūri, **3:**364
Vargas, Getúlio Dornelles, **1:**303, *303*, 304
Varro, Marcus Terentius, **5:**158
Varus, Publius Alfenus, **5:**225
Vashishtha, **5:**265
Vasishtha, **3:**152, 155
  on *smriti*, **5:**264
Vasunandi Indranandi, **3:**364
Vatican I and II. *See under* ecumenical councils
Vattel, Emer (Emmerich) de, **3:**276, 291; **6:**73
  definition of constitution, **2:**120
  on land rights, **1:**312
  on law of nations, **3:**283
Vázquez, Gabriel, **4:**15
Vázquez de Menchaca, Fernando, **3:**134
Veblen, Thorstein, **1:**325
Vedāṅgas, **5:**265
Vedas, **3:**147
Vedic law
  1500–800 B.C.E., **3:**150–151, 179
  environmental law, **2:**452–454
Vegio, Maffeo, **3:**189
Venereal Disease Control Act (U.S., 1938), **3:**144
Venetian Republic, patents in, **3:**269

Venezuela, **6**:73–75
  adoption of Chilean Civil Code in 1859, **1**:398
  Bello, Andrés, in, **1**:286
  slavery abolished in, **5**:254–255
  territorial disputes with Guyana, **3**:138
Vernant, Jean-Pierre, **1**:185
Verona Codex, **5**:155
Verplanck, Gulian, **2**:205
  on contracts, **2**:204
Verri, Alessandro, **1**:285
Verri, Pietro, **1**:285
Versailles, Treaty of, **3**:21
vertical integration, **1**:323
  New Deal views of, **1**:326
Vespasian (Roman emperor), **3**:211; **4**:102
  citizenship under, **5**:139
vested rights, conflict of laws and, **2**:117
vesting clauses, **5**:216
Viana, Oliveira, **1**:304
vicarious liability, **6**:75–78
  agency and, **1**:109–110
  English common law, **6**:75–77
  medieval and post-medieval Roman law, **6**:77–78
Vicarious Liability (Baty), **6**:77
"Vices of the Political Systems of the United States" (Madison), **3**:291–292
Victoria (England), **2**:132; **6**:6
Victoria, Ambrogio Nicandro de, **5**:364
Vietnam, **6**:78–80. *See also* Southeast Asian law
  Chinese law in, **5**:317
  influence of Tang code, **1**:424
  intellectual property, **3**:263
  post-colonial, **5**:314
Vietnam War, **6**:79
  freedom of speech and antiwar protests, **5**:335
  legal education and, **2**:406
  Pentagon Papers and, **3**:411
  protests against, **4**:336
  protests of as free speech, **2**:409
  public opinion and, **5**:83
  war power in, **6**:*89*, 89–90
Vietor, Richard, **5**:97
Vigelius, Nicolaus, **3**:193
Vijñāneśvara, **3**:156, 158
Vikings, **3**:306–307
Village Communities (Maine), **4**:137
villeinage, **5**:250–251; **6**:80–82, 81
Vinaya, **5**:304; **6**:83
  in Sri Lanka, **5**:339
Vinaya Pittaka, **5**:302, 303, 304

Viner, Charles
  abridgements by, **4**:61
  influence on
    Blackstone, William, **1**:297
    United States colonial law, **2**:284
Vinnius, Arnold, **2**:7; **4**:226
Vinnius, Kling Arnoldus, **4**:245
Vinogradoff, Paul, **5**:178
Vinogradoff, Paul G., **5**:163
  on comparative law, **1**:185
Violence Against Women Act (U.S., 1994), **2**:67; **3**:64; **6**:143
  invalidation of, **2**:464
Virginia, **3**:236
Virginia Company, **1**:288
Virginia Justice of the Peace (Webb), **2**:284
Virginia Plan, **2**:149
viscontiel actions in environmental law, **2**:448
Vishnu, **3**:153, 155, 156
Visigoths
  on children, **3**:44
  on fraud, **3**:102
  Germanic provincial administration under, **3**:115
  law codes of, **3**:116
  legislation by, **4**:90
  Spain unified under, **5**:324
Vismara, Giulio, **5**:393
Visuddhimagga (Buddhaghosa), **5**:303
vita canonica, **1**:295
Vitellius, **5**:179
Vitoria, Francisco de, **3**:282
  in Scholasticism, **4**:15, 16–17
Vitória, Francisco de, **5**:299
Vivekananda, **3**:159
Vives, Juan Louis, **3**:9
Vladimir Monomakh (Kievan Grand Prince), **5**:177
Vladimirskii-Budanov, Mikhail, **5**:171
VOC. *See* Dutch East India Company
Voet, Johannes
  on conflict of laws, **2**:112
  on the Digest, **4**:226
  on liability in Roman law, **6**:78
  usus modernus and, **2**:8
Voet, Paul, **2**:112
Vöhmer, Justus Henning, **5**:393
Volksgesetzbuch (People's Code) (Germany, 1942), **4**:394
Vollenhoven, Cornelis van
  on *adat*, **1**:21, 251
  on colonial law, **4**:226

influenced by Grotius, Hugo, **3:**127
in legal anthropology, **4:**59
Vollmer, Howard M., **4:**32
Volpp, Leti, **3:**70
Volstead Act. *See* National Prohibition Act (U.S., 1919)
Voltaire
Beccaria, Cesare, and, **1:**285
influence on Catherine II of Russia, **5:**172
Volumen (medieval civil-law lectures), **2:**399
Volumen parvum. *See Tres libri codicis*
voluntary motherhood, **6:**140–141
voluntary surrender and confession *(zishou)*, **2:**106
Volusius Maecianus, L., **3:**436
Vom Beruf unsrer Zeit für Gesetzgebung und Rechtwissenschaft (Savigny), **2:**48; **5:**159
von Bar, Christian, **2:**496
von Fürst, Chancellor von, **5:**1
Vonnisse von Damme, **4:**150
Voorda, Jacobus, **4:**226
Vorschickung, **3:**80
voting. *See* elections; suffrage
Voting Accessibility for the Elderly and Handicapped Act (U.S., 1984), **2:**335
Voting Rights Act (U.S., 1965), **2:**342
districting based on, **2:**463
racial discrimination and, **4:**339
Reagan, Ronald, on, **2:**343
on special education, **6:**95
on vote dilution, **1:**202
Vulgate, the. *See Digest Vulgate*
Vultejus, Hermann, **2:**303
vyavahāra, **6:82–84**
Arthaśāstra in, **1:**223
in Burma, **5:**320
Vyavahāramayūlja (Nīlakantha), **6:**83
Vyshinskii, Andrei Ia., **5:**178

W

Wächter, Carl Georg von, **4:**277
on conflict of laws, **2:**112
Wade, H. W. R., **2:**443
wadī'a (deposit), **1:**263; **2:**332
Wadih fi-l-sunan, al- (al-Malik ibn Habib), **3:**350
wager of law (compurgation). *See* compurgation
Wages Councils (U.K.), **2:**427
Wagner, Robert, **3:**482
Wagner, Robert Ferdinand, **2:***66*
Wagner, Vincenz August, **6:**163
Wahhabi school of Islamic legal thought, **1:**122–123
Wahid, Abdurrahman, **3:**228

Waitangi, Treaty of (New Zealand, 1840), **4:**227, *227*, 232, 345
on appeal, **4:**231
Australian Aboriginal law and, **1:**3
as basis of government, **4:**147
on Maori law, **4:**145
Waite, Morrison Remick, **5:**117
wājib (duty), *fard* compared with, **2:**376, 377
Wales. *See also* Welsh law
devolution of powers to, **2:**133
feudal law in, **3:**76
justices of the peace in, **3:**453
poor law in, **4:**347–351
wālī. *See* guardianship:Islamic law
Walker, Laurens, **5:**266
Walker, Timothy, **2:**204
Wallace, George, **2:***411*; **4:**344
Wallace, Robert W., **2:**233
Wallace, William
execution, **1:**366
treason by, **4:**205; **6:**2
Wallhausen, Johann Jacob von, **5:**170
Walpole, Robert, **1:**386
Walsingham, Francis, **1:**386
Walter E. Meyer Research Institute of Law, **4:**34
law and society research by, **4:**32
Waltner, Ann, **1:**44, 45
Wamytan, Roch, **4:***173*
Wang Anshi, **1:**197
Wangchuck, Jigme Singye, **1:**290
Wang Huizu, **1:**437
Wang Kentang, **1:**433, 436; **2:**331
Wang Mang, **2:**60
Wangpo, Karma Tenkyong (Tibet), **5:**305
Wang Qiao, **1:**433
Wansharisi, Ahmad ibn Yahya al-Tilimsani al-, **3:**351; **6:**85
fatwas by, **3:**58; **4:**128
Wantage code (Aethelred), **1:**182
waqfs (religious endowments), **2:**37–38, 201
in Africa, **2:**45
Indonesia, **3:**337
Muhammad Qadri Pasha al-Hanafi on, **4:**195
qadi supervision of, **4:**73
war. *See also* war power
Africa, precolonial law on, **1:**74
American devinitions in democratic terms, **2:**16
egalitarian implications of, **2:**17
Enlightment views of, **2:**445
executive power in, **3:**24

Grotius, Hugo, on, **3**:127
impact on government size, **6**:54
"just," **1**:313; **6**:86
military tribunals for war crimes, **4**:177
refugee law
    African contributions to, **1**:107
Scholasticism on just, **4**:16
war and peace in Islamic law, **3**:280; **6:85–87**
waraqat, Al- (Juwayni), **3**:463
Warbeck, Perkin, **4**:205; **6**:4
Ward, Nathaniel, **2**:286
Ward, T. H., **4**:137
wardship, **1**:393
War of 1812, **6**:37
    declaration of war in, **6**:88
    Native Americans in, **4**:208
War of Independence. *See* American Revolution
War of the Roses (England, 1455–1485), **2**:129; **3**:415
    attainder, **6**:5
War on Terror
    declaration of war in, **6**:88
    free speech and, **5**:338
    racial profiling, **2**:344
    war power use in, **6**:90–91
war power, **2**:153–154; **3**:292–293; **6:87–91**
    ancient Rome, Senate in, **5**:212
    separation of powers and, **5**:217–218
War Power Resolution (U.S., 1973), **2**:154
War Production Board, **5**:81
warrants. *See* search and seizure
warranty
    ancient Greek law, **2**:180
    consumer protection and, **2**:168
    in sale contracts, **2**:189
Warren, Charles, **2**:26
Warren, Earl
    civil rights cases, **2**:299, 300
    on desegregation of schools, **2**:153
    on equal protection, **2**:460–462
    on evidence, **3**:11–12
    on federalism, **3**:62–63
    on the political question doctrine, **2**:261
    on statutory interpretation, **5**:361
    Supreme Court term of, **2**:260
Warren, Samuel, **3**:273
Warring States period (China, 475–221 B.C.E.), **2**:57
    collective liability in, **2**:58
Warsaw Pact, **3**:278
wartime, expansion of rights and, **2**:16
Washing Away of Wrongs, **1**:426, 436–437

Washington, George
    administrative agencies under, **1**:25
    on Cumberland Gap Road, **3**:113
    on education, **2**:408
    executive power of, **3**:20
    military tribunals under, **4**:180
    political parties and, **4**:342
    on separation of powers, **5**:220
    Whiskey Rebellion and, **4**:335
Washington Weekly, **2**:422
Wasit fi Sharh al-Qanun al-Madani, al- (al-Sanhuri), **1**:205
    on insurance, **3**:255
Wasps (Aristophanes)
    on arbitration, **1**:212
    on juries, **1**:151
    law depictions in, **1**:148; **4**:111
    on litigiousness of Athenians, **1**:232
Wat byllich unn recht ys (Oldendorp), **4**:261
Watchtower Bible and Tract Society, **5**:117
Water (Prevention and Control of Pollution) Act (India, 1974), **2**:453
watered stock, **1**:326
Watergate scandal, **5**:83, 94
    executive power and, **3**:22–23
    privilege rules and, **3**:11–12
Water Quality Act (U.S., 1965), **2**:454
Waterrecht, **4**:150
WaterrechWisbysches Seerecht, **4**:150
Watson, Alan, **6**:21
Watson, Gregory, **2**:156
Wazir, Muhammad ibn Ibrahim al-, **3**:342; **6**:156
Wealth of Nations (Smith), **2**:175
Webb, George, **2**:284
Webb-Pomerene Act (U.S., 1918), **3**:288
Weber, Max, **2**:297; **5**:110
    on advocates, **1**:58
    on contracts, **2**:193
    on definition of law, **4**:18
    on law and economics, **4**:23
Webster, Daniel, **1**:268
Webster, Noah, **2**:408
Wechsler, Herbert, **4**:65
Week of Islamic Jurisprudence (Damascus, 1961), **2**:61
Wei dynasty (China), **1**:411
    accessory and principal in, **1**:18
    on alcohol and drugs, **1**:119
    appeal in, **1**:194
    on astronomical studies, **4**:252
    collective liability, **2**:58

on deceit, **2**:314
on disrespect *(bujing)*, **4**:251
on lack of filial piety, **3**:85
on penal servitude, **4**:292
Weigel, Erhard, **5**:20
Leibniz, Gottfried Wilhelm, and, **4**:100
weights and measures standardization, **2**:168
in North American colonies, **2**:175
Weihaiwei (Weihai), British leased territory of, **1**:451
Weimarer Reichsverfassung (Imperial Constitution of Weimar, 1919), **2**:121; **4**:475
welfare. *See also* social security in modern Europe; welfare, United States
in absolutism, **1**:8
Brazil, **1**:304
Denmark, **2**:328
elderlaw in, **2**:424–425
England
adoption and, **1**:47
children in, **3**:35–36
feminist legal theory on, **3**:66
India, family networks in, **2**:353; **3**:50
law and science in, **4**:29–30
state constitutions and, **5**:351
Sweden, **5**:417
United Kingdom, **4**:90
women and, **6**:137
welfare, United States, **6**:91–98. *See also* Aid to Dependent Children (ADC); Aid to Families with Dependent Children (AFDC); food stamps; Medicaid; Medicare; poverty (United States)
common-law marriage and, **3**:52
equal protection in, **2**:464
Great Society programs, **3**:62
Welles, Bradford, **4**:86
Wellington, Harry, **4**:65
Well of Loneliness, The (Hall), **1**:381
Welsh Church Act (U.K., 1914), **1**:469; **4**:90; **6**:101
Welsh law, **6**:98–102
law books, **1**:375–376
medieval, **1**:374–375
similarities with Irish law, **1**:374–375
similarities with Irish law, **1**:376–377
Welzel, Hans, **3**:136
Wen (Han emperor)
on disrespect *(bujing)*, **4**:250–251
on mutilation, **4**:197
Wen (King of Shu), **1**:405
Wenceslas IV (Pope), **1**:*293*
Wenck, Karl Friedrich Christian, **4**:277

Wendat Confederacy, **1**:345
Wendi (Sui emperor), **1**:418
Wenger, Leopold, **5**:161
in papyrology, **2**:413
Wenman, T. F., **2**:393
Wentworth, J., **4**:324
Wentworth, Thomas, **3**:310
Wentzel-Teutschental, Carl, **3**:*111*
Wen wu on lack of filial piety, **3**:85
Wenxing tiaoli, **1**:431, 458
Wer, **1**:180
Werbőczy, István, **3**:194
wergild, **1**:182
Wernerius. *See* Irnerius
Wesel Convetn (1568), **1**:350
Wesenbeck, Matthäus, **3**:193
Wesenberg, Gerhard, **5**:163
Wesener, Gunter, **5**:163
Wesley, John, **1**:123
West, Robin, **3**:68
Westbury, Lord, **4**:8, 9
Westermeyer, Joseph J., **4**:14
Western canon law. *See* canon law
Western Depot (palace eunuch agency, China), **1**:432
Western Han dynasty, **1**:363
Western Union, **5**:96
Western Zhou dynasty (China)
corruption in the, **2**:225
disability in, **5**:47
penal servitude in, **4**:292
West Galician Code (1797), **2**:9; **4**:394
West Indies Federation, **1**:369
Westminster Confession (1648), **1**:349
Westminster Hall
Court of Common Please in, **2**:86
King's Bench in, **3**:472
Westminster Review (U.K.)
on land registration, **4**:7
West Pakistan Muslim Personal Law (Shariat) Application Act (Pakistan, 1962), **4**:299
West Papua, **4**:172–173. *See also* Melanesia
Westphalia, Peace of (1648), **2**:120
and control of confession by the princes, **1**:350
international law and, **3**:283
Netherlands independence and, **4**:225–226
and origin of public international law, **3**:276, 291
ratification documents, **3**:*277*
Sweden in, **5**:415
West Publishing, **6**:46
Westropp, C. J., **3**:364

Wetboek van Koophandel (Belgium, 1838), **1:**36
Weytsen, Quintin, **4:**151
Whaddon Folio, **3:**17, 19
Whalan, Douglas J., **4:**8, 9
Wharton, Francis, **2:**442
What Next in the Law (Denning), **2:**330
What Social Classes Owe to Each Other (Sumner), **2:**208
Wheaton, Henry, **3:**293
Wheeler-Howard Act. *See* Indian Reorganization Act
whipping
    Chinese law (*See* beating and whipping in Chinese law)
    in Islamic law, **3:**325
    in the United Kingdom, **1:**394
Whiskey Rebellion (U.S., 1794), **5:**441; **6:**40
    treason charges as a result of, **4:**335
White, Byron, **3:**166, 167; **4:**453
White, Edward D., **1:**189
White, Gardenia, **6:**138–139
White, James Boyd, **2:**160
Whitebread, Charles, **1:**126
Whitehead, Mary Beth, **3:***56*
Whitehead, Richard, **3:***56*
White House Conference on the Care of Dependent Children (1909), **4:**369
White Slave Law. *See* Mann Act
white supremacy, **2:**340
Whitlam, Gough, **1:**3
Whythe, George, **1:**12
Wickershan Commission, **4:**452
widows
    pensions, **6:**137
    right to free bench, **6:**81
Wieacker, Franz, **5:**2, 161, 163
Wiebe, Robert, **2:**209
Wiecek, William, **2:**459
Wigmore, John Henry, **4:**443; **6:**46
    on evidence, **1:**15; **3:**5, 6, 11
    on national evidence law, **3:**10
wilāa (patria potestas), **3:**37
Wilde, Oscar, **4:**106
Wilderness Act (U.S., 1964), **2:**455
Wildlife Protection Act (India, 1974), **2:**453
Wilhelm, Walter, **3:**433
Wilhelm II (Kaiser), **4:**206
Wilhelm Meister (Goethe), **3:**84
Wilkes, John, **4:**143; **5:**203
Wilkie, David, **5:***381*
Wilkie, Harold, **2:***335*
Wilkins, Roy, **2:***342*

Wilkinson, Charles, **4:**211
Willes, James Shaw, **2:**442
Willetts, R. F., **3:**120
William I the Conqueror (England), **1:**385
    Domesday Book ordered by, **1:**178
    ecclesiastical law under, **2:**387
    feudalism under, **3:**72, 74; **5:**425, 448
    on inheritance of the crown, **5:**382
    institutional organization under, **2:**127
    juries under, **3:**437
    land distribution by, **3:**73
    language of law under, **1:**182–183
    legal treatises on, **1:**183
    murder fine by, **1:**182
    Scotland under, **5:**196
    subinfeudation by, **5:**368
    trial by battle under, **6:**6
William II (England; William Rufus)
    feudal law under, **3:**74
    Scotland under, **5:**196–197
    succession after, **5:**382
    tension with St. Anselm, archbishop of Canterbury, **1:**460
William III (England, William of Orange), **2:**132
    judiciary under, **3:**416
    Leiden university founded by, **4:**225
    parliament and, **4:**285
    women under, **6:**120
William I (Scotland; William the Lion)
    grant to Robert Bruce, **3:**76
William I (William the Bad) (Norman king)
    courts under, **2:**251
William of Orange. *See* William III (England)
William of Raleigh
    Bracton, Henry de, and, **1:**301
    on land leases, **4:**11
William Rufus. *See* William II (England)
Williams, Eric, **6:**11
Williams, Glanville L., **2:**443
Williams, Joan, **3:**68
Williams, Patricia J., **2:**301; **3:**69
Williams, Roger, **3:**428
    banishment of, **4:**334
    on religious persecution, **5:**109
    secularization of law and, **5:**110
Williams, Serjeant, **4:**324
William the Conqueror. *See* William I the Conqueror
William the Lion. *See* William I (Scotland)
Williston, Samuel R., **2:**209
    on contracts, **1:**15

Willoughby, Francis, **5**:413
wills, **6:102–107**. *See also* succession
   ancient Greek law, **3**:230–231; **6**:114, 116
      evidence on, **3**:2
      papyri of, **1**:147
   ancient Near Eastern law, **1**:173
   Anglo-Saxon, **1**:178
   Byzantine, **5**:376–377
   Du Moulin, Charles, on, **2**:373
   duress and, **2**:373–376
   England
      ecclesiastical law on, **2**:389
      in estates doctrine, **2**:478
      women in, **6**:123
   English common law, **6:102–105**
   living, **2**:424
   notaries in drawing up, **4**:237
   Roman law, **5**:372–373
      content of, **5**:374
      school disputes over, **3**:476
      by women, **6**:118–119
   Sabinus, Masurius, on, **5**:179
   testamentary disposition in Islamic law, **6:105–107**
   United States, **3**:238; **5**:402–405
      colonial period, **2**:13; **3**:235, 236
      holographic will, **3**:236
Wills Act (England, 1540, 1837)
   on land, **6**:102, 103–104
   minors in, **1**:395
   on succeession, **5**:403
   on witnesses, **6**:104
will theory
   contract law and, **2**:197, 209
   on error and mistake, **2**:474, 476
Wilson, James, **2**:402
Wilson, Michael, **3**:*286*
Wilson, Robert, **4**:7
   on land registration, **4**:8, 9
Wilson, Woodrow
   on antitrust, **1**:189
   in antitrust movement, **1**:324
   corporations under, **5**:78
   on executive power, **3**:20
   foreign policy, **5**:79
   League of Natiosn and, **3**:294
   railroad policy under, **5**:103
   taxation under, **5**:443, 444, 445
   war power under, **6**:89
   on women's suffrage, **6**:135
Wimaladhama (Sri Lanka), **5**:340

Windscheid, Bernhard, **4**:176, 277; **6:107–108**
   on assignment, **1**:228
   commentary on thepandects, **2**:10
   on fraud, **3**:104
   Jhering and, **3**:399
   jurisprudence of concepts and, **3**:433
   on science of pandects, **2**:9
   on systematization, **5**:421
   on vicarious liability, **6**:78
Winfield, Percy, **2**:443
WIPO. *See* World Intellectual Property Organization
Wipo, **4**:90
Wirt, William, **4**:450
Wirz, Henry, **4**:179
wiṣāa (guardian), **3**:37
witchcraft
   Africa
      after independence, **1**:102
      precolonial, **1**:66, 72
   ancient Near Eastern law, **1**:175
   Aztec law, **5**:288
   Chinese law, **4**:251, 252–253
      curses on the emperor, **4**:255–256
      as depravity, **4**:259
   English common law, **3**:176
   Enlightenment views of, **2**:444–445
   Inca law, **5**:289
witch trials, **6:108–110**, *109*
   English common law, **6**:120
   legal procedure against witches, **4**:438
   ordeals for evidence in, **3**:9
   to punish marginal figures, **2**:289
   Sweden, **5**:415
   United States, **3**:428
wite, **1**:182
witenagemot, **2**:128
witnesses. *See also* evidence; false testimony; procedure
   ancient Greece
      Athens, **3**:1–2; **4**:414
      oaths and, **4**:241–242
      slaves as, **5**:245
   ancient Near Eastern law, **1**:170
   Athens, **3**:1–2; **4**:113–115; **6:110–111**
      contracts and, **2**:179
   China, **4**:418
      doubtful cases, **2**:361
      in loans, **4**:117
      recanted, **1**:197
      in enforcement, **2**:431

English common law
   evidence of, **3:**4
fallibility of, **3:**16
medieval and post-medieval Roman law
   class differences in, **3:**8
non-Muslims in Islamic law as, **4:**234
Roman law, **6:**119
scientific expert, **4:**28
social science research on, **5:**269
United States
   reliability/trustworthiness of, **3:**15
   slaves as, **5:**261
unwilling, **3:**1–2
wills, **3:**236; **6:**104, 106
women
   Islamic law, **1:**358; **2:**142; **6:**127, 129
   Ottoman Empire, **6:**129
   Pakistan, **5:**308–309
Wittmann, Roland, **5:**161
Władysław Jagieł, **4:**330
Wolf, Erik, **3:**136
Wolfenden Commission, **3:**110
Wolff, Christian von, **5:**2; **6:111–112**
   on duty and fault, **5:**470–471
   on guilt, **3:**134
   influence of Pufendorf, Samuel von on, **5:**21
   on international law, **3:**283
   on Justinian organization, **2:**400
   on natural law, **3:**118; **4:**217
   Scholasticism and, **4:**17
   on succession, **5:**385
   on systematization, **5:**421
   Vattel, Emer de, and, **6:**73
Wolff, Hans Julius
   on administrative law, **1:**23
   on ancient Greek procedure, **1:**163; **2:**179
   on Egyptian judiciary, **2:**415–416
   in papyrology, **2:**413
   in Symposion, **1:**165
   on unity in Greek law, **1:**164
Wöllnersches Religionsedikt (Prussia, 1788), **1:**351
Wolsey, Thomas (Cardinal)
   Chancery, **2:**468
   Star Chamber, **5:**345, 346
Woman's Christian Temperance Union, **2:**291
woman suffrage movement, **1:**125
women, **6:112–146.** *See also* discrimination, race and sex; feminist legal theory
   Afghanistan, **1:**59
   Africa

after independence, **1:**102–103
circumcision of, **1:**71, 73
discrimination against, **1:**73
precolonial political organizations, **1:**70
ancient Greece
   seclusion of, **6:**114–115
ancient Greek law, **5:**64–66; **6:112–117**
   adoption of, **1:**41
   Athens, **1:**140, 234
   Bachofen, J. J., on, **1:**185
   in divorce, **2:**346–347
   Hellenistic, **1:**159
   homosexual behavior among, **5:**228–229
   legal status of, **5:**357–358
   oaths by, **4:**241–242
   property ownership rights, **4:**456–457
   prostitution, **4:**493–494, 495
   sexual and moral regulation of, **5:**226–227
   as slaves, **5:***243*, 244
   Sparta, **3:**29; **5:**328–329
ancient Near Eastern law, **1:**171
   inheritance by, **1:**173
   in litigation, **1:**169
ancient Rome, **6:117–120**
Australia, **1:**242
barristers, **1:***279*, 280
capacity in Islamic law, **1:**358
Chinese law
   adoption of, **1:**45–46
   exile of, **3:**25, 26
   inheritance law and, **1:**425
   punishment, **5:56–57**
   rape, **5:**66–67
   redemption, **5:**73–74
   in succession, **5:**378
   wounding, **6:**150
   under Yuan empire, **1:**429
Chinese Republic Civil Code
   status, **1:**440
Code of Gortyn on, **3:**122
conveyancing by, **2:**215
in delict, **2:**325–326
dharma of, **2:**333
divorce
   ancient Greece, **6:**113–114
   Ottoman Empire, **6:**128
   United States, **6:**134, 136, 142
duress on, **2:**374
Egypt, guardianship of, **2:**420
in elderlaw, **2:**423

employment and labor law
   England, **2:**426, *427*
   medieval and post-medieval Roman, **2:**430
English common law, **6:120–125**
   dower, **2:**361–363
   Mansfield, Lord, on, **4:**143
   punishment, **5:**30
   rape, **5:**67–69
   in succession, **5:**383
in environmental law, **2:**454
guarantee refused to, **3:**129
Guyana, **3:**137
Hindu law, **4:**479; **6:131–133**
   adoption of, **1:**49–50
India
   adoption, **2:**307, 308
   bride burning, **2:**364–365
   bride price, **2:**308
   inheritance, **2:**307
   Islamic law on, **5:**308
   marriage, **2:**308–309
   as prisoners, **2:**283
   prostitution, **2:**307
   selective abortion and, **1:**5
   in succession, **5:**396–402
   widows, **2:**307
at Inns of Court, **3:**243
in Iranian law, **3:**304
Islamic law, **6:125–130**
   in Arab countries, **1:**207–208
   the body in, **1:**299; **4:**385
   crime and punishment of, **2:**277
   Europe, **2:**484
   in legal education, **2:**397
   legal personality of, **4:**64
   obligations to children, **3:**37
in Isma'ili codes, **2:**38
jihad, **6:**86
jury service by, **3:**440
lawyers, **6:**55
legal education for
   United States, **1:**16; **2:**404, 405
medieval and post-medieval Roman law on
   sexual crimes, **5:**229–231
natural law on, **4:**218
New Zealand, **4:**229
Pakistan, **5:**308–309
property rights
   ancient Greek law, **1:**159
   colonial United States, **2:**14

   Indonesia, **3:**335–336
   Islamic law, **6:**127
   Ottoman Empire, **6:**128–129
   United States, **6:**134, 136
Roman law
   criminal responsibility, **2:**272
   slaves under, **5:**248
   wills by, **5:**372
as solicitors, **5:**273
Southeast Asia, **5:**318
in strict settlements, **5:**365–367
and succession
   in India, **3:**222
Suriname, **5:**414
Sweden, **5:**417
United States, **6:**44–45, 45, **133–146**
   colonial period, **2:**13–14, 289
   educational equal opportunity and, **2:**410–411
   equal protection, **2:**462–463
   labor law on, **3:**479–480
   as lawyers, **4:**49
   in legal profession, **4:**53–54
   punishment of, **2:**290
   suffrage, **4:**339
   women's movement and inheritance law, **3:**237
welfare programs for, **6:**92, 93
in Welsh and Irish laws, **1:**377
wills by, **6:**104
   in ancient Greece, **3:**231
witch trials against, **6:**108
witnesses
   Islamic law, **1:**358; **2:**142; **6:**127, 129
   Ottoman Empire, **6:**129
   Pakistan, **5:**308–309
Women's Charter Ordinance (Singapore, 1961), **5:**318, 321
Women's Equity Action League, **6:**144
Women's India Association, **5:**397
Women's Reservation Bill (India, 2005), **6:***132*
Wong, Andy, **1:***261*
Wood, Edward, **2:**441
Wood, Horace Gay, **1:**115
Wood, Thomas, **2:**394, 441; **3:**252
Wood, William, **1:**219
Woodbine, George, **1:**301
Woodbury, Levi, **5:**263
Wooddeson, Richard, **1:**108; **2:**394
Woodhull, Victoria, **2:***338*
Word to a Drunkard (Wesley), **1:**123
Workable Program for Community Improvement, **3:**186

workers compensation
　environmental law and, **2**:451–452
　industrial accidents and, **3**:480
Work Incentive Program (WIN, U.S.), **4**:372; **6**:93
Works and Days (Hesiod), **3**:401; **4**:109
　on dispute resolution, **1**:138
　on inheritance, **3**:228
Works Progress Administration (U.S.), **1**:27
WorldCom, **5**:95
World Intellectual Property Organization (WIPO), **3**:263, 265
World International Property Organisation, **2**:217
World Trade Organization (WTO)
　India and, **3**:219
　People's Republic of China and, **1**:446
　state sovereignty and, **5**:354
　United States and, **3**:285
World War I
　antitrust, **1**:189
　banking, **1**:272
　consumer protection, **2**:171
　declaration of war in, **6**:88
　expansion of rights as result of, **2**:16
　family disruption in, **2**:348
　Germany tax policy, **5**:438
　influence on universities, **6**:64
　opposition to, **4**:335
　Soviet Union, **5**:175
　treason charges during, **6**:3–4
　United States
　　freedom of speech, **3**:409
　　railroads, **5**:103
　　tax policy, **5**:443–444
　　war power in, **6**:89
　　zoning laws, **3**:182
World War II
　administrative agencies in, **1**:28
　declaration of war in, **6**:88
　expansion of rights as result of, **2**:16–17
　Hungary civil code, **3**:194
　influence on universities, **6**:64
　international law and, **3**:295
　internment of Japanese-Americans during, **6**:58
　Japan, **3**:377–378
　military tribunals after, **6**:90
　military tribunals in, **4**:179
　Poland, **4**:331
　Singapore in, **5**:242
　taxation in England, **5**:447
　United States

　　arbitration in, **3**:486
　　housing, **3**:183, 185
　　labor law and, **3**:482–483
　　martial law in, **4**:180
　　regulations and, **5**:80, 81, 82
　　tax policy, **5**:446–447
　　women's labor in, **2**:338
World Wide Web, trademark and, **3**:272
Wormser, Maurice, **1**:325
worship in Islamic law, **3**:327; **6:146–150**
Worthington, William Henry, **1**:*287*
Wo to Drunkards (Mather), **1**:123
Wounded Knee, **4**:212
wounding in Chinese law, **3**:85; **6:150–152**
WPA. *See* Work Projects Administration; Works Profress Administration
Wray, Christopher, **3**:452
Wray, Kenneth Roberts, **1**:310
Wright, J. Skelly, **2**:210; **3**:186
Wright, Martin, **2**:441
Wright, Robert, **4**:358
writ of account, **2**:196
writ of assistance, **5**:203
writ of *capias ad respondendum*, **4**:175
writ of *capias ad satisfaciendum*, **3**:88–89
writ of covenant, **2**:194–195
　breach of contract and, **1**:305–306
　England
　　in land leases, **4**:12–13
　in environmental law
　　England, **2**:450
writ of debt, **2**:194
　formal contracts and, **2**:195
　informal contracts and, **2**:296
writ of detinue, **2**:196
writ of error, **1**:197
writ of formedon, **5**:70
　estates doctrine and, **2**:478
writ of naifty, **3**:307
writ of right, **3**:307; **5**:69–70, 71
　and battle, **6**:6
writ of trover, **5**:251–252
writs. *See also* novel disseisin, writ of
　abolition of system of, **2**:82
　Anglo-Saxon, **1**:178
　basis of common law, **2**:81
　Chancery and, **1**:388–389
　elegit, **3**:88
　England, **2**:435
　　ecclesiastical law and, **2**:390–391

evidence in, **3:**3
feudal, **3:**74–75
land, **4:**419–420, 473
land leases, **4:**11
mesne process in, **4:**174–175
or right, **3:**75
petty assizes, **4:**315–318
of entry, **5:**70, 71
established by Henry II, **2:**80
of execution, **3:**87–88
final process, **3:**87–88
Glanvill on, **2:**80; **4:**419, 420
in Ireland, **3:**307
quominus, Exchequer and, **3:**17
Scotland, **5:**197
Wales, **6:**100
wrongful judgment in Chinese law, **6:152–153**
Wrongs and Their Remedies (Addison), **2:**442
WTO. *See* World Trade Organization
Wu (China), **4:**116
on mutilation, **4:**197
on witchcraft, **4:**255
Wu (Chinese emperor), **5:**74
Wulfstan, Anglo-Saxon code by, **1:**178
Wu Qi, **1:**412
Württemberg, Protestant church in, **1:**351
Wu Woyao, **1:**195
WvK. *See* Wetboek van Koophandel
Wyse, William, **1:**163
Wythe, George, **2:**402

X

Xenopeithes, **1:**213
Xenophon
on family, **3:**28, 29, 31
on *graphē paranomōn*, **3:**124
on Helots, **5:**245
law depictions by, **1:**148
on Sparta, **1:**143; **5:**327, 328; **6:**115
on theft, **5:**456
Xhosa, **1:**69
Xi, **1:**406, 407
Xia (Chinese king), **5:**57
Xiangang Shilei (Regulations for the Ceremonial System) (China, 1371), **1:**454
Xiao He, **1:**412–413
Xiaowen (Chinese emperor), **1:**421
Xiaozhuang (China), **4:**116
Xing'an huilan (Compendium of Penal Coases), **1:**437
Xing Bu, **1:**196

Xiphilinus, John, **1:**330
Xuexiao geshi (Regulations for the National University and Schools) (China, 1397), **1:**454
Xue Yunsheng. *See* Hsueh Yun-Sheng
Xun Zi, **1:**459
Xunzi, **5:**164
Xu Shiying, **1:**439

Y

yad ḍamān (possession of liability), **2:**332
Yad ha-Chazakah. See Mishneh Torah
Yahya, Yahya ibn, **4:**128
Yahya Hamid al-Din, **6:**156
Yājnavalkya, **3:**153, 155, 156
on *smriti*, **5:**264
Yājñāvalkya, **1:**236
Yājñāvalkyanmrti, **6:**83
Yajnavalkyasmriti, **1:**4
Yajurveda on *śruti*, **5:**344
Yale Law School, **2:**401
faculty-student ratio at, **2:**406
legal process at, **4:**68
legal realism at, **1:**15; **4:**75
realism at, **2:**405
Yan Song, **2:**225
Yaroslav the Wise (grand prince of Kievan Rus), **5:**167
Yaśastilaka (Somadeva Sūri), **3:**364
Yasin, 'Abd Allah ibn, **1:**382
Yates Report, **4:**368
Yearbook of Commercial Arbitration, **1:**129
Year Books, **4:**43–44, 60
of Court of Common Pleas, **2:**86
precedent and, **4:**377, 378, 381; **5:**277
Yegge, Robert, **4:**33, 34
yellow-dog contracts, **3:**480, 481
U.S. Supreme Court and, **2:**26
Yellowstone National Park, **2:**455
Yelverton, William, **4:**377
Yemen, **1:**211; **6:155–157**
alcohol and drugs, **1:**123
capital punishment, **1:**368
of juveniles, **3:**462
conflict of laws, **2:**114
constitution, **3:**317
criminal law, **2:**279
Mansur bi-llah 'Abd Allah ibn Hamza, al-, in, **4:**144
obligatory bequests, **6:**107
personal status laws, **4:**298; **6:**129
Shafi'i, Muhammad ibn Idris al-, in, **5:**235

Shafi'i school of law in, **3**:352
shari'a as principal source of legislation in, **3**:317
zakat, **5**:431
Yemen Arab Republic (YAR), **6**:157
Yew, Lee Kuan, **5**:242
Ye Xiaoxin, **4**:117
YMCA (Young Men's Christian Association), **2**:404
Yngvesson, Barbara, **4**:34
Yntema, Hessel, **1**:15; **4**:74, 75
Yogaśāstra (Hemacandra), **3**:364
Yongping Liu, **1**:408
Yongzheng (Chinese emperor), **1**:434, *438*; **2**:226
 on hereditary debasement, **5**:233
 use of spies, **2**:243
Yorke, Philip. *See* Hardwicke, Lord
Yoro ritsuryo (Japan, 718), **3**:367
Yoruba, **1**:68, 70
Yosemite National Park, **2**:455
Yoshihito (Japanese emperor), **3**:366
Yoshimune (Japanese emperor), **3**:366, 371
Yoshino, Kenji, **3**:69–70
Young, Whitney M., Jr., **2**:*342*
Young Jain Men's Association, **3**:364
Young Offenders Act (Canada, 1985), **1**:341
Youth International Party (Yippies), **4**:337
Yuan dianzhang (Statutes and Precedents of the Yuan), **1**:429
 on ethnic groups, **2**:481
Yuan dynasty (China)
 amnesty, **1**:134
 corruption, **2**:227
 ethnic groups, **2**:481
 exile, **3**:25–26
 foreigners, **3**:91
 illicit sexual intercourse, **5**:231
 judicial precedent, **1**:461
 lack of law codes, **1**:458
 land, **4**:2
  sale of, **5**:187
 loans, **4**:118
 marriage, **4**:157
  remarriage, **4**:160
 Mongols and, **4**:183–184
 offenses against the state, **4**:249
 on review, **1**:196
 structure of law, **1**:429
 succession, **5**:379–380
 wounding, **6**:151
Yuan Shikai, **1**:439; **5**:237
Yudhoyono, Susilo Bambang, **3**:228

Yugoslavia
 Islamic law, **1**:253; **3**:334
 witch trials, **6**:109
Yunis, Ibtihal, **1**:206
Yurchenko, Victor, **1**:*256*
Yvo of Chartres, **4**:263

Z

Zad al-ma'ad (Ibn Qayyim), **3**:199
Zahiri school of Islamic law, **3**:353–354
 on abrogation of legal norms, **1**:6
 Ibn Hazm and, **3**:198
 in Maghrib and al-Andalus, **4**:128
 on wills, **6**:106
Zahir Shah, **1**:*60*
Zaim, Hosni al-, **2**:398
Zaire, **1**:98
zakat (alms), **5**:430–431; **6**:146, 149
Zaleucus, **2**:30
 written law by, **1**:154
Zambia
 constitution, **1**:105
 family law, **1**:104
 independence, **1**:93
 one-party system, **1**:98
Zanardelli code (Italy, 1889), **1**:372
zang, **6**:159–160
Zanji, Muslim bin Khalid al-, **5**:235
Zanobini, Guido, **1**:23
Zanzibar
 abolition of slave trade, **1**:75–76, *76*
 colonialism, **1**:78, 86
 Ibadis in, **3**:349
 independence, **1**:93, 97
 Indian population, **2**:382–383
 penal code, **2**:45
 precolonial, **1**:69
 South Asian law, **2**:382–384
 waqf property, **2**:45
Zarkashi, al-, **3**:353
Zasius, J. U., **6**:160
Zasius, Ulrich, **3**:191; **6**:*160*, 160–161
 in Bourges school, **1**:316
 humanist jurisprudence of, **1**:118
 on succession, **5**:386
Zäsy, Ulrich. *See* Zasius, Ulrich
Zatochnik, Daniil, **5**:177
Zayd, Nasr Hamid Abu, **1**:206
 apostasy conviction of, **2**:421
Zayd ibn 'Ali, **5**:136; **6**:155, **161–162**

Zaydis
  Caspian, **3:**139
  in Yemen, **3:**139, 341; **6:**155–156
Zaydi school of Islamic law, **3:**341–342; **6:**161.
    See also Hadi ila l-Haqq Yahya ibn al-Husayn, al-; Mahdi li-Din Allah Ahmad ibn Yahya al-Murtada, al-; Mansur bi-llah ʿAbd Allah ibn Hamza, al-
  Arabian peninsula, **1:**211
  on duty, **2:**376
  Hadawi school, **3:**139
  on inheritance, **3:**39
  on wills, **6:**106
  in Yemen, **6:**156
Zayn al-Abidin, Ali, **5:**136
Zeger van Espen, Berhnard, **1:**357
Zeiller, Franz von, **6:162–163**
Zeisel, Hans, **4:**32
Zeitschrift für österreichische Rechtsgelehrsamkeit und politische Gesetzkunde (Wagner, ed.), **6:**163
Zeitschrift der Savigny Stiftung, **1:**166
Zelin, Madeleine, **2:**193
Zenger, John Peter, **3:**442; **5:**332
Zeno (Byzantine emperor), **2:**168
  on delict, **2:**324
  Russian translation of the works of, **5:**177
Zhabdrung, **1:**290
Zhang Fei, **1:**419
Zhangsun Wuji, **1:**457
Zhang Yong, **5:**378
Zhao Kyangyin, **1:**425
zhaoxi (seeking extra money), **5:**187, 188
Zhenfan zafan sizui tiaoli (Regulation concerning true and miscellaneous capital crimes), **1:**431
Zhing Fei, **1:**18
Zhiyuan Xinge (New Regulations of the Zhiyuan Era), **1:**428
Zhiyuanxinge (New Statutes of the Zhiyuan Period, 1291), **1:**458
Zhizheng tiaoge (Regulations of the Zhizheng Era), **1:**429
Zhou (Chinese king), **5:**57
Zhou dynasty (1045–221 B.C.E.)
  alcohol and drugs, **1:**119
  appeal, **1:**193
  mutilation, **4:**196
  offenses against the state, **4:**249
  punishment, **5:**24–25, 57
  review, **1:**196
Zhou guan, **4:**196
Zhouli (Confucius), **4:**196; **5:**45, 183
Zhu houcong, **1:**431

Zhusi Zhizhang Gocernment Statutes (China, 1393), **1:**454
Zhu Xi, **1:**425; **4:**157
  on succession, **5:**379
Zhu Yijun, **1:**431
Zhu Youtang, **1:**431
Zhu Yuanzhang, **1:**430
Zia ul-Haq, Muhammad, **2:**141, 142
  Islamization under, **2:**39; **4:**274; **6:**130
Zia ul-Haq, Muhammad Zia ul-
  Islamization under, **5:**308
Zi Chan, **1:**404, 405, 455
Zimbabwe
  constitution, **1:***105*
  independence, **1:**93
Zimmermann, Reinhard, **5:**163
Zivilgesetzbuch (Civil Code, Switzerland, 1907–1912), **2:**49
  employment and labor law, **2:**428
  Huber, Eugen, and, **3:**188
  influence on Hungarian law, **3:**194
  on possession, **4:**360
  on succession, **5:**387, 389, 394
  Turkey adoption of, **6:**15
Ziyadat, al- (Shaybani), **5:**236
Ziyadat-Allah I, **5:**239–240
Zolotinskii, V. T., **5:**172
Zonaras, **1:**348
Zonaras, John
  on canon law, **1:**330
  information on, **1:**333
Zong (slave ship), **5:**252
zoning
  English common law, **2:**449
  local government law, **4:**122
  Native American, **4:**213
  United States, **3:**182
    equal protection and, **2:**460
Zouche, Richard, **3:**283; **5:**156
  in Regius Chair, **2:**393
zouyan (report to higher authority), **5:**214
Zufar, **3:**305
Zufar ibn al-Hudhail, **3:**343
Zuhayli, Wahba, **3:**281
  on lease and tenancy, **4:**55
Zuhri, Ahmad ibn Abi Bakr al, **4:**140
Zuhri, Ibn Shihab al-, **1:**210
  influenced by Malik ibn Anas, **4:**140
Zulueta, Francis de, **5:**161
Zulu nation, **1:**69–70
Zuo Commentary (Zuozhuan), **1:**455, 460; **4:**259
Zweck im Recht, Der (Jhering), **3:**399
Zwingli, Ulrich, **1:**350